Second Edition Revised

ECONOMICS
NEW WAYS OF THINKING

Annotated Teacher's Edition

ROGER A. ARNOLD
California State University San Marcos

EMC Publishing®

ST. PAUL, MINNESOTA

Publisher: Alex Vargas
Managing Editor: Brenda Owens
Production Manager: Bob Dreas
Cover Designer: Leslie Anderson
Text Designers: Hespenheide Design, Jaana Bykonich
Design and Production Specialists: Tammy Norstrem, John Valo, Desktop Solutions
Indexer: Terry Casey
Illustrator: Hespenheide Design

Cover photo: Getty Images/mkakade711@gmail.com

ISBN: 978-1-53383-494-2

© 2019, 2015 by EMC Publishing, LLC
875 Montreal Way
St. Paul, MN 55102
E-mail: educate@emcp.com
Website: www.emcschool.com

Prepare Your Students for the *21ˢᵗ Century!*

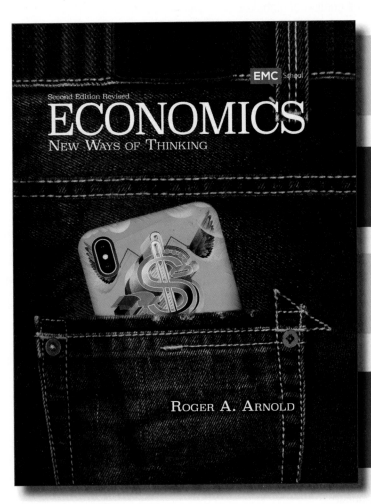

Will the Internet Bring an End to Monopolies?

What's the Price of Playing Video Games?

How Might Leverage Push Banks into Insolvency?

Can a Major Stimulus Bill Boost a Troubled Economy?

"An investment in knowledge always pays the best interest"

—Benjamin Franklin

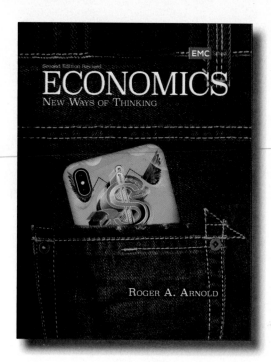

Engage Students with *Real World Features*

Economics: New Ways of Thinking shows students how to find economics in unusual and surprising places. It grabs their attention with **real-world examples** – the NFL draft, rock concert ticket prices, Airbnb – and then provides clear explanations and hundreds of supporting **up-to-date graphs and charts** to teach students solid economic principles. Students learn these basic principles in the context of globalization – the process by which the nations of our world are becoming increasingly integrated. Projects, internet research, and current events lessons keep learning fresh.

- ***Why It Matters*** – Each chapter opens with an explanation of what the subject of that chapter means to economics, society, and students.

- ***Economics Around the Clock*** – Each chapter also opens with short descriptions of daily events that involve economics – accompanied by pertinent questions to help get students thinking.

- ***Economics in the Real World*** – Engaging questions such as "Are you nicer to nice people?" "Why didn't Taylor Swift go to college?" and "Can a soda tax cure obesity?" prompt students to apply economic concepts to real-world situations.

- ***A Student Asks*** – Throughout the text, the author anticipates questions students will have as they read, and answers them in friendly, conversational language.

- ***Economics Facts and Fallacies*** – Identifying common misunderstandings and myths about economics, this feature explains how/why they are inaccurate.

- ***Thinking Like an Economist*** –Examining how an economist might view a situation or problem as opposed to how the general population would view the same scenario.

- ***Quotes*** – Insightful words from economists and economic thinkers provide food for thought and discussion.

- ***Your Personal Economics*** – Topics like the increasing value of education in a global economy, the psychology of credit cards, and how to avoid scams and economic bubbles connect students with economics on a personal level.

- ***Debating the Issues*** – In imaginary conversations, people debate today's economic issues, providing students with opportunities for class discussion.

- ***Photos and Exhibits*** – Current photos and exhibits throughout the text highlight key concepts and pose thought-provoking questions to engage students.

- ***Examples! Examples! Examples!*** – Hundreds of interesting, relevant examples immediately follow the introduction of new concepts to help students master new information.

Motivate Students with *Current Content*

Make Connections to Real-World Economics

Your Personal Economics connects students with economics on a personal level.

Economics in the Real World engages students by asking intriguing economic questions.

Class Multimedia Project Applies 21st Century Skills

Students use the text and outside resources to complete a class project about the effects of a financial crisis.

Teacher resources include project guidelines, correlations to Bloom's taxonomy and multiple intelligences, assessment rubrics, and a checklist of the following 21st Century Skills.

- Collaborative Learning
- Creative Thinking
- Technology Resources
- Presentation Skills

Challenge and Support Students with *Interactive Technology!*

Diverse Teaching Tools

Options to Fit Your Teaching Style

Annotated Teacher's Edition –Semester Pacing Guide, Chapter Planning Guides, and full teacher support

Assessment Book – two separate tests for every chapter, plus section quizzes

Applying the Principles Workbook and Teacher's Edition – multiple activities and exercises for the major economic concepts, with an emphasis on creating and interpreting graphs and charts

Guided Reading and Study Guide and Teacher's Edition – outlining activities and textbook lessons rewritten for students who read below grade level

Finding Economics and Teacher's Edition – fictional short stories embedded with economic principles for students to discover

Lesson Plans Book – detailed lesson plans for every section of the textbook

www.emcpassport.com

Passport®

Passport's unique learning environment seamlessly delivers Economics content and assets along with the latest performance-based learning technologies.

Teachers can...

- access all program resources
- assign homework and tasks
- provide individualized feedback
- track student progress and grades

Students can...

- access materials anytime, anywhere
- complete and submit assignments
- receive immediate feedback
- track their progress

www.emcpassport.com

Connect with Online Resources at www.emcpassport.com

Passport® for Teachers

- Links to the Annotated Teacher's Edition eBook
- Standards Correlations
- Microsoft® PowerPoint® Lectures
- Current Events Lessons
- Additional In the Real World Features
- Economics on the Web activities
- The Global Impact activities
- Avenue™ e-assessment platform

Passport® for Students

- Links to additional Internet resources, including the student eBook and eWorkbook
- Practice Tests
- Study Guides
- Spanish Audio Summaries in print and as MP3s (summaries of key points from each section)
- Tutorials and key-concept videos
- Word Games and Flash Cards (in English and in Spanish)
- Flipgrid™ video discussion platform

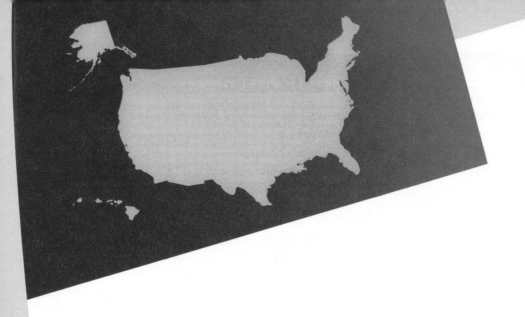

CORRELATION

of the Voluntary National Content Standards in Economics

to Economics:
New Ways of Thinking

Several organizations involved with economics education worked together to produce the Voluntary National Content Standards in Economics as a guide to economics instruction in American schools. These groups included the Council for Economic Education, the Foundation for Teaching Economics, and the National Association of Economic Educators. The table on pages ATE8–ATE11 shows the chapters, sections, and special features in *Economics: New Ways of Thinking* that support the teaching of the 20 Voluntary National Content Standards in Economics. As part of its EconomicsAmerica® program, the Council for Economic Education offers free online lessons that support these standards. The lessons can be accessed at www.emcpassport.com.

State Standards Correlations
Correlations to state standards, including the Common Core State Standards for English Language Arts and Literacy in History/Social Studies & Science, can be accessed at http://econ.myemcp.com/standards.

Content Standards	Chapter and Section Coverage	Special Feature Coverage
Standard 1 **Scarcity** Productive resources are limited. Therefore, people cannot have all the goods and services they want; as a result, they must choose some things and give up others.	Chapter 1, Section 1 Chapter 1, Section 3 Chapter 2, Section 1 Chapter 3, Section 4 Chapter 12, Section 3 Chapter 15, Section 1	▶ Why Didn't Taylor Swift Go to College? 9 ▶ Working After School: What Are the Trade-Offs? 92 ▶ Will You Sleep Less if You Earn More? 263 ▶ Can Economic Growth Stop Political Squabbling? 368
Standard 2 **Decision Making** Effective decision making requires comparing the additional costs of alternatives with the additional benefits. Many choices involve doing a little more or a little less of something; few choices are "all or nothing" decisions.	Chapter 1, Section 2 Chapter 7, Section 3 Chapter 8, Section 1	▶ Why Are There Last-Minute Deals on Cruises? 192 ▶ Did You Get My Text? 202 ▶ Will You Sleep Less if You Earn More? 263
Standard 3 **Allocation** Different methods can be used to allocate goods and services. People acting individually or collectively must choose which methods to use to allocate different kinds of goods and services.	Chapter 2, Section 1 Chapter 3, Section 1 Chapter 3, Section 2 Chapter 15, Section 4	▶ Where Did DVRs, Podcasts, and Blogs Come From? 129
Standard 4 **Incentives** People usually respond predictably to positive and negative incentives.	Chapter 1, Section 2 Chapter 3, Section 1 Chapter 3, Section 2 Chapter 3, Section 3 Chapter 3, Section 4 Chapter 5, Section 1	▶ What Saved the Pilgrims? 70
Standard 5 **Trade** Voluntary exchange occurs only when all participating parties expect to gain. This is true for trade among individuals or organizations within a nation, and among individuals or organizations in different nations.	Chapter 1, Section 2 Chapter 2, Section 2 Chapter 3, Section 1 Chapter 4, Section 1 Chapter 6, Section 1 Chapter 10, Section 1 Chapter 15, Section 1 Chapter 15, Section 3	▶ Would You Hear Rock Music in a Barter Economy? 281 ▶ Might Someone in India Grade Your Homework? 450 ▶ Is Free Trade the Best Policy for the United States? 500
Standard 6 **Specialization** When individuals, regions, and nations specialize in what they can produce at the lowest cost and then trade with others, both production and consumption increase.	Chapter 2, Section 2 Chapter 10, Section 1 Chapter 15, Section 1	▶ To Mow, or Clean, or Both? 440 ▶ Might Someone in India Grade Your Homework? 450

Content Standards	Chapter and Section Coverage	Special Feature Coverage
Standard 7 **Markets and Prices** A market exists when buyers and sellers interact. This interaction determines market prices and thereby allocates scarce goods and services.	Chapter 1, Section 2 Chapter 4, Section 1 Chapter 5, Section 1 Chapter 6, Section 1 Chapter 6, Section 2	▶ What's the Price of Playing Video Games? 107 ▶ How Much Would You Pay for an Ocean View? 147 ▶ What Happened to U.S. House Prices between 2001 and 2009? 153
Standard 8 **Role of Prices** Prices send signals and provide incentives to buyers and sellers. When supply or demand changes, market prices adjust, affecting incentives.	Chapter 2, Section 1 Chapter 4, Section 1 Chapter 4, Section 2 Chapter 5, Section 1 Chapter 5, Section 2 Chapter 6, Section 1 Chapter 6, Section 2	▶ The Price Gap Between Brains and Brawn: Is It Increasing? 50 ▶ Does Elasticity of Demand Pop Up at a Concert? 118 ▶ Are You Nicer to Nice People? 125 ▶ How Do Taxes and Subsidies Change Our World? 131 ▶ If the Prices of Houses Rise, How Many More Houses will be Available for Sale? 136 ▶ How Much Would You Pay for an Ocean View? 147 ▶ Who Feeds Cleveland? 160
Standard 9 **Competition and Market Structure** Competition among sellers usually lowers costs and prices, and encourages producers to produce what consumers are willing and able to buy. Competition among buyers increases prices and allocates goods and services to those people who are willing and able to pay the most for them.	Chapter 2, Section 2 Chapter 3, Section 1 Chapter 3, Section 4 Chapter 7, Section 1 Chapter 8, Section 1 Chapter 8, Section 2	▶ The Price Gap Between Brains and Brawn: Is It Increasing? 50 ▶ Do You Know the Price of an X-Ray or Blood Test? 179 ▶ Is It Sellers Against Buyers or Sellers Against Sellers? 214
Standard 10 **Institutions** Institutions evolve in market economies to help individuals and groups accomplish their goals. Banks, labor unions, corporations, legal systems, and not-for-profit organizations are examples of important institutions. A different kind of institution, clearly defined and enforced property rights, is essential to a market economy.	Chapter 3, Section 1 Chapter 3, Section 5 Chapter 7, Section 1 Chapter 8, Section 3 Chapter 9, Section 2 Chapter 10, Section 2 Chapter 10, Section 4	▶ What Saved the Pilgrims? 70 ▶ What is Money in a Prisoner of War Camp? 288 ▶ What Gives Money Value? 302 ▶ Could You Lose Your Job if Your Bank Loses Money? 336
Standard 11 **Money and Inflation** Money makes it easier to trade, borrow, save, invest, and compare the value of goods and services. The amount of money in the economy affects the overall price level. Inflation is an increase in the overall price level that reduces the value of money.	Chapter 10, Section 1 Chapter 10, Section 2 Chapter 10, Section 3 Chapter 10, Section 4 Chapter 10, Section 5	▶ Spend a Little Now, or a Lot More Later? 24 ▶ Investing in Yourself 138 ▶ Would You Hear Rock Music in a Barter Economy? 281

Content Standards	Chapter and Section Coverage	Special Feature Coverage
Standard 12 **Interest Rates** Interest rates, adjusted for inflation, rise and fall to balance the amount saved with the amount borrowed, which affects the allocation of scarce resources between present and future uses.	Chapter 10, Section 1 Chapter 12, Section 1 Chapter 13, Section 2 Chapter 16, Section 2	▶ Spend a Little Now, or a Lot More Later? 24 ▶ Investing in Yourself 138 ▶ The Psychology of Credit Cards 290 ▶ Is Monetary Policy Sometimes Ineffective? 389
Standard 13 **Income** Income for most people is determined by the market value of the productive resources they sell. What workers earn primarily depends on the market value of what they produce.	Chapter 2, Section 1 Chapter 9, Section 1 Chapter 9, Section 2 Chapter 11, Section 4	▶ Are Entertainers Worth Millions? 253 ▶ Education—It's Like Multiplying Yourself 258 ▶ Will You Sleep Less if You Earn More? 263 ▶ Your Goal: Generic, Not Specific, Human Capital 372
Standard 14 **Entrepreneurship** Entrepreneurs take on the calculated risk of starting new businesses, either by embarking on new ventures similar to existing ones or by introducing new innovations. Entrepreneurial innovation is an important source of economic growth.	Chapter 1, Section 2 Chapter 3, Section 1 Chapter 3, Section 4 Chapter 7, Section 2 Chapter 14, Section 1	▶ Are the Founders of Airbnb Entrepreneurs? 28 ▶ The Price Gap Between Brains and Brawn: Is It Increasing? 50 ▶ Is there a Difference between being Pro-Business and Pro-Free Enterprise? 78
Standard 15 **Economic Growth** Investment in factories, machinery, new technology, and in the health, education, and training of people stimulates economic growth and can raise future standards of living.	Chapter 2, Section 1 Chapter 3, Section 3 Chapter 12, Section 3 Chapter 16, Section 1 Chapter 16, Section 2	▶ Spend a Little Now or a Lot More Later? 24 ▶ Investing in Yourself 138 ▶ Your Goal: Generic, Not Specific, Human Capital 372
Standard 16 **Role of Government and Market Failure** There is an economic role for government in a market economy whenever the benefits of a government policy outweigh its costs. Governments often provide for national defense, address environmental concerns, define and protect property rights, and attempt to make markets more competitive. Most government policies also have direct or indirect effects on peoples' incomes.	Chapter 3, Section 5 Chapter 9, Section 2 Chapter 14, Section 1 Chapter 14, Section 2	▶ Are You Better Off With or Without Speeding Laws? 86 ▶ Should There Be Price Controls on Some Goods at Certain Times? 170 ▶ Should There Be a Minimum Wage? 272 ▶ What Did Keynes Overlook? 384 ▶ What Is Government's Role When It Comes to the Economy? 428

Content Standards	Chapter and Section Coverage	Special Feature Coverage
Standard 17 **Government Failure** Costs of government policies sometimes exceed benefits. This may occur because of incentives facing voters, government officials, and government employees, because of actions by special interest groups that can impose costs on the general public, or because social goals other than economic efficiency are being pursued.	Chapter 14, Section 1 Chapter 14, Section 2 Chapter 15, Section 2	▶ Are You Better Off With or Without Speeding Laws? 86 ▶ Do Voting Rules Matter to Taxing and Spending? 381 ▶ What Did Keynes Overlook? 384 ▶ Are You Paying Someone Else's Taxes? 408 ▶ What Is Government's Role When It Comes to the Economy? 428 ▶ Is Free Trade the Best Policy for the United States? 500
Standard 18 **Economic Fluctuations** Fluctuation in a nation's overall levels of income, employment, and prices are determined by the interaction of spending and production decisions made by all households, firms, government agencies, and others in the economy. Recessions occur when overall levels of income and employment decline.	Chapter 3, Section 1 Chapter 11, Section 1 Chapter 11, Section 2 Chapter 11, Section 3 Chapter 11, Section 4	▶ Is There Real GDP Growth in Your Future? 329 ▶ Did President Kennedy Earn More Than Today's President? 335 ▶ Could You Lose Your Job if Your Bank Loses Money? 336
Standard 19 **Unemployment and Inflation** Unemployment imposes costs on individuals and the overall economy. Inflation, both expected and unexpected, also imposes costs on individuals and the overall economy. Unemployment increases during recessions and decreases during recoveries.	Chapter 11, Section 4 Chapter 12, Section 1 Chapter 12, Section 2	▶ Grade Inflation: When Is a B+ No Better than a C? 352 ▶ Can You Have Too Much Money? 356 ▶ Could You Buy More in 2016 Than in 1964? 361
Standard 20 **Fiscal and Monetary Policy** Federal government budgetary policy and the Federal Reserve System's monetary policy influence the overall levels of employment, output, and prices.	Chapter 10, Section 3 Chapter 13, Section 1 Chapter 13, Section 2 Chapter 13, Section 3 Chapter 14, Section 1	▶ Do Voting Rules Matter to Taxing and Spending? 381 ▶ Is Monetary Policy Sometimes Ineffective? 389 ▶ What Is *The Wizard of Oz* Really About? 391 ▶ Are You Paying Someone Else's Taxes? 408 ▶ Would a Soda Tax Cure Obesity? 411

Semester Pacing Guide

This pacing guide illustrates how you might implement *Economics: New Ways of Thinking* in a standard 90-day semester. The "Regular Schedule" option assumes that you have 90 class periods, each 45 to 50 minutes long; the "Block Schedule" option assumes that you have 45 class periods, each 90 minutes long.

The program consists of 50 sections. These have been divided among the available class days according to both the amount of material they cover and the weight that teachers we surveyed assigned to that material. You may want to vary the time you spend on the sections depending on your state and district standards and curricula, your personal areas of interest and expertise, and your students' needs.

		Number of Days	
		Regular Schedule	**Block Schedule**
Unit I Introduction to Economics			
Chapter 1	**What Is Economics?**		
Section 1	The Foundation of Economics	2	1
Section 2	The Economic Way of Thinking		
Section 3	Basic Economic Language	2	1
Chapter 2	**Economic Systems and the Global Economy**		
Section 1	Economic Systems	2	1
Section 2	Globalization	2	1
Chapter 3	**Free Enterprise**		
Section 1	Characteristics of Free Enterprise		
Section 2	Profit and Loss in Free Enterprise	2	1
Section 3	The Ethics of the Free Enterprise System		
Section 4	Entrepreneurs	2	1
Section 5	The Role of Government in a Free Enterprise Economy	2	1
Unit II The Basics			
Chapter 4	**Demand**		
Section 1	Understanding Demand	2	1
Section 2	The Demand Curve Shifts	2	1
Section 3	Elasticity of Demand	2	1
Chapter 5	**Supply**		
Section 1	Understanding Supply	2	1
Section 2	The Supply Curve Shifts	2	1
Chapter 6	**Price: Supply and Demand Together**		
Section 1	Supply and Demand Together	2	1
Section 2	Supply and Demand in Everyday Life	2	1
Unit III Microeconomics			
Chapter 7	**Business Operations**		
Section 1	About Business Firms	2	1
Section 2	Costs		
Section 3	Revenue and Its Applications	2	1
Chapter 8	**Competition and Markets**		
Section 1	A Perfectly Competitive Market	2	1
Section 2	A Monopolistic Market	2	1
Section 3	A Monopolistic Competitive Market	2	1
Section 4	An Oligopolistic Market	2	1

		Number of Days	
		Regular Schedule	**Block Schedule**
Chapter 9	**Labor, Employment, and Wages**		
Section 1	What Determines Wages?	2	1
Section 2	Labor and Government Regulation	2	1
Unit IV Macroeconomics			
Chapter 10	**Money, Banking, and the Federal Reserve System**		
Section 1	The Origins of Money	2	1
Section 2	The Money Supply	2	1
Section 3	The Federal Reserve System	2	1
Section 4	The Money Creation Process		
Section 5	Fed Tools for Changing the Money Supply	2	1
Chapter 11	**Measuring Economic Performance**		
Section 1	National Income Accounting	2	1
Section 2	Measuring GDP	2	1
Section 3	Real GDP	2	1
Section 4	Measuring Price Changes and the Unemployment Rate	2	1
Chapter 12	**Economic Changes and Cycles**		
Section 1	Inflation and Deflation	2	1
Section 2	Business Cycles	2	1
Section 3	Economic Growth	2	1
Chapter 13	**Fiscal and Monetary Policy**		
Section 1	Fiscal Policy	2	1
Section 2	Monetary Policy	2	1
Section 3	Stagflation: The Two Problems Appear Together	2	1
Chapter 14	**Taxing and Spending**		
Section 1	Taxes	2	1
Section 2	The Budget: Deficits and Debt	2	1
Unit V Trade and Investment			
Chapter 15	**International Trade and Economic Development**		
Section 1	International Trade	2	1
Section 2	Trade Restrictions	2	1
Section 3	The Exchange Rate	2	1
Section 4	Economic Development	2	1
Chapter 16	**Stocks and Bonds**		
Section 1	Stocks	2	1
Section 2	Bonds	2	1
Section 3	Futures and Options	2	1
Total number of days		**90**	**45**

Second Edition Revised

ECONOMICS
NEW WAYS OF THINKING

Second Edition Revised

ECONOMICS

NEW WAYS OF THINKING

ROGER A. ARNOLD

California State University San Marcos

EMC Publishing

ST. PAUL, MINNESOTA

Publisher: Alex Vargas
Managing Editor: Brenda Owens
Production Manager: Bob Dreas
Cover Designer: Leslie Anderson
Text Designers: Hespenheide Design, Jaana Bykonich
Design and Production Specialist: John Valo, Desktop Solutions
Indexer: Terry Casey
Illustrator: Hespenheide Design

Cover photo: Getty Images/mkakade711@gmail.com

Care has been taken to verify the accuracy of information presented in this book. However, the authors, editors, and publisher cannot accept responsibility for Web, email, newsgroup, or chat room subject matter or content, or for consequences from application of the information in this book, and make no warranty, expressed or implied, with respect to its content.

Trademarks: Some of the product names and company names included in this book have been used for identification purposes only and may be trademarks or registered trade names of their respective manufacturers and sellers. The authors, editors, and publisher disclaim any affiliation, association, or connection with, or sponsorship or endorsement by, such owners.

We have made every effort to trace the ownership of all copyrighted material and to secure permission from copyright holders. In the event of any question arising as to the use of any material, we will be pleased to make the necessary corrections in future printings. Thanks are due to the aforementioned authors, publishers, and agents for permission to use the materials indicated.

ISBN: 978-1-53383-309-9

© 2019, 2015 by EMC Publishing, LLC
875 Montreal Way
St. Paul, MN 55102
Email: educate@emcp.com
Website: www.emcschool.com

Printed in the United States of America

26 25 24 23 22 21 20 19 18 17   1 2 3 4 5 6 7 8 9 10

About the Author

Professor Roger Arnold is an experienced teacher, researcher, and writer. He earned his Ph.D. from Virginia Tech. He currently teaches economics at California State University San Marcos. He has also taught at Virginia Tech, California State University Northridge, Hillsdale College, University of Oklahoma, and University of Nevada Las Vegas.

He has written numerous successful textbooks for both high school and college and has written articles and columns for the *Wall Street Journal* and other respected publications.

Dedication

To Sheila, Daniel, and David

Content Reviewers and Program Contributors

Diane Bryant, M.Ed.
Sandusky High School
Sandusky, Ohio

Michael Eggers
Sunnyside High School
Fresno, California

Theresa Fischer
Ridgefield High School
Ridgefield, Connecticut

Debbie Glenn
Upland High School
Upland, California

Clay Heath, M.Ed.
Viroqua High School
Viroqua, Wisconsin

Collette Jackson, M.Ed.
Mountain View High School
Meridian, Idaho

Lars Johannson
McClane High School
Fresno, California

Ken Karrer
LBJ High School
Austin, Texas

Annette King
Colquitt County High School
Moultrie, Georgia

Jeanne Leslie
Avon Grove High School
West Grove, Pennsylvania

Donna McCreadie
Temple City High School
Temple City, California

Jeanne McNamara
Foundation for Teaching Economics
Davis, California

Trent McNeeley
Floyd Central High School
Floyds Knobs, Indiana

Tara O'Brien
Shady Side Academy
Pittsburgh, Pennsylvania

Stephen E. Reilly, PhD
Haverford High School
Havertown, Pennsylvania

Larry Robinette
Broken Arrow High School
Broken Arrow, Oklahoma

Bill Schreier
Wheaton Warrenville South High School
Wheaton, Illinois

Brad Siegel
Scotch Plains-Fanwood School District
Scotch Plains, New Jersey

Paul Trevizo
Townview Magnet High School
Dallas, Texas

Scott Wolla
Senior Economic Education Specialist
Federal Reserve Bank of St. Louis
St. Louis, Missouri

Contents in Brief

Contents

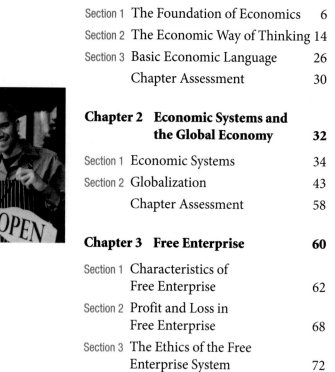

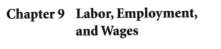

Special Features

Economics *in the* Real World

Your **Personal** Economics

Economic Facts and Fallacies

Thinking Like an Economist

Debating the Issues

Exhibits

Introduction

Economics can be either boring or exciting, depending on how it is presented. Increasingly, I have come to believe that the right way to present economics is to surprise students and readers. Perhaps you come to the study of economics with low expectations; perhaps you think that economics will be a dull and dry subject. If so, you will be surprised when you see that

- economics often occurs in the unlikeliest places;
- what happens on the other side of the world is linked to you through economic channels; and
- economics can answer your questions.

Is it Important to Know about Economics?

People have a sense that economics is important to them because economics is in the news so often. It is hard to go a day without hearing something that has to do with economics or the economy. Unemployment, economic growth, the federal budget deficit, interest rates, the national debt, international trade, the jobs report, wages, business firms, costs and benefits, supply and demand, and a hundred other economic topics are part of the world in which we live.

Now I believe there are really two major reasons for learning economics. The first is to learn why things happen the way they do and the second is to view the world in a new way.

Economics Can Answer Your Questions

So much of our daily lives is affected by economic events. You may ask: Why am I paying more for this product this month than last month? Why are jobs easy to find one month and hard to find the next? What really determines the income of an accountant, physician's assistant, electrician, administrative assistant, professional athlete, or software developer?

Although many people have "economic questions," they often resist learning enough about economics to get answers to those questions. They assume that they will have to work too hard, and study for too long, before they will begin to answer their economic questions. But that is not correct. The truth is, even a small understanding of economics will help you answer these questions. Sometimes even a little economic knowledge goes a long way.

What Happens on the Other Side of the World Is Linked to You Through Economic Channels

You don't live in the same economy that people lived in during the 1920s, or 1950s, or even 1980s. You live in a different kind of economy; you live in a global economy. You live in an economy in which what happens in China or India or Russia can touch your economic life in a matter of seconds.

In addition to providing answers, economics provides you with a new way to look at the world. Economics can do for a person's understanding of the world what eyeglasses do for a person's sight. Instead of wondering why things around the world are occurring, you'll be able to use your knowledge of economics to explain events and global interactions.

Economics Often Occurs in the Unlikeliest Places

Most people think that economics occurs only on Wall Street; in Washington, D.C.; on the factory floor; in a bank; or in a conference room at a major corporation. Economics is in all these places, but it is in many other places too. Economics is in the classroom, at the beach, at a NASCAR race, and at a basketball game. You can find economics at rock concerts, on a reality TV show, mowing the lawn, and even in your sleep. In short, economics can be found nearly everywhere!

Paul Samuelson (1915–2009) was the first American economist to win the Nobel Prize in Economic Sciences. He once said that setting out to explore the exciting world of economics for the first time is a unique thrill. You are about to set out to explore the world of economics, perhaps for the first time. You may not know what awaits you, but those of us who have passed this way before know. I know that you are in for a very special time. You are likely to be surprised at how much you learn about your world in just a few months. And you know something else? You're likely to be pleasantly surprised at how much fun you have along the way.

Second Edition Revised

ECONOMICS
NEW WAYS OF THINKING

Listed below are the chapters included in this unit.

Foundations for the Unit

Unit 1 begins your students' journey into the world of economics. In this unit, your students will learn some of the basic concepts on which the study of economics is built. Among those concepts are scarcity, opportunity cost, supply, demand, and price. As your students work through Unit I, they will also begin to understand how the study of economics can broaden their appreciation of the world around them by helping them engage in the economic way of thinking.

UNIT I
Introduction to Economics

CHAPTER 1

What Is Economics?

CHAPTER 2

Economic Systems and the Global Economy

CHAPTER 3

Free Enterprise

Resources for the Unit

Books

Buchholz, Todd G. *New Ideas from Dead Economists.* New York: Penguin Books, 1989.

Smith, Adam. *An Inquiry into the Nature and Causes of the Wealth of Nations.* London: Strahan and Cadell, 1776. Reprinted with a preface by George J. Stigler and edited by Edwin Cannan. Chicago: University of Chicago Press, 1977.

Articles

Scahill, Edward M. "Did Babe Ruth Have a Comparative Advantage As a Pitcher?" *Journal of Economic Education* 21, no. 4 (1990): 402–410.

Tinari, Frank D. and Kailash Khandke. "From Rhythm 'n' Blues to Broadway: Using Music to Teach Economics," *Journal of Economic Education* 31, no. 3 (2000): 253–270.

> **"It is the business of economics, as of almost every other science, to collect facts, to arrange and interpret them, and to draw inferences from them."**
>
> —Alfred Marshall, economist

3

Introducing the Unit

Introduce Unit I by writing the word *economics* on the chalkboard. Ask students to list the first 10 words that come to their minds when they look at the word *economics*. After they have had a few minutes to compose their lists, ask students to share their lists. You might have a volunteer keep a running list for the class, noting each time a particular word, such as *money*, is mentioned. No matter which words your students name, those terms will likely be related to economics, since economics is a field of study that relates to many areas of our lives.

Performance Project

All students should keep running journals of any purchases they make during the time they study Unit 1. As each chapter is completed, students should write a brief essay that examines one of those purchases using their newly acquired understanding of economics. For example, after studying Chapter 1, each student should examine how the choice to make a particular purchase was influenced by the condition of scarcity and describe his or her opportunity cost in making that choice.

Encourage students to refer to as many economic topics as possible in their essays. Stress that students should use the skills and concepts acquired through the study of the special features found in this unit.

Multimedia

The Art of a Balanced Budget. In *Understanding Free Market Economics: Lessons Learned in the Former Soviet Union.* VHS. Films for the Humanities and Sciences.

Economics at Work. Videos, videodiscs, and simulation software. National Council on Economics Education.

Introductory Economics. 17-part series. Hosted by Ellen Roseman and John Palmer of the University of Western Ontario. Films for the Humanities and Sciences.

Thinking Economics. CDs, simulation software, and study guide. National Council on Economic Education.

Chapter 1 Planning Guide

SECTION ORGANIZER

Section 1
The Foundation of Economics
(pages 6–13)

Learning Objectives	Reproducible Worksheets and Handouts	Assessment
▶ Explain how choice is related to scarcity. ▶ Provide examples of opportunity costs. ▶ Understand a production possibilities frontier. ▶ Describe how competition determines the way rationing devices are distributed.	Section 1 Activity, *Applying the Principles Workbook,* pages 1–4 Outlining Activity, *Guided Reading and Study Guide,* pages 1–2 Just the Facts Handout, *Guided Reading and Study Guide,* page 3	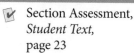 Section Assessment, *Student Text,* page 13 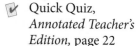 Quick Quiz, *Annotated Teacher's Edition,* page 12 Section Quiz, *Assessment Book,* page 1

Section 2
The Economic Way of Thinking
(pages 14–23)

Learning Objectives	Reproducible Worksheets and Handouts	Assessment
▶ Explain how costs and benefits affect decisions. ▶ Identify incentives. ▶ Distinguish between microeconomics and macroeconomics. ▶ Explain why economists develop theories.	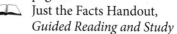 Section 2 Activity, *Applying the Principles Workbook,* pages 5–8 Outlining Activity, *Guided Reading and Study Guide,* pages 4–5 Just the Facts Handout, *Guided Reading and Study Guide,* page 6	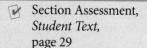 Section Assessment, *Student Text,* page 23 Quick Quiz, *Annotated Teacher's Edition,* page 22 Section Quiz, *Assessment Book,* page 2

Section 3
Basic Economic Language
(pages 26–29)

Learning Objectives	Reproducible Worksheets and Handouts	Assessment
▶ Describe the different ways economists talk about goods. ▶ Identify services. ▶ List the four types of resources. ▶ Explain why labor and entrepreneurship are different categories of resources.	Section 3 Activity, *Applying the Principles Workbook,* pages 9–10 Outlining Activity, *Guided Reading and Study Guide,* page 7 Just the Facts Handout, *Guided Reading and Study Guide,* page 8	Section Assessment, *Student Text,* page 29 Quick Quiz, *Annotated Teacher's Edition,* page 29 Section Quiz, *Assessment Book,* page 3

Reproducible Chapter Resources and Assessment Materials

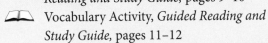 Graphic Organizer Activity, *Guided Reading and Study Guide*, pages 9–10

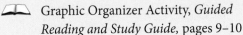 Vocabulary Activity, *Guided Reading and Study Guide*, pages 11–12

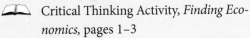 Working with Graphs and Charts, *Guided Reading and Study Guide*, pages 13–14

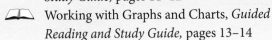 Practice Test, *Guided Reading and Study Guide*, pages 15–17

Critical Thinking Activity, *Finding Economics*, pages 1–3

Chapter Test A, *Assessment Book*, pages 4–7

Chapter Test B, *Assessment Book*, pages 8–12

Student Text Internet Links

Economics: New Ways of Thinking, Second Edition encourages students to use the Internet to find out more about economics. Given the wealth of current, valid information available on websites, students should be encouraged to use the Internet as a research tool. Doing so will likely increase students' interest in and understanding of economics principles and topics. In addition, doing Internet research can help your students form the habit of accessing and using economics information, as well as help them develop investigative skills they will use throughout their educational and professional careers.

To aid your students in achieving these ends, each chapter of *Economics: New Ways of Thinking, Second Edition* includes the addresses of several websites that provide engaging and relevant information. When students type in any of the addresses provided, they will immediately arrive at the intended site. The addresses have been modified so that EMC Publishing can monitor and maintain the proper links—for example, the website http://www.deposit accounts.com/ has been changed to http://econ.emcp.net/accounts. In the event that the address or content of a site changes or is discontinued, EMC's Internet editors will redirect the link to a site with equivalent information.

Activities in the *Annotated Teacher's Edition* often suggest that students search the Internet for information. For some activities, you might want to find reputable sites beforehand and steer students toward them. For other activities, have students do their own searching and then check out the sites they have found and discuss why they might be reliable or unreliable.

Passport® for Economics

Technology resources are available with the *Economics: New Ways of Thinking, Second Edition* program through Passport®. These include:

eBooks for *Economics: New Ways of Thinking, Second Edition*

▸ Student textbook eBook
▸ Interactive Applying the Principles eWorkbook
▸ Finding Economics eBook
▸ Guided Reading and Study Guide eBook
▸ Annotated Teacher's Edition eBook
▸ Lesson Plans eBook
▸ Assessment eBook

Passport® for Students

Students can access helpful resources through Passport® for Economics. Resources include:
▸ Study guides
▸ Practice tests
▸ Flash cards in English and in Spanish
▸ Word games in English and in Spanish
▸ Tutorials and key-concept videos
▸ Spanish print and audio summaries

Passport® for Teachers

Keep your course current and relevant by using the teacher resources provided through Passport® for Economics. In addition to all of the resources on the student side of Passport®, the teacher side contains:
▸ Link to the Annotated Teacher's Edition eBook
▸ Standards correlations
▸ Microsoft® PowerPoint® Lectures
▸ Current Events Lessons
▸ Additional Economics in the Real World features
▸ ExamView® Assessment Suite
▸ PDFs of all print supplements (student and teacher)

Overview

What Is Economics?

This chapter introduces a few of the most important concepts that form the foundation of economics. This is the first of three chapters in which students learn about the basics of economics, economic systems, and free enterprise. The following statements provide brief descriptions of the major concepts covered in each section of this chapter.

SECTION **1** The Foundation of Economics

Section 1 deals with the backbone of all economic thinking, scarcity and choice. Students learn how scarcity of resources creates the need for making choices and how those choices lead to opportunity costs.

SECTION **2** The Economic Way of Thinking

Section 2 explores cost-benefit decisions and the differences between microeconomics and macroeconomics. Students also learn why economists develop theories and what purposes those theories serve.

SECTION **3** Basic Economic Language

Section 3 introduces the four types of economic resources: land, labor, capital, and entrepreneurship.

Why It Matters

Simple arithmetic is both useful and powerful. It is useful because almost every day, you have some reason to add, subtract, multiply, or divide. Just think how much harder your life would be if you did not know simple arithmetic.

Basic arithmetic is powerful because it is the springboard to higher mathematics and to deeper understanding. You could not learn algebra or geometry without knowing how to add, subtract, multiply, and divide. Without algebra and geometry, safe bridges could not be built and satellites could not be put into space.

The economic concepts discussed in this chapter are similar to addition, subtraction, multiplication, and division. How are they similar? First, as with arithmetic, once you learn basic economics, you will be able to use

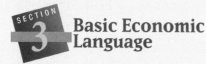

these concepts continually to get more of what you want out of life. Second, these concepts form the basis for the economics you will learn in later chapters. You will not be able to understand economic "algebra," so to speak, without first learning the fundamental economic concepts explained in this chapter.

These shoppers probably can't afford to buy everything they would like, but their choices appear to have been satisfying. In this text, you'll learn how people make these sorts of choices.

4

Teaching Suggestions from the Author

Students come to the study of economics not fully knowing what economics is. They think that economics is a list of topics—unemployment, inflation, deflation, economic growth, interest rates, costs, revenues, and so on. Certainly, economics deals with all these topics and more; however, the essence of economics is not the list of topics but

how the topics are discussed. After all, everyone can talk about unemployment, inflation, and so on, but not everyone talks about these topics the way an economist does.

At the heart of economics is a *way of thinking*. Economists think in terms of scarcity, choices, costs and benefits, unintended effects, supply

Economics Around the Clock

The following events occurred one day in November.

8:33 A.M. Each morning on his way to work, George, 30 years old, drives through a senior citizen community. It usually takes him longer to go one-half mile in the senior citizen community than to go one-half mile anywhere else along his commute. George is currently going 15 mph in a 25 mph zone because the person driving in front of him is driving that speed. George is frustrated because he has no way to get around this slow driver.

- What economic reason might explain why, on average, senior citizens drive slower than 30-year-olds?

5:12 P.M. Jessica is a senior in high school; next year, she hopes to enroll in a college that is very selective. Currently, she is at home filling out one of the many college applications on her desk. The acceptance rate at this particular college is 14 percent. Jessica whispers under her breath, "Why such a low acceptance rate?"

- Why is it so hard to get into certain colleges?

7:43 P.M. José, a junior in high school, is at home studying on a Saturday night. José's mother is surprised because he is usually out with his friends. She asks, "What are you doing home tonight? Do you have a big test next week?" José answers, "No, it's just that Jimmy is sick and Tom is out of town."

- What does José's friends being unavailable have to do with his studying on a Saturday night?

8:45 P.M. David and Elaine Anderson are at home watching TV. They are thinking of buying a new car, so after a Volvo commercial, Elaine says, "I wonder if we should buy a new Volvo, maybe an S80 [starting price, $43,450]." As Dave gets up to get something to drink, he says, "There goes the vacation to Maui."

- What does buying a car have to do with taking a vacation?

5

Introducing the Chapter

Ask students to write a short answer to the following question: What do economists do? Allow students to share their answers. Then explain that economists study markets, prices, costs, production, inflation, unemployment, interest rates, business cycles, budget deficits, trade deficits, exchange rates, and so on. These subjects and others are discussed in this textbook.

This chapter covers some basic elements of economics, including scarcity and opportunity cost. Tell students that although the concepts may sound foreign, we all deal with them every day without even thinking about them. Students should begin to examine things from an economic viewpoint, in the same distinctive way that economists view, interpret, and analyze the world.

Teaching with Visuals

Students will learn about the basics of economics in this chapter. Have them look at the photo on this spread, and ask them to think about what the buying and selling of goods has to do with economics.

and demand, building and testing theories, and much more. In this chapter, students are introduced to the economic way of thinking.

It is a good idea at the beginning of this chapter to tell students to forget about memorizing definitions and outlining topics in a detailed way. Instead, they should concentrate on how econo-

mists approach the study of the world. What do economists focus on? What is important to them? What types of questions do they ask and answer? By approaching the chapter in this way, students will more quickly understand that economics is essentially a way of thinking about the world.

Teacher Support

Focus and Motivate

Section Objectives

After completing this section, students will be able to

▶ explain how choice is related to scarcity;

▶ provide examples of opportunity costs;

▶ understand a production possibilities frontier; and

▶ describe how competition determines the way rationing devices are distributed.

Economics Around the Clock

Kickoff Activity

Instruct students to respond in writing to the 5:12 p.m. scenario in Economics Around the Clock (page 5).

Invite students to share their answers with the class. They should come up with several reasons that certain colleges can be more selective than others.

Activating Prior Knowledge

Have each student describe one thing he or she did last week—such as "Studied history for one hour" or "Talked to my friend for 20 minutes." Then ask students to identify what they would have done during the same period of time, had they not done what they did. In other words, if they had not studied history for one hour, what would they have done during that hour?

 Visit econ.myemcp.com/videos for videos that will help students better understand the key concepts found in this section.

The Foundation of Economics

Focus Questions
▶ What is scarcity?
▶ How is choice related to scarcity?
▶ How is opportunity cost related to choice?
▶ Why are rationing devices needed?
▶ What is the purpose of a production possibilities frontier?
▶ What activity determines how rationing devices are distributed?

Key Terms
want
resource
scarcity
opportunity cost
trade-off
production possibilities frontier
rationing device
economics

Scarcity Exists

People have **wants**—things they desire to have. They do not want just anything, however. They want the things they think will make them happy and satisfied. Most people want cars, houses, haircuts, clothes, entertainment, better health, and countless other things. Few people are completely satisfied, even after getting their initial wants satisfied. Then they want a *bigger* house, a *newer* car, and *more* clothes. All the wants of all the people in the world make the list of wants unlimited.

Resources Are Needed

How do people satisfy their wants? As you probably know, in most cases you cannot get something by just wishing for it. The things we want do not simply appear on our doorsteps because we desire them. Instead, **resources** are needed to produce the goods and services that satisfy our wants. If you want a new desk for your room, it will take wood, tools, and labor (all of which are resources) to produce that desk. Nanette may want a computer, but she is not going to get one by simply wishing for it. Many resources will be needed to produce it.

Resources Are Limited

Unfortunately, the world's supply of resources is limited. So, when you want a new desk or Nanette wants a computer, you both face an ongoing problem in life that we all face—an economic problem. Our wants are unlimited, but the resources available to satisfy these wants are limited. Stated in another way, people's wants are greater than the limited resources available to satisfy them.

This condition in which our wants are greater than the resources available to satisfy them is called **scarcity**. Scarcity is an economic fact of life, much as the law of gravity is a fact of life. In fact, scarcity is such an important, fundamental economic concept that some economists have said that the science of economics wouldn't exist were it not for scarcity.

want
Something that we desire to have.

resource
Anything that is used to produce goods or services. For example, a person's labor may be used to produce computers, TV sets, and much more; therefore, a person's labor is a resource.

scarcity
The condition in which our wants are greater than the resources available to satisfy them.

Differentiating Instruction

Kinesthetic Learners

Help students understand the concept of scarcity by playing musical chairs. Divide the class into three groups. Have each group create a circle of chairs that numbers one fewer than the number of students. Play music briefly and then stop it while everyone tries to sit in a chair. Anyone left standing is eliminated, owing to the scarcity of chairs, and one chair is removed from each set of chairs. Continue until only two students are left in each group. Combine the final six contestants so that they continue with a circle of five chairs. Continue until there is a single winner. Point out that the desire of the contestants (sitting) is always higher than the amount of resources (chairs).

QUESTION: *I know that I must deal with scarcity, but do wealthy people—people like Bill Gates, the multibillionaire—face scarcity too? Bill Gates may have unlimited wants, but doesn't he also have unlimited resources?*

ANSWER: *Both you and Bill Gates have to deal with scarcity. The fact that he can buy more things than you can doesn't mean that he has unlimited resources. Keep in mind that Gates wants more than just goods, such as cars, houses, and vacations; he also wants more friendship, more time to spend with his kids, more time to do some leisurely reading. In addition, he is trying to help solve many of the world's problems by donating millions of dollars to charities. However, not even his vast fortune can provide all the people in the world with everything they want.*

Scarcity Means Making Choices

Wants are unlimited, and resources are limited. Therefore, scarcity exists, and people must make choices. After all, without enough resources to satisfy all our wants (yours, mine, and everybody else's), we have to choose which of our unlimited number of wants we will satisfy.

EXAMPLE Maria earns $1,000 a month. She wants a new outfit, 10 new books, a trip to Hawaii, a new car, and many other things. The problem is that she can't have everything she wants, given her income. She has to choose between the new outfit and the 10 new books. She also has to choose between the trip to Hawaii and a down payment on a new car. ♦

Consider the choices a society makes because scarcity exists. Some groups of people want more health care for the poor, some want more police protection, some want more schools, and some want a cleaner

environment. As we know, wants are not satisfied simply by the asking. Resources are needed to bring these things about. The problem, though, is that even if we could satisfy all the wants just listed, we would be faced with more later. Even if we provided more health care to the poor, hired more police officers, built more schools, and cleaned up the environment, we would still discover other things to do. There are always more wants and never enough resources to satisfy those unlimited wants. Therefore, we must choose how to use our limited resources. We must choose which wants we will try to satisfy and which wants we will leave unsatisfied.

> *"The first lesson of economics is scarcity: there is never enough of anything to satisfy all those who want it."*
> —Thomas Sowell, economist

▲ In a world of scarcity, we must make choices. Would you choose the most expensive or the least expensive shoes? How would this decision affect other decisions?

Discussion Starter

Some people have suggested that one way to eliminate scarcity is to have fewer wants. Ask students if they think this is possible. Which wants would they be willing to give up?

Make sure students understand that not all wants focus on tangible things that can be purchased.

Cause and Effect

The relationship between wants and scarcity is clear: the more people who want a particular item, the scarcer the item. In history, many groups have stated that if you eliminate wants, you gain a sense of understanding and peace. Others have said that someday, far into the future, all wants will be fulfilled. Ask students to think about the following questions: Is it possible that someday all wants could be fulfilled? Is it possible to eliminate all of your wants? What would happen if all wants were fulfilled or eliminated?

Teaching with Visuals

Answers will vary. They should be expressed in terms of limited resources and the costs of choosing the least expensive or most expensive shoes.

To give students a sense of scarcity, share this information with them: In Cebu, in the Philippines, Canadian bird experts captured on video, for the first time, the rarest bird in the world, the Cebu Flowerpecker. This bird was believed to be extinct in the nineteenth century, but a single specimen was spotted on the island in 1992. Since then, experts have determined that there are four living specimens of this rare bird. Encourage students to imagine what it would be like if the Cebu Flowerpecker were the greatest pet bird in the world. If everyone wanted a Cebu Flowerpecker as a pet, how would its incredibly rare nature affect its scarcity and the amount of resources needed to acquire one?

Teaching with Visuals

Direct students to make a list of their opportunity costs for one day. Invite them to share their lists and the choices that underlie them in a class discussion.

Background Information

Students sometimes think that scarcity exists only in poor countries. On the contrary, scarcity is a fact of life—no matter where a person lives. There is scarcity in India, Argentina, Brazil, Russia, the United States, and every other nation. Scarcity "goes around the world" because people's wants (no matter where they live) are always greater than the resources available to satisfy those wants.

Discussion Starter

Scarcity affects everything, even land, air, and water. It may be hard for students to understand that although Earth is more than 70% water, water is scarce in many parts of the world. What choices might have to be made if water were scarce in your area?

EXHIBIT 1-1   Opportunity Cost

What you choose to do	What you might have done	Opportunity cost
Watch television	Read a book	The opportunity cost of watching television is reading a book.
Buy a touchscreen laptop	Buy some new clothes	The opportunity cost of buying a touchscreen laptop is buying some new clothes.
Go to sleep at 9:00 p.m. instead of 11:00 p.m.	Watch a two-hour movie on Netflix	The opportunity cost of sleeping from 9:00 to 11:00 p.m. is watching a two-hour movie on Netflix.

▲ The most valued opportunity or alternative you give up to do something—the next best choice—is that something's opportunity cost.

Making Choices Means Incurring Opportunity Costs

Every time you make a choice, such as choosing to buy a sweater instead of a pair of jeans, you face an *opportunity cost*. The most valued opportunity or alternative you give up (or forfeit) to do something is that something's **opportunity cost**. Thus, the opportunity cost of your choosing to buy a sweater is a pair of jeans. (See Exhibit 1-1 for more examples.)

Economists often say that "Life is full of trade-offs." What do they mean by this statement? The nature of a **trade-off** is that you can get more of one good but only by getting less of another good. Speaking about trade-offs is just another way of speaking about opportunity costs. In other words, saying that "Life is full of trade-offs" is really no different from saying that "Every time we choose one thing over another, we incur an opportunity cost."

> "It is no crime to be ignorant of economics . . . but it is totally irresponsible to have a loud and vociferous opinion on economic subjects while remaining in this state of ignorance."
> —Murray N. Rothbard, economist

opportunity cost
The most highly valued opportunity or alternative given up when a choice is made.

trade-off
A situation in which having more of one thing necessarily means having less of something else.

A Student Asks

QUESTION: *Suppose I decide to spend $50 to buy some used car stereo speakers from a friend. If I hadn't spent the money on the speakers, I could have purchased $50 worth of new clothes, spent $50 on a present for my girlfriend, or given $50 to my mom's favorite charity. Because I could have done any of these things, aren't all of them the opportunity cost of buying the speakers?*

ANSWER: *No. It is necessary to differentiate between what you could have done and what you would have done. Opportunity cost refers to what you would have done if you had not bought the speakers. It's your next best choice— and only that choice. If you would have spent the $50 on your girlfriend's present, then the present— and only the present—is what you actually would have given up to buy the speakers. Your opportunity cost in this case can only be $50 worth of opportunities foregone—not $100, $150, or $200 worth.*

Opportunity costs affect people's decisions every day. In fact, a change in opportunity cost can and often does change a person's behavior. Suppose Sunil has a part-time job at a local grocery store. Each day, he goes to work at 2 p.m. and leaves at 6 p.m. Does he incur an opportunity cost when he chooses to work each day between 2 and 6 p.m.? He certainly does! Whatever he would be doing if he weren't working is the opportunity cost of his working.

Now let's increase the opportunity cost of Sunil's going to work. Suppose that one day Sunil is on his way to work and someone stops him and offers to pay him $300 for doing an easy task, but doing the task will mean that Sunil won't be able to go to work that day. What will Sunil do? Will he continue on his way to work or take the

Cross-Curricular Activity

Tell students to list several major activities in which they have been involved during the last year, such as traveling and buying an expensive item. Then have them create a table that lists each activity, the opportunity cost of the activity, and the approximate monetary cost of the activity.

How does the monetary cost of the activity compare with the monetary cost of the opportunity not taken? Are monetary issues the only concerns when determining what actions are taken? What other concerns should be considered when weighing opportunity costs?

Why Didn't Taylor Swift Go to College?

Taylor Swift was born on December 13, 1989, in Reading, Pennsylvania. Taylor moved to Nashville, Tennessee at the age of 14 to pursue a career in country music. At age 17 her debut album hit number 5 on the Billboard 200. Taylor's second album was released in 2008.

Looking back on her early days in music, Taylor said, "I generally felt that I was running out of time. I wanted to capture these years of my life on an album while they still represented what I was going through."

While Taylor Swift was pursuing her music career, many people the same age were attending college. Why didn't Taylor Swift go to college? She certainly could have afforded the tuition, and would have been accepted had she applied. Could it be that the opportunity cost of attending college was just too high for Taylor Swift to attend college?

To understand, think about what it will cost you to attend college. Let's say that room, board, tuition, books, fees, and living expenses add up to $20,000 a year. Multiplied by four years, that comes to $80,000. Is $80,000

"I generally felt that I was running out of time."
—**Taylor Swift**

really the full cost of your attending college? What would you do if you didn't go to college? Chances are that you'd be earning income

working at a job. For example, perhaps you would work at a full-time job earning $25,000 a year. Multiplied by four years, that's $100,000. Certainly, this forfeited $100,000 is part of the cost of your attending college. Even if you earn some money working part time while in school, you will give up some earnings.

How do the earnings you would give up compare to the earnings that someone like Taylor Swift would give up? Even though the tuition, room, board, and other costs of attending college are roughly the same for everyone who attends the same college, the *opportunity costs* will not be. Some people have higher opportunity costs of attending college than others do. Can you see how it was simply too "costly" for Taylor Swift to attend college?

THINK ABOUT IT You may not be making hundreds of thousands of dollars soon after graduating from high school, but if you decide to go to college, you will have opportunity costs. What will be your opportunity costs of going to college?

Instruct students to read the feature; then tell them to compare the opportunity cost of college for Taylor Swift with the opportunity costs they face by going to college. Ask, How might these costs differ?

ANSWERS TO THINK ABOUT IT Answers will vary. Invite students to share with the class their ideas of what their opportunity costs for going to college might be.

Background Information: Scarcity in Different Cultures

The value of any good, service, or activity may vary over time and across cultures. For instance, in the eighteenth century, a group of colonists offered to "properly educate" some Native American young men at the College of William and Mary, in Williamsburg, Virginia. The Native American elders refused the offer. They had heard that other young men who had been "educated" at colonial schools had returned to their people "neither fit [to be] hunters, warriors, nor councellors [*sic*]; they were totally good for nothing." Remind students that scarcity is related to the value of a good or service for a particular person.

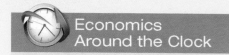
After reading and discussing "Making Choices Means Incurring Opportunity Costs" (pages 8–10), remind students of the 7:43 p.m. scenario in Economics Around the Clock (page 5) and discuss their answers to its question.

Help students understand that when José's friends are unavailable, he has to give up less to study than when his friends are available. In other words, José's opportunity cost for studying is lower when his friends aren't available. We would expect him to study more the lower his opportunity cost for studying happens to be.

Production Possibilities Frontier

Responses will vary but may include the following: A knowledge of opportunity cost grounds us in reality because it helps us to consider that we give up one thing to have something else. Stated differently, no activity, choice, or behavior comes without forfeiting something. Nothing is free or without cost.

$300 and not go to work? An economist would predict that as the opportunity cost of Sunil working at his part-time job increases compared to the benefits of working, Sunil will be less likely to go to work. Based on how economists think about behavior— whether it is Sunil's or your own behavior— the higher the cost of doing something, the less likely it will be done.

EXAMPLE An economics professor at a California college has noticed that more students are absent from class when the surf is good than when it isn't. What might explain these absences? Well, it turns out that quite a few of the professor's students are surfers. When the surf isn't good, the opportunity cost (for the surfer students) is low and they are more likely to come to class. After all, they're not giving up any good waves. But when the surf is good, the opportunity cost for these students is high, and they are less likely to come to class. In other words, the more the students have to give up (in terms of good waves), the higher

production possibilities frontier
A graphic representation of all possible combinations of two goods that an economy can produce.

Economic Facts *and* Fallacies

Production Possibilities Frontier

Suppose a country's economy is located on its production possibilities frontier and is producing 100,000 cars a year and 12 million units of all other goods. A politician running for office claims that if he is elected, he will make sure that national production increases enough to produce more of all goods. Specifically, if he is elected, changes will occur such that, say, 200,000 cars a year are produced along with 14 million units of all other goods. Is this possible?

Given the current production possibilities frontier, it is not possible. If a country's economy is on its production possibilities frontier (such as points A–D in Exhibit 1-2), then it can only move to a point on or below the PPF (such as to E). It cannot move to a point beyond the PPF, such as point F.

Knowing what is and isn't possible in terms of basic economics grounds us in reality and makes us less likely to be swept away by unrealistic promises.

THINK ABOUT IT The PPF helps us to distinguish between what is possible and impossible. What other economic concepts have you learned that can help ground you in reality?

their opportunity cost of attending class, and the less likely they will attend class. The less students have to give up (in terms of good waves), the lower their opportunity cost of attending class, and the more likely they will attend class. ♦

EXAMPLE High school teachers have observed that seniors cut classes more during their final semester than any other time of year. Does this behavior have a "surfer explanation," which is really an opportunity cost explanation?

Yes, the opportunity cost explanation says that by the time seniors' last semester in high school rolls around, many of them have already been admitted to college. In their minds, missing a class here or there won't do much harm to their chances of getting into college. Let's put it the way an economist would: the opportunity cost of going to class is less after a senior has been admitted to college than before he or she has been admitted to college; therefore, we should expect a higher absentee rate (among seniors) when the opportunity cost of attending class is lower.

(Be aware: Some colleges will grant admission but on the condition that a student maintains his or her GPA through the end of the year. In this case, the opportunity cost of attending class is the same before and after the senior is admitted to college.) ♦

One Diagram, Three Economic Concepts

You have probably heard the saying "A picture is worth a thousand words." With that saying in mind, let's look at a diagram that can be used to illustrate the three economic concepts we have discussed thus far: scarcity, choice, and opportunity cost.

The diagram, which is called a **production possibilities frontier** (or PPF, for short), shows all possible combinations of two goods that an economy can produce in a certain period of time. (See Exhibit 1-2.) To keep things simple, we have assumed that only two goods, snowboards and skis, can be produced in an economy. In

Internet Research

Tell students to go to a few commercial websites, such as the sites for their favorite stores or sites that sell discs, and choose products they would like to purchase. Ask students to list the products next to their prices. Then have students list the opportunity cost for each item. What are the most valued opportunities or alternatives students would give up if they bought these items? Are they willing to give up these opportunities for the enjoyment of the products?

Exhibit 1-2(a), you see the four different combinations (A–D) of these two goods that the economy can produce. For example, it can produce 50,000 snowboards and 0 sets of skis, 40,000 snowboards and 20,000 sets of skis, and so on.

We then take each of the four combinations and plot them in Exhibit 1-2(b). If we simply connect these four points, A–D, we have a production possibilities frontier. In other words, the curve you see in Exhibit 1-2(b) is a production possibilities frontier (PPF).

Scarcity and the PPF

Now let's think about scarcity in terms of the PPF. Scarcity, as you know, is the condition in which our wants are greater than the resources available to satisfy them. The PPF—the actual curve in Exhibit 1-2(b)—illustrates this concept. The PPF tells us that certain things are available to us and certain things are not. We can't have everything we want. Any of the points on the PPF is available to us. For example, we can have point B, which represents 40,000 snowboards and 20,000 sets of skis. We can also have the combination of goods represented by any point below the PPF, such as point E. What we can't have—what is unavailable to us because we don't have enough resources to produce it—is the combination of goods represented by point F, which lies beyond the PPF.

Can you see that the PPF (the actual curve) illustrates scarcity by creating two regions? One region—consisting of points on the PPF and below it—represents what is available to us. Another region—consisting of the points beyond the PPF—represents what is unavailable to us. Scarcity tells us we can't have everything we want, and the PPF makes this point visually clear.

Choices and the PPF

Now consider the concept of choice. We stated earlier that because of scarcity, we must make choices. Looking again at Exhibit 1-2(b), we know we cannot be at points A–D at the same time. We must make a choice. Is it going to be A or B or C

or D? Once we make a choice, we are faced with opportunity cost. For example, suppose we narrowed our choices to points B and C and in the end chose point C. What is the opportunity cost of a set of skis over this range? Well, we know that we produce 20,000 more sets of skis by choosing point C over B, but the opportunity cost is producing 15,000 fewer snowboards. In other words, the opportunity cost of 20,000 more sets of skis is 15,000 fewer snowboards.

"There's no such thing as a free lunch."
—Milton Friedman, economist

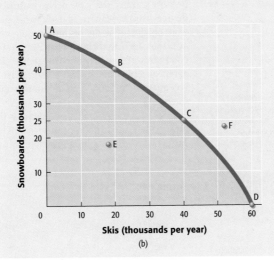

EXHIBIT 1-2 **Production Possibilities Frontier[1]**

Combination	Snowboards	and	Skis
A	50,000		0
B	40,000		20,000
C	25,000		40,000
D	0		60,000

(a)

(b)

[1] The production possibilities frontier is sometimes referred to as a production possibilities curve.

▲ The economy can produce any of the four combinations of snow boards and skis in part (a); these combinations are plotted in part (b). What is the opportunity cost of moving from point A to B? What is the opportunity cost of moving from point C to D? Why is it better for an economy to be at point C than E?

Teaching with Visuals

To ensure that students understand Exhibit 1-2, pick three unlabeled points—perhaps 30,000 snowboards, 15,000 skis, and 25,000 skis—and ask what amounts of snowboards and skis would be produced in these combinations.

Reinforcement Activity

To reinforce understanding of the concepts of choice and opportunity cost, have each student write at the top of one sheet of paper "Buying Choice" and at the top of a second sheet "Opportunity Cost." On the sheet labeled "Buying Choice," the student should draw a picture or paste an advertisement of an item he or she recently purchased. On the sheet labeled "Opportunity Cost," the student should place a picture or advertisement of what he or she could have purchased with the same money.

Prediction Activity

Ask students to suppose that the U.S. Congress makes it illegal to use money (price) as a rationing device. Ask, "Will some other rationing device arise to take its place?"

The answer is yes. Congress can outlaw the use of money (price) as a rationing device, but it cannot eliminate scarcity. It is because of scarcity that there is a need for a rationing device. If price is outlawed as a rationing device, something else will have to arise to ration resources and goods, because scarcity will still exist.

Teaching with Visuals

The opportunity cost of moving from point A to B is 10,000 fewer snowboards. The opportunity cost of moving from point C to D is 25,000 fewer snowboards. It is better for an economy to be at point C than E, because there are more of both snowboards and skis at point C than at point E.

 ## Application Activity

After reading and discussing Section 1, assign the Section Activity in the *Applying the Principles Workbook,* pages 1–4.

Teaching with Visuals

Price is a rationing device in the following sense: if you are willing and able to pay the price, then the good is yours. If you are either unwilling or unable to pay the price, then the good is not yours.

Assess

Quick Quiz

The following true-or-false quiz will help you assess student understanding of the material covered in this section.

1. People have wants—things they desire to obtain. (True)
2. Deep friendship is a tangible good. (False)
3. The concepts scarcity, choice, and competition are linked. (False)
4. Price is a rationing device. (True)
5. Economics is the science that studies the choices of people trying to satisfy their wants in a world of scarcity. (True)

Assessment Book

You will find a quiz for this section in the *Assessment Book,* page 1.

▲ How is the price of jewelry and the price of fruit an example of a rationing device?

A Consequence of Scarcity: The Need for a Rationing Device

Because scarcity exists, we need a **rationing device**—some way to decide who gets what portion of all the resources and goods available. In U.S. society, what is the most common way to determine who gets which goods and how much each person gets? If you guessed "money," you are on the right track.

Price (a certain number of dollars) is the most widely used rationing device in U.S. society. If you are willing and able to pay the price for something, it is yours. If you are either unwilling or unable to pay the price, it won't be yours. By using price, all products are rationed out to the people who are willing and able to pay for them.

If scarcity did not exist, a rationing device would not be necessary. Everyone would get everything he or she wanted.

Another Consequence of Scarcity: Competition

Today's world is very competitive. People compete for jobs, companies compete for profits, and students compete for grades.

rationing device
A means for deciding who gets what portion of the available resources and goods.

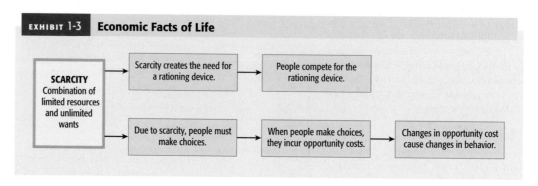

EXHIBIT 1-3	**Economic Facts of Life**

SCARCITY Combination of limited resources and unlimited wants

→ Scarcity creates the need for a rationing device. → People compete for the rationing device.

→ Due to scarcity, people must make choices. → When people make choices, they incur opportunity costs. → Changes in opportunity cost cause changes in behavior.

▲ The science of economics probably would not exist if not for scarcity—an economic fact of life.

Economists believe that competition exists because of scarcity. If enough resources were available to satisfy all our wants, then people would not have to compete for the limited resources.

Economists also believe that competition takes the form of people trying to get more of the rationing device. If price—that is, money or dollars—is the rationing device, people will compete to earn dollars. People compete to earn dollars every day. Suppose three people are up for the same promotion at their business firm. Why do they want the promotion? Certainly, added prestige and responsibility may be part of the answer, but people are more likely to seek and accept promotions that come with more money.

Suppose something other than price—muscular strength, for example—were used as the rationing device. People with more muscular strength would receive more resources and goods than people with less muscular strength. In this scenario,

an economist would predict that people would compete for muscular strength and lift weights each day. The lesson is simple: whatever the rationing device, people will compete for it. See Exhibit 1-3 for a summary of the concepts described in this section.

A Definition of Economics

In this section, you learned about three important and closely related economic concepts: scarcity, choice, and opportunity cost. You also learned something about the way economists think about the world. So, now it's time for a formal definition of the term *economics*. **Economics** is the science that studies the choices people make as they try to satisfy their wants in a world of scarcity. Put another way, you could say that economics is the study of how people use their limited resources to satisfy their unlimited wants.

economics
The science that studies the choices of people trying to satisfy their wants in a world of scarcity.

SECTION 1 ASSESSMENT

Defining Terms

1. Define the following terms:
   a. want
   b. resource
   c. scarcity
   d. opportunity cost
   e. trade-offs
   f. production possibilities frontier
   g. rationing device
   h. economics

Reviewing Facts and Concepts

2. Because scarcity exists, people must make choices. Explain why.

3. Give an example to illustrate how a person may incur an opportunity

cost without paying anyone any money.

4. Is the opportunity cost of attending high school the same for all high school students? Explain why or why not.

5. Describe how the concept of competition relates to the economy.

Critical Thinking

6. If price were not used as a rationing device, would something else have to be used? Why or why not? How might tickets for a concert be rationed without using price?

7. Describe what the world might be like if scarcity did not exist.

8. Explain why choice is a basic economic problem faced by every society.

Applying Economic Concepts

9. Gallagher is planning on going to college in a few months. The tuition is $10,000 a year. Assuming that Gallagher goes to college for four years, is the opportunity cost of his attending college $40,000? Why or why not?

10. Explain how a PPF can be used to illustrate both choice and opportunity cost.

Defining Terms

1. a. **want:** something we desire to have; b. **resource:** anything used to produce goods or services; c. **scarcity:** the condition

in which our wants are greater than the resources available to satisfy those wants; d. **opportunity cost:** the most highly valued opportunity or alternative forfeited, or given up, when a choice is made; e. **trade-offs:** situation in which having more of one thing necessarily means

having less of something else; f. **production possibilities frontier:** a diagram that shows all possible combinations of two goods that an economy can produce; g. **rationing device:** a means for deciding who gets what portion of the available resources and goods;

Reteaching Activity

Guide students in examining choices that they have recently made. For each choice, help students name the scarcity conditions that prompted the choice, the choice made, and the opportunity cost incurred.

Guided Reading

For further reteaching of the key concepts in this section, assign the Outlining Activity and the Just the Facts Handout from the *Guided Reading and Study Guide*, pages 1–3.

h. **economics:** the science that studies the choices of people trying to satisfy their wants in a world of scarcity.

Reviewing Facts and Concepts

2. Scarcity means our wants are greater than the resources available. Because we can't satisfy all our wants, we must choose which ones to satisfy.

3. Answers will vary.

4. No, not all students are giving up the same opportunities to attend high school.

5. Answers will vary.

Critical Thinking

6. As long as scarcity exists, there is a need for a rationing device. Tickets for a concert might be rationed on the basis of first come, first served.

7. People would not have to make choices, rationing devices would not be needed, and people would not need to compete for rationing devices.

8. Answers will vary.

Applying Economic Concepts

9. The opportunity cost of attending college is what a person gives up to attend college. Suppose Gallagher worked full time instead of attending college, earning $23,000 a year. The opportunity cost of attending college would be $92,000 ($23,000 × 4 years). The $40,000 tuition is simply the out-of-pocket expense of attending college.

10. A PPF illustrates scarcity. The choice that must be made because of scarcity reveals the opportunity cost of choosing to produce more of one item than another.

Teacher Support

Focus and Motivate

Section Objectives

After completing this section, students will be able to
- explain how costs and benefits affect decisions;
- identify incentives;
- distinguish between microeconomics and macroeconomics; and
- explain why economists develop theories.

Economics Around the Clock

Kickoff Activity

Direct students to reread the 8:33 a.m. scenario in Economics Around the Clock (page 5) and write their answers to the question that accompanies it. Have them share their responses with the class.

Look for students to mention that some older people have a lower opportunity cost of time. Point out that older people may take their time on the road because they aren't racing to work or other activities.

Activating Prior Knowledge

Tell students to write and share a few sentences describing costs and benefits that they encounter each day. Encourage students to share their sentences with the class.

Visit econ.myemcp.com/videos for videos that will help students better understand the key concepts found in this section.

The Economic Way of Thinking

Focus Questions
- How do costs and benefits affect decisions?
- What are incentives, and why are they important?
- What is the difference between microeconomics and macroeconomics?
- Why do economists develop theories?

Key Terms
marginal
incentive
microeconomics
macroeconomics
theory

Economic Thinking

Economists have a particular way of looking at the world. Just as wearing a pair of sunglasses can change how you view your surroundings (things look darker), so can taking on the economist's way of thinking.

When economists put on their "glasses," they see choices and opportunity costs, as you learned in the last section. Recall that the economics professor saw the surfer students being absent from class because on the day the waves were high, the opportunity cost of attending class was higher than on other days. In other words, in addition to seeing a student, a surfer, the surfboard, the beach, and the waves, the professor "saw" (in his mind's eye) opportunity cost too.

One of the objectives of this book is to get you to understand and use the economist's way of thinking. It is not the only way to look at the world. It is, however, one way of looking at the world that often does help you understand the world you live in. This new way of thinking will also, in many cases, help you get more of what you want in life.

Thinking in Terms of Costs and Benefits

According to an economist, almost everything we do involves costs (negatives, disadvantages) and benefits (positives, advantages). There are costs and benefits to learning economics, eating a hamburger, driving your car, asking a person out on a date, donating your car, taking a vacation, and talking on the telephone.

Making Cost-Benefit Decisions

According to the economist, a person will want to do a particular activity only if the benefits are greater than the costs. For example, a person will buy a computer only if the benefits of buying the computer are expected to be greater than the costs of buying it. If the costs are perceived to be greater than the benefits, then the person will not purchase the computer.

Suppose a student graduates from high school and decides to go to college. In college, she decides to major in psychology. What do we know about her choice of a

Differentiating Instruction

English Language Learners
To help students who are English language learners, the following resources are provided as part of the *Economics: New Ways of Thinking* program:
- a Spanish glossary in the *Student Text*
- Spanish versions of the Chapter Summaries on an audio disc

major? According to the economist, we know that when the student made the decision to major in psychology, she thought the benefits to her of majoring in psychology would be greater than the costs. When economists study a problem by weighing the costs and the benefits, they refer to this process as *cost-benefit analysis.*

EXAMPLE John has been studying four hours for the English test he has tomorrow. It's now 10:30 p.m., and he is considering studying one more hour. The benefits to studying another hour might be a higher grade on the test. The cost of studying another hour is one less hour of sleep, which could negatively affect his ability to concentrate during the test (which, in turn, could negatively affect his grade). John thinks the costs of studying an additional hour are greater than the benefits, so he goes to bed. ♦

Thinking at the Margin

An important economic term will come up throughout this text when discussing costs and benefits. That word is **marginal**, which means "additional."

Why is the term *marginal* so important? It is because economists believe that when people make decisions, they do not think of the *total* costs and benefits involved in the decision. Instead, they think about the *additional,* or *marginal,* costs and benefits.

EXAMPLE You have just eaten two chicken tacos for lunch and are trying to decide whether to go back for a third. You are still hungry, but if you get another taco now, you will have no money left for a snack after school. Are you really that hungry? ♦

In making the decision described above, you are comparing the *marginal benefits* of one more (an additional) taco against the *marginal costs* of one more taco. If you decide that the marginal benefits are greater than the marginal costs, then you will buy the additional taco. If, on the other hand, you decide that the marginal costs are greater than the marginal benefits, then you will keep your money and go without

the additional taco. An economist would say that you were "making decisions at the margin"—a process you will encounter in several of the following chapters.

Thinking in Terms of Incentives

Economists often speak of *incentives* in reference to *actions.* An **incentive** is something that encourages or motivates a person to take action. For example, suppose that Amy lives in a country where every dollar she earns is taxed (by government) at 100 percent. With a tax rate of 100 percent, an economist might argue that Amy does not have an incentive to produce anything for sale. Why work all day to produce a good that is sold for, say $100, when you will have to turn over the full $100 to the government in taxes?

Now let's lower the tax rate in Amy's country from 100 percent to 20 percent. In your mind, should the lower tax rate provide Amy with an incentive to work

marginal
In economics, marginal means "additional."

incentive
Something that encourages or motivates a person to take action.

Teach

Discussion Starter

Tell students to think about decisions that they made recently. Ask if they considered the costs and benefits of the decisions before making them. Invite volunteers to share their decisions and the costs and benefits they have identified. Urge the class to suggest other costs and benefits for those decisions. Finally, ask whether the volunteers would make the same decisions, after considering the additional costs and benefits.

Thinking Like an Economist

Maximizing Net Benefits

You are more likely to see a penny than a $10 bill on the sidewalk, because whereas the cost of picking up a penny and a $10 bill are the same, the benefits of picking up a penny are less than the benefits of picking up a $10 bill.

Reinforcement Activity

Marginal cost is an important concept in economics. Tell students that when they hear or read the word *marginal,* they should think of the word *additional.* In economics, *additional* is a synonym for *marginal.* Suggest that students reread the definition of *marginal cost.*

Cause and Effect

To fully understand economics, students need to understand scarcity. To reinforce the concepts of scarcity and trade-offs, tell students to imagine that they have a big economics test tomorrow and their friends want them to go to a movie tonight. They are busy with other activities until 7:00 tonight, and they need to get up by 7:00 tomorrow morning. Going to the movie will take about four hours. Students need to study at least three hours for the test. They also need to sleep eight hours. Have each student make trade-offs with his or her time tonight: What does the student give up—studying, going out with friends, or sleep? What are the effects of his or her trade-offs?

Economics Around the Clock

Remind students of the 8:45 p.m. scenario in Economics Around the Clock (page 5) and discuss their answers to the question it poses.

Point out that buying a car may make it impossible to take a vacation (especially a vacation in some faraway place). Life is full of trade-offs. More of one thing (a car) often means less of something else (a vacation).

Teaching with Visuals

These images represent the trade-off between government spending for health care and for the military.

Economics *in the* Real World

Yes, there are probably both costs and benefits of "staying in contact with more people." The benefits might be feeling closer to the people in your life, networking with more people (when it comes to getting jobs), and so on. The costs might be the feeling that you have to keep up with so many people, which may be burdensome.

and produce? An economist will say that it should. The lower tax rate should encourage or motivate Amy toward a particular action—working and producing—because it allows her to keep 80 cents out of every dollar she earns.

EXAMPLE Kenneth, who is 15 years old and lives with his parents, does not have an incentive to mow the lawn. There is absolutely nothing that encourages or motivates him to do this work. Then one day, Kenneth's father offers him $10 to mow the lawn. The $10—the money—is an incentive for Kenneth to mow the lawn. It encourages or motivates him to perform this action. ◆

EXAMPLE Jimmy lives in country A, where people are not permitted to own property, so Jimmy rents a house from the government. Adam lives in country B, where people are permitted to own property, so Adam owns his house. Who is more likely to take care of the house he lives in? The answer is Adam. The reasoning is simple: Adam can sell the house he lives in (because he owns it); Jimmy cannot sell the house he lives in. Any damage Adam does to his house will lower the selling price of the house. What's the moral of the story? Private property ownership acts as an incentive to take care of things. ◆

Economics *in the* Real World

Does Social Media Use Make It Easier to Get Groups Together?

The use of social media has lowered the cost of organizing and bringing them together. For example, suppose you want to arrange a Saturday soccer game. You send a group text instead of asking each possible player individually.

Let's say you need an even larger group of participants. You are part of a charity organization and you need many volunteers. You might send the text asking for volunteers to all of your contact list. You may also ask them to pass on the information to people on their contact list. Texting allows

you to speed up the delivery of an old-fashioned chain letter.

With a chain letter, you would send it to 10 people and ask each person to send it to 10 additional people (and so on). It might take weeks to contact 1,000 people.

Consider how much more quickly you can reach 1,000 people if you start with one text to 10 people. They will receive the text in a matter of seconds, and within a few minutes or so, they

will have sent the text to 100 people. Within another few minutes, you will have already reached 1,000 people.

What took a chain letter weeks to do can be accomplished by social media in a matter of minutes. The use of social media has made it very easy and relatively costless to organize a group in a matter of minutes!

THINK ABOUT IT Social networking sites, such as Facebook and Twitter, allow people to stay in contact with more people than they could likely stay in touch with otherwise. Are there both costs and benefits to staying in contact with more people? What might the benefits be? What might the costs be?

Cooperative Learning

Divide students into groups of four or five, and have each group develop one question about something that happens at school. Questions can be as simple as "Why do students bring their lunches when food is available at school?" and "Why do students bring cell phones to school?" Each group should then come up with one theory that answers the question and can be tested in class. Each group should develop a way of testing the theory, predict an outcome for the test, and conduct the test. When groups have finished testing their theories, give them class time to compile the results and to prepare graphs showing their findings. Then have each group share its work with the class. Also mention that the process of proposing and testing a theory and then analyzing and modifying a theory is a description of the scientific method.

Thinking in Terms of Trade-Offs

As you learned in Section 1, trade-offs involve opportunity costs. When more of one thing necessarily means less of something else, we have a trade-off. For example, when we drive our cars, we pollute the air. One way to cut down on the amount of pollution is to drive less. More driving means less clean air, and less driving means more clean air. More of one thing (driving) necessarily means less of something else (clean air). We have a trade-off between driving and clean air.

Individuals Face Trade-Offs

You might notice that when trade-offs arise in life, you sometimes have to stop and think about what course of action you want to take.

EXAMPLE Suppose Mary Ann loves to travel, and she has been given the chance to study abroad in South America during her senior year. She wants to study abroad for two reasons. (1) She has never been to South America and craves new experiences. (2) She wants to become better at speaking Spanish. So, Mary Ann applies to the study abroad program and is accepted. But does Mary Ann face a trade-off? Sure she does. On one hand, if she does go to South America, then she will miss her family and friends (that's bad), but she will get to meet new people and experience new things (that's good). On the other hand, if she doesn't go to South America, she will be able to attend prom and graduation (that's good), but then she misses the opportunity to work on her Spanish-speaking skills (that's bad). No matter what Mary Anne decides, she gets to do something she likes and something she doesn't like. She gets more of one thing (new experiences) and less of another (time with friends) if she chooses to go abroad. If she chooses not to go abroad then she still gets more of one thing (time with friends) and less of another (new experiences). ♦

Societies Face Trade-Offs

Just as individuals face trade-offs, so do societies. At any time, the federal government has only so much money from tax revenues. If more tax dollars are spent on, say, education, then fewer tax dollars can be spent on roads and highways. If more tax dollars go for national defense, then fewer dollars are left for health and welfare.

Trade-offs sometimes lead to conflicts in society. One group may think it's better to spend more money on national defense and less on health and welfare. Another group might prefer the opposite. A conflict arises. In a household, some members of the family might prefer to spend more of the family budget on boats, TVs, and computers. Other members might prefer to spend more of the family budget on education, vacations, and furniture. A conflict arises.

> *"Most of economics can be summarized in four words: people respond to incentives."*
> —Steven Landsburg, economist

Thinking in Terms of What Would Have Been

Economists often think in terms of "what would have been." It is important to be able to think in these terms, because only then do we know the opportunity cost for "what is."

The Story of the Broken Window

The well-known economic journalist Henry Hazlitt once wrote a book in which he told the story of a boy who threw a rock through a baker's shop window. In the story, the townspeople gather around the baker's shop and complain about the actions of today's youth. Then one person offers quite a different perspective. He says that because the boy broke the window, the baker now has to buy a window, which means the window maker will now have more business. And because the window maker has more business, he will earn more money. And because he has more money, he will spend more money. And because he spends more money, someone else in the town will sell

Reinforcement Activity

Instruct each student to select one extracurricular activity or hobby in which he or she participates and then prepare a two-column chart that lists the benefits and costs of this activity or hobby. Invite students to share their charts with the class, and encourage the class to suggest other benefits and costs that could be added to each chart.

Thinking Like an Economist

There are really two lessons in the story about the baker's window, and the lessons are related: (1) Money that is spent to purchase one thing cannot later be used to purchase something else. For example, money that goes to purchase a new window cannot then go to purchase a new suit. (2) To understand things fully, we need to be aware of not only what is but also of what would have been.

Background Information: The United States and the World Market

In recent years, the United States has dominated the world market so strongly that trade embargoes from the United States alone have caused some countries to suffer economically. The United States is so powerful economically that recent crashes in other world markets have barely affected the U.S. economic market. In an effort to combine economic power, some Europeans nations banded together in the European Union. Direct each student to research the European Union and write a one-page report on its policies, focusing on how those policies lead to trade-offs in the world market.

Answers will vary.

Cause and Effect

In the United Kingdom, a regulation specifies that noncitizens with work visas cannot stay in the country beyond a certain period of time. The intended effect of the regulation is to keep the supply of labor in the country lower than it would be if noncitizens were allowed to work in the country indefinitely. An unintended effect of the regulation is that it has created a market for bogus marriages. Now a "fixer" will arrange a marriage between a noncitizen and a citizen, because if married to a citizen, a noncitizen can stay in the country. Soon after this arranged marriage, the husband and wife go their separate ways.

▲ Building and improving highways is expensive. What sorts of things might not exist as a result of this highway being built?

more goods, and on and on. So, says the person with the different perspective, what the boy has done is a good thing: he has generated economic activity for the town. After listening to this different view of the situation, the townspeople are happy. What had at first seemed like a tragedy (a boy breaking a window) now clearly appears to be the beginning of an economic boom for the town.

What do you think? Did the boy set off a chain reaction that will create work, income, and profits for many people in the town? And if so, should the townspeople hope that more boys throw more rocks through more windows?

Before you begin encouraging people to throw rocks in your town, stop and ask, as the economist did, this simple question: if the baker didn't have to buy a new window, what would he have purchased instead? Suppose that he would have spent the money for a new suit. But after paying for a new window, the baker will have no

money for a suit, so the suit maker will earn less money (than otherwise). Without that money, the suit maker will make fewer purchases, which will translate into fewer sales for others, and so on.

Simply put, the economist urges us to see "what would have been" if the boy had not broken the window. The economist urges us to see more than "what will be" because the boy broke the window.

It is easy for all of us to see "what will be": we will actually see with our eyes the window maker selling a window and getting paid for it. It is not so easy, though, to see "what would have been." We can't actually see the suit maker not selling the suit.

Seeing with Your Mind

It takes a certain kind of vision to see "what would have been." It takes your mind (not your eyes) to see what would have been. You have to think your way to understanding that one new window means one fewer suit.

EXAMPLE Suppose the federal government sets aside funds for a new interstate highway system. Thousands of people are hired to work on the project. Local newspapers in the towns along the highway write many stories about all the increased job activity, and soon there are more and better highways in the area. It is easy to see the "what will be" benefits of more jobs and better roads.

We need to remind ourselves, however, that someone—namely, taxpayers—had to pay for the new highway system. What did these taxpayers give up by paying the taxes to fund the new highways? They gave up the opportunity to buy goods for themselves, such as clothes, computers, and books. We now begin to think in terms of all the products that "would have been" produced and consumed had the highways not been built. If, say, more clothes would have been produced instead of highways, more people would have worked in the clothing industry and fewer would have worked in highway construction. ◆

Cross-Curricular Activity

Team with a history teacher to discuss the concept of unintended effects as it relates to the mobilization of women in the U.S. workforce during World War II. During the war, the government supported a campaign of domestic propaganda to make working women appear patriotic. Participation in the workforce by women during the war established a precedent.

The history teacher can discuss the intended effects of the government's efforts to increase female participation in the workplace, allowing you to lead an analysis of some of the unintended effects (increased economic power of women, increased political involvement, the Equal Rights Amendment movement, etc.).

Do Seatbelts Cause Accidents?

Most states have mandatory seatbelt laws for drivers. Seatbelt legislation was passed to save lives. That was its intent.

Soon after states started adopting mandatory seatbelt laws, an economist undertook a study. He wanted to find out if seatbelt laws really do save lives. His study showed that the number of car deaths before seatbelt laws was the same as the number of car deaths after seatbelt laws. This finding perplexed him, because common sense tells us that if you are in an accident, you have a better chance of surviving if you are wearing your seatbelt.

So, what explained the economist's finding? The answer lies in this simple equation:

Number of car deaths = Number of accidents × Probability of being killed in car accident

Seatbelt laws lowered the probability of being killed in a car accident. But if they lowered this probability and the number of car deaths stayed the same (before and after seatbelt laws), then the only thing that can explain this finding is that the number of accidents had to rise.

This is exactly what the economist found. One *unintended effect* of seatbelt laws is that the number of accidents increased.

(Economists are interested in *unintended effects*.)

Why did the number of accidents increase? Some people have suggested that drivers feel safer wearing a seatbelt and that drivers who feel safe are more likely to take risks on the road than drivers who do not feel safe. (Might drivers in large SUVs take more risks than drivers in Honda Civics?) Obviously, to be safe while driving a car, you should wear your seatbelt and drive as carefully as you would if you weren't wearing your seatbelt. In other words, don't let wearing a seatbelt lull you into driving recklessly.

THINK ABOUT IT The intended effect of placing a safety cap on a medication bottle is to prevent children from getting into the medicine and eating it because they mistakenly think it is candy. What might be an unintended effect of placing safety caps on medications?

ANSWERS TO THINK ABOUT IT Answers will vary. Students might suggest that safety caps have made it difficult for some people to open medications.

Clarifying Terms

Check student understanding of the following term by asking them to use it in a sentence: *unintended effects.* Ensure that students recognize that this term means "the result of action that was neither the original intent nor an anticipated consequence."

Internet Research

Tell students to browse the website for Project Vote Smart (http://econ.emcp.net/votesmart) to learn about the spending choices that the federal government has to make each year. Ask each student to write paragraphs answering these questions: What types of spending decisions does the federal government have to make, and how do those decisions relate to the concept of scarcity? On what types of things should the government spend its limited resources?

Thinking in Terms of Unintended Effects

Economists often look for the unintended effects of actions that people take. Has anything ever turned out differently from what you intended?

EXAMPLE On an average day, a shoe store sells 100 pairs of shoes at an average price of $40 a pair, thereby earning $4,000. One day, the store owner decides to raise the price of shoes from an average of $40 to $50. What do you think he expects the effect of his action to be? He probably expects to

> "The art of economics consists in looking not merely at the immediate but at the longer [long-run] effects of any act or policy."
> —Henry Hazlitt, American economic journalist

increase his earnings from $4,000 a day to some greater amount, perhaps to $5,000 (100 pairs of shoes × $50 = $5,000). The store owner might be surprised by the results. At a higher price, it is likely that he will sell fewer pairs of shoes. Suppose that at a price of $50 a pair, the owner sells an average of 70 pairs of shoes a day. What are his average daily earnings now? ($3,500 = 70 pairs of shoes × $50.) The owner did

not intend for things to turn out this way; he intended to increase his earnings by raising the price of shoes. The decrease in his earnings is an unintended effect of his action. ♦

EXAMPLE Suppose that U.S. citizens are buying some Japanese goods (such as Japanese cars) and that Japanese citizens are buying some U.S. goods (such as U.S. computers). Then things change: the Japanese government decides to place a $200 tax on every U.S. computer sold in Japan. People in Japan who buy U.S. computers will have to pay $200 more than they would have paid without the tax. Why might the Japanese government impose this tax? It may want Japanese computers to outsell U.S. computers, and it may want to generate higher profits and greater employment in the Japanese computer industry. To accomplish these goals, the government deliberately makes U.S. computers more expensive than Japanese computers by placing the tax on U.S. computers. This action ends up hurting U.S. computer companies, because they sell fewer computers.

The United States could decide to retaliate by placing a tax on Japanese cars sold in the United States. Japanese cars would be more expensive, and fewer would be sold. This action would hurt Japanese car companies.

Do you see what has happened? Japan takes an action—placing a tax on U.S. computers sold in Japan—hoping that the Japanese people will buy more Japanese computers and fewer U.S. computers (the intended effect of the action). The intended effect is realized: the Japanese people actually do buy more Japanese computers and fewer U.S. computers. But there is an unintended effect too: the United States places a tax on Japanese cars, which ends up hurting Japanese car companies. When the Japanese placed a tax on U.S. computers, they did not intend to harm Japanese car companies. ♦

Do unintended effects matter? The answer is yes, they matter a great deal. That is why, for any action, economists think

▲ Many of these people are unemployed and looking for work. How might unemployment be an example of an unintended effect?

Background Information: Microeconomics and Macroeconomics

Microeconomics is the study of human choices and behavior as they relate to relatively small economic units, and macroeconomics is the study of the way in which choices and behavior relate to far larger economic units, such as the entire U.S. economy. For example, microeconomics examines how a tax change might affect a single firm's output, and macroeconomics examines how that tax change might affect the entire economy's output. Microeconomics studies the individual, the household, the company. Macroeconomics studies whole economic systems and how different sectors interact. National economic policies are part of the study of macroeconomics.

in terms of both intended and unintended effects. Can you see the advantage of being able to think about and anticipate unintended effects when making decisions?

Thinking in Terms of the Small and the Big

Economics is divided into two branches: microeconomics and macroeconomics. In **microeconomics**, economists look at the "small picture." They study the behavior and choices of relatively small economic units, such as individuals and single business firms. Economists who deal with **macroeconomics** look at the "big picture," studying behavior and choices as they relate to the entire economy. (See Exhibit 1-4.)

For example, in microeconomics, an economist would study and discuss the unemployment that exists in a particular industry, such as the car industry; in macroeconomics, an economist would investigate the unemployment that exists in the nation. In microeconomics, an economist would look at the buying behavior of consumers in regard to a single product, such as computers; an economist dealing in macroeconomics would study the buying behavior of consumers in regard to all goods.

We might say that the tools of macroeconomics are telescopes, while the tools of microeconomics are microscopes. Macroeconomics stands back from the trees to see the forest. Microeconomics gets up close and examines the tree itself, including its bark, its branches, and the soil in which it grows. In this book, you will learn to look at the world from both "micro" and "macro" perspectives.

Thinking in Terms of Theories

Some questions have obvious answers, and others do not. For example, if you hold a ball in your right hand and ask someone what will happen if you let go of it, the person will likely say that the ball will drop to the ground. Right answer. If the classroom clock reads 10:12 and you ask

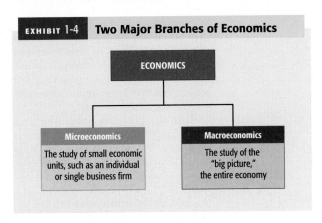

EXHIBIT 1-4   Two Major Branches of Economics

ECONOMICS

Microeconomics
The study of small economic units, such as an individual or single business firm

Macroeconomics
The study of the "big picture," the entire economy

▲ Economists divide economics into two major branches: microeconomics and macroeconomics.

someone in the class what time it is, that person will say 10:12. Again, right answer.

Now suppose you ask someone any of the following questions:

- Why is the crime rate higher in some countries than in other countries?
- What causes the stock market to rise or fall?
- What causes some nations to be rich and others to be poor?

You probably would agree that these questions have no obvious, easy answers.

Because some economic questions do not have obvious answers, economists build theories to explain how things work. A **theory** is an explanation of how something works. Think of a theory as a mechanism that an economist uses to answer a question that has no obvious, easy answer. Here are only five of hundreds of questions for which economists have built theories:

1. What causes inflation?
2. What causes the unemployment rate to rise or fall?
3. How do business firms operate?
4. What causes the prices of goods and services to rise, fall, or remain stable?
5. Why do countries experience good economic times in some years and bad economic times in other years?

microeconomics
The branch of economics that deals with human behavior and choices as they relate to relatively small units—individuals, business firms, and single markets.

macroeconomics
The branch of economics that deals with human behavior and choices as they relate to the entire economy.

theory
An explanation of how something works, designed to answer a question for which there is no obvious answer.

Point out to students that although the word *micro* means "small," microeconomics often deals with very large players in the economy. The activities of a huge corporation such as General Motors are considered a topic of microeconomics, even though the company output exceeds that of some nations.

Discussion Starter

Discuss with students their understanding of the word *theory*. Some students will know the word from science classes. How are the definitions of theory for economists and scientists similar? How are they different?

Reinforcement Activity

Ask students to pose questions for which they have no answers. Then ask how they would go about creating proper theories to form answers to those questions. Also create some questions about situations like those presented in the text (e.g., Why do people get sick after operations?), and ask students to propose theories based on those situations. Remind students that a theory should be judged by how well it predicts the outcome.

Background Information: Economic Theories

Many advancements in technology and science started out as theories. Have each student research one familiar scientific or technological advancement and then present a report on who developed the theory that led to the discovery.

Then present a couple of economic theories from Keynes, Locke, and others to show students that theories are developed in various fields.

After reading and discussing Section 2, assign the Section Activity in the *Applying the Principles Workbook,* pages 5–8.

Assess

Quick Quiz

The following true-or-false quiz will help you assess student understanding of the material covered in this section.

1. There are costs and benefits to almost everything we do. (True)

2. A theory does not explain anything. (False)

3. Economists must think of what would have been. (True)

4. In macroeconomics, economists look at the small picture. (False)

5. Theories should omit everything that is unnecessary. (True)

EXAMPLE Suppose you are living in the days before anyone has heard the word *calorie.* Over a period of three years, you notice that your weight changes. At one time, you weigh 140 pounds, then 145 pounds, and then 155 pounds. You wonder why you are gaining weight.

Then along comes a person who gives you a simplified explanation of what is happening. She says that there are things called "calories" and that we can measure food in terms of how many calories it has. Some foods have more calories than others. She then says that every day you use up, or burn, calories when you walk, run, and clean the house. You even burn them, she says, when you are sitting still on the couch watching television. Finally, she says that your weight depends on how many calories you take in compared to how many you burn. If you consume more calories than you burn, you will gain weight. ◆

▲ Albert Einstein was known for constructing theories—theories of how the physical world works. Economists build theories too, as do sociologists, chemists, and others.

This calorie theory is used to explain one's weight. You will notice that this theory explains how things work (how your body takes in and uses up calories) to answer a question (why do people gain weight?). All theories have this structure. A theory always offers some explanation of how things work to answer a question that does not have an obvious answer.

A Student Asks

QUESTION: *I've always thought that theories were difficult to understand because they contain a lot of mathematics. Is this correct?*

ANSWER: *Some theories contain mathematics, but many do not. Your impression of a theory is the common one. Many people think that a theory has to be abstract, mathematical, and almost impossible to understand. But this is a misconception.*

To a large extent, a theory is simply a "best guess" offered to explain something. Anyone can build a theory; in fact, you may (unknowingly) do so.

Suppose your best friend always eats lunch with you. Then one day, he doesn't. You may wonder what explains his change in behavior.

Once you have a question in your mind—What led to the change in his behavior?—you are on your way to building a theory. Your "best guess" may be that he doesn't like you anymore, that you said something to upset him, or something altogether different. Trying to answer your question by offering your "best guess" is really no different from an economist creating a theory about some aspect of economics. The economist puts forth his or her "best guess" as to what causes inflation, high interest rates, or economic growth.

Is It Reasonable?

Many people evaluate a theory based on whether it seems reasonable. However, many theories that at first seemed very unreasonable to people turned out to be correct. Think about how it might have sounded to you if you had lived before microscopes were invented and someone told you that people were getting sick because of tiny "things" (which today we call *germs*) that no one could see. You might have thought that sounded ridiculous. Or suppose you had lived during the days of the Roman Empire and someone proposed the "round Earth" theory to answer a question. You might have said, "There is no such thing as a round Earth!"

Does It Predict Accurately?

Scientists believe that we should evaluate theories based not on how they sound to us or whether they seem right but on how well they predict. If they predict well, then we should accept them; if they predict poorly, then we should not. No doubt, as you read this text, you will come across an economic theory here or there that you think sounds wrong. You are urged to adopt the scientific attitude and hold off judging any economic theory until you learn how well it predicts.

SECTION 2 ASSESSMENT

Defining Terms

1. Define:
   a. marginal
   b. incentive
   c. microeconomics
   d. macroeconomics
   e. theory
2. Use the term *marginal costs* correctly in a sentence.

Reviewing Facts and Concepts

3. According to economists, almost everything we do has costs and benefits. Identify the costs and benefits of each of the following: getting a dental checkup and getting an extra hour of sleep.

4. Give an example of an unintended effect.
5. What is the difference between microeconomics and macroeconomics?

Critical Thinking

6. If there were zero opportunity costs to everything you did, would you ever face a trade-off? Explain.
7. What do you miss seeing or understanding if you don't think in terms of "what would have been"?
8. Describe the types of economic incentives that you see in your own society.

9. Evaluate the costs and benefits of charitable giving.

Applying Economic Concepts

10. Describe a recent situation in which you weighed the marginal costs versus the marginal benefits to make a decision.
11. Analyze the costs and benefits of the use of personal property (such as a car).
12. Identify the costs and benefits of the disposal of personal property (such as a car).

Assessment Book

You will find a quiz for this section in the *Assessment Book,* page 2.

Reteaching Activity

Use the Section Assessment to gauge which students may need reteaching on this section. Have these students reread the definition of *theory,* think of a question with no obvious answer (e.g., Why is the sky blue?), and pose a theory to explain the phenomenon.

Guided Reading

For further reteaching of the key concepts in this section, assign the Outlining Activity and the Just the Facts Handout from the *Guided Reading and Study Guide,* pages 4–6.

---

unintended effect is that Caroline develops a rash and itching because she is allergic to the antibiotic.)

5. Microeconomics concerns the small picture; macroeconomics concerns the big picture. Microeconomics looks at a component of the economy; macroeconomics looks at the entire economy.

Critical Thinking

6. No. In a trade-off, you give up one thing to get more of another. If there were zero opportunity cost to everything, you would never give up anything to get something else. Hence, you would never encounter a trade-off.
7. You miss understanding that there is an opportunity cost.
8. Answers may vary.
9. Answers will vary.

Applying Economic Concepts

10. Answers will vary.
11. Answers will vary slightly, but students should identify the costs as the cost of insurance, gas, and maintenance; benefits would include access to transportation.
12. Answers will vary slightly, but students should identify that the costs of disposing of personal property could include the removal or recycling fee; benefits could be tax deductions (for donations) or the absence of costs (maintenance, insurance, etc.).

SECTION 2 ASSESSMENT ANSWERS

Defining Terms

1. a. marginal: in economics, "additional"; **b. incentive:** something that encourages or motivates a person to act; **c. microeconomics:** the branch of economics that studies behavior and choices as they relate to small units; **d. macroeconomics:** the branch of economics that studies behavior and choices as they relate to the entire economy; **e. theory:** an explanation of how something works.
2. Answers will vary.

Reviewing Facts and Concepts

3. Answers will vary.
4. Answers will vary. (*Sample answer:* Caroline takes an antibiotic to cure an infection. An

Discussion Starter

Ask students if they have savings accounts. Do students who have savings accounts know how much interest they are earning on their savings? Do they deposit money in their savings accounts on a regular basis? Do students who have not saved any money believe they could have saved some had they made doing so a priority?

Research Activity

After students have read the "Save Now or Save Later?" section in this feature, have them use a compound interest calculator to find out how much they will have if they save $2,000 at various interest rates from ages 22 to 65 (43 years), compounded quarterly. For example, at 4%, they will have $11,074.05; at 3%, $7,230.68; and at 2%, $4,716.20. Emphasize the importance of shopping for the best available interest rate.

Spend a Little Now or a Lot More Later?

Many of us underestimate the power of saving. That's because we don't realize the large gains people can earn by saving—especially if they start saving when they are young.

Save Now or Save Later?

You are probably 17 or 18 years old if you are reading this book. Suppose you go to college and when you are 22, you get your first full-time job, earning $45,000 a year. Also suppose that in that first year after graduating college—and only in that year—you save $2,000 at an annual interest rate of 5 percent, and your interest is compounded quarterly (which means you earn an interest payment every three months). How much money will you have when you retire at age 65? The answer is $16,942. In other words, a one-time savings of $2,000 when you are 22 will turn into $16,942 by the time you are 65.

It is likely, however, that if you are able to save money when you are 22, you will be able to save some when you are 23, 24, and so on. So, let's suppose that instead of saving $2,000 only once, when you are 22, you save $2,000 every year between the ages of 22 and 65. We will assume again that your annual interest rate of return is 5 percent and that interest is compounded quarterly. How much will money will you have at 65? The answer is $319,526.46.

Now, just to show you how much it matters to start saving when you are young, suppose that instead of beginning to save when you are 22, you wait until you are 40 to start saving. At 40 and each year after until you reach 65, you save $2,000. How much money would you have at 65? $106,694.68. So, how important is it to begin saving early? By setting aside just an additional $36,000 ($2,000 a year for each year between age 22 and age 40), you end up with an extra $212,831.78.

▼ Saving now—even if you save only a small amount—will pay off later. **Have you opened a savings account yet?**

Cooperative Learning

After students have read "Smoking or Saving?" on page 25, divide them into groups of three or four. Tell each group to brainstorm a list of items they could give up entirely or reduce in number of purchases and to estimate an amount of savings that would result. After 15 minutes, have the groups report their lists and totals to the class. Discuss realistic expectations for saving.

people think, the same as not spending. Instead, it is postponed spending or future spending. In other words, because you have saved today, you have more money to spend in the future. Your decision is not between spending and saving; your decision is between spending now and spending more later.

Your Personal Economics Activity

1. In a one-page essay, explain how the amount of savings you have can allow you greater flexibility in your life. Provide examples and logical reasoning to support your work.
2. Analyze why understanding interest is important when deciding where to allocate your savings.

▲ Most of us spend small amounts of money every day that could become large amounts later in life. What could you give up in favor of making regular deposits to your savings account?

Smoking or Saving?

Now let's look at saving in a different way. Recently, a person who purchased a pack of cigarettes every other day ended up buying 182 packs a year at a cost of $6 a pack. That's a total of $1,092 per year spent on cigarettes. If that person had simply saved that $1,092 each year, instead of spending it on cigarettes, he or she would have ended up with $37,468.17 after 25 years (at an interest rate of 2 percent, compounded quarterly). What is the opportunity cost to smoking? Is smoking costly? It appears not only to be costly when it comes to your health but also when it comes to your wallet.

One Last Point

If you find it hard to save, then perhaps you need to know what saving really is. It is not, as some

My Personal Economics Action Plan

Here are some points you may want to consider and some guidelines you might want to put into practice:

☑ **1.** The younger you are when you start to save on a regular basis, the more money you'll have when you retire.

Even though I only work part time now, I will begin saving at least part of my income.

☑ **2.** Saving regularly (each year) generates substantially more interest income than saving irregularly (every two or three years).

When I have a full-time job, I will set aside ___ percent of my income every pay period.

☑ **3.** If you are currently spending money on something you would be better off not spending money on (think "cigarettes"), try to save that money instead. Over time, it can add up to quite a hefty sum.

By giving up ___ I will save a minimum of ___ a month.

Note: You can use many of the compound interest calculators on the Web to figure how much your savings will have grown by the time you reach 55, 60, 65, or 70. The calculator used to obtain the numbers you just read is at http://econ.emcp.net/compound_interest. If, by chance, that calculator is not there when you look, simply go to any browser search engine and key in "compound interest calculator." You will have a long list of relevant calculators to choose from.

Teaching with Visuals

Student answers will vary. Examples will likely include entertainment and food (such as movies, concerts, and coffee).

Discussion Starter

To help students realize the power of compound interest and saving, ask them to list the things they might buy with the $106,694.68 that they will have at retirement if they begin saving $2,000 a year at the age of 40. Then ask them to list what they might buy if they begin saving $2,000 a year at age 22 and therefore have $319,526.46 at retirement. Make sure students realize that they will be able to purchase all these additional items as a result of setting aside just an additional $36,000.

My Personal Economics Action Plan Have students survey adults they know to determine how these people are saving money. If students find that the adults are not saving, they should ask whether the adults feel that they could save if they made doing so a priority. Students may want to prepare for the survey by developing a list of items that most people purchase but could do without and then identifying the resulting possible savings. Students could ask the adults which of those items they use and which they might stop purchasing to save money. Ask students to report their survey findings to the class.

Grading Rubric: One-page Essay

1 2 3 4 5   Content identified how savings benefited the account holder.

1 2 3 4 5   Content was supported with examples and logical reasoning.

Grading Rubric: Analysis

1 2 3 4 5   Student identified the importance of interest when allocating savings.

Focus and Motivate

Section Objectives

After completing this section, students will be able to

▶ describe the different ways economists talk about goods;

▶ identify services;

▶ list the four types of resources; and

▶ explain why labor and entrepreneurship are different categories of resources.

Kickoff Activity

Write the following statement on the board: "Write down two particular items in the classroom, and list the materials or resources that were used to produce these goods."

Activating Prior Knowledge

Encourage students to share their responses to the Kickoff Activity. Make sure they understand that the physical makeup of a good is not the only resource that goes into producing it. Explain that when we talk about goods, we should think about all the resources that went into producing them.

Teach

Discussion Starter

Have each student give two examples of each factor of production. Emphasize that in economics, the word *land* means more than just a "plowed field"; it also refers to all the resources found in nature, including water and minerals.

 Visit econ.myemcp.com/videos for videos that will help students better understand the key concepts found in this section.

Basic Economic Language

Focus Questions

▶ What are the different ways that economists talk about "goods"?

▶ What are services?

▶ What are the four types of resources or factors of production?

▶ Why are labor and entrepreneurship different categories of resources?

Key Terms

tangible	services
intangible	land
goods	labor
utility	capital
disutility	entrepreneurship

Goods and Services

tangible
Able to be felt by touch. For example, a book is tangible: you can touch and feel it.

intangible
Not able to be felt by touch. For example, an economics lecture is intangible.

goods
Anything that satisfies a person's wants or brings satisfaction; also, tangible products.

utility
The quality of bringing satisfaction or happiness.

disutility
The quality of bringing dissatisfaction or unhappiness.

services
Tasks that people pay others to perform for them.

If you look closely at all the things people want, you will notice that some are tangible and some are intangible. Something is **tangible** if it can be felt or touched. A computer is tangible; you can touch it. Something is **intangible** if it cannot be felt by touch. Friendship is intangible.

Economists use the term *goods* in different ways. On the most basic level, a **good** is anything that satisfies a person's want—that brings a person satisfaction, **utility**, or happiness. In this sense, a good can be either tangible (such as a candy bar) or intangible (such as the feeling of being safe and secure). It might help you to think of these goods as anything that isn't a *bad*, which is something that brings a person dissatisfaction, **disutility**, or unhappiness.

Economists and others who talk about the economy use the term *goods* in another way, usually when they are talking about how the economy is performing. You have probably read in the newspaper or heard on the television news the phrase *goods and services*. In these cases, people are referring to goods as tangible items only, not both tangible and intangible. They are talking about all the tangible products that have been produced and are available for us to buy in our economy. Toothpaste, alarm clocks, cereal, clothes—all of these items are goods.

Services, on the other hand, are intangible. They are the tasks that you pay other people to perform for you. When people care for you at your doctor's office, wait on you at a local restaurant, or cut your hair at the salon, they are performing services. You will read more about how goods and services are produced and measured in several later chapters.

Resources

Goods and services cannot be produced without resources. Because the world has limited resources (scarcity) and because economics deals with the ways people use these limited resources to satisfy their unlimited wants, economists have spent a lot of time studying and classifying resources.

Internet Research

Tell students to search the Internet for sites discussing or promoting resources in land, labor, and capital for a particular industry. For example, students might find the official website of a national forest, a site for a union representing workers in the logging industry, and a site for a company that sells machinery used in the logging process. Ask each student to explain, in writing, how each site represents the land, labor, and capital resources for that industry. Then have each student explain what a person needs to do to demonstrate entrepreneurship—the fourth economic resource, in this industry.

▲ Both the oil refinery on the left and the newly planted forest on the right represent resources, or *factors of production*, as economists often call resources. Into which of the four major categories of resources would you place oil and wood? In what way are these two resources different?

In economics, a synonym for *resources* is *factors of production*. Resources, or factors of production, are what people use to produce goods and services. For example, corn, other natural substances, and many different machines are resources that were used to produce the cereal that you ate for breakfast this morning. Economists place resources in four broad categories: land, labor, capital, and entrepreneurship.

Sometimes economists differentiate between renewable and nonrenewable resources. A *renewable resource* is one that can be drawn on indefinitely if it is replaced. For example, wood, or timber, is a renewable resource, because once trees have been cut down, new trees can be planted. In other words, timber can be renewed to maintain a certain supply of it.

A *nonrenewable* (or exhaustible) *resource* is obviously a resource that cannot be replenished. For example, oil and natural gas are nonrenewable resources. There is no way to "plant" more oil, the way you can plant more trees. Using a certain quantity of oil means that you've reduced the remaining supply by exactly that much.

Land

When the word **land** is mentioned, you may picture an acre of woods or a plowed field in your mind's eye. The resource *land* is more, however. It includes all the natural resources found in nature, such as water, minerals, animals, and forests.

Labor

Labor refers to the physical and mental talents that people contribute to the production of goods and services. For example, a person working in a factory is considered to be the resource *labor*. A TV weatherperson telling you what the weather will be like tomorrow is considered to be the resource *labor*. Your economics teacher is a resource —a labor resource.

Capital

In economics, **capital** refers to produced goods that can be used as resources for further production. Such things as machinery, tools, computers, trucks, buildings, and factories are all considered to be capital,

land
All the natural resources found in nature. Acres of wheat fields, mineral deposits, and water in a stream are all considered land.

labor
The physical and mental talents that people contribute to the production of goods and services.

capital
Produced goods that can be used as resources for further production. Such things as factories, machines, and farm tractors are capital.

Teaching with Visuals

An economist would place wood and oil in the land category. Wood is renewable; oil is nonrenewable.

Thinking Like an Economist

Tell students that before the introduction of the steam engine, work could be performed only by humans, animals, wind, or moving water. To use wind or moving water, people had to go where these resources could be found. Thus, early factories had to be located in the countryside, where wind and water (streams) were most likely to be found. The goods produced in factories were then carried to markets. By the time the goods were produced and transported to the cities, their prices were so high that only the richest could afford to buy them.

In 1769, James Watt developed a steam engine that could run anywhere. Ask students how this might have affected producers' labor and transportation costs. How, in turn, would this have affected the price of the goods?

Cooperative Learning

Divide the class into four groups. Assign each group one of the four factors of production. Each group should complete the following assignments for its resource:

1. Develop a one-minute oral report describing the factor of production and its importance.

2. Using images clipped from magazines or newspapers, images found online and printed out, or original artwork, create a collage depicting the resource. Have the groups take turns sharing their work with the rest of the class.

ONLINE
emcp.com

Practice Tests and Study Guide

Are there economic reasons behind the strategies used by British troops during the American Revolution? To explore this question, invite students to go to www.emcschool.net /Economics2e, select Chapter 1, and read the Economics in the Real World feature titled **"Why Did British Troops Wear Bright Red Uniforms?"**

Answers will vary. David Friedman argues that a formation of neat rows made it easy to see any soldier who broke ranks and tried to desert.

Reinforcement Activity

The concept of dressing in distinctive clothing is not uncommon. Urge students to think of groups who dress distinctively to stand out from the general population. Ask, Should everyone have a distinctive set of clothing to show his or her cultural and personal designations? What would we lose if everyone had a prescribed set of clothing? What might we gain? Encourage students to include economics losses and gains in their answers.

Discussion Starter

Students may think that finding and taking advantage of new opportunities sounds imaginative, creative, and financially rewarding. However, not all entrepreneurs are successful. And even successful entrepreneurs are not successful all the time. Ask each student to

Are the Founders of Airbnb Entrepreneurs?

Airbnb is essentially a website. Here is how things work at the website. One person wants to rent a room in a house, or an entire house, or say a couch in the living room of someone's house for a night, a week, or more. Another person, with a room or a house or a couch in the living room, is willing to accommodate this person. What Airbnb essentially does is put these two people in contact with each other and Airbnb charges both persons a fee. In a way, you could say that Airbnb is a hotel, but owns no rooms.

Now what many people think when first learning about Airbnb is to ask themselves: Why didn't I think of that? How ingenious to start your own hotel business but not own any rooms.

The founders of Airbnb are entrepreneurs. They had that "special talent for searching out and taking advantage of new business opportunities and for developing new products and new ways of doing things." Essentially, what they recognized is that people could be brought together in a profitable way.

Airbnb knows that there are people who want to rent a room or a house in, say, Miami Beach for a day or a week and other people who want to rent out their room or a house in Miami for a day or a week. Airbnb brings these two sets of people together.

So, how does one come up with entrepreneurial business ideas? Basically these ideas have to do with trying to answer this question: *How do I bring together people who want to trade with each other, but who are not currently trading with each other?* That is the question the founders Airbnb asked and answered, with respect to lodging. Are there other instances where people who want to trade with each are just waiting to be brought together?

THINK ABOUT IT Might some people simply be born with entrepreneurial talent, in much the same way that some people might be born with a good singing voice, or do you think that a person can be taught how to be an entrepreneur?

or *capital goods.* Each capital good is used to produce some other good or service. For instance, computers are used to produce books and magazines, trucks are used to carry groceries to your local supermarket, and factories produce most, if not all, of the items you see in your classroom.

A Student Asks

QUESTION: *I thought the word* capital *referred to money. When my uncle said he needed more capital to invest in his business, wasn't he talking about needing more money?*

ANSWER: *Maybe your uncle did use the word* capital *as a synonym for* money. *But to an economist,* capital *refers to such things as machinery, tools, and so on—things that can be used as resources for further production. So, when an economist says a firm wants to buy more capital, he is saying that the firm wants to buy more machinery and tools.*

Entrepreneurship

If someone asked you to point to the resource *land,* you might point to a forest. For the resource *labor,* you might point to yourself as an example. To show *capital,* you

identify a different entrepreneur and research her or his efforts. Then discuss whether the various entrepreneurs have been successful in all their endeavors.

 ## Application Activity

After reading and discussing Section 3, assign the Section Activity in the *Applying the Principles Workbook,* pages 9–10.

might point to a computer. But what would you point to if someone asked you to give an example of *entrepreneurship*? This resource is not so easy to identify.

Entrepreneurship refers to the special talent that some people have for searching out and taking advantage of new business opportunities, as well as for developing new products and new ways of doing things. For example, Steve Jobs, one of the developers of the first personal computer, exhibited entrepreneurship. He saw a use for the personal computer and developed it, and hundreds of thousands of customers then purchased his product—the Apple computer. In recent years, billions of dollars in revenue have been generated by Apple products such as the iPhone and iPad.

A Student Asks

QUESTION: *Since only people can exhibit entrepreneurship, why isn't entrepreneurship considered a type of labor? In short, why aren't there only three resources—land, labor, and capital—instead of four?*

ANSWER: *Economists consider entrepreneurship sufficiently different from the ordinary talents of people to deserve its own category. Consider this explanation: both the star player on your high school basketball team and LeBron James fall into the category "basketball player," just as entrepreneurs and laborers both fall into the category "people." But are they the same in terms of the impact they can have on the success of a team? Even if the star of your team is an outstanding player, he is not likely as talented as LeBron James. LeBron James is considered a superstar—he has extraordinary basketball talents. So it is with labor and entrepreneurship: the ordinary mental and physical talents of people are considered labor. The special talents that are directed toward searching out and taking advantage of new business opportunities, products, and methods are considered entrepreneurship.*

entrepreneurship
The special talent that some people have for searching out and taking advantage of new business opportunities and for developing new products and new ways of doing things.

SECTION 3 ASSESSMENT

Defining Terms
1. Define:
   a. tangible
   b. intangible
   c. goods
   d. utility
   e. disutility
   f. services
   g. land
   h. labor
   i. capital
   j. entrepreneurship
2. The resource that involves goods used to produce other goods is _____.

Reviewing Facts and Concepts
3. Identify the following resources. Write "Ld" for land, "Lb" for labor, "C" for capital, and "E" for entrepreneurship.
   a. Francis's work as a secretary
   b. iron ore
   c. a farm tractor
   d. a computer used to write a book
   e. a comedian telling jokes on a television show
   f. someone inventing a new product

Critical Thinking
4. Entrepreneurship is sometimes the "forgotten resource." Why do you think it's easier to forget entrepreneurship than, say, labor or capital?
5. Someone says that goods are more important to buyers than services. Do you agree or disagree? Explain your answer.

Applying Economic Concepts
6. Some economists will talk about the resource *time*. Under what category of resource (land, labor, capital, or entrepreneurship) would you most likely place *time*? Explain your answer.

Assess

Quick Quiz
The following true-or-false quiz will help you assess student understanding of the material covered in this section.

1. A synonym for *resources* is *factors of enterprise*. (False)
2. The four categories of resources include labor. (True)
3. An intangible good is something that can be touched. (False)
4. A good is anything that satisfies a person's wants. (True)
5. Services are intangible. (True)

Assessment Book
You will find a quiz for this section in the *Assessment Book*, page 3.

Reteaching Activity
Assign students to work with partners to create pictorial charts depicting the four types of resources.

Guided Reading
For further reteaching of the key concepts in this section, assign the Outlining Activity and the Just the Facts Handout from the *Guided Reading and Study Guide*, pages 7–8.

Reviewing Facts and Concepts
3. **a.** Lb; **b.** Ld; **c.** C; **d.** C; **e.** Lb; **f.** E.

Critical Thinking
4. Entrepreneurship is easier to forget because it is more difficult to identify.
5. Disagree. What is important to buyers is *utility*, or satisfaction, and both goods and services are capable of giving buyers utility. If good A gives a person more utility than service B, then good A is more important to the person. Alternatively, if service B gives the person more utility than good A, service B is more important to the person.

Applying Economic Concepts
6. Answers will vary. Students might say land, because time is a natural resource that is used along with labor and capital to produce goods.

Defining Terms
1. a. tangible: something that can be felt or touched; **b. intangible:** something that cannot be felt by touch; **c. goods:** anything that satisfies a person's wants; **d. utility:** the quality of bringing satisfaction or happiness; **e. disutility:** the quality of bringing dissatisfaction or unhappiness; **f. services:** tasks people pay others to perform for them; **g. land:** all the natural resources found in nature; **h. labor:** the physical and mental talents people contribute to the production of goods and services; **i. capital:** produced goods that can be used as resources for further production; **j. entrepreneurship:** the special talent some people have for searching out and taking advantage of new business opportunities.
2. capital.

Assessment Answers

Economics Vocabulary

1. scarcity; 2. wants; 3. production possibilities frontier; 4. Opportunity cost;
5. Economics; 6. microeconomics;
7. theory; 8. tangible; 9. intangible;
10. disutility.

Understanding the Main Ideas

1. Scarcity is the condition in which people's wants are greater than the resources available to satisfy those wants.
2. Because scarcity exists, people must *choose* which of their many wants they will satisfy.
3. By making a choice, people give up something; in other words, they incur an opportunity cost.
4. Scarcity implies the need for some rationing device. People will compete for the rationing device.
5. The opportunity cost of attending high school is what one would be doing if not attending high school. Opportunity costs exist even when tuition does not.
6. It is preferable to think in terms of costs and benefits rather than just benefits because most things in life (activities, purchases, and so on) have both costs and benefits connected with them.
7. The PPF illustrates scarcity by showing which items are available and which are not.
8. You cannot be at different points on the PPF at the same time; you must make a choice to be at only one point on the PPF.
9. Two lessons may be learned from the story about the baker's window:
(1) Money that is spent to purchase one thing cannot be used later to purchase something else. For example, money that goes to purchase a new window cannot then go to purchase a new suit.
(2) To understand things fully, we need to be aware not only of what is but also of what would have been.

Chapter Summary

Section 1

▶ People have unlimited wants, but resources are limited. The condition in which our wants are greater than the limited available resources is known as *scarcity*.
▶ Because of scarcity, people must make choices, which means they must incur *opportunity costs* (highly valued opportunities or alternatives given up when the choice is made).
▶ A production possibilities frontier shows all the possible combinations of two goods that an economy can produce.
▶ Rationing devices are needed to decide who gets what portion of the available goods. Because people compete for the rationing device, competition is a consequence of scarcity.

Section 2

▶ Economists often consider both the costs and benefits of an activity.
▶ Economists believe that people act as they do in response to incentives.
▶ Individuals and societies must deal with trade-offs.
▶ Economists try to see "what would have been" as well as "what will be."
▶ Decisions and actions often have important unintended effects.
▶ Economics is divided into two branches: microeconomics and macroeconomics.
▶ Economists construct theories to answer economic questions.

Section 3

▶ *Utility* means the same thing as *satisfaction* or *happiness*; *disutility* means the same thing as *dissatisfaction* or *unhappiness*.
▶ Goods are tangible items; services are tasks that people perform for others.
▶ The four categories of resources, or factors of production, are land, labor, capital, and entrepreneurship.

Economics Vocabulary

To reinforce your knowledge of the key terms in this chapter, fill in each of the following blanks on a separate piece of paper with the appropriate word or phrase.

1. The condition in which wants are greater than the resources available to satisfy those wants is called _____.
2. Things that we desire to have are called _____.
3. A(n) _____ represents the possible combinations of two goods that can be produced in a certain time period.
4. _____ is the most highly valued, or next best, alternative that is forfeited when a choice is made.
5. _____ is the science that studies the choices of people trying to satisfy their wants in a world of scarcity.
6. The branch of economics that deals with human behavior and choices as they relate to relatively small units is called _____.
7. A(n) _____ is an explanation of how something works and is designed to answer a question that has no obvious answer.
8. A good that can be touched is considered to be _____.
9. A service is not tangible but _____.
10. Another word for *dissatisfaction* or *unhappiness* is _____.

Understanding the Main Ideas

Review the main ideas in this chapter by writing answers to the following questions on a separate sheet of paper.

1. What is scarcity?
2. Explain this statement: "Because scarcity exists, choices must be made."
3. Describe the connection between choices and opportunity costs.
4. Explain the link between scarcity and competition.
5. If you attend a public high school, you are not charged admission fees or tuition. Does it follow, then, that you face no opportunity cost in attending school? Explain your answer.
6. Why is it preferable to think in terms of costs and benefits rather than in terms of benefits only?

10. Economists believe that in making decisions, people think in terms not of total costs but of marginal costs and benefits.
11. No. The benefits of building (and using) the schools may outweigh the costs. Even though the costs will be high, the benefits may be higher.
12. An unintended effect of this law might be that a typical apple seller's income actually falls. People might buy fewer apples at 75 cents or more apiece than they did at 50 cents. As a result, a seller's income might be lower at 75 or more cents an apple than at 50 cents an apple.
13. When we evaluate a theory according to whether it sounds right or reasonable, we are prejudging the theory before testing it to see if it is a good or bad theory. The problem with this approach is that what sounds right or reasonable often turns out to be wrong, and what

7. Explain how scarcity is illustrated by a production possibilities frontier.

8. Why do the points on a production possibilities frontier represent choices?

9. What lesson is to be learned from the story in this chapter about the boy and the broken window?

10. What does it mean to think "at the margin"?

11. Suppose it is costly to build more schools in your city or town. Does it necessarily follow that the schools should not be built? Explain your answer.

12. Suppose apples are currently selling for 50 cents each. Someone says that apple sellers can't make a decent living if they sell their apples so cheaply. He says there should be a law stating that no one can sell an apple and no one can buy an apple for less than 75 cents. He intends for the law to raise the income of apple sellers. What might be an unintended effect of this law? Explain your answer.

13. Why is it better to judge theories by how well they predict than by whether they sound right or reasonable to us?

14. Identify some trade-off that you face.

15. How does entrepreneurship differ from labor?

Doing the Math

Do the calculations necessary to solve the following problems.

1. Bill decided to buy six books on history instead of four books on politics. It follows, then, that the opportunity cost of each history book was _____ books on politics.

2. The owner of a movie theater decides to raise ticket prices from $10 to $12 a ticket. Since he sells an average of 789 tickets a day, he might expect to collect _____ more per day in ticket sales. Why might he be disappointed?

Solving Economic Problems

Use your thinking skills and the information you learned in this chapter to find solutions to the following problems.

1. Apply. The recent college graduates who created Instragram, a free photo-sharing application for smartphones, did so because they saw a need for people quickly to upload and share their photos online. Within two years they sold Instagram to Facebook for a billion dollars. Would you say that they were exhibiting entrepreneurship? Explain your answer.

2. Apply. Think like an entrepreneur. Identify a new product or service that you believe many people will want to buy. List the land, labor, and capital that will be needed to produce this new product or service, and explain why you think people will want to buy it.

3. Analyze. Explain how scarcity is related to each of the following: (1) choice, (2) opportunity cost, and (3) a rationing device.

4. Identify Cause and Effect. "Because we have to make choices, there is scarcity." What is wrong with this statement?

5. Analyze. What does a college classroom that gets filled to capacity quickly have to do with scarcity?

6. Analyze. WRITING Because scarcity exists, rationing devices are needed. Do you think some rationing devices are better than others? Explain your answer.

7. Find the Main Idea. WEB Go to http://econ.emcp.net/library_essays and read the essay "I, Pencil," by Leonard E. Read. Then, in a paragraph, summarize and explain the main idea of the essay.

8. Analyze. MEDIA Find an example in your local newspaper of one effect of scarcity. Your example may come from an article, editorial, or advertisement.

Project or Presentation

A Real-World Example. Write and present a 1½- to 2-page paper in which you give a real-world example (from your life) of each of the following economic concepts: opportunity cost, trade-off, a marginal cost–marginal benefit decision, thinking in terms of what would have been, and using money as a rationing device.

ONLINE
emcp.com

Practice Tests and Study Guide

Go to **www.emcschool.net/Economics2e** and choose *Economics: New Ways of Thinking*, **Chapter 1,** if you need more help in preparing for the chapter test.

---

sounds wrong or unreasonable may turn out to be right. Knowing this, we can see that it is better to judge theories by how well they perform (how well they predict) and not to prejudge them.

14. Answers will vary.

15. *Labor* refers to the physical and mental talents that people contribute to the production of goods and services. *Entrepreneurship* refers to a special talent (that not everyone has) for searching out and taking advantage of new business opportunities, developing new products, and so on.

Doing the Math

1. For every history book Bill purchased, he could have purchased two-thirds of a book on politics (*calculation:* Cost of 6 history books = cost of 4 politics books; Cost of ⁶⁄₆ history books = cost of ⁴⁄₆ politics books; Cost of 1 history book = ⁴⁄₆ politics books; Cost of 1 history book = ⅔ politics books).

2. $1,578 (*calculation:* Average daily increase in ticket sales = daily increase in price per ticket × average number of tickets sold per day = ($12 − $10) × 789 = $2 × 789 = $1,578). He might be disappointed because demand might fall as the price goes up.

Solving Economic Problems

1. Yes. The definition of entrepreneurship refers to "searching out and taking advantage of new business opportunities."

2. Answers will vary. Students should realize just how hard it is to think up a new and good product.

3. (1) Scarcity is the condition in which our wants outstrip the resources available so we must choose which of our wants will and will not be satisfied or which will be satisfied to a greater degree. (2) Scarcity implies choice, and choice implies opportunity cost. To choose X, for example, is to not choose Y, so Y is the opportunity cost of X. (3) People need resources to satisfy their wants, so there needs to be a way of deciding who gets what resources and in what quantities. Hence, there is a need for a rationing device.

4. It is the other way around: because scarcity exists, we have to make choices.

5. Because the classroom gets filled to capacity quickly, it could be the case that more people want to take the course than there is room available.

6. Some rationing devices are better than others. For example, if money is used as the rationing device for cars, sellers receive payment and are likely to continue producing and selling cars. If "First come, first served" is used, sellers receive nothing and are not likely to continue producing and selling cars.

7. The main idea is that no one person knows how to make a pencil, yet thousands of pencils get made each day. It is important to know that many products are made by individuals who specialize in certain tasks and coordinate their specialized activities with others.

8. Answers will vary.

Project or Presentation

Answers will vary.

Chapter 2 Planning Guide

Economic Systems
(pages 34–42)

Globalization
(pages 43–55)

	Learning Objectives	Reproducible Worksheets and Handouts	Assessment
Section 1	▶ List three economic questions every society must answer. ▶ Distinguish among free enterprise, decentralized socialism, and communism. ▶ Explain what an economic system is. ▶ Describe what Adam Smith said about self-interest. ▶ Describe what Friedrich Hayek said about social planning. ▶ Define the labor theory of value.	Section 1 Activity on economic systems, *Applying the Principles Workbook*, pages 11–13 Section 1 Activity on the visions, *Applying the Principles Workbook*, pages 14–16 Outlining Activity, *Guided Reading and Study Guide*, pages 18–19 Just the Facts Handout, *Guided Reading and Study Guide*, pages 20–21	☑ Section Assessment, *Student Text*, page 42 ☑ Quick Quiz, *Annotated Teacher's Edition*, pages 41–42 ☑ Section Quiz, *Assessment Book*, page 13
Section 2	▶ Define globalization and explain its causes. ▶ Describe the evidence that indicates globalization is taking place. ▶ Describe the benefits and costs of globalization. ▶ Explain why the trend toward globalization is likely to continue.	Section 2 Activity, *Applying the Principles Workbook*, pages 17–21 Outlining Activity, *Guided Reading and Study Guide*, pages 22–23 Just the Facts Handout, *Guided Reading and Study Guide*, pages 24–25	☑ Section Assessment, *Student Text*, page 55 ☑ Quick Quiz, *Annotated Teacher's Edition*, page 54 ☑ Section Quiz, *Assessment Book*, page 14

Reproducible Chapter Resources and Assessment Materials

 Graphic Organizer Activity, *Guided Reading and Study Guide*, pages 26–27

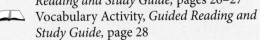 Vocabulary Activity, *Guided Reading and Study Guide*, page 28

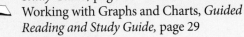 Working with Graphs and Charts, *Guided Reading and Study Guide*, page 29

☑ Practice Test, *Guided Reading and Study Guide*, pages 30–32

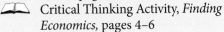 Critical Thinking Activity, *Finding Economics*, pages 4–6

☑ Chapter Test A, *Assessment Book*, pages 15–17

☑ Chapter Test B, *Assessment Book*, pages 18–21

Student Text Internet Links

Economics: New Ways of Thinking, Second Edition encourages students to use the Internet to find out more about economics. Given the wealth of current, valid information available on websites, students should be encouraged to use the Internet as a research tool. Doing so will likely increase students' interest in and understanding of economics principles and topics. In addition, doing Internet research can help your students form the habit of accessing and using economics information, as well as help them develop investigative skills they will use throughout their educational and professional careers.

To aid your students in achieving these ends, each chapter of *Economics: New Ways of Thinking, Second Edition* includes the addresses of several websites that provide engaging and relevant information. When students type in any of the addresses provided, they will immediately arrive at the intended site. The addresses have been modified so that EMC Publishing can monitor and maintain the proper links—for example, the website http://www.deposit accounts.com/ has been changed to http://econ.emcp.net/accounts. In the event that the address or content of a site changes or is discontinued, EMC's Internet editors will redirect the link to a site with equivalent information.

Activities in the *Annotated Teacher's Edition* often suggest that students search the Internet for information. For some activities, you might want to find reputable sites beforehand and steer students toward them. For other activities, have students do their own searching and then check out the sites they have found and discuss why they might be reliable or unreliable.

Passport® for Economics

Technology resources are available with the *Economics: New Ways of Thinking, Second Edition* program through Passport®. These include:

eBooks for *Economics: New Ways of Thinking, Second Edition*

▶ Student textbook eBook
▶ Interactive Applying the Principles eWorkbook
▶ Finding Economics eBook
▶ Guided Reading and Study Guide eBook
▶ Annotated Teacher's Edition eBook
▶ Lesson Plans eBook
▶ Assessment eBook

Passport® for Students

Students can access helpful resources through Passport® for Economics. Resources include:
▶ Study guides
▶ Practice tests
▶ Flash cards in English and in Spanish
▶ Word games in English and in Spanish
▶ Tutorials and key-concept videos
▶ Spanish print and audio summaries

Passport® for Teachers

Keep your course current and relevant by using the teacher resources provided through Passport® for Economics. In addition to all of the resources on the student side of Passport®, the teacher side contains:
▶ Link to the Annotated Teacher's Edition eBook
▶ Standards correlations
▶ Microsoft® PowerPoint® Lectures
▶ Current Events Lessons
▶ Additional Economics in the Real World features
▶ ExamView® Assessment Suite
▶ PDFs of all print supplements (student and teacher)

This chapter discusses the two major economic systems in the world: free enterprise and socialism. Students will also learn about globalization, which has made the world a much smaller place. The following statements provide brief descriptions of the major concepts covered in each section of this chapter.

SECTION 1 Economic Systems

Section 1 explains what an economic system is and describes the details of both the free enterprise vision and the socialist vision.

SECTION 2 Globalization

Section 2 covers globalization, including what it is, what caused it, and how people are affected by it.

CHAPTER 2
Economic Systems and the Global Economy

Why It Matters

Understanding this chapter is important to understanding the world today. Some countries that used to be socialist are currently experimenting with free enterprise, or capitalism. Their transition away from socialism to capitalism cannot be understood without understanding economic systems. So, in the first section of the chapter, you will learn about economic systems—what they do, what the two major types are, and how the two major types differ in how they answer key economic questions.

The end of the Cold War, breakthroughs in technology, and a movement toward free enterprise have all made it possible for more and more people around the globe to trade with each other. As journalist Thomas Friedman once stated, "The relevant market today is planet Earth."

Understanding economic systems is a necessary part of understanding globalization, which is the main topic in this chapter. Globalization is an economic process that many countries of the world are now undertaking. It is also a process that will probably continue for much of your life. It is important for you to understand what it is, what caused it, and how it will affect you.

Teaching Suggestions from the Author

There are many countries in the world but principally only two economic systems: free enterprise (or capitalism) and socialism. Students are usually familiar with the terms *capitalism* and *socialism* and come to class with a bias in favor of one or the other. As suggested in other chapters, it is better if students can set aside their biases while they read and study this chapter.

One of the things we try to do in this chapter is to get students to realize that economic systems are created by people. This means that people's ideas or visions (of how the world works) are the foundation stones upon which economic systems are built. In other words, certain ideas form

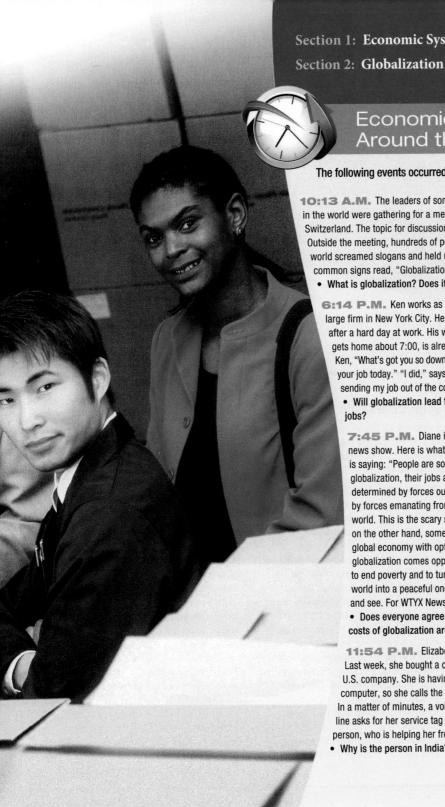

Economics Around the Clock

The following events occurred one day in September.

10:13 A.M. The leaders of some of the richest countries in the world were gathering for a meeting in a small town in Switzerland. The topic for discussion: economic globalization. Outside the meeting, hundreds of people from all over the world screamed slogans and held up signs. One of the most common signs read, "Globalization hurts the poor."
- **What is globalization? Does it hurt the poor?**

6:14 P.M. Ken works as a software engineer for a large firm in New York City. He just walked into his house after a hard day at work. His wife, Alexis, who usually gets home about 7:00, is already at home. She says to Ken, "What's got you so down? You look as if you lost your job today." "I did," says Ken. "The company is sending my job out of the country."
- **Will globalization lead to some people losing jobs?**

7:45 P.M. Diane is watching a television news show. Here is what the TV news reporter is saying: "People are somewhat afraid that with globalization, their jobs and their livelihoods will be determined by forces outside their control, perhaps by forces emanating from halfway around the world. This is the scary side of globalization. But on the other hand, some people look upon this new global economy with optimism. They say that with globalization comes opportunities—opportunities to end poverty and to turn a turbulent and hostile world into a peaceful one. We'll just have to wait and see. For WTYX News, this is Tabitha Sherman."
- **Does everyone agree what the benefits and costs of globalization are?**

11:54 P.M. Elizabeth lives in Kentucky. Last week, she bought a computer online from a U.S. company. She is having a little trouble with the computer, so she calls the customer service number. In a matter of minutes, a voice on the other end of the line asks for her service tag number. She gives it to the person, who is helping her from a call-in center in India.
- **Why is the person in India?**

33

Introducing the Chapter

To introduce Chapter 2, write the word *socialism* on the board. Ask students, What do you think of when you see the word *socialism?* Allow students to share responses. It might be helpful for you to know what preconceived notions and predilections students bring to the study of economic systems and the discussion of globalization.

Tell students to read the chapter title: "Economic Systems and the Global Economy." To what do they think "Economic Systems" refers in this title? Explain that in this chapter, they will learn about a different economic system, socialism, and comparing it with the system they live under, free enterprise.

Stress that this comparison is only part of the chapter. In addition, this chapter examines how individuals and businesses are affected by events in other parts of the world—that is, by globalization.

Teaching with Visuals

Ask students, Why do you think many former socialist countries are currently experimenting with free enterprise? How does this trend relate to globalization?

the basis of socialism and certain ideas form the basis of capitalism. In this chapter, we try to make this clear to students.

You may want to begin by asking students these questions: What ideas or visions underlie capitalism? Is one foundation stone the idea that private property is sacred? the idea that people have the right to trade with others? What ideas underlie socialism? Is one basis the idea of equality? the idea that economic plans are efficient?

Teacher Support

Focus and Motivate

Section Objectives
After completing this section, students will be able to
- list three economic questions every society must answer;
- distinguish between free enterprise and socialism;
- explain what an economic system is;
- describe what Adam Smith said about self-interest;
- describe what Friedrich Hayek said about social planning; and
- define the labor theory of value.

Kickoff Activity
Read the following quote from Aristotle: "What is common to many is taken least care of, for all men have greater regard for what is their own than for what they possess in common with others." Invite students to identify from their daily lives examples of the truth of this statement.

Activating Prior Knowledge
Instruct students to list the first four words that come to mind when you say the word *vision*. Encourage them to share their lists. Explain that in this section, the class will talk about the free enterprise, or capitalist, vision and the socialist vision. Mention that for the purposes of this discussion, a *vision* is a sense of how the world works.

Teach

Discussion Starter
Pose the following question: who or what decides what goods should be produced by a society and in what quantities? Mention that this question must be answered by every society. Some people might think that more artwork and houses need to be produced. Other people might think that more medical services should be produced. Somehow, a society as a whole must address such issues.

Economic Systems

Focus Questions
▶ What are three economic questions every society must answer?
▶ What are the major differences between free enterprise and socialism?
▶ What are the major differences between decentralized socialism and communism?
▶ What is an economic system?
▶ What did Adam Smith say about self-interest?
▶ What did Friedrich Hayek say about social planning?
▶ What is the labor theory of value?

Key Terms
economic system
free enterprise
socialism
economic plan
income distribution
mixed economy
vision
labor theory of value
surplus value

Three Economic Questions
All nations in the world share something fundamental: each of them must decide how to answer three economic questions about the production and distribution of goods.

- *What goods will be produced?* The first economic question every nation has to answer concerns what goods to produce. Because of scarcity, no country can produce every good it wants in the quantity it would like. More of one good (say, TVs) leaves fewer resources to produce other goods (such as cars). No matter what nation we are talking about—the United States, China, Japan, India, Russia, Cuba, or Brazil—each must decide what goods will be produced.
- *How will the goods be produced?* The next question every nation has to answer deals with the ways in which people produce the goods. Will farmers use modern tractors or primitive tools to produce food? Will the food be produced on private farms, where production decisions are made by individual farmers, or will it be produced on collective farms, where production decisions are made by people in the government?
- *For whom will the goods be produced?* This question relates to who gets the goods. Will anyone who is able and willing to pay for the goods be able to obtain them, or will the government decide who will have the goods?

Two Major Economic Systems
How a nation answers these three economic questions defines its **economic system**. The two major economic systems are free enterprise and socialism. **Free enterprise** is an economic system in which individuals own most, if not all, the resources and control their use; current examples include Hong Kong, Australia, and the United States. In **socialism**, the government controls and may own many of the resources; current examples include North Korea, Cuba, and Venezuela. Sometimes, free enterprise is called *capitalism*, a free market, or a *market economy*. In this book, we will mainly use

economic system
The way in which a society decides what goods to produce, how to produce goods, and for whom goods will be produced.

free enterprise
An economic system in which individuals (not the government) own most, if not all, the resources and control their use. The government plays only a small part in the economy.

socialism
An economic system in which the government controls and may own many of the resources.

Cooperative Learning

Divide students into groups of three or four. Ask each group to choose a country at random. (Pulling a name out of a hat or pinning a flag on a world map could be fun.) Then have the groups research the goods that their selected countries produce and the goods that those countries trade (import and export) most often. Each group should give a short presentation about its country that answers the three economic questions:

- What goods are produced?
- How are the goods produced?
- For whom are the goods produced?

In addition, each group should describe the economic system under which the country runs: enterprise, socialism, or mixed.

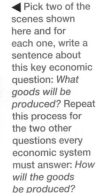

◀ Pick two of the scenes shown here and for each one, write a sentence about this key economic question: *What goods will be produced?* Repeat this process for the two other questions every economic system must answer: *How will the goods be produced?* and *For whom will the goods be produced?*

the term *free enterprise*, but occasionally, we will speak of a *capitalist economic system* or a *market economy*. Socialism is sometimes loosely referred to as a *command economy*. To be more accurate, a command economy is a particular type of socialist economic system.

A Student Asks

QUESTION: *I thought there were more than two economic systems. For example, isn't communism an economic system?*

ANSWER: *Yes, communism is sometimes considered an economic system. So why are we talking essentially about two economic systems instead of three, four, or five? Essentially, all other systems are variations of one of the two major systems. Think of all the different kinds of food in the world, such as bread, meat, and fruit. If we were to ask how many different types of food are in the world, one answer would be "many." But another way of looking at things says that there are only two types of food: food from plants and food from animals. Instead of talking about all the various minor modifications in economic systems (for example, some with slightly more government control than others), we choose to talk about the two major and distinctly different economic systems: free enterprise and socialism. Communism,*

then, goes in the socialism category, in that it is a type of socialism—a system with extensive government control over economic matters. For a broader discussion of socialism versus communism, see page 38.

Major Differences Between Free Enterprise and Socialism

Let's look at the major differences between free enterprise and socialism in a few areas.

Resources

Resources are used to produce goods and services. In a free enterprise economic system, resources are owned and controlled by private individuals. In a socialist economic system, the government controls and may own many of the resources. For example, in the former Soviet Union, the central government owned many of the resources in the country. Today, in North Korea, the government owns almost all the resources in the country.

Incentives

Under free enterprise, most individuals have a strong incentive to produce goods and services that customers want to buy, because individuals benefit monetarily by doing so. Under a socialist economic system, where private property is not as important

Teaching with Visuals

Answers will vary. Students should write about two of the scenes, and for each scene they should address all three economic questions.

Reinforcement Activity

Make sure that students remember that the terms *free enterprise*, *free market*, *capitalism*, and *money market* are synonyms, by asking them to describe the U.S. economic system using different terms.

A Student Asks

You may want to use this A Student Asks to make sure that students understand that *communism* is not only an economic system but also a political system.

Thinking Like an Economist

Some people look at countries and see differences. For example, they might note that citizens speak French in France and English in the United States or that the crime rate is higher in the United States than in Belgium. Economists look at countries and see similarities. For example, they might note that the United States, China, Russia, Mexico, Egypt, and other countries all make different decisions about what goods will be produced, how those goods will be produced, and for whom the goods will be produced.

Have each student choose two or three countries, making sure that the class covers Canada, Sweden, Finland, Cuba, Vietnam, Australia, and India. Instruct students to search the Internet, current reference texts, and other sources to discover which economic system (free enterprise, socialism, or a mixed economy) is used in each of their selected countries. Display a chart with the column heads "Free Enterprise," "Socialism," and "Mixed Economy," and enter the results of the class's research in the chart. Discuss the class's findings and possible reasons for them. Make sure students can locate their countries on a world map.

 Visit econ.myemcp.com/videos for videos that will help students better understand the key concepts found in this section.

Differentiating Instruction

Visual and English Language Learners

If students have difficulty understanding free enterprise and socialism, ask them to create collages for both systems. Suggest that they include photos, graphs, headlines, quotes, and so on for each characteristic of each system:

- free enterprise—small role of government in economic decisions, no economic plan, little

attention to income distribution, economic incentives, competition, no price control, private property

- socialism—large role of government in economic decisions, government control of resources, economic plan, more attention to income distribution, price control, public (government-owned) property

After students have read this feature, ask if they believe that only people who advocate for social progress pay attention to social media. Or do governmental agencies follow social media too?

Teaching with Visuals

After students have read this feature, ask if they think that technological developments in manufacturing in the United States will result in fewer jobs overall. Discuss the possibility that although there may be fewer manufacturing labor jobs in factories, these jobs may be replaced by jobs in design and technology. More education and training will be required for workers to fill these higher level manufacturing jobs.

ANSWERS TO THINK ABOUT IT The correct answer is that no, it doesn't follow. It is possible that the number of jobs declined in an industry without impacting that particular industry's output; the decline in total output could have been caused by a different industry. Just because two things happen at about the same time, it doesn't follow that one thing caused the other.

Reinforcement Activity

Ask students to describe how incentives appear in a free enterprise economy compared to a socialist economy. Students may research and identify the countries in the world that impose price controls on goods (examine current socialist economic systems). Students should search to see if producers are freely producing and supplying those goods and how these controls may be affecting incentives compared to countries that do not impose price controls. Ask students to draw conclusions about the relationship between incentives and price controls and share their views in a class discussion.

---

or revered and price controls often exist, producers would not have as strong of an incentive to produce. Why produce a good if the government has imposed a price control on it, stating that it can only be sold for a certain price? What if that price is below the cost the producer incurs to produce the good? In that case, the incentive to produce the good would not exist.

Do Fewer Manufacturing Jobs Mean Less Manufactured Output?

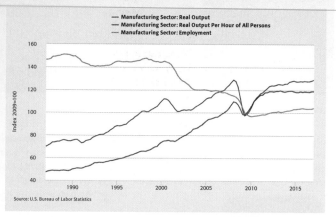

Source: U.S. Bureau of Labor Statistics

One of the criticisms of globalization is that it has led to fewer manufacturing jobs in the United States. Fact is, there are fewer manufacturing jobs in the United States today than there have been in the past. For instance, between 2000 and 2017, the number of manufacturing jobs declined by about 5 million in the United States.

Keep in mind, though, that the number of jobs in a particular sector of the economy (such as manufacturing) can decrease, but that does not necessarily mean the output produced in that sector must decline too. It could very well be that fewer people working in a particular sector are producing more goods.

Consider a case in which this has happened. There used to be time in the United States when a fairly high percentage of the labor force was in agriculture (they were farmers). But today only a small percentage (1.2 percent) of the labor force is in agriculture. In other words, the country has lost agriculture jobs; it has lost many of its farmers. But does it follow that because there is a small percentage of workers in agriculture today – as well as a smaller absolute number

of farmers – that there is less food produced in the United States today than in the past. The answer is no. In fact, more food is produced in the country today with fewer farmers than was the case in the past with more farmers. One of the key reasons that fewer farmers have been able to produce more food is due to advancements in technology in agriculture.

Could that be the case in manufacturing, too? Could it be that there have been technological developments in manufacturing in the United States, such that fewer workers in manufacturing can produce the same number or more manufacturing goods as it took more workers to produce in the past? It certainly could be. In fact, you can see for yourself in the exhibit, which comes from data provided by the U.S. Bureau of Labor Statistics. Notice what has

happened to real output (production of goods) in manufacturing between, say, 1990 and 2015. It has gone up (see blue line). This increase in output happened at the same time that employment in manufacturing declined (see green line). In other words, fewer people working in manufacturing, fewer manufacturing jobs, does not necessarily mean less manufacturing output being produced.

THINK ABOUT IT Suppose the dollar amount of total output produced in a country, adjusted for price changes, is $500 billion in year 1 and $490 billion in year 2. Also suppose that in year 2 that the number of jobs in one particular industry declined from 1,000 to 900. Does it follow that the number of jobs declining in one particular industry was the cause of the decline in total output produced?

Background Information: Socialism

In 1848, two Germans, Karl Marx and Friedrich Engels, wrote a treatise called *The Communist Manifesto*. Marx and Engels were distressed at the extremely poor conditions in which people worked in factories. They wrote that the cause of these deplorable conditions was the system of industrial capitalism and the ruling class that it created, called the *bourgeoisie*. They proposed that the *proletariat*, or the working class, would someday violently overthrow the bourgeoisie and organize the means of production. From this socialist revolution, a classless society would develop, in which economic differences among people would be abolished.

Government's Role in the Economy

In a free enterprise economic system, the government plays a small role in the economy. It does not make decisions on things like what goods and services will be produced or how they will be produced. But under socialism, the government may make those decisions. For example, in the United States, the federal government doesn't decide how many pairs of shoes will be produced in the country or how many cars, TVs, or computers. These decisions are made by individuals in private firms. In contrast, in North Korea today, the government sets production levels for almost all products.

Economists tell a story about the days of the Soviet Union when a Soviet official visited the United States. He asked to meet his counterpart in the United States—the person who decided what goods would be produced—and was shocked when his hosts told him no such person existed. He couldn't understand how things got done if no one issued economic orders.

Economic Plans

Under socialism, government decision makers may write an **economic plan**, which specifies the direction economic activities will take. A plan may state that over the next five years, the nation's economy will produce more manufactured goods (such as cars and trucks) and fewer agricultural goods (such as wheat and corn). A free enterprise economic system doesn't have such a plan.

Competition

One of the key things that government can do to increase the amount of competition between producers and sellers is to allow firms to enter any industry they see fit to enter. Suppose there are 10 firms in industry X, each earning high profits. Under free enterprise, any firm that is currently not in industry X can enter industry X and produce the good that is earning high profits. Government is not standing at the entrance way to the industry preventing firms from entering the industry. Under socialism, however, the government often plays a bigger economic role in the economy

▲ Rice paddy farmers tend to their crop. In a socialist economy, who would determine the production levels that these workers would be expected to achieve?

economic plan
A government plan specifying economic activities, such as what goods will be produced and what prices will be charged.

income distribution
The way all the income earned in a country is divided among different groups of income earners.

than is the case under free enterprise. Socialist governments often do dictate who can and cannot enter a particular industry.

Income Distribution

Income distribution refers to how all the income earned in a country is divided among different groups of income earners.

Economic Facts *and* Fallacies

Income Distribution and Unequal Taxes

Like many Americans, you may be misinformed about the amounts of taxes paid by different income groups in the general population. What percentage of the country's total income do you think is earned by the top 1 percent of income earners? *(Answer: In a recent representative year, 20.58 percent.)* What percentage of federal income taxes do you think is paid by the top 1 percent of income earners? *(Answer: In that same year, 39.48 percent.)* What percentage of federal income taxes do you think is paid by the top 10 percent of income earners in the country? *(Answer: 70.88 percent.)* Finally, what percentage of total income do you think the top 50 percent of income earners earn and what percentage of total federal income taxes does that group pay? *(Answer: 88.73 percent and 97.25 percent.)*

THINK ABOUT IT How do these inequalities in federal tax payments affect the distribution of income in the United States?

Source: The data percentages are for 2014.

Analyzing

Form pairs of students and direct each pair to find a financial news article on the Internet; one source of such articles is the CNN/Money website. Ask one partner to summarize the article from the perspective of a capitalist thinker (which is probably the perspective from which the article was written), and ask the other partner to summarize the article from the perspective of a socialist thinker. Then allow the pair to debate the issue. After the debate, ask the partners to write a brief summary answering this question: how do the two analyses differ?

Teaching with Visuals

The government of a socialist economy often determines the production levels that workers are expected to achieve.

Economic Facts *and* Fallacies

Unequal Taxes

People who earn high incomes pay higher percentages in taxes, and those taxes benefit everyone, including people who earn less and pay lower percentages in taxes. Overall, this system helps to even out overall incomes and benefits. People who earn more keep a little less of their income, and people who earn less keep a little more. Everyone gains from the programs supported by taxes, and in fact, poorer people may gain more because they qualify for additional income subsidies.

Marxist thought dominated the world for most of the twentieth century. Communism, the antithesis of capitalism, formed the basis for much of the hysteria that drove U.S. foreign policy during the Cold War. Communism contributed an ideological edge to the existing military threat of the Soviet Union after World War II. After the Russian Revolution of 1917, the United States experienced two so-called Red Scares, in which constitutional freedoms were curtailed to protect the country from communism. Most Americans understood the fear but had little understanding of what communism actually was.

Reinforcement Activity

Assign each student to write a paragraph on how the three economic questions are answered in a free enterprise economy, in a socialist economy, and in a mixed economy. Each student should also identify who decides how the four types of resources are allocated in each type of economic system.

Teaching with Visuals

Answers will vary. Students might say that employment tends to be less stable at factories owned by individuals or companies, because private owners might be more vulnerable to market fluctuations for the goods they produce.

For example, the top 10 percent of income earners may earn 20 percent of the total income of the country, whereas the bottom 10 percent of income earners may earn just 4 percent. In a free enterprise economic system, less attention is paid to income distribution than in a socialist economic system. Under socialism, decision makers are more likely to use government's powers to redistribute income, usually directing it away from society's high earners.

Controlling Prices

In a free enterprise economic system, prices are allowed to fluctuate—that is, to go up and down. The government does not attempt to control prices. In a socialist economic system, government decision makers do control prices, although not all socialist systems control prices to the same extent. For example, government decision makers may say no one can buy or sell bread for more than $1.50 a loaf. Or they may say wage rates for unskilled labor are too low at $4 an hour and forbid anyone from "buying" or "selling" unskilled labor for less than $6 an hour.

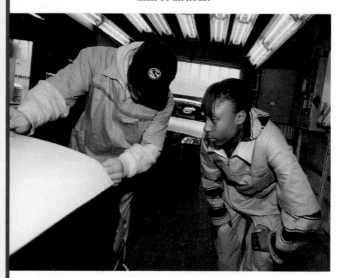

▲ These quality-control inspectors work at a Toyota plant in the United States. What are the advantages and disadvantages of factories being owned by individuals or companies, as opposed to being owned by the government?

Private Property

Under free enterprise, private property is sacred. The proponents of free enterprise believe that if you own something yourself—if, say, your house is your private property—you are more likely to take care of it than if it is owned communally by you and others or owned by the government.

The proponents also believe that having private property encourages individuals to use their resources in a way that benefits others. For example, suppose Johnson owns a factory that is her private property. If Johnson wants to maximize her income, she will have to use her factory to produce goods that people are willing and able to buy. If she does otherwise and produces something that people are unwilling and unable to buy, she will not benefit the people or earn an income.

The socialist view of things is different. Socialists believe that those who own property will end up having more political power than those who do not own it. Furthermore, individual property owners will use their greater political power to their advantage and to the disadvantage of others. According to socialists, it is better for the government to own most of the nonlabor property in the economy (such as factories, raw materials, and machinery). Government will be more likely than private individuals to make sure this property is used to benefit the many instead of the few.

Decentralized Socialism Versus Communism

Within the broad category of socialism as an economic system, there are sometimes variants. In other words, not all socialist economic systems behave exactly the same way or have exactly the same characteristics. To illustrate, let's compare and contrast decentralized socialism with communism. Although both are variants of socialism, they are usually at the opposite ends of the socialism spectrum. We can argue that *decentralized socialism* is a somewhat weaker form of socialism and that *communism* is a particularly strong form.

Cooperative Learning

Divide the class into three groups, and have each group research feudalism as it existed in Europe (from 600s to 1300s), in medieval Japan (1300s–1900s), or in the Aztec civilization (1600s). Each group should report on political, social, and economic developments as well as cultural achievements. Have each group prepare a presentation to share the information it has obtained, emphasizing economic developments. Students within each group should have both individual and group responsibilities. After the presentations, lead a class discussion on the groups' findings, and compare similarities and differences, especially of the economic systems.

Resources

In both decentralized socialism and communism, the government owns the nonlabor factors of production. However, in decentralized socialism, there is a much greater market allocation of resources than in communism, where the government largely allocates resources. Under decentralized socialism, people are freer to decide where they will work and for whom they will work.

Private Property and the Private Sector

There is a greater attempt to take away private property rights under communism than under decentralized socialism. In both decentralized socialism and communism, many economic activities take place in the public sector as opposed to the private sector.

Government's Role

In decentralized socialism, the government oversees much that occurs in the economy but does not control every aspect of the economy. In communism, by contrast, the government comes close to controlling all legal economic activities.

In both decentralized socialist and communist economic systems, individuals often attempt to engage in what are considered unlawful economic activities. For example, under communism, it is not uncommon for people to try to buy and sell goods at uncontrolled (free, market) prices. In many cases, these activities would be considered lawful (and even desirable) in a free enterprise economic system.

Mixed Economies

You might be wondering whether we can easily place each country's economy in either the free enterprise or the socialism category. The answer is no. In reality, a country's economic system may contain some ingredients of free enterprise and some ingredients of socialism too. For example, the United States is considered to have a free enterprise economic system. After all, most of the resources are owned by private individuals, and no overall economic plan determines the use of those

EXHIBIT 2-1	Economic Freedom Scores	
Rank	City/Country	Freedom Score
1	Hong Kong	89.8
2	Singapore	88.6
7	Canada	78.5
17	United States	75.1
19	Sweden	74.9
40	Japan	69.6
70	Mexico	63.6
98	Nicaragua	59.2
111	China	57.4
178	Cuba	33.9
180	North Korea	4.9

Source: 2017 Index of Economic Freedom, a publication of the Heritage Foundation.

resources. However, the U.S. government plays a larger role in the economy than it would play in a *pure* free enterprise system, and some prices are controlled. Thus, while the United States is considered a free enterprise nation, it has a few features of socialism.

A similar point can be made for other nations. For example, China is considered to be a communist country. However, since 1978, China has experimented with numerous market, or free enterprise, practices; so to say that China is 100 percent socialist is incorrect.

Economies with features of both free enterprise and socialism are called **mixed economies**. If we were to adopt this terminology, we would have to say that both the U.S. and Chinese economies are mixed economies. However, saying that would be misleading. It would make them sound alike (even identical) when they are not. The United States has much more free enterprise than China, and China has much more socialism than the United States; the economies of these two nations are different. It is clearer to refer to the United States as a free enterprise nation and to China as principally a socialist nation, while noting some socialist practices occur in the United States and some free enterprise practices take place in China.

Each year, the Heritage Foundation ranks countries according to how much economic freedom and free enterprise exist in the country. In 2017, they scored 180 countries on a scale of 1 to 100. The closer

▲ Countries were scored according to economic freedom on a scale of 1 to 100. The higher the score, the more economic freedom in the country; the lower the score, the less economic freedom.

mixed economy
An economy that is neither purely capitalist nor purely socialist; an economy that has some elements of both capitalism and socialism. Most countries in the world have mixed economies.

Teaching with Visuals

If students want to learn more about economic freedom scores, tell them to check out the description of this tool at the Heritage Foundation website (http://econ.emcp.net/heritage).

Reinforcement Activity

Point out North Korea's score in Exhibit 2-1. Ask each student to write a one-page paper summarizing the key features of North Korea's economy. Tell students to include some background information about how North Korea arrived at the economic system it has today.

Discussion Starter

Ask students how their lives might be different if they lived in a country with decentralized socialism or communism. Would they choose their own careers? Would they choose their own houses or apartments?

Reinforcement Activity

Lead a discussion of why some countries still have decentralized socialist or communist economies. Ask students to list the advantages of living in a decentralized socialist or communist economy. Then have them list the disadvantages.

Background Information: Traditional Economies

The Hadza people of Tanzania have a nomadic hunting culture and therefore live without a fixed location or many material possessions. In addition, they live in a land occupied by fierce and powerful predators, and while they hunt for their own food, they might be hunted as well. Fewer than 1,000 Hadza remain in the Tanzanian bush.

They build no shelters, have no chieftains, and have no economic structures. What they do have is a traditional economy based on thousands of years of life in the same region, hunting the same animals and having only a few outside goods introduced, such as Western clothes.

Reinforcement Activity

Explain that Adam Smith was one of the first economists to discuss and comment on the benefits of a free enterprise system. One of the key points Smith made was that free enterprise was not only an efficient economic system that could produce numerous goods and services but that it was also an ethical system because it was grounded in human freedom and personal liberty. Smith was also one of the first economists to address the question of what the government should and should not do. The government was to be limited to providing national defense, a system of justice, and public works.

Reinforcement Activity

Explain that Adam Smith's philosophy underlies the capitalist system, which allows people to own telephones, computers, and automobiles. Smith believed that competition among merchants could act as a regulator of the economic system. Ask students to explain what Smith meant by that thought. He also felt that private enterprise would stimulate fair distribution of wealth in a country. Ask, Have you noticed this to be true in the United States? Why or why not?

Reinforcement Activity

Consider reading to students the following passage translated from Karl Marx's *Das Kapital:* "The directing motive, the end and aim of capitalist production, is to extract the greatest possible amount of surplus-value, and consequently to exploit labour-power to the greatest possible extent" (Karl Marx, *Capital,* vol. 1, New York: International Publishers, 1975, p. 331). Ask for student volunteers who can answer the following question: what is the aim of capitalist production?

Here is another quote translated from *Das Kapital:* "As the number of cooperating labourers increases, so too does their resistance to the domination of capital, and with it, the necessity for capital to overcome this resistance by counter-pressure" (ibid.). Ask students, According to Marx, what happens as the number of laborers increases?

a country's economic freedom number is to 100, the more economic freedom and free enterprise in the country; the closer a country's economic freedom number is to 1, the less economic freedom in the country.

Keep in mind that different organizations sometimes rank countries differently in terms of their levels of economic freedom. We show rankings and freedom score numbers for selected countries in Exhibit 2-1. (Hong Kong had the most economic freedom and North Korea the least.)

The Visions Behind Free Enterprise and Socialism

Both free enterprise and socialism are the products of certain **visions**—ways of looking at, understanding, and explaining the world. Adam Smith, the eighteenth century economist, is a major thinker whose ideas are fundamental to free enterprise. For Smith, free enterprise is not only the economic system that produces the most economic wealth (the most goods and services), but it is also the most ethical of the economic systems.

vision
A sense of how the world works.

▶ The ideas of Adam Smith and Karl Marx have changed the world. What impact do you think Adam Smith had on getting individuals to see the benefits of a free enterprise economic system?

In contrast, the ideas of Karl Marx, a nineteenth century economist, are at the heart of socialism (and communism). It was Marx who pointed out what he believed were many of the failures and injustices of free enterprise. In his major work, *Das Kapital*, he presents his vision for an alternative system.

How important are the ideas of these two men? Consider that in late 1999, *Life* magazine created a list of the 100 most important people of the second millennium (1000–1999). Both Smith and Marx were on the list. (See Exhibit 2-2 for more information about both Smith and Marx.)

To get a sense of how these two economists' visions differed and therefore how the two major economic systems differ, let's take a closer look at one major idea from each. For Smith, it is the idea that self-interest can lead to good things not only for the individual but for others too.

Self-Interest

Smith said that from the minute we enter this world until the day we go to our graves, we feel a desire to make ourselves better off.

EXHIBIT 2-2 Two Economic Visionaries

Topic	Adam Smith	Karl Marx
Born–Died	1723–1790	1818–1883
Place of birth	Kircaldy, Scotland	Trier, Germany (Rhineland)
University	Universities of Glasgow and Oxford	Universities of Bonn, Berlin, and Jena
Major work	*An Inquiry into the Nature and Causes of the Wealth of Nations*; published 1776	*Das Kapital*; volume 1 published 1867
Economic system based on his ideas	Free enterprise, capitalism	Socialism, communism
Some ideas contributing to his vision	• Self-interest causes people to work hard and take risks, which benefits society. • The division of labor creates greater productivity and wealth. • Competition keeps prices down and quality up. • Government should provide national defense, a system of justice, and public works.	• All value in produced goods comes from labor. • Capitalists exploit laborers. • Nations will progress through six stages of development, from primitive to pure communism.

Cooperative Learning

Divide the class into small groups. Have each group research a country that has a primarily socialist economic system. (Students might use economic freedom scores to identify these countries.) Each group should present its findings, including information about resource ownership and allocation; the government's role in the economy; the economic plan, if there is one; income distribution policies; price controls; private versus public property; and trade policies and figures. The group should also provide a map of the country, recent news photos, and brief descriptions of current events, particularly those related to economics. Allow class time for students to give their presentations.

Smith felt that self-interest is a major part of who we are. He believed that our self-interest prompts us to work hard, take risks, and in the end, benefit others through our activities.

How can we benefit *others* through *our* self-interest? After all, doesn't a person's self-interest pit him or her against the best interests of others? Smith believed that if people want to serve their own self-interest, they have to serve others first. In a passage from his major work, *The Wealth of Nations*, Smith says:

It is not from the benevolence of the butcher, the brewer, or the baker, that we expect our dinner, but from their regard to their own interest. We address ourselves, not to their humanity but to their self-love, and never talk to them of our own necessities but of their advantages.

In other words, the butcher, brewer, and baker do not give us our dinner because they love us or because they want to assist us. They give us our dinner because they cannot get what they want from us until they first give us what we want. According to Smith, we are led by an "invisible hand" to do good for others. In probably the most famous passage in *The Wealth of Nations*, he says:

Every individual…neither intends to promote the public interest, nor knows how much he is promoting it…he intends only his own gain, and he is in this, as in many other cases, led by an invisible hand to promote an end which was no part of his intention.

Labor Theory of Value

Karl Marx saw things very differently. He didn't see self-interest as leading to good things; instead, he saw it as hurting others. Marx believed that capitalists, in pursuing their self-interests, actually exploited the workers. How does this happen?

Marx argued in his **labor theory of value** that all value in produced goods comes from labor. The value of any item, he said, is determined by the necessary labor time needed to produce it. For example, if it takes 5 hours of labor time to produce a chair and 10 hours to produce a table, then the table is twice as valuable as the chair.

Marx believed that the owners of factories and businesses exploit the workers by paying them far less than they are worth. For example, suppose a worker produces $100 a day worth of value for the factory owner but is only paid $20. The difference between the total value of production ($100) and the wages paid to the worker ($20) is what Marx called **surplus value** ($80). According to Marx, this surplus should go to the worker, but instead, it is stolen by the capitalist for himself.

> "By virtue of exchange, one man's prosperity is beneficial to all others."
> —Frédéric Bastiat, economist

Ideas That Changed the World

The ideas of both Smith and Marx have been with us for many years. Smith's ideas compose much of the foundation on which free enterprise rests, while Marx's ideas provide much of the foundation for socialism. Their ideas have changed the world and will probably continue to have a major impact on the world for years to come.

Friedrich Hayek and the Road to Serfdom

Friedrich Hayek (1899–1992) was an Austrian-born economist who won the Nobel Prize in Economics in 1974. In 1944, he published a book titled *The Road to Serfdom*. In 1976, the book was reissued with a subtitle: *A Classic Warning Against the Dangers to Freedom Inherent in Social Planning.*

Hayek dedicated *The Road to Serfdom* to "the socialists of all parties." By doing this, he was essentially indicating that he believed an inclination or bias toward socialism could be found not only in people who called themselves socialists but in many who did not. Hayek wrote the book because he was surprised at how fast many European countries had forgotten the virtues of a free society and the free enterprise economic system. He thought the same thing could likely happen in the United States.

According to Hayek, countries that had once practiced free enterprise were moving

labor theory of value
The belief that all value in produced goods is derived from labor.

surplus value
The difference between the total value of production and the subsistence wages paid to workers.

Application Activity

After reading and discussing "The Visions Behind Free Enterprise and Socialism," assign the Section Activity on the visions in the *Applying the Principles Workbook,* pages 14–16.

Discussion Starter

Ask students to imagine that they are responsible for central planning. What types of products would they produce more of? What products that they see in stores would they produce less of? Ask other students if they agree or disagree with the initial students' suggestions.

Assess

Quick Quiz

The following true-or-false quiz will help you assess student understanding of the material covered in this section.

1. A traditional economic system uses customs, traditions, and beliefs to answer the three economic questions. (True)
2. The two dominant economic systems are traditional and free enterprise. (False)
3. Our economic vision is our sense of how the world works. (True)
4. A socialist thinks price should be set and controlled by the government. (True)
5. All nations must answer three basic economic questions. (True)

Differentiating Instruction

Enrichment and Extension

Instruct students to prepare to role-play either Adam Smith or Karl Marx and to review the chapter until they have a good understanding of that person's viewpoint. Also ask each student to write a question he or she would like to ask the other economist. Gather students acting as Smith on one side of the room and students acting as Marx on the other side. Call on a Smith to read a question and a Marx to answer it, and list the main points made by the respondent. Next, call on a Marx to read a question and a Smith to answer it. After everyone has had a chance to ask a question and respond to a question, encourage students to explain what they learned from this exercise.

Reteaching Activity

Write the terms *free enterprise* and *socialism* at opposite ends of the board, and then draw a line connecting the terms. Make sure students understand that all economies exist somewhere along this line.

Guided Reading

For further reteaching of the key concepts in this section, assign the Outlining Activity and the Just the Facts Handout from the *Guided Reading and Study Guide,* pages 18–21.

Defining Terms

1. a. economic system: the way in which a society decides what goods to produce, how to produce them, and for whom to produce them; **b. free enterprise:** an economic system in which individuals own most, if not all, the resources and control their use; **c. socialism:** an economic system in which the government controls and may own many of the resources; **d. economic plan:** a government plan that specifies economic activities; **e. income distribution:** the way all the income earned in a country is divided among different groups of income earners; **f. mixed economy:** an economy that has some elements of both capitalism and socialism; **g. vision:** a sense of how the world works; **h. labor theory of value:** the belief that all value in produced goods is derived from labor; **i. surplus value:** the difference between the total value of production and wages paid to workers.

Reviewing Facts and Concepts

2. What goods will be produced? How will they be produced? For whom will they be produced?

3. In a free enterprise system, property is owned by individuals. In a socialist

▲ Friedrich Hayek is well known for his book *The Road to Serfdom.*

the information they needed to succeed. How did they know what goods and services people would want to buy and in what quantities? That is the kind of information that is found only through the market process.

In Hayek's view, examples of central planning in the Soviet Union were notorious for failing to meet the demands of the population. It was not uncommon for a planned economy to end up with too much of some goods (that individuals didn't want to buy) and too little of other goods (that individuals did want to buy).

In the end, said Hayek, central or government planning led to a kind of dictatorship. It led to government officials deciding—and then dictating—what goods were produced and consumed and who produced what, when, and where. A planned economy, Hayek argued, is an unfree society; it is a society in which the people are essentially serfs, being told what to do. For Hayek, socialism was the road to serfdom, and free enterprise was the road to freedom.

toward central or government planning of the economy—a definite characteristic of socialism. Hayek believed that central planning was doomed to fail. Planning an economy was impossible, he argued. Government planners simply did not have

Defining Terms

1. Define:
   a. economic system
   b. free enterprise
   c. socialism
   d. economic plan
   e. income distribution
   f. mixed economy
   g. vision
   h. labor theory of value
   i. surplus value

Reviewing Facts and Concepts

2. What are the three economic questions every nation must answer?

3. What is the difference between free enterprise (or capitalism) and socialism as each relates to private property?

4. Are all mixed economies the same? Explain your answer.

5. What is Smith's position on self-interest?

6. Explain Marx's labor theory of value.

7. What was Hayek's impact on the U.S. free enterprise system?

Critical Thinking

8. Why are most economies mixed economies instead of purely capitalist or purely socialist economies?

9. How might someone else's self-interest benefit you economically?

Applying Economic Concepts

10. Choose a current economic issue or policy measure, and then contrast the way a proponent of capitalism would discuss it versus the way a proponent of socialism would discuss it.

system, the government owns much of the property.

4. No. Some have more aspects of capitalism, and others have more aspects of socialism.

5. Smith believed that society benefited from self-interest and that in pursuing their own needs, people are guided by an "invisible hand" to act in ways that benefit society.

6. Marx said that all value in produced goods comes from labor.

7. Hayek's work is often viewed as providing an intellectual case for capitalism or the free enterprise system and against government that stifles or greatly constrains economic freedom in the marketplace.

Critical Thinking

8. Answers will vary.

9. If a self-interested person wants something (such as money) from you, he or she must offer you something you want (such as a product or service to buy).

Applying Economic Concepts

10. Answers will vary.

Globalization

Focus Questions
▶ What is globalization?
▶ What are the causes of globalization?
▶ What evidence indicates that globalization is taking place?
▶ What are the benefits of globalization?
▶ What are the costs of globalization?
▶ Is the trend toward globalization likely to continue?

Key Terms
globalization
offshoring

What Is Globalization?

From the 1950s through the 1980s, it was common to hear people talk about a "capitalist" or "free enterprise" country versus a "socialist" or "communist" country. It was as if each country in the world was definitely one or the other. It was also the case that for the most part, countries only associated (politically and economically) with their "own kind."

Things have changed. Today, few countries can clearly be labeled "capitalist" or "socialist," and countries that never communicated in the past have become major trading partners. Why? Well, according to many thinkers, it's because of *globalization*.

So, what is this thing called **globalization**? Many economists define it as a process by which individuals and businesses in any part of the world are much more affected by events elsewhere in the world than they used to be. Globalization can also be defined as the growing integration of the national economies of the world. Some believe that

this integration may eventually lead to the existence of a single worldwide economy. Let's take a closer look at some of the key features of globalization.

A Smaller World

The first definition of globalization emphasizes that economic agents (individuals, businesses, governments) in any given part of the world are affected by events elsewhere in the world. In other words, living in the United States you are affected not only by what happens in the United States, but also by what happens in Brazil, Russia, and China.

EXAMPLE In 2015, the Chinese government was taking much of the money it earned in trade with the United States and buying bonds issued by the U.S. government. As a result of Chinese purchases of U.S. bonds, interest rates in the United States ended up being lower than they would have been. Are you affected by interest rates? Sure you are, whenever you buy a car, a house, or anything else you take out a loan to purchase. ◆

globalization
A phenomenon by which economic agents in any given part of the world are affected by events elsewhere in the world; the growing integration of the national economies of the world to the degree that they could merge and operate as a single worldwide economy.

Focus and Motivate

Section Objectives

After completing this section, students will be able to
▶ define globalization and explain its causes;
▶ describe the evidence that indicates globalization is taking place;
▶ describe the benefits and costs of globalization; and
▶ explain why the trend toward globalization is likely to continue.

Economics Around the Clock

Kickoff Activity

Direct students to read the 10:13 a.m. scenario in Economics Around the Clock (page 33) and then write their answers to the accompanying question. Invite students to share their answers with the class. Draw attention to the ways their thoughts on globalization differ. Explain that globalization is a fairly recent phenomenon, which students will explore in this chapter.

Activating Prior Knowledge

Have students read the definition of *globalization* on this page and then write a few sentences describing how free enterprise and socialist economies might react differently to globalization. Encourage volunteers to share their sentences with the class.

Visit econ.myemcp.com/videos for videos that will help students better understand the key concepts found in this section.

Differentiating Instruction

Enrichment and Extension

Robert Burton, an English clergyman, wrote, "A dwarf standing on the shoulders of a giant may see farther than a giant himself." Burton meant that people who build on the ideas of others often develop more astute and comprehensive concepts.

Ask each student to research a capitalist or socialist thinker and to record information about the person's name, dates of birth and death, birth-

place, education, economic vision (capitalist or socialist), and significant works, theories, and ideas. Post students' summaries in chronological order by when the thinkers lived. Give students time to view the resulting time line and jot notes about any trends or relationships that strike them. As a class, discuss what students found in their research and in their viewing of the time line.

Teaching with Visuals

Answers will vary. If students have trouble responding to the question, ask what they would say if trading at the Tokyo Stock Exchange were less expensive than trading at the New York Stock Exchange; in that case, they might expect more people to trade at the Tokyo Stock Exchange.

Discussion Starter

Urge students to think about the clothes and shoes they have purchased recently. Do they know where the items were made? Do they usually pay more, less, or the same for clothes or shoes that were made outside the United States? Ask students to consider how the trend toward globalization might have affected the costs of these items.

Reinforcement Activity

Have students reread the quote from Thomas Friedman in paragraph 2. Note that Friedman believes globalization represents the spread of free market capitalism. Ask students to think of reasons that globalization represents the spread of capitalism rather than socialism.

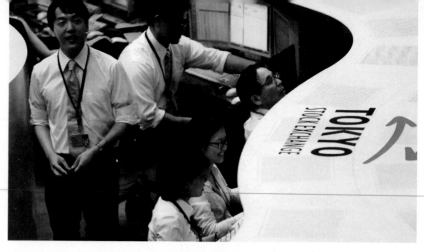

▶ These financial workers are making and recording trades at the Tokyo Stock Exchange. Do you expect more or fewer Americans to buy and sell shares traded on this exchange in the years to come? Explain.

Can you see how, in a sense, globalization makes the world smaller? China hasn't moved physically; it isn't any closer to the United States (in terms of distance) than it was 100 years ago. Still, because of globalization, what happens in China today has the same effect on you as what might happen 10 or 100 miles away from you. For all practical purposes, we live in a smaller world today than people did 100 years ago.

A Free Enterprise World

Globalization is closely aligned with a movement toward more free enterprise, freer markets, and more freedom of movement for people and goods. According to Thomas Friedman, author of several books on globalization, "Globalization means the spread of free-market capitalism in the world." There is no doubt that many countries are moving toward greater free enterprise practices.

What does this trend mean for our study of economic systems? Speaking of various economic systems made sense when national economies were the most important economies. With globalization, however, the world is moving from hundreds of national economies toward *one large world economy*. In a world of one, it does not make sense to speak of "different" economic systems. It makes sense to speak of "the" economic system for that one world economy. And the economic system that best describes what is happening in the world economy is free enterprise, or capitalism.

A Student Asks

QUESTION: *What specifically is the difference between a national economy and a global economy?*

ANSWER: *Think of an invisible string as connecting you and everyone with whom you have an economic relationship. If you buy something from someone, a string connects the two of you; if you work for someone, a string connects you. Now, perhaps the best way to think of a national economy is to think of strings linking only those people who reside in the same country. In a world or global economy, however, strings link individuals with people in their own country and in other countries too. In other words, their economic relationships extend beyond the nation's borders. In the past, a few strings extended outside country borders, but only a few, and for a long time, the strings went only to certain countries. With globalization, more and more strings—a seemingly unlimited number of strings—are being connected across borders. And these strings are connecting people in more and more countries.*

Cooperative Learning

Direct each student to find a news article about globalization and write a brief summary of it. Then divide the class into groups of three or four and pose the following questions for group discussions: In what ways do the articles relate to globalization? Do they cast globalization in a good or bad light? Ask each group to write a paragraph explaining how its articles reflect the trend away from thinking in terms of national economies and toward thinking in terms of one large, world economy. As the groups share their summaries, list their main points on the board, focusing on evidence that supports or disputes the trend toward globalization and evidence that casts globalization in a good or bad light.

Movement Toward Globalization

How did we come to live in a global economy? Did someone push a button years ago and start the process of globalization? No, things don't happen that way.

Early History

Globalization did not just occur on the world stage two decades ago. In fact, the world has gone through different globalization periods. For example, globalization occurred during the period from the mid-1800s to the late 1920s. Some people today refer to it as the First Era of globalization. In some ways, that world was a freer world when it came to the movement of people than the world today, as evidenced by the fact that many people moved from country to country without passports, which were not required.

That early era of globalization was largely ended by the two world wars (World War I and World War II) and the Great Depression. Even though all three of these events were over by 1945, globalization did not start anew. The Cold War essentially divided the world into different camps (free versus unfree, capitalist versus communist), which led to relatively high political and economic barriers. The visible symbol of these barriers—the Berlin Wall—separated not only East from West Germany, but it also separated one group of countries living under one political and economic system from another group of countries living under a different political and economic system.

Recent Causes

Several factors have led to the most recent period of globalization. Let's look at a few of the most frequently mentioned factors.

The End of the Cold War The Cold War intensified after World War II and, most people agree, ended with the visible fall of the Berlin Wall in 1989. This event occurred while the Soviet empire was beginning to crumble and many of the communist Eastern European countries were breaking away from Soviet control.

As some explain it, the end of the Cold War resulted in turning two different worlds (the capitalist and communist worlds) into one world. It resulted in a thawing of not only political but also economic relations between former enemies.

Why was this important economically? People are reluctant to trade with their enemies, but once conflicts with those individuals or countries have been resolved, the barriers begin to fade away. The Cold War acted as a political barrier between certain groups of countries. Once it ended, a giant barrier standing in the way of trade was no longer there.

▼ In the past, we traded exclusively with certain people, in certain countries. Today, with the movement toward globalization and worldwide free enterprise, we are more closely connected through trade with people all around the globe.

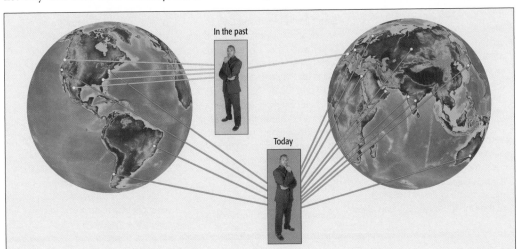

In the past

Today

The fall of the Berlin Wall reflects the often close relationship between politics and economics. Assign each student to write a one-page paper discussing how political differences limited trade between nations before the collapse of the Soviet Union. Each student should also explain how the removal of those political barriers affected trade after the Soviet Union's collapse.

As an alternative, have students to work individually or in pairs to create a political cartoon illustrating the economic effects of removing one of those political barriers. Post students' artworks. Then instruct each student to choose a cartoon created by a classmate and to write a sentence or two summarizing its meaning.

Teaching with Visuals

The lower part of this visual represents the growing number of strings, or ties, that appear between people and nations as barriers to trade fall away.

Internet Research

Ask each student to find an online news article about a formerly communist nation of Eastern Europe and how the fall of the Berlin Wall affected that nation economically. Have each student write a brief report describing what items were produced in the nation under communism and then explaining how the nation's economy has changed in the past 20-plus years. Tell students to be sure to explain in their reports whether the economic changes resulted from globalization or from other forces.

After students have read this feature, ask them to consider barriers that musicians might still face, even in a world of increased globalization.

ANSWERS TO THINK ABOUT IT Answers will vary. Students might suggest that the greater number of students in larger high schools likely means a wider variety of interests, which probably leads to a wider variety of clubs. Also, one of the benefits of a free enterprise system is that it provides consumers with choices. Specifically, it is the competition among producers for consumers' dollars that brings about these choices. If one producer offers consumers one variety of soft drink, other producers will try to compete by offering substitutes, such as other varieties of soft drinks. When producers are allowed to compete, the outcome is often providing more options for consumers.

Discussion Starter

Ask students to think about the types of businesses that are well positioned to benefit from globalization. Suggest that students consider businesses that offer goods or services that appeal to people in a variety of countries.

Will Globalization Change the Sound of Music?

Suppose you have only 100 people to whom you can sell some specific good. Given this small number, if you want to be successful, you had better sell something that some of these 100 people want to buy. For example, if these 100 people don't like fruit salad, then you had better not produce and offer to sell fruit salad; if some of these 100 people like bread, then perhaps you should produce and offer to sell bread.

Now, increase the number of people from 100 to 1 million. Is it more or less likely that some people within a group of 1 million will like fruit salad, compared to a group of 100 people? It's more likely. As the size of the potential customer base increases, the number of things you can sell increases too. In a world of 100 people, you can only sell bread, but in a world of 1 million people, you can sell fruit salad and bread.

Suppose you are a musician, and you can play different styles of music: jazz, pop, classical, hard rock, metal, hip-hop, and so on. If you are limited to selling your music to the people in one state of the United States, you can offer to sell fewer styles of music than if you can sell your music to all of the people in the nation.

The general point is a simple one: the larger the size of the potential customer base (simply put, the more people you can possibly sell to), the greater the variety of goods that can be offered.

Globalization is, to a large degree, expanding everyone's ability to potentially sell to more people. American companies aren't limited to selling only to Americans; they can sell to others in the world too. Chinese firms aren't limited to selling only to the Chinese; they can sell to others in the world too.

As an example, consider a musician in the United States who is experimenting with a new style of music. If the musician's potential customer base is only the population of the United States (approximately 327 million), then she might not get enough actual customers to make it

worth producing and offering to sell this particular, unique, and narrowly defined music. However, if the musician can draw on the population of the world (population 7.5 billion), then she might be able to find enough people who are willing to buy this particular new type of music.

As we move toward a world economy, we see a greater variety within almost every category of goods that you can think of: a greater variety of music to listen to, books to read, types of TV shows to watch, and so on. Today, the greater variety of goods you see in your world is an effect of globalization.

THINK ABOUT IT A greater variety of student clubs can usually be found in large high schools than in small high schools. Does this difference have anything to do with the issue of globalization we discussed in the feature? Explain. Explain how this is an example of a benefit of a free enterprise system.

Background Information: GATT

A number of international trade agreements have helped to bring about globalization. The most important agreement of the post–World War II era was the General Agreement on Tariffs and Trade (GATT) of 1947. Twenty-three nations signed this agreement. Several rounds of talks followed the signing, and over the next 40 years, tariffs were reduced to enhance free trade. Nations also worked to reduce other barriers to trade, such as quotas and licensing requirements. In 1995, GATT was superseded by the World Trade Organization (WTO).

Advancing Technology In the past, innovations such as the internal combustion engine, steamship, telephone, and telegraph led to increased trade between people in different countries. All of these inventions led to lower transportation or communication costs, and lower costs mean fewer barriers to trade.

EXAMPLE In 1930, the cost of a three-minute telephone call from New York to London was $250. In 1960, it was $60.42; in 1980, it was $6.32; and in 2000, it was 40 cents. Today, it is even less. As the costs of communicating continue to fall, the obstacle of physical distance (to trade) is overcome, in some sense. Businesspeople in the United States, for example, can more cheaply talk with businesspeople in China. ♦

EXAMPLE What would a computer have cost in 1960 that is comparable to the desktop computers that many people today have at home? The answer is $1.8 *million*. (Yes, you read that right—$1.8 million.) That computer cost $199,983 in 1970, $27,938 in 1980, $7,275 in 1990, and only $300 in 2018. People today use computers not only to do their work but also to communicate with others via the Internet. Having computers and Internet technology makes it possible for people to communicate with others over long distances, thus increasing the probability that people will trade with each other. ♦

Policy Changes Governments have the power to slow down the process of globalization, if they want. Suppose that two countries, A and B, have free economic relations with each other. Neither country prevents its citizens from going to the other country to live and work, and neither country hampers its citizens from investing in the other country. Then, one day, for whatever reason, the government of country A decides to limit its citizens from traveling to and investing in country B. In other words, the government of country A decides to close its political and economic "door."

Just as the government of one country can close the door to another country, it can open that door too. It can open that door a

▲ How is variety an example of globalization?

little, more than a little, or a lot. In recent decades, governments of many countries have opened their doors to other countries. China has opened its door; India has opened its door; Russia has opened its door.

In Exhibit 2-3, you will find a list of the top 10 globalized countries in the world in 2016. Beside the name of each country, you will see a number. The closer that number is to 100, the more globalized that country is said to be.

▼ What are some possible reasons that the United States was not one of the top 10 globalized countries in 2016?

EXHIBIT 2-3 Top 10 Globalized Countries in 2016

Rank	Country	Globalization Index
1	Netherlands	91.70
2	Ireland	91.64
3	Belgium	90.51
4	Austria	89.83
5	Switzerland	87.01
6	Singapore	86.93
7	Denmark	86.44
8	Sweden	85.92
9	Hungary	85.78
10	Canada	85.67

Source: KOF Index of Globalization

Background Information

The International Monetary Fund (IMF) is an international organization that provides economic advice and temporary funds to nations with economic difficulties. If a nation requests assistance, the IMF might submit a list of economic reforms for the nation to follow in exchange for a loan from the IMF.

Discussion Starter

Stimulate a class discussion on the costs and benefits of a global economy by asking students the following questions: What examples of international trade do you find in your everyday lives? What do the countries involved gain or lose in each exchange? Supplement this discussion by bringing to class the business section from a newspaper and allowing students to find articles or statistics related to international trade.

Discussion Starter

In recent years, China has opened up its economy to globalization. Its communist government, however, maintains tight control over the nation. Urge students to consider how the increasing economic freedom in China might affect the nation's political structure in the future.

Teaching with Visuals

After students review Exhibit 2-4, ask them to consider what, if any, factors other than globalization might contribute to increased life expectancy.

Here are a few of the things considered when ranking countries according to how globalized they are:

- sum of imports and exports as a percentage of the country's total income
- tariff rate (the lower the rate, the more globalized the country)
- number of Internet users per 1,000 persons
- share of households with a television set
- number of embassies in the country

> *"Globalization is the process by which markets integrate worldwide."*
> —Michael Spence, winner of the 2001 Nobel Prize in Economics

In 2017, the United States was the twenty-seventh most globalized country in the world.

EXHIBIT 2-4 Globalization and Life Expectancy

▲ The globalization index (prepared by *Foreign Policy* magazine) was compared to the life expectancy for various countries. There is a strong correlation between the degree to which a country is globalized and the life expectancy of its citizens.

The Costs and Benefits of Globalization

Some people believe that globalization is, in general, a good thing and that its benefits outweigh its costs. Other people take the opposite view: that the costs of globalization are greater than the benefits. Let's look at what benefits are pointed out by those who favor globalization and what costs are noted by those who oppose it. As you read, you will probably begin to form your own opinion.

Benefits

Following are some of the major benefits of globalization.

Trade   To say that the world is undergoing globalization is really no more than saying that people are trading with more people and at greater distances. People are also trading different things: money for goods, labor services for money, savings for expected returns, and so on. In other words, globalization is about extending the benefits of trading to people with whom one might not have traded earlier.

Standard of Living   As both India and China opened up their economies to globalization in recent decades, they experienced increases in income per person. For example, between 1980 and 2000, income per person doubled in India. Between 1940 and 2000, income per person increased by 400 percent in China, with much of this increase coming in latter years. According to the International Monetary Fund, these dramatic increases in income per person accompanied the expansion of free international trade (which is a key component of globalization).

Also according to the International Monetary Fund, in the last 40 years, hunger and child labor have been cut in half and life expectancy has increased dramatically in developing countries. According to the World Bank, 200 million people in the world were raised up out of poverty in the past 30 years.

People in the United States have benefited as well. Researchers found that

Internet Research

Tell students to search the Web for information about how India's economy has changed during the last 20 years. Ask students to pay particular attention to the relationship between U.S. businesses and Indian businesses. For example, students might look for answers to these questions: How has the availability of computer training in India affected the Indian economy? Why have many U.S. companies developed relationships with Indian companies and workers in recent years?

globalization increases U.S. income by roughly $1 trillion a year, or $10,000 per household. This means that if the United States didn't participate in globalization, Americans would be poorer by $1 trillion a year.

Another benefit to globalization seems to be longer life expectancy. One study compared life expectancy, as computed by the United Nations, with the globalization index, a rating based on how globalized a country is—the higher the number, the more globalized the country. The study found that in general, the more globalized a country is, the greater the life expectancy of its people (see Exhibit 2-4).

A Student Asks

QUESTION: *How do we know that the benefits you say are a result of globalization are, in fact, caused by globalization? Couldn't they be caused by something else?*

ANSWER: *Economists are fairly sure that globalization leads to increases in standard of living, based on their comparisons of countries with similar characteristics. In fact, globalization has produced that effect for quite awhile now, as measured by changes in total output per person in specific countries. For example, in the 1990s, the World Bank reported that less-globalized countries experienced a decline of about 1 percent in average annual output per person. In comparison more-globalized countries experienced an average increase of 5 percent in annual output per person.*

Also consider the case of North Korea versus South Korea. The two countries share a people and a culture, but North Korea avoided the process of globalization during the period in which South Korea embraced it. Today, South Koreans enjoy a much higher standard of living than North Koreans.

▲ East Indian American Express employees work at their computer in Delhi, India. Name at least one possible cost and one possible benefit of American Express offshoring work to India.

Reinforcement Activity

Divide the class into two groups to debate whether the benefits of globalization outweigh the costs. Assign one group to present the benefits and the other group to address the costs. Tell students to prepare for the debate by collecting evidence to support their assigned sides of the issue. Also tell students that particular topics for the debate will be trade, standard of living, increased income inequality, loss of American jobs, and the power of corporations. As you conduct the debate, use a chart on the board to note the major points made by each side. At the end of the debate, attempt to reach a class consensus on the issue.

Teaching with Visuals

One cost of American Express's hiring people in India is that some Americans have lost their jobs. One benefit may be that American Express has reduced its expenses, which probably has increased its profits.

Cross-Curricular Activity

Invite a government teacher to speak to your class about the political impact that globalization has had on the United States. Ask the teacher to explain whether the loss of American jobs has been a major issue in political campaigns in the United States. Also suggest that the teacher discuss whether the issue resulted in laws designed to protect American jobs and, if so, what effects those laws have had.

After students have read this feature, ask why higher education is increasingly valuable in a globalized economy. List students' responses on the board, and then ask each student to choose one reason and create a billboard, public service announcement, jingle, or other creative advertising tool to convey that message.

ANSWERS TO THINK ABOUT IT Answers will vary. Students might suggest that competition will grow because more people will be competing for scarce resources.

Background Information

The Indian Institutes of Technology (IITs) were founded in 1946 when a committee was created to explore the creation of institutions to support post-war industrial development in India. The committee called for the creation of several campuses across India. The first of the IITs opened in May 1950 in Hijli, Kharagpur, in the eastern part of India. Like the institutes in other parts of India, IIT Kharagpur has grown rapidly. Today, it employs some 450 teachers and serves several thousand students.

The Price Gap Between Brains and Brawn: Is It Increasing?

The Indian Institutes of Technology (IITs)—a group of universities located across India—are some of the hardest universities in the world to be admitted to, largely because of their reputation. In an average year, about 178,000 high school seniors in India take the exam necessary to apply to the IITs, but just over 3,500 students are admitted. In other words, only 1.96 percent of all applicants are admitted. In comparison, the admission rate of Harvard University is 7 percent.

Like the IITs, prestigious U.S. universities such as Princeton, Stanford, and Duke have very selective admission criteria. Each year, students who have the top-level grade point average and standardized test scores to be considered for admission to these universities are turned away. And this trend has developed at the same time that college tuition has skyrocketed. For example, during the period from 1995 to 2015, college tuition went up by 179 percent—considerably more than the costs of medical care, housing, and food. Around the world at other prestigious schools, we see the same pattern: the admission rate is usually low, and the cost is usually high.

As you know, grades (one admissions criterion) and money function as rationing devices. In the last chapter, you learned that because of scarcity, some mechanism has to ration the available resources, goods, and services. Still, we have to ask: Why have both of these rationing devices—grades and money—become stiffer when it comes to being admitted to the top universities in the world? Why the demand for ever-higher grades and ever-more money? The answer is twofold.

First, the population of the world has increased dramatically, but the number of Harvards has not. There are only a handful of universities at this level: for instance, Harvard in the United States, Oxford in the United Kingdom, the IITs in India. We can easily produce more computers, houses, and dining room chairs as the population of the world increases, but it seems more difficult to produce more Harvards. So, over time, we are faced with an increasing scarcity of top-notch educational institutions. As a result, the rationing devices for such institutions must do more work to ration, which essentially means that it will become harder and more expensive to get admitted to such schools.

The second reason for this pattern involves globalization. One of the things that pays a high dividend in a global economy is education. "Brains" seem to matter more than "brawn," which will increase the overall demand for a college education—not just at Harvard but at all levels of higher education.

So, will the premium currently being placed on education in a global economy cause the demand for admission at the most prestigious schools to rise at a faster rate than at other colleges? The likely answer is yes. With a growing world population and with the global economy paying a high premium to those who are well educated, we can expect admission to the world's best institutions of higher learning to become even more difficult.

THINK ABOUT IT Some people suggest that the competition to be the best in a world economy will be much stiffer than the competition to be the best in a national economy. Do you think this suggestion is true? Explain your answer.

Internet Research

Encourage students to look online for information about how other nations are preparing their young people for the global economy. Assign each student a country to research, or let him or her pick one. Pose questions like these to guide students' study: What steps is the country taking to prepare students for life after school? How will students' postgraduate experiences differ from their school experiences? Invite students to share their findings in brief oral reports. Then ask the class whether they feel ready to compete in the global economy and, if not, what they need to do to prepare.

Costs

Following are some of the costs associated with globalization.

Increased Income Inequality Critics of globalization often point out that globalization seems to go hand in hand with increased income inequality in the world. Has income inequality increased? Yes, it has. One hundred years ago, people in rich countries had about 10 times more income than people in poor countries. Today, they have about 75 times more income. Without a doubt, globalization and income inequality (between rich and poor countries) are strongly correlated. The question, though, is whether globalization *causes* the income inequality. The critics of globalization say it does; the supporters say it does not.

Losing American Jobs Many critics of globalization argue that it may result in Americans losing certain kinds of jobs. Suppose a U.S. company hires engineers in India to do jobs that once were done by Americans. This practice of hiring people in other countries is often called **offshoring**. (You will study *offshoring* and *outsourcing* in detail in Chapter 15).

It is true that some Americans may lose their jobs to workers in other countries due to globalization. It has already happened. Over the past few years, a major New York securities firm has replaced its team of 800 American software engineers, each of whom earned about $150,000 per year, with an equally competent team in India, each of whom earns about $20,000 a year. Offshoring is also relocating jobs in some medical professions. In the coming years, the number of radiologists in the United States is expected to fall significantly, because it is now possible to send the data that U.S. radiologists analyze over the Internet to Asian radiologists, who can analyze it at a fraction of the cost.

Also, while some Americans are losing jobs due to globalization, we must remember that jobs are always being lost (and found) in an economy responding to market changes. Even if the degree of

Rank	Country/Region	Exports (billions of dollars)
1	European Union	$ 2,259
2	China	$ 2,011
3	United States	$ 1,471
4	Germany	$ 1,283
5	Japan	$ 641
6	Korea, South	$ 509
7	France	$ 505
8	Hong Kong	$ 487
9	Netherlands	$ 460
10	Italy	$ 436

EXHIBIT 2-5 Top 10 Countries According to Exports (in billions of dollars)

Source: World Fact Book, 2016

▲ One measure of globalization is the dollar amount of exports for a region or country. Some economists say that the greater the dollar amount of exports, the greater the degree of globalization. Here is the list of the top 10 regions and countries in terms of dollar exports. The dollar amount for the European Union is for 2014; all other dollar amounts are for 2016.

offshoring in the United States were zero, people would still be losing old jobs and getting new jobs every day.

offshoring
The term used to describe work done for a company by persons other than its employees in a country other than the one in which the company is located.

A Student Asks

QUESTION: *I have heard of the word* outsourcing *but not* offshoring. *Do these two words mean the same thing?*

ANSWER: *Yes and no.* Offshoring *is a particular kind of outsourcing.* Outsourcing *refers to any work done for a company by people other than the company's employees. More and more companies are outsourcing work to people who live in other countries. This special kind of outsourcing is called* offshoring. *Sometimes people use the word* outsourcing *when the correct word is* offshoring. *It is not uncommon to hear "Yes, many U.S. companies are outsourcing jobs to India and China." The correct word is* offshoring.

A Student Asks

Use this A Student Asks to make sure that students understand the difference between *outsourcing* and *offshoring*.

Economics Around the Clock

Remind students of the 6:14 p.m. scenario in Economics Around the Clock (page 33), and discuss their answers to the question posed there.

The answer is yes. Globalization is not a static process, in which everything stays the same from day to day. One result of globalization is that some people will lose jobs. However, even without globalization, some people will lose jobs. Even in a country that never trades with other countries, people's preferences for certain goods and services will change, and some people will lose their jobs as a consequence.

Researching and Analyzing Activity

Richard Cobden (1804–1865) was a prominent nineteenth century politician who had strong feelings about international trade. Ask students to use library and Internet sources to research Cobden's life and ideas. Each student should write a one- to two-page paper addressing this question: if Cobden were alive today, would he support economic globalization efforts? Students should support their theses with details from their research. (Answer to the research question: Cobden was a strong advocate of free trade. He believed that international trade was necessary between major powers if war was to be avoided. If he were alive today, he would likely support economic globalization efforts.)

Reinforcement Activity

Remind students that the benefits of globalization are often less obvious than the costs. Ask students to think of some of the hard-to-see benefits of globalization. Work with the class to create a list of such benefits.

Economics Around the Clock

Instruct students to reread the 7:45 p.m. scenario in Economics Around the Clock (page 33). Call on students to name all the benefits of globalization mentioned in the scenario, listing their responses as they are offered. Do the same for all the costs mentioned in the scenario. Invite students to add to both lists from their own experiences.

Teaching with Visuals

Answers to the photo question on this page will vary. Students might say that the presence of Japanese-made games in the American marketplace points to the greater choices available to American consumers because of globalization. Students might also mention that competition from Japanese-made games pushes U.S. manufacturers to improve technology and lower prices and that profits from sales of Japanese-made games in the United States help increase the standard of living in Japan.

Thinking Like an Economist

Costs Versus Benefits

The economist is likely to ask, "What are the benefits?" Likely responses are that it increases the variety of products available and that it may increase the standard of living for some people by increasing incomes and life expectancy and decreasing hunger and child labor.

Thinking Like an Economist

Costs Versus Benefits

An economist often thinks in terms of costs and benefits, or disadvantages and advantages, or pros and cons. If you tell the economist that there are benefits to, say, going on vacation, the economist will ask, "What are the costs?" If you tell an economist that there are costs to eliminating pollution, the economist will ask, "What are the benefits?" In short, the economist usually thinks in terms of two sides of a coin: one side reads "benefits," the other side reads "costs."

THINK ABOUT IT If you tell an economist that there are certain costs to globalization, what is the economist likely to ask? What might you answer?

▼ These U.S. consumers are trying a new virtual reality game. How might this scene represent the hidden benefits of globalization?

More Power to Big Corporations Many of the critics of globalization argue that the process will simply "turn over" the world (and especially the developing countries of the world) to the large corporations headquartered in wealthier countries, such as the United States, the United Kingdom, and France. In fact, in the minds of many people, globalization is not as we have defined it in this chapter; rather, it is the process of *corporatizing* the world. Instead of governments deciding what will and will not be done, large corporations will have that responsibility.

The proponents of globalization often point out a major difference between a corporation and a government. First, a government can force people to do certain things (pay taxes, join the military). No corporation can do this; instead, corporations can simply produce goods that they hope customers will buy. Additionally, the proponents of globalization often argue that the critics overestimate the influence and reach of large transnational companies.

The Continuing Globalization Debate

To a large degree, whether someone supports or criticizes globalization seems to depend on where that person is sitting, so to speak. Globalization doesn't affect everyone in the same way, and often, *how* it affects someone determines how he or she feels.

EXAMPLE Suppose Sanders, an American worker living in New York, loses his job to an Indian worker living in New Delhi, India, who will do the same job for less pay. In this case, Sanders incurs real costs, but what about Sanders's company and the company's customers? For the company, this change means lower costs and higher profits. For the company's customers, it may result in lower prices for the company's products. So, in this case, Sanders is probably a strong opponent of offshoring, while his company and its customers are probably supporters. ♦

When it comes to globalization, it is often much more difficult to see the benefits than the costs. For example, the supporters of globalization argue that it brings greater economic wealth, lower prices, more innovation, and less poverty. Yet it is sometimes difficult for us to see all these benefits. When you buy cheaper goods or different goods because of globalization, you probably never say, "Wow, I can't believe all the benefits I get from globalization!" In fact, you might not even connect the lower-priced goods with globalization. The benefits of globalization tend to be difficult to see, partly because they are so widely dispersed.

Cooperative Learning

Divide students into groups of three or four. Ask each group to look into whether globalization could be more accurately described as the *corporatizing* of the world. Ask students to find out why some people see globalization as the corporatization of the world. What evidence exists to support this point of view? What evidence supports the opposing view?

Economics *in the* Real World

Can Sticking Chopsticks Straight Up In a Bowl Cost You Money?

Customs and traditions differ among countries, even sometimes when it comes to conducting business. Not knowing the proper way to conduct business in a country can act as a barrier to getting it done.

With globalization bringing together U.S. and Chinese businesspeople in growing numbers, it is becoming increasingly important for Americans to understand Chinese etiquette. For example, if you are in China and someone offers you a business card (which is a very common occurrence), accept it with both hands, read it immediately, and then present your own card in return. Be sure that your business card is printed in English on one side and Chinese on the other, and hand it to the other person with the Chinese side up. Also be sure that you always have business cards on hand. In both China and Hong Kong, it is considered impolite to run out of business cards.

When you get dressed for a meeting in China, keep in mind your host country's traditions for business dress. Most men wear a suit and tie. Most women dress conservatively, wearing neutral colors and shoes with no heel or a low heel.

Also consider your use of gestures. Chinese generally do not speak with their hands, so making large gestures while talking is often considered distracting. If you need to point to something, do not use one finger (because that gesture is often used when dealing with dogs); instead, use an open hand.

When invited to a meal, do not start eating before the host or hostess. And as a cultural courtesy, taste all the dishes you are offered. If you use chopsticks, never place them on the bowl (which is considered bad luck) and never stick them straight up in the bowl (because upright sticks often represent death). Also, it is customary to leave a small amount of food on your plate. Eating everything on the plate is a sign that your host or hostess did not provide you with enough food and will cause embarrassment.

THINK ABOUT IT Why might it be easier to do business in a foreign country if you know that country's traditions and customs?

 Application Activity

After reading and discussing Section 2, assign the Section Activity in the *Applying the Principles Workbook*, pages 17–21.

Economics *in the* Real World

ANSWERS TO THINK ABOUT IT Often, the people you do business with are used to certain customs, manner of dress, and so on. They find their common practices comfortable and often perceive those who have adopted to their customs and manners to be more acceptable, trustworthy, and motivated to do business with them.

Differentiating Instruction

English Language Learners

To help students who are English language learners, use the following resources, which are provided as part of the *Economics: New Ways of Thinking* program:

- a Spanish glossary in the *Student Text*
- Spanish versions of the Chapter Summaries on an audio disc

Quick Quiz

The following true-or-false quiz will help you assess student understanding of the material covered in this section.

1. In part because of globalization, few countries can be easily labeled "capitalist" or "socialist." (True)

2. The early era of globalization began during the two world wars. (False)

3. Innovations have helped to lower trade barriers. (True)

4. The practice of hiring people in other countries is often called *offshoring*. (True)

5. It is often easier to see the benefits of globalization than the costs. (True)

"Globalization presumes sustained economic growth. Otherwise, the process loses its economic benefits and political support."
—Paul Samuelson, winner of the 1970 Nobel Prize in Economics

The costs of globalization, in contrast, are more visible, often because they are so concentrated. A person who loses a job because of freer international trade in the world knows exactly what is to blame for the predicament he or she is in. At a later point, this person can surely receive some benefits from globalization (in the role of a consumer), but for a time, he or she will incur some rather high costs from globalization (as an unemployed worker). This person will likely know of the costs but be unaware of the benefits.

Globalization and the Financial Crisis

The forces propelling the world toward greater globalization are not always equally strong. In fact, they often wax and wane.

Some economists argue that the financial crisis in the United States and other countries (2007–2009) has placed a damper on globalization forces, with the consequence that globalization may not proceed as quickly or strongly in each of the next two decades as it did in the last decade. Some have gone further and argued that globalization is merely a fad or passing trend that will eventually fade away.

Whatever happens, there is one basic force behind globalization that will probably not be overcome, no matter what the political and economic climate might be: the human inclination to trade. The founder of modern economics, Adam Smith, noticed more than 200 years ago that human beings want to trade with each other. In fact, it is the desire to trade that separates us from all other species, he said. In Smith's words, "Man is an animal that makes bargains: no other animal does this—no dog exchanges bones with another."

In other words, we want to trade with people. We want to trade with our next-door neighbor, the person on the other side of town, the person in the next state, the person on the other side of the country, and finally, the person on the other side of the world.

Three Fallacies About Globalization

A number of the economic ideas that are tied up with the issue of globalization are incorrect or based on poor reasoning. Let's talk about three of these fallacies.

Fallacy 1

A country is always better off if it exports many goods and imports very few goods. So, for example, if globalization leads to the United States importing more goods, then it has to be bad for the United States.

Fact What matters to the wealth of a country is how much it produces, not how much it exports or imports. In fact, Adam Smith argued this point against the mercantilists of the 1600s–1700s in England. His opponents believed in the economic doctrine called *mercantilism*. Under mercantilism, it was thought that to become wealthy, a country had to export a lot of goods and import very few goods. At that time, the difference between exports and imports was paid in gold. And it was gold, the mercantilists thought, that made a country wealthy.

EXAMPLE Suppose that in a given year, a country exports goods worth 400 gold ounces and imports goods worth 50 gold ounces. This means that the residents of the country gain 350 gold ounces in that year. ◆

Smith argued that having more gold does not necessarily make people wealthier. He reasoned that if gold is money and there is more money in a country, all that will happen is that the prices of goods (clothes, houses, horses, food, books, and so on) will rise. Having more gold does not necessarily mean having more goods. The wealth of a nation, Smith argued, is not to be found in the total amount of gold in the country but in how much people produce and can therefore consume. The more houses, clothes, grain, meat, and books people have, the wealthier they are.

Fallacy 2

Through globalization, some countries will be made better off economically, but other countries will necessarily be made worse off.

Fact This idea captures what is called the *zero-sum mentality*. This is the belief that for every winner, there has to be a loser and, moreover, that whatever the winner wins, the loser loses. In the end, the sum of all wins and losses is zero.

EXAMPLE The card game of blackjack is a zero-sum game. What one person wins, another loses. ♦

But globalization is not blackjack. All countries can be made better off through globalization. To understand how, consider the fact that at the heart of globalization is international trade. A more globalized world is a world in which there is more trading going on between countries. Clothes are made in China and sold in the United States; computers are made in the United States and sold in China. Rugs are made in Turkey and sold in the United Kingdom; phones are made in the United Kingdom and sold in Turkey. As we learned in Chapter 1, just as individuals expect to improve their situation through voluntary trade or exchange, so they expect to be better off if they trade with people in other countries.

Fallacy 3

In a globalized world, business will necessarily gravitate toward the countries where wages are low. Someone might say, "No company is going to stay in the United States and pay high wages when it can go to, say, India, or Mexico, or China and pay lower wages."

Fact The person who makes a statement like this overlooks the fact that workers in some countries receive higher wages than workers in other countries because their productivity is higher.

EXAMPLE Suppose a person in the United States can produce 10 chairs at a day and is paid $200. In contrast, a person in Chile can produce 2 chairs a day and is paid $60. Clearly, the person in Chile is receiving a lower daily wage than the person in the United States, but that does not mean that a U.S. chair manufacturer will want to hire the Chilean worker. It's actually cheaper to hire the American worker. If we divide the wage paid to each person by the number of chairs produced, the American worker is being paid $20 per chair and the Chilean worker is being paid $30 per chair. So, even though the American's daily wage is more than three times that of the Chilean worker, the American worker is five times as productive. ♦

Assessment Book

You will find a quiz for this section in the *Assessment Book,* page 14.

Reteaching Activity

Use the Section Assessment to gauge which students may need reteaching on this section. Have those students reread the first part of the section and then explain why the world is becoming both smaller and freer economically.

Guided Reading

For further reteaching of the key concepts in this section, assign the Outlining Activity and the Just the Facts Handout from the *Guided Reading and Study Guide*, pages 22–25.

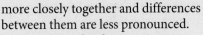

SECTION 2 ASSESSMENT

Defining Terms

1. Define:
   a. globalization
   b. offshoring

Reviewing Facts and Concepts

2. Identify two costs and two benefits of globalization.

3. Why does it make less sense to speak of different economic systems in a global economy than in a world of national economies?

4. What does changing technology have to do with globalization?

Critical Thinking

5. Why might it be easier to recognize the costs of globalization than the benefits?

6. (a) Do you think globalization is a fad, or is it here to stay? (b) How would Adam Smith answer this question? Explain both answers.

Applying Economic Concepts

7. If globalization continues over the next few decades, how might your life be different?

SECTION 2 ASSESSMENT ANSWERS

Defining Terms

1. a. globalization: a phenomenon by which individuals and businesses in any part of the world are affected by events elsewhere in the world; also, the growing integration of national economies of the world; **b. offshoring:** the practice by which a company located in one country hires workers located in other countries.

Reviewing Facts and Concepts

2. Two costs of globalization are increased income inequality and loss of American jobs; two benefits are increased trade and improved standard of living.

3. With globalization, almost all economies are tied much more closely together and differences between them are less pronounced.

4. Changing technology can improve communication and lower trade barriers, thereby helping globalization.

Critical Thinking

5. The benefits tend to be widely dispersed and thus difficult to see.

6. (a) Answers will vary. (b) Adam Smith believed that people have a deep desire to trade with each other—no matter where they reside. He would likely say that individuals will continue to push for globalization. Whether governments will permit them to push, we cannot know.

Applying Economic Concepts

7. Answers will vary. Look for mention of situations affected by the benefits of trade and increases in standard of living and by the costs of income inequality, global movement of jobs, and corporatization.

Discussion Starter

Begin by asking students whether they have thought about attending college after they graduate. Ask them to shout out how much they expect college to cost. Do they expect it to be expensive? Do they know what resources are available to them to help them pay for college? Most students will be familiar with loans, but they may not know about the other financial assistance that is available to them. Ask students to identify the options that they know about already.

Research Activity

After students have read the first section in the text about the average yearly tuition, have them research a post-secondary college or university and identify the yearly tuition costs. Have them identify whether their selection was above or below the national average.

Reinforcement Activity

Remind students that they learned about costs and benefits in Chapter 1. After students have identified a college, university, or other postsecondary institution that interests them, tell them to list the costs and benefits of attending this school and then give an oral presentation about why they chose this school. Presentations must include five benefits and five costs related to attending this particular institution.

Paying for College

According to The College Board at http://econ.emcp.net/college_costs_faqs, the average yearly tuition (with fees) is $3,440 for a two-year college; $9,410 for in-state students and $23,890 for out-of-state students at a public four-year college; and $32,410 at a private four-year college Thankfully there are a number of ways in which you can get assistance with paying for college.

Free Application for Federal Student Aid (FAFSA)

College financial aids programs are provided by both federal and state governments and individual colleges and universities, but to qualify for one of these programs, you will need to complete a Free Application for Student Aid (FAFSA) application. Fill out the form at the U.S. Department of Education FAFSA website at http://econ.emcp.net/form. Make sure that you arrive at the U.S. Department of Education's website. You will find a number of FAFSA-related sites online. Many of these are private companies that will help you fill out the FAFSA application for a fee, but this is assistance that you likely don't need. The form is really quite easy to fill out.

Once at the FAFSA.gov website, you will have to provide your first and last name, your social security number, and your date of birth. You will then create a password in case you want to return at a later date to complete your FAFSA application. The application contains numerous questions for you to answer, such as your address, your parents' names and social security numbers, and so on. Expect to spend about 30 minutes filling out the application.

File a FAFSA application as soon as possible. Deadlines do exist in different states and with different educational institutions. Also, the amount of financial aid funding available is not limitless, so the earlier you apply, the better.

Federal Student Aid

You may want to visit the website for the Federal Student Aid office of the U.S. Department of Education at http://econ.emcp.net/StudentAid. There you will find information on types of financial aid, who can qualify for aid, and more. Generally, there are three types of financial aid: (1) grants and scholarships, (2) loans, and (3) work-study jobs.

Grants and Scholarships

Grants and scholarships are usually called "gift aid," because they award money that does not have to be repaid. (You may have to repay a part of a grant if you withdraw from school before finishing the designated enrollment period). Grants are usually given out based on financial need, while scholarships are usually awarded based on merit. Grants and scholarships can come from the federal government, state government, a college or career school, or from a private business or nonprofit organization.

One example of a federal grant is the Federal Pell Grant, which is awarded to undergraduate college students who have not yet earned a bachelor's or professional degree on the basis of their financial need. The amount of the grant depends on the cost of attending the student's college, his or her status as a part- or full-time student, and the length of time he or she plans to attend college (a full academic year or less).

Another federal grant is the Federal Supplemental Educational Opportunity Grant (FSEOG), which is reserved for undergraduate students with exceptional financial need. These grants are administered by the financial aid office at each participating school, and are often referred to as campus-based aid. Check with each individual college you are interested in to find out if they offer the FSEOG.

Another grant is the TEACH grant. TEACH stands for Teacher Education Assistance for College and Higher Education. This grant is different from other federal student grants in that it requires you to take certain kinds of classes, and then do a certain job for a certain period of time after you graduate (such as teaching in a school that serves students from low-income families).

Cooperative Learning

Divide the classroom into groups to locate and identify programs and organizations in their state or community that provide scholarships to students who want to attend college. Each group should identify and research 3-4 different scholarship opportunities and create an informative presentation to deliver to the rest of the class. Students within each group should have individual as well as group responsibilities. You may choose to assign organizations to each group to ensure that duplicate information is avoided.

Loans

A loan is money that must be repaid with interest. The largest federal student loan program is the William D. Ford Direct Loan Program, for which the lender is the U.S. Department of Education.

The Federal Perkins Loan Program is a school-based loan program for students with great financial need. Under this program, the school is the lender.

In addition to federal student loans, private student loans are also available. Private student loans are issued by a bank or a credit union and usually require a credit check. The advantage of federal student loans is that they offer low fixed-interest rates, deferment options (such as if the student returns to school), income-based repayment, and cancellations based on types of employment. For these reasons, students and parents should always exhaust federal student loan options before considering a private loan.

Your college or career school will send you a financial aid offer based on your submitted FAFSA application. This offer may include a federal student loan.

Work-Study Jobs

Federal Work-Study provides part-time jobs for undergraduate and graduate students based on financial need, allowing these students to earn money to help pay for their college expenses. Work-Study is administered by schools that participate in the Federal Work-Study program. All work-study jobs pay at least the current federal minimum wage.

FAFSA4caster

FAFSA4caster is a free financial aid calculator that will give you an early estimate of your eligibility for federal student aid. Keep in mind that FAFSA4caster is not an application for aid; it is simply a planning tool. You can access the FAFSA4caster at http://econ.emcp. net/fafsa4caster.

State Information

The U.S. Department of Education's website provides online resources and links to financial aid information provided by different states. You can access this information at http://econ.emcp.net/StateLinks.

Nontraditional Methods

Nontraditional payment methods also exist. These include loans from family members, non-work-study employment, and military service (education assistance benefits), to name a few.

Your Personal Economics Activity

1. Create a document (such as a spreadsheet) to research, track, and evaluate opportunities for financial aid. Include scholarships, grants, loans (both private and federal), and possible alternative (or non-traditional) methods.
2. Write a FAFSA application how-to guide that other students could use as a reference when completing the form. Start by identifying the benefits of completing the form and then provide a step-by-step plan.

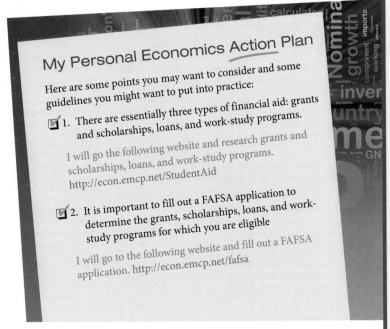

My Personal Economics Action Plan

Here are some points you may want to consider and some guidelines you might want to put into practice:

☑ 1. There are essentially three types of financial aid: grants and scholarships, loans, and work-study programs.

I will go the following website and research grants and scholarships, loans, and work-study programs. http://econ.emcp.net/StudentAid

☑ 2. It is important to fill out a FAFSA application to determine the grants, scholarships, loans, and work-study programs for which you are eligible

I will go to the following website and fill out a FAFSA application. http://econ.emcp.net/fafsa

Reinforcement Activity

Encourage students to use the FAFSA4caster tool to identify their own options for financial aid. Either assign or use as an extra-credit opportunity to encourage early investigation.

Discussion Starter

Once students have read about the various loans, scholarships, and grants available to them, ask "What are some alternative methods for funding college?" These might include enlisting in the armed forces, working part time, or taking time off to work and save money. After students have brainstormed these options, ask whether they prefer one method over another and why.

My Personal Economics Action Plan Assign students the task of doing additional research to identify what options are available to them. Students should complete the FAFSA application form if possible. Invite students to report back what they have discovered and discuss any additional financial aid options that weren't discussed in class.

Grading Rubric: Document

1 2 3 4 5   Document was thorough and complete.

1 2 3 4 5   Student evaluated multiple methods to finance their post-secondary plans.

Grading Rubric: How-to Guide

1 2 3 4 5   Guide was clear and easy to follow.

1 2 3 4 5   Guide accurately explained the FAFSA application process.

Economics Vocabulary

1. mixed economy; **2.** economic system; **3.** Free enterprise; **4.** Socialism; **5.** income distribution; **6.** economic plan; **7.** Globalization; **8.** vision; **9.** labor theory of value; **10.** offshoring.

Understanding the Main Ideas

1. An economics system is how a society answers the three basic economic questions. Free enterprise and socialism are the two major economic systems today.

2. Most of the resources are controlled by individuals and companies in free enterprise and by the government in socialism; socialist governments prepare economic plans; and prices are allowed to fluctuate in a free enterprise system.

3. Their self-interest in getting something from us motivates them to offer us dinner.

4. Marx saw self-interest as harmful to society. He believed that capitalists, in pursuing their self-interests, exploit workers.

5. The end of the Cold War eliminated many trade barriers that had previously existed. Advancing technology led to lower transportation and communication costs, and lower costs meant fewer barriers to trade. Governments of many nations have changed policies to encourage globalization.

6. Globalization has increased U.S. income by roughly $1 trillion per year.

7. Yes. Some people might lose their jobs because of globalization.

8. The benefits of globalization tend to be more widely dispersed than the costs, so they can be more difficult to recognize.

9. People might be less inclined to attack trading partners.

10. Hayek was saying that there are socialists in many political parties—not just the socialist party. In other words,

Chapter Summary

Section 1

▶ All nations must answer three economic questions: What goods will be produced? How will the goods be produced? For whom will the goods be produced?

▶ The two main economic systems are free enterprise and socialism.

▶ Free enterprise, also known as capitalism or a market economy, is an economic system in which individuals own most, if not all, the resources and control their use.

▶ In socialism, the government controls and may own many of the resources.

▶ In decentralized socialism, the government oversees much that occurs in the economy but does not control every aspect of it.

▶ In communism, the government comes close to controlling all legal economic activities.

▶ The ideas of Adam Smith provided the foundation for capitalism, or free enterprise.

▶ Karl Marx proposed an alternative to free enterprise and helped formulate the vision for socialism and communism.

Section 2

▶ Globalization is a growing integration of the national economies of the world into a single worldwide economy and is closely aligned with free enterprise, freer markets, and greater movement of people and goods.

▶ The end of the Cold War, advancing technologies, and changes in governments' policies all contributed to the growth of globalization.

▶ Benefits of globalization include greater trade, increases in standard of living, lower prices, and growing innovation.

▶ Costs of globalization include increased income inequality, greater corporate power, and lost jobs for some people.

▶ Three fallacies concerning globalization are that a country is always better off if it exports many goods and imports few; that some countries are better off and others must be worse off; and that companies move to countries with low wages.

Economics Vocabulary

Reinforce your knowledge of the key terms in this chapter by writing the appropriate word or phase for each blank on a separate piece of paper.

1. A(n) _____ is an economy with a mixture of capitalist and socialist elements.

2. A(n) _____ is the way in which a society decides what goods to produce, how to produce them, and for whom to produce them.

3. _____ is an economic system in which individuals (not the government) own most, if not all, the resources and control their use.

4. _____ is an economic system in which the government controls and may own many of the resources.

5. The _____ is the way all the income in a country is divided among groups of income earners.

6. A(n) _____ is a government program that specifies economic activities, such as what goods will be produced and what prices will be charged.

7. _____ refers to the integration of economic activities across national borders; a phenomenon by which economic agents in any part of the world are affected by events elsewhere in the world; and the extension of the division of labor and specialization beyond national borders.

8. Karl Marx and Adam Smith each had a _____, or a certain way of explaining the world.

9. The _____ states that any value in produced goods comes from the labor used to produce those goods.

10. _____ refers to work being done for a company by people other than its employees if the people live in a country other than the one in which the company is located.

Understanding the Main Ideas

Review the main ideas in this chapter by writing answers to these questions on a separate sheet of paper.

1. What is an economic system? What are the two major economic systems in the world today?

2. List three ways in which free enterprise (or capitalism) and socialism are different.

there can be Democrats who are socialists, Republicans who are socialists, and so on.

11. What matters to businesses is how productive labor is and what labor costs. It could be that the country in which wages are low is also the country in which labor isn't very productive.

12. No, they are not. Some characteristics are common to all socialist economic systems, such as government ownership of nonlabor resources and government oversight over the economy, but not all socialist economies practice the same degree of government control over the economy. For example, under a decen-

3. According to Adam Smith, why do the butcher, brewer, and baker provide food for us to buy?

4. How would Marx respond to Smith's claim that self-interest is vital to a productive economy?

5. Identify and explain each of the three causes of globalization.

6. By how much (per year) has globalization affected U.S. income?

7. Might globalization benefit some residents of a country more than others? Explain your answer.

8. Why might it be easier to recognize the costs of globalization than the benefits?

9. Explain how increased globalization might lessen intolerance and conflict in the world.

10. When Friedrich Hayek dedicated his book *The Road to Serfdom* to "socialists of all parties," what thought was he trying to communicate?

11. Why don't businesses always move to countries where labor is the cheapest?

12. Are all socialist economies the same? Explain.

Working with Graphs and Tables

1. In Exhibit 2-3, on page 47, what is the eighth most globalized country?

2. In Exhibit 2-4, on page 48, what can we conclude about Venezuela when it comes to globalization and life expectancy? What can we conclude about Canada?

Solving Economic Problems

Use your thinking skills and the information from this chapter to find solutions to these problems.

1. Apply. Do you think that a typical family operates more like a free enterprise economy or a socialist economy? Might different families operate differently? Explain.

2. Analyze. How is Adam Smith's comment that "Man is an animal that makes bargains: no other animal does this—no dog exchanges bones with another" related to globalization?

3. Identify Cause and Effect. In this chapter, we identified three recent causes of globalization. Which of the three causes do you think has

played the biggest role in promoting globalization? Explain.

4. Compare and Contrast. WRITING Imagine life in two different worlds. In the first, countries are completely open to one another when it comes to trade, movement of people, and so on. In the second, countries are closed to these things. Write a two-page essay explaining how life would be different in the two worlds.

5. Summarize. MEDIA Find a recent newspaper or magazine article that addresses the issue of globalization. Write a one-page essay summarizing the article. Be sure to attribute ideas and information to your source material.

6. Find the Main Idea. MEDIA Find a news story that addresses capitalism, socialism, private property, or global economic forces. Identify the major ideas of the story. Describe these ideas to your class in the form of a televised news report.

Project or Presentation

Economic Systems Today We have identified the two major types of economic systems in this chapter: free enterprise (capitalism) and socialism. One type of socialism is communism. China, North Korea, and Cuba are often described as communist countries. Research one of these three countries. Use the Internet and the library to research the country's economic system. Try to find out who decides what goods will be produced in the country, what industries government controls, how prices are determined, and generally research the standard of living of the people who live in the country. Prepare a two- to three-minute oral presentation on your findings. Include graphs, audio, video, presentation slides, and other media to engage your audience. As you present your oral report, monitor your speech and pronounce new and difficult words slowly and carefully.

ONLINE
emcp.com
Practice Tests and Study Guide

Go to **www.emcschool.net/Economics2e** and choose *Economics: New Ways of Thinking*, Chapter 2, if you need more help in preparing for the chapter test.

---

tralized economic system, people generally have more freedom to work for whom they want than under a communist economic system. Also, there is a greater attempt to delegitimize private property rights under communism than under decentralized socialism.

Working with Graphs and Tables

1. Denmark
2. About 20 percent in 1980 and about 29 percent in 2010.

Solving Economic Problems

1. Answers will vary. Some students might say that families are more like socialist economies, because the parents (the government) own the property and decide how the three basic economic questions are answered.

2. Smith's words mean that people have an inherent desire to trade.

3. Answers will vary. Students might say that the end of the Cold War played the biggest role in promoting globalization, because it not only removed political barriers to trade, but it also opened up communication between nations and increased exposure to other economies and to the variety of goods and services available worldwide.

4. Students' essays should describe differences between the two worlds.

5. Students should submit their articles along with their essays. Students' essays should accurately summarize their articles.

6. Answers will vary.

Project or Presentation

Answers will vary.

Chapter 3 Planning Guide

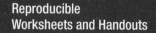

SECTION ORGANIZER

Learning Objectives	Reproducible Worksheets and Handouts	Assessment
Characteristics of Free Enterprise (pages 62–67)		

SECTION 1

Characteristics of Free Enterprise
(pages 62–67)

- ▶ Explain what goods will be produced in a free enterprise economy.
- ▶ Tell who decides what goods will be produced in a free enterprise economy.
- ▶ Explain for whom goods will be produced in a free enterprise economy.
- ▶ List five major features of free enterprise.
- ▶ Describe the circular flow of economic activity.

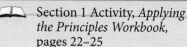 Section 1 Activity, *Applying the Principles Workbook,* pages 22–25

Outlining Activity, *Guided Reading and Study Guide,* page 33

Just the Facts Handout, *Guided Reading and Study Guide,* pages 34–35

☑ Section Assessment, *Student Text,* page 67
☑ Quick Quiz, *Annotated Teacher's Edition,* page 66
☑ Section Quiz, *Assessment Book,* page 22

SECTION 2

Profit and Loss in Free Enterprise
(pages 68–71)

- ▶ Describe the roles that profits and losses play in a free enterprise economy.
- ▶ Explain what profits, losses, and resources have to do with one another.
- ▶ Describe how profits and losses operate as signals to business firms.

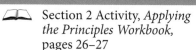 Section 2 Activity, *Applying the Principles Workbook,* pages 26–27

Outlining Activity, *Guided Reading and Study Guide,* page 36

Just the Facts Handout, *Guided Reading and Study Guide,* page 37

☑ Section Assessment, *Student Text,* page 71
☑ Quick Quiz, *Annotated Teacher's Edition,* pages 70–71
☑ Section Quiz, *Assessment Book,* page 23

SECTION 3

The Ethics of the Free Enterprise System
(pages 72–76)

- ▶ Identify some of the qualities and characteristics of an ethical economic system.
- ▶ List some of the freedoms in free enterprise.
- ▶ Explain what economic principles are stated in the Bill of Rights, the Constitution, and the Declaration of Independence.
- ▶ Describe some of the responsibilities people have in a free enterprise system.

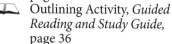 Section 3 Activity, *Applying the Principles Workbook,* pages 28–30

Outlining Activity, *Guided Reading and Study Guide,* page 38

Just the Facts Handout, *Guided Reading and Study Guide,* pages 39–40

☑ Section Assessment, *Student Text,* page 76
☑ Quick Quiz, *Annotated Teacher's Edition,* page 75
☑ Section Quiz, *Assessment Book,* page 24

SECTION 4

Entrepreneurs
(pages 77–79)

- ▶ Describe what an entrepreneur is.
- ▶ Explain how consumers benefit from the actions of entrepreneurs.
- ▶ Describe how a law that limited profits would affect future entrepreneurs.
- ▶ Explain why entrepreneurs are willing to risk their time and money.

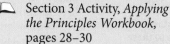 Section 4 Activity, *Applying the Principles Workbook,* pages 31–32

Outlining Activity, *Guided Reading and Study Guide,* page 41

Just the Facts Handout, *Guided Reading and Study Guide,* page 42

☑ Section Assessment, *Student Text,* page 79
☑ Quick Quiz, *Annotated Teacher's Edition,* page 79
☑ Section Quiz, *Assessment Book,* page 25

SECTION 5

The Role of Government in a Free Enterprise Economy
(pages 80–87)

- ▶ Describe what would happen if government did not enforce contracts.
- ▶ Describe a public good.
- ▶ Explain why individuals in a free enterprise economy will not produce nonexcludable public goods for sale.
- ▶ Define negative and positive externalities.

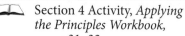 Section 5 Activity, *Applying the Principles Workbook,* pages 33–36

Outlining Activity, *Guided Reading and Study Guide,* page 43

Just the Facts Handout, *Guided Reading and Study Guide,* pages 44–45

☑ Section Assessment, *Student Text,* page 87
☑ Quick Quiz, *Annotated Teacher's Edition,* page 86
☑ Section Quiz, *Assessment Book,* page 26

Reproducible Chapter Resources and Assessment Materials

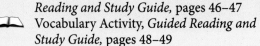 Graphic Organizer Activity, *Guided Reading and Study Guide,* pages 46–47

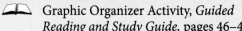 Vocabulary Activity, *Guided Reading and Study Guide,* pages 48–49

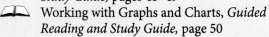 Working with Graphs and Charts, *Guided Reading and Study Guide,* page 50

Practice Test, *Guided Reading and Study Guide,* pages 51–53

Critical Thinking Activity, *Finding Economics,* pages 7–8

Chapter Test A, *Assessment Book,* pages 27–30

Chapter Test B, *Assessment Book,* pages 31–34

Student Text Internet Links

Economics: New Ways of Thinking, Second Edition encourages students to use the Internet to find out more about economics. Given the wealth of current, valid information available on websites, students should be encouraged to use the Internet as a research tool. Doing so will likely increase students' interest in and understanding of economics principles and topics. In addition, doing Internet research can help your students form the habit of accessing and using economics information, as well as help them develop investigative skills they will use throughout their educational and professional careers.

To aid your students in achieving these ends, each chapter of *Economics: New Ways of Thinking, Second Edition* includes the addresses of several websites that provide engaging and relevant information. When students type in any of the addresses provided, they will immediately arrive at the intended site. The addresses have been modified so that EMC Publishing can monitor and maintain the proper links—for example, the website http://www.deposit accounts.com/ has been changed to http://econ.emcp.net/accounts. In the event that the address or content of a site changes or is discontinued, EMC's Internet editors will redirect the link to a site with equivalent information.

Activities in the *Annotated Teacher's Edition* often suggest that students search the Internet for information. For some activities, you might want to find reputable sites beforehand and steer students toward them. For other activities, have students do their own searching and then check out the sites they have found and discuss why they might be reliable or unreliable.

Passport® for Economics

Technology resources are available with the *Economics: New Ways of Thinking, Second Edition* program through Passport®. These include:

eBooks for *Economics: New Ways of Thinking, Second Edition*

► Student textbook eBook
► Interactive Applying the Principles eWorkbook
► Finding Economics eBook
► Guided Reading and Study Guide eBook
► Annotated Teacher's Edition eBook
► Lesson Plans eBook
► Assessment eBook

Passport® for Students

Students can access helpful resources through Passport® for Economics. Resources include:
► Study guides
► Practice tests
► Flash cards in English and in Spanish
► Word games in English and in Spanish
► Tutorials and key-concept videos
► Spanish print and audio summaries

Passport® for Teachers

Keep your course current and relevant by using the teacher resources provided through Passport® for Economics. In addition to all of the resources on the student side of Passport®, the teacher side contains:
► Link to the Annotated Teacher's Edition eBook
► Standards correlations
► Microsoft® PowerPoint® Lectures
► Current Events Lessons
► Additional Economics in the Real World features
► ExamView® Assessment Suite
► PDFs of all print supplements (student and teacher)

Today, many of us take life's conveniences for granted—washing machines to clean our clothes, radios to provide music in our cars, TVs to inform and entertain us, and computers at home, school, and on the job. These things and others that make our lives easier and more pleasant were developed mainly in free enterprise economies. This chapter considers what the free enterprise system is, how it operates, and what ethical basis it has. Students will also learn the roles that government and entrepreneurs play in a free enterprise system. The following statements provide brief descriptions of the major concepts covered in each section of this chapter.

Characteristics of Free Enterprise

Section 1 explains how a free enterprise economy answers the three economic questions. Students will also learn the five major features of free enterprise and will be able to explain the circular flow of economic activity and how government actions affect this model.

Profit and Loss in Free Enterprise

Section 2 explains the roles that profits and losses play in a free enterprise economy. Students will learn how to calculate total revenue, total cost, and average costs for businesses.

The Ethics of the Free Enterprise System

Section 3 covers the characteristics of an ethical economic system. Students will also learn some of the freedoms allowed by the free enterprise system and what responsibilities people have in this type of economic system.

Why It Matters

Free enterprise can be examined in two ways. One way is to look at it the way Winston Churchill, a former prime minister of Great Britain, looked at democracy. Churchill's view was that it's not that democracy is so good but that the other political systems are so bad. In other words, democracy is far from perfect, but it's the best system we have. Some people feel the same way about free enterprise: it's not that free enterprise is so good but that it's the best system we have.

Others take a different view. To them, free enterprise is good in an absolute sense. Free enterprise is not only an economic system that puts the "bacon on the table" but also a system that does so in an ethically desirable way.

These shop owners can own the property on which their business is built, make their own business decisions, and enjoy the profits of their hard work if their business is successful. The economic system that provides them with these opportunities is free enterprise.

No matter what you think of free enterprise, it is an economic system to reckon with. As you know from reading Chapter 2, in the late 1980s and early 1990s, countries that had not yet adopted free enterprise ways began to do so. As an economic system, free enterprise has always played a major role in the development of economic wealth in the world. As globalization spreads in the twenty-first century, free enterprise promises to play an even bigger role.

60

Teaching Suggestions from the Author

If your car drives well, you rarely question how it does what it does. You just go on about your business, happy that your car is doing what you want it to do.

It's much the same with economic systems. If the economic system under which you live does a good job of putting bread on the table and generally gives you a good life, you rarely question how it works. This is the attitude that most people have toward the free enterprise system. It gets the job done, so what is there to discuss?

In this chapter, we take some time to examine free enterprise. What is it? Most people think they know, but often they do not. They might

Economics Around the Clock

The following events occurred one day in May.

7:38 A.M. Danielle is reading a story in her local newspaper about a billionaire who hired a major rock band for his son's twelfth birthday party. The total cost for the party was more than $1 million. Danielle thinks, "It is absolutely ridiculous. I mean, people in the world are starving, and this guy spends $1 million on a birthday party?"
- **What does a $1 million party have to do with free enterprise?**

11:02 A.M. James wants to buy a new pair of shoes. He's found a pair that are nice, and he'd like to buy them, but the price is a little high. A salesman asks James if he can help him. James says that he is just looking and decides to look for shoes at another store.
- **What does deciding to go to another store have to do with free enterprise?**

2:33 P.M. Tory's economics teacher is talking about the role of the entrepreneur in the economy. He says, "The entrepreneur is one of the most important persons in the economy. Without the entrepreneur, we wouldn't have many of the goods and services we enjoy." Tory wonders whether she should study economics in college if she wants to be an entrepreneur.
- **What should you study if you want to be an entrepreneur?**

6:42 P.M. Lisa is in her car delivering pizzas. Her radio is turned up loud, the windows of her car are rolled down, and she is singing along with the song. When Lisa stops at an intersection, the driver in the car next to hers wishes she would turn down the music. Lisa doesn't even notice him. She just keeps on singing. The light turns green, and Lisa drives away.
- **What does listening to a song have to do with free enterprise?**

61

SECTION 4 — Entrepreneurs

Section 4 explains what an entrepreneur does and how an entrepreneur is affected by a free enterprise system.

SECTION 5 — The Role of Government in a Free Enterprise Economy

Section 5 explores the differences between a public good and a private and between an excludable and a nonexcludable public good. Students will also learn why individuals in a free enterprise economy will not produce nonexcludable public goods.

Introducing the Chapter

Ask students to list five words or phrases that come to mind when they hear the words *free enterprise.* Allow volunteers to share their answers.

Explain that the economic system of the United States is a free enterprise system. Tell students that the free enterprise system is something that many Americans hold dear because it is a part of the framework of this nation. Explain to students that in this chapter, they will explore the nature of the free enterprise system and discuss the ethics of this economic system.

Teaching with Visuals

One hallmark of free enterprise is choice—of stores, brands of products, and prices. Discuss with students how their lives as consumers might be different without the element of choice.

say, "Free enterprise is about letting people do what they want to do" or "Free enterprise is about businesses producing the goods that consumers want to buy." Both these statements represent elements of free enterprise but are woefully incomplete.

In this chapter, we put the free enterprise system under the microscope and examine it carefully. One of the things students may be surprised to learn is that free enterprise is about more than buying and selling. It is about private property, ethics, entrepreneurs, and much more.

Teacher Support

Focus and Motivate

Section Objectives

After completing this section, students will be able to

▶ explain what goods will be produced in a free enterprise economy;

▶ tell who decides what goods will be produced in a free enterprise economy;

▶ explain for whom goods will be produced in a free enterprise economy;

▶ list five major features of free enterprise; and

▶ describe the circular flow of economic activity.

Economics Around the Clock

Kickoff Activity

Ask students to reread and respond in writing to the 7:38 a.m. scenario in Economics Around the Clock (page 61). Students should specify how they think an expensive party relates to free enterprise.

Activating Prior Knowledge

Allow students to share their responses to the Kickoff Activity with the rest of the class. Tell them that the term *free enterprise* refers to the ability to act as you want in an economic system.

Teach

Discussion Starter

Tell students that dictionaries typically define *enterprise* as "a project or undertaking that is difficult, complicated, or risky." What does this definition suggest about the nature of the free enterprise system?

Characteristics of Free Enterprise

Focus Questions

▶ What goods will be produced in a free enterprise economy?

▶ Who decides what goods will be produced in a free enterprise economy?

▶ For whom will goods be produced in a free enterprise economy?

▶ What are the five major features of free enterprise?

▶ What is the circular flow of economic activity?

Key Terms

private property
public property
household
circular flow of economic activity

How Does Free Enterprise Answer the Three Economic Questions?

We discussed the three key economic questions that every economic system must answer in Chapter 2. Now, let's look at how these questions are answered in a free enterprise economy.

What Goods Will Be Produced?

In a free enterprise economy, business firms will produce the goods that consumers want to buy. For example, suppose consumers are willing and able to buy goods A, B, and C at prices and quantities that will earn profits for business firms. Also suppose that consumers are either unwilling or unable to buy goods D, E, and F at prices and quantities that will result in profits for the businesses that produce the goods. Business firms will produce goods A, B, and C, but they will *not* produce D, E, and F.

EXAMPLE In the United States, the Ford Motor Company decides what style of car it will produce. The company bases its production on what it thinks the car-buying public wants to buy. ◆

How Will These Goods Be Produced?

The individuals who own and manage business firms decide how goods will be produced. For example, if the owners and managers of an automobile company want to use robots to produce cars, then they will purchase the robots and produce cars with them. If a company prefers that its workers use computers produced by Apple instead of computers produced by Hewlett-Packard, the workers will use computers produced by Apple.

For Whom Will the Goods Be Produced?

In a free enterprise economy, goods are produced for those people who are willing and able to buy them. Notice that it takes both *willingness* to buy and *ability* to buy. A person has the ability to buy a $25,000 car if he or she has $25,000 to spend, but if the

Differentiating Instruction

Visual Learners

Students might have difficulty understanding the characteristics of free enterprise from only reading the text. Ask students who have trouble to create visual collages. Students must find or create visuals of all the characteristics of the free enterprise system: private property, economic incentives, competition, voluntary exchange, and freedom to choose. Finding concrete, pictorial examples will help both visual learners and English language learners to better grasp the concepts in this section of the text.

same person is unwilling to spend $25,000 for the car, then he or she will not purchase the car. Also, no purchase will occur if a person is willing to buy something but is unable to do so. For example, Shelly may be willing to spend $800 to buy a computer but unable to do so because she currently does not have the money.

QUESTION: *Aren't some of the goods and services produced in a free enterprise economy unnecessary and even harmful? Wouldn't we be better off without pornography and drugs and showy, extravagant products like $20,000 watches, $1 million diamond rings, and solid gold bathroom faucets? Should these goods and services be produced?*

ANSWER: *Probably everyone can find some good or service produced, bought, and sold in a free enterprise economy that he or she thinks we would be better off without. Some people dislike hip-hop and think the country would be better without it; some people think that big SUVs on the road are things we would be better off without. The free enterprise economic system doesn't really make value judgments about what is produced; it simply produces goods and services that individuals (maybe not all individuals) want to buy. Look at it this way: you might be in favor of free speech but still not like everything that people say. Similarly, you might be in favor of free enterprise but still not like everything that people produce, sell, and buy.*

Five Features of Free Enterprise

Five major features, or characteristics, define free enterprise: private property, choice, voluntary exchange, competition, and economic incentives. (See Exhibit 3-1.)

Characteristics of Free Enterprise

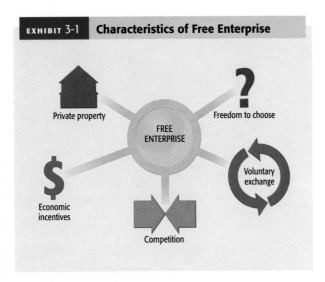

Private property

Freedom to choose

FREE ENTERPRISE

Economic incentives

Voluntary exchange

Competition

▲ Economic systems are often defined by their characteristics. Five characteristics that define free enterprise are private property, choice (or freedom to choose), voluntary exchange, competition, and economic incentives.

Private Property

Any good—such as a car, house, factory, or piece of machinery—that is owned by an individual or a business is referred to as **private property**. Any good that is owned by the government—such as the Statue of Liberty—is referred to as **public property**. Under free enterprise, individuals and businesses have the right to own property. Furthermore, they may own as much property as they are willing and able to purchase, and they may sell whatever property they own.

The right to own private property is not, however, absolute in all cases. Suppose the government wants to run a new road through the private property of some homeowners. The government offers to buy the property from the homeowners, but a few owners refuse to sell. What happens next? Generally, under the right of *eminent domain*, the government can take ownership of the land even without

private property
Any good that is owned by an individual or a business.

public property
Any good that is owned by the government.

You may want to use this A Student Asks to emphasize that a free enterprise economic system does not make value judgments. Rather, the free enterprise system simply provides goods and services.

Reinforcement Activity

After students have read the subsection on free enterprise and the three economic questions, guide them in a discussion of the answers that the free enterprise system provides to the questions. Do students feel that the answers are reasonable or unreasonable? For example, for the question "What goods will be produced?" students might believe the answer provided is unreasonable, because in their view, businesses don't really know what consumers want to buy.

 Visit econ.myemcp.com/videos for videos that will help students better understand the key concepts found in this section.

Internet Research

Ask each student to use an online news source to find an article on a new or popular product and the company producing it. The product might be a new technological gadget or a new line of clothing by a popular fashion designer. Have students analyze the article and explain how it relates to each of the five features of free enterprise: private property, choice, voluntary exchange, competition, and economic incentives. Ask students how their selected products and companies fit into the free enterprise model.

▲ Why is this car, rather than a different model, being produced? Who decided how it should be built? For whom is it being built?

the consent of the owner. In such cases, the government will compensate owners for the loss of their land.

Choice (or Freedom to Choose)

Choice is a key element of free enterprise. Workers have the right to choose what work they will do and for whom they will do it. Businesses have the right to choose the products they will produce and offer for sale. Buyers have the right to choose the products they will buy.

EXAMPLE Morgan, living in a free enterprise economy, wants to buy some vitamins, tofu, and barbells, plus a classic novel by William Faulkner. Ashley, also living in a free enterprise economy, wants to buy an album by Pharrell Williams, a tattoo of an eagle, a book by Ayn Rand, and a motorcycle. Both Morgan and Ashley can buy what they want in a free enterprise economy. ♦

Voluntary Exchange

In free enterprise, individuals have the right to make exchanges or trades they believe will make them better off. For example, suppose Mei has $10, Michael has a book, and they trade. We conclude that Mei believes she is better off having the book than the $10 and that Michael believes he is better off having the $10 than the book. Individuals make themselves better off by entering into exchanges—by trading what they value less for what they value more.

Competition

Under free enterprise, individuals are free to compete with one another. Suppose you live in a town with five bakeries. You think you would like to open your own bakery and compete for customers with the other five bakeries. In a free enterprise system, no person or law can stop you.

As a consumer living in a free enterprise system, you will likely benefit from competition between sellers. You will probably have a bigger selection of products from which to choose, and sellers will compete for your dollars by increasing the quality of the goods they sell, offering lower prices, providing better service, and so on. Although consumers in a free enterprise system may still have justified consumer complaints, they usually enjoy major advantages. The system may also have some disadvantages, which may or may not be present in other economic systems.

As a worker in a free enterprise economy, you may benefit from competition in another way. The competition between employers for your labor services may result in your earning a higher wage or income than you would earn without competition. For example, suppose you are an accountant working for one of the five accounting firms in town. A person opens up another accounting firm and wants you to come to work for her. How might she get you to quit your present job and come to her firm? She may offer you more money than you are currently earning.

Economic Incentives

As we learned in Chapter 1, an incentive is something that encourages or motivates a person toward action. Under free enterprise, money acts as an incentive to produce. If you produce goods and services that people are willing and able to buy, you receive money in return. As we learned in Chapter 2, Adam Smith wrote about the usefulness of economic (or monetary) incentives in a free enterprise economy. He explained that business owners are interested in making themselves better off. This desire to earn an income strongly motivates them to produce for others.

Laws, Institutions, and Regulations

A free enterprise economy (such as the U.S. economy) does not operate in a vacuum. Exactly how free enterprise operates is affected by the laws, institutions, and regulations of the country in which it exists. What a particular country's legal system permits and prohibits affects the so-called economic climate of that country and determines, to a large degree, how free enterprise operates there.

Legal systems and institutions can help or hinder free enterprise. For example, imagine a country in which the banking sector is somewhat undeveloped and private property is *not* viewed as important. In this country, the free enterprise system will have a difficult time operating (and doing what it does well). In a country such as the United States, however, laws have been developed to regulate banking and protect private property, which helps promote free enterprise.

As you read along in this text, you will learn how some of the institutions and laws in the United States influence the economy. For example, the last section of this chapter introduces the government's role in free enterprise; Chapter 8 discusses antitrust laws; Chapter 9 describes certain business regulations; and Chapter 10 examines the banking system.

The Circular Flow

Much of what characterizes a free enterprise economy relates to how the key economic sectors—government, businesses, and **households**—deal with each other. Does the government play a big role in the economy or a small role? Are businesses free to produce what they want? What goods do businesses produce to sell to the households?

> *"Some see private enterprise as a target to be shot, others as a cow to be milked, but few are those who see it as a sturdy horse pulling the wagon."*
> —Winston Churchill, former prime minister of Great Britain

A Snapshot of an Economy

Looking at a picture of an economy in action might help us answer these questions. Look at Exhibit 3-2, which shows the **circular flow of economic activity** in the U.S. economy. This diagram shows the key players in the economy, the relationships they have with each other, and the ways

household
An economic unit of one person or more that sells resources and buys goods and services.

circular flow of economic activity
The economic relationships that exist between different economic groups in an economy.

Thinking Like an Economist

The Circular Flow and the Rest of the World

Economists often discuss the circular flow of economic activity in one of two ways, depending upon what they want to focus on. One way is in terms of a domestic economy that does not trade with other countries; the other is in terms of a domestic economy that does trade with other countries.

Look at it this way: there is always buying and selling going on in an economy. In a domestic economy without international trade, all the buying is done by domestic households and all the selling is done by domestic businesses. For example, American households are buying the goods being sold by only American businesses, located in the United States.

In a domestic economy with international trade, the buying is done by both domestic and foreign households and the selling is done by both domestic and foreign businesses. For example, American households and, say, French, Mexican, and Chinese households are buying the goods being sold by American businesses and French, Mexican, and Chinese businesses too.

Reinforcement Activity

According to economist Adam Smith, even if a country had a lot of gold, it wasn't necessarily rich. Instead, a country was rich according to "the achievement of an abundance of the necessities of life." In other words, a country was rich if it had the necessities—houses, clothes, food. Having necessities makes a country rich; having money doesn't.

Activating Prior Knowledge

Share with students the fact that if a company offers its employees incentives, then those employees are likely to continue to work there. Discuss some common incentives at various jobs. (Examples include money, holidays and vacation time, social contacts, and health benefits.)

Background Information

Free enterprise countries trade more with other free enterprise countries than with socialist countries. In recent years, however, some formerly socialist countries have turned to free enterprise. We can expect the United States to enter into more trade with these countries.

Critical Thinking

Ask students to discuss how the circular flow model would be affected by the rest of the world. Help students determine that the rest of the world (including the firms and consumers in the rest of the world) interact with U.S. businesses and households. For example, consumers in the rest of the world buy goods from U.S. firms. Also, firms in the rest of the world sell goods to U.S. consumers. One of the things that a circular flow model shows is the interactions between households and businesses. Just as U.S. households interact with U.S. businesses, so do foreign businesses interact with U.S. households and foreign households interact with U.S. businesses. The circular flow model would, therefore, include many more arrows representing these relationships.

Differentiating Instruction

Enrichment and Extension

Allow selected students to present a discussion of Adam Smith and his views on free enterprise, either as an oral report or a multimedia presentation. One student could prepare an oral report or poster describing the economic conditions in England during Adam Smith's lifetime that led to his writing *An Inquiry into the Nature and Causes of the Wealth of Nations* (1776). Another student or a group of students could create a slide or PowerPoint presentation describing how Smith's work was received in the years after its publication.

Teaching with Visuals

The circular flow diagram in Exhibit 3-2 represents the economic activity of the United States. Lead students in a discussion of how the diagram might be different when considering another country.

Cause and Effect

Ask students how the arrows in Exhibit 3-2 are related. What would happen if one of the arrows (and the good it represents) increased in size? (*Answer:* Another arrow would probably change in size as well.) Encourage students to describe the relationships among the parts of the diagram.

Problem Solving

Have each student create a new circular flow diagram that increases the amount of money, goods, or services flowing from one point to another point. The student can choose which arrow to increase. Remind the class that as one of these areas increases, others will be affected. Allow volunteers to share their new diagrams with the class.

Application Activity

After reading and discussing Section 1, assign the Section Activity in the *Applying the Principles Workbook*, pages 22–25.

Assess

Quick Quiz

The following true-or-false quiz will help you assess student understanding of the material covered in this section.

1. In a free enterprise system, businesses are free to choose which goods to produce. (True)
2. Any good owned by the government is referred to as a *public good*. (True)
3. Under free enterprise, only certain individuals are able to compete in certain markets. (False)
4. In a free enterprise system, there is competition for your labor. (True)
5. Under free enterprise, money is an incentive to produce. (True)

▶ The circular flow of economic activity shows the relationships between different economic groups. For example, in this circular flow diagram, we see that households buy goods from businesses and sell resources to businesses. We also see that both businesses and households pay taxes to government and receive benefits from government.

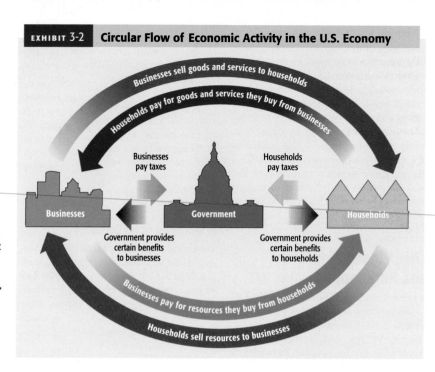

EXHIBIT 3-2   Circular Flow of Economic Activity in the U.S. Economy

Businesses sell goods and services to households

Households pay for goods and services they buy from businesses

Businesses pay taxes

Households pay taxes

Businesses

Government

Households

Government provides certain benefits to businesses

Government provides certain benefits to households

Businesses pay for resources they buy from households

Households sell resources to businesses

in which they interact. At first glance, the diagram looks like it has lines going every which way, but those lines tell a story.

- As mentioned earlier, it is customary to think of an economy as composed of businesses, government, and households. In the exhibit, businesses, government, and households are represented in the center of the diagram.
- An economic relationship exists between businesses and households. Businesses sell goods and services to households (purple arrow), for which households must make monetary payments (blue arrow). For example, a consumer decides to buy a sofa from a furniture company.
- Businesses and households have another economic relationship: individuals in households sell resources (such as their labor services) to business firms (red arrow), and in return, businesses pay individuals for these resources (green arrow). For example, a business pays a worker a day's wage.

- Both businesses and households have economic relationships with the government. Households pay taxes to the government (yellow arrow) and in return receive certain goods and services (gray arrow). For example, the government provides individuals with roads, schools, and national defense. The same kind of relationship holds between businesses and the government: businesses pay taxes to the government (orange arrow), and the government provides certain goods and services to businesses (brown arrow).

Now look at Exhibit 3-2 as a whole, rather than focusing on any of its parts. Notice in particular the relationships between different economic individuals, businesses, and institutions.

- *Businesses and households.* Households sell resources to businesses, and businesses pay for those resources. In addition, businesses sell goods and services to households, and households pay for those goods and services.

Differentiating Instruction

Visual and English Language Learners
Either create and post a larger version of the circular flow diagram or show one using a projector. Ask students to cite specific examples of each entity and arrow on the diagram. Completing this activity will show students how the diagram relates directly to their lives.

Next, instruct students to draw circular flow diagrams and provide specific examples in the arrows. For example, in the bottom right-pointing arrow, students might add "A cereal company pays workers to put cereal in boxes," and in the bottom left-pointing arrow, students might add "The Diaz family buys a box of cereal."

- *Government and households.* House-holds pay taxes to the government, and the government provides goods and services to households.
- *Government and businesses.* Businesses pay taxes to the government, and the government provides goods and services to businesses.

Why Is the Circular Flow Diagram Useful?

Suppose you are watching the news one night on TV. An economist who works for the president of the United States says that the president is seriously considering raising people's taxes. Look at Exhibit 3-2 and ask yourself which arrow will be affected by this action. It is the yellow arrow labeled "Households pay taxes," which goes from households to the government. If all other things remain the same, this arrow will grow larger, because more tax dollars will flow through it.

Next, ask yourself this question: if more tax dollars flow through the yellow arrow from households to government, will fewer dollars flow through some other arrow? The answer is yes. Fewer dollars will flow through the blue arrow, which moves from households to businesses. In other words, when households pay more of their income in taxes, they have less of their income to buy things such as TVs, cars, and computers. The circular flow diagram helps us see how a change in one economic activity (such as paying taxes) will lead to a change somewhere else in the economy (such as the amount households spend on goods and services produced by businesses).

SECTION 1

ASSESSMENT

Defining Terms

1. Define:
   a. private property
   b. public property
   c. household
   d. circular flow of economic activity
2. Use the word *incentive* correctly in a sentence.

Reviewing Facts and Concepts

3. According to the circular flow of economic activity, in what economic activities is the government engaged? (Look at Exhibit 3-2 to help you answer the question.)
4. In Exhibit 3-2, both households and businesses are identified. Often we think of the households as U.S. households and the

businesses as U.S. businesses. Would this still be the case if countries traded with each other? Explain.
5. In a free enterprise economy, how would you answer this question: *For whom are goods produced?*
6. How does voluntary exchange benefit a person?
7. What advantages do consumers get from the competition between sellers?
8. Explain the basic characteristics of the U.S. free enterprise system, including incentives, economic freedom, competition, and the limited role of government.

Critical Thinking

9. Would Adam Smith agree that the benefits of free enterprise are a consequence of the human desire to make life better for others? Explain.
10. In country A, people are not allowed to have private property. In country B, they are. In which country will individuals have a greater incentive to produce goods? Why?

Applying Economic Concepts

11. Teachers want students to do their homework completely, carefully, and on time. Identify an incentive that will increase students' efforts toward reaching these objectives.

SECTION 1

ASSESSMENT ANSWERS

Defining Terms

1. a. private property: any good that is owned by an individual or a business; **b. public property:** any good that is owned by the government; **c. household:** an economic unit of one person or

more that sells resources and buys goods and services; **d. circular flow of economic activity:** the economic relationships that exist between different economic groups in an economy.

2. Answers will vary. Students should write sentences that show that they clearly understand the economic use of the term.

Reviewing Facts and Concepts

3. The government is involved in the economic activities of receiving taxes and providing certain benefits to households and to businesses.

4. No. In an economy with international trade (e.g., the U.S. trades with Mexico, Italy, and China), then the households in

the circular flow diagram would be American, Mexican, Italian, and Chinese households and the businesses would be American, Mexican, Italian, and Chinese businesses.

5. In a free enterprise economy, goods are produced for those people who are willing and able to buy them.

6. When a person trades, he or she exchanges something of less value to him or her for something of greater value.

7. Consumers will likely have a larger selection of products from which to choose. They are also likely to have higher-quality goods, pay lower prices, and receive better service.

8. Answers will vary.

Critical Thinking

9. No. According to Adam Smith, good things happen under free enterprise because people can't make themselves better off unless they help others first.

10. Individuals will have a greater incentive to produce goods in country B. Without private property, goods are not your own to sell. If you can't sell the goods you produce, then you have little reason to produce them in the first place.

Applying Economic Concepts

11. Answers will vary. Compile a list of student suggestions on the board and discuss them.

Assessment Book

You will find a quiz for this section in the *Assessment Book,* page 22.

Reteaching Activity

Guide students in examining their favorite aspects of the free enterprise system. Is it competition between employers for a worker's labor service? Is it the fact that businesses produce the goods consumers want to buy? Ask volunteers to share the reasons for their favorites.

Guided Reading

For further reteaching of the key concepts in this section, assign the Outlining Activity and the Just the Facts Handout from the *Guided Reading and Study Guide,* pages 33–35.

Focus and Motivate

Section Objectives

After completing this section, students will be able to
- describe the roles that profits and losses play in a free enterprise economy;
- explain what profits, losses, and resources have to do with one another; and
- describe how profits and losses operate as signals to business firms.

Economics
Around the Clock

Kickoff Activity

Tell students to reread the 11:02 a.m. scenario in Economics Around the Clock (page 61) and respond in writing.

Allow volunteers to share their answers with the class. Students should explain how deciding to go to another store relates to free enterprise.

Activating Prior Knowledge

Profit pulls resources toward itself. To help students understand this concept, make an analogy between profit and a magnet. A magnet pulls things toward itself, too. Ask students to describe what profit is pulling toward itself. (*Answer:* resources.)

Teach

Discussion Starter

Ask how many students have jobs in retail stores. Ask those students if they are aware of the wholesale costs (average costs of goods) of the items they sell in the stores.

Profit and Loss in Free Enterprise

Focus Questions
- What roles do profits and losses play in a free enterprise economy?
- What do profits, losses, and resources have to do with one another?
- How do profits and losses operate as signals to business firms?

Key Terms
profit
loss

Profits and Losses

In a free enterprise economy, there are no guarantees. A business can succeed or fail. Whether a business is successful or not depends on whether it generates profits or losses.

Profits

Suppose that a computer company spends $800 to produce a computer and then sells the computer for $1,200. In this case, the company earns $400 in profit. **Profit** is the amount of money left over after all the costs of production have been paid.

Profit can also be described in terms of total revenue and total cost. *Total revenue* is the price of a good times the number of units of the good sold:

profit
The amount of money left over after all the costs of production have been paid. Profit exists whenever total revenue is greater than total cost.

loss
The amount of money by which total cost exceeds total revenue.

$$\text{Total revenue} =$$
$$\text{Price of a good} \times \text{Number of units sold}$$

For example, suppose you sell cell phones at a price of $50 apiece. On Monday, you sell five cell phones, so the total revenue for Monday is $250.

Total cost is the *average cost* of a good times the number of units of the good sold:

$$\text{Total cost} =$$
$$\text{Average cost of a good} \times \text{Number of units sold}$$

Suppose the average cost of the five cell phones you sell is $30 per phone. The total cost is $150. For the five cell phones, the difference between total revenue ($250) and total cost ($150) is $100. This $100 is profit.

Losses

Notice that profit results any time total revenue is greater than total cost. When the opposite is true—when total cost is greater than total revenue—a *loss* occurs. A **loss** stated in terms of the amount of money by which total cost exceeds total revenue. For example, suppose that in a given year, a clothing store has a total revenue of $150,000 and total costs of $200,000. If we subtract the store's costs from its revenues, we get –$50,000, a loss for the year.

Profit = Total revenue > Total cost
Loss = Total cost > Total revenue

Cross-Curricular Activity

Invite a history teacher to speak to your class about how the profit motive was a factor in the American Revolution. Ask the history teacher, for example, to put the Boston Tea Party into an economic context. Many patriots believed that Great Britain was infringing on their economic rights, as well as other rights and liberties. Ask students to think about how closely related economic rights can be to other rights, such as the right to freedom of speech.

Profit and Loss as Signals

At any time in a free enterprise economy, some business firms are earning profits and some are taking losses. Profits and losses serve as signals not only to the firms actually earning the profits and taking the losses but also to firms standing on the sidelines.

Suppose the NBC television network airs a comedy show on Thursday night that earns high ratings. Because companies will pay more to advertise on high-rated shows, the comedy show creates more profits for NBC. The CBS network airs a crime show on Thursday night that receives low ratings and therefore losses. What are NBC and CBS likely to do now?

NBC will probably do nothing different; it will continue doing what it has been doing. The comedy show is earning high ratings, and the network is earning high profits. CBS, in contrast, will probably cancel its crime show, because the public doesn't like it. CBS might replace the crime show with a comedy, because NBC has shown that a comedy does better than a crime show.

So far, the third major network, ABC, has remained on the sidelines watching what is happening to NBC and CBS on Thursday night. ABC is thinking about developing a new program. Will what has happened to NBC and CBS influence ABC's decision about what type of program it will develop? Probably. ABC will be more likely to develop a comedy than a crime show.

Let's summarize what happened:

- The people at home decide what they want to watch on TV.

▲ In a free enterprise economy, there is no guarantee that a new business will succeed. Why do you think more than 3 million businesses fail each year?

◄ *The Big Bang Theory* is a profitable show on CBS. How do one company's profits affect decisions made by its competitors?

69

Teaching with Visuals

Businesses fail because they experience too many losses.

Activating Prior Knowledge

Instruct each student to write one sentence that relates profit to total cost and total revenue—for example, "Profit exists whenever total revenue is greater than total cost."

Thinking Like an Economist

Some people believe that if you favor a free enterprise economy, you must be in favor of everything that businesspeople do. Economists think differently. They know that businesspeople might want to hamper the free enterprise economy. For example, suppose a U.S. car company wants the government to restrict the number of new foreign cars that can be imported into the country to be sold. In doing so, the U.S. car company hopes to lessen the competition it faces from foreign car companies. This act isn't consistent with free enterprise, which promotes competition. In other words, being pro-business is not the same as being pro-free enterprise. Being pro-free enterprise is usually more consistent with being pro-consumer and pro-competition. Invite students to identify another instance in which a business wants to stifle the free enterprise economy.

Teaching with Visuals

One company's profits signal to its competitors that perhaps they should copy what the successful company has done.

Visit econ.myemcp.com/videos for videos that will help students better understand the key concepts found in this section.

Cooperative Learning

Write the following sentences on the board: "Some people believe that profit benefits only those people who earn it. Others say that profit has a social function, too. This means that it provides some good to society."

Divide the class into two groups: one for each side of this issue. Ask the members of each group to work together to prepare a presentation supporting its side. Tell students that they will need to explain why their viewpoint is correct or best.

After students have read this feature, ask them to compare their experiences of owning private property with their experiences of using common property. Which experience do they prefer?

ANSWERS TO THINK ABOUT IT Students' answers will vary. Let them share their ideas about in which scenario they will be more likely to take good care of the car.

Reinforcement Activity

The role of profits and losses in free enterprise can be defined in many relationships in an economic system. Instruct students to identify the role of profits and losses in various sectors of the economic world in which they live. To make sure they can see the impact of these economic factors on their daily lives, ask them to describe ways in which profit and loss affect them every day.

 Application Activity

After reading and discussing Section 2, assign the Section Activity in the *Applying the Principles Workbook,* pages 26–27.

Economic Facts *and* Fallacies

FALSE
TRUE

The expectation is that the higher the interest rate one can earn on a savings account, the more of one's wealth one will hold in cash.

Assess

Quick Quiz

The following true-or-false quiz will help you assess student understanding of the material covered in this section.
1. Total revenue is the average cost of a good divided by the number of units of the good sold. (False)

What Saved the Pilgrims?

Private property is one of the features of free enterprise. Many advocates of free enterprise argue that without private ownership property, free enterprise could not produce as much wealth as it does.

Private property is not without its critics, though. Some people argue that owning private property breeds greed and selfishness. Common property—that is, property owned together by the community—motivates people to be more civic minded, peaceful, and caring, critics say. The advocates of private property retort that this notion of common property is idealistic and wrong. The truth is, they say, that common property often leads to poverty and unhappiness.

With this background, consider the Pilgrims in the early 1600s. When the Pilgrims left the Old World, they formed a partnership in a joint-stock company with some London merchants. When the Pilgrims landed off the coast of Massachusetts in 1620, they followed the advice of the company and declared that all pastures and produce would be common property. The result was chaos and starvation; after the first winter, half the colonists had died.

Bad weather is often blamed for what happened to the Pilgrims, but the governor of the Plymouth colony, William Bradford, believed otherwise. He thought it had a lot to do with the fact that the Pilgrims held common property instead of private property. Bradford, therefore, assigned every family in the colony a private parcel of land, on which they could produce food that they sold for profit. In his diary, Bradford wrote that privatizing the land "had very good success for it made all the hands very industrious, as much more corn was planted than otherwise would have been." He also noted how unsuccessful the common property scheme had turned out to be when he said, somewhat philosophically, that it had proved the "vanity of that conceit of Plato's . . . that the taking away of [private] property and bringing community into a commonwealth [of common property] would make them happy and flourishing." It seemed that common property had made people poor and hungry, not happy and flourishing.

Some historians say that it was probably Bradford's decision to turn common property into private property (and not just a change in the weather) that produced the first plentiful harvest in the Plymouth colony: a plentiful harvest that was subsequently celebrated as Thanksgiving.

THINK ABOUT IT To get an idea of how owning private property affects people's incentives, consider two scenarios. In the first scenario, you and five of your friends share ownership of a car. In the second scenario, you are the only owner of the car. In which scenario are you more likely to take care of the car (for example, to make sure it is clean and in good running order)? Explain your answer.

Differentiating Instruction

English Language Learners

To help students who are English language learners, use the following resources, which are provided as part of the *Economics: New Ways of Thinking* program:

- a Spanish glossary in the *Student Text*
- Spanish versions of the Chapter Summaries on an audio disc

- Many more people watch the NBC comedy show (giving it high ratings) than the CBS crime show (giving it low ratings).
- Companies pay more to advertise on high-rated shows than low-rated shows, so NBC earns profits on its Thursday show and CBS takes losses.
- NBC realizes that it has a winning show, so it keeps the comedy show on the air. CBS realizes it has a losing show, so it takes the crime show off the air.
- ABC, waiting on the sidelines, decides to copy NBC instead of CBS.

You recall that resources consist of land, labor, capital, and entrepreneurship. When CBS decides to take its crime show off the air and replace it with a comedy show, what happens to the resources that were used to produce the crime show? An economist would say the resources are being *reallocated*—moved from one place to another, or used differently. Some of the resources used to produce the crime show—such as the crew that worked on the show, the cameras used to film the show, the accountants who kept the books—will probably be used to work on a comedy show instead of a crime show. Simply put, resources flow toward profit; resources flow away from loss. Profit is like a big magnet: it pulls resources toward it. Loss is like a big wind: it pushes resources away.

EXAMPLE In the early days of VCRs, DVD players, personal calculators, and personal computers, profits were relatively

high for the relatively few companies that produced these new products. These high profits attracted competitors. It was as if the high profits were saying, "Look, I'm over here, come and get me." Soon, numerous companies were producing VCRs, DVD players, calculators, and personal computers, instead of only few. As a result, the prices of these goods came down—and so did the profits. ♦

Economic Facts *and* Fallacies

Money and Wealth

Some people assume that money is wealth. The fact is, however, that money is just one form of wealth. One's wealth consists of all those things that one owns which have value. A person's wealth might consist of her car, house, clothes, computer, watch, and artwork. Money has value too, so if a person has $5,000 in cash, either on hand or in a checking account, this $5,000 is part of a person's overall wealth. Now, is it possible to be wealthy and not have any money? The answer is yes! Consider the person who owns 10 houses worth a total of $10 million, paintings worth $3 million, and cars worth $1 million, yet doesn't have any cash in his wallet or checking account. This is an example of a wealthy person who has no money. Of course, if this person wanted to, he could obtain money by, say, selling one of his houses.

THINK ABOUT IT Money in one's wallet does not earn interest, but money in a savings account does. Do you think that changes in the interest rate one can earn on a savings account will influence how much of their wealth people hold in terms of cash? Explain your answer.

SECTION 2 ASSESSMENT

Defining Terms
1. Define:
   a. profit
   b. loss

Reviewing Facts and Concepts
2. Explain how profits and losses affect where resources will be used.
3. If a business is currently earning high profits producing lamps, what

are other firms that observe this fact likely to do? Explain your answer.
4. If the price is $40, the number of units sold is 450, and the average cost is $33, what is the profit?
5. If the average cost is $423, the price is $399, and the number of units sold is 23, what is the loss?

Critical Thinking
6. Many people think that a profit benefits only the person who earns it; in other words, a profit provides no social function. Do you agree or disagree? Explain your answer.
7. What role do losses play in a free enterprise system? Are losses as important as profits to free enterprise? Explain.

2. Resources flow toward losses. (False)
3. When total cost is greater than total revenue, there is a loss. (True)
4. Profit is the price of a good times the number of units of the good sold. (False)
5. Goods that earned profits in the past always earn profits in the future. (False)

Assessment Book
You will find a quiz for this section in the *Assessment Book,* page 23.

Reteaching Activity
Guide students in examining profit. Write the following chart on the board and ask, What is the profit in each case?

	Total Cost	Total Revenue
A.	$100	$120
B.	$75	$100
C.	$1,250	$1,550

The answers are **A.** $20; **B.** $25; **C.** $300. Review these answers with students to ensure they understand how to determine profit.

Guided Reading
For further reteaching of the key concepts in this section, assign the Outlining Activity and the Just the Facts Handout from the *Guided Reading and Study Guide,* pages 36–37.

Critical Thinking
6. Answers will vary, but an economist would disagree with this statement. Profit does benefit the person who earns it, but it does more. It directs resources in ways that people want resources directed. To illustrate, suppose good X earns high profits on its production and sale. In a sense, what buyers are saying by rewarding the firm with profits is, "We want more Xs. Use resources to produce Xs." Some firms that currently are not producing good X will begin to produce it. In short, firms will respond by producing those goods for which profit can be earned.
7. Losses indicate that firms' resources were used to produce goods or services that individuals did not want to buy at the prices specified. Losses are as important as profits. Both tell firms what to produce more of (profits) and less of (losses).

SECTION 2 ASSESSMENT ANSWERS

Defining Terms
1. a. profit: the amount of money left over after all the costs of production have been paid—in other words, total revenue minus total costs; **b. loss:**
the amount of money by which total cost exceeds total revenue.

Reviewing Facts and Concepts
2. Profits and losses significantly affect the distribution of resources. Resources gravitate toward activities that generate profits. Resources move away

from activities that generate losses.
3. Other firms are likely to start producing lamps. The reason for this is that they want to try to capture some of the profits that can be made in the lamp market.
4. $3,150.
5. $552.

Teacher Support

Focus and Motivate

Section Objectives

After completing this section, students will be able to

- describe some of the qualities and characteristics of an ethical economic system;
- list some of the freedoms in free enterprise;
- explain what economic principles are stated in the Bill of Rights, the Constitution, and the Declaration of Independence; and
- describe some of the responsibilities people have in a free enterprise system.

Kickoff Activity

Write the following sentences on the board and ask students to answer the questions: "The word *ethics* is usually associated with people. Do you think that an economic system can be considered ethical? For example, do you think free enterprise is ethical?"

Activating Prior Knowledge

In the last section, students learned that there are no guarantees in a free enterprise economy. A business can either fail or succeed. Ask students to think about whether this might create pressure in some instances for people to act unethically and to cite examples. Discuss how people might respond differently in these situations to ensure ethical behavior.

 Visit econ.myemcp.com/videos for videos that will help students better understand the key concepts found in this section.

The Ethics of the Free Enterprise System

Focus Questions

- What are some of the qualities or characteristics of an ethical economic system?
- What are some of the freedoms in free enterprise?
- What economic principles are stated in the Bill of Rights, the Constitution, and the Declaration of Independence?
- What are some of the responsibilities people have in a free enterprise system?

Key Term

ethics

Ethics and Free Enterprise

Ethics consist of the principles of conduct, such as right and wrong, moral and immoral, good and bad. We often evaluate people as being ethical or not. Can we do the same thing for an economic system? For example, can we determine whether free enterprise is an ethical economic system? Another way of approaching this question is to ask what characteristics or qualities free enterprise would need to have to be an ethical system. What goals would it need to meet? (See Exhibit 3-3.)

People Can Choose

In arguing that free enterprise is an ethical economic system, supporters begin by pointing out that it allows individuals to choose their occupations or professions. An ethical system, they say, does not force people to do jobs or tasks they would rather not do. On this count, the supporters of free enterprise argue that it is an ethical system because no one is forced to work at a job he or she does not want. People are free to choose the types of work they want to do.

ethics
The principles of conduct, such as right and wrong, morality and immorality, good and bad.

A Variety of Products

Supporters of free enterprise argue that an ethical economic system produces the goods and services preferred by both the majority and the minority. Under that economic system, if the majority of the people want to buy medium-sized SUVs that have Bluetooth and GPS, then manufacturers will produce those kinds of vehicles. (After all, they do not want to produce goods that

---

EXHIBIT 3-3 An Ethical Economic System

- Allows individuals to choose their own occupations or professions

- Produces goods and services preferred by both the majority and the minority

- Rewards or punishes producers based on how well or poorly they respond to the buying public

- Supports the right of the individual to be free, including the freedom to acquire property, work where you choose, and start your own business

Cooperative Learning

The characteristics of an ethical free enterprise system are sometimes difficult to understand. To help students better grasp these characteristics, divide the class into groups of three or four. Ask each group to choose a characteristic from Exhibit 3-3 and then research real-world examples of it. Ask the groups to present their findings to the class.

consumers are not willing to buy.) If a few people want big SUVs instead of medium-sized SUVs, then it is likely that some big SUVs will be produced too. If other people want small SUVs, then some small SUVs will probably be produced.

Think of free enterprise at work in the restaurant business. In most U.S. cities of moderate size, many different types of restaurants serve particular styles of food: home cooking, fast food, and ethnic foods, for example. A wide variety of goods and services are available because free enterprise responds both to the majority and to minorities.

Rewards Depend on Performance

An ethical economic system rewards (or punishes) producers according to how well (or poorly) they respond to the preferences of the buying public. Free enterprise fits this description. Sellers that continue to give consumers what they want to buy in terms of the type of good, quality of good, and price of good will likely earn profits and stay in business. Sellers that do not respond to public preferences end up taking losses and going out of business.

Numerous Freedoms

The proponents of free enterprise argue that no economic system can be ethical if it limits people's freedom. In free enterprise, they say, people have numerous freedoms: the freedom to work where they want to work, the freedom to start their own businesses if they want, the freedom to acquire property, the freedom to buy and sell the goods they want to buy and sell, and even the freedom to fail.

EXAMPLE Suppose Harris takes his entire savings and opens a shoe store. Six months later, he shuts down his business and declares bankruptcy. Harris's problem was that few people wanted to buy shoes from him. ♦

Despite the advantages offered by the U.S. free enterprise system, businesses close every day. Free enterprise gives us the freedom to spend our money as we choose, and sometimes that freedom

▲ These students are learning about career possibilities. Why is this something they can do in a free enterprise economy, but not in some other economic systems?

results in business failures for other people. Individuals must accept the consequences of their decisions. Free enterprise does not offer any guaranteed outcomes; rather, it offers freedoms.

A Student Asks

QUESTION: *Having the freedom to do something is different from having the ability to do it. What use is having the freedom to start your own business if you do not have the money to do it? Without the ability, the freedom seems useless.*

ANSWER: *No economic system can provide people with the ability to do anything, such as write a great novel, run a four-minute mile, or be a successful entrepreneur. However, economic systems may or may not give individuals the opportunity to realize their potential.*

Teaching with Visuals

One of the freedoms that people living in a free enterprise economy enjoy is the freedom to choose a career.

Discussion Starter

Ethics may be a difficult concept for students to comprehend. Dictionaries commonly define *ethics* as "a set of moral principles or values, a theory or system of moral values, and a guiding philosophy." Ask, Where do ethics come from? What are your personal ethics? How would you apply your own values to an economic system?

Analyzing

A freedom in free enterprise that's often overlooked is the freedom to fail. Explain to students that some people fail in their business efforts in a free enterprise economy because other people have the freedom to spend their money as they choose. Ask students why being able to fail is considered a freedom.

Reinforcement Activity

Ask students if they see the importance of ethics in a free enterprise economic system. Have them identify examples of both ethical behavior in the free enterprise system and unethical behavior, such as monopolies and fixed pricing.

Cross-Curricular Activity

Invite a history teacher to speak to your class about "rags to riches" stories in U.S. history. Suggest to the teacher that he or she include stories that reflect the ethnic diversity of your school's community. Also suggest that the teacher address what features of the U.S. economy made these successes possible. Consider asking students to prepare, individually or in groups, one-page reports about Americans who can be considered economic success stories.

Reinforcement Activity

Help students to see the relationship between rights and responsibilities; that is, if a person has the right to do something, then he or she should assume the responsibility that goes along with that right. Ask students to discuss what rights they have in today's society. They may mention the right to drive a car (after a person has reached a certain age and obtained a license) or the right to buy and sell goods and services. Once students have identified specific rights in their daily lives, ask them to develop a list of the responsibilities that go along with those rights. For example, if someone has the right to drive a car, he or she also has the responsibility of operating the car in a safe and legal manner.

Teaching with Visuals

The Bill of Rights and the Declaration of Independence helped solidify free enterprise as the economic system for the United States.

The supporters of free enterprise argue that free enterprise does provide people with the opportunity, or freedom, to start a business. They also argue that free enterprise gives individuals the opportunity to strengthen and develop their abilities.

Suppose a person does not currently have the money or the knowledge to open up her own business and is currently working at a low-wage job. Is she destined never to start her own business? Not necessarily. She can begin today doing those things that are necessary to start her own business in the future. Those steps might include working hard in her current job, saving some money, attending school to learn about the business she wants to start, and obtaining a business loan.

The economic history of the United States under free enterprise is full of stories of people who were poor and uneducated (and, in many cases, did not know the English language) yet went on to start their own businesses and become economically successful.

Economic Principles in Key Documents

The Constitution, the Bill of Rights, and the Declaration of Independence hold a special place in the hearts and minds of most Americans. It can also be argued that these three documents have a special significance to free enterprise: each document has free enterprise economic principles contained within it.

Remember that private property, choice, and competition are important features of free enterprise and that the essence of free enterprise is freedom. It is not difficult to find evidence that the Constitution, the Bill of Rights, and the Declaration of Independence are also about private property, choice, competition, and freedom, among other things.

Bill of Rights

The Bill of Rights, for example, notes that "private property [shall not] be taken for public use, without just compensation." In other words, if the government wants some land that you own to put in a road, it cannot simply take that land from you. It must justly compensate, or pay, you for that land. This right shows the high regard for private property in the Bill of Rights.

Declaration of Independence

The signers of the Declaration of Independence listed many complaints against the king of Great Britain, George III. One complaint was that the king had prevented the 13 colonies from "trad[ing] with all parts of the world." Surely, the signers of the Declaration of Independence were angry at King George III for not allowing them to practice free trade—an essential ingredient of free enterprise—with the rest of the world.

▶ The signing of the Constitution in Philadelphia in 1787 helped establish the principles of free enterprise in the United States. **What other key documents helped solidify free enterprise as the economic system for the young nation?**

Background Information: Founding Documents

The political and economic ideals expressed in the U.S. Constitution are still relevant today. For instance, the Constitution still dictates the structure of the U.S. government. It also guarantees many of the economic freedoms we all enjoy.

The Constitution has affected not only the United States but many other countries and world organizations as well. These countries and organizations have used the Constitution as a model in developing their own political and economic rights.

Does an "Invisible Hand" Guide Individuals in Free Enterprise?

Adam Smith, the father of modern economics, lived in Scotland and England from 1723 to 1790. One of his economic concepts was something he called the "invisible hand." He said that individuals in a market or free enterprise setting (where buyers are free to buy what they want and sellers are free to produce and sell what they want) are led by an invisible force—an invisible hand—"to promote an end which was not part of their intention."

To illustrate this concept, suppose there is a producer/seller of some product who is very self-interested. His only goal is to earn as much money as possible. How will he proceed? According to Adam Smith, the producer/seller will be guided by the invisible hand to produce and sell only those things that buyers want to buy. In other words, if people only want to buy canned fruit and vegetables, then he will produce canned fruit and vegetables. If they don't want to buy donuts, then he won't produce donuts.

But in producing and offering to sell what others want to buy, he is "promoting an end which was not his intention." Recall that his intention was to make as much money as possible, and to achieve that, he had to produce something that others wanted to buy. He had to offer others what they wanted before they would give him what he wanted (money). That is the market process at work—or as Adam Smith might say, that is the invisible hand at work.

THINK ABOUT IT Adam Smith thought that self-interest was similar to a resource or factor of production (such as land, labor, or capital). Just as you need certain resources, such as land and labor, to produce a good, you might also need self-interest to produce a good. Self-interest is often the motivation for producing goods and services for others. Does a pharmaceutical company produce medicines for people out of its sense of altruism or self-interest? Does a builder build a house to sell to a family out of his sense of altruism or self-interest? Adam Smith was somewhat unique in that he clearly understood that a person's self-interest within a free enterprise system could very well work to the advantage of others. Do you think self-interest works the same way in all other economic systems? Explain your answer.

The Constitution

Article 1, Section 8, of the U.S. Constitution says that "no tax or duty shall be laid on articles exported from any State." The Constitution favors preserving competition; if states had been allowed the right to impose taxes on other states' goods, then competition within individual states would have been lessened. To preserve competition—an important feature of free enterprise—it was important to deny states the right to tax each other's goods.

ANSWERS TO THINK ABOUT IT Answers will vary here, but generally speaking we would expect that those economic systems in which one could only make himself better off by first making others better off would be more likely to direct self interest into serving others than in economic systems that did not.

Reinforcement Activity

Currently, the 50 states cannot tax each other's goods. For example, North Carolina cannot impose a special tax on a good that is produced in Virginia and sold in North Carolina. Divide the class into groups of four or five students, and ask them to discuss how life might be different if states could tax each other's goods.

Application Activity

After reading and discussing Section 3, assign the Section Activity in the *Applying the Principles Workbook,* pages 28–30.

Assess

Quick Quiz

The following true-or-false quiz will help you assess student understanding of the material covered in this section.

1. In an ethical economic system, people can choose whatever job they wish. (True)
2. An ethical economic system produces nothing for the minority. (False)
3. An ethical economic system does not punish producers. (False)
4. An ethical economic system gives producers the freedom to fail. (True)
5. Rights rarely come without responsibilities. (True)

Ask students to imagine how their lives would be different if the colonists had not rebelled against British rule and if the Constitution had never been written. Ask student volunteers to express in their own words how knowing more about the Constitution helps them understand the free enterprise system. Also encourage students to think broadly about the Constitution's impact worldwide. How would the world be different if the U.S. Constitution didn't exist?

Assessment Book

You will find a quiz for this section in the *Assessment Book,* page 24.

Reteaching Activity

Have students work in pairs to create charts that depict individual rights and responsibilities in a free enterprise system.

Guided Reading

For further reaching of the key concepts in this section, assign the Outlining Activity and the Just the Facts Handout from the *Guided Reading and Study Guide,* pages 38–40.

ASSESSMENT ANSWERS

Defining Terms

1. ethics: principles of conduct, such as right and wrong, morality and immorality, good and bad

Reviewing Facts and Concepts

2. Disagree. If the minority is willing and able to buy certain goods, producers will find it in their best interest to produce those goods. Stated differently, if the minority is willing and able to pay a price for a good that will return a profit to the producer, the producer is very likely to produce that particular good.

3. Disagree. Free enterprise doesn't guarantee anyone economic success.

4. a. the responsibility of giving the other person involved in the exchange accurate information about what is being exchanged; **b.** the responsibility of using one's property only for legal purposes; **c.** the responsibility to act in a truthful, legitimate manner.

Critical Thinking

5. Answers will vary. (*Sample answer:* Even if we agree that under free enterprise, more trashy novels will be published and sold than serious, soul-inspiring works of literature, it doesn't follow that free enterprise is unethical. Maybe more people are will-

Economic Rights and Responsibilities in a Free Enterprise Economy

People have certain rights in a free enterprise economy, but rights rarely come without responsibilities. What responsibilities do people have in a free enterprise economy?

Open Disclosure

Many people argue that the right to voluntary exchange comes with the responsibility to give the other person accurate information about what is being exchanged. Suppose that Steve wants to exchange (sell) his 12-year-old house for the $270,000 that Roberto is willing and able to pay for it. In a free enterprise economic system, Steve and Roberto have the economic right to complete this exchange, but Steve also has the responsibility to tell Roberto the particulars about the house. For example, if the house has termites or faulty plumbing, Steve should tell Roberto this fact. In other words, Steve has the responsibility of truthfully relating to Roberto the facts about the product he is considering buying. This disclosure is a matter of simple fairness or justice.

"If you wish to prosper, let your customer prosper."
—Frédéric Bastiat, economist

Obeying the Law

Consider another economic right in a free enterprise economy: the right to private property. The responsibility associated with this right is the responsibility of using one's property only for legal purposes; it is a responsibility to respect and abide by the law. Suppose that Isabella owns a car. She certainly has the right to use that car to drive to and from work, go on vacations, pick up friends at school, and so on. But Isabella also has some responsibilities—for example, to obey the speed limit, to know and follow all other traffic laws, and to drive carefully.

Being Truthful

Finally, consider the economic right to compete in a free enterprise system. The responsibility attached to this right is to compete in a truthful, legitimate manner. If Tushar and Yolanda both own pizzerias in town and are thus in competition with each other, then each has the responsibility to be truthful about the other's business. Tushar should not lie to his customers by telling them that Yolanda's pizzeria was cited by the health examiner for having insects in the kitchen. Yolanda should not lie and say that Tushar uses less cheese in his pizzas than he actually does.

ASSESSMENT

Defining Terms
1. Define:
   a. ethics

Reviewing Facts and Concepts
2. "Under free enterprise, only the majority of people can buy the goods they prefer; the minority always end up buying those goods they would prefer not to buy." Do you agree or disagree with this statement? Explain your answer.
3. "Free enterprise guarantees economic success." Do you agree or disagree with this statement? Explain your answer.
4. Explain what responsibility goes with each of the following rights:
   a. the right to voluntary exchange
   b. the right to private property
   c. the right to compete

Critical Thinking
5. "In a free enterprise system, more trashy novels could be published and sold than serious, soul-inspiring works of literature. Any system that produces this outcome can't be ethical." Do you agree or disagree? Explain.
6. How would your economic life be different if the U.S. economy was not based on the economic principles expressed in the Bill of Rights, the Declaration of Independence, and the Constitution?

ing and able to buy trashy novels than serious literature. Free enterprise may simply reflect this fact—in short, responding to people's preferences. Doing so is not unethical. If tomorrow, people began to prefer serious literature to trashy novels, then free enterprise would deliver more serious literature and fewer trashy novels. Free enterprise doesn't decide which preferences are right or wrong or good or bad; its goal is to satisfy consumers' preferences.)

6. Americans would have limited economic opportunities if the economy was not based on these principles. All three documents speak to elements of free enterprise. The Bill of Rights speaks to private property, the Declaration of Independence to free trade, and the Constitution to competition.

Entrepreneurs

Focus Questions
- ► What is an entrepreneur?
- ► How might the actions of an entrepreneur benefit you?
- ► How would future entrepreneurs be affected by a law that limits profits?
- ► Why are entrepreneurs willing to risk their time and money?

Key Term
entrepreneur

Imagine Being an Entrepreneur

An **entrepreneur** is a person who has a special talent for searching out and taking advantage of new business opportunities, as well as developing new products and new ways of doing things. To get some idea of what being an entrepreneur is like, try to imagine that you are one.

New Opportunities

How would you search out new business opportunities? No single source of information, whether a book or a website, will tell you exactly how and where to find business opportunities. Even if such a source existed, the information would be out of date before it was published or posted. When most people are confronted with the task of finding a new business opportunity, they end up scratching their heads. Most people are not entrepreneurs; entrepreneurs are a tiny minority of the population.

New Products

Think about the second task of an entrepreneur: developing new products. What new product can you think of developing? Most of us are accustomed to thinking in terms of products that already exist, such as TVs, computers, and cars. Thinking of a new product is not easy, especially a product with a high potential for sales.

entrepreneur
A person who has a special talent for searching out and taking advantage of new business opportunities.

▲ Entrepreneurs feel that they have new and better ways of satisfying customers. **What sort of business might you want to start someday?**

Cooperative Learning

Divide the class into groups of no more than four. Tell each group that they are entrepreneurs who will develop something for a new business opportunity. They need a rough sketch of the new product and, if possible, a prototype of the product.

One group member should write a description of the product, and then together, group members should list the benefits and risks involved in developing this product.

Teacher Support

Focus and Motivate

Section Objectives

After completing this section, students will be able to
- ► describe an entrepreneur;
- ► explain how consumers benefit from the actions of entrepreneurs;
- ► describe how a law that limited profits would affect future entrepreneurs; and
- ► explain why entrepreneurs are willing to risk their time and money.

Kickoff Activity

Write this instruction on the board for students to answer: "Identify five products that make your life easier or more enjoyable."

Activating Prior Knowledge

Invite students to discuss their responses to the Kickoff Activity. Explain that entrepreneurs developed many of the goods they listed. Invite students to find out who developed these products and when.

Teach

Cause and Effect

When entrepreneurs develop new products or processes, they stand to earn huge profits. Other people also benefit. Invite students to discuss how these products benefit others: the streetlight, plastic, and the telephone.

Reinforcement Activity

Ask each student to think of a popular product from the past year and research its creator. Ask, What is the creator's entrepreneurial history? What background or training might one need to become this type of entrepreneur?

Teaching with Visuals

Answers will vary.

After students have read this feature, ask what they know about the history of the U.S. auto industry. In the early days (before 1960), there were multiple U.S. companies. Slowly, all of them were taken over by the remaining three, producing limited competition and innovation. Beginning in the 1960s and really accelerating in the 1980s, many foreign companies entered the U.S. market, producing intense competition. U.S. auto makers were slow to respond to the competition, and by 2010, two of the three major companies were in bankruptcy and being supported by the U.S. government.

ANSWERS TO THINK ABOUT IT Being pro-business generally refers to acting in ways that help particular businesses (by restricting competition for a particular business, giving a business tax advantages not enjoyed by others, etc.). In contrast, being pro-free enterprise refers to supporting competition in a market setting, even if doing so isn't advantageous to a particular business. The misconception that being pro-business is the same as being pro-free enterprise has likely developed because business leaders preach the values of free enterprise yet willingly overlook them in serving their own interests.

Economics Around the Clock

After discussing the section on entrepreneurs, remind students of the 2:33 p.m. scenario in Economics Around the Clock (page 61), and discuss their answers to the question that accompanies it.

Answers will vary. Students may suggest that they study economics, business, accounting, and current product trends.

Visit econ.myemcp.com/videos for videos that will help students better understand the key concepts found in this section.

Is There a Difference Between Being Pro-Business and Pro-Free Enterprise?

Suppose that a privately owned, domestic (U.S.) auto manufacturer is having a hard time selling cars in the country because of intense foreign competition. In other words, auto manufacturers from countries such as Japan, Germany, and Italy are selling a lot of cars in the United States. In its frustration, this domestic company hires lobbyists to go to Washington, D.C., to convince elected representatives to place a high tariff (tax) on imported cars. Specifically, what the domestic car company wants is, say, a tariff of $2,000 on every foreign car offered for sale in the country. So, if a foreign car ordinarily sells for $24,000, it will now sell for $26,000.

The reason the domestic car manufacturer has asked the U.S. government to apply this tariff is clear: it wants to make it harder for its foreign competitors to sell cars, making it easier to sell its own cars. If the government agrees to the tariff, then the domestic car company will have succeeded in penalizing its foreign competitors and benefitting itself.

Is this free enterprise in action? Some people think that it is, because a private company has asked for a favor that the U.S. government grants. But this is not an example of free enterprise. This is an example of a government working with a domestic, private company to stifle foreign competition and to push citizens toward buying from domestic manufacturers. This is also an example of a private business benefitting at the expense of domestic consumers. Remember, under free enterprise, individuals are free to compete with others. Imposing a tariff on foreign car companies prevents fair competition between foreign and domestic manufacturers.

What does economist Milton Friedman think about doing business this way? He states the following:

You must separate out being "pro free-enterprise" from being "pro-business." The two greatest enemies of the free enterprise system, in my opinion, have been on one hand my fellow intellectuals, and on the other hand, the big businessmen—for opposite reasons.

Almost every businessman is in favor of free enterprise for everybody else, but special privilege and special government protection for himself. As a result, they have been a major force in undermining the free enterprise system. Stop kidding yourself into thinking you can use the business community as a way to promote free enterprise. Unfortunately, most of them are not our friends in that respect.

THINK ABOUT IT What is the difference between being pro-free enterprise and being pro-business? Which view do you support?

New Processes

As for the third task of an entrepreneur—developing new ways of doing things—ask yourself *what* things people would want to do differently. Then ask *how* people could do these things differently. You'll probably find that these questions are difficult to answer. Indeed, entrepreneurs must overcome obstacles, solve problems, and answer challenging questions.

Internet Research

The Global Impact

Remind students that entrepreneurs can come from any country. In fact, the word *entrepreneur* is from the French words *entre prendre*, which mean "to undertake." Have students use the Internet to research a list of foreign entrepreneurs and their contributions. Can students see the connections among all parts of the global free enterprise system?

Milton Friedman's Impact

Ask students to research Milton Friedman and to analyze his importance as an economic philosopher and his work's impact on the U.S. free enterprise system.

Who Benefits?

If an entrepreneur succeeds in coming up with an idea for a new product, develops and produces it, and then offers it for sale, how are you made better off? Think of entrepreneurs whose new products have helped you. For example, think about Steve Jobs, who was the co-founder and CEO of Apple. He helped develop the personal computer and devices such as the iPod, iPad, and iPhone. Was your life affected positively or negatively as a result of his entrepreneurship? Most people would say that they benefited from the introduction of, say, the personal computer. Entrepreneurs, it seems, play an important role in society by taking risks to develop new products or new ways of doing things that benefit the public. From a consumer's point of view, having more risk-taking entrepreneurs in a society likely means having more choices of goods and services in that society.

EXAMPLE Twitter is an online social networking and microblogging service. The users of Twitter send and receive tweets, which are text messages limited to 140 characters. Twitter was created in March 2006 by Jack Dorsey, Evan Williams, Biz Stone, and Noah Glass and it officially launched in July 2006. The creators of Twitter are entrepreneurs. They identified a demand for short, quick comments, and connections. Then they set out to satisfy that demand. According to the Twitter website, the number of active monthly users of Twitter is 313 million and there are 1 billion unique visits monthly to sites with embedded tweets. Twitter is one of the ten most visited websites in the world. What was the first tweet? It was written and sent by Jack Dorsey. He tweeted: "just setting up my twtrr." ♦

Entrepreneurs, Profit, and Risk

"You can't get something for nothing." This saying is certainly true for entrepreneurship. People can't be expected to risk their own time and money, to try to develop new products, and to innovate unless they can potentially earn a profit. With this in mind, how would you respond to someone who says, "Look at that entrepreneur. He's a billionaire; he's earned high profits for years. We ought to pass a law that people can earn no more than 5 percent profit on anything they produce and sell"?

> *"American prosperity and American free enterprise are both highly unusual in the world, and we should not overlook the possibility that the two are connected."*
> —**Thomas Sowell, economist**

You may be inclined to agree, thinking that with a law that limited profits, you would be able to buy goods and services at lower prices. Less profit for the billionaire entrepreneur, in other words, would mean more money in your own pocket.

Things don't always work this way, however. If *potential* entrepreneurs knew that they could earn only a 5 percent profit at best, they might not be willing to take the risks necessary to become *actual* entrepreneurs. With fewer entrepreneurs, there would be fewer new goods and services and fewer innovations available for your benefit.

Not all entrepreneurs are successful, of course. In fact, many of them risk their time and money and end up with nothing. Only a few end up with millions or even billions of dollars. It is the prospect of striking it rich that motivates entrepreneurs to assume the risks inherent in entrepreneurship.

SECTION 4 ASSESSMENT

Defining Terms
1. Define:
   a. entrepreneur

Reviewing Facts and Concepts
2. What does an entrepreneur do?
3. How might an entrepreneur's risk-taking activities benefit society?

Critical Thinking
4. Economists speak of four categories of resources: land, labor, capital, and entrepreneurship. Suppose country A has much more land, labor, and capital than country B but no entrepreneurs. Country B has many entrepreneurs. In which country would you prefer to live? Why?
5. How do entrepreneurs make your life better?

Section 4 Entrepreneurs **79**

SECTION 4 ASSESSMENT ANSWERS

Defining Terms

1. a. entrepreneur: a person who has a special talent for searching out and taking advantage of new business opportunities

Reviewing Facts and Concepts
2. An entrepreneur searches out and takes advantage of new business opportunities, develops new products, or develops new ways of doing things.
3. If an entrepreneur takes a risk, society may obtain a product that it didn't have before—a product that could make people's lives more enjoyable, more interesting, or easier. (Ask students to think of products they have that improve their lives and were developed by entrepreneurs.)

Critical Thinking
4. Answers will vary. A country that has a lot of land, labor,

---

After reading and discussing Section 4, assign the Section Activity in the *Applying the Principles Workbook,* pages 31–32.

Application Activity

Assess

Quick Quiz

The following true-or-false quiz will help you assess student understanding of the material covered in this section.

1. Entrepreneurs develop new products. (True)
2. No entrepreneur can make people better off. (False)
3. Less profit for entrepreneurs means more money in our pockets. (False)
4. Entrepreneurs risk their own time and money. (True)

Assessment Book

You will find a quiz for this section in the *Assessment Book,* page 25.

Reteaching Activity

Use the Section 4 Assessment to gauge which students may need reteaching. Ask students to list the three things that entrepreneurs do.

Guided Reading

For further reteaching of the key concepts in this section, assign the Outlining Activity and the Just the Facts Handout from the *Guided Reading and Study Guide,* pages 41–42.

and capital isn't guaranteed to be rich. A lot depends on how these resources are used. For example, labor that's used to dig and fill up ditches isn't as valuable as labor that's used to produce medicines, computers, and so on. Without entrepreneurs, land, labor, and capital are not as valuable. Entrepreneurs contribute significantly to the economy because they use land, labor, and capital in new and innovative ways.
5. Answers will vary. One correct answer is that entrepreneurs try to develop and produce new products that many individuals will want to purchase.

Teacher Support

Focus and Motivate

Section Objectives

After completing this section, students will be able to

▶ describe what would happen if government did not enforce contracts;

▶ describe a public good;

▶ explain why individuals in a free enterprise economy will not produce nonexcludable public goods for sale; and

▶ define negative and positive externalities.

Kickoff Activity

Write the following questions on the board and ask students to answer them: "What role should government play in a free enterprise economy? Why do you think so?"

Activating Prior Knowledge

Allow students to discuss their responses to the Kickoff Activity. Explain that in this section, they will discuss the role of government in a free enterprise economy.

Teach

Discussion Starter

Guide students in a discussion of situations in which they made a contract with someone. Ask whether students lived up to their side of the agreement and what repercussions they faced if they did not. Also ask whether the other party fulfilled her or his part of the agreement and what repercussions were involved.

The Role of Government in a Free Enterprise Economy

Focus Questions

▶ What would happen if government did not enforce contracts?

▶ What is a public good?

▶ In a free enterprise economy, why won't individuals produce nonexcludable public goods for sale?

▶ What is a negative externality? What is a positive externality?

Key Terms

contract
private good
public good
excludable public good
nonexcludable public good
free rider
negative externality
positive externality

---

contract
An agreement between two or more people to do something.

private good
A good for which one person's consumption takes away from another person's consumption.

public good
A good for which one person's consumption does not take away from another person's consumption.

excludable public good
A public good that individuals can be excluded (physically prohibited) from consuming.

nonexcludable public good
A public good that individuals cannot be excluded (physically prohibited) from consuming.

Government as Enforcer of Contracts

Think of what life would be like in a nation without government—no city government, no state government, no federal government. Suppose you own a construction company and regularly purchase supplies from people. On Tuesday, you enter into a **contract** with another person (an agreement between the two of you to do something). You agree to pay her $1,000 today if she delivers a shipment of wood to you on Friday. Friday comes, and no wood is delivered. Saturday, no wood. Sunday, no wood. On Monday, you call the person to ask what happened. She says that she has no intention of delivering the wood to you. "But you took my $1,000. That is theft!" you say. She just laughs at you and hangs up the telephone.

What do you do now? You can't turn to the police, because police services are part of government, which doesn't exist. You can't take the person to court, because the court system also is a part of government.

You can see the need for some institution to enforce contracts. In our society today, the government stands ready to punish persons who break their contracts.

Who is better off and who is worse off with government standing ready to enforce contracts? Just about everybody is better off. Only the contract breakers are worse off, because they can no longer break agreements without at least the threat of punishment.

Could the free enterprise system function without a government to enforce contracts? Most economists believe that it could function but not nearly as well as it does now. In fact, it would be severely crippled. Without government to enforce contracts, economists argue, the risk of going into business would be too great for many people. (Would you go into business if you knew people could break their contracts with you and not be punished?) Only a few people would assume the high risks of producing such items as TVs, houses, cars, and computers. The economy would be much smaller. Some economists believe that a free enterprise system will be a large, thriving economy when government acts to enforce contracts and a small, sluggish economy when it does not.

Cross-Curricular Activity

To clarify the role government plays in a free enterprise system, invite a government or civics teacher to speak to the class. Ask the teacher to discuss how the government's role in the economy has changed since World War II. He or she might also address the fact that while government and economics are connected in many ways (more than discussed in this chapter), the role of government *preferred* by free enterprise economists is a limited one.

Government as Provider of Nonexcludable Public Goods

Goods are categorized as two major types: private goods and public goods. A **private good** is a good for which one person's consumption takes away from another person's consumption. For example, an apple and a computer are both private goods. If Micala takes a bite of an apple, then less of the apple is available for someone else to consume. If Bill is working on the computer, then Janey cannot also be on the computer; in other words, Bill's use of the computer takes away from Janey's use of the computer.

In contrast, a **public good** is a good for which one person's consumption does not take away from another person's consumption. A movie in a theater and a lecture in college are public goods. If the movie is showing in a theater, then the fact that Vernon is watching the movie does not detract from Xavier's watching the movie. Both men can view the same movie to the same degree. If a teacher in college is lecturing on biology to 30 students, one student's consumption of the lecture does not take away anything from any other student's consumption.

Not all public goods are alike, however. They are both **excludable public goods** and **nonexcludable public goods**. A public good is *excludable* if individuals can be excluded (physically prohibited) from consuming it. A public good is *nonexcludable* if individuals cannot be excluded from consuming it.

Excludable Public Goods

Again, consider the movie in the theater. It is an excludable public good, because movie theater owners can (and do) prevent people from watching the movie. If you go to the movie theater and refuse to pay the ticket price, then the theater owner will not permit you to enter the theater. The owner will exclude you from viewing the movie.

What about a lecture in a college classroom? It is also an excludable public good. If you do not get admitted to the college or do not pay your tuition, the college can see to it that you can't sit in the college classroom and listen to the lecture.

▲ Free enterprise would be less effective if there were no legal system to enforce contracts. Can you describe a situation in which a trial would be necessary to prevent one business from dealing unfairly with another?

▲ This college lecture is a public good. Is it an excludable or non-excludable public good?

Teaching with Visuals

Answers will vary. Students might say that a trial would be necessary if one party to the contract refuses to live up to its part of the agreement.

Prediction Activity

Tell students that a country has decided to change its economic system from socialism to free enterprise. There is one problem, though: the country has a very poor institutional mechanism for enforcing contracts. Ask students to predict whether free enterprise will flourish in this country. Why or why not? (*Answer:* It will not flourish because for free enterprise to be successful, people have to be sure that contracts will be enforced.)

Teaching with Visuals

A college lecture is an excludable public good, because people who are not students in the course can be excluded from attending.

 Visit econ.myemcp.com/videos for videos that will help students better understand the key concepts found in this section.

Differentiating Instruction

Kinesthetic and Visual Learners

To reinforce students' understanding of the concepts of public goods and private goods, assign half the class to find and copy photographs of public goods from a newspaper or magazine. The remainder of the class will find and copy photographs of private goods. Students should then work together to create a bulletin board display that depicts public and private goods. Each picture in the display should be labeled appropriately.

▲ Is a bridge a private good, a nonexcludable public good, or an excludable public good?

Nonexcludable Public Goods

The classic example of a nonexcludable public good is national defense, which consists of missiles, soldiers, tanks, and so on. Suppose that the U.S. government produces a certain amount of national defense. National defense is definitely a public good, because one person's consumption of it does not detract from another person's consumption. In this way, national defense is like a movie or a lecture.

In another way, however, national defense is not like a movie or a lecture. The seller of a movie or a lecture can exclude people from consuming what he or she has to sell, but the producer of national defense cannot exclude people from consuming the good it produces. The U.S. government cannot exclude anyone in the United States from consuming its national defense, because it is physically impossible or prohibitively costly to do so.

For example, suppose an enemy's missiles are headed for the United States. The U.S.

free rider
A person who receives the benefits of a good without paying for it.

government's military decides to take action and fire on the incoming missiles. When it fires and destroys the incoming missiles, it protects Yang, who lives in a rather large city, and it also (automatically) protects many other people. It cannot work any other way.

To make the matter even more stark, suppose that one of the spies of the country that launched the attack against the United States lives in the same city as Yang. The U.S. government may not want to protect this spy from the incoming missile attack, but it must. It is physically impossible to protect some people and not others.

Who Will Produce Nonexcludable Public Goods?

Economists believe that in a free enterprise economy, people will be willing to produce private goods and excludable public goods, but no one will want to produce nonexcludable public goods. Why not? Because once a nonexcludable public good is produced, no one will pay for it. People will not pay for something they cannot be excluded from consuming.

Suppose a company builds a dam to stop the flooding of people's property. After the dam is built, representatives of the company ask the people if they want to buy the dam's services (flood prevention). Each person says, "The dam is already in place, I am benefiting from it, and there is no physical way you can exclude me from benefiting from it. So why should I pay?" Economists call people who receive the benefits of a good without paying for it **free riders**.

People know that they can't usually get others to voluntarily pay for a nonexcludable public good, so they decide not to produce it. (Looking back, we can now see that the company that produced the dam in our example would probably never produce the dam in real life.) In contrast, though, people in a free enterprise economy will be quite willing to produce and offer to sell private goods and excludable public goods. First, all private goods are excludable. If you do not pay for an apple, computer, car, or book, then you do not get the good; you are excluded from it. If you do not pay for a movie or lecture, you do not get to consume these excludable public goods. In short, people in a free enterprise economy will produce those things that they can withhold from buyers if they do not get paid for producing them.

The Political Process

A free enterprise economy will produce private goods and excludable public goods, but it will not produce nonexcludable public goods. Suppose, though, that people still want nonexcludable public goods, such as national defense and flood protection. If the free enterprise economy will not produce these goods, who will?

The government will provide nonexcludable public goods and pay for them with taxes. Many economists argue that the government *should* provide nonexcludable public goods because no one else will. The framers of the Constitution recognized the legitimate role of government in providing nonexcludable public goods, such as national defense, in the Preamble:

We, the People of the United States, in Order to form a more perfect Union, establish Justice, insure domestic Tranquility, provide for the common defence, promote the general Welfare, and secure the Blessings of Liberty to ourselves and our Posterity, do establish this Constitution for the United States of America. (Emphasis added.)

How do people communicate to the government what nonexcludable public goods and how much of these goods it should provide? In the U.S. system of government, one way people communicate what types and amounts of nonexcludable public goods they want is through the political process.

U.S. citizens have the right to vote, and they can influence what government does through the ballot box. For example, suppose the majority of the people want the U.S. government to provide less instead of more national defense. They will likely vote for politicians who voice this same preference and vote against politicians who do not share their preference. U.S. citizens

also have the right to lobby their elected representatives directly, by writing letters or talking to them in person.

A Student Asks

QUESTION: *I am used to thinking that any good the government provides is a public good, but that thought is wrong, isn't it?*

ANSWER: *Yes, it's wrong. Remember, we are talking here about three kinds of goods: (1) private goods, (2) excludable public goods, and (3) nonexcludable public goods. A free enterprise economy*

▲ As you know, a free enterprise system may not produce nonexcludable public goods. How can you voice your opinion as to which nonexcludable public goods the government should produce?

Reinforcement Activity

Ask each student to write a sentence that identifies the two roles that advocates of free enterprise feel government should play in the economy.

Analyzing

Ask students to think about excludability in the context of unauthorized downloading of music and video games. Then ask, How is excludability of these products affected when people can obtain them illegally? How might musicians or video game developers be affected?

Teaching with Visuals

People can voice their opinions about nonexcludable public goods by exercising the right to vote, lobbying, and talking to their government representatives.

Economics *in the* Real World

How do producers respond to consumers who are trying to economize on time? To explore this question, invite students to go to www.emcschool.net /Economics2e, select Chapter 3, and read the Economics in the Real World feature titled **"Why Does McDonald's Put Hash Browns in Half-Sized Bags?"**

After students have read this feature, ask if any of them gets stuck in traffic on a regular basis. As the feature explains, this is a common experience for many working people. Ask students to think of ideas for products that might make someone's commute more productive.

ANSWERS TO THINK ABOUT IT Answers will vary.

Cooperative Learning

Divide students into groups of three or four. Ask each group to find an example of a nonexcludable public good. Then have group members work together to prepare an oral presentation about the political process that led to the creation or continued existence of that good and whether people agreed or disagreed about the value of the good. Ask students to present both sides of the issue. Suggest that they include visual aids in the presentation to help clarify the issue.

Give students the following assignment: "Using your own words, write a definition of the word *external* and use the word in a sentence." Allow volunteers to share their definitions and sentences with the rest of the class. Explain that one definition of *external* is "situated outside." This definition relates to the economic definition of *externality*.

Background Information

California banned smoking in most restaurants and bars in 1995. The law was passed in response to complaints from employees of the establishments. Their health was affected by the negative externality of the secondhand smoke. Since then, some establishments have reported significant losses in revenue, as smoking consumers have stayed away. This action created a positive externality for some and a negative externality for others.

Thinking Like an Economist

Ask student to list and then discuss two institutional changes they would like to see that would make their lives better. Also ask them to list and discuss two institutional changes that would make their lives less pleasant if implemented. Examples of the former include the city, state, or national government making college more affordable, increasing public rapid transit, enlarging the military forces, and reducing sales taxes on products of interest to teenagers. Examples of the latter include the city or state government stopping building highways, reducing police forces, and eliminating public schools.

---

negative externality
An adverse side effect of an act that is felt by others.

positive externality
A beneficial side effect of an action that is felt by others.

will produce both private goods (shirts, shoes, computers) and excludable public goods (movies in theaters, music at a rock concert). What a free enterprise economy will not produce is nonexcludable public goods. So, if nonexcludable public goods are going to be produced, they must be produced by the government. However, it doesn't follow that the government will necessarily restrict itself to producing only nonexcludable public goods. For example, the U.S. government is

Thinking Like an Economist

The Importance of Institutions

Why are some countries rich and other countries poor? Why do some people say they are content with their lives but others say they are not? To the economist, the answers to these and similar questions have to do with the economic and political systems under which people live. As economists sometimes say, "Institutions matter." What they mean by the term *institutions* includes a country's (a) property rights structure, (b) legal system, and (c) economic system.

Economists know that these systems and property rights structures matter. Not every economic system generates wealth for its people, and not just any legal system keeps people free or instills in them the sense that justice is being served. A legal system that has general rules (which are applied to all people) and that preserves basic human and economic rights will do better in keeping people free than a system that has different rules for different people and that diminishes basic human and economic rights.

Ask yourself where you would want to be born if you could choose the country of your birthplace. Would it be a country in which the government controlled the economy, trampled on basic human and economic rights, and controlled people's personal and economic lives, or would it be a country in which the government was limited to protecting and preserving people's basic human and economic rights and perhaps to providing various nonexcludable public goods? If you have a clear preference in making this choice, then you are acknowledging that the type of institutions you live under *do* matter to your life.

---

involved in delivering mail, building roads, collecting social security taxes and writing out checks to social security recipients, and much more. None of these things falls into the category of a nonexcludable public good.

Externalities

Suppose that it is 3 a.m. and you are fast asleep. Suddenly, you awaken to the sounds of a radio blasting away. You get up, open the window of your bedroom, and realize that the loud music is coming from your neighbor's house. Your neighbor is taking an action—playing the radio loudly—that has an adverse side effect on you. Economists call this adverse side effect a **negative externality**, or a negative third-party effect.

EXAMPLE The owners of a house rarely mow their lawn or trim their shrubs. The people who live in the houses nearby complain that not only is this property not kept up and therefore unpleasant to look at but also that the condition of the property lowers the value of their own houses. One neighbor, who lives across the street, says, "I need to sell my house, but I'm going to have a hard time doing it because the people across the street don't keep up their property. No one wants to live across from an eyesore. I will probably have to lower the price of my house before anyone will start to think about buying it." Undoubtedly, the owners of the property that is not kept up are acting in a way that adversely affects their neighbors. The adverse side effect is a negative externality. ◆

Externalities are not always negative. For example, Erica is a beekeeper, who lives near an apple orchard. Erica's bees occasionally fly over to the orchard and pollinate the blossoms of the apple trees, in the process making the orchard more productive. In this situation, Erica takes an action—keeping bees—that benefits another person, the orchard owner. Because Erica's beekeeping activity results in an externality that benefits someone else, it is referred to as a **positive externality**, or a positive third-party effect.

Internet Research

Although less than 3% of the U.S. workforce is employed in agriculture, it continues to be one of the most regulated and assisted industries in the U.S. economy. Direct students to visit the United States Department of Agriculture (USDA) website and research the services the USDA provides to American farmers. Tell students to pretend they are farmers who need assistance. Their assignment is to write a one-page proposal outlining the services they would request from the government based on the types of economic assistance available for the agriculture industry.

EXAMPLE Yolanda visits a physician and is inoculated against polio. Now, she can be sure that she will not become sick with polio. Yolanda's actions also benefit other people: people who come into contact with Yolanda are protected from getting polio from her. As far as the community is concerned, Yolanda's getting inoculated against polio is a positive externality. ◆

Government and Positive Externalities

Some people argue that education generates positive externalities. They say that when you attend school, you not only learn things that will directly help you in life and in the workplace, but you also become a better citizen and a more informed voter. Becoming a better citizen and a more informed voter ends up benefiting more people than just you.

Let's analyze your own case. You are in high school and taking this economics course. Because of the course, it is hoped, you will become more knowledgeable about economics issues than you would have been otherwise. One day, you watch a TV program on which two politicians running for the U.S. Senate from your state are debating some economics issues. One politician makes inaccurate statements about almost all the issues, while the other accurately discusses the issues. You decide to vote for the politician who is accurate about the issues, because you feel she will more likely end up promoting economic policies that are good for the United States.

Your informed vote increases (by a tiny percentage) the probability that the politician who understands economics will get elected. If she is elected, whom did you help? You helped yourself, no doubt, but you also helped all the other people who will now benefit by having a person knowledgeable about economics, instead of an uninformed person, shape government policy. In this case, your education produced a positive externality.

Some people argue that because your education can help other people, those other people should pay something for the benefits they derive from your education. One solution might be to have members of society pay taxes to support the schools

▲ Buses, classrooms, books, and teachers' salaries all contribute to the thousands of dollars required each year to provide you with an education. Should other people have to pay for part of your education? Why or why not?

you attend. In other words, because the public benefits from your education and the education of other persons like you, it should pay toward that education. The U.S. public school system is a result of this thinking.

Persons who attend public schools do not directly pay for the education they receive (although they indirectly pay if their parents pay property taxes). Instead, their education is paid for with taxpayer money. That is, the education of public school students is subsidized. Some people argue that the government should subsidize all activities that generate positive externalities for society at large.

Government and Negative Externalities

If you are on the receiving end of a negative externality—for instance, if you are awakened at 3 a.m. by loud music or the smoke that a factory emits is getting into your lungs—you will probably feel that negative externalities are bad. But what can be done about them? Some people argue that it is the government's duty to minimize the bad in society—in other words, to reduce the negative externalities.

Government can do so in three principal ways: through the court system, regulation, and taxation.

Teaching with Visuals

Answers will vary, but students might say that in addition to students, other people benefit from public education.

Reinforcement Activity

List on the board half a dozen negative and positive externalities. Don't separate them into two groups—just jumble them together. One of the best ways for students to learn the difference between negative and positive externalities is to identify them from a large group of items. The criteria are simple: if the action affects someone in a positive way, it's a positive externality; if it affects someone in a negative way, it's a negative externality.

Discussion Starter

Ask students if they believe that their education generates a positive externality for others. If they believe this is true, ask them to give examples of how others benefit from their education.

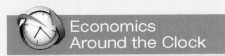

Economics Around the Clock

Now that students have a general grasp of free enterprise, ask them to reconsider the 6:42 p.m. scenario in Economics Around the Clock (page 61), and discuss their answers to the question it poses.

In this case, Lisa's choice of music has a negative externality on the driver next to her. If there are government-regulated noise restrictions in the neighborhood, Lisa will be forced to lower the volume.

Cooperative Learning

Divide the class into groups of four or five. Have each group take a piece of paper and divide it down the middle. On one side of the paper, students should write "Positive Externalities," and on the other side, "Negative Externalities." Then have each group make a list of the positive and negative externalities that its members have experienced in the last three days. Remind students that *externalities* are the actions of people or groups that produce side effects that are felt by others. After students have finished this activity, instruct them to start a new piece of paper. This time, they should list the positive and negative externalities they have caused for others in the last three days.

Ask students if they believe that in a society with no speeding laws, people would keep a promise to obey posted speed limits for safety's sake. Discuss whether or not speed limits would be followed by all citizens if government doesn't play the role of the enforcer.

ANSWERS TO THINK ABOUT IT Answers will vary. Most students will say yes. Even though the person complains, it could be that he realizes he is better off if he has to obey speeding laws, and others do too, because then he will face less risk driving than he would in a world without speeding laws that are enforced.

Problem Solving

Explain to students that one of the jobs of the court system is to deal with cases of negative externalities. In these cases, one person usually claims to have the right to do something that another person claims she or he does not have the right to do. In other words, the first person is negatively affecting the second person. Ask students to look through newspapers and magazines to find examples of court decisions in cases of negative externalities. Then, using the example on this page, have students act as a court. What should be a outcome of the case?

 Application Activity

After reading and discussing Section 5, assign the Section Activity in the *Applying the Principles Workbook,* pages 33–36.

Assess

Quick Quiz

The following true-or-false quiz will help you assess student understanding of the material covered in this section.

1. A contract is a good shared by two or more people. (False)
2. A private good is a good for which one person's consumption takes away from another person's consumption. (True)
3. National defense is an excludable public good. (False)
4. Regulation and taxation are always positive externalities. (False)
5. Government responses to negative externalities can sometimes have unintended effects. (True)

Are You Better Off With or Without Speeding Laws?

Consider that you are part of a society that had no speeding laws. Living in this society, you could drive as fast or as slow on the roads as you want to. If you want to drive 90 miles on an interstate highway, you could without penalty. If you want to drive 5 miles an hour in a residential area you could. Of course, you could also drive 60 miles an hour in the residential area (which could be dangerous for you and others).

Do you think that you would like to live in such a society, where there are no speeding laws? Part of you may say yes, because then you are not confined to how fast you could drive. But part of you may say no, because if you can drive as fast as you want, so can everyone else, and having everyone else drive as fast as they want may not be the best thing for you. In fact, the situation in which everyone can drive as fast as they want may put your life in danger.

Other people may agree. So what might happen in such a society is that people would soon figure out

that it is not really to their benefit to allow everyone to drive as fast as they want and so they might get together, discuss the issue at hand, and agree that what is the best thing for them to do is for them to post speed limits on the roads. Also, they all promise to obey the speed limits.

But without an agency to actually enforce the speed limits – without an agency to stop people who are speeding, give them a ticket, and demand that they show up in court to face the charges of speeding – it is very likely that even with posted speed limits, people would, in time, fall back to not obeying the posted speed limits.

This is where government may provide a solution to the peoples' problems. Government could play the role of the enforcer of speed limits. Government can have its police force enforce the posted speed limits that the people themselves want enforced, but don't seem to be able to enforce themselves. In other words, they don't seem to enforce speeding laws without government.

Some people argue that here is one of the key reasons for

government existence: to enforce agreements between people that the people themselves actually want enforced but don't seem to be able to enforce without government.

THINK ABOUT IT A person is driving 65 miles per hour in a 50 miles per hour zone. He gets pulled over by a police officer who writes him a ticket for $230. Afterward, the person complains about the cost of the ticket, the fact that he got pulled over, and generally argues that the police should have better things to do than pull him over for speeding. Even though the person complains about the speeding ticket, might he still prefer to live in a world where there are speeding laws that are enforced than one in which there are no speeding laws or one in which there are speeding laws that are not enforced?

The Court System Suppose a firm owns a factory near where you live that is emitting smoke and pollutants into the air. As far as you are concerned, the polluted environment is a negative externality. You think you should be able to breathe unpolluted air, so you sue the firm. Obviously, the firm will hire a lawyer to counter your suit. In the end,

a court will decide who has the right to do what. Does the firm have the right to emit smoke and pollutants into the air, or do you have the right to breathe unpolluted air?

Regulation Sometimes, the government creates regulations to deal with negative externalities. For example, most states

 Assessment Book

You will find a quiz for this section in the *Assessment Book,* page 26.

Reteaching Activity

Use the Section Assessment to gauge which students may need reteaching. Have a student read

the definitions of *positive* and *negative externalities* on page 84. Then ask students to list some negative and positive externalities.

 Guided Reading

For further reteaching of the key concepts in this section, assign the Outlining Activity and the Just the Facts Handout from the *Guided Reading and Study Guide,* pages 43–45.

require motor vehicles to meet pollution standards, and federal laws limit the amount of pollution that factories can emit into the air and dump into the rivers and lakes.

Taxation Suppose a business firm is producing steel. As a by-product, pollutants are discharged into the air through a smokestack. Instead of imposing an environmental regulation on the steel-producing firm to clean up the air, the government decides to impose a tax. For every ton of steel produced, the firm has to pay $100 in taxes.

As a result of the tax, the business firm will find it costlier to produce steel. The firm is likely to produce less steel, which means fewer pollutants will be discharged into the air. In other words, placing a tax on steel indirectly reduced the amount of negative externality (pollutants in the air) by making the production of steel more costly.

We have to be careful in our analysis, though. Taxation, like regulation, sometimes has unintended consequences. For example, let's say that in year 1, the automobile industry pays no taxes. In year 2, the government places a tax of $500 per car on the auto industry. In other words, for every new car a firm produces, it must pay the government $500 in taxes. Do you think the auto industry will produce more cars in year 1 or year 2? The correct answer is year 1, all other things remaining the same. Taxes

of the sort described here raise the cost of producing and selling cars, and car firms will likely react by producing fewer cars.

At this point, you might point out that fewer cars mean less pollution. This statement overlooks something important, though. Although fewer new cars are produced and purchased, people may simply drive their old cars longer, and old cars emit more pollution than new cars. Thus, the tax on the production of new cars reduces the number of new cars on the road compared to the number of old cars. In this case, if miles driven do not change, we can expect more, not less, pollution from cars. Taxation, like regulation, does not always have its intended effect.

▲ What negative externality is represented in this photograph? How does the government attempt to minimize this negative externality?

Defining Terms
1. Define:
   a. contract
   b. private good
   c. public good
   d. excludable public good
   e. nonexcludable public good
   f. free rider
   g. positive externality
   h. negative externality

Reviewing Facts and Concepts
2. Identify each of the following as a public or a private good: (a) a pair of shoes, (b) sunshine, (c) a pen, and (d) a pizza.
3. Why won't a private business produce a non-excludable public good?
4. How are nonexcludable public goods paid for?
5. Explain how taxes can be applied to deal with negative externalities.

Applying Economic Concepts
6. Give and explain an example of a setting in which a free rider is present.
7. National defense is a nonexcludable public good. Does this mean that every individual gets the type of national defense he or she prefers? Explain.

Teaching with Visuals

It appears that the police officer has stopped the driver of the car for some infraction—such as speeding. Speeding can be viewed as a negative externality in that it can adversely affect others. The police place a "cost on speeding" to get drivers to take the negative externality into account when deciding how to behave.

externality: a beneficial side effect felt by others.

Reviewing Facts and Concepts
2. (a) private good; (b) public good; (c) private good; (d) private good.
3. A private business won't produce nonexcludable public goods because it won't be able to collect any payment for them. To illustrate, once a nonexcludable public good is produced and provided to one person, it will be available to all other people as well. Because all these other people can have the benefits of the good without paying for it, many of them will choose not to pay for it.
4. Nonexcludable public goods are paid for through taxes.
5. Taxes can be used to make an activity that generates negative externalities more costly. As a result, less of that activity will be performed.

Applying Economic Concepts
6. Answers will vary. (*Sample answer:* Ortiz lives across the street from Desai. Ortiz creates a beautifully landscaped lawn, which Desai enjoys but doesn't pay for. Desai is a free rider.*)
7. No. The problem with a nonexcludable public good is that "one size has to fit all," even though one size will never be everyone's preferred choice. For instance, some people will want a bigger national defense, while others will want a smaller national defense.

Defining Terms

1. a. free rider: a person who receives the benefits of a good without paying for it; **b. contract:** an agreement between two or more people to do something; **c. private good:** a good for which one person's consumption takes away from another person's consumption; **d. public good:** a good for which one person's consumption does not take away from another person's consumption; **e. excludable public good:** a public good that individuals can be excluded (physically prohibited) from consuming; **f. nonexcludable public good:** a public good that individuals cannot be excluded (physically prohibited) from consuming; **g. negative externality:** an adverse side effect felt by others; **h. positive**

Discussion Starter

Ask students if any of them plan to take out a loan in the near future (for school, a business, or for a big purchase). Pose these questions: What do you know about loans? What happens when you can't pay back a loan? What is bankruptcy and who does it protect?

Background Information

Students may be interested to know that the concept of filing for bankruptcy is a relatively new one. For example, in ancient Greece, if a man owed money and could not pay, he and his wife and children were forced into debt slavery until the creditor had recouped his losses through physical labor.

Your Obligations as a Borrower

The ability to borrow money from a bank or other financial institution is a valuable resource that can give you the opportunity to purchase important items that would otherwise be out of your reach. However, the obligations and responsibilities that accompany borrowing money should be carefully considered before doing so.

Types of Loans

When you borrow money, you take out a loan, but not all loans are the same. An *open-ended loan* is a loan that you can take out over and over again. For example, if you have a credit card, you have an open-ended loan. To illustrate, suppose your credit card has a limit of $5,000. You buy something with your credit card for $5,000. In time, you pay off the balance, which means that you can once again borrow up to $5,000.

In contrast, a *close-ended loan* is a loan that cannot be taken out again once it has been repaid. For example, a car loan is a close-ended loan. Once you have paid off the loan, you need to apply for another loan if you want to borrow more money. Student loans for college are another example of close-ended loans.

A *secured loan* is a loan for which a person has pledged some asset (e.g., a car or property) as collateral. In other words, if the person does not pay back the loan, the creditor can take the asset as payment instead. Because secured loans come with collateral, their interest rates are often lower than the rates for *unsecured loans* which, of course, do not require an asset as collateral.

When it comes to mortgage loans (a loan taken out to buy a house or other property), you will often hear of both unconventional and conventional loans. An *unconventional loan* is a loan insured or guaranteed by a government agency. Veteran Affairs (VA) loans are examples of unconventional loans. With an unconventional loan, it is possible to borrow the full amount of the value of the house one wants to purchase. If a down payment is made with an unconventional loan, it is often lower than what is required for a conventional loan. *Conventional loans* are not insured by a government agency, but they do adhere to specific guidelines. Requiring a down payment is one of these guidelines. Suppose you want to buy a house priced at $300,000. Depending on your credit rating, you may need to make a 20 percent down payment of $60,000 in order to get a $240,000 conventional mortgage loan. Generally, conventional loans come with lower interest rates than unconventional loans.

Finally, a *payday loan* is a short-term loan that is made using your next paycheck as a guarantee. Even though their terms are short, payday loans often come with very high interest rates. Most financial planners advise against taking out payday loans.

Borrower Obligations and Responsibilities

When you apply to borrow money, you must report to the lender all other loans and all regular financial commitments you have, such as rent, mortgage payments, and so on. You must also identify for (and prove to) the lender your monthly income. These measures are necessary so that your lender can estimate your ability to repay the loan for which you are being considered. If you are accepted for the loan, you also agree to certain responsibilities as a borrower. Chief among these responsibilities is to do your best to pay back your loan. When you take out a loan, you have entered into a contract with the lender. This contract says that the lender will lend you a certain amount of money for a certain period of time at a given interest rate, and that in return you agree to pay back the money owed with interest according to the predetermined schedule. This contract constitutes a "legal promise." Your responsibility is to keep your promise.

What happens if you can't keep up your end of the deal by paying back your loans? For secured loans, this might mean that you lose whatever you put up as collateral (such as your car). For unsecured loans, after a certain amount of missed payments, you would

Cooperative Learning

Divide students into groups of three or four. Each group should research a current bankruptcy case involving a company or high-profile individual. Using the Internet and other resources, identify the type of bankruptcy sought, what that would mean for the individual or group seeking bankruptcy, and whether any issues arose (such as accusations of fraud). Groups should report their findings to the rest of the class. If desired, you may choose to assign a specific type of bankruptcy to each group.

begin to hear from creditors or the department in charge of seeking reimbursement. Aside from causing late penalties to accrue on top of the money you already owe, missing loan payments will also lower your credit score. If there is no possible way to repay your loans and honor your commitments, you may be forced to file for bankruptcy.

Bankruptcy

Bankruptcy exists, according to the U.S. Supreme Court, to give debtors a fresh start. In a 1934 decision, the Supreme Court said of bankruptcy that "it gives to the honest unfortunate debtor . . . a new opportunity and clear field for future effort, unhampered by the pressure and discouragement of preexisting debt."

What is bankruptcy exactly? Bankruptcy is a legal proceeding involving a person or business that is unable to repay outstanding debts. Declaring bankruptcy begins with a petition filed by the debtor (which is very common) or on behalf of creditors (much less common). Next, all the assets of the debtor (the person declaring bankruptcy) must be disclosed to the court, whether or not the debtor believes the asset has a marketable value. If assets are omitted by the debtor, serious ramifications can occur. Bankruptcy fraud is a federal crime in the United States.

Four types of bankruptcy filings exist in the United States. Two of the more common are Chapter 7 and Chapter 13 bankruptcy filings. Filing bankruptcy under Chapter 7 means that all of the assets of a debtor that are not protected

or exempt by bankruptcy law are subject to being collected and sold for the purposes of paying a portion of the debt owed to the creditor. State laws declare which assets are exempt and not exempt. One of the major costs of declaring bankruptcy under Chapter 7 is that petitioners often lose important and even priceless items such as their homes or family items that have been passed down through generations. Bankruptcy under Chapter 7 also has a very serious negative effect on one's credit score, which will be detrimental to any future attempts to borrow money. It is often very difficult for persons who have declared bankruptcy under Chapter 7 to get creditors to lend to them.

Many persons will file bankruptcy under Chapter 13 in the hopes of retaining a family home, a car, or other possessions. Chapter 13 bankruptcy reduces the debt obligation of petitioners while

allowing them to keep the bulk of their possessions. In exchange for these more lenient terms, the petitioner must adhere to a payment plan and agree to live under court-ordered financial guidelines during the entire period of debt repayment. These guidelines often include no accrual of additional debt and drastic cut backs to personal expenditures.

Your Personal Economics Activity

1. Research and identify the different types of loans available to you as a consumer and explain the responsibilities and obligations associated with borrowing money.

2. In an informative essay, evaluate the costs and benefits of declaring personal bankruptcy. Support your views with evidence and logical reasoning.

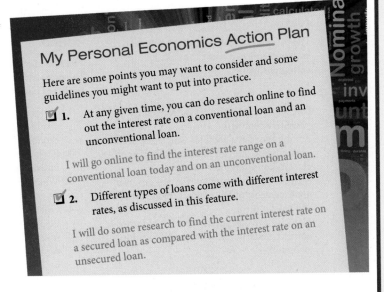

My Personal Economics Action Plan

Here are some points you may want to consider and some guidelines you might want to put into practice.

☑ **1.** At any given time, you can do research online to find out the interest rate on a conventional loan and an unconventional loan.

I will go online to find the interest rate range on a conventional loan today and on an unconventional loan.

☑ **2.** Different types of loans come with different interest rates, as discussed in this feature.

I will do some research to find the current interest rate on a secured loan as compared with the interest rate on an unsecured loan.

Grading Rubric: Research

| 1 2 3 4 5 | Student accurately identified borrower obligations |
| 1 2 3 4 5 | Student identified available loans. |

Grading Rubric: Essay

| 1 2 3 4 5 | Evaluation of bankruptcy costs and benefits was logical. |
| 1 2 3 4 5 | Essay was complete and well written. |

Assessment Answers

Economics Vocabulary

1. total revenue; **2.** incentive; **3.** Ethics; **4.** public property; **5.** entrepreneur; **6.** loss; **7.** free riders; **8.** contract; **9.** public good; **10.** private; **11.** positive externality.

Understanding the Main Ideas

1. The individuals who own and manage the business firms will decide how goods will be produced.

2. Consider two individuals, Muong and Sally. Muong has $1, and Sally has a pen. If they exchange—that is, trade $1 for the pen—we assume that each one has been made better off through the exchange, or he or she would not have made the exchange in the first place.

3. The five major features of a free enterprise economy are private property, choice, voluntary exchange, competition, and economic incentives.

4. a. $78 (profit); **b.** $232 (loss); **c.** $442,868 (profit).

5. The message is that company Z is using resources to produce a good that people don't want to buy at the price that Z is charging.

6. Profit attracts resources into the production of the good from which the business is earning a profit. For example, if company B is earning a profit on the production and sale of good X, then other companies currently not producing good X will shift resources to produce it.

7. Entrepreneurs search out and take advantage of new business opportunities, develop new products, and develop new ways of doing things.

8. Government should be limited to enforcing contracts and providing nonexcludable public goods. Contract enforcement provides security and ensures high levels of exchange and economic activity. Government should provide nonexcludable public goods because the private sector will not provide them. The private sector won't provide these goods because once they

Chapter Summary

Be sure you know and remember the following key points from the chapter sections.

Section 1

▶ In a free enterprise economy, business firms will produce the goods that consumers want.

▶ Five major features define free enterprise: private property, choice, voluntary exchange, competition, and economic incentives.

Section 2

▶ Profit is the money left over after the costs of production are paid.

▶ Loss is the money spent when total cost exceeds total revenue.

▶ Profits and losses are signals to business firms.

Section 3

▶ An ethical economic system allows individuals to choose their occupations, produces goods and services preferred by buyers, rewards (or punishes) producers according to how well (or poorly) they respond to buyer preferences, and does not limit individual freedom in making choices.

Section 4

▶ The prospect of making great profits motivates entrepreneurs to assume the risks inherent in entrepreneurship.

Section 5

▶ One of government's roles in free enterprise is to enforce contracts.

▶ A public good is a good for which one person's consumption does not take away from another person's consumption.

▶ A free enterprise economy will not produce nonexcludable public goods, because no one will pay for them.

▶ Many believe that government should provide nonexcludable public goods and adjust for externalities.

Economics Vocabulary

To reinforce your knowledge of the key terms in this chapter, fill in each of the following blanks on a separate piece of paper with the appropriate word or phrase.

1. The price of a good times the number of units of the good sold equals _____.

2. A(n) _____ is something that encourages or motivates a person toward an action.

3. _____ relates to principles of right and wrong, moral and immoral, good and bad.

4. Any good that is owned by the government is considered _____.

5. A(n) _____ is a person with a special talent for developing new businesses, new products, and new ways of doing things.

6. If a product's total cost is greater than total revenue, the firm incurs a(n) _____.

7. One reason a private business firm will not supply a nonexcludable public good is because it cannot collect payment from _____.

8. A(n) _____ is an agreement between two or more people to do something.

9. One person's consumption of a(n) _____ does not take away from another's.

10. A computer is an example of a(n) _____ good.

11. A(n) _____ is a beneficial side effect of an action that is felt by others.

Understanding the Main Ideas

Review the main ideas in this chapter by writing answers to the following questions on a separate sheet of paper.

1. How is the question "How will goods be produced?" answered in a free enterprise economy?

2. Explain how voluntary exchange can make individuals better off.

3. What are the five major features of a free enterprise economy?

4. Calculate the profit (+) or loss (−) in each of the following situations. (TR stands for total revenue, and TC stands for total cost.)
   a. TR = $400; TC = $322
   b. TR = $4,323; TC = $4,555
   c. TR = $899,765; TC = $456,897

have been provided, there is no way to collect payment for them.

9. Exhibit 3-2 shows the economic relationships in an economy. It's useful because a change somewhere in the economy can be shown to have effects at other places in the economy.

10. Government can deal with a negative externality in three ways: the court system; regulation; and taxation. Court rulings and regulations

can curtail negative externalities. Taxation can also be used to make certain activities more costly.

11. Public school students aren't the only people who benefit from public education. Students will one day be voters. Because they have been educated, they will presumably cast votes for candidates and policies that will benefit all of society.

5. Company Z produces men's clothes. For the past 18 months, the company has been taking a loss. What is the loss "saying" to company Z?

6. An economist would say that "Profit attracts resources." What does this statement mean? You may want to give an example.

7. What do entrepreneurs do?

8. According to supporters of free enterprise, what should the government do? Why?

9. What does the circular flow diagram provided in Exhibit 3-2 show, and how is it useful?

10. Identify and explain the three ways that the government may deal with a negative externality.

11. Justify providing a public school system in terms of producing positive externalities.

Doing the Math

Do the calculations necessary to solve the following problems.

EXHIBIT 3-4

Price	Quantity produced and sold	Average cost	Total cost	Profit
$10	100	$ 4	A	B
$15	C	$ 7	$ 700	$ 800
$12	10	$10	$ 100	D
E	F	$50	$1,000	$2,000
$ 4	G	$ 3	H	$ 100

1. For each letter (A through H) in Exhibit 3-4, provide the correct number or dollar amount.

2. A business firm earns a $5,000 profit by selling 1,000 units of a good for $6.99 each. What is the average cost of the good?

Working with Graphs and Tables

1. Look back at the circular flow diagram in Exhibit 3-2 and answer the following questions.
   a. Where do households get the funds to buy goods and services from businesses?
   b. Where do businesses get the funds to pay for the resources they purchase from households?

   c. Where does the government get the funds to provide benefits to businesses and households?

2. Look at the circular flow diagram in Exhibit 3-2. Suppose you are a member of the household sector, and you have to pay $100 in taxes to the government. You sign your name on a $100 bill and give it to the government. Could that same $100 bill ever be back in your hands again? Explain your answer.

Solving Economic Problems

Use your thinking skills and the information you learned in this chapter to find solutions to the following problems.

1. **Analyze.** "Some mechanism is necessary to decide where resources will be used in an economy. Free enterprise is such a mechanism." Explain what this statement means.

2. **Analyze.** Five features of free enterprise were discussed in this chapter. If you had to pick the most important two features, which two would you pick? Explain your answer.

3. **Identify Cause and Effect.** In Chapter 2, you read this quote from Adam Smith: "It is not from the benevolence of the butcher, the brewer, or the baker, that we expect our dinner, but from their regard to their own interest." Why do we "get our dinner," in Smith's opinion?

Project or Presentation

Negative Externalities. Write a 1½- to 2-page magazine article in which you identify three negative externalities in your life. After identifying each externality, propose a solution to deal with it. Illustrate your article with photos and graphics. Compile your class's articles into a magazine featuring negative externalities.

ONLINE   *Practice Tests and Study Guide*
emcp.com

Go to **www.emcschool.net/Economics2e** and choose *Economics: New Ways of Thinking*, Chapter 3, if you need more help in preparing for the chapter test.

Working with Graphs and Tables

1. a. Households get the funds from selling resources to businesses. Also, households receive certain benefits from the government. If these are money benefits, we conclude that households also get funds from the government. **b.** Businesses get their funds from the households that buy their goods and services. Also, businesses receive certain benefits from the government. If these are money benefits, we conclude that businesses also get funds from the government. **c.** The government gets funds from businesses and households that pay taxes.

2. Yes. The diagram shows that the government provides benefits to households and businesses. One way for the $100 bill to get back in your hands would be for the government to provide you with $100 in money benefits. (In other words, you give the $100 bill to the government via the yellow arrow in the exhibit, and the government gives it back to you via the purple arrow.) Alternatively, the government could provide a business with $100 in money benefits (brown arrow), in which case business has the $100 bill. The business may buy some resources from you (say, your labor) and pay you with the $100 bill (green arrow).

Solving Economic Problems

1. No one doubts that under free enterprise, there are both profits and losses. Resources are linked to profits and losses in the following way: resources move toward activities that are generating profits and away from activities that are generating losses.

2. Answers will vary. This question should lead to a good classroom discussion.

3. The butcher, brewer, and baker provide us with our dinner not because they like us or they want us to be happy and full but because they know that the only way they can get what they want from us is to give us what we want. They are motivated by self-interest to provide us with our dinner.

Project or Presentation

Answers will vary. Invite volunteers to create a cover, a table of contents, and an introduction for the magazine.

Doing the Math

1. A. $400 (*calculation:* Total cost = quantity sold × average cost); **B.** $600 (*calculation:* Profit = (price × quantity sold) − total cost); **C.** 100 (*calculation:* Total cost ÷ average cost = quantity sold); **D.** $20 (*calculation:* Profit = (price × quantity sold) − total cost); **E.** $150 (*calculation:* Price = (total cost + profit) ÷ quantity); **F.** 20 (*calculation:* Quantity sold = total cost ÷ average cost); **G.** 100 (*calculation:* Quantity sold = profit ÷ (price − average cost); **H.** $300 (*calculation:* Total cost = quantity sold × average cost).

2. $1.99. Because total revenue minus total cost equals profit, we know that $6,990 − x = $5,000, so total cost = $1,990. If we divide $1,990 by the number of units (1,000), we see that the average cost is $1.99.

Debating the Issues

Discussion Starters

1. Ask how many students have or have had after-school jobs. Allow volunteers to share their personal experiences about how working affected their schoolwork and what they have learned from having jobs.

2. Ask what outside factors might influence a student's decision to get an after-school job? (*Answer:* parents' opinions, peers' opinions, family financial situation.)

3. Ask whether any students feel that they have missed out because they have never had an after-school job. If so, discuss what they feel they have missed and how this has affected their lives. (*Examples:* They may not have had opportunities to learn life skills such as developing a good work ethic and managing a budget, and they may not have had extra money to spend for personal items.) Ask students to brainstorm other examples of knowledge and experiences that young people miss out on by not working after school.

4. Ask whether any students who have had after-school jobs feel that they have missed out on anything because of working. If so, what? Discuss how working has affected their lives. (*Examples:* They may have had less sleep and rest, a diminished social life, less time and energy for schoolwork, and less time to participate in school and leisure activities.) Discuss whether students would rethink the trade-off and make a different decision about having an after-school job.

Debating the Issues

Working After School: What Are the Trade-Offs?

Through our study of economics, we learn that there are trade-offs in life. More of one thing often means having less of something else. Spending more money on clothes means having less money for entertainment. More time spent studying means less time to hang out with your friends.

High school students must think about the trade-offs that come with working or not working after school. Some people argue that high school students should get jobs and work after school; others argue against it, saying students' time is better spent studying. Let's hear what five people have to say.

Rebecca, a junior in high school

I work after school and on the weekends at a fast-food restaurant here in town. It may be hard to believe, but I actually like the work. I meet a lot of nice people, I earn some money, and I am developing a good work ethic. When I first went to work, I thought it was going to be easier than it turned out to be. I thought I was just going to have some fun and make some money. But I've learned that to do a job well, you have to be conscientious, follow orders closely, and focus on what you are doing. These are qualities that I think will benefit me throughout my life. I think I am a better person because I work. My parents are concerned about how work takes time away from my studies, but I never was much of a student. If I weren't working, I might be just wasting my time. I might even get into some trouble.

Tommy, a senior in high school

I know I could work after school, but I choose not to. Working after school would come at too high a price for me. If I worked after school, I wouldn't have as much time to study. I want to get into a really good college, and to do that I need to have high grades. If I worked, I probably couldn't get the A's that I am currently getting in my courses. The way I look at it, I will have 40 or 50 years to work. I am young now and I like learning, and the more I learn, the brighter my future will be. I think I would be sacrificing my future if I worked after school now.

My older brother didn't work at a job when he was in high school. He spent most of his time studying. As a result, he got high grades and a good score on the SAT. What is even more important is that he got into Yale. He received a top-quality education at Yale and made many good future business contacts. In fact, he now works in a company owned by the father of one of his best friends at Yale.

Some of my friends talk about the money they make in their after-school jobs. They can buy a lot of things that I can't. They buy better clothes, and some of them have even bought a car. I'd like to have a car, too, but I don't want to take away from my studies right now to get a job just so I can buy a car.

Bob, parent

I think it is important for teens to develop a sense of responsibility, and that's why I have urged my daughter to get a job after school and on the weekends. I worked when

---

Enrichment and Extension

1. Form small groups, and have each group create a short skit demonstrating the positive and negative aspects of having an after-school job. Ideas include, but are not limited to, a workplace scenario, discussion with family about a job, and a classroom being affected by students' working.

2. Ask students to pretend that they are writing a feature article for the school newspaper about the pros and cons of after-school jobs. Students might interview other students or a supervisor at a company that employs high school students.

I was her age, and I learned a lot from what I did. Mainly, I learned the value of a dollar. I know that people say teens should not work, that they should devote more time to their education, but the truth of the matter is, there are different types of education. There is the book-learning type of education, where a person learns geometry, calculus, English literature, and history. And then there is the education that you receive from getting out in life and working. When you work, you learn how to get along with people. You learn to persevere in order to get a job done. These are important things to learn. In the long run, they'll be more important to my daughter than learning how to solve calculus problems.

Nancy,
guidance counselor

I think working after school is good for some students and not for others. It really depends on the trade-offs the particular student faces. For instance, I often get students in my office who work but who are doing poorly in their courses. I tell them they would be better off if they didn't work but instead spent their time after school studying and trying to get their grades up.

But I've got other students who are doing well in their courses and feel they can continue to do well even though they get jobs. I see working as a good idea. Not only will they learn some things in their work that they might not otherwise learn, but they will have a little extra spending money too. There are things they want to do and buy, and working gives them the opportunity to do those things.

I think that whether or not a student should work depends on the individual student. Not all students face the same trade-offs. What is right for one student may not be right for another.

Amy,
college student

I worked all through high school, and I really regret it now. I worked for all the wrong reasons. I worked simply to get the money to buy the same things my friends were buying. My friends were spending a lot of money on clothes, so I thought I had to too. I worked to get a down payment for a car. Once I bought the car, I had to continue to work so I could make the payments and keep it running. There were many weekends when I was dead tired from working. I'd come home Sunday night, after working all day Saturday and all day Sunday, and have to study for a biology or calculus test. I can't tell you how many times I just went to bed, telling myself I would get up early and study. The alarm clock would ring, and I'd shut it off. I paid the price in lower grades.

I got into college, and I am doing better now, but college hasn't been easy for me. I think if I had worked less in high school and studied more, college would have been more enjoyable and easier.

I've learned that it is extremely important to prioritize—a person just can't do too many things and do them well. The world we live in values education a lot. You can't cut corners when it comes to your education. Working just gets in the way. My advice to any high school student is that if you don't have to work, don't. Study more, work less. You'll be glad you did in the long run.

What Do You Think?

1. Which person's opinion most closely matches your own?
2. Is there a trade-off between education and work? Explain your answer.

1. For a class survey, ask students to "vote with their feet" and physically move to labeled points at the front of the room. The group of students that meets at each point should spend five minutes listing their reasons for voting for that opinion; then each group should spend one minute presenting its reasons to the class. Hold another class vote, and see if there is any change in the voting.

2. Tell students to make lists of the positives and negatives of working after school. Assign a short persuasive essay, in which each student takes a position and defends it with examples from his or her list.

Closure

Instruct each student to write a paragraph that explains whether having an after-school job is right for him or her. If the student's opinion has changed over the course of this discussion, he or she should include that information, along with what prompted the change.

Listed below are the chapters included in this unit.

Foundations for the Unit

Unit 2 focuses on two key concepts of economics: demand and supply. Students will see how supply and demand play out in markets. As students work through this unit, they should also begin to understand the effects that markets have on their lives. Like everyone else, students are affected by prices. In this unit, they will learn how prices are determined by the interplay of supply and demand.

UNIT II
The Basics

94

Resources for the Unit

Books

Fischer, David Hackett. *The Great Wave: Price Revolutions and the Rhythm of History.* New York: Oxford University Press, 2000.

Heilbroner, Robert L. *The Worldly Philosophers: The Lives, Times, and Ideas of the Great Economic Thinkers.* New York: Touchstone Books, 1999.

Ott, Rick. *Creating Demand.* Richmond, VA: Symmetric Systems, 1999.

Thurow, Lester, and Robert Heilbroner. *Economics Explained.* New York: Touchstone Books, 1998.

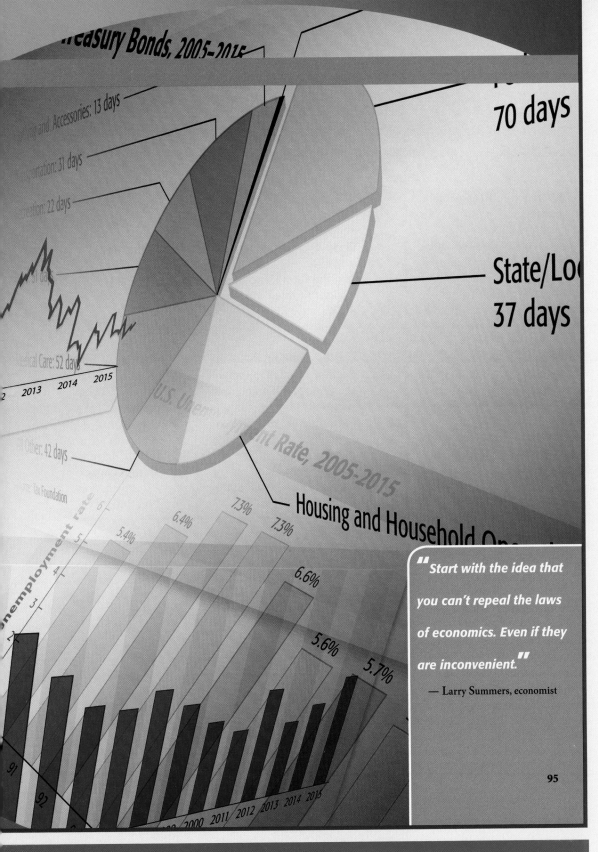

Treasury Bonds, 2005–2015

70 days

...ng and Accessories: 13 days

...portation: 31 days

...ation: 22 days

State/Lo...
37 days

...cal Care: 52 days

...ll Other: 42 days

...x Foundation

U.S. Une... ...nt Rate, 2005–2015

Housing and Household O...

Unemployment rate

6

5.4%

6.4%

7.3%

7.3%

6.6%

5.6%

5.7%

91

92

...00 2000 2011 2012 2013 2014 2015

2013 2014 2015

"**Start with the idea that you can't repeal the laws of economics. Even if they are inconvenient."**

— Larry Summers, economist

95

Introducing the Unit

To introduce Unit 2, ask students if they have recently had a *willingness* to purchase a new CD, video game, or other item? Did they also have the *ability* to purchase the item? Tell students that willingness and ability to purchase are both necessary to create demand. Creating demand is a step in creating the price for a good or service. Ask for student volunteers to suggest what happens to price if demand increases. Also ask why students think this occurs.

Performance Project

Divide students into groups of three or four to learn about the relationship among demand, supply, and price. Have each group choose a product and research how demand for that good has affected its price. Ask each group to consider the factors that affected demand for the good. For example: Did demand change seasonally? in response to a competitor's actions? Invite each group to present an oral report of its findings to the class.

Article

Hailing, Zang. "Time Takes Its Toll: Getting in First Does Not Ensure Market Success," *TIME World,* May 29, 2000. Available online at http://content.time.com/time/world/article/0,8599,2051061,00.html

Multimedia

Economics at Work. Videos, software, and print materials. National Council on Economics Education.

Exchanging. Videotape and teacher's guide. Films for the Humanities and Sciences.

Chapter 4 Planning Guide

SECTION ORGANIZER

SECTION 1

Understanding Demand
(pages 98–103)

Learning Objectives	Reproducible Worksheets and Handouts	Assessment
▸ Define the term *demand*. ▸ Describe the difference between demand and quantity demanded. ▸ Discuss why price and quantity demanded move in opposite directions. ▸ Explain the law of diminishing marginal utility. ▸ Distinguish between a demand schedule and a demand curve.	Section 1 Activity, *Applying the Principles Workbook,* pages 37–39 Outlining Activity, *Guided Reading and Study Guide,* page 54 Just the Facts Handout, *Guided Reading and Study Guide,* page 55	☑ Section Assessment, *Student Text,* page 103 ☑ Quick Quiz, *Annotated Teacher's Edition,* page 102 ☑ Section Quiz, *Assessment Book,* page 35

SECTION 2

The Demand Curve Shifts
(pages 104–109)

Learning Objectives	Reproducible Worksheets and Handouts	Assessment
▸ Explain why a demand curve shifts to the right or the left. ▸ Distinguish among normal, inferior, and neutral goods. ▸ List the factors that can change demand. ▸ Identify the factor that can change the quantity demanded.	Section 2 Activity, *Applying the Principles Workbook,* pages 40–44 Outlining Activity, *Guided Reading and Study Guide,* pages 56–57 Just the Facts Handout, *Guided Reading and Study Guide,* pages 58–59	☑ Section Assessment, *Student Text,* page 109 ☑ Quick Quiz, *Annotated Teacher's Edition,* page 108 ☑ Section Quiz, *Assessment Book,* page 36

SECTION 3

Elasticity of Demand
(pages 112–119)

Learning Objectives	Reproducible Worksheets and Handouts	Assessment
▸ Describe elasticity of demand. ▸ Explain how to compute elasticity of demand. ▸ Distinguish among elastic, inelastic, and unit-elastic demand. ▸ List the factors that can change the elasticity of demand. ▸ Describe the relationship between an increase in price for a good and higher total revenue.	Section 3 Activity, *Applying the Principles Workbook,* pages 45–49 Demand Practice Activity, *Applying the Principles Workbook,* pages 50–53 Outlining Activity, *Guided Reading and Study Guide,* page 60 Just the Facts Handout, *Guided Reading and Study Guide,* pages 61–62	☑ Section Assessment, *Student Text,* page 119 ☑ Quick Quiz, *Annotated Teacher's Edition,* page 118 ☑ Section Quiz, *Assessment Book,* page 37

Reproducible Chapter Resources and Assessment Materials

 Graphic Organizer Activity, *Guided Reading and Study Guide,* page 63

Vocabulary Activity, *Guided Reading and Study Guide,* pages 64–65

Working with Graphs and Charts, *Guided Reading and Study Guide,* page 66

Practice Test, *Guided Reading and Study Guide,* pages 67–68

Critical Thinking Activity, *Finding Economics,* pages 9–12

Chapter Test A, *Assessment Book,* pages 38–41

Chapter Test B, *Assessment Book,* pages 42–45

Student Text Internet Links

Economics: New Ways of Thinking, Second Edition encourages students to use the Internet to find out more about economics. Given the wealth of current, valid information available on websites, students should be encouraged to use the Internet as a research tool. Doing so will likely increase students' interest in and understanding of economics principles and topics. In addition, doing Internet research can help your students form the habit of accessing and using economics information, as well as help them develop investigative skills they will use throughout their educational and professional careers.

To aid your students in achieving these ends, each chapter of *Economics: New Ways of Thinking, Second Edition* includes the addresses of several websites that provide engaging and relevant information. When students type in any of the addresses provided, they will immediately arrive at the intended site. The addresses have been modified so that EMC Publishing can monitor and maintain the proper links—for example, the website http://www.deposit accounts.com/ has been changed to http://econ.emcp.net/accounts. In the event that the address or content of a site changes or is discontinued, EMC's Internet editors will redirect the link to a site with equivalent information.

Activities in the *Annotated Teacher's Edition* often suggest that students search the Internet for information. For some activities, you might want to find reputable sites beforehand and steer students toward them. For other activities, have students do their own searching and then check out the sites they have found and discuss why they might be reliable or unreliable.

Passport® for Economics

Technology resources are available with the *Economics: New Ways of Thinking, Second Edition* program through Passport®. These include:

eBooks for *Economics: New Ways of Thinking, Second Edition*

▶ Student textbook eBook
▶ Interactive Applying the Principles eWorkbook
▶ Finding Economics eBook
▶ Guided Reading and Study Guide eBook
▶ Annotated Teacher's Edition eBook
▶ Lesson Plans eBook
▶ Assessment eBook

Passport® for Students

Students can access helpful resources through Passport® for Economics. Resources include:
▶ Study guides
▶ Practice tests
▶ Flash cards in English and in Spanish
▶ Word games in English and in Spanish
▶ Tutorials and key-concept videos
▶ Spanish print and audio summaries

Passport® for Teachers

Keep your course current and relevant by using the teacher resources provided through Passport® for Economics. In addition to all of the resources on the student side of Passport®, the teacher side contains:
▶ Link to the Annotated Teacher's Edition eBook
▶ Standards correlations
▶ Microsoft® PowerPoint® Lectures
▶ Current Events Lessons
▶ Additional Economics in the Real World features
▶ ExamView® Assessment Suite
▶ PDFs of all print supplements (student and teacher)

Overview

This chapter introduces and discusses a very important concept in economics: demand. This is the first of three chapters in which students learn about demand, supply, and the ways demand and supply work together in markets. The following statements provide brief descriptions of the major concepts covered in each section of this chapter.

SECTION **1** Understanding Demand

Section 1 discusses the basic concepts that underlie the law of demand. It also introduces the elements of the demand curve.

SECTION **2** The Demand Curve Shifts

Section 2 explores the factors that cause the demand curve to shift, including income, preferences, prices of related goods, number of buyers, and buyers' expectations of future price. Section 2 also explains the difference between a change in demand and a change in quantity demanded.

SECTION **3** Elasticity of Demand

Section 3 covers the relationship between the percentage change in quantity demanded and the percentage change in price. That relationship is the elasticity of demand.

Demand

Why It Matters

Certain people and institutions play important roles in your life. For example, your parents, teachers, and friends all play key roles. Government is an institution that plays an important part in your life. It determines such things as when you can get a driver's license, how much you will pay in taxes, and when you will be able to vote.

Markets also have a major impact on your life. A market is any place people come together to buy and sell goods or services. Markets determine what prices you pay for computers, cars, TVs, mobile devices, books, and clothes. Markets also determine what people earn as teachers, truck drivers, TV and movie stars, baseball players, and nurses. How much money you earn in the future will depend on the markets.

If you are interested in the prices you pay for the goods and services you buy or why some people are paid higher salaries than others, then you will be interested in learning how markets work. The first step is to learn about demand, the subject of this chapter.

Shopping for a more powerful computer and the latest software program can be fun. Whether these shoppers decide to make a purchase will depend on their willingness and ability to buy—conditions you will learn more about in this chapter.

96

Teaching Suggestions from the Author

This is the first chapter of the book in which diagrams are used in a big way. Most students will be unaccustomed to translating what they know into diagrams. For example, in this chapter, we discuss the law of demand and a demand schedule and then translate each into a demand curve. Students seem to have little trouble understanding what the law of demand states, and they understand the numbers in a demand schedule. But when it comes to understanding what a demand curve represents, they tend to go blank.

I know of no better way of getting students to understand a diagram than to have them repeatedly state using their own words what the diagram

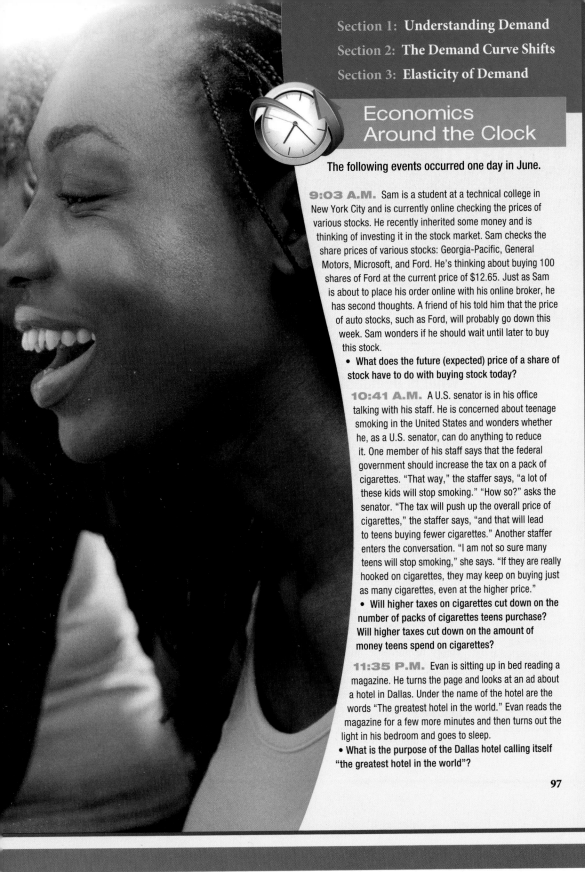

Economics Around the Clock

The following events occurred one day in June.

9:03 A.M. Sam is a student at a technical college in New York City and is currently online checking the prices of various stocks. He recently inherited some money and is thinking of investing it in the stock market. Sam checks the share prices of various stocks: Georgia-Pacific, General Motors, Microsoft, and Ford. He's thinking about buying 100 shares of Ford at the current price of $12.65. Just as Sam is about to place his order online with his online broker, he has second thoughts. A friend of his told him that the price of auto stocks, such as Ford, will probably go down this week. Sam wonders if he should wait until later to buy this stock.

• **What does the future (expected) price of a share of stock have to do with buying stock today?**

10:41 A.M. A U.S. senator is in his office talking with his staff. He is concerned about teenage smoking in the United States and wonders whether he, as a U.S. senator, can do anything to reduce it. One member of his staff says that the federal government should increase the tax on a pack of cigarettes. "That way," the staffer says, "a lot of these kids will stop smoking." "How so?" asks the senator. "The tax will push up the overall price of cigarettes," the staffer says, "and that will lead to teens buying fewer cigarettes." Another staffer enters the conversation. "I am not so sure many teens will stop smoking," she says. "If they are really hooked on cigarettes, they may keep on buying just as many cigarettes, even at the higher price."

• **Will higher taxes on cigarettes cut down on the number of packs of cigarettes teens purchase? Will higher taxes cut down on the amount of money teens spend on cigarettes?**

11:35 P.M. Evan is sitting up in bed reading a magazine. He turns the page and looks at an ad about a hotel in Dallas. Under the name of the hotel are the words "The greatest hotel in the world." Evan reads the magazine for a few more minutes and then turns out the light in his bedroom and goes to sleep.

• **What is the purpose of the Dallas hotel calling itself "the greatest hotel in the world"?**

97

Introducing the Chapter

Open the chapter by telling students that many objects, such as buildings and computers, are composed of separate parts or "building blocks." Ask them to provide examples of objects and their component parts. Then tell them that a subject like economics is similar to those objects and that a major building block of economics is demand. Also mention that another key component of economics is supply, which students will learn about in the next chapter. Write the definition of *demand* (see page 98) on the board, stressing the two parts of that definition: *willingness* and *ability*.

Teaching with Visuals

Students will likely be familiar with the general concept of demand, but the term *demand* may be new to them as it's used in economics. Have students look at the photo on this spread and explain how it shows demand at work. Students will probably say that the buyers want the goods they are buying. An economist would say that the buyers are expressing their demand for the goods—their willingness and ability to purchase the goods.

says. What does a demand curve say? What does a movement from one point on a demand curve to another point say? What does a shift rightward in the demand curve say? What does a shift leftward say? Only by repeatedly interpreting the diagram using their own words will students come to understand that a diagram is essentially a form of shorthand. For example, simply drawing a rightward shift in a demand curve is a visual way of saying, "Buyers are willing and able to buy more units of the good or service at each and every price." One shift in a curve is the equivalent of 19 words of explanation. (Perhaps economists use diagrams because they like to economize.)

Teacher Support

Focus and Motivate

Section Objectives

After completing this section, students will be able to
- define the term *demand*;
- describe the difference between demand and quantity demanded;
- discuss why price and quantity demanded move in opposite directions;
- explain the law of diminishing marginal utility; and
- distinguish between a demand schedule and a demand curve.

Economics
Around the Clock

Kickoff Activity

Tell students to reread the 9:03 a.m. scenario in Economics Around the Clock (page 97) and then write their answers to the accompanying question.

Invite students to share their answers with the class. Guide students to see that there is a direct relationship between price and quantity demanded.

Activating Prior Knowledge

Students often instinctively understand demand and the law of demand. They refer to the willingness to pay for a product and the understanding that as price increases, demand decreases. Ask students to identify situations in which the price of a good or service increased and their own demand for that good or service decreased or vice versa.

Visit econ.myemcp.com/videos for videos that will help students better understand the key concepts found in this section.

Understanding Demand

Focus Questions
▶ What is demand?
▶ What is the difference between demand and quantity demanded?
▶ Why do price and quantity demanded move in opposite directions?
▶ What is the law of diminishing marginal utility?
▶ What is the difference between a demand schedule and a demand curve?

Key Terms
market
demand
law of demand
quantity demanded
law of diminishing marginal utility
demand schedule
demand curve

What Is Demand?

A **market** is any place people come together to buy and sell goods or services. Economists often say that a market has two sides: a buying side and a selling side. In economics, the buying side is referred to as *demand*, and the selling side is referred to as *supply*. In this chapter, you will learn about demand; in the next chapter, you will learn about supply.

The word **demand** has a specific meaning in economics. It refers to the willingness and ability of buyers to purchase different quantities of a good at different prices during a specific time period. *Willingness* to *purchase* a good refers to a person's want or desire for the good. Having the *ability* to *purchase* a good means having the money to pay for the good. Both willingness and ability to purchase must be present for demand to exist. It is important for you to remember that if either one of these conditions is absent, there is no demand.

EXAMPLE Cruz doesn't have the $34,000 needed to buy a particular car. If she did have the money, though, she says that she certainly would buy the car. Notice that Cruz has the willingness (she wants the car) but not the ability (not enough money) to buy the car. Under these circumstances (willingness but not ability to buy), Cruz does not have a demand for the car. ◆

EXAMPLE Molly is shopping for a new cell phone. The one she likes is $129, which is within her price range. She was worried that she wouldn't have enough money, but she has set aside just enough for the new phone. Because Molly has the willingness and the ability to buy the cell phone, demand does exist. ◆

What Does the Law of Demand "Say"?

Suppose the average price of a movie theater ticket rises from $10 to $15. Will customers want to buy more or fewer tickets at the higher price? Most people would say that customers will buy fewer tickets.

Now suppose the average price of a movie theater ticket falls from $10 to $5. Will customers want to buy more or fewer

market
Any place people come together to buy and sell goods or services.

demand
The willingness and ability of buyers to purchase different quantities of a good at different prices during a specific time period.

law of demand
A law stating that as the price of a good increases, the quantity demanded of the good decreases, and that as the price of a good decreases, the quantity demanded of the good increases.

Differentiating Instruction

English Language Learners

This chapter contains a number of terms that are difficult for English language learners and others who have difficulty reading English. Assign these students to work in pairs, and have each pair make a list of key terms. Students should define the terms both in English and in their native languages, if appropriate, and then write new sentences that show that they understand the meanings of the words and how to use them correctly in English. You might also ask students to provide clear, concrete examples of the terms on their lists. Ask students to turn in their lists to you or make a copy for you so that you can quiz them individually on the terms at the end of the study of the chapter.

tickets at the lower price? Most people would say more.

If you answered the questions the way most people would, you instinctively understand the **law of demand**. This law says that as the price of a good increases, the quantity demanded of the good decreases. The law of demand also says that as the price of a good decreases, the quantity demanded of the good increases. In other words, price and quantity demanded move in opposite directions. This relationship (which you have probably heard referred to as an *inverse relationship* in your math classes) can be shown in symbols:

Law of Demand

If $P\uparrow$ then $Q_d\downarrow$

If $P\downarrow$ then $Q_d\uparrow$

(where P = price and Q_d = quantity demanded)

If you were reading closely, you probably noticed two words that sound alike: *demand* and *quantity demanded*. Don't make the mistake of thinking they mean the same thing. *Demand*, as you learned earlier, refers to both the willingness and ability of buyers to purchase a good or service. For example, if an economist said that Karen had a *demand* for popcorn, you would know that Karen has both the willingness and ability to purchase popcorn.

Quantity demanded is a new and different concept. It refers to the *number of units* of a good purchased at a specific price. For example, suppose the price of popcorn is $5 a bag and Karen buys two bags. In this case, two bags of popcorn is the *quantity demanded* of popcorn at $5 a bag. As you work your way through this chapter, you will see why it is important to know the difference between demand and quantity demanded.

Why Do Price and Quantity Demanded Move in Opposite Directions?

The law of demand says that as price rises, quantity demanded falls and that as price falls, quantity demanded rises. Why? According to economists, it is because of

▲ The cronut, which is part croissant and part doughnut, was invented by Dominique Ansel, a chef. In many places, the cronut is a popular item in high demand. Time magazine identified the cronut as one of the 25 best inventions of 2013. Can you think of two things you can put together and come up with a new item (much the way the croissant and doughnut were put together to come up with the cronut)?

the **law of diminishing marginal utility**, which states that as a person consumes additional units of a good, the utility or satisfaction gained from each additional unit of the good will eventually decrease. For example, you may receive more utility (satisfaction) from eating your first hamburger at lunch than your second and, if you continue, more utility from eating your second hamburger than your third.

"The main reason economists believe so strongly in the law of demand is that it is so plausible, even to noneconomists."

— David R. Henderson, economist and public policy adviser

What does this have to do with the law of demand? Economists state that the more utility you receive from a unit of a good, the higher the price you are willing to pay for it, and the less utility you receive from a unit of a good, the lower the price you are willing to pay for it. According to the law of diminishing marginal utility, individuals eventually get less utility from obtaining additional units of a good (such as hamburgers), so it follows that they will buy larger quantities of a good only at lower prices. And this is what the law of demand states.

quantity demanded
The number of units of a good purchased at a specific price.

law of diminishing marginal utility
A law stating that as a person consumes additional units of a good, the utility gained from each additional unit of the good will eventually decrease.

Clarifying Terms

Students might confuse the meanings of the words *want* and *demand,* perhaps thinking of them as synonymous. For example, a person who says "I want the TV" can be interpreted as saying "I demand the TV." In economics, however, *want* and *demand* mean two different things. The person who demands something is expressing a willingness and ability to pay for it. The person who wants something is expressing a desire, not a willingness and ability to pay. For example, a person may say "I want a car," but that doesn't mean he or she has the ability to buy a car.

Teaching with Visuals

Answers will vary.

Background Information: Diminishing Marginal Utility and Advertising

Students have probably not paid much attention to the concept and pricing associated with diminishing marginal utility—a key economic concept in this section. To emphasize this concept, ask each student to spend the next week keeping a log of goods and services that seem to have diminishing marginal utility in stores, advertisements, and other places. For example, a supermarket may offer 3 pounds of oranges for $2 and charge $1 per pound for any smaller quantity. Ask students to create visuals to accompany their logs and to present both to the class. After students have given their presentations, guide them in a discussion of diminishing marginal utility and advertising practices.

After students read this feature, invite them to describe personal experiences at amusement parks and other recreational sites. Ask if they enjoyed their visits more, the same, or less on each succeeding hour or day. Find out if they agree or disagree with the theory of diminishing marginal utility.

ANSWERS TO THINK ABOUT IT Answers will vary. Encourage students to share their personal experiences with the class.

Reinforcement Activity

Direct students to create price change examples from their own everyday experiences that demonstrate the law of demand. Begin by urging them to imagine that the prices of movie tickets at local theaters have dropped from over $7 to below $5 and to decide whether this price decrease will make them more likely to go to the movies. Then ask students to name several goods and services they typically purchase, imagine specific price change situations for each good and service, and describe how those changes would affect the quantities they would demand.

Can the Law of Diminishing Marginal Utility Explain Boredom?

Can the law of diminishing marginal utility explain why we sometimes get bored? Perhaps. Recall that the law of diminishing marginal utility states that as a person consumes additional units of a good, the utility or satisfaction he or she gains from each additional unit eventually decreases.

Think of what happens when you take a long trip in a car. You might start out feeling excited about the coming adventure. But after you have "consumed" the first mile, then the second, the third, the fourth, and so on, you may feel less enthused.

Often, as a trip moves along, people say they are getting bored. This might be because they get less utility from the one-hundredth mile driven than the tenth mile driven—especially if each mile looks pretty much the same. In other words, boredom may be a reflection of diminishing marginal utility.

Consider another example. Many people say they don't like to watch a TV program more than once. You might want to see a new episode of a program but not want to watch it again as a rerun. Why?

Maybe the first time you see a show, you are surprised or shocked or learn something new. Whatever the case, you get more out of it than you do the second or third or fourth time. Again, less utility leads to boredom.

THINK ABOUT IT In what settings have you said that you are bored? Can your boredom be explained by the law of diminishing marginal utility? Explain your answer.

The Law of Demand in Numbers and Pictures

The law of demand can be represented both in numbers and in pictures. Look at Exhibit 4-1(a), which has a "Price" column and a "Quantity demanded" column. Notice that as the price falls (from $4 to $3 to $2 to $1), the quantity demanded rises (from 1

demand schedule
The numerical representation of the law of demand.

to 2 to 3 to 4). Do you see that price and quantity demanded are moving in opposite directions? The economic term for this type of numerical chart showing the law of demand is **demand schedule**.

Now let's see how you would illustrate the law of demand in picture form. The simple way is to plot the numbers from a demand schedule in a graph. Look at Exhibit

---

Differentiating Instruction

Kinesthetic Learners

The law of diminishing marginal utility is a fun economic concept to show students. Call on five student volunteers to come to the front of the class. Give each volunteer a breath mint and then offer all of them additional mints. Continue to offer mints until one student has had enough. Ask your volunteers if they noticed any difference between their level of satisfaction from the first, to the second, and so on to the last mint. (You might post a chart with a 10-point "Enjoyment" scale on the vertical axis and "Number of Mints" on the horizontal axis and then ask each volunteer to plot his or her satisfaction level after each mint.) Explain that this activity demonstrates the law of diminishing marginal utility.

4-1(b), which shows how the combinations of price and quantity demanded in Exhibit 4-1(a) are plotted. The first combination (a price of $4 and a quantity demanded of 1) is labeled as point A. The second price and quantity demanded combination ($3 and a quantity demanded of 2) is labeled B. The same process continues to plot points C and D. If we connect all four points, from A to D, we have a line that slopes downward from left to right. This line, called a **demand curve**, is the graphic representation of the law of demand.

You might be wondering why we use the word *curve* when, as you can see in Exhibit 4-1(b), we ended up drawing a straight line to represent demand. The answer has to do with the standard practice in economics, which is to call the graphic representation of the relationship between price and quantity demanded a *demand curve*, whether it is a curve or a straight line.

A Student Asks

QUESTION: *Where will I see demand curves in the real world?*

ANSWER: *If you go outside and look up into the sky, you're not going to see a demand curve. If you look under your bed or in the school auditorium, you won't see a demand curve. This doesn't mean, though, that demand curves don't exist in the real world. (You also can't see a virus with your naked eye, but that doesn't mean viruses don't exist.)*

The data (numbers) that make up a demand curve—combinations of price and quantity demanded—do exist in the real world. When people buy more of a good (such as a can of soda or new pair of jeans) at a lower price than at a higher price, they are expressing the law of demand, which is graphically portrayed as a demand curve (in a textbook). So what do you think? Do demand curves exist in the real world?

demand curve
The graphical representation of the law of demand.

Teaching with Visuals

The law of demand says that price and quantity demanded move in opposite directions. Exhibit 4-1(a) shows this in a chart or table, and 4-1(b) shows this as a graph.

A Student Asks

You may want to expand the discussion from this A Student Asks to make sure students are not confused by the fact that some demand "curves" are actually straight lines.

The Global Impact

Some students think that the law of demand and the downward-sloping demand curve hold true only in the United States, only in rich countries, or only in free enterprise countries. This isn't true. The law of demand and the downward-sloping demand curve are relevant in economies all over the world. Whenever the price of a good rises, people will buy fewer units of the good. The law of demand is universal.

EXHIBIT 4-1 | **Demand Schedule and Demand Curve**

Price (in dollars)	Quantity demanded (in units)
$4	1
3	2
2	3
1	4

(a)

(b)

◀ (a) A demand schedule for a good. Notice that as price decreases, quantity demanded increases. (b) Plotting the four combinations of price and quantity demanded from part (a) and connecting the points gives us a demand curve. Price, on the vertical axis, represents price per unit of a good. Quantity demanded, on the horizontal axis, always applies to a specific time period (a week, a month, a year, and so on).

Section 1 **Understanding Demand** **101**

Internet Research

Direct each student to find an online news article, online press release, or corporate web page describing a new technological product. The student should then name two or three related products and services and explain how the advancement in technology will affect demand curves for those products and services. Ask, How will this product facilitate the production of other items or help people provide better services?

Economic Facts and Fallacies

Answers will vary.

Teaching with Visuals

A market demand curve is the sum of individual demand curves. To further illustrate the point made in Exhibit 4-2, have students work in groups of three or four to create individual and market demand curves for similar goods. Arrange for groups to share their demand curves with the class.

 Application Activity

After reading and discussing Section 1, assign the Section Activity in the *Applying the Principles Workbook*, pages 37–39.

Assess

Quick Quiz

The following true-or-false quiz will help you assess student understanding of the material covered in this section.

1. Both willingness and ability to purchase must be present for demand to exist. (True)
2. As the price of a good or service decreases, the quantity demanded decreases. (False)
3. The more utility you receive from a good, the higher the price you are willing to pay for it. (True)

Economic Facts and Fallacies

Demand Is Not *Want*

Some people think that in economics, the word *demand* means the same thing as the word *want*. For example, they believe that saying "She wants a new coat" is the same as saying "She demands a new coat." That is not actually the case, though.

When we say that someone *demands* a good, we mean that he or she is willing and able to purchase different quantities of the good at different prices. If we say "She demands a new coat," we mean that she is willing to pay a certain amount (say, $80) to buy one new coat.

The word *want*, on the other hand, does not imply willingness and ability to pay. If we say "She wants a new coat," we might mean that she would like a new coat, but if she cannot afford the coat at any price or is not willing to spend even a penny on the coat, she is not demanding a new coat.

THINK ABOUT IT What is something that you currently want? Do you demand that item? Explain your answer.

Individual Demand Curves and Market Demand Curves

An individual demand curve and a market demand curve are different. An individual demand curve is what it sounds like: the demand curve that represents an individual's demand. For example, Harry's demand curve represents Harry's (and only Harry's) demand for, say, DVDs. A market demand curve is simply the sum of all the different individual demand curves added together.

EXAMPLE Suppose that the whole world has only three buyers of DVDs: Harry, Sally, and Elizabeth. At a price of $10 per DVD, the quantity demanded is 2 for Harry, 1 for Sally, and 3 for Elizabeth. As a result, the *market demand curve* will include a point representing a price of $10 per DVD and a market quantity demanded of 6 DVDs $(2 + 1 + 3)$.

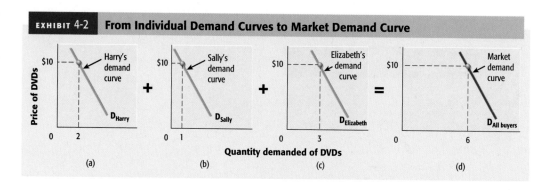

EXHIBIT 4-2 **From Individual Demand Curves to Market Demand Curve**

▲ Parts (a) through (c) show the individual demand curves for Harry, Sally, and Elizabeth. The market demand curve, shown in part (d), is simply the sum of the individual demand curves. Stated differently, we know that at a price of $10 per DVD, the quantity demanded of DVDs is 2 for Harry, 1 for Sally, and 3 for Elizabeth. It follows that all three buyers together would like to buy 6 DVDs at a price of $10 per DVD. This point is identified on the market demand curve in part (d).

To see this graphically, look at Exhibit 4-2. In parts (a) through (c), you see the *individual* demand curves for Harry, Sally, and Elizabeth, respectively. (To keep things simple, we identify only one point on the demand curve for each person.) Now look at part (d). Here, you can see the *market* demand curve (for all buyers—Harry, Sally and Elizabeth—of DVDs). Notice that the point we identify on the market demand curve simply represents the quantity demanded of all three buyers together if the price of a DVD is $10. ♦

ASSESSMENT

Defining Terms

1. Define:
   a. market
   b. demand
   c. law of demand
   d. quantity demanded
   e. law of diminishing marginal utility
   f. demand schedule
   g. demand curve
2. Use the terms *demand* and *quantity demanded* correctly in a sentence about concert tickets.

Reviewing Facts and Concepts

3. State the law of demand.
4. Give an example of a demand schedule.

Critical Thinking

5. Yesterday, the price of a good was $10 and the quantity demanded was 100 units. Today, the price of the good is $12 and the quantity demanded is 87 units. Did the quantity demanded fall because the price increased, or did the price increase because the quantity demanded fell?
6. What does the law of diminishing marginal utility have to do with the law of demand?

Applying Economic Concepts

7. Assume that the law of demand applies to theft. What might community leaders do to reduce the number of thefts committed in the community?

ASSESSMENT ANSWERS

Defining Terms

1. a. market: any place people come together to buy and sell goods or services; **b. demand:** the willingness and ability to purchase a good; **c. law of demand:** a law stating that as the price of a good increases, the quantity demanded of the good decreases, and that as the price of the good decreases, the quantity demanded of the good increases; **d. quantity demanded:** the number of units of a good purchased at a certain price; **e. law of diminishing marginal utility:** a law stating that as a person consumes additional units of a good, the utility gained from each unit will eventually decrease; **f. demand schedule:** the numerical representation of the law of demand; **g. demand curve:** the graphical representation of the law of demand.

2. Answers will vary.

Reviewing Facts and Concepts

3. As the price of a good increases, the quantity demanded of the good decreases and vice versa.

4. Answers will vary. Ensure that the student provides a numerical representation.

Critical Thinking

5. The increase in price (from $10 to $12) is the cause, and the fall in quantity demanded (from 100 units to 87 units) is the effect.

6. The law of diminishing marginal utility states that individuals eventually obtain less utility from additional units of a good, so it follows that they will buy larger quantities of a good only at lower prices. The law of demand states that individuals will buy more of a good at lower prices.

Applying Economic Concepts

7. Answers will vary. Students might mention that increasing the punishment for a crime (price) is likely to decrease people's willingness to commit the crime (demand).

Assessment Book

You will find a quiz for this section in the *Assessment Book,* page 35.

Reteaching Activity

Guide students in examining the definitions of *demand, quantity demanded, law of demand,* and *law of diminishing marginal utility.* Then instruct students to create and share with the class their own sentences using these terms.

Guided Reading

For further reteaching of the key concepts in this section, assign the Outlining Activity and the Just the Facts Handout from the *Guided Reading and Study Guide,* pages 54–55.

Focus and Motivate

Section Objectives

After completing this section, students will be able to

▶ explain why a demand curve shifts to the right or the left;

▶ distinguish among normal, inferior, and neutral goods;

▶ list the factors that can change demand; and

▶ identify the factor that can change the quantity demanded.

Kickoff Activity

Before instructing students to open their books to this page, explain that economists often tell economic stories with graphs. For example, a demand curve tells a story about the relationship between the price of a good and the quantity demanded of that good. Ask each student to draw a picture of a demand curve and to illustrate what happens to that curve when demand increases and when demand decreases.

Activating Prior Knowledge

Tell students that to learn how to tell stories with graphs, as economists do, they can start by describing graphs in the text using their own words. Have each student pick a graph from the preceding section and tell its story in his or her own words.

Visit econ.myemcp.com/videos for videos that will help students better understand the key concepts found in this section.

The Demand Curve Shifts

Focus Questions

▶ What does it mean when a demand curve shifts to the right?

▶ What does it mean when a demand curve shifts to the left?

▶ What is a normal good? An inferior good? A neutral good?

▶ What factors can change demand?

▶ What factor can change quantity demanded?

Key Terms

normal good
inferior good
neutral good
substitute
complement

When Demand Changes, the Curve Shifts

Demand can go up, or demand can go down. For example, the demand for orange juice can rise or fall. The demand for jeans can rise or fall. Every time the demand changes for a good, any good, the demand curve for that good shifts. By *shift*, we mean that it moves to the right or the left.

For example, if the demand for orange juice increases, then the demand curve for orange juice shifts to the right. If the demand for orange juice decreases, then the demand curve for orange juice shifts to the left. We can express this shifts as follows:

Demand increases → Demand curve shifts rightward
Demand decreases → Demand curve shifts leftward

We can understand the shifts in demand curves better with the aid of Exhibit 4-3. Look at the curve labeled D_1 in the exhibit. Suppose this demand curve represents the original and current demand for orange juice. Notice that the quantity demanded

at a price of $1 is 400 quarts of orange juice. Now suppose that the demand for orange juice increases. For some reason, people want to buy more orange juice. This increase in demand is shown by the demand curve D_1 shifting to the right and becoming D_2.

What does it mean for a demand curve to shift to the right? The answer is easy if you again look at Exhibit 4-3. (Focus on the horizontal axis and the numbers on it, along the bottom of the graph.) What is the quantity demanded on curve D_2 at the price of $1? The answer is 600 quarts of orange juice. In other words, we can describe an increase in demand (or a shift rightward in the demand curve) by saying, "Buyers want to buy more of a good at each and every price." In our example, buyers want to buy more quarts of orange juice at $1.

How can we graphically represent a decrease in demand? In Exhibit 4-3, let's suppose again that D_1 is the original and current demand curve. A decrease in demand will then be represented as a shift leftward in the demand curve from D_1 to D_3. A decrease in demand means that buyers

---

Differentiating Instruction

Kinesthetic Learners

To help kinesthetic learners understand the factors that create shifts in demand curves, prepare a felt or sticky board and provide materials for students to create demand curves and symbols representing the factors that cause the curves to shift. Kinesthetic learners could manipulate these curves and factors to better understand their functions. You might put each factor on a scale to show it rising and falling and encourage students to demonstrate the changes in the demand curve.

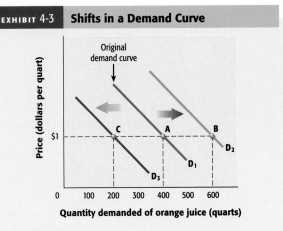

EXHIBIT 4-3 **Shifts in a Demand Curve**

Price (dollars per quart)

Original demand curve

$1

C   A   B

D₃   D₁   D₂

0   100 200 300 400 500 600

Quantity demanded of orange juice (quarts)

◀ Moving from D₁ (original demand curve) to D₂ represents a rightward shift in the demand curve. Demand has increased. Moving from D₁ to D₃ represents a leftward shift in the demand curve. Demand has decreased.

want to buy less of the good at each and every price. Specifically, if we look at the price of $1, we see that buyers once wanted to buy 400 quarts of orange juice at $1 a quart, but now, they want to buy only 200 quarts at $1 a quart.

A Student Asks

QUESTION: *Is saying that demand has increased for a good the same as saying that buyers are buying more of the good?*

ANSWER: *Yes, but with one important qualification. Buyers are buying more of the good at the same price at which they bought less earlier. For example, suppose that on Monday, buyers bought 100 units of a good at $3 per unit. Then on Tuesday, they bought 150 units of the same good at $3 per unit. An economist would say that demand for the good increased between Monday and Tuesday, because buyers bought more at the same price. If the good's price changed, the economist would describe the situation differently. The economist would say that the quantity demanded changed, rather than mention a change in demand.*

What Factors Cause Demand Curves to Shift?

Demand curves do not shift to the right or left without cause. They shift because of changes in demand, which can result from changes in several factors. Those factors include income, buyer preferences, prices of related goods, number of buyers, and future price.

Income

As a person's income changes, he or she may buy more or less of a particular good. You might think that if income goes up, demand will go up, and if income goes down, demand will go down. This is not necessarily the case, however. Much of what happens depends on what goods are involved.

If a person's income and demand change in the same direction (both go up or both go down), then the good is called a **normal good**. For example, if Robert's income rises and he buys more video games, then video games are a normal good for Robert. If, however, income and demand go in different directions (one goes up, while the other goes down), the good is called an **inferior good**. If a person buys the same amount of the good when his or her income changes, the good is called a **neutral good**.

normal good
A good for which the demand rises as income rises and falls as income falls.

inferior good
A good for which the demand falls as income rises and rises as income falls.

neutral good
A good for which the demand remains unchanged as income rises or falls.

Teaching with Visuals

To make sure that students understand Exhibit 4-3, display a new graph—perhaps showing the demand curve for kayaks or bungee cords. Illustrate both a rightward shift and a leftward shift in the demand curve. Call on student volunteers to explain what is happening with demand as the curve shifts.

A Student Asks

You may want to use this A Student Asks to make sure students understand the difference between *demand* changing and *quantity demanded* changing.

Thinking Like an Economist

An economist believes that if the demand rises for a good, there must be a cause. Prompt students to identify the most popular holiday gifts from last year. Ask, What are some of the reasons that the demand for these items was so high last year? Do you think the demand will be as high again this year? Why or why not?

Reinforcement Activity

Divide the class into groups of four or five students. Have group members determine what they consider a normal good, an inferior good, and a neutral good. Then have volunteers share their findings with the class. You might chart the students' responses and note any trends.

Cooperative Learning

Divide the class into groups, and tell each group to create an advertisement that will increase the demand for a good of its choice. The advertisement should address the factors that cause demand curves to shift. For example, "Buy a tennis racket, and get a free tube of tennis balls!" reflects the connection between two goods as complements. The advertisement may take the form of a TV or radio piece (either of which can be acted out in front of the class or videotaped and played for the class), a print piece, a billboard, an Internet pop-up—anything that might catch the consumer's eye. Each group should provide a written copy or outline of its presentation for your evaluation.

Teaching with Visuals

The demand for fuel will increase.

Discussion Starter

Brainstorm with students a list of goods that they demand, and write their responses on the board. Help the class create a list of substitute goods for these items. Then guide the class in developing a list of complements. Discuss the differences to make sure students understand both categories.

The Global Impact

A change in the price of a good produced and sold in a foreign country can change the demand for a related good produced and sold in the United States. To illustrate: Suppose X and Y are substitute goods, and X is produced and sold in Mexico and Y is produced and sold in the United States. Now suppose the price of X rises. Consequently, the demand for Y rises. It rises because people in Mexico are likely to switch from buying the higher-priced X to buying (importing) the lower-priced Y.

 Application Activity

After reading and discussing "What Factors Cause Demand Curves to Shift?" (pages 105–108), assign the Section 2 Activity in the *Applying the Principles Workbook,* pages 40–44.

◄ If Southwest Airlines expects the price of fuel to rise and decides to buy fuel now instead of later, what will happen to the current demand for fuel?

substitute
A similar good. With substitutes, the price of one and the demand for the other move in the same direction.

EXAMPLE In a typical month, Simon bought and consumed five hot dogs, one steak, and one tube of toothpaste when he was a college student earning $100 a week. Now that he has graduated from college and is earning $700 a week, he buys two hot dogs, three steaks, and one tube of toothpaste a month. During this time, prices have been stable (meaning they have not changed). So for Simon, hot dogs are an inferior good (he buys *less* as his income *rises*), steak is a normal good (he buys *more*

as his income *rises*), and toothpaste is a neutral good (he buys the *same amount* as his income *rises*). ♦

If you're wondering if a good can be a normal good for one person and an inferior good for another person, the answer is yes. People, not economists, decide whether a good is normal or inferior or neutral for them. If Bob's income goes up and he buys fewer potato chips, then potato chips are an inferior good for Bob. If Georgia's income goes up and she buys more potato chips, then potato chips are a normal good for Georgia.

Buyer Preferences

People's preferences affect how much of a good they buy. A change in preferences in favor of a good shifts the demand curve to the right. A change in preferences away from a good shifts the demand curve to the left.

EXAMPLE People today favor (prefer) small, gas-efficient cars more than they did in the past. As a result, the demand curve for small, gas-efficient cars has shifted to the right. At the same time, people have begun to favor mobile devices (smartphones, tablets, and laptops) over large desktop computers. As a result, the demand curve for desktop computers has shifted to the left. ♦

Prices of Related Goods

The demand for goods is affected by the prices of related goods. The two types of related goods are substitutes and complements.

When two goods are **substitutes**, the demand for one good moves in the *same* direction as the price of the other good. In other words, if the price for a good (say, peanuts) goes up, the demand for that good's substitute (say, pretzels) will also go

Thinking Like *an* Economist

Changing Demand, Changing Jobs

Can changes in the demand for a good or service hurt your job prospects? The answer is yes—at least in the short term.

To illustrate, think back to the days before the personal computer. For years, people used typewriters at home and at work. Then one day, the personal computer was unveiled, and people started using it instead. The demand for typewriters declined, and as a result, the demand for people to work in companies producing typewriters declined too. Many of those workers found themselves out of jobs. But if you think like an economist, you know that this was not the end of the story.

An economist knows that the demand for any particular good or service isn't likely to remain constant over time. People change their preferences for goods, and as they do, demand curves shift. When demand curves shift, resources get reallocated. In our typewriter example, the workers who left the typewriter industry ended up in other industries—some of them in the personal computer industry!

106 Chapter 4 Demand

Internet Research

Tell students that some products, such as books, are increasingly being sold online. Have them visit two major online booksellers, Amazon.com and Barnesandnoble.com, and compare their prices and offerings. Students will probably find the sites very similar. Ask them to discuss the factors that could contribute to a change in the demand curve for books sold online. What might make people buy more or fewer books on the Internet? What can these booksellers do to increase the demand for books on their sites?

Economics *in the* Real World

What's the Price of Playing Video Games?

Millions (billions?) of people like to play video games. In fact, there is a demand for playing video games. There is also a demand *for* video games. Did you catch that? There is a demand *for* video games as well as a demand *for playing* video games. What is the difference?

The demand *for* video games is the willingness and ability to buy different quantities of video games at different prices. For example, if video games are $20 each, you might buy 3 video games, but if video games are $5 each, you might buy 7 video games. In other words, the lower the price you have to pay for a video game, the more video games you will buy. In graphic terms, your demand curve for video games is downward sloping (left to right).

Now consider the demand *for playing* video games. Suppose you have already purchased 5 video games, and now you have to decide how much time to spend playing them. Will you spend 5 hours a week playing video games? 10 hours? 15 hours? Will you spend the same amount of time every week? Like most people, you will probably play more

hours some weeks than others. Why?

The answer has to do with the "price" you pay to play a video game. We are not talking about a dollar price, because when you play a video game that you own or that a friend owns, no one charges you. But price doesn't always mean "dollars." There is such a thing as a nonmoney price, and the nonmoney price of playing a video game is what you have to give up to do it. Do you have to give up studying for an exam or watching TV? Do you have to give up sleeping or eating a snack?

Is it true that the lower the nonmoney price of playing a video game, the more time you will spend playing the game? The law of demand would say yes, it's true.

You might be willing to spend more time playing video games if you have to give up less when you play. If you have to give up

studying for your upcoming biology test and thus risk the chance of getting a bad grade, you may decide that the nonmoney price for playing a video game is too great to spend any time at all doing it. But if you have to give up watching TV and end up seeing three hours of reruns of programs that you found boring the first time around, you may very well decide that the nonmoney price is low enough to justify playing for the whole three hours.

THINK ABOUT IT Think of the nonmoney price you pay for hanging out with a friend, talking on the phone, or watching a movie on an iPad. Is it true that the lower the nonmoney price for doing each of these activities, the more time you are willing and able to spend doing it? Explain your answer.

ANSWERS TO THINK ABOUT IT In general, the less someone has to pay to do something—whether that payment is in money or nonmoney terms—the more of that thing he or she does. This is true because people generally do those things for which they receive net benefits (benefits minus costs), and the greater the net benefits, the more they want to do it. When the price of something declines, the "cost" of someone doing it also declines, but the benefits remain constant and the net benefits increase. Therefore, as the net benefits increase, the more of this thing someone will likely want to do.

Reinforcement Activity

The difference between a change in demand and a change in quantity demanded may be difficult for students to grasp. Have them cite particular situations that show a change in demand and others that show a change in quantity demanded. Ensure that students understand the difference and can articulate it.

Differentiating Instruction

English Language Learners

To help students who are English language learners, use the following resources, which are provided as part of the *Economics: New Ways of Thinking* program:

- a Spanish glossary in the *Student Text*
- Spanish versions of the Chapter Summaries on an audio disc

Prediction Activity

Present students with a comparison between a local bookstore (at the mall perhaps) and an online bookstore. Ask students to predict what will happen to the demand for books at the local bookstore if the online store offers the same titles at lower prices. (*Answer:* Demand will fall at the local store.)

Reteaching Activity

Direct students to work in pairs to list five examples of goods that are substitutes and five examples of goods that are complements. Ask each pair to prepare a brief statement describing what will happen to demand if prices increase on the substitute goods and on the complement goods. Ask one pair to share its statements, and invite the class to fine-tune them if necessary.

Assess

Quick Quiz

The following true-or-false quiz will help you assess student understanding of the material covered in this section.

1. When the demand curve shifts to the right, demand has decreased. (False)
2. Demand has increased when the demand curve shifts to the right. (True)
3. The prices of related goods affect the demand curve. (True)
4. A change in the number of buyers creates a change in the quantity demanded. (True)

up. For many people, coffee is a substitute for tea. Thus, if the *price* of coffee increases, the *demand* for tea increases as people substitute tea for the higher-priced coffee.

EXAMPLE Jessica is in the supermarket looking at soft drinks. She usually buys a six-pack of Coke a week, but today, she notices that the price of Coke has risen from what it was last week. So instead of buying a six-pack of Coke, she buys a six-pack of Pepsi. For Jessica, Coke and Pepsi are substitutes, which means that as the price of Coke goes up, so does Jessica's demand for Pepsi. ♦

Two goods are **complements** if they are consumed together. For example, tennis rackets and tennis balls are used together to play tennis. With complementary goods, the demand for one moves in the *opposite* direction as the price of the other. As the price of tennis rackets rises, for example, the demand for tennis balls falls. Other examples of complements (or complementary goods) include cars and tires, lightbulbs and lamps, and golf clubs and golf balls.

Number of Buyers

The demand for a good in a particular market is related to the number of buyers in the market. The more buyers, the higher the demand; the fewer buyers, the lower the demand. The number of buyers may increase because of a higher birthrate, increased immigration, or the migration of people from one region of the country to another. Factors such as a higher death rate and the migration of people can also cause the number of buyers to decrease.

Future Price

complement
A good that is consumed jointly with another good. With complements, the price of one and the demand for the other move in opposite directions.

Buyers who expect the price of a good to be higher in the future may buy the good now, thus increasing the current demand for the good. Buyers who expect the price of a good to be lower in the future may wait until the future to buy the good, thus decreasing the current demand for the good.

EXAMPLE Suppose Brandon is willing and able to buy a house (demand exists), but he thinks the average price of a house will be lower next month. As a result, Brandon is likely to hold off on making a purchase, which has the effect of decreasing current demand.

What Factor Causes a Change in Quantity Demanded?

We identified the factors (income, buyer preferences, etc.) that can cause *demand* to change, but what can cause *quantity demanded* to change? Only one factor: price. For example, the only thing that can cause customers to change their quantity demanded of orange juice is a change in the price of orange juice; the only thing that can cause a change in the quantity demanded of pencils is a change in the price of pencils.

As we stated earlier, a change in demand is represented as a shift in the demand curve: right or left. (See Exhibit 4-4[a].) So how do we represent a change in quantity demanded? When quantity demanded changes, the curve doesn't move right or left. Instead, the only movement is to a different point *along* a given demand curve, which stays in the same place on the graph. (See Exhibit 4-4[b].)

EXAMPLE Ian notices that the price of bananas has fallen; as a result, he goes from buying 3 bananas a week to buying 5 bananas a week. An economist would say that Ian's *quantity demanded* of bananas has increased (from 3 to 5) as a result of the price of bananas falling. ♦

EXAMPLE The price of a book was $10 in July, and Jeff bought 3. The price was $10 in August, and Jeff bought 4. Economists would say that Jeff's *demand* for books increased between July and August. ♦

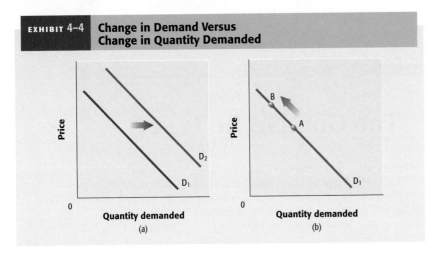

EXHIBIT 4-4 Change in Demand Versus Change in Quantity Demanded

(a)

(b)

▲ (a) A change in demand refers to a shift in the demand curve. A change in demand can be brought about by a change in one of several of factors (income, buyer preferences, prices of related goods, number of buyers, future price). (b) A change in quantity demanded refers to a movement along a given demand curve, which is brought about only by a change in the price of the good.

Assessment Book

You will find a quiz for this section in the *Assessment Book,* page 36.

Guided Reading

For further reteaching of the key concepts in this section, assign the Outlining Activity and the Just the Facts Handout from the *Guided Reading and Study Guide,* pages 56–59.

SECTION 2

ASSESSMENT

Defining Terms

1. Define:
   a. normal good
   b. inferior good
   c. neutral good
   d. substitute
   e. complement

Reviewing Facts and Concepts

2. Explain what it means to say that "demand increases."

3. Jerry Seinfeld, a comedian, started out doing stand-up comedy and went on to perform on a hit TV series. As he went from stand-up comedian to TV star, his income increased substantially. During this time, he bought more cars (specifically, Porsches) to add to his collection. For Jerry, what kind of good is a Porsche?

Critical Thinking

4. Identify a good that is a substitute for one good and a complement for another.

5. How does the expectation of a good's future price affect the good's current demand?

Applying Economic Concepts

6. In recent years, the price of a computer has fallen. What effect is this price change likely to have on the demand for software? Explain your answer.

7. Graph the following:
   a. an increase in demand
   b. a decrease in demand

SECTION 2

ASSESSMENT ANSWERS

Defining Terms

1. a. normal good: a good for which demand rises as income rises and falls as income falls; **b. inferior good:** a good for which demand falls as income rises and rises as income falls; **c. neutral good:** a good for which demand remains unchanged as income rises or falls; **d. substitute:** a similar good; **e. complement:** a good that is consumed jointly with another good.

Reviewing Facts and Concepts

2. Answers will vary. Students might say it means that buyers want to buy more of the good at each and every price. They also might mention the factors that cause a shift in demand: income, preferences, prices of related goods, number of buyers, and expectations of future prices.

3. A normal good.

Critical Thinking

4. Answers will vary.

5. If people expect the future price of a good to be higher than the current price, they will demand more of the good now (when it is cheaper). As their demand for the good rises, so does the current price.

Applying Economic Concepts

6. Computer hardware and software are complements. With complements, the price of one is inversely related to the demand for the other. Thus, as the price of computers falls, the demand for software is predicted to rise.

7. a. An increase in demand is represented by a rightward shift in a demand curve, such as from D_1 to D_2 in Exhibit 4-3. **b.** A decrease in demand is represented by a leftward shift in a demand curve, such as from D_1 to D_3 in Exhibit 4-3. (Ensure that students label both the axes and all relevant demand curves in their diagrams. They must also show, with arrows, how the demand curve shifts.)

Your **Personal** Economics

Too Good to Be True?

You just learned that buyers' expectations about future prices can affect current demand. If computer buyers think the price of a computer will be higher next year, they might buy their computers now (at the lower price) instead of next year (at the higher price). Buyers who think the price of a computer will be lower next year might hold off buying this year, thinking they will pay a lower price next year.

The Tulip Example

Similar thinking has affected prices and demand for goods for hundreds of years. In the 1600s in Holland, for example, a tulip craze became so frenzied that some people sold their businesses and family jewels just to buy a few tulip bulbs.

Why would people behave in this way? The answer has to do with what they believed about the future price of tulips. They believed that if they bought tulips today at a relatively lower price, they could sell the tulips at a higher price in the future.

Don't Forget Beanie Babies

In 1998 many people in the United States bought Beanie Babies (small stuffed animals).

They believed that Beanie Babies would become collectors' items and that the future price of Beanie Babies would be higher than the current price. They thought that if they bought Beanie Babies in 1998, they could turn around and sell them at a higher price in 1999, 2000, or some later year.

Then Came the Internet Bubble

One more example: Internet stocks in the late 1990s. Everyone seemed to believe that the prices were going to be higher next week or next month, and so they bought up the stocks as quickly as possible. Even though many experts said the stocks were overpriced, people kept buying, thinking that the prices would continue to climb. Many people even borrowed money to buy the stocks.

Housing Prices

Well, Beanie Babies, tulips, and many Internet stocks all crashed in price. Beanie Babies that once sold for $100 sold for $5; tulips that sold for hundreds of thousands of dollars ended up being sold for (the equivalent of) a few pennies; and Internet stock prices in some cases went from $400 a share to a few cents a share.

In the early 2000s, house prices in the United States rose dramatically. From 2001 to 2005 in many places around the country, all anyone heard was how house prices were destined—yes, *destined*—to keep on rising.

It was as if some natural law kept pulling prices up, much like the law of gravity pulls things down. In California, it was not uncommon to hear people say, "There is no way that houses near the coast are going to go down in price. After all, there's only so much coast to go around."

At the time, many people were buying houses not to live in but to speculate on. In other words, they bought a house in 2003 because they were "certain" they would be able to sell it for a higher price in 2004.

Then came the crash. In mid-2006, house prices in much of the country hit their peak and began to plummet. From mid-2006 to May 2009, prices fell 32.2 percent. From the first quarter of 2008 to the first quarter of 2009 alone, they dropped 19 percent. As shown in Exhibit 4–5, between April 2007 and April 2008, house prices in a selection of metropolitan areas declined.

One Last Point

Consider George. George watches as the prices of houses plummet. He also notices that house prices are dropping much more rapidly than

HOME FOR SALE

FORECLOSURE

◀ As house prices fell after 2006, an increasing number of sellers could not find buyers and lost their properties to foreclosure. **Can economists predict when real estate prices will rise or fall?**

house rents. Based on the difference between the rate of change in house rents and the rate of change in house prices, he is quite sure that sometime in the future, house prices will rise (perhaps very quickly).

What George doesn't know is *when* house prices will start to rise. Will the price rise begin next week, next month, next year, or five years from now? It is much harder to predict the timing of an event than it is to predict the event. (The doctor

can tell the pregnant woman that she is going to have a baby but be unsure of the day and time. The weather forecaster may be fairly sure that it will rain in the next 24 hours but be unable to say if the rain will start at 7:08 a.m. or at 9:32 a.m.)

Your Personal Economics Activity

Imagine that you had $10,000 that you were required to invest in a single venture. In a page-long essay, describe where you would invest your money. Explain your reasoning and support your choice with reliable sources.

EXHIBIT 4–5	**House Prices Decline**
Metropolitan Area	**One Year Change (%)**
Atlanta	−5.6%
Boston	−4.6
Chicago	−8.5
Cleveland	−9.2
Dallas	−4.1
Denver	−5.5
Detroit	−16.5
Las Vegas	−22.8
Los Angeles	−19.4
Miami	−21.7
Minneapolis	−12.5
New York	−6.6
Phoenix	−20.8
Portland	−2.0
San Diego	−19.2
San Francisco	−17.2
Seattle	−2.7
Tampa	−17.5
Washington	−13.0

Source: Standard & Poor's.

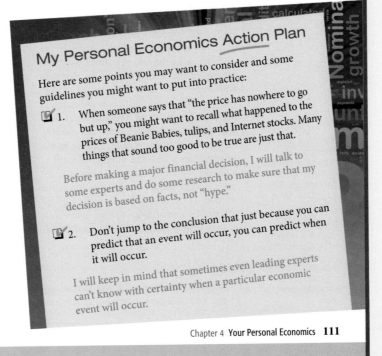

My Personal Economics Action Plan

Here are some points you may want to consider and some guidelines you might want to put into practice:

1. When someone says that "the price has nowhere to go but up," you might want to recall what happened to the prices of Beanie Babies, tulips, and Internet stocks. Many things that sound too good to be true are just that.

   Before making a major financial decision, I will talk to some experts and do some research to make sure that my decision is based on facts, not "hype."

2. Don't jump to the conclusion that just because you can predict that an event will occur, you can predict when it will occur.

   I will keep in mind that sometimes even leading experts can't know with certainty when a particular economic event will occur.

Chapter 4 Your Personal Economics **111**

Grading Rubric: Essay

1 2 3 4 5 Essay identified and described an investment opportunity.

1 2 3 4 5 Student supported his or her choice with logical reasoning and sources.

Teaching with Visuals

Economists research the housing market to determine how big the demand for real estate is, when supply is likely to equal or exceed demand, and what other factors might affect prices and then make predictions based on their findings. However, even leading economists can't be certain that their predictions will be correct. Also, when many economists make a similar prediction, the act of predicting can affect the actual outcome, although not always in the direction of the prediction.

Discussion Starter

To help students understand that it is harder to predict the timing of an event than the occurrence of the event, suggest that they consider the prices of cars. Ask, Do you think car sticker prices will go up or down in the future? On what is your opinion based? On a scale of 1 to 10, with 1 meaning "Very Unsure" and 10 meaning "Very Sure," how certain are you of your answer? Record students' ratings and calculate the class average.

Now ask, When do you think prices will change? On what do you base this opinion? How sure are you of this answer? Again, record their ratings and calculate the class average.

Compare the average ratings of certainty for the two opinions. The class as a whole should be more sure of its response to the first question; if it isn't, point out that the students' responses are an anomaly, and try to find out why they didn't follow the usual pattern.

My Personal Economics Action Plan Ask each student to identify the next major financial decision he or she might make. Have each student describe in writing what research is needed to gather facts and what experts could provide information and advice about the decision. Encourage students to carry out the research and make at least tentative decisions. Invite students to report their plans and decisions back to the class, if they feel comfortable doing so.

Teacher Support

Focus and Motivate

Section Objectives

After completing this section, students will be able to

► describe elasticity of demand;

► explain how to compute elasticity of demand;

► distinguish among elastic, inelastic, and unit-elastic demand;

► list the factors that can change the elasticity of demand; and

► describe the relationship between an increase in price for a good and higher total revenue.

Economics Around the Clock

Kickoff Activity

Have students reread the 11:35 p.m. scenario in Economics Around the Clock (page 97) and then write their answers to the question that accompanies it.

Invite students to share their answers with the class. Look for responses indicating that the hotel is attempting to increase its value to Evan, so that he might be willing to pay a higher price for a room.

Activating Prior Knowledge

Instruct each student to write two or three sentences that explain the differences in meaning between the terms *elastic* and *inelastic* and that guess at the meanings of the terms *elastic demand,* *inelastic demand,* and *unit-elastic demand.*

Visit econ.myemcp.com/videos for videos that will help students better understand the key concepts found in this section.

Elasticity of Demand

Focus Questions

► What is elasticity of demand?

► How is elasticity of demand computed?

► What does it mean to say that the demand for a good is elastic? Inelastic? Unit elastic?

► What factors can change the elasticity of demand?

► Does an increase in price for a good necessarily bring about a higher total revenue?

Key Terms

elasticity of demand
elastic demand
inelastic demand
unit-elastic demand

What Is Elasticity of Demand?

Suppose Jimmy loves chewing gum so much that he buys as many as four or five packs a week. One day he notices that the price of his favorite gum has gone up a quarter. Jimmy will probably now buy less chewing gum. But *how much* less?

This question about Jimmy's gum buying is the kind of question that you will learn how to answer as you study our next economic concept: *elasticity of demand.* **Elasticity of demand** deals with the relationship between price and quantity demanded. It is a way of measuring how a price change affects the number of units of a good people buy. In some cases, a small price change causes a major change in the number of units of a good people buy. In other cases, a small price change causes little change in how many units of a good people buy.

Elastic Demand

Economists have created a way to measure these relationships between price and quantity demanded. They compare the percentage change in quantity demanded of a good to the percentage change in the price of that good. In mathematical terms, here is what elasticity of demand looks like:

$$\text{Elasticity of demand} = \frac{\text{Percentage change in quantity demanded}}{\text{Percentage change in price}}$$

In the equation, the numerator is *percentage change in quantity demanded* and the denominator is *percentage change in price.* **Elastic demand** exists when the quantity demanded (the numerator) changes by a greater percentage than the price (the denominator).

For example, suppose the quantity demanded of lightbulbs falls by 15 percent as the price of lightbulbs increases by 10 percent. An economist would say that because the numerator (15%) is greater than the denominator (10%), the demand for lightbulbs is *elastic.* Another way that an economist might state this relationship is that the elasticity of demand is greater than 1, because if you divide 15% by 10%, you get 1.5, which is greater than 1.

elasticity of demand
The relationship between the percentage change in quantity demanded and the percentage change in price.

elastic demand
The type of demand that exists when the percentage change in quantity demanded is greater than the percentage change in price.

112 Chapter 4 Demand

Internet Research

Instruct each student to use the Internet to find products for which there is high demand, low demand, elastic demand, and inelastic demand—one product for each category. For each product, the student should write a brief description, state reasons for the level of demand, and identify factors that might change the level of demand. Have students create pictures, charts, and graphs showing the results of their research.

Inelastic Demand

Inelastic demand exists when the quantity demanded changes by a smaller percentage than the price—that is, when the numerator changes by less than the denominator. Suppose the quantity demanded of salt falls by 5 percent as the price of salt rises by 10 percent. In this case, the numerator (5%) is less than the denominator (10%), so the demand for salt is inelastic. An economist might say that the elasticity of demand is less than 1 (because if you divide 5% by 10% you get 0.5, which is less than 1).

Unit-Elastic Demand

Unit-elastic demand exists when the quantity demanded changes by the same percentage as the price—that is, when the numerator changes by the same percentage as the denominator. For example, suppose the quantity demanded of picture frames decreases by 10 percent as the price of picture frames rises by 10 percent. The numerator (10%) is equal to the denominator (10%), so the demand for picture frames is unit elastic. According to an economist, elasticity of demand is equal to 1 (10% divided by 10% equals 1).

When elasticity of demand is greater than 1, we say that demand is elastic. When it is less than 1, we say that demand is inelastic. And finally, when it is equal to 1, we say that demand is unit elastic. (See Exhibit 4-6.)

Elastic or Inelastic?

So, you're probably wondering what products are elastic and what products are inelastic? One economics study identified oysters, restaurant meals, and automobiles as goods with elastic demand. For these goods, price changes have a strong impact on how much customers will buy. In the same study, coffee, gasoline (for your car), physicians' services, and legal services were identified as goods with inelastic demand. For these products, changes in price had less impact on how much customers will buy.

EXHIBIT 4-6	Elasticity of Demand
If demand is . . .	**That means . . .**
Elastic	Quantity demanded changes by a larger percentage than price. For example, if price rises by 10 percent, quantity demanded falls by, say, 15 percent.
Inelastic	Quantity demanded changes by a smaller percentage than price. For example, if price rises by 10 percent, quantity demanded falls by, say, 5 percent.
Unit elastic	Quantity demanded changes by the same percentage as price. For example, if price rises by 10 percent, quantity demanded falls by 10 percent.

EXAMPLE A university raises its tuition by 10 percent. As a result, the number of students that apply to the university falls by 2 percent. In this situation, we would say that the demand for education at this particular university is inelastic. Why? The percentage change in quantity demanded (2%) is less than the percentage change in price (10%). ◆

What Determines Elasticity of Demand?

The demand for some goods (coffee, gasoline at the local gas station, physicians' services) is inelastic, while the demand for other goods (oysters, restaurant meals, cars) is elastic. But why? Four factors affect the elasticity of demand: (1) the number of substitutes available, (2) whether something is a luxury or a necessity, (3) the percentage of income spent on the good, and (4) time.

Number of Substitutes

Let's look at two goods: heart medicine and soft drinks. Heart medicine has relatively few substitutes, and many people must have it to stay well. Even if the price of heart medicine went up by 50, 100, or 150 percent, the quantity that people demanded probably would not fall by much. Is the demand for heart medicine more likely to be elastic or

inelastic demand
The type of demand that exists when the percentage change in quantity demanded is less than the percentage change in price.

unit-elastic demand
The type of demand that exists when the percentage change in quantity demanded is the same as the percentage change in price.

Clarifying Terms

After students read the definitions of the terms *elasticity of demand, elastic demand, inelastic demand,* and *unit-elastic demand* on pages 112–113, tell them to restate the definitions in their own words. Students may think the terms refer just to the pliability of demand. If that's the case, emphasize that the terms refer to relationships between quantity demanded and price.

Reinforcement Activity

Tell students to list five goods on which they spend a small percentage of their income. Then tell them to list five goods on which they spend a large percentage of their income. Next, ask them what the percentage of income they spend on each good has to do with the elasticity of their demand for that good. For example, students may say that because they spend a very small amount of money on pencils, their demand for pencils is relatively inelastic.

Cross-Curricular Activity

Mathematical calculations are made throughout this section on the elasticity of demand. To ensure students' understanding, review some of the equations with them. If students have trouble with the math involved, especially with the percentages, walk them through the equations using a demand graph that you have drawn on the board.

Show, through markings on the graph, the changes that create the percentage changes in quantity demanded and price. Create percentages that are easy to recognize (10%, 50%, etc.). Then have students tell you whether each ratio is elastic, inelastic, or unit elastic.

Tell students that many people believe that the more money someone has, the more expensive the version of a product he or she will buy. Point out that these people are assuming that someone who has the ability to buy something also has the willingness to buy it. An economist doesn't think this way. He or she knows that most people try to find the best deal available to them.

Encourage students to survey family members and friends to find out whether they buy the most expensive items available when they can afford them or look for the best buys. Discuss the findings, focusing on willingness and ability as the key elements of demand.

Economic Facts and Fallacies

Demand, Elasticity, and the Price of Rugs

Some people believe that if a seller raises the price of a good, he or she will necessarily earn more revenue. This may not be true. It all depends on the elasticity of demand for the seller's good. Suppose that a rug seller raises her price from $200 to $400 per rug. If the demand for rugs is elastic between the prices of $200 and $400, then the seller will earn less revenue selling rugs at $400 than at $200. When the demand is elastic, lowering the price is the way to earn greater total revenue.

inelastic? The answer is inelastic. Do you see the reasoning here? The fewer substitutes for a good, the less likely the quantity demanded will change much if the price rises.

In contrast, a particular soft drink (say Sprite) has many substitutes (Pepsi, Mountain Dew, etc.). Therefore, if the price of Sprite rises, we would expect the quantity demanded to fall greatly, because people can choose many other soft drinks. Is the demand for a particular soft drink more likely to be elastic or inelastic? The answer is elastic, because the more substitutes there are for a good, the more likely people will buy much less of it if the price rises.

Luxuries Versus Necessities

Luxury goods (luxuries) are goods that people feel they do not need to survive. For example, a $70,000 car is a luxury good for most people. Necessary goods (necessities), in contrast, are goods that people feel they need to survive. Heart medicine is a necessity for some people. Food is a necessity for everyone.

Generally speaking, if the price of a necessity (such as food) increases, people cannot cut back much on the quantity demanded. (They need a certain amount of food to live.) However, if the price of a luxury good increases, people are more able to cut back on the quantity demanded. The demand for luxuries tends to be elastic; the demand for necessities is more likely to be inelastic.

Percentage of Income Spent on the Good

Claire has a monthly income of $2,000. Of this amount, she spends $10 on magazines and $400 on dinners at restaurants. In percentage terms, she spends 0.5 percent of her monthly income on magazines and 20 percent of her monthly income on dinners at restaurants. Suppose the price of magazines and the price of dinners at restaurants both double. What will Claire be more likely to cut back on: the number of magazines or the number of dinners at restaurants?

She will probably reduce the number of dinners at restaurants, don't you think? Claire will feel this price change more strongly, because it affects a larger percentage of her income. She may shrug off a doubling in the price of magazines, on which she spends only 0.5 percent of her income, but she is not likely to shrug off a doubling in the price of dinners at restaurants, on which she spends 20 percent.

In short, buyers are more responsive to price changes for goods on which they spend larger percentages of their incomes. In these cases, the demand is likely to be elastic. In contrast, the demand for goods on which consumers spend small percentages of their incomes is more likely to be inelastic.

Time

As time passes, buyers have greater opportunities to change the quantity demanded in response to a price change. For example, if the price of electricity went up today and you knew about it, you probably would not change your consumption of electricity much today. But by three months from today, you would probably have changed your consumption more. As time passes, you have more chances to change your consumption by finding substitutes (natural gas), altering your lifestyle (buying more blankets and turning down the thermostat at night), and similar actions. The less time you have to respond to a price change in a good, the more likely your demand for that good will be inelastic.

Background Information: Elasticity and Total Revenue

The relationship between elasticity and total revenue is a basic formulator of price in a free enterprise economy. The law of demand—which specifies that price and quantity demanded move in opposite directions—is based on the assumption that when price changes, *nothing else changes*.

In Latin, the term used to denote that nothing else changes is *ceteris paribus* (pronounced "set eris pair abis"). As long as every other part of the equation stays the same *(ceteris paribus),* knowing the nature of this relationship allows a seller to learn the best price at which to sell a good or service.

Is the Demand for Health Care Elastic?

Consider a health care system in which the customers have to pay some percentage of their health-care bill and taxpayers pay the remainder. For example, it could be that, for every $100, the customer pays $30 and taxpayers pay $70. We'll call this system the 30-percent co-pay system (because the customer has a 30 percent co-payment).

Now, suppose someone argues that the 30 percent co-payment is too high; he supports bringing it down to 10 percent. So, for every $100, the customer pays $10 and the taxpayers pay $90. Will this decline in what the customer pays (from $30 to $10) result in an increase or decrease in the total dollar amount spent on health care? The answer depends on the whether the demand for health care is elastic or inelastic.

First, suppose the demand for health care is elastic. In this case, a lower price for health care (a lower co-payment) will lead to a percentage increase in the quantity demanded of health care that is greater than the percentage decrease in price. This will result in an increase in the total dollar amount spent on health care.

Now, some studies have shown that the demand for health care is fairly elastic. In other words, small declines in price (that customers pay) are going to increase the quantity demanded much more than proportionally. For example, if price elasticity of demand is, say, 2.22, then a 10 percent decline in price is going to increase quantity demanded of health care by 22.2 percent. Some economists have wondered whether the hospitals and doctors could deal with all the extra work. Would some kind of non-price rationing device have to be instituted?

In one study, it was noted that if customers paid much less than 30 percent of their own health care bills, the demand for health care was highly elastic. What would this observation mean for the taxpayers in our health care

system? It would mean that they would end up paying much larger bills for health care because, if demand is highly elastic and price is lowered, then the total amount spent on health care is going to increase dramatically. (Think of this situation in terms of total revenue for a good: If demand is elastic and price declines, total revenue will rise. Similarly, if demand is elastic for health care at low prices, and the price the customer pays drops, then the total amount of spending on health care—much of which will have to be picked up by the taxpayer—will definitely increase.)

THINK ABOUT IT Suppose the demand for health care is elastic and the price the customer pays for health care rises. What will happen to the total amount of money spent on health care?

ANSWERS TO THINK ABOUT IT Answers will vary. Students should recognize that if demand is elastic and price rises, then the total amount of money spent on health care declines.

Reinforcement Activity

Instruct students to clip or copy from magazines and newspapers pictures of products they believe are luxuries. Then have them do the same thing for products they believe are necessities. Create a bulletin board display with the items provided by students.

So, when the law of demand states that as the price of an item falls, people will buy more of that item, the assumption is that nothing else changes.

Instruct each student to find an advertisement for a sales event in the newspaper and to write a short summary of the advertisement. Then divide the class into groups of three or four and direct each group to decide how the concept of *ceteris paribus* is reflected in the sales events examined by the group members.

Teaching with Visuals

If the producer of laptop computers has just raised the price of laptops and demand for laptops is inelastic, then total revenue will rise.

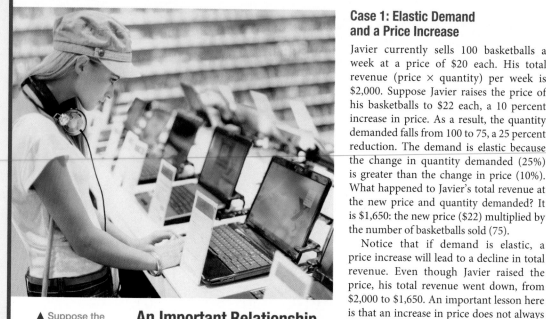

▲ Suppose the producer of laptop computers has just raised the price of laptops and demand for laptops is inelastic. What will happen to total revenue?

"Price and total revenue don't always travel in the same direction."
— Anonymous

An Important Relationship Between Elasticity and Total Revenue

Demand is elastic for one good and inelastic for another good. Does it matter? As you just read, it can matter to you as an individual, and it definitely matters to the sellers of goods. In particular, it matters to a seller's total revenue (the money a seller receives for selling his or her goods). To see how elasticity of demand relates to a business's total revenue, let's consider four cases in detail. The cases look at both elastic and inelastic goods and at what happens to each when the price rises and when the price falls. See Exhibit 4-7 for a summary of the four types of relationships between elasticity and revenue.

Case 1: Elastic Demand and a Price Increase

Javier currently sells 100 basketballs a week at a price of $20 each. His total revenue (price × quantity) per week is $2,000. Suppose Javier raises the price of his basketballs to $22 each, a 10 percent increase in price. As a result, the quantity demanded falls from 100 to 75, a 25 percent reduction. The demand is elastic because the change in quantity demanded (25%) is greater than the change in price (10%). What happened to Javier's total revenue at the new price and quantity demanded? It is $1,650: the new price ($22) multiplied by the number of basketballs sold (75).

Notice that if demand is elastic, a price increase will lead to a decline in total revenue. Even though Javier raised the price, his total revenue went down, from $2,000 to $1,650. An important lesson here is that an increase in price does not always bring about an increase in total revenue.

Elastic demand + Price increase = Total revenue decrease

Case 2: Elastic Demand and a Price Decrease

In Case 2, as in Case 1, demand is elastic. This time, however, Javier lowers the price of his basketballs from $20 to $18, a 10 percent reduction in price. We know that if price falls, quantity demanded rises. Also, if demand is elastic, the percentage change in quantity demanded is greater than the percentage change in price. Suppose quantity demanded rises from 100 to 130, a 30 percent increase. Total revenue at the new, lower price ($18) and higher quantity demanded (130) is $2,340. Thus, if demand is elastic and price decreases, total revenue will increase.

Elastic demand + Price decrease = Total revenue increase

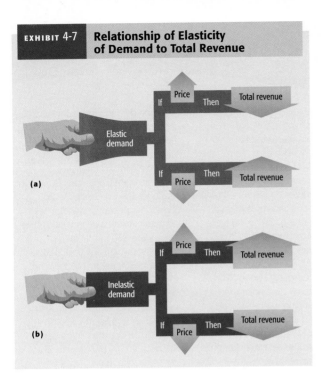

EXHIBIT 4-7 Relationship of Elasticity of Demand to Total Revenue

(a)

(b)

◀ (a) If demand is elastic, price and total revenue move in opposite directions: as price goes up, total revenue goes down, and as price goes down, total revenue goes up. (b) If demand is inelastic, price and total revenue move in the same direction: as price goes up, total revenue goes up, and as price goes down, total revenue goes down.

Case 3: Inelastic Demand and a Price Increase

Now let's assume that the demand for basketballs is inelastic, rather than elastic, as it was in Cases 1 and 2. Suppose Javier raises the price of his basketballs to $22 each, a 10 percent increase in price. If demand is inelastic, the percentage change in quantity demanded must fall by less than the percentage rise in price. Suppose the quantity demanded falls from 100 to 95, a 5 percent reduction.

Javier's total revenue at the new price and quantity demanded is $2,090, which is the new price ($22) multiplied by the number of basketballs sold (95). Notice that if demand is inelastic, a price increase will lead to an increase in total revenue. Javier's total revenue went from $2,000 to $2,090 when he increased the price of basketballs from $20 to $22.

Inelastic demand + Price increase = Total revenue increase

Case 4: Inelastic Demand and a Price Decrease

Demand is again inelastic, but Javier now lowers the price of his basketballs from $20 to $18, a 10 percent reduction in price. We know that if demand is inelastic, the percentage change in quantity demanded is less than the percentage change in price. Suppose quantity demanded rises from 100 to 105, a 5 percent increase. Total revenue at the new, lower price ($18) and higher quantity demanded (105) is $1,890. Thus, if demand is inelastic and price decreases, total revenue will decrease.

Inelastic demand + Price decrease = Total revenue decrease

Discussion Starter

Have students reread the case studies concerning the relationship between elasticity and total revenue on pages 116–117. Call on student volunteers to explain each case study in turn. You might invite volunteers to act out the case studies and graph them on the board.

Economics Around the Clock

After discussing "An Important Relationship Between Elasticity and Total Revenue," remind students of the 10:41 a.m. scenario in Economics Around the Clock (page 97) and discuss their answers to its questions.

Students should note that according to the law of demand, the higher the price charged for a good, the fewer the units that will be purchased. Higher taxes on cigarettes will raise the price, so teens will buy fewer of them. Whether this reduces the amount of money teens spend on cigarettes depends on whether their demand for this good is elastic or inelastic. If it's inelastic, then a higher price means greater total revenue (or more spent on cigarettes); if it's elastic, then a higher price means lower total revenue (or less spent on cigarettes).

Teaching with Visuals

After students study Exhibit 4-7, instruct them to create their own visuals to explain the relationship between elasticity of demand and total revenue. Suggest that students think of things that are elastic or stretchy and incorporate them into the illustrations. Urge students to be creative; they might come up with cartoon characters, three-dimensional models, or Flash presentations, for example.

After students read this feature, ask them to describe personal experiences in which they have attended popular concerts. Ask whether they agree that musicians need to know about elasticity of demand and to explain their responses.

Ask if students know of any direct connection between economics and Mick Jagger, lead singer for the Rolling Stones. Savvy students might know that he attended the London School of Economics.

ANSWERS TO THINK ABOUT IT Answers will vary. Understanding elasticity of demand will be important if the student wants to increase total revenue in his or her business.

Application Activity

After reading and discussing Section 3, assign the Section Activity and the Demand Practice Activity in the *Applying the Principles Workbook*, pages 45–53.

Assess

Quick Quiz

The following true-or-false quiz will help you assess student understanding of the material covered in this section.

1. Demand is always inelastic. (False)
2. Unit-elastic demand exists when the quantity demanded is less than the percentage change in price. (False)
3. Time affects the elasticity of demand. (True)
4. The demand for a good considered a necessity is likely inelastic. (True)
5. It doesn't matter to sellers if demand is elastic, inelastic, or unit elastic. (False)

Assessment Book

You will find a quiz for this section in the *Assessment Book*, page 37.

Does Elasticity of Demand Pop Up at a Concert?

Performing musicians need to know more than how to write and play music. They also need to know about elasticity of demand. In fact, a large part of their earnings will depend on whether they know about elasticity of demand.

Suppose you are a professional musician. You write songs, record them, and spend 150 days each year on the road performing.

Let's say that tonight, you will be performing in Chicago. The auditorium there seats 30,000 people. Will you earn more income if all 30,000 seats are sold or if only 20,000 seats are sold?

This question seems a little silly. The obvious answer is that you will be better off if you sell more tickets. Certainly, selling 30,000 is better than selling 20,000—isn't it?

The obvious answer here is not necessarily correct. The answer really depends on an understanding of elasticity of demand. Let's say that to sell all 30,000 seats, the price per ticket has to be $30. At this ticket price, total revenue (which is the number of tickets sold multiplied by the price per ticket) is $900,000.

If the demand for your Chicago performance is inelastic, a higher ticket price will actually raise total revenue. (Remember: Inelastic demand + Price increase = Increase in total revenue.) Suppose you raise the ticket price to $50. At this higher price, you will not sell as many tickets as you would if the price were $30 per ticket.

Let's say you sell only 20,000 tickets at $50 each. You have not "sold out" the auditorium, but it doesn't matter. At a price of $50 per ticket and 20,000 seats sold, total revenue is $1 million—or $100,000 more than if you had set the price at $30 per ticket and sold out the auditorium.

So, is a sold-out auditorium better than an auditorium that is not sold out? You might think so, but an understanding of elasticity of demand informs us that it may be better to sell fewer tickets at a higher price than to sell more tickets at a lower price. Who would have thought it?

THINK ABOUT IT Even if you are not a concert-performing musician, you may run your own business someday. Explain why it will be important for you to understand elasticity of demand.

Note: This example assumes that only one ticket price, $30 or $50, can be charged. If more than one ticket price can be charged, then some seats may be sold for $30, some for $40, some for $50, and so on.

▲ Carrie Underwood performing in Oklahoma City, OK.

Differentiating Instruction

Enrichment and Extension

Present this puzzle: A musical group is going to play at an auditorium Friday night. The owner of the auditorium must sell each ticket for the same price. Will the owner necessarily be better off if the entire auditorium is filled? What does this scenario have to do with elasticity? *(Answer:* The owner will not necessarily be better off if the auditorium is filled.

Achieving that will probably mean selling the tickets for a lower price, and the total revenue will then be lower. Suppose the auditorium holds 10,000 people and the owner can sell 10,000 tickets at $10 each, for a total revenue of $100,000. Also suppose that if the owner increases ticket prices to $20 each, he or she can sell 7,500 tickets, for a total revenue of $150,000.)

Defining Terms

1. Define:
   a. elasticity of demand
   b. elastic demand
   c. inelastic demand
   d. unit-elastic demand

Reviewing Facts and Concepts

2. Does an increase in price necessarily bring about a higher total revenue? Why or why not?

3. The price of a good rises from $4.00 to $4.50, and as a result, total revenue falls from $400 to $350. Is the demand for the good elastic, inelastic, or unit-elastic? Why?

4. Good A has 10 substitutes, and good B has 20 substitutes. The demand is more likely to be elastic for which good? Explain.

Critical Thinking

5. How is the law of demand (a) similar to and (b) different from elasticity of demand?

Applying Economic Concepts

6. Do you think the elasticity of demand for oil will increase or decrease over the next 40 years? Explain.

7. A hotel chain advertises its hotels as "The Best Hotels You Can Find Anywhere." Does this ad have anything to do with elasticity of demand? If so, what?

Reteaching Activity

Direct pairs of students to create their own versions of Exhibit 4-5. The pairs may use the same descriptions on their charts, but they should create examples of specific goods or services that illustrate elastic, inelastic, and unit-elastic demand.

Guided Reading

For further reteaching of the key concepts in this section, assign the Outlining Activity and the Just the Facts Handout from the *Guided Reading and Study Guide,* pages 60–62.

---

3. Elastic.

4. The demand for good B is more likely to be elastic. The more substitutes a good has, the higher the likelihood that the quantity demanded will fall off greatly as the price rises. And the higher the likelihood that the quantity demanded will fall off greatly, the higher the likelihood that the percentage change in quantity demanded will be greater than the percentage change in price (which is the definition of *elastic demand*).

Critical Thinking

5. (a) The law of demand and the elasticity of demand deal with the same two variables: price and quantity demanded. (b) The law of demand specifies the *direction* that quantity demanded changes as price changes. The elasticity of demand deals with the *amount* that quantity demanded changes as price changes.

Applying Economic Concepts

6. If the price of oil rises over the next 40 years, entrepreneurs will find it increasingly profitable to find substitutes for oil. The more substitutes they find, the greater the elasticity of demand will be. Given this reasoning, we should expect the elasticity of demand for oil to increase.

7. When a firm advertises its hotels as "the best," it's saying there are few substitutes for its hotels. After all, there can be only one "best."

Defining Terms

1. a. elasticity of demand: the relationship between the percentage change in quantity demanded and the percentage change in price;

b. elastic demand: the type of demand that exists when quantity demanded changes by a larger percentage than price.

c. inelastic demand: the type of demand that exists when quantity demanded changes by a smaller percentage than price; **d. unit-elastic demand:** the type of demand that exists when quantity demanded changes by the same percentage as price.

Reviewing Facts and Concepts

2. No. The effect on total revenue depends on if the demand is elastic, inelastic, or unit elastic.

Assessment Answers

Economics Vocabulary

1. market; **2.** inferior; **3.** quantity demanded; **4.** law of demand; **5.** law of diminishing marginal utility; **6.** inelastic; **7.** law of demand; **8.** normal; **9.** substitutes; **10.** unit elastic.

Understanding the Main Ideas

1. The demand for margarine rises.
2. a. The demand curve for apples shifts to the right. **b.** The demand curve for apples shifts to the right. **c.** The demand curve for apples shifts to the right.
3. a. elastic; **b.** elastic.
4. a. Total revenue falls. **b.** Total revenue falls. **c.** Total revenue rises. **d.** Total revenue rises.

Doing the Math

1. 0.583 (*calculation*: 0.07 ÷ 0.12 = 0.583).
2. $1,045 (*calculation*: $9.50 × 110 = $1,045).

Working with Graphs and Charts

1. (a) an increase in demand, or a rightward shift in the demand curve; (b) a decrease in demand, or a leftward shift in the demand curve; (c) a movement along a demand curve, or a decrease in quantity demanded.
2. (a) inelastic; (b) unit elastic; (c) inelastic

Solving Economic Problems

1. It's better to buy stock in a company that produces a normal good. If income is expected to rise, then the demand for a normal good will rise. It's better to buy stock in a company that you expect will have more sales than in one that you expect will have fewer or the same sales (which would be the case with an inferior good or a neutral good, respectively).
2. Students should disagree. If demand is elastic, an increase in price will lower total revenue.

Chapter Summary

Be sure you know and remember the following key points from the chapter sections.

Section 1

▶ Demand is the willingness and ability of buyers to purchase different quantities of a good at different prices during a specific time period.
▶ A market is any place people come together to buy and sell goods and services. There are two sides to a market: demand and supply.
▶ The law of demand says that price and quantity demanded move in opposite directions.
▶ A demand curve graphically represents the law of demand.

Section 2

▶ An increase in demand for a good causes the demand curve to shift to the right.
▶ A decrease in demand for a good causes the demand curve to shift to the left.
▶ A change in demand may be caused by changes in income, buyers' preferences, prices of related goods, number of buyers, and future price expectations.
▶ A change in price is what causes quantity demanded to change.

Section 3

▶ Elasticity of demand is based on the relationship between price and quantity demanded.
▶ Demand is elastic when quantity demanded changes by a greater percentage than price.
▶ Demand is inelastic when quantity demanded changes by a smaller percentage than price.
▶ Elasticity of demand is affected by available substitutes, whether the good is a luxury or necessity, percentage of income spent on the good, and time.

3. In their essays, students should identify that a rise in the price causes the quantity demanded to decline. People respond to changes in price.

Project or Presentation

Answers will vary.

Economics Vocabulary

To reinforce your knowledge of the key terms in this chapter, fill in each of the following blanks on a separate piece of paper with the appropriate word or phrase.

1. A(n) _____ is any place people come together to buy and sell goods or services.
2. If as income rises, demand for a good falls, then that good is a(n) _____ good.
3. According to the law of demand, as the price of a good rises, the _____ of the good falls.
4. According to the _____, price and quantity demanded are inversely related.
5. According to the _____, as a person consumes additional units of a good, the utility he or she gains from each additional unit of the good eventually decreases.
6. Demand is _____ if the percentage change in quantity demanded is less than the percentage change in price.
7. A downward-sloping demand curve is the graphic representation of the _____.
8. For a(n) _____ good, the demand increases as income rises and falls as income falls.
9. If as the price of good X rises, the demand for Y increases, then X and Y are _____.
10. When demand is _____, the percentage change in quantity demanded is the same as the percentage change in price.

Understanding the Main Ideas

Review the main ideas in this chapter by writing answers to the following questions on a separate sheet of paper.

1. Margarine and butter are substitutes. What happens to the demand for margarine as the price of butter rises?
2. Explain what happens to the demand curve for apples as a consequence of each of the following:
   a. More people begin to prefer apples to oranges.
   b. The price of peaches rises (because peaches are a substitute for apples).
   c. People's incomes rise (and apples are a normal good).

3. For each of the following, identify whether the demand is elastic, inelastic, or unit elastic:
   a. The price of apples rises 10 percent as the quantity demanded falls 20 percent.
   b. The price of cars falls 5 percent as the quantity demanded rises 10 percent.
4. State whether total revenue rises or falls in each of the following situations:
   a. Demand is elastic and price increases.
   b. Demand is inelastic and price decreases.
   c. Demand is elastic and price decreases.
   d. Demand is inelastic and price increases.

Doing the Math

Do the calculations necessary to solve the following problems.

1. If the percentage change in price is 12 percent and the percentage change in quantity demanded is 7 percent, what is the elasticity of demand?
2. The price falls from $10.00 to $9.50, and the quantity demanded rises from 100 units to 110 units. What does total revenue equal at the lower price?

Working with Graphs and Charts

Use Exhibits 4-7 and 4-8 to answer questions 1 and 2. (P = Price and Q_d = Quantity demanded)

1. What does each part of Exhibit 4-7 represent?
2. In Exhibit 4-8, a downward-pointing arrow (↓) means a decrease, an upward-pointing arrow (↑) means an increase, and a bar (—) means the variable remains constant (unchanged). Fill in the blanks for parts (a) through (c).

EXHIBIT 4-7

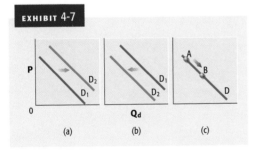

EXHIBIT 4-8

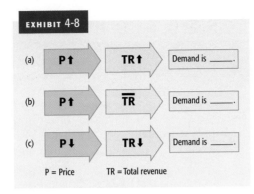

Solving Economic Problems

1. **Apply.** Income in the nation's economy is expected to grow over the next few years. You are thinking about buying stock. Is it better to buy stock in a company that produces a normal, inferior, or neutral good? Explain.
2. **Evaluate.** "Sellers always prefer higher prices to lower prices." Do you agree or disagree? Explain.
3. **Identify Cause and Effect. WRITING** Suppose that quantity demanded for a product rises and price declines. Write a one-page essay that answers this question: Does the decline in price cause quantity demanded to rise, or does the decline in quantity demanded cause price to rise? Include examples and support for your answer.

Project or Presentation

Elasticity of Goods. Choose eight goods and identify all the substitutes you can think of for each. Then put the goods in order from highest elasticity of demand to lowest, according to the number of substitutes. Compile a class chart listing everyone's findings, and discuss the results.

ONLINE emcp.com — *Practice Tests and Study Guide*

Go to **www.emcschool.net/Economics2e** and choose *Economics: New Ways of Thinking*, Chapter 4, if you need more help in preparing for the chapter test.

Chapter 5 Planning Guide

SECTION ORGANIZER

SECTION 1
Understanding Supply
(pages 124–127)

Learning Objectives	Reproducible Worksheets and Handouts	Assessment
▶ Define the term *supply*. ▶ Describe supply curves. ▶ Differentiate between a supply schedule and a supply curve.	Section 1 Activity, *Applying the Principles Workbook*, pages 54–56 Outlining Activity, *Guided Reading and Study Guide*, page 69 Just the Facts Handout, *Guided Reading and Study Guide*, page 70	Section Assessment, *Student Text*, page 127 Quick Quiz, *Annotated Teacher's Edition*, pages 126–127 Section Quiz, *Assessment Book*, page 46

SECTION 2
The Supply Curve Shifts
(pages 128–137)

Learning Objectives	Reproducible Worksheets and Handouts	Assessment
▶ Explain the meaning of a supply curve's shifting to the right. ▶ Explain the meaning of a supply curve's shifting to the left. ▶ Identify the factors that can change supply. ▶ Identify the factors that can change quantity supplied.	Section 2 Activity, *Applying the Principles Workbook*, pages 57–62 Supply Practice Activity, *Applying the Principles Workbook*, pages 63–66 Outlining Activity, *Guided Reading and Study Guide*, pages 71–72 Just the Facts Handout, *Guided Reading and Study Guide*, pages 73–74	Section Assessment, *Student Text*, page 137 Quick Quiz, *Annotated Teacher's Edition*, page 136 Section Quiz, *Assessment Book*, page 47

Reproducible Chapter Resources and Assessment Materials

 Graphic Organizer Activity, *Guided Reading and Study Guide,* page 75

Vocabulary Activity, *Guided Reading and Study Guide,* page 76

Working with Graphs and Charts, *Guided Reading and Study Guide,* page 77

Practice Test, *Guided Reading and Study Guide,* pages 78–80

Critical Thinking Activity, *Finding Economics,* pages 13–15

Chapter Test A, *Assessment Book,* pages 48–51

Chapter Test B, *Assessment Book,* pages 52–56

Student Text Internet Links

Economics: New Ways of Thinking, Second Edition encourages students to use the Internet to find out more about economics. Given the wealth of current, valid information available on websites, students should be encouraged to use the Internet as a research tool. Doing so will likely increase students' interest in and understanding of economics principles and topics. In addition, doing Internet research can help your students form the habit of accessing and using economics information, as well as help them develop investigative skills they will use throughout their educational and professional careers.

To aid your students in achieving these ends, each chapter of *Economics: New Ways of Thinking, Second Edition* includes the addresses of several websites that provide engaging and relevant information. When students type in any of the addresses provided, they will immediately arrive at the intended site. The addresses have been modified so that EMC Publishing can monitor and maintain the proper links—for example, the website http://www.deposit accounts.com/ has been changed to http://econ.emcp.net/accounts. In the event that the address or content of a site changes or is discontinued, EMC's Internet editors will redirect the link to a site with equivalent information.

Activities in the *Annotated Teacher's Edition* often suggest that students search the Internet for information. For some activities, you might want to find reputable sites beforehand and steer students toward them. For other activities, have students do their own searching and then check out the sites they have found and discuss why they might be reliable or unreliable.

Passport® for Economics

Technology resources are available with the *Economics: New Ways of Thinking, Second Edition* program through Passport®. These include:

eBooks for *Economics: New Ways of Thinking, Second Edition*

► Student textbook eBook
► Interactive Applying the Principles eWorkbook
► Finding Economics eBook
► Guided Reading and Study Guide eBook
► Annotated Teacher's Edition eBook
► Lesson Plans eBook
► Assessment eBook

Passport® for Students

Students can access helpful resources through Passport® for Economics. Resources include:
► Study guides
► Practice tests
► Flash cards in English and in Spanish
► Word games in English and in Spanish
► Tutorials and key-concept videos
► Spanish print and audio summaries

Passport® for Teachers

Keep your course current and relevant by using the teacher resources provided through Passport® for Economics. In addition to all of the resources on the student side of Passport®, the teacher side contains:
► Link to the Annotated Teacher's Edition eBook
► Standards correlations
► Microsoft® PowerPoint® Lectures
► Current Events Lessons
► Additional Economics in the Real World features
► ExamView® Assessment Suite
► PDFs of all print supplements (student and teacher)

Overview

A market has a buying side and a selling side. The previous chapter discussed demand, which is the buying side of the market. This chapter discusses supply, the selling side. The following statements provide brief descriptions of the major concepts covered in each section of this chapter.

SECTION 1 Understanding Supply

Section 1 introduces the economic concept of supply. Students will learn the difference between supply and quantity supplied and the differences between a supply schedule and a supply curve.

SECTION 2 The Supply Curve Shifts

Section 2 explores the factors that cause a supply curve to shift. These factors include resource prices, technology, taxes, subsidies, quotas, number of sellers, future price, and, in some cases, weather.

Supply

Why It Matters

Just as a coin has two sides, so does a market. A coin has heads and tails; a market has a buying side and a selling side. The previous chapter discussed demand, which is the buying side of the market. This chapter discusses supply, the selling side.

In your life, you will be both a buyer and a seller. You will buy many goods, and you will also sell some goods. You will certainly end up selling a resource—your labor. In Chapter 4, we learned about you as a buyer. In this chapter, we will learn about you as a seller.

These autographed guitars are being examined before being offered for sale in an auction. How might the supply of these specialty guitars affect the price that people will pay for them?

122

Teaching Suggestions from the Author

Students learned about demand in the last chapter, and in this chapter they will learn about supply. I've found that one of the best ways to help students understand supply, the law of supply, and the factors that shift a supply curve is to ask them to put themselves in the shoes of a supplier of some good. Perhaps they produce and sell

computers or furniture. Once students adopt the mindset of a supplier, they have an easier time understanding what will make them undertake certain actions.

It is important that students use economic terms in discussing and explaining economic concepts. They have been studying economics for at

Economics Around the Clock

The following events occurred one day in April.

7:04 A.M. Tara has young twin boys, Dave and Quentin. She has tried repeatedly to get both boys to be more well behaved. Yesterday, she promised to take them to a movie if they behaved better. Dave ended up behaving a lot better, but Quentin behaved only slightly better. Right now, Tara is asking Quentin why his behavior didn't improve as much as his brother's.

- What does the concept elasticity of supply have to do with the twins?

9:10 A.M. Georgia and Tom are riding on a train that is traveling from East Hampton, New York, to downtown Manhattan. Georgia is reading an article about taxes in the newspaper that says the government wants to place a tax on the production of cigarettes. For every pack of cigarettes produced, the government wants cigarette manufacturers to pay a $2 tax. Georgia tells Tom about the article. "What do you think of that?" she asks. Tom responds, "I think that tax is going to end up reducing the supply of cigarettes."

- Will the tax reduce the supply of cigarettes?

11:03 A.M. Angie owns a small oil company in Texas. She believes the price of a barrel of crude oil will be higher in three months than it is today and is thinking about not selling her current oil supply until the price goes up. She knows she will lose the interest on the revenue she would have if she sold the oil now, but she thinks selling at a higher price in three months might more than compensate for lost interest.

- Would you advise Angie to wait until later to sell her oil?

2:38 P.M. Frank and Pete are having coffee at their local Starbuck's. Frank owns a construction company, and Pete is his business manager. Frank says, "I'm not sure how many more people will want to work for us if we pay a higher wage. No matter how much money we offer, people just don't want to work in construction the way they once did." Pete just says, "I don't know. Money is a powerful motivator."

- Will more people want to work in the construction industry if Frank increases the wage rate (dollars per hour) he pays his employees?

123

Introducing the Chapter

The previous chapter discussed one-half of the foundation of economics: demand. This chapter will cover the other half: supply. It is impossible to study economics without understanding these key concepts. While demand deals with the buying side of the market (which students may be more involved in), supply deals with the selling side of the market. Students may initially be unfamiliar with the supply side the market, but once they have learned both sides, the study of economics will be much easier.

Teaching with Visuals

Students are probably familiar with the word *supply* and may use it to refer to their belongings—for example, a supply of pens and paper. However, in the study of economics, supply takes on a different meaning. Economists define *supply* as the willingness and ability to produce and sell goods. Invite students to predict how the supply of these autographed guitars will affect the prices that people will pay for them in the auction. Many students will correctly predict that having a limited supply of autographed guitars will increase the prices of the instruments.

least several weeks now, and they should begin to use the language of economics. If asked what the law of supply states, a student may answer, "It says that people sell more goods as price goes up." This answer isn't wrong, of course, but it's phrased slightly differently than the answer an economist would provide. An economist would say, "The law of supply holds that as price rises, quantity supplied rises, and as price falls, quantity supplied falls." It is important that students begin to use the phrase *quantity supplied* and to understand the difference between it and *supply*.

Teacher Support

Focus and Motivate

Section Objectives

After completing this section, students will be able to
- define the term *supply*;
- describe supply curves; and
- distinguish between a supply schedule and a supply curve.

Kickoff Activity

Ask each student to write an answer to the following question: If the price of a good that a supplier sells goes up, will the supplier want to sell more or fewer units of the good? Explain your answer.

Activating Prior Knowledge

Although the reason that sellers always want to produce and sell more when the price goes up might seem obvious, some students may not understand it. Now that students are familiar with using graphs to analyze demand, they may find it easier to understand supply if they see a graph illustrating it.

Teach

Discussion Starter

Ask students about factors that might affect a seller's ability and willingness to supply a good or service. These might include resource availability and cost, technology, taxes, quotas, and future price.

Visit econ.myemcp.com/videos for videos that will help students better understand the key concepts found in this section.

Understanding Supply

Focus Questions
- What is supply?
- Are all supply curves upward sloping?
- What is the difference between a supply schedule and a supply curve?

Key Terms
supply
law of supply
direct relationship
quantity supplied
supply schedule
supply curve

What Is Supply?

Like the word *demand*, the word **supply** has a specific meaning in economics. It refers to the willingness and ability of sellers to produce and offer to sell different quantities of a good at different prices during a specific time period. The supply of a good or service requires both a supplier's *willingness* and *ability* to produce and sell. *Willingness* to produce and sell means that the person wants or desires to produce and sell the good. *Ability* to produce and sell means that the person is capable of producing and selling the good.

> **EXAMPLE** Jackie is willing to build and sell wooden chairs, but unfortunately, she doesn't know *how* to build chairs. In other words, she has the willingness but not the ability. Outcome: Jackie will not supply chairs. ♦

What Does the Law of Supply Say?

Suppose you are a supplier, or producer, of TV sets, and the price of a set rises from $300 to $400. Would you want to supply more or fewer TV sets at the higher price? Most people would say more. If you did, you instinctively

supply
The willingness and ability of sellers to produce and offer to sell different quantities of a good at different prices during a specific time period.

law of supply
A law stating that as the price of a good increases, the quantity supplied of the good increases, and as the price of a good decreases, the quantity supplied of the good decreases.

direct relationship
A relationship between two factors in which the factors move in the same direction. For example, as one factor rises, the other rises too.

quantity supplied
The number of units of a good produced and offered for sale at a specific price.

understand the **law of supply**, which says that as the price of a good increases, the quantity supplied of the good increases, and as the price of a good decreases, the quantity supplied of the good decreases. In other words, price and quantity supplied move in the same direction. This **direct relationship** can be shown using symbols:

Law of Supply
If $P\uparrow$ then $Q_s\uparrow$
If $P\downarrow$ then $Q_s\downarrow$
(where P = price and Q_s = quantity supplied)

When economists use the term *supply*, they mean something different from what they mean when they use the term *quantity supplied*. Again, supply refers to the willingness and ability of sellers to produce and offer to sell different quantities of a good at different prices. For example, a supply of new houses in the housing market means that firms are currently willing and able to produce and offer to sell new houses.

Quantity supplied refers to the number of units of a good produced and offered for sale at a specific price. Let's say that a seller will produce and offer to sell five hamburgers when the price is $2 each. Five is the quantity

124 Chapter 5 Supply

Cooperative Learning

Ask students to form groups of three and brainstorm lists of manufacturing and supply companies in the local area. Have a member of each group contact the public relations department of one of the companies to set up an interview with an executive from its manufacturing department. The class as a whole should prepare questions that relate to how supply is determined. Have

each group meet with its executive, and if possible, videotape or audiotape the interview. After the interview, have the group write a paragraph or two summarizing the executive's answers and present its findings to the class. Then have the class discuss the differences among their interviews.

Are You Nicer to Nice People?

Business firms supply cars, clothes, food, computers, and much more. The quantity of each good or service they supply depends on the price. According to the law of supply, the higher the price, the greater the quantity supplied. In other words, the higher the price of notebooks, the greater the quantity supplied of notebooks.

Do you think the law of supply is true in personal situations, as well as business situations? Do people behave differently toward others depending on how others react to their emotions and behavior? Let's look at some examples of one "product" that people can supply to a greater or lesser degree: niceness.

Wouldn't you say that people can supply different amounts of niceness? Think about your own behavior: you can be very nice to a person, moderately nice, a little nice, or not nice at all. What determines how much niceness you supply to people? (In other words, why are you nicer to some people than to others?)

One factor that may determine how nice you are to someone is how much someone "pays" you to be nice. It may be a stretch, but think of yourself as selling niceness, in much the same way you might think of yourself as selling shoes, T-shirts, corn, or computers. The quantity of each item you supply depends on how much the buyer pays you.

If people want to buy niceness from you, what kind of payment will they offer? A person could come up to you and say, "I will pay you $100 if you will be nice to me," but usually things don't work that way. People buy, and therefore pay for, niceness not with the currency of dollars and cents but with the currency of niceness. In other words, the nicer they are to you, the more they are paying you to be nice to them.

Suppose a person can pay three prices of niceness: the very-nice price (high price), the moderately nice price, and the little-nice price (low price). Now consider two persons, Caprioli and Turen. Caprioli pays you the very-nice price, and Turen pays you the little-nice price. Will you be nicer to Caprioli, who pays you the higher price, or to Turen, who pays you the lower price?

If you answer that you will be nicer to Caprioli, you are admitting that you will supply a greater quantity of niceness to the person who pays you more to be nice. You have found the law of supply in your behavior. Again, you are nicer to those persons who pay you more (in the currency of niceness) to be nice.

THINK ABOUT IT When it comes to the quantity supplied of niceness, do most people behave in a manner consistent with the law of supply?

Have students read this feature and make lists of the people to whom they are very nice, moderately nice, a little nice, and not nice at all. Ask students why they are nicer to some people than others. Encourage students to think about whether they are ever paid for being nice in "currency" other than niceness. For example, parents may award students with privileges. Point out that someone who is nice to get more privileges is still obeying the law of supply.

ANSWERS TO THINK ABOUT IT Answers will vary. Invite volunteers to share their experiences with the class.

Reinforcement Activity

Ask students to think about how they treat their friends. Are they nicer to friends who are nice to them? Encourage them to be completely honest. What are some specific acts of niceness they have recently witnessed?

Cause and Effect

Discuss with students the cause and effect relationship presented in the Economics in the Real World on this page. Use the following questions to generate discussion: If people always respond to niceness by being nice, why would anyone not be nice? What are the costs and benefits of being nice to other people?

Clarifying Terms

Ask students to explain the difference between *quantity supplied* and *supply*. Students should recognize that quantity supplied is the number of goods or services actually supplied, and supply is the willingness and ability of sellers to produce and offer goods or services.

Prediction Activity

Present students with two scenarios: In the first, high school students are not paid to get A's. In the second, they are paid $50 for each A. In which scenario will there be more A's? How does this relate to the law of supply? The answer is that there will be more A's in the second scenario. As the price the student receives for supplying an A rises from $0 to $50, so will the quantity of A's supplied.

---

supplied at this price. As you work your way through this chapter, you will see why it is important to know the difference between supply and quantity supplied.

The Law of Supply in Numbers and Pictures

We can represent the law of supply in numbers, just as we did the law of demand. The law of supply states that as price rises, quantity supplied rises. (See Exhibit 5-1[a].)

As the price goes up from $1 to $2 to $3 to $4, the quantity supplied goes up from 10 to 20 to 30 to 40. A numerical chart like this one that illustrates the law of supply is called a **supply schedule**.

We can also show the law of supply in picture form by plotting the data in the supply schedule, as in Exhibit 5-1(b). Point A is the first combination of price and quantity supplied from the supply schedule, with a price of $1 and a quantity supplied of 10. Point B represents a price of $2 and a

supply schedule A numerical chart illustrating the law of supply.

Differentiating Instruction

Visual Learners

There are many different visual representations of supply curves in the supplemental materials for *Economics: New Ways of Thinking*. You might use the *Applying the Principles Workbook* or the *Daily Lectures: Overheads and Notes*. You might also have students practice creating and reading supply curves using the *Working with Graphs and Charts* disc.

Economics Around the Clock

After reading and discussing the law of supply, refer students to the 2:38 p.m. scenario in Economics Around the Clock (page 123) and discuss their answers to the question that accompanies it.

If necessary, remind students that the law of supply states that as the price of a good rises, the quantity supplied rises. If the law of supply applies to workers, then as the wage rate offered to workers rises, more workers will offer to work. For example, if the wage rate is $10 an hour, 1,000 individuals might be willing to work, but if the wage rate rises to, say, $20 an hour, then 1,500 individuals might be willing to work.

Teaching with Visuals

Direct students to Exhibit 5-1. Beginning with point A, ask students to tell you the price and quantity that corresponds with each point. These specifics provide concrete examples of the law of supply: price and quantity supplied move up and down together.

Ask students why the supply curves in Exhibit 5-2 are vertical. They should understand that the supply of these items cannot increase. See the Background Information box below for more information.

Reinforcement Activity

Ask students if they have ever saved money to buy a special item only to watch its price increase while they are saving. How did they feel about this experience? What factors might have accounted for the price increase?

 Application Activity

After reading and discussing Section 1, assign the Section Activity in the *Applying the Principles Workbook,* pages 54–56.

Assess

Quick Quiz

The following true-or-false quiz will help you assess student understanding of the material covered in this section.

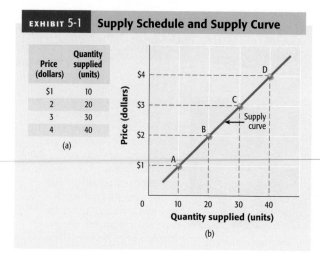

EXHIBIT 5-1 Supply Schedule and Supply Curve

Price (dollars)	Quantity supplied (units)
$1	10
2	20
3	30
4	40

(a)

(b)

▲(a) A supply schedule for a good. Notice that as the price increases, the quantity supplied increases. (b) Plotting the four combinations of price and quantity supplied from part (a) and connecting the points yields a supply curve.

supply curve
A graph that shows the amount of a good sellers are willing and able to sell at various prices.

► When additional units cannot be produced or there is no time to produce more, the supply curve is vertical.

quantity supplied of 20; point C, a price of $3 and a quantity supplied of 30; and point D, a price of $4 and a quantity supplied of 40. Connecting points A through D creates a **supply curve**, a line that slopes upward (from left to right) and shows the amounts of a good sellers are willing and able to sell at various prices. The upward-sloping supply curve in Exhibit 5-1(b) is the graphic representation of the law of supply.

A Vertical Supply Curve

The law of supply—which states that as the price rises, the quantity supplied rises—does not hold true for all goods, nor does it hold true over all time periods. For example, it does not hold for goods that cannot be produced any longer, such as Stradivarius violins. These violins were made by Antonio Stradivari more than 250 years ago, and it is impossible for additional "Strads" to be produced today, because Stradivari died in 1737. No matter how high the price goes, the quantity supplied cannot increase to more than the total number of Stradivarius violins that currently exist. Thus, the supply curve of Stradivarius violins is not upward sloping but vertical, straight up and down, as shown in Exhibit 5-2(a).

In another example, a theater in St. Louis is sold out for tonight's play. Increasing ticket prices from $40 to $50 will not create additional seats for tonight's play, because time does not allow enlarging the theater to add more seats. For tonight's performance, the supply curve of theater seats is vertical, as illustrated in Exhibit 5-2(b).

A Firm's Supply Curve and a Market Supply Curve

Most of the goods supplied in the United States are supplied by business firms. For example, computers are supplied by Apple, Dell, Hewlett-Packard, and so on. A firm's

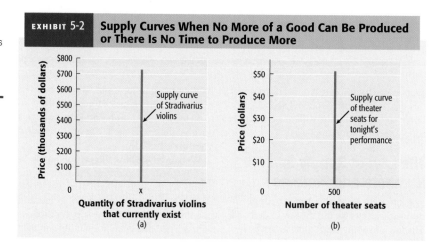

EXHIBIT 5-2 Supply Curves When No More of a Good Can Be Produced or There Is No Time to Produce More

(a) Supply curve of Stradivarius violins — Quantity of Stradivarius violins that currently exist

(b) Supply curve of theater seats for tonight's performance — Number of theater seats

126 Chapter 5 Supply

Background Information: Vertical Supply Curves

Students may be familiar with products that have vertical supply curves. Antiques, tickets to sold-out concerts, and so on, will have vertical supply curves. While copies could be made of some items, copies would not affect the prices of the original. Ask students the following questions:

Do you or your family own items that might have vertical supply curves? How do you feel about these items? Why might collecting goods that have a fixed supply (like old baseball cards) be so popular?

EXHIBIT 5-3 **From Firms' Supply Curves to the Market Supply Curve**

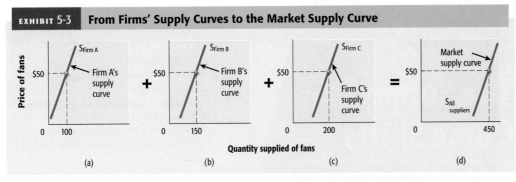

▲ In parts (a) through (c) we show the supply curve for firms A, B, and C, respectively. The market supply curve, shown in part (d), is simply the sum of the firms' supply curves. Stated differently, we know that at a price of $50 per fan, firm A's quantity supplied of fans is 100, firm B's is 150, and firm C's is 200. It follows that all three firms together will offer 450 fans at a price of $50 per fan. This point is identified on the market supply curve in part (d).

supply curve is different from a market supply curve. A firm's supply curve is what it sounds like: it is the supply curve for a particular firm. A market supply curve is the sum of all firms' supply curves.

EXAMPLE Suppose that only three suppliers of fans exist in the whole world: firm A, firm B, and firm C. At a price of $50 a fan, the quantity supplied is 100 for firm A, 150 for firm B, and 200 for firm C. As a result, the *market supply curve* will have

a point representing a price of $50 per fan and a market quantity supplied of 450 fans (100 + 150 + 200).

To see this concept graphically, look at Exhibit 5-3 above. Parts (a) through (c) show the supply curves for firms A, B, and C, respectively. (To keep things simple, we identify only one point on the supply curve for each firm.) Now look at part (d). It shows the market supply curve, which is the combination of all the individual market supply curves. ♦

SECTION
1
ASSESSMENT

Defining Terms

1. Define:
   a. supply
   b. law of supply
   c. direct relationship
   d. quantity supplied
   e. supply schedule
   f. supply curve

2. Use the term *quantity supplied* correctly in a sentence. Use the word *supply* correctly in a sentence.

Reviewing Facts and Concepts

3. **a.** State the law of supply.
   b. Explain the direct relationship between the price of a good and the quantity supplied.

4. Do all supply curves graphically represent the law of supply? Explain your answer.

5. Identify a good that has an upward-sloping supply curve. Explain your choice.

Critical Thinking

6. Three months ago, the price of a good was $4, and the quantity supplied was 200 units. Today, the price is $6, and the quantity supplied is 400 units. Did the quantity supplied rise because the price increased, or did the price rise because

the quantity supplied increased?

7. Identify three goods that have a vertical supply curve. Explain your choices.

Applying Economic Concepts

8. Suppose three McDonald's restaurants operate in your town, and each pays its employees $7.25 per hour. If McDonald's started paying $9 per hour, would more, fewer, or the same number of people want to work for McDonald's, according to the law of supply?

SECTION
1
ASSESSMENT
ANSWERS

Defining Terms

1. a. supply: the willingness and ability to produce and sell a good; **b. law of supply:** as the price of a good increases, the quantity supplied increases, and as the price of a good decreases,

the quantity supplied decreases; **c. direct relationship:** one in which two factors move in the same direction; **d. quantity supplied:** the number of units produced and offered for sale at a specific price; **e. supply schedule:** a numerical chart that illustrates the law of supply;

f. supply curve: a graph that shows the amount of a good sellers are willing and able to sell at various prices.
2. Answers will vary.

Reviewing Facts and Concepts

3. a. The law of supply states that price and quantity supplied

1. The law of supply states that as price goes up, quantity supplied decreases. (False)
2. Quantity supplied is the number of units of a good produced and offered for sale at a specific price. (True)
3. A supply schedule is a numeric chart that illustrates the law of supply. (True)
4. A supply curve is a graphic representation of the law of supply. (True)
5. A vertical supply curve shows that supply is limited. (True)

Assessment Book

You will find a quiz for this section in the *Assessment Book,* page 46.

Guided Reading

For further reteaching of the key concepts in this section, assign the Outlining Activity and the Just the Facts Handout from the *Guided Reading and Study Guide,* pages 69–70.

move in the same direction. Specifically, as price rises, quantity supplied rises, and as price falls, quantity supplied falls. **b.** Price and quantity supplied move in the same direction.
4. No, only upward-sloping supply curves represent the law of supply. For example, the supply curve in Exhibit 5-1 represents the law of supply. Vertical supply curves, such as those in Exhibit 5-2, do not represent the law of supply.
5. Answers will vary. Any good that can be produced over time will have an upward-sloping supply curve. Any good that can no longer be produced and almost any good for which there is no time to produce more will have a vertical supply curve.

Critical Thinking

6. The price increased because the quantity supplied increased.
7. Answers will vary. Each good should be one that is no longer produced or that cannot be produced in the time allotted.

Applying Economic Concepts

8. If the wage rate increases from $6 to $9 per hour, the law of supply predicts that more people will want to work at McDonald's.

SECTION **2**

Teacher Support

Focus and Motivate

Section Objectives

After completing this section, students will be able to

▶ explain the meaning of a supply curve's shifting to the right;

▶ explain the meaning of a supply curve's shifting to the left;

▶ identify the factors that can change supply; and

▶ identify the factors that can change quantity supplied.

Economics Around the Clock

Kickoff Activity

Direct students to reread the 11:03 a.m. scenario in Economics Around the Clock (page 123) and write their answers to its question.

Call on volunteers to share their answers with the class. Students should see that Angie needs to wait until later to sell her oil to maximize her revenue.

Activating Prior Knowledge

To review some of the concepts presented in the previous chapter, ask students to discuss the conditions that must be present for demand to exist: willingness to purchase and ability to purchase. Students will notice that the same conditions are necessary for supply.

Teach

Teaching with Visuals

Exhibit 5-4 shows what happens to the quantity supplied when the supply curve shifts to the right. Have students brainstorm ideas as to why the quantity of computers supplied increases.

The Supply Curve Shifts

Focus Questions

▶ What does it mean when a supply curve shifts to the right?

▶ What does it mean when a supply curve shifts to the left?

▶ What factors can change supply?

▶ What factor can change quantity supplied?

Key Terms

technology advancement in technology
per-unit cost
subsidy
quota
elasticity of supply
elastic supply
inelastic supply
unit-elastic supply

When Supply Changes, the Curve Shifts

Supply can go up, and it can go down. Every time the supply of a good changes, the supply curve for that good shifts. By *shift*, we mean that it moves, it moves either to the right or to the left.

For example, if the supply of computers increases, the computer supply curve will shift to the right. If the supply of computers decreases, the supply curve will shift to the left.

We can better understand shifts in supply curves with the help of Exhibit 5-4. Look at the curve labeled S_1. Suppose this supply curve represents the original (and current) supply of computers. Notice that the quantity supplied at a price of $1,000 is 4,000 computers. Now suppose the supply of computers increases. For whatever reason, sellers want to produce more computers. This increase in supply is shown by the supply curve S_1 shifting to the right and becoming S_2.

What does it mean for a supply curve to shift rightward? The answer is easy if you again look at Exhibit 5-4 and focus on the horizontal axis (along the bottom of the graph) and the numbers on it. What is the quantity supplied on curve S_2 at the price of $1,000? The answer is 6,000 computers.

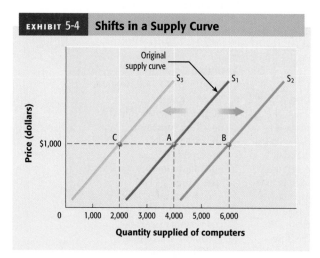

EXHIBIT 5-4   Shifts in a Supply Curve

◀ Moving from S_1 (the original supply curve) to S_2 represents a rightward shift in the supply curve. Supply has increased. Moving from S_1 to S_3 represents a leftward shift in the supply curve. Supply has decreased.

Internet Research

Direct students to the Old Farmer's Almanac website to look at the long-range weather forecast for their region. If this forecast is accurate, what might students expect to see happen to the supply of agricultural products from their region? How might prices be affected?

This means that we can describe an increase in supply (or a shift rightward in the supply curve) by saying "Sellers want to sell more of a good at each and every price." In our example, sellers want to sell more computers at $1,000.

How can we graphically represent a decrease in supply? In Exhibit 5-4, let's suppose again that S_1 is our original (and current) supply curve. A decrease in supply is represented as a shift leftward in the supply curve from S_1 to S_3. This decrease in supply means that sellers want to sell less of the good at each and every price. Specifically, if we look at the price $1,000, we see that sellers who once wanted to sell 4,000 computers now want to sell 2,000 computers:

Supply increases → Supply curve shifts rightward
Supply decreases → Supply curve shifts leftward

Economics *in the* Real World

Where Did DVRs, Podcasts, and Blogs Come From?

It is important to distinguish between *increasing the supply* of a good that has existed for some time (say, corn, paper, or shoes) and *creating the supply* of a good that has never existed before. Many goods that we have today—digital video recorders (DVRs, first introduced by TiVo), podcasts, and blogs, for example—weren't available to us in the past. Where did these goods and the ideas for them come from?

Two answers come to mind: new technology and entrepreneurship. To illustrate how these two factors sometimes work together, consider a blog. A blog, or weblog, is a personal website with a dated *log* (diary-like) format that contains commentary and links to other websites. In 1999, there were only about 30 blogs, but today you can find millions. The first blogs were hand-coded by web developers who taught themselves HTML (a markup language designed to create web pages). Then, programmers created new software programs (a technological development), and entrepreneurs responded to the unfulfilled demand for posting items on the Web, leading to the vast supply of blogs today.

Similarly, no digital video recorder could exist before the software had been developed to provide programming information and encode data streams. The DVR was a new product brought to us through an advancement in technology and by the entrepreneurs who saw that the TV-viewing public wanted more control over what programs they could watch and when.

Podcasting, which delivers recorded audio programs through the Internet to iPods, other portable music players, or smartphones, would not exist without the software that makes it easy to beam a podcast from a home computer to someone who has signed up to receive it. It would also not exist without the entrepreneurs who saw an unfulfilled demand on the part of consumers for more choices and greater control over their entertainment.

New technology and entrepreneurship are the catalysts behind the *supply* of new products. And because of how quickly technology changes, new products are soon replaced with even newer products.

THINK ABOUT IT Do you think that some new products for which the technology exists aren't being developed because entrepreneurs think no one will buy them? What might undeveloped products do? Will they brush your teeth for you? Make your bed? If you were an entrepreneur, what new products would you supply?

Economics *in the* Real World

Have students read this feature, and then ask them to create their own lists of other new products similar to TiVo, podcasts, and blogs. What new technology enabled the development of each product? What unfulfilled demand did an entrepreneur see that prompted him or her to develop each product?

ANSWERS TO THINK ABOUT IT Answers will vary. Invite students to share with the class new products they would develop.

Background Information

A change in resource prices can change the supply of a good and thus shift the supply curve of the good. Suppose good X is produced in the United States, but one of the resources that is used to produce it (resource Y) is produced in Bolivia. It follows, then, that what happens in Bolivia can affect the market in the United States. Here's how: The price of the resource (in Bolivia) rises. This causes the supply of good X (in the United States) to fall, because producers of X are not willing or able to produce as many of X. Consequently, the price of good X in the United States rises. In other words, if you are a buyer of good X, you will now pay a higher price for it. What has happened in Bolivia affects you, even though you are in the United States.

 Visit econ.myemcp.com/videos for videos that will help students better understand the key concepts found in this section.

Clarifying Terms

Remind students that economists use specialized language—for example, "The supply curves shifts to the right." Ask students to translate this phrase into one that everyone can understand. Students might say that "Sellers offer more of a good or service at each and every price."

Reinforcement Activity

Ask students to discuss the meaning of the term *technology* in other areas, such as live entertainment, sports, and road construction.

Economics Around the Clock

Have students reread the 9:10 a.m. scenario in Economics Around the Clock (page 123) and then write their answers to its question.

The answer is yes. The type of tax identified here will reduce the supply of cigarettes. A tax on production makes it more costly to produce goods—in this case, cigarettes. As a result, firms are less willing to produce the good, and so the supply curve (for the good) shifts leftward.

What Factors Cause Supply Curves to Shift?

Supply curves do not shift to the right or left without cause. They shift because of changes in several factors, including resource prices, technology, taxes, subsidies, quotas, number of sellers, future price, and even weather, in some cases.

Resource Prices

Chapter 1 identified four resources, or factors of production: land, labor, capital, and entrepreneurship. For now, concentrate on land, labor, and capital. These resources are used to produce goods and services.

When resource prices fall, sellers are willing and able to produce and offer to sell more of the good (which means the supply curve shifts to the right). Why? It is cheaper to produce the good. In contrast, when resource prices rise, sellers are willing and able to produce and offer to sell less of the good (which means the supply curve shifts to the left). It is more expensive to produce the good.

EXAMPLE Suppose wage rates rise for employees working for a car manufacturer, while everything else remains the same. Wage rates rise from, say, $20 an hour to $22 an hour. As a result, the car manufacturer will produce and offer to sell fewer cars; the supply curve shifts leftward. ♦

Technology

Technology is the body of skills and knowledge used in production. For example, the technology of farming is much different today that it was 200 years ago. Today, farmers use tractors, pesticides, and special fertilizers to grow crops.

An **advancement in technology** is the ability to produce more output with a fixed amount of resources. Again, consider farming. By using fertilizers and pesticides, farmers today can produce much more on an acre of land than they could years ago. This advancement in technology, in turn, lowers the **per-unit cost**, or average cost, of

production. Farmers respond to lower per-unit costs by being willing and able to produce and offer to sell more output. In other words, the supply curve shifts to the right.

Taxes

Some taxes increase per-unit costs. Suppose a shoe manufacturer must pay a $2 tax for each pair of shoes it produces. This extra cost of doing business causes the manufacturer to supply less output. (It is similar to the price of a resource rising and thus making it more expensive and less profitable for the producer to manufacture the good. As a result, the producer produces less output.) The supply curve shifts to the left. If the tax is eliminated, the supply curve will shift rightward to its original position.

Subsidies

Subsidies have the opposite effect of taxes. A **subsidy** is a financial payment made by the government for a certain action. Suppose the government subsidizes the production of corn by paying farmers $2 for every bushel of corn they produce. Farmers will want to produce more corn at every price, which means the supply curve of corn will shift rightward. Removing the subsidy will cause the supply curve to shift to the left, back to its position prior to the subsidy.

Quotas

A **quota** is a restriction on the number of units of a foreign-produced good (import) that can enter a country. Suppose that Japanese producers are currently sending and want to continue to send 100,000 cars to the United States each year. Now suppose that the U.S. government imposes a quota on Japanese cars at 80,000 a year. This quota means that no more than 80,000 Japanese cars can be imported into the United States. A quota decreases the supply, so the supply curve shifts to the left. The elimination of a quota causes the supply curve to shift rightward, back to its original position.

technology
The body of skills and knowledge concerning the use of resources in production.

advancement in technology
The ability to produce more output with a fixed amount of resources.

per-unit cost
The average cost of a good. For example, if $400,000 is spent to produce 100 cars, the average, or per-unit, cost is $4,000.

subsidy
A financial payment made by government for a certain action.

quota
A legal limit on the number of units of a foreign-produced good (import) that can enter a country.

Background Information: Taxes, Tariffs, and the Great Depression

The text discusses both taxes and subsidies as factors that affect supply. A tariff is a tax on foreign-produced (imported) goods.

In June 1930, the Smoot-Hawley Tariff Act became law. It included higher tariffs on many imported goods. Some people thought that the higher tariffs would result in Americans buying fewer imports and more goods being produced in the United States. Many people worried that

other countries would retaliate with their own high tariffs (which they did) and that global trade would diminish, thus hurting the U.S. economy.

The Smoot-Hawley Tariff Act was enacted shortly after the stock market crashed in 1929. Many economists believe that the Smoot-Hawley Tariff Act made the Great Depression last longer than it would have otherwise.

How Do Taxes and Subsidies Change Our World?

Economists tend to agree that if you *tax* something, you will get *less* of it, and if you *subsidize* something, you will get *more* of it.

Recall that some taxes increase the per-unit costs of producing a good, thus causing the producer to make less of the good and shifting the supply curve to the left. A subsidy has the opposite effect. If producers receive a subsidy to produce a good, they will likely make more of it and the good's supply curve will shift to the right.

Many environmentalists want to use this principle to help protect the environment. For example, pollution is considered bad and therefore gives us disutility or dissatisfaction. So how can we get less pollution? One way is to tax those activities or products that produce pollution.

Consider a factory that produces a product but in the process creates air pollution by spewing smoke and particles into the air. One way to reduce the levels of these pollutants is to place a tax on what is being produced in the factory. Doing this will make the factory owners want to produce less of the product, which will lead to less pollution.

Keep in mind, however, that while we might get less pollution because of the tax, we will also get less of the good. And eventually, this reduction in supply will increase the price of the good.

In the next chapter, you will learn how this process works. Specifically, reducing the supply of a good will cause its price to rise, just as increasing the demand for a good will cause its price to rise. So, in the end, charging the tax may reduce the amount of pollution, but it will also mean having less of the good and paying more for it.

Now, let's consider the effects of paying a subsidy.

Suppose a high school English teacher wants her students to read more classic books. In fact, she wants her students to read more classic books than are currently recommended by the curriculum. To get her students to read more classics, she subsidizes their reading by offering to add one extra point to the final course grade for each additional book a student reads. In other words, if a student reads two extra books, then the teacher will add two points to his or her final grade. So instead of earning, say, an 89 (B+) in the course, the student would earn a 91 (A-).

Will this subsidy work? Will it encourage at least some students to read more books? Probably.

In sum, a tax is a disincentive. If you tax an activity, people will have less reason (a disincentive) to engage in it. In contrast, a subsidy is an incentive. If you subsidize an activity, people will have more reason (an incentive) to engage in it.

THINK ABOUT IT Sometimes in our own lives, we end up "subsidizing" the wrong things—things we want less of instead of things we want more of. What examples can you provide?

ANSWERS TO THINK ABOUT IT Examples will vary. One student example could be subsidizing people who are unemployed. The negative effect of this is that paying people when they are unemployed may result in them being unemployed for longer than if they weren't paid. A second student example could be subsidizing farmers to encourage them to produce more of some agricultural good. The negative impact of this is that it could lead to a surplus of the good.

Thinking Like an Economist

Economists think in terms of incentives and disincentives. More importantly, they believe that individuals respond to changes in incentives in predictable ways. Recall the discussion of taxes and subsidies with respect to supply. A tax on the production of a good is a disincentive to produce that good. Consequently, economists believe that fewer units of that good will be produced. In contrast, a subsidy on the production of a good is an incentive to produce that good. Consequently, economists believe that more units of that good will be produced. Ask students to think of incentives and disincentives they have received for such acts as earning good grades and breaking their curfews.

Cross-Curricular Activity

Ask students to research how natural disasters—such as earthquakes, hurricanes, and floods—can affect the supply curve. You might invite a geography teacher to discuss the devastation caused by natural disasters to help students understand the powerful influence of nature on the supply of goods and services. Discuss all the different effects of weather, including reallocation of resources, increased taxes, the likelihood of subsidies, and the number of sellers.

Reinforcement Activity

The United States has a long tradition of creating and then reducing or eliminating tariffs. Assign students to research particular trade restrictions to determine whether each had a positive or negative effect on the economy and why.

Reinforcement Activity

Assign students to use newspapers or magazines to find changes in any of the factors mentioned—resource prices, technology, taxes, subsidies, quotas, number of sellers, or weather—that have affected the supply of a particular good. Direct each student to give an oral report on his or her findings.

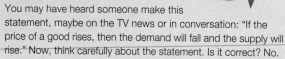

Thinking Like *an* Economist

Supply and Demand Versus Quantity Supplied and Quantity Demanded

You may have heard someone make this statement, maybe on the TV news or in conversation: "If the price of a good rises, then the demand will fall and the supply will rise." Now, think carefully about the statement. Is it correct? No.

Remember from the last chapter and this chapter that there is a difference between (a) demand and (b) quantity demanded and between (c) supply and (d) quantity supplied. A change in price will *not* change demand or supply; rather, it will change quantity demanded and quantity supplied.

Let's rewrite the statement correctly: "If the price of a good rises, then the quantity demanded will fall and the quantity supplied will rise."

Obviously, waiting a few months or even a year to sell a house won't change its quality.

That wouldn't be the case for a perishable good, such as eggs. An egg seller might believe that the future price of eggs will be higher than the current price and want to wait and sell his eggs later. He can't really do that, though, because eggs spoil if kept too long. ♦

Number of Sellers

If more sellers begin producing a particular good, perhaps because of high profits, then supply will increase and the supply curve will shift to the right. If some sellers stop producing a particular good, perhaps because of losses, the supply will decrease and the supply curve will shift to the left.

> *"What is wrong with our world is that love is in short supply."*
> —Anonymous

Future Price

Sellers who expect the price of a good to be higher in the future may hold back the good now and supply it to the market later. Sellers who expect the price of a good to be lower in the future may supply the good now instead of later.

EXAMPLE Ricky is thinking of selling his house and just heard that the price of houses is expected to rise over the next three months. Instead of putting his house up for sale today, he decides to wait. Why? Ricky believes the future price of a house will be higher than the current price of a house.

Notice that we are talking about a nonperishable good here (houses).

Weather (in Some Cases)

Weather can affect the supply of a good. Bad weather reduces the supply of many agricultural goods, such as corn, wheat, and barley. Unusually good weather can increase the supply. Weather can also impact the supply of nonagricultural products, as happens when a hurricane damages fishing boats, shipping docks, and coastal oil refineries.

EXAMPLE Monica is the owner of a dairy farm. She has had three successful years, but a drought has made it difficult for her to find affordable grain for her cows. The farmers who sell her grain blame the high prices on the weather. ♦

What Factor Causes a Change in Quantity Supplied?

We identified the factors (resource prices, technology, etc.) that can cause *supply* to change. As we stated earlier, a change in supply is represented as a shift in the supply curve. The curve moves either right or left. (See Exhibit 5-5[a].)

But what factor(s) can cause a change in *quantity supplied*? Only one: *price*. For example, the only thing that can cause sellers to change the quantity supplied of computers is a change in the price of computers. A change in quantity supplied is shown as a movement along a given supply curve. (See Exhibit 5-5[b].)

Many people are, at first, confused about what leads to a change in quantity supplied and what leads to a change in supply. To many, it seems as if changes in quantity supplied and supply are the same thing.

Cooperative Learning

Put students in groups of four or five. Have each group choose a good or service that it wants to produce or provide. The group should then develop a list of specific factors that would shift the supply curve of its good or service to the left, decreasing supply. Then the group should brainstorm ways to overcome the various factors that shifted the supply curve.

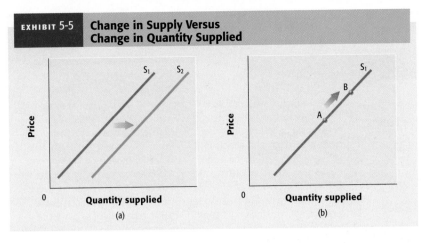

EXHIBIT 5-5 Change in Supply Versus Change in Quantity Supplied

(a)

(b)

▲ (a) A change in supply refers to a shift in the supply curve. A change in supply can be brought about by a number of factors. (b) A change in quantity supplied refers to a movement along a given supply curve. A change in quantity supplied is brought about only by a change in a good's price.

To make sure you understand the difference, let's look back at a couple of examples in this chapter. Turn back to Exhibit 5-1 on page 126 and look at point A. There, you see a price of $1 and a quantity supplied of 10. Now ask yourself what must happen before you can move from a quantity supplied of 10 to 20, or from point A to B. Stated differently, what has to change before a move from A to B will happen? The answer is that the price (on the vertical axis) must increase from $1 to $2. In other words, the only factor that will change the quantity supplied of a good is a change in price: the factor on the vertical axis.

Now let's move over to Exhibit 5-4 on page 128. Take a look at S_1. Ask yourself what has to happen before S_1 shifts to its right and becomes S_2. Does price (on the vertical axis) have to change? No, as you can see in the exhibit, the price never changes from $1,000. So, then, you know that a change in a good's actual price isn't what will cause a shift in the supply curve. What does cause such a shift? The answer is changes in resource prices, technology, taxes, and so on.

Economic Facts *and* Fallacies

FALSE
TRUE

The Price of Oil

Some people believe that even if the price of oil goes up, the quantity of oil supplied by producers will *not* change. In other words, no matter what the price of oil, producers will continue to supply the same amount of oil to the market—say, 30 million barrels a day—to maximize their profits.

If this is true, then the supply curve of oil is vertical: straight up and down. But what we see more often is an upward-sloping supply curve. This means that as the price of oil rises, the quantity supplied *also* rises. What explains this relationship?

It makes better monetary sense for oil producers (1) to work to discover more oil deposits and (2) to reopen oil wells that were not profitable at lower oil prices. For example, some oil wells might not be worth using if the price of oil is $50 a barrel but might be worth using if the price is $100 a barrel.

The higher the price of oil, the greater the incentive producers have to find and pump oil. At a price of $2 a barrel, almost no one will pump oil, but at a price of $110 a barrel, a lot of people will be interested in pumping oil.

What this shows is that the dollar price—whether for oil or anything else—is not only something that consumers have to pay. It is also an incentive for producers to produce.

Direct students to read the feature and share their opinions on whether the current system of buying back tickets from airline passengers is superior or inferior to the old system of bumping airline passengers off of flights if those flights were filled.

ANSWERS TO THINK ABOUT IT Airlines try to get some idea of how many people might cancel a given flight at the last minute, or not show up for a given flight. For example, if on flight 1 (from location X to Y) usually 5 ticket holders cancel or do not show up, then the airlines might overbook by 5 passengers. However, if on flight 2 (from location B) usually 10 ticket holders cancel or do not show up, then the airlines might overbook by 10 passengers.

The Case of Selling Airline Tickets and Then Buying Some of Them Back

Airlines often overbook flights; that is, they accept more reservations than they have seats available on a flight. In terms of the supply of seats, suppose there are 100 seats on an airplane. The airlines then may end up selling 105 tickets instead of 100. That's because airlines know that a certain (usually small) percentage of individuals with reservations will not show up. An empty seat means that the airline's cost per actual passenger on board is higher than it would be if the seat were occupied by a paying passenger. So airlines try to make sure to have few empty seats. One way to reduce the number of empty seats is to overbook.

In the past, when more people with reservations showed up for a flight than there were seats available, the airline simply "bumped" passengers. In other words, the airline would tell some passengers that they could not fly on that flight. Understandably, the bumped passengers were disappointed and angry.

One day while shaving, economist Julian Simon (1932–1998) came up with a better way to deal with overbooking. He argued that the airline should enter into a market transaction with the ticket holders who had reserved seats for an overbooked flight. Instead of bumping people randomly, an airline should ask passengers to sell back their seats to the airline. Passengers who absolutely had to get from one city to another would not sell their seats, but passengers who did not have to fly right away might be willing to sell their tickets for, say, first class on a later flight or some other compensation, such as a $300 discount on any trip they take in the future on the airlines.

Simon wrote the executives of various airlines and outlined the details of his plan. He even told them that the first airline which enacted the plan would likely reap larger sales. The airline could, after all, guarantee its passengers that they would not get bumped. Most airline executives wrote back and told him that his idea was a reasonably good one but was unworkable.

Then Alfred Kahn, an economist, was appointed chairman of the Civil Aeronautics Board. Simon contacted Kahn with his plan, and Kahn liked it. According to Simon, "Kahn announced something like the scheme in his first press conference. He also had the great persuasive skill to repackage it as a 'voluntary' bumping plan, and at the same time to increase the penalties that airlines must pay to involuntary bumpees, a nice carrot-and-stick combination."

The rest, as they say, is history. Simon's plan has been in operation since 1978.

THINK ABOUT IT What do you think it is that determines the degree to which an airlines might overbook a flight? For example, if there are 100 seats on each of two flights, an airlines might sell 105 tickets on one flight and 110 on the other. Why not the same on both flights?

Elasticity of Supply

Chapter 4 discussed elasticity of demand, which deals with the relationship between price and quantity demanded. **Elasticity of supply** is the relationship between the percentage change in quantity supplied and the percentage change in price. We can look at this relationship as an equation:

$$\text{Elasticity of supply} = \frac{\text{Percentage change in quantity supplied}}{\text{Percentage change in price}}$$

Notice that the equation has a numerator (percentage change in quantity supplied) and a denominator (percentage change in price). **Elastic supply** exists when the quantity supplied changes by a greater percentage than the price—that is, when the numerator changes by more than the denominator. For example, suppose the price of lightbulbs increases by 10 percent, and the quantity supplied of lightbulbs increases by 20 percent. The numerator (20%) changes by more than the denominator (10%), so the supply of lightbulbs is elastic. **Inelastic supply** exists when the quantity supplied changes by a smaller percentage than the price—that is,

when the numerator changes by less than the denominator. Finally, **unit-elastic supply** exists when the quantity supplied changes by the same percentage as the price—that is, when the numerator changes by the same percentage as the denominator. Exhibit 5-6 reviews the definitions of elastic, inelastic, and unit-elastic supply.

EXAMPLE Firm A currently produces 400 skateboards a day at $50 a skateboard. After the price of skateboards increases to $55 a skateboard, the firm starts producing 420 skateboards a day. Because the quantity supplied of skateboards goes up (5%) by a smaller percentage than the price of skateboards (10%), the supply of skateboards is *inelastic*. ◆

◄ Suppose the overall price of skateboarding rises by 12 percent (not just the price of the skateboard, but the price of elbow and knee pads that might be worn, the price of getting to and from a skateboard park, and so on). But, as a result, only a tiny percentage of skateboarders reduce the frequency of skateboarding. Is the demand for skateboarding elastic, inelastic, or unit elastic?

EXHIBIT 5-6	Elasticity of Supply
If supply is . . .	**That means . . .**
Elastic	Quantity supplied changes by a larger percentage than price. For example, if price rises by 10 percent, quantity supplied rises by, say, 15 percent.
Inelastic	Quantity supplied changes by a smaller percentage than price. For example, if price rises by 10 percent, quantity supplied rises by, say, 5 percent.
Unit elastic	Quantity supplied changes by the same percentage as price. For example, if price rises by 10 percent, quantity supplied rises by 10 percent.

elasticity of supply
The relationship between the percentage change in quantity supplied and the percentage change in price.

elastic supply
The kind of supply that exists when the percentage change in quantity supplied is greater than the percentage change in price.

inelastic supply
The kind of supply that exists when the percentage change in quantity supplied is less than the percentage change in price.

unit-elastic supply
The kind of supply that exists when the percentage change in quantity supplied is equal to the percentage change in price.

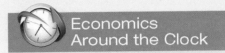

Economics Around the Clock

After reading and discussing "Elasticity of Supply" (page 135), direct students to the 7:04 A.M. scenario in Economics Around the Clock (page 123) and invite them to discuss which boy's supply of good behavior is more likely to be elastic.

The answer is that Dave's quantity of good behavior is more likely to be elastic than Quentin's. Both Dave and Quentin behave better, but Dave behaves a lot better and Quentin behaves only a little better. In other words, Dave's "quantity supplied of good behavior" increases by more than Quentin's. Dave's supply of good behavior is more likely to be elastic (to change in quantity supplied is greater than the change in price).

Teaching with Visuals

The demand for skateboards is likely to be inelastic, since only a tiny percentage of skateboarders reduce the frequency of their skateboarding.

Economics *in the* Real World

THINK ABOUT IT Local politicians would weigh the concerns of all residents. Some residents would likely prefer building restrictions that do not allow more houses to be built in their neighborhood. These residents would lobby the city council for such building restrictions. In contrast, developers, who have the opportunity to make money from building houses, and people who want to buy new houses in the neighborhood would likely lobby for fewer restrictions.

Application Activity

After reading and discussing Section 2, assign the Section Activity and the Supply Practice Activity in the *Applying the Principles Workbook,* pages 57–66.

Assess

Quick Quiz

The following true-or-false quiz will help you assess student understanding of the material covered in this section.

1. Supply has decreased when the curve shifts to the left. (True)

2. Resource prices affect the supply curve. (True)

3. Advancement in technology will cause the supply curve to shift to the right. (True).

4. Subsidies have the same effect on the supply curve as taxes. (False)

5. Quotas are restrictions on the number of units of a foreign good that can enter the country. (True)

If House Prices Rise, How Many More Houses Will Be Available for Sale?

Think of an upward-sloping supply curve for houses. What this curve tells us is that as the price of houses rises, the quantity supplied of houses also rises. Is the concept of elasticity of supply relevant to the increase of supplied houses as the price rises? The answer is yes.

To illustrate, suppose the price of houses in Dallas, Texas, rises by 10 percent. Will the quantity supplied of houses rise by 10 percent, less than 10 percent, or more than 10 percent? Unfortunately, we don't know for sure. Any of these outcomes might occur.

Now let's say that during a given year in Dallas, house prices went up by 10 percent and the quantity supplied (houses available for sale) went up by 15 percent. We can conclude that during that year, the supply of houses in Dallas was elastic.

If the supply of houses in Dallas is elastic, does the supply of houses in every other city in the United States have to be elastic too? Is the supply necessarily elastic in Tampa, Florida; Norman, Oklahoma; and Tucson, Arizona?

Of course not. For a given 10 percent rise in house prices in, say, Tucson, the quantity supplied of houses in Tucson might go up only 2 percent, so that the supply of houses in this city is inelastic.

In many parts of the country, even when house prices go up by a large percentage, the quantity supplied of houses does not increase significantly. In many cases, this happens because it's harder for builders to build new houses in some parts of the country than others. In other cases, the quantity supplied doesn't increase because of other factors, such as the lack of vacant land (new homes are usually built on vacant land), minimum lot size restrictions (lots may be required to be a certain size), limits on the number of allowed building permits, open space laws, and so on.

How might restrictions on building affect the quantity supplied of houses given house price increases? Consider California. Before 1970, house prices in California were much like prices in the rest of the country, but today, house prices in California are nearly three times higher than in the rest of the country.

What caused house prices in California to change? Most economists point to government restrictions that directly or indirectly began affecting California builders in 1970. One example is that construction was prohibited on three-quarters of the land in Monterey County, California, and on two-thirds of the land in San Mateo County, California. These restrictions were put in place to preserve open spaces within these two areas.

In comparison, consider a place that has many fewer house-building restrictions, such as Houston, Texas. A much greater percentage change in quantity supplied of houses can occur here than in San Mateo County, California. This means that the supply of houses in Houston (where there are fewer restrictions) will likely be elastic, whereas the supply of houses in San Mateo (where there are more restrictions) will likely be inelastic.

THINK ABOUT IT Economists often talk about trade-offs. Only one trade-off is involved in our discussion: namely, the trade-off between having more open spaces that people can enjoy and having more houses that people can occupy. People like having open spaces, but they also need homes to live in. How might local politics come into play when making laws that restrict the construction of new houses? Explain your answer.

Differentiating Instruction

English Language Learners

To help students who are English language learners, use the following resources, which are provided as part of the *Economics: New Ways of Thinking* program:

- a Spanish glossary in the *Student Text*
- Spanish versions of the Chapter Summaries on an audio disc

Defining Terms

1. Define:
   a. technology
   b. advancement in technology
   c. per-unit cost
   d. subsidy
   e. quota
   f. elasticity of supply
   g. elastic supply
   h. inelastic supply
   i. unit-elastic supply

Reviewing Facts and Concepts

2. Explain what happens to a given supply curve as a result of each of the following:
   a. Resource prices fall.
   b. Technology advances.
   c. A quota on importing a good is repealed.
   d. A tax on producing a good is repealed.

3. If supply increases, does the supply curve shift to the right or to the left?
4. Determine whether a given supply curve will shift to the right or the left as a result of each of the following:
   a. Resource prices rise.
   b. A quota is placed on a good.
5. Give a numerical example that illustrates elastic supply.

Critical Thinking

6. If a supply curve is vertical, does this mean that supply is (a) elastic, (b) inelastic, (c) unit elastic, or (d) none of the above? Explain your answer.
7. What is wrong with this statement: "As price rises, so does supply"?

Graphing Economics

8. Graph the following:
   a. an increase in supply
   b. a decrease in supply
   c. an increase in the supply of good X that is greater than the increase in the supply of good Y

Assessment Book

You will find a quiz for this section in the *Assessment Book*, page 47.

Reteaching Activity

Use the Section Assessment to gauge which students need reteaching. Have those students work with partners to create charts like Exhibit 4-4 on page 109 for elasticity of supply. Review with each pair of students the chart they created.

Guided Reading

For further reteaching of the key concepts in this section, assign the Outlining Activity and the Just the Facts Handout from the *Guided Reading and Study Guide*, pages 71–74.

than price; **i. unit-elastic supply:** the kind of supply that exists when the percentage change in quantity supplied is equal to the percentage change in price.

Reviewing Facts and Concepts

2. a. shifts to the right; **b.** shifts to the right; **c.** shifts to the right; **d.** shifts to the right.
3. The supply curve shifts to the right.
4. a. to the left; **b.** to the left.
5. Answers will vary. The percentage change in quantity supplied must be greater than the percentage change in price.

Critical Thinking

6. Supply is (b) inelastic, because quantity supplied changes by a smaller percentage than price. If the supply curve is vertical, quantity supplied doesn't change no matter how the price changes. Therefore, the percentage change in quantity supplied (0%) is less than the percentage change in price.
7. The word *supply* should be *quantity supplied*.

Graphing Economics

8. a. The shift from S_1 to S_2 in Exhibit 5-4 represents an increase in supply. **b.** The shift from S_1 to S_3 in Exhibit 5-4 represents a decrease in supply. **c.** The rightward shift in the supply curve for good X should be greater than the rightward shift in the supply curve for good Y.

Section 2 The Supply Curve Shifts **137**

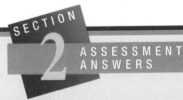

ASSESSMENT ANSWERS

Defining Terms

1. a. technology: the body of skills and knowledge concerning the use of resources in production; **b. advancement in technology:** the ability to produce more output with a fixed amount of resources; **c. per-unit cost:** the average cost of a good; **d. subsidy:** a financial payment made by government for certain actions; **e. quota:** a legal limit on the number of units of a foreign-produced good (import) that can enter a country; **f. elasticity of supply** the relationship between percentage change in quantity supplied and percentage change in price; **g. elastic supply:** the kind that exists when quantity supplied changes by a larger percentage than price; **h. inelastic supply:** the kind that exists when quantity supplied changes by a smaller percentage

Your **Personal** Economics

Discussion Starter

Ask students the following questions: What does it mean to "invest in yourself"? In what ways do you presently invest in yourself? How could you increase your investment in yourself?

Research Activity

After students have read "How You Spend Your Time," have each individual record the number of hours spent on each activity every day for a week. Ask students whether they might reallocate time toward something that could provide them with a higher return.

Investing in Yourself

When most people think of investing, they think of buying things such as stocks, bonds, and real estate. Also, most people want to earn a high return from their investments.

We rarely think of investing in ourselves, but in fact, it's one of the most important things we can do. What can you invest in today—as a high school student—that will provide you with a high return tomorrow?

Before we tell you what that is, let's look at how the average 15- to 17-year-old spends his or her time each week.

How You Spend Your Time

According to a University of Michigan study, each week the average 15- to 17-year-old spends 29 hours and 33 minutes in school, 7 hours and 26 minutes socializing or visiting with friends, 3 hours and 32 minutes playing sports, 49 minutes reading, 5 hours and 8 minutes on the computer, 6 hours and 25 minutes eating, 5 hours and 52 minutes doing household work, and 15 hours watching TV.

Let's focus on the 15 hours a week of watching TV. Can some of this time be redirected toward activities that might provide a higher return? For example, as a high school student, you might be thinking of attending college. Getting into a good college could be the stepping stone to a good-paying job in the future. According

to recent data, college graduates earn substantially more over their lifetimes than those with only high school diplomas. (See Exhibit 5-7.)

You Are Preparing for College, Aren't You?

So, how can you get into a good college? First, you need to have good high school grades. Second, you need to have a reasonably high score on one of the two standardized tests that college-bound high school juniors and seniors take: the SAT and ACT.

Many high school students take these standardized tests without studying for them. They simply get a good night's sleep the night before the test and then go in and take it. But think of another way to go about this. Suppose that at the end of your sophomore year or the beginning of your junior year of high school, you start watching 2 hours less of TV a week and spend that time studying for the SAT or ACT.

Now, ask yourself how many hours most juniors spend studying for the SAT or ACT. Many will say no more than 5 hours. This isn't very much time when you think about the

importance of these test scores for getting into college.

If you have already taken the SAT and ACT, apply the following suggestions to college courses and tests you'll take in the future. If you are a senior and haven't taken the SAT and ACT, then it's not too late to plan and prepare to take them.

Is 100 Hours Too Much Study Time?

What if instead of spending only 5 hours studying for the SAT or ACT, a student spends 100 hours studying. Finding those 100 hours would be easy if the average 15- to 17-year-old would simply cut back on TV viewing. If you are the average 15- to 17-year-old and watch 15 hours of TV a week, consider cutting that down to 13 hours. Then use that freed-up 2

EXHIBIT 5-7	Median Weekly Earnings by Level of Education
No high school diploma	$493
High school diploma	$678
Some college, no degree	$738
Associate's degree	$798
Bachelor's degree	$1,137
Master's degree	$1,341
Ph.D. degree	$1,623

Source: Bureau of Labor Statistics, 2016

Cooperative Learning

After students have studied Exhibit 5-7, divide them into groups of three or four. Tell each group to develop a list of careers they are interested in pursuing. Then ask them to predict the level of education needed for each career and the median

weekly earnings of people in that career. After 15 minutes of brainstorming, invite groups to report their lists of careers, education, and earnings to the class. Discuss the relationship between annual earnings and education level.

hours to study for the SAT or ACT. In 50 weeks, you will have studied 100 hours. Studying diligently for 2 hours a week for 50 weeks will likely boost your overall score.

By investing this time, will you "earn a high return" at the end of the 100 hours? We can't guarantee how much you will improve your score by studying versus not studying, but the increase could certainly be substantial. And earning a high score on the SAT or ACT could pave the way to attending a good college and everything else that may follow.

The Best Use of Your Time

So, how should you proceed if you are convinced that investing 2 hours in yourself each week might bring a higher return than watching an additional 2 hours of TV? Begin by going online to see what each test looks like. Go to http://econ.emcp. net/SAT for the SAT, and go to http://econ.emcp.net/ACT for the ACT.

We also strongly urge you to purchase one or two SAT or ACT test preparation books, which you can find at almost any bookstore. Most of these prep books provide not only sample tests but also with plenty of study material.

After you have purchased these books, study the information they contain slowly and carefully. Don't just take the sample tests and put the books away.

Most of these books offer guidelines for test taking—for instance, how to make good use of the available time. In addition, the books include sections on grammar, vocabulary, critical reading, essay writing, and more. Read each section carefully,

and then read it again. Do all the exercises, and then do them again. Take the sample tests, and then figure out what you got wrong on each test. Then take more sample tests.

If you cut out 2 hours of television a week and devote that time to studying for the SAT or ACT, you will be surprised at how much you learn. You may also enjoy getting a fantastic return on your investment by boosting your test score.

Your Personal Economics Activity

Consider the cause-and-effect relationship of studying to improve a test score. Analyze and identify other cause-and-effect relationships that exist in your everyday life and how you might better invest in your future.

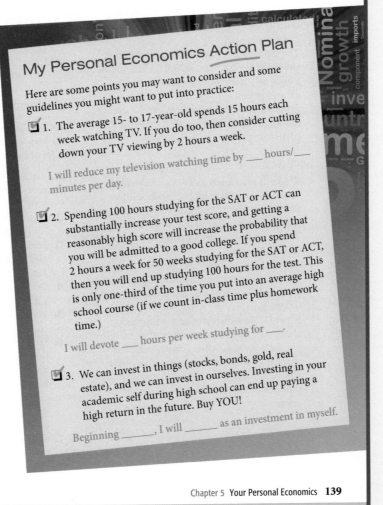

My Personal Economics Action Plan

Here are some points you may want to consider and some guidelines you might want to put into practice:

☑ 1. The average 15- to 17-year-old spends 15 hours each week watching TV. If you do too, then consider cutting down your TV viewing by 2 hours a week.

I will reduce my television watching time by ___ hours/___ minutes per day.

☑ 2. Spending 100 hours studying for the SAT or ACT can substantially increase your test score, and getting a reasonably high score will increase the probability that you will be admitted to a good college. If you spend 2 hours a week for 50 weeks studying for the SAT or ACT, then you will end up studying 100 hours for the test. This is only one-third of the time you put into an average high school course (if we count in-class time plus homework time.)

I will devote ___ hours per week studying for ___.

☑ 3. We can invest in things (stocks, bonds, gold, real estate), and we can invest in ourselves. Investing in your academic self during high school can end up paying a high return in the future. Buy YOU!

Beginning _____, I will _____ as an investment in myself.

Chapter 5 **Your Personal Economics** **139**

To help students realize the power of investing in themselves, have them compare items that can be purchased with the income of someone with a high school diploma with items that can be purchased with the income of someone with a four-year college degree. Make sure students realize that reallocating a small amount of time now might provide a higher return in the future.

My Personal Economics Action Plan Have each student survey adults he or she knows to determine how their average annual earnings relate to their education levels. Encourage students to ask follow-up questions, including what these adults did to invest academically in themselves when they were 17 or 18 years old. Allow students to report back to the class.

Grading Rubric: Cause-and-Effect

1 2 3 4 5 Student identified other cause-and-effect relationships that exist in his or her everyday life.

1 2 3 4 5 Student identified how to better invest in his or her future.

Assessment Answers

Economics Vocabulary

1. supply schedule; **2.** supply curve; **3.** quantity supplied; **4.** elastic; **5.** inelastic; **6.** Quantity supplied.

Understanding the Main Ideas

1. *Supply* refers to the willingness and ability of sellers to produce and offer to sell a good or service. *Quantity supplied* refers to the number of units of a good produced for sale at a specific price.
2. (a) As the price of a good increases, the quantity supplied of the good increases; as the price of a good decreases, the quantity supplied of the good decreases. (b) If P↑ then Q$_s$↑; if P↓ then Q$_s$↓. (c) See Exhibit 5-1(b).
3. No, Luisa is not a supplier of plastic cups. To be a supplier, one must be both willing and able to produce and offer to sell. Luisa is willing but not able.
4. No. When the supply of a good cannot be increased or there is not enough time to increase it, the supply curve is vertical.
5. Answers will vary. However, the price of the good and the quantity supplied should always go up and down together.
6. a. vertical; **b.** vertical; **c.** upward sloping; **d.** upward sloping; **e.** vertical.
7. When a supply curve shifts to the right, it means that sellers are willing and able to sell more of a good at all prices. When a supply curve shifts to the left, it means sellers are willing and able to sell fewer units of a good at all prices.
8. Any change in price in this range—say, from $10 to $11—will result in a smaller percentage change in quantity supplied.
9. a. The supply of TVs shifts to the right. **b.** The supply of TVs shifts to the right. **c.** The supply of TVs shifts to the left.
10. This chapter discussed seven factors that can change supply: resource prices, advancements in technology, taxes on production, subsidies, quotas, the number of sellers, and weather (in some

Chapter Summary

Be sure you know and remember the following key points from the chapter sections.

Section 1

▶ The supply of a good or service requires both a supplier's *willingness* and *ability* to produce and sell.
▶ The law of supply says that price and quantity supplied move in the same direction: as price increases, so does quantity supplied, and vice versa. This is called a *direct relationship*.
▶ *Quantity supplied* refers to the number of units of a good produced and offered for sale at a specific price.
▶ The supply curve is an upward-sloping line (from left to right) that shows the amount of a good sellers are willing and able to sell at various prices.
▶ A market supply curve represents the sum of all individual firms' supply curves for a particular good.

Section 2

▶ Resource prices, advances in technology, subsidies, quotas, number of sellers, future price expectations, and weather are all factors that can cause a shift in the supply curve.
▶ The factor that causes a change in the quantity supplied is price.
▶ The elasticity of supply measures the relationship between the percentage change in price and the percentage change in quantity supplied.
▶ Supply is elastic when quantity supplied changes by a greater percentage than price.
▶ Supply is inelastic when quantity supplied changes by a smaller percentage than price.
▶ Unit-elastic supply exists when quantity supplied changes by the same percentage as price.

Economics Vocabulary

To reinforce your knowledge of the key terms in this chapter, fill in each of the following blanks on a separate piece of paper with the appropriate word or phrase.

1. A(n) _____ is the numerical representation of the law of supply.
2. A(n) _____ is the graphic representation of the law of supply.
3. According to the law of supply, as price increases, _____ rises.
4. Supply is _____ if the percentage change in quantity supplied is greater than the percentage change in price.
5. Supply is _____ if the percentage change in quantity supplied is less than the percentage change in price.
6. _____ refers to the number of units of a good produced and offered for sale at a specific price.

Understanding the Main Ideas

Review the main ideas in this chapter by writing answers to the following questions on a separate sheet of paper.

1. Explain the term *supply* as it applies to economics. What is the difference between supply and quantity supplied?
2. Express the law of supply in (a) words, (b) symbols, and (c) graphic form.
3. Luisa is willing but not able to produce and sell plastic cups. Is Luisa a supplier of plastic cups? Explain your answer.
4. Do all supply curves slope upward? Why or why not?
5. Write out a supply schedule for four different combinations of price and quantity supplied.
6. Determine whether the supply curve for each of the following is vertical or upward sloping:
a. seats in your classroom at this moment
b. seats at a football stadium at this moment
c. TV sets over time
d. Hewlett-Packard computers over time
e. Picasso paintings (*Hint*: Picasso died in 1973.)
7. What does it mean when a supply curve shifts to the right? To the left?

cases). Only one factor can change quantity supplied: price. In other words, the only factor that can change the quantity supplied of apples is the price of apples.
11. a. elastic; **b.** unit elastic; **c.** elastic.
12. Price is the factor that causes movement along a supply curve.

Doing the Math

1. $100,000. Average cost, or per-unit cost, is the total cost of producing something divided by the number of units produced.
2. Both stores are charging $500 for game systems. This should be reflected in the graph.
3. 2 (*calculation:* 10% ÷ 5% = 2).

8. "Between the price of $10 and $14, supply is inelastic." What does this statement mean?

9. Explain what happens to the supply curve of TV sets as a consequence of the following:
  a. Resource prices fall.
  b. A technological advancement occurs in the TV industry.
  c. A tax is placed on the production of TV sets.

10. Identify the factors that can change supply and that can change quantity supplied.

11. For each of the following, determine if the supply of goods is elastic, inelastic, or unit elastic:
  a. The price of books increases 10 percent, and the quantity supplied increases 14 percent.
  b. The price of bread increases 2 percent, and the quantity supplied increases 2 percent.
  c. The price of telephones decreases 6 percent, and the quantity supplied decreases 8 percent.

12. What factor causes movement along a supply curve?

Doing the Math

Do the calculations necessary to solve the following problems.

1. A house-building company spends $40 million to produce 400 houses. What is the average cost, or per-unit cost, of a house?

2. Firm A sold 400 game systems for a total of $200,000, and firm B sold 550 game systems for a total of $275,000. Which firm is charging more per unit? Graph the market supply curve.

3. If the percentage change in price is 5 percent and the percentage change in quantity supplied is 10 percent, what is the elasticity of supply?

4. The price of a good is $10, and the quantity supplied is 300 units. For every $1 increase in price, quantity supplied rises by 5 units. What is the quantity supplied at a price of $22?

Working with Graphs and Charts

Use Exhibit 5-8 to answer the following questions. P = price, and Q_s = quantity supplied.

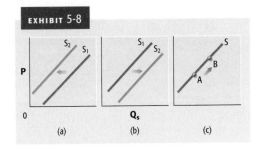

EXHIBIT 5-8

(a)   (b)   (c)

1. What does Exhibit 5-8(a) represent?
2. Which part of Exhibit 5-8 represents a change in supply due to technological advancement?
3. What does Exhibit 5-8(c) represent?
4. Which part of Exhibit 5-8 represents a change in supply due to an increase in resource prices?

Solving Economic Problems

Use your critical thinking skills and the information you learned in this chapter to find solutions to the following problems.

1. Apply. The law of supply can be applied to many goods. Design an experiment to test whether studying for an economics test is subject to the law of supply.

2. Identify Cause and Effect. Explain the process that occurs when a tax is applied to the production of a good and changes the supply of the good.

Project or Presentation

Supply and Demand on TV. List all the types of TV shows you can think of (such as crime, reality, and so on). Identify one type that you think will increase in supply over the next five years and one that might decrease. What factors will lead to the increase and decrease? Present your work to the class.

ONLINE emcp.com — *Practice Tests and Study Guide*

Go to www.emcschool.net/Economics2e and choose *Economics: New Ways of Thinking*, Chapter 5, if you need more help in preparing for the chapter test.

Solving Economic Problems

1. Answers will vary. (*Sample answer*: A student keeps a journal of the number of hours she or he studies for an economics test. Let's say the student currently studies an average of 4 hours for every economics test. Next, the teacher increases the reward for a certain performance on the test. Instead of getting only an A for a perfect test, the reward will be an A+, something else the student values. If the law of supply holds for studying for an economics test, the student will study more than 4 hours for the next test.)

2. If a tax is applied to the production of a good, the good becomes more expensive to produce. As a result, producers will earn lower profits on the good and thus want to produce fewer units of it. At every given price, quantity supplied will decrease. If quantity supplied decreases at every given price, supply will fall.

Project or Presentation

Answers will vary.

---

4. 360 units (*calculation:* Increased quantity supplied = current quantity supplied + [5 units × (increased price − current price)] = 300 + [5 units × (22 − 10)] = 300 + [5 units × 12] = 360).

Working with Graphs and Charts

1. Exhibit 5-8(a) represents a decrease in supply, or a leftward shift in the supply curve.

2. Exhibit 5-8(b) could represent a change in supply due to technological advancement.
3. Exhibit 5-8(c) represents movement along a supply curve, or an increase in quantity supplied.
4. Exhibit 5-8(a) could represent a change in supply due to an increase in resource prices.

Chapter 6 Planning Guide

SECTION ORGANIZER

Supply and Demand Together
(pages 144–155)

Learning Objectives	Reproducible Worksheets and Handouts	Assessment
▸ Explain how supply and demand together determine price. ▸ Describe what happens to price when the market has a surplus. ▸ Describe what happens to price when the market has a shortage.	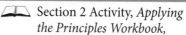 Section 1 Activities, *Applying the Principles Workbook*, pages 67–72 Outlining Activity, *Guided Reading and Study Guide*, pages 81–83 Just the Facts Handout, *Guided Reading and Study Guide*, pages 84–85	Section Assessment, *Student Text*, page 155 Quick Quiz, *Annotated Teacher's Edition*, page 154 Section Quiz, *Assessment Book*, page 57

Supply and Demand in Everyday Life
(pages 156–165)

Learning Objectives	Reproducible Worksheets and Handouts	Assessment
▸ Provide examples of how supply and demand affect everyday life. ▸ Describe how shortages, surpluses, and equilibrium affect special events. ▸ Understand why the prices of goods differ from city to city. ▸ Explain the relationship between traffic congestion and supply and demand. ▸ Identify necessary conditions for earning a high income.	Section 2 Activity, *Applying the Principles Workbook*, pages 73–77 Outlining Activity, *Guided Reading and Study Guide*, pages 86–88 Just the Facts Handout, *Guided Reading and Study Guide*, pages 89–90	Section Assessment, *Student Text*, page 165 Quick Quiz, *Annotated Teacher's Edition*, page 165 Section Quiz, *Assessment Book*, page 58

Reproducible Chapter Resources and Assessment Materials

Graphic Organizer Activity, *Guided Reading and Study Guide*, page 91

Vocabulary Activity, *Guided Reading and Study Guide*, page 92

Working with Graphs and Charts, *Guided Reading and Study Guide*, page 93

Practice Test, *Guided Reading and Study Guide*, pages 94–95

Critical Thinking Activity, *Finding Economics*, pages 16–18

Chapter Test A, *Assessment Book*, pages 59–61

Chapter Test B, *Assessment Book*, pages 62–66

Student Text Internet Links

Economics: New Ways of Thinking, Second Edition encourages students to use the Internet to find out more about economics. Given the wealth of current, valid information available on websites, students should be encouraged to use the Internet as a research tool. Doing so will likely increase students' interest in and understanding of economics principles and topics. In addition, doing Internet research can help your students form the habit of accessing and using economics information, as well as help them develop investigative skills they will use throughout their educational and professional careers.

To aid your students in achieving these ends, each chapter of *Economics: New Ways of Thinking, Second Edition* includes the addresses of several websites that provide engaging and relevant information. When students type in any of the addresses provided, they will immediately arrive at the intended site. The addresses have been modified so that EMC Publishing can monitor and maintain the proper links—for example, the website http://www.deposit accounts.com/ has been changed to http://econ.emcp.net/accounts. In the event that the address or content of a site changes or is discontinued, EMC's Internet editors will redirect the link to a site with equivalent information.

Activities in the *Annotated Teacher's Edition* often suggest that students search the Internet for information. For some activities, you might want to find reputable sites beforehand and steer students toward them. For other activities, have students do their own searching and then check out the sites they have found and discuss why they might be reliable or unreliable.

Passport® for Economics

Technology resources are available with the *Economics: New Ways of Thinking, Second Edition* program through Passport®. These include:

eBooks for *Economics: New Ways of Thinking, Second Edition*

▶ Student textbook eBook
▶ Interactive Applying the Principles eWorkbook
▶ Finding Economics eBook
▶ Guided Reading and Study Guide eBook
▶ Annotated Teacher's Edition eBook
▶ Lesson Plans eBook
▶ Assessment eBook

Passport® for Students

Students can access helpful resources through Passport® for Economics. Resources include:
▶ Study guides
▶ Practice tests
▶ Flash cards in English and in Spanish
▶ Word games in English and in Spanish
▶ Tutorials and key-concept videos
▶ Spanish print and audio summaries

Passport® for Teachers

Keep your course current and relevant by using the teacher resources provided through Passport® for Economics. In addition to all of the resources on the student side of Passport®, the teacher side contains:
▶ Link to the Annotated Teacher's Edition eBook
▶ Standards correlations
▶ Microsoft® PowerPoint® Lectures
▶ Current Events Lessons
▶ Additional Economics in the Real World features
▶ ExamView® Assessment Suite
▶ PDFs of all print supplements (student and teacher)

Overview

Price: Supply and Demand Together

This chapter discusses demand and supply together, looks at markets and how they function, and explains how markets determine prices. The following statements provide brief descriptions of the major concepts covered in each section of this chapter.

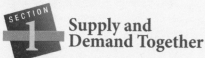

SECTION 1 Supply and Demand Together

Section 1 explains how supply and demand work together to determine price. Students will learn how an equilibrium price is established, what happens to price when there is a surplus or shortage in the market, and how price controls affect supply and demand.

SECTION 2 Supply and Demand in Everyday Life

Section 2 examines real-world scenarios to demonstrate the market forces of supply, demand, and price. Students will attain a deeper understanding of supply and demand by examining how they work in settings with which students are familiar.

Why It Matters

Markets and prices are a little like the air you breathe—they are everywhere. Anytime you buy or sell something, you do so at a price and in a market.

Supply and demand work together to determine price. What determines the price of the car you buy? Answer: supply and demand. What determines the price you sell your labor services for? Answer: supply and demand. What determines the price of the house you buy? Answer: supply and demand.

We will learn about supply and demand together in this chapter by looking at several examples from everyday life. We will also learn about price, which is the outcome of demand and supply working at the same time.

This dealer is an expert in fine-crafted art from all over the world. An important part of his job is to arrive at the right price for each artwork.

Teaching Suggestions from the Author

In my mind, this is the most important chapter in the book. All the fundamentals of supply and demand are covered here, and the model of how free, competitive markets work is presented. I present the theoretical material in this chapter by asking questions such as the following: What happens in a market if price is above the equilibrium level? What happens in a market if price is below the equilibrium level? What happens if there is a shortage in a market? What happens if there is a surplus in the market? What is so significant about equilibrium price and quantity?

Section 1: **Supply and Demand Together**

Section 2: **Supply and Demand in Everyday Life**

Economics Around the Clock

The following events occurred one day in June.

8:45 A.M. Gordon is online checking the price of a stock he's thinking of buying. Ten minutes ago, the price was $43.23 per share. Right now, it's $42.18. Gordon wonders whether he should buy the stock now or wait another 10 minutes, or 20 minutes, or several hours.
- What causes the price of a share of stock to drop $1.05 in 10 minutes?

8:47 A.M. Jennifer is driving to work. With so many cars on the road, she is only moving 15 mph. As she crawls along, she listens to a song on the radio and wonders why traffic is so bad during the morning commute.
- What does traffic congestion have to do with supply and demand?

2:17 P.M. Malcolm is watching a baseball game on his smartphone while waiting for his flight to board. The sports announcer is talking about the player who is currently at bat, who earns $7 million a year. Malcolm wonders why someone can earn so much by playing a game.
- Why do some baseball players earn millions of dollars a year?

8:13 P.M. Alice and Parker are at home watching their favorite TV show. Alice says, "You know, I read that this show has really high ratings." "Good," says Parker, "that means it won't be canceled anytime soon."
- How are TV ratings like the economic concept of price?

9:05 P.M. After hearing a knock at the door, Evelyn walks over and opens it. It's the pizza delivery guy. He takes a large pizza out of the case and says that she owes him $15.75. Evelyn gives him a $20 bill. After receiving her change, she gives the pizza delivery guy a $3 tip.
- Why was the price of the pizza $15.75? Why wasn't it $12 or $18?

143

Introducing the Chapter

In previous chapters, students learned about two of the building blocks of economics: supply and demand. In this chapter, they will learn what supply and demand create: price. Write the word *price* on the board. Ask students to discuss how important prices are to both buyers and sellers. After the class discussion, explain to students that this chapter will explore how supply and demand work together in our free enterprise economy to determine the prices we pay for goods and services.

Teaching with Visuals

Price is a concept with which students are familiar. Have them look at the photo on this spread and explain how price is important to the art dealer in the photo. Students will probably say that the dealer must be knowledgeable about the value of art from all over the world to determine the right price for each object.

Then, after students understand the theory of supply and demand and how markets equilibrate, it is time to have some fun with these concepts by examining real-world applications. Students will see theory in action and use it to understand their everyday world. After you teach the applications in the chapter, invite students to think up their own supply and demand applications. Spending a few days on this exercise will likely pay high dividends.

Teacher Support

Focus and Motivate

Section Objectives

After completing this section, students will be able to

▶ explain how supply and demand together determine price;

▶ describe what happens to price when the market has a surplus; and

▶ describe what happens to price when the market has a shortage.

Economics Around the Clock

Kickoff Activity

Have students read the 8:45 a.m. scenario in Economics Around the Clock (page 143) and write their answers to the accompanying question.

Invite students to share their answers with the class. Students may predict that changes in the price of a share of stock are determined by changes in the supply and demand of that stock. Obviously, one or the other changed to make the price drop in 10 minutes. For example, the supply of the stock available for sale might have increased, thus causing the price to fall.

Activating Prior Knowledge

To review concepts presented in the previous chapter, give students time to address the following question and create a visual: What is the relationship between the price of a good and the quantity supplied? Each student should draw a supply curve.

Visit econ.myemcp.com/videos for videos that will help students better understand the key concepts found in this section.

Supply and Demand Together

Focus Questions

▶ How do supply and demand work together to determine price?

▶ What happens to price when the market has a surplus?

▶ What happens to price when the market has a shortage?

Key Terms

surplus
shortage
equilibrium
equilibrium quantity
equilibrium price
inventory
price ceiling
price floor

Moving to Equilibrium

Imagine a pair of scissors. Which blade does the cutting: the top blade or the bottom? It's impossible to say, isn't it? In much the same way, it's impossible to say whether demand or supply is responsible for the prices we pay for goods and services. The fact is, supply and demand work together to determine price.

To understand exactly how supply and demand work together, imagine that you are at an auction where 40,000 bushels of corn are being sold. All the potential buyers are sitting in front of computers. At any given price, the buyers simply key in the number of bushels of corn they want to buy. The auction begins with the auctioneer calling out a price of $6. (Follow along in Exhibit 6-1 as you read about what is happening at the auction.)

surplus
The condition in which the quantity supplied of a good is greater than the quantity demanded. Surpluses occur only at prices *above* the equilibrium price.

• At $6 a bushel, the potential buyers think for a second, and then they all enter into their computers the numbers of bushels they want to buy at that price. The total that the buyers enter is 20,000 bushels, which is the quantity

demanded of corn at $6 per bushel. (See Exhibit 6-1.) The quantity supplied, though, is 40,000. In economics, when the quantity supplied is greater than the quantity demanded, a **surplus** exists. At a price of $6 per bushel, the surplus equals 20,000 bushels (the difference between the quantity supplied and the quantity demanded). So, what do you think will happen next? The auctioneer realizes that 20,000 bushels of corn will go unsold at $6 and decides to lower the price to $5.

• At $5 a bushel, the buyers again key in the numbers of bushels they want to buy, and the total increases to 30,000 bushels. This amount still leaves a surplus of corn—specifically, 10,000 bushels. So, what will the auctioneer do? Again, he lowers the price—this time, to $2.

• At only $2 a bushel, the buyers want to buy a lot more corn, and the total quantity demanded jumps to 60,000 bushels. At first, this sounds like a good thing, but do you see why it's a problem? (Look again at Exhibit 6-1.) The quantity demanded is now greater

Internet Research

Guide students in finding online real estate listings for their city or region and comparing the prices for two- or three-bedroom apartments or homes in different neighborhoods. Bring city maps to class so students can see where the listings are actually located. What factors affect the prices?

Why does supply and demand differ among neighborhoods? Encourage students to think not only about the overall desirability of living in certain neighborhoods but also about factors such as available land, housing density, and zoning restrictions that may affect housing supply.

than the quantity supplied. Economists call this condition a **shortage**. The auctioneer, realizing that he can't sell 60,000 bushels of corn when he only has 40,000, decides to raise the price to $3.

- As we would expect, when the price goes up from $2 to $3 a bushel, the buyers want less corn. The quantity demanded falls to 50,000 bushels, but there is still a shortage. The auctioneer again raises the price—this time, to $4.
- At $4 a bushel, the buyers key in a total of 40,000 bushels, which is exactly the same amount the auctioneer has to sell. The quantity demanded equals the quantity supplied. The auction stops. At this point economists say that the corn market is in equilibrium. A market is said to be in **equilibrium** when the quantity demanded of a good equals the quantity supplied. In this example, 40,000 bushels is the **equilibrium quantity** (the quantity of a good bought and sold in a market that is in equilibrium), and the price of $4 is the **equilibrium price** (the price at which a good is bought and sold in a market that is in equilibrium). Here are the symbolic expressions of these conditions:

Relationship of quantity supplied (Q$_s$) to quantity demanded (Q$_d$)	Market condition
$Q_s > Q_d$	Surplus
$Q_d > Q_s$	Shortage
$Q_d = Q_s$	Equilibrium

When the price was $6 a bushel and there was a surplus of corn, the auctioneer lowered the price. When the price was $2, resulting in a shortage, he raised the price. The behavior of the auctioneer can be summarized this way: if a surplus exists, lower the price; if a shortage exists, raise the price. In this way, the auctioneer moved the corn market into equilibrium.

Not all markets have auctioneers. (When was the last time you saw an auctioneer in the grocery store?) Still, many markets act *as if* an auctioneer is calling out higher and lower prices until the equilibrium price is reached. In many real-world markets, prices

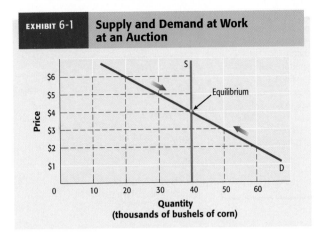

EXHIBIT 6-1 **Supply and Demand at Work at an Auction**

▲ Only at a price of $4 is the quantity demanded equal to the quantity supplied, with neither a surplus nor a shortage.

fall when a surplus occurs and rise when a shortage occurs.

Why Does Price Fall When a Surplus Occurs?

With a surplus, suppliers will not be able to sell all they had hoped to sell, so their **inventories** (stocks of goods on hand) grow beyond the normal level. Storing extra goods can be costly and inefficient; thus, sellers want to reduce their inventories. Some will lower prices to do so; some will cut back on producing output; others will do a little of both. As shown in Exhibit 6-2 on the next page, price and output tend to fall until equilibrium is achieved.

Why Does Price Rise When There Is a Shortage?

With a shortage, buyers will not be able to buy all they had hoped to buy. Some buyers will offer to pay a higher price to get sellers to sell to them, rather than other buyers. The higher prices will motivate suppliers to start producing more output. Thus, in a shortage, the tendency is for price and output to rise until equilibrium is achieved. (See Exhibit 6-2.)

shortage
The condition in which the quantity demanded of a good is greater than the quantity supplied. Shortages occur only at prices *below* the equilibrium price.

equilibrium
In a market, the point at which the quantity of a good that buyers are willing and able to buy is equal to the quantity that sellers are willing and able to produce and offer for sale (quantity demanded equals quantity supplied).

equilibrium quantity
The quantity of a good that is bought and sold in a market that is in equilibrium.

equilibrium price
The price at which a good is bought and sold in a market that is in equilibrium.

inventory
The stock of goods that a business or store has on hand.

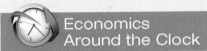

Teaching with Visuals

Draw a supply and demand diagram on the board, as in Exhibit 6-2. Label the vertical axis "Price" and the horizontal axis "Quantity." Put in an equilibrium price that corresponds to the intersection of the supply and demand curves. Invite students to come to the board and shift the supply or demand curve in one direction or the other. Ask students to explain what happens to supply or demand and to identify the new equilibrium quantity and price.

Reinforcement Activity

Tell students to ask one or two store owners whether they lower the price when they have a surplus of a good and raise the price when they have a shortage of a good. Allow students to report their findings to the class.

Prediction Activity

Suppose that a company stock sells for $110 per share. The company produces a product that it sells in many countries. One day, the company receives some bad economic news: Congress has passed legislation prohibiting it from selling its product in five countries to which it currently sells. Ask students to predict what will happen to the share price of this stock.

Students should predict that the share price will decline because the demand for the stock will decrease, and as demand decreases, price will fall.

▶ If a surplus occurs, the price and quantity of output fall. If a shortage happens, the price and quantity of output rise. A price of $10 means neither a surplus nor a shortage, so neither the price nor quantity of output changes.

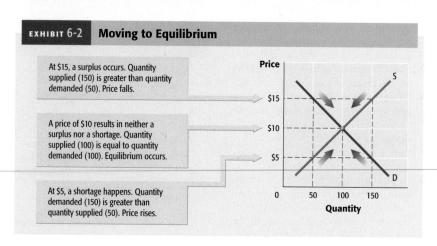

EXHIBIT 6-2 **Moving to Equilibrium**

At $15, a surplus occurs. Quantity supplied (150) is greater than quantity demanded (50). Price falls.

A price of $10 results in neither a surplus nor a shortage. Quantity supplied (100) is equal to quantity demanded (100). Equilibrium occurs.

At $5, a shortage happens. Quantity demanded (150) is greater than quantity supplied (50). Price rises.

EXAMPLE We know what a shortage and a surplus look like on a graph, but what do they look like in the real world? Suppose it's Friday night and your school's football team is playing at home. Your school stadium seats 2,000 people, but only 500 people are in the stands (350 from your school and 150 from your opponent's school), resulting in a surplus of seats. In other words, the number of people who want to be at the game is a smaller than the number of seats available in the stands. Suppose, however, that at another game, 2,500 people want to attend, but the stadium still has only 2,000 seats. Now, there is a shortage of seats. Maybe some people will have to stand, or maybe some will not be admitted to the game. ◆

EXAMPLE Before the collapse of the Soviet Union (pre-1989), very few people were seen in some of the shops in Moscow, but long lines of people were seen waiting inside and outside other shops. At the time, Soviet officials set the prices of the goods and services sold in the country. Often, those prices were not equilibrium prices—prices at which quantity demanded equaled quantity supplied. When officials set the price of a good higher than the equilibrium price (say, 100 rubles was the equilibrium price and the price was set at 250 rubles), there was a surplus of that good. The surplus became evident by less of the good being purchased than was available for sale,

and therefore, by seeing stores with few customers. When officials set the price of a good lower than equilibrium price (say, 100 rubles was the equilibrium price and the price was set at 30 rubles), there was a shortage of that good. A shortage was demonstrated by a long line of people waiting to buy a good that was likely to be sold out before they reached the front of the line. ◆

What Causes Equilibrium Prices to Change?

You now know that the equilibrium price is determined by both supply and demand. Can you guess what might cause an equilibrium price to change? You probably guessed right: for the equilibrium price to change, either supply or demand has to change.

Before looking at changes to equilibrium prices, let's review your ability to read graphs showing supply and demand curves. Having practice reading these graphs will help you use graphs to determine shortages, surpluses, and ultimately, equilibrium prices.

Look at Exhibit 6-2 above. Start at a price of $15 on the vertical (or price) axis. To find the quantity demanded, follow the dotted horizontal line over to the demand curve (D). Then follow the dotted vertical line down to the horizontal (or quantity) axis (50). In doing this, you'll find that the *quantity demanded* at $15 is 50.

Background Information: Equilibrium Prices

In the mid- to late 1980s, real estate prices in Tokyo were very high. The demand for land and the supply of land in Tokyo were intersecting at a high equilibrium price. Then, in the early to mid-1990s, real estate prices fell dramatically. What happened? Obviously, the supply of land did not change, since it is constant. Rather, the demand for land fell, lowering the equilibrium price of land. Direct students to research house prices in their neighborhoods. Overall, have house values gone up, gone down, or stayed the same during the last 25 years?

To find the *quantity supplied* at $15, again start at the price of $15 on the vertical axis, and follow the dotted horizontal line over to the supply curve (S). Then follow the dotted vertical line down to the horizontal axis. The number there is 150, so the quantity supplied at $15 is 150.

So, at $15, does a surplus or a shortage occur? Because the quantity supplied (150) is greater than the quantity demanded (50), the result is a surplus.

Now let's look at some graphs to see what happens when either supply or demand changes.

How Much Would You Pay for an Ocean View?

Once upon a time, a man bought a house. The house was built on a high cliff overlooking the Atlantic Ocean. The man got up every morning and drank his coffee as he gazed out over the ocean.

One day, a friend visited the man. The friend asked the man how much he thought he had paid for the ocean view he enjoyed daily. The man said, "I didn't pay anything for the view. I bought the house. The view was just there."

The friend asked the man if any houses in the neighborhood were similar to his house but without an ocean view. The man said that a house right down the street was exactly like his house but without an ocean view. "Was the price of the house down the street the same as the price of your house?" the friend asked. "No," said the man, "it was $200,000 cheaper."

"Then *that* is what you paid for the ocean view," the friend said. "If the only difference between your house and the house down the street is the ocean view, then the price difference between the houses is the price of the view."

Of course, another way of putting this relationship is to say that the demand for the man's house was greater than the demand for the house down the street, because the man's house came with an ocean view and the house down the street didn't. The higher demand for the house with the view meant that a higher price was paid for it.

The man knew that his friend was right. All this time, he had thought that he simply paid more for his house. Instead, he paid the same dollar price for his house as the person down the street paid for the identical house, and then he "purchased" the ocean view for $200,000.

Now ask yourself if you have ever been in the same situation as the man. Do you buy and pay for things that you are unaware of? If you have ever paid more for designer jeans than for the identical (and it must truly be "identical") nondesigner jeans, then the price difference is what you paid for the name on the back of the jeans. If you ever paid more for Bayer aspirin than for generic aspirin, then the price difference is what you paid for the name "Bayer."

We are not urging you to stop buying designer jeans or Bayer aspirin. Similarly, we are not saying that it's somehow wrong to buy a house with an ocean view. We are simply pointing out what you are paying for.

THINK ABOUT IT People who live in areas with good climates often talk about the nice weather being "free." Someone might say, "Aren't we lucky to live here? And to think, we don't have to pay a penny for all this good weather." Is it true that they don't pay anything for the good weather?

Have students read this feature and brainstorm other situations in which they pay for something without knowing that they are doing so.

ANSWERS TO THINK ABOUT IT The answer is no. As with houses with ocean views, houses in areas with good climates are likely more expensive than houses in areas with other climates, all other things being equal.

Background Information

Perhaps no other scholar introduced the economics profession to as many widely used microeconomic "tools" as British economist Alfred Marshall (1842–1924). Two of the most important tools are supply and demand. Marshall compared supply and demand to the two blades of a pair of scissors. Just as it is impossible to say which blade does the actual cutting, it is impossible to say whether demand or supply is responsible for the market price. Some economists before Marshall thought that only the cost of production (reflected in supply) determined price; others thought that only demand determined price. Marshall, however, said that both supply and demand determine price. It is widely acknowledged today that Marshall was right.

Differentiating Instruction

Kinesthetic and Visual Learners

Allow kinesthetic learners to manipulate the supply and demand curves to find the equilibrium price. Use a sticky board with materials for curves, or direct students to create their own three-dimensional graphs with supply and demand curves. Ask students to show what happens as supply and demand increase and decrease. Students who create the most imaginative displays should have their work exhibited in the classroom.

Discussion Starter

Invite students to imagine that they want to sell an item on an online auction site. Ask them whether they can set any price they like for this item. From the discussion of supply and demand, students should understand that although a seller can set any price, he or she cannot determine the quantity demanded at that price. Ask students what would happen if they set the price too high. Students should recognize that the item will not sell; in other words, the quantity of even one item will not be demanded.

Reinforcement Activity

From time to time, celebrity property is auctioned off at one of the major auction houses. Suggest that students create a list of five things they would be willing to bid on in a celebrity auction and the prices they would be willing to pay for those items. Ask whether they would pay more if someone bid against them; then point out that another bidder increases the demand for the item, increasing the price.

Teaching with Visuals

Learning how the supply and demand curves shift as the two factors change is very important. Students can probably name 10 different situations in which the price of something suddenly increased or they wanted to buy something but the store had run out of its supply. Tell students to prepare their own supply and demand curves based on real-world situations.

Demand Changes Cause Changes to Equilibrium Price

Exhibit 6-3(a) below shows the demand for and supply of TVs. The original demand curve is D_1, the supply curve is S_1, equilibrium is at point 1, and the equilibrium price is $300. Now suppose the demand for TVs increases. (Recall from Chapter 4 the factors that can shift the demand curve for a good: income, preferences, prices of related goods, number of buyers, and future price.) The demand curve shifts to the right, from D_1 to D_2. D_2 is now the relevant demand curve. At $300 per TV, the quantity demanded (using the new demand curve, D_2) is 300,000, and the quantity supplied (using the one and only supply curve, S_1) is 200,000.

Because the quantity demanded is greater than the quantity supplied, a shortage exists in the TV market. Then the price begins to rise. As it does, the TV market moves to point 2, where it is in equilibrium again. The new equilibrium price is $400. We conclude that an increase in the demand for a good will increase the price, all other things remaining the same.

Now suppose the demand for TVs decreases, as shown in Exhibit 6-3(b). The demand curve shifts to the left, from D_1 to D_2. At $300, the quantity demanded (using the new demand curve, D_2) is 100,000, and the quantity supplied (again using S_1) is 200,000. Because quantity supplied is greater than quantity demanded, a surplus exists. Now the price begins to fall. As it does, the TV market moves to point 2, where it is in

▶ A change in equilibrium price can be brought about by (a) an increase in demand, (b) a decrease in demand, (c) an increase in supply, or (d) a decrease in supply.

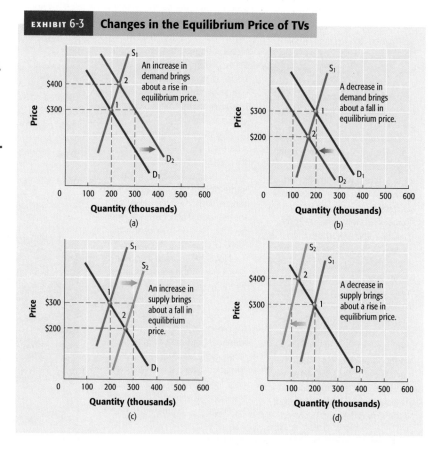

EXHIBIT 6-3   Changes in the Equilibrium Price of TVs

equilibrium again. The new equilibrium price is $200. A decrease in the demand for a good will decrease the price, all other things remaining the same.

EXAMPLE If you go to the Boston Red Sox website, you will be able to buy tickets (that some ticket holders want to sell) for various games played at Fenway Park. On the day we checked, the price of a seat in Section 36, Row 19 was $105 if you wanted to see the game between the Boston Red Sox and the Atlanta Braves. If you wanted to see a game between the Boston Red Sox and the New York Yankees, the price of a seat in the same section and row was $205. The number of seats in Fenway Park is the same for all games. In other words, the supply curve of seats at Fenway Park is vertical at a little more than 36,000 seats. The demand for games at Fenway differs from game to game, though. For example, the demand for a game with the Yankees is usually greater than the demand for a game with the Braves. (That is, the demand curve for a Yankees game lies to the right of the demand curve for a Braves game.) As a result, the ticket price for a Red Sox–Yankees game is usually higher than the ticket price for a Red Sox–Braves game. ♦

EXAMPLE A hotel in Miami Beach charges $150 a night for a room in June but $250 a night in January. Why the difference? A room is a room is a room, isn't it? Well, yes, a room is a room, but the demand for the room is different at different times of the year. Winter is the "high season" in Miami Beach, because people all over the United States want to vacation there and escape the cold weather where they live. Higher demand translates into higher price. ♦

Supply Changes Cause Changes to Equilibrium Price

Now let's return to Exhibit 6-3. Suppose the supply of TVs increases. (Recall the discussion in Chapter 5 of the factors that can shift the supply curve for a good, including resource prices, technology, taxes, and so on.) The supply curve in

Exhibit 6-3(c) shifts to the right, from S_1 to S_2. At $300, the quantity supplied (using the new supply curve, S_2) is 300,000, and the quantity demanded (using D_1) is 200,000. The quantity supplied is greater than the quantity demanded, so a surplus exists in the TV market. When the price begins to fall, the TV market moves to point 2, where it is in equilibrium again. The new equilibrium price is $200. Thus, an increase in the supply of a good will decrease the price, all other things remaining the same.

Now suppose the supply of TVs decreases, as in Exhibit 6-3(d). The supply curve shifts left, from S_1 to S_2. At $300, the quantity supplied (using S_2) is 100,000, and the quantity demanded (using D_1) is 200,000. Because the quantity demanded is greater than the quantity supplied, a shortage exists in the TV market. The price begins to rise, and the TV market moves

Thinking Like an Economist

Markets on the Move: Seeking Equilibrium

When economists think of supply and demand at work in a market setting, they immediately think of three things: shortage, surplus, and equilibrium. Specifically, economists know that at any time, a particular market must be in one of three states: a shortage state, a surplus state, or an equilibrium state.

In addition, if a market is in a shortage or surplus state, economists know that it will not stay there—as long as the market is a free market (that is, a market without a price ceiling or price floor). Change will occur because both shortages and surpluses are temporary states in a free market. In other words, if a shortage exists, economists know what will happen next: the price will rise and the market will move into equilibrium, so that the quantity supplied equals the quantity demanded. Or if a surplus exists, economists know that the price will soon fall and the market will move into equilibrium. To a large degree, equilibrium is the state to which free markets are always moving.

THINK ABOUT IT Suppose there has been a shortage in a given market for nearly a year. Is this evidence that free markets do *not* move to equilibrium? Explain.

Discussion Starter

Students may understand the reasons for changes in equilibrium prices and not even realize it. Ask students the following questions about sales they have seen in the last few days or weeks: What might have happened to supply and demand to cause the sale? How does this change the way you feel about sale prices, if at all?

Cause and Effect

Ask students to bring in advertisements for sales of goods. Most advertisements list both the sale price and the original price. Direct each student to graph the supply and demand curves of a sale good and to write a short description of what has happened to supply and demand for that good.

Reinforcement Activity

Street markets and farmers markets are becoming increasingly common in the United States. Ask students to recall a time when they negotiated a lower price from a seller at a market or to imagine a time they might have done so. Have each student write a sentence about how this negotiation contributed to the forces of supply and demand.

Thinking Like an Economist

Markets on the Move: Seeking Equilibrium

ANSWERS TO THINK ABOUT IT No, this is not evidence that free markets do not move to equilibrium. It could very well be the case that a price ceiling has been imposed on the market, thus making it impossible for the market to attain equilibrium.

Reinforcement Activity

Direct each student to write a sentence that explains how supply and demand relate to equilibrium. The student might write that equilibrium exists in a market when the quantity of a good that buyers are willing and able to buy is equal to the quantity of the good that sellers are willing and able to produce and offer for sale. That is, quantity demanded equals quantity supplied.

Discussion Starter

Invite students to imagine the two worlds discussed on page 150 and discuss the following questions: What would it be like to live in a world that is at complete equilibrium price? What would it be like to live in a world with no markets at equilibrium? Which world would you rather live in? Why?

Thinking Like an Economist

Economists know that competitive markets, if left alone, eventually reach equilibrium. They also know that not all competitive markets reach equilibrium at the same speed. For example, the stock market may go from shortage to equilibrium in a matter of seconds or minutes, whereas the housing market may take months to make a similar move.

---

to point 2, where it is again in equilibrium at the new equilibrium price of $400. We conclude that a decrease in the supply of a good will increase the price, all other things remaining the same.

EXAMPLE The supply of oranges produced in Florida and California is greater in year 2 than in year 1. As a result, the supply curve of oranges in year 2 lies to the right of the supply curve of oranges in year 1. If the demand curve for oranges in both years is the same, then the price of oranges will be lower in year 2 than in year 1. ♦

Changes in Supply and in Demand at the Same Time

"Teach a parrot to say 'supply and demand,' and you've got an economist."
— Economics joke

Until now, we have looked at cases in which either demand changed and supply remained constant or supply changed and demand remained constant. In the real world, of course, both demand and supply can change at the same time. Let's review one case to see how equilibrium price changes as a result.

Look at Exhibit 6-4. Suppose that D_1 and S_1 represent the initial situation in the market, and the resulting equilibrium price is $300. Then, both demand and supply increase. Demand increases from D_1 to D_2, and supply increases from S_1 to S_2. Notice that the increase in demand is greater than

▶ Sometimes, supply and demand change at the same time. Here, although both demand and supply increase, demand increases more than supply. As a result, the equilibrium price increases.

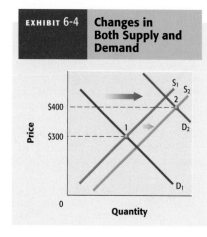

EXHIBIT 6-4 Changes in Both Supply and Demand

the increase in supply. In other words, the demand curve shifts further right (from D_1 to D_2) than the supply curve shifts right (from S_1 to S_2). As we can see in the exhibit, the equilibrium price rises from $300 to $400. So, if both demand and supply increase but demand increases more than supply, the equilibrium price increases.

The change in equilibrium price will be determined by which changes more, supply or demand. If demand increases more than supply, the equilibrium price will go up. If supply increases more than demand, the equilibrium price will go down.

Does It Matter If Price Is at Its Equilibrium Level?

Think of two different worlds. World 1 has 10 markets, each of which is in equilibrium. If all the markets are in equilibrium, then there are no shortages or surpluses of any good or service. In this world, buyers and sellers have no complaints. Everyone is happy.

World 2 also has 10 markets, but in 5 of the markets, price is below equilibrium price and in 5 of the markets, price is above equilibrium price. In other words, half the markets are in surplus, and half are in shortage. In this world, both buyers and sellers are complaining.

Which world would you prefer to live in? Can you see why economists think it is important to study and understand price and equilibrium?

Price Is a Signal

You are probably beginning to see that price performs certain important jobs in the marketplace. One such job is to provide information, which price does in a kind of "market conversation." For example, suppose for two goods—clocks and books— buyers' preferences one day shift against clocks and in favor of books. We know that a change in preferences affects the demand for both clocks and books. The demand for clocks will fall, and the demand for books will rise.

Background Information: Supply, Demand, and the California Gold Rush

The California Gold Rush provides an excellent example of how a dramatic change in supply or demand can lead to equally dramatic changes in prices. Before the discovery of gold at Sutter's Mill, a metal pan sold for 20 cents, which is the equivalent of $3.60 today. After gold was discovered, the demand for metal pans (which were used to mine for the gold) increased sharply. The price increased, as well, rising to $15 (equivalent to $270 today). Real estate that cost $16 (the equivalent of

What happens to the price in each case? As a result of the decreased demand for clocks, the price of clocks falls. Because of the lower price for clocks, the quantity supplied of clocks falls. In other words, clock sellers will respond to the lower price for clocks by offering to sell fewer clocks. (The quantity supplied of clocks is lower at a lower price than at a higher price.)

As a result of the increased demand for books, the price of books rises. Because of the higher price for books, book sellers will offer to sell more books. In other words, book sellers will respond to the higher price of books by offering to sell more books. (The quantity supplied of books is higher at a higher price than at a lower price.)

Notice how buyers are communicating with sellers. Buyers aren't saying "Produce fewer clocks and produce more books," but the result is the same. Instead, buyers are simply lowering the demand for clocks and raising the demand for books. As a result, the price goes down for clocks and up for books. Sellers see these price changes and respond to them. They decrease the quantity supplied of clocks and increase the quantity supplied of books. Price, then, acts as a signal that is passed along by buyers to sellers. As the price goes down, buyers are saying to sellers "Produce less of this good." As the price goes up, buyers are saying to sellers "Produce more of this good."

In this example, price is a signal that directs the allocation of resources away from clocks and toward books.

What Are Price Controls?

Sometimes, the government prevents markets from reaching an equilibrium price. For example, suppose that the equilibrium price for a good is $10. It is possible for government officials to pass a law setting the price lower—say, $8. A legislated price that is below the equilibrium price is called a **price ceiling**. A price ceiling is like a ceiling in a room. Just as you cannot go higher than the ceiling in a room, buyers and sellers cannot legally buy and sell a good for a price higher than the price ceiling.

In addition, the government can and sometimes does legislate a higher (than equilibrium) price—say, $12. A legislated price that is above the equilibrium price is called a **price floor**. A price floor is like a floor in a room. Just as you cannot go lower than the floor in a room, buyers and sellers cannot legally buy and sell a good for a price lower than the price floor.

Let's look at both a price ceiling and a price floor graphically. Exhibit 6-5(a) shows a price ceiling. In the exhibit, $10 is the equilibrium price of the good. Also notice that the equilibrium quantity is 80. The price ceiling of $8 is below the equilibrium price. What is an effect of a price ceiling? One effect is that it creates a shortage in the market. Notice that at $8, the quantity demanded (100) is greater than the quantity supplied (60), which is the definition of a shortage. Because suppliers want to supply only 60 units at $8, only 60 units are bought and sold. (Sure, buyers may want to buy 100 units at $8, but because suppliers want to sell

price ceiling
A legislated price—set below the equilibrium price—above which buyers and sellers cannot legally buy and sell a good.

price floor
A legislated price—set above the equilibrium price—below which buyers and sellers cannot legally buy and sell a good.

Economic Facts and Fallacies

FALSE   TRUE

The Many Jobs of Price

Some people think the only job price performs is to decide who can and cannot buy a particular item. Said differently, the only job price performs is to ration goods and services among people.

Suppose your neighbor offers to sell you her used car for $10,000. If you are willing and able to pay that price for the car, then it will be yours. But if you are not willing or not able to pay that price for the car, the car won't be yours and your neighbor will offer it to someone else.

But price does more than simply ration goods and services. It also serves as a signal and provides information. This job is described in the section "Price Is a Signal," which shows how price communicates to clock sellers and book sellers what consumers want to buy.

Price also acts as an incentive to produce. Think of the companies that produce cars. Why do they produce cars? They want to sell them for some dollar price and then use the dollars to buy what they want.

In summary, price is three things: a rationing device, a signal that communicates information from consumers to sellers, and an incentive to produce. Clearly, price does a lot in a market setting. Think of that the next time someone says that price is only a number with a dollar sign in front of it.

What are some benefits of learning to speak Economics? Invite students to go to http://emcschool.net/economics2e, select Chapter 6, and read the Economics in the Real World feature titled **"Do You Speak Economics?"**

After reading this feature, students should list the benefits of learning to speak Economics. Ask how learning the language of economics might help them make informed decisions on significant financial issues in the future.

ANSWERS TO THINK ABOUT IT Answers will vary. Invite volunteers to share their "econospeak" with the class.

Reinforcement Activity

Ask students to explain how responsive prices are a benefit of the U.S. free enterprise system and whether imposed price controls help or hinder that process.

$288 today) before gold was discovered jumped to more than $40,000 (more than $750,000 today). Near the mines, a loaf of bread cost 75 cents ($13.50 today). Eggs sold for about $2 each ($36 today), and boots were $100 a pair ($1,800 today).

Travelers trekking westward often found water in short supply. It was common for them to pay $1 for a glass of water ($18 today). In some cases, the price for a glass of water rose to $100 ($1,800 today).

Use this A Student Asks to make sure students understand the difference between price ceilings and price floors. Then direct students to the Debating the Issues feature on pages 170–171 to read arguments for and against price controls in a specific situation. After reading and discussing the feature, lead students in brainstorming other situations in which price controls might be used, and choose one situation for a class discussion on possible positive and negative effects of such controls.

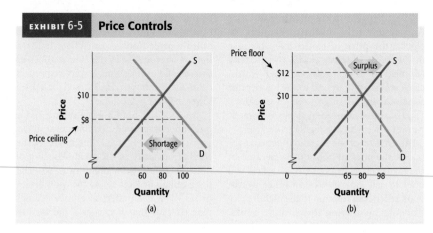

EXHIBIT 6-5 **Price Controls**

▲ The two types of price controls are price ceilings and price floors. (a) A price ceiling creates a shortage and reduces the quantity of the good bought and sold from what it would be in equilibrium. (b) A price floor creates a surplus and reduces the quantity of the good bought and sold from what it would be in equilibrium.

only 60 units, suppliers decide how much is bought and sold. You can't make suppliers sell more of a good than they want to.)

Now look at Exhibit 6-5(b). It shows a price floor of $12. What is an effect of a price floor? One effect is that it creates a surplus in the market. Notice that at $12, the quantity supplied (98) is greater than the quantity demanded (65), which is the definition of a surplus. With the price floor, fewer units are bought and sold. Because buyers want to buy only 65 units at $12, only 65 units are bought and sold.

QUESTION: *Why does the government sometimes impose price controls, such as price ceilings and price floors?*
ANSWER: *Sometimes, the government imposes a price ceiling on a good to make the good cheaper for consumers to buy. For example, suppose the price of a particular medicine is $200 for a month's supply. By imposing a price ceiling on this medicine of, say,*

$100, the government could make the medicine more affordable to more people. Of course, the unintended effect of this lower-than-equilibrium price might be that a shortage will result. In that case, some of the people who need the medicine might not be able to buy it at $100 because it isn't available.

Sometimes, the government imposes a price floor to assist a certain group of producers. For example, farmers sometimes argue that they need to receive higher dollar prices for what they sell. Suppose that the equilibrium price for a bushel of corn is $3. Farmers may argue that they can't make a decent living at $3 a bushel, so the government may impose a price floor of $4 on corn. This means that no one can buy or sell corn for less than $4 a bushel. The intended effect of the price floor is to help farmers, but the unintended effect is to hurt the buyers of corn (who have to pay a higher price). Also, setting a price floor can lead to a surplus of corn.

152 Chapter 6 Price: Supply and Demand Together

Differentiating Instruction

English Language Learners

To help students who are English language learners, use the following resources, which are provided as part of the *Economics: New Ways of Thinking* program:
- a Spanish glossary in the *Student Text*
- Spanish versions of the Chapter Summaries on an audio disc

Economics *in the* Real World

What Happened to U.S. House Prices Between 2001 and 2009?

Many consumers believe that producers of goods determine the prices of those goods by simply adding a certain percentage to the costs of producing the goods. For example, if the cost of producing a clock is $10, then the price charged for the clock is 10 percent higher—or $11.

The assumption that some percentage formula is used to determine price is wrong. To see why, consider something other than the price of clocks.

From 2001 to mid-2006, house prices in the United States rose rapidly—by as much as 30 percent a year in some cities. No one who was trying to sell a house said something like this: "Let's see, I bought the house for $200,000, so I guess I should add on 10 percent and therefore sell the house for $220,000." Instead, house sellers were trying to charge as high a price as they could. If the new market-determined price was 30, 40, or 50 percent higher than the price they paid for the house, well then, so be it. That was the price for which they would sell the house.

The rise in house prices turned around in mid-2006. House prices fell, especially during the period 2007–2009. During this time, some people ended up selling their houses for less than they paid for them.

A case in point: a house that a couple bought for $400,000 in 2005 sold for 30 percent less (or $280,000) in 2009. The couple wanted to sell the house for the cost they paid ($400,000) plus 10 percent, but the market didn't let them. They had to sell the house for 30 percent less or not sell the house at all.

The idea that prices are set by some formula such as "Price = Costs (per unit) + 10 percent" is incorrect. Countless examples in everyday life prove that there is no such formula. The "formula," to the degree that one exists, is the formula of supply and demand—as we can see from recent changes in the housing market.

> **THINK ABOUT IT** Suppose the price of one unit of good X is $10, which happens to be 10 percent higher than the cost of producing one unit of good X. Does it necessarily follow that the price of good X is determined by the formula Price = Cost (per unit) + 10 percent?

After completing this feature, lead the class in identifying three items that are in high demand and three that are in low demand. Divide the class into six groups and assign each group one of the items. Instruct each group to find out as much as they can about the economics of their assigned item—including actual demand and supply, price, costs, and price as a percentage of costs. Invite each group to present its findings. As a class, compare and contrast the results.

ANSWERS TO THINK ABOUT IT No. It could simply be that the supply and demand price for good X is 10 percent higher than the per-unit cost of producing the good. What looks like "Price = Costs (per unit) + 10 percent" could simply be supply and demand at work.

Background Information

There are many different currencies in the world: Mexican pesos, Russian rubles, British pounds, Japanese yen, and so on. If you want foreign currency, you have to buy it much the same way you have to buy a computer. The value of a foreign currency is based on the supply or demand for that currency, just like any other good. Whenever the demand for or the supply of a currency changes, its price changes too. A foreign currency is very similar to any other good: the equilibrium price will be reached by the market as long as nothing else interferes.

Reinforcement Activity

Ask each student to write a sentence that explains the likely effect of long lines of buyers on the equilibrium price of a product.

Cooperative Learning

Divide the class into groups of four or five. Each group member should scan newspapers and newsmagazines for an article or a feature that illustrates supply and demand working together. As a group, students should choose the best article and complete the following tasks:

1. Write a summary of the article.
2. Evaluate how this condition affects the local economy.
3. Create a graph illustrating the supply and demand issue in the selected article.

Groups should present their findings to the class.

Application Activity

After reading and discussing Section 1, you may want to assign the Section Activities in the *Applying the Principles Workbook,* pages 67–72.

Assess

Quick Quiz

The following true-and-false quiz will help you assess student understanding of the material covered in this section.

1. When quantity supplied is greater than quantity demanded, a surplus exists. (True)
2. A shortage occurs when quantity demanded is greater than quantity supplied. (True)
3. The price at which a good is bought and sold in a market that is in equilibrium is called the *equilibrium price.* (True)
4. The stock of goods on hand is called the *inventory.* (True)
5. If price is too high, there is a surplus; if price is too low, there is a shortage. (True)

 Assessment Book

You will find a quiz for this section in the *Assessment Book,* page 57.

Reteaching Activity

Use the Section Assessment to gauge which students may need reteaching on this section. Guide those students in examining Exhibit 6-2. First, ask students to define the words *surplus, shortage,* and *equilibrium.* Then invite students to explain at what prices there is a surplus and at what prices there is a shortage, and why.

Price Controls and the Amount of Exchange

Price controls (price ceilings and price floors) bring about less exchange (less trade) than would occur without them. In Figure 6-5(a), the equilibrium quantity traded was 80, but the price ceiling reduced this level to 60. In Figure 6-5(b), the equilibrium quantity traded was 80, but the price floor reduced it to 65.

With this relationship in mind, let's go back to something you learned about voluntary exchange (or trade) in Chapters 2 and 3. In those chapters, you learned that exchange is something that makes people better off. If John exchanges his $15 for Yvonne's book, John is, through his actions, saying that he is better off with the book than the $15. At the same time, Yvonne is saying that she is better off with the $15 than she is with the book. In other words, exchange is something that makes both parties (the buyer and the seller) better off. If price controls decrease the amount of exchange that occurs, we must conclude that price controls limit the opportunities that people have to make themselves better off.

Price and Speculators

Suppose you read an online news story stating that speculators are buying up corn and holding it off the market. As a result of these actions, the price of corn increases, which means consumers have to pay more for corn and corn products. The story ends

by saying that these speculators are hurting consumers. You wonder if that's true.

Let's see if we can figure out whether the conclusion makes sense by taking the story apart piece by piece and examining the pieces using some of the economics we know. First, if the speculators are buying up corn and holding it off the market, they are in effect reducing the supply of corn. A reduction in the supply of corn will naturally cause the equilibrium price of corn to rise. So far, then, what the news story reported is accurate.

But the news story does not say *why* the speculators are buying up corn and holding it off the market. They must have some reason. Speculators do things they hope will earn them profits. For example, they will buy corn today at a low price if they think they will be able to sell it later for a higher price. It would make economic sense for them to buy corn today at $4 a bushel if they believe they can sell the same corn next year at $6 a bushel. However, it would make no sense for them to buy corn today at $6 a bushel if they expect to have to sell it next year for $4 a bushel. So, if speculators are buying corn today and holding on to it, they must believe that the price of corn will be higher in the future.

So, what might make speculators think the price of corn will be higher in the future? Here's what: a weather report predicting that there will likely be a drought in the next growing season, meaning less corn will be harvested. If you were a speculator and had reason to believe that next year's crop of corn will be less than this year's crop of corn, you would also immediately think that next year's price of corn will be higher than today's price. And what is the best thing for you to do? Buy corn today and wait until next year to sell it.

Now let's look at what might happen to the price of corn if there *is* a drought—in a world without spectators and in a world with speculators:

- **Without speculators.** In year 1, consumers buy just what they need, and

◄ Higher expected corn prices (in the future) can lead to rising current corn prices.

the price of corn is $4 a bushel. In year 2, there is a drought. Farmers harvest less corn than consumers demand, and the price of corn is $8 a bushel.

- **With speculators.** Suspecting that a drought is coming, speculators buy more corn than they really need in year 1, thus decreasing the supply of corn from what it would have been in a world without speculators. The price of corn in year 1 is therefore higher than $4 a bushel—say, $6 a bushel. The speculators do not use the corn in year 1; instead, they hang on to it. In year 2, the speculators release the corn, thus increasing the supply of corn from what it would have been without speculators, and the price of corn in year 2 is therefore lower than $8 a bushel—say, $6 a bushel.

Year 1 in a world with speculators is what the news story described. What the story did not cover, though, is what happens when speculators move some of the corn from year 1 to year 2, thus increasing the supply of corn in year 2. The full story is that the speculators will make the supply of corn in

year 1 less than it would have been without them, and they will make the supply of corn in year 2 more than it would have been without them. They will decrease the supply of corn in year 1, causing the price of corn to be higher, and they will increase the supply of corn in year 2, causing the price to be lower.

Without speculators, the price of a bushel of corn will vary greatly from $4 in year 1 to $8 in year 2. With speculators, the price of a bushel of corn will not vary as much; in fact, it may remain steady at $6 in both years.

This is what speculators do: they reduce the variability in prices from one year to the next by reallocating supply between years. Do speculators earn a profit by doing this? If they guess correctly, they do—but there is no guarantee that they will guess correctly. Do speculators serve any social purpose? Most economists would say that they do: they prepare and adjust for expected changes (such as a possible drought) in the marketplace. In the corn example, speculators are a little like squirrels. They collect food in good times and save it for bad times.

SECTION 1 ASSESSMENT

Defining Terms
1. Define:
   a. surplus
   b. shortage
   c. equilibrium
   d. equilibrium quantity
   e. equilibrium price
   f. inventory
   g. price ceiling
   h. price floor

Reviewing Facts and Concepts
2. If demand increases and supply is constant, what happens to the equilibrium price?
3. If supply decreases and demand is constant, what happens to the equilibrium price?

4. If supply increases and demand is constant, what happens to the equilibrium price?
5. If the shortage is 40 units and the quantity supplied is 533 units, what is the quantity demanded?
6. If supply decreases by more than demand decreases, what happens to the equilibrium price?

Critical Thinking
7. A producer makes 100 units of good X at $40 each. He decides that under no circumstances will he sell the good for less than $40. Do you agree or disagree with his decision? Explain.

8. Do price controls cause shortages, or do shortages cause price controls? Explain.
9. What does a speculator have to do with the current supply of a good and the future supply of the same good?

Graphing Economics
10. Graph the following:
   a. Demand increases in a market.
   b. Supply decreases in a market.
   c. Demand decreases in a market.
   d. Demand increases by more than supply increases in a market.

SECTION 1 ASSESSMENT ANSWERS

Defining Terms

1. a. surplus: exists when the quantity supplied of a good is greater than the quantity demanded; **b. shortage:** exists when the quantity demanded

of a good is greater than the quantity supplied; **c. equilibrium:** exists when the quantity supplied of a good equals the quantity demanded of the good; **d. equilibrium quantity:** the quantity of a good that is bought and sold in a market that is in equilibrium; **e. equilibrium**

price: the price at which a good is bought and sold in a market that is in equilibrium; **f. inventory:** the stock of goods that a business or store has on hand; **g. price ceiling:** a legislated price set below the equilibrium price; **h. price floor:** a legislated price set above the equilibrium price.

Guided Reading

For further reteaching of the key concepts in this section, assign the Outlining Activity and the Just the Facts Handout in the *Guided Reading and Study Guide,* pages 81–85.

Reviewing Facts and Concepts

2. Equilibrium price rises.
3. Equilibrium price rises.
4. Equilibrium price falls.
5. Quantity demanded equals 573 units, or quantity supplied plus the shortage.
6. Equilibrium price rises.

Critical Thinking

7. Students should disagree. Imagine that on Monday, the equilibrium price of good X is $50. A producer decides to produce 100 units of good X, which takes from Monday through Thursday. During this time, demand for good X falls, so the new equilibrium price is $35. On Friday, the producer must decide whether to sell the good at $35 per unit even though it cost $40 per unit to produce the good or not to sell the good at all. The producer can lose $40 or $5 (*calculation:* $40 − $35 = $5) per unit.
8. Price controls cause shortages. If a price is set below the equilibrium price, the quantity demanded will be greater than the quantity supplied. In other words, a shortage will occur.
9. The objective of a speculator is to buy low and sell high. Suppose that the current supply is large and the price of the good is $3. The future supply is expected to be small, however, so the future price of the good is expected to be $7. If they can, speculators will purchase some of the current supply at a relatively low price, move it to the future when the price is expected to be higher.

Graphing Economics

10. a. See Exhibit 6-3(a). b. See Exhibit 6-3(d). c. See Exhibit 6-3(b). d. See Exhibit 6-4.

Teacher Support

Focus and Motivate

Section Objectives

After completing this section, students will be able to

- provide examples of how supply and demand affect everyday life;
- describe how shortages, surpluses, and equilibrium affect special events;
- understand why the prices of goods differ from city to city;
- explain the relationship between traffic congestion and supply and demand; and
- identify necessary conditions for earning a high income.

Kickoff Activity

Read the following scenario to students and have them answer the questions in a written paragraph: Suppose tickets to a popular show go on sale at 8 a.m. Monday morning for $50 each. When the booth opens, there is a long line of people waiting to buy tickets. Some people at the far end of the line end up not being able to buy tickets at all. Was the $50 price for a ticket too high, too low, or just right? Explain your answer.

Activating Prior Knowledge

Invite students to share their responses to the Kickoff Activity. Explain to them that running out of tickets is an indicator of a shortage. A shortage occurs only at a price below equilibrium price.

Teach

Discussion Starter

Urge students to think about purchases they have made recently. Ask them to explain how supply and demand affected those purchases and whether they would make the same purchases again, knowing what they do about how price is set.

Supply and Demand in Everyday Life

Focus Questions

- Why do people wait in long lines to buy tickets for some rock concerts?
- Why does a house cost more in San Francisco than in Louisville, but a candy bar costs the same in both cities?
- Why does it cost more to go to the movies on Friday night than on Tuesday morning?
- What does traffic congestion have to do with supply and demand?
- What does trying out for a high school sports team have to do with supply and demand?
- What is the necessary condition for earning a high income?

Why the Long Lines for Concert Tickets?

Suppose tickets for a rock concert go on sale at 8 a.m. on Saturday. A long line of people forms even before the ticket booth opens. The average person has to wait an hour to buy a ticket. Some people don't get to buy tickets at all, because the concert sells out before they get to the ticket booth.

Why do so many people wait in line to buy tickets to a rock concert? You don't see a long line of people waiting to buy food at the grocery store or TVs at the electronics store. Also, why will some of the people waiting to buy tickets to the rock concert be turned away? No one who wants to buy bread is turned away at the grocery store, and no one who wants to buy a TV set is turned away at the electronics store. The market for the rock concert tickets (at least in this instance) must be different in some way, but how?

In economic terms, when some people go away without being able to buy what they came to buy, it means that the quantity demanded exceeds the quantity supplied, resulting in a shortage in the market. You learned earlier that a market shortage causes the price to rise. Eventually, it will rise to

its equilibrium level. The problem in the rock concert example, though, is that the tickets were bought and sold before the seller realized a shortage of tickets would occur. In hindsight, the seller realizes that the price charged for the tickets was too low, and this pricing caused a shortage. If the seller had charged the equilibrium price, he would have encountered no shortage, no long lines, and no one being turned away without a ticket.

As shown in Exhibit 6-6, the seller charged $40 a ticket. At this price, the quantity demanded (12,500) was greater than the quantity supplied (10,000). If the price had been $60 a ticket, the quantity supplied (10,000) would have equaled the quantity demanded (10,000), and no shortage would have occurred. Why didn't the seller charge the higher equilibrium price, instead of a price that was too low? The seller might have charged the equilibrium price had he known it.

Think back to the auctioneer example. Recall that the auctioneer didn't call out the equilibrium price at the start of the auction. He called out $6, which was too high a price and thus created a surplus. Later, he called out $2, which was too low a price and thus caused a shortage. It was only through trial

Internet Research

Direct students to go to the website for Project Vote Smart, look for information on current legislation, and pick as many as three bills that, if passed, might affect the price of some good.

Students should briefly summarize the intent of each bill and explain how and why it could affect prices. Then allow students to discuss whether they would pass the bills if they were legislators.

and error that the auctioneer finally hit on the equilibrium price.

Because people go to the grocery store and electronics store to buy goods every day, those stores have countless opportunities to learn by trial and error and adjust their prices to reach equilibrium. The seller of the rock concert tickets didn't have the same opportunity.

QUESTION: *At a concert I attended last month, scalpers were selling tickets for at least $50 more than the original price. Tickets that had initially sold for $60 were being sold for $110. Aren't the scalpers, in a way, like the auctioneer?*

ANSWER: *Yes. Look again at Exhibit 6-6. We can see that the equilibrium ticket price (for this particular concert) is $60, but the initial ticket seller sells tickets for only $40. What will happen in this case is that someone will likely buy a ticket (or two, or three, or four) for $40 and then resell it for $60, earning a profit of $20 per ticket. Now ask yourself whether this buying and reselling of tickets would happen if all the tickets were sold for $60 in the first place. The answer is no. Lesson learned: Scalpers (people who buy and resell tickets at higher prices) enter the picture only when the good in question was not originally sold at its equilibrium price.*

Look around you. You don't see scalpers when it comes to milk, computers, rugs, shirts, turkey sandwiches, or cups of coffee. No person stands outside a coffee shop and offers to sell you a cup of coffee for $2 more than you can pay for it inside the shop. The reason you don't see scalpers in any of these cases is that the prices of the goods are at equilibrium.

Still, you will see scalpers for rock concerts, as well as some sporting events and even some plays. Why? Because in these cases, the price initially charged for the event was below the equilibrium price; that is, the price was below the price at which the quantity demanded equals the quantity supplied.

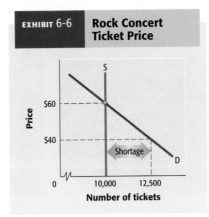

EXHIBIT 6-6 **Rock Concert Ticket Price**

◄ The seller of rock concert tickets sells 10,000 tickets at a price of $40 each. At this price, a shortage occurs; the seller charged too low a price. A price of $60 per ticket would have achieved equilibrium in the market.

The Differences in Prices for Candy Bars, Bread, and Houses

In general, no matter where you go in the United States, the price of a candy bar (pick your favorite brand) is approximately the same. A candy bar in Toledo, Ohio, is approximately the same price as a candy bar in Miami, Florida. This consistency is also mostly true for many other goods, such as loaves of bread.

But is it true for all goods? What about real estate prices—in particular, the price of a house in San Francisco, California, and the price of a similar house in a similar neighborhood in Louisville, Kentucky? In fact, the house in San Francisco will sell for approximately three to four times the price of the house in Louisville. Why, when it comes to candy bars and bread, does a good sell for approximately the same price no matter where it's purchased in the United States, but when it comes to houses, a house in San Francisco is much more expensive than a similar house in Louisville? It's all about supply and demand.

Let's imagine for a second that the price of a candy bar is *not* the same in Toledo as in Miami. At a particular time, the price for candy bars is $2 in Toledo and $1 in Miami, because the demand for candy bars is higher in Toledo. Knowing what you know now about supply and demand, what do you think will happen?

Remind students that the vertical supply curve means that the supply of tickets is fixed. Supply cannot be shifted left or right.

Use this A Student Asks to review how supply and demand establish price equilibrium and how the market changes when price changes.

Discussion Starter

Many of the situations in this section will be very familiar to students. Have them share their experiences as each situation is discussed. Ask students how economic thinking is changing the way they think about these common situations.

Reinforcement Activity

Ask students to explain the following scenario in terms of supply and demand: A popular recording artist is on tour. Tickets to see her perform in a large sports arena in St. Louis, Missouri, cost $40. In Providence, Rhode Island, she is performing in a small club, and tickets cost $75. What accounts for the difference in ticket prices?

 Visit econ.myemcp.com/videos for videos that will help students better understand the key concepts found in this section.

Background Information: Equilibrium Price

Economists talk about the *law of one price,* meaning that a particular good will sell for the same price no matter where it is sold (exclusive of transportation costs). To illustrate: If prices for cars are higher in Topeka than in Chicago, automakers will send more cars to Topeka; doing this will flood the market in Topeka and drive down prices there. Once prices settle, they should be the same in both cities. The law of one price does not hold true for goods that cannot be moved. For example, the price of a piece of land in Malibu (on the coast in southern California) is higher than that of a comparable piece of land in Dallas, because it would be impossible to move the Malibu land (with its view, climate, and so on) to Dallas.

Teaching with Visuals

The price of housing is dependent not only on the size and condition of the house but also on the amount of land and location. Products that do not differ in price from location to location are cars, clothing, and household goods. Unlike real estate, these items can be moved from location to location.

Discussion Starter

Ask students where they would live if housing costs were the same all over the world. What are some of the factors that increase the demand for houses in various areas of the world?

Background Information

The price of oil is affected by international trade and economic activity. In 1999, members of the Organization of Petroleum Exporting Countries (OPEC) and non-OPEC oil producing countries were concerned when the price of oil fell to approximately $13 a barrel. They decided that each of their countries would cut back on the supply of oil in the hope that the price would rise. Soon the price of oil was in the range of $15 to $17 a barrel. Motorists in the United States noticed a rise in the price of gasoline at the pump, from around $1.05 a gallon to about $1.30 a gallon. For this tactic to be successful, the members of OPEC must live up to their cut-back agreements. When they do, the oil supply falls and prices rise.

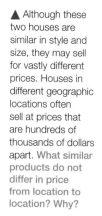

▲ Although these two houses are similar in style and size, they may sell for vastly different prices. Houses in different geographic locations often sell at prices that are hundreds of thousands of dollars apart. What similar products do not differ in price from location to location? Why?

Given the price difference, the suppliers of candy bars will prefer to sell more of their product in Toledo than in Miami, so the supply of candy bars will increase in Toledo and decrease in Miami. Then what will happen? The price of a candy bar will decrease (say, from $2 to $1.50) in Toledo and increase (say, from $1 to $1.50) in Miami. Only when the prices of candy bars are the same in Toledo and Miami will suppliers no longer have an incentive to rearrange the supply in the two cities. The same type of activity would affect the price of bread in the two cities. When suppliers can shift supply from one location to another, price will tend to be uniform for products.

Now consider houses in different cities. House prices are much higher in San Francisco than in Louisville, because the difference between demand and supply (more demand, less supply) in San Francisco is greater than it is in Louisville. If houses were candy bars or loaves of bread, suppliers would shift their supplies from Louisville to San Francisco. However, houses are built on land, and the price of the land is part of the price of a house. Naturally, suppliers cannot pick up an acre of land in Louisville and move it to San Francisco.

So, what have we learned? When the supply of a good cannot be moved in response to a difference in price between cities, then the prices for this good are likely to remain different in these cities.

Supply and Demand at the Movies

Have you noticed that the prices for movie tickets can vary? A movie on Friday night may cost $11, but to see the same movie at 11:00 a.m. on Tuesday, you may have to pay only $6.50. The difference depends on supply and demand. The supply of seats in the theater is the same Friday night as Tuesday morning. The higher demand makes for a higher price.

Supply and Demand on a Freeway

Supply and demand are easy to see at a movie theater or grocery store. But they also appear in places we might not think to look, such as a freeway. Suppose the supply of freeway space consists of a certain number of lanes and miles, and the demand is equal to the number of people who want to use that space.

The demand to drive on a freeway is not always the same, of course. The demand is higher at 8 a.m. on Monday, when people are driving to work, than at 11 p.m. (See Exhibit 6-7[a].) The supply curve, S_1, represents the supply of freeway space (say, four lanes for 150 miles). The demand curve D (11 p.m.) represents the demand for freeway space at 11 p.m. on Monday, and the demand curve D (8 a.m.) represents the demand for freeway space at 8 a.m. on Monday. You will notice that the demand at 8 a.m. is greater than the demand at 11 p.m.

What do most people have to pay to drive on the freeway? For most freeways in the United States, the price is zero; most freeways do not have tolls.[1] In Exhibit 6-7(a), you will notice that zero price is the equilibrium price at 11 p.m. on Monday. The demand curve for freeway space and the supply curve for freeway space intersect at zero price at 11 p.m. on Monday. In other words, at this time neither a shortage nor a surplus of freeway space exists. People are using the freeway, and traffic is moving freely without congestion.

Now look at the situation at 8 a.m. At zero price—no toll—the quantity demanded of freeway space is greater than the quantity supplied, resulting in a shortage of freeway space. In everyday language, the freeway is congested. If you have ever been in a major traffic jam, you can probably understand that a congested freeway means a shortage of freeway space.

[1] People do pay taxes to build freeways, but this fact is not relevant here. People are not paying a price to drive on freeways, at least not nontoll freeways.

Ask students the following questions: How many of you have stood in line at a movie theater waiting to buy tickets? Why didn't you leave and return at a time there was less demand? In other words, what intangibles made viewing the movie more attractive at that particular time than at other less busy times?

Discussion Starter

Ask students the following questions: How many of you have stood in line at a movie theater waiting to buy tickets? Why didn't you leave and return at a time there was less demand? In other words, what intangibles made viewing the movie more attractive at that particular time than at other less busy times?

Economics Around the Clock

After students have read about various situations in Section 2, you may want to refer them to the 8:47 a.m. scenario in Economics Around the Clock (page 143) and discuss their answers to the question posed there.

Traffic during rush hour is caused by high demand (more people on the road) for a limited supply of space on the road.

EXHIBIT 6-7 **Supply and Demand on a Freeway**

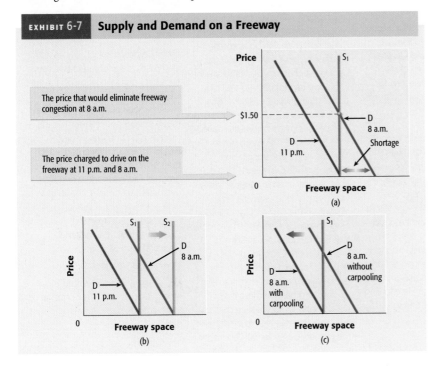

The price that would eliminate freeway congestion at 8 a.m.

The price charged to drive on the freeway at 11 p.m. and 8 a.m.

◄ Freeway congestion can be solved by (a) charging a toll, (b) increasing supply, or (c) reducing demand.

Internet Research

Direct students to go to the website for Ticketmaster and find three events they would like to attend. They should choose a mix of music, sporting, and other events. Have students record the prices for these events, and ask them to discuss why they think the prices for these three events differ (if they do) and the reasons why tickets are selling for these prices. What factors might change the pricing of these tickets in the future?

Ask students the following questions: Have you ever driven on a toll road? If so, why did you choose the toll road over a road you could have driven on for free? Point out that the purpose of toll roads is to lessen traffic and save travel time, as well as to raise revenue for transportation improvements.

Prediction Activity

Present students with the following scenario: Suppose every freeway or highway in your state is turned into a toll road. Furthermore, suppose the toll is mistakenly set at $2 above equilibrium price. What will happen as a result?

The answer is that relatively few people will drive on the freeways and highways. Instead, they will drive on free surface streets. There will be a surplus of space on freeways, but there may be a shortage of space (congestion) on surface streets.

Economics *in the* Real World

Have students read this feature, and then ask them to consider how supply and demand affects them at the grocery store. Do they hear their parents comment on the price of groceries, or do their parents buy certain items only at certain times?

ANSWERS TO THINK ABOUT IT Answers will vary. The invention of supply and demand would have been comparable in importance to inventions such as the wheel and fire. However, the invention (or ability to manage) fire is more fundamental to human existence at a more basic and primitive level.

What is the solution to freeway congestion? Two common solutions are building more freeways and having people carpool. When people say that more freeways should be built, they want to push the supply curve (of freeway space) to the right, as shown in Exhibit 6-7(b). If the supply of freeway space shifts from S_1 to S_2, then the freeway space is able to meet the quantity demanded at zero price at 8 a.m. The problem of freeway congestion is solved.

If more people carpool, then for all practical purposes, the demand for freeway space will fall, as shown in Exhibit 6-7(c). That is, if people carpool to such an extent that the demand for driving on the freeway drops by as much as shown in the exhibit, then freeway space is able to meet the quantity demanded at zero price at 8 a.m. Once again, the shortage of freeway space is eliminated.

Of course, as is probably evident now, freeway congestion can be eliminated a third way—and it has nothing to do with building more freeways or carpooling. Freeway congestion can be eliminated by charging tolls. The tolls bring the freeway market into equilibrium. As shown in Exhibit 6-7(a), charging a toll of $1.50 would eliminate freeway congestion at 8 a.m.

Economics *in the* Real World

Who Feeds Cleveland?

Rarely does anyone ask who feeds Cleveland or who feeds the people in any other city in the world, for that matter. Most of us take it for granted that we somehow get fed. We go to the grocery store, we select certain items off the shelves, we pay for those items, and then we go home and eat the food. What more do we need to think about?

To understand just how much is involved, suppose you have the job of feeding Cleveland. You need to tell farmers how much corn, wheat, and soybeans to grow. You need to decide what prices to charge for Cheerios and ketchup and milk. (How do you figure out these prices?) You need to send so many boxes of orange juice to various grocery stores. (Might you send too much orange juice to one grocery store and not enough to another?)

To get the right amount of food to your local grocery store, literally hundreds of decisions have to be made along the way. Yet no giant computer decides how much corn and wheat will be grown and how much orange juice will be sent to the grocery store at the corner of 13th Street and Main. No government bureaucracy in Washington, D.C., decides such things. As far as we know, we cannot point to a single person in the world and say, "She feeds Cleveland."

Well, if no one feeds Cleveland, then how does Cleveland get fed? The answer is that supply and demand feeds Cleveland. That's right, supply and demand, or what we have come to know as "the market." If the demand for Cheerios rises, the price rises, which prompts the manufacturer of Cheerios to produce more Cheerios. If the demand for corn rises, the price rises, which prompts corn farmers to plant and harvest more corn. If the demand for fat-free ice cream falls, then fat-free ice cream stays in the grocery cases longer, and soon the price drops, which signals to ice cream manufacturers that they shouldn't produce as much fat-free ice cream.

A famous economist once said that if supply and demand or the market didn't naturally exist, it would have to be invented—and then it would be hailed as the greatest invention the world had ever seen. Of course, the market was not invented; it just is.

Who feeds Cleveland, Tulsa, Biloxi, Nashville, Miami, and Denver? And who feeds you?

THINK ABOUT IT If the market had been invented, how would it compare in importance to inventions such as the wheel and fire?

Differentiating Instruction

Kinesthetic and Visual Learners

Students will probably be unaccustomed to thinking of freeway space as a good. Help them visualize this concept by creating a freeway and using toy cars. Use a large plank (perhaps 3 by 5 feet) and draw two freeways on it: one marked as a toll road, the other as free. Put as many of the toy cars on the "free" freeway as possible. Leave the toll road empty. How many drivers are willing to spend money to drive without bumper-to-bumper traffic? How much are they willing to spend? Start at 25 cents per 10 miles and raise the price to see how the demand for traffic-free driving decreases as the price for using the toll road increases.

Supply and Demand on the Gridiron

Suppose you want to try out for a high school sport, such as football, volleyball, or golf. How competitive do you have to be to get on the team? It depends on how many positions are open on the team you want to try out for, as well as how many people are going to try out for those positions. How competitive you must be is a matter of the supply of positions and the demand for them.

Suppose you want to try out for tight end on the high school football team. The coach has decided he will have three tight ends on the team. In economic terms, we can say that the quantity supplied of tight end positions is three. Suppose that 30 people want to try out for the position of tight end. The quantity demanded of tight end positions is 30. Because the quantity demanded is greater than the quantity supplied, a shortage of tight end positions results.

When a shortage of anything occurs in a competitive market, the price of that thing rises. Of course, the football coach is not going to accept money from the students who want to try out for the team. What he will do is raise the "price" of being a tight end in a different way. People will have to "pay" to be a tight end with hard work and skill. The players who pay more—the ones who demonstrate more skill and work harder—will be the ones to make the team as tight ends.

Would these players have to be as good to get on the team if only five people wanted to be tight ends? Not at all. In that case, the shortage of tight end positions would be smaller, and the "price" of being a tight end would not rise as much to bring supply and demand into equilibrium.

Supply and Demand on the College Campus

As you probably know, you don't need the same grade point average (GPA) or standardized test score (SAT or ACT) to get into every college. One college may require a GPA of 3.0 and an SAT score of 1090, while another college may require a GPA of 3.8 and an SAT score of 1350. Why the differences? Again, the answer is supply and demand. The higher the demand to get into a particular college, the higher that school's entrance requirements.

Take two colleges, college A and college B. Each college will admit 2,000 students to its first-year class next year, and each college charges $5,000 a semester in tuition. The quantity supplied of open spots and the tuition are the same at both colleges, but suppose the demand to go to college A is three times the demand to go to college B. At college B, 4,000 students apply for 2,000 spots, but 12,000 students apply for 2,000 spots at college A. The shortage at college A is greater than the shortage at college B, so the "price" to get into college A will rise by more than it will at college B.

The "price" of getting into college is usually measured in terms of high school academic performance (in other words, GPA and SAT or ACT scores). The greater the demand to get into a college compared with the supply, the higher the GPA and test score required to be selected—or the higher the "price" a student must pay in terms of grades.

EXAMPLE Suppose a university charges tuition of $12,000 a year and requires a 3.0 GPA and an SAT score of 1100 or higher for admission. Currently, 7,000 students apply for admission each year and 2,000 are admitted. Time passes and the number of applicants rises to 10,000. We know that the rise in the number of applicants means that demand to attend the university has increased.

Our study of supply and demand teaches us that if demand rises, tuition will rise too. It might rise to $16,000 a year. Suppose the university chooses not to raise tuition; instead, it maintains tuition at $12,000 a year. Will the standards of admission rise instead? The answer is yes. The university might start requiring a GPA of 3.3 and an SAT score of 1200 or higher. ♦

▲ What factors determine how hard this player has to work and how skilled he has to be to win a position on the team?

Background Information: Supply, Demand, and the Job Market

Many students will have experienced competitive situations in sports, drama, and other extra-curricular activities for which a limited number of positions are available. Tell students that the same situation occurs when they apply for a job. A manager will review applications and résumés from several people who have applied for the same position and then choose the best-qualified individual. The more applicants, the more likely that a very qualified, capable person will be hired. Assign students to research the number of applicants for jobs at your school or in the community, and ask them how their findings affect their plans for finding work.

ANSWERS TO THINK ABOUT IT Movie theaters do not allocate seats in the same way that colleges and universities allocate seats in classrooms. Movie theaters charge higher prices at those times of the day when the demand to see the movie is higher.

Why Is It So Hard to Get into a 10 a.m. College Class?

Suppose you have been accepted at your first-choice college (yay!) and you are ready to register for your first course—Econ 101. You sign in to the online registration site and see that four sections of the course are available: at 8 a.m., 10 a.m., 3 p.m., and 8 p.m. Which section do you want?

If you are like most college students, you want the 10 a.m. class. For some reason, many college students don't like to take classes too early in the day (say, 8 a.m.) or too late in the day (say, 8 p.m.), but they do like to take classes in the late morning.

Now suppose that each of the four sections of Econ 101 is held in the same classroom, which seats 50 students. In other words, the supply of seats for the four sections is the same—always 50 seats. The demand for the different sections is not the same, however. Given that college students really like to take late-morning classes, the demand for the 10 a.m. section of Econ 101 is greater than the demand for the other sections of the course.

Even though the demand for the 10 a.m. section is higher than the demand for the other sections, the supply of seats in each section is the same. This means that the "equilibrium price" for the 10 a.m.

section must be higher than the equilibrium prices for the other sections. If classes were "sold" at equilibrium prices, then the equilibrium price to get into the 10 a.m. class might be $20 for a given day and the equilibrium price to get into the other sections might be less at $15 for the same day.

But of course, equilibrium prices are not used to set tuition rates for particular sections of college courses. Colleges don't charge more to enroll in one section of Econ 101 than to enroll in another. The price or tuition for one section is the same as it is for all the other sections.

If the demand for a particular section is higher than the supply and the price of all the sections is the same, what will happen to the market for the popular section? The market will experience a state of shortage.

Now ask yourself this: if one section of Econ 101 is going to experience a shortage, which section will it likely be? The answer is the 10 a.m. section for three reasons: the demand to enroll in that section is higher than the demand to enroll in any other

section, the supply of seats for all the sections is the same, and colleges don't charge equilibrium prices or tuition for individual sections. If by chance the 3 p.m. section is in equilibrium (with 50 students wanting to enroll in the section and 50 seats available), it follows that the 10 a.m. section can't possibly be in equilibrium, because for that section, demand is higher. (There might be 70 students who want to enroll in the section and only 50 seats available.)

What will happen if there is a shortage of spots for the 10 a.m. section? Since the seats in the classroom are not rationed by price or tuition, they must be rationed by something—perhaps timing (first come, first served), seniority (priority registration for fourth-year students), major (priority registration for students with economics, business, and accounting majors), or some other device.

What does this mean for you? If you decide to go to college, you will find it harder to enroll in some classes than others. And more often than not, it's going to be hard to enroll in classes that meet in the late morning. Knowing that this problem occurs because classes are not sold on an equilibrium basis will not help you find a solution, but it will help you understand what's going on.

THINK ABOUT IT Movie theaters often charge different ticket prices depending on the time of day. Do they allocate seats in the movie theater the same way that colleges and universities allocate seats in classrooms? Explain your answer.

Cooperative Learning

After students have read the "Economics in the Real World" feature, divide them into groups and ask them to brainstorm different examples of supply and demand shifting through the course of a day. Allow time for groups to come up with as many examples as possible and then discuss each example as a class.

Necessary Conditions for a High Income: High Demand, Low Supply

As consumers, we are used to paying prices. We pay a price to buy a computer, a soda, or a shirt. We sometimes receive prices too. As the seller of a good, we receive the price that the buyer pays.

Many people do not sell goods; instead, they sell their labor services. The person who works at a fast-food restaurant after school or the attorney who works at a law firm is selling labor services. The "price" employees receive for what they sell is usually called a *wage*. A wage, over time, can be referred to as a *salary* or *income*. A person who earns a wage of $10 an hour receives a monthly income of $1,600 if he or she works 160 hours a month.

Wages are determined by supply and demand, just like the prices of oranges, apples, and TVs. It follows, then, that for someone to receive a high wage, the demand must be high and the supply low. The higher the demand relative to the supply, the higher the wage will be.

To earn a high wage, then, is to perform a job that's in great demand and that not many other people can do. If few people know how to do it, then the supply will be low. Low supply combined with high demand means you will receive a (relatively) high wage.

Consider the wage of a restaurant server versus a computer scientist. The demand is great for both servers and computer scientists. However, there is a large supply of servers and a not-so-large supply of computer scientists, which means computer scientists earn more than servers.

EXAMPLE In 2017, Clayton Kershaw was a pitcher for the Los Angeles Dodgers. His base salary that year was $33 million. Why was his salary so high? The answer: high demand, low supply. The demand to watch a good pitcher play in a Major League Baseball game is high. The number of people who can throw a baseball the way Clayton Kershaw does is small. High demand and low supply is the winning combination for a high salary. ◆

▲ Whether your future occupation is auto mechanic, teacher, doctor, or anything else, your income will be determined by supply and demand. How do supply and demand impact wages?

Behavioral and Experimental Economics

Both behavioral and experimental economics are relatively new fields in economics. *Behavioral economics* studies the role that social, cognitive, and emotional factors have on economic decision making. *Experimental economics* applies experimental methods to study economic decision-making. Consider the following experiments.

Experiment 1: The Ultimatum Game

The ultimatum game consists of two people, A and B. Person A is given $100 and told to split the money between Person B and himself any way he chooses. For example, Person A can keep $99 for himself and give $1 to B, or keep $60 for himself and give $40 to B, and so on. *However*, once A proposes the split, B gets to decide whether to accept the split or not. If B accepts the proposed split, then both A and B receive the amount of money identified by the split. If B rejects the split, then neither A nor B receive any money.

Suppose that you are Person B and Person A proposes to give you $1 and to keep $99. Do you accept the offer or reject it?

The *rational-actor model* in economics, which assumes that people are rational and would choose to receive $1 versus receiving nothing, would predict that B would accept the proposed split. Instead, however, most people in the position of B reject the $99 to $1 split. In fact, most people reject the split until it gets to $80 to $20, and then only some people accept it. Most people accept a $60 to $40 split. Why might this be?

Behavioral economics suggests that people turn down lopsided offers because they view the split as unfair or that Person A is taking advantage of them. They may even feel that they are punishing Person A

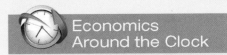
Economics Around the Clock

After reading and discussing "Necessary Conditions for a High Income: High Demand, Low Supply" refer students to the 2:17 p.m. scenario in Economics Around the Clock (page 143) and discuss their answers to its question.

Students should understand that paying baseball players high salaries is a matter of supply and demand. The demand for major league baseball players is high, and the supply is low because few people have the skills required. High demand and low supply are the recipe for a high salary.

Some student might point out that if Major League Baseball expanded the number of teams, then the demand for players would decrease, supply would increase, and the average salary would decrease.

Teaching with Visuals

The answer to the photo question is that supply and demand determine equilibrium price. In the work world, equilibrium price is equal to salary.

 Application Activity

After reading and discussing Section 2, you may want to assign the Section Activity in the *Applying the Principles Workbook,* pages 73–77.

Background Information: Radio Host Incomes

The necessary conditions for high income—high demand, low supply—apply to the career of radio host. The salary range for radio hosts is wide. Hosts in small markets generally earn very little, whereas those in large markets might earn millions of dollars.

Many more people want to work in radio than there are positions available. Those who do get

jobs usually have a college degree in speech, communications, journalism, business, or public relations or a degree from a broadcasting school. They also have a good, clear, likable voice; creativity; and the ability to be spontaneous on the air. Many begin as assistants or interns at small stations, gaining the experience they will need as a host.

Discussion Starter

In the ultimatum game experiment, many people reject a lopsided split (such as $99 to $1). We conclude that they are willing to punish themselves (by rejecting $1) to punish others, if they believe they have been cheated, treated unfairly, or been taken advantage of. Do you think they are more likely to behave this way if they think they can influence the other person's behavior in the future (perhaps into making a more nearly even split)?

by rejecting the split. This behavior (and the behavior shown in many other experiments) indicates that people are not always rational.

Experiment 2: The Disease Problem

A group of people are told to respond to a hypothetical disease that can kill up to 600 people. Everyone is asked to consider and select a way to combat the disease based on a set of options. The first two options, A and B, are identified in terms of the *number of lives saved*.

> Option A (the sure thing option): 200 people will be saved.

> Option B (the gamble option): One-third probability that 600 people will be saved and a two-thirds probability that no one will be saved.

Now in the experiment, 72 percent of the people chose option A and 28 percent of the people chose option B. In other words, when the options are worded in terms of "number of lives saved" most people choose the sure thing option over the gamble (certain probabilities) option.

Notice, however, that the number of people expected to be saved is the same in either option. In option A, we know that 200 people will be saved. This is the same number of people that will be saved in option B since one-third of 600 people is 200 people.

The experiment is then conducted again, but this time instead of wording the options in terms of number of lives *saved*, it is worded in terms of number of lives *lost* or the "number of people who will die".

> Option C (the sure thing option): 400 lives will be lost (400 people will die).

> Option D (the gamble option): One-third probability that nobody will die and two-thirds probability that 600 people will die.

Again notice that the options are really the same because in both options the expected number of people who will die is 400. In option C, 400 people will die, and in option D there is a two-thirds probability that 600 people will die, which is 400 people. (Also, keep in mind, that in all our options, A through D, 200 people end up saved (or not dying) and 400 people are not saved (or will die)).

When the options are worded in terms of lives lost 22 percent of the people choose option C, the sure thing option, and 78 percent choose option D, the gamble option.

In economics, the term *framing* refers to how a problem is presented. Notice that options A and B were framed differently than options C and D. Options A and B were framed in terms of lives saved; options C and D were framed in terms of lives lost. What the experiment shows is that how options are framed will influence how people choose. Most people choose the sure thing option when the options are worded in terms of lives saved, but when the options are worded in terms of lives lost, most people choose to go with the gamble option.

The persons who conducted this experiment, Daniel Kahneman and Amos Tversky, have stated that "rational choice [rationality] requires that preferences between options should not reverse with changes of frame." But, of course, the experiment points out that peoples' choices did reverse with a change of frame. People decide differently based on how a situation is framed.

Experiment 3: Coffee Mugs

This experiment starts with 40 people divided into two equal size groups (A and B). Each person in group A is given a new coffee mug. No one in group B is given a coffee mug. Then group A is asked what the lowest price is for which they would be willing to selling their coffee mug. Group B is asked what the highest price is that they would be willing to pay for a coffee mug.

In the experiment, it turns out that the people with the coffee mugs (group A) want a higher price than the people without the coffee mugs (group B) are willing to pay. To illustrate, group A might say they are unwilling to sell at a price lower than $10 per mug while the people without the mugs say they are unwilling to pay more than $8 per mug.

Since the groups were assigned randomly, there is no reason to believe that group A people value coffee mugs more or less than group B people. What the experiments shows, though, is that somehow owning something automatically makes it more valuable.

This pattern of behavior—that people want much more to give up an object than they would be willing to pay for it—is called the *endowment effect*. The endowment effect is often present when buying and selling a house. A person isn't willing to buy a house for even $1 more than $300,000. However, if the same person owns the house, he or she is unwilling to sell it for $1 less than $350,000.

Is the endowment effect consistent with individuals being rational? The answer is no. Rational action dictates that a person's willingness to pay for a good should be equal to that person's willingness to accept compensation in exchange for that good. In other words, if a person is willing to pay $50 for item X, then he or she should be willing to sell the same good for $50. But that, of course, is not what we would infer from the coffee mugs experiment.

Instinct and Choice

Mainstream economics is often described as a science of choice because economists study the choices of buyers, sellers, producers, borrowers, lenders, and so on. We can change "choice" to "rational choice" since so much of mainstream economics assumes that people are rational.

To a degree, behavioral economists have begun to challenge mainstream economics and rational choices by pointing out that the people they observe in their experiments are making some irrational choices; they are choosing in a way that is inconsistent with the rational-actor model in economics. The question then becomes: are people, at times, making irrational choices, or are they simply responding to instinct? For example, if we return to the ultimatum game experiment, and you wouldn't have accepted the lopsided $99 to $1 division of the $100 in experiment 1, were you responding on instinct? If you were, then maybe many of our choices in everyday life (even our economic choices) are based on instinct. Some have argued that if behavioral economics continues to find that people are not always rational, then economics will become more a science of instincts and less a science of choice.

SECTION 2 ASSESSMENT

Reviewing Facts and Concepts

1. Even on the same freeway, the traffic is sometimes congested and other times very light. Explain why.
2. Housing prices are higher in city X than in city Y. Using the concepts of supply and demand, explain why.
3. Determine if a shortage, surplus, or equilibrium exists in each of the following situations:
   a. Fewer students apply for the first-year class at college X than there are spaces available.
   b. People who want to attend a baseball game are told that the tickets sold out the day before.
   c. Houses for sale used to stay on the market six months before selling. Now, they stay on the market only two months.
4. Provide an example of someone who expresses the endowment effect.

Critical Thinking

5. Carmelo says, "A movie theater charges the same price for a popular movie as it does for an unpopular movie. Obviously, the movie theater doesn't charge more when demand for the movie is higher than when it is lower." Shelby counters by saying, "Movie theaters often call the more popular movies 'special engagements' and do not accept any discount tickets for them." Does Shelby's point negate Carmelo's? Explain.
6. If high demand–low supply leads to high wages, then what leads to low wages? Explain.

Applying Economic Concepts

7. This section stated that people will earn high incomes if they can supply labor services that not many other people can supply and for which demand is great. If you go to college, what will happen to your supply position?

Quick Quiz

The following true-and-false quiz will help you assess student understanding of the material covered in this section.

1. If there is a shortage in the market, price will fall to equilibrium price. (False)
2. Housing prices vary because of fixed demand. (False)
3. Toll roads alleviate traffic congestion by reducing demand. (True)
4. Movie tickets cost different prices at different times because the supply changes. (False)
5. The demand to drive on freeways is not always the same. (True)

 ### *Assessment Book*

You will find a quiz for this section in the *Assessment Book,* page 58.

Reteaching Activity

Use the Section Assessment to gauge which students may need reteaching on this section. Write *shortage* and *price* on the board. Explain that a shortage exists when quantity demanded exceeds quantity supplied. Ask students to explain how price helps eliminate shortages.

 ### Guided Reading

For further reteaching of the key concepts in this section, assign the Outlining Activity and the Just the Facts Handout in the *Guided Reading and Study Guide,* pages 86–90.

SECTION 2 ASSESSMENT ANSWERS

Reviewing Facts and Concepts

1. The supply of freeway space is always the same (same number of miles), as is the price to drive on a freeway ($0). The demand is not always the same, though. Traffic congestion is evidence that there is a shortage of freeway space. If there is very little traffic, we might say there is a surplus of freeway space.

2. The reason for the price difference may be that demand for housing is higher in city X than in city Y, that supply is smaller in city X than in city Y, or both.

3. a. surplus; **b.** shortage; **c.** surplus.

4. Answers will vary.

Critical Thinking

5. Yes. By not accepting any discount tickets for special engagements, the theater ensures that the average price of seeing a special-engagement movie is higher than that of other movies.

6. Low demand–high supply leads to low wages. If you produce a good or service for which there is low demand and you are one of many who can produce it, your wages will likely be low.

Applying Economic Concepts

7. A person who goes to college acquires certain skills, information, and knowledge that other people do not have. In effect, it decreases the number of people who can do what you do. As a result, your income will be higher.

Discussion Starter

Ask students if any of them regularly searches the World Wide Web for information about goods and services they are interested in buying. Invite those who do to explain the most successful ways of finding the information they need. Encourage students who do not have much Internet experience to think of a purchase they would like to make and to search the Web for information about it, using the tips provided by their classmates.

Research Activity

After students have read the "New Car Purchases" scenario in the text, have them decide what kinds of cars they would like to purchase. Ask them to look on the Internet for information on those cars. Next, have students research safe cars for teenage drivers and compare that information with their findings on the cars they would like to purchase. Now that they have collected this information, ask students what decision they would make about the purchase of a car.

The Web Can Help You Get More for Less

Information is something people will pay to have. We see it a hundred times a day. A person who wants to sell her house will pay a real estate agent to inform her about buyers who want to buy her house. A person who wants to buy bonds and stocks might pay a financial analyst to inform him of the best stocks and bonds to buy. Just as people buy goods and services every day, they also buy information every day.

The World Wide Web

The introduction of the World Wide Web has made it cheaper and easier to acquire certain information. You just need to know where to look.

New Car Purchases Suppose that Jimmy wants to buy a new Honda Accord. The list price of the car is $24,100, but Jimmy wants to know the invoice price—what the dealer paid for the car. He can go to http://econ.emcp.net/autobytel and find that the invoice price is $21,788. Knowing the invoice price gives Jimmy information that he didn't have before. This information will be useful to him when he is negotiating the price he will pay for the car.

Suppose Jimmy wants to know what cars are especially safe.

▶ If you want to get the best deal possible, you have to do some research.

He can go to http://econ.emcp. net/safe_cars and view lists of the best and worst cars in terms of safety. He will also find lists of recommended cars that have advanced safety features and good crash-test results.

Consumer Price Comparisons

Suppose Katherine wants to buy a TV. Instead of going from store to store to price TVs, she can go to http://econ.emcp.net/television_prices. There, she can click on the "Price Checker" for TVs and in two seconds, she will see a list of stores in her area that sell the TV she is looking at and at which prices.

Suppose Ivan wants to find out where he can buy gas for as little as possible. He can go to http://

econ.emcp.net/gas_prices and key in his city, state, and ZIP code. A list of gasoline stations will appear with gas prices per gallon listed at each station.

Background Checks Suppose Melissa is thinking about having a medical operation. She wants to know something about the surgeon she's talked to about performing the operation. What's his education? Is he a good surgeon? Is he board certified? Have any disciplinary actions been taken against him? All Melissa needs to do is go to http://econ.emcp.net/healthgrades and key in her doctor's name in the search box. There, she can purchase a full report on her surgeon.

Cooperative Learning

Read "College Professor Reviews" with students, and then divide the class into groups of three or four. Tell students to decide what information they want to know about specific colleges. Then have them access the Web to get that information. After 15 minutes of searching, have the groups report their findings to the class.

College Professor Reviews

Suppose it is Oliver's first year at college, and he wants to know what students at his school think about some of the professors whose courses he wants to take. He can go to http://econ.emcp.net/rate_professors and find out. Once at the site, all he has to do is choose the state, the college, and then the professor. Here's what he finds written about one professor: "All we did was watch videos. Don't take this class." And here's what he finds written about another: "Best class I've ever had. Her lectures are clear and she is always there to help you."

Caveat Emptor

When it comes to buying goods and services, it is sometimes good to remember the expression "*caveat emptor*," which means "Let the buyer beware." It means that you, as a buyer, have the responsibility of watching out for yourself. Sellers won't always tell you everything you want to know. For instance, a car salesperson isn't likely to tell you how poorly the car you're looking at did in national crash tests. Likewise, a surgeon isn't likely to tell you that he has two disciplinary actions pending, and a gas station isn't likely to advertise that it has some of the highest gas prices in the county.

Free Credit Reports Many companies advertise that you can get a "free" credit report from them. An ad might read: "Want to know what your credit report says? Come to our website and you'll get a free credit report in minutes."

The fact is, many companies that advertise "free" credit reports don't deliver free credit reports.

Often, once you go to their sites, they try to get you to sign up for subscription-based services sold by credit bureaus.

Your Personal Economics Activity

Practice using the Internet to compare prices online. Select an item that you would like to buy in the near future (such as an article of clothing or electronic device). Research that item online and gather information including the vendor, cost of the item, shipping costs, and so on. Categorize the information using a data or text document and then identify which website has the best deal for the product you want to purchase.

▲ With so much valuable information available on the Web, there are few excuses for making poor buying decisions.

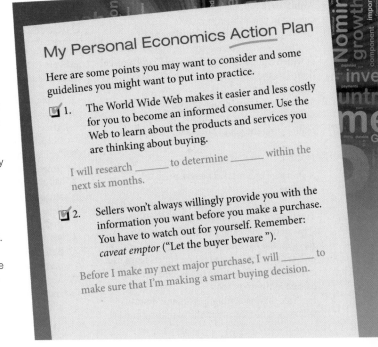

My Personal Economics Action Plan

Here are some points you may want to consider and some guidelines you might want to put into practice.

☑ 1. The World Wide Web makes it easier and less costly for you to become an informed consumer. Use the Web to learn about the products and services you are thinking about buying.

I will research _____ to determine _____ within the next six months.

☑ 2. Sellers won't always willingly provide you with the information you want before you make a purchase. You have to watch out for yourself. Remember: *caveat emptor* ("Let the buyer beware ").

Before I make my next major purchase, I will _____ to make sure that I'm making a smart buying decision.

Research Activity

To help students realize the power of being an informed consumer, ask them to name an item they want to save money on when they buy it. Then have them research that item on the Web. Ask whether the information they found has influenced how they will purchase the item.

My Personal Economics Action Plan Ask students to survey their peers about their use of the Web to research purchases. Students should ask peers which purchases they typically research online and which they don't. Students may find their peers are more likely to get information from the Web on some specific items but not on others. Invite students to report back to the class. Compile the class results into a chart and discuss the overall findings.

Grading Rubric: Research

1 2 3 4 5	Student identified cost and vendor information.
1 2 3 4 5	Information was presented in a data or text document.
1 2 3 4 5	Student selected website based on the collected data.

Assessment Answers

Economics Vocabulary

1. surplus; 2. shortage; 3. equilibrium; 4. equilibrium price; 5. equilibrium quantity; 6. inventory; 7. price floor; 8. price ceiling.

Understanding the Main Ideas

1. If there is a surplus, buyers do not demand the entire quantity produced. To sell the quantity produced, sellers must lower the price until the equilibrium price is reached.

2. A surplus exists at $5 and $6. The equilibrium price is $4, and the equilibrium quantity is 40,000 bushels.

3. Disagree. Markets are sometimes in surplus or shortage. Markets move to equilibrium over time.

4. Answers will vary. Students might say that prices are likely to rise as a result of a shortage.

5. Pens can be moved from city 1, where prices are low, to city 2, where prices are high. This move results in a fall in the supply of pens in city 1 and increase in the supply of pens in city 2. Prices will adjust: the price of pens will rise in city 1 and fall in city 2. Houses and the land they occupy cannot be moved, so the supply doesn't shift from one city to another.

6. Marshall's point was that just as two blades (not one alone) of a pair of scissors are needed to cut something, both supply and demand (not one alone) are needed to determine price.

7. a. equilibrium price and quantity rise; b. equilibrium price and quantity fall; c. equilibrium price falls and equilibrium quantity rises; d. equilibrium price rises and equilibrium quantity falls.

8. The manager checks the shelves. If he puts item X on the shelves at noon and it is sold out by later that day (nothing is left on the shelves), there is a shortage of X. If he puts 25 units of item Y on the shelves at noon and three days later, only 2 units of Y have been purchased, he has some evidence to believe there is a surplus of Y.

Chapter Summary

Section 1

▶ Supply and demand work together to determine price.

▶ A surplus exists when the quantity supplied is greater than the quantity demanded.

▶ A shortage exists when the quantity demanded is greater than the quantity supplied.

▶ A market reaches equilibrium when the quantity of a good that buyers are willing and able to buy is equal to the quantity of the good that sellers are willing and able to produce and offer for sale.

▶ Equilibrium is shown as the intersection of the supply and demand curves.

▶ The cost of storing inventory is part of the reason the price decreases when a surplus occurs.

▶ A shift in the demand curve will cause a change in price.

▶ A shift in the supply curve will also cause a change in price.

▶ Governments sometimes legislate price controls: a price ceiling sets the highest price at which a good can legally be sold, and a price floor sets the lowest price at which a good can legally be sold.

▶ Speculators often reduce the variability in prices from one year to the next by reallocating the supply between years.

Section 2

▶ A shortage in a market causes price to increase.

▶ A surplus in a market causes price to decrease.

▶ The laws of supply and demand affect many areas of our lives: the prices of goods and services, the likelihood of getting into a certain university or making a certain sports team, the amount of traffic on the roads, and the wages earned in different jobs.

▶ In a free market setting, prices and quantity will always move toward the equilibrium level.

Economics Vocabulary

To reinforce your knowledge of the key terms in this chapter, fill in each of the following blanks on a separate piece of paper with the appropriate word or phrase.

1. A(n) _____ exists when the quantity supplied is greater than the quantity demanded.
2. A(n) _____ exists when the quantity demanded is greater than the quantity supplied.
3. A market is in _____ when the quantity demanded equals the quantity supplied.
4. The price that exists when the quantity demanded equals the quantity supplied is the _____.
5. The quantity that exists when the quantity demanded equals the quantity supplied is the _____.
6. If the quantity supplied is greater than the quantity demanded, then a firm's _____ is/are above normal levels.
7. A(n) _____ is a legislated price below which legal sales cannot be made.
8. A(n) _____ is a legislated price above which legal sales cannot be made.

Understanding the Main Ideas

Review the main ideas in this chapter by writing answers to the following questions on a separate sheet of paper.

1. Explain why price falls when a surplus occurs.
2. Look at the prices listed in Exhibit 6-1. At what prices does a surplus occur? What are the equilibrium price and the equilibrium quantity?
3. "All markets are necessarily in equilibrium at all times." Do you agree or disagree? Explain.
4. What tangible event might we see when a shortage occurs in a market?
5. Pens sell for about the same price in every city in the country, but houses do not. Why?
6. Alfred Marshall, the British economist, compared supply and demand to the two blades of a pair of scissors. Explain his thinking.
7. Identify what will happen to the equilibrium price and equilibrium quantity in each of the following:
   a. Demand rises and supply is constant.
   b. Demand falls by more than supply rises.
   c. Supply rises by more than demand rises.
   d. Supply falls and demand is constant.

9. If demand rises by the same amount that supply rises, then price remains constant. This point is illustrated in Exhibit 6-4.

10. High salaries are a result of high demand and low supply. The basketball players supply a certain level of basketball performance that very few people in the world can supply. Combine this low supply with the high demand for watching basketball, and we now understand why professional basketball players are paid high salaries.

11. Suppose we consider the price of corn in year 1 and year 2. There is news that there will be a drought in year 2. Sensing a higher price for corn in year 2 (because of the drought), speculators move some of the current supply of corn in year 1 to year 2 (when they will sell the corn). As a result, the price of corn in year 1 is higher than

8. How does a grocery store manager know which goods are in shortage? In surplus?

9. Both the demand for and supply of a good rise. Under what condition will the price of the good remain constant?

10. Some professional basketball players receive annual incomes of several million dollars. Explain their salaries in terms of supply and demand.

11. Explain how speculators can reduce the variability in the price of a good over time.

Doing the Math

Do the calculations necessary to solve the problem.

1. The price is $10, the quantity demanded is 100 units, and the quantity supplied is 130 units. For each dollar decline in price, quantity demanded rises by 5 units and quantity supplied falls by 5 units. What is the equilibrium price?

Working with Graphs and Tables

1. Identify the exhibit in the chapter that illustrates each of the following:
   a. an increase in demand, supply constant
   b. a decrease in supply, demand constant
2. Graphically represent the following:
   a. a decrease in demand, supply constant
   b. an increase in supply, demand constant
   c. a decrease in demand equal to a decrease in supply
3. Explain what is happening in each part, (a)–(d), of Exhibit 6-8.

Solving Economic Problems

Use your thinking skills and the information you learned in this chapter to solve these problems.

1. Analyze. Suppose that in 2013, the average price of a meal at a restaurant was $20, and 50,000 restaurant meals were bought and sold. In 2014, the average price was $22, and 60,000 meals were bought and sold. Which of the following events explains the price increasing and more meals being bought and sold? Explain.
   a. The supply of restaurant meals increased.
   b. The demand for restaurant meals decreased.
   c. The demand for restaurant meals increased.
2. Identify Cause and Effect. Suppose that the equilibrium price of bread is $2 a loaf. The federal government mandates that no bread can

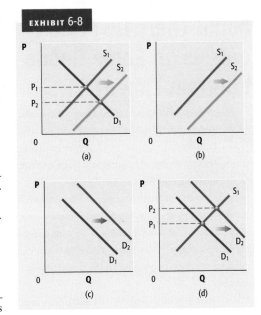

EXHIBIT 6-8

(a)

(b)

(c)

(d)

be sold for more than $1 a loaf. How will the market for bread be different from when bread could be purchased and sold for $2? Explain.

3. Identify Cause and Effect. A person notices two things at nearly the same time: a price ceiling on some good and a shortage of that good. He says, "Shortages always seem to bring about price ceilings." Has he identified cause and effect correctly? Explain.

Project or Presentation

Teaching Supply and Demand. Suppose you have been asked to explain supply and demand to a group of middle school students. Create an electronic presentation, web page, or other presentation that explains how these concepts apply to a good, service, or situation of high interest to the students. Include supply and demand curves and other visuals.

ONLINE
emcp.com

Practice Tests and Study Guide

Go to www.emcschool.net/Economics2e and choose *Economics: New Ways of Thinking*, Chapter 6, if you need more help in preparing for the chapter test.

Working with Graphs and Tables

1. a. Exhibit 6-3(a); **b.** Exhibit 6-3(d).
2 a. See Exhibit 6-3(b). **b.** See Exhibit 6-3(c). **c.** See Exhibit 6-7(b). **3.** (a) An increase in supply lowers the equilibrium price from P_1 to P_2. (b) Supply increases. (c) Demand increases. (d) Demand increases, and equilibrium price rises from P_1 to P_2.

Solving Economic Problems

1. If event a or event b occurred, the price of a restaurant meal and the number of meals purchased and sold would have fallen. Only with event c would the price rise and more meals be purchased and sold.

2. At $2 a loaf, the quantity demanded of bread equals the quantity supplied. But at $1 a loaf, the quantity demanded is greater than the quantity supplied. (You may want to have students graphically show this.) In short, at $1 there will be a shortage of bread, but at $2 there will be neither a shortage nor a surplus. The lesson here is that below-equilibrium prices (such as $1 for bread, in our example) generate shortages. The federal government may not have intended to create a shortage by mandating a $1 price for bread; from its perspective, the shortage may be an unintended effect.

3. No, he has not identified cause and effect correctly. He sees a shortage as the cause of the price ceiling. In other words, he believes that when shortages exist, the government imposes price ceilings. In fact, the cause and effect is the opposite of what he has stated. That is, the government-imposed price ceilings cause shortages. It is the lower-than-equilibrium price (the price ceiling) that causes the quantity demanded of a good to be greater than the quantity supplied, which is the definition of a shortage.

Project or Presentation

Answers will vary.

it would be without the speculators and the price of corn in year 2 is lower than it would be without the speculators. Because the price of corn in year 1 rises and the price of corn in year 2 falls (in relation to what each would be without speculators), the gap between the two prices in the two years is smaller than it would be without the speculators. As a result, there is less variability in corn prices.

Doing the Math

1. $7. At this price, quantity demanded equals quantity supplied, which equals 115 units.

Discussion Starters

1. Ask students to summarize the arguments for and against price ceilings. Students should recognize that price ceilings can help provide equal access to goods for people with less money, including, in this case, disaster victims. However, price ceilings can also create shortages and long lines. Give students a moment to think of goods they use frequently. Which trade-off would they be willing to make to continue buying those particular goods and why?

2. Ask students to imagine a particular natural disaster that they might experience and to list several economic concerns they might face in that event.

3. Ask students if they think their opinions on price controls would change if they lost their way of life to a natural disaster. If so, how would their opinions change and why?

4. What steps might a nation need to take to rebuild its economy after a natural disaster changes demand for a particular good? You might offer a specific example—such as the shortage of natural gas following the flooding of refineries during Hurricane Katrina—and lead the class in a discussion about ways the government could help manage demand for that good.

Debating the Issues

Should There Be Price Controls on Some Goods at Certain Times?

Hurricane Harvey was a category 4 hurricane that hit land (such as Rockport and Houston, Texas) on August 25, 2017. It was estimated that Hurricane Harvey would end up doing billions of dollars' worth of damage along the coast of Texas.

In the aftermath of Hurricane Harvey, Texans saw huge jumps in the prices of many goods and services—such as water, gasoline, and hotel rooms. A case of water was selling for $99, many hotels tripled the daily rates for their rooms, and the price of gasoline at the pump tripled or quadrupled.

Often, when a natural disaster hits and prices begin to rise, people demand that something be done. Some people argue for placing price ceilings on gas, certain food items, and water, but other people argue against price ceilings. Here is what a few people had to say as they discussed the topic about a week after Hurricane Harvey hit.

**Gilberto,
marketing manager of
a fast-food chain**

Gasoline prices have skyrocketed in just the last week. This is getting ridiculous! I used to pay around $4 for a gallon of gas. Now I have to pay $5, $10, or more. For many people, this spike in gas prices is adding $200 to $300 more to the amount of money they have to spend. That is a lot of money. What am I supposed to do? After all, I have to do a lot of driving in my job. What do I do, buy less food for my family? My daughter needs braces badly. Does she go without braces? I think the federal government should impose a price ceiling on gas. Maybe the ceiling should be set at 20 cents or 30 cents more than the price used to be, so the oil companies can make some money. Don't get me wrong. I don't usually favor government controls. But sometimes, I think they are necessary. Why should some people have so much when they are just taking from others?

**Winifred,
economics teacher at
Jefferson High School**

I'm not sure I agree with Gilberto's assumption. He seems to assume that the oil companies—and others who sell gas—can raise the price of gas to anything they want. But if they could do that, why weren't they charging more when the price of gas at the pump was under $3 a gallon? They didn't, I expect, because they couldn't. Supply and demand determine gasoline prices—not the big oil companies. Supply and demand are impersonal forces; they don't have an office anywhere in some building. But people always seem to want to blame someone for their predicament. It is just so easy to blame the oil companies.

Well, suppose the federal government does place a price ceiling on gas when it is rising rapidly. If that price ceiling is below the equilibrium price, then simple economics tells us that we are going to have some problems. At a price below equilibrium price, shortages will arise. And with shortages, long lines. I read about things back in the late 1970s, when the federal government did place a price ceiling on gas at the pump. Sometimes, people had to wait for an hour in line to get gas. I don't want to go back to that.

Cooperative Learning

Divide the class into groups of three or four. Have the groups brainstorm natural disasters that could strike where they live and the effects such disasters might have on certain goods. What goods would likely be in high demand because of the disaster? What trade-offs would the group be willing to make to ensure that people could obtain the goods they want and need? Have the groups share their work with the class.

Patrick,
graduate student in physics

Maybe sometimes a long line is better than a high price. Take what happened after Hurricane Katrina occurred back in 2005 or after any natural disaster. All of a sudden, the price of water rises. What the day before cost $2 to buy now costs $5 or more to buy.

After Katrina hit, many people had to leave their homes. Some went to Houston, Baton Rouge, Atlanta, and other cities. In many of the cities near where cities were devastated, hotel and motel rooms went for higher daily rates. Some of these motel and hotel owners must have said to themselves, "Well, here come all the people leaving New Orleans, so our motel rooms are going to be in high demand, so now is the time to raise the daily rate." It seems to me that these people who raise prices dramatically after a natural disaster are profiting on human misery. They see someone in trouble, they see someone who has no choice but to pay the prices they charge, and they sock it to them.

Maybe there should be a law that after a natural disaster, no one can raise the price of anything for at least a month. I think I would be in favor of such a law. We shouldn't allow some people to benefit because other people are in a miserable situation.

Doug,
salesman

Patrick talks as if price is only there to take money away from some and give to others. Price is a rationing device; that is what all economists teach you. If the demand for water or motel rooms or gasoline is high and there is only so much supply, then something is going to have to ration these goods. What should the motel owner do? Ration by brute force: if you are stronger than someone else, you get the motel room? By appearance: the prettier you are, the more likely you will get a room?

Patrick seems to forget that price has a job to do and if we don't let it do its job—which is rationing—something else is going to do the job. Patrick didn't suggest what should become the rationing device for water, or gas, or motel rooms. He simply points a finger at sellers and scolds them.

Anabelle,
high school student

I think some good points have been made on both sides of the issue. I guess I would argue that if people can help one another during a natural disaster, they should. If that means holding prices down, they ought to. After all, presumably, the sellers of gasoline made money on the day before Hurricane Harvey hit by charging, say, $3.80 per gallon of gas. Why can't they make money after the hurricane if they charge the same rate?

What Do You Think?

1. Whom do you most nearly agree with? Why?
2. What are the strong points of the debate here? The weak points?

Activities for What Do You Think?

1. Conduct a class survey of students' answers to the first question. Chart their opinions to find out the position of the class on price controls on some goods at certain times.
2. Direct students to make lists of the strong points and weak points of the debate. Invite them to share their lists with the class and debate which side of the issue has the most merit.

Closure

Direct each student to write a paragraph describing how his or her opinion on price controls was affected by reading and discussing this Debating the Issues feature. Have students share their paragraphs with the class. Ask students what particular pieces of information influenced their thinking.

Cooperative Learning

Divide the class into groups of three or four. Assign each group a different natural disaster—for example, a hurricane, blizzard, volcanic eruption, superflood, extreme drought, or massive fire. Have each group identify a part of the United States likely to be hit by their assigned disaster. Instruct each group to assume the role of a team of federal officials and to establish guidelines for placing price controls on particular goods at certain times. Have the groups share their guidelines with the class. Discuss similarities and differences in the plans. You might want to outline a general plan that the government could use in deciding price controls with all natural disasters.

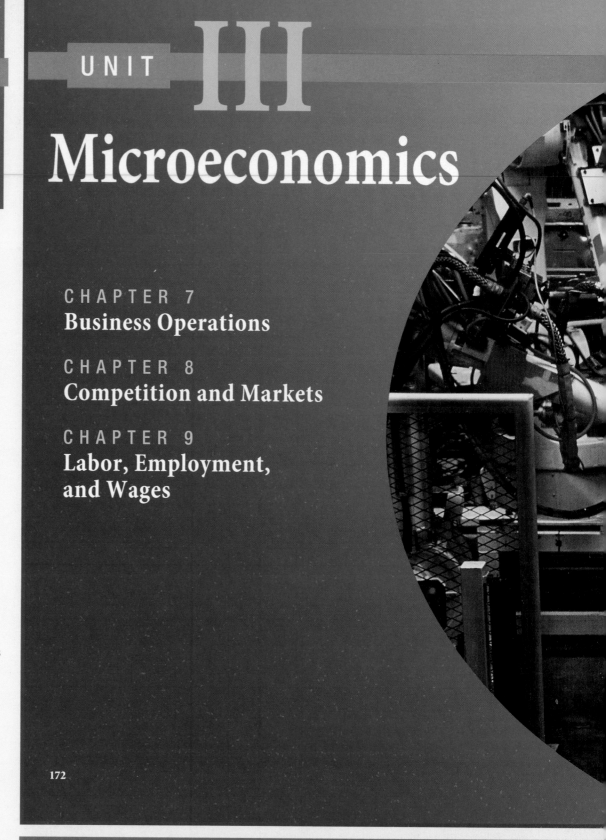

UNIT III
Microeconomics

Listed below are the chapters included in this unit.

Foundations for the Unit

Unit III concentrates on microeconomics. As pointed out in Chapter 1, the tools of microeconomics have been referred to as "microscopes," and the tools of macroeconomics have been referred to as "telescopes." In this unit, students will look through "microscopes" to examine microeconomics—to see a side of the world of business that they may never have seen before. They will begin to see that business decisions are shaped by economic forces that are identifiable and in many cases predictable.

172

Resources for the Unit

Books

Allen, Frederick. *Secret Formula: How Brilliant Marketing and Relentless Sales Made Coca-Cola the Best Known Product in the World*. New York: Harper Business, 1995.

Geiss, Charles R. *Monopolies in America: Empire Builders and Their Enemies from Jay Gould to Bill Gates.* London, England: Oxford University Press, 2000.

Ortega, Robert. *In Sam We Trust: The Untold Story of Sam Walton and Wal-Mart, the World's Most Powerful Retailer*. New York: Times Books, 1999.

Yates, Michael D. *Why Unions Matter*. New York: Monthly Review Press, 1998.

Articles

Ackerman, Elise. "Picking Up the Pace," *U.S. News and World Report,* February 22, 1999.

> **"Productivity is what makes us rich. Specialization is what makes us productive."**
> —Charles Wheelan, economist

173

Introducing the Unit

You might want to introduce Unit III by writing the word *microeconomics* on the board. Ask students to recall how this word was defined in Chapter 1. Ensure students understand that microeconomics is the branch of economics that deals with human behavior and choices as they relate to relatively small units—the individual, the business firm, the single market. Stress that students should find the material in Unit III useful and informative, because each of them, as an individual, represents one of the "relatively small units" studied in microeconomics.

Performance Project

Assign students to work in small groups to learn about successful businesses. Each group should choose a specific company or firm to focus on. For each chapter in this unit, students should gather pertinent information about that company. For Chapter 7, students might explain why the company is structured the way it is. Other topics include strategies that the firm uses to maximize profits, an analysis of the firm's competition, and how the firm manages its employees. Each group should write a summary of what its members have learned, including a graph that shows the company's profits for the last few years. Each group should also predict how the competitive environment of its firm might change in the future and what the firm might do to respond to this challenge.

Allen, Jodie T. "These Are the Good Old Days," *U.S. News and World Report,* January 31, 2000.

Slatalla, Michelle. "Online Shopper: Boxed In: Exploring a Big Box Store Online," *New York Times,* January 27, 2000. Available online at http://www.nytimes.com/2000/01/27/technology/online-shopper-boxed-in-exploring-a-big-box-store-online.html

Multimedia

Branded: The Power of Brand Names. Three-part series. VHS. British Broadcasting Corporation.

Branding: The Marketing Advantage. Seven-part series. VHS. Films for the Humanities and Sciences.

Market Failure: Externalities and *Market Failure: Monopoly.* In *Introductory Economics.* VHS. Films for the Humanities and Sciences.

Producing. VHS and printed teacher's guide. Films for the Humanities and Sciences.

Chapter 7 Planning Guide

SECTION ORGANIZER

	Learning Objectives	Reproducible Worksheets and Handouts	Assessment
 About Business Firms (pages 176–189)	▶ Explain why business firms exist. ▶ Describe a sole proprietorship. ▶ Explain how partnerships and corporations are similar and different.	Section 1 Activity, *Applying the Principles Workbook,* pages 78–81 Outlining Activity, *Guided Reading and Study Guide,* pages 96–98 Just the Facts Handout, *Guided Reading and Study Guide,* pages 99–100	☑ Section Assessment, *Student Text,* page 189 ☑ Quick Quiz, *Annotated Teacher's Edition,* page 188 ☑ Section Quiz, *Assessment Book,* page 67
 Costs (pages 190–193)	▶ Describe fixed and variable costs. ▶ Explain what total costs equal. ▶ Explain how to compute fixed cost, variable cost, average total cost, and marginal cost.	Outlining Activity, *Guided Reading and Study Guide,* page 101 Just the Facts Handout, *Guided Reading and Study Guide,* page 102	☑ Section Assessment, *Student Text,* page 193 ☑ Quick Quiz, *Annotated Teacher's Edition,* page 192 ☑ Section Quiz, *Assessment Book,* page 68
 Revenue and Its Applications (pages 196–203)	▶ Explain what total revenue and marginal revenue are. ▶ Explain why a business firm compares marginal revenue with marginal cost when deciding how many units of a good to produce.	Sections 2 and 3 Activity, *Applying the Principles Workbook,* pages 82–84 Outlining Activity, *Guided Reading and Study Guide,* pages 103–104 Just the Facts Handout, *Guided Reading and Study Guide,* pages 105–106	☑ Section Assessment, *Student Text,* page 203 ☑ Quick Quiz, *Annotated Teacher's Edition,* page 202 ☑ Section Quiz, *Assessment Book,* page 69

Reproducible Chapter Resources and Assessment Materials

- Graphic Organizer Activity, *Guided Reading and Study Guide,* page 107
- Vocabulary Activity, *Guided Reading and Study Guide,* pages 108–109
- Working with Graphs and Charts, *Guided Reading and Study Guide,* pages 110–111
- Practice Test, *Guided Reading and Study Guide,* pages 112–114
- Critical Thinking Activity, *Finding Economics,* pages 19–21
- Chapter Test A, *Assessment Book,* pages 70–72
- Chapter Test B, *Assessment Book,* pages 73–76

Student Text Internet Links

Economics: New Ways of Thinking, Second Edition encourages students to use the Internet to find out more about economics. Given the wealth of current, valid information available on websites, students should be encouraged to use the Internet as a research tool. Doing so will likely increase students' interest in and understanding of economics principles and topics. In addition, doing Internet research can help your students form the habit of accessing and using economics information, as well as help them develop investigative skills they will use throughout their educational and professional careers.

To aid your students in achieving these ends, each chapter of *Economics: New Ways of Thinking, Second Edition* includes the addresses of several websites that provide engaging and relevant information. When students type in any of the addresses provided, they will immediately arrive at the intended site. The addresses have been modified so that EMC Publishing can monitor and maintain the proper links—for example, the website http://www.deposit accounts.com/ has been changed to http://econ.emcp.net/accounts. In the event that the address or content of a site changes or is discontinued, EMC's Internet editors will redirect the link to a site with equivalent information.

Activities in the *Annotated Teacher's Edition* often suggest that students search the Internet for information. For some activities, you might want to find reputable sites beforehand and steer students toward them. For other activities, have students do their own searching and then check out the sites they have found and discuss why they might be reliable or unreliable.

Passport® for Economics

Technology resources are available with the *Economics: New Ways of Thinking, Second Edition* program through Passport®. These include:

eBooks for *Economics: New Ways of Thinking, Second Edition*

- Student textbook eBook
- Interactive Applying the Principles eWorkbook
- Finding Economics eBook
- Guided Reading and Study Guide eBook
- Annotated Teacher's Edition eBook
- Lesson Plans eBook
- Assessment eBook

Passport® for Students

Students can access helpful resources through Passport® for Economics. Resources include:
- Study guides
- Practice tests
- Flash cards in English and in Spanish
- Word games in English and in Spanish
- Tutorials and key-concept videos
- Spanish print and audio summaries

Passport® for Teachers

Keep your course current and relevant by using the teacher resources provided through Passport® for Economics. In addition to all of the resources on the student side of Passport®, the teacher side contains:
- Link to the Annotated Teacher's Edition eBook
- Standards correlations
- Microsoft® PowerPoint® Lectures
- Current Events Lessons
- Additional Economics in the Real World features
- ExamView® Assessment Suite
- PDFs of all print supplements (student and teacher)

Overview

This chapter discusses business firms. It explains why they exist and describes the different types of firms. It also discusses how a business firm decides what number of units of a good to produce and how many employees to hire.

SECTION 1 About Business Firms

Section 1 explains why business firms exist and describes the different kinds of business firms.

SECTION 2 Costs

Section 2 covers the difference between fixed and variable costs. It also explores how fixed costs, variable costs, average total costs, and marginal costs are computed.

SECTION 3 Revenue and Its Applications

Section 3 examines total and marginal revenue. It also covers how cost and revenue together determine quantity produced by a firm.

Business Operations

Why It Matters

To understand the life you are living, it is important to understand the institutions that play a big role in our society. One of those institutions is business. Almost every day, you come into contact with some kind of business—when you stop for lunch at a fast-food restaurant, buy new shoes at the mall, go online to or purchase your favorite musician's new album. If you have a part-time job, you are probably working for a business that is located near where you live. This chapter begins to examine business—the institution we all deal with so often.

The owner of this bakery appears pleased with her efforts to maximize profits, the goal of all business owners.

Teaching Suggestions from the Author

Some students will go on to major in business administration in college. For these students in particular, this chapter is critical because it presents the basics of business decisions. The student who understands these basics will have a keener understanding of why businesses do what they do.

I usually begin this chapter by asking students what they think the business world is like. I ask questions such as these: Why are some businesses big and others small? Why are there few businesses in some industries and many in other industries? How do businesses decide how many units of goods to produce? For example,

Economics Around the Clock

The following events occurred one day in November.

11:09 A.M. Carl and Vernon are retired. They meet each Wednesday morning at a local restaurant to have breakfast and talk. Carl says, "I'm not sure what is happening to this country. It looks to me like American firms are just shipping jobs overseas." Vernon nods in agreement and then says, "I guess it's a lot cheaper to hire people in other countries than it is to hire people here. You know, when you can hire someone in another country for $2 an hour, why in the world would you pay $14 an hour here?" Carl says, "I guess it's just good economics to go where your labor cost is low." "I guess," says Vernon.

- Do U.S. companies always hire workers in countries where the wages are low?

12:44 P.M. Bob is eating his lunch at a small restaurant near his workplace. He gets a full hour for lunch each day. He looks at his watch and then calls the server over to order a small dessert. (Bob is trying to lose weight, but now is not the time.) The server comes over and asks, "So, are you going to have some dessert today?" Bob says, "I'll have a slice of chocolate cake with vanilla ice cream." "Not in a rush to get back to work?" the server asks. "No," says Bob, "I don't have to punch in."

- Would Bob be less likely to order dessert if the hours he worked were recorded by a time clock?

1:07 P.M. Uri has a hot dog stand in Manhattan. Each day, he sells between 300 and 400 hot dogs for $5 each. He just sold a hot dog to one of his regular customers, Sam. As Sam pays for his hot dog and drink, he says, "You know, Uri, I bet you'd sell a lot more hot dogs if you charged $7.50." Uri just looks at Sam and says, "It's not about selling more hot dogs."

- If it's not about selling more hot dogs, then what is it about?

175

Introducing the Chapter

Ask students to list three firms or stores with which they have done business in the last month. Call on students to share their lists of businesses.

Explain that, as students know, there are different types of businesses. In a free enterprise economy, however, there are only three basic forms of business ownership: sole proprietorships, partnerships, and corporations.

In this chapter, students will learn about these three basic forms of business ownership and look at the advantages and disadvantages of each one.

Teaching with Visuals

Business owners face many choices. Where should the business be located, what goods and services are most profitable, and how should it be organized? Today, of course, businesses face an additional question: should they be online, traditional, or a combination of both? If these questions are answered well and the business prospers, everyone will be smiling, as shown in this photo.

how does a car company know to produce, say, 10,000 cars instead of 20,000?

When students try to answer these questions, they begin to realize that owning and operating a business requires specific skills and knowledge. It takes much more than coming up with a good product. It also involves knowing what resources to buy, how many employees to hire, what price to charge, how many units of a good to produce, and so on.

I often tell students that there is a science of business, just as there is a science of physics, chemistry, and biology. This chapter begins to unlock the secrets of the science of business.

Teacher Support

Focus and Motivate

Section Objectives

After completing this section, students will be able to

▸ explain why business firms exist;

▸ describe a sole proprietorship; and

▸ explain how partnerships and corporations are similar and different.

Kickoff Activity

Instruct students to pretend they work at a convenience store, along with three other employees. For employees to get paid, each task on a set list must be completed. If the tasks aren't done, no one gets paid. One day, one employee decides not to do any more work. How does this action affect the other employees?

Activating Prior Knowledge

Discuss students' responses to the Kickoff Activity, and explain that in this section, students will learn how business firms are set up to minimize the kind of shirking of responsibilities shown by the lazy employee.

Teach

Discussion Starter

Ask students the following questions: Do you know anyone who owns a business? What is his or her business? How many employees does she or he have? Is the business a sole proprietorship or a partnership? Invite several local business owners to talk to your class about their businesses and why they formed them as they did.

 Visit econ.myemcp.com/videos for videos that will help students better understand the key concepts found in this section.

About Business Firms

Focus Questions

▸ Why do business firms exist?

▸ What is a sole proprietorship?

▸ What is a partnership?

▸ What is a corporation?

Key Terms

business firm
shirking
sole proprietorship
partnership
corporation
stockholder
asset

limited liability
board of directors
franchise
franchiser
franchisee
asymmetric information

Why Do Business Firms Exist?

A **business firm** is an organization that uses resources to produce goods and services that are sold to consumers, other businesses, or the government. Businesses typically are formed when someone has an idea about how he or she can earn profits by producing and selling a good or service. While many new businesses begin with just one person, most businesses exist because people working together can produce more than the sum of what someone working alone can produce.

"When I started the business, I hardly went home. I became very driven about work and about my career."
—Calvin Klein, fashion designer

Suppose 10 individuals each fish for a living. Each day, each person catches 100 fish. The daily sum of fish caught is therefore 1,000 fish. One day, one individual says to the others, "Instead of fishing alone, why don't we form a team and fish together? We can specialize in doing different things. One person will make the nets, another will navigate the boat, some will cast the nets, and so on. I think that if we work together, we will be able to catch 2,000 fish a day."

business firm
An organization that uses resources to produce goods and services that are sold to consumers, other firms, or the government.

Let's suppose this person is correct. Ten people working together can catch more fish (2,000) than the sum of these 10 people working alone (1,000 fish). This would be reason enough for the people to form a team. Another name for this team is a *business firm*. A business firm of people working together can be more effective than a group of people all working individually.

Why Are Bosses Necessary?

Business firms need bosses and employees: people who give the orders and people who carry out the orders. Why are businesses structured this way? Why doesn't everyone have an equal say in what happens in the firm? To answer this question, let's return to our team of fishers.

Suppose that our 10 fishers agree to form a firm and fish together each day. They also agree to split their catch evenly among the 10 of them. If they catch 2,000 fish a day, for example, each person will get 200 fish to sell. Each fish sells for $1, so each person's income will be $200 a day, double the amount he or she was earning individually.

Cooperative Learning

To own part of a corporation, all one has to do is buy stock in it. Some corporations perform well, and their stock prices and value go up. Other businesses perform poorly, and their stock prices fall. Bring in a copy of the newspaper financial pages that contain the corporations listed on the NASDAQ and the New York Stock Exchange. Divide students into groups of three or four.

Allow each group to choose a corporation. On a weekly basis, invite students to check the stock prices of their corporations. Ask them if they had purchased real stock, would they have made money or would they have lost some of their original investment? You might have students make charts showing the fluctuations in the prices of their stocks.

▶ Few businesses can operate successfully without a boss or bosses. **Can you explain why?**

Shirking

Things go smoothly for a while. Each day, the 10 fishers work together catching fish, and each day, they catch 2,000 fish. Then one day, one of the 10 individuals, Jake, feels lazy. He comes to work late, takes long breaks, and generally doesn't work as hard as he should. Jake is **shirking**, or putting forth less than the agreed-to effort. Because of Jake's shirking, the fish catch falls to 1,800. Divided 10 ways, each person receives 180 fish, or an income of $180, that day.

Notice that only one person shirked, but all 10 people had to pay for his shirking. Everyone's income fell by $20 because Jake shirked. When he shirked, Jake received the full benefits of shirking (longer breaks, less work), but he paid only one-tenth of the costs of shirking. Nine-tenths of those costs were paid by the remaining nine persons in the fishing firm, none of whom shirked.

How would you have responded if you were one of the other nine fishers and Jake continued to shirk? Do you think you might have begun shirking? When a person receives the full benefits of shirking but pays only a fraction of the costs, shirking is likely to increase. No doubt, more people will be shirking than Jake, and this slacking off will further reduce the fish catch. In other words, instead of 1,800 fish a day, the catch will fall to 1,600 as more people shirk, then to 1,400 as even more people shirk, and so on. The increased fish catch (2,000 instead of 1,000), however, was the reason the 10 individuals came together to form a business firm in the first place. Without the added fish, the reason for the firm to exist is gone.

Monitors

How can the 10 fishers stop the shirking and continue to enjoy the benefits of the larger fish catch? One way is to have one of them to be the monitor—the person in the firm who coordinates team production and seeks to reduce shirking (the boss, in other

Thinking Like an Economist

Seeking Answers to Basic Questions

Most of us deal with business firms every day. We buy groceries from business firms, we buy cars from business firms, and we buy clothes, cell phones, and tablets from business firms.

Because we deal with business firms so often, we take them for granted. And usually, when we take something for granted, we don't think about what purpose it serves. This is where the economist steps in and asks the young child's question: "Why? Why do business firms exist?" An adult may want to respond by saying "Just because," but that is not a very helpful answer. By asking and trying to answer this question, we can learn things about business firms that we wouldn't learn otherwise.

Consider money. Since early childhood, we have used money—to buy toys, to buy food, to buy TV sets—but most of us never ask: "Why does money exist?" The economist asks this question. By asking and then answering it, the economist learns much more about money than would otherwise have been learned.

What's the lesson here? Sometimes, it's useful to "play the child" and ask the kinds of questions that small children ask. Sometimes, we learn quite a lot by trying to answer these very basic questions.

Who would think to ask "Why do business firms exist?" An economist. An economist often wants to know why things are the way they are.

words). To be effective, this boss must have the ability to hire and fire people. (Can you see the reason for having a boss now?) If Jake is shirking, the boss must be able to fire him and replace him with someone who will

shirking
The behavior of a worker who is putting forth less than the agreed-to effort.

Reinforcement Activity

Ask the sole proprietor of a business in your community to give a short talk to students. To prepare students for the presentation, tell them about the business and the person coming to visit. Ask each student to develop a list of two or three questions he or she would like the business owner to answer. After the owner has spoken, ask each student to write a one-page paper describing what he or she learned.

Background Information

Many people think that of the three types of business firms—sole proprietorship, partnership, and corporation—corporations are the most numerous. People may think this because they hear and read more about major corporations than the other two types. Point out that sole proprietorships are far more common than corporations, but corporations account for a much larger percentage of total business revenues.

Economics Around the Clock

After reading and discussing "Why Are Bosses Necessary?" (pages 176–178), direct students to the 12:44 p.m. scenario in Economics Around the Clock (page 175).

Answers will vary. Students may say that if Bob's work time isn't monitored by a time clock, it's easier for him to shirk without being caught. If he is caught shirking, he might lose his job.

Teaching with Visuals

Advantages of sole proprietorships: easy to form and dissolve; all decision-making power resides with the sole proprietor; profit is taxed only once. Disadvantages: unlimited liability; limited ability to raise funds for expansion; the business usually ends with the retirement or death of the owner.

---

sole proprietorship
A business that is owned by one individual, who makes all of the business decisions, receives all of the profits or takes all of the losses of the firm, and is legally responsible for the debts of the firm.

▼ Many small retail businesses, like this bicycle shop, are sole proprietorships. What are the advantages and disadvantages of a sole proprietorship compared to other types of business ownership?

---

not shirk. The threat of dismissal is what reduces shirking in a firm.

How can the monitor, or boss, be kept from shirking? One possibility is to give the monitor an incentive not to shirk by making him or her a *residual claimant* of the firm. A residual claimant receives the excess of revenues over costs (profits) as income. If the monitor shirks, then profits are likely to be lower (or even negative); therefore, the monitor will receive less income.

A Student Asks

QUESTION: *You say, "Once a firm is formed, people in the firm will shirk." You say it as though you know it will happen. How can you be so sure?*

ANSWER: *We can't say that everybody will shirk if he or she gets a chance, but most people will likely shirk under the right circumstances. Why? Because people value leisure, and someone who shirks is essentially enjoying some leisure. Also, once some people shirk, others naturally begin to feel that they should shirk too. Otherwise, they will end up doing more than their share and getting paid for less of their share.*

Ask yourself whether you are more likely to shirk in some settings than others. If you are like most people, you are more likely to shirk when the costs of shirking (to you) are low and that you are less likely to shirk when the costs of shirking (to you) are high.

For example, in the classroom environment, some students say they end up doing less work and taking things a little easier when a substitute teacher leads the class. Why? Often, students think that the substitute is here today and gone tomorrow, so they can pretty much do what they want and get away with it. In anticipation of this behavior, the regular teacher will ask the substitute teacher to give a graded quiz to the students. Giving the quiz is supposed to get the students to take the substitute more seriously.

Three Types of Firms

Business firms commonly fall into one of three legal categories: sole proprietorships, partnerships, and corporations. Let's look at the similarities and differences of these three types of ownership.

Sole Proprietorships

A **sole proprietorship** is a business that is owned by one individual, who makes all of the business decisions, receives all of the profits or takes all of the losses of the firm, and is legally responsible for the debts of the firm. Many family farms are sole proprietorships, as are many other businesses, such as barbershops, restaurants, and carpet-cleaning services. About 22.6 million sole proprietorships operate in the United States.

Advantages of Sole Proprietorships Certain advantages come with organizing a business as a sole proprietorship:

1. Sole proprietorships are easy to form and to dissolve. To start a sole proprietorship, you only need to meet certain broadly defined government regulations. Some firms must meet

---

Cross-Curricular Activity

Invite a business teacher to speak to your class about partnerships. Before his or her visit, discuss with students the economic advantages and disadvantages of partnerships, and ask them to list partnerships in your community. The business teacher should discuss the basics of partnerships and partnership law, such as liability and fiduciary relationships. You might ask the business teacher to bring samples of partnership agreements to show your class.

Do You Know the Price of an X-Ray or Blood Test?

Suppose you stop at a gas station to buy gas. Do you know the price of gas per gallon before you buy it? Sure you do: the price is posted on a sign at the gas station. Suppose you go into a store and are looking at shirts. You see one that you would like to buy. Do you know the price of it before you buy it? Sure you do: the price is identified on a tag attached to the shirt. For most of the goods you buy, you know the price of the good before you decide to buy it or not.

Now think of a good or service that you might not know the price of before you buy it. Suppose you go to see the doctor because you are not feeling well. The doctor examines you and then tells you that you need to get a few X-rays taken of your back and that you need to have a few blood tests taken. You get both the X-rays and blood tests taken. Later that day someone asks you how much the X-rays and blood tests cost. Would you know the answer? Were the prices of the X-rays and blood tests posted somewhere for you to see? Did the doctor or X-ray technician inform you that the X-ray would be so many dollars? Did the lab technician tell you the price for the blood test? Probably not.

So, why are some prices posted – such as the price of gas, or the price of a shirt – and other prices not? Well, notice that the prices of

those goods are posted that you buy directly. You buy the gas and the shirt with your money – from your wallet to the seller of the good. But you don't really buy the X-ray or blood test directly with your money. If you have health insurance, the health insurance company pays for it, although there may be a co-payment that you incur. Because a third-party – the insurance company – pays for the X-rays or blood tests, you don't have as strong an incentive to know the price of what it is that you are buying. And because you do not have as strong an incentive to know the price of what it is that

you are buying – and because you are unlikely to do as much comparison shopping when you are not directly paying the price of what is being purchased – it is likely that prices will be higher than if you and hundreds of thousands of others were asking what the X-ray or blood test cost, and you and others were comparison shopping. To a degree, this helps us to understand why the prices of health care procedures and services are as high as they are.

Enter some medical partnerships that are attempting to do things differently. Consider both the Surgery Center of Oklahoma and Clinica Mi Pueblo in southern California. If you go to the website for each, you will see the prices of medical

procedures listed. The day we visited the Clinica Mi Pueblo website, an X-ray was $80, an ultrasound was between $130 and $180, a MRI was $350, a general medical visit was $30 and a glucose blood test was $10. These were much lower prices that one would have to pay for these services at many other places (that do not list their prices). For example, the national average price for an MRI is $2,611 compared with Clinica Mi Pueblo's price of $350. It is interesting to note that Clinica Mi Pueblo does not take insurance, which tells us something about the prices of medical services when people pay directly for them (out of pocket) compared to what they are when they don't. Clinica Mi Pueblo will, however, give patients all the paperwork they need to submit claims to their insurance companies if they have insurance.

On the day we checked at Surgery Center of Oklahoma website, the prices of numerous medical procedures were identified – such as Achilles heel repair for $5,730, cataract surgery for $4,000, and pacemaker placement for $11,400.

Is more transparent pricing of medical services in the future? Much will depend upon how successful medical clinics and organizations are that actually do post their prices. The early signs, though, are positive.

THINK ABOUT IT Besides not knowing the price of an X-Ray or blood test, are there any other goods or services (outside the medical field) of which you do not know the price before you purchase? Are these goods connected with insurance in any way?

Ask students to think about other situations that involve both cooperation and competition.

ANSWERS TO THINK ABOUT IT Answers will vary. Students should be able to back up their opinions with examples.

Discussion Starter

After studying the advantages and disadvantages of sole proprietorships, have students discuss whether they would like to be sole proprietors. Ask what goods or services they would provide.

Reinforcement Activity

Tell students to imagine they are sole proprietors of their own businesses. Instruct each student to write a letter to another person encouraging him or her to begin a business. The student should explain what good or service his or her business offers and describe how he or she runs the business (performing accounting tasks, marketing, and so on). Each student should also explain how he or she manages personnel.

Cooperative Learning

Divide students into groups of four or five. Tell group members to view themselves as partners in a partnership. Each group should decide what type of business it is, such as law, medical, or accounting. Then the group should write five to seven questions that its partnership would need to answer—for example: How are we going to

generate business? How are we going to decide what our salaries are? How are we going to decide what materials we need to buy? Allow each group to present its questions to the class and explain why it considers these questions important to forming a partnership.

Activating Prior Knowledge

Discuss with students the concept of liability. Compare the definition given in the text with definitions written by students. Explain that liability is a legal term that has to do with the responsibility to pay debts. Point out that in this chapter, students will read about liability as it refers to the owners of differently organized businesses.

Critical Thinking

If one person in a partnership incurs business debts, all the other partners are responsible for those debts. Problems in partnerships may not always occur, but partners need to be prepared for them. Ask students what qualities would make someone a good partner.

Reinforcement Activity

Direct students to clip articles from the newspaper that relate to failed sole proprietorships, partnerships, and corporations. Assign a short essay in which each student summarizes what went wrong with the business and offers suggestions for how to fix these problems.

---

health and zoning regulations; for example, if you are starting a restaurant, you must be sure that the restaurant is clean (a health regulation) and that it is located in an area in which restaurants are permitted (a zoning regulation). Also, you need to register the name of the business with local governmental officials. To dissolve a sole proprietorship, you need only to stop doing business.

2. **All decision-making power resides with the sole proprietor.** If you are the owner of a sole proprietorship, you alone can make all of the business decisions. Having no stockholders or partners means that you decide whether to expand your business, buy more supplies, advertise on the radio, and so on. Decisions can be made quickly and easily, since only one person has a say in them—the sole proprietor.

3. **The profit of the firm is taxed only once.** Among the different types of taxes in the United States are sales taxes, property taxes, corporate income taxes, and personal income taxes. If you are the owner of a sole proprietorship, the profit you earn is counted as your income, and only personal income taxes (taxes paid on your income) apply. Proprietorships do not pay corporate income taxes (taxes paid on a corporation's profits). As you will see, neither do partnerships. Only corporations pay corporate income taxes.

Disadvantages of Sole Proprietorships Sole proprietorships have disadvantages too:

1. **The sole proprietor faces unlimited liability.** Liability is a legal term that has to do with the responsibility to pay debts. Saying that sole proprietors have *unlimited liability* means that their personal assets may be used to pay off the debts of the firm. For example, suppose Arzlani opens her own cookie shop in the mall. A year passes, and she is taking a loss on the business. She is also in debt to her suppliers—the person from whom she buys flour, the person

partnership
A business owned by two or more co-owners, called partners, who share profits and are legally responsible for debts.

from whom she rents the shop, and so on. Because Arzlani has unlimited liability, her personal assets (such as her car and her house) may have to be sold to pay off her business debts.

2. **Sole proprietors have limited ability to raise funds for business expansion.** Sole proprietors do not find borrowing funds easy, because lenders are not eager to lend funds to a business firm whose success depends on one person. The sole proprietor's sources of money are often limited to his or her personal funds and the funds of close friends and family members.

3. **Sole proprietorships usually end with the retirement or death of the proprietor; they have a limited life.** When the owner of a sole proprietorship dies, the business "dies" as well. From the point of view of the business community and the firm's employees, this factor is a disadvantage. Employees usually like to work for firms that offer some permanency and the possibility of moving upward.

Partnerships

A **partnership** is a type of business that is owned by two or more co-owners, called *partners*, who share any profits the business earns and are legally responsible for any debts incurred by the firm. You may think of a partnership as a proprietorship with more than one owner. Partnerships include such businesses as medical offices, law offices, and advertising agencies. Approximately 3.1 million partnerships operate in the United States.

Advantages of Partnerships The advantages of partnerships include the following:

1. In a partnership, the benefits of specialization can be realized. If, for example, one partner in an advertising agency is better at public relations and the other is better at artwork, each can work at the task for which he or she is best suited. This way, the ad agency has a better chance of succeeding than if only one person ran it.

Internet Research

Send students to the Internet to learn which large corporations maintain offices or are headquartered in their community. Ask, Do you know people who work for these companies? How significant are these companies to the local economy? How many companies are headquartered in this region? How many corporations have only branches here? Which companies are involved in economic activities that are unique to the region (such as mining)? Which are involved in global activities?

2. The profit of the partnership is the income of the partners, and only personal income taxes apply to it. The owners of a partnership, like the owner of a sole proprietorship, pay only personal income taxes. Corporate income taxes do not apply.

Disadvantages of Partnerships Partnerships also have some disadvantages:

1. There are two types of partners: general partners and limited partners. *General partners* are responsible for the management of the firm. They face unlimited liability, just as sole proprietors do. However, unlimited liability is even more of a disadvantage in a partnership than it is in a sole proprietorship. In a sole proprietorship, the proprietor incurs his or her own debts and is solely responsible for them. In a partnership, one general partner might incur the debts, but all of the general partners are responsible for them. For example, suppose partner Matson incurs a debt by buying an expensive piece of medical equipment without the permission of partners Bradbury and Chan. This is too bad for Bradbury and Chan. They are still legally responsible for the debts incurred by Matson.

   Although a general partner has unlimited liability, a limited partner does not. The liability of a *limited partner* is restricted to the amount he or she has invested in the firm. Limited partners usually do not participate in the management of the firm or enter into contracts on behalf of the firm.

2. Decision making in a partnership can be complicated and frustrating. Suppose that Smithies, a partner in a law firm, wants to move the partnership in one direction to specialize in corporate law. Yankelovich wants to move it in another direction to specialize in family law. Who makes the decision in this tug-of-war? Possibly, no one will make the decision, and things will stay as they are, which may not be a good thing for the growth of the partnership.

▲ Sergey Brin (left) and Larry Page (right) co-founded Google, Inc., in September 1998 in Menlo Park, California. What reasons might they have had for forming a corporation?

Corporations

A **corporation** is a legal entity that (1) can conduct business in its own name in the same way that an individual does and (2) is owned by its stockholders. **Stockholders** are people who buy shares of *stock* in a corporation. A share of stock represents a claim on the assets of the corporation. (An **asset** is anything of value to which the firm has legal claim.) A share of stock gives the purchaser a share of the ownership of the corporation. About 5.8 million corporations operate in the United States and account for about 82 percent of all business receipts.

What does it mean when we say that a corporation is a legal entity that can conduct business in its own name? For purposes of the law, a corporation is a living, breathing entity (like an individual), even though in reality, this is not the case. Let's say that 1,000 people want to form a corporation and call it XYZ Corporation. The law treats XYZ Corporation as if it were a person. We can see what this treatment means through an example. Suppose XYZ Corporation has a debt of $3 million and only $1 million with which to pay the debt. Legally, the remainder of the debt ($2 million) cannot be obtained from the owners (stockholders) of the corporation. It is the corporation that owes the money, not the owners of the corporation. The owners of the corporation have limited liability.

Advantages of Corporations The advantages of corporations include the following:

corporation
A legal entity that can conduct business in its own name in the same way that an individual does.

stockholder
A person who owns shares of stock in a corporation.

asset
Anything of value to which the firm has a legal claim.

Teaching with Visuals

By forming a corporation, Google's founders could avoid personal liability, the corporation could continue even if they left it, and they could more easily raise funds by using the corporate structure.

Reinforcement Activity

Assign each student to pick one major corporation (such as General Motors, Microsoft, or Xerox) and then find out the number of stockholders in that particular corporation, as well as its current stock price. Students can do their research in the library, on the Internet, or by calling the corporation for the information. They might wish to use *Fortune* magazine and check its *Fortune* 500 listing. Have students share their findings in small groups.

Discussion Starter

Growing numbers of individuals own stocks. Ask students if they know people who own stock in a corporation or if they own stock. Ask, Why do people invest in the stock market? What are the advantages and disadvantages of owning stock?

Background Information: Double Taxation

We point out in this section that corporations are subject to double taxation, whereas sole proprietorships and partnerships are not. When considering only the taxation issue, both sole proprietorships and partnerships seem better off than corporations. We have also noted in this chapter that whereas the owners of sole proprietorships and partnerships have unlimited liability, the owners of corporations have limited liability. Some people have suggested that the owners of corporations have paid for the advantage of limited liability through double taxation.

Discussion Starter

Corporations are often involved in local community activities. Direct students to find the names of the top five corporations in their state according to sales revenue. Ask, Are these corporations involved in their communities? In what ways? What motivates corporations to assist communities? What are the benefits and disadvantages of a corporation? Refer students to the views of Milton Friedman and Ralph Nader (pages 186–187) for more information on this topic.

Reinforcement Activity

Suggest to students that one evening as they are watching TV, they study advertising. On the left side of a piece of paper, each student should note the product advertised in each commercial he or she saw during one hour. On the right side of the paper, the student should note the sole proprietorship, partner-ship, or corporation that produces the product. For example, the student might see a commercial for Ford cars. On the left side of the paper, he or she should write "Ford cars" and on the right side, "Ford Motor Corporation." Students may need to conduct research to find out the names of the business firms that make the products they see in commercials. Allow volunteers to share their findings in class.

Teaching with Visuals

Advantages of partnerships: benefits of specialization can be realized; only personal income taxes apply to it. Disadvantages: partners in some types of partnerships face unlimited liability; decision making can be complicated and frustrating.

limited liability
A condition in which an owner of a business firm can lose only the amount he or she has invested (in the firm).

▼ Mark Zuckerberg is the co-founder and chief executive of Facebook, Inc What advantages would Mark Zuckerberg have enjoyed operating his company as a partnership? What would have been the disadvantages? As a corporation, what advantages would he enjoy?

1. The owners of the corporation (the stockholders) are not personally liable for its debts; they have limited liability. To say that the stockholders have **limited liability** means that they cannot be sued for the corporation's failure to pay its debts. They are not personally responsible for these debts. For example, if Turner is a stockholder in Corporation X and the corporation cannot pay off its creditors, Turner does not have to sell her personal assets (her house, car, and so on) to pay those debts. She can lose only her investment and nothing more. For example, if she bought 50 shares of stock in the corporation at a price of $10 each, her investment is $500. She may never see this $500 again, but she will not lose any more.

2. A corporation continues to exist even if one or more owners sell their shares or die. The corporation is a legal entity. Its existence does not depend on the existence of its owners.

3. Corporations are usually able to raise large sums of money by selling stock. Because of limited liability, people are more willing to invest in a corporation than in other business forms. The price of a share of stock may be low, so many more people can afford to invest. Furthermore, they can invest as much or as little as they want—whether 10 shares or 1,000 shares of stock in a corporation. In addition, because corporations can sell bonds and issue stock, they have ways of raising money that do not exist for proprietorships and partnerships.

Disadvantages of Corporations The disadvantages of corporations include the following:

1. Corporations are subject to double taxation. Suppose XYZ Corporation earns $3 million profit this year. This profit is subject to the corporate income tax. If the corporate income tax rate is 25 percent, then $750,000 is paid in taxes and $2.25 million remains for dividends and other uses. (*Dividends* are shares of the corporation's profits distributed to stockholders.)

   Suppose that half of the $2.25 million profit after taxes is distributed to stockholders as dividends. This distribution is considered income for the stockholders and is taxed at personal income tax rates. In short, the $3 million profit was subject to both the corporate income tax and the personal income tax—two taxes, or double taxation. Contrast this situation with the profit earned by a proprietorship, which is subject to only one tax, the personal income tax. Exhibit 7-1 shows after-tax profits per dollar of sales in different types of corporations in the fourth quarter of 2016.

2. A corporation is complicated to set up. Corporations are more difficult to organize than sole proprietorships and partnerships, as we discuss next.

Exhibit 7-2 summarizes the advantages and disadvantages of corporations and compares them with the advantages and disadvantages of proprietorships and partnerships.

Background Information: Corporations

Corporations originated from joint-stock companies. Medieval guilds and monasteries were the earliest forms of corporations. Business corporations were formed in England in the sixteenth century to further the country's mercantilist policies. In the late nineteenth century, industrialization required large sums of capital that could be acquired most easily through the formation of corporations, and the number of new corporations quickly grew. As large corporations emerged, so did monopolies, including Standard Oil and United States Steel. This led, in turn, to the creation of antitrust laws, which were meant to control monopoly power and to preserve and promote competition. See the discussion of antitrust laws in Chapter 8 (pages 220–225) for more information.

EXHIBIT 7-1 — After-Tax Profits per Dollar of Sales, Various Types of Corporations

Type of Corporation	After-tax profits per dollar of sales (in cents) 2016
Manufacturing	8.9
Information	11.3
Wholesale trade	1.6
Nondurable goods	8.3
Durable goods	8.2

Source: U.S. Census Bureau News, March 2017

◄ Which type of corporation had the highest profits per dollar of sales? Which type of corporation had the lowest per dollar of sales?

EXHIBIT 7-2 — Advantages and Disadvantages of Different Types of Business Firms

Type of business firm	Examples	Advantages	Disadvantages
Sole proprietorship	• Local barbershop • Many restaurants • Family farm • Carpet-cleaning service	• Easy to form and dissolve. • All decision-making power resides with the sole proprietor. • Profit is taxed only once.	• Proprietor faces unlimited liability. • Have limited ability to raise funds. • Usually ends with retirement or death of proprietor.
Partnership	• Some medical offices • Some law offices • Some advertising agencies	• Benefits of specialization can be realized. • Profit is taxed only once.	• Partners face unlimited liability. • Decision making can be complex and frustrating.
Corporation	• Hewlett-Packard • Intel • Walt Disney	• Owners (stockholders) have limited liability. • Corporation continues if owners sell their shares of stock or die. • Usually able to raise large sums of money.	• Profit is taxed twice (double taxation). • Corporations are complicated to set up.

◄ A summary of the advantages and disadvantages of the three types of business firms. Would there be more sole proprietorships if proprietors had limited liability instead of unlimited liability? Explain your answer.

The Corporate Structure As a group, the stockholders are the most important people in a corporation. They are its owners, and they elect the members of its board of directors. Voting for the board of directors is usually an annual event, with each stockholder having the right to cast as many votes as he or she has shares of stock. For example, a person with 1 share of stock has 1 vote, whereas a person with 10,000 shares of stock has 10,000 votes.

Remind students that the organization chart shown in Exhibit 7-3 is hierarchical. Stockholders are placed at the top, because they own the company and vote on which directions it will take. Many new companies, especially those involved in e-commerce, have organizational structures that are quite different than the one shown here. Ask students to describe or create organizational structures of nonhierarchical companies. Ask, How might the products or flow of work differ in a nonhierarchical company? What factors might cause a business to organize in a nonhierarchical structure?

Discussion Starter

Ask students whether they know the difference between stocks and bonds. Point out that bonds and stocks are two very different instruments. When an individual buys a bond, he or she is lending money. When an individual buys stock, he or she becomes part owner of a corporation.

The **board of directors** is an important decision-making body in a corporation and determines corporate policies and goals. The board decides what products the corporation will produce and sell, what percentage of the profits of the firm will go to stockholders (as stock dividends), and what percentage will go for modernization and expansion. Also, the board of directors appoints the corporation's top officers, including the president, one or more vice presidents, the secretary, and the treasurer. These officers carry out the day-to-day operations of the corporation. To do so, they often appoint other vice presidents, as well as department heads, who supervise all of the employees in their departments. Exhibit 7-3 shows this structure.

board of directors
An important decision-making body in a corporation. It decides corporate policies and goals, among other things.

Financing Corporate Activity All types of firms—proprietorships, partnerships, and corporations—can raise money by borrowing from banks and other lending institutions. Only corporations, however, have two other means of raising money. They can sell bonds (sometimes referred to as *issuing debt*), and they can issue (or sell) additional shares of stock.

Think of a *bond* as a statement of debt issued by a corporation—an IOU, or written promise to pay back the debt. For example, when AT&T issues a bond, it is promising to pay bondholders a certain amount of money at a certain time. Here is the process at work:

1. Quentin buys a bond issued by AT&T in the year 2018 for $10,000. The $10,000 is now in the possession of AT&T (which might use the money to buy new equipment), and the bond (a piece of paper) is in the possession of Quentin.

2. The bond that Quentin has in his hands has a few things written on it. For one thing, it has a dollar figure written on it, called the *face value* (or *par value*) of the bond. We'll say it is $10,000. The percentage written on the bond is called the *coupon rate*. The coupon rate is the percentage of the face value of a bond that is paid out regularly to the bondholders. For Quentin's bond, we'll say the coupon rate is 8 percent. Finally, the *maturity date* written on the bond is the date it matures, or is paid off by AT&T. We'll say this date is 2028.

3. The bond is a legal promise that AT&T makes to Quentin. The promise has two parts. First, AT&T promises to pay the face value of the bond at the maturity date. Second, it promises to pay the coupon rate times the face value of the bond each year until the maturity date. The coupon rate is 8 percent, and the face value is $10,000; 8 percent of $10,000 is $800, so Quentin receives $800 in the year 2018 and in each year through 2028. (This $800 is called the *annual coupon payment*.) In 2028, Quentin receives not only $800 but also the face value of the bond ($10,000), because 2028 is the maturity date of the bond.

Instead of selling bonds, AT&T could issue stock to raise money. Remember that a share of stock is a claim on the assets of

EXHIBIT 7-3 **Structure of a Typical Corporation**

▲ Stockholders occupy the top position in a corporation. They elect the board of directors, which in turn appoints the corporation's top officers (the president and others). Why do you think stockholders are placed at the top of the corporate structure?

Differentiating Instruction

English Language Learners

Guide students in examining Exhibit 7-3, Structure of a Typical Corporation. Allow student volunteers to suggest what each person listed might do or be responsible for. For example, the department head for research and development researches existing products and new technologies to develop new products for the company. Reviewing this chart with the class should be beneficial for students who are English language learners, as well as auditory learners.

▲ Members of the board of directors are elected to their positions by a vote of the stockholders. What do you think are the major responsibilities of the board of directors?

Teaching with Visuals

Boards of directors determine corporate policies and goals, such as what percentage of the firm's profits will go to stockholders and what percentage will go for modernization and expansion.

Discussion Starter

Ask students if they would expect bonds with high ratings to offer a lower coupon rate than bonds with low ratings. Recall that the corporation that issues a bond promises to pay the coupon rate times the face value of the bond each year until the maturity date.

Analyzing

Remind students to read the information concerning the difference between stocks and bonds carefully and critically. Then ask each student to make a list of the advantages and disadvantages of buying and owning both stocks and bonds.

the corporation that gives the purchaser a share of the ownership of the corporation. Whereas the buyer of a corporate bond is lending funds to the corporation, the buyer of a share of stock is acquiring ownership in the corporation. So, if you buy a bond from a corporation, you are a lender, not an owner. If you buy shares of stock in a corporation, you are an owner, not a lender.

The key difference between bondholders and stockholders is that the corporation is under no legal obligation to pay stockholders. Bond purchasers, in contrast, have lent money to the corporation, so the corporation must pay them back and make extra payments (such as the $800 Quentin received each year) to them for the use of their money. Stockholders do not lend funds to the corporation; instead, they buy a part of it. If the corporation does well, the value of its stock will rise, and stockholders will be able to sell it at a price higher than the price they paid for it. However, if the corporation does not do well, the value of its stock will fall, and stockholders will most likely have to sell it for less than they paid for it.

A Student Asks

QUESTION: *I'd like to go back to the example of Quentin buying the bond. He buys the bond in 2018 and the bond matures in 2028—10 years later. Suppose Quentin wants to get the money out of the bond before the 10 years has passed. Can he do this?*

ANSWER: *Yes, he can sell the bond (to anyone willing to buy it) at any time. He doesn't have to wait the full 10 years before cashing in the bond. Nothing guarantees, though, that Quentin will be able to sell his bond for the price he paid for it or for more. He might have to sell the bond for less than the purchase price. Why? New bonds might have a higher coupon rate than the coupon rate on the bond that Quentin purchased. So, he will have to sell his bond for less to compete with the new bonds that are offering a higher coupon rate.*

Background Information: Corporate Workplaces

Some recently published books and online sources identify what some authors believe to be the best corporations for which to work. Ask each student to list what he or she would find most important in a corporate employer. Some people say corporations have a responsibility to produce a high-quality product, sell it at a reasonable price, help the community, and protect the environment. Others may want high pay and substantial benefits, such as childcare and gym memberships. Tell students to prioritize the items on their lists and then try to find corporations that closely match their priorities. You might have students share results of their research in pairs or small groups.

Teaching with Visuals

Answers will vary. Students might say that franchisees benefit from having national advertising campaigns, a proven and successful business model, and assistance in training personnel.

Cause and Effect

Guide students in a discussion of the success of some national franchises. Certainly, marketing campaigns account for a certain degree of success of these franchises. Ask students to name other reasons for this success (location, convenience, name recognition, standard quality of food). Help students to see that multiple causation better explains the effect (success) than a single cause.

Reinforcement Activity

Tell students to work in pairs to list the advantages and disadvantages of managing a chain store (such as The Gap, Barnes & Noble bookstore, or Ann Taylor) versus owning a franchise. When partners have finished their lists, compile a class list. Direct students who would prefer to manage a retail store to move to one side of the room, and direct students who would prefer to own their own franchise to the other side of the room. Allow a few minutes for discussion within groups, and then ask one representative from each side to explain the group's reasoning to the class.

▲ McDonald's opened its first franchise restaurant in Illinois in 1955. The company continues to be a premier franchiser, with more than 36,000 restaurants in 120 countries. If you were going to open a restaurant, why might you consider becoming part of a franchise operation such as McDonald's?

The Franchise

The franchise is a form of business organization that has become more common in the last 25 years. A **franchise** is a contract by which a firm (usually a corporation) lets a person or group use its name and sell its goods or services. In return, the person or group must make certain payments and meet certain requirements. For example, McDonald's Corporation offers franchises. Individuals can buy the right to use McDonald's name and to sell its products, as long as they meet certain requirements. The corporation, or parent company, is called the **franchiser**; it is the entity that offers the franchise. The person or group that buys the franchise is called the **franchisee**.

Franchises are available in many different types of businesses. A few well-known U.S. franchises are McDonald's, Subway, Dunkin' Donuts, the UPS Store, Sport Clips, Planet Fitness, and Ace Hardware.

How It Works

A franchise agreement works this way: The franchisee pays an initial fee. In addition, the franchisee often pays a royalty (percentage of the profits) to the franchiser for a number of years—say, 12 percent. Usually,

franchise
A contract by which a firm (usually a corporation) lets a person or group use its name and sell its goods in exchange for making certain payments and meeting certain requirements.

franchiser
The entity that offers a franchise.

franchisee
The person or group that buys a franchise.

the franchisee must agree to meet certain quality standards set by the franchiser. In return, the franchisee receives from the franchiser the right to use the parent company name, the right to sell a certain product, assistance with financial matters and training employees and personnel, and national advertising.

Advantages and Disadvantages

Franchises offer several advantages to franchisees. For many franchisees, national advertising is especially important. Consider how many hours of national TV advertising McDonald's buys every year. This advertising benefits franchisees from Maine to California. Furthermore, with a well-established company such as McDonald's or Subway, the franchisee buys a business that has been proved successful. Consider the risk of starting your own restaurant compared with the risk of opening a McDonald's or a Subway. The U.S. Department of Commerce reports that the failure rate is about 12 times higher for independently owned businesses than for franchises.

Of course, franchise business arrangements are not always smooth sailing. Sometimes, the franchiser fails to provide the financial and training support the franchisee expects, and occasionally, the franchisee does not provide the quality of service and product that the franchiser expects.

What Ethical and Social Responsibilities Do Businesses Have?

Do businesses have ethical and social responsibilities, and if so, what are they? Here are some different views.

The Nader View

Ralph Nader, a long-time consumer advocate, thinks that businesses do have ethical and social responsibilities. For example, Nader believes that businesses have the responsibility to provide their customers with full information about the products they sell. In addition, says Nader, ethical companies often encourage their

---

Background Information: The Small Business Administration

In 1997, President Clinton appointed Aida Alvarez to serve as administrator of the U.S. Small Business Administration (SBA). She was the first Hispanic woman to serve in any presidential cabinet. The SBA has begun to tap into the extraordinary potential of the increasingly diverse U.S. business community, expand the competitiveness of small businesses, and help ensure that small businesses play a larger role in the global marketplace. Since 1992, the SBA has backed more than $70 billion in small business loans. It has also tripled the number of loans to minorities and women, granting $15 billion to minority-owned businesses and providing $10 billion in loans to women.

customers to shop around to make sure they are getting exactly what they want.

According to Nader, businesses should also treat their employees well. For example, businesses should take employee grievances seriously and provide a safe place to work. In addition, when possible, businesses should consider quality-of-life issues, such as flextime and parental leave. Nader is also in favor of businesses donating funds to meet social needs in the community.

The Friedman View

According to Milton Friedman, the winner of the 1976 Nobel Prize in economics, "There is one and only one social responsibility of business—to use its resources and engage in activities designed to increase its profits so long as it stays within the rules of the game, which is to say, engages in open and free competition, without deception or fraud." According to Friedman, if a company tries to use government to stifle its competition, that company is not engaging in open and free competition and therefore is acting unethically. If a company lies to the buying public about its product, saying the product provides certain benefits that it actually does not provide, it is acting unethically.

After a business meets these ethical standards, says Friedman, its job is simple: it should earn as much profit as possible by selling the public something it wants to buy. A business should forget about giving money to the Red Cross, the homeless, or the children's wing of a hospital, in Friedman's opinion. Supporting organizations like these is outside its social responsibility.

"Drive thy business or it will drive thee."
—Benjamin Franklin

Asymmetric Information

Asymmetric information exists when one party to a transaction has information that another party does not have. For example, suppose you are planning to buy a used car from Jack. If Jack has some information about the car that he doesn't pass on to

asymmetric information
Exists when one party to a transaction has information that another party does not have.

▲ Actors Jeffrey Dean Morgan, Annabella Sciorra, and Mary Louise Parker, model Helena Christensen, and chef Mario Batali helped promote Starbucks' partnership with (RED). A portion of all sales from (RED) products goes to the Global Fund to fight HIV/AIDS in Africa. Numerous companies have (RED) products, including Apple, Coca-Cola, Bed Bath & Beyond, Bank of America, and more.

After students have read the material in the text about asymmetric information, ask them to provide other examples. Find out whether students believe that the employer described in the text has an ethical responsibility to disclose accurate and complete information to potential employees.

 Application Activity

After reading and discussing Section 1, assign the Section Activity in the *Applying the Principles Workbook*, pages 78–81.

Teaching with Visuals

Additional movement will not increase the number of customers for either firm; thus, there is no incentive to move away from this location.

Assess

Quick Quiz

The following true-or-false quiz will help you assess student understanding of the material covered in this section.

1. Business firms exist whenever people working together can produce more than the sum of what an individual working alone can produce. (True)
2. The person in the firm who shirks his or her duty is called the *monitor*. (False)
3. Under a sole proprietorship, all decision-making power resides with the board of directors. (False)
4. In a partnership, the benefits of specialization can be realized. (True)
5. Corporations are subject to triple taxation. (False)

you (the potential buyer), then asymmetric information exists. The information Jack withholds could affect your decision to buy the car. Maybe the car has been in an accident, and you don't want to buy a car that has been damaged. Unless Jack gives you this piece of information, you might end up buying a car you don't really want to buy.

Asymmetric information can exist in employer–employee situations too. For example, suppose you are being interviewed for a job, and the person interviewing you doesn't mention that a few employees have gotten sick working at the company because of certain pollutants in the air. This is another case of asymmetric information. The person representing the employer has some information about the job that he or she isn't passing along to you. Suppose also you wouldn't take the job if you had this information, but without it, you do.

The general consensus today is that businesses have social and ethical responsibilities to tell their customers and employees everything that is relevant to buying a product or taking a job, respectively.

▼ Competition for customers often drives similar firms toward each other. The process by which this happens is described on this page and the next. Why does movement stop once the two firms are located next to each other?

Where Will Firms Locate?

Economists often want to know what factors firms consider when deciding where to locate. For example, suppose you wanted to go into the farming business. Where will you locate? Obviously, you might want to locate where farmland is plentiful and the climate is conducive to growing what you want to grow (wheat, corn, etc.). Or suppose you want to open a car dealership. Where will you locate?

At First, Far Apart

To better understand how firms make location decisions, let's look at a hypothetical situation, as shown in Exhibit 7-4(a). In the exhibit, the letters A through Z represent customers and their locations (say, along a road). You will notice that Customers A–Z are evenly distributed along this road. The numbers *1* and *2* represent competing firms, which sell the same goods. They are currently located at opposite ends of the road. If a customer wants to buy a good sold by either Firm 1 or 2, the customer will go to the firm located closer to him or her. This means that Customers A–M will buy from Firm 1 and Customers N–Z will buy from Firm 2. If you count the number of customers that each firm sells to, you will find the number is 13.

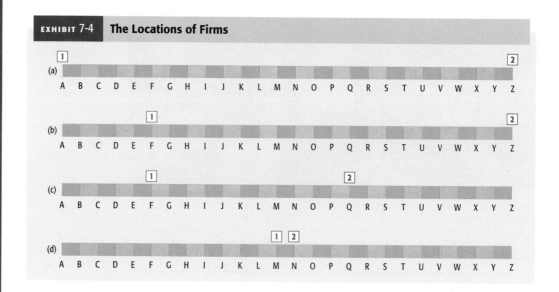

EXHIBIT 7-4 **The Locations of Firms**

Differentiating Instruction

English Language Learners

To help students who are English language learners, use the following resources, which are provided as part of the *Economics: New Ways of Thinking* program:

- a Spanish glossary in the *Student Text*
- Spanish versions of the Chapter Summaries on an audio disc

One Firm Moves, Then the Other

Now suppose that one day, Firm 1 moves to a different location, as shown in part (b). How does moving serve the firm's best interest? The answer is that Firm 1 can take away customers from Firm 2. Now Customers A–O are closer to Firm 1 than Firm 2, so these customers will buy from Firm 1. Customers Q–Z will buy from Firm 2. (P isn't counted; he's the same distance from 1 and 2.) In short, moving puts Firm 1 closer to 15 customers instead of 13 customers, leaving 10 customers for Firm 2.

Do you think Firm 2 will try to counter Firm 1's move? Probably. After all, the firms are competing for customers. Firm 2 moves to a new location, as shown in part (c). Now Customers L–Z go to Firm 2, leaving Customers A–K to go to Firm 1. Firm 1 now has only 11 customers and Firm 2 has 15.

A Pattern Develops

If you look at what has happened in parts (a) through (c) of the exhibit, you will notice a pattern. The two firms were located at opposite ends of the road initially, but the competition for customers made them move closer together. The competition continues. In the end, the two firms will likely be located next to each other, as shown in part (d). At this point, Firm 1 will have Customers A–M (13 customers) and Firm 2 will have Customers N–Z (13 customers)— exactly the number of customers each firm started out with in part (a).

What is our conclusion? Similar firms have an incentive to locate near each other. What drives them to this position? The competition for customers.

In the Real World?

Does our theory hold up in the real world? Think about how often you see gas stations located near each other (perhaps four at an intersection). Also think about how often restaurants are located in a certain part of town, many even right next to each other. If you look at major financial firms, you will notice that many of them are headquartered in New York City. In fact, not only are they in the same city but in the same neighborhood of the same city (near the lower end of Manhattan).

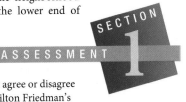
"The only way to know how customers see your business is to look at it through their eyes."
—Daniel R. Scroggin, founder of TGI Friday's

SECTION 1

ASSESSMENT

Defining Terms

1. Define:
   a. business firm
   b. shirking
   c. sole proprietorship
   d. partnership
   e. corporation
   f. stockholder
   g. asset
   h. limited liability
   i. board of directors
   j. franchise
   k. franchiser
   l. franchisee
   m. asymmetric information

Reviewing Facts and Concepts

2. What makes individuals want to form a business firm?
3. The owners of which types of business organizations face unlimited liability?
4. Which type of business organization accounts for the largest share of total business revenue?
5. Why would a company make a boss a residual claimant of the firm?

Critical Thinking

6. Do you think that all franchises charge the same initial fee? Why or why not?

7. Do you agree or disagree with Milton Friedman's position on the ethical and social responsibilities of businesses? Explain.

Applying Economic Concepts

8. If the face value of a bond is $10,000 and the coupon rate is 5 percent, what is the annual payment to the bondholder?
9. Go to http://econ.emcp .net/stories, click "Business and Finance," and choose an article to read. Write two paragraphs explaining the article and how it relates to the concepts discussed in this section.

SECTION 1

ASSESSMENT ANSWERS

Defining Terms

1. a. business firm: an organization that uses resources to produce goods and services that are sold to consumers, other firms, or the government; **b. shirking:** the behavior of a worker who is putting forth less than the agreed-to effort; **c. sole proprietorship:** a business that is owned by one individual, who makes all of the business decisions, receives all of the profits or takes all of the losses of the firm, and is legally responsible for the debts of the firm; **d. partnership:** a business owned by two or more co-owners, called partners, who share profits and are legally responsible for debts; **e. corporation:** a legal entity that can conduct business in its own name in the same way that an individual does; **f. stockholder:** a person who owns shares of stock in a corporation; **g. asset:** anything of value to which the firm has a legal claim; **h. limited liability:** a condition in which an owner of a business firm can lose only the amount he or she has invested (in the firm); **i. board of directors:** an important decision-making body in a corporation; **j. franchise:** a contract by which a firm lets a person or group use its name and sell its goods in exchange for making certain payments and meeting certain requirements; **k. franchiser:** the entity that offers a franchise; **l. franchisee:** the person or group that buys a franchise; **m. asymmetric information:** when one party to a transaction has information that another party does not have.

Reviewing Facts and Concepts

2. Individuals will form a firm if the sum of what they can produce working together is greater than what they can produce working alone.
3. Sole proprietorships and partnerships.
4. Corporations.
5. The boss will receive more money if the company is more profitable; thus, the boss is less likely to shirk.

Critical Thinking

6. No. The initial fee would be determined by supply and demand. The demand for some franchises would be higher than others, so the initial fee for those franchises would be higher.
7. Answers will vary.

Applying Economic Concepts

8. $500 (*calculation:* $10,000 × 0.05 = $500).
9. Answers will vary.

Assessment Book

You will find a quiz for this section in the *Assessment Book,* page 67.

Reteaching Activity

Divide students into groups of three for a debate. Each member of the group should choose a different type of business organization and argue that his or hers is the optimal type.

Guided Reading

For further reteaching of the key concepts in this section, assign the Outlining Activity and the Just the Facts Handout from the *Guided Reading and Study Guide,* pages 96–100.

Teacher Support

Focus and Motivate

Section Objectives

After completing this section, students will be able to
- describe fixed and variable costs;
- explain what total costs equal; and
- explain how to compute fixed cost, variable cost, average total cost, and marginal cost.

Kickoff Activity

Since students know what *costs* are and what *fixed* and *variable* mean, let them guess the meanings of these vocabulary terms: *fixed costs* and *variable costs*.

Activating Prior Knowledge

Allow volunteers to share their definitions of *fixed costs* and *variable costs* with the rest of the class. Ask them to think of examples of fixed and variable costs for various businesses.

Teach

Reinforcement Activity

As a classroom activity, ask each student to identify the annual costs that the school incurs. Students may cite such things as teachers' salaries, heat and electricity, paper, chalk, food, and so on. Once students have compiled individual lists of 10–15 items, ask them to go back to their lists and identify which items are variable costs and which are fixed costs.

 Visit econ.myemcp.com/videos for videos that will help students better understand the key concepts found in this section.

Costs

Focus Questions
- What are fixed costs?
- What are variable costs?
- What do total costs equal?
- How do we compute fixed cost, variable cost, average total cost, and marginal cost?

Key Terms
fixed cost
variable cost
total cost
average total cost
marginal cost

Fixed and Variable Costs

All businesses have costs, but not all costs are the same. For example, suppose Maria Torres owns a business that produces a certain kind of toy. In her business, Torres needs a plant, or factory, in which the toy can be produced. She also needs employees, machines, and certain materials (such as plastic and rubber) to produce the toy, as well as insurance, paper, pens, computers, electricity, and much more to run the business. Consider one of the many things Torres needs: a plant. Currently, she rents a plant from Terry Adams. The rental contract specifies that Torres will pay Adams $2,000 each month for 12 months.

Suppose that after three months, Torres doesn't want to rent the plant anymore. Must she pay rent for the remaining nine months? Given the contract that Torres entered into with Adams, the answer is yes. No matter if Torres produces 1 toy, 1,000 toys, 10,000 toys, or even 0 toys in the plant each month, she still has the legal obligation to pay rent of $2,000, and she must continue to pay this rent for 12 months.

A cost, or expense, that is the same no matter how many units of a good are

fixed cost
A cost, or expense, that is the same no matter how many units of a good are produced.

variable cost
A cost, or expense, that changes with the number of units of a good produced.

produced is called a **fixed cost**. The $2,000 rent is a fixed cost for Torres for a period of 12 months.

EXAMPLE Bobby pays a business tax of $1,000 a year no matter how many boxes he produces and sells. The business tax is a fixed cost. Taryn pays $1,500 in insurance for her small store each year no matter how much she sells. The $1,500 insurance payment is a fixed cost. ◆

Now suppose Torres employs 10 workers and pays each worker $50 a day. Her labor cost per day is $500. One day, she gets a special order for hundreds of toys. To meet the order, she hires 5 additional workers at $50 per day. As a result, her weekly labor cost increases by $250, to a total of $750. Notice that the increase in labor cost goes along with the increase in number of toys produced. A cost, or expense, that changes with the number of units of a good produced is called a **variable cost**.

Internet Research

Instruct students to imagine they are setting up their own businesses in their community. These are the questions they will answer: What type of businesses will you open? What will your fixed costs be? What will your variable costs be? Students should find web pages for local businesses and agencies that will provide the things they will need to open a business, such as office space, office supplies, and telephone service. Then students should answer the following: What will your startup costs be, and approximately how much will your fixed and variable costs be for the first few months? What factors will influence your variable costs?

If we add fixed costs to variable costs, we have **total cost**:

Total cost = Fixed costs + Variable costs

Suppose we want to compute total costs for a month. If fixed costs are $2,000 and variable costs are $750, then total costs are $2,750 for the month.

EXAMPLE Jimmy pays $2,000 rent a month on the factory and $1,800 a month for each of the 20 employees he hired. His fixed costs are $2,000 a month, and his variable costs are $36,000 a month. It follows, then, that his total costs are $38,000 a month. ♦

Average Total Cost

Suppose a teacher gives a test to five students, and the grades are as follows: 80, 90, 100, 60, and 75. The total number of points—the sum of the individual grades—is 405. To find the average grade, we divide the total (405) by the number of students (5). The average grade on the test is 81.

Similarly, to compute the **average total cost** (ATC), or per-unit cost, we simply divide the total cost (TC) by the quantity of output (Q):

$$\text{Average total cost (ATC)} = \frac{TC}{Q}$$

For example, if the total cost is $6,000 and 1,000 units of a good are produced, then the average total cost is $6 ($6,000 ÷ 1,000 = $6).

Marginal Cost: An Important Cost Concept

Marginal cost is an important cost concept in economics. As you will see later, it is one of the two factors a business must know about when deciding how much of a good to produce. For now, though, to illustrate what marginal cost is, suppose Torres currently produces 1,000 units of a toy, and the total cost is $6,000. She then decides to produce an additional unit of the toy; in other words, she produces one more toy. As a result, the total cost rises from $6,000 to $6,008. What is the change in total cost that results from this change in output?

▲ Do these workers at a pineapple cannery likely represent fixed or variable costs?

Well, if the total cost was $6,000 and rose to $6,008, the change in total cost (from $6,000 to $6,008) must be $8. In other words, the total cost has changed by (increased by) $8. The change in total cost that results from producing an additional unit of output is called the **marginal cost**. (Every time you read the word *marginal* in economics, you should think "additional.") In other words, *the marginal cost is the cost of producing an additional unit of a good.* In our example, the marginal cost is $8. When you think about marginal cost, focus on the word *change*. The marginal cost describes a change in one thing (total cost) caused by a change in something else (quantity of output).

In economics, the Greek letter *Delta*, which is a triangle symbol (Δ), means "change in." Thus, when we write

$$\text{Marginal cost (MC)} = \frac{\Delta TC}{\Delta Q}$$

we mean "Marginal cost equals the change in total cost divided by the change in quantity of output." We can place the numbers from our example in this equation. The change in total cost (ΔTC) is $8 ($6,008 − $6,000 = $8). The change in quantity produced (ΔQ) is 1 (1,001 − 1,000 = 1):

$$\text{Marginal cost (MC)} = \frac{\$8}{1} = \$8$$

total cost
The sum of fixed costs plus variable costs.

average total cost
The total cost divided by the quantity of output.

marginal cost
The cost of producing an additional unit of a good; the change in total cost that results from producing an additional unit of output.

Teaching with Visuals

The workers most likely represent variable costs, because they may be paid differently for flexible schedules or because a company may not know how many workers it needs until the work begins.

Discussion Starter

Lead students in brainstorming on the following questions: What are the advantages and disadvantages of a business that has only fixed costs? only variable costs? Could either of these types of business really exist?

Critical Thinking

After students have defined fixed cost, variable cost, and total cost, tell them to find average total cost for the example given on this page (*calculation:* 6,008 ÷ 1,000 = 6.01). Ask students why a business firm would be interested in finding its average total cost. (Students should be aware that after a business finds its average total cost, it knows what costs it incurs on a per-unit basis.)

Background Information

Explain to students that there are costs and benefits to purchasing any property—personal or business. The costs of purchasing a business property (a store, a factory, a building) are obvious. They include the time and money required to actually purchase the property (including the price of the property, the fees for the attorney who is looking over the purchase agreement, and so on). Costs of using business property can include utility bills and taxes. The benefits of the property are largely viewed in terms of the profits that can be earned from owning and operating a business within the confines of the business property.

Critical Thinking

Ask students to brainstorm the costs and benefits of purchasing business property. Encourage the group to identify when they would consider it important for a business to own property.

Differentiating Instruction

Visual Learners

To illustrate fixed and variable costs, average total costs, and marginal costs, hold a pair of shoes in front of your class. Tell students that the fixed cost to produce 1,000 pairs of shoes was $30,000 for rent and machines. The variable cost was $10,000 for payroll and equipment maintenance.

Ask students to find the total cost and the average total cost for a pair of shoes. (*Answers:* Total cost = fixed cost + variable cost = $40,000. Average total cost = $40,000 ÷ quantity = $40.) Tell students that if they want to produce one more pair of shoes, the total cost will increase by $50. Ask, What is the marginal cost of this one pair? (*Answer:* $50.)

Economics *in the* Real World

ANSWER TO THINK ABOUT IT Hotels and airlines commonly offer discount rates and tickets at the last minute. Sometimes the hotels and airlines offer these lower rates and ticket prices themselves, and sometimes they end up selling discounted rooms and trips to a company like Priceline.com, which offers them to the public.

Teaching with Visuals

To reinforce the concepts shown in Exhibit 7-5 (page 193), ask students to work in pairs to write two problems for each of the five types of costs. Have pairs exchange papers and then solve the 10 math problems. (*Example:* If rent for a firm is $1,000 per month, utilities cost $150, and insurance is $75, what are the fixed monthly costs?)

Assess

Quick Quiz

The following true-or-false quiz will help you assess student understanding of the material covered in this section.

1. All businesses have costs, and all costs are the same. (False)
2. Expenses that are the same, no matter how many units of a good are produced, are called *fixed costs*. (True)
3. Expenses that change with the number of units produced are called *total costs*. (False)
4. Average total cost is total cost divided by variable costs. (False)
5. Marginal cost is the cost of producing one additional unit of a good. (True)

Why Are There Last-Minute Deals on Cruises?

Cruise ship companies often advertise discount fares a week before the ship is supposed to set sail, and the discounted fare is sometimes hundreds or even thousands of dollars less than the regular fare. So, instead of paying, say, $7,000 for a Caribbean cruise, you might end up paying only $1,200.

Why do cruise ship companies cut fares so drastically shortly before the departure date? The answer has to do with occupancy rate and marginal cost.

Suppose that a week before the scheduled departure, passengers have booked 98 percent of the available space on the ship. The cruise ship company would prefer to have 100 percent of the space booked, because that occupancy rate would mean greater revenue.

But of course, the real question is what costs the company will incur to generate the additional revenue. In other words, what is the marginal cost of adding another passenger at the last minute?

The fact is, the fuel costs of the cruise ship will be the same with or without the additional passenger, so there is no additional fuel cost. What about the cabin cost? If the additional passenger doesn't go on the cruise, there will be an empty cabin. What is the cost of cleaning one more cabin? It is probably very low.

As it turns out, the marginal cost of adding a passenger is so low that we can, for all practical purposes, say it is zero. Many of the costs associated with the cruise will stay the same regardless of whether another passenger is on board.

Cruise ship company executives will reason this way: The company earns more revenue with an additional passenger than without an additional passenger, and the marginal cost of adding a passenger is zero. The best business move, therefore, is to try to add a passenger, as long as he or she pays the company a positive amount—even as little as $100.

So, why not discount the fare for the cruise to get that additional passenger? It's better to get $1,200 for the cruise than nothing, even if the full price of the fare was $7,000.

THINK ABOUT IT What other businesses and companies offer last-minute deals? Do you think they offer these discounts because the marginal cost of adding a customer is quite low? Explain your answer.

The marginal cost is $8. Exhibit 7-5 reviews the five cost concepts discussed in this section.

EXAMPLE Harry produced 10 chairs for a total cost of $1,000. Harry went on to produce one more chair (the eleventh chair) and his total cost rose to $1,088. The marginal cost of a chair is $88—the cost of producing the additional chair (in this case, the eleventh chair). ♦

EXAMPLE Flight 23 is almost ready to depart for Miami. Currently, 98 of the 100 seats are occupied. Jones walks up to the ticket agent and asks to get on the plane. The ticket agent tells him that the ticket price is $400. Jones says, "That is an outrageous price to pay to get on a plane that is headed to Miami whether I get on it or not! In fact, the marginal cost for me to travel on the plane is probably near zero. The airline doesn't have to pay any more for gas, it doesn't have to pay the pilot any more, it doesn't have to pay the flight attendants any more, and so on. The only thing it has to do is give me a free Coke if I ask for it, and to tell you the truth, I don't mind paying for the Coke myself. Here's $1.50." Is Jones right? Is the marginal cost of his traveling on the airplane close to zero for the airline?

Yes, he's right. Still, the ticket agent isn't going to be too happy about the $1.50.

What is the lesson from this example? The price you pay to travel on an airplane is not necessarily equal to the marginal cost of traveling on the airplane. ♦

EXHIBIT 7-5

Exhibit 7-5 Five Cost Concepts

Type of cost	Description	Example
Fixed cost (FC)	Cost, or expense, that does not change as output changes	A firm's monthly rent is a fixed cost.
Variable cost (VC)	Cost, or expense, that changes as output changes	The amount a firm spends on employees' wages is usually a variable cost.
Total cost (TC)	Fixed costs plus variable costs (FC + VC)	If fixed costs equal $2,000 and variable costs equal $4,000, then total cost equals $6,000.
Average total cost (ATC)	Total cost divided by quantity of output $\left(\dfrac{TC}{Q}\right)$	If total cost equals $6,000 and quantity equals 1,000 units, then average total cost equals $6.
Marginal cost (MC)	Change in total cost divided by change in quantity of output $\left(\dfrac{\triangle TC}{\triangle Q}\right)$	If total cost equals $6,000 when quantity equals 1,000 units and total cost equals $6,008 when quantity equals 1,001 units, then marginal cost equals $8.

Assessment Book
You will find a quiz for this section in the *Assessment Book*, page 68.

Reteaching Activity
Use the Section Assessment to gauge which students may need reteaching on this section. Have those students re-examine Exhibit 7-5. Make sure that each student understands all of the equations and symbols used in the exhibit before you move on to Section 3.

Guided Reading
For further reteaching of the key concepts in this section, assign the Outlining Activity and the Just the Facts Handout from the *Guided Reading and Study Guide*, pages 101–102.

SECTION 2

ASSESSMENT

Defining Terms
1. Define:
   a. fixed cost
   b. variable cost
   c. total cost
   d. average total cost
   e. marginal cost

Reviewing Facts and Concepts
2. Give an example of a fixed cost and a variable cost.
3. A firm produces 125 units of a good. Its variable costs are $400, and its total costs are $700. Answer the following questions:

   a. What are the firm's fixed costs?
   b. What is the average total cost?
   c. If variable costs are $385 when 124 units are produced, then what is the total cost at 124 units?

Critical Thinking
4. This section discussed both average total cost and marginal cost. What is the key difference between these two cost concepts?
5. When are fixed costs equal to total costs?

Applying Economic Concepts
6. An airline has 100 seats to sell on a plane traveling from New York to Los Angeles, and it's charging $450 a ticket. Ninety-seven tickets are sold at this price. Just as the plane is about to take off, a person without a ticket says he is willing to pay $150 to get on the plane. The cost of adding this passenger (to the airline)—that is, the marginal cost—is $100. Is it in the airline's best interest to sell this person a ticket for $150? Explain your answer.

Section 2 Costs **193**

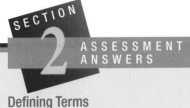

SECTION 2

ASSESSMENT ANSWERS

Defining Terms
1. a. fixed cost: a cost (or expense) that is the same no matter how many units of a good are produced; **b. variable cost:** a cost (or expense) that changes with the number of units produced; **c. total cost:** the sum of fixed costs plus variable costs; **d. average total cost:** the total cost divided by the quantity of output; **e. marginal cost:** the cost of producing an additional unit of a good. Alternatively, it is the change in total cost that results from producing an additional unit of a good.

Reviewing Facts and Concepts
2. Answers will vary. (*Sample answer:* Rent is a fixed cost; wages are a variable cost. There are other examples in the text.)

3. a. $300 (*calculation:* $700 − $400 = $300); **b.** $5.60 (*calculation:* Average total cost = $700 ÷ 125 = $5.60); **c.** $685 (*calculation:* Total cost at 124 units = $300 + $385 = $685).

Critical Thinking
4. With marginal cost, we are considering a change in total cost, given a change in quantity of output. The emphasis is on "change in." With average total cost, we are not concerned with change. Total average cost is the average cost of producing one unit of a good.
5. When variable costs are zero.

Applying Economic Concepts
6. Yes. The airline receives more in additional benefits ($150) than it incurs in additional costs ($100), so it is better off selling the ticket for $150. If the airline sells the seat, it will make $50.

Discussion Starter

Ask students if they know the importance of insurance and ask for volunteers to explain why people buy insurance (such as for a car, home, or personal property). Encourage students to discuss the positive and negative aspects of having insurance.

Internet Research

Divide students into pairs and have them research various insurance companies (for health insurance, car insurance, and otherwise), and to take note of the companies that are available to them online or in their communities.

The Value of Insurance

In Section 2, you learned that a business firm has various costs. One of those costs relates to buying insurance for protection against losses caused by events such as fire or theft. Individuals also purchase insurance. In fact, individuals often buy a variety of different kinds of insurance. Each type of insurance is a means of protection against a certain form of potential loss.

Buying Insurance

When you buy insurance from an insurance company, you enter into a contract with that company. Your part of the contract says that you will make regular payments (called premiums) in exchange for the promise that the company will pay you for a certain kind of loss or damage, should it occur. All of the details of this contract (including the type of insurance, what it covers, and the premium rate) are explicitly stated in the insurance agreement.

Premiums & Deductibles

Insurance premiums are determined based on a variety of different factors (depending on the type of insurance), and they are not the same for everyone. Premiums may be due monthly or twice a year. Suppose you have paid the premiums on your car insurance for a few years, and then an accident occurs whereby you need to collect on the insurance. The total bill to fix the car is $3,000, but the insurance

company will likely not cover this entire amount. The amount the insurance company will pay depends on your deductible, which is the dollar amount you have to pay before the insurance company will cover the rest. For example, if your deductible is $200, you pay $200 and the insurance company pays the remainder, or $2,800, to fix the car. Usually, the higher your premium, the lower your deductible. For example, if your monthly premium is $400, your deductible might be $200, but if your monthly premium is $500, your deductible might be $100.

Types of Insurance

Individuals commonly buy three types of insurance: car, life, and health insurance. Deciding which types to buy and not buy can be a personal choice or be based on a legal requirement.

Some people think insurance is a waste of money if you never collect on it, but everyone buys insurance hoping not to use it. No one buys car insurance hoping to have an accident; no one buys fire insurance hoping that his or her house will catch fire; and no one buys health insurance hoping to get sick. We buy insurance because it helps to give us peace of mind in an uncertain world.

Automobile Insurance

Several types of car insurance coverage are available. Liability

insurance is required by law in many states and is broken into two types. Bodily injury liability insurance pays for losses due to death or injury in a car accident that is the insured driver's fault, and property damage liability insurance covers damage done to another person's car or property.

Medical payments insurance pays for medical expenses resulting from a car accident, no matter who is at fault. Uninsured motorist protection insurance covers you if you get into an accident with an uninsured motorist or are harmed by a hit-and-run driver. Collision insurance pays for the damage to your car if it is in an accident, no matter who is responsible, and comprehensive insurance is a companion to collision insurance that covers everything else, such as if the car is stolen, vandalized, or catches fire.

Health Insurance

Medical costs for major illnesses and injuries are often far beyond what the average family can afford. Because of this, health insurance is a necessity for most people. Individuals can buy health insurance directly from providers, or they may get it at a discount through a group plan with their employer.

If you are currently in high school, you likely have health insurance through your parents' or guardians' health policy. At a later time, you will be responsible

for finding your own coverage. As stated earlier, many employers provide health insurance to their employees at a major discount, so keep this in mind when looking for a job. If you need to purchase your own health insurance, you may want to explore local Health Maintenance Organizations (HMOs), which offer members comprehensive medical care for a low monthly or yearly fee. While HMOs do limit you by requiring members to receive medical care from a selected group of doctors and hospitals, an HMO is often one of the more economical options for health insurance.

Life Insurance

Life insurance guarantees payment of a certain sum to a specified person—the beneficiary—when the policyholder dies or reaches a certain age. People buy this type of insurance to financially protect loved ones in case of an unexpected death. There are two major types of life insurance: term life and whole life insurance.

With term life insurance, you pay premiums to the insurance company, and, in turn, your beneficiaries are paid a certain sum of money if you die during a specific period. When this period ends, your coverage ends, and you receive no payments. When you buy term life insurance, you are buying insurance only for the term of the policy, which makes it considerably cheaper than whole life insurance.

As the name implies, whole life insurance covers a person until his or her death. One important feature of whole life insurance is its cash

value, or the amount of money policyholders would receive if they decided to redeem their policy. The cash value is what makes whole life insurance more expensive than term life insurance.

Your Personal Economics Activity

1. Research online or contact a car insurance company to identify the rates and coverage options available to you. What costs and benefits are associated with this type of insurance? Write a two-

paragraph essay that analyzes the costs and benefits of having health insurance.

2. Summarize your opinion on the value of health insurance for yourself and others.

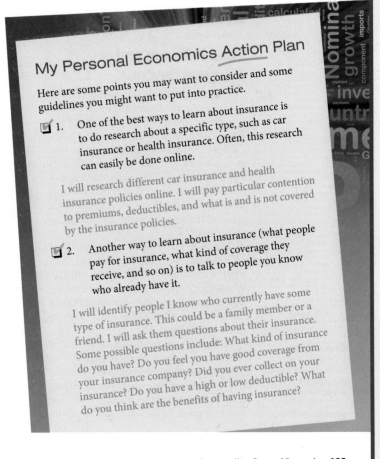

My Personal Economics Action Plan

Here are some points you may want to consider and some guidelines you might want to put into practice.

☑ 1. One of the best ways to learn about insurance is to do research about a specific type, such as car insurance or health insurance. Often, this research can easily be done online.

I will research different car insurance and health insurance policies online. I will pay particular contention to premiums, deductibles, and what is and is not covered by the insurance policies.

☑ 2. Another way to learn about insurance (what people pay for insurance, what kind of coverage they receive, and so on) is to talk to people you know who already have it.

I will identify people I know who currently have some type of insurance. This could be a family member or a friend. I will ask them questions about their insurance. Some possible questions include: What kind of insurance do you have? Do you feel you have good coverage from your insurance company? Did you ever collect on your insurance? Do you have a high or low deductible? What do you think are the benefits of having insurance?

Research Activity

To help students identify the benefit of insurance, encourage students to ask their parents or guardians if they know of anyone who benefited from having insurance and how that person benefited.

My Personal Economics Action Plan Assign the "My Personal Action Plan" and ask students to survey adults about their insurance choices and to research for themselves the different types of insurance available to them.

Grading Rubric: Analysis

1 2 3 4 5 Student identified the costs and benefits of insurance options.

Grading Rubric: Opinion Summary

1 2 3 4 5 Student clearly summarized their opinion on the value of insurance.

Focus and Motivate

Section Objectives

After completing this section, students will be able to

► explain what total revenue and marginal revenue are; and

► explain why a business firm compares marginal revenue with marginal cost when deciding how many units of a good to produce.

Kickoff Activity

Ask each student to write the definition of *revenue*. If students have forgotten, tell them to refer to the glossary. Then, ask them to define *marginal revenue*.

Activating Prior Knowledge

Allow volunteers to share their definitions of *marginal revenue* with the rest of the class. Based on what they learned in the previous section, students should have clear, sound definitions. Tell students that in this section, they will apply the word *marginal* to both costs and revenues.

Teach

Discussion Starter

Just as there are two sides to a market, a buying side and a selling side, there are two sides to a business firm, a cost side and a revenue side. The cost side was covered in the previous section of this chapter. Tell students that the revenue side of the relationship will be discussed in this section.

Visit econ.myemcp.com/videos for videos that will help students better understand the key concepts found in this section.

Revenue and Its Applications

Focus Questions

► What is total revenue?
► What is marginal revenue?
► Why does a business firm compare marginal revenue with marginal cost when deciding how many units of a good to produce?

Key Terms

marginal revenue
law of diminishing marginal returns

Total Revenue and Marginal Revenue

In Chapter 3, total revenue was defined as the price of a good times the quantity sold. For example, if the price of a book is $15 and 100 are sold, then total revenue is $1,500. Consider the following: Harris sells toys for a price of $10 each and currently sells 1,000 toys a year. This means that Harris's total revenue is $10,000. If Harris sells one more toy for $10, what is the change in total revenue that results from the change in output sold?

To answer this question, we first calculate what the total revenue is when Harris sells 1,001 instead of 1,000 toys; it is $10,010. We conclude that the total revenue changes from $10,000 to $10,010 when an additional toy is sold. In other words, the change in total revenue equals $10.

The change in total revenue (TR) that results from selling an additional unit of output is **marginal revenue (MR)**. In other words, marginal revenue is the additional revenue that's earned from selling one more unit of a good. In the example, $10 is the

marginal revenue
The revenue from selling an additional unit of a good; the change in total revenue that results from selling an additional unit of output.

marginal revenue. We can express this relationship like this:

$$\text{Marginal revenue (MR)} = \frac{\Delta TR}{\Delta Q}$$

Marginal revenue equals the change in total revenue divided by the change in the quantity sold.

Firms Have to Answer Questions

Suppose you start a business producing and selling T-shirts. To operate that business successfully, you will have to answer several key questions. For instance, how many T-shirts are you going to produce each month? Will you make 100, 1,000, or 10,000? Also, how will you decide how many T-shirts to produce? Will you simply put a bunch of different numbers in a hat and draw one out? Whatever number you draw, will that be how many T-shirts you produce? Of course not! The question of how much to produce is one that every business firm has to answer.

Cooperative Learning

Divide the class into groups of three or four students. Instruct groups to identify situations in which they have said something is "not worth the effort." Ask what they were talking about. When they say something is not worth the effort, they are saying that the marginal revenue acquired isn't worth the additional energy expended. With-

out even thinking about it, students have been finding marginal revenue for years. Tell groups to pair off and present situations to one another. Their goal is to determine if what is gained (the change in total revenue) is worth the cost (the change in quantity).

▲ What questions might these business executives be trying to answer?

Suppose you decide to produce 1,000 T-shirts a month. Now, you have another question to answer: What price will you charge for each T-shirt? Are you going to charge $10, or $10.50, or $15? How will you decide how much to charge for each T-shirt? The question of what price to charge is a second key question that every business firm has to answer.

How Much Will a Firm Produce?

As the owner of a T-shirt business, what two pieces of information do you need before you can decide how many T-shirts to produce? If you think about it, the answer is fairly simple. You need to know the marginal cost and the marginal revenue for the T-shirts. Suppose you are presented with the following data (which are representative of many real-world businesses):

T-shirts	MR	MC
1st	$10	$4
2nd	10	6
3rd	10	8
4th	10	9.99
5th	10	11

What is the correct number of T-shirts for you to produce? Four. In other words, you should keep producing T-shirts as long as the marginal revenue (revenue of producing the additional T-shirt) is greater than the marginal cost (cost of producing one additional T-shirt). As long as what comes in through the "revenue door" is greater than what leaves through the "cost door," you should keep producing T-shirts. Look at it this way:

$$MR > MC \rightarrow Produce$$
$$MC > MR \rightarrow Do\ not\ produce$$

If you want to produce as long as MR is greater than MC and you don't want to produce if MC is greater than MR, ask yourself when you should stop producing. For example, you've already produced, say, 10,000 hats. Should you produce one more? The answer is yes as long as the marginal revenue is greater than the marginal cost—even if the difference between marginal cost and marginal revenue is one penny (as it was for the fourth T-shirt in the example).

Now, suppose the difference is half a penny. Should you still produce the good? Again, the answer is yes. What about one-fourth of a penny? Yes, produce it.

You can perhaps see where we are going with this discussion. Essentially, economists say that it is beneficial to produce as long as the marginal revenue is greater than the marginal cost, even if the difference is extremely small. For all practical purposes, then, economists recommend that a business firm should continue to produce additional units of its good until the marginal revenue (MR) is equal to the marginal cost (MC).

In the T-shirt example, we didn't find any unit of production at which this occurred, but we did find one in which there was only a penny difference. We stopped producing after the fourth T-shirt because it was as close to MR = MC as we could get.

> *"When you innovate, you've got to be prepared for everyone telling you you're nuts."*
> —Larry Ellison, founder/CEO of Oracle

Teaching with Visuals

Automobile manufacturers know that they need to continue producing cars until marginal revenue is no longer greater than marginal cost. They should maximize profits by finding the production level that gives them the most marginal revenue.

Discussion Starter

Ask students if they think that most companies want to be as large as possible. Some students may say yes, thinking that with greater size come greater revenues and greater profits. Point out that the objective of a company isn't to become as large as possible but to maximize profits. Sometimes, growth can actually diminish a company's profit.

Critical Thinking

Explain that some stores earn more (per store and per square foot) than others. For example, at one time, Abercrombie and Fitch earned an average of $2,766,639 per store and $379 per square foot. Sharper Image earned a similar amount per store ($2,509,051) but a much higher amount per square foot ($627). At the same time, Wal-Mart earned an average of $422 per square foot and $55,924,898 per store, while Krispy Kreme earned $859 per square foot but only $3,952,000 per store.

Ask students to consider why a business might want to track its revenue per square foot. (*Answer:* Many stores rent their property by the square foot. If a store can cut down on the number of square feet it rents, it might be able to decrease its fixed cost of rent. Decreasing that fixed cost could increase profitability.)

▲ All companies want to maximize profits and generate the kinds of results reported in newspapers and business magazines. How do automobile manufacturers know how many cars to produce, and what does that have to do with maximizing profits?

A Student Asks

QUESTION: *I've known some people who owned businesses, and to tell you the truth, I don't think any of them even knew what marginal revenue and marginal cost are. You can't expect me to believe that these business owners were producing the quantity of output for which MR = MC if they didn't even know what MR and MC are. Please comment.*

ANSWER: *You don't always have to understand how to do something to do it. For example, not many people understand how their legs move to make them walk or how their lungs behave to make them breathe, but they still walk and breathe. Our guess is that a bird doesn't really understand aerodynamics (which is the study of forces and the resulting motion of objects through the air), but birds can fly.*

A business owner may not know what marginal revenue and marginal cost are, but here is what he or she does know: whether more money is coming in than is going out. And, of course, this is what marginal revenue and marginal cost really are. The additional money coming in is marginal revenue, and the additional money going out is marginal cost. As long as a business owner can count, he or she will naturally end up producing the level of output at which MR = MC.

Having said all this, let's add that sometimes taking a course in economics or business formalizes all of these business practices more effectively. A person who has studied economics will be less likely to make a mistake when determining what quantity of a good to produce than a person who has not studied economics.

What Every Firm Wants: To Maximize Profit

In Chapter 3, we stated that profit is the difference between total revenue and total cost. For example, if total revenue is $400,000 and total cost is $320,000, then profit is $80,000. In most cases, a business firm wants its profit to be as large as possible. An economist states it this way: the business firm wants to maximize profit.

Another way of saying that a firm wants to maximize profit is to say that it wants the biggest difference possible between its total revenue and total cost. For example, given a choice of a total revenue of $1 million or $2 million, a firm will likely prefer a total revenue of $2 million (all other things being equal). Or given a choice between a total cost of $250,000 or $500,000, a business firm will probably prefer a total cost of $250,000 (all other things being equal). So, maximizing profit is consistent with a firm getting the largest possible difference between its total revenue and its total cost.

Background Information: Thomas Malthus

Thomas Malthus, a British economist who lived from 1766 to 1834, developed the law of diminishing returns. Malthus argued that land is a fixed resource and that when a variable resource (such as labor) is applied to it, the return from the additional quantity of the variable resource will eventually decrease. Malthus was careful to say that his theory was applicable only under the technology of his day. Modern-day economists have tried to disprove the theory by applying current technology—developments that Malthus could never have foreseen.

Now, here is something else to think about: is getting the largest possible difference between total revenue and total cost the same thing as producing the quantity of output at which MR = MC? Yes, it is. To prove it, again suppose that a business firm's total revenue is $400,000, total cost is $320,000, and profit is $80,000. The firm produces and sells one additional unit of a good. The revenue from selling this additional unit of the good (marginal revenue) is $40, and the cost of producing this additional unit of the good (marginal cost) is $10. Total revenue will rise to $400,040 ($400,000 + $40 = $400,040), and total cost will rise to $320,010 ($320,000 + $10 = $320,010). What will happen to the profit? It will increase to $80,030 ($400,040 − $320,010 = $80,030). Thus, whenever the firm produces and sells an additional unit of a good and marginal revenue is greater than marginal cost, it is adding more to its total revenue than to its total cost and therefore maximizing profit.

How to Compute Profit and Loss

When a firm computes its profit or loss, it determines the total cost and total revenue and then finds the difference:

1. To compute total cost (TC), add fixed cost (FC) to variable cost (VC):

$$TC = FC + VC$$

2. To compute total revenue (TR), multiply the price of the good (P) times the quantity of units (Q) of the good sold:

$$P \times Q = TR$$

3. To compute profit (or loss), subtract total cost (TC) from total revenue (TR):

$$\text{Profit (or loss)} = TR - TC$$

EXAMPLE Suppose variable cost is $100 and fixed cost is $400. It follows that total cost is $500. Now suppose that 100 units of

---

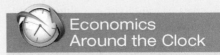
a good are sold at $7 each; total revenue is now $700. If we subtract total cost ($500) from total revenue ($700), we are left with a profit of $200. ♦

How Many Workers Should the Firm Hire?

Walmart has more than 2 million employees—actually, about 2.3 million employees. How does Walmart know how many employees to hire? Did the president of the company simply say one day, "I think 2.3 million employees sounds like the right number of employees, so let's go with it"? Probably not.

The fact is, every business has to decide how many employees it will hire (just as we learned that every business has to decide how much it will produce). Let's begin the discussion of how a firm decides how many employees to hire by discussing the **law of diminishing marginal returns**.

The name of this economic law sounds worse than it is. (If you understood the law of diminishing marginal utility, back in Chapter 4, you shouldn't have too much trouble understanding the law of diminishing marginal returns.) It states that if we add additional units of a resource

law of diminishing marginal returns
A law that states that if additional units of one resource are added to another resource in fixed supply, eventually the additional output will decrease.

Reinforcement Activity

To show students exactly how profit and loss are determined, provide several examples. Supply the class with the fixed cost, variable cost, price, and quantity produced of an imaginary good. Have students work in pairs to find the total cost, total revenue, and profit or loss. Perhaps create a game in which teams and students race to find the answers.

Economics Around the Clock

After reading and discussing how much firms should produce, refer students to the 1:07 p.m. scenario in Economics Around the Clock (page 175), and discuss their answers to its question.

Help students understand that if it were just about selling more hot dogs, or more cars, or more of anything, then sellers would lower their prices dramatically. More hot dogs will be sold at $2 than at $3 a dog; more cars will be sold at $4,000 than at $40,000 a car; and so on. It is not about selling more but about earning a profit. Selling more does not create more profit if the revenue earned on the unit of the good (the marginal revenue) is less than the cost incurred on the unit of the good (the marginal cost).

Discussion Starter

Review with students the benefits of hiring additional workers. Ask, What are some of the other benefits to the entire economy when more workers are employed? Are there any disadvantages? If so, what? Also guide students in a discussion of what happens to workers when the demand for goods produced by their company declines.

Background Information

Businesses want to hire qualified employees who are well suited for the jobs that need to be filled. To facilitate this process, businesses hire human resources specialists who recruit and interview employees and advise on hiring decisions. Human resources specialists also provide training and deal with employee compensation, benefits, and so on.

In the late 1990s, so-called HR specialists held about 544,000 jobs and were employed in every industry in the United States. To fill HR jobs, employers usually look for college graduates with majors in business administration, communication, and public administration, among other fields. Many colleges have programs that offer degrees in personnel, human resources, or labor relations.

(such as labor) to another resource (such as capital) that is in fixed supply, the additional output produced (as a result of hiring an additional worker) will eventually decrease.

The best way to illustrate this law is with numbers. Take a look at Exhibit 7-6. Reading across the first row, we see that with zero workers, no output occurs. When one worker is added, the quantity of output (shown in the second column) is 5 units. The third column shows the additional output produced as a result of hiring an additional worker. If output is 0 units with no workers and 5 units with one worker, we can conclude that hiring an additional (the first) worker increased output by 5 units.

> "In the business world the rearview mirror is always clearer than the windshield."
> —Warren Buffet

When a second worker is added, the quantity of output (shown in column 2) increases to 11 units. How much did output increase as a result of an additional (the second) worker? The answer is 6 units, as shown in column 3. If a third worker is added, output rises to 18 units, and the additional output produced as a result of the hiring of an additional (the third) worker is 7 units, as shown in column 3.

Before we go on, notice what is happening in column 3: the numbers are increasing, from 0 to 5, then 6, then 7. Notice that when a fourth worker is added, output increases to 23 units; the additional output produced is 5 units, which is *less* than the output produced as a result of adding the third worker.

What we are observing here is the law of diminishing marginal returns, which states that eventually, the additional output produced (as a result of hiring an additional worker) will decrease. We added another worker (the fourth worker) here, and the additional output (shown in column 3) decreased from 7 to 5 units. In short, diminishing marginal returns set in with the addition of the fourth worker.

So what does the law of diminishing marginal returns have to do with hiring employees? Everything, once we turn the factors into dollars. To understand this concept, ask yourself whether you would hire the fourth worker if you owned a business. To really be able to answer this question, you first have to ask yourself these two questions:

1. What do I sell each unit of output for?
2. What do I have to pay to hire the fourth worker?

Suppose you sell each unit of output for $30 and you will have to pay the fourth worker a wage of $70. Would you hire the fourth worker? One way to figure out the answer is to calculate how much comes in the door with the fourth worker compared to how much goes out the door with the fourth worker. The worker produces 5 more units of output, and you can sell each unit for $30, so the worker really comes in the door with $150. You have to pay the fourth worker $70, so the worker goes out the door with this amount. Would you be willing to pay someone $70 to get $150 in return? Sure you would, so you should hire the fourth worker.

EXHIBIT 7-6 **The Law of Diminishing Marginal Returns**

(1) Workers	(2) Quantity of output (units) produced each day	(3) Additional output (units) produced (each day) as a result of hiring an additional worker	
0	0 units	0 units	
1	5	5 (5 – 0 = 5)	
2	11	6 (11 – 5 = 6)	Diminishing returns set in with the addition of the fourth worker.
3	18	7 (18 – 11 = 7)	
4	23	5 (23 – 18 = 5) ←	
5	26	3 (26 – 23 = 3)	

▲ As more workers are added (column 1), the quantity of output produced each day rises (column 2). It isn't until the fourth worker is added that diminishing marginal returns are said to set in.

Background Information: U.S. Firms and Mexico

In many foreign countries, workers are paid lower wages than in the United States. Because of this, U.S. firms benefit by doing business in a foreign country and hiring foreign labor. However, firms face drawbacks, as well.

Have students consider the following scenario: If a U.S. firm operates in the United States and hires U.S. workers, it will have to pay $10 an hour in

wages. If it goes to Mexico and hires Mexican labor, it will have to pay $5 an hour in wages. Wages are twice as high in the United States than in Mexico, so why wouldn't the U.S. firm head for Mexico? The answer is that labor productivity may not be as high in Mexico as in the United States. In the United States, the average worker, working with various capital equipment, produces 30 units of good X

What is the general rule now for hiring employees? As long as the output produced by the additional worker multiplied by the price of the good is greater than the wage you have to pay the worker, then you should hire the worker. If the output produced by the additional worker multiplied by the price of the good is less than the wage you have to pay the worker, then don't hire the worker.

EXAMPLE If Bob hires Marianne, output will increase by 7 units a day. Bob can sell each unit of output for $50. To hire Marianne, Bob will have to pay her $200 a day. Should Bob hire Marianne? Yes. Output increases by 7 units a day and Bob sells each unit for $50, so Marianne brings in $350 a day to Bob. Bob has to pay Marianne only $200 a day. Who wouldn't spend $200 to get $350? ◆

Reread the previous example from Marianne's point of view. Is Bob cheating Marianne by paying her only $200 a day? After all, she brings in $350 a day to Bob. Shouldn't Marianne get more than $200 a day if she makes Bob $350 a day?

Keep in mind that things are a little more complicated than we have made them out to be. Marianne could very well be working with other employees and with certain machines. Not all of what Marianne produces for Bob is the result of her work and her work alone. In fact, Marianne's working with other employees and with certain machinery or tools is what ends up producing $350 a day more for Bob.

To illustrate, suppose someone goes to work on a farm and 100 more bushels of wheat are harvested on a given day. Is it that new worker that harvests those 100 additional bushels, or is it the new worker using a tractor (which is a capital good) that harvests those 100 additional bushels of wheat? The answer is that it's the new worker using the tractor. The same explanation can be used for Marianne. People don't usually work in isolation from others or without using certain capital goods.

Thinking Like *an* Economist

Recognizing a Profitable Company

Suppose you read about a company that earns $10,000 in total revenue each second of each 12-hour day, which is $432 million a day, or $157.68 billion a year. Also, this company earned $8 billion in profit for the year. These are certainly large dollar amounts, and most people would say that a company that earns $8 billion in profit has earned a lot of money. We might even conclude that this is an enormous profit.

Let's divide the profit ($8 billion) by the total revenue ($157.68 billion) to see how much profit the company is earning on each dollar of total revenue. In other words, out of every $1 that the company takes in from its customers or clients, how much does it get to keep in profit? The answer is 5.07 cents.

Now, think about this: Suppose we had started out by saying that the company earns a profit of 5.07 cents on every dollar of revenue, not by stating its total revenue and profit. What would you have thought about the company then? More than likely, you would have thought that the company isn't doing very well. So, you would have drawn the opposite conclusion about the company.

But, of course, that is not the way we started; instead, we started by telling you that this company earns $10,000 in total revenue every second of every 12-hour day. Now earning $10,000 a second sounds like the company is one super-profitable company, doesn't it?

Clearly, we can come away with different opinions about a company depending on what values we examine. Earning $10,000 in revenue every second of every 12-hour day gives a completely different impression than earning 5.07 cents in profit from every $1 in revenue. Here are some selected industries, identified by profit (in cents) per $1 dollar of revenue:

- Publishing (Books): 10.5 cents
- Data Storage Services: 9.6 cents
- Broadcasting (TV): 8.8 cents
- Lodging: 8.0 cents
- Toys and Games: 7.8 cents
- Restaurants: 7.5 cents
- Home Furnishing Stores: 7.10 cents
- Office Supplies: 6.30 cents

*Source: Yahoo! Finance, February 2017.

THINK ABOUT IT Sometimes, it's necessary to look beyond the single fact that's presented to get a clear picture of what's happening with a company. This can be true of other things in life, as well. When have you formed a different opinion about something after getting more information about it?

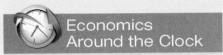

Economics Around the Clock

After reading and discussing "How Many Workers Should the Firm Hire?" direct students to reread the 11:09 a.m. scenario in Economics Around the Clock (page 175) and consider its question.

Labor costs in other countries may be lower, but workers' output is sometimes low, as well. Companies should set up where they can produce the most output per dollar.

Thinking Like *an* Economist

Answers may vary. Some students may say that they changed their opinions after learning more about political candidates or topics, sporting and or entertainment topics, or something about someone they know.

---

every hour. In Mexico, the average worker produces 10 units of good X every hour.

The firm needs to compute its output per dollar of labor cost, which it can do by dividing labor productivity by the hourly wage (*calculation:* Output per dollar of labor cost = number of units labor produces per hour ÷ wage rate).

In the United States, the company pays a worker $10 an hour and receives 30 units of good X in return; it produces 3 units per $1 of labor cost. In Mexico, the firm pays a worker $5 an hour and receives 10 units of good X in return; it produces 2 units per $1 of labor cost. The firm produces more output per dollar in the United States than in Mexico.

In personal terms, it is probably more costly to call your supervisor and report that you are sick and will miss work than it is to email a similar message. Thus, more reports of "sickness" with email messages than with phone messages are to be expected.

Application Activity

After reading and discussing Sections 2 and 3, assign the activity for those sections in the *Applying the Principles Workbook,* pages 82–84.

Assess

Quick Quiz

The following true-or-false quiz will help you assess student understanding of the material covered in this section.

1. Marginal revenue is the additional revenue from selling an additional unit of a good. (True)
2. Marginal revenue equals the change in total cost divided by the change in total revenue. (False)
3. A firm will produce a good only if it can earn a profit. (True)
4. The difference between total cost and total revenue is profit or loss. (True)
5. Seeing an increase in total revenue after hiring one more worker is an example of the law of diminishing returns. (False)

Assessment Book

You will find a quiz for this section in the *Assessment Book,* page 69.

Did You Get My Text?

Just as a business firm has to keep an eye on both its costs and its revenues, individuals have to keep an eye on both their costs and their benefits. There are costs and benefits to almost everything we do, and when the costs of doing something go down, we usually do more of it. With this in mind, consider what has happened in recent years to the cost of asking someone for personal information.

Suppose you want to ask someone for some very personal information. How might you go about this? Three ways come to mind: you can ask for the information in a face-to-face encounter, over the telephone, or in a text message or email. If the information being requested is truly personal, then the most difficult and thus "costly" way of asking for it is a face-to-face encounter. In such an encounter, you will have to stand in front of the person and speak to him or her directly. The person will see you and hear you, which will likely make you feel awkward and embarrassed.

The second-hardest way to ask for personal information (and thus a somewhat less costly way) is via telephone. Not having to see the other person will make asking for the information less "costly" for you. But he or she will still hear your voice, making the exchange somewhat awkward.

Next, consider a text message. In this type of exchange, you can ask for and receive the information without having to see or talk to the other person. In a way, it's as if you are invisible or anonymous. Handling the exchange this way is of little or no cost to you.

What should we expect then? If the least costly way of asking someone for personal information is by texting or emailing, then more personal information will be exchanged that way than face to face or over the telephone. But we are looking at only the cost on the "asking" side of the encounter. What about the "answering" side? Is it easier to answer a request for personal information—or perhaps to refuse to answer—via text than, say, face to face or via telephone? When you say no via text, the person you are responding to neither sees nor hears you. The cost to you is little or nothing. Saying no is difficult for many people, but texting makes it less difficult.

Have you ever heard of a person in a relationship breaking up with someone via text? We can understand that texting might be the chosen method because it's

so much easier and less costly to break up that way—until, of course, you discover that what you've done is socially frowned on and others view your actions as cowardly and rude.

Notice what's being done here: the individuals who frown on the idea of breaking up via text are indirectly raising the cost of doing so. If you're the texter, you won't have any trouble writing and sending the message, and you won't have to face the recipient. You will, however, have to incur the cost of others thinking of you in a negative way.

Think about this issue in the setting of the workplace. If an employee is sick and plans to stay home, is it more costly to call his or her employer with this news or to email him or her? If email were an acceptable way to report an illness to one's employer, do you think more people would end up emailing in sick than currently call in sick?

Cooperative Learning

Students sometimes have difficulty understanding the law of diminishing returns. Here's an example that may help them: Suppose that a student is at home at night reading a textbook. His objective is to learn certain information to help him write a major term paper. In the first hour he learns 10 pieces of information. In the second hour he learns 15 pieces of information. In the third hour he learns 12 pieces of information, but in the fourth hour he learns only 8 pieces, and in the fifth hour he learns just 6 pieces of new information. Have students work in groups to create diagrams that illustrate this example. Also have them brainstorm other examples that demonstrate the law of diminishing marginal returns.

▲ People wait in line at an internship job fair held by the Miami Marlins at Marlins Park in Miami. What economic principle might the hiring manager use in deciding how many of the applicants they will hire as paid interns?

Teaching with Visuals

The Miami Marlins hiring manager should use the law of diminishing marginal returns.

Reteaching Activity

Use the Section Assessment to gauge which students may need reteaching on this section. Guide those students in rereading the definitions of *marginal revenue* and the *law of diminishing returns*. Make sure that students understand these terms. Pay particular attention to the definition of the *law of diminishing returns* to stress that this law applies when one resource is fixed in supply.

 Guided Reading

For further reteaching of the key concepts in this section, assign the Outlining Activity and the Just the Facts Handout from the *Guided Reading and Study Guide,* pages 103–106.

SECTION 3 ASSESSMENT

Defining Terms

1. Define:
   a. marginal revenue
   b. law of diminishing marginal returns

Reviewing Facts and Concepts

2. The output obtained by adding an additional worker is 50 units, and each unit can be sold for $2. Is it worth hiring the additional worker if she is paid $150 a day? Explain.

3. The price is $20 per unit no matter how many units a firm sells. What is the marginal revenue for the fiftieth unit? Explain.

Critical Thinking

4. Profit is computed by determining the total cost and total revenue and then finding the difference. Suppose a firm wants to compute its profit per unit. In other words, instead of computing how much profit it earns in total, the firm wants to know how much profit it earns per unit. How can the firm go about computing profit per unit? (*Hint:* The answer deals with average total cost.)

5. When does maximizing profit give a firm the same result as maximizing total revenue? What conditions are necessary?

Graphing Economics

6. Suppose the marginal benefit of playing tennis is constant for each minute of the first 20 minutes and then steadily declines for each additional minute. The marginal cost of playing tennis is constant. Furthermore, the marginal cost is equal to the marginal benefit at the forty-fifth minute. Create a diagram that represents the marginal benefit versus the marginal cost of playing tennis.

Section 3 Revenue and Its Applications **203**

SECTION 3 ASSESSMENT ANSWERS

Defining Terms

1. a. marginal revenue: the revenue from selling an additional unit of a good, or the change in total revenue that results from selling an addi-

tional unit of a good; **b. law of diminishing marginal returns:** a law that states if additional units of one resource (such as labor) are added to another resource in fixed in supply (such as capital), eventually the additional output will decrease.

Reviewing Facts and Concepts

2. No. Hiring the additional worker creates $100 in benefits but costs $150. Because the costs are greater than the benefits, it is not worth hiring another worker.

3. $20. Total revenue for 49 units is $980, or price ($20) × 49 units. Total revenue for 50

units is $1,000, or price ($20) × 50 units. Because marginal revenue is the change in total revenue that results from selling an additional unit of output, it is $20.

Critical Thinking

4. Average total cost is sometimes called *per-unit cost.* The firm simply subtracts the average total cost from the price it charges for each good to compute profit (or loss) per unit. For example, if price is $10 and average total cost is $9, then per-unit profit is $1.

5. Profit is the difference between total revenue and total cost—that is, Profit = total revenue − total cost. If there are no variable costs, then total cost is simply fixed costs. We can rewrite profit as P = TR − FC. We know that FC is constant over output. It follows that if TR rises by $1, P also rises by $1. In short, maximizing TR is the same as maximizing P. Every time TR rises, P rises by the same amount.

Graphing Economics

6. Students' diagrams should show a steady horizontal line to the 20-minute mark; then the line should decline evenly to the 45-minute mark.

Assessment Answers

Economics Vocabulary

1. unlimited, limited; **2.** board of directors; **3.** fixed cost; **4.** marginal cost; **5.** law of diminishing marginal returns; **6.** per-unit cost; **7.** franchiser; **8.** coupon rate; **9.** asset; **10.** personal income.

Understanding the Main Ideas

1. The owners of a partnership have unlimited liability, whereas the owners of a corporation have limited liability. Also, the profit of the partnership is the income of the partners, and only the personal income tax is applied to it. The profit of a corporation provides income for the owners, but both the owners and the corporation pay taxes on it.

2. A proprietorship may have one owner and a partnership at least two. For both a proprietorship and partnership, profit is taxed only once and both proprietors and partners face unlimited liability

3. A proprietor faces unlimited liability whereas the owners of corporations face limited liability. A proprietorship may not continue after the death of a proprietor, but corporations can "live on" indefinitely.

4. Profits of a corporation are taxed as profits (corporate income tax) and as income (dividends to owners/stockholders). The two taxes are the corporate income tax and the personal income tax.

5. $800 (*calculation:* $10,000 × 0.08 = $800).

6. If the sum of what individuals can produce working together (as a team in a firm) is greater than the sum of what they can produce working alone, then a firm will be formed.

7. Mayang is more likely to shirk in setting 2. In setting 1, Mayang obtains all the benefits of her shirking and pays all the costs. In setting 2, she obtains all the benefits of her shirking and pays only one-fifth of the costs. Individuals are more likely to shirk in settings where they pay a lower fraction of the costs

---

Chapter Summary

Be sure you know and remember the following key points from the chapter sections.

Section 1

▶ A business is an organization that uses resources to produce goods and services to sell to customers.

▶ A business needs a boss to efficiently coordinate and direct the activities of others in the organization.

▶ A sole proprietorship is a business owned by one person who makes the decisions, receives the profits earned, and is liable for the debts of the business.

▶ A partnership is a business owned by two or more partners who share in the profits and are responsible for any liabilities it incurs.

▶ A corporation is a legal entity formed to conduct business and is owned by individuals who buy shares of the organization.

Section 2

▶ Fixed costs are expenses that are the same no matter how many units of a good are produced.

▶ Variable costs are expenses that vary according to the number of units produced.

▶ Total costs = Fixed costs + Variable costs

▶ Marginal cost is the cost of producing an additional unit of a good.

Section 3

▶ Firms must answer two key questions: How much should we produce? and What price should we charge?

▶ Marginal revenue is the change in total revenue that results from selling an additional unit of output.

▶ A firm wants to maximize profit, which requires it to produce a quantity of output at which marginal revenue equals marginal cost.

Economics Vocabulary

1. In both a sole proprietorship and a partnership, owners have _____ liability, whereas in a corporation, owners have _____ liability.

2. The stockholders of the firm choose the _____.

3. Total cost equals _____ plus variable cost.

4. The cost of producing an additional unit of a good is called _____.

5. The _____ states that if additional units of a resource are added to a resource that is fixed in supply, the additional output produced will eventually decrease.

6. Another term for average total cost is _____.

7. The entity that offers a franchise is called the _____.

8. Ten percent of the face value of a bond is paid out regularly, so 10 percent is the _____ of the bond.

9. A(n) _____ for a firm is anything to which the firm has a legal claim.

10. The tax that a person pays on his or her income is called the _____ tax.

Understanding the Main Ideas

1. List and explain two major differences between a corporation and a partnership.

2. Compare and contrast a partnership with a sole proprietorship.

3. Compare and contrast a sole proprietorship with a corporation.

4. To what taxes are we referring when we say that corporations are "taxed twice"?

5. Suppose a bond has a face value of $10,000 and a coupon rate of 8 percent. What is the dollar amount of each annual coupon payment?

6. Specify the condition under which a business firm will likely be formed.

7. In setting 1, Mayang works for herself. She gets to keep or sell everything she produces. In setting 2, Mayang works with five individuals. She gets to keep one-fifth of everything she produces and of everything everyone else produces. In which setting is Mayang more likely to shirk? Explain your answer.

8. What is the relationship between a bondholder and the firm that issued the bond? What is the

---

of shirking. The lower the cost of shirking, the more people will shirk.

8. The bondholder is a lender to the firm. The stockholder is an owner of the firm. Below them in the company hierarchy are the board of directors, president, vice presidents, department heads, and employees. Exhibit 7-3 (page 184) shows this structure.

9. Fixed costs are constant over output, and variable costs are not. In other words, as output rises, fixed costs remain the same. This isn't the case with variable costs, which rise as output rises.

10. Marginal revenue is additional revenue, and marginal cost is additional cost. As long as additional revenue is greater than additional cost, it's worth producing and selling a good. More is coming into the firm than going out.

relationship between a stockholder and the firm that issued the stock?

9. In general, what is the difference between fixed costs and variable costs?

10. Explain why a firm continues to produce those units of a good for which marginal revenue is greater than marginal cost.

11. A firm will produce and sell units of a good if marginal revenue is greater than marginal cost. Does this strategy have anything to do with the firm's objective to maximize profit? Explain.

12. How does a firm compute its profit or loss?

Doing the Math

1. Calculate the marginal cost for the additional unit produced in each of the following cases. (TC = total cost, and Q = quantity of output.)
  a. Q = 100, TC = $4,322; Q = 101, TC = $4,376
  b. Q = 210, TC = $5,687; Q = 211, TC = $5,699
  c. Q = 547, TC = $10,009; Q = 548, TC = $10,123

2. Calculate the average total cost in each of the following cases. (TC = total cost, and Q = quantity of output.)
  a. Q = 120, TC = $3,400
  b. Q = 200, TC = $4,560
  c. Q = 150, TC = $1,500

3. The marginal benefit of playing chess (in money terms) is $10 for the first game of chess, $8 for the second, $6 for the third, $4 for the fourth, $2 for the fifth, and $0 for the sixth. The marginal cost of playing chess (in money terms) is always $5. What is the right number of games of chess to play? Explain your answer.

4. Look at Exhibit 7-6 on page 200. Suppose it costs a firm $45 a day to hire the fifth worker. What price must be charged for the good the firm produces before it is worth hiring the fifth worker?

Working with Graphs

In Exhibit 7-7, Q = quantity of the good, MC = marginal cost, and MR = marginal revenue. Which part or parts (a–c) illustrate the following?

1. Jim pays more to produce the second unit of the good than the first, more for the third than the second, and so on.

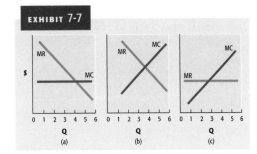

EXHIBIT 7-7

2. The additional benefit of producing the fourth unit of the good is the same as the additional benefit of producing the fifth.

3. Marginal revenue is constant over a specific quantity of the good produced.

4. Marginal revenue declines as the firm sells additional units of the good.

Solving Economic Problems

1. *Apply.* When Dairy Queen first began, it did not require franchisees to handle all of the company's products. In contrast, McDonald's requires its franchisees to handle all of its products. If you were a franchiser, what kind of agreement would you want? Why?

2. *Apply.* Suppose a firm is neither incurring a loss nor earning a profit. What is the relationship between the firm's total revenue and total cost?

Project or Presentation

A Profitable Debate. A firm earns profit when its total revenue is greater than its total cost. This means there are two ways to earn more profit: (1) raise total revenue and (2) lower total cost. Hold a class debate about this statement: raising total revenue is the easier way to increase profit.

ONLINE emcp.com
Practice Tests and Study Guide

Go to **www.emcschool.net/Economics2e** and choose *Economics: New Ways of Thinking*, Chapter 7, if you need more help in preparing for the chapter test.

$22.80); **c.** $10 (*calculation*: $1,500 ÷ 150 = $10).

3. Three games. For the first three games, marginal benefits are greater than marginal costs. With the fourth game, marginal costs are greater than marginal benefits, so you wouldn't want to play this game.

4. $15.01. The firm will hire the fifth worker only if it expects greater benefits than costs. Its costs are $45. The fifth worker increases output by 3 units. If the firm can sell each unit for $15, then it will break even on hiring the fifth worker and therefore be indifferent about hiring or not hiring the worker. One penny more ($15.01 per unit), and the firm will benefit from hiring the fifth worker.

Working with Graphs

1. parts (b) and (c).
2. part (c).
3. part (c).
4. parts (a) and (b).

Solving Economic Problems

1. Answers will vary. Many students will realize the advantages of consistency across all franchises (like McDonald's). Customers will know what they are getting if they stop at any franchise. If they don't know, they might be less likely to stop. This is an argument for all of the franchises to be the same.
2. Total revenue is equal to total cost: TR = TC.

Project or Presentation

Lead the class in a formal or informal debate on the topic. Education World provides debate guidelines and options at http://econ.emcp.net/debateoptions.

---

11. Yes. As long as the firm's marginal revenue is greater than its marginal cost, it's adding more to its revenue than to its costs. Therefore, the difference between the two, which is profit, is getting larger.

12. First, a firm computes its total cost by summing its fixed and variable costs. Then, it computes its total revenue by multiplying the price of the good it sells times the number of units it sells. Finally, it subtracts total cost from total revenue to find profit or loss.

Doing the Math

1. a. $54 (*calculation*: $14,376 − $4,322 = $54);
  b. $12 (*calculation*: $5,699 − $4,322 = $12);
  c. $114 (*calculation*: $10,123 − $10,009 = $114).
2. a. $28.33 (*calculation*: $3,400 ÷ 120 = $28.33); **b.** $22.80 (*calculation*: $4,560 ÷ 200 =

Chapter 8 Planning Guide

SECTION ORGANIZER

	Learning Objectives	Reproducible Worksheets and Handouts	Assessment
A Perfectly Competitive Market (pages 208–214)	▶ Identify the characteristics of a perfectly competitive market. ▶ Provide examples of perfectly competitive markets. ▶ Explain what it means to say that a firm "has no control over price." ▶ Describe the role that profit plays in a perfectly competitive market.	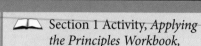 Section 1 Activity, *Applying the Principles Workbook,* pages 85–86 Outlining Activity, *Guided Reading and Study Guide,* pages 115–116 Just the Facts Handout, *Guided Reading and Study Guide,* pages 117–118	☑ Section Assessment, *Student Text,* page 214 ☑ Quick Quiz, *Annotated Teacher's Edition,* page 214 ☑ Section Quiz, *Assessment Book,* page 77
A Monopolistic Market (pages 215–225)	▶ Identify the characteristics of a monopolistic market. ▶ Provide some examples of barriers to entry. ▶ Explain whether monopolists ever face competition. ▶ Explain the purpose of antitrust laws. ▶ List some major antitrust laws.	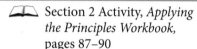 Section 2 Activity, *Applying the Principles Workbook,* pages 87–90 Outlining Activity, *Guided Reading and Study Guide,* pages 119–121 Just the Facts Handout, *Guided Reading and Study Guide,* pages 122–123	☑ Section Assessment, *Student Text,* page 225 ☑ Quick Quiz, *Annotated Teacher's Edition,* page 224 ☑ Section Quiz, *Assessment Book,* page 78
A Monopolistic Competitive Market (pages 228–232)	▶ Identify the characteristics of monopolistic competition. ▶ Provide some examples of monopolistic competition. ▶ Explain whether monopolistic competitors are price takers or price searchers. ▶ Describe how monopolistic competitors answer questions about how much to produce and what price to charge. ▶ Explain the ways in which the products of monopolistic competitors differ.	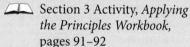 Section 3 Activity, *Applying the Principles Workbook,* pages 91–92 Outlining Activity, *Guided Reading and Study Guide,* page 124 Just the Facts Handout, *Guided Reading and Study Guide,* page 125	☑ Section Assessment, *Student Text,* page 232 ☑ Quick Quiz, *Annotated Teacher's Edition,* page 231 ☑ Section Quiz, *Assessment Book,* page 79
An Oligopolistic Market (pages 233–241)	▶ Identify the characteristics of an oligopolistic market. ▶ Provide some examples of an oligopolistic market. ▶ Explain whether sellers in an oligopolistic market are price takers or price searchers. ▶ Explain what cartel agreements are.	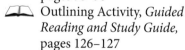 Section 4 Activity, *Applying the Principles Workbook,* pages 93–95 Outlining Activity, *Guided Reading and Study Guide,* pages 126–127 Just the Facts Handout, *Guided Reading and Study Guide,* pages 128–129	☑ Section Assessment, *Student Text,* page 241 ☑ Quick Quiz, *Annotated Teacher's Edition,* page 240 ☑ Section Quiz, *Assessment Book,* page 80

Reproducible Chapter Resources and Assessment Materials

 Graphic Organizer Activity, *Guided Reading and Study Guide,* page 130

 Vocabulary Activity, *Guided Reading and Study Guide,* pages 131–132

 Working with Graphs and Charts, *Guided Reading and Study Guide,* page 133

☑ Practice Test, *Guided Reading and Study Guide,* pages 134–135

 Critical Thinking Activity, *Finding Economics,* pages 22–23

☑ Chapter Test A, *Assessment Book,* pages 81–83

☑ Chapter Test B, *Assessment Book,* pages 84–86

Student Text Internet Links

Economics: New Ways of Thinking, Second Edition encourages students to use the Internet to find out more about economics. Given the wealth of current, valid information available on websites, students should be encouraged to use the Internet as a research tool. Doing so will likely increase students' interest in and understanding of economics principles and topics. In addition, doing Internet research can help your students form the habit of accessing and using economics information, as well as help them develop investigative skills they will use throughout their educational and professional careers.

To aid your students in achieving these ends, each chapter of *Economics: New Ways of Thinking, Second Edition* includes the addresses of several websites that provide engaging and relevant information. When students type in any of the addresses provided, they will immediately arrive at the intended site. The addresses have been modified so that EMC Publishing can monitor and maintain the proper links—for example, the website http://www.deposit accounts.com/ has been changed to http://econ.emcp.net/accounts. In the event that the address or content of a site changes or is discontinued, EMC's Internet editors will redirect the link to a site with equivalent information.

Activities in the *Annotated Teacher's Edition* often suggest that students search the Internet for information. For some activities, you might want to find reputable sites beforehand and steer students toward them. For other activities, have students do their own searching and then check out the sites they have found and discuss why they might be reliable or unreliable.

Passport® for Economics

Technology resources are available with the *Economics: New Ways of Thinking, Second Edition* program through Passport®. These include:

eBooks for *Economics: New Ways of Thinking, Second Edition*

▶ Student textbook eBook
▶ Interactive Applying the Principles eWorkbook
▶ Finding Economics eBook
▶ Guided Reading and Study Guide eBook
▶ Annotated Teacher's Edition eBook
▶ Lesson Plans eBook
▶ Assessment eBook

Passport® for Students

Students can access helpful resources through Passport® for Economics. Resources include:
▶ Study guides
▶ Practice tests
▶ Flash cards in English and in Spanish
▶ Word games in English and in Spanish
▶ Tutorials and key-concept videos
▶ Spanish print and audio summaries

Passport® for Teachers

Keep your course current and relevant by using the teacher resources provided through Passport® for Economics. In addition to all of the resources on the student side of Passport®, the teacher side contains:
▶ Link to the Annotated Teacher's Edition eBook
▶ Standards correlations
▶ Microsoft® PowerPoint® Lectures
▶ Current Events Lessons
▶ Additional Economics in the Real World features
▶ ExamView® Assessment Suite
▶ PDFs of all print supplements (student and teacher)

Overview

This chapter describes the four market structures: perfect competition, monopoly, monopolistic competition, and oligopoly. The following statements provide brief descriptions of the major concepts covered in each section of this chapter.

SECTION 1
A Perfectly Competitive Market

Section 1 introduces the characteristics of a perfectly competitive market.

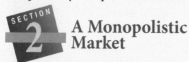

SECTION 2
A Monopolistic Market

Section 2 examines monopoly, which is the opposite of perfect competition. Students will learn the characteristics of a monopoly and how monopolies come into being, as well as the difference between a government monopoly and a market monopoly.

SECTION 3
A Monopolistic Competitive Market

Section 3 explores monopolistic competition—a middle ground between the markets of monopoly and perfect competition. Students will also learn the three conditions that characterize monopolistic competition.

SECTION 4
An Oligopolistic Market

Section 4 covers oligopoly. Students will learn the characteristics of an oligopoly and explore the relationship between oligopolies and cartels.

Competition and Markets

Why It Matters

Sometimes, you can negotiate the price you pay for a good. Suppose you are buying a car, for example. The sticker price is $25,000. You offer the car dealer $23,000, and he comes back with $24,500. You say $24,200, and the dealer accepts your offer.

Other times, you can't negotiate the price you pay. Suppose you want to buy a shirt at a store in the mall, and the price is $30. You wouldn't say to the clothing salesperson, "I'll pay $25 for the shirt." Instead, you pay $30.

The lesson here is that not all goods are sold in identical types of markets. In some markets, you negotiate the price; in others, you don't. Some markets are competitive; others are not. Understanding the material in this chapter will help you better realize why markets function in different ways.

This farmer operates in a market that economists call *perfectly competitive*, which means that he is a price taker. You will learn about four different kinds of markets in this chapter.

206

Teaching Suggestions from the Author

Students often find this an odd chapter. They come to it thinking that business is business is business. But that is not true. Every business finds itself in a particular market, and markets are not all alike. For example, there is more competition in some markets than in other markets. There are more sellers in some markets than in other markets. There are more barriers to entering some markets than other markets.

In this chapter, we want students to understand that the market in which a firm finds itself will determine how that firm will act. In other words, the type of market affects the behavior of the firm.

You might want to ask students to identify the

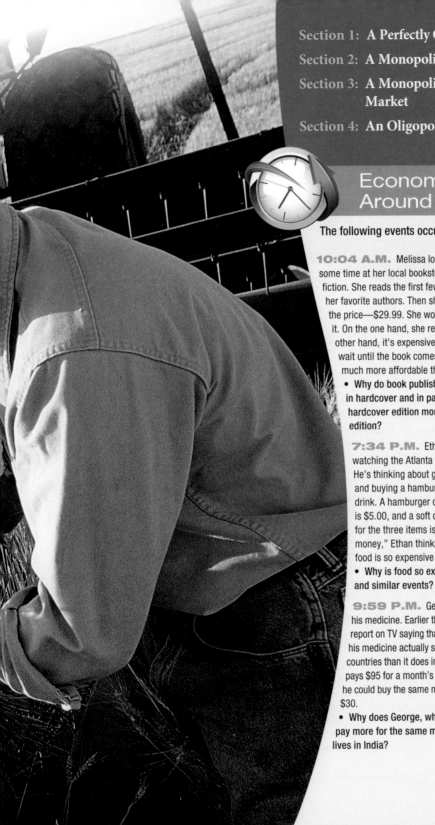

Economics Around the Clock

The following events occurred one day in July.

10:04 A.M. Melissa loves to read and is enjoying some time at her local bookstore looking at the newest fiction. She reads the first few pages of a book by one of her favorite authors. Then she closes the book and checks the price—$29.99. She wonders whether she should buy it. On the one hand, she really wants the book. On the other hand, it's expensive and she knows that she could wait until the book comes out in paperback. It will be much more affordable then.

• **Why do book publishers publish the same book in hardcover and in paperback but release the hardcover edition months before the paperback edition?**

7:34 P.M. Ethan is at the baseball park watching the Atlanta Braves play the Chicago Cubs. He's thinking about going to the concession stand and buying a hamburger, some peanuts, and a soft drink. A hamburger costs $6.50, a bag of peanuts is $5.00, and a soft drink is $3.75. The total price for the three items is $15.25. "That is a lot of money," Ethan thinks to himself. "I don't know why food is so expensive at a baseball game."

• **Why is food so expensive at baseball games and similar events?**

9:59 P.M. George is getting ready to take his medicine. Earlier this evening, he saw a news report on TV saying that the company that produces his medicine actually sells it for much less in foreign countries than it does in the United States. George pays $95 for a month's supply, but if he lived in India, he could buy the same medicine for the equivalent of $30.

• **Why does George, who lives in the United States, pay more for the same medicine than a person who lives in India?**

207

Introducing the Chapter

Remind students that the previous chapter discussed the three types of business firms. Several of the activities asked students to identify examples of businesses that represent each of these types. Explain to students that they might keep the same businesses in mind as they examine competition and markets in Chapter 8.

Also remind students that economics often applies very specific meanings to commonly used words. In this chapter, students will learn about the specific meaning that economics applies to the word *competition*.

Teaching with Visuals

Students will learn about a variety of markets in this chapter. Have them look at the photo on this spread and think about the differences between wheat and, say, automobiles. What does it mean to say that "these products belong to different markets"?

market structures of well-known firms. In what kind of market structure does Microsoft find itself? For instance, in what kind of market structure does General Motors find itself? After addressing these questions, ask students how a firm that finds itself in a monopolistic market might behave if it found itself in an oligopolistic market or in a perfectly competitive market.

Finally, it is always important to talk about competition when discussing market structures. Ask students if the nature of competition differs between a perfectly competitive market and a monopolistic competitive market or between a monopolistic market and a monopolistic competitive market.

Teacher Support

Focus and Motivate

Section Objectives

After completing this section, students will be able to

▶ identify the characteristics of a perfectly competitive market;

▶ provide examples of perfectly competitive markets;

▶ explain what it means to say that a firm "has no control over price"; and

▶ describe the role that profit plays in a perfectly competitive market.

Activating Prior Knowledge

Invite students to list the three types of business firms they studied in Chapter 7. Tell them that each type of firm operates in a market structure.

Teach

A Student Asks

Use this A Student Asks to make sure that students understand that economists can distinguish between markets and that students will learn to distinguish one market from another, as well.

 Visit econ.myemcp.com/videos for videos that will help students better understand the key concepts found in this section.

A Perfectly Competitive Market

Focus Questions

▶ What are the characteristics of a perfectly competitive market?

▶ What are some examples of perfectly competitive markets?

▶ What does it mean to say that a firm "has no control over price"?

▶ What role does profit play in a perfectly competitive market?

Key Terms

market structure
perfectly competitive market
price taker

Four Types of Markets

There are more than 25 million businesses in the United States, and they include car companies, bookstores, clothing stores, grocery stores, hair salons, restaurants, and more. Not every one of these 25 million businesses operates in the same kind of market, however.

Economists talk about the different types of market structures. **Market structures** are defined by their characteristics, such as the number of sellers in the market, the product that sellers produce and sell, and how easy or difficult it is for new firms to enter the market. You will learn about four types of markets in this chapter:

market structure
The setting in which a seller finds itself. Market structures are defined by their characteristics, such as the number of sellers in the market, the product that sellers produce and sell, and how easy or difficult it is for new firms to enter the market.

- perfectly competitive
- monopolistic
- monopolistic competitive
- oligopolistic

For now, think of the four kinds of markets the way you might think of four different rooms in a house. Each room is both similar to and different from every other room. All of the rooms have floors and ceilings, for example, but not all of the rooms are painted the same color or are the same size.

It's the same with markets. They have some things in common (such as buyers and sellers), and a few things that differ. Let's begin by discussing our first market: the perfectly competitive market.

A Student Asks

QUESTION: *For me, as a buyer, almost all markets seem the same. For example, I can't tell much difference between the market for books and the market for skateboards. In both markets, if I want to buy something, I pay the price that is charged. What do economists look at to distinguish one market from another?*

ANSWER: *What you've implied about markets—they all seem the same— can be said about other things too. Someone might say that he can't tell much difference between two shirts. But if he looks more closely, he might find that one shirt is cotton and the other polyester or that one is a short-sleeve*

Differentiating Instruction

English Language Learners

Students with limited English proficiency might have difficulty with a number of terms in this chapter. Assign these students to work in pairs to make their own lists of key terms. Students should define the terms both in English and in their native languages, if appropriate. Then, indi-

vidual students should write sentences that show they understand both the meanings of the words and how to use them correctly in English. You might also ask students to provide clear, concrete examples of the terms on their lists. When you have finished the chapter, quiz these students on the words on their lists.

shirt and the other a long-sleeve shirt. It's the same with markets: the closer you look at them, the more differences you can find. Economists look at a variety of things to distinguish between markets, such as how many sellers there are in a market (many, a few, only one), how many buyers there are in a market, and whether sellers sell the same good or slightly differentiated goods. You will learn about more of the differences as you progress through this chapter.

Characteristics of a Perfectly Competitive Market

Economists categorize markets according to their characteristics. Here are four characteristics of a **perfectly competitive market**:

1. The market has many buyers and many sellers.
2. All firms sell identical goods.
3. Buyers and sellers have relevant information about prices, product quality, sources of supply, and so on.
4. Firms have easy entry into and exit out of the market.

EXAMPLE Jones is a wheat farmer, or a producer and seller of wheat. Does Jones sell his wheat in a perfectly competitive market? In other words, is the wheat market a "perfectly competitive market"? To answer this question, we have to determine whether the wheat market has the four characteristics of a perfectly competitive market. First, does it have many buyers and many sellers of wheat? The answer is yes, so the first characteristic holds for the wheat market.

Second, do all wheat sellers sell the same wheat? For a given type of wheat, the answer is yes. It would be impossible, for example, to tell Jones's wheat from any other farmer's wheat. So, the second characteristic of a perfectly competitive market holds.

Third, do buyers and sellers of wheat possess information on the quality of wheat, prices of wheat, and so on? The answer is yes. For example, wheat farmers often check the daily wheat report. They know what

▲ In a typical mall, many different kinds of stores sell many different kinds of products. Do you think any of the markets represented by these stores and products are perfectly competitive markets? If so, what four characteristics must be present?

price wheat is selling for on that given day. So, the third characteristic of a perfectly competitive market holds.

Fourth, is entry into and out of the wheat market easy? In other words, is it easy for Jones to leave the farming business if he wants to, and would it be easy for others to get into the farming business if they wanted to? The answer is yes. Nothing prevents Jones from deciding to no longer be a farmer, and nothing prevents you or anyone else from being a wheat farmer. If an accountant at an accounting firm wants to quit his job tomorrow, buy some land in Kansas, and start wheat farming, she is free to do just that. You might say that it's expensive to get into farming, so doesn't that make it hard to get started? It may be expensive, but what economists mean when they say that there is "easy entry and exit" is that no entity prevents entry into or exit from a market. For example, the government doesn't prevent individuals from going into farming if they want. So, the fourth characteristic of a perfectly competitive market is met. We can conclude that the wheat market is a perfectly competitive market. ◆

perfectly competitive market
A market structure characterized by (1) many buyers and many sellers, (2) all firms selling identical goods, (3) all relevant information about buying and selling activities being available to buyers and sellers, and (4) easy entry into and easy exit out of the market.

Section 1 A Perfectly Competitive Market **209**

Background Information: Perfect Competition

Sometimes people believe that sellers can sell their goods at any prices they desire. A discussion of perfect competition will reveal that this is not the case. For example, a firm that finds itself in a perfectly competitive market can sell its goods only at the market price. Point out to students that the market price has been determined by the impersonal forces of supply and demand. Thousands of sellers and thousands of buyers collectively determine the equilibrium or market price through quantity demanded and quantity supplied. No single seller or buyer sets price. The entire market does.

Teaching with Visuals

Student answers will vary. If they answer yes, then they should list the four characteristics of a perfectly competitive market.

Discussion Starter

Guide students in a discussion of the word competition. Ask them to define the word in as many ways as they can, and record the definitions on the board. Then explain that in this chapter, students will look at competition from an economist's point of view.

Discussion Starter

Guide students in a discussion of the characteristics of perfect competition. Have students identify examples of markets that might be perfectly competitive. Examine each example in light of the four characteristics to determine if it qualifies.

Discussion Starter

Write the following statement on the board: "In a perfectly competitive market, there is only one price." Ask students if they agree or disagree with this statement. Students should understand that while the possibility of multiple prices exists, only one price will maximize profit and bring demand.

Reinforcement Activity

The markets for agricultural goods (such as wheat and corn) are considered perfectly competitive markets. Direct each student to prepare a short essay on one of these markets. The essay should describe what a farmer must do to produce the product, the price of the product, who buys this product, and any variable conditions that might affect quantity and/or price. If your students live in an agricultural area, this could be a particularly interesting project.

Clarifying Terms

Perfectly competitive firms are price takers: sellers who can sell all of their output at the equilibrium price but none of it at a higher price. These firms must take the price that the market offers; if they try to sell at a higher price, they will be unable to sell any of their output.

Teaching with Visuals

The markets for corn and wheat are perfectly competitive, because they meet the four characteristics. Because sellers of these commodities must sell at the equilibrium or market price, they are price takers.

Sellers in a Perfectly Competitive Market Are Price Takers

Because of the four characteristics of a perfectly competitive market, sellers in this market end up being **price takers**. It is similar to saying that a person who exercises daily, eats healthfully, and always gets enough sleep will end up being healthier than a person who doesn't do these things. Certain things follow from certain characteristics.

When it comes to the perfectly competitive market, its characteristics determine that a seller in this market will be a price taker: a seller that can only sell his or her goods at the equilibrium price. (Think back to Chapter 6, where we explained how the equilibrium price comes to exist.) In other words, suppose Jones, the farmer, is a price taker. What does this mean for him? It means that he gets up in the morning; turns on the radio, TV, or computer; and finds out today's equilibrium price for wheat. If it is, say, $5 a bushel, Jones will have to sell his wheat at this price and no other price.

Now consider another price taker—this time, in a market other than the wheat market. Consider Brown, who owns 1,000 shares of Disney stock. One day, Brown decides to sell her stock (just like Jones might have decided to sell his wheat). Brown goes

price taker
A seller that can sell all its output at the equilibrium price but can sell none of its output at any other price.

▼ Sellers of commodities such as corn and wheat are price takers. Can you explain why?

online and checks the current (equilibrium) price of Disney stock. If it is $80.07, then this is the price Brown must take if she wants to sell her stock. She won't be able to sell her stock for even one penny more.

QUESTION: *Aren't all sellers price takers? Doesn't every seller have to sell his or her goods at the equilibrium price determined by supply and demand?*

ANSWER: *No. Think of the difference between the seller of stock or wheat and the seller of, say, books. The stock seller can only sell her stock at one price—the equilibrium price. Charge one penny higher, and she can't sell any stock. The wheat seller can only sell his wheat at one price—the equilibrium price. Charge one penny higher, and he can't sell any wheat. But the seller of books can sell books at various prices, although he or she can't sell as many books at a higher price as at a lower price.*

Can Price Takers Sell for Less than the Equilibrium Price?

So, we've learned that if Jones, the farmer, and Brown, the stock seller, want to sell what they own (wheat and stock), they will have to sell at the equilibrium prices in their respective markets, not at one penny more. What happens if they want to sell for one penny less? If the equilibrium price of Disney stock is $110.00, can't Brown sell her stock at $109.70 (for 30 cents less)? Yes, she can. No buyer is going to turn down a lower price. The point is that Brown has no reason to offer to sell her stock at a price lower than the equilibrium price. After all, she can sell all of her stock at the equilibrium price of $110.00. So, two points are true for every price taker:

1. He or she cannot sell for a price higher than the equilibrium price.
2. He or she will not sell for a price lower than the equilibrium price.

Divide students into groups of four or five, and ask each group to develop a product that could exist in a perfectly competitive market. Once each group has developed and named its product, have it set an initial price and identify the fac-

tors they considered to determine that price. Once each group has determined an equilibrium price, ask group members to explain what would happen to its place in the market if they raised its price and if they lowered its price.

EXAMPLE Patty owns 10 ounces of gold that she wants to sell. She checks the daily (equilibrium) price for gold on a particular day; it is $1,200. She will have to sell her gold for $1,200 an ounce. If, by chance, she charges a higher price—say, $1,280—she won't sell even an ounce of gold. Patty is a price taker. ♦

Must a Perfectly Competitive Market Have All Four Characteristics?

Recall that a perfectly competitive market has four characteristics. Is a real-world market still a perfectly competitive market if it doesn't perfectly match these four characteristics? For example, suppose a market has characteristics 1, 2, and 4 but only slightly satisfies characteristic 3. (You may want to look back to refresh your memory on the four characteristics of a perfectly competitive market.) Does it follow that because this market doesn't satisfy all four characteristics 100 percent, it isn't a perfectly competitive market? The answer is no.

Think about this old saying "If it looks like a duck and quacks like a duck, it is probably a duck." The same thing holds for markets too. If a seller is a price taker—that is, if he or she can sell only at the equilibrium price—then for all practical purposes, this seller is operating in a perfectly competitive market. Rephrasing the duck saying, "If a seller is a price taker, then it is operating in a perfectly competitive market."

What Does a Perfectly Competitive Firm Do?

As we said in the previous chapter, every firm has to answer these two key questions:

1. How much of our product should we produce?
2. What price should we charge for our product?

How does a perfectly competitive firm answer the first question of how much to produce? It answers it the same way any firm

would answer it: it produces the quantity of output at which marginal revenue (MR) equals marginal cost (MC). How does a perfectly competitive firm answer the second question of what price to charge? Because it is a price taker, it has no choice in the matter: it sells its product for the equilibrium price determined in the market. If the equilibrium price is $10, then that is the price it charges, not $10.01 or $9.99.

So, to summarize the answers to the two questions: (1) perfectly competitive firms produce the quantity of output at which marginal revenue equals marginal cost; (2) they charge the equilibrium price for their product.

EXAMPLE Market A is a perfectly competitive market. Currently, the equilibrium price is $10. The total revenue and marginal revenue data for one seller in this market look like the following:

Units of output	Total revenue	Marginal revenue
1	$10	$10
2	20	10
3	30	10

This firm's total cost and marginal cost data look like the following:

Units of output	Total cost	Marginal cost
1	$6	$6
2	14	8
3	24	10

▲ If this manufacturer operates in a perfectly competitive market, how does it decide what price to charge for its products?

Teaching with Visuals

The manufacturer has no choice in the matter; it checks the equilibrium price and must accept it.

Reinforcement Activity

Ask students if they would like to be sellers in a perfectly competitive market. What would be the advantages for price takers? What would be the disadvantages? If the market price does not change and all sellers' products are the same, is this a good market in which to be? Then ask students if they would like to be buyers in a perfectly competitive market. What would be the advantages and disadvantages?

Critical Thinking

Firms in a perfectly competitive market must answer the two questions of how much of a good to produce and how much to charge for that good. No matter what the firm decides, the market has already set the equilibrium price. Ask students to identify ways that a business can deviate from perfect competition to make more profits and what might happen if it takes those steps. Students should realize that as soon as a business differentiates its product, it is no longer competing in a perfectly competitive market, because it no longer fits the third characteristic of a perfectly competitive market.

Cooperative Learning

The stock market and the commodities markets are great examples of perfectly competitive markets. Divide the class into groups of three or four. Have each group track a particular stock or commodity for a week. Does the price change during the week? What quantity of stock or commodity is sold during the week? If possible, have a stock-broker or commodities trader come to your class to discuss how these markets work. Have the groups prepare questions the day before the visit so that both the class and your guest speaker are prepared.

Application Activity

After reading and discussing Section 1, you may want to assign the Section Activity in the *Applying the Principles Workbook*, pages 85–86.

Now ask what quantity of output this firm will produce. You know that it wants to produce the quantity of output at which marginal revenue equals marginal cost: MR = MC occurs at a quantity of 3 units. Now ask what price it will charge for each of the 3 units it sells. Because the firm is a price taker, it takes the equilibrium price of $10. So, it produces 3 units and charges a price of $10 for each unit.

> *"Designing your product for monetization first, and people second, will probably leave you with neither."*
> —Tara Hunt, online marketing pioneer

How much profit does this firm earn? We know that profit is the difference between total revenue and total cost. When the firm produces 3 units of output, its total revenue is $30 and its total cost is $24, so it follows that this firm's profit is $6. ♦

A Student Asks

QUESTION: *How did you get the dollar amounts in the marginal revenue (MR) and marginal cost (MC) columns?*

ANSWER: *Remember from Chapter 7 that marginal revenue is the revenue from producing an additional unit of a good. Notice that when the firm sells 1 unit of the good, its total revenue is $10, and when it sells 2 units of a good, its total revenue is $20. What is the revenue generated from selling the additional unit (the second unit)? Obviously, the answer is $10. The same holds going from selling 2 units to 3 units. The total revenue for the firm when it sells 2 units is $20 and it is $30 when it sells 3 units; therefore, the revenue from selling the additional unit is $10. Here is the MR equation from Chapter 7:*

$$\text{Marginal revenue (MR)} = \frac{\Delta TR}{\Delta Q}$$

As to the dollar amounts in the marginal cost (MC) column, we just made them up. Often, in the real world, marginal cost rises as a firm produces additional units of a good, so we had the marginal cost dollar amounts rise in our example.

Profit Is a Signal in a Perfectly Competitive Market

Suppose 200 sellers operate in market X, a perfectly competitive market. Each of the sellers produces good X and sells it for its current equilibrium price, $10. Furthermore, all 200 firms earn profits. Will things stay as they are? Not likely.

Recall that the fourth characteristic of a perfectly competitive market is easy entry. In other words, firms that are not currently in market X can easily get into it. Nothing is holding them out. As long as sellers are earning profits in that market, new firms will enter it.

As new firms enter market X, the number of firms in the market increases, say, from 200 to 250. With more firms, the supply of good X increases. (Remember from Chapter 5 that as the number of sellers increases, the supply of the good increases too—the supply curve shifts rightward.) When the supply of a good rises, the equilibrium price falls. Furthermore, as the price falls, so does profit. Profit, remember, is total revenue (price times number of units sold) minus total cost. In this case, as the price falls, so do total revenue and profit.

▲ What will likely happen if this fast-food restaurant's profits begin to climb?

Differentiating Instruction

English Language Learners

To help students who are English language learners, use the following resources, which are provided as part of the *Economics: New Ways of Thinking* program:

- a Spanish glossary in the *Student Text*
- Spanish versions of the Chapter Summaries on an audio disc

How long will new firms keep entering market X? Until they see no reason to do so—that is, until the competition eliminates the profit. When profit falls to zero and total revenue equals total cost, firms will no longer have a monetary incentive to enter market X.

In a perfectly competitive market, profit acts as a signal to firms that are not in the market. It says, "Come over here and get me." As new firms gravitate toward the profit, they increase the supply of the good earning the profit and thus lower its price. As the price goes down, the profit disappears. The process ends when firms no longer see an incentive to enter the market to obtain profit:

Profit exists → New firms enter the market →
Supply rises → Price falls →
Price falls until firms no longer see an
incentive to enter the market

A Student Asks

QUESTION: *What are some examples of profit that signals other firms to enter the market, ultimately reducing the price that consumers pay?*

ANSWER: *Think about the prices you sometimes pay for new goods (goods that have just been introduced). When the VCR was introduced, for instance, its price was more than $1,000. The profit in the VCR market acted as a signal to new firms to enter that market. As they did, the supply of VCRs went up and the price of VCRs fell. You can buy one today for about $60. The same thing happened in the market for calculators (the early ones with numerous functions sold for about $400), the market for personal computers, the market for DVD players, and many more markets.*

Economic Facts *and* Fallacies

FALSE
TRUE

Profits Are Not Like Periods in a Sentence

Many people view profits in much the same way they view periods in a sentence: they see profits as coming at the ends of production and selling processes, much like periods come at the ends of sentences. In fact, profits are more like commas in that things come after them. Profits lead to new firms entering the market, which leads to supply rising, which leads to price falling until there is no longer an incentive for new firms to enter the market.

Profits May Be Taxed Away

Suppose we go back to the point when the 200 firms in market X were all earning profits. Now, suppose a member of Congress says, "The firms in market X are earning huge profits. They do not deserve them; they just happened to be in the right place at the right time. The government needs some additional money for some new programs, so we should tax these profits. I propose a special tax on these profits of 100 percent."

Congress goes along with this member, enacts a special tax on the profits of the firms in market X, and taxes away these profits. With the profits taxed away, the reason for firms not currently in market X to enter it is gone. If no new firms enter market X, the supply of good X will not rise, and the price of good X will not fall. This situation leaves consumers paying a higher price than they would have paid if the profits of the 200 firms had not been taxed away.

The intended effect was to tax away the profits of the 200 firms and to generate new revenue for the government. The unintended effect was that consumers ended up paying a higher price for good X.

Assessment Book

You will find a quiz for this section in the *Assessment Book,* page 77.

Reteaching Activity

Use the Section Assessment to gauge which students may need reteaching on this section. Ask those students whether sellers in a perfectly competitive market have control over price, and work with them to write explanations of their answers.

Guided Reading

For further reteaching of the key concepts in this section, assign the Outlining Activity and the Just the Facts Handout from the *Guided Reading and Study Guide,* pages 115–118.

Discussion Starter

The feature on the next page discusses competition. Competition between sellers can be quite obvious. In recent years, the two major soft drink companies have developed advertising campaigns directed against one another. Invite students to name other markets in which the sellers have used advertising to downgrade their competition.

Economics *in the* Real World

ANSWERS TO THINK ABOUT IT The existing restaurants will likely see the new restaurant as more competition. If the restaurants provide similar types of goods to their customers, then a new restaurant becomes a substitute for many of the already existing restaurants. Thus, existing restaurants will view the new restaurant as just more substitutes for what they provide. They may say, "just more competition for us."

Assess

Quick Quiz

The following true-or-false quiz will help you assess student understanding of the material covered in this section.

1. In a perfectly competitive market, there are few buyers and many sellers. (False)
2. In a perfectly competitive market, all firms sell identical goods. (True)
3. All firms are price takers in a perfectly competitive market. (True)
4. Only three of the four characteristics must be met for a market to be considered perfectly competitive. (False)
5. If price falls in a perfectly competitive market, firms will enter it. (False)

SECTION 1 ASSESSMENT ANSWERS

Defining Terms

1. a. market structure: the setting in which a seller finds itself; characteristics include number of sellers, the product produced and sold, and so on;
b. perfectly competitive market: a market structure with these four characteristics: (1) many buyers and many sellers; (2) all firms sell identical goods; (3) buyers and sellers have all relevant information about buying and selling activities; and (4) easy entry into and exit out of the market; **c. price taker:** a seller that can sell all its output at the equilibrium price but can sell none of its output at any other price.

Reviewing Facts and Concepts

2. Easy entry and easy exit mean that there is nothing stopping firms from getting into a market or leaving it.
3. A perfectly competitive firm produces the quantity of output at which marginal revenue equals marginal cost. It charges the equilibrium price as determined in the market by supply and demand.

Economics *in the* Real World

Is It Sellers Against Buyers or Sellers Against Sellers?

It might seem like buyers and sellers are always at odds with each other. Sellers want to sell their goods and services at high prices, and buyers want sellers to sell their goods and services at low prices. This situation naturally pits buyers and sellers against each other. Each wants the price to go in a different direction.

But buyers and sellers are not always on opposite sides over prices. Suppose firms in a perfectly competitive market are earning profits. Firms that are not currently in this perfectly competitive market will try to enter it to obtain some of those profits. Will the firms that are already in the market welcome the new firms trying to enter the market? Not at all. The existing firms will see the new firms as trying to take their profits away from them. Here, we have existing firms (sellers) at odds with new firms (also sellers).

Now ask yourself, who is being helped by the new firms entering the market? Buyers. When new firms enter the market, the supply curve of the good or service shifts to the right, thus lowering the price for buyers. So, the new firms benefit the buyers.

To recap, in a perfectly competitive market, when profits are being earned, existing firms are at odds with new firms entering the market, and new firms entering the market actually benefit buyers. It isn't a case of all sellers being against all buyers; instead, some sellers are working against other sellers, and some sellers (the new ones) are helping buyers.

THINK ABOUT IT Suppose there are 10 restaurants in a particular part of town, and each restaurant is only 1,000 yards from another restaurant. Then a new restaurant comes into the market and locates in the same area. Will the existing restaurants likely welcome the new restaurant, or will they likely see the new restaurant as more competition? Explain your answer.

SECTION 1 ASSESSMENT

Defining Terms
1. Define:
  a. market structure
  b. perfectly competitive market
  c. price taker

Reviewing Facts and Concepts
2. What is easy entry into a market and easy exit out of the market?
3. What quantity of output does a perfectly competitive firm produce? What price does it charge for its product?

Critical Thinking
4. Some of the firms in market X (a perfectly competitive market) are incurring losses. How will these losses influence (a) exit out of the market, (b) the supply of the good produced, and (c) the price of the good?

5. In this section, we said profit is a signal. Is loss a signal too? If so, for what?

Applying Economic Concepts
6. How can a seller determine whether it is a price taker?
7. Go to http://econ.emcp.net/quotecorn and find the current price of corn. Is corn produced in a perfectly competitive market? Explain.

Critical Thinking

4. The firms that incur losses will (a) exit the market, because exit is easy in a perfectly competitive market. This will lead to (b) a reduction in the supply of the good produced in the market, which will lead to (c) a higher price for the good.
5. Yes. Loss is a signal to firms to get out of a market. Firms follow profits and move away from losses.

Applying Economic Concepts

6. It can offer to sell its product for a price above equilibrium price. If it can sell some of its product at this price, then it is not a price taker. If it cannot sell anything above equilibrium price, then it is not a price taker.
7. Yes, corn is produced in a perfectly competitive market. It has a single market price, and all sellers must sell at that price.

A Monopolistic Market

Focus Questions

► What are the characteristics of a monopolistic market?
► What are examples of barriers to entry?
► Do monopolists ever face competition?
► What purpose do antitrust laws serve?
► What have been some of the major antitrust laws?

Key Terms

monopolistic market
barrier to entry
price searcher
public franchise
natural monopoly
antitrust law

Focus and Motivate

Section Objectives

After completing this section, students will be able to

► identify the characteristics of a monopolistic market;
► provide some examples of barriers to entry;
► explain whether monopolists ever face competition;
► explain the purpose of antitrust laws; and
► list some of the major antitrust laws.

Kickoff Activity

Have students brainstorm associations with the word *monopoly*. Most students will think of the famous board game Monopoly.

Activating Prior Knowledge

Invite students to share the ideas they generated during the Kickoff Activity. Most will mention the board game, and many will already have a simplistic understanding of what a monopoly is in economic terms. Explain to students that in this section, they will learn what an economist associates with the word *monopoly*.

Characteristics of a Monopoly

A **monopolistic market** has these three characteristics:

1. It consists of one seller.
2. The single seller sells a product that has no close substitutes.
3. The **barriers to entry** are high, which means that entry into the market is extremely difficult.

How Monopolists Differ from Perfect Competitors

A perfectly competitive firm is a price taker, but a monopoly firm (or monopolist) is a **price searcher**. In contrast with a price taker, a price searcher can sell some of its product at various prices (for example, at $12, $11, $10, $9, and so on). Whereas a price taker has to take one price—the equilibrium price—and sell its product at that price, the price searcher has a list of prices from which to choose. The price searcher "searches" for the best price—the price that generates the greatest profit or, in some cases, the price that minimizes losses.

Which of the many possible prices is the best price? To answer this question, back up and consider the questions that the monopoly firm, like any firm, has to answer: (1) How much should we produce? (2) How much should we charge? The monopoly firm, like any firm, will produce that quantity of output at which marginal revenue equals marginal cost.

Now suppose that for a monopoly firm, that quantity is 20,000 units. What is the best price to charge for each unit? The best price turns out to be the highest price at which all 20,000 units can be sold. If only 15,000 units of the 20,000 units will be sold at a price of $14, then $14 is not the best price. But if at $13, all 20,000 units will be sold, then $13 is the best price. Again, the monopoly firm seeks to charge the best price possible, which is the highest price at which it can sell its entire output.

Here is the problem for the monopolist: it does not know what its best price is. So, it has to search for it through a process of trial and error. It may charge one price this week, only to change the price next week. Over time, a monopoly firm finds the highest price at which it can sell its entire output.

monopolistic market
A market structure characterized by (1) a single seller, (2) the sale of a product that has no close substitutes, and (3) extremely high barriers to entry.

barrier to entry
Anything that prohibits a firm from entering a market.

price searcher
A seller that can sell some of its output at various prices.

Teach

Discussion Starter

Direct students to read aloud the characteristics of a monopoly listed on this page. Ask them to think of markets that might qualify as monopolies. Examples include utilities such as gas, electricity, and cable in regions where only one company is permitted to provide these goods.

Background Information: The Monopoly Game

The game that we know and play today as Monopoly has a very cloudy past. While some people say it was invented in the 1930s, others can show a direct line back to a game invented by a young woman in 1903. What is not in doubt is the fact that Monopoly has sold over 200 million copies worldwide. The blocks on the original board are representations of streets in Atlantic City, New Jersey, but versions of the game have been developed for many cities all over the world—and even for the Star Wars universe!

► How might the owner of this small, neighborhood store have a monopoly? How might the introduction of online stores remove this monopoly position?

Teaching with Visuals

The store might have a local monopoly if it is the only such store in the area. If people want to buy something from a store close to where they live, then this store might be considered a monopolist within, say, a two-square-mile radius. Of course, online stores could remove this store from its monopoly position by offering people in the neighborhood a way to buy without venturing far from where they live.

Cause and Effect

In its position as a price searcher, the monopoly firm will adjust the price of its good or service to find the equilibrium price for the quantity supplied. Ask students to describe how supply and demand affect the selling price of a monopolistic good or service.

Discussion Starter

Ask students which market they would rather sell their products in: a perfectly competitive market or a monopolistic market. What are the advantages and disadvantages of each type of market?

 Visit econ.myemcp.com/videos for videos that will help students better understand the key concepts found in this section.

EXAMPLE Suppose you are taking a long drive along a route that has only one gas station. A sign at the station reads, "Last Chance for Gas for 100 Miles." Gasoline is a product with very few substitutes. You can't put water in your gas tank and hope that the car will run. This gas station is a local monopolist. Although it's not the only gas station in the world, it's the only gas station in a certain small part of the world. The gas station owner has decided that the best quantity of gas for her to sell is 400 gallons. Now, of course, she wants to find the highest price per gallon at which she can sell all 400 gallons. She may have to "search" for this price. Is $3.26 too low? Is $4.50 too high? Through trial and error, she will eventually figure out the highest price at which she can sell all 400 gallons of gas. ◆

A Student Asks

QUESTION: *You mentioned that the gas station is a local monopolist. I am interested in the word "local" here. Do you mean to imply that a seller might be a monopolist in one area but not in another?*

ANSWER: *Yes. Think of a small grocery store instead of a gas station. The small grocery store might be the only grocery store in 10 square miles but not the only grocery store in 20 square miles.*

Or think of a bookstore on a university campus. Many university campuses have only one bookstore that sells the textbooks that students buy. Some would consider the bookstore in this setting a monopolist. Of course, with the introduction of the Internet, this bookstore isn't as much a monopolist today as it might have been in the past. Today, students can buy many of their textbooks online, either directly from the publisher or from an online bookstore.

How Selling Corn or Stock Differs from Selling Cable TV Service

Perhaps nothing brings home the difference between a perfectly competitive seller (a price taker) and a monopoly seller (a price searcher) than placing yourself in the role of each. First, suppose you are a corn farmer in Iowa. You just harvested 100,000 bushels of corn, and you want to sell them as quickly as possible. It's easy to determine at what price you will sell your corn: you just check the newspaper or listen to the crop report on the radio or TV news to see what price corn is selling at. That's the price you will take for your corn.

Now, suppose you own a cable TV company. In many towns, only one cable

216 Chapter 8 Competition and Markets

Cross-Curricular Activity

The U.S. economic system is based on the principles of free enterprise. At times, certain businesses have grown into monopolies. Invite a history teacher to your class to discuss the development of monopolies in the United States, especially focusing on the late–nineteenth century

"barons of business," John D. Rockefeller, J. P. Morgan, and Andrew Carnegie. If possible, also have the history teacher discuss the laws and regulations that have limited the growth of monopolies in the United States.

company is allowed to serve a certain geographic area; therefore, you are a monopolist. (With Internet and satellite TV, however, the local cable company is probably less of a monopolist than it once was.) The cable wire has been laid across town, and you are ready for business. What will you charge for your cable service? The answer is not so easy this time. No "cable TV report" provides the market with information, the way a crop report does. So, even though it's rather easy for firms to determine their selling prices in perfectly competitive markets, determining prices is not so easy in monopolistic markets.

Is the Sky the Limit for the Monopolist?

Suppose a pharmaceutical company recently invented a new medicine that cures arthritis. With respect to this medicine, the company is a monopolist; it is the only seller of a medicine that has no close substitutes. Can it charge any price it wants for the medicine? For example, can it charge $5,000 for one bottle (30 pills)? If your answer is yes, ask yourself whether it can charge $10,000 for one bottle. If your answer is still yes, ask yourself whether it can charge $20,000 for one bottle.

The purpose of these questions is to get you to realize that monopolists do face a limit as to how high a price they can charge. (The sky is not the limit!) At some of the high prices in our example, no one—not even someone who suffers greatly from arthritis pain—will be willing to buy the medicine.

The monopolist is limited by the "height" of the demand curve it faces. What does this mean? Suppose the demand curve in Exhibit 8-1 is for the medicine that cures arthritis and the pharmaceutical company has decided to produce 500,000 bottles of medicine. The highest price (per bottle) that can be charged for each bottle of 500,000 bottles is determined by the height of the demand curve, or $100 per bottle. Thus, the height of the demand curve (at the quantity of output the firm wants to sell) is the limit.

A Monopoly Seller Is Not Guaranteed Profits

Most people think that if a firm is a monopoly seller, it is guaranteed to earn profits. This assumption is not true, however; no monopoly seller is guaranteed profits. A firm earns profits only if the price for which it sells its good is above its average total cost. For example, if a firm sells its good for $10 and its average total cost (per-unit cost) is $6, then it earns $4 profit per unit. If it sells 1,000 units, its profit is $4,000.

"Efficiency is doing better what is already being done."
—Peter Drucker, management consultant

The monopolist sells its product for the highest price possible, but nothing guarantees that this price will be greater than the monopoly seller's average total cost. If it isn't greater, the monopoly seller doesn't earn any profits. If average total cost for the monopoly seller is actually higher than the highest possible price for which it sells its product, the monopoly seller will earn a loss (not a profit). If this situation continues, the monopoly seller will go out of business.

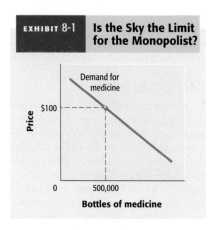

EXHIBIT 8-1 | **Is the Sky the Limit for the Monopolist?**

▲ Once a monopoly firm decides on its quantity of output, it is limited to the highest price it can charge (per unit) for the product. Specifically, it is limited by the height of the demand curve. In this case, the monopoly firm decides to produce 500,000 bottles of medicine. The highest price it can charge (per unit) and sell this output is $100 per bottle.

Reinforcement Activity

The example of the medical monopolist is a good one for students to think about. If a company discovers a new cure for a previously incurable disease, can it charge as much as $1 million for each dose? Assign students to research discoveries of new cures to determine whether the discovering company or individual set a price that dramatically increased profits. Ask students why a company or individual might not set such a high price.

Discussion Starter

Prompt students to identify situations in which the equilibrium price for a good produced by a monopolist is less than its average cost. Ask them why a monopoly seller might continue to produce in a market in which it is not making a profit. Students might mention start-up monopolistic companies with new products for which demand is small but growing. These companies might tolerate losses in a particular market to drive competitors out of business.

Teaching with Visuals

Use Exhibit 8-1 to make sure students understand that monopolistic markets do have limits on the prices they can charge for their products.

Cooperative Learning

Direct students to work in pairs to identify three monopolies. Students should refer to the three characteristics of a monopoly listed on page 215. Examples of monopolies include local public utility companies. In many areas, there is only one water company, one gas company, and one electric company. Encourage students to look beyond public utilities and try to find other examples of monopolies in the U.S. economy.

Often, one existing barrier to entry is that local governments prevent more than one company from serving a given area.

Critical Thinking

Assign students to research monopolies that have existed in the United States, including those discussed by the history teacher in the Cross-Curricular Activity at the bottom of page 216. As part of their research, urge students to consider whether each business created barriers to prevent competitors from entering the market or whether barriers were created by an outside force.

Reinforcement Activity

Direct each student to list the three characteristics of a monopoly and give one example of a monopolistic market.

▶ A cable TV company may have a monopoly in a certain geographic area. What are the likely barriers to entry here?

EXAMPLE Tony has gone into business; he sells a good that no one else sells. Because he is the only one who sells this particular good, his friend refers to him as a monopolist. Is Tony guaranteed profit because he is the only seller of a particular good? Not necessarily. It turns out that no one demands the good that Tony sells. In other words, a seller can be a monopolist but not sell anything. The objective many sellers set for themselves is to be a monopolist with respect to a good for which demand is high. ◆

Barriers to Entry

Suppose firm X is a monopolist. It is currently charging a relatively high price for its product and earning large profits. Why don't other businesses enter the market and produce the same product as firm X? As noted earlier, one of the three characteristics of a monopolistic market is high barriers to entry. They include legal barriers, a monopolist's extremely low average total costs, and a monopolist's exclusive ownership of a scarce resource.

Legal Barriers

public franchise
A right granted to a firm by the government that permits the firm to provide a particular good or service and excludes all others from doing so.

Legal barriers to entry in a monopoly market include public franchises, patents, and copyrights. A **public franchise** is a right granted to a firm by the government that permits the firm to provide a particular good or service and excludes all others from

doing so. Potential competition is thus eliminated by law.

For example, as stated earlier, in many towns, only one cable company is allowed to service a particular geographic area. This company has been given the exclusive right to produce and sell cable TV service. If an organization other than the designated company starts producing and selling cable TV service, it will be breaking the law. Another example of a legal barrier is the restriction the U.S. government has placed on private mail carriers. Only the U.S. Postal Service can deliver first-class mail. Also, some towns make it illegal for more than one company to collect trash.

In the United States, a *patent* is granted to the inventor of a product or process for 20 years. For example, a pharmaceutical firm may have a patent on a medicine. During this time, the patent holder is shielded from competitors; no one else can legally produce and sell the patented product or process.

Copyrights give authors or originators of literary or artistic productions the right to publish, print, or sell their intellectual productions for a period of time. With books, either the author or the company that publishes the book holds the copyright. For example, the publishing company holds the copyright to this textbook—it owns the right to reproduce and sell copies of this book. Anyone else who copies the book or large sections of it to sell or simply to avoid buying a copy is breaking the law.

Extremely Low Average Total Costs (Low Per-Unit Costs)

Chapter 7 described the average total cost as the total cost divided by the quantity of output, also called per-unit cost. For example, if the total cost is $1,000 and the quantity of output is 1,000 units, then the average total cost is $1 per unit.

In some industries, one particular firm will have an average total cost that is extremely low—so low that no other firm can compete with it. To see why, let's consider the relationship of average total cost and price. A business will earn a per-unit profit when it sells its product for a price that is higher than

Internet Research

Have students search the Internet for an example of a patent or a copyright that has helped to provide an individual or company with a monopoly. Ask each student to write a one-page paper about that person or company. Ask the student to examine how copyright or patent law provides a legal barrier to entry by the monopolist. Also ask the student to identify the time limitation on the copyright or patent. Have the student predict what will happen to the market for the product after this copyright or patent expires.

its average total cost. For example, if the price is $10 and the average total cost is $4, then the per-unit profit is $6.

Some companies may have such low average total costs that they are able to lower their prices to very low levels and still earn profits. Consequently, competitors may be forced out of business. Suppose 17 companies are currently competing to sell a good. One of the companies, however, has a much lower average total cost than the others. Say company A's average total cost is $5, whereas the other companies' average total cost is $8. Company A can sell its good for $6 and earn a $1 profit on each unit sold. Other companies can't compete with it. In the end, company A—because of its low average total cost—is the only seller of the good. Such a firm is called a **natural monopoly**.

natural monopoly
A firm with such a low average total cost (per-unit cost) that only it can survive in the market.

Will the Internet Bring an End to Monopolies?

Many college campuses have only one bookstore. Professors tell the campus bookstore manager what books they want their students to buy, and the bookstore orders the books. During the first weeks of classes, students usually go to the bookstore and buy the books they need. They often complain about the high prices of textbooks; it is not uncommon for individual textbooks to sell for $100 or more.

Many college students feel that, to a large degree, the campus bookstore acts as a monopolist. It is a single seller of a good (required textbooks) that has no substitutes (the student must buy the book the professor is using in class, not a similar book). Usually, the university administration won't allow more than one bookstore on campus (so barriers to entry are high). In a way, we might consider the campus bookstore a local or geographic monopoly: it is the single seller of a good with no substitutes and high barriers to entry in a certain location.

Enter the Internet, which has destroyed many local or geographic monopolies. College students no longer have to buy their textbooks from the campus bookstore. They can buy books from an online bookstore, such as Amazon.com. The Internet has essentially eliminated the barrier to entering any campus's textbook market.

Similarly, some people think that the Internet has eliminated local monopolies in selling cars, although the case is less strong here. Suppose you live in a town with only one Ford dealership. It's true that the dealership may be the sole seller of Fords within a certain area (say, a radius of 40 miles), but substitutes for Fords (for example, Hondas) are available. Nevertheless, it is possible for a single Ford dealership to have a certain degree of monopoly power. If you want a Ford, you will be inclined to go to that Ford dealership.

Again, the Internet changes the situation in several ways. First, at various online sites, you can obtain the invoice price of any car you are thinking about buying. Second, via the Internet, you can contact Ford dealers in nearby towns and ask if they are willing to sell you a Ford for, say, $1,500 over invoice price. Now, instead of negotiating with the only Ford dealership in town, you can negotiate with several dealerships over the Internet.

THINK ABOUT IT The existence of the Internet has weakened local (or geographic) monopolies in textbooks and cars. What other kinds of local monopolies are threatened by the Internet?

After students read this feature, ask them why some college administrations grant monopolies to college bookstores. Students might suggest that the campus has space for only one bookstore or that the college is getting some benefit from the bookstore to enforce barriers to entering the market.

ANSWERS TO THINK ABOUT IT Answers will vary. Students should spend some time searching the Internet to help them answer this question. Ask students to share the results of their research with the class.

Background Information

Is the Internet the enemy of geographic monopolies? Imagine that you live in a small town in Italy, Japan, or the United States and that this town has only one bookstore. The bookstore can be said to be a geographic monopoly—that is, it is the only seller of books within a certain geographical area. Enter the Internet! Now, there is a substitute for the one bookstore in town (assuming you have an Internet connection), and the local store no longer has a monopoly.

Internet Research

Have students find out how to apply for or register a patent and a copyright. They should visit the websites of the U.S. Patent and Trademark Office and the U.S. Copyright Office. Ask students to list the steps to take to apply for a patent and a copyright and to explain the reasons these protections exist and how they affect competition.

Teaching with Visuals

Answers will vary, but students might say that the barriers to entry are necessary to allow companies to recover their research costs.

Reinforcement Activity

Ask each student to write a one-page essay answering the following question: What are the benefits and costs of a patent law that gives the inventor of a product or process a monopoly position for 20 years? Why would this law be important to inventors? Students should see that patents provide incentives for inventors by virtually guaranteeing that they will be able to sell their inventions at higher prices than they could charge in a perfectly competitive market.

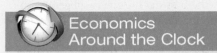

Economics Around the Clock

After reading and discussing the first part of Section 2, direct students to reread the 7:34 p.m. scenario in Economics Around the Clock (page 207) and write answers to the question that accompanies it.

Students should see that the concession companies that operate at baseball stadiums and other arenas have a monopoly on the sale of food. Each company is a price searcher and can charge the highest price at which people are willing and able to purchase a sufficient amount of each type of food.

▲ Research companies often obtain patents on their products, which prevents other companies from entering the market for a specified time period. Are such barriers to entry necessary? Explain.

EXAMPLE Three companies—A, B, and C—all sell a particular good. The per-unit costs of company A are $4 while the per-unit costs of B and C are $7. Currently, all three companies sell their good for a price of $10. In time, company A lowers its price to $6, but companies B and C cannot follow suit. For them to lower the price to $6 would mean incurring a $1 per-unit loss on each item they produce and sell. Because of the lower price, customers start buying from company A instead of from B and C. In time, companies B and C go out of business. ♦

Exclusive Ownership of a Scarce Resource

It takes oranges to produce orange juice. If one firm owns all the oranges, it can be considered a monopoly firm. The classic example of a monopolist controlling a resource is the Aluminum Company of America (Alcoa). For a long time, Alcoa controlled almost all of the sources of bauxite (the main source of aluminum) in the United States, making it the sole producer of aluminum in the country from the late nineteenth century until the 1940s.

antitrust law
Legislation passed for the stated purpose of controlling monopoly power and preserving and promoting competition.

Government Monopoly and Market Monopoly

Sometimes, high barriers to entry exist because competition is legally prohibited, and sometimes, these barriers exist for other reasons. When a barrier takes the form of a public franchise, patent, or copyright, competition is legally prohibited. In contrast, when a barrier takes the form of one firm's low average total cost or exclusive ownership of a resource, competition is not legally prohibited. In this case, no law keeps rival firms from entering the market and competing, even though they may choose not to do so.

Some economists use the term *government monopoly* to refer to a monopoly that is legally protected from competition. Economists use the term *market monopoly* to refer to a monopoly that is not legally protected from competition.

Antitrust and Monopoly

One of the stated objectives of the U.S. government is to encourage competition so that monopolists do not have substantial control over the prices they charge. Let's look briefly at some of the issues involved in maintaining competition.

Antitrust Laws

The U.S. government tries to meet its objectives through its **antitrust laws**: laws meant to control monopoly power and to preserve and promote competition. Following are descriptions of some of the major antitrust laws throughout history. Exhibit 8-2 provides a timeline for the implementation of these laws.

The Sherman Antitrust Act The Sherman Antitrust Act (or simply, the Sherman Act) was passed in 1890, a time when numerous mergers were occurring between companies. In a merger, one company buys more than half the stock in another company, putting two companies under the same management. At the time of the Sherman Act, the organization that two companies formed by combining to act as a

Cross-Curricular Activity

Team with a history teacher from your school to discuss both the economics and the technology involved in a historical example of government monopoly and market monopoly.

The history teacher might discuss the evolution of the steam engine from the first one built in 1712 by Thomas Newcomen to the ones that powered steamboats, such as Robert Fulton's steamboat (1807), and later steam locomotion.

You might encourage students to look at the economic impact of each of these innovations and at the resources that were used to produce these products.

monopolist was called a *trust*, which in turn gave us the word *antitrust*.

The Sherman Act contains two major provisions:

1. "Every contract, combination in the form of trust or otherwise, or conspiracy, in restraint of trade or commerce . . . is hereby declared to be illegal."
2. "Every person who shall monopolize, or attempt to monopolize, or combine or conspire with any other person or persons to monopolize any part of the trade or commerce . . . shall be deemed guilty of a misdemeanor."

Together, these two provisions state that attempting to become a monopolist and trying to restrain trade are both illegal.

The Clayton Act   The Clayton Act of 1914 made certain business practices illegal when their effects "may be to substantially lessen competition or tend to create a monopoly." Here are two practices prohibited by the act:

1. *Price discrimination.* Price discrimination occurs when a seller charges different buyers different prices for the same product and when the price differences are not related to cost differences. For example, if a company charges you $10 for a product and charges your friend $6 for the same product and there is no cost difference for the company in providing the two of you with this product, then the company is practicing price discrimination. (You will learn more about price discrimination near the end of the chapter.)
2. *Tying contracts.* A tying contract is an arrangement whereby the sale of one product depends on the purchase of some other product or products. For example, suppose the owner of a company that sells personal computers and computer supplies agrees to sell computers to a store only if the store owner agrees to buy paper, desk furniture, and some other products too. This agreement is a tying contract, and it's illegal under the Clayton Act.

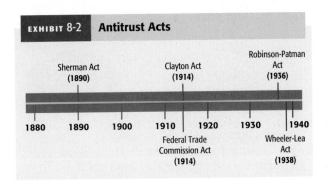

EXHIBIT 8-2   Antitrust Acts

Sherman Act (1890) — Clayton Act (1914) — Robinson-Patman Act (1936)

1880 1890 1900 1910 1920 1930 1940

Federal Trade Commission Act (1914) — Wheeler-Lea Act (1938)

▲ Major antitrust acts in U.S. history include the Sherman Act, the Clayton Act, the Federal Trade Commission Act, the Robinson-Patman Act, and the Wheeler-Lea Act.

The Federal Trade Commission Act   The Federal Trade Commission Act, passed in 1914, declared that "unfair methods of competition in commerce" are illegal. In particular, the act was designed to prohibit aggressive price-cutting acts, sometimes referred to as "cutthroat" pricing.

EXAMPLE   Suppose you own a business that produces and sells tires. A competitor begins to drastically lower the prices of the tires it sells. From your viewpoint, your competitor may be engaged in cutthroat pricing. From the viewpoint of the consumer, your competitor is simply offering a good deal. The FTC officials, who enforce the Federal Trade Commission Act, will have to decide. If the officials believe your competitor is cutting its prices so low that you go out of business and that it intends to raise its prices later, when you're gone, they may decide that your competitor is violating the act. ◆

Some economists have noted that the Federal Trade Commission Act, like other antitrust acts, contains vague terms. For instance, the act does not precisely define what "unfair methods of competition" consist of. Suppose a hotel chain puts up a big, beautiful hotel across the street from an old, tiny, run-down motel, and the old motel ends up going out of business. Was the hotel chain employing "unfair methods of competition"?

Allow students to look through newspapers and magazines for articles that mention antitrust activities. Two of the best newspapers and magazines for this activity are the *Wall Street Journal* and *Fortune* magazine. Invite students to report their findings to the class.

Thinking Like an Economist

Eroding the Monopoly on First-Class Mail

Economists often remark that "Technology can change a market." To illustrate, consider the market for the delivery of first-class mail. The federal government prohibits private firms from competing with the U.S. Postal Service (USPS) when it comes to the delivery of first-class mail. This makes it illegal for a private company to deliver first-class mail the way the USPS does. Because of this, the USPS had a true monopoly on the delivery of first-class mail for many years.

But then a series of technological changes brought about email. Now you can type a letter, attach it to or copy it into an email, click Send, and the letter is delivered to the recipient almost immediately. There's no need to purchase and attach a postage stamp, to put the letter in a mailbox, or to wait for postal workers to pick up, transport, and deliver the letter. All you need is an email account and access to a computer connected to the Internet. Email is so convenient and low in cost that it has effectively eroded the monopoly position of the USPS when it comes to the delivery of first-class letters.

▲ Maureen K. Ohlausen is the acting chair of the Federal Trade Commission, whose mission is to protect consumers by preventing anticompetitive, deceptive, and unfair business practices.

The Robinson-Patman Act The Robinson-Patman Act was passed in 1936 in an attempt to decrease the failure rate of small businesses by protecting them from the competition of large and growing chain stores. At that time in U.S. economic history, large chain stores were brand new. They bought goods in large amounts and were sometimes offered price discounts from their suppliers. When the chain stores began to pass on the price discounts to their customers, the small businesses (who were not being offered the discounts) found it increasingly difficult to compete. The Robinson-Patman Act prohibited suppliers from offering special discounts to large chains unless they also offered the discounts to everyone else.

Many economists believe that rather than preserving and strengthening competition, the Robinson-Patman Act limited it. The act, they say, seemed more concerned about a particular group of competitors (small businesses) than about the process of competition.

The Wheeler-Lea Act The Wheeler-Lea Act, passed in 1938, empowered the Federal Trade Commission (FTC), a government agency, to deal with false and deceptive acts and practices by businesses. Major actions by the FTC in this area have involved advertising that the agency has deemed false and deceptive.

The Issue of Natural Monopoly

Instead of applying antitrust laws to natural monopoly, the government often imposes some kind of regulation on the natural monopolist. For example, instead of allowing the natural monopoly to charge any price it wants, the government often sets the price that the natural monopoly can charge. Alternatively, sometimes the government specifies a certain rate of profit that the natural monopoly can earn.

Government regulation of natural monopolists often produces unintended effects. For example, suppose the government states that the natural monopolist can charge a price of only $2 above costs. If the natural monopolist

Background Information: Price Discrimination

Price discrimination occurs when a seller charges different buyers different prices for the same product and the price differences are not related to cost differences. The Clayton Act deems price discrimination illegal when it substantially lessens competition. Students may find it interesting and fun to look for examples of price discrimination.

Also ask students to come up with examples of when price discrimination should be allowed. For example, some people might say that if a medical doctor wants to charge a poor person for a medical visit, the doctor should be allowed to do so—even if this is an act of price discrimination. Ask students what they think about this.

What Have Uber and Lyft Done to the Taxicab Business in New York City?

It is easy for new firms to enter some markets and difficult for them to enter others. Difficulty in entering a market is usually caused by the existence of some barrier. Of course, not all barriers to entry are the same. One kind is created through legal means. For example, when the government prohibited private firms from competing with the U.S. Postal Service in the delivery of first-class mail, it effectively created a legal barrier to entering this business. Are there similar government-created barriers to entry in other businesses?

Consider the taxicab business in New York City before Uber and Lyft, two-riding services, came on the scene. To operate a taxicab in New York City, the Taxi and Limousine Commission requires you to have a taxi license, called a taxi medallion. How much does it cost? In 2014, the price of a medallion was $1.3 million. The high price of a taxi medallion acts as a barrier to entering the taxicab business in New York City.

Who wins and who loses with such a system? The winners are clearly the current owners of taxicab businesses. Because of such a high barrier to entering the business, the supply of taxis on the streets of New York City is less than it otherwise would be. If the supply is lower than it would be, then prices are higher. In other words, taxi rides are higher in price than they would be. So, current taxicab businesses win, taxi riders lose, and people who want to enter the taxicab business lose too.

But that was in 2014. Today, Uber and Lyft have entered the New York City market and provided stiff competition for taxicab owners and drivers. Instead of taking a taxi from one location to another in New York City, people today have the option of taking a ride-share service such as Uber and Lyft instead. What would you predict that the introduction of Uber and Lyft into the New York City market would do to the price of a taxi medallion? Fact is, the price of taxi medallion has fallen dramatically. In 2017, medallions were in the $500,000 range with one listed for sale at $250,000. That is down from a high of $1.3 million just three years earlier.

THINK ABOUT IT What do Uber and Lyft have to do with supply and demand?

After students have read this feature, ask them to think about why the barriers to entry are so high and why this situation hasn't changed.

ANSWERS TO THINK ABOUT IT Answers will vary. Students should note that Uber and Lyft increase the supply of taxi-like services--the service of a car taking people from one location to another--thus, lowering the price of a ride.

Reinforcement Activity

Have each student research the cost of beginning and maintaining a taxi service in his or her own community. Does the owner need a taxi medallion?

► What would a company have to do to be guilty of antitrust violations?

knows that it can always charge a price of $2 higher than costs, then it will have little, if any, incentive to keep its costs down. In the end, consumers may end up paying high prices, because the natural monopolist knows that no matter what its costs are, it can always charge only $2 more (than costs). Similarly, if a natural monopoly is guaranteed a certain rate of profit, it will have little incentive to hold down its costs.

Are Antitrust Laws Always Applied Properly?

People are inclined, perhaps, to believe that when the government enforces antitrust laws, it does so properly. Government may be seen as riding into the market on a white horse, preventing monopolies from running roughshod over consumers. In reality, though, the record of government in this area is mixed. Sometimes, through its enforcement of antitrust laws, the government promotes and protects competition, and sometimes it does not.

EXAMPLE In 1967, the Salt Lake City–based Utah Pie Company charged that three of its competitors in Los Angeles

were practicing price discrimination, which is deemed illegal by the Clayton Act. Specifically, the three competitors were charged with selling pies for lower prices in Salt Lake City than in Los Angeles. The U.S. Supreme Court ruled in favor of Utah Pie.

What were the facts? Were the three Los Angeles competitors running Utah Pie out of business? Were they hurting consumers by charging low prices? Some economists have noted that Utah Pie actually charged lower prices for its pies than did its competitors and that it continued to increase its sales volume and earn a profit during the time its competitors were supposedly exhibiting anticompetitive behavior. These economists suggest that Utah Pie was simply trying to use the antitrust laws to hinder its competition. ◆

EXAMPLE Now consider a case in which most economists believe antitrust laws were applied properly. For many years, the upper-level administrators of some of the top U.S. universities—Brown, Columbia, Cornell, Dartmouth, Harvard, MIT, Princeton, University of Pennsylvania, and Yale—met to discuss such things as tuition, faculty salaries, and financial aid. Evidence seemed to show that these meetings occurred because the universities were trying to align tuition, faculty raises, and financial need. For example, one of the universities wanted to raise faculty salaries by more than the others but was persuaded not to do so. Also at these meetings, the administrators compared lists of applicants to find the names of students who had applied to more than one of their schools (for example, someone who had applied to Harvard, Yale, and MIT). The administrators then adjusted their financial aid packages for that student so that no university offered him or her more than another.

The U.S. Justice Department charged the universities with a conspiracy to fix prices. Eight of the universities settled the case by agreeing to cease colluding (making secret agreements that effectively reduce competition) on tuition, salaries, and financial aid. MIT pursued the case to the U.S. Supreme Court. In 1992, the Supreme Court ruled against MIT, saying that it had violated antitrust laws. ♦

SECTION 2 ASSESSMENT

Defining Terms
1. Define:
   a. monopolistic market
   b. barrier to entry
   c. price searcher
   d. public franchise
   e. natural monopoly
   f. antitrust law

Reviewing Facts and Concepts
2. When it comes to determining the quantity of goods to produce, how is a monopolist like a perfect competitor?
3. A monopolist is a price searcher. For what price is the monopolist searching?
4. Suppose that a company advertises its product in a deceptive manner. Which antitrust act applies to this action?

Critical Thinking
5. Firm A is a perfectly competitive firm, and firm B is a monopoly firm. Both are earning profits. Which is less likely to be earning profits in the future? Explain.

6. Many people mistakenly believe that a monopolist must earn profits. Explain why this is not necessarily the case.

Applying Economic Concepts
7. The demand for the good that firm A sells does not rise or fall during the month. Firm A raises its price at the beginning of the month and lowers its price at the end of the month. What might explain firm A's behavior?

SECTION 2 ASSESSMENT ANSWERS

Defining Terms

1. a. **monopolistic market:** a market structure with these three characteristics: (1) a single seller; (2) the sale of a product with no close substitutes; and (3) extremely high barriers to entry; b. **barrier to entry:** anything that prohibits a firm from entering a market; c. **price searcher:** a seller that can sell some of its output at various prices; d. **public franchise:** a right granted to a firm by the government that permits it to provide a particular good or service and excludes all others from doing so; e. **natural monopoly:** a firm with such a low average total cost (per-unit cost) that it alone can survive in a market; f. **antitrust law:** legislation passed to control monopoly power and preserve and promote competition.

Guided Reading

For further reteaching of the key concepts in this section, assign the Outlining Activity and the Just the Facts Handout from the *Guided Reading and Study Guide,* pages 119–123.

Application Activity

After reading and discussing Section 2, you may want to assign the Section Activity in the *Applying the Principles Workbook,* pages 87–90.

Reviewing Facts and Concepts

2. Both a monopolist and a perfect competitor produce the quantity of output at which marginal revenue equals marginal cost.
3. The monopolist is searching for the best price to charge for the product it produces and sells. The best price is the highest per-unit price at which the monopolist can sell its entire output.
4. The Wheeler-Lea Act prohibits false advertising.

Critical Thinking

5. Firm A, the perfectly competitive firm, is less likely to earn profits in the future. In perfect competition, there is easy entry into the market, whereas in monopoly, there are high barriers to entering the market. This difference matters. Firms will enter the perfectly competitive market, and firm A's profits will eventually decrease. Firms will be unable (or unlikely) to enter the monopoly market and take away firm B's profits.

6. To earn a profit, a monopolist must sell at a price that is greater than its average total cost. Nothing guarantees that the highest price for which a monopolist can sell its product will be greater than its average total cost. After all, the height of the demand curve the monopolist faces is only so high.

Applying Economic Concepts

7. Firm A may be a price searcher; changing the price of the good it sells may reflect its search for the best price.

Your **Personal** Economics

Discussion Starter

Ask students if any of them has ever seen a suspicious offer on the Internet or received a suspicious offer in a letter or email. What kind of offer was it? What seemed suspicious about it?

Research Activity

Have each student survey several adults to determine whether any has seen a scam, such as the type discussed in the feature. Students should find out the nature of each scam and whether any of the people they surveyed were victimized. Have each student compile his or her data and report back to the class.

Don't Fall for an Old Scam

One day, you receive a letter in the mail. It's from an investment advisor who says that he can predict what will be good investments in the near future.

The Setup

At this point, you are skeptical, like most people would be. Having anticipated your skepticism, the investment advisor goes on to say in his letter that he's going to make a prediction about next week's price of gold. He predicts that it will rise. It costs you nothing to wait to see if the price of gold rises, so you do.

Next week, the price of gold rises. Soon after, you get another letter from the investment advisor. He reminds you that he wrote you last week and predicted a rise in the price of gold. He reminds you that things happened as he said they would. Just to prove to you, once again, that he can predict increases and decreases in the price of gold, he tells you that next week, the price of gold will fall. Sure enough, the price of gold does fall the next week.

Again, you get a letter from the advisor. Again, he reminds you that he correctly predicted the change in the price of gold in two consecutive weeks. He makes a third prediction: that next week, the price of gold will rise again. Sure enough, he is right a third time.

The Hook

The final letter you get from the advisor reminds you that he correctly predicted the change in gold in three consecutive weeks. He asks whether you are convinced that he can predict what will and will not be good investments. He also asks you for $1,000, after which he promises to send you a weekly update of his investment advice. He says that if you follow his "crystal-ball advice," you will turn a little money into a lot.

Don't Be Fooled

Now, if you are thinking that you should go along and send in the $1,000, think again. What the investment advisor has just done is make a promise to you that he can't possibly keep. He can't really predict good investments time after time.

But he's done it, you say. You saw him do it with your own two eyes. He didn't just *say* he could predict the change in the price of gold; he *did* it.

How It Works

Here's how he did it. Before you got your first letter from the investment

◄ Be skeptical of any get-rich-quick offers you receive in the mail or online. If something sounds too good to be true, it probably isn't true.

Cooperative Learning

Divide students into groups of three or four. Have each group look through magazines and newspapers to find three advertisements for questionable business ventures. Each group should discuss the characteristics of the offers. Next, have the groups compare and contrast the advertisements. How are they different? How are they similar?

▲ Even reputable newspapers and magazines contain ads for questionable business ventures. Investigate a company before giving it your money.

the price of gold rose, he wrote the people who got the "price-is-going-up" letter—one of whom was you—and told you how he had predicted things correctly three times in a row. Then came the request for money: he urged you to pay him $1,000 for his investment advice.

So you see, the investment advisor never really predicted anything. He just wrote a lot of letters, making completely opposite predictions to two unknowing groups of people. To the people who received the "correct

prediction," he wrote again. He wasn't predicting the future: he was covering all of his bases. He was running a scam.

Your Personal Economics Activity

Consider ways that you can be a wise investor and how you will decide which personal investment options to pursue. Record your plans in a two- to three-paragraph financial plan.

advisor, he wrote 10,000 letters. Half of the letters predicted an increase in the price of gold next week, and half predicted a decrease. The investment advisor kept a record of the people to whom he sent each letter. When the price of gold went up the next week, he wrote again to the people who got the "price-is-going-up" letter. He did not write to the "price-is-going-down" people.

In the second round of letters, he predicted a rise in price to half the people and a decline in price to the other half. When the price of gold went down, he wrote again to the people who got the "price-is-going-down" letter but not to the "price-is-going-up" people.

He repeated this process one more time. To half of the people receiving the third round of letters, he predicted another fall in the price of gold. To the other half, he predicted a rise in the price of gold. When

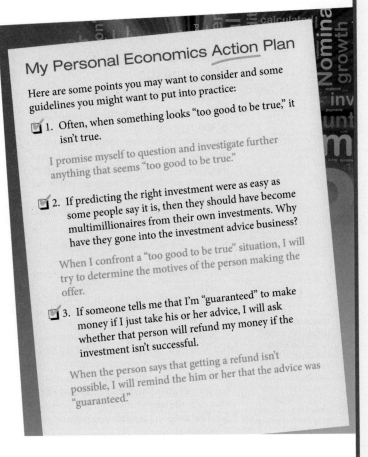

My Personal Economics Action Plan

Here are some points you may want to consider and some guidelines you might want to put into practice:

☑ 1. Often, when something looks "too good to be true," it isn't true.

I promise myself to question and investigate further anything that seems "too good to be true."

☑ 2. If predicting the right investment were as easy as some people say it is, then they should have become multimillionaires from their own investments. Why have they gone into the investment advice business?

When I confront a "too good to be true" situation, I will try to determine the motives of the person making the offer.

☑ 3. If someone tells me that I'm "guaranteed" to make money if I just take his or her advice, I will ask whether that person will refund my money if the investment isn't successful.

When the person says that getting a refund isn't possible, I will remind the him or her that the advice was "guaranteed."

Grading Rubric: Financial Plan

1 2 3 4 5   Student identified a plan for investing.

1 2 3 4 5   Financial plan was two to three paragraphs in length.

A Monopolistic Competitive Market

Focus Questions

▶ What are the characteristics of monopolistic competition?
▶ What are some examples of monopolistic competition?
▶ Are monopolistic competitors price takers or price searchers?
▶ How do monopolistic competitors answer questions about how much to produce and what price to charge?
▶ What are some ways in which the products of monopolistic competitors differ?

Key Term

monopolistic competitive market

Focus and Motivate

Section Objectives

After completing this section, students will be able to

▶ identify the characteristics of monopolistic competition;
▶ provide some examples of monopolistic competition;
▶ explain why monopolistic competitors are price searchers;
▶ describe how monopolistic competitors answer questions about how much to produce and what price to charge; and
▶ explain the ways in which the products of monopolistic competitors differ.

Kickoff Activity

Define the term *oxymoron* as "a combination of contradictory words." Ask students to make a list of five to ten oxymoronic expressions, such as "make haste slowly" and "a cruel kindness."

Activating Prior Knowledge

The previous section explained that there is little or no competition in a monopoly. The title of this section, however, is not an oxymoron. Point out to students that *monopolistic competition* has a very specific definition in economics. Also, *monopolistic* is an adjective; monopoly is most commonly used as a noun.

Teach

Discussion Starter

Ask students to read the characteristics of monopolistic competition. Then have them try to identify existing markets that have all these characteristics.

Characteristics of a Monopolistic Competitive Market

Between perfect competition, at one end of the types-of-markets continuum, and monopoly, at the other, there are two other markets: monopolistic competitive and oligopolistic. In this section, we will learn about monopolistic competition, and in the next section, we will examine oligopolies.

The three characteristics of a **monopolistic competitive market** are as follows:

1. The market includes many buyers and many sellers.
2. Firms produce and sell slightly different products.
3. Firms have easy entry into and exit out of the market.

Notice that two of the characteristics (the first and third) are the same as those for a perfectly competitive market. (A perfectly competitive market has many buyers and sellers and easy entry and exit.) However, the second characteristic does not describe either a perfectly competitive or a monopolistic market.

monopolistic competitive market
A market structure characterized by (1) many buyers and many sellers, (2) the production and sale of slightly different products, and (3) easy entry into and exit out of the market.

Monopolistic Competitive Firms Are Price Searchers

Firms in a monopolistic competitive market are price searchers. Why do we consider them price searchers? Because they sell slightly different products.

Suppose firm A is a monopolistic competitive firm or seller. It is currently producing and selling good A at $40 per unit. At this price, the firm sells 1,000 units a week. If it raises its price to $45, it will still likely sell some of its product (say, 700 units), because what it sells is a bit different from every other product in the market. In other words, consumers will not be able to stop buying good A and start buying an identical good.

EXAMPLE Many cities and towns have a good number of Italian and Mexican restaurants. One restaurant that serves Italian-style food may be similar but not identical to another restaurant that serves Italian-style food. These restaurants operate in a monopolistic competitive market. ◆

Cooperative Learning

Divide the class into groups of three or four. Have each group research a business that functions in a monopolistic competitive market and then describe how the market demonstrates the three characteristics of monopolistic competitive markets. Once all the groups have presented their research, lead a class discussion that focuses on the similarities and differences among the businesses.

What Do Monopolistic Competitive Firms Do?

Like perfectly competitive firms and monopoly firms, monopolistic competitive firms have to answer two questions: (1) How much should we produce? and (2) What price should we charge? They answer the first question the same way every firm answers it: they produce the quantity of output at which marginal revenue equals marginal cost. They answer the second question the same way monopoly sellers answer it: by searching for the highest price per unit at which they can sell their entire output. If they produce 10,000 units of their good, they search for the highest per-unit price at which they can sell all 10,000 units.

QUESTION: *What use is it to me to know that one seller (say, a wheat farmer) operates in a perfectly competitive market and another seller (a restaurant) operates in a monopolistic competitive market?*

ANSWER: *This information helps you understand why the prices you pay are what they are. Suppose a number of sellers are selling a particular good for the same price. (Every seller is charging $100.) When some people see different sellers all charging the same price, they jump to the conclusion that the sellers agreed to do this. In other words, people think the sellers colluded on price. Of course, another explanation that you learned from our discussion of a perfectly competitive market is that sellers all sometimes sell the good for the same price because they have no other choice. The sellers haven't colluded; rather, they are operating in a perfectly competitive market.*

Suppose you wonder why some medicines are priced as high as they are. Some of the high prices have to do with the patents that pharmaceutical companies hold—patents that hold

other sellers out of the market (for a period of time). Or suppose you learn that in your town, only one company has the right to provide cable TV services. Would you have known how this type of monopoly would affect your monthly cable bill? Now you know that limiting entry to a market (for good reasons or bad reasons) always results in higher prices than would have existed had entry not been limited.

We don't expect that, as the years pass, you will go around in your daily life pointing out which companies are perfectly competitive companies, which companies are monopolists, and so on. That's not the reason for learning this material. The reason is to understand how things work in a part of the world that you might not have understood before.

How Are Monopolistic Competitors' Products Different?

When we say that one product is slightly *different* from another product, what do we mean? When we say that McDonald's hamburgers are slightly different from Burger King's hamburgers, for example,

▲ Do you think the owner of this restaurant is a price taker or a price searcher?

the word *different* refers to taste and appearance. McDonald's hamburgers look and taste slightly different (to most people) from Burger King's hamburgers.

Products can differ in other ways too. For example, consider a particular brand of gasoline that's sold at a gas station at Third Avenue and Main Street and at a gas station at Ninth Avenue and Main Street. Is the gasoline at the two stations identical? Certainly, the physical properties are the same, but the gasoline is sold at different locations, and the locational differences may affect the choices of the people who buy gasoline. For example, suppose the gas station at Third and Main is in a dangerous neighborhood, and the gas station at Ninth and Main is in a safe neighborhood. Consumers may perceive the gas sold in a safe neighborhood as slightly different from the gas sold in a dangerous neighborhood. The location at which a product is sold may be enough to differentiate one physically identical product from another.

▼ Customers have many different features to choose from when buying a new cell phone. In what ways might the phones differ, in addition to the physical features of the phones themselves?

Monopolistic competitors' products, then, can be different in any way that is perceived as different by consumers. If location makes a difference to consumers, then two physically identical products sold at different locations are slightly different products. If different credit terms, sales service, or delivery options make two physically identical products different in the minds of consumers, then they are slightly different products. In short, the physical properties of a product may not be all that matters to consumers. How the product is packaged, where it is purchased, from whom it is purchased, and whether it is delivered may all make a difference to consumers.

Many Monopolistic Competitors Would Rather Be Monopolists

Suppose you own a business that is considered a monopolistic competitive firm. Your business is one of many sellers, you sell a product that's slightly different from the products of your competitors, and entry into and exit from the industry are easy. Would you rather your business was a monopolist firm instead? Wouldn't it be better for you to be the only seller of a product than to be one of many sellers?

Most business owners would say it is indeed better to be a monopolist firm than a monopolistic competitive firm, because they believe that as a monopolist, they would face less competition. How do monopolistic competitors go about trying to become monopolists?

Some monopolistic competitors use advertising. If a monopolistic competitor can, through advertising, persuade the buying public that its product is more than slightly different from the products of its competitors, it stands a better chance of becoming a monopolist. For example, many firms produce men's and women's jeans, and many people think the jeans produced by these firms look very much alike. How, then, does any one of the firms differentiate its product from the pack? Some companies add designer labels to their jeans to suggest that they are unique and thus desirable.

QUESTION: *Are you suggesting that it's wrong or uneconomical to buy designer jeans?*

ANSWER: *Not at all. People may get utility or satisfaction from wearing designer jeans. It isn't the job of the economist to tell consumers how they should get their satisfaction. Sometimes people buy, say, designer clothes because they feel it sets them apart from others, because their friends are wearing designer clothes, or because they feel better about themselves if they are wearing a particular item with a monogram. We aren't saying that any of these motivations is wrong. We are simply pointing out that sellers sometimes try to differentiate their products (from their competitors' products) by adding a particular label, coming up with a particular motto ("Just Do It"), and other such things. It's up to the consumer to decide whether the designer label, motto, or anything else is worth the (sometimes) higher price. It might be a bland world, indeed, if all shirts were green, all jeans were the same cut, and all MP3 players had the same features.*

What Matters Is How Much Competition a Seller Faces

One of the major differences between sellers in different types of markets is how much competition they face. How much competition a seller faces—much, some, very little, none—depends primarily on two factors: how close to unique the seller's product is and how easy it is for new sellers to enter the market.

In a perfectly competitive market, a seller does not produce and sell a unique product at all: it produces and sells a product *identical* to that of other sellers. This means the seller is in a competitive position. If it raises the price of its product by only one penny over the equilibrium price, consumers can turn to other sellers to purchase the identical product. A seller in a perfectly competitive market faces stiff competition from other sellers currently in the market, as well as potentially stiff competition from new sellers who may join the market. After all, a perfectly competitive market allows easy entry.

Things are somewhat different for the monopolistic competitive seller. This seller does not face as much competition from current sellers, because it produces and sells a product that is slightly different from the products of other sellers. A rise in the price of its good will not cause all of its customers to leave it and head for its competitors. Still, the monopolistic competitor has the same problem as the perfect competitor when it comes to potential competitors because of easy entry into a monopolistic competitive market, just as in a perfectly competitive market. New sellers can be just around

 Why might a jeans manufacturer create a designer label for its product?

Explore the value that students place on various company logos and mottos by asking students how much more they are willing to pay to get a brand-name product.

Teaching with Visuals

Some companies add designer logos to suggest that their jeans are uniquely desirable—in other words, to differentiate them in the market.

Teaching with Visuals

In response to the photo on page 232, students should say that the painkiller market is monopolistic competitive. Types of painkillers are slightly differentiated and sell for different prices.

Application Activity

After reading and discussing Section 3, you may want to assign the Section Activity in the *Applying the Principles Workbook*, pages 91–92.

Assess

Quick Quiz

The following true-or-false quiz will help you assess student understanding of the material covered in this section.

1. There are many buyers and sellers in monopolistic competitive markets. (True)
2. Monopolistic competitive firms are price searchers. (True)
3. Location can be a differentiating factor between two products. (True)
4. Most monopolistic competitors would rather be monopolies. (True)
5. A monopoly seller faces less competition than a monopolistic competitor. (True)

Cooperative Learning

Divide the class into groups of three or four, and have each group pick a type of good or service. Encourage students to look not only at physical products, such as hats and bicycles, but also at services, such as movie theaters and auto repair shops. Then have each group list the ways that monopolistic competitors differentiate their versions of this good or service. If students notice that companies—for example, movie theaters—sell the same good for different prices, ask them how this can be. Have each group present its findings to the class.

Reteaching Activity

Use the Section Assessment to gauge which students may need reteaching on this section. Have those students create a chart that shows the conditions for each type of market. In both markets, there are many sellers and buyers, and entry into and exit from the market are easy. The difference is that in monopolistic competition, firms produce slightly different products, whereas in perfect competition, the products are identical.

Guided Reading

For further reaching of the key concepts in this section, assign the Outlining Activity and the Just the Facts Handout from the *Guided Reading and Study Guide,* pages 124–125.

▲ How would you categorize the painkiller market: as perfectly competitive, monopoly, or monopolistic competitive? Explain.

the corner, waiting to take away some of a current monopolistic competitor's business.

How much competition does a monopoly seller face? It faces less competition than either a perfect competitor or a monopolistic competitor. It sells a product that has no close substitutes. Consumers buying from monopoly sellers have fewer options than consumers buying from perfect competitors or monopolistic competitors. For example, if a monopolistic competitor raises its price too high, provides poor service, or lowers quality, many consumers will choose to walk away and buy from the seller's competition. It's not that easy to walk away from a monopoly seller, because no sellers sell a close substitute for the monopoly seller's product. In short, the monopoly seller does not have to be afraid of competition, because it really doesn't have much. Furthermore, competition is not likely to increase because of barriers to entering the monopoly market.

SECTION 3 ASSESSMENT

Defining Terms
1. Define:
   a. monopolistic competitive market

Reviewing Facts and Concepts
2. What are the three characteristics of a monopolistic competitive market?
3. How might monopolistic competitors' products be slightly different?

4. A monopolistic competitive market shares some characteristics with a perfectly competitive market and some with a monopolistic market. Explain.

Critical Thinking
5. In what way or ways are a monopolist, a monopolistic competitor,

and a perfect competitor alike?
6. In what way or ways is a monopolist different from a monopolistic competitor?

Applying Economic Concepts
7. Identify an action of a real-world monopolistic competitor that is trying to turn itself into a monopolist.

SECTION 3 ASSESSMENT ANSWERS

Defining Terms

1. a. monopolistic competitive market: a market structure with these three characteristics: (1) many buyers and sellers; (2) the production and sale of slightly different products; and (3) easy entry into and exit out of the market.

Reviewing Facts and Concepts

2. Monopolistic competitive markets are characterized by many buyers and many sellers, slightly differentiated products, and easy entry into and exit from the market.
3. They can be different in any way that is perceived as different by consumers. Factors may include location, service, and perceived quality.

4. In both monopolistic competition and perfect competition, there are many buyers and many sellers, along with easy entry into and exit from the market. In both monopolistic competition and monopoly, firms are price searchers.

Critical Thinking

5. All three try to maximize profit, try to minimize cost, want to sell their output for the highest price possible, and produce the quantity of output at which marginal revenue is equal to marginal cost.

6. A monopolist's good has no close substitutes; a monopolistic competitor's good may have close substitutes. A monopolist is protected from competitors because of barriers to entry; a monopolistic competitor is not.

Applying Economic Concepts
7. Answers will vary.

An Oligopolistic Market

Focus Questions
▶ What are the characteristics of an oligopolistic market?
▶ What are some examples of an oligopolistic market?
▶ Are sellers in an oligopolistic market price takers or price searchers?
▶ What are cartel agreements?

Key Terms
oligopolistic market
cartel agreement
price discrimination

Characteristics of an Oligopolistic Market

An **oligopolistic market** has these three characteristics:

1. It has few sellers.
2. Firms produce and sell identical or slightly different products.
3. The barriers to entry are significant, which means entering the market is difficult.

Exhibit 8-3 on page 234 identifies the characteristics of the four types of markets discussed in this chapter.

Oligopolistic Firms Are Price Searchers

Like monopolistic and monopolistic competitive firms, oligopolistic firms are price searchers. In other words, they have some control over the prices they charge. An oligopolistic firm can raise the price of the good it produces and still sell some of it (which is not the case for price takers).

How Much Competition Do Oligopolists Face?

In the last section, we developed a way to think about sellers in various markets. We categorized sellers according to how much competition they face. In turn, how much competition a seller faces depends on how close to unique its product is and how easily new sellers can enter the market and compete with it. With this information as background, let's discuss oligopoly.

How close to unique is an oligopolist's product? Based on the characteristics of oligopoly, the product is not unique. Some oligopolists produce identical goods (steel), and others produce slightly different products (cars). We would expect, then, that an oligopolistic seller faces fairly intense competition from current sellers. For example, Ford faces stiff competition from General Motors. In the world market for cars, Ford also faces extremely stiff competition from Japanese car companies, such as Toyota, Nissan, Honda, and Mitsubishi.

oligopolistic market
A market structure characterized by (1) few sellers, (2) the production and sale of identical or slightly different products, and (3) significant barriers to entry.

Cooperative Learning

Divide the class into three groups, and assign each group one of these industries to research: breakfast cereal, farm machinery, and soaps and detergents. Each group should research how well its industry meets the three conditions that char-

acterize oligopoly. The group should also identify the firms that dominate this particular industry and some of the products produced along with specific prices. Encourage the groups to prepare oral reports with visual aids.

Teacher Support

Focus and Motivate

Section Objectives

After completing this section, students will be able to
▶ identify the characteristics of an oligopolistic market;
▶ provide some examples of an oligopolistic market;
▶ explain whether sellers in an oligopolistic market are price takers or price searchers; and
▶ explain what cartel agreements are.

Kickoff Activity

Write the following statement on the board for students to respond to: "Write the names of five U.S. car manufacturers."

Activating Prior Knowledge

List the names of U.S. car manufacturers on the board as students volunteer them. Point out to students that relatively few manufacturers produce the vast number of cars in the United States. Explain to students that these manufacturers are oligopolists, and tell them that in this section, they will learn more about oligopoly markets.

Teach

Discussion Starter

For each characteristic of oligopoly, ask students if it is more closely associated with perfect competition or monopoly. Refer students to Exhibit 8-3 to review the characteristics of the four types of markets.

 Visit econ.myemcp.com/videos for videos that will help students better understand the key concepts found in this section.

Critical Thinking

In class, invite students to name between 10 and 20 large and small items found in most households, including automobiles, TVs, washing machines, and toothbrushes. Ask students to decide in which market structure each item is sold.

Teaching with Visuals

Oligopolistic. The smartphone market has few sellers (including Apple, Samsung, and Motorola), the products are slightly differentiated (all offer a similar array of features, though with some differences), the barriers to entry are significantly high (high costs of research and production), and some legal controls affect the price.

Reinforcement Activity

One of the most famous oligopolies in the U.S. economy is the soft drink market. Two companies, the Coca-Cola Company and PepsiCo, control approximately 75% of the soft drink market through a pure oligopoly. These companies control the majority of brand names that you see in restaurants and supermarkets. To show that an oligopoly can sell identical to slightly differentiated products, stage the famous blind cola taste test. Ask students how different the products actually are and how these companies truly differentiate their products.

► Which of the four markets in this table describes the market for smartphones? Explain.

A Student Asks

Ask students to think of examples of ways that competition keeps sellers "in line."

EXHIBIT 8-3 Characteristics of Various Markets

Market	Number of sellers	Type of product	Barriers to entry	Control over price	Examples of products and services sold
Perfectly competitive	Many	Identical	No barriers	No control	Wheat, corn, stocks
Monopolistic	One	Unique	Extremely high barriers	Considerable amount of control	Water, electricity, delivery of first-class mail
Monopolistic competitive	Many	Slightly different	No barriers	Yes, but not as much as in monopoly	Clothing, meals at restaurants
Oligopolistic	Few	Identical or slightly different	Significantly high barriers	Yes, but not as much as in monopoly	Cars, cereal

Where the oligopolistic seller does not face too much competition is from potential sellers. It's difficult to enter an oligopolistic market, so current oligopolistic sellers are shielded from competition from new sellers to some degree.

A Student Asks

QUESTION: *I always thought that the more sellers in a given market (for example, the more sellers of computers), the more competition in that market. Now it sounds like there can be quite a bit of competition in a market even with only two or three sellers. Is this correct?*

ANSWER: *Yes. Competition can exist in a market with 3 or 300 sellers. For example, think back to the days of only three TV networks: ABC, NBC, and CBS. The three networks stiffly competed with each other. Today, there is more competition in the TV market largely because of cable channels and, increasingly, because of online streaming services (like Netflix). Still, there was strong competition in the TV market before cable and streaming.*

Identifying Oligopolistic Industries

Economists determine whether a market is oligopolistic by looking at the percentage of sales made by the top four firms in the industry. If only a few firms account for a large percentage of sales, then the market is considered oligopolistic. For example, suppose an industry has ten firms, and the total revenue of the industry is $100 million. The four firms with the highest sales generate $80 million of that revenue. In other words, the top four firms account for 80 percent of total revenue in the industry (because $80 million is 80 percent of $100 million), so clearly, the industry is dominated by these four firms. This is an example of an oligopolistic market. Some real-world examples of oligopolistic markets include industries that produce cars (such as General Motors and Ford), cigarettes (e.g., Phillip Morris and R.J. Reynolds), tires and inner tubes (e.g., Bridgestone Corporation and Goodyear Tire & Rubber Company), breakfast cereals (e.g., Malt-o-Meal Company and General Mills, Inc.), farm machinery (e.g., Deere & Company [John Deere] and Vermeer Corporation), and soap and detergents (e.g., Proctor & Gamble Co. and Johnson & Johnson).

Differentiating Instruction

Kinesthetic and Visual Learners

Invite students to create their own versions of the table in Exhibit 8-3. Encourage students to use visuals to trigger their memories of characteristics of each market. For example, students might create three-dimensional tables with actual products as samples. Decorate your room with these representations of the exhibit.

Oligopoly and Interdependence: Looking over Your Shoulder

Oligopoly differs from other market structures in terms of the number of sellers. Both perfectly competitive and monopolistic competitive markets include many sellers, and a monopolistic market has just one seller. Only an oligopolistic market consists of a *few* sellers.

Will a seller act differently if it is one of only a few sellers than if it is one of many sellers? Some evidence indicates that when a seller is one of only a few sellers, it is more likely to base its behavior on what other sellers do than if it is one of many sellers. Consider the airline market, which is considered to be oligopolistic. If one airline lowers its ticket prices, other airlines are likely to do the same.

Cartels

It's easier for the few sellers in an oligopolistic market to get together and discuss common issues than for the many sellers in a perfectly competitive or a monopolistic competitive market to do the same. Why would sellers that compete with each other want to get together in the first place? One of the various reasons may be that they want to eliminate or reduce the competition among them.

Each year, the three major U.S. car companies (Ford, General Motors, and Chrysler) compete on such things as price, quality, style, and service. Over the years, they have realized that the competition among them actually helps car buyers and hurts them. More than likely, the chief executive officer (CEO) of any of these companies tells the board of directors: "Every time our competitors lower prices, we have to do the same thing. Every time they come up with a new sport utility vehicle or a better or safer sedan, we have to do the same thing. All this competition is great for the consumer, but it's not so good for our profits."

Suppose the CEO calls a meeting with the CEOs at the other two major car companies.

They get together for a nice lunch and talk over their problems. At the end of the lunch, they all agree that the competition among them is helpful to consumers but not to them, so they should try to reduce some of this competition. Specifically, they decide to keep prices where they currently are (no more discounts) and to stop coming up with new car models for the next two years.

The three CEOs have entered into a **cartel agreement**—an agreement that specifies they will act in a coordinated way to reduce the competition among them and (they hope) raise their profits. In the United States, cartel agreements are illegal. But suppose they were not illegal, so nothing would prevent the CEOs from making a cartel agreement. What then? Many people would say that the CEOs would be successful at reducing their competition and increasing their profits. In other words, the cartel agreement would hurt consumers and help the three car companies.

This answer assumes that the three car companies would actually hold to the cartel agreement. In fact, though, firms that enter into cartel agreements often break them. To see why, put yourself in the place of one of the three automobile company CEOs. You return to your office after having lunch with

cartel agreement
An agreement that specifies how the firms that entered into the agreement will act in a coordinated way to reduce the competition among them.

▲ The cereal market is an oligopolistic market. Can you name the firms that dominate this market?

Internet Research

Tell students to visit http://econ.emcp.net/autobytel and search by make of car. Each student should choose one or two makes and compare the cars made by different companies. How similar or different are the cars in each category? What characteristics of oligopoly does the student notice when comparing these car models? Have each student find one car that appears significantly different from the others and determine how the manufacturer differentiated this car from others manufactured by companies in the oligopoly.

Teaching with Visuals

Answers will vary, but students might say that cartels reduce competition and harm consumers.

Discussion Starter

Invite students to imagine that they are major producers of personal and hand-held computers. Ask them to identify the advantages and disadvantages that would be associated with forming a computer cartel.

▲ The Organization of the Petroleum Exporting Countries (OPEC) is a cartel. Here we see the opening of an OPEC meeting at OPEC headquarters in Vienna. **Why do you think cartels are illegal in the United States?**

"People of the same trade seldom meet together, even for merriment and diversion, but the conversation ends in a conspiracy against the public, or in some contrivance to raise prices."
—Adam Smith, economist

price discrimination
The practice by which a seller charges different prices to different buyers for the product it sells when the price differences do not reflect cost differences.

the other CEOs. You start to think about the cartel agreement you just entered into and say to yourself, "I know I promised not to lower prices and not to develop any new model cars, but suppose I forget what I promised. Suppose I develop new car models and release them to the market next year. If my competitors hold to the cartel agreement and don't release new models next year, then I'll be the only car company with new models. My company should be able to take business away from its competitors. Instead of not competing with my competitors, why don't I just try to run them out of business?"

Each CEO feels a strong monetary incentive to break the promise made with the other CEOs. Each is likely to break the agreement in the hope of getting rid of the competition, once and for all. If all three CEOs break the agreement out of self-interest, the agreement will no longer exist. The three car companies will be back where they started, competing with each other.

Even if cartel agreements were not illegal, they probably would not have much effect on consumers. Certainly, sellers in the same market might try to make cartel agreements and would want them to hold, but it's not likely they would hold. After all, once the agreement was made, each seller would feel a sharp monetary incentive to break the agreement and make itself much better off at the expense of its competitors. It's nearly impossible for companies to ignore the chance to get rid of their competition.

Price Discrimination

Price discrimination exists when a seller charges different prices to different buyers and the price differences do not reflect cost differences. Suppose a movie theater charges children $5 to see a movie and adults $10 to see a movie. If the movie theater experiences absolutely no cost difference when it comes to children and adults, this situation is an example of price discrimination.

Now suppose a company runs two small grocery stores: one on the east side of town and one on the west side of town. In the grocery store on the east side of town, the company charges $3 for a loaf of bread, but on the west side of town, it charges $2.50 for the same loaf of bread. Is this an example of price discrimination? Well, it could be but not necessarily. In this town, the crime rate is higher on the east side than on the west side, which means insurance rates for the company are higher on the east side of town. As a result, it may be more costly to sell bread on the east side of town than on the west side of town, and this higher cost is reflected in the higher price of bread on the east side of town. The difference in price here is not an example of price discrimination.

When price discrimination does occur, though, we need to ask two important questions: (1) Why would a seller want to price discriminate? (2) Under what conditions can a seller price discriminate?

Differentiating Instruction

Enrichment and Extension

The Organization of the Petroleum Exporting Companies (OPEC) is one of the most powerful cartels in the world. It controls a large percentage of the world's oil supply and has done so since the 1960s. Assign some of your more advanced students to research the OPEC countries and see what effects OPEC has had on the world's oil market. Allow students to share their results with the class.

How Is a New Year's Resolution Like a Cartel Agreement?

When a seller enters into a cartel agreement, it joins other sellers. Often, the parties agree to modify their behavior if others do the same. For example, one seller may agree to stop discounting prices if the other sellers do the same, or one may agree to reduce supply if the others do the same.

When you make a New Year's resolution—say, to exercise more or study harder—you are essentially entering into an agreement with yourself. One part of you (the part that wants to sit on the couch and watch TV or hang out with friends and play video games) makes an agreement with another part of you (the part that wants to exercise more or study harder) to behave differently.

The problem with both cartel agreements and resolutions is that they are easy to break. A cartel agreement can be broken by any seller that decides to compete with the other sellers even though it has agreed not to. And once one member of the cartel decides to compete, the others will hear about it and decide to compete too. Pretty soon, the sellers that agreed not to compete with each other are back where they started: competing with each other.

Resolutions are just as easy to break. At any time, the part of you that wants to watch TV or hang out with friends instead of work out or study can become stronger than the part that wants to hold to the resolution.

Both cartel agreements and resolutions need some kind of enforcement—something to make them stick. Following through with a resolution may take a lot of personal willpower or the help of friends and family. Suppose Rashad resolves to give up smoking and asks his sister Inas to help him by demanding that he pay $5 every time he lights up. Inas serves as the enforcer of the resolution. (Of course, having an enforcer does not guarantee that Rashad will stop smoking; he may simply ignore Inas when she asks for $5.)

Sometimes, the sellers who enter into a cartel agreement need the government to enforce their agreement. The stated position of the U.S. government is that it will not enforce cartel agreements because they are illegal. Yet sometimes, what the government does amounts to enforcing a cartel agreement.

Consider the Civil Aeronautics Board (CAB), which operated in the days of airline regulation (1938–1984). The CAB was created to protect airlines from cutthroat competition and had the power to set fares, allocate routes, and prevent new carriers from entering the airline industry. The federal government's General Accounting Office estimates that in the days of regulation, airfares would have been as much as 52 percent lower if the CAB had not been regulating them. In this case, a striking conclusion presents itself: the CAB was doing for the airlines what a cartel agreement would have done—preventing crippling competition by preventing fare wars, dividing up routes, and keeping new firms out of the market.

THINK ABOUT IT In the Economics in the Real World feature "What Have Uber and Lyft Done to the Taxicab Business in New York City" on page 223, we made mention of the New York Taxi and Limousine Commission. Do you think the commission was doing something for current taxi owners that they could not do for themselves -- namely, prevent others from entering the taxi business? Explain your answer.

ANSWERS TO THINK ABOUT IT The answer is yes. By requiring that individuals who want to operate taxis in New York City have taxi medallions and by restricting the number of medallions issued, the Taxi and Limousine Commission effectively facilitates competition amongst current taxi owners.

Remind students of the 9:59 p.m. scenario in Economics Around the Clock (page 207), and discuss their answers to the question that accompanies it.

Help students see that pharmaceutical companies try to price discriminate. If the highest price that people in relatively poor countries are willing and able to pay for medicine is lower than the highest price that people in rich countries are willing and able to pay, then a pharmaceutical company may end up charging individuals in the rich country a higher price for the same medicine.

Teaching with Visuals

Answers will vary, but students might say that because the store has locations across the nation, it can more easily discriminate according to median income.

Why Discriminate?

A seller would want to price discriminate if it increased total revenue. Look at the following three points on a market demand curve:

Point	Price	Quantity demanded
A	$10	1
B	8	2
C	6	3

As you can see, price and quantity demanded move in the opposite direction according to the law of demand, which says that more is purchased at lower prices than at higher prices.

Now suppose the seller can charge only one price and wants to sell 3 units of the good. What price will the seller charge? The answer is $6, because only at $6 will 3 units of the good be purchased. (If the seller charges $8, only 2 units will be purchased.) The total revenue for this seller is $18, which is the price of the good ($6) times the quantity bought (3).

Now suppose this seller can price discriminate, or charge one price to one

▲ How might this major retailer, which sells men's and women's fashions at its website and in stores across the country, practice price discrimination?

buyer and a different price to another buyer. The seller will charge one buyer $10 (because from our table, we know that at least one buyer is willing and able to pay $10 for the good—after all, we can see that the quantity demanded is 1 at a price of $10). Then, the seller will charge a second buyer $8 (because we know that the price of the good has to be $8 before another person will buy it) and a third buyer $6 (because we know that the price of the good has to be $6 before a third person will buy it). What is the seller's total revenue now? It is the sum of $10 and $8 and $6, or $24.

So, if the seller does not (or cannot) price discriminate and charges the same price to all customers, total revenue is $18. But if the seller can and does price discriminate, charging different prices to different customers, total revenue increases by $6 to a total of $24.

It would seem, then, that every seller in the world would want to price discriminate. In fact, every seller does want to price discriminate—but not every seller can. Certain conditions must be present.

Factors Allowing Price Discrimination

First, different customers must be willing and able to pay different prices for a good. For example, one person is willing and able to pay $10 for the good, but another person is willing and able to pay only $8 for the good.

Second, the seller must have a way to tell who is willing to pay $10 and who is willing to pay $8. (By the way, buyers don't willingly give up this information.)

Third, it has to be impossible (or extremely costly) for the good that is purchased by one customer to be resold to another. For example, suppose the person who bought the good at $6 (in the example earlier) could buy 3 units of the good at this price. This buyer could then sell one unit of the good to another buyer for, say, $10, and one unit of the good to still another buyer for $8. Instead of the seller capturing the $6 of added revenue from price discrimination, it goes instead to one buyer.

Background Information: Price Discrimination and the Clayton Antitrust Act

The Clayton Antitrust Act of 1914 made certain business practices, including price discrimination, illegal. The law prohibited "any person engaged in commerce…to discriminate in price between different purchasers of commodities of like grade and quality…where the effect of such discrimination may be substantially to lessen competition or

tend to create a monopoly in any line of commerce."

The Clayton Act was passed to supplement the Sherman Antitrust Act. Many legal cases were brought under the Clayton Act to curb price discrimination and other conduct considered unlawful under its provisions.

Do You Sometimes Choose to Pay Higher Prices?

As you know, one of the conditions of price discrimination is that the seller be able to distinguish among customers who are willing to pay different prices.

Ask yourself whether people who highly value their time are more willing to pay a higher price for a product than people who do not. Some sellers think so. They argue that people who place a high value on their time want to spend less time shopping for products. If sellers want to price discriminate between these two types of customers—charging more to customers who value their time more and charging less to customers who value their time less—then they must determine the category into which each customer falls.

How would you go about making this determination if you were a seller? What many sellers do is place cents-off coupons in newspapers and magazines. They think that people who value their time relatively little will spend it clipping and sorting coupons. People who place a relatively high value on their time will not.

In effect, the process works in a similar way at your local grocery store:

- The posted prices for all products are the same for all customers.
- Both Linda and Josh put the same cereal in their shopping carts.
- When Josh goes through the checkout, the clerk asks if he has any coupons. Josh says no, so Josh pays the posted price.
- When Linda goes through the checkout, the clerk asks if she has any coupons. She says yes. She hands the clerk the coupon for the cereal and so she pays a lower price than Josh paid.

THINK ABOUT IT Are people in their thirties more or less likely to use coupons than people in their late sixties? Explain your answer.

Where Does Price Discrimination Occur?

Think of the places you might see price discrimination. Often, restaurants will sell a dinner to an older person for less than it will sell the same dinner to a younger person. In other words, the older person gets the "senior discount." This is an example in which the good the older person buys is not usually resold. We wouldn't likely see an older person in a restaurant buy the salmon and vegetables for $15 and then try to sell it for $20 to the person at the next table.

As mentioned earlier, we sometimes see price discrimination at movie theaters.

Children are often charged less than adults. Again, little if any reselling is going on here. A child won't typically buy 100 tickets for $5 each and then stand outside the movie theater and sell them for, say, $10 each.

We also sometimes see price discrimination at pharmacies. An older person may pay a lower price for a medicine than a younger person. Here again, reselling is unlikely. Older people (and younger people too) seem to buy only the medicine they need.

"If you wish to prosper, let your customer prosper."
—Frédéric Bastiat, economist

Cases were brought by individuals who alleged that they had suffered from anticompetitive activities or by the federal government.

After passing the Clayton Act, Congress created the Federal Trade Commission (FTC) to enforce antitrust law. The FTC can temporarily halt suspected anticompetitive activities pending investigation and potential legal action by the Department of Justice.

After students have read this feature, ask them to suggest reasons that some people believe coupon clipping is not worth their time. How might such people otherwise spend their time?

ANSWERS TO THINK ABOUT IT Answers will vary, but students might suggest that people in their late sixties are more likely to use coupons because many are on fixed incomes and because they typically have more free time than people in their thirties.

Clarifying Terms

Check students' understanding of the following term by asking them to use it in a sentence: *discrimination* (to show prejudice against someone or something). Challenge students to use the term in a way that is not necessarily negative.

Economics Around the Clock

After reading the introductory paragraphs to the section "Price Discrimination" (page 236), direct students to reread the 10:04 a.m. scenario in Economics Around the Clock (page 207) and to write answers to its question.

Students may point out that when a publisher produces a more expensive hardcover edition first, it hopes to attract both buyers who are willing to pay the higher price and buyers who would rather pay less for a paperback but don't want to wait for it to come out. By later offering the paperback edition to satisfy those who are willing to wait for it, the publisher covers a broad market and maximizes revenue.

A Student Asks

After reading the feature on page 241, make sure students understand that sellers engage in price discrimination to maximize revenue, not to make up for revenue lost by selling to some groups at lower prices.

After students have read this feature, ask them to provide reasons that colleges and universities practice price discrimination.

ANSWERS TO THINK ABOUT IT Answers will vary.

Discussion Starter

Ask students what problem could arise if several universities charged the same tuition, paid the same salaries, and gave identical financial aid packages. Students should see that without competition, prospective university students will face higher prices, among other issues.

Teaching with Visuals

Answers to the caption question on page 241 will vary. Students might say that because medical providers treat some people at lower prices, they need to make up lost revenue by setting higher prices for other people. An economist would say that medical providers charge the highest prices they can to each group they serve.

 Application Activity

After reading and discussing Section 4, you may want to assign the Section Activity in the *Applying the Principles Workbook*, pages 93–95.

Assess

Quick Quiz

The following true-or-false quiz will help you assess student understanding of the material covered in this section.

1. Entry into and exit from an oligopolistic market is easy. (False)
2. Oligopolistic firms can control the prices they charge. (True)
3. Cartel agreements are designed to maximize competition. (False)
4. Competition between sellers helps keep their interests aligned with buyers' interests. (True)
5. The primary purpose of price discrimination is to maximize revenue. (True)

Economics *in the* Real World

Do Colleges and Universities Price Discriminate?

Do you know that colleges and universities often practice price discrimination? Consider the example of two students, Alana and Ruby, who are admitted to the same public university. Alana comes from a family that has a rather low income, and Ruby comes from a family with a rather high income. The university gives a financial aid package to Alana but not to Ruby.

By giving financial aid to one student but not the other, the university is price discriminating. How so? The cost of educating each student is probably the same. So by giving one student financial aid and not the other, the university is essentially charging them different "prices" (tuition) for the same product (education).

To illustrate, let's say that the tuition is normally $20,000 a year.

That's the amount Ruby will pay. But if Alana receives $15,000 a year in financial aid, then her tuition will be $5,000. In short, Alana and Ruby will pay different dollar amounts for the education they receive. (We aren't saying that the two students *shouldn't* pay different amounts, only that they *will* pay different amounts. Economists often argue that the should-versus shouldn't part of the issue comes down to personal opinion.)

There are also other examples of price discrimination at colleges and universities. Suppose the same university offers students academic and sports scholarships. Providing scholarships is another way of charging different students different amounts of tuition. If another student, Henry, receives a sports scholarship of $5,000 a year, he will pay $15,000 in tuition, compared with Alana's $5,000 and Ruby's $20,000.

Hotels sometimes price discriminate too. Some hotels charge lower rates to people who

are veterans, senior citizens, or members of an automobile club. Some restaurants and movie theaters price discriminate by offering discounts to senior citizens and children.

Now, consider an organization that does *not* usually price discriminate: the local police. If you get a ticket for driving 20 miles per hour over the speed limit in your community, chances are you will have to pay the same fine as everyone else who committed the same offense. It doesn't matter what kind of car you drive, how long you've been driving, or how much money you make.

THINK ABOUT IT Identify at least two examples of price discrimination that are not discussed in this feature. How does each illustrate price discrimination?

Why Not Higher Prices for Everyone?

Here's something to consider, though: why does the seller charge a lower price to some customers than others? For example, if the older person would pay $20 for the salmon and vegetables, why charge $15? If the young child would pay $10 to get into the movie, why charge $5? The answer is because the seller believes that older people (on average) won't pay $20 for the salmon

and vegetables and that young children (on average) won't pay $10 for a movie.

It's not that the seller is trying to do a favor for the older person or the young child. It's that the seller has some reason to believe that the older person won't buy the dinner unless it's priced at, say, $15. How does the seller know? It might be because at $20 a dinner, very few seniors show up to buy the meal, but at $15 a dinner, many

---

Cooperative Learning

Divide students into groups of three or four. Ask each group to find an example of price discrimination in your community. Ask the groups to answer two questions: Why does the seller discriminate, and What conditions make it possible for the seller to do so? Explain to students that these two questions are essential to understanding why price discrimination occurs.

do. The situation is similar with the movie theater. If the price is $10 for adults and for children, then few children will go to the movies. Parents might leave their kids at home or with a babysitter if they have to pay $10 for every ticket, but will bring their kids along if the children's ticket price is $5.

QUESTION: *Does one buyer end up paying a higher price because another buyer has paid a lower price? For example, does some 30-year-old pay more for a dinner because an older person has been given a "senior discount"?*

ANSWER: *No, but most people seem to think it works this way. The seller wants to charge both the 30-year-old and the older person the highest prices they are willing and able to pay. If possible, the seller would charge the older person $20 for the dinner instead of $15. But charging the older person $5 more wouldn't make the seller feel like charging the younger person less—say, $18 instead of $20. The seller would still charge the 30-year-old $20 for the dinner. Again, the objective is to charge everyone the highest price he or she is willing and able to pay, no matter what someone else pays.*

Price Discrimination and the Law

The general perception is that price discrimination is illegal in the United States, but in fact, it is illegal under certain conditions. For example, it is illegal if a seller price discriminates and, as a result, injures competition (which usually means reducing the amount or intensity of competition in the market). It is also usually illegal if one of the discriminating sales crosses state lines (for example, when a seller sells a good for less in one state than in another state and the difference in price is not warranted by a difference in costs). Price discrimination is not usually deemed illegal by government authorities if no injury occurs to competition or if the seller can show that charging a lower price to some customers is necessary to adequately compete in the market.

▲ Do you think some people pay more for medical procedures because others pay less? How might an economist answer this question?

SECTION 4 ASSESSMENT

Defining Terms
1. Define:
   a. oligopolistic market
   b. cartel agreement
   c. price discrimination

Reviewing Facts and Concepts
2. Why might a firm that voluntarily entered into a cartel agreement decide to cheat on (or breach) the agreement?
3. Why are oligopolistic firms price searchers?
4. What conditions are necessary for a seller to practice price discrimination?

Critical Thinking
5. If perfectly competitive firms are price takers, and monopolistic, monopolistic competitive, and oligopolistic firms are price searchers, then it follows that three times as many firms in the real world are price searchers than are price takers. Do you agree or disagree? Explain.

6. Evaluate this statement: "The more sellers there are of a particular good, the more competition there is between sellers."

Applying Economic Concepts
7. Someone tells you that the firms in a particular industry are all selling their products for the same prices. Does it follow that the firms have entered into a cartel agreement? Why or why not?

 Assessment Book

You will find a quiz for this section in the *Assessment Book,* page 80.

Reteaching Activity

Use the Section Assessment to gauge which students may need reteaching on this section. Invite each student to create an imaginary company and explain why its market is oligopolistic. Then invite the student to explain how and why his or her company might use price discrimination and whether doing so would be legal in its case.

Guided Reading

For further reteaching of the key concepts in this section, assign the Outlining Activity and the Just the Facts Handout from the *Guided Reading and Study Guide,* pages 126–129.

Before, the firm might have wanted the agreement to reduce its competition. After, it might realize that it can benefit by violating the agreement.
3. Oligopolistic firms are price searchers because they can sell some of their output at various prices.
4. Different customers must be willing and able to pay different prices for a good; the seller must be able to tell how much different customers are willing to pay; and it has to be impossible or extremely costly for the good purchased by one customer to be resold to another.

Critical Thinking
5. Students should disagree. The question does not specify the percentage breakdown among the four types of firms. The statement is true only if firms are distributed equally among the four market types, which is not necessarily the case.
6. This is probably true—all other things being the same. But strong competition can exist with even two sellers.

Applying Economic Concepts
7. No. Firms may sell their products for the same prices without having a cartel agreement. For example, perfectly competitive firms must sell their products for the same equilibrium price.

SECTION 4 ASSESSMENT ANSWERS

Defining Terms
1. a. oligopolistic market: a market structure with these three characteristics: (1) few sellers; (2) firms produce and sell identical or slightly differentiated products; and (3) are significant barriers to entry; **b. cartel agreement:** an agreement that specifies how the firms that entered into the agreement will act in a coordinated way to reduce the competition among them; **c. price discrimination:** the practice by which a seller charges different prices to different buyers for the same product when the price differences do not reflect cost differences.

Reviewing Facts and Concepts
2. The firm might find itself in a different position after the agreement than before it.

Assessment Answers

Economics Vocabulary

1. price taker; **2.** monopoly; **3.** price searcher; **4.** government monopoly; **5.** natural monopoly; **6.** monopolistic competition; **7.** oligopoly; **8.** cartel; **9.** public franchise.

Understanding the Main Ideas

1. A perfectly competitive market has many sellers of identical products. Furthermore, buyers have all relevant information that relates to price. It follows that if firm A tries to sell its product for one penny more, buyers will know this, and they will simply buy from one of the many other sellers.
2. A monopoly seller is a price searcher because it can sell some of its product at various prices. This means that it can raise its price and still sell some of its product.
3. Students should agree. A perfectly competitive firm sells its product for the equilibrium price, which is the highest price for which it can sell its product. A monopoly firm tries to sell the quantity of output it has produced for the highest price possible.
4. Per-unit profit is the difference be-tween price and average total cost (or per-unit cost). For example, if price is $10 and per-unit cost is $4, then profit per unit is $6. Suppose there are 10 firms, A through J. Firm A has an average total cost of $2, and every other firm has an average total cost of $6. It follows that firm A can lower its price to, say, $5, earn a profit per unit of $3, and eliminate its competition (which cannot lower the price to $5 and still earn a profit). Thus, once firm A has eliminated its competition, its low aver-age total costs act as a barrier for other firms entering the market.
5. Other firms find it difficult to enter the monopoly market and compete away the profits of the monopoly seller because of extremely high barriers to entry.

Chapter Summary

Be sure you know and remember the following key points from the chapter sections.

Section 1

▶ The four types of market structures are perfectly competitive, monopolistic, monopolistic competitive, and oligopolistic.
▶ A perfectly competitive market has many buyers and sellers who have relevant information about prices, quality, and other factors; its firms sell identical goods; and market entry and exit are easy.

Section 2

▶ A monopolistic market consists of one seller in a market with high barriers to entry that produces and sells a good that has no good substitutes.
▶ A monopoly firm searches for the price at which it can maximize its profits.
▶ Some of the barriers to entry into a monopolistic market are legal barriers.

Section 3

▶ A monopolistic competitive market includes many buyers and sellers, its firms produce and sell slightly differentiated products, and market exit and entry are easy.
▶ Monopolistic competitive firms are price searchers because their products are slightly different.
▶ Like other firms, monopolistic competitive firms must answer the questions of how much to produce and what price to charge.

Section 4

▶ An oligopolistic market has few sellers, its firms sell identical or slightly different goods, and market entry and exit are difficult.
▶ Oligopolistic firms have some control over the prices they charge.
▶ The barriers to market entry limit the amount of potential competition for oligopolistic firms.

Economics Vocabulary

1. A(n) _____ is a seller that can sell all its output at the equilibrium price but none at one penny higher.
2. The characteristics of _____ include one seller, no close substitutes for the good the seller sells, and high barriers to entry.
3. A(n) _____ can sell some of its output at various prices, although it sells less output at higher prices.
4. A(n) _____ is a monopoly that is legally protected from competition.
5. A company that ends up being the only seller of a good because of its low average total cost is called a(n) _____.
6. The characteristics of _____ include many buyers and sellers, firms that sell slightly differentiated products, and easy entry into and exit from the market.
7. The characteristics of _____ include few sellers, firms that produce and sell identical or slightly different products, and significant barriers to entry.
8. An agreement among firms that specifies they will act in a coordinated way to reduce the competition between them is called a(n) _____ agreement.
9. A(n) _____ is a right granted to a firm by the government that permits the firm to provide a particular good or service and excludes all others from doing so.

Understanding the Main Ideas

1. Firm A is a perfectly competitive firm. Why can't it sell its product for one penny more than the equilibrium price?
2. Why is a monopoly seller a price searcher?
3. "In at least one sense, a perfectly competitive firm is like a monopoly firm: each firm sells its product for the highest price possible." Do you agree or disagree? Explain your answer.
4. How can low average total costs (per-unit costs) act as a barrier to entry?
5. What keeps any profits the monopoly seller earns from being competed away?

6. A tying contract is an arrangement whereby the sale of one product depends on the purchase of some other product or products. Tying con-tracts are prohibited by the Clayton Act.
7. They can be different in terms of features, loca-tion, proximity, accompanying services, and so on.
8. The two determinants are how close to unique a seller's product is and how easy it is for new sellers to enter the market and compete with the seller.

9. There are few sellers in oligopoly and many sellers in monopolistic competition. It is easier for a few sellers to reach an agreement than for many sellers to reach an agreement. For example, it is easier to get three car companies together than hundreds of clothing companies.
10. A firm would break a cartel agreement to make itself better off. The opportunity to elimi-nate the competition is too hard for most firms to pass up.

6. What is a tying contract, and which antitrust act deems it illegal?

7. Firms in a monopolistic competitive market produce slightly different products. In what ways might these products differ?

8. What are the two principal determinants of how much competition a seller in a market faces?

9. Why might a cartel agreement be more likely in an oligopolistic market than in a monopolistic competitive market?

10. Explain why a firm that entered into a cartel agreement would break that agreement.

11. Can every seller price discriminate? Explain.

Doing the Math

1. A monopoly seller produces and sells 1,000 units of a good at a price of $49.99 per unit. Its total cost is $30,000. How much profit does the seller earn?

2. A firm can sell one unit of good X at $40, and it can sell one additional unit for every $1 reduction in price. Its marginal cost is constant at $34. How many units of the good should the firm produce?

Working with Graphs and Tables

1. Exhibit 8-4(a) partly illustrates what happens in a competitive market when firms earn high profits. Fill in the missing details for A through C.

2. Exhibit 8-4(b) partly illustrates what happens in a competitive market when firms in a market earn losses. Based on your knowledge of what happens when firms earn high profits, fill in the missing details for D and E.

Solving Economic Problems

1. **Apply.** Lam goes to a car dealership to look at cars, and the salesperson asks what he does for a living. What is the economic reason for asking this question?

2. **Analyze.** Firm A has been producing and selling good A in market A for 10 years. Recently, other firms have moved into market A and started to produce good A. Firm A has

EXHIBIT 8-4

Firms in market A earn high profits	Firms in market A are incurring losses
A	Some firms in market A leave the market
Supply in market A increases	D
B	Price rises
C	E
(a)	(b)

asked the government to restrict the number of firms that can enter the market. Why?

3. **Synthesize.** Suppose the government decides to limit the profit that firms in perfectly competitive market X can earn. How will this affect entry into the market?

Project or Presentation

Charting Your Personal Consumption. List 10 products you buy or consume on a regular basis. For each, identify the market in which it is produced and sold as perfectly competitive, monopolistic, monopolistic competitive, or oligopolistic. Write a two-page essay that evaluates each product and presents your answers. Support your work with examples and logical reasoning.

ONLINE
emcp.com

Practice Tests and Study Guide

Go to www.emcschool.net/Economics2e and choose *Economics: New Ways of Thinking*, Chapter 8, if you need more help in preparing for the chapter test.

---

11. Not every seller can price discriminate. Three conditions must be met: different customers must be willing and able to pay different prices for a good; the seller must be able to tell how much different customers are willing to pay; and it has to be impossible or extremely costly for the good purchased by one customer to be resold to another.

Doing the Math

1. $19,990. Total revenue from the sale of 1,000 goods at $49.99 each is $49,990. Profit = total revenue − total cost, or $19,990.

2. 4 units. To find out how many units a firm should produce, the student needs to find that quantity of output at which marginal revenue is equal to marginal cost. In the problem, marginal cost is given at $34, which leaves the student to

find marginal revenue. At 1 unit and a price of $40, total revenue is $40. At 2 units and a price of $39, total revenue is $78 and marginal revenue is $38 ($78 − $40 = $38). At 3 units and a price of $38, total revenue is $114, and marginal revenue is $36 ($114 − $78 = $36). At 4 units and a price of $37, total revenue is $148, and marginal revenue is $34. Because marginal revenue equals marginal at 4 units, that is what the firm should produce.

Working with Graphs and Tables

1. A. New firms enter the market.
B. Price falls. C. Profit declines.
2. D. Supply falls. E. Losses decline, or losses turn into profits.

Solving Economic Problems

1. The economic reason for asking the question is to gauge the price Lam can pay for the car. The car dealership wants to sell every car for the highest price possible, but it does not know what that price is. The salesperson may want to get a sense of how high a price a person can pay. Finding out what the person does for a living (and thus how much the person probably makes) may help in this regard. Of course, ability to pay and willingness to pay are two different things. It does not necessarily follow that because a person can pay a higher price, he or she will do so.

2. Easy entry into the market means firm A faces greater competition and lower profits. Firm A may want to restrict entry into market A so that if it does earn profits, it can continue to earn profits instead of having them competed away by new firms entering the market and producing the same good.

3. By limiting the profit that firms can earn, the government is indirectly limiting the number of firms that enter the market. Indirectly, then, the government is limiting both the supply of the good in the market and the decline in the price of the good that would arise from firms entering the market.

Project or Presentation

Answers will vary.

Chapter 9 Planning Guide

SECTION ORGANIZER

What Determines Wages?
(pages 246–257)

Learning Objectives	Reproducible Worksheets and Handouts	Assessment
▸ Describe what the demand curve for labor looks like. ▸ Describe what the supply curve for labor looks like. ▸ Explain why wage rates differ. ▸ Explain nonmoney benefits and how they factor into comparisons of jobs. ▸ Identify factors that determine how much a person earns.	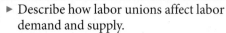 Section 1 Activity, *Applying the Principles Workbook*, pages 96–100 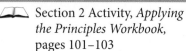 Outlining Activity, *Guided Reading and Study Guide*, pages 136–137 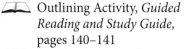 Just the Facts Handout, *Guided Reading and Study Guide*, pages 138–139	☑ Section Assessment, *Student Text*, page 257 ☑ Quick Quiz, *Annotated Teacher's Edition*, page 256 ☑ Section Quiz, *Assessment Book*, page 87

Labor and Government Regulation
(pages 260–269)

Learning Objectives	Reproducible Worksheets and Handouts	Assessment
▸ Describe how labor unions affect labor demand and supply. ▸ Explain what union and closed shops are. ▸ Identify states that have right-to-work laws. ▸ Provide examples of the unintended effects of regulation.	Section 2 Activity, *Applying the Principles Workbook*, pages 101–103 Outlining Activity, *Guided Reading and Study Guide*, pages 140–141 Just the Facts Handout, *Guided Reading and Study Guide*, pages 142–143	☑ Section Assessment, *Student Text*, page 269 ☑ Quick Quiz, *Annotated Teacher's Edition*, pages 268–269 ☑ Section Quiz, *Assessment Book*, page 88

Reproducible Chapter Resources and Assessment Materials

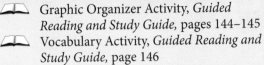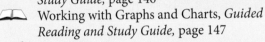

- Graphic Organizer Activity, *Guided Reading and Study Guide,* pages 144–145
- Vocabulary Activity, *Guided Reading and Study Guide,* page 146
- Working with Graphs and Charts, *Guided Reading and Study Guide,* page 147
- Practice Test, *Guided Reading and Study Guide,* pages 148–150
- Critical Thinking Activity, *Finding Economics,* pages 24–25
- Chapter Test A, *Assessment Book,* pages 89–91
- Chapter Test B, *Assessment Book,* pages 92–94

Student Text Internet Links

Economics: New Ways of Thinking, Second Edition encourages students to use the Internet to find out more about economics. Given the wealth of current, valid information available on websites, students should be encouraged to use the Internet as a research tool. Doing so will likely increase students' interest in and understanding of economics principles and topics. In addition, doing Internet research can help your students form the habit of accessing and using economics information, as well as help them develop investigative skills they will use throughout their educational and professional careers.

To aid your students in achieving these ends, each chapter of *Economics: New Ways of Thinking, Second Edition* includes the addresses of several websites that provide engaging and relevant information. When students type in any of the addresses provided, they will immediately arrive at the intended site. The addresses have been modified so that EMC Publishing can monitor and maintain the proper links—for example, the website http://www.deposit accounts.com/ has been changed to http://econ.emcp.net/accounts. In the event that the address or content of a site changes or is discontinued, EMC's Internet editors will redirect the link to a site with equivalent information.

Activities in the *Annotated Teacher's Edition* often suggest that students search the Internet for information. For some activities, you might want to find reputable sites beforehand and steer students toward them. For other activities, have students do their own searching and then check out the sites they have found and discuss why they might be reliable or unreliable.

Passport® for Economics

Technology resources are available with the *Economics: New Ways of Thinking, Second Edition* program through Passport®. These include:

eBooks for *Economics: New Ways of Thinking, Second Edition*

▶ Student textbook eBook
▶ Interactive Applying the Principles eWorkbook
▶ Finding Economics eBook
▶ Guided Reading and Study Guide eBook
▶ Annotated Teacher's Edition eBook
▶ Lesson Plans eBook
▶ Assessment eBook

Passport® for Students

Students can access helpful resources through Passport® for Economics. Resources include:

▶ Study guides
▶ Practice tests
▶ Flash cards in English and in Spanish
▶ Word games in English and in Spanish
▶ Tutorials and key-concept videos
▶ Spanish print and audio summaries

Passport® for Teachers

Keep your course current and relevant by using the teacher resources provided through Passport® for Economics. In addition to all of the resources on the student side of Passport®, the teacher side contains:

▶ Link to the Annotated Teacher's Edition eBook
▶ Standards correlations
▶ Microsoft® PowerPoint® Lectures
▶ Current Events Lessons
▶ Additional Economics in the Real World features
▶ ExamView® Assessment Suite
▶ PDFs of all print supplements (student and teacher)

Overview

There are many markets in the economy. This chapter discusses the labor market—the market in which wages are determined. This chapter also discusses the demand for and supply of labor and how wages are determined. It also discusses the history of the labor union movement in the United States.

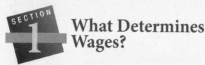

SECTION 1 What Determines Wages?

Section 1 deals with labor, which, like any other resource, exists within a market. Students will learn how the forces of supply and demand affect the labor market. These forces determine an equilibrium price (or wage) for labor. Students will also learn what money and nonmoney benefits are and how they affect wages.

SECTION 2 Labor and Government Regulation

Section 2 explores the organization of workers into labor unions, which changed the market for labor. Students will learn the history of labor unions and how they affect the labor market.

CHAPTER 9

Labor, Employment, and Wages

Why It Matters

Millions of people go to work every day. They work as cab drivers, attorneys, computer programmers, salespersons, construction workers, and accountants, among other things. Just as the work these people do differs from job to job, so does the pay. Workers' pay is determined by supply and demand.

All of the workers just mentioned are part of the civilian labor force. The civilian labor force consists

of men and women at least 16 years old and who are working at jobs or actively searching for jobs. One day soon, you will be part of the civilian labor force, if you are not already. When that day arrives, you will probably think a lot about what you are paid in the labor market. This chapter will help you understand the labor market and why people get paid what they do.

These emergency room doctors and nurses are awaiting the arrival of a patient being flown to the hospital by helicopter. In this chapter, you will learn why some people earn more than others and how wage rates reach equilibrium.

244

Teaching Suggestions from the Author

One way to get students interested in the material in this chapter is to start with this question: how many of you are interested in the amount of money you will earn on a job? Tell students that in this chapter, they will learn about factors that determine wage rates.

Alternatively, you can start by asking students to give reasons that baseball stars, basketball stars, and movie stars earn the high incomes that they do. This question can often stimulate a classroom discussion. Some students will say that baseball stars are not worth what they are

Section 1: **What Determines Wages?**

Section 2: **Labor and Government Regulation**

Economics Around the Clock

The following events occurred one day in September.

7:14 A.M. Blake is up and watching television. He hears a story about professional basketball players and the high salaries they earn. Blake, an avid basketball fan, wonders why some people end up making so much money.

- Is Blake part of the reason that professional basketball players earn high incomes?

8:44 A.M. Emily is talking to her friend, Karen, about a conversation she recently had with her grandfather. Her grandfather was talking about when he was a young man, just starting out in his career, and earning $100 a week as a salary. "Nowadays," he said, "people earn a lot more than that. But back then, $100 a week was a lot of money."

- What would make $100 "back then" a lot of money to earn a week, but today not so much?

10:56 A.M. Jill works as an accountant in Atlanta, and her annual salary is $82,000. She just got off the phone with an accounting firm in Milwaukee. The vice president of that firm has offered her a salary of $100,000 to work for the firm. The Milwaukee firm has a reputation for having disgruntled employees, so Jill is thinking of turning down the offer.

- Would Jill be wrong to turn down the job in Milwaukee?

5:03 P.M. Stephen is 16 years old and works at a grocery store every day after school. He earns the minimum wage. Right now, he is cleaning up in the back room of the store. When a coworker enters the room, Stephen asks him how much he is getting paid. The coworker says, "Same as you, minimum wage." "I wish I made a little more at this job," Stephen says. "So do I," says the coworker.

- Would Stephen likely have a job at the grocery store if the minimum wage went up?

245

Introducing the Chapter

Write the word *labor* on the board. Ask students to name the first three words that come to mind when they think of labor. Note that many times, students' responses will reflect negative connotations.

To give students a balanced perspective on labor, you might point out that President Ulysses S. Grant said, "Labor disgraces no man; unfortunately you can occasionally find men who disgrace labor."

Ask students what they think Grant meant by this statement. Explain that this chapter looks at the labor force, examining both people who are employed and people who are unemployed.

Teaching with Visuals

Workers in specialized fields, such as the medical industry, are in high demand. Due to low supply, these workers are able to command high salaries. Ask your students to name other occupations for which the demand for skilled workers is greater than the supply. Ask students how this affects wage rates. Using their knowledge of supply and demand, students should conclude that as demand for labor increases, wage rates increase and vice versa.

paid. Other students may argue that baseball stars are worth what they are paid. Ask these students to explain why.

You may also want to ask students how much discretion employers have over the salaries they pay their employees. For example, can an employer pay an employee less than the market-determined wage, or are employers forced to pay the mar-

ket-determined wage?

Finally, it's always good to ask students to think about what they need to do early in life to earn a good salary as an adult. Examine the correlation between education and wages, as well as between work experience and wages. What factors are most important in determining wages? Have students explain why.

Teacher Support

Focus and Motivate

Section Objectives

After completing this section, students will be able to

▶ describe what the demand curve for labor looks like;

▶ describe what the supply curve for labor looks like;

▶ explain why wage rates differ;

▶ explain nonmoney benefits and how they factor into comparisons of jobs; and

▶ identify factors that determine how much a person earns.

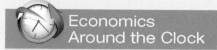

Economics Around the Clock

Kickoff Activity

Instruct students to respond in writing to the 8:44 a.m. scenario in Economics Around the Clock (page 245).

Invite students to share their answers with the class. Students should recognize that $100 "back then" was likely to be a higher real wage than it is today. One's real wage is equal to one's nominal wage divided by the CPI. Back then"—in Emily's grandfather's time—the CPI was lower than it is today, so that $100 divided by a low CPI would give one a higher real wage than $100 divided by a high CPI.

Activating Prior Knowledge

To review the supply and demand concepts presented in previous chapters, ask each student to create a visual aid explaining the relationship between wages and supply and demand. Divide students into small groups to present their visual aids.

Visit econ.myemcp.com/videos for videos that will help students better understand the key concepts found in this section.

SECTION 1

What Determines Wages?

Focus Questions

▶ What does the demand curve for labor look like?

▶ What does the supply curve for labor look like?

▶ Why do wage rates differ?

▶ What are nonmoney benefits and how do they factor into comparisons of jobs?

▶ What factors will determine how much you will earn?

Key Terms

wage rate
derived demand
minimum wage law

Supply and Demand in the Labor Market

In Chapters 4 and 5, you learned about demand and supply. In particular, you learned how both supply and demand affect prices for goods or products—such things as apples, cars, and houses. Supply and demand can also be used to analyze how we determine the price of a resource, or factor of production, such as labor.

People who demand labor are usually referred to as *employers*, and people who supply labor are *employees*. Looking at employers and employees in this way, we can create a demand curve and a supply curve that show the price of labor. The price of labor is called the **wage rate**.

The demand curve for labor is downward sloping (left to right), as shown in Exhibit 9-1. A downward-sloping demand curve indicates that employers are willing and able to hire more people at lower wage rates than at higher wage rates. For example, employers are willing and able to hire more workers if the wage rate is $7 per hour than if the wage rate is $10 per hour.

wage rate
The price of labor.

EXAMPLE Jack owns a small hotel. Currently, he employs four persons to clean rooms. He pays each person $80 a day. If he could pay each worker only $60 a day, he would hire five persons instead of four to clean rooms. ◆

The supply curve for labor, in contrast, is upward sloping (left to right), as shown in Exhibit 9-2. More people are willing and able to work at higher wage rates than at lower wage rates. In the exhibit, more people are willing and able to work if the wage rate is $10 per hour than if the wage rate is $7 an hour. For example, Pam is not willing to work as a salesperson in a clothing store if the store pays $7 an hour. However, she is willing to do that job if the store pays $10 an hour.

How the Equilibrium Wage Rate Is Established

Recall from Chapter 6 that the equilibrium price is the price at which the quantity demanded of a good equals the quantity supplied. Suppose $14 is the equilibrium price of DVDs; at this price, the number of

---

Background Information: Supply, Demand, and Teen Labor

Students may be interested to know how supply and demand affect teen labor. In recent years, teens have had difficulty getting jobs. Employment rates seem to vary across gender and racial/ethnic groups, but millions of teens looking for summer and year-round employment have remained unemployed or ended up underemployed.

Recent studies indicate a clear need to provide job opportunities for teens on a year-round basis. Some experts have suggested that Congress should expand job opportunities for teens by proposing programs such as increased job placement efforts and a targeted job stimulus bill.

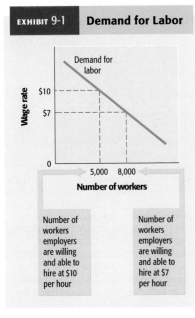

EXHIBIT 9-1 Demand for Labor

▲ A downward-sloping demand curve indicates that employers are willing and able to hire more people at lower wage rates.

Does a decrease in the wage rate cause the demand or the quantity demanded of labor to change?

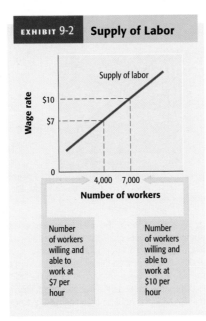

EXHIBIT 9-2 Supply of Labor

▲ An upward-sloping supply curve indicates that more people are willing and able to work at higher wage rates.

DVDs that sellers are willing and able to sell equals the number of DVDs that buyers are willing and able to buy.

Similarly, in the labor market, the equilibrium wage rate is the wage at which the quantity demanded of labor equals the quantity supplied of labor. Stated differently, it is the wage rate at which the number of people employers are willing and able to hire is the same as the number of people who are willing and able to be hired. In Exhibit 9-3(a) on the next page, when the wage rate is $9, the number of people who are willing and able to work (quantity supplied equals 7,000) is greater than the number of people employers are willing and able to hire (quantity demanded equals 3,000). It follows that $9 is not the equilibrium wage rate; at $9, the market has a surplus of labor.

In Chapter 6, you learned that when a surplus of a good occurs, the price of the good falls. Things are similar in a competitive labor market. When the market has a surplus of labor, the wage rate falls:

Quantity supplied of labor > Quantity demanded of labor = Surplus of labor

Surplus of labor → Wage rate falls

Now consider Exhibit 9-3(b). The wage rate is $7, and the number of people employers are willing and able to hire (6,000) is greater than the number of people who are willing and able to work (4,000). Thus, $7 is not the equilibrium wage rate. At $7, the market experiences a shortage of labor, so the wage rate rises:

Quantity demanded of labor > Quantity supplied of labor = Shortage of labor

Shortage of labor → Wage rate rises

If students have difficulty understanding the three charts shown in Exhibit 9-3, review how equilibrium prices are established. Remind students that labor is a good, or commodity, with variable rates. The price for labor is established just as the equilibrium price is established for other goods.

Teaching with Visuals

If the demand for labor increases, the equilibrium wage rate will rise.

Reinforcement Activity

Instruct students to copy and share with the class articles from newspapers or magazines that relate to people earning different incomes. For example, one student may find an article from a newspaper stating that a business executive earns $100,000 per year or that a professional baseball player earns $5 million per year. Ask students to offer economic explanations for the salaries. You might make a bulletin-board display of the articles.

Some people believe that a celebrity who earns a very high annual income is not worth that much money. An economist would say, however, that this person's income is a reflection of supply and demand forces. Ask students to consider whether they agree or disagree that supply and demand is at work as they present their articles to the class. Also ask students whether they believe it's fair or unfair to allow supply and demand to operate in the labor market.

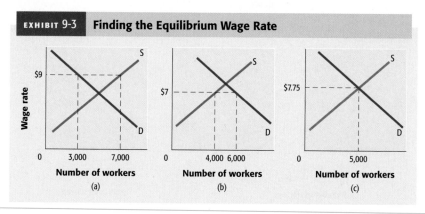

EXHIBIT 9-3   Finding the Equilibrium Wage Rate

▲ (a) At $9 per hour, the number of people willing and able to work (7,000) is greater than the number employers are willing and able to hire (3,000). We conclude that $9 is not the equilibrium wage rate. (b) At $7 per hour, the number of people employers are willing and able to hire (6,000) is greater than the number willing and able to work (4,000). We conclude that $7 is not the equilibrium wage rate. (c) At $7.75 per hour, the number of people willing and able to work (5,000) is the same as the number employers are willing and able to hire (5,000). We conclude that $7.75 is the equilibrium wage rate. What will happen to the equilibrium wage rate if the demand for labor increases?

In Exhibit 9-3(c), the wage rate is $7.75, and the number of people employers are willing and able to hire (5,000) equals the number of people who are willing and able to work (5,000). We conclude that $7.75 is the equilibrium wage rate. At this level, the wage rate neither rises nor falls because the market has neither a shortage nor a surplus of labor.

Why Do Some People Earn More than Others?

If you convert a daily or monthly salary into hours, you can find out how much a person earns on an hourly basis. This figure is that person's wage rate. For example, suppose someone earns $4,000 per month and works 160 hours a month. Her wage rate is $25 an hour.

Of course, some people earn higher wage rates than others. For example, some people earn $100 an hour while other people earn $8 an hour. Why the big difference? Supply and demand help us to understand why some people earn higher wages than others. First, suppose that the demand for every type of labor is the same—the demand for accountants is the same as the demand for construction workers and so on. Also suppose that we learn the equilibrium wage rate for accountants is higher than that for construction workers. If demand for the two types of labor is the same, how can we explain the difference in wage rates? Obviously, the supply of accountants and the supply of construction workers must not be the same. If accountants earn more than construction workers, it must be because the supply of accountants is less than the supply of construction workers. We conclude that *wage rates can differ because the supply of different types of labor is not the same.*

Suppose instead that the supply of different types of labor is the same—for example, the supply of bank tellers is the same as the supply of grocery store cashiers. If grocery store cashiers earn more than bank tellers, then what can possibly explain the difference? Obviously, the demand for bank tellers and grocery store cashiers must not be the same. We conclude that *wage rates can differ because the demand for different types of labor is not the same.*

"Pleasure in the job puts perfection in the work."
— Aristotle, ancient Greek philosopher

248   Chapter 9 Labor, Employment, and Wages

Differentiating Instruction

Kinesthetic and Visual Learners
If students have difficulty understanding the information presented in Exhibit 9-3, have them make their own three-dimensional graphs with materials they can manipulate upward and downward. Then ask students to explain what wages and number of workers are at various points along the curves.

QUESTIONS: *Many physicians earn less than many Major League Baseball players, but shouldn't they earn more? After all, Major League Baseball players are just playing a game. Physicians are trying to save lives.*

ANSWER: *Your question takes us beyond the confines of economics. It's sort of like asking a physicist if we would be better off if dynamite didn't blow up. Some things just are. It's a fact that the average Major League Baseball player earns more than the average physician, and it isn't so much the economist's job to pass judgment on this point as it is to explain why. The reason has to do with supply and demand. If a lot more people could do what Major League Baseball players do (thus increasing the supply of Major League Baseball players), you can be sure that ball players would earn less than they currently do. Or suppose, for example, that people stopped watching baseball games (lowering the demand for baseball games); again, baseball salaries would decline. As things are now, though, the demand for Major League Baseball players is high and the supply of them is low, and so they earn more than most people earn.*

Are Money Benefits the Only Thing That Matters?

Suppose Smith is offered two jobs, A and B. In job A, he will earn an annual income of $100,000 and in job B, $40,000. Which job will he choose? Most people will say that Smith will choose job A because it pays a higher income. Smith won't necessarily choose job A, however, because a higher income (more money per year) isn't the only thing that matters to people. Also important are what people do in their jobs, who their coworkers are, where they have to work, how many hours a week they have to work, how much vacation time they receive, and more. In short, if everything between the two jobs, A and B, is the same except the income (job A pays $100,000 and job B pays $40,000), then certainly Smith will choose job A over job B. But usually, not everything is the same between two jobs.

Suppose Smith chooses job B (the lower-paying job) over job A because he likes it much more. In job B, he is doing something that he has always wanted to do, works with nice people, gets one month of vacation each year, and is enormously stimulated by the work. In contrast, in job A, he would have done something both boring and tedious to him, worked with people he did not really like (especially his boss), and had only two weeks of vacation each year. On top of all this, he would have had to work 10 more hours each week and had much less job security. So, although job A pays more than job B, it does not have the nonmoney benefits that job B has.

All jobs come with both money benefits and nonmoney benefits. Look at it this way:

$$\text{Benefits in a job} =$$
$$\text{Money benefits (income)} + \text{Nonmoney benefits}$$

> *"Find a job you like and you add five days to every week."*
> —H. Jackson Brown Jr.,
> **author of inspirational books**

▼ Being able to afford a trip to a seaside resort is of no value if your job prevents you from getting away. **What are some nonmoney benefits of different jobs?**

Use this A Student Asks to make sure that students understand how supply and demand determine the salaries of Major League Baseball players.

Discussion Starter

Guide students in a discussion of non-money benefits. Create a class list of nonmoney benefits other than those listed in the text.

Critical Thinking

Ask students to imagine that they have just been offered three jobs. The first one is in their hometown and pays $30,000 a year. The second job pays $50,000 but is more than two thousand miles from their hometown. The third job pays only about $25,000, but it's in the most beautiful location in the nation. Ask, Which job would you choose? Would you need any other information before making a decision? How much does the location of the job (a nonmoney benefit) have to do with your accepting it?

Teaching with Visuals

Answers will vary. Students should be able to list several nonmoney benefits of different jobs.

Differentiating Instruction

English Language Learners

To help students who are English language learners better understand this information, tell them to read through this chapter and list the words that are unfamiliar to them. This chapter uses many terms and phrases that may be difficult for students to comprehend. Create a list of these terms and phrases, and then work through them with students. Have students make flash cards and work in pairs to quiz each other on these concepts before moving on to the next chapter.

After students have read this feature, ask if they have had a personal experience in which their productivity was closely linked to monetary benefits. Ask if they think it's fair for some people to receive higher wages for lower productivity.

ANSWERS TO THINK ABOUT IT Answers will vary.

Discussion Starter

Ask each student to identify his or her single most important nonmoney benefit. Ask how much money each student would be willing to give up to attain this benefit.

Economics Around the Clock

After students have read and discussed "Are Money Benefits the Only Thing That Matters?" (pages 249–251), instruct them to discuss their answers to the 10:56 a.m. scenario in Economics Around the Clock (page 245).

You might point out that when deciding whether to accept the job, Jill considers both the money benefits and the nonmoney benefits, not just one or the other. Students can think of it this way: Jill isn't wrong to turn down a job that pays more, because the nonmoney benefits she receives in her current job may more than compensate her for any money income she will lose.

Do You Want the 1st or the 43rd Pick in the NFL Draft?

Each year, the National Football League (NFL) conducts a draft in which the 32 teams take turns picking the best college players. Most people assume that the players picked early in the draft are the best players. For this reason, when a player is picked in the draft largely determines his starting salary: the earlier the player is chosen, the higher the salary.

After studying the NFL draft, two economists argue that a player's value to a team depends on how productive he is and how much he is paid. For example, player 1 might perform better than player 2 but be paid *twice* as much. Unless player 1 is twice as valuable on the field as player 2, then either player 1 is being overpaid or player 2 is being underpaid.

The economists collected data from the last 17 drafts and tried to figure out which draft picks were the best for the amount of money they were paid. The economists tried to identify not the best overall player but the best per-dollar player.

What did they discover? The best per-dollar player isn't usually the first pick in the first round. Instead, it's usually the 43rd person picked, which is the 11th pick in the second round.

In 2011, this pick went to the Minnesota Vikings, who took tight end Kyle Rudolph. Rudolph's rookie season included 26 receptions, 249 receiving yards, and 3 touchdowns. In 2012, he was selected to the pro-bowl and was named MVP of the game. And what did Rudolph's four-year contract cost the Vikings? $3.9 million with a $1.8 million signing bonus. (This is very reasonable, considering the first pick of the 2011 draft, Cam Newton, received a four-year deal worth over $22 million.)

The strategy outlined by the economists—go with lower-priced players in the second round rather than higher-priced players in the first round—is said to have been used in the 1960s by General Manager Bobby Beathard of the Washington Redskins. He often traded away his first-round picks for lower-priced picks in later rounds. The team Beathard built using this strategy won three Super Bowls. In more recent years, the New England Patriots won three Super Bowl titles in four years led by quarterback Tom Brady, who wasn't drafted until the sixth round.

So, if the economists are right, why are many teams paying so much for some of the early picks in the draft? Some have speculated that it's difficult to correctly estimate an athlete's worth over time, compared to other types of employees. For example, could you estimate a receptionist's productivity over time? His or her work environment and skills might improve a little, but will probably remain fairly constant from one year to the next.

The productivity of football players, on the other hand, seems very different. A football player usually plays with different team members and for different coaches from one year to the next, both of which impact his performance. In addition, injuries and age can have a major impact on a player's performance, much more significantly than in other occupations.

Since the two economists published their research, a number of NFL teams have contacted them for advice. It will be interesting to see which teams, if any, continue to overpay top picks. And by the way, how did your favorite team do in recent drafts?

THINK ABOUT IT We might expect that productivity is more closely linked to pay in some fields than in others. For example, we would expect productivity and pay to be closely linked in a field where it is easy to measure productivity and less closely linked in a field where it is hard to measure productivity. In what fields might be hard to measure productivity?

Cooperative Learning

Divide the class into small groups, and ask each group to select and research three occupations. For each occupation, students should find out the skills required, working conditions, employment opportunities, training and advancement, and earnings. Direct students to the website of the Bureau of Labor Statistics (http://econ.emcp.net/BLS), which is an agency of the U.S. Department of Labor.

Certainly, job A comes with higher money benefits (higher income) than job B, but (as far as Smith is concerned) it also comes with lower nonmoney benefits than job B. Because Smith chose job B (the $40,000 job) over job A (the $100,000 job), the nonmoney benefits in job B must have been higher than the nonmoney benefits in job A.

How much higher must they have been, in a dollar amount? The answer is at least $60,000 higher. To understand why, consider what Smith has "paid" by choosing job B over job A. He has paid $60,000 a year, because he has given up the opportunity to earn $60,000 more a year in job A. Therefore, the nonmoney benefits of job B must have been worth at least $60,000 to Smith. This means that job B "pays" more, as long as we understand that a person in a job is paid in terms of both money and nonmoney benefits.

EXAMPLE Kevin will graduate from college in a year and knows that his father has always wanted him to go to medical school. One of the reasons his father wants him to go to medical school is that doctors earn relatively high salaries. An orthopedic surgeon, for example, can earn $600,000 a year. Kevin doesn't really want to go to medical school. It's not that he thinks he would find being a doctor uninteresting; it's just that he doesn't want to work as hard as is needed to become a physician. He would have to go to four years of medical school, serve an internship and residency, and then work 60 to 80 hours a week for years. According to Kevin, "There is more to life than just money."

Here, then, is an example of a person who considers more than just the money benefits in a job; Kevin considers the nonmoney benefits too. Even though being a medical doctor comes with high money benefits, it doesn't come with enough nonmoney benefits for Kevin. Obviously, he is willing to trade off some of the money benefits he would receive as a doctor for greater nonmoney benefits in another job. ◆

Thinking Like an Economist

Money Versus Nonmoney Costs and Benefits

Many people assume that economists view the benefits and costs of something (a job, a vacation, an education) as it relates to money—that is, money benefits and money costs. But this common assumption is not true.

Economists know that many things have both money and nonmoney benefits and costs. For example, there are money benefits of working at a job (the income you receive), but there are probably nonmoney benefits too (working with people you like, doing what you really like to do, and so on).

Money benefits and costs aren't the only things that motivate people. Nonmoney benefits and costs motivate people too. Economists want the full picture of what motivates people, not just a half picture. That's why economists always consider nonmoney benefits and costs when they exist.

A Student Asks

QUESTION: *I thought economics was about money—specifically, the more money, the better. Am I wrong here?*

ANSWER: *It is one thing to say "the more money, the better" and quite another to say "the more money, the better, all other things being equal." The economist will make the second statement but not the first. What the economist means is that if two jobs, A and B, are exactly alike except for the fact that job A pays more than B, then job A is a better job than job B.*

The Demand for a Good and Wage Rates

Eva works in a factory that manufactures mp3 players. Suppose the demand for mp3 players decreases, as shown in Exhibit 9-4(a) on the next page. What do you think will happen to Eva? If the demand decreases, mp3 player manufacturers will not need to hire as many workers, so the demand for

Background Information

Some people believe that labor productivity is lower in one country or one part of the country than in another. The perception is that people don't work as hard in some areas as they do in others. Actually, labor productivity has more to do with incentives, education, and whether factories are highly industrialized and well equipped than with the innate productivity of the people who live and work in a particular region.

A Student Asks

Use this A Student Asks to make sure students understand the significance of the phrase "all things being equal."

Reinforcement Activity

One of the factors that determine how much money you earn is the location of your job. Students may not be aware of the large salary differences that sometimes exist for the same types of jobs based solely on geographic location. For example, a tax manager for a bank in the Midwest makes, on average, $57,200. On the West Coast, the same position pays, on average, $62,300. Assign students to research two or three jobs and find the differences in salaries in various areas of the nation. Some of this information is available on the Internet.

Cooperative Learning

Divide the class into groups of three or four. Ask each group to select a particular industry or factory and research the average wages of the workers in that industry or factory over the past five years. Each group should prepare demand curves based on the salaries and output of the chosen industry or factory. If salaries have varied, group members should write an explanation of the changes. Groups should be prepared to share their visuals (demand charts) with the class and give oral reports of their findings. After students have finished, lead them in analyzing which industries have had the most variance and the least variance, and ask them to suggest what factors might account for this.

Teaching with Visuals

Discuss with students both charts in Exhibit 9-4 to ensure that everyone comprehends them. Have students recreate both (a) and (b) on their own paper and add quantity and dollar amounts. Then ask students to plot particular points along the curves.

Prediction Activity

Ask students to consider this scenario: Jim is offered two jobs, A and B. Job A pays $50,000 a year, and job B pays $60,000 a year. The nonmoney benefits for the two jobs are the same. Cindra is offered two jobs, C and D. Job C pays $50,000 a year, and job D pays $60,000 a year, but the nonmoney benefits for the two jobs are not the same. Is it as easy to predict which job Cindra will choose as it is to predict which job Jim will choose? Why or why not?

(*Answer:* It is easier to predict which job Jim will choose. He will likely choose job B, because it has the same nonmoney benefits as job A but offers more money. It is impossible to predict accurately which job Cindra will pick. Job C pays less than job D, but the nonmoney benefits for job C might be much greater than the money benefits for job D. If this is the case, then Cindra will most likely choose job C. We don't know, however, the value (in dollars) of the nonmoney benefits for each job.)

Reinforcement Activity

Productivity is measured both for individuals and for nations. Assign each student to compare a particular nation's productivity figures with those of the United States. Ask, Which is higher? Why? Encourage students to prepare oral reports with visuals to share with the class.

Teaching with Visuals

Answers will vary. Students should include factors such as demand for labor services, supply of labor offered, productivity, education level, and skill development.

▶ The demand for mp3 players affects the demand for the workers who produce the players and their wages. In this example, when the demand for mp3 players falls, the demand for workers also falls, causing the wage rate to fall from $18 to $15 per hour.

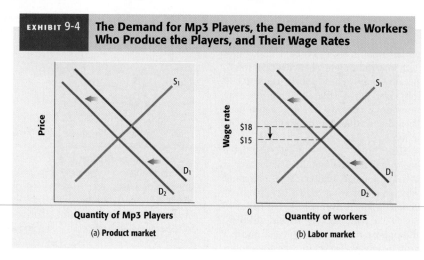

EXHIBIT 9-4 The Demand for Mp3 Players, the Demand for the Workers Who Produce the Players, and Their Wage Rates

(a) **Product market**

(b) **Labor market**

derived demand
A demand that is the result of some other demand.

▶ How much do you think you would earn as an automobile mechanic? What are some of the factors that would determine your wage rate?

252 Chapter 9

workers will decrease, as shown in Exhibit 9-4(b). As the demand for these workers decreases and the supply stays constant, the wage rate will decrease as well.

Because the demand for labor depends on the demand for the good or service the labor produces, the demand for labor is often referred to as a **derived demand**. A derived demand is one that is the result of some other demand.

EXAMPLE Carl plays ice hockey. If the demand to watch hockey games falls (perhaps people switch from watching hockey to watching basketball), then the demand for hockey players will fall too. As a result, Carl's wage rate will fall. ◆

What Will You Earn?

If you are reading this book as part of a high school course, you are likely somewhere between the ages of 14 and 18. Let's jump ahead 15 years, when you will be between 29 and 33 years old. At that time, you will be working at some job and earning some wage rate or salary. You could be earning anywhere between, say, $40,000 and $500,000 a year. What will determine the amount you will earn?

Your wage rate (and salary) depends on a number of things, one of which is the demand for your labor services. That demand may be high, low, or medium. The higher the demand for you, the higher your wage rate will be. Obviously, you want the demand for you to be as high as possible.

Two factors will make the demand for your labor services high: (1) the demand for the good you produce and (2) your productivity. The greater the demand for the product you produce, the greater the demand for your labor services. If you produce attorney services and attorney services are in high demand, then you will be in high demand too. If you produce telephones and telephones are in low demand, then you will be in low demand too.

The second factor that relates to the demand for you as an employee is your productivity. The more productive you are

---

Background Information: Gender and Wages

Gender is another significant factor that accounts for wage differences in the United States. For example, in 2003, women who worked full time earned only 80 cents for every dollar earned by men. In 1980, the difference was even greater; women earned only 60% as much as men. Gender differences in wages exist in other countries as well. For example, in South Korea, women earn 60% as much as men; in France, 80%; in the Philippines, 91%; and in Australia, 102%. Ask students to list factors that might explain why women often make less than men but why they tend to make more than men in Australia.

Are Entertainers Worth Millions?

A TV news anchor announces a particular sports star's new salary: $10 million a year. The anchor goes on to say that a particular TV star will earn $1 million per episode, and a movie star will get $20 million for his next movie.

When hearing about these large salaries, it's natural to ask whether the people who receive them are worth the money. Is *anyone* worth $1 million to act in one episode or $10 million to play one season of baseball? Would an economist say these high salaries are justified? Let's explore the question by laying out a possible set of facts.

Suppose you are the president of NBC television and a star of one of your hit shows is asking for $1 million per episode. Whether you pay it depends on whether the star is worth that much. But how do you determine that?

First, you ask yourself what will happen to the ratings of the show if the star no longer appears on it. Suppose you think the ratings will drop. If they do, you won't be able to charge as much for a 30-second commercial that runs during the star's show. The cost of a 30-second commercial can range from a low of $30,000 to a high of $700,000 or more (if we are dealing with the Super Bowl). Let's say that for a fairly successful show, a 30-second commercial costs $260,000. For 10 30-second

commercials, the revenue amounts to $2.6 million.

Suppose you think that ratings will drop so much that you can charge only $80,000 for a 30-second commercial. With 10 commercials, this price will reduce revenue to $800,000.

In short, with the star appearing in the show, the network earns revenue of $2.6 million an episode, and without the star, it will earn only $800,000 per episode. So, if the star leaves the show, revenue will drop by $1.8 million.

Is it worth paying $1 million to the star to prevent losing $1.8 million in revenue? The answer is yes. As long as the additional revenue that the star generates (in this case, $1.8 million) is greater than the star's salary (in this case, $1 million), then the star is worth what she is paid.

THINK ABOUT IT In 2017–2018, LeBron James, a professional basketball player for the Cleveland Cavaliers, earned $33.2 million. His teammate Edy Tavares earned $1.4 million. What explains such a large difference between the two players' earnings?

at what you do, the greater the demand for you. Suppose that two people can produce accounting services. One, however, can produce twice as many accounting services per hour as the other. It follows, then, that the more productive accountant will be in greater demand by accounting firms.

A number of factors can influence your productivity. One factor is your innate ability; you may simply have been born

with a great ability to organize people, play baseball, sing a song, or write a story. A second factor is how much effort you put into developing your skills. You may have worked hard developing and perfecting your ability to produce a service, whether attorney services, teaching services, or medical services. Third, your productivity is affected by the quality and amount of your education. The higher the quality of your

Prompt students to think of their favorite athlete or TV star and to guess what he or she earns annually. Ask if students think the high salaries of such people are justified.

ANSWERS TO THINK ABOUT IT Answers will vary. Students should understand that a highly paid star presumably brings in much higher revenue for the team than other players on the team.

Economics Around the Clock

After reading and discussing "Are Entertainers Worth Millions?" ask students to discuss their answers to the 7:14 a.m. scenario in Economics Around the Clock (page 245).

Basketball players in the NBA earn high salaries because the demand for them is high and the supply of them is low. One of the reasons the demand is high is that many people enjoy watching professional basketball—one of whom is Blake. If basketball had fewer fans like Blake, basketball players wouldn't earn as much as they do.

Discussion Starter

The salaries for professional athletes and Hollywood stars are so high that many people cannot fathom the amounts of money that these individuals earn. The idea that a professional basketball star makes $15 million in one season is inconceivable. When that salary is broken down over an 82-game season, it comes to approximately $182,926.83 a game, $3,810.90 a minute, and $63.50 a second. Make sure students understand that despite the shock value of these enormous numbers, the market of supply and demand supports these salaries.

Internet Research

Assign students to go online to find the 10 to 20 highest-paid executives in the United States. Ask each student to select one of these executives and conduct online research about the company for which he or she works. If possible, the student should also find a biographical sketch of the person. In small groups, allow students to share the results of their research and explain why they believe these executives earn such high salaries.

Answers will vary. Students should see that Lawrence's high wages are a result of high demand combined with low supply.

Discussion Starter

Ask, Can the demand for football in other countries affect the salary of a football player in the United States? It certainly can. To illustrate, consider the Super Bowl, which is broadcast around the world. There seems to be a demand by people in other countries for watching American football. If that demand were to fall, foreign TV ratings of the Super Bowl would fall, reducing the amount firms would pay to advertise during the Super Bowl. This would reduce the earnings of the football teams, and teams would not be willing to pay the same salaries to football players. Players would earn less.

Reinforcement Activity

Instruct each student to write a sentence that defines the role of the equilibrium wage rate in the supply and demand for labor.

▲ Jennifer Lawrence is a successful star of movies that do well at the box office. What qualities do you think contribute to Jennifer's earning more than most people her age?

"I'm living so far beyond my income that we may almost be said to be living apart."
— e. e. cummings, poet

---

minimum wage law
A federal law that specifies the lowest hourly wage rate that can be paid to workers.

education and the more education you have, the more productive you will be (all other things being equal). In fact, statistics show that as a person's educational level rises, so does his or her income. In summary, the demand for you (as an employee) will rise with the demand for the product or service you produce and your productivity.

Of course, your wage (or salary) in the future depends not only on how high or low the demand for you is in the future but also on the number of people who can do what you do. In short, it also depends on supply. For example, the demand for you may be high, but if the supply is high too, then you won't be as likely to earn a high wage. High wages are the result of high demand combined with low supply.

Why is supply high in some labor markets and low in others? The supply of labor offered in a particular labor market is the result of a number of factors, one of which is the ability to perform a particular

service. For example, more people can work as restaurant servers than as brain surgeons. Similarly, more people can drive trucks than can argue and win difficult law cases before the U.S. Supreme Court. These statements do not put a value judgment on work as a restaurant server or truck driver. They simply report the fact that some tasks can be completed by more people than others. All other things being equal, the fewer people who can do what you do, the higher your wage (or salary) will be.

EXAMPLE Orthopedic surgeons earn a relatively high income because they meet the three requirements for generating a high income. First, they are part of a (medical) team that produces health services, which are in high demand. Second, orthopedic surgeons are productive. Third, not many people can do what they do (supply is low). In short, as was stated earlier, the combination of high demand for the good or service produced, high productivity, and a situation in which not many people can do what one does results in a high salary. ◆

Government and the Minimum Wage

The **minimum wage law** sets a wage floor—that is, a level below which hourly wage rates are not allowed to fall. The law, passed during the Great Depression of the 1930s, initially established a minimum wage of 25 cents an hour. In 2017, the federal minimum wage was $7.25 an hour. Many states set their minimum wage rate higher than the federal rate.

The U.S. Congress determines the minimum wage. Earlier, however, you read that supply and demand determine wage rates. So what really does determine wage rates—the government or supply and demand? The fact is that supply and demand usually but not always determine wages.

Suppose that in a particular labor market, the equilibrium wage rate is $6.10 an hour. In other words, the demand curve and the supply curve of labor intersect at a wage rate of $6.10. Congress then argues that a wage

Cooperative Learning

Divide students into small groups, and assign each group a job category in which people tend to earn high salaries (entertainment, music, athletics, TV, journalism). Each group should identify five to ten well-known people in that field and research the annual salaries of these individuals. Each group should also create a visual documenting the salaries. Ask groups to prepare and present oral reports to show their visuals and provide explanations for salary differences among the people they have researched.

 This worker is paid the minimum wage at a sporting goods store near his home. **How might he be affected if the government raises the minimum wage by $2 an hour?**

rate of $6.10 an hour is too low and orders employers to pay employees at least $7.25 an hour. That rate is now the minimum wage. It becomes unlawful to pay an employee less than this hourly wage.

Many people agree with Congress that a wage of $6.10 an hour is simply too low. Economists, however, are not as interested in whether Congress is justified in setting a minimum wage as they are in knowing the *effects* of setting the minimum wage rate above the equilibrium wage rate. They know what the intended effects are, but they also wonder about the unintended effects. For example, will employers hire as many workers at the minimum wage rate of $7.25 as they would at the equilibrium wage rate of $6.10? Remember, the demand curve for labor is downward sloping (from left to right). As the wage rate falls, employers will hire more workers, and as the wage rate rises, they will hire fewer workers. Thus, Congress's setting a minimum wage rate above the equilibrium wage rate will result in employers being willing and able to hire fewer workers.

A Student Asks

QUESTION: *Without a minimum wage law, wouldn't employers pay next to nothing for unskilled labor?*

ANSWER: *Suppose 100 people are working and earning the minimum wage of $7.25 an hour. First, ask whether these people are worth $7.25 an hour. The answer has*

to be yes, because no employer would pay an employee $7.25 an hour unless he or she was worth that much.

Next, let's ask ourselves whether the people who are not worth $7.25 an hour to an employer are working when this is the minimum wage. The answer is no. For example, Jack, 16 years old, may be worth $6.00 an hour but not $7.25, so if the employer has to pay Jack $7.25 an hour, he will not hire Jack in the first place.

What happens if the minimum wage is scrapped? Do the 100 people who were earning $7.25 find themselves earning only $2.00 an hour? Not at all. If they were hired when the wage rate was set at $7.25, then they truly must be worth $7.25 an hour. If someone offers them $2.00 an hour, they will simply move to work for someone who pays them their market wage of $7.25 an hour.

Scrapping the minimum wage law won't lower the wage rate for workers currently earning the minimum wage; instead, it will bring people into the labor force who weren't previously worth the minimum wage. It will bring Jack into the market, for instance, because an employer will be willing to hire Jack if he can pay him $6.00 an hour. Most likely, Jack will acquire new skills in time that will make him worth more (to an employer), and then he will earn a higher wage.

Teaching with Visuals

Student answers will vary. Students should understand that if the minimum wage is raised, employers might hire fewer workers.

Economics Around the Clock

After reading and discussing "Government and the Minimum Wage" (pages 254–255), instruct students to discuss their answers to the 8:44 a.m. scenario in Economics Around the Clock (page 245). The effects that immigration has on wages depend on whether immigration increases the supply of labor by more than, less than, or equal to how much it increases the demand for labor.

Cause and Effect

Many students may think that the minimum wage only increases earnings and has no effect on employment rates. Have students evaluate this scenario and determine the effect on wages and employment rates: A company has enough money to pay $38 an hour in wages. It has five employees, all of whom make $7.60 an hour working full time. What will happen if the government raises the minimum wage to $9 an hour? to $10 an hour? How will such an increase affect the company and its workers?

A Student Asks

Use this A Student Asks to make sure students understand the intended and unintended effects of the minimum wage law.

Cooperative Learning

Some students may have already worked at full-time jobs in the summer and perhaps hold down jobs during the school year. Divide the class into groups, making sure that each group includes at least one student who has worked. Assign groups to create lists of costs and benefits of working, including the lost time from school studies and the chance to make their own money. Stress that you are not necessarily endorsing working during school. Rather, guide students to see that at some point, they will all have jobs and will have to give up other things to work.

Prediction Activity

Ask students to think about the following question: what will happen to real wages in the near future if the prices of goods and services are rising but nominal wages are not rising at the same pace. (*Answer:* Because it costs more in nominal wages to purchase goods and services, real wages will fall.)

Teaching with Visuals

The answer to the question accompanying the photo on page 257 is that increasing prices at the pump will cause this person's real wages to fall.

 Application Activity

After reading and discussing Section 1, you may want to assign the Section Activity in the *Applying the Principles Workbook,* pages 96–100.

Assess

Quick Quiz

The following true-or-false quiz will help you assess student understanding of the material covered in this section.

1. The price of labor is called the *derived demand.* (False)
2. The equilibrium wage rate is established when the quantity demanded of labor equals the quantity supplied of labor. (True)
3. Location can be a nonmoney benefit. (True)
4. If the demand for a good increases, the wage for the producers of that good decreases. (False)
5. The minimum wage law sets a wage floor. (True)

 Assessment Book

You will find a quiz for this section in the *Assessment Book,* page 87.

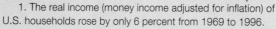

The Number of Persons in a Household Matters

Consider two statements, both of which are true:

  1. The real income (money income adjusted for inflation) of U.S. households rose by only 6 percent from 1969 to 1996.

  2. The average real income per person in the United States rose by 51 percent from 1969 to 1996.

Again, both statements are true, but the they seem to say different things, don't they? The first statement makes it sound like real income is close to stagnant in the United States, whereas the second statement makes it sound like real income is rising appreciably. How can both statements be true?

The first statement talks about "households" and the second statement talks about "per person." The average number of persons that make up a household varies over time. So, if a household consists of five persons one time and four persons another time, it's possible for the real income of the household to go down as the income per person goes up.

Let's illustrate this. Suppose there are five persons in a household, and each person has a real income of $50,000. That means the household income is $250,000. Now let's suppose that the average U.S. household has gotten smaller, so that it includes only four persons, but each person earns $60,000. On a per-person basis, real income has risen from $50,000 to $60,000, but the real income of a household has fallen to $240,000. In other words, household income in the United States has gone down as per-person income has risen.

Two Types of Wages: Nominal and Real

Suppose Patel earns $9 an hour in 2016 and $12 an hour in 2017. Is she better off in 2016 or in 2017? The obvious answer seems to be that she is better off in 2017, when she earns the higher wage rate. This answer assumes, however, that the prices of the goods and services she buys in 2016 and 2017 are the same, which may not be true. Prices may be higher in 2017 than 2016. Whether Patel is better off in 2017 than 2016 depends on how much her wages have increased compared to the increases in prices.

We can measure a person's wage rate in terms of money (for example, $9 or $11 per hour) or in terms of what the wages will buy.

Measuring a person's wage rate in terms of money gives us the person's *nominal wage* (sometimes called the *money wage*). Measuring a person's wage rate in terms of what it buys gives us the person's *real wage.* Can a person's nominal wage rise while his or her real wage falls? Let's look at an example.

EXAMPLE Suppose the only good that Patel buys is chocolate bars. In 2016, chocolate bars sell for $1 a bar. With a wage rate of $9 an hour, Patel can buy 9 chocolate bars an hour. In 2017, chocolate bars are $2 a bar; with a wage rate of $12 an hour, Patel can buy 6 chocolate bars an hour. Patel went from earning $9 to $12 an hour, but her real wage fell from 9 chocolate bars an hour to 6 chocolate bars an hour. Everyone talks in terms of nominal wages ("I earn $10 an hour"), but the real wage is far more important, because it measures what we can do with the nominal wage we receive.

We are paid in nominal wages, obviously. So, how can we compute our real wages and then determine how much buying power we have from one period to the next? We computed Patel's real wage in 2016 versus 2017 by simply dividing the nominal wage in each year by the price of a chocolate bar in each year. In the real world, of course, people do not simply buy chocolate bars; they buy a variety of goods. The government measures the average price of these goods (usually called a *price index*). One particularly well-known price index is the *Consumer Price Index,* or *CPI*. Perhaps you've heard a TV newscaster say, "The government reported today that the CPI rose by 4 percent over the year." This means that prices, on average, are 4 percent higher this year than last year.

The government computes the CPI on an annual basis. Therefore, we can compute our real wage by simply dividing our nominal wage in a given year by the CPI in the same year:

$$\text{Real wage} = \frac{\text{Nominal wage}}{\text{CPI}}$$

For example, suppose that in 2016, a person earned a wage rate of $20 an hour and the CPI was 200. The person's real

---

Differentiating Instruction

English Language Learners

To help students who are English language learners, use the following resources, which are provided as part of the *Economics: New Ways of Thinking* program:

• a Spanish glossary in the *Student Text*
• Spanish versions of the Chapter Summaries on an audio disc

wage was 0.10. In percentage terms, it is 10 percent—but 10 percent of what? In the chocolate bar example, it would be 10 percent of one chocolate bar. But we aren't talking about chocolate bars here; we are talking about many goods. Think of the 0.10, then, as 10 percent of one unit of a composite good. This composite good is a little food, a little housing, and a little entertainment all rolled up into one. With $20 an hour, then, a person can purchase 10 percent of one unit of the composite good.

Now suppose that in 2017, the person's wage rate rises to $30 and the CPI goes up to 210. What is the person's real wage now? If we divide $30 by 210, we get 0.1428, or 14.28 percent of one unit of a composite good.

Is the person's real wage higher in 2016 or in 2017? The answer is 2017. In 2016, the real wage rate is 10 percent of one unit of a composite good, and in 2017, it is 14.28 percent of one unit of a composite good. ♦

▲ How does increasing gas prices at the pump affect this person's real wage?

ASSESSMENT — SECTION 1

Defining Terms

1. Define:
   a. wage rate
   b. derived demand
   c. minimum wage law
2. Give an example of a nominal wage and a real wage.

Reviewing Facts and Concepts

3. In a competitive labor market, suppose the quantity demanded of labor is greater than the quantity supplied. What will happen to the wage rate? Explain.

4. John is paid $7 an hour, and Kimsan is paid $23 an hour. Why does Kimsan likely earn more than John?

5. Mauricio accepts a job that pays $35,000 a year instead of a job that pays $80,000 a year. What do the nonmoney benefits in the $35,000 job equal (at minimum)? Explain your answer.

Critical Thinking

6. If Major League Baseball becomes less popular, what will happen to players' salaries? Explain your answer.

7. Is nominal wage or real wage more important in determining a person's material standard of living? Explain.

Applying Economic Concept

8. Over the past three years, Rachel's nominal wage has increased 10 percent and prices have increased 13 percent. Has Rachel's real wage increased, decreased, or remained stable? Explain your answer.

Section 1 What Determines Wages? **257**

Your Personal Economics

Education—It's Like Multiplying Yourself

Here is what possibly could be one of the most important tables you will ever see. It's from the U.S. Bureau of Labor Statistics.

More Money, More Security

This table shows the median weekly earnings in 2016 for individuals with various levels of education. For example, the average person with some high school but no diploma earned $493. Now notice what happens as a person's educational level rises. His or her weekly earnings rise as well.

In fact, as you get more education, it is like multiplying yourself.

To see how, let's suppose you compare your earnings under two scenarios. In the first, you have some high school (but no diploma). In the second case, you earn a master's degree.

Education attained	Median weekly earnings in 2016
Doctoral degree	$1,623
Master's degree	1,341
Bachelor's degree	1,137
Associate degree	798
Some college, no degree	738
High school graduate	678
Some high school, no diploma	493

▼ Are the financial benefits of all college diplomas the same? No, some degrees are worth more than others. Go to http://econ.emcp.net/degrees and identify the five best undergraduate college degrees by salary.

258 Chapter 9 Labor, Employment, and Wages

Cooperative Learning

Divide students into groups of three or four. Tell each group to draw the same comparisons as the text, using median weekly earnings of the current year. Each group should calculate lifetime earnings for an 18-year-old working for 48 years, for someone with a bachelor's degree working for 43 years, and for someone with a master's degree working for 41 years. After 15 minutes, let all the groups report their calculations to the class.

An Important Comparison

Let's assume that you have some high school (only), and you start working when you are 18 and stop working when you are 65. You will earn an average of $25,636 per year for 48 years. This yields a total of $1,230,528 in lifetime earnings (before taxes).

Now let's assume you have a master's degree. Getting this degree means that you will work for fewer years because you must go to college to earn a bachelor's degree (that's 4 or 5 years) and then on to graduate school to earn a master's degree (let's say 2 years). So, in total, you will work 6 to 7 years less. You will earn, then, an average of $69,732 a year for, say, 41 years. The total ends up being $2,859,012 in lifetime earnings (before taxes).

Now we know that your lifetime earnings with a master's degree ($2,859,012) is more than two times your lifetime earnings with only some high school ($1,230,528). What does this comparison mean? Simply that having a master's degree gives you the ability to create more of yourself. In other words, when you go into the labor market with only some high school, it's like one of you going to work. But when you go into the labor market with a master's degree, it's like you and another person going to work.

Your Personal Economics Activity

What type of post-secondary program would interest you? Research three post-secondary options and identify how much each option would cost per year. Then, investigate and analyze student financial services (such as loans, scholarships, or government aid) that might help you pay for your post-secondary education. Record this information in a chart or text document.

My Personal Economics Action Plan

Here are some points you may want to consider and some guidelines you might want to put into practice:

☑ 1. The more education you have, the higher your lifetime earnings likely will be.

I will graduate from high school with the highest possible grade point average.

☑ 2. The more education you have, the less likely you will be unemployed.

After graduating from high school, I will enroll in _____ to get a degree in _____.

☑ 3. Going from a high school diploma to a master's degree is equivalent to creating more of yourself in terms of earning power.

After graduating from _____, I will assess my options for graduate school and make a decision to obtain a graduate degree in _____ by the time I am _____ years old.

☑ 4. Some people say they don't like school and would rather go to work as soon as possible. Look at it this way: whether you are in school or working at a job, you have something to do eight hours a day. It's not a choice between going to school and doing nothing; the choice is between learning eight hours a day or working eight hours a day. Sometimes, learning looks a lot better when you see at it as a substitute for working (instead of leisure).

I will substitute learning for working _____ hours a day for _____ years so that I can earn twice as much money in my lifetime.

Discussion Starter

To help students realize the power of using education to multiply themselves, ask them to list necessities that can be purchased with wages, such as a house, a car, and food. Invite students to put a dollar amount on each necessity. Then instruct them to calculate how much money is left from weekly earnings after subtracting money for necessities. Ask them to do this for each of the three educational levels. Then have students compare the money left from the weekly earnings at each level of education. Ask students if this information has changed their minds about education. Ask what they can do now as teens to earn good salaries as adults.

My Personal Economics Action Plan Ask each student to survey several adults to determine if they experience the same pattern of more education bringing a higher income. Students may want to ask follow-up questions to determine what kinds of situations break the pattern. Allow students to report their findings in small groups.

Grading Rubric: Research

1 2 3 4 5 Student identified and evaluated three post-secondary options.

1 2 3 4 5 Research was identified in a data or text document.

Teacher Support

Focus and Motivate

Section Objectives

After completing this section, students will be able to

▶ describe how labor unions affect labor demand and supply;

▶ explain what union and closed shops are;

▶ identify states that have right-to-work laws; and

▶ provide examples of the unintended effects of regulation.

Kickoff Activity

Invite students to respond in writing to the following question: what is a labor union? Allow volunteers to share their answers with the rest of the class. Knowing how well your students understand labor unions and their activities will be helpful as you decide how best to present this material.

Activating Prior Knowledge

To an economist, the minimum wage law is neither a good law nor a bad law. It is a law that has consequences; specifically, because of it, fewer persons will have jobs than would have jobs without it. Ask students' opinions on whether the law is worth keeping.

Teach

Discussion Starter

Ask students if they know anyone who belongs to a labor union. One student may say her father belongs to a labor union. Another may say his next-door neighbor belongs to a labor union. Invite students to share what they know about labor unions. Ask if labor unions help working men and women and if so, in what ways.

Labor and Government Regulation

Focus Questions

▶ How do labor unions affect labor demand and supply?

▶ What is a union shop? Closed shop?

▶ How many states have right-to-work laws?

▶ What are some of the unintended effects of regulation?

Key Terms

labor union
closed shop
Taft-Hartley Act
union shop
strike
right-to-work law

Some Practices of Labor Unions

One objective of a **labor union** may be to obtain higher pay for its members. To achieve that goal, the union must direct its activities to increasing the demand for its labor, decreasing the supply of its labor, or both.

The Demand for Union Labor

As stated earlier, if the demand for a good decreases, then the demand for the labor that produces the good decreases too. For example, if the demand for cars decreases, then the demand decreases for the workers who produce cars. If the demand for cars increases, of course, the demand increases for the workers who produce cars.

With that relationship in mind, suppose you are a union worker in the U.S. automobile industry, centered in Detroit, Michigan. Would you want the demand for American-made cars to increase, stay constant, or decrease? Obviously, you would want the demand for American-made cars to increase, because you know

labor union
An organization that seeks to increase the wages and improve the working conditions of its members.

that if it increases, the demand for your labor increases too. As the demand for your labor increases, your wage rate increases, all other things remaining the same.

For this reason, your labor union might try to increase the demand for the product it produces. It might launch an advertising campaign urging people to purchase only union-produced goods. For example, TV commercials in the past have urged people to "look for the union label"—in other words, buy union-made goods. Also, when U.S. union workers are in competition with workers in other countries (for example, U.S. car workers are in competition with Japanese car workers), an advertising campaign might urge people to buy goods "made in the U.S.A."—another union slogan in the recent past.

The Supply of Union Labor

Just as a labor union tries to increase the demand for its labor, it also tries to decrease the labor supply. Suppose you work as a truck driver. Would you prefer to be one of a thousand truck drivers in the United States or one of ten thousand truck drivers?

Internet Research

Direct students to visit the websites of several major labor unions, such as the Teamsters and the United Auto Workers. Assign them to find out what services the unions provide for their members and in what activities and actions unions are involved. Have each student write a page explaining how these services and activities might affect wages for both union and nonunion workers in these industries.

Your answer probably is one of a thousand, because you know that the lower the supply of truck drivers, the higher your wage rate, all other things remaining the same.

Some people criticize labor unions for trying to control the supply of labor at times. In the past, some unions supported **closed shops**: organizations that hire only union members. To work for one of these companies, people would first have to join the labor union. The labor union, in turn, might hold down the number of workers who could join (and thus work in the particular industry) to keep the supply of workers in that industry low and to keep wage rates high. The union could do this by limiting membership or requiring long training periods. Today, the closed shop is illegal. It was prohibited by the **Taft-Hartley Act**, passed by the U.S. Congress in 1947.

The *union shop*, however, is legal in many states. A **union shop** does not require individuals to be union members to be hired, but it does require employees to join the union within a certain period of time after being hired. Labor unions favor union shops, because if everyone working in a particular trade or industry has to become a member of the union within a certain period of time, the labor union gains greater control

over the supply of labor. For example, consider the **strike**: a work stoppage called by union members to put pressure on an employer. It is easier for the union to call a strike if everyone in a particular trade or industry is a member of the union.

Today, 28 states have passed **right-to-work laws**, which make it illegal to require union membership for purposes of employment. In short, in states with right-to-work laws, the union shop is illegal.

 ▲ Union and non-union citizens protest legislation that they believe will be damaging to U.S. workers and consumers.

closed shop
An organization that hires only union members.

Taft-Hartley Act
An act, passed in 1947 by the U.S. Congress, that made the closed shop illegal and allowed states to pass right-to-work laws. These laws prohibit employers from making union membership a condition of employment.

union shop
An organization that requires employees to join the union within a certain period after being hired.

strike
A work stoppage called by union members to put pressure on an employer.

right-to-work law
A state law that prohibits the practice of requiring employees to join a union to work.

▼ Union shops are illegal in the 28 states with right-to-work laws.

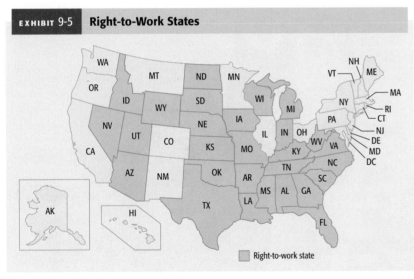

| EXHIBIT 9-5 | **Right-to-Work States** |

□ Right-to-work state

Discussion Starter
Strikes and work slowdowns have become common tools for organized labor. What other tools might labor unions employ to improve working conditions for their members?

Reinforcement Activity
The Taft-Hartley Act is discussed briefly on page 261. Ask students to research this act. Instruct them to either turn in their work or share their findings with the rest of the class. Remind students to include what happened in that period of U.S. history that caused the government to pass this act. Stress the importance of placing legislative acts in the correct historical perspective.

Visit econ.myemcp.com/videos for videos that will help students better understand the key concepts found in this section.

Background Information: Strikes

Strikes have generally been peaceful, but there have been exceptions Review the history of the strike at the McCormick Harvester Works in Chicago on May 3, 1886, when one worker was killed and several were injured. A public meeting was called at Chicago's Haymarket Square the next day to protest the killing of the worker. That rally ended in violence. When police marched into the square to break up the meeting, someone in the crowd threw a dynamite bomb. Seven people were killed by the bomb, and four more were killed in the ensuing exchange of gunfire between the police and armed men in the crowd. At least 60 people were injured.

Exhibit 9-5 shows the states with right-to-work laws. Also, today approximately 10.7 percent of all workers are members of unions.

Unions' Effects on Union and Nonunion Wages

On average, do union workers receive higher pay than comparable nonunion workers? (By saying *comparable nonunion workers*, we are comparing union and nonunion workers who do essentially the same work.) One important economics study concluded that over the period from 1920 to 1979, the average wage of union members was 10 to 15 percent higher than that of comparable nonunion labor. That is, for every $100 earned by nonunion labor, comparable union labor earned between $110 and $115. In 2016, the U.S. Bureau of Labor Statistics reported that mean weekly earnings for union workers were about 22 percent higher than for nonunion workers.

An economic reason supports these results. Suppose the labor force has 100 persons; 25 are members of a union, and 75 are not. We assume that each of the 100 persons can work in either the union or the nonunion part of the economy. Furthermore, we assume that each of the 100 persons currently earns a wage rate of $20.

Suppose now that the labor union (of which 25 persons are members) calls a strike and ends up bargaining its way to a wage rate of $25. At $25 per hour, the businesses that currently employ union labor workers do not wish to employ as many persons as they wished to employ at a wage rate of $20, so a few of the union workers get fired. Let's say that 5 workers get fired.

The 5 union workers who were fired seek jobs in the nonunion part of the economy. As a result, the supply of persons in the nonunion part rises (from 75 to 80). An increase in the supply of labor puts downward pressure on wage rates in the nonunion part of the economy. The wage rate moves down from $20 to $18. Can you see from this example how unions are likely to affect the wages of both union and nonunion workers?

Two Views of Labor Unions

There are two major views of how labor unions affect production and efficiency. The traditional view holds that labor unions are an obstacle to establishing reasonable work standards and thus make companies that employ union labor less competitive. For example, suppose some members of a plumbers' union work for a manufacturing company. The union may insist that in this

► Members of the Amalgamated Transit Union picket Veola Transportation Services in Phoenix, AZ. **How might this type of activity benefit the union workers?**

Will You Sleep Less If You Earn More?

Do you remember from Chapter 1 that the opportunity cost of something is the most valued opportunity or alternative you have to give up (or forfeit) to do it? For example, if you were not reading this chapter right now, you might be talking to a friend on the telephone; thus, "talking to a friend on the telephone" is the opportunity cost to you of reading this chapter.

Let's see if we can tie together opportunity cost, education, and wage rates with the number of hours a person sleeps. We know that as educational achievement rises, a person's wage rate rises. It's possible to view a person's wage rate as the opportunity cost of not working. In other words, a person who earns $20 an hour when she is working is forfeiting this amount when she chooses not to work. It follows, then, that

people who earn relatively high wages have higher opportunity costs of not working than do people who earn relatively low wages. For example, the person with the doctorate forfeits more than the person with only the high school diploma when that person doesn't work.

One of the things we do when we don't work is sleep. It follows that the opportunity cost of sleeping is higher for the person with more education and higher wages than for the person with less education and lower wages. An economist would predict that the higher the opportunity cost of sleeping, the less a person will sleep. If the economist is correct, we should see that individuals who are more educated and earn higher incomes sleep less than those who

are less educated and earn lower incomes.

More education → Higher wages → Higher opportunity cost of not working → Higher opportunity cost of sleeping → Sleep less

Two economists, J. Biddle and D. Hammermesh, did present evidence that, on average, sleep is related to education and wage rates. They found that more-educated people earn more and sleep less than less-educated, lower-earning people. A person sleeps 14 minutes less for each year of additional schooling. In short, more education may be good for your wallet, but it's not so good for your sleep.

THINK ABOUT IT Consider this evidence: Blackwell has a high school diploma, earns $20 an hour, and sleeps 8 hours a night. Nitobe has a doctorate, earns $100 an hour, and sleeps 8 hours and 30 minutes a night. Both Blackwell and Nitobe are the same age. If our evidence is correct, does it mean that the Biddle and Hammermesh evidence must be incorrect?

Ask students to estimate the number of hours of sleep they get each night during a school week. Ask if they get less sleep during the week because they are studying.

Students are likely to get less sleep during the school week than during the weekend because the opportunity cost sleeping is higher during the week (because of homework assignments that need to be completed, tests that need to be taken, etc.)

ANSWERS TO THINK ABOUT IT Biddle and Hammermesh present evidence that the higher one's hourly wage, the less one sleeps. The observation of Blackwell (who earns $20 an hour and sleeps 8 hours a night) and Nitobe (who earns $100 an hour and sleeps 8 hours and 30 minutes a night) is inconsistent with the evidence presented by Biddle and Hammermesh. In short, it is not so much that the Biddle and Hammermesh evidence is definitely wrong, but that it is contrary to the evidence of Blackwell and Nitobe.

Analyzing

We have presented two views of labor unions: the traditional view and the new view. Ask each student to write a one-page essay defending one of the two views and pointing out the weaknesses of the other view. Alternatively, ask students to find examples (in books, magazines, newspapers, or the Internet) of the two views. Invite students to report their findings to the class.

Discussion Starter

Instruct students to discuss their views on labor unions after reading this section. Some students may have family members who have been involved in unions. In any case, make sure students can support their opinions on whether labor unions have a positive or a negative effect on the U.S. economy.

---

company, only a plumber (and no one else) can change the washer on a leaky faucet. Union critics argue that such rigid staffing requirements are unreasonable and make these companies less competitive in a world economy. When a company loses its competitive edge, it may go out of business.

A newer view says that the labor union is a valuable collective voice for its members. Evidence in some industries

indicates that union firms have a higher rate of productivity than nonunion firms. Economists explain this difference by saying that the labor union acts as a collective voice for its members. Without a labor union, some argue, workers who are disgruntled with their jobs, who feel taken advantage of by their employers, or who feel unsafe in their work will leave their jobs and seek work elsewhere. This "job exiting"

---

million people supporting the grape boycott, the growers signed an agreement with the NFWA; the strike had lasted five years. Today Chavez is recognized for bringing to the attention of the U.S. public the poor working conditions of migrant workers and for initiating the process that led to improved working conditions.

Reinforcement Activity

This part of the text highlights an interesting period in U.S. history. Instruct students to research different organizations or laws discussed on these pages. For example, students might research the American Federation of Labor, the Wagner Act, and the Congress of Industrial Organizations. Point out to students that the history of labor unions is mixed. At times, labor unions seem to have been mistreated, but at other times, they have taken harsh actions against certain industries and businesses.

Analyzing

For the most part, only labor has been unionized, but there are notable exceptions. More than 1 million teachers belong to the American Federation of Teachers, a union. Some engineers belong to the International Association of Mechanics and Aerospace Workers, and some doctors and dentists belong to the Union of American Physicians and Dentists. Guide students in a discussion about why highly educated professionals might choose to join a union.

Teaching with Visuals

Discuss with students the impact that images such as this may have had on people's opinions of unions.

comes at a cost. It raises training costs for the firm and results in lengthy job searches, during which those persons searching for jobs are not producing goods. Such costs can be reduced, it is argued, when a labor union provides a collective voice for its members. Instead of individual employees discussing sensitive employment matters with their employers, the labor union does it for them. Overall, the labor union makes employees feel more confident, less intimidated, and more secure in their work. Such positive feelings usually mean happier, more productive employees.

A Brief History of the Labor Movement

National unionism began to emerge in the United States after the Civil War. Because labor unions greatly affect the U.S. economy, you should be aware of some of the key events in their development.

The Knights of Labor

In 1869, a union called the Knights of Labor was organized. Seventeen years later, in 1886, its membership totaled approximately

▶ Dozens of people were killed at the Haymarket Riot in Chicago in 1886. Many Americans came to associate unions with violence and radical ideas as a result of events such as this, although no wrongdoing by the union was ever proved.

800,000. The Knights of Labor welcomed anyone who worked for a living—farmers, skilled workers, and unskilled workers— with a few exceptions, such as liquor dealers. The group called for higher wages and an eight-hour working day.

On May 4, 1886, approximately 100,000 members of the Knights of Labor demonstrated in front of the McCormick Harvester Works in Haymarket Square in Chicago. Someone tossed a bomb into the crowd, causing a riot in which several people were killed. Public sentiment soon turned against the Knights of Labor, although no wrongdoing on its part was proved. The union began to lose membership, and in 1917 it collapsed.

The American Federation of Labor

The American Federation of Labor (AFL) was formed in 1886 under the leadership of Samuel Gompers, who ran the organization until his death in 1924. Gompers believed that the AFL should consist mainly of skilled workers. Membership was approximately 2 million in 1904, rising to 5 million in 1920 and then falling to 3 million in 1930. The union's activities were almost solely directed

Cross-Curricular Activity

Invite a government teacher from your school to join you in class for a discussion of labor unions. While you discuss the economic effects of labor unions have the government teacher address labor unions' impact on the political world, the free-speech issues that relate to strikes and picket lines, and labor unions as interest groups. Both you and the government teacher should encourage students to share their perceptions of unions and union membership.

to lobbying for better pay and improved working conditions for its members.

Early Court Decisions

In the early days of the labor union movement, the courts treated unions as illegal conspiracies. Union leaders were regularly prosecuted and sued for damages. For example, in an important case decided by the Supreme Court of Massachusetts in 1842, the court ruled that unions were not illegal but that certain union practices were. Later, the Sherman Antitrust Act, which was passed by Congress in 1890, began to be applied to labor unions, although many people said that Congress had intended it to be applied only to businesses. The Sherman Act declared that "every person who shall . . . combine or conspire with any other person or persons, to monopolize any part of the trade or commerce . . . shall be guilty of a misdemeanor."

During the early 1900s, *injunctions* were used against labor unions to prevent strikes and some other activities. (Injunctions are court orders that were originally designed to prevent damage to property when it was thought that other court processes would be too slow.) Because of the use of injunctions by employers during this period, labor unions found it difficult to strike.

The Norris-LaGuardia and Wagner Acts

The legal climate in which labor unions operated changed dramatically in 1932 with passage of the Norris-LaGuardia Act by the U.S. Congress. The main purpose of the act was to restrain the use of injunctions. It declared that workers should be "free from the interference, restraint, or coercion of employers" in choosing their union representatives.

In 1935, Congress passed the Wagner Act, which required employers to bargain in good faith with workers; the act also made it illegal for employers to interfere with their employees' rights to organize or join a union. In addition, the act set up the National Labor Relations Board (NLRB) to investigate unfair labor practices. Union

◀ John L. Lewis formed the Congress of Industrial Organizations (CIO). What difference of opinion led Lewis and others to split with the AFL and form the CIO?

membership grew by leaps and bounds as a result of the Norris-LaGuardia and the Wagner Acts.

The Congress of Industrial Organizations

Labor unions enjoyed a better legal climate after passage of the Norris-LaGuardia and Wagner Acts, and so they pushed to unionize major industries, such as steel and automobiles. This trend caused some discontent within the AFL. The union was largely made up of craft unions—unions of individuals who practice the same craft or trade (for example, carpenters). Some people within the AFL wanted to unionize people only into craft unions. Others wanted industrial unions—unions that include everyone in a particular industry, regardless of whether they all practice the same craft. For example, people doing many different jobs in the automobile industry would belong to the same union. In 1938, John L. Lewis of the United Mine Workers broke with the AFL and formed the Congress of Industrial Organizations (CIO). The CIO successfully unionized the steel, rubber, textile, meatpacking, and automobile industries along industrial union lines.

For a time, the AFL and the CIO increased their memberships. After World War II, however, membership in the CIO began to decline. Some thought the bickering between

> *"Far and away the best prize that life has to offer is the chance to work hard at work worth doing."*
> —Theodore Roosevelt, U.S. president (1901–1909)

Teaching with Visuals

Some AFL members wanted industrial unions, while others believed unions should remain associated with particular crafts and trades. John L. Lewis and others formed the CIO, which unionized along industrial lines. The AFL unionized people mainly into craft unions.

Discussion Starter

Ask students if they would rather live in a country without labor unions or in a country with labor unions and to state reasons for their positions. Students may state that unions can make working conditions more secure and democratic than they may otherwise be. Other students may point out that labor unions can cause inefficiencies and that they sometimes employ questionable tactics to achieve their goals.

Reinforcement Activity

Ask students the following questions: What is a union shop? What does it have to do with a right-to-work state?

Background Information: PATCO

Students may not realize that air traffic controllers used to be unionized. In 1981, 13,000 members of the Professional Air Traffic Controllers Organization (PATCO) walked off their jobs. President Reagan had little sympathy for labor unions and warned the striking workers to return to their jobs or face dismissal. The workers were dismissed and initially replaced by military personnel. The resulting change in personnel resulted in major delays in air travel, which caused the public to lose sympathy for the striking members of PATCO. Discuss with students the importance of having public support for strikes and striking workers, if a strike is to be successful.

Instruct students to research one of these two regulatory agencies: the Occupational Safety and Health Administration (OSHA) or the Consumer Products Safety Commission (CPSC). Students should research when each agency was formed, what duties it performs, and so on. Each student should pair up with someone who studied the other agency and share findings.

Discussion Starter

How much government regulation is enough? How much is too much? Direct students who believe that the government has too many regulations to stand on one side of the classroom. Then direct students who believe that the government has just enough or too few regulations to stand on the other side of the classroom. Allow students on both sides to take turns sharing their opinions about government regulations. If a student's argument persuades another student to change his or her opinion, the student with the changed opinion may change sides of the room. It will be interesting to note how many students change their opinions about government regulation and whether most students favor a lot of regulation or less regulation.

---

the two unions was the cause. In 1955, the AFL, a craft union, and the CIO, an industrial union, merged under the leadership of George Meany into the AFL-CIO.

The Taft-Hartley Act

The congressional sentiment that made the Wagner Act possible in 1935 began to shift after World War II. A few particularly damaging strikes in 1946 set the stage for the Taft-Hartley Act in 1947. This act allowed states to pass right-to-work laws.

The Landrum-Griffin Act

Congress passed the Landrum-Griffin Act in 1959 with the intent of policing the internal affairs of labor unions. The act called for regular union elections and secret ballots, and it required union leaders to report on their unions' finances. It also prohibited former convicts and communists from holding union office. The Landrum-Griffin Act was passed because the U.S. public became concerned during the late 1950s that some labor union leaders had misappropriated funds and were involved in corruption.

The Growth in Public Employee Unions

A public employee union is a union whose members work for the local, state, or federal government. By far the most important development in the labor movement in the 1960s and 1970s was the sharp growth in public employee union membership. The main issue associated with public employee unions is the right to strike. These unions feel they should be able to exercise this right, but their opponents argue that public sector strikes—by police officers or firefighters, for example—could have a crippling effect on society.

Government Regulation

In the United States, government often regulates business and labor practices. In Chapter 8, we discussed how the government might regulate a natural monopoly firm. In Chapter 3, we discussed how the government often regulates business when it comes to issues such as air quality.

The government also regulates labor markets, with regard to issues such as hiring practices and safety regulations. For example, the Occupational Safety and Health Administration (OSHA) is concerned with protecting workers from injuries and illnesses on the job. The Consumer Product Safety Commission (CPSC) specifies minimum standards for potentially unsafe products. Unsafe toys get a lot of attention, because these products are marketed to children. The Environmental Protection Agency (EPA) regulates the amount of pollution that business firms can emit into the air or rivers.

Not everyone agrees on the value of government regulation. Critics argue that most regulation is too costly to taxpayers, and proponents counter that even though the costs are high, the benefits are higher. They say, for example, that highway fatalities would be 40 percent higher without the automobile safety features that have been mandated by regulation. Similarly, mandated childproof lids have resulted in 90 percent fewer child deaths caused by accidental swallowing of poisonous substances. Proponents of regulation also say that restrictions on the use of asbestos save between 630 and 2,553 persons from dying of cancer each year.

EXAMPLE In 1987, Beech-Nut Nutrition Corporation, a baby food manufacturer, pleaded guilty to 215 felony counts. (A felony is a major crime.) The company had sold millions of containers of sugar water and flavoring that it had labeled "100 percent apple juice." ♦

EXAMPLE Cordis Corporation produced and sold thousands of pacemakers that it knew were defective. Many of the pacemakers failed, and the company ended up pleading guilty to 25 criminal violations. ♦

Government regulation—whether it has to do with prices and profits, consumer information, or working standards—continues to be a major topic of debate. The next section explains why.

Cooperative Learning

Organize a union day in your classroom to show students how unions work. Divide the class into three groups, and have each group select a name for its union, along with two or three leaders. Instruct each union to draw up a mission statement and list its particular goals for improving conditions in the school or classroom. Each union should set a membership fee and present it along with arguments for joining the organization. Then have the unions compete for members. Students can change unions, joining the union that appeals to them most. Discuss with each student which union he or she joined and why. Ask how the benefits promised by that union compared with the fee charged for membership.

How Much Does an Occupation Pay?

Many people know what they want to do in life before they even graduate from high school. Others require time and effort to identify the career they want to pursue. Having information is important when making such a major decision. Thankfully, occupational information is available.

The Bureau of Labor Statistics, an agency of the U.S. Department of Labor, publishes information about jobs in the annual Occupational Outlook Handbook (OOH). You can find this publication online at http://econ.emcp.net/ooh. This site profiles hundreds of occupations, providing details about wages, education and training needed, work environment, and so on.

The OOH site also identifies trends in the job market. For example, you can find out what jobs are expected to be in demand in the future and what they pay. For 2014–2024, three of the top five fastest-growing occupations are all expected to be in health care: occupational therapy assistants, physical therapy assistants, and physical therapy aides.

The highest-paying occupations are identified on the OOH site as well. In 2015, the top five occupations were all surgeon and physician occupations.

Another trend you might want to check out is which fields are expected to add the greatest number of new jobs. During the period 2014–2024, more new jobs (458,100) will be created for personal care aides than for any other occupation.

One of the most useful things about the OOH is that it identifies the educational and training requirements for each job. To become a biomedical engineer, for example, you need a bachelor's degree in biomedical engineering.

To get a complete picture of what information is available on the OOH site, let's look into a specific job. Let's say you want to become an accountant.

What do accountants do? Accountants (a) examine financial statements to ensure they are accurate and comply with laws and regulations; (b) compute taxes owed, prepare tax returns, and ensure that taxes are paid properly and on time; (c) inspect account "books" and accounting systems for efficiency and use of accepted accounting procedures; (d) organize and maintain financial records; (e) assess financial operations and make best-practices recommendations to management; and (f) suggest ways to reduce costs, enhance revenues, and improve profits

How much are accountants paid? The median annual wage for accountants is $67,190 (2015 data).

Where do accountants work? Accountants work in finance, insurance, accounting, manufacturing, and service firms and in local, state, and federal government.

What kind of education does an accountant need? To become an accountant, a person needs a bachelor's degree in accounting or some business-related field. Some employers prefer to hire individuals with a master's degree in accounting or in business administration with a concentration in accounting.

What is the outlook for accounting jobs? Employment of accountants is expected to grow 11 percent from 2014 to 2024 (which is faster than average of all occupations). Accountants who earn professional recognition, especially as Certified Public Accountants (CPAs), have the best job prospects.

THINK ABOUT IT Have you decided what you want to do after you leave high school? Will you get a job right away or go to college? Will you get a job after college? To help plan your future career, spend some time on the OOH website and identify what you will need to pursue your career and income goals.

Ask students what their plans are after high school. Also ask students to state what salaries they would like to earn in the future. Then have students name two cities in which they would like to live. Ask, In which city would your salary buy more?

ANSWERS TO THINK ABOUT IT For the first part of the question, answers will vary. For the second part, students should see that salaries are higher in some cities than in others.

Discussion Starter

Ask students to think of people they know who live in an apartment or a house rented from someone else. Ask if students are aware of how much notice these people have to give if they want or need to move out. Assign students to research how much apartments and houses cost to rent around your school or city. Ask, How would the level of rent be affected by a change in regulations that reduced the length of notice a renter is required to give?

Reinforcement Activity

Public utility commissions are government groups that regulate public utility companies. Tell students that it has been argued that if a public utility commission sets a certain limit on the profit rate a public utility can earn, the public utility will have little incentive to hold down its costs. Ask students whether they agree or disagree, and have them explain their answers.

Discussion Starter

Rules and regulations are not foreign topics to students. Ask, What rules and regulations can you think of? (*Sample answers:* dress codes, curfews, and rules of the road.) What kinds of activities are these rules and regulations intended to regulate?

Cooperative Learning

Divide students into small groups, and assign each group a different union to research. Each group should find the union's mission statement, history, number of members, dues or fees, and the requirements and process for joining. Each group should also find out if the union has ever gone on strike or used a work stoppage to try to get better conditions for its members. Have each group prepare visuals to explain and support their research, and invite them to present their findings to the class.

Answers will vary. Students should see that there are costs and benefits of government regulation that affect goods and services.

Background Information

Costs and benefits of government regulation have a global impact. The owners of firms will pick up and leave a country if that country's regulations become too stiff. There is an old saying that "People vote with their feet." What this means is that if people don't like something in one place and believe things are better in some other place, they will simply move to that place. If regulations become too stiff in Canada, Canadian firms will move to other countries (such as the United States). If regulations become too stiff in the United States, some U.S. firms will no doubt move to other countries.

Teaching with Visuals

Answers will vary. Students should be able to identify environmental regulations—for example, requirements that businesses purchase antipollution devices and that car manufacturers improve their products' fuel economy.

 Application Activity

After reading and discussing Section 2, you may want to assign the Section Activity in the *Applying the Principles Workbook,* pages 101–103.

Assess

Quick Quiz

The following true-or-false quiz will help you assess student understanding of the material covered in this section.

1. A union can raise the demand for a product through advertising. (True)
2. Labor unions try to increase the labor supply. (False)
3. On average, union workers receive higher pay than comparable nonunion workers. (True)
4. The Knights of Labor represented factory owners during labor disputes. (False)

▶ An Audi employee checks a finished Audi A3 at a factory in Ingolstadt, Germany. Have government regulations in the United States impacted the sales of imported cars?

The Costs and Benefits of Government Regulation

Suppose a business firm is polluting the air with smoke from its factories. The government passes an environmental regulation that requires this business to install antipollution devices that reduce the smoke emitted into the air. What are the benefits of this kind of regulation?

First is cleaner air, which may reduce the medical problems people face in the future. For example, in some U.S. cities, the pollution from cars and factories causes people to cough, feel tired, and experience eye discomfort. Some people have continuing medical problems from constantly breathing dirty air. Government regulation that ends up reducing the amount of pollution in the air surely helps these people, reducing lost work time and health care costs.

Regulation may also benefit the environment and thus the people who enjoy nature and being outdoors. For example, some air pollution harms birds and destroys certain types of plants and trees. Having cleaner air may ensure there are plenty of birds and trees to enjoy.

Although regulation creates benefits, it comes with costs too. For example, a business firm that is required to install antipollution devices will experience a rise in its overall costs of production. As a result, the firm may produce fewer units of its product, which raises its product price and results in some workers losing their jobs.

If you are a worker who loses your job, you may view the government's regulation of firms that cause air pollution differently from someone who has weak lungs. If you have weak lungs, less pollution may be the difference between your feeling well or sick. If you work at a factory, less pollution may end up costing you your job. Ideally, you

▼ What has the government done to solve problems such as poor air quality?

Internet Research

Direct students to the websites of federal regulatory agencies, such as the Environmental Protection Agency (EPA) and the Food and Drug Administration (FDA). Each student should choose an agency and learn about the kinds of regulations it creates. Then the student should choose three regulations and write an oral report outlining the costs and benefits of each. Allow students to share their findings with the class.

may prefer to have less pollution in your neighborhood, but not at the cost of losing your job.

Where do economists stand on these issues? Are they for or against government regulation of air pollution and similar problems? They are neither for nor against such regulation. The job of the economist is to point out both the benefits and the costs of regulation. To the person who sees only the costs, the economist asks, "But what about the benefits?" And to the person who sees only the benefits, the economist asks, "But what about the costs?" The economist then goes on to outline the benefits and costs as accurately as possible.

Unintended Effects of Regulation

In addition to outlining the benefits and costs of regulation, the economist tries to point out the sometimes unintended consequences of regulation. For instance, the government often regulates manufacturers of automobiles by imposing fuel economy standards on cars—perhaps requiring new cars to get an average of 40 miles per gallon instead of, say, 30 miles

per gallon. Many people believe that this regulation is good. They reason that if car companies are required to produce cars that get better mileage, people will not need to buy and burn as much gasoline. And if less gasoline is burned, less pollution will be produced.

There's no guarantee that things will work out this way, though. If car companies produce cars that are more fuel efficient, people will have to buy less gasoline to take them from one place to another. The cost per mile of traveling will fall, so people might travel more. Leisure driving on Saturday and Sunday might become more common, people might begin to drive farther on vacations, and so on. If people travel more, the gasoline saving that resulted from the higher fuel economy standards might be offset or even outweighed. More gasoline consumption due to more travel will mean more gas being burned and more pollutants ending up in the air. In other words, a regulation requiring car companies to produce cars that get better fuel mileage might have an unintended effect.

"Everything comes to him who hustles while he waits."
—Thomas Edison, inventor

SECTION 2 ASSESSMENT

Defining Terms

1. Define:
  a. labor union
  b. closed shop
  c. Taft-Hartley Act
  d. union shop
  e. strike
  f. right-to-work law
2. What is the difference between a union shop and a closed shop?

Reviewing Facts and Concepts

3. Labor union A wants to increase the demand for its member workers. Identify two things the union can do to try to achieve this outcome.

4. Are union shops illegal in right-to-work states?
5. What did the Norris-LaGuardia Act accomplish?
6. How does the economist view government regulation?

Critical Thinking

7. In the early days of unions, was it right for the courts to issue injunctions to prevent strikes and other union activities? Why or why not?
8. "If the government imposes higher fuel economy standards, the amount of pollution

produced by automobiles will undoubtedly become less." Do you agree or disagree? Explain.

Applying Economic Concepts

9. The members of labor union X produce cars in the United States for sale only in the United States. The U.S. Congress is contemplating imposing a quota, restricting the number of foreign-produced cars that can be sold in the country. Will members of labor union X likely support this action? Explain.

SECTION 2 ASSESSMENT ANSWERS

Defining Terms

1. a. labor union: an organization that seeks to increase the wages and improve the working conditions of its members;
b. closed shop: an organization that hires only union members;
c. Taft-Hartley Act: an act that made closed shops illegal and allowed states to pass right-to-work laws;
d. union shop: an organization that requires employees to join the union within a certain period of time after being hired;
e. strike: a work stoppage called by union

members to put pressure on an employer;
f. right-to-work law: a state law prohibiting the practice of requiring employees to join a union to work.
2. A closed shop hires only union members. A union shop doesn't require membership to be hired, but employees must

join within a certain period after being hired.

Reviewing Facts and Concepts

3. The labor union can gain greater control over the supply of labor, and it can increase demand for the product it produces.
4. Yes, union shops are illegal in these states.
5. The Norris-LaGuardia Act restrained the use of injunctions, giving workers the freedom to choose their union representatives.
6. The economist isn't for or against government regulation but points out the costs and benefits of regulation.

Critical Thinking

7. Answers will vary.
8. Answers will vary. Students should see that imposing higher fuel economy standards may produce unintended effects.

Applying Economic Concepts

9. Members of labor union X will likely support the quota on foreign-produced cars, because when supply decreases for foreign cars, demand for union X cars should increase.

5. The Wagner Act required employers to bargain in good faith with workers. (True)

Assessment Book

You will find a quiz for this section in the *Assessment Book,* page 88.

Reteaching Activity

Use the Section Assessment to gauge which students may need reteaching on this section. Ask those students to explain the difference between a closed shop and a union shop. Go over the answers with students. After you are sure that students understand the distinction, remind them that closed shops were outlawed by the Taft-Hartley Act.

Guided Reading

For further reteaching of the key concepts in this section, assign the Outlining Activity and the Just the Facts Handout from the *Guided Reading and Study Guide,* pages 140–143.

Assessment Answers

Economics Vocabulary

1. minimum wage law; **2.** closed shop; **3.** strike; **4.** wage rate; **5.** union shop; **6.** Taft-Hartley Act.

Understanding the Main Ideas

1. If there is a surplus of labor, the wage rate will fall. If there is a shortage of labor, the wage rate will rise.

2. Disagree. The supply of John's labor services could be lower than the supply of Wilson's services.

3. Agree. The demand curve for labor is downward sloping. Fewer people will be hired at higher wages than at lower wages.

4. Most studies conclude that unions raise the wages for union labor and decrease the wages for comparable non-union labor. Unions reduce the supply of workers in the union sector and indirectly increase the supply of workers in the nonunion sector.

5. Demand can be changed by the productivity of labor and the change in the demand for the good or service that labor produces.

6. Yes. If price decreases, then the real wage can increase even if the nominal wage decreases. For example: If a person's nominal wage rate is $10 an hour and the price of the only good the person buys, X, is $1, then the person's real wage is 10 units of X. If the person's nominal wage rate falls to $8 an hour and the price of X falls to $0.50, then the person's real wage increases to 16 units of X.

7. The traditional view identifies labor unions as an obstacle to establishing reasonable work standards; it generally sees labor unions in negative terms. The new view sees labor unions in a positive light. Unions serve as a collective-voice mechanism for their members, representing workers in negotiations with management. This representation makes workers feel more comfortable

Chapter Summary

Be sure you know and remember the following key points from the chapter sections.

Section 1

▶ People who demand labor are employers.
▶ People who supply labor are employees.
▶ The price of labor is called the wage rate.
▶ The equilibrium wage rate occurs at the point at which the quantity of labor supplied equals the quantity of labor demanded.
▶ Wage rates differ because the supply and the demand for different types of labor are not the same.
▶ A job has both money and nonmoney benefits.
▶ Labor is a derived demand—the result of the demand for a good.
▶ The minimum wage rate is a government-set wage floor.
▶ Nominal wages are the actual dollars received for doing a job.
▶ Real wages are the value of the dollars in terms of what they buy.
▶ The Consumer Price Index (CPI) is the average price, or index, of a group of goods.

Section 2

▶ A labor union seeks to increase the wages and improve the working conditions of its members.
▶ A closed shop is an organization that hires only union members; the Taft-Hartley Act made closed shops illegal.
▶ A union shop requires joining the union within a certain period after taking a job.
▶ Right-to-work laws, in place in many states, make it illegal to require union membership to get a specific job.
▶ Unions emerged in the United States after the Civil War and have had both successes and setbacks in labor's history.

Economics Vocabulary

To reinforce your knowledge of the key terms in this chapter, fill in each of the following blanks on a separate piece of paper with the appropriate word or phrase.

1. The _____ sets a level below which wage rates are not allowed to fall.

2. A(n) _____ is an organization that hires only union members.

3. A _____ is a tactic used by unions to put pressure on employers by having workers refuse to work.

4. The price of labor is called the _____.

5. A(n) _____ is an organization that requires employees to join the union within a certain period of time after being hired.

6. The _____, which was passed in 1947, allowed states to pass right-to-work laws.

Understanding the Main Ideas

Review the main ideas in this chapter by writing answers to the following questions on a separate sheet of paper.

1. In a competitive labor market, what happens to the wage rate when a surplus of labor occurs? When a shortage of labor occurs?

2. "John earns a higher wage rate than Wilson. It necessarily follows that the demand for John's labor services is greater than the demand for Wilson's labor services." Do you agree or disagree? Explain your answer.

3. "If the minimum wage rate is higher than the equilibrium wage rate, fewer people will be hired because the cost of labor is too high." Do you agree or disagree? Explain your answer.

4. What are unions' effects on union wages? On nonunion wages? Explain your answers.

5. Identify two factors that can change the demand for labor.

6. Can a person's nominal wage decrease at the same time his or her real wage increases? Explain.

7. Outline the traditional view and the new view of labor unions.

8. Outline the details of the Wagner Act.

9. What is a public employee union?

in their jobs, more productive, and less likely to quit their jobs.

8. The Wagner Act required employers to bargain in good faith with workers and made it illegal for employers to interfere with their employees' rights to organize or join a union. The act also it set up the National Labor Relations Board to investigate unfair labor practices.

9. It is a union whose members work for the local, state, or federal government.

10. Wages will remain the same.

11. Disagree. Economists are neither for nor against regulation of business and labor. Their job is to point out the costs and benefits of regulation.

10. If the demand for labor increases by the same amount as the supply of labor increases, will wages rise, fall, or remain the same?

11. "Economists are against regulation of business and labor." Do you agree or disagree? Explain.

Doing the Math

1. Alicia turned down a job that pays $60,000 a year for a job that pays $32,000 a year. The nonmoney benefits in the lower-paying job equal at least what dollar amount?

2. In year 1, Bob earns $1,000 a month when the CPI is 130. In year 2, Bob earns $1,500 a month when the CPI is 135. In which year is Bob's real income higher? What percentage higher?

Working with Graphs and Tables

Graphically represent the following.

1. The equilibrium wage rate is currently $10 an hour. The demand for labor increases by more than the supply of labor increases. The new equilibrium wage rate is $12. (Be sure to label the axes.)

2. The demand for labor falls by more than the supply of labor rises.

3. The demand for labor rises by the same amount as the supply of labor rises.

4. In Exhibit 9-6, the original demand and supply curves are labeled D_1 and S_1 and the new demand and supply curves are labeled D_2 and S_2. In parts (a) through (d), identify what will happen to the equilibrium wage as a result of the change in demand, supply, or both.

Solving Economic Problems

1. **Apply.** Suppose you are an economist hired by a labor union that is currently negotiating wages with management. Current union members are paid $18 an hour. The labor union executives want to make sure that over the next year, members' wages do not fall in real terms. The CPI in the current year is 179, and the CPI expected next year is 190. What nominal wage is needed to maintain the real wage of union members?

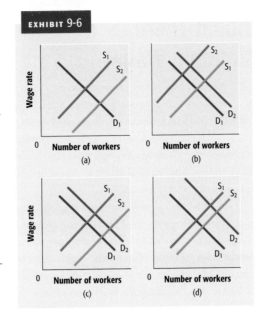

EXHIBIT 9-6

(a) (b) (c) (d)

2. **Analyze.** Three jobs all pay the same salary: $70,000 a year. What additional information do you need to decide which of the three jobs is the best job for you?

3. **Apply.** Suppose you are offered two similar jobs that pay the same. One is in San Francisco, California, and the other is in Des Moines, Iowa. What should you consider in deciding which job to take?

Project or Presentation

Compare Occupations. Go to http://econ.emcp.net/jobs, choose a job you might like, and outline details such as salary and educational requirements. Share your findings in a small group. Write an essay comparing and contrasting the jobs discussed.

ONLINE
emcp.com

Practice Tests and Study Guide

Go to www.emcschool.net/Economics2e and choose *Economics: New Ways of Thinking*, Chapter 9, if you need more help in preparing for the chapter test.

Working with Graphs and Tables

1.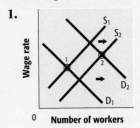

2.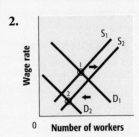

3.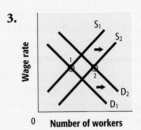

4. (a) The wage rate will fall; (b) The wage rate will rise; (c) The wage rate will fall; (d) The wage rate will rise.

Solving Economic Problems

1. The current real wage is $18 ÷ 179, or 0.10. If the CPI (the divisor) next year will be 190, then the nominal wage must be $19 to keep the real wage (0.10) constant.

2. You need to know the dollar value of the nonmoney benefits in each job. The best job for you is the one with the highest overall benefits, as measured by you.

3. One thing you should consider is the costs of living in the different cities. House prices are often different in different cities, so one thing to find out is the price of houses in each city. Other things you should consider include which city offers more opportunity for job advancement, which offers more entertainment value, and which has a more appealing climate.

Project or Presentation

Answers will vary.

Doing the Math

1. $28,000 (*calculation*: $60,000 − $32,000 = $28,000).

2. Real income per month in year 1 is $1,000 ÷ 130, or 7.69. Real income per month in year 2 is $1,500 ÷ 135, or 11.11. Thus, real income per month in year 2 is 44.47% higher.

Discussion Starters

1. Ask how many students have worked for the minimum wage. Allow volunteers to share their personal experiences working at jobs that paid the minimum wage.

2. Ask students how productivity relates to the minimum wage. Ask them to consider the following scenario: Student A is motivated to attract the attention of his or her employer by being a "self-starter" and demonstrating high productivity. Student B does the minimum to meet the job description, knowing that he or she will collect the minimum wage. If you were an employer, which student would you want to work for you? Which student's work ethic would encourage you to pay him or her more than the minimum wage?

3. Ask students the following questions: Does an employee's value to an employer depend on the minimum wage? What other things make an employee valuable to an employer? Does an employee's worth increase just because the minimum wage increases? How could an employee become worth more to an employer, justifying an increase in pay?

4. What are some trade-offs of having a minimum wage in effect?

Should There Be a Minimum Wage?

Like many high school students, you may have a job and work after school. If so, there's a good chance that you earn the minimum wage, which is set by the U.S. Congress. It's against the law for employers to pay workers less than the minimum wage. If the minimum wage is $7.25 an hour, then it's unlawful for an employer to pay an employee less than this amount.

Do you think having a minimum wage is good for workers and good for the economy too? Some people argue in favor of it; others argue against it. Some people argue that the minimum wage should be raised; others argue that it should not be. Let's listen in on a conversation between Mike and Mrs. Peters. Mrs. Peters owns a small bakery in town. Mike, 17 years old, works at the hardware store three doors down from the bakery. Mike currently earns the minimum wage.

Mrs. Peters: How are you doing today, Mike? What can I get for you?

Mike: I'll have a chocolate éclair and a milk. And, by the way, I'm doing pretty well today. On my way to work, I heard that Congress is thinking of raising the minimum wage. That will mean more money for me.

Mrs. Peters: I think the minimum wage is something that sounds better than it is.

Mike: What do you mean? What could possibly be wrong with the minimum wage?

Mrs. Peters: Well, for one thing, it goes against the whole idea of free enterprise. Under free enterprise, employers and employees should be able to make their own deals. They shouldn't have the government telling them how much to pay.

Mike: But if there weren't a minimum wage, employers would pay their employees next to nothing. Instead of earning $7.25 an hour, I might earn $3 an hour.

Mrs. Peters: Okay, let's say that you are earning $7.25 an hour. Along comes the government and tells your employer that he has to pay you $11.50 an hour. Jim may decide to fire you. It may be worth it for Jim to pay you $7.25 an hour but not $11.50 an hour. Has the minimum wage helped you? I don't think so. I think it has priced you out of a job.

Mike: But it's possible that I'll keep my job as the wage goes from $7.25 to $11.50. Fact is, I may be worth $11.50 an hour, but Jim is paying me only $7.25 an hour so he can earn higher profits. The minimum wage forces Jim to pay me what I'm worth.

Mrs. Peters: If you were really worth $11.50 an hour, you would be earning $11.50 an hour right now. The boss who thinks you are worth $11.50 an hour would simply offer you that amount to come work for him instead of working for Jim. That's how he would compete you away from Jim.

But let's go with what you say. Let's suppose that Congress tells your employer he has to pay you $11.50 an hour. And let's suppose you keep your job. That doesn't mean some people won't lose their jobs. Everyone knows that employers hire more people at lower wages than at higher wages. As wages go up, employers are going to hire fewer people. In other words, some of the people working at the lower wages will be fired.

Differentiating Instruction

Enrichment and Extension

1. Instruct each student to prepare and conduct a survey of adults that asks whether there should be a minimum wage. After collecting data, have each student create a visual that displays the results of the survey. You might create a class bulletin board for these visuals.

2. Assign each student to write a rap song or poem that expresses his or her opinion of the minimum wage. Allow class time for volunteers to present their songs and poems. After the presentations, let the class vote on the best song or poem, and allow its writer to teach it to the class.

Mike: I don't think anyone has to lose his job as the wage goes up. Employers will simply end up with lower profits.

Mrs. Peters: That might work if you're talking about Microsoft or General Motors, but what about Joe's Pizza or the corner deli? Some companies are just squeaking by, so any mandated cost increase will hurt them. They will try to cut their costs by firing some people.

Also think about this: not all businesses face the same set of circumstances. Circumstances may differ from one region of the country to another. The economy may be booming in the Southwest and businesses can easily pay higher wages. But the economy may be sluggish in the Midwest and businesses can't pay higher wages. Setting a minimum wage that every business has to pay, no matter what its circumstances, doesn't take this into account.

Mike: I don't know. I hear what you're saying, but I still think that without the minimum wage, too many employers would squeeze their employees.

Mrs. Peters: Mike, there are whole industries in this country in which the minimum wage isn't relevant. No one who works for an accounting firm is paid the minimum wage; no one who works as a computer scientist is paid the minimum wage; no one who works as an attorney is paid the minimum wage. All these people earn much more than the minimum wage. Do they earn more because the government has ordered companies to pay them more than the minimum wage? Not at all. The government hasn't said a thing. The companies simply pay these people more because they can't hire them without paying more. It's a matter of supply and demand, Mike. Companies have to pay the wages that are determined in the market by the forces of supply and demand.

Mike: Oh, come on. You know there is a big difference between what an attorney earns and what I earn. The minimum wage law isn't there to protect attorneys, accountants, and computer scientists. It's there to protect the little guy—the guy without much skill or experience.

Mrs. Peters: But that's just the point! The minimum wage doesn't protect this person. It often just prices him out of a job. You can't make an employer pay more for a person than that person is worth to him. If a person is worth only $7 an hour to an employer and the government says you have to pay this person $12 an hour, you know what's going to happen? That person is going to go without a job.

What Do You Think?

1. Who do you think makes the stronger argument, Mike or Mrs. Peters? Defend your answer.
2. What are Mike's strong points? Weak points? What are Mrs. Peters's strong and weak points?
3. Should the minimum wage be raised, left where it currently is, or eliminated altogether? Explain your answer.

Activities for What Do You Think?

1. Label three different areas in the room with the following signs: "Minimum Wage Should Be Raised," "Minimum Wage Should Be Left Alone," and "Minimum Wage Should Be Eliminated." Then have students move to the labels with which they most agree. Allow students five minutes to list the reasons that they chose their labels. Let each group present its reasons to the class, and then vote again to see if opinions change.
2. Divide students into groups of three or four, and ask them to create skits to act out. Skits should show real-life examples of the minimum wage either working or failing. Allow time for groups to present their skits to the class.

Closure

Assign students to write short essays describing their current opinions on the minimum wage. They should describe any previous opinions, along with what factors changed their minds. Allow students to share these essays with partners.

Preview

Macroeconomics

Listed below are the chapters included in this unit.

Foundations for the Unit

In Unit IV, we shift our focus from microeconomics to macroeconomics. We put away the "microscopes" we used to examine the discrete components of economics and take out "telescopes" to see the aggregate picture of economics. Throughout this unit, encourage students to watch nightly newscasts and to read the front pages of daily newspapers. Many macroeconomic topics are highlighted in headlines and discussed in news stories.

274

Resources for the Unit

Books

Beard, Charles A. *An Economic Interpretation of the Constitution of the United States.* New York: Free Press, 1986.

DuBoff, Richard B. *Accumulation and Power: An Economic History of the United States.* Armonk, NY: M. E. Sharpe, 1989.

Galbraith, John Kenneth. *The Affluent Society.* New York: Houghton Mifflin, 1998.

Morris, Charles R. *Money, Greed and Risk: Why Financial Crises and Crashes Happen.* New York: Times Books, 1999.

> **"** *The ideas of economists . . . are more powerful than is commonly understood. Indeed the world is ruled by little else.* **"**
>
> —John Maynard Keynes, economist

275

Introducing the Unit

You might introduce Unit IV by calling for students to demonstrate by a show of hands whether they have already taken a government course. Point out that students who have already taken this type of course will probably be familiar with many of the concepts discussed in this unit. Explain that macroeconomics deals with the state of a nation's economic health. That economic health is usually a topic of great concern for both people who are serving in public office and people who hope to be elected to public office.

Performance Project

Assign students to work in small groups to create their own portraits of the nation's economic health. For each chapter in this unit, students should collect and analyze pertinent national economic statistics. For Chapter 10, students might collect figures relating to the current money supply. Each group should present these figures graphically; write a summary of what is presented in the graphs, including calculations showing the percentage changes and so on; and write an analysis stating what the figures mean in terms of the United States' economic health. Other topics might include the current discount rate, the current gross domestic product and consumer price index, the current inflation rate and unemployment rate, and the current national debt.

Articles

Gergen, David. "No Time for Complacency," *U.S. News and World Report,* March 29, 1999.

Grant, James. "Future Shock at the Fed," *New York Times,* October 26, 2005.

Greenman, Catherine. "Filing Your Taxes Online: It's Faster, More Accurate and Welcomed by I.R.S.," *New York Times,* January 27, 2000.

Healey, Matthew. "This Pile of Scrap Once Cast a Fortune in Notes," *New York Times,* December 19, 2005.

Multimedia

Economics U$A: The Banking System. VHS. The Annenberg/CPB Projects.

Chapter 10 Planning Guide

SECTION ORGANIZER

	Learning Objectives	Reproducible Worksheets and Handouts	Assessment

SECTION 1
The Origins of Money
(pages 278–284)

Learning Objectives
- Describe what a barter economy is.
- Explain how money emerged from a barter economy.
- Describe what money is.
- Explain what gives money its value.
- Identify the functions of money.

Reproducible Worksheets and Handouts
- Section 1 Activity, *Applying the Principles Workbook*, pages 104–108
- Outlining Activity, *Guided Reading and Study Guide*, pages 150–152
- Just the Facts Handout, *Guided Reading and Study Guide*, pages 153–154

Assessment
- Section Assessment, *Student Text*, page 284
- Quick Quiz, *Annotated Teacher's Edition*, page 283
- Section Quiz, *Assessment Book*, page 95

SECTION 2
The Money Supply
(pages 285–289)

Learning Objectives
- Explain what the money supply consists of.
- Explain what a Federal Reserve note is.
- Describe what *money* is and what it is not.
- Explain what causes interest rates to change.

Reproducible Worksheets and Handouts
- Section 2 Activity, *Applying the Principles Workbook*, pages 109–111
- Outlining Activity, *Guided Reading and Study Guide*, pages 155–156
- Just the Facts Handout, *Guided Reading and Study Guide*, pages 157–158

Assessment
- Section Assessment, *Student Text*, page 289
- Quick Quiz, *Annotated Teacher's Edition*, page 288
- Section Quiz, *Assessment Book*, page 96

SECTION 3
The Federal Reserve System
(pages 294–297)

Learning Objectives
- Explain what the Federal Reserve System is.
- State how many persons sit on the Board of Governors of the Federal Reserve System.
- Describe the major responsibilities of the Federal Reserve System.
- Explain how the check-clearing process works.

Reproducible Worksheets and Handouts
- Section 3 Activity, *Applying the Principles Workbook*, pages 112–114
- Outlining Activity, *Guided Reading and Study Guide*, page 159
- Just the Facts Handout, *Guided Reading and Study Guide*, pages 160–161

Assessment
- Section Assessment, *Student Text*, page 297
- Quick Quiz, *Annotated Teacher's Edition*, page 296
- Section Quiz, *Assessment Book*, page 97

SECTION 4
The Money Creation Process
(pages 298–303)

Learning Objectives
- Explain what total reserves equal.
- Explain what required and excess reserves are.
- Describe how banks use checking accounts to increase the money supply.
- Describe what banks do with excess reserves.
- Calculate the maximum change in the money supply that results from bank loans.

Reproducible Worksheets and Handouts
- Section 4 Activity, *Applying the Principles Workbook*, pages 115–117
- Outlining Activity, *Guided Reading and Study Guide*, pages 162–163
- Just the Facts Handout, *Guided Reading and Study Guide*, pages 164–165

Assessment
- Section Assessment, *Student Text*, page 303
- Quick Quiz, *Annotated Teacher's Edition*, page 302
- Section Quiz, *Assessment Book*, page 98

SECTION 5
Fed Tools for Changing the Money Supply
(pages 304–311)

Learning Objectives
- Explain how a change in the reserve requirement changes the money supply.
- Explain how an open market operation changes the money supply.
- Explain how a change in the discount rate changes the money supply.

Reproducible Worksheets and Handouts
- Section 5 Activity, *Applying the Principles Workbook*, pages 118–119
- Outlining Activity, *Guided Reading and Study Guide*, pages 166–167
- Just the Facts Handout, *Guided Reading and Study Guide*, pages 168–169

Assessment
- Section Assessment, *Student Text*, page 311
- Quick Quiz, *Annotated Teacher's Edition*, page 310
- Section Quiz, *Assessment Book*, page 99

Reproducible Chapter Resources and Assessment Materials

 Graphic Organizer Activity, *Guided Reading and Study Guide,* pages 170–173

 Vocabulary Activity, *Guided Reading and Study Guide,* pages 174–175

Working with Graphs and Charts, *Guided Reading and Study Guide,* page 176

 Practice Test, *Guided Reading and Study Guide,* pages 177–179

Critical Thinking Activity, *Finding Economics,* pages 26–28

Chapter Test A, *Assessment Book,* pages 100–102

Chapter Test B, *Assessment Book,* pages 103–106

Student Text Internet Links

Economics: New Ways of Thinking, Second Edition encourages students to use the Internet to find out more about economics. Given the wealth of current, valid information available on websites, students should be encouraged to use the Internet as a research tool. Doing so will likely increase students' interest in and understanding of economics principles and topics. In addition, doing Internet research can help your students form the habit of accessing and using economics information, as well as help them develop investigative skills they will use throughout their educational and professional careers.

To aid your students in achieving these ends, each chapter of *Economics: New Ways of Thinking, Second Edition* includes the addresses of several websites that provide engaging and relevant information. When students type in any of the addresses provided, they will immediately arrive at the intended site. The addresses have been modified so that EMC Publishing can monitor and maintain the proper links—for example, the website http://www.deposit accounts.com/ has been changed to http://econ.emcp.net/accounts. In the event that the address or content of a site changes or is discontinued, EMC's Internet editors will redirect the link to a site with equivalent information.

Activities in the *Annotated Teacher's Edition* often suggest that students search the Internet for information. For some activities, you might want to find reputable sites beforehand and steer students toward them. For other activities, have students do their own searching and then check out the sites they have found and discuss why they might be reliable or unreliable.

Passport® for Economics

Technology resources are available with the *Economics: New Ways of Thinking, Second Edition* program through Passport®. These include:

eBooks for *Economics: New Ways of Thinking, Second Edition*

► Student textbook eBook
► Interactive Applying the Principles eWorkbook
► Finding Economics eBook
► Guided Reading and Study Guide eBook
► Annotated Teacher's Edition eBook
► Lesson Plans eBook
► Assessment eBook

Passport® for Students

Students can access helpful resources through Passport® for Economics. Resources include:
► Study guides
► Practice tests
► Flash cards in English and in Spanish
► Word games in English and in Spanish
► Tutorials and key-concept videos
► Spanish print and audio summaries

Passport® for Teachers

Keep your course current and relevant by using the teacher resources provided through Passport® for Economics. In addition to all of the resources on the student side of Passport®, the teacher side contains:
► Link to the Annotated Teacher's Edition eBook
► Standards correlations
► Microsoft® PowerPoint® Lectures
► Current Events Lessons
► Additional Economics in the Real World features
► ExamView® Assessment Suite
► PDFs of all print supplements (student and teacher)

This chapter defines *money*, including the history of money and the purposes that it serves today. This chapter also explains banking, the Federal Reserve System, and how the changing money supply affects our lives. The following statements provide brief descriptions of the major concepts covered in each section of this chapter.

SECTION 1 The Origins of Money

Section 1 teaches students about the origins of a money economy and explains the various functions of money.

SECTION 2 The Money Supply

Section 2 explores the components of the money supply and the difference between M1 and M2. Students learn to determine whether savings accounts, credit cards, and debit cards are money.

SECTION 3 The Federal Reserve System

Section 3 discusses the major responsibilities of the Federal Reserve System and explains the system's role in the U.S. economy.

SECTION 4 The Money Creation Process

Section 4 explores the ways modern banks work. Students learn the differences among total reserves, required reserves, and excess reserves.

SECTION 5 Fed Tools for Changing the Money Supply

Section 5 combines what was taught in Sections 3 and 4. Students learn about the Fed's tools for changing the monetary supply and enacting monetary policy.

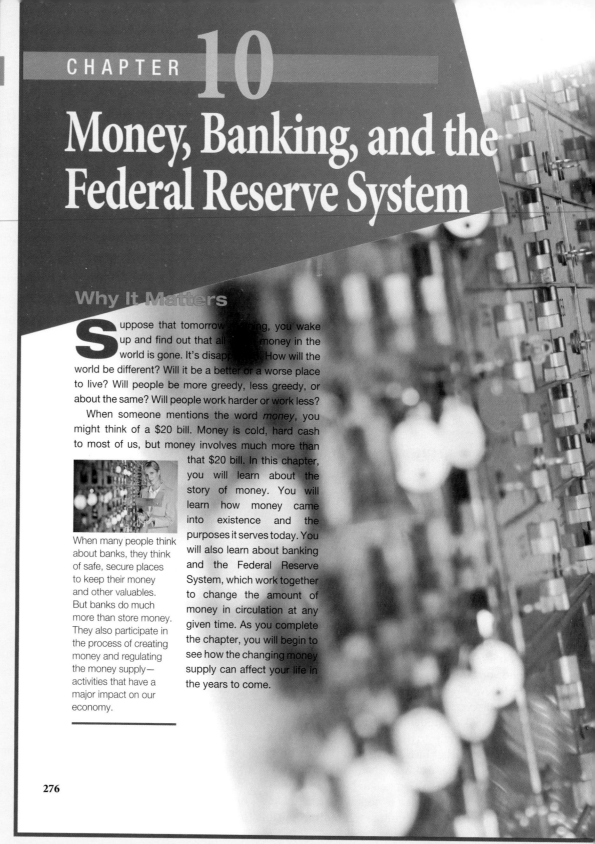

Money, Banking, and the Federal Reserve System

Why It Matters

Suppose that tomorrow morning, you wake up and find out that all the money in the world is gone. It's disappeared! How will the world be different? Will it be a better or a worse place to live? Will people be more greedy, less greedy, or about the same? Will people work harder or work less?

When someone mentions the word *money*, you might think of a $20 bill. Money is cold, hard cash to most of us, but money involves much more than that $20 bill. In this chapter, you will learn about the story of money. You will learn how money came into existence and the purposes it serves today. You will also learn about banking and the Federal Reserve System, which work together to change the amount of money in circulation at any given time. As you complete the chapter, you will begin to see how the changing money supply can affect your life in the years to come.

When many people think about banks, they think of safe, secure places to keep their money and other valuables. But banks do much more than store money. They also participate in the process of creating money and regulating the money supply— activities that have a major impact on our economy.

276

Teaching Suggestions from the Author

Most students are naturally interested in a chapter that is concerned with money. I usually tell students that in this chapter, we are going to put money under a microscope and examine it. We are going to try to explain why money came into existence, what gives money value, and so on.

One of the first things I do to get students' attention and to show them that there's more to money than they know is to take out a dollar bill and ask, "What is this called?" They will often say, ""It's called a dollar bill." Then I point out the actual words at the top of the bill: Federal Re-

Economics Around the Clock

The following events occurred one day in February.

8:15 A.M. The members of the Federal Open Market Committee (FOMC), in Washington, D.C., will start their meeting at 9 a.m. The FOMC has a lot to say about whether the money supply of the United States increases, decreases, or remains constant. Many people would like to hear what goes on at these meetings. If you knew what was discussed, you might be able to profit from it. So right now, the room in which the meeting will take place is being swept for electronic bugs.

• **What specifically does the FOMC do that is so important?**

9:00 A.M. Mrs. Harris teaches English literature at Monroe High School and is talking about the book *The Strange Case of Dr. Jekyll and Mr. Hyde*. She reads from the book: "It was on the moral side, and in my own person, that I learned to recognize the thorough and primitive duality of man: I saw that, of the two natures that contended in the field of my consciousness, even if I could rightly be said to be either, it was only because I was radically both."

• **What does Robert Louis Stevenson's *The Strange Case of Dr. Jekyll and Mr. Hyde* have to do with the material in an economics text?**

5:29 P.M. At NBC Studios in New York City, Jimmy Fallon, host of *The Tonight Show Starring Jimmy Fallon*, is getting ready to go on. He tapes his show every weekday at this time. As the announcer of the show warms up his voice, Jimmy goes over his first two jokes in his head.

• **What does Jimmy Fallon have to do with material in an economics text?**

277

Introducing the Chapter

Draw a large dollar symbol on the board, and underneath the symbol write the word "money." Next to the symbol, write this question: "How many of you expected money to be the basic subject of this course?" Many students will respond in the affirmative. Point out that money was not even mentioned in the definition of economics given in Chapter 1. (That definition states that *economics* is the science that studies the choices that people make when trying to satisfy their wants in a world of scarcity.)

Explain to students that just as the definition of economics may have turned out to be different from what they expected, so might the study of money in this chapter hold some surprises.

Teaching with Visuals

Students are probably familiar with many of the services offered by banks. The rental of safety deposit boxes is only one such service. Ask students to suggest other services offered by banks.

serve Note. Sometimes, I describe all the national symbols on the dollar bill. Most students have never considered these words and symbols. This activity shows students that they do not know as much about money as there is to know. I often find that they become much more interested in the material in this chapter after doing this simple activity. You might also display a credit card and lead students in a discussion of whether it is money and what value it actually has.

Teacher Support

Focus and Motivate

Section Objectives

After completing this section, students will be able to

- describe what a barter economy is;
- explain how money emerged from a barter economy;
- describe what money is;
- explain what gives money its value; and
- identify the functions of money.

Kickoff Activity

Before class, write the following instruction on the board: "Describe what you think life would be like in a world where money did not exist." (Essentially, you are asking students to describe what life would be like in a barter economy.) When class begins, tell students to write out their answers.

Activating Prior Knowledge

Ask for student volunteers to share their responses to the Kickoff Activity. Explain that in a barter economy or in a world with no money, it would take longer to make daily transactions than it does today in our money economy.

Visit econ.myemcp.com/videos for videos that will help students better understand the key concepts found in this section.

The Origins of Money

Focus Questions

- What is a barter economy?
- How did money emerge out of a barter economy?
- What is money?
- What gives money its value?
- What are the functions of money?

Key Terms

barter economy
transaction costs
money
medium of exchange
unit of account
store of value
fractional reserve banking

What's It Like Living in a Barter Economy?

A **barter economy** is an economy with no money. The only way you can get what you want in a barter economy is to trade something you have for it. Suppose you have apples and want oranges. You might trade two apples for three oranges.

Life in a barter economy can be difficult. It can take a lot of time and effort to get what you want. Suppose you produce utensils, such as forks, spoons, and knives. No one can live on utensils alone, so you set out to trade your utensils for bread, meat, and other necessities. You come across a person who bakes bread and ask if he is willing to trade some bread for some utensils. He says, "Thank you very much, but no. I have all the utensils I need." You ask him what he would like instead of utensils. He says he would like to have some fruit and that if you had fruit, he would be happy to trade bread for fruit.

What makes living in a barter economy difficult is that many of the people you want to trade with don't want to trade with you.

barter economy
An economy in which trades are made in goods and services instead of money.

transaction costs
The costs associated with the time and effort needed to search out, negotiate, and complete an exchange.

In this type of economy, trade is time consuming. It could take all day, if not longer, to find a person who wants to trade bread for utensils. Economists state the problem this way: the *transaction costs* of making exchanges are high in a barter economy. Think of the **transaction costs** as the time and effort you have to spend before you can make an exchange. If the transaction costs could somehow be lower, trading would be easier.

A Student Asks

QUESTION: *I've heard of both a commodity money and fiat money. Are these the same thing?*

ANSWER: *No. Let's start with an example. Gold is an example of a commodity money; paper dollar bills are an example of a fiat money. A commodity money is a money whose value initially came from the commodity of which it was made. In short, a commodity money has an*

Cooperative Learning

Ask each student to bring to class something he or she no longer needs, uses, or wants. You might want to put a value limit (say, $10) on each item students bring. (Used discs might be good tools for this exercise.) Once you have discussed the text information on bartering, tell students you are going to allow 15 minutes for them to barter with classmates to secure items they want that someone else has brought to sell. When the time has ended, ask students to share their experience. Have each student tell how many trades it took to actually get the item he or she wanted.

intrinsic value (gold has value even if it is not used as money – for example, it can be used to make jewelry) and a value as money too. Historically, all the first monies were commodity monies. A fiat money is a money that has been deemed by government edict or order to be money. In Latin, fiat means "let it be (done)." Fiat money has no intrinsic value of its own (as a commodity money does).

How and Why Did Money Come to Exist?

How can an individual living in a barter economy reduce the transaction costs of making exchanges? In a barter economy with, say, 100 goods, some goods are more readily accepted in exchange than others. For example, good A might be accepted (on average) every tenth time it is offered in exchange, while good B might be accepted every seventh time. If you are going out today to trade in a barter economy, which good, A or B, would you prefer to have in your possession? The answer is B, because it is more likely to be accepted in a trade than A. In other words, to reduce the transaction costs of making exchanges, it is better to offer B than A.

Before you can offer B, though, you have to have it. So suppose someone offers to trade good B for your utensils. You don't really want to consume good B (in the same way that you want to consume bread), but you realize that good B will be useful in making exchanges. You accept the trade because later, you will use good B to lower the transaction costs of getting what you want.

Once some people begin accepting a good because it reduces the transaction costs of exchange, others will follow. After you accepted good B, it had greater acceptability than it used to have. Because you accepted it (even though it wasn't the good you really wanted), perhaps it will be accepted every sixth time now instead of every seventh time. This greater acceptability makes good B more useful to other people than it was previously. Then, when the next person

▲ These Native Americans are trading furs with explorer Henry Hudson. What are some disadvantages of living in a barter economy?

accepts good B, it is even more likely that someone else will accept good B.

Can you see what is happening? Your accepting good B made it more likely that the next person would accept it. That person's accepting good B made it more likely that someone else would accept it. Eventually, everyone will accept good B in exchange. When this happens—when good B is widely accepted in exchange—good B is called money. **Money** is any good that is widely accepted in exchange and in the repayment of debt. Historically, goods that evolved into money have included gold, silver, copper, rocks, cattle, and shells, to name only a few.

EXAMPLE You are on an island with 10 other people and without money. You start to make trades with the others on the island: some shells for some mango; two small, bluish fish for one large, reddish fish; some rocks for some seaweed. One day, you learn that of all of the things on the island, coconuts are more widely accepted in exchange than anything else. In fact, if you have a coconut to trade, 6 out of every 10 people will trade with you, but for other items (shells, fish, rocks), 4 or fewer out of every 10 people will trade with you. You realize that having coconuts will make it a whole lot easier to trade: "I had better always accept a coconut (in a trade) when someone offers one to me, because then, I can use the coconut to get what I want from others."

money
A good that is widely accepted in exchange and in the repayment of debt.

Teaching with Visuals

Some disadvantages of living in a barter economy are that bartering takes a lot of time and effort and transaction costs are high.

Discussion Starter

Ask students to define the term *barter economy*. You might want to read aloud the section "What's It Like Living in a Barter Economy?" (pages 278–279). Explain that a barter economy is a system in which people trade goods for goods, goods for services, and services for services. Ask students to identify some of the problems of living in a barter economy. Try to help them understand that making everyday exchanges in a barter economy would be very time consuming.

Cause and Effect

Although some people believe that the government created money, money actually emerged out of the need for a simpler, more expedient method of exchange. Bartering was slow and at times tedious. The need for a more effective method of exchange caused paper and coin money to evolve. Instruct students to research the history of money to discover when the shift from bartering to a simpler method of exchange occurred and what other changes this shift caused.

Reinforcement Activity

A barter economy does not have to be countrywide. Whenever students trade a good or service for a good or service from another person, that is bartering. Ask students to think about the last time they bartered with someone. Have them describe the situation and decide whether the exchange was equal in value—that is, a fair exchange—for both parties.

Cross-Curricular Activity

Invite a world or U.S. history teacher to your class to discuss bartering as it took place in another time period. For instance, you could ask the visiting teacher to discuss bartering or commodity money used by the early colonists. Students may be interested in information such as what was considered a valuable commodity to be used for trade and what items were scarce and in high demand during that period. You may want to assign a project in which individual students or groups of students research that historical period and expand on the information they gained from the lecture.

A few items that people have used for money are silver, copper, rocks, cattle, and shells.

Critical Thinking

Pose this scenario to students: Suppose you woke up tomorrow morning and no money existed. How would your life be different? What good or goods do you think would evolve as money? Students might suggest that their discs and other such items would take on greater value in a barter economy.

Critical Thinking

Ask students what gives money its value. Some may say that gold backing gives money its value. However, the U.S. dollar is no longer backed by gold. What gives money its value is the fact that other people will accept it for purposes of exchange. Point out that an intangible—something that exists even if we cannot see it or touch it—gives money its value.

Economic Facts and Fallacies

FALSE / TRUE

Money Is Money...Except When It Isn't

ANSWERS TO THINK ABOUT IT No, a prepaid gift card is not money. A gift card is not widely accepted for purposes of exchange (imagine trying to give a bus driver a prepaid gift card to an electronics store in exchange for a ride to the mall), and it is not widely accepted for the repayment of debt (you could not, for example, pay your phone bill with a prepaid gift card to your favorite restaurant).

▲ This woodcut shows men panning for gold in California in the 1850s. **What materials, other than gold, have people used for money?**

So you start accepting coconuts in trade, even though you don't like coconuts, and because you do, the acceptability of coconuts is now even greater than before. Then someone else sees that the acceptability of coconuts is on the rise, and so she begins accepting coconuts in all trades. This continues until almost everyone realizes that it's in his or her best interests to accept coconuts. Coconuts are now money. ◆

Economic Facts and Fallacies

FALSE / TRUE

Money Is Money...Except When It Isn't

Some people believe that only cash—paper bills and coins—is money, but that's not true. Money is any good that is widely accepted in exchange and in the repayment of debt.

Is a $10 bill money? Yes, because it's widely accepted in exchange and in the repayment of debt. What about a personal check? Is it money? Yes, because it's widely accepted in exchange (people write checks to buy goods and services every day) and in the repayment of debt (people write checks to pay what they owe on their credit cards, for example). So both cash and personal checks are money.

We can make one quibble with the economic fact that a personal check is money. If a mugger stops you on the street and shouts, "Give me your money!" he is definitely demanding cash. A mugger isn't asking you to write him a check—even though, as we have said, a personal check is money.

THINK ABOUT IT Is a prepaid gift card money? Explain.

What Gives Money Value?

Forget coconuts. Let's turn to a $10 bill. Is a $10 bill money? The $10 bill is widely accepted for purposes of exchange, of course, so therefore, it is money.

What gives money (say, a $10 bill) its value? Like good B and the coconuts in the earlier examples of a barter economy, our money today has value because of its general acceptability. Money has value because you know that you can use it to get what you want. However, you can use it this way only because other people will accept it in exchange for what they have.

EXAMPLE Suppose that Ryan is walking to a local shopping center. On the way, he stops by the convenience store to buy a doughnut and milk. He tries to pay for the food with two $1 bills. The owner of the store says that he no longer accepts dollar bills in exchange for what he has to sell. This story repeats itself all day with different store owners. No one is willing to accept dollar bills for what he or she has to sell. Suddenly, dollar bills have little or no value to Ryan. If he cannot use them to get what he wants, they are simply paper and ink, with no value at all. ◆

EXAMPLE During the Civil War, Confederate notes had value because this newly created form of money was accepted by people in the South for purposes of exchange. Today in the South, Confederate money has little value (except to collectors), because it is not widely accepted in exchange. For example, you cannot pay for gasoline at a service station in Alabama with Confederate notes. ◆

Are You Better Off Living in a Money Economy?

The transaction costs of exchange are lower in a money economy than in a barter economy. In a barter economy, not everyone you want to trade with wants to trade with you. In a money economy, however, everyone you want to buy something from wants what you have: money. In short, having a willing trading partner lowers the transaction costs of making an exchange.

Internet Research

Direct students to search for websites that allow users to trade goods and services in a virtual barter economy and to find answers to questions like these: What types of goods and services are being traded? Does making this type of site available seem like a good idea? What are the advantages and disadvantages of trading versus using money to buy something over the Internet? Have students discuss their responses or write them down. Then challenge pairs of students to design their own barter websites, identifying particular products and services for inclusion and explaining their choices.

Would You Hear Rock Music in a Barter Economy?

Suppose that one of today's rock artists lived in a barter economy. Would he still be a rock artist?

Before we answer this question, let's look at what an average day is like for a rock artist living in a money economy. He writes songs, rehearses, plans for a tour, works on a video, and so on. Much of his day is wrapped up in the highly specialized work of being a rock artist.

Would he be engaged in the same activities if he lived in a barter economy? Probably not. A typical day might go like this: he wakes up, eats breakfast, and then sees if he can trade a little of his rock music for some goods. He meets a woman with bread and asks if she is willing to trade some bread for a little music. The woman tells the rock artist that she isn't interested in making a trade. She says she doesn't care much for rock music.

Onward the rock artist goes, trying to find someone who will trade goods for rock music. He might run into a few people who are willing to trade with him, but we can be sure that by the end of the day, he will have found it fairly hard to make simple exchanges: a song for some steak, a song for some fruit, a song for a shirt.

What's likely to happen to the rock artist? He will quickly recognize how difficult it is to make trades and decide to make a lot of what he needs to survive by himself. He might start making his own bread and his own clothes instead of trying to trade rock music for these goods. In short, in a barter economy, because trade is so difficult and time consuming, people will likely try to produce for themselves the things they need. In the end, the rock artist will be so busy making bread, clothes, and so on that he really won't have much time to work on his music. As a result, rock will likely go by the wayside. Soon, the rock artist will no longer be only a musician but another person producing many of the things he needs.

What's the lesson here? Few people would specialize in a barter economy to the degree they do in a money economy. After all, what is the probability that everyone whose goods you want will want the one thing that you produce?

▲ Would Beyoncé still be a successful artist in a barter economy?

In a money economy, in contrast, everyone is willing to trade what he or she has for money. The risk in specializing is less than in a barter economy, so people produce one thing (rock songs, attorney services, corn, and so on), sell it for money, and then use the money to make their preferred purchases.

THINK ABOUT IT Is specialization more likely in a large city (such as New York City) or a small city (some city with a population under 7,000 persons, for example)? Explain your answer. Also, does being able to buy goods online make it more likely or less likely that you will specialize? Explain your answer.

Lower transaction costs translate into less time needed to trade in a money economy than in a barter economy. Using money, then, frees up some time for you. With that extra time, you can produce more of whatever it is you produce (accounting services, furniture, computers, or novels), consume more leisure, or both. In a money economy, then, people produce more goods and services and consume more leisure than they would in a barter economy. The residents of money economies are therefore richer in goods, services, and leisure than the residents of barter economies.

Background Information: Barter Economies

The Internet is causing a resurgence of bartering. Corporations are now using several websites that allow trading of products as diverse as office furniture and hotel rooms and charge a small trading fee. Some 250,000 U.S. companies already barter independently or through barter exchanges. Until 1982, business-to-business bartering was an underground economy that encouraged tax evasion. In 1982, President Reagan signed the Tax Equity and Fiscal Responsibility Act, which opened the door to corporate bartering. Some experts suggest that it might be possible for big corporations to stop using cash altogether!

Background Information

Over the years, many different items have been used as mediums of exchange and as stores of value. This was especially true in the preindustrial world. For example, obsidian (a type of volcanic glass) was used for making stone tools. It occurs in only a few areas, so people had to trade for it. Sometimes, a piece of obsidian was traded hundreds of miles away from its source before it reached its final destination. Instruct students to form groups of three or four and research other forms of money that were used in earlier periods. Ask the groups to present their findings in class.

After students have read this feature, ask them what other goods and services that we enjoy today might not be available in a barter economy.

ANSWERS TO THINK ABOUT IT Answers will vary. Students might say that specialization is more likely in a large city, where the variety of people may be interested in a variety of goods and services. The ease of buying and selling goods online also encourages specialization by making those goods available to a wider population with broader interests.

Economics Around the Clock

Refer students to the 9:00 a.m. and 5:29 p.m. scenarios in Economics Around the Clock (page 277), and discuss their answers to the accompanying questions.

Lead students to understand that Robert Louis Stevenson would probably never have written *The Strange Case of Dr. Jekyll and Mr. Hyde* had he not lived in a money economy. Likewise, Jimmy Fallon would not likely be a comedian if he did not live in a money economy. If Stevenson and Fallon had lived in a barter economy, they would have been too busy making trades and trying to be self-sufficient to specialize in writing a book and creating comedy. Specialization often is the result of living in a money economy.

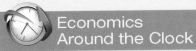

Teaching with Visuals

This transaction would be much more difficult without money, because each party would have to have something the other wanted.

Discussion Starter

The text details the three functions of money. To help students gain a better understanding of this concept (which is that money is more than just a means by which they can purchase a new disc), ask them to think of a time that they exercised each of the three functions in the past two weeks. (*Possible answer:* medium of exchange: purchased a disc; unit of account: priced a certain pair of jeans or game system; store of value: chose to save for a particular purchase in the future.) Invite students to share their experiences with the class.

Reinforcement Activity

Every day, students use money in each of the three ways discussed in the text. They pay for their lunches, compare prices, and maybe put money in a savings account. Tell each student to create a chart with three columns: "Medium of Exchange," "Unit of Account," and "Store of Value." Then assign students to keep track of the ways they use money for three days by logging this information in their charts. At the end of the three days, discuss students' results.

▲ Money lowers the transaction costs of making exchanges. How much more difficult would this transaction be without money?

medium of exchange
Anything that is generally acceptable in exchange for goods and services.

unit of account
A common measurement used to express value.

store of value
Something with the ability to hold value over time.

The residents of money economies are more specialized too. If you lived in a barter economy, you would find it both difficult and time consuming to make everyday transactions. You probably would produce many things yourself rather than deal with the hardship of producing only one good and then trying to exchange it for so many other goods. In other words, the higher the transaction costs of trading, the less likely you will want to trade and the more likely you will produce the goods that you would otherwise have obtained via trading.

In a money economy, however, it is neither difficult nor time consuming to make everyday transactions. The transaction costs of exchange are low compared with what they are in a barter economy. You have the luxury of specializing in the production of one thing (fixing faucets, writing computer programs, teaching students), selling that one thing for money, and then using the money to buy whatever goods and services you want to buy.

In today's world, bartering is still practiced in very few places. In those places, you will find that the people have a low standard of material living and that they are not nearly as specialized as they are in money economies.

What Are the Three Functions of Money?

Money has three major functions: serving as a medium of exchange, a unit of account, and a store of value.

Money as a Medium of Exchange

A **medium of exchange** is anything that is generally acceptable in exchange for goods and services. As we have seen, then, the most basic function of money is as a medium of exchange. Money is part of (present in) almost every exchange that's made.

Money as a Unit of Account

A **unit of account** is a common measurement used to express value. Money functions as a unit of account, which means that all goods can be expressed in terms of money. For example, we express the value of a house in terms of dollars (say, $280,000), the value of a car in terms of dollars (say, $30,000), and the value of a computer in terms of dollars (say, $1,000).

Money as a Store of Value

A good is a **store of value** if it maintains its value over time. Money serves as a store of value. For example, you can sell your labor services today, collect money in payment, and wait for a future date to spend the money on goods and services. You don't have to rush to buy goods and services with the money today; it will store value to be used at a future date.

To say that money is a store of value doesn't mean that it's necessarily a constant store of value. Let's say that the only good in the world is apples, and the price of an apple is $1. Julio earns $100 on January 1, 2018. If he spends the $100 on January 1, 2018, he can buy 100 apples. Suppose he decides to hold the money for one year, until January 1, 2019. Suppose also that the price of apples doubles during this time to $2. On January 1, 2019, Julio can buy only 50 apples. What happened? The money lost some of its value between 2018 and 2019. If prices rise, the value of money declines.

When economists say that money serves as a store of value, they don't mean to imply that money is a *constant* store of value or that it always serves as a store of value equally well. Money is better at storing value at some times than at other times. (Money is bad at storing value when prices are rising rapidly.)

For a summarized comparison of the three major functions of money, see Exhibit 10-1.

Visual and English Language Learners

Students are learning about the three major functions of money. Ask them to create posters using pictures to exhibit all the functions of money. Each picture should be labeled by function along with a short description of it. This activity will be particularly useful for visual learners and those who have difficulty comprehending English.

QUESTION: *Can money lose its value very quickly over a short period of time?*

ANSWER: *Money will lose its value fairly quickly (and therefore not be a good store of value) whenever prices rise quickly over a short period of time. A classic example is Germany in 1923, when prices rose so dramatically and money lost its value so quickly that workers were paid (with money) three times a day. They might be paid in the morning, use the money right away to buy goods, be paid again in the afternoon, use that money right away to buy goods, and so on. If workers waited too long to use the money they were paid, they wouldn't be able to buy much because prices would have risen so high. So they ended up spending their money almost as quickly as they received it.*

Who Were the Early Bankers?

Our money today is easy to carry and transport, but it wasn't always that way. For example, at one point, our money was principally gold coins, and carrying it was neither easy nor safe. Gold is heavy, and the equipment needed to transport thousands of gold coins could easily draw the attention of thieves. Thus, individuals wanted to store their gold in a safe place. The person that most individuals turned to was the goldsmith—someone already equipped with safe storage facilities. Goldsmiths were the first bankers. They took in other people's gold and stored it for them.

To acknowledge that they held deposited gold, goldsmiths issued *warehouse receipts* to their customers. For example, Adam might have a receipt stating that he deposited 400 gold pieces with the goldsmith Turner. Before long, people began to circulate the warehouse receipts in place of the gold. (Gold was not only inconvenient for customers to carry, but it was also inconvenient for merchants to accept.) For instance, if Adam wanted to buy something for 400 gold pieces, he might give a warehouse receipt to the seller instead of going to the goldsmith, obtaining the gold, and then delivering it to the seller. Using the receipts was easier than dealing with the gold itself for both parties. In short, the warehouse receipts circulated as money—that is, they became widely acceptable for purposes of exchange.

Goldsmiths began to notice that on an average day, few people redeemed receipts for gold. Most people simply traded the receipts for goods. At this stage, warehouse receipts were fully backed by gold. The receipts simply represented the actual gold in storage.

"When the people find they can vote themselves money, that will herald the end of the republic."
—Benjamin Franklin, colonial statesman and inventor

EXHIBIT 10-1	**Major Functions of Money**	
Function	**Definition**	**Example**
Medium of exchange	Anything that is generally acceptable in exchange for goods and services	John uses money to buy haircuts, books, food, DVDs, and computers. Money is the medium of exchange.
Unit of account	Common measurement used to express value	The price of a candy bar is $1, and the price of a book is $14. The exchange values of both goods are measured by dollars (unit of account). Notice that exchange values can be compared easily when money is used. In this example, the book has 14 times the exchange value of the candy bar.
Store of value	Something able to hold its value over time	Phil has a job and gets paid $400. He could use $200 to buy a ski jacket that he wants, but he decides not to. Instead, he saves the $400 and buys the ski jacket six months later. For Phil, money has acted as a store of value over the six-month period.

◀ This table summarizes the three major functions of money.

Teaching with Visuals

Encourage students to re-create Exhibit 10-1 using their own words and examples. Then display their examples on a bulletin board in the classroom.

Teaching with Visuals

The answer to the question accompanying the illustration on page 284 is that goldsmiths were among the first bankers because they kept gold for others, in the process passing out receipts that began to circulate. Eventually, goldsmiths began to lend out gold to earn interest.

 Application Activity

After reading and discussing Section 1, you may want to assign the Section Activity in the *Applying the Principles Workbook*, pages 104–108.

Assess

Quick Quiz

The following true-or-false quiz will help you assess student understanding of the material covered in this section.

1. Bartering is difficult because not everyone wants to trade for what you have to offer. (True)
2. The money economy appeared because of individual self-interest. (True)
3. Money has value because you can use it to get the things you want. (True)
4. The most basic function of money is as a medium of exchange. (True)
5. Banks create money by holding on reserve all the money deposited with them and lending none of it. (False)

Internet Research

Instruct students to locate the websites for banks in their community and to find out about the different types of accounts that are offered. Encourage students to create brochures for other teenagers that explain their banking options. The brochures should help students understand the ways that having a bank account can help them save and earn money.

▲ A goldsmith's shop in the sixteenth century. Why were goldsmiths essentially the first bankers?

fractional reserve banking
A banking arrangement in which banks hold only a fraction of their deposits and lend out the remainder.

Some goldsmiths, however, began to think, "Suppose I lend out some of the gold that people have deposited with me. If I lend it to others, I can charge interest for the loan. And since receipts are circulating in place of the gold, I will probably never be faced with redeeming everyone's receipts for gold at once." Some goldsmiths did lend out some of the gold deposited with them and collected interest on the loans. The consequence of this lending activity was an increase in the supply of money, measured in terms of gold and paper receipts. Remember, both gold and paper warehouse receipts were widely accepted for purposes of exchange.

A numerical example can show how the goldsmiths' activities increased the supply of money. Suppose the world's entire money supply is made up of 100 gold coins. Also suppose the owners of the gold deposit their coins with the goldsmith. To keep things simple, let's say the goldsmith gives out

1 paper receipt for each gold coin deposited. In other words, if Flores deposits 3 coins with a goldsmith, she receives 3 warehouse receipts, each representing a coin.

The warehouse receipts begin to circulate instead of the gold itself, so the money supply consists of 100 paper receipts, whereas before it consisted of 100 gold coins. Still, the number is 100. So far, so good.

Now the goldsmith decides to lend out some of the gold and earn interest on the loans. Suppose Robert wants to take out a loan for 15 gold coins. The goldsmith grants the loan. Instead of handing over 15 gold coins, though, the goldsmith gives Robert 15 paper receipts.

What happens to the money supply? Before the goldsmith went into the lending business, the money supply consisted of 100 paper receipts. Now, though, the money supply has increased to 115 paper receipts. The increase in the money supply (as measured by the number of paper receipts) is a result of the lending activity of the goldsmith.

The process described here was the beginning of **fractional reserve banking**. We live under a fractional reserve banking system today. Under a fractional reserve banking system, such as the one that currently operates in the United States, banks (like the goldsmiths of years past) create money by holding on reserve only a fraction of the money deposited with them and lending the remainder.

SECTION 1 ASSESSMENT

Defining Terms
1. Define:
   a. barter economy
   b. transaction costs
   c. money
   d. medium of exchange
   e. unit of account
   f. store of value
   g. fractional reserve banking

Reviewing Facts and Concepts
2. What gives money its value?
3. Money serves as a unit of account. Give an example to illustrate what this means.
4. What does it mean to say that the United States has a fractional reserve banking system?

Critical Thinking
5. Is specialization more or less likely to occur in a money economy than in a barter economy? Explain your answer.
6. Would your everyday life be harder in a barter economy or in a money economy? Explain your answer.

The Money Supply

Focus Questions
▶ What does the money supply consist of?
▶ What is a Federal Reserve note?
▶ What is and what is not money?
▶ What causes interest rates to change?

Key Terms
money supply
currency
Federal Reserve note
demand deposit
savings account
loanable funds market

What Are the Components of the Money Supply?

The most basic **money supply**—sometimes referred to as M1 ("M-one")—consists of three components, which we will soon identify. Other money supplies besides M1 include a broader measure of the money supply called M2 ("M-two"). For purposes of simplicity, when we discuss the money supply in this text, we are referring to M1.

The M1 in the United States is composed of these three components:

1. *Currency*. **Currency** includes both coins (such as quarters and dimes) minted by the U.S. Treasury and paper money. The paper money in circulation consists of **Federal Reserve notes**. If you look at a dollar bill, you will see at the top the words "Federal Reserve Note." The Federal Reserve System, which is the central bank of the United States (discussed in a later section), issues Federal Reserve notes.

2. *Checking accounts*. Checking accounts are accounts in which funds are deposited and can be withdrawn simply by writing checks. Sometimes checking accounts are referred to as **demand deposits**, because the funds can be converted to currency on demand and given to the person to whom the check is made payable. For example, suppose Malcolm has a checking account at a local bank with a balance of $400. He can withdraw up to $400 currency from his account, or he can transfer any dollar amount up to $400 to someone else simply by writing a check to him or her.

3. *Traveler's checks*. A traveler's check is a check issued by a bank in any of several denominations ($10, $20, $50, and so on) and sold to a traveler (or to anyone who wishes to buy it), who signs it at the time it is issued by the bank and then again in the presence of the person cashing it.

In February 2017, $1,433 billion in U.S. currency was in circulation, along with $1,936 billion in checking accounts and $2 billion in traveler's checks. Altogether, the money supply equaled $3,371 billion. (See Exhibit 10-2.)

money supply
The total supply of money in circulation, composed of currency, checking accounts, and traveler's checks.

currency
Coins issued by the U.S. Treasury and paper money (called *Federal Reserve notes*) issued by the Federal Reserve System.

Federal Reserve note
Paper money issued by the Federal Reserve System.

demand deposit
An account from which deposited funds can be withdrawn in currency or transferred by a check to a third party at the initiative of the owner.

Focus and Motivate

Section Objectives

After completing this section, students will be able to
▶ explain what the money supply consists of;
▶ explain what a Federal Reserve note is;
▶ describe what *money* is and what it is not; and
▶ explain what causes interest rates to change.

Kickoff Activity

Prompt students to name all the ways that they pay for goods and services and collect payments from others. Without comment or discussion, list the responses on the board as students call them out.

Activating Prior Knowledge

Refer to the list you compiled during the Kickoff Activity. Ask students which of the items listed can be considered money. Put an *M* next to each of these items. Then go back through the list and discuss why students' responses are correct and incorrect.

Some students may say that credit cards are money. Acknowledge that like money, credit cards are widely accepted for purposes of exchange. But also explain that only money can ultimately be used to pay off debts. A credit card is an instrument that allows a person to take out a loan from the bank that issued the card. A credit card is not money.

Discussion Starter

Where do cashier's checks, money orders, and certified checks fit in with the money supply? *Answer:* The monies may come out of checkable deposits or savings. The money is in a checkable account before it turns into a cashier's check, money order, or certified check.

Many students think of money as only currency (paper bills and coins). Ask, What is the money supply? Read aloud the definition of *money supply* from page 285 of the text. Stress that the money supply is more than just currency. It is currency, checking accounts, and traveler's checks combined. All three are money. Some students may have questions or ask about credit cards. Tell them they will learn more about credit and debit cards in this section.

Discussion Starter

Ask students if they have savings accounts. Did they set up these accounts themselves, or did their parents set up the accounts? Do students know how much money is in their accounts? How often do they check their balances? What interest rates are they earning? If some students have trouble answering these questions, encourage them to find out more about saving money.

Reinforcement Activity

Encourage students to contact various banks to get information about minimum balances, interest rates, incentives, and benefits of opening and maintaining a savings account. Invite students to bring in brochures from the banks or printouts from the banks' websites. After everyone has looked through the materials, ask each student to choose the bank that offers the best savings account for him or her. Direct each student to write a paragraph that identifies the bank and explains why he or she selected it.

 Visit econ.myemcp.com/videos for videos that will help students better understand the key concepts found in this section.

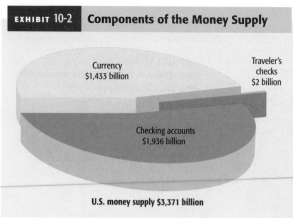

EXHIBIT 10-2 Components of the Money Supply

Currency
$1,433 billion

Traveler's checks
$2 billion

Checking accounts
$1,936 billion

U.S. money supply $3,371 billion

Source: St. Louis Federal Reserve.

▲ The money supply consists of currency, checking accounts (balances), and traveler's checks. The amounts shown represent the money supply in February 2017.

You might be wondering why debit cards aren't mentioned; after all, you can buy products with a debit card in the same way you can with currency. Debit cards aren't included in our list because these funds are already represented in checking accounts. When you use a debit card, money is removed from your checking account in the same way that it is when you write a check.

Another card that people in the future might think of as currency is the smart card. A *smart card* (also commonly called a *chip card*) resembles a credit card in shape and size, but it isn't just a simple piece of plastic the way a credit card is. Inside it is an embedded eight-bit microprocessor. A smart card can be used for many things, and it can hold significant amounts of data. For our purposes here, though, we need to point out that a monetary value can be placed on a smart card (much like a monetary value can be placed on a card at a video arcade), and then the card can be used to make on-the-spot purchases (much like currency is used in the same way).

A Student Asks

QUESTION: *I am used to thinking that only the cash and change I have in my wallet are money. Are we saying that cash is only one component of money?*

savings account
An interest-earning account.

ANSWER: *Yes, that is exactly what we are saying. Remember that money is anything generally accepted in exchange and in the repayment of debt. The cash and change in your wallet (that is, the currency) is generally accepted in exchange and in the repayment of debt, so it is money. The check you might write out for $100 is also accepted in exchange and in the repayment of debt, so it is money. Traveler's checks are also generally accepted in exchange and in the repayment of debt, so they are money too. In summary, money consists of currency plus checking accounts plus traveler's checks.*

Moving Beyond M1 to M2

M1 is the narrowest definition of the money supply. M2 is a broader measure, including everything in M1 plus savings deposits, small-denomination time deposits, money market deposit accounts, and retail money market mutual fund accounts.

A savings deposit (sometimes called a *regular savings deposit*, or **savings account**) is an interest-earning account at a commercial bank or thrift institution. Some savings accounts have check-writing privileges; others do not.

A time deposit is an interest-earning deposit with a specified maturity date. Time deposits are subject to penalties for early withdrawal. Small-denomination time deposits are those under $100,000.

A money market deposit account (MMDA) is an interest-earning account at a bank or thrift institution. Usually, a minimum balance is required for an MMDA. Most MMDAs offer limited check-writing privileges. For example, the owner of an MMDA might be allowed to write only a certain number of checks each month, and/or each check may have to be above a certain dollar amount.

A money market mutual fund (MMMF) is essentially the same thing as an MMDA, except it is with a mutual fund company. There are two varieties of MMMFs: retail and institutional. Only retail MMMFs are part of M2.

286 Chapter 10 Money, Banking, and the Federal Reserve System

Internet Research

Direct students to the website of the Federal Deposit Insurance Corporation (FDIC) to find out when the agency was established, why it exists, and what it does. Ask students to imagine that the FDIC suddenly ceased to exist. What might be the consequences? Tell students to write essays examining these possibilities.

Are Credit Cards Money?

You're out on a Friday night with your friends eating pizza. Someone asks, "Does anyone here have any money?" You say, "I have a credit card." Your friends say, "Good enough."

Is a credit card money? After all, it is often referred to as "plastic money," and most retailers accept credit cards as payment for purchases. On closer examination, we can see that a credit card is not money.

Consider Tina, who decides to buy a pair of shoes. She hands the shoe clerk her Visa card and signs for the purchase. Essentially, what the Visa card allows Tina to do is take out a loan from the bank that issued the card. The shoe clerk knows that this bank has, in effect, promised to pay the store for the shoes. At a later date, the bank will send Tina a credit card bill. At that time, Tina will be required to reimburse the bank for the shoe charges, plus interest (if her payment is made after a certain date). Tina is required to discharge her debt to the bank with money, such as currency or a check written on her checking account.

Can you see that a credit card is not money? Money has to be both generally used for exchange and used in the repayment of debt. A credit card is not used to repay debt but rather to incur it. It is an instrument that makes it easier for the holder to obtain

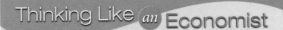

Thinking Like an Economist

Good Money Versus Bad Money

Have you ever heard the expression "Don't throw good money after bad"? For most people, this means "Don't spend more money on something you've already wasted money on." This idiom suggest that "good money" is money that produces a good result and "bad money" is money that produces a bad result.

Economist define good money and bad money differently. For most economists, good money maintains its purchasing power or value, and bad money does not. To illustrate, suppose there are two countries in the world, A and B. In country A, dollars are used as money, and in country B, euros are used as money. In country A, a dollar buys, say, 10 apples in year 1, year 2, year 3, and so on. In other words, in country A, dollars maintain their purchasing power or value over time. However, in country B, euros lose their purchasing power or value over time. A euro buys 10 apples in year 1, but in year 2, it takes two euros to buy 10 apples; in year 3, it takes 10 euros to buy 10 apples; and so on. For economists, good money is money that is reliable, in the sense that its purchasing power or value is relatively stable over time.

THINK ABOUT IT Would you prefer for the money you use (U.S. dollars) to maintain its purchasing power over time or to decline in value over time? In other words, do you want $1 to buy the same thing today and tomorrow that it bought yesterday, or do you want what cost $1 yesterday to cost $2 today and $3 tomorrow?

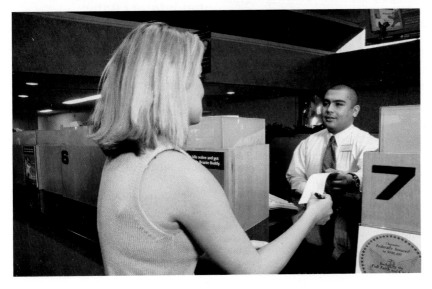

◀ Today, you can deposit and withdraw money in person, using an ATM, or through online banking services. Are the funds you deposit with a bank M1 or M2?

How does a society decide what constitutes money?

After students have read this feature, ask them to suggest why cigarettes rather than some other item became "money" in prison camps.

ANSWERS TO THINK ABOUT IT The prisoners accepted cigarettes as money because they were universally recognized as having value. The prisoners set the exchange rates for other goods to cigarettes.

Teaching with Visuals

The answer to the question for the photograph on page 289 is that credit cards cannot be used to pay a debt; credit cards incur debt.

Application Activity

After reading and discussing Section 2, you may want to assign the Section Activity in the *Applying the Principles Workbook*, pages 109–111.

Assess

Quick Quiz

The following true-or-false quiz will help you assess student understanding of the material covered in this section.

1. One component of the money supply is traveler's checks. (True)
2. Of the three major components of the money supply, the currency component was the largest in August 2005. (True)
3. A nonchecking savings account is considered money. (False)
4. A credit card is money. (False)
5. Using a credit card put a person in debt, which needs to be paid off with money. (True)

Assessment Book

You will find a quiz for this section in the *Assessment Book*, page 96.

What Is Money in a Prisoner of War Camp?

During World War II, a British soldier named Richard A. Radford was captured and placed in a prisoner of war (POW) camp. During his captivity, he noticed that the Red Cross distributed packages to the prisoners from time to time that contained goods such as cigarettes, toiletries, chocolate, cheese, margarine, and tinned beef. Radford also noticed that not all of the prisoners had the same preferences for the items in the packages: some liked chocolate but not cigarettes, whereas others liked cigarettes but not cheese. The other

▲ Cigarettes were money in prisoner of war camps and were used to purchase other goods, like chocolate and cheese.

prisoners also noticed this and began to barter with each other. For instance, a prisoner who had extra cigarettes and wanted more chocolate would trade goods with a prisoner who had extra chocolate and wanted more cigarettes.

Soon, the prisoners no longer bartered but exchanged goods using money instead. (Recall from earlier in this chapter that bartering is more time consuming and difficult than trading with money.) The money was not U.S. dollars, French francs, German marks, or British pounds, however. In fact, it was not any national form of money at all. Instead, cigarettes were used as the money in the POW camp. Cigarettes were generally accepted for purposes of exchange. With the emergence of this form of money, chocolate bars, cheese, and other goods were quoted in cigarette prices: 10 cigarettes for a chocolate bar, 20 cigarettes for cheese, and so on.

THINK ABOUT IT Why do you think that cigarettes, rather than chocolate or cheese, became money in the POW camp?

---

a loan. Using a credit card places a person in debt, which he or she then has to repay with money.

Don't think of the card as money because it isn't money. Think of it as what it is: a piece of plastic that allows you to take out a loan from the bank that issued the card.

In other words, when you hand the credit card to the cashier to pay for the pizza, or shoes, or new DVD, it is you and the bank standing up there in front of the cashier—not just you alone. The bank is saying to you, "Here, we are going to lend you some 'money' to pay for the item. Oh, and by the way, we want you to pay us back later, with interest."

To get a better understanding of credit cards, turn to page 290 and read about "The Psychology of Credit Cards" in the "Your Personal Economics" feature.

loanable funds market
The market for loans. There is a demand for loans (stemming from borrowers) and a supply of loans (stemming from lenders). The loanable funds market is where the interest rate is determined.

Borrowing, Lending, and Interest Rates

As you know, when a person uses a credit card, he or she is actually borrowing funds from a bank. In other words, the person is a borrower and the bank is a lender. Often, when a loan is made, an interest rate must be paid for the loan.

If we look at the interest rates for loans over time, we see that rates are higher than at some times than others. For example, in the 1970s, interest rates were relatively high, but in 2017, interest rates were relatively low.

Why are interest rates high at some times and low at other times? The answer has to do with supply and demand, which are concepts you learned about in Chapters 4 through 6. Interest rates are determined in the **loanable funds market** in much the

---

Kinesthetic Learners and Enrichment and Extension

For one week, create an imaginary bank with accounts for your class. Each student should have a savings account and a checking account (with checkbook and debit card). Instruct students to make imaginary purchases with their imaginary checkbooks and debit cards and to keep track of their balances. Set a minimum balance on their savings accounts, and then allow students to transfer money from their savings accounts into their checking accounts. At the end of the week, have students prepare statements like the monthly statements that banks send to customers and turn in their checkbooks, passbooks, and statements for evaluation.

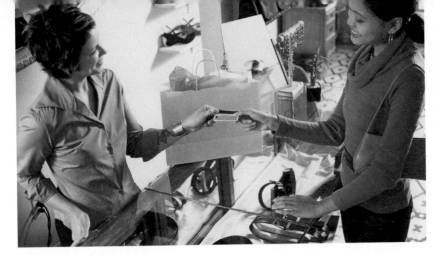

 Credit cards are not money. They cannot be used to repay debt. What is the relationship between credit cards and debt?

same way that apple prices are determined in the apple market, computer prices are determined in the computer market, and house prices are determined in the housing market.

The loanable funds market includes a demand for loans and a supply of loans. The demanders of loans are called *borrowers*; the suppliers of loans are called *lenders*. Through the interaction of the demand for and supply of loans, the interest rate is determined.

What happens if the demand for loans rises? Obviously, if the demand for loans rises and the supply remains constant, the price of a loan (which is the interest rate), will rise. What happens if the demand for loans falls? The interest rate falls. What happens if the supply of loans rises? The interest rate falls. What happens if the supply of loans falls? The interest rate rises.

Sometimes, people make a distinction between short-term interest rates and long-term interest rates. The terms short and long refer to the time period of the loan. For example, if you took out a six-month loan, it would likely be referred to as a short-term loan, in contrast to, say, a 30-year loan, which would be referred to as a long-term loan. The interest rate you paid (as a borrower) for the six-month loan would be referred to as a short-term interest rate; the interest rate you paid for the 30-year loan would be referred to as a long-term interest rate.

> *"There is only one way to have your cake and eat it too: Lend it out at interest."*
> — Anonymous

SECTION 2 ASSESSMENT

Defining Terms
1. Define:
   a. money supply
   b. currency
   c. Federal Reserve note
   d. demand deposit
   e. savings account
   f. loanable funds market

Reviewing Facts and Concepts
2. What is the official name for a dollar bill? (*Hint:* Look at what is written at the top of a dollar bill.)
3. Suppose people move funds from their savings accounts to their checking accounts. Does M1 rise? Does M2 rise?

Critical Thinking
4. Credit cards are widely accepted for purposes of exchange, yet they are not money. Why?
5. Is money currency? Explain your answer.

Applying Economic Concepts
6. Take a look at a Federal Reserve note. On it, you will see the following words: "This note is legal tender for all debts, public and private." What part of the definition of money does this message refer to?

Section 2 The Money Supply **289**

SECTION 2 ASSESSMENT ANSWERS

Defining Terms
1. a. money supply: the total supply of money in circulation, composed of currency, checking accounts, and travel-er's checks; **b. currency:** coins issued by the U.S. Treasury and paper money issued by the Federal Reserve System; **c. Federal Reserve note:** paper money issued by the Federal Reserve System; **d. demand deposit:** an account from which deposited funds can be withdrawn in currency or transferred by a check to a third party at the initiative of the owner; **e. savings account:** an interest-earning account; **f. loanable funds market:** the market for loans, which is where the interest rate is determined.

Reviewing Facts and Concepts
2. A dollar bill is officially called a Federal Reserve note.
3. M1 rises, because it consists of currency, checking accounts, and traveler's checks, so more dollars in checking accounts. M2 does not rise, because both savings accounts and checking accounts are part of M2; so when dollars move from savings accounts to checking accounts, M2 remains constant.

Critical Thinking
4. To be money, a good has to be widely used for purposes of exchange and must be used in the repayment of debt. Credit cards are not used to repay debt; they are used to obtain loans. When you receive a loan, you have incurred a debt, and you have to repay the debt with money.
5. No. Money is more than currency. Money consists of currency, checking accounts, and traveler's checks. Stated differently, currency is a subset of money.

Applying Economic Concepts
6. Money is any good that is widely used for purposes of exchange and in the repayment of debt. The inscription on the Federal Reserve note refers to the latter part of the definition (the repayment of debt).

Section 2 The Money Supply **289**

Discussion Starter

Ask students if they know individuals who incurred large debts because they were careless with credit cards. (Caution students not to name names.) Ask how these people found themselves in this situation.

Teaching with Visuals

Answers will vary. Students may say that their decision will depend on whether they paid for the original ticket with cash or a credit card and on whether they will purchase a replacement with cash or a credit card.

The Psychology of Credit Cards

If you work to earn $50, do you use the money in the same way that you would use a $50 gift? Many economic studies have shown that people often are more serious with money they earn than with money they win or receive as a gift. In reality, a dollar is a dollar is a dollar, no matter from where it came. But in everyday life, we see a dollar earned as somehow different from a dollar won or gifted.

$100 "Out the Window"

Suppose you plan to go to a concert, and the ticket costs $100. You buy the ticket on Monday to attend the concert on Friday. When Friday night comes, you realize that you've lost the ticket. Assuming that tickets are still available, will you buy another? (Answer this question before reading further.)

Now let's change the circumstances. Suppose that instead of buying the ticket on Monday, you plan to buy it on Friday, right before the concert. At the ticket window on Friday night, you realize that on your way to the concert, $100 fell out of your wallet. You brought plenty of cash, so you still have enough to buy the ticket. But will you buy it?

The Economist Says…

According to economists, the two situations described here present

you with the same choice. In both cases, you have to spend another $100 to see the concert. Because the two situations present you with the same choice, economists argue that you will behave the same way in both. If you decide not to buy another ticket in the first situation, then you won't in the second either. If you decide to buy another ticket in the first situation, then you won't in the second.

…But in Real Life

People don't seem to behave the way that economists predict,

▼ If you lost your ticket to this concert, would you buy another?

Cooperative Learning

Divide the class into groups of three or four. Direct each group to compare credit cards offered by three different companies. Ask students to note the cards' interest rates, late fees, annual fees, and fees for cash advances. Tell students to be sure that they read the fine print of the credit card agreements. Which card offers the best deal? What in the fine print surprised the group? Allow the groups to summarize their findings for the class.

▲ You must either pay for something when you buy it or pay for it later. If you pay later, you often pay more.

however. When asked the two questions in this example, many people say that they wouldn't buy a second ticket if they lost the first ticket, but they would buy a ticket if they lost $100. Why? These people argue that spending an additional $100 on a second ticket is like spending $200 to see the concert, which is too much to pay. However, they don't see themselves spending $200 to see the concert when they lose $100 on the way to the concert and pay $100 for a ticket. To these people, the situations are completely different.

Economists say that the people who answer the two questions differently (although both settings offer the same basic choice) are *compartmentalizing*. They are treating the two $100 amounts differently, as if the amounts come from two different compartments. The concert ticket example shows that people do compartmentalize when it comes to money. They don't always treat a dollar in the same way.

Cash Versus Credit Cards

With this example in mind, let's compare using cash to using a credit card. Say a person has both $500 in cash and a credit card in her wallet. She wants to purchase something that costs $480. She could use the cash to make the purchase, or she could put the purchase on her credit card (and pay off the credit card later). In this situation, many people will say that it's somehow easier to use the credit card than to pay cash. When they pay cash, they say, they have a harder time making the decision to purchase the item. Somehow, it seems more real to them; somehow, the purchase seems more expensive.

You and Your Lending Partner

It may be easier to use a credit card than to pay cash, but it certainly isn't cheaper. In fact, it can be more expensive. If you don't pay off credit card balances monthly, you will end up paying interest on the loan the bank provided you via your credit card purchase.

In a sense, when you buy something with a credit card, two people, not one, stand in front of the cashier making the purchase. First is you, handing over your credit card. Second, standing next to you, is your "partner," which is the bank. This imaginary partner is there with you, issuing you a loan to make the purchase with the credit card. Later, your partner will come back to you and ask to be repaid for the loan, with interest. In other words, a $100 item will cost you $100 if you pay in cash, but it could cost you $110 if you pay with a credit card

($100 for the purchase and $10 interest paid for the $100 loan).

An Expensive Lesson

Making a credit card purchase might be easier (for you) than a cash purchase of the same amount, but it's often a more costly purchase. Not realizing this can lead to serious financial trouble, as far too many people have learned the hard way.

Consider Kevin (a real person whose name has been changed). He went off to college with a credit card. The first two months at college, he used the credit card for all of his purchases—many purchases. Kevin purchased new clothes, took his friends out to eat regularly, and bought an expensive TV for his dorm room.

When Kevin received the credit card bill, he was shocked at just how much he had spent. (It seemed so easy to spend when he was out with his friends having a good time.) He said he felt as if someone else had spent the money. In his words, "At the time, it felt like I was getting things for free." Now, Kevin certainly was smart enough to know that he wasn't getting anything for free; it just seemed that way. Looking back, he realized that his compartmentalizing caused him to buy a lot more than he would have if he had paid in cash. In the end, he had to work many extra hours to pay off his credit card bill.

Your Personal Economics Activity (A)

In a brief essay, examine the positive and negative aspects of credit cards.

Grading Rubric: Essay

1 2 3 4 5 Student explained the positive aspects of credit cards.

1 2 3 4 5 Student explained the negative aspects of credit cards.

Research Activity

Assign students to research how many credit cards the average American has. Have each student answer questions like these: Has this number increased or decreased during the last 10 years? Has individual credit card debt increased or decreased during this period? What effects have these changes had on the economy? on society as a whole? on individual people? Compare students' findings in a class discussion.

Credit card use is widespread in our modern market economy. People use credit cards every day to buy groceries, clothes, computers, furniture, and more. Knowing what a credit card is and how it can be both used and abused is an important part of your personal economic education.

How to Avoid Credit-Card Debt

Every time you use a credit card—to buy gas, clothes, or an airline ticket—you incur a debt. That's because using a credit card is equal to taking out a loan. When you buy a shirt, a pair of shoes, or a watch with your credit card, you are essentially taking out a loan from the credit card company to buy the shirt, shoes, or watch. Later, you will have to pay back the loan you took out from the credit card company.

A good way to remember that using your credit card is the same as taking out a loan and therefore incurring a debt is to say, quietly in your mind, as you purchase anything with a credit card: I have just incurred a debt that must be repaid.

Although every purchase you make on a credit card is considered a debt, the term credit card debt refers to debt that you carry over from one payment period to the next—that is, debt that incurs interest. What is the best way to avoid credit card debt? Obviously, the surest way is to never use a credit card. But, for most of us, that

is not a feasible solution. We need to use credit cards because they are a convenient way to make many of our purchases, among other reasons.

Aside from avoiding using credit cards altogether, the best way to avoid credit card debt is to pay off the debt, also known as the balance, in full each month. Let's consider the case of Yvonne, who has just used her credit card to buy $300 worth of clothing. A month later, her credit card company sends her a statement asking her to pay off the debt she owes to them, which, currently, is $300. If she pays off the full $300, she has reduced her credit card debt to zero. If she pays only the minimum amount due on her credit card bill (say, $30), then not only will she still owe $270, and thus still be in debt, but interest payments will begin to accrue on the amount she still owes. Now, depending on her interest rate, instead of owing $270, she might owe $287.

While paying off your full credit card balance each month sounds like a good idea, you might say it is easier said than done. What if you buy a $5,000 item with your credit card and don't have the $5,000 to repay to the credit card company at the end of the month? Obviously you will not be able to eliminate your debt right away.

When using a credit card, it is especially important to carefully consider what you can and cannot afford. You should make every

effort to avoid purchasing with a credit card those things that you cannot pay for with cash when the credit card bill comes due (usually within 30 days). This may not be something that most people want to hear, but it is a smart rule to live by. Just because you have access to credit does not mean you should use it. When you buy more than your income allows, you will end up literally paying for it, with interest.

How to Eliminate Credit-card Debt

Let's say that you didn't follow the advice offered earlier and you ended up buying more than you could afford, causing you to amass a large amount of credit card debt. What is the best way to reduce or eliminate this debt? The answer is to cut back on your spending and direct the saved funds to paying off the debt. Instead of making only the minimum monthly payment on your credit card, double or triple it. The more debt you pay off this month, the less interest you will end up owing next month.

Some might argue that one of the best ways to begin to eliminate credit card debt is to transfer the balance from one credit card to another one with a lower interest rate. To illustrate, suppose you owe $5,000 on one credit card and are paying an interest rate of 10 percent. You now have the chance to transfer the $5,000 debt you owe to a new card on which you would pay an interest rate of 8 percent.

Differentiating Instruction

Reinforcement Activity

Help reinforce the concept of how debt owed on a credit card, in effect, increases the cost of items purchased with that card. Instruct students to identify a purchase they would like to make in the near future (such as concert tickets, clothing, and

so on). After they have identified the cost of the item assign the task of determining how much the same item would be if he or she paid for it using a credit card with an interest rate of 14% and it took six months to pay off the item.

Should you do it? The answer depends on whether or not the 8 percent is a temporary or teaser rate (a low introductory interest rate that will go up in time) or a permanent rate. It also depends upon whether you will have to pay a balance transfer fee and how much this fee is. If you will not be able to pay off the balance before the interest rate rises, or if the balance transfer fee will negate the savings on interest you would gain by transferring the balance, you should keep your existing credit card as you work to pay off the balance.

Becoming a Low-Risk Borrower

A low-risk borrower is a borrower who creditors believe is likely to repay a loan. Stated differently, a low-risk borrower is a borrower with a high credit score. A credit score indicates the degree of credit worthiness of a person; the higher the score, the greater the person's credit worthiness, or likelihood of paying off a debt, is considered to be.

Why might you want to become a low-risk borrower? One reason is that low-risk borrowers are often charged lower interest rates by lenders, since the costs of lending to them are lower. Low-risk lenders are also able to get loans for higher amounts—a privilege that will come in handy when it comes time to buy a house or car.

How do you become a low-risk borrower? Start by paying off current credit card debt each month, and do not miss any payments. Make managing your credit card payments a priority so that you can create a long positive credit history, which indicates you have consistently and over a long time period paid what you owe. Keep your credit card balance below your limit (somewhere in the range of 45-55 percent of your limit) and, if you take out any other loans, be able to show that you have consistently worked toward paying back what you owe on those debts as well.

Your Personal Economics Activity (B)

Apply critical thinking skills to examine how you might avoid credit card debt in the future; and if you incur credit card debt, how you would go about eliminating it. Write a two-page credit how-to plan that explores these topics. Next, consider strategies you might implement to become a low-risk borrower and raise your credit score. Identify these strategies at the end of your credit how-to plan.

My Personal Economics Action Plan Encourage students to identify scenarios in which it might not be a good idea to use a credit card. Also suggest that they identify circumstances under which using a credit card might be acceptable. Arrange for students to report their thoughts to the class.

My Personal Economics Action Plan

Here are some points you may want to consider and some guidelines you might want to put into practice.

☑ 1. Someone once said that "If you know where the holes are, you are less likely to step in them." Does this observation apply to using credit cards? If you know that credit cards are easy to abuse, then you are less likely to get into financial trouble using them.

I will not use a credit card instead of a check or cash until I am _____ years old and have proven to myself that I am financially responsible.

☑ 2. Keep in mind that people sometimes compartmentalize. To them, a dollar is not always a dollar. In fact, these people are deceiving themselves: a dollar is a dollar is a dollar.

In the future, I will spend only _____ percent of money gifts I receive, and I will save _____ percent.

☑ 3. If you use a credit card to buy something that costs $100, you may end up paying more than $100 for the item. Generally speaking, using a credit card to buy something makes that item costlier than using cash.

I will not use a credit card unless I know for sure that I will be able to pay my bill in full when it comes.

Grading Rubric: How-to Plan

1 2 3 4 5   Student explained how to avoid credit card debt.

1 2 3 4 5   Student identified strategies to become a low-risk borrower.

The Federal Reserve System

Focus Questions
▸ What is the Federal Reserve System (the Fed)?
▸ How many persons sit on the Board of Governors of the Federal Reserve System?
▸ What are the major responsibilities of the Federal Reserve System?
▸ How does the check-clearing process work?

Key Terms
Federal Reserve System (the Fed)
Board of Governors of the Federal Reserve System
Federal Open Market Committee (FOMC)
reserve account

Focus and Motivate

Section Objectives

After completing this section, students will be able to

▸ explain what the Federal Reserve System is;

▸ state how many persons sit on the Board of Governors of the Federal Reserve System;

▸ describe the major responsibilities of the Federal Reserve System; and

▸ describe how the check-clearing process works.

Kickoff Activity

Write the following statement and question on the board: "The central bank of the United States, called the Federal Reserve System, serves as the lender of last resort. What do you think this statement means?" Give students five minutes to think about the question.

Activating Prior Knowledge

Invite students to share their responses to the Kickoff Activity. Ensure students understand that the Federal Reserve System is an important part of the U.S. government. As a *lender of last resort,* its function is to lend money to banks that are suffering cash management problems. Ask why other banks might not loan money to banks with cash management problems.

Teach

Discussion Starter

Ask whether students have heard "the Fed" being discussed in the news and what they think the Fed does.

What Is the Federal Reserve System?

In 1913, Congress passed the Federal Reserve Act. This act set up the **Federal Reserve System**, which began operation in 1914. (The popular name for the Federal Reserve System is "**the Fed**.") The Fed is a *central bank*, which means it is the chief monetary authority in the country. A central bank has the job of determining the money supply and supervising banks, among other things. Today, the principal components of the Federal Reserve System are (1) the Board of Governors, and (2) the 12 Federal Reserve district banks.

Board of Governors

Federal Reserve System (the Fed)
The central bank of the United States.

Board of Governors of the Federal Reserve System
The governing body of the Federal Reserve System.

The **Board of Governors of the Federal Reserve System** controls and coordinates the Fed's activities. The board is made up of seven members, each appointed to a 14-year term by the president of the United States with Senate approval. The president also designates one member of the board as chairperson for a 4-year term. The offices of the Board of Governors are located at

20th Street N.W. and Constitution Avenue in Washington, D.C.

> **A Student Asks**
>
> **QUESTION:** *Do other countries have a Federal Reserve System?*
>
> **ANSWER:** *As stated earlier, the Federal Reserve System is a central bank, and other countries do have central banks. In the United States, we call our central bank the* Federal Reserve System, *but in most other countries, the central bank is either called* the central bank *or* the bank *of that particular country—for example, the Bank of Japan, the Bank of Ghana, the Central Bank of Iceland, and so on.*

The 12 Federal Reserve District Banks

The United States is divided into 12 Federal Reserve districts, as shown in Exhibit 10-3. Each district has a Federal Reserve district bank. (Think of the district banks as "branch offices" of the Federal Reserve System.)

Cooperative Learning

Students often learn and retain information best through firsthand exposure to a concept. If you live near a Federal Reserve district bank, contact the bank and schedule a tour for your class. Before the trip, have students work in groups of three or four to develop specific questions they would like to ask. In the class period following the visit, tell the groups to write short reports on what they learned and to describe specifically anything they discovered about a Federal Reserve bank or the Federal Reserve System that was not discussed in the text.

EXHIBIT 10-3 Federal Reserve Districts and Federal Reserve Bank Locations

◀ What Fed district do you live in?

Minneapolis ⑨

Cleveland

Boston ①

②

Chicago ⑦

New York

⑫ San Francisco

⑩ Kansas City

④

③

Philadelphia

St. Louis

⑧

Board of Governors (Washington, D.C.)

⑤

Richmond

Dallas ⑥

⑪

Atlanta

Alaska and Hawaii are part of the San Francisco District

Each Federal Reserve district bank has a president. Which Federal Reserve district do you live in?

An Important Committee: The FOMC

The major policy-making group within the Fed is the **Federal Open Market Committee (FOMC)**. We will consider what the FOMC does later in this chapter, but for now, note that the FOMC is made up of 12 members. Seven of the 12 members are the members of the Board of Governors. The remaining 5 members come from the ranks of the presidents of the Federal Reserve district banks.

What Does the Fed Do?

The Fed has six major responsibilities:

1. *Control the money supply.* A full explanation of how the Fed controls the money supply comes later in the chapter.
2. *Supply the economy with paper money (Federal Reserve notes).* As stated in an earlier section, the pieces of paper money we use are Federal Reserve notes. Federal Reserve notes are printed at the Bureau of Engraving and Printing in Washington, D.C. The notes are issued to the 12 Federal

Reserve district banks, which keep the money on hand to meet the demands of the banks and the public. For example, suppose it is the holiday season, and people are going to their banks and withdrawing greater than usual numbers of $1, $5, and $20 notes. Banks need to replenish their supplies of these notes, and they turn to their Federal Reserve district banks to do so. The Federal Reserve district banks meet this cash need by supplying more paper money. (Remember, the 12 Federal Reserve district banks do not print the paper money; they only supply it.)

3. *Hold bank reserves.* Each commercial bank that is a member of the Federal Reserve System is required to keep a **reserve account** (think of it as a checking account) with its Federal Reserve district bank. For example, a bank located in Durham, North Carolina, is located in the fifth Federal Reserve district, which means it deals with the Federal Reserve Bank of Richmond (Virginia). The local bank in Durham must have a reserve account with this reserve bank. Soon, we will look at the function of a bank's reserve account with the Fed in increasing and decreasing the money supply.

Federal Open Market Committee (FOMC)
The 12-member policy-making group within the Fed. This committee has the authority to conduct open market operations.

reserve account
A bank's "checking account" with its Federal Reserve district bank.

Teaching with Visuals

Exhibit 10-3 shows the Federal Reserve districts and the cities in which the Fed banks are located. Ask, Which district is our community in? Where is the closest Federal Reserve bank?

Discussion Starter

Tell students that one bank is more important than all the other banks in the United States: the central bank of the United States, the Federal Reserve System. Ask students what they think a central bank does that a regular commercial bank does not or cannot do. In other words, what makes a central bank special? Point out that one major feature is that a central bank has the ability to control the money supply.

 Visit econ.myemcp.com/videos for videos that will help students better understand the key concepts found in this section.

Internet Research

Suggest that students visit additional websites to enhance their study of this chapter. Have them go to the website of the Board of Governors of the Federal Reserve System to find out more about the structure and functions of the Fed. Encourage students to make posters or diagrams that clearly illustrate the Fed's different roles. The visuals should be geared toward a general audience that doesn't know anything about the Fed and its functions. You might arrange for pairs or groups of students to give brief presentations about the Fed to classes of younger students.

Critical Thinking

Ask students to think about why China might be interested in opening up its banking sector. See The Global Impact feature on the book website at www.emcschool.net/Economics2e.

ANSWERS TO ECONOMIC THINKING Answers will vary. Students might suggest that efforts to increase international trade motivate nations to open up their banking sectors.

Teaching with Visuals

Instruct students to re-create Exhibit 10-4 for specific banks in their Federal Reserve district. Or suggest that students look at a check that has cleared and use the signatures and stamps on it to trace the check's path through the clearing process.

 Application Activity

After reading and discussing Section 3, you may want to assign the Section Activity in the *Applying the Principles Workbook*, pages 112–114.

Assess

Quick Quiz

The following true-or-false quiz will help you assess student understanding of the material covered in this section.

1. The Federal Reserve Act was passed by Congress in 1913. (True)
2. The president of the Board of Governors is elected by the people. (False)
3. There are 15 Federal Reserve districts in the United States. (False)
4. The major policy-making group in the Fed is the FOMC. (True)
5. The Fed has six major responsibilities. (True)

Teaching with Visuals

To answer the question with the image on page 297, the Bureau of Engraving and Printing is responsible for printing paper money in the United States.

---

4. *Provide check-clearing services.* When someone in Cincinnati (Ohio) writes a check to a person in Columbus (Ohio), what happens to the check? The process by which funds change hands when checks are written is called the *check-clearing process.* The Fed plays a major role in this process. Here is how it works (see Exhibit 10-4):

a. Suppose Harry writes a $1,000 check on his Cincinnati bank and sends it by mail to Ursula in Columbus. To record this transaction, Harry reduces the balance in his checking account by $1,000. In other words, if his balance was $2,500 before he wrote the check, it is $1,500 after he writes the check.

b. Ursula receives the check in the mail. She takes the check to her local bank, endorses it (signs it on the back), and deposits it into her checking account. The balance in her account rises by $1,000.

c. Ursula's Columbus bank sends the check to its Federal Reserve district bank, which is located in Cleveland. The Federal Reserve Bank of Cleveland increases the reserve account of the Columbus bank (Ursula's bank) by $1,000 and decreases the reserve account of the Cincinnati bank (Harry's bank) by $1,000.

d. The Federal Reserve Bank of Cleveland sends the check to Harry's bank in Cincinnati, which

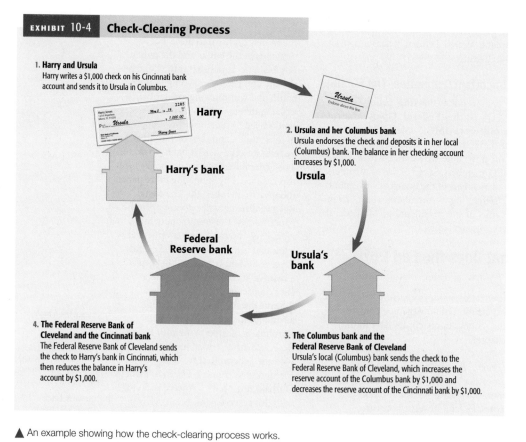

EXHIBIT 10-4 **Check-Clearing Process**

1. Harry and Ursula
Harry writes a $1,000 check on his Cincinnati bank account and sends it to Ursula in Columbus.

Harry

Harry's bank

2. Ursula and her Columbus bank
Ursula endorses the check and deposits it in her local (Columbus) bank. The balance in her checking account increases by $1,000.

Ursula

Ursula's bank

Federal Reserve bank

4. The Federal Reserve Bank of Cleveland and the Cincinnati bank
The Federal Reserve Bank of Cleveland sends the check to Harry's bank in Cincinnati, which then reduces the balance in Harry's account by $1,000.

3. The Columbus bank and the Federal Reserve Bank of Cleveland
Ursula's local (Columbus) bank sends the check to the Federal Reserve Bank of Cleveland, which increases the reserve account of the Columbus bank by $1,000 and decreases the reserve account of the Cincinnati bank by $1,000.

▲ An example showing how the check-clearing process works.

Differentiating Instruction

English Language Learners

To help students who are English language learners, use the following resources, which are provided as part of the *Economics: New Ways of*

Thinking program:

- a Spanish glossary in the *Student Text*
- Spanish versions of the Chapter Summaries on an audio disc

 The Federal Reserve controls the nation's money supply, but the Fed does not actually print money. What government agency is responsible for printing our paper money?

then reduces the balance in Harry's checking account by $1,000. Harry's bank in Cincinnati either keeps the check on record or sends it along to Harry with his monthly bank statement.

5. *Supervise member banks.* Without warning, the Fed can examine the books of member commercial banks to see what kinds of loans they have made, whether they have followed bank regulations, how accurate their records are, and so on. If the Fed finds that a bank has not followed established

banking standards, it can pressure the bank to do so.

6. *Serve as the lender of last resort.* A traditional function of a central bank is to serve as the "lender of last resort" for banks suffering cash management problems. For example, let's say that bank A has lost millions of dollars and finds it difficult to borrow from other banks. At this point, the Fed may step in and act as lender of last resort to bank A. In other words, the Fed may lend bank A the funds it wants to borrow when no one else will.

SECTION 3 ASSESSMENT

Defining Terms

1. Define:
   a. Federal Reserve System (the Fed)
   b. Board of Governors of the Federal Reserve System
   c. Federal Open Market Committee (FOMC)
   d. reserve account

Reviewing Facts and Concepts

2. In what year did the Fed begin operating?

3. Explain how a check is cleared.

4. What does it mean when we say the Fed is the "lender of last resort"?

Critical Thinking

5. Economists speak about printing, issuing, and supplying paper money. How are these different functions? Where is each function performed?

6. Would it make much difference if there were 20

Federal Reserve districts instead of 12? Explain

Applying Economic Concepts

7. Do you think banks need the Fed to act as the "lender of last resort" more often during good economic times or bad economic times? Explain your answer.

SECTION 3 ASSESSMENT ANSWERS

Defining Terms

1. a. Federal Reserve System (the Fed): the central bank of the United States; **b. Board of Governors of the Federal Reserve System:** the governing body of the Federal Reserve System; **c. Federal Open Market Committee (FOMC):** the 12-member policy-making group within the Fed, which has the authority to conduct open market operations; **d. reserve account:** a checking account that a commercial bank has with its Federal

Reserve district bank.

Reviewing Facts and Concepts

2. The Fed began operating in 1914.
3. See Exhibit 10-4 on page 296 for the explanation.
4. As the "lender of last resort," the Fed has the responsibility of lending banks money when no one else will.

Section 3 The Federal Reserve System **297**

 Assessment Book

You will find a quiz for this section in the *Assessment Book*, page 97.

Reteaching Activity

Use the Section Assessment to gauge which students may need reteaching on this section. Ask those students to list the six major responsibilities of the Federal Reserve System. (*Answer:* Control the money supply, supply the economy with paper money, hold bank reserves, provide check-clearing services, supervise member banks, and serve as the lender of last resort.)

Guided Reading

For further reaching of the key concepts in this section, assign the Outlining Activity and the Just the Facts Handout in the *Guided Reading and Study Guide*, pages 159–161.

Critical Thinking

5. "Printing" has to do with producing money, "issuing" with sending money to various banks, and "supplying" with the banks passing along the money to the public. Printing, issuing, and supplying paper money are different functions. In the United States, paper money is printed (produced) by the Bureau of Engraving and Printing in Washington, D.C. It is then issued by the Bureau of Engraving and Printing to various Federal Reserve district banks. For example, the Bureau of Engraving and Printing may issue (send) $200 million of paper money to the Federal Reserve District Bank of San Francisco. The district bank then supplies the paper money to commercial banks, which supply it to the public.
6. No. What matters are the functions of the districts, not so much the size and number of the districts.

Applying Economic Concepts

7. Banks most likely need the Fed as a "lender of last resort" during bad economic times. If people and businesses cannot repay their loans, banks will lose money and need assistance from the Fed.

Teacher Support

Focus and Motivate

Section Objectives

After completing this section, students will be able to

▶ explain what total reserves equal;

▶ explain what required and excess reserves are;

▶ describe how banks use checking accounts to increase the money supply;

▶ describe what banks do with excess reserves; and

▶ calculate the maximum change in the money supply resulting from bank loans.

Kickoff Activity

Write the following question on the board before students come to class, and tell them to answer it in writing: "What's the first thing you think of when you hear the phrase 'creating money'?"

Activating Prior Knowledge

Allow time for students to share their responses to the Kickoff Activity. Students may say that the first thing that comes to their minds is printing money. Some may think of counterfeiting money. Make the point that banks do not have the ability or the right to print money. Guide students to distinguish between printing money and creating money. One can create money without printing currency by creating checking accounts or demand deposits. Remind students once again that money is more than currency.

 Visit econ.myemcp.com/videos for videos that will help students better understand the key concepts found in this section.

The Money Creation Process

Focus Questions

▶ What do total reserves equal?

▶ What are required reserves? Excess reserves?

▶ How do banks use checking accounts to increase the money supply?

▶ What do banks do with excess reserves?

▶ Knowing the reserve requirement, how can you calculate the maximum change in the money supply that results from bank loans?

Key Terms

total reserves
required reserves
reserve requirement
excess reserves

Different Types of Reserves

Now, you are going to learn how the money supply in the United States is increased (more money) and decreased (less money). Before you can understand the difference, it is important to know the different types of bank reserves. The following points and definitions are crucial to understanding how the money supply rises and falls:

total reserves
The sum of a bank's deposits in its reserve account at the Fed and its vault cash.

required reserves
The minimum amount of reserves a bank must hold against its deposits, as mandated by the Fed.

reserve requirement
The regulation that requires a bank to keep a certain percentage of its deposits in its reserve account with the Fed or in its vault as vault cash.

1. The previous section mentioned that each member bank has a reserve account, which is like a checking account with its Federal Reserve district bank. If we take the dollar amount of a bank's reserve account and add it to the cash the bank has in its vault (called, simply enough, *vault cash*), we have the bank's **total reserves**.

   Total reserves = Deposits in the reserve account at the Fed + Vault cash

   EXAMPLE The president of bank A, a small commercial bank, notes that the bank has $15 million in its vault. (In other words, if the bank were robbed right now, the most the thieves would get is $15 million.) The bank president also notes that the bank has $10 million in its reserve account at the Fed. If we add the vault cash of $15 million (the money in the vault) to the $10 million deposit in the reserve account, we get a total of $25 million. This dollar sum—$25 million—is the bank's total reserves. ◆

2. A bank's total reserves can be divided into two types: required reserves and excess reserves. **Required reserves** are the amount of reserves a bank must hold against its checking account deposits, as ordered by the Fed. For example, suppose bank A holds checking account deposits (checkbook money) for its customers totaling $100 million. The Fed requires, through its **reserve requirement**, that bank A hold a percentage of this total amount in the form of reserves—that is, either as deposits in its reserve account at the Fed or as vault cash (because both of these are reserves). If the reserve requirement is 10 percent, bank A is

---

Internet Research

Counterfeiting has a long history in the United States. Early on, banks often issued their own money, and it was difficult for people to know which bills were real and which were fake. Experts have estimated that by the time of the Civil War, one-third of all currency in the United States was counterfeit. In 1863, the government adopted a national currency in an attempt to solve the problem, but the number of forgeries continued to grow. The U.S. Secret Service was established in 1865 to deal with counterfeiting. Modern counterfeiters use computers, scanners, and digital imaging software to create realistic fakes. For more information, direct students to the website of the Secret Service.

required to hold 10 percent of $100 million, or $10 million, in the form of reserves. This $10 million is called *required reserves*.

Required reserves = Reserve requirement × Checking account deposits

3. **Excess reserves** are the difference between total reserves and required reserves. For example, if total reserves equal $25 million and required reserves equal $10 million, then excess reserves are $15 million. See Exhibit 10-5 for a review of these points.

Excess reserves = Total reserves − Required reserves

4. Banks can make loans with their excess reserves. For example, if bank A has excess reserves of $15 million, it can make loans of $15 million.

(You may not realize it, but you just read a very important section of this chapter. In this short section, you were introduced to four new terms: *total reserves, required reserves, reserve requirement,* and *excess reserves.* If you are not absolutely sure what each term means, you should go back and read this section again. These four terms will be used often in the discussion that follows. You don't want to be in the thick of the discussion asking yourself, "What are required reserves again?")

How Banks Increase the Money Supply

Earlier, we said that the money supply is the sum of three components: currency (coins and paper money), checking account deposits, and traveler's checks. For example, having $710 billion in currency, $619 billion in checking account deposits, and $7 billion in traveler's checks means that the money supply is $1,336 billion. Recall that checking account deposits are sometimes referred to as *demand deposits* because checking accounts contain funds that can be withdrawn not only by a check but also on demand.

Banks (such as your local bank down the street) are not allowed to print currency. Your bank cannot legally print a $10 bill, for example. However, banks can create checking account deposits (checkbook money), and if they do, they increase the money supply. The following discussion explains the process.

Creating Checking Account Deposits

To see how banks use checking account deposits to increase the money supply, let's imagine a fictional character named Fred. (His name rhymes with Fed for a reason you will learn later.) Fred is somewhat of a magician: he can snap his fingers and create a $1,000 bill out of thin air. On Monday morning at 9:00, outside bank A, Fred snaps his fingers and creates a $1,000 bill. He immediately walks into the bank, opens

excess reserves
Any reserves held beyond the required amount.

◀ A summary of the different types of reserves.

EXHIBIT 10-5 **Reserves: Total, Required, and Excess**

Kind of reserves	What it equals	Numerical example
Total reserves	Total reserves = Deposits in the reserve account at the Fed + Vault cash	Deposits in the reserve account = $10 million Vault cash = $15 million **Total reserves = $25 million**
Required reserves	Required reserves = Reserve requirement × Checking account deposits	Reserve requirement = 10% Checking account deposits = $100 million **Required reserves = $10 million**
Excess reserves	Excess reserves = Total reserves − Required reserves	Total reserves = $25 million Required reserves = $10 million **Excess reserves = $15 million**

Discussion Starter

After students read the section "Different Types of Reserves" and the definition of *excess reserves,* ask, Why do you think it's important for a bank to know the amount of excess reserves it has available? How could a bank increase its excess reserves? Why would a bank choose to increase its excess reserves?

Reinforcement Activity

To help students grasp the concept of how money is created, ask them to research the subject. Encourage them to visit local banks or conduct Internet research to gather data. Ask each student to write a one-page report or share his or her findings orally in class.

Teaching with Visuals

Suggest that students re-create Exhibit 10-5 on their own paper to keep as a reference while studying this chapter. Remind students that excess reserves are the amount of money the bank can lend. Bankers need to monitor their excess reserves very carefully.

Differentiating Instruction

Kinesthetic Learners

Bring a set of Monopoly money to class to teach students the differences among total reserves, required reserves, and excess reserves. Urge students to imagine that the play money is a bank. Give several students two random bills, and tell them to deposit these amounts in the bank. Then instruct students to find the total reserves of the bank, the required reserves for the new accounts, and the excess reserves from the initial deposits. Call on each student to go through this process so that everyone becomes familiar with these terms. You might divide the class into groups for this activity, appointing one student in each group to serve as the banker.

Cause and Effect

There is an obvious cause-and-effect relationship between total reserves and excess reserves. Have students create their own examples that illustrate the relationship between changes in total reserves and excess reserves.

Research and Report

Mayer Amschel Bauer Rothschild (quoted on page 303) was the founder of international banking. Encourage students to research his life and ideas, choose specific topics from that research, and prepare short presentations on their findings. Compile the presentation materials into a class project on the man.

Teaching with Visuals

Students may find it hard to understand that a deposit of $1,000 results in the creation of $10,000. Guide the class in a discussion in which individual students explain specific parts of Exhibit 10-6. Guide students in explaining the diagram in their own words and in re-creating it on the board.

up a checking account, and tells the banker that he wants the $1,000 deposited into his checking account. The banker gladly complies. Entry (a) in Exhibit 10-6 shows this deposit.

Now what does the bank physically do with the $1,000 bill? It places the bill into its vault, which means the money found its way into vault cash, which is part of total reserves. (Total reserves = Deposits in the reserve account at the Fed + Vault cash.) Thus, if vault cash goes up by $1,000, total reserves increase by the same amount. (If you need to check back to the earlier equations to see this total, do it now.)

To keep things simple, let's assume that bank A had no checking account deposits before Fred walked into the bank. Now, it has $1,000. Also, let's say that the Fed set the reserve requirement at 10 percent. What are bank A's required reserves? Required reserves equal the reserve requirement multiplied by checking account deposits. Bank A's $1,000 × 10 percent = $100, which is the amount bank A has to keep in

reserve form—either in its reserve account at the Fed or as vault cash. Look at entry (b) in Exhibit 10-6.

Currently, however, bank A has more than $100 in its vault; it has the $1,000 that Fred handed over to it. What, then, do its excess reserves equal? Because excess reserves equal total reserves minus required reserves, the bank's excess reserves equal $900—the difference between $1,000 (total reserves) and $100 (required reserves), as in entry (c) in Exhibit 10-6.

What Does the Bank Do with Excess Reserves?

What does bank A do with its $900 in excess reserves? It creates new loans with the money. For example, suppose Alexi walks into bank A and asks for a $900 loan. The loan officer at the bank asks Alexi what she wants the money for. She tells the loan officer she wants a loan to buy a new TV, and the loan officer grants her the loan.

Some people may think that at this point, the loan officer of the bank simply walks

▶ Follow this diagram and the explanation in the text to see how banks increase the money supply.

EXHIBIT 10-6 **The Banking System Creates Checking Account Deposits (Money)**

Bank	New checking account deposits (new reserves)	Required reserves	Excess reserves, new loans, or new bank-created checking account deposits
	This amount was created by Fred.		
A	$1,000 (a)	$100 (b)	$900 (c)
B	$900 (d)	$90 (e)	$810 (f)
C	$810	$81	$729
D	$729	$72.90	$656.10
E	⋮	This amount was created by the banks.	
Totals	$10,000	$1,000	$9,000
	Created by Fred	Created by banking system	Created by Fred and banking system
	$1,000 +	$9,000 =	$10,000

Cross-Curricular Activity

Invite a U.S. history teacher to your class to talk about the details of the depression of 1893, the fight for metals, and the election of 1896. These historical events relate directly to how the money supply should or should not be handled. There are many interesting angles to this story that students can relate to the information in this chapter. If you wish, ask each student to prepare a short oral presentation on one person or event of the time (accepted by you) and to deliver their presentations when the history teacher is present. The teacher can then give helpful hints on the history, and you can evaluate students' performances.

over to the bank's vault, takes out $900 in currency, and hands it to Alexi. It doesn't happen this way, though. Instead, the loan officer opens up a checking account for Alexi at bank A and informs her that the balance in the account is $900. See entry (c) in Exhibit 10-6. In other words, banks give out loans in the form of checking account deposits. (This point is important to remember as we continue.)

What has bank A done by opening up a checking account (with a $900 balance) for Alexi? It has, in fact, increased the money supply by $900. Remember that the money supply consists of (1) currency, (2) checking account deposits, and (3) traveler's checks. When bank A opens up a checking account (with a balance of $900) for Alexi, the dollar amount of currency has not changed, nor has the dollar amount of traveler's checks. The only thing that has changed is the dollar amount of checking account deposits, or checkbook money. It is $900 higher, so the money supply is $900 higher too.

At this point, you might ask, "But isn't the $900 Alexi receives from the bank part of the money that Fred deposited in the bank?" To say that Fred does not have the $1,000 anymore but that Alexi has $900 of it is not exactly correct. Fred does not have the $1,000 in currency anymore, but he does still have $1,000. In other words, he doesn't have the $1,000 on him, in his wallet. It is now in the bank vault. He does have a checking account with a balance of $1,000, and Alexi has $900 in her checking account—an additional $900 created by the bank that did not exist before.

A Student Asks

QUESTION: *Does the bank have to create loans with its excess reserves?*

ANSWER: *No, banks don't have to create loans with their excess reserves, but lending money is what banks do. That is how banks generate income. A bank is a business like any other business, trying to make a profit. Banks extend loans to customers to earn income in*

much the same way that farmers grow and sell corn to earn income. If a bank held on to its excess reserves, it would be ignoring an opportunity to earn income.

▲ Bank employees must decide what to do with the bank's excess reserves. The bank's success depends on these people being able to make good loans with the excess reserves.

What Happens After a Loan Is Granted?

So far, Alexi has been given a loan in the form of a $900 balance in a new checking account. She now goes to a retail store and buys a $900 TV set. She pays for the TV by writing out a check for $900 drawn on bank A. She hands the check to the owner of the store, Roberto.

At the end of the business day, Roberto takes the check to bank B. For simplicity's sake, we will assume that the checking account deposits in bank B equal zero. Roberto, however, changes this situation by depositing the $900 into his checking account. See entry (d) in Exhibit 10-6.

At this point, the check-clearing process (described earlier) kicks in. Bank B sends the check to its Federal Reserve district bank, which increases the balance in bank B's reserve account by $900. At the same time, the Federal Reserve bank decreases the funds in bank A's reserve account by $900. Once the Federal Reserve bank increases the balance in bank B's reserve account, total reserves for bank B rise by $900. (Total reserves = Deposits in the reserve account

Section 4 **The Money Creation Process** **301**

Reinforcement Activity

To reinforce students' understanding of how banks create money, ask them to read the explanation in the text and then go to one other source (to visit someone in a local bank or research the Internet) to ask for further information or details. Ask students to describe the process, in their own words, in one-page written reports or oral presentations.

Critical Thinking

In the numerical examples in this section, banks always create loans (new checking account deposits) equal to the amounts of excess reserves they hold. For example, if bank A has $900 in excess reserves, it will create new loans equal to $900, not less. In reality, banks may not lend every dollar of their excess reserves, but they usually come close. Why would a bank want to lend out nearly all (if not all) of its excess reserves? (*Answer:* When a bank lends money, it can charge interest. Banks try to generate interest earnings by creating loans with excess reserves.)

Economics *in the* Real World

Economic concepts can be found in surprising places—even in the languages we speak. Invite students to go to www.emcschool.net/Economics2e, select Chapter 10, and read the Economics in the Real World feature titled **"How Is the English Language Like Money?"**

After students have read this feature, ask them for reasons that companies outside the English-speaking world might be interested in hiring people who can speak English.

Teaching with Visuals

Answers will vary. Students might mention that they are more likely to communicate with someone who speaks the same language that they speak, because doing so requires less time and effort.

ANSWERS TO THINK ABOUT IT Answers will vary. Students might say that more and more people are using English.

Background Information: Lending Practices

The fine line between increasing the money supply and engaging in dangerous lending practices might have been crossed in the Great Depression. By 1934, more than 6,000 banks had stopped doing business. The shutdowns created a national crisis as depositors tried to recoup their losses and people stood in large groups outside closed banks trying to get the money they had deposited in savings and checking accounts. To control this so-called run on the banks, President Franklin D. Roosevelt declared a bank holiday on March 6, 1933. Have students research this period of banking history. Guide the class in a discussion of the role of reserve requirements and federal regulations in the banking industry.

Direct students to read the feature and express their opinions on whether or not it is better to live in a barter economy or money economy.

ANSWERS TO THINK ABOUT IT Answers will vary. Keep in mind, though, that if something other than money did have widespread acceptability, it would be money. For example, if, for some reason, sea shells had widespread acceptability – that is, they were widely accepted in exchange for goods and services – then sea shells would be money.

Discussion Starter

Students may find it difficult to understand that banks can create money simply by creating checking accounts or demand deposits for customers. Perhaps this is hard to understand because students often think of money only as currency. Remind students that checks are also money. The money supply consists of currency, plus checking accounts and traveler's checks.

 Application Activity

After reading and discussing Section 4, you may want to assign the Section Activity in the *Applying the Principles Workbook*, pages 115–117.

Assess

Quick Quiz

The following true-or-false quiz will help you assess student understanding of the material covered in this section.

1. Total reserves can be divided into required reserves and excess reserves. (True)

2. Banks are allowed to print currency. (False)

3. When banks create demand deposits, there is more money in the economy. (True)

4. The money supply consists of currency, checking accounts, and traveler's checks. (True)

5. A bank creates new loans with excess reserves. (True)

What Gives Money Value?

Consider two different monetary systems. In the first, there is paper money (say, dollar bills) that the government promises to redeem for gold. In other words, if you have, say, $500, and you want gold instead, you can take the $500 to the government and get it exchanged for so much gold.

In the second monetary system, you cannot redeem paper money for gold. In this second monetary system, there is no gold-backing for paper money.

Now in the days when there was gold-backing for paper money, sometimes people would ask: What gives paper money value? The answer always seemed to be "paper money is backed by gold." In other words, paper money had value because it was backed by gold. Almost no one asked the follow-up question, "But what gives gold value?"

Today there is no gold backing for our paper money. Our money has value because of its *widespread acceptability*. For example, you

accept the dollar bill in payment for your goods and services because you know others will accept the dollar bill in payment for their goods and services. It sounds odd, but think about it.

Suppose one day the grocery store cashier doesn't accept the paper dollars you have in your wallet as payment for the groceries you want to buy. And neither the plumber nor the gas station attendant accepts your paper dollars for fixing your kitchen drain or for gas. If this were to happen, would you be as likely to accept paper dollars in exchange for what you sell? We think not. You accept paper dollars because you know that other people will accept paper dollars when you try to spend them. Money is valued by you, and by others, because it is widely accepted in exchange for goods and services.

Let's return to our original question: What gives money value? The answer, once again, is that money has value because of its widespread acceptability – the fact that people accept money for what they want to buy and sell is what gives money value.

THINK ABOUT IT Can you think of something other than money that has widespread acceptability?

---

at the Fed + Vault cash.) Again, see entry (d) in Exhibit 10-6.

What happens to the checking account deposits at bank B? They rise to $900 too. Bank B is required to keep a percentage of the checking deposits in reserve form. If the reserve requirement is 10 percent, then $90 has to be maintained as required reserves, as in entry (e) in Exhibit 10-6. The remainder, or excess reserves ($810), can be used by bank B to extend new loans or create new checking account deposits (which are money), as in entry (f) in Exhibit 10-6. The

story continues in the same way with other banks (banks C, D, E, and so on).

A Student Asks

QUESTION: *So far in the story, bank A created a loan, then bank B created a loan, then bank C created a loan, and so on. Does this process ever stop?*

ANSWER: *Yes, it stops when the dollar amounts that banks can lend out become tiny. For example, notice that bank A created a loan of $900, but bank*

Cooperative Learning

Divide the class into two equal groups. The first person in group 1 should ask the first person in group 2 a question that relates to the information in Section 4—for example, What are total reserves? or What are excess reserves? Students should give examples to illustrate their answers. If the first person in group 2 gets the correct an-swer, that group gets one point. If not, that group neither loses nor gains a point. The process continues with the first person in group 2 asking the first person in group 1 a question, and so on. At the end of the allotted time, the side with the most points wins.

> *B created a loan of only $810, and bank C created a still smaller loan of $729. In other words, the loans become smaller and smaller. At some point, the dollar amount becomes so small that it doesn't make sense to create a loan.*

How Much Money Was Created?

So far, bank A has created $900 in new loans or checking account deposits, and bank B has created $810 in new loans or checking account deposits. If we continue by bringing in banks C, D, E, and so on, we will find that all of the banks together—that is, the entire banking system—have created $9,000 in new loans or checking account deposits (money) as a result of Fred's deposit. This dollar amount is boxed in Exhibit 10-6. This $9,000 is new money—money that did not exist before Fred snapped his fingers, created $1,000 out of thin air, and then deposited it into a checking account in bank A. The facts can be summarized as follows:

1. Fred created $1,000 in new paper currency (money) out of thin air.
2. After Fred deposited the $1,000 in bank A, the banking system as a whole created $9,000 in additional checking account deposits (money).

Thus, Fred and the banking system together created $10,000 in new money. Fred created $1,000 in currency, and the banking system created $9,000 in checking account deposits. Together, they increased the money supply by $10,000.

You can use the following simple formula to find the (maximum) change in the money supply ($10,000) brought about in the example:

> "Give me control of a nation's money and I care not who makes its laws."
> — Mayer Amschel Bauer Rothschild, eighteenth-century banker

Change in money supply = (1 ÷ Reserve requirement) × Change in reserves of first bank

In the example, the reserve requirement was set at 10 percent (0.10). The reserves of bank A, the first bank to receive the injection of funds, changed by $1,000. Put the data into the formula:

Change in the money supply =
(1 ÷ 0.10) × $1,000 = $10,000

The idea here is that $1,000 created by Fred ended up increasing the money supply by a specific multiple (in this example, the multiple is 10).

Defining Terms

1. Define:
   a. total reserves
   b. required reserves
   c. reserve requirement
   d. excess reserves

Reviewing Facts and Concepts

2. Fred creates $2,000 in currency with the snap of his fingers and deposits it in bank A. The reserve requirement is 10 percent. By how much does the money supply increase?

3. Bank A has checking account deposits of $20 million, the reserve requirement is 10 percent, vault cash equals $2 million, and deposits in the reserve account at the Fed equal $1 million. What do required reserves equal? What do excess reserves equal?

Critical Thinking

4. In recent years, the Fed has begun to pay interest on the excess reserves held by a bank. What

might this do to banks' incentive to create loans?

5. If vault cash rises, does it necessarily follow that total reserves also rise? Explain.

Applying Economic Concepts

6. Is a $100 check money? Explain.

Defining Terms

1. a. total reserves: the sum of a bank's deposits in its reserve account at the Fed and its vault cash; **b. required reserves:** the minimum amount of reserves a bank must hold against its deposits, as mandated by the Fed; **c. reserve requirement:** the regulation that requires a bank to keep a certain percentage of its deposits in its reserve account at the Fed or in its vault as vault cash; **d. excess reserves:** any reserves held beyond the required amount.

Reviewing Facts and Concepts

2. $20,000 (*calculation:* Change in the money supply = 1 ÷ 0.10 × $2,000 = $20,000).

3. Required reserves = required reserve requirement × checking account deposits = 0.10 × $20 million = $2 million. Excess reserves = Total reserves − required reserves = $3 million − $2 million = $1 million

Critical Thinking

4. Paying interest on excess reserves diminishes the incentive for banks to create loans, especially if the rates on loans are not much higher than the rate on excess reserves.

5. No. Total reserves = deposits in the reserve account at the Fed + vault cash. A bank can lower its reserve deposits and increase its vault cash by the same amount, leaving total reserves unchanged.

Applying Economic Concepts

6. Yes. Money is anything that is widely accepted for purposes of exchange and in the repayment of debt. Checks are widely accepted for purposes of exchange (you can use a check to buy a TV, a computer, or groceries) and in the repayment of debt; therefore, checks are money.

Reteaching Activity

Use the Section Assessment to gauge which students may need reteaching on this section. Write these terms on the board: "total reserves," "required reserves," and "excess reserves." Assign students to work with partners to define each term. Then reread the material on the money creation process to these students, having them supply their definitions each time one of these words is used.

Guided Reading

For further reteaching of the key concepts in this section, assign the Outlining Activity and the Just the Facts Handout from the *Guided Reading and Study Guide*, pages 162–165.

Teacher Support

Fed Tools for Changing the Money Supply

Focus and Motivate

Section Objectives

After completing this section, students will be able to

► describe how a change in the reserve requirement changes the money supply;

► explain how an open market operation changes the money supply; and

► explain how a change in the discount rate changes the money supply.

Activating Prior Knowledge

At the beginning of class, ask students to write answers to the following question: What do you think the term *monetary policy* means? Allow time for students to share their answers. Explain that in this section, students will learn that the term *monetary policy* refers to the deliberate control of the money supply by the Fed.

 Visit econ.myemcp.com/videos for videos that will help students better understand the key concepts found in this section.

Focus Questions

► How does a change in the reserve requirement change the money supply?

► How does an open market operation change the money supply?

► How does a change in the discount rate change the money supply?

Key Terms

open market operations
federal funds rate
discount rate
federal funds rate target

Changing the Reserve Requirement

Think of the Fed as having three "buttons" to push. Every time it pushes one of the buttons, it either raises or lowers the money supply.

The first button is the reserve requirement button. To understand how a change in the reserve requirement can change the money supply, let's consider three cases. In each case, the money supply is initially zero, and $1,000 is created out of thin air. The difference in the three cases is the reserve requirement, which is 5 percent in the first case, 10 percent in the second, and 20 percent in the third. Let's calculate the change in the money supply in each of the three cases. For these calculations, we will use the formula you learned in the last section:

$$\text{Change in money supply} = (1 \div \text{Reserve requirement}) \times \text{Change in reserves of first bank}$$

Case 1: (Reserve requirement = 5%); Change in money supply = $(1 \div 0.05) \times \$1,000 = \$20,000$

Case 2: (Reserve requirement = 10%); Change in money supply = $(1 \div 0.10) \times \$1,000 = \$10,000$

Case 3: (Reserve requirement = 20%); Change in money supply = $(1 \div 0.20) \times \$1,000 = \$5,000$

Note that the money supply is largest ($20,000) when the reserve requirement is 5 percent and smallest ($5,000) when the reserve requirement is 20 percent. You can see that the smaller the reserve requirement, the bigger the change in the money supply. So, what happens to the money supply if the reserve requirement is lowered? Obviously, the money supply must rise. What happens to the money supply if the reserve requirement is raised? Obviously, the money supply must fall.

Thus, the Fed can increase or decrease the money supply by changing the reserve requirement. If the Fed decreases the reserve requirement, the money supply increases; if the Fed increases the reserve requirement, the money supply decreases:

Lower reserve requirement → Money supply rises
Raise reserve requirement → Money supply falls

304 Chapter 10 Money, Banking, and the Federal Reserve System

Cooperative Learning

Divide students into an even number of groups of four or five. Ask half of the groups to find a reason for the Fed to increase the money supply, and ask the other half to find a reason for the Fed to decrease the money supply. Have each group develop a role-play that demonstrates its reasoning and decision. Discuss the possible economic conditions of these actions. Challenge students to determine the current economic conditions, and ask them if they think the Fed should increase, decrease, or maintain the money supply. Students should justify their answers with logic and reasoning.

QUESTION: *Why would the Fed want to increase or decrease the money supply? Why not simply leave the money supply alone?*

ANSWER: *You are asking a question about monetary policy, a topic we will discuss more fully in a later chapter. For now, though, let's just say that the Fed may increase or decrease the money supply to deal with some economic problem. For example, if businesses are not doing well and the unemployment rate is rising, the Fed might increase the money supply to stimulate consumer spending.*

Open Market Operations

The second "button" the Fed can push to change the money supply is the open market operations button. Remember that earlier we mentioned an important committee in the Federal Reserve System: the Federal Open Market Committee (FOMC). This committee of 12 members conducts **open market operations**, which are simply the buying and selling of government securities by the Fed. Before we discuss open market operations in detail, we need to provide some background information that relates to government securities and the U.S. Treasury.

The U.S. Treasury is an agency of the U.S. government. The Treasury's job is to collect the taxes and borrow the money needed to run the government. Suppose the U.S. Congress decides to spend $1,800 billion on various federal government programs. The U.S. Treasury has to pay the bills. It notices that it collected only $1,700 billion in taxes, which is $100 billion less than Congress wants to spend. It is the Treasury's job to borrow the $100 billion from the public. To borrow this money, the Treasury issues or sells government (or Treasury) securities to members of the public. A government security (or bond) is no more than a piece of paper promising to pay a certain dollar amount of money in the future; think of it as an IOU statement.

The Fed (which is different from the Treasury) may buy government securities from any member of the public or sell securities to the public. When the Fed buys a government security, it is said to be conducting an *open market purchase*. When it sells a government security, it is said to be conducting an *open market sale*. These operations affect the money supply.

Open Market Purchases

Let's say that you own a government security, which the Fed offers to purchase for $10,000. You agree to sell your security to the Fed. You hand it over, and in return, you receive a check for $10,000.

It's important to realize where the Fed gets this $10,000. It gets the money out of thin air. Remember Fred, who could snap his fingers and create a $1,000 bill out of thin air? Obviously, no individual has this power, but the Fed does—it can create money out of thin air.

How does the Fed create money out of thin air? Think about the answer in this way: You have a checking account, and the Fed has a checking account. Each account has a certain balance (amount in the account). The Fed can take a pencil and increase the balance in its account at will—legally. You, on the other hand, cannot. If you pencil in a new balance and then write a check for an amount you don't have in your checking account, your check will bounce and you will have to pay the bank a penalty. Fed checks do not bounce. The Fed can and does create money at will out of thin air.

Let's return to the example of an open market purchase. Once you have the $10,000 check from the Fed, you take it to your local bank and deposit it in your checking account. The total dollar amount of checking account deposits in the economy is now $10,000 more than before the Fed purchased your government security.

open market operations
Buying and selling of government securities by the Fed.

▼ This person at the Chicago Board of Trade is buying and selling U.S. Treasury bonds. Why does the U.S. Treasury issue bonds?

Teach

Discussion Starter

Ask students if they know how the Fed controls the money supply. Ensure that they know that the Fed can do this in one of three ways: by changing the reserve requirement, by conducting open market operations, or by changing the discount rate. All three ways are discussed in this section. Open market operations is the tool most commonly used by the Fed to change the money supply. Changing the discount rate and changing the reserve requirement are used less often. Remind students that the Federal Open Market Committee (FOMC) is the committee that conducts open market operations.

Economics Around the Clock

Direct students to reread the 8:15 a.m. scenario in Economics Around the Clock (page 277) and then write their answers to its question.

Allow students to share their answers with the class. Ensure that they know that the FOMC buys and sells government securities. Ask why they think secrecy is so important for the committee's meeting.

Teaching with Visuals

The U.S. Treasury issues bonds to raise revenue for the federal government.

▲ The Federal Reserve Bank of Chicago. **What are some of the functions this bank performs for the commercial banks in its district?**

federal funds rate
The interest rate one bank charges another for a loan.

discount rate
The interest rate the Fed charges a bank for a loan.

Because no other component of the money supply (not currency or traveler's checks) is less, the overall money supply has increased:

Open market purchase → Money supply rises

Open Market Sales

Suppose the Fed has a government security that it offers to sell you for $10,000. You agree to buy the security. You write out a check to the Fed for $10,000 and give it to the Fed. The Fed, in return, turns the government security over to you. Next, the check is cleared, and a sum of $10,000 is removed from your account in your bank and transferred to the Fed. Once this sum is in the Fed's possession, it is removed from the economy altogether. It disappears from the face of the earth. As you might have guessed, the Fed also has the power to make money disappear into thin air.

The total dollar amount of checking account deposits is less than before the Fed sold you a government security. An open market sale reduces the money supply:

Open market sale → Money supply falls

Changing the Discount Rate

The third "button" the Fed can push to change the money supply is the discount rate button. Suppose bank A wants to borrow $1 million. It can borrow this dollar amount from another bank (say, bank B), or it can borrow the money from the Fed. If bank A borrows the money from bank B, bank B will charge an interest rate for the $1 million loan. The interest rate charged by bank B is called the **federal funds rate**. If bank A borrows the $1 million from the Fed, the Fed will charge an interest rate called the *primary credit rate* or the **discount rate**.

Whether bank A borrows from bank B or from the Fed depends on the relationship between the federal funds rate and the discount rate. If the federal funds rate is lower than the discount rate, bank A will borrow from bank B instead of from the Fed. (Why pay a higher interest rate if you don't have to?) If, however, the discount rate is lower than the federal funds rate, bank A will probably borrow from the Fed.

Whether bank A borrows from bank B or from the Fed has important consequences. If bank A borrows from bank B, no new money will enter the economy. Bank B will simply have $1 million less, and bank A will have $1 million more; the total won't change. If, however, bank A borrows from the Fed, the Fed will create new money in the process of granting the loan. Here is how it works: the bank asks for a loan, and the Fed grants it by depositing the funds (created out of thin air) into the reserve account of the bank. Suppose the bank has $4 million in its reserve account when it asks the Fed for a $1 million loan. The Fed will simply change the reserve account balance to $5 million.

If the Fed lowers its discount rate so that it's lower than the federal funds rate and if banks then borrow from the Fed, the money supply will increase:

Lower the discount rate → Money supply rises

If the Fed raises its discount rate so that it's higher than the federal funds rate, banks will begin to borrow from each other rather than from the Fed. At some point, though, the banks must repay the funds they borrowed from the Fed in the past (say, funds they borrowed many months ago), when the discount rate was lower. When the banks repay these loans, money is removed from the economy and the money supply drops. We conclude that if the Fed raises its discount rate relative to the federal funds rate, the money supply will eventually fall:

Raise the discount rate → Money supply falls

See Exhibit 10-7 for a review of how these tools affect the money supply.

In October 2008, the United States was in the midst of a financial crisis. Much of the crisis had to do with the worsening condition in which banks found themselves. To understand what was happening, we first need to note that banks have assets and liabilities.

Recall that *assets* are things a bank owns that generate income for it. For example, a loan that a bank gives to Smith is an asset for the bank. When Smith makes monthly payments on the loan, the bank receives a certain income. *Liabilities* are what a bank owes. For example, if you have a checking account with a bank, that account is a liability for the bank. The bank owes you the money from that account when you ask for it.

For a bank to be profitable, its assets must be greater than its liabilities. In October 2008, some banks found their assets declining in value. This occurred partly because many banks had made loans in the real estate market and some of those loans were not being repaid. As the banks' assets dropped in value, the banks became less profitable—and they also fell dangerously close to the point where their liabilities would become greater than their assets. When a bank reaches that point, it can go out of business.

To stay in business, banks started cutting back on their lending activity. They did so largely because they thought that in the current economy, the money they did lend wasn't as likely to be repaid. The Fed saw the banks cutting back on lending and reasoned that this action could lead to a decline in consumer and business spending—which could lead to fewer consumer

EXHIBIT 10-7 Fed Monetary Tools and Their Effects on the Money Supply

Fed monetary tool	Money supply
Open market operation	
Buys government securities	Increases
Sells government securities	Decreases
Reserve requirement	
Raises reserve requirement	Decreases
Lowers reserve requirement	Increases
Discount rate	
Raises discount rate (relative to the federal funds rate)	Decreases
Lowers discount rate (relative to the federal funds rate)	Increases
Federal funds rate target	
Sets federal funds rate target below the actual federal funds rate	Increases
Sets federal funds rate target above the actual federal funds rate	Decreases

▲ This table summarizes the ways in which the Fed can change the money supply.

purchases, lower output production, higher unemployment, and a general decline in economic activity.

In an attempt to keep all this from happening, the Fed started to increase reserves in the banking system, hoping that banks would use the extra reserves to make loans. The banks did make some loans with the new reserves, but not as many as the Fed had wanted.

The Federal Funds Rate Target

We know that the federal funds rate is the interest rate one bank charges another bank for a loan. What the second bank lends to the first bank is the second bank's reserves. Now recall what reserves are: bank deposits at the Fed plus vault cash. We can conclude the following: (1) If the federal funds rate is the interest rate one bank charges another bank for a loan and (2) what banks lend each other is their reserves, then it follows that (3) the federal funds rate is the interest rate one bank charges another bank for a certain dollar amount of reserves. Think of it this way: Bank A calls up bank B and says, "We would like to borrow $10 million in reserves. What is the federal funds rate you will charge for this loan?" Bank B answers, "We will charge a federal funds rate of 5 percent."

After students have studied Exhibit 10-7, ask them to use the Internet to find out which two of the various monetary tools are most often used by the Fed today.

The answer is open market operations and the federal funds rate target.

After students have read the caption on this page, invite them to do additional research on the components that make up a dollar bill. Ask, What do all of the different numbers, phrases, and symbols mean on a dollar bill?

▲ On dollar bills, you will find a Federal Reserve emblem.

federal funds rate target
The rate the Fed would like the federal funds rate to be.

One of the ways the Fed can change the money supply is to set the federal funds rate target. **The federal funds rate target** is exactly what it sounds like: it is the rate the Fed would like the federal funds rate to be. To illustrate, suppose the actual federal funds rate is 4 percent and the Fed would like it to be 2 percent. Well, then, 2 percent is the federal funds rate target.

If the actual federal funds rate is 4 percent and the federal funds rate target is 2 percent, what can the Fed do to get the 4 percent rate down to 2 percent? It can conduct an open market purchase. Specifically, it can purchase government securities from banks. As the banks turn over the securities to the Fed, they receive increases in reserves. In other words, the Fed adds to the deposits in the banks' reserve accounts.

With a greater supply of reserves in the banking system, the interest rate one bank has to pay another bank to borrow reserves will drop. In our example, the actual federal funds rate will eventually drop from 4 percent to 3 percent. The Fed will keep buying government securities until the federal funds rate falls to the target rate of 2 percent.

Will lowering the actual federal funds rate to the target rate affect the money supply? Yes, because to lower the federal funds rate to the target rate, the Fed has to conduct an open market purchase and, as we discussed earlier, an open market purchase leads to a rise in the money supply:

Set the federal funds rate target below the actual federal funds rate → Conduct an open market purchase → Money supply rises

Now suppose the Fed sets the federal funds rate target above the actual federal funds rate. To illustrate, say the actual federal funds rate is 4 percent and the target rate is 6 percent. To raise the rate, the Fed can conduct an open market sale, or sell government securities to banks. As the banks pay for these government securities, the balances in their reserve accounts will decline; thus, they will have fewer reserves. When the supply of reserves in the banking system falls, the federal funds rate rises.

What will happen to the money supply in this scenario? Since the Fed had to conduct an open market sale to get the federal funds rate to rise to its target rate, the money supply will fall:

Set the federal funds rate target above the actual federal funds rate → Conduct an open market sale → Money supply falls

The Discretion of the Fed

The Fed has the power today to increase and decrease the money supply of the country by any amount, even a large amount. If the Fed wanted, it could increase the money supply by 10 percent, 20 percent, or more. In short, the Fed has discretionary power to change the money supply

Some economists argue that this kind of power can be abused. It would be better, they say, if the Fed had to abide by some monetary rule. Consider this rule: the Fed cannot increase the money supply by more than 3 percent a year. Or this rule: the Fed cannot increase the money supply by more than the annual increase in the output that is produced in the country. For example, if the output (of goods and services) rises by 3 percent in a given year, then the Fed can increase the money supply by 3 percent—but no more.

Background Information: Preventing Counterfeit Bills

In 2013, the Federal Reserve began circulating new $100 bills that include more security features: a blue 3D security ribbon (containing images of bells and 100s) and a color-changing bell in an inkwell. These features are meant to help deter counterfeit bills and to help the average consumer recognize a counterfeit bill.

The redesign was created in partnership by the Federal Reserve, U.S. Department of the Treasury, U.S. Bureau of Engraving and Printing, and the U.S. Secret Service. For more information go to: http://econ.emcp.net/newmoney.

There are two reasons that some (but certainly not all) economists think a monetary rule should be followed to limit the Fed's power. The first reason has to do with politics. Some economists argue that without a rule, the Fed is subject to politics. That is, if politicians want the money supply to rise by some large percentage, then the Fed might fall in line and do the bidding of the politicians. In this case, politics, not sound economic theory or policy, might dictate increases and decreases in the money supply.

The second reason some economists advocate using a monetary rule is that they believe a monetary rule can be more effective than the Fed's discretionary power. They argue that we would get better economic performance—better economic growth, more stable prices, less variation in unemployment rates—if the Fed followed a solid monetary rule rather than decided what the money supply should be at any time.

A Gold Standard

Sometimes, people who advocate using a monetary rule, rather than allowing the Fed full discretion, mention a gold standard as a kind of monetary rule. We do not have a gold standard today in the United States. Furthermore, our paper money is not backed by gold. But if we did decide to use a gold standard, how might it work?

There are different varieties of gold standards, but here is how one particular gold standard might work. First, the government pegs (sets) the price of gold at some dollar amount, which becomes the official price of gold. Many proponents of a gold standard say that the official price of gold should be pegged at the current price of gold. Let's say that price is $1,000 an ounce.

Second, the government promises to buy and sell gold at the official or pegged price. Suppose that after the government pegs the price of gold at $1,000, months pass and the market price of gold rises to $1,100. Now, people can buy gold from the government for $1,000 and sell it in the gold market for $1,100.

As people buy gold from the government, they reduce either the amounts of cash they have or the dollar balances in their checking accounts. Since the M1 money supply is currency plus checking accounts plus traveler's checks, the money supply declines. As the money supply declines, there is less demand in the economy for goods and services, so the prices of goods and services decline. One of the prices that declines is the price of gold. The price of gold falls because as people buy gold from the government and sell it on the market, the market supply of gold rises. (Recall that as the supply of a good rises, its price falls.) The process stops when the market price of gold (which, when we left it last, was $1,100) has fallen by enough to equal the official, pegged price of gold (which is $1,000).

Now, let's reverse things. Suppose the market price of gold falls to $900 and the official, pegged price of gold is $1,000.

▲ On a gold standard, the monetary authority of the country stands ready to buy and sell gold at an official or pegged price.

Discussion Starter

Ask students how close we ever get to imposing some kind of control over the Fed and how a monetary rule might be put in place. Is this something the president might mandate, or would Congress decide?

Teaching with Visuals

If there is a sudden and rapid increase in the supply of gold, the price of gold will decline.

Assess

Quick Quiz

The following true-or-false quiz will help you assess student understanding of the material covered in this section.

1. The FOMC conducts open market operations, buying and selling government securities. (True)
2. When the Fed buys and sells government securities, it does not affect the money supply. (False)
3. The Fed and the Treasury are actually the same governmental department. (False)
4. An open market sale reduces the money supply. (True)
5. If bank A borrows money from the Fed, the interest rate is called the *federal funds rate*. (False)

Assessment Book

You will find a quiz for this section in the *Assessment Book*, page 99.

Application Activity

After reading and discussing Section 5, you may want to assign the Section Activity in the *Applying the Principles Workbook*, pages 118–119.

▲ If there is a sudden and rapid increase in the supply of gold, what will happen to the market price of gold?

What do people do now? They buy gold in the market for $900 and sell it to the government for $1,000. (Remember, the government has promised to buy and sell gold at $1,000.)

What happens when people sell gold to the government and thus reduce the amount of gold on the market? Two things happen. First, the government issues new money to pay the people for the gold. This action increases the money supply. We can then expect the demand for goods and services in the economy to rise, thus raising their prices. Second, because people have taken gold from the market and sold it to the government, the market supply of gold falls and the market price of gold rises. The process stops when the market price of gold (which, when we started, was $900) rises to equal the official, pegged price of gold ($1,000).

Notice that in both scenarios—the first, in which people bought gold from the government and the second, in which they sold gold to the government—the price of gold and the prices of other goods and services fall and rise together. In other words, as the market price of gold goes up and down, so do the prices of other goods and services. It's as if the market price of gold and the prices of other goods and services are tracking each other. If this is always the case, then the gold standard automatically stabilizes (pegs) the general price level (or the average price of all other goods and services).

This is often claimed to be a major advantage of a gold standard: it stabilizes prices. Stated differently, the gold standard stabilizes the value of the dollar in terms of what a dollar can purchase.

Critics of a gold standard often argue that the price-stabilizing effect of the gold standard will be upset if there is a major gold discovery. How so? Suppose a major gold discovery increases the supply of gold on the gold market, thus reducing the price of gold to $700. People will buy a lot of gold in the market and sell it to the government for $1,000. The government will have to create a lot of new money to buy the gold. This will lead to a large rise in the money supply and thus to a substantial increase in the prices of goods and services.

How do proponents of a gold standard respond to such critics? They often argue that major discoveries of gold are uncommon. Although it's possible that a major gold discovery may occur, it isn't likely.

Cooperative Learning

After reading "A Gold Standard," divide students into groups of four to five students. Assign half of the groups the position of supporting the gold standard and the other half the position of opposing the gold standard. Instruct each group to investigate and find evidence that supports their assigned view. Then hold a class debate on the issue.

◀ The United States Federal Reserve Building located in Washington, D.C.

Reteaching Activity

Use the Section Assessment to gauge which students may need reteaching on this section. Ask students to look at Exhibit 10-7 on page 307. As students review the ways the Fed can increase or decrease the money supply, invite them to explain some of these processes in greater detail.

Guided Reading

For further reteaching of the key concepts in this section, assign the Outlining Activity and the Just the Facts Handout in the *Guided Reading and Study Guide*, pages 166–169.

SECTION 5 ASSESSMENT

Defining Terms

1. Define:
   a. open market operations
   b. federal funds rate
   c. discount rate
   d. federal funds rate target

Reviewing Facts and Concepts

2. The Fed wants to increase the money supply:
   a. What can it do to the reserve requirement?
   b. What type of open market operation can it conduct?
   c. What can it do to the discount rate?

3. Suppose the Fed conducts an open market sale. Does the money for which it sells the government securities stay in the economy? Explain your answer.

Critical Thinking

4. When the Fed conducts an open market purchase, it buys government securities. As a result, the money supply rises. Could the Fed raise the money supply by buying something other than government securities? For example, if the Fed bought apples instead of government securities, would the apple purchases raise the money supply? Explain.

5. Suppose the Fed wants to undo an open market purchase. How can it do this?

Applying Economic Concepts

6. If the Fed sets the federal funds rate target below the actual federal funds rate, what must it do to move the actual federal funds rate down to the target level? Explain.

7. Could the Fed make the money supply rise by a ridiculously high percentage—say, 1 million percent? Explain.

SECTION 5 ASSESSMENT ANSWERS

Defining Terms

1. a. open market operations: buying and selling of government securities by the Fed; **b. federal funds rate:** the interest rate one bank charges another bank for a loan; **c. discount rate:** the interest rate the Fed charges a bank for a loan; **d. federal funds rate target:** the rate the Fed would like the federal funds rate to be.

Reviewing Facts and Concepts

2. a. lower the reserve requirement; **b.** an open market purchase; **c.** lower the discount rate relative to the federal funds rate. **3.** No. When the Fed sells a government security, it collects the funds from the purchaser and removes those funds from the economy. It is as if the funds do not exist. They are not in anyone's checking account, they do not belong to any bank, and no one has ownership over them. For all practical purposes, the funds have disappeared.

Critical Thinking

4. Apple purchases by the Fed would increase the money supply. The Fed buys whatever it buys with money created out of thin air. It simply changes the balance in its account to whatever dollar amount it wants. **5.** An open market purchase leads to an increase in the money supply. To undo the increase, the Fed can conduct an open market sale, raise the reserve requirement, or raise the discount rate.

Applying Economic Concepts

6. It must buy government securities from banks, thus increasing reserves in the banking system. Having greater reserves will lower the federal funds rate. **7.** Yes. Nothing was said in the chapter to indicate that there is a limit to how much money the Fed can create. How does the Fed raise the money supply? By lowering the reserve requirement, lowering the discount rate, or conducting an open market purchase.

Assessment Answers

Economics Vocabulary

1. barter economy; **2.** medium of exchange; **3.** fractional reserve banking; **4.** money supply; **5.** open market operation; **6.** Board of Governors; **7.** excess reserves; **8.** Required reserves; **9.** federal funds rate; **10.** discount rate.

Understanding the Main Ideas

1. In this case, money is functioning principally as a medium of exchange.

2. In a barter economy, goods were traded for goods, services were traded for services, and so on. To try to make their daily trading easier, individuals began to accept the good that was more acceptable than other goods. As some people did this, others began to do this as well, until the good was widely accepted for purposes of exchange. At this point, it was considered money.

3. The funds in the checking account belong to the owner and can be obtained on demand.

4. Currency consists of paper money and coins.

5. The check-clearing process is shown in Exhibit 10-4, page 296.

6. Boston, New York City, Philadelphia, Cleveland, Richmond, Atlanta, Chicago, St. Louis, Minneapolis, Kansas City, Dallas, and San Francisco.

7. a. Total reserves = deposits in the reserve account at the Fed + vault cash; **b.** Required reserves = reserve requirement × checking account deposits; **c.** Excess reserves = total reserves – required reserves.

8. The obligation of a borrower is to repay the loan amount with interest.

9. (a), (c), and (e).

10. To understand what this means, consider the following scenario: Bank A has a reserve account with the Fed. The balance in the account is $10 million. Next, the Fed buys government securities worth $2 million from bank A. Bank A turns over the securities to the Fed, and the Fed must now pay

Chapter Summary

Section 1

▶ Transaction costs are high in a barter economy.
▶ Money is any good that is generally accepted in exchange and in repayment of debts.
▶ The value of money comes from its general acceptability in exchange.
▶ Money has three major functions: a medium of exchange, a unit of account, and a store of value.
▶ Early bankers were goldsmiths.

Section 2

▶ M1 ("M-one"), the most basic money supply, consists of currency, checking accounts, and traveler's checks.
▶ Currency is coins and paper money (or Federal Reserve notes).
▶ Checking accounts funds can be deposited and then withdrawn by writing checks.
▶ Traveler's checks are issued by banks in specific denominations and sold to travelers.
▶ M2 is a broader measure of the money supply, including everything in M1 plus savings deposits, small-denomination time deposits, MMDAs, and retail MMMFs.
▶ Credit cards are not money.

Section 3

▶ As a central bank, the Federal Reserve System is the chief monetary authority in the country.
▶ The Federal Reserve's main activities include the following: control the money supply, supply paper money, hold bank reserves, provide check-clearing services, supervise member banks, and act as lender of last resort.

Section 4

▶ A bank's total reserves can be divided into two types: required and excess reserves.
▶ Excess reserves are used to make loans.
▶ Banks create money by making loans.

Section 5

▶ The Fed can change the money supply by changing the reserve requirement, conducting open market operations, changing the discount rate, or changing the federal funds rate target.

Economics Vocabulary

To reinforce your knowledge of the key terms in this chapter, fill in each of the following blanks on a separate piece of paper with the appropriate word or phrase.

1. A(n) _____ is an economy in which trades are made in terms of goods and services instead of money.
2. Anything that is generally accepted in exchange for goods and services is a(n) _____.
3. A banking arrangement in which banks hold only a fraction of the deposits and lend out the remainder is referred to as _____.
4. The _____ is composed of currency, checking accounts, and traveler's checks.
5. When the Fed buys or sells government securities, it is conducting a(n) _____.
6. The governing body of the Federal Reserve System is the _____.
7. Total reserves minus required reserves equals _____.
8. _____ are the minimum amount of reserves a bank must hold against its checking account deposits, as mandated by the Fed.
9. The interest rate that one bank charges another bank for a loan is called the _____.
10. The interest rate that the Fed charges a bank for a loan is called the _____.

Understanding the Main Ideas

Review the main ideas in this chapter by writing answers to the following questions on a separate sheet of paper.

1. Suppose a person goes into a store and buys a pair of shoes with money. Is money functioning principally as a medium of exchange, a store of value, or a unit of account?
2. Explain how money emerged out of a barter economy.
3. Why is a checking account sometimes called a *demand deposit*?
4. What is currency?
5. Explain how a check clears. Illustrate this process using two banks in the Federal Reserve district in which you live.
6. List the locations of the 12 Federal Reserve district banks.

the bank. How does the Fed pay the bank? It simply goes to the reserve account of the bank and changes the balance to $12 million ($2 million more than previously existed). Where did the Fed get the $2 million it deposited into the bank's reserve account? Out of thin air.

11. The Fed buys government securities and pays for them by creating money out of thin air. (See the answer to question 10 for an explana-

tion of what this means.) Doing so increases the reserves of banks, which means they have excess reserves that they loan out. As they create new loans, they create new checking account deposits, and those deposits are money.

12. As the reserve requirement is lowered, the money supply increases; as the reserve requirement is increased, the money supply decreases.

7. State what each of the following equals:
   a. total reserves
   b. required reserves
   c. excess reserves
8. Explain the obligations of a borrower.
9. Determine which of the following Fed actions will increase the money supply: (a) lowering the reserve requirement, (b) raising the reserve requirement, (c) conducting an open market purchase, (d) conducting an open market sale, (e) lowering the discount rate relative to the federal funds rate, (f) raising the discount rate relative to the federal funds rate.
10. What do we mean when we say that the Fed can create money "out of thin air"?
11. Explain how an open market purchase increases the money supply.
12. How is the reserve requirement related to changes in the money supply?
13. Suppose the Fed sets the discount rate much higher than the existing federal funds rate. What message is the Fed sending to banks?
14. If the Fed sets the federal funds rate target below the actual federal funds rate, is the Fed trying to increase or decrease the money supply? Explain.

Doing the Math

1. A tiny economy has the following money in circulation: 25 dimes, 10 nickels, 100 one-dollar bills, 200 five-dollar bills, and 40 twenty-dollar bills. In addition, traveler's checks equal $500, balances in checking accounts equal $1,900, and balances in savings accounts equal $2,200. What is the money supply? Explain your answer.
2. A bank has $100 million in its reserve account at the Fed and $10 million in vault cash. The reserve requirement is 10 percent. What do total reserves equal?
3. The Fed conducts an open market purchase and increases the reserves of bank A by $2 million. The reserve requirement is 20 percent. By how much does the money supply increase?

Working with Graphs and Tables

1. In Exhibit 10-8, fill in the blanks (a), (b), and (c).

EXHIBIT 10-8

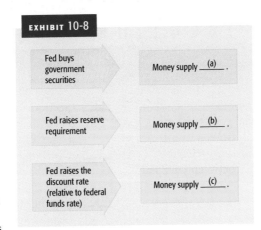

Fed buys government securities	→	Money supply ___(a)___ .
Fed raises reserve requirement	→	Money supply ___(b)___ .
Fed raises the discount rate (relative to federal funds rate)	→	Money supply ___(c)___ .

Solving Economic Problems

1. **Identify Cause and Effect.** In year 1, reserves equal $100 billion and the money supply equals $1,000 billion. In year 2, reserves equal $120 billion and the money supply equals $1,200 billion. Did the greater money supply in year 2 cause the higher dollar amount of reserves, or did the higher dollar amount of reserves cause the greater money supply? Explain.
2. **Identify Cause and Effect.** WRITING Write a one-page paper about something you enjoy that would not exist in a barter economy. Explain why it would not exist.
3. **Synthesize.** Can a country operate without a central bank, such as the Fed? Explain.

Project or Presentation

Illustrated History of the Fed. Go to http://econ.emcp.net/fedhistory and read the history of the Fed. Create a detailed time line of your findings, including illustrations and examples.

ONLINE
emcp.com

Practice Tests and Study Guide

Go to **www.emcschool.net/Economics2e** and choose *Economics: New Ways of Thinking*, Chapter 10, if you need more help in preparing for the chapter test.

---

2. $110 million (*calculation:* Total reserves = deposits in the reserve account at the Fed + vault cash = $100 million + $10 million = $110 million).
3. $10 million (*calculation:* Change in money supply = (1 ÷ reserve requirement) × change in reserves of first bank = (1 ÷ 0.20) × $2 million = 5 × $2 million = $10 million).

Working with Graphs and Tables

1. (a) rises or increases; (b) falls or decreases; (c) falls or decreases.

Solving Economic Problems

1. The higher dollar amount of reserves caused the greater money supply. Here is how it works: The Fed does something to increase reserves in the banking system (say, it undertakes an open market purchase). With more reserves, banks end up with greater excess reserves. With greater excess reserves, they can offer more loans. More loans mean more checking account deposits, and more checking account deposits mean more money.
2. Each student will write a one-page paper about something he or she enjoys that would not exist in a barter economy. The paper should explain why the item would not exist.
3. Yes. The United States operated without a central bank until 1914, when the Fed was established.

Project or Presentation

Dates and events should match the history outlined on the website. You might want to assign this as a group or class project and have students on a mural-size time line or an electronic presentation of the history.

---

13. The Fed is sending the message that it does not want to increase the money supply.
14. The Fed is trying to increase the money supply. By setting the target rate below the actual rate, the Fed wants the actual rate to decline. To achieve this, the Fed will conduct an open market purchase, thus increasing reserves in the banking system and lowering the actual federal funds rate.

Doing the Math

1. The money supply, as defined in the text, is equal to currency plus checking accounts plus traveler's checks. In this problem, currency equals $1,903, checking account balances equal $1,900, and traveler's checks equal $500. It follows that the money supply equals the sum of these dollar amounts, or $4,303.

Chapter 11 Planning Guide

SECTION ORGANIZER

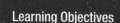

	Learning Objectives	Reproducible Worksheets and Handouts	Assessment
SECTION 1 **National Income Accounting** (pages 316–320)	▶ Define GDP. ▶ Explain why only final goods and services are computed in GDP. ▶ Identify what is omitted from GDP. ▶ Explain the difference between GDP and GNP.	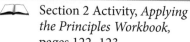Section 1 Activity, *Applying the Principles Workbook*, pages 120–121 Outlining Activity, *Guided Reading and Study Guide*, page 180 Just the Facts Handout, *Guided Reading and Study, Guide*, pages 181–182	✔ Section Assessment, *Student Text*, page 320 ✔ Quick Quiz, *Annotated Teacher's Edition*, page 319 ✔ Section Quiz, *Assessment Book*, page 107
SECTION 2 **Measuring GDP** (pages 321–326)	▶ Identify the four sectors of the economy. ▶ Describe consumption, investment, government purchases, export spending, and import spending. ▶ Explain how GDP is measured. ▶ Define per capita GDP.	Section 2 Activity, *Applying the Principles Workbook*, pages 122–123 Outlining Activity, *Guided Reading and Study Guide*, pages 183–184 Just the Facts Handout, *Guided Reading and Study Guide*, pages 185–186	✔ Section Assessment, *Student Text*, page 326 ✔ Quick Quiz, *Annotated Teacher's Edition*, page 325 ✔ Section Quiz, *Assessment Book*, page 108
SECTION 3 **Real GDP** (pages 327–330)	▶ Identify the two variables involved in calculating GDP. ▶ Explain whether we would automatically know why GDP is higher in one year than another. ▶ Describe the difference between GDP and real GDP. ▶ Explain how economists go about computing real GDP.	Section 3 Activity, *Applying the Principles Workbook*, page 124 Outlining Activity, *Guided Reading and Study Guide*, page 187 Just the Facts Handout, *Guided Reading and Study Guide*, page 188	✔ Section Assessment, *Student Text*, page 330 ✔ Quick Quiz, *Annotated Teacher's Edition*, page 329 ✔ Section Quiz, *Assessment Book*, page 109
SECTION 4 **Measuring Price Changes and the Unemployment Rate** (pages 331–337)	▶ Explain what the consumer price index is and how it is calculated. ▶ Distinguish between an aggregate demand curve and an aggregate supply curve. ▶ Explain how the employment rate and unemployment rate are calculated.	Section 4 Activity, *Applying the Principles Workbook*, pages 125–127 Outlining Activity, *Guided Reading and Study Guide*, pages 189–191 Just the Facts Handout, *Guided Reading and Study Guide*, pages 192–193	✔ Section Assessment, *Student Text*, page 337 ✔ Quick Quiz, *Annotated Teacher's Edition*, page 336 ✔ Section Quiz, *Assessment Book*, page 110

Reproducible Chapter Resources and Assessment Materials

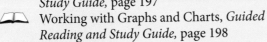
Graphic Organizer Activity, *Guided Reading and Study Guide*, pages 194–196

Vocabulary Activity, *Guided Reading and Study Guide*, page 197

Working with Graphs and Charts, *Guided Reading and Study Guide*, page 198

Practice Test, *Guided Reading and Study Guide*, pages 199–201

Critical Thinking Activity, *Finding Economics*, pages 29–31

Chapter Test A, *Assessment Book*, pages 111–114

Chapter Test B, *Assessment Book*, pages 115–118

Student Text Internet Links

Economics: New Ways of Thinking, Second Edition encourages students to use the Internet to find out more about economics. Given the wealth of current, valid information available on websites, students should be encouraged to use the Internet as a research tool. Doing so will likely increase students' interest in and understanding of economics principles and topics. In addition, doing Internet research can help your students form the habit of accessing and using economics information, as well as help them develop investigative skills they will use throughout their educational and professional careers.

To aid your students in achieving these ends, each chapter of *Economics: New Ways of Thinking, Second Edition* includes the addresses of several websites that provide engaging and relevant information. When students type in any of the addresses provided, they will immediately arrive at the intended site. The addresses have been modified so that EMC Publishing can monitor and maintain the proper links—for example, the website http://www.deposit accounts.com/ has been changed to http://econ.emcp.net/accounts. In the event that the address or content of a site changes or is discontinued, EMC's Internet editors will redirect the link to a site with equivalent information.

Activities in the *Annotated Teacher's Edition* often suggest that students search the Internet for information. For some activities, you might want to find reputable sites beforehand and steer students toward them. For other activities, have students do their own searching and then check out the sites they have found and discuss why they might be reliable or unreliable.

Passport® for Economics

Technology resources are available with the *Economics: New Ways of Thinking, Second Edition* program through Passport®. These include:

eBooks for *Economics: New Ways of Thinking, Second Edition*

▶ Student textbook eBook
▶ Interactive Applying the Principles eWorkbook
▶ Finding Economics eBook
▶ Guided Reading and Study Guide eBook
▶ Annotated Teacher's Edition eBook
▶ Lesson Plans eBook
▶ Assessment eBook

Passport® for Students

Students can access helpful resources through Passport® for Economics. Resources include:
▶ Study guides
▶ Practice tests
▶ Flash cards in English and in Spanish
▶ Word games in English and in Spanish
▶ Tutorials and key-concept videos
▶ Spanish print and audio summaries

Passport® for Teachers

Keep your course current and relevant by using the teacher resources provided through Passport® for Economics. In addition to all of the resources on the student side of Passport®, the teacher side contains:
▶ Link to the Annotated Teacher's Edition eBook
▶ Standards correlations
▶ Microsoft® PowerPoint® Lectures
▶ Current Events Lessons
▶ Additional Economics in the Real World features
▶ ExamView® Assessment Suite
▶ PDFs of all print supplements (student and teacher)

Overview

This chapter discusses several of the measurements that economists consider when determining the health of the economy. One measurement is total output, or the total market value of all goods and services in the United States. Another measurement is overall prices in the economy. The following statements provide brief descriptions of the major concepts covered in each section of this chapter.

SECTION 1 National Income Accounting

Section 1 explains what the gross domestic product is and how it reflects the health of the nation's economy.

SECTION 2 Measuring GDP

Section 2 explores the four sectors of the economy and how per-capita GDP is determined.

SECTION 3 Real GDP

Section 3 deals with calculating real GDP. This calculation is necessary for tracking the growth of GDP precisely from one year to the next.

SECTION 4 Measuring Price Changes and the Unemployment Rate

Section 4 introduces the consumer price index, which shows how prices change over time.

Measuring Economic Performance

Why It Matters

If you go to the doctor for a checkup, she will take your vital signs—your temperature, your blood pressure, and your pulse rate. When it comes to the economy, economists do much the same. This chapter discusses many of the measurements that economists make to determine the "health" of the economy.

Economists measure the total output of the economy. They want to measure the total market value of all the goods and services produced annually in the United States. Think of it in this way: each year, people in the United States produce goods and services—

cars, houses, computers, attorney services, and so on. Economists want to know the total dollar value of all these goods and services.

This relatively small transaction is but one of millions that economists account for each year to measure the economy's activity.

Another vital sign that economists want to monitor is prices. Are prices in the economy rising? If so, how fast and by how much? Are they rising by 1 percent, 3 percent, or 5 percent? Are prices falling? If so, how fast and by how much?

As you read this chapter, think of the economy as a patient in a doctor's office. Instead of the doctor checking out the patient, an economist is taking the economy's "pulse," "height and weight," and other vital signs. In later chapters, you will learn more about the "remedies" economists prescribe for an unhealthy economy.

314

Teaching Suggestions from the Author

I've found that one of the best ways to get students interested in the material in this chapter is to first get them to see why it's so important to measure a few particular items.

Every student has something he or she feels is important to measure. It may be her performance on a biology test or his performance on the baseball field. It may be the temperature outside or the number of days until semester break. I ask students why it's important for them to measure and quantify certain things. Often, they say it's so that they can plan their lives better, add some certainty to their lives, or simply to know what is going on.

Economics Around the Clock

The following events occurred one day in June.

1:13 P.M. Jones, the plumber, is just finishing up the job at Kevin's apartment. Kevin asks Jones how much he owes. Jones says, "$210." "Okay," says Kevin as he takes out his checkbook. "Oh, and by the way," Jones adds, "could you pay me in cash?"

• **Why does Jones want to be paid in cash?**

1:34 P.M. The economics professor is telling her class that China has one of the highest gross domestic products of any country in the world. A student remarks, "Does having a high gross domestic product (GDP) make China a rich country? Or can a country have a high gross domestic product and still not be a rich country?"

• **Can a country have a high GDP and be poor?**

2:34 P.M. Beverlee Smith picks up the phone to call her parents, both of whom are retired. When her father answers the phone, Beverlee blurts out, "I got the job! And I got the salary I asked for—$60,000." Her father replies, "That's a great salary—you're rich. After all, your mother and I lived comfortably on my first salary of $8,000."

• **What mistake is Beverlee's father making in comparing his first salary from years ago with Beverlee's salary today?**

11:03 P.M. Sam is watching a report on the 11 o'clock news about the growth rate in per capita real GDP in the United States over the last year. Sam is nearly bored to tears. He says under his breath, "Who really cares about these things? This stuff doesn't affect anyone."

• **Is Sam right that the growth rate in per capita real GDP doesn't affect anyone?**

315

Introducing the Chapter

Before you begin to teach this chapter, hold up a ruler for the class to see. Ask students to tell you what this tool is used for. Then ask them to name other devices that are used for measurement purposes. Explain that in this chapter, students will look at some of the tools that economists use to measure factors related to the economy. Tell them that just as we have many tools to help us measure things like distance, economists have a variety of tools to measure factors that indicate the health of the economy.

Teaching with Visuals

The terms *gross domestic product*, *consumer price index*, and *real gross domestic product* might seem foreign to students. However, students will learn that every time they go shopping, they contribute to the GDP.

The same reasons apply when economists measure GDP, real GDP, and prices. They want to be better able to plan and to know what is going on. Ask students to keep this in mind as they read the chapter.

You might also want to discuss with students how certain things are measured. Determining baseball scores is very different from counting days until the holidays, and different ways of measuring or keeping track of the measurements are needed.

Teacher Support

Focus and Motivate

Section Objectives

After completing this section, students will be able to
▶ define GDP;
▶ explain why only final goods and services are computed in GDP;
▶ identify what is omitted from GDP; and
▶ explain the difference between GDP and GNP.

Kickoff Activity

Write the following on the board for students to think about and then answer while attendance is being taken: "Suppose the government wants to measure all the production that occurs in the U.S. economy. How do you think the government might do this?"

Activating Prior Knowledge

Allow volunteers to share their responses to the Kickoff Activity. Students may have a difficult time answering this question. To simplify it, ask students to think of their classroom as a mini-economy. Each student produces and sells something in the mini-economy and buys goods from other students. Ask students how they can measure the total output produced in their mini-economy. For example, suppose that in their mini-economy, they produce 25 bicycles, 3 cars, and 4 bushels of wheat. The way to measure the total production of this economy is to take each quantity of goods, multiply it by its particular price, and then add all of the amounts to get a total.

National Income Accounting

Focus Questions
▶ What is GDP?
▶ Why are only final goods and services computed in GDP?
▶ What is omitted from GDP?
▶ What is the difference between GDP and GNP?

Key Terms
gross domestic product (GDP)
double counting

What Is Gross Domestic Product?

A family has an income. For example, the annual income of the Smith family might be $90,000. A country has an income too, but we don't call it an income. Instead, we call it *gross domestic product*. **Gross domestic product (GDP)** is the total market value of all final goods and services produced annually in a country. (Note: Sometimes GDP is referred to as *nominal* GDP. This is sometimes done to distinguish it from *real* GDP, which we will discuss later.)

Suppose that in a tiny economy, only three goods are produced in these quantities: 10 computers, 10 cars, and 10 watches. We'll say that the price of a computer is $2,000, the price of a car is $20,000, and the price of a watch is $100. If we wanted to find the GDP of this small economy—that is, if we wanted to find the total market value of the goods produced during the year—we would multiply the price of each good times the quantity of the good produced and then add the dollar amounts.

gross domestic product (GDP) The total market value of all final goods and services produced annually in a country.

Here's how we would do that (see also Exhibit 11-1):

1. *Find the market value for each good produced.* Multiply the price of each good times the quantity of the good produced. For example, if 10 computers are produced and the price of each is $2,000, then the market value of computers is $20,000.

2. *Sum the market values.* Here are the calculations:

Market value of computers =
$2,000 × 10 computers = $20,000

Market value of cars =
$20,000 × 10 cars = $200,000

Market value of watches =
$100 × 10 watches = $1,000

Gross domestic product =
$20,000 + $200,000 + $1,000 = $221,000

This total, $221,000, is the gross domestic product, or GDP, of the tiny economy.

Differentiating Instruction

Visual Learners

For students who have difficulty understanding the terms *gross domestic product, final goods,* and *intermediate goods,* assign them to make three-part pictorials or collages. One section should be labeled "GDP," and students should draw or affix 10 to 20 pictures of items included in the GDP. Then students should pictorially distinguish between final and intermediate goods, showing in their illustrations the relationships between the intermediate and final goods.

EXHIBIT 11-1 **Gross Domestic Product (GDP)**

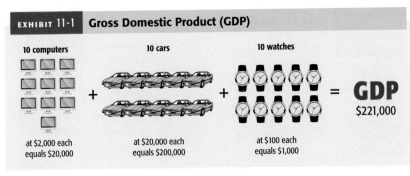

10 computers

10 cars

10 watches

+ + = **GDP**
$221,000

at $2,000 each
equals $20,000

at $20,000 each
equals $200,000

at $100 each
equals $1,000

◄ In our example of a tiny economy, the only goods produced are computers, cars, and watches. To calculate the GDP, we multiply the quantity of each good by its price and then sum the dollar amounts.

EXAMPLE A tiny economy has two goods, A and B. It produces 100 units of A and 200 units of B this year. The price of A is $4 and the price of B is $6. It follows that GDP is $1,600. We got this dollar figure by finding the market value of A ($4 × 100 units = $400) and the market value of B ($6 × 200 units = $1,200) and then adding the two values. ♦

Why Count Only Final Goods?

The definition of GDP specifies "final goods and services"; GDP is the total market value of all *final* goods and services produced annually in a country. Economists often distinguish between a *final good* and an *intermediate good.*

A final good is a good that's sold to its final user. When you buy a hamburger at a fast-food restaurant, for example, the hamburger is a final good. You are the final user; no one uses (eats) the hamburger other than you.

An intermediate good, in contrast, has not reached its final user. For example, consider the bun that the restaurant buys and on which the hamburger is placed. The bun is an intermediate good at this stage, because it isn't yet in the hands of the final user (the person who buys the hamburger). Rather, it's in the hands of the people who run the restaurant, who use the bun, along with other goods (lettuce, mustard, hamburger meat), to produce a hamburger for sale.

When computing GDP, economists count only final goods and services. If they counted both final and intermediate goods and services, they would be **double counting**, or counting a good more than once.

Suppose that a book is a final good and that paper and ink are intermediate goods used to produce the book. In a way, we can say that the book is paper and ink (book = paper + ink). If we calculate the GDP by adding together the value of the book, the paper, and the ink (book + paper + ink), we will, in effect, be counting the paper and ink twice. Because the book is paper and ink, after we count the book, we have automatically counted the paper and the ink. It is not necessary to count them again.

EXAMPLE A car is made up of many intermediate goods: tires, engine, steering wheel, radio, and so on. When computing GDP, we count only the market value of the car, not the market value of the car plus the market value of the tires, engine, and other intermediate goods. ♦

"A study of economics usually reveals that the best time to buy anything is last year."
—Marty Allen, comedian

A Student Asks

QUESTION: *I assume that each country in the world computes its GDP. Why is GDP so important?*

ANSWER: *Countries are interested in computing their GDPs for much the same reason that individuals are interested in knowing their incomes. Just as knowledge of your income from one year to the next lets you know how you're doing, knowing GDP does much the same for a country. Exhibit 11-2 on the next page shows the GDPs for certain countries and for the world in 2016.*

double counting
Counting a good more than once in computing GDP.

Answers will vary.

Reinforcement Activity

Write the name of each student on a separate slip of paper and put all the names into a hat. Pull out the first name and ask that student why one of the factors is omitted from the GDP—for example, Why are illegal goods and services omitted from the GDP? Why are the sales of used goods omitted from the GDP? If the student answers the question correctly, keep his or her name out of the hat. If the student answers incorrectly, put his or her name back in the hat. Choose another name, and continue until all the factors have been identified.

Economics Around the Clock

Lead students in a discussion of their answers to the 1:13 p.m. scenario in Economics Around the Clock (page 315).

Help them see that if Kevin pays Jones in cash, there will be no record of this transaction, which means it will not be counted in the GDP. Jones might want to do this because if the amount isn't reported to the government as income, he might decide not to pay taxes on it.

▶ Why might a country want to keep track of its GDP?

GDPs for the World and Selected Countries (2016)

Country or World	GDP (in trillions of dollars)
World	$75.27
United States	18.65
China	10.73
Japan	4.73
Germany	3.49
United Kingdom	2.65
France	2.48
India	2.25
Brazil	1.77
Canada	1.53
Russia	1.26
Australia	1.25
Mexico	1.06

Source: CIA World Factbook, 2017.

Does GDP Omit Anything?

Some exchanges that take place in an economy are omitted from the GDP. The following are not included when calculating GDP.

Illegal Goods and Services

For something to be included in the calculation of GDP, it must be capable of being counted. Illegal trades are not capable of being counted, for obvious reasons. For example, when someone makes an illegal purchase, no record is made of the transaction. In fact, the criminals involved in the transaction do everything in their power to prevent anyone from knowing about it.

EXAMPLE As you know, it is illegal in the United States to buy and sell drugs such as cocaine, heroin, and methamphetamine. Suppose a person pays $400 to buy an illegal drug. This $400 is not counted in GDP. If, however, the person spends $40 to buy a book, this $40 is counted in GDP. It is not illegal to buy a book. ◆

A Student Asks

QUESTION: *Obviously, illegal transactions occur in the United States every day (such as dollars exchanged for illegal drugs), and other transactions that occur are "under the table" (such as a person being paid for his services in cash instead of with a check). Do economists know what percentage of all transactions these types of transactions account for?*

ANSWER: *Both illegal transactions and legal transactions that government authorities do not know about (such as cash transactions that do not include receipts) make up what is called the underground economy. Some economists estimate that the underground economy in the United States is about 13 percent of the regular economy. In other words, for every $100 transaction in the regular economy, there is a $13 transaction in the underground economy. Keep in mind, though, that it's difficult to get a good estimate of the underground economy because, by definition, it's largely invisible to economists. It's difficult to count what people are trying to hide from you.*

Transactions of Legal Goods and Services with No Record

Suppose a gardener goes to someone's house and offers to mow the lawn and prune the shrubbery for $60 a week. The person agrees. The gardener then asks that he be paid in cash instead of by check and that no written record of the transaction be made. In other words, no sales receipt is to be provided. Again, the person agrees. The payment for these gardening services does not find its way into GDP. Making a cash payment and not providing a sales receipt means that there's no evidence a transaction was made.

Some Nonmarket Goods and Services

Some goods and services are traded but not in an official market setting. Let's say that Eileen Montoya cooks, cleans, and takes

Background Information: Nonmarket Goods and Services

Currently, nonmarket goods and services are not counted in the GDP. For example, if a man or woman stays at home and cooks and cleans, the value of these services is not figured into the GDP. Some people have said that by not counting these services in the GDP, we devalue the work of these people. For example, society does not perceive a homemaker's work in the home as being as valuable as a person's work in the marketplace. Ask students if they would be in favor of counting nonmarket goods and services in the GDP, assuming that it is possible to do so. Ask them to give reasons for their positions.

care of all financial matters in the Montoya household. She does not receive a weekly salary from the family for doing these things. Because she is not paid, the value of the work she performs is not counted in GDP.

EXAMPLE Jayne has three sons and she cuts their hair every few weeks. The market value of these haircuts is not counted in GDP. However, if Jayne took her boys to a barber for haircuts, what the barber charged for haircuts would be counted in GDP. ♦

Sales of Used Goods

Suppose you buy a used car tomorrow. Will this purchase be recorded in this year's GDP statistics? No, the sale of a used car does not enter into the current year's statistics because the car was counted when it was originally produced.

EXAMPLE Mario just sold his 2013 Toyota to Jackson for $7,000. This $7,000 is not counted in GDP. ♦

Stock Transactions and Other Financial Transactions

Suppose Elizabeth buys 500 shares of stock from Keesha for a price of $100 a share. The total price is $50,000. The transaction is not included in GDP, because GDP is a record of goods and services produced annually in an economy. A person who buys stock is not buying a product but rather an ownership right in the firm that originally issued the stock. For example, when a person buys Coca-Cola stock, he is becoming an owner of the Coca-Cola Corporation.

Government Transfer Payments

In everyday life, one person usually makes a payment to another in exchange for a good or service. For example, Enrique may pay Harriet $40 to buy her old DVD player.

When the government makes a payment to someone, it often does not get a good or service in exchange. When this happens, the payment is said to be a *government transfer payment*. For example, the social security check that 67-year-old Frank Simmons receives is a government transfer payment. Simmons, who is retired, is not currently supplying a good or service to

the government in exchange for receiving social security. Because GDP accounts only for current goods and services produced and a transfer payment has nothing to do with current goods and services produced, transfer payments are properly omitted from GDP statistics. See Exhibit 11-3 for a review of items omitted from GDP.

EXHIBIT 11-3 What GDP Omits

Item	Example
Illegal goods and services	A person buys an illegal substance.
Legal goods and services with no record of the transaction	A gardener works for cash, and no sales receipt exists.
Some nonmarket goods and services	A family member cooks, cleans, and mows the lawn.
Used goods	You buy a used car.
Stock transactions and other financial transactions	You buy 100 shares of stock in a company.
Government transfer payments	Frank Simmons receives a social security check.

Thinking Like an Economist

The "Average" Person

Suppose someone says, "The average person in the country earns $40,000 a year." Is there anything wrong with making a statement like this? Yes, from the viewpoint of an economist.

We might argue whether there really is such a thing as an "average person." However, there is such a thing as an "average income."

For instance, suppose we have two people. One person earns $50,000 a year, and the other person earns $100,000 a year. What is the average income of these two people? The answer is $75,000. Note that neither person actually earns $75,000, so it would be wrong for us to say that "The average person earns $75,000." Rather, $75,000 is the *average income* of these individuals.

Now suppose each person earns $80,000. Their average income is, of course, $80,000. Does either person earn $80,000? Yes, both of them do. So now, can we accurately say that "The average person earns $80,000"? No, not really. It's more accurate to say that "The average income is $80,000, and there are two people who earn the average income."

Teaching with Visuals

Exhibit 11-3 lists examples of items that are not included in the GDP. Have students re-create this table for themselves, listing the same items but providing different examples.

Application Activity

After reading and discussing Section 1, you may want to assign the Section Activity in the *Applying the Principles Workbook*, pages 120–121.

Assess

Quick Quiz

The following true-or-false quiz will help you assess student understanding of the material covered in this section.

1. GDP is the total market value of all final goods and services produced monthly in an economy. (False)
2. A final good is a good sold to its final user. (True)
3. When a restaurant pays for steak, this is a final good. (False)
4. Sales of used goods are omitted from the GDP calculations. (True)
5. GDP measures economic activity only within the boundaries of the country it is measuring. (True)

Cooperative Learning

Divide the class into groups of four or five. Tell each group that it will be looking at the concept of final goods and services and double counting. Instruct each group to choose a final good that it can bring to class or find around the room. (You might encourage students to bring in appropriate goods that are not of excessive value.) As a group, members should examine the good and try to name what other goods went into producing it. For example, if the good is a radio, some of the goods used to produce it might be plastic and wires. Each group should make a list of the goods used in producing its final good. Have each group choose a speaker to report its findings to the class.

Reteaching Activity

Use the Section Assessment to gauge which students may need reteaching on this section. For those students, write the following on the board: "The gross domestic product is the total market value of final goods and services produced annually in an economy. The gross domestic product is often simply called the GDP." Ask students to explain each statement. Go over their answers to be sure they understand the meaning of GDP.

Guided Reading

For further reteaching of the key concepts in this section, assign the Outlining Activity and the Just the Facts Handout from the *Guided Reading and Study Guide*, pages 180–182.

Defining Terms

1. a. gross domestic product (GDP): the total market value of all final goods and services produced annually in a country; **b. double counting:** counting a good more than once in computing GDP.

Reviewing Facts and Concepts

2. $1,690 (*calculation:* 10 pens × $4 = $40; 20 shirts × $30 = $600; 30 radios × 35 = $1,050; $40 + $600 + $1,050 = $1,690).
3. If we count intermediate goods as well as final goods and services, we will count some goods twice, which is double counting.
4. None of the items listed is included in calculating the GDP.

GNP

Total market value of final goods and services produced by U.S. citizens (wherever they reside: the United States, France, Mexico, etc.)

≠

GDP

Total market value of final goods and services produced within the borders of the United States (by both citizens and noncitizens)

▲ The producer's *citizenship* matters in computing GNP. The producer's place of residence matters in computing GDP.

The Difference Between GDP and GNP

Economists, government officials, and members of the public talk about GDP when they want to discuss the overall performance of the economy. They might say, "GDP has been on the rise" or "GDP has been declining a bit." It was not always GDP that these individuals talked about, though. They used to talk about GNP, the *gross national product*. (In some international publications, you will read about *gross national income*, or GNI, instead of gross national product, GNP.)

What is the difference between GDP and GNP? GNP measures the total market value of final goods and services produced by U.S. citizens, no matter where in the world they reside. GDP, in contrast, is the total market value of final goods and services produced within the borders of the United States, no matter who produces them.

Suppose a U.S. citizen owns a business in Japan. The value of the output she produces in Japan is counted in GNP because she is a U.S. citizen, but it is not counted in GDP because it was not produced within the borders of the United States. Now suppose a Canadian citizen produces goods in the United States. The value of his output is not counted in GNP because he is not a U.S. citizen, but it is counted in GDP because it was produced within the borders of the United States. (See Exhibit 11-4.)

EXAMPLE José is a Mexican citizen working in the United States. The dollar value of what he produces is counted in the U.S. GDP. Sabrina is a U.S. citizen living and working in Brazil. The dollar value of what she produces (in Brazil) is counted in U.S. GNP. ◆

SECTION 1 ASSESSMENT

Defining Terms

1. Define:
  a. gross domestic product (GDP)
  b. double counting

Reviewing Facts and Concepts

2. In a simple economy, three goods are produced during the year, in these quantities: 10 pens, 20 shirts, and 30 radios. The price of pens is $4 each, the price of shirts is $30 each, and the price of radios is $35 each. What is GDP for the economy?
3. Why are only final goods and services computed in GDP?

4. Which of the following are included in calculating this year's GDP?
  a. Twelve-year-old Bobby mowing his family's lawn
  b. Terry buying a used car
  c. Barbara buying 100 shares of Chrysler Corporation stock
  d. Sidwhali receiving a social security check
  e. An illegal sale at Elm and Jefferson

Critical Thinking

5. What is the difference (for purposes of measuring GDP) between buying a new computer and buying 100 shares of stock?
6. Can a country's GDP rise even if no more goods and services are produced from one year to the next? Explain.

Applying Economic Concepts

7. The government does not now include the housework that a person does for his or her family as part of GDP. Suppose the government were to include housework. How might it go about placing a dollar value on housework?

Critical Thinking

5. The computer purchase is part of the GDP, but the stock purchase is not. A person who buys stock isn't buying a good that was produced. Instead, he or she is buying an ownership right in a company that produces certain goods and services.
6. Yes. GDP is the product of prices and quantity of output. If prices rise and quantity of output is constant, GDP will rise.

Applying Economic Concepts

7. The government could find out how much a person would have to pay someone to do his or her housework. How much would Jones, for example, have to pay someone to wash his clothes, tidy up his house, cook his meals, and so on? This dollar amount would be added to the GDP.

Measuring GDP

Focus Questions
► What are the four sectors of the economy?
► What are consumption, investment, government purchases, export spending, and import spending?
► How is GDP measured?
► What is per capita GDP?

Key Terms
consumption
investment
government purchases
export spending
import spending

How Is GDP Measured?

The GDP of the United States today is more than $16 trillion. How did economists come up with this figure? What exactly do they do to determine GDP?

First, economists break the economy into four sectors: the household sector, the business sector, the government sector, and the foreign sector. Next, they state a simple fact: the people in each of these sectors buy goods and services—that is, they make expenditures.

Economists give names to the expenditures made by each sector. The expenditures made by the household sector (consumers) are called **consumption**. The expenditures made by the business sector are called **investment**, and expenditures made by the government sector are called **government purchases**. (Government purchases include purchases made by all three levels of government: local, state, and federal.) Finally, the expenditures made by the residents of other countries on goods produced in the United States are called **export spending**. Exhibit 11-5 on the next page gives examples of goods purchased by

households, businesses, government, and foreigners.

Consider all of the goods and services produced in the U.S. economy in a year: houses, tractors, watches, restaurant meals, cars, computers, plasma TV sets, DVDs, iPads, cell phones, and much, much more. Suppose someone from the household sector buys a DVD. This purchase falls into the category of *consumption*. When someone from the business sector buys a large machine to install in a factory, the purchase is considered an *investment*. If the U.S. government purchases a tank from a company that produces these vehicles, the purchase is considered a *government purchase*. If a person living in Sweden buys a U.S.-produced sweater, this purchase is considered spending on U.S. exports and is therefore registered as *export spending*.

All goods produced in the economy must be bought by someone in one of the four sectors of the economy. If economists simply sum the expenditures made by each sector—that is, if they add up consumption, investment, government purchases, and export spending—they will be close to computing the GDP.

consumption
Expenditures made by the household sector.

investment
Expenditures made by the business sector.

government purchases
Expenditures made by the government sector. Government purchases do not include government transfer payments.

export spending
The amount spent by the residents of other countries on goods produced in the United States.

Differentiating Instruction

Visual Learners

Divide the class into four groups. Each group will create a poster for one sector of the economy. Students can bring in photographs or small items that represent their assigned sector and glue them to the posters. Once the posters are completed, display them in the classroom. Group members should identify the items on their poster and explain why the items within that particular sector of the economy. Ask, Do any items appear in more than one sector? If so, how is this possible? Is it possible for a good to appear in all four sectors of the economy? Why or why not?

Teacher Support

Focus and Motivate

Section Objectives

After completing this section, students will be able to
► identify the four sectors of the economy;
► describe consumption, investment, government purchases, export spending, and import spending;
► explain how GDP is measured; and
► define per capita GDP.

Kickoff Activity

Write the following question on the board for students to answer: "Do you think people who live in a country with a large GDP are better off than people who live in a country with a small GDP? Explain your answer."

Activating Prior Knowledge

Allow volunteers to share their responses to the Kickoff Activity. Students' answers should touch on the idea that neither is necessarily better, because GDP does not take into account nonmaterial goods and services. Similarly, GDP does not take into account how goods and services are distributed among the population.

Teach

Discussion Starter

Invite students to discuss the products they have purchased in the last month. Do these items reflect consumption or import spending?

 Visit econ.myemcp.com/videos for videos that will help students better understand the key concepts found in this section.

Reinforcement Activity

Obtain a copy of the *Economic Report of the President* from your school library or the Internet. Ask students to locate in that document current dollar figures for the components of the GDP: consumption, investment, government expenditures, and imports and exports.

Critical Thinking

What goes on in the United States affects the GDP in, say, Mexico, and what goes on in Mexico affects the GDP in, say, the United States. This is obvious once we note that the GDP for any country is equal to C + I + G + EX − IM. When Mexicans buy more goods from the United States, exports in the United States (EX) rise and the U.S. GDP rises. When Americans buy more goods from Mexico, exports in Mexico rise and the Mexican GDP rises. In short, by affecting the exports of a country, importing countries affect the exporting country's GDP.

A Student Asks

Use this A Student Asks to make sure that students understand the difference between the two meanings of the word *investment*.

EXHIBIT 11-5 Expenditures Made by the Four Sectors of the Economy

Sector of the economy	Name of expenditures	Definition	Examples
Household	Consumption	Expenditures made by the household sector on goods for personal use	TVs, telephones, clothes, lamps, cars
Business	Investment	Expenditures made by the business sector on goods used in producing other goods; also includes business inventories	Tools, machines, factories
Government	Government purchases	Expenditures made by federal, state, and local governments	Paper, pens, tanks, planes
Foreign	Exports	Expenditures made by foreigners for American-made goods	Cars, wheat, computers
	Imports	Expenditures made by Americans for foreign-made goods	Cars, radios, computers

Economists will only be close, however; they will still need to adjust for U.S. purchases of foreign-produced goods. For example, if Cynthia in Detroit purchases a Japanese-made TV for $500, this $500 purchase will not be included in GDP because GDP is a measure of goods and services produced annually in a country. Specifically, the U.S. GDP is a measure of the goods and services produced annually in the territorial area we know as the United States. Cynthia's TV was not produced in the United States, so it is not part of U.S. GDP. Spending by Americans for foreign-produced goods is called **import spending**.

To compute U.S. GDP, then, economists need to sum consumption (C), investment (I), government purchases (G), and export spending (EX) and then subtract import spending (IM). We can now write how to calculate GDP in equation form:

$$GDP = C + I + G + EX - IM$$

For example, in 2016, consumption in the United States was $12.82 trillion, investment was $3.01 trillion, government purchases were $3.28 trillion, export spending was $2.27 trillion, and import spending was $2.73 trillion. Thus, we can calculate GDP to be $18.65 trillion. (See Exhibit 11-6.)

import spending
The amount spent by Americans for foreign-produced goods.

A Student Asks

QUESTION: *Earlier, you stated that investment is defined as expenditures made by the business sector. For example, if a business buys a new machine, the purchase of the machine is considered an investment. I think in the everyday world, people use the word investment a little differently than the word is being used here. Am I right?*

ANSWER: *Yes, you are right. For example, in the everyday world, someone might say, "I made a good investment last week. I bought stock in the stock market." The economist, however, does not use the word investment in this way. Again, what an economist means when he or she uses the word investment is the expenditures made by a business—for example, a business buying a factory, more robotics, and so on.*

Is Every Good Produced Also Sold?

Our definition of GDP is the total market value of all final goods and services *produced* annually in an economy. However, we measured the GDP by finding out how much

Cooperative Learning

Divide students into groups of two or three, and let each group choose a U.S. state other than their own. Tell students that people often have misconceptions about the industries that are most important in a state. For example, many people assume that there are only two major industries in Texas (oil and cattle), but in fact, its major products and services also include natural gas, cotton and other crops, steel, banking, insurance, and tourism. Instruct each group to find out the largest and most important industries for their chosen state and the GDP of that state. Then provide students with the same information for their own state. Ask, How do the industries and GDP of our own state compare with those of the states you have researched?

EXHIBIT 11-6 **Computing GDP (2016, in trillions of dollars)**

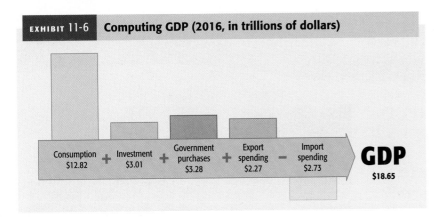

◀ To calculate GDP, we add several expenditures and then subtract one expenditure. **What expenditure do we subtract rather than add?**

| Consumption $12.82 | + | Investment $3.01 | + | Government purchases $3.28 | + | Export spending $2.27 | − | Import spending $2.73 | → | **GDP** $18.65 |

the four sectors of the economy *spend* on goods and services. Suppose something is produced but not purchased. Is it included in GDP? For example, a car company produces 10,000 new cars this year, but the household sector chooses to buy only 8,900 of the 10,000 cars. That means that some cars (1,100) were produced but not sold. Do these cars get counted in GDP?

The answer is yes, because the government statisticians who measure GDP assume that everything that is produced is purchased by someone. For purposes of calculating GDP, the government statisticians assume that the car company "purchased" the 1,100 cars that the car company did not sell.

EXAMPLE Nigel owns his own sock factory. Last year, he produced 100,000 pairs of socks and sold 80,000 pairs to people. That left 20,000 pairs of socks produced but unsold (as far as Nigel is concerned). Government statisticians view these 20,000 pairs of socks as having been "purchased" by Nigel. How many pairs of socks are counted in GDP: 80,000 or 100,000? Answer: 100,000. ◆

QUESTION: *How do government statisticians know about the 20,000 pairs of socks that Nigel has in inventory? After all, they would have to know about them to count them in GDP.*

ANSWER: *To produce the 100,000 pairs of socks, Nigel had to pay workers. These workers earned incomes that were reported to the government for tax purposes. By comparing expenditures with incomes, the government statisticians can get a rough idea of what was produced but not sold. Suppose you paid $1,000 to workers but sold goods totaling only $40. This difference indicates the production of some goods that were not later sold.*

Teaching with Visuals

We subtract import spending. To help students understand the calculations involved in determining GDP, bring in objects that represent all the factors in the equation. You might use bread for consumption, a stapler for investment, a ream of paper for the government (all those forms), a toy car for export spending, and anything from a foreign country for import spending. Guide students in a discussion of how these items are reflected in the GDP.

Economics Around the Clock

After students have read Section 2, ask them to discuss their answers to the 1:34 p.m. scenario in Economics Around the Clock (page 315).

Answers may vary. Students might suggest that just because a country has a high GDP, it might not have a high per capita GDP. China has a very large population, so its per capita GDP might be smaller than that of another country.

New technology has made it possible to produce the same product (food, clothing, etc.) more quickly.

ANSWERS TO THINK ABOUT IT The invention of agricultural machines, such as tractors, has allowed a single farmer to do the same amount of work in less time than farmers in years past.

Economics *in the* Real World

Is Declining Employment in Manufacturing Cause for Concern?

In 1840, 70 percent of Americans employed in the private sector worked in agriculture. That means that most of the people who didn't work for the government (in the public sector) had jobs related to producing food.

By 1900, employment in agriculture had fallen to 40 percent, and by 1950, it had fallen to 10 percent. Today, only about 1.2 percent of all private sector employment in the United States is in agriculture.

Does the fact that fewer Americans work in agriculture today than ever before mean that the United States produces less foodstuff than it used to? Not at all. What has happened in agriculture is that productivity has skyrocketed. Today, it takes many fewer farmers to produce the amount of food that it took many more farmers to produce even decades ago. It's as if 10 farmers today can produce what 100 farmers produced in the past.

Now consider how employment in manufacturing has changed in the United States over time. In 1948, only slightly more people were employed in providing services than in manufacturing goods, but today, the numbers aren't even close. Today, about 80 percent of Americans working in the private sector are engaged in providing services while slightly fewer than 20 percent are engaged in manufacturing goods.

The same trend that occurred in agriculture throughout the 1800s and 1900s has affected manufacturing in recent decades. That is, increased productivity has resulted in fewer jobs.

You might have read newspaper articles with headlines such as "What has happened to all the manufacturing jobs in America?" and "Where have all the manufacturing jobs gone?" But remember, the same kinds of headlines could have been applied to jobs in agriculture many years ago. "Where did all the farmers go?"

The fact is, any area of the economy (such as agriculture or manufacturing) can end up losing jobs when productivity and output rise. For example, if you look at manufacturing productivity (as measured by output per hour) during the period of 1965–2012, you will notice that overall, productivity increased tremendously. In some years, though, productivity in manufacturing actually decreased. Also, if you look at the period 1983–2005, you will notice that U.S. exports of manufactured goods increased by 407 percent during this time.

The point is this: If you look at the number of jobs in any business or industry over time, you may see declining employment. But this isn't necessarily a sign of weakness. What matters more than employment in any business or industry is productivity and output. It's possible for fewer people to work in a business or industry yet produce greater output than more people did in previous years.

THINK ABOUT IT What likely made productivity in agriculture increase so much that today, one farmer can produce what it took many farmers to produce in years past?

Cooperative Learning

Divide students into groups to develop lists of the industries they feel are important in their community. Have a volunteer list the industries on the board. Then, as a class, try to rank the industries in terms of number of employees. To follow up on this activity, you might ask students to contact the local Chamber of Commerce or Board of Trade to check the accuracy of the list. Ask students to research these questions: Were any industries left off this list? Are there any industries on the list that really do not belong? Perhaps arrange to have a representative from one of the industries visit your class and discuss the role and importance of that industry in the community.

GDP Versus Quality of Life

In 2017, the U.S. GDP was over five times larger than the GDP of Germany. Given this difference in GDP, does it follow that Americans are better off than Germans? If your answer is yes, then you have made the mistake of equating a higher GDP with being better off or having greater well-being. Greater production of goods and services is only one of the many factors that contribute to being better off or having greater well-being.

Look at the issue on an individual basis. Franklin has $1 million in the bank, owns a large home, drives a luxury car, and works 70 hours a week. He has little time to enjoy his family or hobbies. In contrast, Harris has $100 in the bank, owns a small home, drives an old car, and works 30 hours a week. He has a lot of time to enjoy life.

Who is better off—Franklin or Harris? In terms of expensive goods, Franklin certainly has more than Harris; in this one respect, Franklin benefits more than Harris. In terms of leisure time, though, Harris is better off than Franklin. In overall terms—taking everything into account—we cannot say who is better off.

Similarly, we simply cannot say whether Americans are better off than Germans on the basis of their countries' GDPs. All we can say for sure is that Americans live in a country that produces more goods and services. Being better off takes into account much more than simply how much output is produced.

In assessing a country's GDP, its population also must be considered. Suppose country X has double the GDP of country Y, but its population is three times as large. This would mean that on a per-person basis (the same as a *per capita* basis), each person has fewer goods and services (on average) in country X than in country Y. In short, a bigger national GDP does not necessarily mean a bigger per capita GDP. Per capita GDP is calculated using this equation:

$$\text{Per capita GDP} = \frac{\text{GDP}}{\text{Population}}$$

Economic Facts *and* Fallacies

A Rising GDP May Not Indicate the Production of More Goods

Suppose a country's GDP is higher in year 2 than in year 1. Based on this, someone says, "The country produced more goods and services in the second year than it did in the first year." Is this necessarily true?

No, it's not. GDP can rise for a number of reasons. One of those reasons is that prices rise while the quantity of goods and services produced remains constant.

A rise in GDP means very little unless you know what caused it to rise. Did it rise because the production of goods and services increased? Did it rise because prices went up? Did it rise both because the production of goods and services increased and prices went up? Or did it rise because prices went up by more than the production of goods and services went down? Knowing what caused the rise in GDP is key to understanding its significance.

A Student Asks

QUESTION: *What are some countries that have high per capita GDPs?*

ANSWER: *According to the World Bank, the following countries had some of the highest per capita GDPs in 2016: Luxembourg ($101,936), Norway ($69,296), Singapore ($87,082), Switzerland ($59,376), United States ($57,294), Australia ($48,806), Austria ($47,856). To find the current rank ordering of countries according to GDP, go to http://econ.emcp.net/GDP.*

Section 2 Measuring GDP **325**

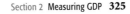

Application Activity

After reading and discussing Section 2, you may want to assign the Section Activity in the *Applying the Principles Workbook,* pages 122–123.

Assess

Quick Quiz

The following true-or-false quiz will help you assess student understanding of the material covered in this section.

1. Economists break the economy into three sectors: household, government, and business. (False)
2. If a person living in Sweden purchases a U.S.-produced TV, this purchase is regarded as U.S. import spending. (False)
3. According to GDP figures, every good that's produced by the economy is sold. (True)
4. Living in a nation with a higher GDP necessarily means a happier life. (False)
5. Americans are better off than the French on the basis of the two countries' GDPs. (False)

Assessment Book

You will find a quiz for this section in the *Assessment Book,* page 108.

Reteaching Activity

Use the Section Assessment to gauge which students may need reteaching on this section. Guide those students in using the formula on page 322 to compute the GDP. Write the equation on the board as you discuss it, so students can better make the connection. Give students various sample problems, and have them calculate the GDPs with numbers you supply.

Guided Reading

For further reteaching of the key concepts in this section, assign the Outlining Activity and the Just the Facts Handout from the *Guided Reading and Study Guide,* pages 183–186.

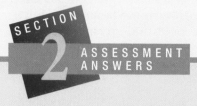

SECTION 2 ASSESSMENT ANSWERS

Defining Terms

1. a. consumption: expenditures made by the household sector; **b. investment:** expenditures made by the business sector; **c. government purchases:** expenditures made by the government sector; **d. export spending:** the amount spent by the residents of foreign countries on goods produced in the United States; **e. import spending:** the amount spent by Americans for foreign-produced goods.

Reviewing Facts and Concepts

2. Imports are not produced in the United States, and to find the GDP, we must subtract what Americans spend on foreign-produced goods.
3. $3,850 billion (*calculation:* C + I + G + EX − IM = $2,000 billion + $700 billion + $1,200 billion + $100 billion − $150 billion = $3,850 billion).
4. Government statisticians say that if any goods are produced by a company but are not sold, the remaining goods are considered to be purchased by the company itself.

SECTION 2 ASSESSMENT

Defining Terms

1. Define:
   a. consumption
   b. investment
   c. government purchases
   d. export spending
   e. import spending

Reviewing Facts and Concepts

2. In computing GDP, why is import spending subtracted from the sum of consumption, investment, government purchases, and export spending?

3. Suppose consumption is $2,000 billion, investment is $700 billion, government purchases are $1,200 billion, export spending is $100 billion, and import spending is $150 billion. What does GDP equal?

4. A computer company produces 25,000 computers this year and sells 22,000 to its customers. According to government statisticians, however, all 25,000 computers have been purchased. How do the statisticians reach this conclusion?

Critical Thinking

5. Suppose country X has a GDP that is three times larger than that of country Y. Are the people in country X better off than the people in country Y? Explain your answer.

6. Suppose country A has a per capita GDP of $10,000. Does it follow that every person in the country has $10,000? Explain your answer.

Applying Economic Concepts

7. A family has six people, five of whom produce goods and services that are sold directly to consumers. One person in the family is too young to work. How would you go about measuring the family's "GDP"?

Critical Thinking

5. Not necessarily. *Better off* is a subjective term. Even if everyone in country X has three times as many goods and services as everyone in country Y, the people in country X are not necessarily better off. Maybe the people in country X have to work long hours and have very little leisure time. Furthermore, if the population of country X is four times that of country Y, then the per capita GDP is lower in country X than country Y.
6. No. Per capital GDP is an average. Some people might have more than $10,000, and some might have less.

Applying Economic Concepts

7. GDP is the total market value of all final goods and services produced annually in an economy. For a "family economy," we compute the market value of what each family member produces and then sum the values.

Focus Questions

▶ What two variables are involved in calculating GDP?

▶ If GDP is higher in one year than another, do we automatically know why it is higher?

▶ What is the difference between GDP and real GDP?

▶ How do economists go about computing real GDP?

Key Terms

base year
real GDP

The Two Variables of GDP: P and Q

When we computed GDP in a simple, one-good economy, we multiplied two variables: price (P) and quantity (Q). If one of the two variables rises and the other remains constant, GDP will rise.

To see how this relationship works, look at the following chart:

Price	Quantity	GDP
$10	2	$20
15	2	30
10	3	30

With a price of $10 and a quantity of 2, GDP is $20. When the price rises to $15 but the quantity is held constant at 2, GDP rises to $30. Finally, if the price is constant at $10 and the quantity increases to 3, GDP again is $30. Clearly, an increase in either price or quantity will raise GDP.

Suppose someone then told you that GDP was $20 one year and $30 the next year. You would have no way of knowing whether GDP increased because the price increased, because the quantity of output increased, or because both the price and quantity increased. But what if the price was held constant and GDP increased? Would you know what caused the rise in GDP? If the price is held constant, then any rise in GDP must be due to a rise in quantity, of course.

How can we keep price constant? Economists do it by computing GDP for each year—2003, 2004, 2005, and so on—using the prices that existed in one particular year in the past. That year, called the **base year**, is chosen as a point of reference for comparison. Economists who compute GDP this way are said to be computing *real GDP* (GDP measured in base-year, or constant, prices). GDP is equal to price in the current year times quantity in the current year, but **real GDP** is equal to price in the base year times quantity in current year.

Let's again assume that we have a simple, one-good economy that produces only watches. In Exhibit 11-7 on the next page, column 1 lists several years, column 2 gives the prices of watches in these years, and column 3 gives the quantities of watches

base year
In general, a benchmark year—a year chosen as a point of reference for comparison. When real GDP is computed, the outputs of different years are priced at base-year levels.

real GDP
Gross domestic product (GDP) that has been adjusted for price changes; GDP measured in base-year, or constant, prices.

Focus and Motivate

Section Objectives

After completing this section, students will be able to

▶ identify the two variables involved in calculating GDP;

▶ explain whether we would automatically know why GDP is higher in one year than another;

▶ describe the difference between GDP and real GDP; and

▶ explain how economists go about computing real GDP.

Kickoff Activity

Ask students to respond in writing to the following question while attendance is being taken: What two things can increase GDP?

Activating Prior Knowledge

Invite students to discuss their responses to the Kickoff Activity. Students' answers should reflect that if prices go up, GDP will increase, and/or if output goes up, GDP will increase.

Teach

Discussion Starter

Ask students for a reason that most economists use real GDP instead of GDP when talking about the economy. Students should recognize that most economists do so because an increase in prices and/or output will increase GDP, whereas only an increase in output will increase real GDP.

 Visit econ.myemcp.com/videos for videos that will help students better understand the key concepts found in this section.

Background Information: Real GDP

If students question the importance of the information about real GDP, tell them the following: When choosing the base year, economists choose a year in which sharp changes in major economic factors do not appear. For example, if prices skyrocket in one year and are stable in another year, economists are much more likely to pick the second as the base year—the year against which other years are measured.

Cause and Effect

To show the relationship between price and quantity, write the following problem on the board: "The given price for 1,000 units of a good produced last year was $5. This year, the price is $5.50 and the quantity produced is 750." Ask students which year has the higher GDP. (*Answer:* Last year's GDP of $5,000 is higher than this year's GDP of $4,125.) Ask students which is the higher real GDP. (*Answer:* The real GDP of last year, $5,000, is higher than that of this year, $3,750.) What will happen to the comparison if the quantity produced in the second year is 1,200? (*Answer:* Both GDP and real GDP will increase.)

Economics Around the Clock

Instruct students to reread and discuss their answers to the accompanying question to the 11:03 p.m. scenario in Economics Around the Clock (page 315).

Help students understand that Sam is not right. A small increase in the per capita real GDP growth rate can make a huge difference in people's standard of living.

Reinforcement Activity

Ask students to demonstrate their understanding of this section by writing sentences that explain how real GDP differs from GDP. Students' answers should reflect that while GDP is the total market value of all final goods and services produced annually in the economy, real GDP makes adjustments for changes in price and output.

EXHIBIT 11-7 Computing GDP and Real GDP in a Simple, One-Good Economy

(1) Year	(2) Price of watches	(3) Quantity of watches produced	(4) GDP	(5) Real GDP
2005	$20	—	Price in current year × Quantity in current year	Price in 2005 × Quantity in current year
2016	$50	1,900	$50 × 1,900 = $95,000	$20 × 1,900 = $38,000
2017	$60	2,000	$60 × 2,000 = $120,000	$20 × 2,000 = $40,000
2018	$70	1,855	$70 × 1,855 = $129,850	$20 × 1,855 = $37,100

▲ In column 4, the GDP is computed for a simple, one-good economy. The price in the current year is multiplied by the quantity produced in the current year. In column 5, real GDP is computed by multiplying the price in 2005 (the base year for purposes here) by the quantity produced in the current year. Economists prefer working with real GDP to working with GDP because they know that if real GDP in one year is higher than real GDP in another year, output is greater in the year with the higher real GDP.

---

produced in these years. Column 4 shows GDP for each year. (GDP equals the current-year price times the current-year quantity of watches.)

Real GDP is shown in column 5. To calculate it, we multiply the price of watches in our chosen base year of 2005 by the current-year quantity. For example, to get real GDP in 2016, we take the quantity of watches produced in 2016 and multiply it by the price of watches in 2005.

A quick look at real GDP figures tells us that because real GDP in 2017 ($40,000) is higher than that in 2016 ($38,000), the quantity of watches produced in 2017 must have been greater than the quantity produced in 2016. A look at the quantities in column 3 confirms this observation. Also, because the real GDP figure for 2018 ($37,100) is lower than that for 2017 ($40,000), the quantity of watches produced in 2018 must have been lower than the quantity produced in 2017. Again, column 3 confirms this lower level of production.

Finally, in computing real GDP for 2016, 2017, and 2018, we multiplied the quantity of watches produced in each year times the price of watches in 2005, the base year. Thus, another way to define real GDP is

GDP in base-year prices or, if 2005 is the base year, for example, *GDP in 2005* prices.

EXAMPLE A country produces one good, X, which it sells for $4 in 2010, $8 in 2013, and $10 in 2018. It produces 40 units of X in 2010, 45 units in 2013, and 40 units in 2018. If 2010 is designated as the base year, what is the real GDP in each of the three years we designated: 2010, 2013, and 2018?

To find out, we simply multiply the quantity of X the country produces each year by the price it sells X for in the base year. For example, the real GDP in 2010 is $4 times 40 units, which equals $160. The real GDP in 2013 is $4 times 45 units, which equals $180. The real GDP in 2018 is equal to $4 times 40 units, which is $160. Notice that the real GDP is the same in both 2010 and 2018. ◆

You may be wondering how economists decide what year will be the base year when calculating real GDP. Unfortunately, there is no easy answer to this question. The base year must be a year in the past but not too far in the past. For example, no economist would choose 1865 as a base year, because that's too long ago. The economic world then was much different from today.

Background Information: Healthy Laborers

One way of producing more goods and services (and therefore increasing real GDP), is to increase the number of people working. Obviously, this was not possible in the past, when many people died young, often of conditions that are readily cured today.

Consider the case of Nathan Rothschild, who in 1836 was said to be the richest man in the world.

At the time, he suffered from an inflammation that a German physician had diagnosed as a boil. When Rothschild got steadily worse, a surgeon opened and cleaned the wound, but it was too late. The "boil" was an abscess, and the poison from it had gotten into Rothschild's body. On July 28, 1836, Rothschild died of an infection that today would be routinely cured by antibiotics.

Is There Real GDP Growth in Your Future?

Suppose you heard on the news that per capita real GDP grew by 2.3 percent last year in the United States. Does this percentage matter to you? Life will go on pretty much the same way, right? You didn't get a pay raise at your part-time job; nobody bought you a new car; you still have to go to school every day and do homework. So what does it matter?

Well, real GDP growth in one year may not matter much, but how much it grows over time should matter to you. How much per capita real GDP grows during your lifetime will greatly influence the kind of life you live.

You may be a bit skeptical about this, so let's take a quick

look at the history of real GDP. Little per capita real GDP growth occurred from the year A.D. 1 to about 1500. A person living in, say, 1300 didn't have a much different standard of living from a person living in the year 70. It was fairly common during the years of little to no growth in per capita real GDP for a son or daughter to have the same standard of living as his or her great-great-great-great grandmother or grandfather.

Today, it's different. For example, your standard of living is much higher than the standards of living of the people who lived in the United States during the Revolutionary War, Civil War, World War I, and World War II. And we are not just talking about the fact that you enjoy some goods today that people in the Revolutionary War did not (such as cell phones, computers, and so on).

Now let's think about the standard of living that can be expected by someone who is born today. If the annual growth rate of per capita real GDP is 1.1 percent, this person will be 63 years old before his or her standard of living (as measured by per capita real GDP) will have doubled. But if the annual growth rate

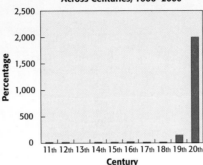

Growth in Material Wealth Across Centuries, 1000–2000

Source: Figure courtesy of Brad de Long, University of California–Berkeley.

of per capita real GDP is just 1 percent higher (2.1 percent), this person will only be 33 years old when his or her standard of living has doubled. If the person lives to be 66 years old, he or she will have seen his or her standard of living double twice.

Think of what this doubling means for you. You are, say, 17 years old. If you live to the age of 83, your standard of living will have doubled twice if the annual per capita real GDP growth rate is 2.1 percent, but it will have doubled only once if the rate is 1.1 percent. In other words, just a little more growth in per capita real GDP can make a huge difference in the life you live.

THINK ABOUT IT A well-known economist once said that if he had to pick a country for his children to be born in, it would be a country with a high annual growth rate in per capita real GDP. What does the economist want for his grandchildren?

Economics *in the* Real World

Ask students to study the chart in this feature. Allow volunteers to suggest reasons that material wealth grew so rapidly during the twentieth century.

ANSWERS TO THINK ABOUT IT Answers will vary. Students should say that the economist wants his grandchildren to experience a high standard of living. He knows that a country with a high annual growth rate in per capita real GDP will have a high standard of living.

Application Activity

After reading and discussing Section 3, you may want to assign the Section Activity in the *Applying the Principles Workbook,* page 124.

Assess

Quick Quiz

The following true-or-false quiz will help you assess student understanding of the material covered in this section.

1. To find real GDP, you must know a good's current price. (False)
2. Real GDP is more accurate than GDP because it holds price constant. (True)
3. If real GDP is higher in one year than another, it means the price for the good increased. (False)
4. Real GDP shows the change in quantity. (True)
5. The base year is the year from which price is taken to calculate real GDP. (True)

Assessment Book

You will find a quiz for this section in the *Assessment Book,* page 109.

Rothschild's fate was not uncommon in the early 1800s. People also commonly died of gastrointestinal infections, which were often transmitted from human waste to hands to food to digestive tracts. The main reasons for this transmission were wearing woolen underwear (which caused people to itch) and a lack of mass-produced soap.

Two chief products of the Industrial Revolution were cheap, washable cotton (which does not scratch) and mass-produced soap. These products dramatically reduced the transmission rates of gastrointestinal infections. After the introduction of these products, people lived longer and worked longer, which meant they produced more goods and services.

Reteaching Activity

Use the Section Assessment to gauge which students may need reteaching on this section. The difference between real GDP and GDP can be difficult for some students to understand. Review Exhibit 11-7 (page 328) with those students, and give them some new sample numbers for columns (2) and (3) to provide more practice finding GDP and real GDP. Two variables are used to compute GDP: price and quantity. Real GDP takes into account price changes to paint a more accurate portrait of any change in the quantity of final goods and services produced in an economy in one year. In other words, with real GDP, economists can see if the number of final goods and services has grown or shrunk.

 Guided Reading

For further reteaching of the key concepts in this section, assign the Outlining Activity and the Just the Facts Handout from the *Guided Reading and Study Guide,* pages 187–188.

SECTION 3 ASSESSMENT ANSWERS

Defining Terms

1. a. base year: a benchmark year—a year chosen as a point of reference for comparison; **b. real GDP:** GDP that has been adjusted for price changes; GDP measured in base-year, or constant, prices.

Reviewing Facts and Concepts

2. No, output is not necessarily higher in the second year than in the first. Prices could be higher.
3. Economists compute real GDP because they want to see what happens to production over time. The GDP does not provide that information.
4. When real GDP increases, the variable Q increases. The variable P is held constant.

Critical Thinking

5. Yes, GDP can go up at the same time that real GDP goes down. GDP is price × quantity, and real GDP is simply

Economists generally want the base year to be a year in the near past in which no major economic events occurred. They try not to pick a year in which there were large increases in prices or high unemployment, for example. Aside from those factors, however, choosing the base year is somewhat arbitrary. Several years in the immediate past might meet the basic conditions, but one will be chosen over the others.

SECTION 3 ASSESSMENT

Defining Terms
1. Define:
   a. base year
   b. real GDP

Reviewing Facts and Concepts
2. Gross domestic product is $6 trillion one year and $6.5 trillion the next year. Is output necessarily higher in the second year than in the first? Explain your answer.

3. Why do economists compute real GDP?
4. When real GDP increases, which variable, P or Q, has also increased?

Critical Thinking
5. Can GDP go up at the same time that real GDP goes down? Explain your answer.
6. If the current year is 2018, would it be better to use 2001 or 1778 as a base year for calculating real GDP? Explain.

Applying Economic Concepts
7. An economist wants to know whether the "average person" in country X has more goods and services to consume than the "average person" in country Y. Do you recommend that the economist look at per capita GDP or per capita real GDP? Explain your answer.

quantity (holding prices constant). If quantity goes down, then real GDP falls. The GDP does not necessarily fall, though, because prices can go up by more than quantities go down.
6. A base year is used as a benchmark against which to compare the current year.

Ideally, the base year and current year have similar goods and services. The closer the base year is to the current year, the more likely this will be the case.

Applying Economic Concepts
7. The economist should look at per capita real GDP, because

real GDP measures output, whereas GDP measures output and prices. In short, increases in GDP and per capita GDP do not ensure that more output will be available for people to consume. When real GDP rises, in contrast, there must be more output.

Measuring Price Changes and the Unemployment Rate

Teacher Support

Focus Questions

▶ What is the consumer price index?
▶ How is the consumer price index calculated?
▶ What is the aggregate demand curve?
▶ What is the aggregate supply curve?
▶ How do we calculate the unemployment rate?
▶ How is the employment rate calculated?

Key Terms

price index
consumer price index (CPI)
aggregate demand curve
aggregate supply curve
unemployment rate
employment rate

Focus and Motivate

Section Objectives

After completing this section, students will be able to

▶ explain what the consumer price index is and how it is calculated;
▶ distinguish between an aggregate demand curve and an aggregate supply curve; and
▶ explain how the employment rate and unemployment rate are calculated.

Kickoff Activity

Ask students the following questions at the beginning of class: Did you hear on the news that prices are 5% higher this year than last year? How do you think government goes about measuring the change in prices from one year to the next?

Activating Prior Knowledge

Invite students to share their responses to the Kickoff Activity. They will learn on page 332 that government workers use a representative group of goods called the *market basket*. They compare the prices of this basket from year to year.

Calculating the Change in a Single Price

Suppose that in 2015, a Honda Accord was priced at $20,000, and in 2016, a Honda Accord was $21,500. By what percentage did the price of a Honda Accord increase? Here is the formula we use to determine the percentage change in price:

$$\text{Percentage change in price} =$$

$$\frac{\text{Price in later year} - \text{Price in earlier year}}{\text{Price in earlier year}} \times 100$$

If we fill in the numbers, we get the following:

$$\text{Percentage change in price} =$$

$$\frac{\$21{,}500 - \$20{,}000}{\$20{,}000} \times 100 = 7.5\%$$

The Consumer Price Index

In the previous example, the percentage increased in a single price from one year to the next. Economists are much more interested, though, in what happens to prices in general than in what happens to a single price. Before they can calculate the change in prices from one year to the next, they need to compute a **price index**, or average price level. The most widely used price index is the **consumer price index (CPI)**. You might have heard a newscaster say, "Today, it was reported in Washington that the consumer price index has risen 3.2 percent on an annual basis." Let's look at how the CPI is computed and what it means.

EXAMPLE In February 2007, the CPI was 203.4 and in February 2017 it was 243.6. How much had prices changed from 2007 to 2017? To calculate the change in prices (as measured by the CPI) we subtract 203.4 from 243.6 and then divide by 203.4 and then multiply by 100. Here is the calculation [(243.6 − 203.4) ÷ 203.4] x 100. This gives us 19.76 percent. This means that something that cost $1 in 2007 would cost approximately $1.20 in 2017. ◆

price index
A measure of the price level, or the average level of prices.

consumer price index (CPI)
The most widely used price index.

Teach

Reinforcement Activity

To give students more practice with determining price changes, bring a weekend advertisement into class that shows original prices and sale prices. Have students find the percentage change in price for each item.

Cooperative Learning

Divide the class into groups of three or four students. Instruct groups to research the consumer price index (CPI). Ask them to consider how changes in the CPI affect their lives and their parents' lives. For example, students might explore how buying power is affected by a rise in the CPI. Allow groups to present their findings in class.

Reinforcement Activity

Assign students to look through newspapers for reports of a change in prices of all goods in an economy or any mention of the consumer price index (CPI). Instruct them to share their findings in small groups.

Teaching with Visuals

To provide students more practice with calculating the CPI and to help ensure that they understand this concept, create your own market basket of items and discuss it with the class. Make sure you have clear base-year prices and current-year prices. Then tell students to do the same with five to ten products whose base-year prices they know or can find. Invite students to share their information, what they included in their market baskets, and what they used as base-year prices. As a class, compare students' individual CPIs. Are they all in the same range?

 Visit econ.myemcp.com/videos for videos that will help students better understand the key concepts found in this section.

The CPI is calculated by the U.S. Bureau of Labor Statistics. The bureau surveys thousands of households and determines what these consumers paid for a representative group of goods called the market basket. This amount is compared with what a typical *consumer unit* paid for the same market basket in 1982–1984. (A consumer unit is a household of related or unrelated individuals who pool their money. In the last survey, the average consumer unit was made up of 2.5 people.)

The CPI is calculated using the following process (see also Exhibit 11-8):

1. Calculate the total dollar expenditure on the market basket in the base year and the total dollar expenditure on the market basket in the current year.

▶ If you have some basic information, you can use these steps to calculate the CPI.

EXHIBIT 11-8 **Calculating the Consumer Price Index**

Step 1: Calculate the total dollar expenditure on the market basket in the base year and the current year. These amounts are calculated in column 3 ($150) and column 5 ($180), respectively.

(1) Goods in the market basket	(2) Price in base year	(3) Base-year expenditure (1) × (2)	(4) Price in current year	(5) Current-year expenditure (1) × (4)
10 DVDs	$13	10 × $13 = $130	$15	10 × $15 = $150
5 T-shirts	$4	5 × $4 = $20	$6	5 × $6 = $30
		$150		$180

Total dollar expenditure on the market basket in the base year

Total dollar expenditure on the market basket in the current year

Step 2: Divide the total dollar expenditure on the market basket in the current year by the total dollar expenditure on the market basket in the base year, and then multiply by 100.

$$CPI_{current\ year} = \frac{\text{Total dollar expenditure on the market basket in current year}}{\text{Total dollar expenditure on the market basket in base year}} \times 100$$

$$= \frac{\$180}{\$150} \times 100$$

$$= 120$$

Cooperative Learning

Divide the class into groups of three or four students each. Direct the students to the Bureau of Labor Statistics CPI databases website at http://econ.emcp.net/cpi. Students should then use the "Top Picks" column to gather data to the following questions: (1) What was the (current series) CPI in January 2013, using 1982–1984 as the base year? [230.280]. (2) What was the CPI for urban and clerical workers in January 2013, using 1982–1984 as the base year? [226.520]. (3) Under "Average Price Data" find the dollar price of a gallon of gasoline in February 2014 [$3.422].

2. Divide the total current-year expenditure by the total base-year expenditure, and multiply by 100.

Exhibit 11-8 provides an example. To simplify things, we'll say that the market basket is made up of only two goods instead of the hundreds of items that it actually contains. Our market basket contains 10 DVDs and five T-shirts.

To find the total dollar expenditure on the market basket in the base year, we multiply the quantity of each good in the market basket (column 1) times the price of that good in the base year (column 2). A look at column 3 shows us that $130 was spent on DVDs and $20 was spent on T-shirts, for a total dollar expenditure of $150.

Next, to find the total dollar expenditure on the market basket in the current year, we multiply the quantity of each good in the market basket (column 1) times the price of that good in the current year (column 4). A look at column 5 shows us that $150 was spent on DVDs and $30 was spent on T-shirts, for a total dollar expenditure of $180.

Now, we divide the total current-year expenditure ($180) by the total base-year expenditure ($150) and then multiply by 100:

$$\frac{\$180}{\$150} \times 100 = 120$$

The CPI for the current year (in our example) is 120.

Note that the CPI is just a number. What does this number tell us? By itself, the CPI number tells us little. It's only when we compare one CPI with another that we learn something. For example, in the United States in 2015, the CPI was 236.5. One year later, in 2016, the CPI was 241.4. The two CPI numbers can be used to figure out the percentage by which prices increased between 2015 and 2016 in the same way we determined the percentage increase for a single price:

Percentage change in CPI =

$$\frac{\text{CPI}_{\text{later year}} - \text{CPI}_{\text{earlier year}}}{\text{CPI}_{\text{earlier year}}} \times 100$$

If we fill in the numbers, we get the following:

Percentage change in CPI =

$$\frac{241.4 - 236.5}{236.5} \times 100 = 2.07\%$$

Determining the Quantity of Goods and Services and the Price Level

Chapter 4 explained that every market has two sides: a demand side and a supply side. We represent the demand in a market with a downward-sloping demand curve (left to right) and the supply in a market with an upward-sloping supply curve (left to right). As you may recall, the equilibrium price and quantity in a market (the point at which the demand curve and the supply curve intersect) are determined by the forces of supply and demand.

What holds for a market holds for an economy too. Every economy has a demand side and a supply side, as illustrated in Exhibit 11-9. The demand side is represented by the **aggregate demand curve**, which shows the quantity of goods and services that buyers are willing and able to buy at different price levels. (Sometimes, the quantity of goods and services is simply referred to as *output* or *real GDP*.) The supply side is represented by the **aggregate supply curve**, which shows the quantity of goods and services (or *output*) that producers are willing and able to supply at different price levels. The equilibrium price level and equilibrium quantity of goods and services are determined by the forces of aggregate demand and aggregate supply.

The forces of aggregate demand and supply determine the equilibrium price level and equilibrium quantity of goods and services (*equilibrium output*) in an economy. The equilibrium price level (P_E in Exhibit 11-9) and the equilibrium quantity of goods and services, or output (Q_E in Exhibit 11-9), come to exist over time. For example, at P_1, the quantity demanded

aggregate demand curve
A curve that shows the quantity of goods and services that buyers are willing and able to buy at different price levels.

aggregate supply curve
A curve that shows the quantity of goods and services that producers are willing and able to supply at different price levels.

Teaching with Visuals

In this chapter, we have studied three major topics: GDP, real GDP, and the CPI. All three are represented in Exhibit 11-9 on page 334 (the price level is on the vertical axis; the quantity of goods and services, or real GDP, is on the horizontal axis; and GDP is simply the product of what is on the vertical axis (P) and the horizontal axis (Q)).

Discussion Starter

Ask students to define the terms *aggregate demand curve* and *aggregate supply curve*. Encourage them to use their own words and to give examples. The aggregate demand/aggregate supply framework is used often in economics. Tell students that understanding this concept is very important and that they will use it in a future chapter.

▶ Equilibrium in an economy is produced by the economic forces of aggregate demand (AD) and aggregate supply (AS). The economy is in equilibrium at point A in the exhibit.

EXHIBIT 11-9 **Aggregate Demand and Aggregate Supply**

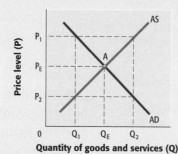

	When price level is	Buyers are willing and able to buy	Sellers are willing and able to sell	Remarks
Look at AD only	P_1	Q_1	—	Buyers are willing and able to buy more at lower price levels than at higher price levels.
	P_2	Q_2	—	
Look at AS only	P_1	—	Q_2	Sellers are willing and able to produce and sell more at higher price levels than at lower price levels.
	P_2	—	Q_1	
Look at AD and AS together	P_1	Q_1	Q_2	Buyers are willing and able to buy less than sellers are willing and able to produce and sell.
	P_2	Q_2	Q_1	Buyers are willing and able to buy more than sellers are willing and able to produce and sell.
	P_E	Q_E	Q_E	At equilibrium, buyers are willing and able to buy the same amount as sellers are willing and able to produce and sell.

of goods and services (Q_1) is less than the quantity supplied (Q_2), resulting in a surplus of goods and services. As a result, the price level drops. At a lower price level, people buy more goods and services and producers produce less. The surplus begins to disappear because of these actions on the part of buyers and sellers. (Buyers help to eliminate the surplus by buying more, and sellers help by producing less.)

At P_2, the quantity demanded of goods and services (Q_2) is greater than the quantity supplied (Q_1), resulting in a shortage of goods and services.

"There are plenty of good five-cent cigars in the country. The trouble is they cost a quarter. What this country needs is a good five-cent nickel."
—Franklin Pierce Adams, twentieth-century newspaper columnist

Thus, the price level rises, people buy fewer goods and services, and producers produce more. The shortage begins to disappear because of the actions of buyers and sellers. (Buyers help eliminate the shortage by buying less, and sellers help by producing more.) Only at P_E is the quantity of goods and services supplied equal to the quantity of goods and services demanded. Both are Q_E.

Aggregate supply and demand are influenced by a number of factors and act as influences on some other factors. One of the factors that aggregate supply and demand influence is unemployment, which we discuss next.

Internet Research

Instruct students to browse online news sources to find examples of current events that can change the aggregate supply and aggregate demand curves. Ask them to list their findings and explain how each event might affect either of the curves. Ask students to use the specific information about supply and demand that they have learned from their textbook.

Did President Kennedy Earn More Than Today's President?

Today, the president of the United States earns an annual salary of $400,000. In 1962, when John F. Kennedy was president, the salary was $100,000. Does this mean that the president today is paid four times more than President Kennedy was paid?

The answer is yes if we consider only the actual dollar amounts. We need to keep in mind, however, that when Kennedy was president, the prices of goods and services were much lower than they are today. In 1962, $100,000 bought much more than $100,000 will buy today. The question is, would it buy four times as much in 1962 as it will buy today?

To get some idea of what a $100,000 salary in 1962 would equal in today's dollars, economists use the following formula:

$$\text{Salary in today's dollars} = \text{Salary in earlier year} \times (\text{CPI}_{today} \div \text{CPI}_{1962})$$

Suppose that by *today*, we mean 2017. We want to find out what Kennedy's 1962 salary is equal to in 2017 dollars. The CPI in February 2017 was 243.6, and the CPI in 1962 was about 30. Filling in the formula, we see that Kennedy's salary in 1962 is equivalent to earning $812,000 in 2017:

$$\text{Salary in today's dollars} = \$100,000 \times (243.6 \div 30) = \$812,000$$

Based on these calculations, we can see that President Kennedy earned considerably more than the president today earns, in terms of purchasing

power. Kennedy earned the equivalent of $812,000 in today's (2017) dollars, compared to the current president earnings of $400,000. In other words, Kennedy was paid the equivalent of $412,000 more than the president today is being paid.

THINK ABOUT IT Suppose a house cost $45,000 in 1970, and the CPI in 1970 was 38.8. What is the price of the house in 2017 dollars (CPI in 2017 = 243.6)?

Who Are the Unemployed?

Look at Exhibit 11-10 on page 337 which shows the employment status of the entire United States population. Notice the total population, which is divided into two broad groups. One group consists of persons who are under 16 years of age, in the armed forces, or in a mental or correctional facility. The other group, which consists of all others in the total population, is called the *noninstitutional adult civilian population*.

Now take the noninstitutional adult civilian population and divide it into two groups: persons *not in the labor force* and

persons in the *civilian labor force*. Persons not in the labor force are those who are neither working nor looking for work. Retired persons fall into this category, as do homemakers and persons who choose not to work.

Finally, persons in the civilian labor force can be divided into two groups: they are either *employed* or *unemployed*.

> *"The study of economics won't necessarily keep you out of the unemployment line, but at least if you're there, you'll understand why."*
> — Anonymous

$$\text{Civilian labor force} = \text{Unemployed persons} + \text{Employed persons}$$

Background Information: Movie Sales

Once students have worked on the CPI formula for calculating current dollars, they should be able to apply it to anything, including blockbuster movies of the past. Some Disney movies—including *Snow White and the Seven Dwarfs, Fantasia, 101 Dalmatians, Bambi, Mary Poppins,* and *Sleeping Beauty*—are among the highest-grossing movies of all time in current dollars. Ask students why they think these movies have grossed so much money. (The answer is that copies of these movies continue to sell in stores, while other classic movies do not have current sales.)

This feature may be a good beginning point for comparing prices of various products over time. One fun way to do this is to assign students to look at old newspapers or catalogs for prices and then have them use the CPI formula to find how much the product would cost today. This can be even more interesting when the product still exists and is manufactured by the same firm.

ANSWERS TO THINK ABOUT IT If a house cost $45,000 in 1970, the price of the house in 2017 dollars would be approximately $282,525 (*calculation:* $45,000 × (243.6 ÷ 38.8).

Economics Around the Clock

Discuss students' answers to the 2:34 p.m. scenario in Economics Around the Clock (page 315).

Help students realize that Beverlee's father needs to convert both his salary and Beverlee's salary into today's dollars and then compare them. We practice doing this in the Economics in the Real World feature on President Kennedy's salary.

Historical information can help us to understand what's happening to the economy now and to plan for the future. But comparing economic data from different years can be difficult, because price levels change over time. Invite students to explore this issue by going to http://emcschool.net /Economics2e, selecting Chapter 10, and reading the Economics in the Real World feature titled **"What Is the All-Time Top-Grossing Movie?"**

After students have read this feature, ask if they were surprised to learn that *Gone with the Wind* is the top-grossing movie of all time. Which movie did they think would be the top earner?

ANSWERS TO THINK ABOUT IT Answers will vary.

Students may wonder what the economic crisis has to do with them. Point out that the economy affects real people in real ways. This feature explains how the financial health of banks can affect individuals at a most basic level: their jobs.

ANSWERS TO THINK ABOUT IT Consider two banks, A and B. Bank A has assets of $100, liabilities of $97, and net worth of $3. Bank B has assets of $100, liabilities of $90, and net worth of $10. A 4% decline in assets (from $100 to $96 will move bank A into insolvency. But it will take an 11% decline in assets (from $100 to $89) to do the same to bank B, because it has a bigger net worth and thus a bigger buffer against insolvency.

Application Activity

After reading and discussing Section 4, you may want to assign the Section Activity in the *Applying the Principles Workbook,* pages 125–127.

Assess

Quick Quiz

The following true-or-false quiz will help you assess student understanding of the material covered in this section.

1. The average price level is known as the *price appendix.* (False)
2. The consumer price index is calculated by the U.S. Treasury. (False)
3. The quantity of goods and services is simply referred to as *output.* (True)
4. An upward-sloping aggregate supply curve indicates that producers are willing and able to produce and offer to sell a greater quantity of goods at higher price levels than at lower price levels. (True)
5. The forces of aggregate demand and supply determine the equilibrium price level and equilibrium quantity of goods and services in an economy. (True)

Could You Lose Your Job if Your Bank Loses Money?

▲ If the business you work for closes its doors, you will be out of a job.

The answer is yes. But how? To understand how, start by looking at the financial crisis of 2007–2009 as a balance sheet problem.

A bank's *balance sheet* lists three things: assets, liabilities, and net worth (or capital). *Assets* consist of things that are owned by the bank (such as government securities) and things that generate income for the bank (such as loans granted to others).

Liabilities consist of things the bank owes to others. For example, the bank owes the money in your checking account to you.

The difference between a bank's assets and liabilities constitutes the bank's *net worth*, or *capital*. A bank is *solvent* if its assets are greater than its liabilities. A bank is *insolvent* if its liabilities are greater than its assets.

In the financial crisis of 2007–2009, some banks found that they were insolvent or fast approaching insolvency. Many were in this situation because their assets were declining in value. Which assets in particular? Subprime mortgage loans[1] and mortgage-backed securities (which were backed by subprime loans).

During the crisis, many people who had taken out subprime mortgages from banks didn't pay them back. After many of these loans went bad, banks' assets declined in value, moving the banks closer to insolvency.

Consider a bank with $35 million in assets, $29 million in liabilities, and $6 million in net worth. Suppose the bank's assets decline in value to $28 million. Now the bank will have a net worth of *minus* $1 million, making it insolvent.

When banks approach or reach insolvency, they cut back on lending. As lending is reduced, spending in the real sector of the economy often declines. As a result, economic activity generally slows down. In the end, some companies go out of business, and some people lose their jobs.

THINK ABOUT IT Having a large net worth is often said to be a buffer against insolvency. Why?

1. A *subprime* loan is a nontraditional loan, which means that the borrower must meet less strict standards than are established for obtaining a traditional loan. Some people received subprime loans without going through a thorough credit check and without making the traditional 20 percent down payment. In some cases, the down payment was 1 or 2 percent of the selling price of the house.

Differentiating Instruction

English Language Learners

To help students who are English language learners, use the following resources, which are provided as part of the *Economics: New Ways of Thinking* program:

* a Spanish glossary in the *Student Text*
* Spanish versions of the Chapter Summaries on an audio disc

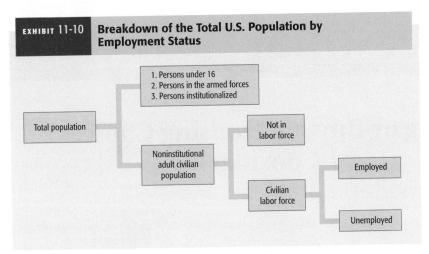

EXHIBIT 11-10 Breakdown of the Total U.S. Population by Employment Status

Total population
- 1. Persons under 16
- 2. Persons in the armed forces
- 3. Persons institutionalized
- Noninstitutional adult civilian population
  - Not in labor force
  - Civilian labor force
    - Employed
    - Unemployed

 In which of the boxes shown in the exhibit do you belong? Think of different people you know and try to determine which categories they are currently in.

The Unemployment and Employment Rates

The **unemployment rate** is the percentage of the civilian labor force that is unemployed. It is equal to the number of unemployed persons divided by the civilian labor force:

$$\text{Unemployment rate} = \frac{\text{Unemployed persons}}{\text{Civilian labor force}}$$

For example, if the civilian labor force totals 10 million and the number of persons unemployed is 1 million, then the unemployment rate is 10 percent.

The **employment rate** is the percentage of the noninstitutional adult civilian population that is employed. It is equal to the number of persons employed divided by the number of persons in the noninstitutional adult civilian population:

$$\text{Employment rate} = \frac{\text{Employed persons}}{\text{Noninstitutional adult civilian population}}$$

unemployment rate
The percentage of the civilian labor force that is unemployed.

employment rate
The percentage of the noninstitutional adult civilian population that is employed.

SECTION 4 ASSESSMENT

Defining Terms
1. Define:
   a. price index
   b. consumer price index (CPI)
   c. aggregate demand curve
   d. aggregate supply curve
   e. unemployment rate
   f. employment rate

Reviewing Facts and Concepts
2. Suppose the CPI was 143 in year 1 and 132 in year 2. Did prices rise or fall between year 1 and year 2?

3. The noninstitutional adult civilian population is 120 million, the number of unemployed is 5 million, and the number of employed is 60 million. What is the unemployment rate?

Critical Thinking
4. What can cause the equilibrium price level to rise? What can cause the equilibrium quantity of goods and services (in the economy) to fall? (*Hint*: Look at Exhibit 11-9.)

5. If the number of unemployed people drops, can the unemployment rate rise? Explain.

Applying Economic Concepts
6. Smith earned $40,000 in 2003 and $50,000 in 2004. The CPI was 184.0 in 2003 and 188.9 in 2004. Using the data presented, how can Smith figure out whether his earnings went up by more than, less than, or equal to the change in prices?

SECTION 4 ASSESSMENT ANSWERS

Defining Terms
1. **a. price index:** a measure of the price level, or the average level of prices; **b. consumer price index (CPI):** the most widely cited price index; **c. aggregate demand curve:** shows the quantity of goods and services that buyers are willing and able to buy at different price levels; **d. aggregate supply curve:** shows the quantity of goods and services that producers are willing and able to supply at different price levels; **e. unemployment rate:** the percentage of the civilian labor force that is unemployed; **f. employment rate:** percentage of the noninstitutional adult civilian population that is employed.

Reviewing Facts and Concepts
2. Prices fell.

Assessment Book

You will find a quiz for this section in the *Assessment Book,* page 110.

Reteaching Activity

Use the Section Assessment to gauge which students may need reteaching on this section. With those students, review the paragraph on page 333 that begins "Note that the CPI is just a number." Make sure that students understand the usefulness of the CPI for tracking prices over time.

Guided Reading

For further reteaching of the key concepts in this section, assign the Outlining Activity and the Just the Facts Handout from the *Guided Reading and Study Guide,* pages 189–193.

3. The unemployment rate is 7.7% (*calculation:* UR = 5 million ÷ 65 million = 0.0768=7.7%).

Critical Thinking
4. The equilibrium price level will rise if (a) the aggregate demand curve shifts to the right or (b) the aggregate supply curve shifts to the left. The equilibrium quantity of goods and services will fall if (a) the aggregate demand curve shifts to the left or (b) the aggregate supply curve shifts to the left.

5. The unemployment rate is equal to the number of unemployed persons divided by the civilian labor force. If the number of unemployed persons drops by, say, 2 percent, but the civilian labor force declines by a greater percentage (say, 10 percent), the unemployment rate will rise.

Applying Economic Concepts
6. Smith needs to figure out the percentage increase in his earnings from one year to the next (*calculation:* ($50,000 − $40,000) ÷ $40,000 × 100% = 25%). Next, he must figure out the percentage increase in prices from one year to the next (*calculation:* 188.9 − 184 ÷ 184 × 100% = 2.66%). From there, he needs to compare the percentage increase in his earnings with the percentage increase in prices. Smith will see that his earnings went up by a greater percentage than prices increased.

Your **Personal** Economics

Discussion Starter

Ask students if they plan to rent or buy their housing in the future. If so, why do they hope to do so? Many students may not have considered whether they want to rent or buy housing. This feature will help them evaluate the benefits and costs of both home ownership and renting.

Research Activity

Ask students to look in a newspaper or online for housing prices in their area (both renting and buying prices). This information will be helpful to put some of the concepts of the "Your Personal Economics" feature into context.

Renting or Buying: Housing Choices to Consider

One of the most important financial decisions an individual can make is whether to rent or buy housing.

We use the term "housing" because it covers a wide variety of dwellings, including apartments, condominiums, and single-family houses. So, how do you know whether it is smarter to rent or buy housing? And which type of housing is best to rent or buy? There are a lot of different options to consider. Many people believe that buying is better because, unlike renting, buying is an investment that can potentially pay off; however, it is important to consider a wide range of factors when making this decision.

Comparing Apples to Apples Rather than Oranges

When considering whether it is better to buy or rent, it is important to compare homes with similar characteristics. For example, compare renting a 1,500-square-foot dwelling with buying a 1,500-square-foot dwelling. That's because comparing homes that are very different (for example, comparing renting a 750-square-foot apartment with buying a 4,000-square-foot house) is like comparing apples to oranges—there is too much of a difference between the objects

to make it a helpful exercise. The monthly mortgage payments for a 4,000-square-foot house are almost guaranteed to be much higher than the monthly rent on a 750-square-foot apartment.

The Price-Rent Ratio

When it comes to deciding whether to rent or buy, calculating the price-rent ratio can be a helpful exercise. The price-rent ratio is equal to the median price for housing in an area divided by the annual rent for a similar dwelling.

$$\frac{\text{Median Price of Housing}}{\text{Annual Rent of Equivalent Housing}} = \text{Price Rent Ratio}$$

Suppose the median price for a house in city X is $100,000. (This means that half the houses in that city sell for more than $100,000 and the other half sell for less than $100,000.) Now, suppose that the total annual rent on a house similar to those priced at $100,000 is also $100,000. This would make the price-rent ratio 1. Does it make more sense to buy or rent the house? Most people will say that it is better to buy the house. After all, it would take the same amount of money to buy the house as it would take to rent it for one year.

Now suppose we change the median price of housing to

$200,000 and leave the annual rent for a similar house at $100,000. This bumps up the price-rent ratio to 2. It may *still* be better to buy than to rent, but the benefit is not quite as strong as it was when the price-rent ratio was 1.

In general, the lower the price-rent ratio, all other things being equal, the better it is to buy than rent.

Predicting House Prices

You may choose to examine historical price-rent ratios to see if it is a good time to buy. Suppose that the price-rent ratio in a given city over a twenty-year period is 18, which means that the median price of a house is 18 times the annual rent for a similar house. Then, all of a sudden, the price-rent ratio rises to 21, then 25, and then finally to 27! This rise means that the median home price jumped to 21 times greater than the annual rent, and then to 25 times greater, and finally to 27 times greater. When the price-rent ratio rises dramatically above its long-run average, many economists will argue that there is a "bubble" in the housing market in that city. In other words, house prices are out of line with rents, and there is likely to be a return to what is "normal" (in this case, 18).

Comparing a long-run price-rent ratio with the current price-rent ratio

Cooperative Learning

Divide students into small groups and ask them to discuss which housing option is better: buying or renting? Start by having each group brainstorm a list of pros and cons for each option. Groups should either do additional research or consult the

price information from the research assignment (listed in the column above). Finally, ask students to vote (as individuals) which option they would recommend and discuss the options as a class.

for a city can give you some idea about whether house prices will continue to rise or are likely to fall. It is better to buy when the price-rent ratio is not historically high so that you will not lose money on your investment if prices fall (which they are likely to do).

During the years 2000–2006 in the United States, the price-rent ratios in many cities increased.

City	Pre-2000 average price-rent ratio	2005 price-rent ratio
San Francisco	24	40
Minneapolis	12	21
Tampa	12	24
Atlanta	13	20
Phoenix	11	25

What eventually happened in these cities (and in many more cities across the country) was that housing prices declined rapidly and appreciably, and the price-rent ratios moved back toward their long-run averages.

Is a House a Good Investment?

Many people think of the house they own as not just a place to live, but also as an investment. Such people will argue that you "throw money away" when you rent, and that when you buy, you are investing in something that you can sell at a later date at a higher price. In other words, the house you buy today for $200,000 can be sold at a later date for $250,000 or $300,000.

Since 1975, housing prices in the United States have appreciated by an average of 4.5 percent per year. When you look at housing appreciation over a longer period of time—since 1890—there has been a 3 percent annual increase in the nominal (or dollar) value of housing. But once the dollar value has been adjusted for inflation, the real (or inflation-adjusted) return on housing is just slightly above zero.[1]

In other words, the house you buy today may go up in price, say, from $200,000 to $300,000, which is an increase of 50 percent. But that doesn't mean buying the house is a good investment. If inflation has advanced by 50 percent during the time you bought and then sold the house, the real (inflation-adjusted) return on the house is zero.

House Prices and the Return on Equity

Another factor to consider when deciding to buy or rent housing is how much of a down payment you can put toward the property. Suppose a house is priced at $250,000. A person makes a 20 percent down payment ($50,000) and takes out a mortgage loan of $200,000 to buy the house. This means that his or her *equity* in the house is $50,000, since equity is equal to the difference between what the house is worth (what it sold for) and how much the owner

1 See "Should You Buy a House or Rent?" by Bill Conerly, Forbes magazine, November 11, 2013 at https://www.forbes.com/sites/billconerly/2013/11/11/should-you-buy-a-house-or-rent-the-economics-of-homeownership/#29c25efe5f14

of the house still owes on the mortgage loan.

Now suppose the price of the house rises by 3 percent to $257,500. This causes the person's equity in the house to rise from $50,000 to $57,500—a positive difference of $7,500.

If we divide $7,500 by the original amount of equity in the house ($50,000), we get the *return on equity*, which, in this case, is 15 percent. In other words, a 3 percent increase in the sales price of the house has increased the owner's equity by 15 percent, which demonstrates that even small increases in value can have significant effects on equity. What this example points out is that borrowing to buy a house (taking out a mortgage loan) is a sound investment as long as home prices continue to rise.

Suppose instead that housing prices had decreased by 3 percent. This would cause the value of the house to drop from $250,000 to $242,500, and cause the owner's equity to decline from $50,000 to $42,500—a decrease of $7,500, or a negative difference of 15 percent.

In other words, it works both ways: a small decrease in the price of a house can also cause a relatively large decline in the owner's equity. What percentage decrease in the price of the house would completely eliminate the owner's equity? The answer is 20 percent, since $50,000 is 20 percent of $250,000. In short, with a 20 percent down payment,

Research Activity

Assign students the task of finding the price-rent ratio for their area. Students should use online resources and data collected in class to support their findings. Emphasize how the results can help them decide whether renting or buying housing would be wise.

Research Activity

Ask students to identify their own housing needs. Where do they want to live? How many rooms would they require? Should their housing be pet friendly? How many square feet do they want? Once students have identified their list of wants, instruct students to look in a newspaper or online for housing prices in their preferred area. Encourage students to identify what housing options are currently available in the area to rent and to buy and how these prices differ. Emphasize the importance of comparing similar housing options when they look at prices. Encourage students to report their findings to the class.

a 20 percent decline in price will eliminate the person's entire equity in the house. The smaller the down payment, the more likely it is than a small downturn in the housing market will cause a total loss of equity.

What is the lesson to be learned? If housing prices are rising, then a small down payment on a house will produce a bigger gain in equity than a large down payment. But, of course, if housing prices fall, a small down payment will produce a greater loss in equity than a large down payment.

The Benefits and Costs of Renting

Let's now consider the costs and benefits of renting. One of the benefits is that maintenance on the property is handled by the owner or landlord. If the hot water heater breaks down or the roof leaks, the landlord has to have it fixed—at no cost to you.

Another benefit of renting is that it allows for flexibility should you not be sure of your living arrangements or plans. Owning a home prevents you from moving quickly, since you have to list and sell your home before you can leave. Although you will usually have to sign a relatively short-term lease agreement, renting gives you much greater freedom to pack up and move if your job changes, you realize you don't like the area, or you need more or less space.

Renting is also beneficial if price-rent ratios are very high where you live. As discussed earlier, this

means that housing prices are likely to decline relatively soon, and so it is better to wait to buy a house until this happens, and rent in the interim.

Another benefit of renting is that the money that would have been used for a down payment to buy a house can now be used in a different way – perhaps to buy stock, bonds, gold coins, and so on.

In addition to the rent itself, costs associated with renting include rental insurance and security deposits (which can be sizeable, as they are usually equal to one month's rent). In addition to these monetary amounts, there are also other costs to consider. One of the downsides of renting is that the property you inhabit is not yours, so you are limited when it comes to making changes. For example,

if you want to paint the bedrooms a different color, you have to get permission from the landlord to do so. Another potential cost to consider is that even if you want to renew your rental contract when it expires (say, for another six months or a year), the landlord could say no. You may end up having to move when you would rather stay, and moving can be quite expensive on its own.

The Benefits and Costs of Buying

Some people say that one of the key benefits of owning a house is the feeling that comes with knowing it is yours. People often feel a sense of accomplishment when they are able to buy their house. Owning a home also fosters a sense of security: no one can tell you to move (as could be the case if you are renting and the landlord does not renew your contract).

Another benefit to owning a home is the home mortgage interest deduction (a tax break based on your mortgage interest payments during that year). Note, however, that this benefit only applies to those individuals who itemize their tax deductions.

The costs of buying a home include the down payment, maintenance costs, home insurance, and property taxes. Besides the costs of owning a house, there are costs associated with selling a house, such as the real estate broker's commission, paying for the house to be inspected, closing costs, and so on.

One of the risks associated with buying a property is that housing prices are subject to change. As discussed earlier, if housing prices rise, your return on equity is positive and you reap a gain, but if housing prices fall, your return on equity is negative, and you incur a loss.

The Transition from Renting to Owning

In addition to losing benefits you received as a renter (such as calling a landlord to make repairs on your housing), the financial costs of transitioning from renting to home ownership include the financial expenses of relocating yourself and your property. This could include airfare, movers, gas, and/or truck rental.

Your Personal Economics Activity

Evaluate the costs and benefits of owning your own home. How do they compare to the costs and benefits of renting a home? Investigate the options in your current area and consider the price-rent ratio when supporting your evaluation. Also assess the financial aspects of transitioning from renting to owning and include this information in your evaluation.

My Personal Economics Action Plan

Here are some points you may want to consider and some guidelines you might want to put in practice:

☑ 1. Housing prices don't always rise (especially when they are adjusted for inflation), and taking out a big mortgage loan to reduce your income taxes is not always worthwhile.

When I hear someone say that "housing prices always rise" or that "it's best to take out a big mortgage loan so that I can reduce my income taxes," I will do my homework, which consists of finding out if house prices always rise and figuring out how much I have to pay in interest payments to reduce my income taxes by a specified dollar amount.

☑ 2. Keep in mind that the historical record of price-rent ratios can give you some idea of whether housing prices are likely to rise or fall in the near future. Remember, the lower the price-rent ratio, the more beneficial it is to buy. For example, a price-rent ratio of 2 means that the price to own a median-priced house is twice the annual rent of a similar house, but a price-rent ratio of 33 means that the price to own a median-priced house is 33 times the annual rent of a similar house.

I will do some research (usually this can be done online) on the price-rent ratio in the city in which I want to reside. I will compare the current price-rent ratio in the city with the long-run average price-rent ratio in the city. If the current price-rent ratio is substantially higher than the long-run average, I will consider waiting to buy instead of buying now.

Discussion Starter

Ask students whether investing in a home or owning property is a good investment in their current location. How would the conditions need to change to make the opposite true? Emphasize the fact that factors can change quickly for many investments.

My Personal Economics Action Plan Instruct students to identify their future housing goals (renting vs. owning). Tell them to describe in writing what factors they should consider before deciding to rent or buy housing. Encourage students to carry out the necessary research and to tentatively identify if their preferred housing plan is supported by the price-rent ratio in their desired location.

Economics Vocabulary

1. GDP; **2.** GNP; **3.** double counting; **4.** consumption; **5.** investment; **6.** base year; **7.** aggregate demand curve; **8.** Aggregate demand, aggregate supply; **9.** Real GDP; **10.** government purchases; **11.** export spending; **12.** employment rate.

Understanding the Main Ideas

1. Government transfer payments are unrelated to the production of goods and services.

2. GDP measures output produced within the borders of a country; GNP measures the output produced by the citizens of a country, no matter where they reside. The GDP is relevant to geography; the GNP is relevant to citizenship.

3. There are no records of illegal transactions.

4. Stock transactions simply bring about a change in the ownership of assets; there is no production.

5. A final good is in the hands of a consumer or end user of the good. An intermediate good is not.

6. Real GDP figures have been adjusted for price changes. When an economist sees that the real GDP is higher in year 2 than in year 1, she knows why: quantity of output is higher in year 2. But when an economist sees that the GDP is higher in year 2 than in year 1, she doesn't know why. It could be because quantity of output is higher, because prices are higher, or because both are higher. An economist has greater certainty with real GDP than with GDP.

7. Exhibit 11-6 (page 323) shows that consumption is the largest spending component of GDP.

8. Because GDP = C + I + G + EX − IM, if import spending (IM) rises and nothing else changes, then GDP will fall.

9. The unemployment rate is the percentage of the civilian labor force that is not employed. Unemployment

Chapter Summary

Be sure you know and remember the following key points from the chapter sections.

Section 1

▶ Gross domestic product (GDP) is the total market value of all final goods and services produced annually in a country.

▶ Some exchanges, such as illegal transactions and those that are not recorded, are omitted from GDP.

Section 2

▶ Economists divide the economy into four sectors: household, business, government, and foreign.

▶ To compute U.S. GDP, we need to sum consumption (C), investment (I), government purchases (G), and export spending (EX) and then subtract import spending (IM).

▶ Greater production of goods and services (higher GDP) is a factor that contributes to people being better off.

Section 3

▶ Real GDP is equal to price in the base year times quantity in the current year.

▶ Economists often use a base year to separate out changes in output from prices.

Section 4

▶ To calculate the change in prices from one year to the next, economists compute a price index.

▶ The consumer price index (CPI) is calculated by surveying households to determine what consumers paid for a group of goods called the *market basket*.

▶ The forces of an economy's aggregate demand and supply determine the equilibrium price level and equilibrium quantity of goods and services.

▶ The unemployment rate equals the number of unemployed persons divided by the number of persons in the civilian labor force.

Economics Vocabulary

1. The total market value of all final goods and services produced annually in an economy is called _____.

2. The total market value of all final goods and services produced annually by the citizens of a country, no matter where in the world they reside, is called _____.

3. Counting a good more than once in computing GDP is called _____.

4. The household sector makes expenditures called _____.

5. The business sector makes expenditures called _____.

6. Real GDP is measured in _____ prices.

7. The _____ shows the quantity of goods and services that buyers are willing and able to buy at different price levels.

8. _____ and _____ go together to determine the equilibrium price level and equilibrium quantity of goods and services in an economy.

9. _____ is GDP that has been adjusted for price changes.

10. _____ refers to expenditures made by the government sector.

11. Expenditures made by the people in foreign countries who are buying U.S.-produced goods are called _____.

12. The _____ is the percentage of the noninstitutional adult civilian population that is employed.

Understanding the Main Ideas

1. Why does the GDP omit government transfer payments?

2. What is the difference between GDP and GNP?

3. Why does GDP omit illegal transactions?

4. Why does GDP omit stock transactions?

5. What is the difference between an intermediate good and a final good?

6. Why does an economist prefer to work with real GDP figures over GDP figures?

7. Which spending component of GDP is the largest?

8. What happens to GDP if import spending rises and no other spending component of GDP changes?

---

rate = unemployed persons ÷ civilian labor force. The employment rate is the percentage of the noninstitutional adult civilian population that is employed. Employment rate = employed persons ÷ noninstitutional adult civilian population.

10. No, it is not possible. Unemployment rate = unemployed persons ÷ civilian labor force.

Doing the Math

1. $6 trillion (*calculation:* $3.2 trillion + $1.2 trillion + $1.9 trillion + $1.5 trillion − $1.8 trillion = $6 trillion).

2. 162.5 (*calculation:* for the base year, x = 10 × $1 = $10; y = 15 × $2 = $30; and x + y = $10 + $30 = $40; for the current year, x = 10 × $2 = $20; y = 15 × $3 = $45; and $20 + $45 = $65. $65 ÷ 40 × 100 = 162.5).

9. What is the unemployment rate? The employment rate?

10. Is it possible for the unemployment rate to rise as the number of unemployed persons falls? Explain.

Doing the Math

1. Using the following data, compute the GDP: consumption = $3.2 trillion; government purchases = $1.2 trillion; export spending = $1.9 trillion; import spending = $1.8 trillion; and investment = $1.5 trillion.

2. A tiny economy produces 10 units of good X and 15 units of good Y. Base-year prices for these goods are $1 and $2, respectively. Current-year prices for these goods are $2 and $3. What is the CPI?

3. Using the data in question 2, what does real GDP equal?

4. In Exhibit 11-8, change the prices in column 2 to $14 for DVDs and $6 for T-shirts. Change the prices in column 4 to $17 for DVDs and $8 for T-shirts. Now calculate the CPI.

5. The CPI is 143 in year 1 and 132 in year 2. By what percentage have prices fallen?

6. Total population = 145 million; noninstitutional adult civilian population = 135 million; persons not in the labor force = 10 million; unemployed persons = 7 million. Using these data, compute the following:
a. The unemployment rate
b. The employment rate
c. The civilian labor force

Solving Economic Problems

1. Identify Cause and Effect. Does a higher GDP cause higher prices, or do higher prices cause a higher GDP? Explain your answer.

2. Summarize. WRITING Find a recent copy of the Economic Report of the President in your library or at www.gpo.gov/fdsys/browse/collection.action?collectionCode=ERP. Click on the most recent year under "About the

---

EXHIBIT 11-11

Goods in market basket	Price in base year	Base-year expenditure	Price in current year	Current-year expenditure
10 X	$4	(b)	(c)	$50
12 Y	(a)	$120	$12	(d)

Total dollar expenditure on market basket in current year = (e)

Total dollar expenditure on market basket in base year = (f)

Economic Report of the President," and from that page, review the Table of Contents for the report. The report contains chapters on different economic topics. Choose one chapter to read; then write a two-page paper that summarizes the content.

3. Find the Main Idea. MEDIA Find a story or article in your local newspaper that addresses one of the following: GDP, real GDP, CPI, unemployment rate, consumption spending, investment spending, or government spending. Find the main idea and describe what was said in the story or article.

4. Analyze. What is wrong with this statement: "Individuals were worse off in 1960 because they didn't earn as much as individuals earn today"?

Working with Graphs and Tables

Look at Exhibit 11-11. Identify the correct dollar amount for each blank, (a) through (f).

Project or Presentation

The Happiness Quotient. Does real GDP per person bring happiness? Create an essay, poem, skit, short story, or song in response to this question. Present your work to the class.

ONLINE   *Practice Tests and Study Guide*
emcp.com

Go to www.emcschool.net/Economics2e and choose *Economics: New Ways of Thinking*, Chapter 11, if you need more help in preparing for the chapter test.

Solving Economic Problems

1. Price is a component of GDP; GDP is not a component of price. It follows, then, that higher prices cause a higher GDP.

2. Answers will vary.

3. Answers will vary.

4. The statement mentions only what individuals earn; it doesn't mention the prices in 1960 versus today. People in 1960 might have earned less, but they paid lower prices for what they bought (in comparison to people today). How well off individuals are depends on two things: what they earn and what prices they pay.

Working with Graphs and Tables

(a) $10 (*calculation:* $120 ÷ 12 = $10);
(b) $40 (*calculation:* 10 × $4 = $40);
(c) $5 (*calculation:* $50 ÷ 10 = $5);
(d) $144 (*calculation:* 12 × $12 = $144);
(e) $194 (*calculation:* $50 + $144 = $194); (f) $160 (*calculation:* $40 + $120 = $160).

Project or Presentation

Responses will vary.

---

3. $40 (*calculation:* Real GDP for good X = $1 × 10 units = $10; Real GDP for good Y = $2 × 15 units = $30; Total real GDP for both X and Y = $10 + $30 = $40).

4. 123.53 (*calculation:* Total dollar expenditure (TDE) for base year = ($10 × $14) + ($5 × $6) = $140 + $30 = $170; TDE for current year = ($10 × $17) + ($5 × $8) = $170 + $40 =

$210; (Total current year expenditure ÷ total base year expenditure) × 100 = ($210 ÷ $170) × 100 = 123.53).

5. 7.69% (*calculation:* ($132 − $143) ÷ $132 × 100 = 7.69).

6. a. 5%; **b.** 87%; **c.** $125 million.

Chapter 12 Planning Guide

SECTION ORGANIZER

Inflation and Deflation
(pages 346–357)

Learning Objectives

- ▶ Explain what inflation is.
- ▶ Explain how inflation is measured.
- ▶ Identify causes of inflation.
- ▶ Explain what deflation is.
- ▶ Identify causes of deflation.

Reproducible Worksheets and Handouts

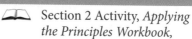

- Section 1 Activity, *Applying the Principles Workbook*, pages 128–131
- Outlining Activity, *Guided Reading and Study Guide*, pages 202–204
- Just the Facts Handout, *Guided Reading and Study Guide*, pages 205–207

Assessment

- ☑ Section Assessment, *Student Text*, page 357
- ☑ Quick Quiz, *Annotated Teacher's Edition*, page 356
- ☑ Section Quiz, *Assessment Book*, page 119

Business Cycles
(pages 358–363)

Learning Objectives

- ▶ Explain what a business cycle is.
- ▶ Explain how economists forecast business cycles.
- ▶ Identify some economic indicators.
- ▶ Identify some causes of business cycles.
- ▶ Explain how politics cause upward and downward movements in the economy.

Reproducible Worksheets and Handouts

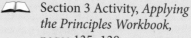

- Section 2 Activity, *Applying the Principles Workbook*, pages 132–134
- Outlining Activity, *Guided Reading and Study Guide*, pages 208–210
- Just the Facts Handout, *Guided Reading and Study Guide*, pages 211–212

Assessment

- ☑ Section Assessment, *Student Text*, page 363
- ☑ Quick Quiz, *Annotated Teacher's Edition*, page 362
- ☑ Section Quiz, *Assessment Book*, page 120

Economic Growth
(pages 364–371)

Learning Objectives

- ▶ Differentiate between absolute real economic growth and per capita real economic growth.
- ▶ Explain the purpose of the Rule of 70.
- ▶ Explain whether small differences in economic growth rates matter.
- ▶ Identify causes of economic growth.
- ▶ Explain arguments against economic growth.

Reproducible Worksheets and Handouts

- Section 3 Activity, *Applying the Principles Workbook*, pages 135–138
- Outlining Activity, *Guided Reading and Study Guide*, pages 213–214
- Just the Facts Handout, *Guided Reading and Study Guide*, pages 215–216

Assessment

- ☑ Section Assessment, *Student Text*, page 371
- ☑ Quick Quiz, *Annotated Teacher's Edition*, page 370
- ☑ Section Quiz, *Assessment Book*, page 121

Reproducible Chapter Resources and Assessment Materials

 Graphic Organizer Activity, *Guided Reading and Study Guide*, pages 217–219

Vocabulary Activity, *Guided Reading and Study Guide*, page 220

Working with Graphs and Charts, *Guided Reading and Study Guide*, page 221

Practice Test, *Guided Reading and Study Guide*, pages 222–224

Critical Thinking Activity, *Finding Economics*, pages 33–34

Chapter Test A, *Assessment Book*, pages 122–125

Chapter Test B, *Assessment Book*, pages 126–129

Student Text Internet Links

Economics: New Ways of Thinking, Second Edition encourages students to use the Internet to find out more about economics. Given the wealth of current, valid information available on websites, students should be encouraged to use the Internet as a research tool. Doing so will likely increase students' interest in and understanding of economics principles and topics. In addition, doing Internet research can help your students form the habit of accessing and using economics information, as well as help them develop investigative skills they will use throughout their educational and professional careers.

To aid your students in achieving these ends, each chapter of *Economics: New Ways of Thinking, Second Edition* includes the addresses of several websites that provide engaging and relevant information. When students type in any of the addresses provided, they will immediately arrive at the intended site. The addresses have been modified so that EMC Publishing can monitor and maintain the proper links—for example, the website http://www.deposit accounts.com/ has been changed to http://econ.emcp.net/accounts. In the event that the address or content of a site changes or is discontinued, EMC's Internet editors will redirect the link to a site with equivalent information.

Activities in the *Annotated Teacher's Edition* often suggest that students search the Internet for information. For some activities, you might want to find reputable sites beforehand and steer students toward them. For other activities, have students do their own searching and then check out the sites they have found and discuss why they might be reliable or unreliable.

Passport® for Economics

Technology resources are available with the *Economics: New Ways of Thinking, Second Edition* program through Passport®. These include:

eBooks for *Economics: New Ways of Thinking, Second Edition*

► Student textbook eBook
► Interactive Applying the Principles eWorkbook
► Finding Economics eBook
► Guided Reading and Study Guide eBook
► Annotated Teacher's Edition eBook
► Lesson Plans eBook
► Assessment eBook

Passport® for Students

Students can access helpful resources through Passport® for Economics. Resources include:
► Study guides
► Practice tests
► Flash cards in English and in Spanish
► Word games in English and in Spanish
► Tutorials and key-concept videos
► Spanish print and audio summaries

Passport® for Teachers

Keep your course current and relevant by using the teacher resources provided through Passport® for Economics. In addition to all of the resources on the student side of Passport®, the teacher side contains:
► Link to the Annotated Teacher's Edition eBook
► Standards correlations
► Microsoft® PowerPoint® Lectures
► Current Events Lessons
► Additional Economics in the Real World features
► ExamView® Assessment Suite
► PDFs of all print supplements (student and teacher)

This chapter identifies some causes and effects of inflation and deflation and discusses business cycles and economic growth. The ups and downs of business cycles, changes in real gross domestic product (GDP), and changing standards of living create the economic environment in which we spend much of our lives.

SECTION 1 Inflation and Deflation

Section 1 discusses the concepts of inflation and deflation. Students will learn what causes inflation and deflation, how they are measured, and what effects they have.

SECTION 2 Business Cycles

Section 2 examines the business cycle, which is one of the predictive tools used by economists. Students will learn the phases of the business cycle and how economists use various indicators to forecast business cycles.

SECTION 3 Economic Growth

Section 3 explores economic growth. Students will learn the difference between absolute real economic growth and per capita economic growth. They will also discover how the production possibilities frontier shows what absolute real economic growth looks like.

Economic Changes and Cycles

Why It Matters

People often say that you can't do anything about the weather. If it's snowing, raining, or sleeting today—so be it. Some people also think that certain economic events—such as inflation, deflation, the business cycle, and economic growth—are natural, unavoidable events. However, these upturns and downturns in the economy are not really natural economic events. Also, they are not inevitable in the same sense that rain in Seattle or snow in Buffalo is inevitable. Inflation, for example, doesn't have to happen—certain conditions make it more or less likely.

Ski vacations are fun—and expensive. The topics covered in this chapter—inflation, business cycles, and economic growth—play a large part in determining our standard of living.

Economists say that an understanding of economics won't necessarily keep you out of the unemployment line, but if you find yourself there, at least you will understand why. The same is true for economic occurrences such as inflation. Having a better understanding of inflation won't help you avoid rising prices, but at least you will know why they are rising.

344

Teaching Suggestions from the Author

This chapter presents the main topics of concern for macroeconomists: inflation, deflation, business cycles, and economic growth.

I like to begin the discussion of inflation and deflation by asking students to define each term and to identify what causes it. It's then a good idea to talk about the personal costs of each.

How are people harmed by inflation? Are people harmed by deflation? Does the state of the economy affect people's standard of living? Does it affect people's happiness?

Increasingly, business cycles and economic growth are the most important topics of study in macroeconomics. Economists know that people's

Economics Around the Clock

The following events occurred one day in December.

9:00 A.M. Emma and Blake Stevens are driving around various neighborhoods looking at houses. They want to sell the house they currently live in and buy another one. Emma says, "The prices of houses have really gone up in the last few years." "They sure have," adds Blake. "I guess you could say there has been a lot of inflation over the last few years."

• **Is Blake using the word** *inflation* **correctly?**

10:13 A.M. Frank is viewing an online newscast. The reporter says, "About 16,000 people die every day from hunger or hunger-related causes. This number is down from 35,000 15 years ago, and 41,000 25 years ago. Three-fourths of the deaths are children under the age of five."

• **What does death from hunger have to do with economic growth?**

3:34 P.M. Willie graduated from college in June, six months ago, but he's still living at home with his parents. So far, he hasn't found a good-paying job. At the moment, he is waiting for the interviewer at a small auto parts company to call him into the office. Willie is reading a magazine and thinking, "I hope I get this job. I really need to move out of my parents' home."

• **What does the likelihood of Willie getting a job have to do with the business cycle?**

7:32 P.M. Harry is in the grocery store looking at the different varieties of salad dressing. He counts 37 and says underneath his breath, "Whatever happened to the good ol' days when there was just blue cheese, Italian, ranch, and French?"

• **Why are so many varieties of salad dressing available today?**

345

Introducing the Chapter

To introduce Chapter 12, ask students to focus on the importance of inflation, deflation, business cycles, and economic growth as political issues. Ask students to identify some of the larger issues facing the United States today. Students may state such issues as crime, violence, racism, drugs, poverty, homelessness, AIDS, and so on. Have a volunteer list students' responses on the board.

After you have compiled a reasonably lengthy list, have students read Why It Matters on page 344. Point out that inflation, deflation, business cycles, and economic growth can be difficult to understand at first but knowing how the economy changes over time may give students peace of mind when economic fluctuations affect them. Some economists, such as Ray Fair of Yale University, think that the economy is directly linked to the person that Americans elect as president. Encourage students to see that many social issues are linked to inflation and unemployment. For example, some people believe there is a direct link between the crime rate and the unemployment rate.

Teaching with Visuals

Many families like to take vacations on a regular basis. Ask students if they think there is a direct relationship between a family's standard of living and the kinds of vacations the family takes. In what ways might a family's standard of living affect how family members spend their leisure time?

standard of living depends largely on the economy's growth rate. Adam Smith, the famous eighteenth-century economist, wanted to know why some nations are rich and some nations are poor. This has been a key macroeconomic question for over two centuries. Ask students what they think determines the wealth and poverty of nations.

Teacher Support

Focus and Motivate

Section Objectives

After completing this section, students will be able to

▶ explain what inflation is;

▶ explain how inflation is measured;

▶ identify causes of inflation;

▶ explain what deflation is; and

▶ identify causes of deflation.

Economics Around the Clock

Kickoff Activity

Direct students to read the 9:00 a.m. scenario in Economics Around the Clock (page 345) and write their answers to the question. Invite them to share their answers with the class.

Students should see that Blake isn't using the word *inflation* correctly. Inflation is an increase in the general level of prices, not an increase in the price of one good. Blake and Emma are talking about the prices of houses. An increase in housing prices doesn't necessarily indicate that the average prices of goods and services in general have risen.

Activating Prior Knowledge

Students often instinctively understand inflation and the effects of inflation. They may know of times when their families' incomes haven't changed but the costs of goods and services has increased. Ask students to identify situations in which they were aware of inflation and its effects on them personally.

Visit econ.myemcp.com/videos for videos that will help students better understand the key concepts found in this section.

Inflation and Deflation

Focus Questions

▶ What is inflation?
▶ How is inflation measured?
▶ What causes inflation?
▶ What is deflation?
▶ What causes deflation?

Key Terms
inflation
demand-side inflation
supply-side inflation
velocity
simple quantity theory of money
hedge
deflation

What Is Inflation?

Each good produced and sold in the economy has a price. The average of all of these prices is called the *price level*.

When someone says that the price level has increased, it means that the prices of goods produced and sold in the economy are

"Inflation: everyone's illusion of wealth."
—Anonymous

higher *on average* than they were previously. This does not necessarily mean that every single price in the economy is higher—only that on average, prices are higher. **Inflation** is an increase in the price level.

EXAMPLE Suppose an economy has three goods (A, B, C), and their prices are $1, $2, and $3, respectively. The average price is $2. Now suppose the prices change to $1.50, $2.99, and $2.50, respectively. Note that two prices increased and one decreased. The new average price is $2.33. Because the new average price is higher than the old average price, we have inflation. Notice that inflation is possible even if some prices fall. ◆

inflation
An increase in the price level, or average level of prices.

How Do We Measure Inflation?

How do we determine whether an economy experienced inflation? If the price level increased, then inflation occurred; if it did not increase, then no inflation occurred.

Chapter 11 explained that the consumer price index (CPI) is used to measure the price level. Suppose the CPI last year was 230, and the CPI this year is also 230. Did inflation occur between the two years? The answer is no, because the price level (as measured by the CPI) did not increase. Suppose, though, that the CPI was 230 last year and is 235 this year. The increase in the CPI means that inflation occurred between the two years.

It is usually not enough just to know whether inflation occurred. People often want to know how much inflation occurred; that is, they want to measure the rate of inflation. We can find the inflation rate between two years by using the same formula we used in Chapter 11 to find the percentage change in the CPI:

Differentiating Instruction

English Language Learners

Some students may have difficulty understanding the difference between inflation and an increase in the price of a particular item—in other words, between *price* and *price level*. When the price of houses or tires or cars goes up, it doesn't neces-

sarily follow that inflation is occurring. As the price of cars or tires or houses goes up, the prices of other goods may be coming down, so there is no net increase in the price level. It's only when the price level (that is, prices on average) increases that inflation is indicated.

Inflation rate =

$$\frac{\text{CPI later year} - \text{CPI earlier year}}{\text{CPI earlier year}} \times 100$$

Filling in the numbers from our example, we get the following:

Inflation rate =

$$\frac{235 - 230}{230} \times 100 = 2.17\%$$

A positive change (rise) in the CPI means inflation occurred; the inflation rate is 2.17 percent.

Exhibit 12-1 shows the CPI over the period 1913–2017. As you can see, the CPI rose only slightly from 1913 to 1968 but then began to increase substantially after that date. One way to interpret this graph indicates what happens to the value of the dollar over time: when the CPI rises, a dollar buys less than it used to buy. So, as the CPI rises (in Exhibit 12-1), the value of the dollar falls.

Exhibit 12-2 on the next page shows the inflation rate in the United States during the period 1960–2017. Notice the sharp increases and decreases in the inflation rate in the late 1970s and early 1980s compared with the less dramatic changes in recent decades.

Demand-Side Versus Supply-Side Inflation

Chapters 4 and 5 discussed supply and demand in a market setting. When the demand for a good increases and supply remains the same, price increases, and when the supply of a good decreases and demand remains the same, price increases. Chapter 11 introduced the concept of supply and demand in an economy. The demand side of the economy was represented by *aggregate demand*, and the supply side of the economy was represented by *aggregate supply*.

Inflation, which is an increase in the price level, can originate on either the demand side or the supply side of the economy. Consider Exhibit 12-3(a) on the next page, which depicts an aggregate demand curve (AD_1) and an aggregate supply curve (AS_1). The equilibrium price level is P_1. Suppose aggregate demand increases; the aggregate

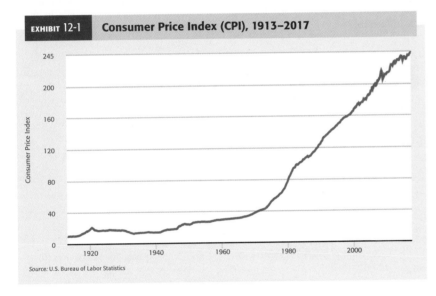

EXHIBIT 12-1 Consumer Price Index (CPI), 1913–2017

Consumer Price Index (y-axis: 0, 40, 80, 120, 160, 200, 245; x-axis: 1920, 1940, 1960, 1980, 2000)

Source: U.S. Bureau of Labor Statistics

◀ How would you describe the relationship between the value of the dollar and the CPI?

Background Information: Inflation and Long Lines

In some countries, prices and wages are set by the government. Markets don't determine prices and wages through the forces of supply and demand; government officials do.

When aggregate demand rises or aggregate supply falls in these countries, price level can't rise. Therefore, because of inflation, people wait in long lines to buy goods. Instead of prices serving to ration goods, the first-come-first-served (FCFS) rule rations goods. People must wait in line for their turn to get served. The longer the line is, the higher the inflation rate must be.

Section 1 Inflation and Deflation **347**

Teach

Discussion Starter

Inflation is an increase in the average level of prices. Students may more easily see this phenomenon on a large scale. Explain that prices have changed a lot since 1950 for products that students still purchase, such as soft drinks, shirts, and automobiles. Ask students if they believe the general price level has risen in the last 50 years or only the prices of a few particular goods and services.

Teaching with Visuals

Students should understand that when the CPI rises, the value of the dollar falls.

Reinforcement Activity

Allow students to look through current newspapers (if the inflation rate is high) or newspapers from earlier years, particularly the late 1970s (if the inflation rate isn't high), to find stories about inflation. Have students write reports on their findings, or ask them to present findings to the class.

Teaching with Visuals

Exhibit 12-3 shows the two ways the price level can increase: through increase in aggregate demand or through a decrease in aggregate supply. Help students understand how these increases in the price level originate.

▶ This graph charts the annual inflation rate for the period 1960–2017.

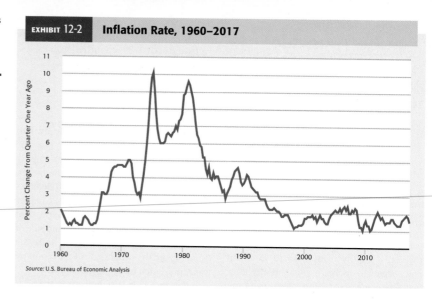

EXHIBIT 12-2 Inflation Rate, 1960–2017

Source: U.S. Bureau of Economic Analysis

demand curve shifts rightward from AD_1 to AD_2. Consequently, the price level increases from P_1 to P_2. The increase in the price level indicates that inflation has occurred. We conclude that if aggregate demand increases and aggregate supply stays the same, inflation will occur. When an increase in the price level originates on the demand side of the economy, economists call it **demand-side inflation**.

One of the things that can cause demand-side inflation is an increase in the money supply. For example, suppose the Fed increases the money supply. The result is having more money in the economy, and so people end up buying more goods and services. In other words, aggregate demand in the economy rises. As a consequence of the increased aggregate demand, the price level increases.

demand-side inflation
An increase in the price level that originates on the demand side of the economy.

▶ An increase in the price level can be caused by an increase in aggregate demand (AD) as shown in part (a), or by a decrease in aggregate supply (AS) as shown in part (b).

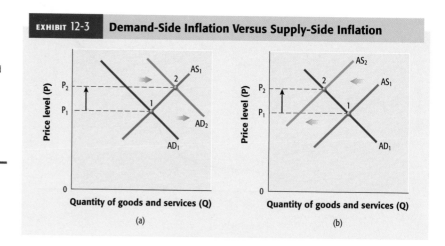

EXHIBIT 12-3 Demand-Side Inflation Versus Supply-Side Inflation

Internet Research

Direct students to use Exhibit 12-2 to examine inflation rates over the period 1960–2013. Then have them write paragraphs explaining what most likely happened to unemployment rates during these years and why. Finally, direct students to the website of the U.S. Department of Labor, Bureau of Labor Statistics, to check their predictions against actual unemployment statistics. Tell students to summarize their findings by writing second paragraphs.

Exhibit 12-3(b) shows a decrease in aggregate supply from AS_1 to AS_2. As a result of this decrease, the price level increases from P_1 to P_2. Again, the increase in price level indicates that inflation has occurred. Thus, if aggregate supply decreases and aggregate demand stays the same, inflation will occur. An increase in the price level that originates on the supply side of the economy is called **supply-side inflation**. One of the things that can cause supply-side inflation is a major drought that lowers the output of agricultural goods. As a result, the supply of goods in the economy is smaller, and the price level increases.

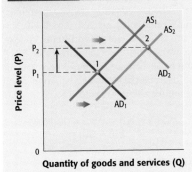

EXHIBIT 12-4 **Aggregate Demand Increases by More Than Aggregate Supply**

◄ When aggregate demand (AD) increases by more than aggregate supply (AS), the price level (P) increases, causing inflation.

Quantity of goods and services (Q)

A Student Asks

QUESTION: *What if both aggregate demand and aggregate supply increase? Will this cause inflation?*
ANSWER: *It depends on how much aggregate demand increases compared with a specific increase in aggregate supply. For example, look at Exhibit 12-4. Initially, the economy is at point 1, and the price level is P_1. Then both aggregate demand and aggregate supply increase, so both the AD and AS curves shift rightward, to AD_2 and AS_2, respectively. Notice, though, that aggregate demand increases more; its curve shifts rightward more than the aggregate supply curve shifts rightward. In this case, the increase in the price level from P_1 to P_2 indicates inflation.*

The Simple Quantity Theory of Money

The simple quantity theory of money presents a clear picture of what causes inflation. Before examining this theory, though, we must know something about velocity and the exchange equation.

Velocity

The average number of times a dollar is spent to buy final goods and services is called **velocity**. To illustrate the concept of velocity, consider a tiny economy with only five $1 bills. In January, the first of the $1 bills moves from Maria's hands to Nancy's hands to buy a newspaper. Then, in June, it goes from Nancy's hands to Bob's hands to buy a bagel. And in December, it goes from Bob's hands to Tu's hands to buy a used paperback book. Over the course of the year, this $1 bill has changed hands three times. The other $1 bills also change hands during the year. The second bill changes hands five times; the third, six times; the fourth, three times; and the fifth, three times.

Given this information, we can calculate the number of times the average dollar changes hands in purchases. We do so by finding the sum of the times each dollar changed hands (3 + 5 + 6 + 3 + 3 = 20 times) and then dividing by the number of dollars (5). The answer is 4, which is the velocity in this example.

The Exchange Equation

In the exchange equation

$$M \times V = P \times Q$$

M stands for the money supply, V stands for velocity, P stands for the price level or average price, and Q stands for the quantity of output (quantity of goods and services). M times V must equal P times Q. To see why, think of the equation on a personal basis.

supply-side inflation
An increase in the price level that originates on the supply side of the economy.

velocity
The average number of times a dollar is spent to buy final goods and services in a year.

Background Information: The Simple Quantity Theory of Money

The simple quantity theory of money was proposed by classical economists. One of the leading proponents of the simple quantity theory of money was Irving Fisher (1867–1947), an American economist and mathematician. Many of the ideas of these early economists have been updated by modern economists and now serve as the building blocks of modern economic theory. Some economists today still adhere to the simple quantity theory of money.

Teaching with Visuals

Exhibit 12-4 illustrates inflation as it would occur when aggregate demand increases by more than aggregate supply. Ask students to explain why this causes inflation.

Critical Thinking

Assign students to come up with a visual representation of velocity. Students might perform a role-play like the following one: Three people stand in front of the class. The first person has a dollar in her hand. She gives it to the second person, and then the second person gives it to the third person. Ask the class what the velocity is in this example. (*Answer:* 2.)

Reinforcement Activity

Write the exchange equation on the board. Provide values for the variables in the equation, and ask students to find the remaining values. For example, if you write P = 7, Q = 10, and M = 14, then students should find V, which equals 5.

Reinforcement Activity

To reinforce inflation concepts, have students work with partners to complete the following sentences. Answers are given for your reference.

1. Demand-side inflation is an <u>increase</u> in the price level that originates on the demand side of the economy.
2. An increase in the <u>price</u> level that originates on the <u>supply</u> side of the economy is called supply-side inflation.

Prediction Activity

Ask students to predict what will happen to the price level as a result of each of the following occurrences:

1. The money supply decreases.
2. Velocity increases.
3. The quantity of goods and services decreases.

(*Answers:* **1.** Price level decreases. **2.** Price level increases. **3.** Price level increases.)

Reinforcement Activity

Ask students how inflation is like theft. Some people have suggested that inflation robs people of the purchasing power of their money. To illustrate, suppose you have $100. With a 10% inflation rate, your $100 will buy less than it would have with 0% inflation. You can no longer purchase the goods that you could have purchased without inflation. Ask students whether those goods were stolen from you in a sense.

Clarifying Terms

Help students understand the phrase *strictly proportional. Strictly* means "exactly" or "precisely," and *proportional* means "having the same or a constant ratio." To ensure students' understanding of the phrase, invite volunteers to use it in a couple of original sentences.

Teaching with Visuals

Since Exhibit 12-5 begins with the exchange equation, review with students the variables used in the equation: M = money, V = velocity, P = price level or average price, and Q = quantity of output (quantity of goods and services).

Suppose you have $40; this amount is your money supply (M). You spend the $40 one time, so velocity (V) is 1. You spend the $40 on 5 books, so 5 is the quantity of goods and services you purchase; it is your Q in the exchange equation. Now ask yourself what P must equal, given that M is $40, V is 1, and Q is 5. If you spend $40 on 5 books, the average price per book must be $8. P must be $8, because $8 times 5 books equals $40. Here is the exchange equation using the numbers in this example:

$$M(\$40) \times V(1) = P(\$8) \times Q(5 \text{ books})$$
$$\$40 = \$40$$

Explaining Inflation

simple quantity theory of money
A theory that predicts that changes in the price level will be strictly proportional to changes in the money supply.

The **simple quantity theory of money** is used to explain inflation. The theory begins by making two assumptions: that velocity (V) is constant and that the quantity of output or goods and services (Q) is constant.

▶ This exhibit outlines the basics of the simple quantity theory of money. Start with M × V = P × Q. Then, if V and Q are held constant, it follows that a change in the money supply (M) will lead to a strictly proportional change in the price level (P).

EXHIBIT 12-5 Simple Quantity Theory of Money

M × V = P × Q	Let M = $500
	V = 2
	P = $10
	Q = 100 units
	so
	$500 × 2 = $10 × 100
	$1,000 = $1,000

| Hold V and Q constant. In other words, V stays at 2, and Q stays at 100. | |

Increase M from $500 to $1,000.	M = $1,000
	V = 2
	so
	M × V = $2,000

If M × V = $2,000 and Q = 100, then P must rise to $20.	M = $1,000
	V = 2
	P = $20
	Q = 100 units
	so
	$1,000 × 2 = $20 × 100
	$2,000 = $2,000

Conclusion: If V and Q are held constant, a doubling of the money supply (M) from $500 to $1,000 leads to a doubling of the price level (P) from $10 to $20.

Let's set V at 2 and Q at 100 units. These numbers will remain constant throughout our discussion.

Suppose the money supply (M) equals $500. If V is 2 and Q is 100 units, then the price level must equal $10:

$$M(\$500) \times V(2) = P(\$10) \times Q(100 \text{ units})$$
$$\$1,000 = \$1,000$$

Now suppose the money supply doubles, increasing from $500 to $1,000. As stated earlier, velocity and output are constant. Velocity (V) is still 2, and output (Q) is still 100 units. The price level (P), however, increases to $20:

$$M(\$1,000) \times V(2) = P(\$20) \times Q(100 \text{ units})$$
$$\$2,000 = \$2,000$$

In other words, if the money supply doubles (from $500 to $1,000), the price level doubles (from $10 to $20; see Exhibit 12-5).

In Theory The simple quantity theory of money states that changes in the money supply will bring about *strictly proportional changes* in the price level. For example, if the money supply increases by 100 percent, the price level will increase by 100 percent, and if the money supply increases by 20 percent, the price level will increase by 20 percent.

Real-World Application In the real world, the strict proportionality between changes in the money supply and the price level doesn't usually hold. An increase in the money supply of, say, 10 percent doesn't usually bring about a 10 percent increase in the price level.

What we do see in the real world is that the greater the increase in the money supply, the greater the increase in the price level. For example, a nation that increased its money supply by 30 percent would usually have a greater increase in its price level (its inflation rate) than a nation that increased its money supply by 20 percent. This finding is consistent with the central idea of the simple quantity theory of money. After all, the theory says that changes in the money supply bring about strictly

Cross-Curricular Activity

Team with a math teacher to discuss inflation. Open the lesson by helping students recall and understand the definitions of important terms, such as *velocity, quantity of output, money supply,* and *price.* The math teacher can then walk students through the equations in this chapter, helping them with the basic math concepts inherent in each equation. Give students time to create their own problems with these variables, and then have them exchange problems with other students in the class.

proportional changes in the price level. It follows, therefore, that larger changes in the money supply should bring about larger changes in the price level.

EXAMPLE The money supply in country A rises by 10 percent, and the money supply in country B rises by 2 percent. Let's also assume that velocity is constant and the output of goods and services in each country is constant. In which country would we predict the higher inflation rate: A or B? Well, according to the simple quantity theory of money, the greater the increase in the money supply, the greater the inflation rate, so we would predict a higher inflation rate in country A. ◆

A Student Asks

QUESTION: *How long after the money supply rises does the price level rise? Is it the next day?*
ANSWER: *A lag occurs between the time the money supply rises and the time the price level rises. That lag is usually 10 months to 18 months. In other words, if the money supply rises in January, prices might not go up until October.*

The Effects of Inflation

We tend to think that inflation affects only the buyer of goods, as when a person pays $60 instead of $50 a week for groceries. In truth, however, people are affected by inflation in many other ways as well.

Inflation and Individuals on Fixed Incomes

Denise has lived on a fixed income for the last 10 years; that is, every year for the past 10 years, her income has been the same. However, each year for the past 10 years, the price level has increased and inflation has occurred. Because of inflation, Denise has less purchasing power. She can buy fewer units of goods with a given amount of money than she could previously, and her material standard of living is reduced.

Economic Facts and Fallacies

When More Money *Doesn't* Mean Higher Prices

FALSE / TRUE

Some people say that if the money supply rises, the price level will rise. Is this true? Does more money necessarily mean higher prices? No, this isn't true. But why isn't it true?

The answer can be found in the exchange equation. According to the equation, if the money supply rises by 2 percent and velocity declines by 2 percent, the price level will remain unchanged. A decline in velocity can offset an increase in the money supply. Suppose the money supply rises by 2 percent and the quantity of output rises by 2 percent. Again, there will be no change in the price level. A rise in the quantity of output can also offset an increase in the money supply.

Inflation and Savers

On January 1, Lorenzo puts $2,000 into a savings account that pays 6 percent interest. On December 31, he removes $2,120 from the account ($2,000, which is the original amount, plus $120 in interest). Suppose that during the year, prices did not increase at all—an inflation rate of 0 percent. Saving money made Lorenzo better off, because at the end of the year, he can purchase $120 more of goods and services than he could at the beginning of the year.

Now suppose that during the year, prices increased by 10 percent—an inflation rate of 10 percent. How much money would Lorenzo need at the end of the year to buy exactly what $2,000 could buy at the beginning of the year? If prices increased by 10 percent, he would need 10 percent more money, or a total of $2,200. Instead of having $2,200, Lorenzo has only $2,120 from his savings account. He must settle for purchasing $80 less of goods and services than he could have at the beginning of the year. Because the inflation rate of 10 percent was greater than the interest rate of 6 percent that Lorenzo earned on his savings, he ended up worse off. Clearly, inflation hurts savers.

If inflation persists, however, it is customary for financial institutions to compete for

A Student Asks

Make sure students understand that an increase in the money supply doesn't immediately result in higher prices.

Reinforcement Activity

Invite students to consider the following scenario: Someone tells you that she paid $30,000 for a house in 1960. That sounds like very little to pay for a house, but 1960 was a long time ago, when prices weren't as high as they are today.

To figure out what you would have to pay today for the same house, visit the U.S. Bureau of Labor Statistics website and go to the Consumer Price Index Inflation Calculator. Fill in the calculator with the relevant data and then answer this question: for the most recent year identified, what would you have to pay to buy the same house that sold for $30,000 in 1960?

Critical Thinking

Guide students in a discussion of inflation rates versus savings rates. In the example given in the text, Lorenzo does lose some purchasing power. Ask, What might Lorenzo and others do to protect themselves against high inflation rates? Students might say that individuals can put their money in an investment account that typically yields an interest rate comparable to or higher than the rate of inflation.

Differentiating Instruction

English Language Learners

Students who have difficulty reading English and those who have difficulty understanding graphs and mathematical formulas may have difficulty understanding Exhibit 12-5. Pair students to practice solving for one of the four variables by substituting different money supplies, velocities, prices, and quantities.

Ask students if they have experienced grade inflation and, if so, whether they were aware that their relative standing in school had not gone up. Discuss similarities and differences between grade inflation and price inflation.

Discussion Starter

Ask students to vote on whether they would like to have their grades inflated. Then have students give reasons for their answers and write the reasons on the board in two columns: Pro and Con. After you have listed all the reasons, take another vote to see how many students still would like to have their grades inflated. Lead students in explaining why their vote changed or stayed the same.

Reinforcement Activity

Grade inflation may seem like a good idea to students. However, it can create a false sense of security: "I am getting better grades without studying harder, so why put in the effort?" Students should understand that an inflated grade doesn't indicate knowledge of the subject matter or an ability to use its concepts out in the world. Ask students to compare the subjects in which they studied hard and truly learned in school with subjects in which they may have received a good grade but learned very little.

Problem Solving

People often talk about inflation in negative terms—as if it's a bad thing. In light of this, discuss with students the following question: what is so bad about inflation? Students may answer that it makes it difficult for people to budget and plan their spending. For example, someone may plan to buy a house in three years at a price of $150,000, but by then, with inflation, the price of houses may have risen to a level they can't afford.

customers by offering an interest rate that has been adjusted upward by the inflation rate. Suppose financial institutions will offer a 4 percent interest rate next year if prices are going to stay the same as this year (meaning no inflation). However, they anticipate a 5 percent inflation rate during the year. Many institutions will begin to compete for customers by offering a 9 percent interest rate, the sum of the interest rate they would offer if prices did not change plus the anticipated inflation rate (4% + 5% = 9%).

Grade Inflation: When Is a B+ No Better Than a C?

The effects of inflation can sometimes be deceptive. Suppose Lavotka produces and sells motorcycles, and the average price for one of his bikes is $10,000. Unknown to Lavotka, the Fed increases the money supply. Months pass, and then one day, Lavotka notices that the demand for his motorcycles has increased. He raises the price of his motorcycles and earns a higher dollar income.

Lavotka is excited about earning more income, but he soon realizes that the prices of many of the things he buys have increased too. Food, clothing, and housing prices are all higher. Lavotka is earning a higher dollar income, but he is also paying higher prices. In relative terms, his financial position may be the same as it was before he increased the price of his motorcycles. For example, if his income went up 10 percent and prices also increased 10 percent, he will be no better off.

Grade inflation also exists. Suppose that instead of teachers using the full range of grades, A through F, they start to use only grades A through C. As a result, the average grade given out rises, resulting in grade inflation. (Just as price inflation is a higher average price, grade inflation is a higher average grade.)

The effects of grade inflation can be just as deceiving as those of price inflation. Suppose you get higher grades without studying more. Your average grade goes from a C to a B+. Your relative standing in school has not gone up, however, unless only your grades (and no one else's grades) have risen (or your grades have risen more than other persons' grades). Because everyone is getting higher grades, you may just be maintaining your relative position. In other words, if you are now earning a B+ instead of a C, other people may be earning an A instead of a B+.

In a class of 30 students, with the teacher giving out the full range of grades (A through F), you might have been ranked tenth in the class. Now, in the same class of students, with the teacher only using grades A through C, you might be earning higher grades but still be ranked tenth in the class.

THINK ABOUT IT What do you think might be the cause of grade inflation? What might be the effects of grade inflation?

Internet Research

A good activity to get students to think globally is to have them research inflation rates in other countries. After locating this data, students should then find data on the growth rates in the money supply in the same countries and determine whether higher rates in the money supply correspond to higher inflation rates. Students should research how the inflation rates of other countries affect people in the United States.

Inflation and Past Decisions

Inflation often turns past decisions into mistakes. Consider the building contractor who last year signed a contract to build a shopping mall for $30 million. He agreed to this dollar figure based on his estimates of what it would cost to buy the materials and hire the labor to build the mall. He estimated $28 million in costs. All of a sudden, inflation hits. Prices of labor, concrete, nails, tile, and roofing all rise. Now the contractor realizes it will cost him $31 million to build the mall. He looks back on his decision to build the mall for only $30 million as a mistake—a costly mistake for him.

Inflation and Hedging Against Inflation

What do individuals in an inflation-prone economy do that individuals in a stable-price economy do not? They try to **hedge** against inflation. In hedging, people try to avoid or lessen a loss by taking some counterbalancing action. For instance, they try to figure out what investments offer the best protection against inflation. Would gold, real estate, or fine art be the best hedge? People also travel to distant cities to hear so-called experts talk about inflation and subscribe to numerous newsletters that claim to predict future inflation rates accurately.

All of these actions obviously require an expenditure of resources. Resources, we remind ourselves, that are expended in the effort to protect against inflation can no longer be used to build factories or produce houses, shoes, or cars. Thus, one effect of inflation is that it causes individuals to try to hedge against it, thereby diverting resources away from being used to produce goods.

What Is Deflation?

Deflation is the opposite of inflation. **Deflation** is a decrease in the price level, or the average level of prices. We measure deflation the same way we measure inflation: by finding the percentage change in prices or the CPI between years. For

example, suppose the CPI in year 1 is 180, and it is 175 in year 2. What is the change in the CPI? Here is the formula again:

$$\text{Deflation rate} = \frac{\text{CPI later year} - \text{CPI earlier year}}{\text{CPI earlier year}} \times 100$$

Filling in the numbers yields the following:

$$\text{Deflation rate} = \frac{175 - 180}{180} \times 100 = -2.8\%$$

A negative (downward) change in the CPI indicates deflation. The deflation rate is 2.8 percent.

Note that when we calculate the deflation rate, we use a minus sign. However, when we speak of a deflation rate, we don't usually mention the minus. In other words, we do not say, "The deflation rate is minus 2.8 percent." It is understood that deflation refers to a decrease in the price level, so we simply say, "The deflation rate is 2.8 percent."

▲ Many senior citizens live on fixed incomes. How would their grocery shopping be affected by the combination of a fixed income and inflation?

hedge
To try to avoid or lessen a loss by taking some counterbalancing action.

deflation
A decrease in the price level, or average level of prices.

> *"By a continuing process of inflation, governments can confiscate, secretly and unobserved, an important part of the wealth of their citizens."*
> — John Maynard Keynes, twentieth-century economist

Thinking Like an Economist

Discussion Starter

Prompt students to brainstorm events and developments that might cause deflation. Students might mention a stock market crash, a sharp decrease in the money supply by the Fed, and a technological development that dramatically increases aggregate supply.

Reinforcement Activity

Ask students to define the term *deflation* and show how to find the deflation rate.

Critical Thinking

Tell students that we often read and hear about inflation, but we rarely hear about deflation. Ask, Why don't people talk about deflation? (*Answer:* We don't often talk about deflation for a simple reason—there hasn't been any deflation for some time. In the recent economic history of the United States, we have not had a period of deflation; instead, we have had an extended period of low inflation, including some years of disinflation.)

Suggest that students go back to Exhibit 12-2, on page 348, and notice that in every year, inflation or disinflation—not deflation—occurred. Perhaps we should ask why inflation—but not deflation—has occurred so frequently in the U.S. economy. Much of the answer to this question has to do with increases in the money supply (M) compared with increases in output (Q). The Fed often increases the money supply at a faster rate than the rate at which output increases.

Thinking Like an Economist

Total Spending Can Be Greater Than the Money Supply

Suppose you stop someone on the street and tell him that the total money supply in the economy is $1 trillion. If you ask this person how much total spending can be in the economy, he will probably say $1 trillion. The fact is that most people believe total spending can never be more than the amount of money available to spend.

However, an economist knows that total spending in an economy can be greater than the money supply. Why? Because money changes hands and can be spent again and again and again. The $1 that's spent by Joe today can be spent by Katherine tomorrow and by Suki the day after that. Because velocity in the economy can be greater than 1, total spending can be greater than the money supply.

The exchange equation explains this possibility. According to the exchange equation, if we multiply the money supply (M) times the velocity (V), we have the total dollar amount of spending in the economy (P x Q). So if the money supply is equal to $1 trillion and velocity is equal to 3, then total spending in the economy is $3 trillion. That is, $3 trillion is spent to buy goods and services in the economy.

THINK ABOUT IT What is total spending in the economy if the money supply is $4 trillion and velocity is 5?

Demand-Side Versus Supply-Side Deflation

Just like inflation, deflation can originate on either the demand side or the supply side of the economy. Consider Exhibit 12-6(a), which shows an aggregate demand curve (AD_1) and an aggregate supply curve (AS_1). The equilibrium price level is P_1. Suppose the aggregate demand curve decreases and shifts from AD_1 to AD_2. Consequently, the price level decreases from P_1 to P_2. Because the price level decreased, deflation occurred. We conclude that if aggregate demand decreases and aggregate supply stays the same, deflation will occur. One of the things that can cause aggregate demand to fall is a decrease in the money supply, so a decrease in the money supply can cause deflation.

Next, consider an increase in aggregate supply from AS_1 to AS_2. (See Exhibit 12-6[b].) As a result, the price level drops from P_1 to P_2. Again, because the price level decreased, deflation occurred. If aggregate supply increases and aggregate demand stays the same, deflation will occur. One of the things that can cause deflation (from the supply side) is an increase in technology that makes it possible to produce more goods and services with the same level of resources.

▶ Deflation can be caused by a decrease in aggregate demand, as shown in part (a), or by an increase in aggregate supply, as shown in part (b).

EXHIBIT 12-6 Demand-Side Deflation Versus Supply-Side Deflation

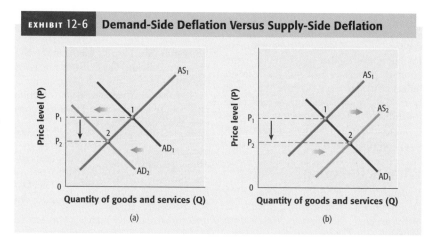

(a)

(b)

Cross-Curricular Activity

Students can have difficulty understanding what it's like to live in a period of deflation. Invite a history teacher to class to talk about deflationary periods in U.S. history. The teacher might focus on the deflation that occurred during the financial panic of 1893 or the Great Depression of the 1930s. After the teacher's presentation, ask students to search the Internet or the library for first-hand testimony of what it was like to live during a deflationary period. Ask students to share what they have learned with the class.

QUESTION: *If the rate of inflation falls from 4 percent to 1 percent, are we still experiencing inflation or are we experiencing deflation?*

ANSWER: *Actually, we are experiencing disinflation. Disinflation is a decrease in the inflation rate. It occurs when prices are rising but not as fast as they have risen in the recent past. Let's explain by using numbers. Suppose that in year 1 the CPI is 110, in year 2 it is 120, and in year 3 it is 125. Since the price level rises over all three years, we say inflation occurs during the period from year 1 to year 3. After all, inflation is defined as an increase in the price level. But note this: The inflation rate (the rate or percentage at which prices are rising) is greater between years 1 and 2 (when it is 9.09 percent) than it is between years 2 and 3 (when it is 4.16 percent). In other words, between years 2 and 3, there is disinflation.*

QUESTION: *I have noticed that the price of LCD high-definition TVs has been decreasing in recent years. Is this an example of deflation?*

ANSWER: *The price of one good falling does not constitute deflation. Remember, you need a decline in the price level, or in the average price of goods, before you can say deflation occurred.*

Simple Quantity Theory of Money and Deflation

Just as the simple quantity theory of money can be used to explain inflation, it can be used to explain deflation too. Suppose the money supply (M) equals $500, velocity (V) equals 2, and the quantity of goods and services (Q) is 100 units. We know that M × V must equal P × Q, so the price level (P) must equal $10:

$$M(\$500) \times V(2) = P(\$10) \times Q(100 \text{ units})$$
$$\$1,000 = \$1,000$$

Suppose the money supply drops to $250, and all other things remain the same. What happens to the price level? It must drop to $5:

$$M(\$250) \times V(2) = P(\$5) \times Q(100 \text{ units})$$

In other words, a fall in the money supply will bring about deflation (assuming that velocity and the quantity of goods and services do not change).

A Major Effect of Deflation

When prices fall, they do not all fall at the same time. This situation often presents a problem.

For example, suppose Latoya produces wooden tables. To produce these tables, she needs wood, glue, and laborers. In short, in her business, Latoya is interested in four prices: the prices of wooden tables, wood, glue, and laborers. She is interested in the price of wooden tables because it relates to her total revenue. For example, if the price of wooden tables is $100 and she sells 50 tables, her total revenue will be $5,000. If the price of wooden tables is only $40, her total revenue will be $2,000. Latoya is also interested in the prices of wood, glue, and laborers because these prices relate to her total cost. The higher these prices, the higher her overall costs.

Suppose that the money supply in the economy drops, and deflation occurs. Furthermore, not all prices fall at the same time. The price of wooden tables falls first, and the prices of wood, glue, and laborers fall many months later.

What happens to Latoya as a result of the price of wooden tables falling but the prices of wood, glue, and laborers staying constant (for a few months)? Her total revenue falls, but her total costs stay the same. As a result, her profits fall—so much that Latoya ends up getting out of the business of producing wooden tables. She closes up shop, lays off the workers she currently employs, and looks for different work.

In short, when prices do not fall at the same time, deflation can lead to firms going out of business and workers being laid off. Because it is unusual for all prices to fall at the same time, these results are common in deflation.

Reinforcement Activity

Direct students to Exhibit 12-1 on page 347. Challenge them to use the CPI figures to determine which years had an inflationary economy and which years had a deflationary economy.

Cause and Effect

Divide the class into pairs, and give each pair time to invent their own imaginary business similar to Latoya's wooden table business in "A Major Effect of Deflation." Then have each pair imagine what would happen if deflation struck. First, have them suppose that the prices of the goods they need for their operation fell before the price of the good they sell fell. Then have them imagine that the price of the good they sell dropped first. What would happen to their business in each scenario?

Quote on Deflation

Ben Bernanke, the former chairman of Board of Governors of Federal Reserve System, once said: "The sources of deflation are not a mystery. Deflation is in almost all cases a side effect of a collapse of aggregate demand…a drop in spending so severe that producers must cut prices on an ongoing basis in order to find buyers."

Cooperative Learning

Divide the class into three groups to study instances of hyperinflation. Assign one group to 1920s Germany, one to 1940s Hungary, and one to 1980s Brazil. Each group should create a chart or graph to show the rate of inflation and the rate of growth in the money supply. Allow each group to present to the class its visuals during an oral report on the causes of the hyperinflation and the methods the government used to deal with it.

After students read this feature, ask if they think they could ever have too much money. Invite them to para-phrase the reason that it's possible for a country to have too much money.

ANSWERS TO THINK ABOUT IT Answers will vary.

Teaching with Visuals

The answer to the question accompany-ing the photograph on page 357 is that deflation might hurt the construction company if the prices of the houses it's building fall more quickly than the prices of the supplies it needs to build the houses.

 Application Activity

After reading and discussing Section 1, assign the Section Activity in the *Applying the Principles Workbook,* pages 128–131.

Assess

Quick Quiz

The following true-or-false quiz will help you assess student understanding of the material covered in this section.

1. Inflation is an increase in the price level. (True)
2. Inflation can originate on either the supply side or the demand side. (True)
3. Deflation can only originate on the supply side of the economy. (False)
4. Inflation generally hurts savers. (True)
5. A negative change in the consumer price index leads to deflation. (True)

Economics *in the* Real World

Can You Have Too Much Money?

Suppose someone has $20,000 and we ask him if he would prefer to have $50,000 instead. His first response is to question what he has to do to get the extra money. We say, "Nothing." He quickly smiles and says, "Sure, I'll take the extra money."

No one, it seems, turns down money for doing nothing in return. More money is always better than less money.

Now, what's odd is that even though an individual may never have too much money, the sum of individuals (society) may have too much money. To understand how, we need two things: first, a short history lesson, and second, an understanding of the simple quantity theory of money.

In 1923, prices were rising quite rapidly in Germany—not by 10 percent or 20 percent a year but by 41 percent a day. In 1946 in Hungary, prices were tripling each day. Both situations are examples of hyperinflation.

To understand the effects of such a dramatic level of inflation, consider a modern-day example. Suppose a hamburger costs $2 today, but its price is going to triple every day. In just nine days, a hamburger will cost $13,122. Think of what this level of inflation would do to a person with a

savings account of $13,122. It would surely reduce the buying power of that money.

Ask yourself what would happen in a society that experienced this kind of hyperinflation. History has shown us that such societies tend to be composed of fearful, uncertain individuals who cannot predict what tomorrow will bring. One economist argued that the hyperinflation in Germany destroyed much of the wealth of the nation's middle class and made it easier for the Nazis to gain power. If he is correct, rapid increases in prices are more destructive than anyone could imagine.

What caused the hyperinflation in Germany? The answer is simple: too much money. The German government had been increasing the money supply at an astronomical rate; that's what caused prices to soar. Prices rose by *854 billion percent* in the five-month period from July to November 1923.

You might think you could never have too much money. But what many of us forget is that when we think that we can never get enough money, we are assuming that the nation's money supply remains constant. In other words, we are assuming that we have $4 million more and that collectively everyone else has $4 million less.

Think of the difference in effects between (1) your having $4 million more and collectively everyone else having $4 million less and (2) you and everyone else having $4 million more. In the first case, the nation's money supply stays the same and so do prices. It's just that you have $4 million more to spend for goods whose prices have not changed. In the second case, the nation's money supply increases by $4 million times the population. In the United States, we would multiply $4 million times a population of about 327 million. That means the money supply would increase by 130 followed by 13 zeroes. In this scenario, prices would rise so fast and so high that soon, you'd be paying hundreds of thousands of dollars for a hamburger.

What is the lesson here? For the individual, there may not be such a thing as too much money. But for the sum of individuals—that is, for a society—there is.

THINK ABOUT IT In what other situations might having more of something be better for the individual but not necessarily for the sum of individuals, or society?

▲ The company developing this section of new homes must invest considerable resources to purchase the land, materials, and labor needed to build the homes. **How might deflation create a financial hardship for the company?**

Defining Terms

1. Define:
   a. inflation
   b. demand-side inflation
   c. supply-side inflation
   d. velocity
   e. simple quantity theory of money
   f. hedge
   g. deflation

Reviewing Facts and Concepts

2. The CPI is 167 in year 1 and 189 in year 2. What is the inflation rate between the two years?

3. The CPI is 180 in year 1 and 174 in year 2. What is the deflation rate between the two years?

4. "An increase in the money supply is more likely to cause supply-side inflation than demand-side inflation." Do you agree or disagree with this statement? Explain your answer.

5. Explain how changes in aggregate demand and aggregate supply can cause deflation.

Critical Thinking

6. A theory that predicts that changes in the money supply will bring about strictly proportional changes in the price level also predicts that larger changes in the money supply will bring about larger changes in the price level. Do you agree or disagree with this theory? Explain your answer.

7. Use the exchange equation—and some variable other than the money supply—to explain deflation.

Applying Economic Concepts

8. The simple quantity theory of money assumes that velocity and the quantity of goods and services are constant. Suppose we drop the second assumption, and the quantity of goods and services in the economy falls. What will happen to the price level?

Defining Terms

1. a. inflation: an increase in the price level, or average level of prices; **b. demand-side inflation:** an increase in the price level that originates on the demand side of the economy; **c. supply-side inflation:** an increase in the price level that originates on the supply side of the economy; **d. velocity:** the average number of times a dollar is spent to buy final goods and services in a year; **e. simple quantity theory of money:** a theory that predicts that changes in the price level will be strictly proportional to changes in the money supply; **f. hedge:** to try to avoid or lessen a loss by taking some counterbalancing action; **g. deflation:** a decrease in the price level, or average level of prices.

Reviewing Facts and Concepts

2. 13.17%. See the formula on page 347.
3. 3.33%. See the formula on page 353.
4. Students should disagree. An increase in the money supply is more likely to cause demand-side inflation.
5. A decrease in aggregate demand will cause deflation. An increase in aggregate supply will also cause deflation.

Critical Thinking

6. Students should agree. This theory predicts that a 10% increase in the money supply will cause a 10% rise in the price level and that a 20% increase in the money supply will cause a 20% rise in the price level.
7. Deflation is a decrease in P. P declines if V declines, Q rises, or M falls. The answer is "V declines" or "Q rises."

Applying Economic Concepts

8. The price level will rise. If M and V are constant and Q falls, P must rise.

You will find a quiz for this section in the *Assessment Book,* page 119.

Reteaching Activity

Use the Section Assessment to gauge which students may need reteaching on this section. With those students, review the concepts of CPI, aggregate supply, and aggregate demand. Then help students create graphs showing how increases and decreases in aggregate supply and aggregate demand affect inflation and deflation.

Guided Reading

For further reteaching of the key concepts in this section, assign the Outlining Activity and the Just the Facts Handout from the *Guided Reading and Study Guide,* pages 202–207.

SECTION 2

Teacher Support

Focus and Motivate

Section Objectives

After completing this section, students will be able to

▶ explain what a business cycle is;

▶ explain how economists forecast business cycles;

▶ identify some economic indicators;

▶ identify some causes of business cycles; and

▶ explain how politics cause upward and downward movements in the economy.

Economics Around the Clock

Kickoff Activity

Direct students to read "What Is a Business Cycle?" on pages 358–359, followed by the 3:34 p.m. scenario in Economics Around the Clock (page 345). Then discuss the answer to the question that follows that scenario.

Students should remember that a business cycle has five stages. If Willie looks for a job during the contraction stage of the business cycle, his chances of getting one are less than if he looks during the expansion stage of the business cycle.

Activating Prior Knowledge

Many students will have heard the terms *economic recovery, recession,* and *depression.* Ask them to discuss their associations with these terms.

 Visit econ.myemcp.com/videos for videos that will help students better understand the key concepts found in this section.

SECTION 2

Business Cycles

Focus Questions

▶ What is a business cycle?

▶ How do economists forecast business cycles?

▶ What are some economic indicators?

▶ What causes business cycles?

▶ How does politics cause upward and downward movements in the economy?

Key Terms

business cycle
recession

What Is a Business Cycle?

Chapter 11 discussed both GDP and real GDP. As you recall, GDP is the total market value of all final goods and services produced annually in a country. Real GDP is simply GDP adjusted for price changes. To calculate real GDP, we take the quantity of goods and services produced in a country in a current year and multiply by the prices that existed in a base year:

$$\text{Real GDP} = P_{\text{Base Year}} \times Q_{\text{Current Year}}$$

If real GDP is on a roller-coaster—rising and falling and rising and falling—the economy is said to be experiencing a **business cycle**. Economists usually talk about four or five phases of a business cycle. Five phases are identified here and in Exhibit 12-7:

1. *Peak.* At the peak of a business cycle, real GDP is at a temporary high (Q_1 in Exhibit 12-7).

2. *Contraction.* If real GDP decreases, the economy is said to be in a contraction. If real GDP declines for

business cycle
Recurrent swings (up and down) in real GDP.

recession
A slowdown in the economy marked by real GDP falling for two consecutive quarters. (Also see footnote 1.)

two consecutive quarters (there are four quarters in a year), the economy is said to be in a **recession**.[1] Usually, when the economy contracts (real GDP falls), the unemployment rate rises. A higher unemployment rate not only hurts those who are unemployed, but it hurts the economy (and thus the country) as a whole. More unemployment means fewer goods and services are being produced, which means people's overall material standard of living declines.

3. *Trough.* The trough is the low point in real GDP, just before it begins to turn up.

4. *Recovery.* The recovery is the period when real GDP is rising; it begins at the trough and ends at the initial peak. For example, the recovery in Exhibit 12-7

---

1 The National Bureau of Economic Research has defined a *recession* as "a significant decline in economic activity spread across the economy, lasting more than a few months, normally visible in real GDP, real income, employment, industrial production, and wholesale-retail sales." However, many economists use the definition provided in this book (a decline in real GDP lasting for two consecutive quarters) when referring to a recession.

Cooperative Learning

To help students better understand business cycles of the past, have them research the Great Depression and the New Deal legislation that was intended to increase demand and spur economic activity. After students have completed their research, have them work in pairs to create posters showing the business cycle from the peak of the 1920s through the Great Depression to the boom period of World War II. You may want students to indicate on this cycle the names of the major pieces of New Deal legislation that apply.

EXHIBIT 12-7 **Phases of the Business Cycle**

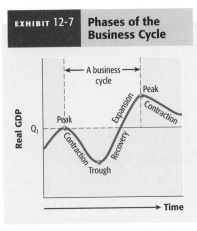

▲ The phases of a business cycle include the peak, contraction, trough, recovery, and expansion. A business cycle is measured from peak to peak.

extends from the trough to where real GDP is again at Q_1.

5. *Expansion.* The expansion period includes increases in real GDP beyond the recovery. In Exhibit 12-7, it refers to increases in real GDP above Q_1.

An entire business cycle is measured from peak to peak. Between 1854 and 2009, the U.S. economy has experienced 33 business cycles.

Forecasting Business Cycles

Economists try to predict changes in the economy. Comparing the economy to your health might help you see how economists go about making their predictions.

Think of yourself when you have the flu. Your illness usually has three stages: (1) when you are coming down with the flu, (2) when you have the flu, and (3) when you are getting over the flu but don't yet feel like your old self. Each stage includes signs or indicators of what is happening.

Flu Signs

In the first stage, when you are coming down with the flu, you feel a little sluggish and tired. We might call this condition a *leading*

indicator of the flu, in that it precedes the flu; it lets you know what's coming.

In the stage when you have the flu, you feel achy, and you might have a fever. We could call these signs *coincident indicators* of the flu, in that they coincide with having the flu.

Finally, during the period when you are getting over the flu, your temperature returns to normal. You are also slightly more alert, but you do not have all your energy back. We could call these leftover effects *lagging indicators* of the flu. In sum, knowing about these indicators of health and sickness helps you recognize when an illness is coming on and what to expect as it runs its course.

Economic Indicators

Similarly, economists have devised a few indicators of the health and sickness of the economy: *leading*, *coincident*, and *lagging* indicators. These indicators do what their names suggest: *lead* economic upturns or downturns (in real GDP), *coincide* with

BILL PROUD!

"Sorry, I don't do financial advice."

Background Information

To help students understand a business cycle, share the following scenario with them: Suppose there is an economic contraction in Asia. As a result, incomes in Asia are falling. With lower incomes, Asians buy fewer goods from the United States, and so U.S. exports decline. Since GDP = C + I + G + (EX − IM), a decline in exports (EX) will lower U.S. GDP. In short, because of the economic contraction in Asia, U.S. GDP declines.

A Student Asks

Use this A Student Asks to make sure students understand the difference between a recession and a depression.

Reinforcement Activity

The National Bureau of Economic Research (NBER) is a private, nonprofit, nonpartisan research organization that's "dedicated to promoting a greater understanding of how the economy works." One of the many things the NBER does is determine the dates of the different phases of the business cycle. For example, it might determine that the peak of a given business cycle was in a certain month and year. Go to the NBER website at http://econ.emcp.net /businesscycles to find the business cycle that took place during the Great Depression. According to the NBER, how many months was the Great Depression, from peak to trough? The answer is 43 months; in other words, the contraction phase known as the Great Depression lasted for 43 months.

---

economic upturns or downturns, and *lag* behind economic upturns and downturns.

We would expect a leading indicator to rise before an upturn in real GDP and to fall before a downturn in real GDP. A coincident indicator should reach its high point at the same time as a peak of a business cycle and reach its low point with the trough of a business cycle. Finally, we would expect a lagging indicator to reach its high sometime after the peak of a business cycle and to reach its low sometime after the trough.

Leading economic indicators tend to be mentioned in the news more often than coincident and lagging indicators, perhaps because people seem particularly interested in predicting or forecasting the future. They want to know what lies ahead—contraction or expansion. What will the economic future hold?

Key leading indicators include stock prices, the money supply (in inflation-adjusted dollars), consumer expectations, and average weekly hours worked in manufacturing. For example, a stock market that is up generally reflects good economic times ahead, and a stock market that is down generally reflects bad economic conditions to come.

Similarly, an increase in average weekly hours worked reflects good times ahead. The reasoning is that when good things are happening in the economy—when sales and profits are expected to rise—companies increase the number of hours their employees work before hiring more people. In contrast, a decline in average weekly hours worked reflects bad times ahead. When this indicator goes down, it usually means that sales and profits are expected to fall, and companies are cutting back on the number of hours their employees work.

A Student Asks

QUESTION: *Is an economic contraction the same thing as a recession?*
ANSWER: *The term contraction refers to a declining period of real GDP. In Exhibit 12-7, the declining parts of the curve are contractions. When the decline is relatively mild (like a slide with only a slight incline), we often call the*

---

contraction a recession. For example, if real GDP drops by 2 percent for two consecutive quarters, we say the economy is in a recession. If the decline in real GDP is sharp (like a steep slide), we usually call the contraction a depression.

What Causes Business Cycles?

Since the end of World War II, the United States has gone through 11 business cycles. What causes business cycles? As you might expect, different economists identify different causes.

Money Supply

Some economists believe that changes in the money supply cause economic contractions and expansions. For example, when either the absolute money supply drops (say, from $2.20 trillion to $2.15 trillion) or the growth rate in the money supply declines (say, from 5 percent to 1 percent), people end up buying fewer goods and services, and the economy falls into a contraction. In contrast, an increase in the money supply means more buying and leads to an economic expansion.

These economists say the ups and downs of the business cycle are caused by the erratic behavior of the monetary authorities or the Fed. Sometimes, the Fed puts the monetary "accelerator" to the floor, dramatically increasing the money supply and causing expansion. At other times, it slams on the monetary "brakes", causing the money supply to drop and the economy to dive into a contraction.

EXAMPLE Suppose the money supply goes up in one six-month period, down in the next six-month period, and then up again in the next six-month period. This up-and-down movement in the money supply is what causes the ups and downs in economic activity (real GDP), according to some economists. In a way, increasing the money supply acts as a "stimulant" to the economy, and reducing the money supply acts as a "depressant" on the economy. ♦

Background Information: Real GDP

Most economists use *real* GDP instead of GDP when talking about the economy. They do so because an increase in prices and/or output will increase GDP, whereas only an increase in output will increase real GDP. The difference between real GDP and GDP can be difficult for some students to grasp. Remind them that two variables are used to compute GDP: price and quantity. It's important to understand that real GDP takes into account price changes to paint a more accurate picture of any change in the quantity of final goods and services produced in an economy in one year.

Could You Buy More in 2016 Than in 1964?[1]

Back in 1964, a person could buy a Sears Silvertone entertainment center that consisted of a 21 inch color TV set, a phonograph, and an AM-FM radio for $750. In the last chapter, we learned how to convert a dollar amount in the past into today's dollars. If we convert $750 in 1964 into 2016 dollars, we get $5,891. In other words, buying the entertainment center in 1964 for $750 is the same as spending $5,891 in 2016.

But keep this in mind. In 2016, one could buy much more

than an entertainment center (that consisted of a TV set, phonograph, and AM-FM radio) for $5,891. In fact, for $5,891, you could buy all the items listed here:

▶ a freezer for $450
▶ a refrigerator for $670
▶ a gas stove and oven for $675
▶ a washer and dryer for $900
▶ a laptop computer for $400
▶ a Garmin GPS for $118
▶ a camera for $600
▶ a Blu-Ray home theater system for $600
▶ a 55 inch HDTV for $500
▶ an iPod MP3 player for $285
▶ an iPhone 7 Plus for $620
▶ a graphing calculator for $73

To summarize, with $750 in 1964 (which was equivalent to $5,891

in 2016) a person could buy one entertainment center. But with $5,891 in 2016, one could buy so much more. Would you rather have had $750 to spend in 1964 or its 2016-equivalent of $5,891 to spend in 2016?

In addition, consider the point that the price one pays to buy a good or service can be measured in dollars or in labor time. To illustrate, back in 1964, the average hourly wage was $2.56. This means that person earning the average hourly wage in 1964 would have had to work 293 hours to earn the $750 needed to buy the entertainment center with the 21 inch color TV set. In contrast, in 2016, the average hourly wage was $21.73, which means the person earning the average hourly wage in 2016 would have had to work 23 hours to earn the $500 needed to buy the 55 inch HDTV. Was it easier for the average hourly wage earner to buy a TV set in 1964 or in 2016?

THINK ABOUT IT If an average hourly wage of $2.56 in 1964 sounds low to you, consider that it was equivalent to an average hourly wage of $20.13 in 2016. Of what benefit is it to convert dollar amounts this way?

[1] This feature is based on The 'Magic of the Global Marketplace' and the 'Miracle of Global Manufacturing': Christmas 1964 vs. Today" by Mark J. Perry, Carpe Diem blog, December 22, 2016.

Direct students to read the feature and identify what goods they would purchase from the list if they had, say, $1,000 to spend. Ask them why they chose the goods they chose over the ones they did not choose.

ANSWERS TO THINK ABOUT IT One possible answer is that when we convert dollars in the past into today's dollars, it is as if we are translating things from a language we don't understand that well into a language we do understand. It's somewhat like translating things from a foreign language into one's own language. Understanding is often gained as a result.

Discussion Starter

Economists use economic indicators to make educated guesses about how the economy will react to various stimuli. Ask students if they can think of another subject in school in which they must gather data to support making an educated guess. Discuss whether economics is a science or an art.

Reinforcement Activity

Invite one or two students to give oral reports on how the economic policy of the United States both contributed to and alleviated the Great Depression. Then assign all students to graph the business cycle in the United States from 1925 to 1945. Discuss with students the impact of the Depression and World War II on the business cycle.

Background Information: Economist Irving Fisher and the Depression

How hard is it to predict downturns in the economy? It was rather hard for American economist Irving Fisher (1867–1947), which says a lot about how hard it is for others.

Fisher, who taught at Yale University, was one of the most respected economists of his day. But not even he predicted the Great Depression. Just

two days before the October 1929 stock market crash, the "first shot" of the Great Depression, Fisher said that the stock market would continue to rise and that no problems lay ahead for the economy. Taking his own advice, Fisher invested a lot of money in the stock market, which he lost in the crash.

Teaching with Visuals

Answers will vary, but students should see that an increase in government spending on road construction will create jobs for people and that those people will spend money on goods and services, potentially leading to an increase in economic activity.

Cause and Effect

Invite students to brainstorm events that might affect the current economic situation (for instance, an oil embargo, invention of a new microprocessor, presidential election, natural disaster, etc.) and then determine the effect of each event on the business cycle.

Prediction Activity

Have students consider this scenario and the questions that follow it: The chair of the Board of Governors of the Federal Reserve System goes before Congress and says that the Fed is likely to sharply cut back the growth rate of the money supply in the next few months. What do you predict will happen to real GDP? to the unemployment rate?

Students should predict an economic contraction. This means that real GDP will decline and that the unemployment rate will rise.

 Application Activity

After reading and discussing Section 2, assign the Section Activity in the *Applying the Principles Workbook,* pages 132–134.

Assess

Quick Quiz

The following true-or-false quiz will help you assess student understanding of the material covered in this section.

1. The length of a typical business cycle is 10 years. (False)
2. The three types of economic indicators are leading, lasting, and coincident. (False)
3. The money supply and politics both cause business cycles. (True)
4. Stock prices are leading indicators. (True)

▲ How might changes in government spending on road construction affect the economy?

> "One good thing can be said for inflation: without it there would be no football."
> —Martin Ragaway, comedy writer

Business Investment, Residential Construction, and Government Spending

Some economists point to changes in business investment (firms have cut back on buying factories and machinery), residential construction (contractors are building fewer homes), or government spending (government spending has been cut substantially) as the cause of a business cycle. For example, a contraction might result from a cutback in business investment or government spending that lowers aggregate demand in the economy. With lower aggregate demand, firms do not sell as many goods and services, so they end up firing workers. Fired workers do not have the income they once had, so overall income in the economy falls. With lower incomes, people do not buy as many goods. Thus, the initial cut in spending results in even further declines in spending, and the economy falls deeper into recession. Things

are reversed when either the business sector or government starts to spend more.

EXAMPLE Suppose the federal government is spending $3.5 trillion a year and then cuts back to $3.1 trillion. According to some economists, this cutback in government spending can reduce the overall demand for goods and services in the economy and lead to a decline in economic activity. Similarly, they argue that a rise in government spending can lead to a rise in economic activity. ♦

Politics

Some economists believe that at least some business cycles have been caused by politicians trying to get reelected to office. Suppose it's a year or so before the members of Congress will be running for reelection. They know their chances of getting reelected are better if the economy is in good shape on election day. To this end, they pass more spending bills in Congress, hoping to increase aggregate demand in the economy. With greater aggregate demand, they reason, firms will sell more goods and services and hire more workers. People will have jobs and income. When times are good, voters are more likely to reward the people in office who (they believe) made this possible.

Of course, things may get out of hand after the election. The greater aggregate demand can cause inflation (as we saw in earlier in the chapter). Congress may then reverse its strategy by trying to cut spending to lower aggregate demand and slow down the economy. If Congress cuts spending too much, though, the economy may slide into a contraction.

EXAMPLE Every two years, all of the members of the House of Representatives and one-third of the members of the Senate are up for reelection. Suppose that as election day nears, the economy is contracting: real GDP is declining, more people are becoming unemployed, and so on. The members of Congress are afraid that if election day comes during poor economic times, they will not be reelected to office. So, before election day, they decide to pass various spending bills, including more

Background Information: Economist Irving Fisher and the Depression

Was Fisher a bad economist? Not at all. In fact, he is regarded as one of the best economists who ever lived. Clearly, even the best economists have trouble making consistently accurate economic predictions.

If all economists could make consistently accurate predictions about the stock market, what would you expect to see in the world? (*Answer:* You would expect to see a lot of wealthy economists!)

money for national defense, Medicare, education, and for highway development. As a result, some economists argue that economic activity will pick up, but they also point out that the motivation for the pickup in economic activity was Congress members' desire to get reelected. ♦

Innovation

Some economists believe that major innovations lay the way for business cycles. For example, suppose one company develops a major new technology or product, and its sales skyrocket. To stay competitive, other companies try to copy what the innovator has done or come up with a better innovation themselves. For a time, these copycat firms invest heavily to maintain their market positions relative to the innovator. In time, though, investment spending tends to decrease, and the economy slows down.

Supply Shocks

Some economists argue that the contraction phase of the business cycle is brought about by major supply-side changes in the

 In 2012, Hurricane Sandy caused more than 280 deaths and billions of dollars in damage to the United States, Jamaica, Cuba, and the Bahamas. Known as "Superstorm Sandy," it affected the entire eastern seaboard of the U.S. What impact can such an event have on the economy?

economy that reduce the capacity of the economy to produce. For example, a war can lower an economy's productive capacity by destroying its factories and killing its people. Consider the effects of a major cutback in oil production brought on by conflict in the Middle East. With less oil, which is an important resource in the production process, the productive capability of the economy declines. Firms end up producing less, so they fire some of their workers. Real GDP goes down, and the unemployment rate goes up.

ASSESSMENT

SECTION 2

Defining Terms

1. Define:
   a. business cycle
   b. recession

Reviewing Facts and Concepts

2. What are the five phases of a business cycle?
3. Suppose the initial peak of a business cycle was January 1, year 1; the trough was July 1, year 2; and the final peak was July 1, year 4. How long was the contraction (in months)?

4. What is a coincident indicator?

Critical Thinking

5. One leading indicator is average weekly hours worked. If this indicator rises, what does it suggest about the future performance of the economy? Explain.
6. Real GDP was $100 billion in year 1 and $130 billion in year 3. Was there a business cycle during this period?

Applying Economic Concepts

7. One explanation of the business cycle is that it's caused by changes in business investment, residential construction, or government spending. If this explanation is correct, how can you use it to determine whether it's a good time or bad time to buy stocks in the stock market?

Section 2 Business Cycles **363**

SECTION 2 ASSESSMENT ANSWERS

Defining Terms

1. a. business cycle: recurrent swings (up and down) in real GDP; **b. recession:** a slowdown in the economy marked by real GDP falling for two consecutive quarters.

Reviewing Facts and Concepts

2. The five phases are peak, contraction, trough, recovery, and expansion.
3. The contraction lasted 18 months.
4. A coincident indicator is an indicator that reaches its high when the economy is at the

peak of a business cycle and its low when the economy is at the trough of a business cycle.

Critical Thinking

5. It suggests that the future economic performance will likely be good. That is, the economy will be in recovery or

---

5. Real GDP goes up during the contraction phase of the business cycle. (False)

Teaching with Visuals

Hurricane Sandy affected the economy by restricting needed imports, interrupting industrial production, and knocking out city services that maintain healthy living conditions.

Assessment Book

You will find a quiz for this section in the *Assessment Book,* page 120.

Reteaching Activity

Use the Section Assessment to gauge which students may need reteaching on this section. Direct those students to examine Exhibit 12-7. On their own paper, have them list the five phases of the business cycle shown in the exhibit and, next to each, an event in history that will remind them of that phase.

Guided Reading

For further reteaching of the key concepts in this section, assign the Outlining Activity and the Just the Facts Handout from the *Guided Reading and Study Guide,* pages 208–212.

expansion. If firms expect greater sales and profits in the future, they will ask their present workforce to work longer hours. This is what the indicator suggests.
6. It's impossible to tell if there was a business cycle. A business cycle runs from peak to peak. We can't be sure that year 1 and year 3 were peaks. Year 1 could have been a trough and year 3 an expansion.

Applying Economic Concepts

7. If spending is down, then the economy is headed downward. If spending is far enough down, perhaps a contraction is in the future. A contraction would be bad for businesses and the stocks that they issue. Now is probably not a good time to buy stocks. Instead, now might be a good time to sell stocks. Conversely, if spending is up, the economy may be about to improve, in which case buying stocks would be a good idea.

Section 2 Business Cycles **363**

Focus and Motivate

Section Objectives

After completing this section, students will be able to

► differentiate between absolute real economic growth and per capita real economic growth;

► explain the purpose of the Rule of 70;

► explain whether small differences in economic growth rates matter;

► identify causes of economic growth; and► explain arguments against economic growth.

Economics Around the Clock

Kickoff Activity

Have students reread the 7:32 p.m. scenario in Economics Around the Clock (page 345) and suggest answers to the question given. Help students see that having a wide selection of products often indicates economic growth.

Activating Prior Knowledge

Review the phases of the business cycle. Then ask students how the business cycle might be affected by inflation and deflation. Note that if inflation is caused by an increase in the money supply, allowing people to buy more, then economic growth may result. Deflation might have the opposite effect.

Visit econ.myemcp.com/videos for videos that will help students better understand the key concepts found in this section.

Focus Questions

► What is the difference between absolute real economic growth and per capita real economic growth?

► What is the purpose of the Rule of 70?

► Do small differences in economic growth rates matter?

► What causes economic growth?

► Why might someone argue against economic growth?

Key Terms

absolute real economic growth
per capita real economic growth
human capital

What Is Economic Growth?

So far in this chapter, we have talked about inflation (increase in the price level), deflation (decrease in the price level), and the business cycle (real GDP on a roller-coaster ride, going up and down).

Economic growth occurs whenever people take resources and rearrange them in ways that are more valuable."

—Paul Romer, economist

absolute real economic growth
An increase in real GDP from one period to the next.

per capita real economic growth
An increase from one period to the next in per capita real GDP, which is real GDP divided by population.

The last topic we need to discuss is economic growth. Specifically, we can talk about absolute real economic growth and per capita real economic growth. **Absolute real economic growth** is an increase in real GDP from one period to the next. For example, if real GDP was $10.2 trillion in year 1 and $11.1 trillion in year 2, the economy experienced absolute real economic growth. Exhibit 12-8 illustrates real GDP over the period 1947–2017. **Per capita real economic growth** is an increase from one period to the next in per capita real GDP, which is real GDP divided by the population:

$$\text{Per capita real GDP} = \frac{\text{Real GDP}}{\text{Population}}$$

For example, if per capita real GDP is $23,000 in year 1 and $25,000 in year 2, then the economy experienced per capita real economic growth.

Per Capita Real GDP Growth and the Rule of 70

In Chapter 11, the Economics in the Real World feature on page 329 explained the effects of real GDP growth. In that feature, we looked at what happens when the annual growth rate of per capita real GDP is 1.1 percent. A person born today will be 63 years old before his or her standard of living (as measured by per capita real GDP) will have doubled. But if the annual growth rate of per capita real GDP is just 1 percent higher, or 2.1 percent, this person will be only 33 when his or her standard of living will have doubled. If this person lives to 66 years old, his or her standard of living will have doubled twice.

How do we know that a person will be 63 years old before his or her standard of living will have doubled (assuming per capita real GDP grows at a rate of 1.1 percent)? We use

Internet Research

Direct students to the website of the U.S. Department of Commerce Bureau of Economic Analysis to view the chart showing the GDP for the past few years. Ask students to print out this chart or re-create it on their own paper. Students should label the different phases of the business cycle and identify the phase the country appeared to be in during the last financial quarter shown on the chart. Ask students to share their charts with the class.

EXHIBIT 12-8   **Real GDP, 1947–2017**

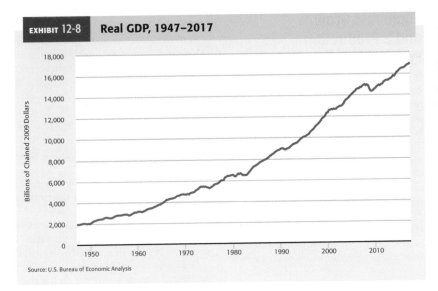

◀ Which would an economist likely say is more important: increases in GDP or increases in real GDP? Explain.

Source: U.S. Bureau of Economic Analysis

the Rule of 70, which says that the way to find out the time required for any variable to double is simply to divide its percentage growth rate (expressed as a whole number, not a decimal) into 70:

$$\text{Rule of 70} = \frac{70}{\text{Growth rate}} =$$

Number of years for a variable to double

Suppose you earn an annual interest rate of 5 percent on a savings account. How many years will it take for the money you deposit into the account to double? The answer is 14 years, because 70 divided by 5 is 14. Or suppose your weight increases by 2 percent per year. How many years will it be before your weight doubles? The answer is 35 years, because 70 divided by 2 is 35.

◀ Based on what you have learned about real GDP and standard of living, do you think this farmer lives in a country with relatively high or low economic growth?

Background Information: The Rule of 70

The Rule of 70 is a valuable tool for students to understand and apply. It can be used to project population growth, investment performance, and so on. Just divide 70 by the known growth rate, and you can determine the amount of time it will take for the variable to double. Students need to realize, however, that they must use annual growth rates or compounded interest rates in this formula. They must also realize that the Rule of 70 is based on the assumption that the growth rate will remain constant. Allow students to experiment with this formula using the economic growth rates of various countries.

Teach

Teaching with Visuals

Students' explanations may vary. Increases in real GDP are more important to economists, because they present a more accurate picture of actual increases in products and services.

Discussion Starter

Ask students if absolute real growth or per capita real growth is a better indicator of a country's standard of living. They will probably say that per capita economic growth is a better indicator, because it keeps pace with the growth of the population. If population grows at a faster rate than absolute real economic growth, the country will experience negative per capita economic growth.

Clarifying Terms

If students have difficulty understanding the meanings of *absolute real economic growth*, *per capita real economic growth*, and *production possibilities frontier*, you might discuss each term as a class. Then ask students to write definitions for the terms in their own words.

Discussion Starter

Ask students if a country that experiences more economic growth than another country is better off, and if so, how. Students will probably say that economic growth benefits a country by providing its residents with more goods and services, access to more jobs, and so on.

Background Information

The Kirov Factory in St. Petersburg, Russia (formerly the Putilov Iron Works), once produced military equipment and now produces farm machinery. This change may have a positive impact on economic growth in Russia. With advanced machinery, farmers' productivity increases. With increased productivity, the country can better serve the needs of its own people and export excess crops.

Teaching with Visuals

Students will probably say the farmer lives in a country with low economic growth.

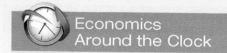
After reading and discussing the first part of this section, refer students to the 10:13 a.m. scenario in Economics Around the Clock (page 345) and discuss their answers to the question that accompanies it.

Help students realize that economic growth, especially per capita real economic growth, is generally associated with less hunger. Hunger and hunger-related diseases are often found in countries that have experienced low per capita real economic growth.

Critical Thinking

Economic growth may produce consequences that students have not considered. Some economists say that a country that experiences great economic growth not only has more goods and services to consume but also provides more effectively for those who cannot provide for themselves. A rich country has a greater ability to provide for people who are poor and homeless than a poor country does, if it has the will to do so. Ask students whether they agree with this view, and encourage them to think of other consequences of economic growth.

Reinforcement Activity

Production possibility frontiers show the opportunity costs of producing one product over another. Direct students to reread the section in Chapter 1 on opportunity cost (pages 8–10).

Economic Growth and a Production Possibilities Frontier

In Chapter 1, we defined the *production possibilities frontier (PPF)*. You might remember that the PPF shows all of the possible combinations of two goods that an economy can produce in a certain period of time. (If you have forgotten how we derived the PPF, you might want to go back to Chapter 1 and review the material. We are assuming in our discussion here that you remember the details of a PPF.)

Using a PPF, we can show what absolute real economic growth looks like. As shown in Exhibit 12-9, economic growth can occur from a position either below or on the PPF.

Economic Growth from a Position Below the PPF

An economy can be located on or below its PPF. For example, an economy could be located at either point A or point B in Exhibit 12-9(a). Suppose an economy is located at point A—a point below the PPF. Obviously, at this point, some resources in the economy remain unused, because only when the economy is on the PPF are all resources fully used. At point A, the economy is producing 100 units of X and 100 units of Y, but it can produce more with the resources it has. It can produce 150 units of X and 200 units of Y by using all of its resources and producing at point B.

A movement from point A to point B is evidence of economic growth. More of both goods are produced at point B than at point A. This means that real GDP is higher at point B than point A.

Economic Growth from a Position on the PPF

Now suppose the economy is located at point B in Exhibit 12-9(b), on PPF₁, which means it's producing 150 units of X and 200 units of Y. How does an economy that's currently on its PPF experience economic growth?

The only way for the economy to achieve growth is to shift its PPF to the right—say, from PPF_1 to PPF_2. In other words, if an economy is already on its PPF, it can experience economic growth only if its PPF shifts rightward. Then, as we see in Exhibit 12-9(b), the economy can move from point B to point C, where more goods are produced and the real GDP is higher.

What Causes Economic Growth?

What factors cause economic growth of the type shown in Exhibit 12-9(b)—that is, economic growth brought on by a rightward shift in the PPF? A few factors can affect growth, such as natural resources, labor, capital, human capital, technological advances, and incentives.

▶ Economic growth can occur from a position below the PPF, as shown in part (a), or from a position on the PPF, as shown in part (b).

EXHIBIT 12-9 **Economic Growth from Positions Below and On the PPF**

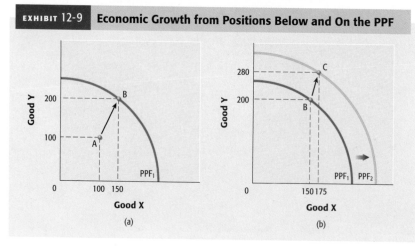

Background Information: Global Economic Growth

Students might find it interesting to compare the economic growth in other countries with that in the United States during the same period. Have students find this information by consulting the *Economic Report of the President* in the school or city library or on the Internet. Alternatively, students may want to look at the *Statistical Abstract of the United States* for this information. (Both are annual publications.) Ask students to prepare written reports or create graphs that clearly show the similarities and differences in the economic growth of various countries.

◀ Capital investment can lead to increases in productivity and growth. **Explain** how investment in capital has made workers in this photograph more productive than the farmer shown on page 365.

the farmer shown on page 365.

Teaching with Visuals

Capital investment causes economic growth by combining workers and capital goods to increase productivity. In the photograph, the workers with the construction equipment are more productive than the farmer who works without machinery.

Background Information

Remind students that although using capital goods (such as machines) increases productivity, such goods are expensive. Poor nations are in a so-called catch-22: they usually have inexpensive (but often untrained) labor but scarce capital to purchase the machines needed to become more productive and thus profitable when competing against capital-intensive labor.

Natural Resources

When a country has more natural resources, it can produce more goods and services. For this reason, people often think that countries with plentiful supplies of natural resources experience economic growth, whereas countries that are short of natural resources do not. In reality, however, some countries with abundant natural resources have experienced rapid economic growth in the past (such as the United States), and some have experienced no growth or only slow growth. Also, some countries that are short of natural resources (such as Singapore) have grown quickly in the past.

Natural resources are neither sufficient nor necessary for economic growth. However, it is still more likely for a country rich in natural resources to experience growth, all other things being equal. In other words, if two countries, A and B, are the same in nearly all aspects except that A has more natural resources than B, then A is more likely to have economic growth than B.

Labor

With more labor, it is possible to produce more output. Clearly, we can get more output with 100 people working than with 70 people working. More labor, by itself, however, is not what matters most to economic growth. More important is the productivity of the labor. Government statisticians measure labor productivity by dividing the total output produced by the number of hours it takes to produce the output:

$$\text{Labor productivity} = \frac{\text{Total output produced}}{\text{Total hours it takes to produce total output}}$$

For example, if $6 trillion of output is produced in 200 billion labor hours, then labor productivity is $30 per hour.

An increase in labor productivity causes economic growth. The real question, then, is how an economy can achieve an increase in labor productivity. One way is through increased education and training of workers. Another way is through capital investment. Providing workers with more capital goods tends to increase their labor productivity. For example, a farmer with a tractor is more productive than a farmer without one, and an accountant with a computer is more productive than an accountant without one.

Internet Research

Assign each student a particular country. Have him or her find the country's investment as percentage of GDP for the current year and, if possible, for the 1990–2000 decade. Students might begin their investigations using the Internet search engines of their choice. As part of this assignment, you might invite volunteers to describe the steps they took to find this data.

After students have read this feature, ask if they know of any squabbles between politicians over economic issues. Invite volunteers to describe these situations. Then choose one or two situations and discuss how economic growth might have satisfied both sides.

ANSWERS TO THINK ABOUT IT Answers will vary. Some students might say that economic growth can make political differences irrelevant only for a while.

Analyzing

Point out that the Fed sometimes increases the money supply even though doing so will likely cause inflation. Ask students the following questions: Given what you know about the relationship between capital and economic growth, why does the Fed increase the money supply? How does doing this help the economy? Students may say that increasing the money supply increases available capital and thus fuels economic growth.

Discussion Starter

After students have read the section "Human Capital" is an outstanding time to remind them of the importance of an educated workforce. The better educated an individual is, the higher his or her productivity will be, and the greater his or her income will likely be. On a larger scale, an educated workforce leads to higher economic growth.

Can Economic Growth Stop Political Squabbling?

Liberal and conservative politicians sometimes want different things for the voters in their districts and for society as a whole. Sometimes, it seems as if politicians are at opposite ends of a rope, each pulling the rope in a different direction and engaging in a political tug-of-war.

Suppose the U.S. production possibilities frontier is PPF$_1$ in Exhibit 12-10. The economy is currently at point A, producing and consuming 10 units of good X and 10 units of good Y.

Political liberals would prefer to be at point L, producing and consuming 15 Y and only 5 X. Political conservatives, however, would prefer to be at point C, producing and consuming 15 X and only 5 Y. In other words, the liberals are pulling in the direction of L, and the conservatives are pulling in the direction of C. Both are trying to influence politicians and citizens to vote for a different combination of goods than currently exists at point A.

If no economic growth occurs and the economy remains on PPF$_1$, the liberals won't be able to get what they want without making the conservatives unhappy. Similarly, without economic growth, the conservatives won't be able to get what they want without making the liberals unhappy.

Both liberals and conservatives can get what they want, however, with economic growth. As we know, economic growth shifts the PPF rightward from PPF$_1$ to PPF$_2$. In fact, it's possible for an economy to move from point A (on PPF$_1$) to point B (on PPF$_2$). Notice that at point B, both liberals and conservatives get what they want. Liberals get 15 Y, and conservatives get 15 X. In other words, economic growth can end the political tug-of-war between liberals and conservatives for awhile.

We say "awhile" because soon after the economy is located at point B, it's likely that liberals will want to move up PPF$_2$ to get more Y and conservatives will want to move down PPF$_2$ to get more X.

THINK ABOUT IT What specific goods and services do you think liberals want more of? What specific goods and services do you think conservatives want more of? Might economic growth eventually make these political differences irrelevant? Why or why not?

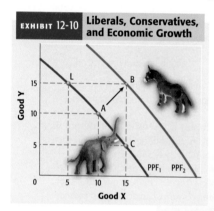

EXHIBIT 12-10 Liberals, Conservatives, and Economic Growth

Cooperative Learning

The text discusses some factors that affect economic growth—natural resources, labor, capital, human capital, technological advances, and incentives. Divide the class into six groups, and assign each group one of these six factors. Each group should brainstorm examples of the factor it has been assigned and report its ideas to the class.

Teaching with Visuals

Electrical workers represent human capital because their knowledge and experience are required to complete the work safely and accurately.

Reinforcement Activity

The world is in danger of running out of the natural resources. Guide students in creating a list of natural resources and determining which are renewable.

Analyzing

In Chapter 2, students learned about the differences between free enterprise and socialism. In this chapter, they are learning that incentives affect economic growth. Ask students how the incentives structure likely differs between free enterprise and socialism and how this difference might affect the economic growth rates of the two economic systems. You might also ask students whether they think incentives other than money can stimulate economic growth and to name other incentives if they can think of any.

Capital

As just mentioned, capital investment can lead to increases in labor productivity and therefore to increases in output or real GDP. However, more capital goods do not just fall from the sky. Recall from an earlier chapter that getting more of one thing often means having less of something else. To produce more capital goods, which are not directly consumable, the present level of consumption must be reduced.

Consider Robinson Crusoe, alone on an island and fishing with a spear. To take the time to weave a net (a capital good) and learn how to use it to catch more fish, he must give up some of his time catching (and consuming) fish.

Human Capital

Production of goods and services requires not only physical or tangible capital (a machine, for example) but also human capital. **Human capital** consists of the knowledge and skills that people get from education, on-the-job training, and work experience. It also consists of such things as honesty, creativity, and perseverance—traits that lend themselves to finding and keeping a job. Human capital is part of a person and cannot be separated from him or her the way physical or tangible capital can be. (You can separate a person from a machine, but you cannot separate a person from his or her education, skills, and other personal qualities.)

Many economists argue that human capital is related to economic growth. Generally speaking, the more human capital a group of people have, the greater economic growth will be. It is important to point out how important human capital is to economic growth. Some countries that lack resources have experienced economic growth by relying on a well-trained, educated, hardworking, and conscientious labor force. For example, the so-called Asian tigers (Hong Kong, Singapore, South Korea, and Taiwan) have experienced economic growth in this way.

> *"In a modern economy, human capital is by far the most important form of capital increasing wealth and growth."*
> **Gary Becker, economist**

Technological Advances

Technological advances make it possible to obtain more output from the same amount of resources. Compare the amount of work that can be done by a business that uses computers with the amount accomplished by a business that does not.

Technological advances may be the result of new capital goods or new ways of producing goods. The use of computers is an example of a technological advance that

▲ How do these electrical line workers represent human capital?

human capital
The knowledge and skills that people use in the production of goods and services; also includes honesty, creativity, and perseverance—traits that lend themselves to finding and keeping a job.

Background Information: Journalism and Business Cycles

Newspaper journalists are members of the educated workforce. Many major in journalism, English, history, economics, or political science, and they have good listening and writing skills. They gather information and write stories about local, state, national, and international events and present points of view on various current issues.

Journalists have to research stories quickly to meet deadlines and go places they may not want to go. Their working hours vary, and they may work long into the night. They also get to meet interesting people and act as current-day historians.

Ask students to explain how a newspaper journalist's job is linked to the ups and downs of a business cycle.

▶ What potential costs of economic growth come to mind as you look at this photograph?

resulted from a new capital good. New and improved management techniques are an example of a new way of producing goods.

Technological advances usually result from companies and countries investing in research and development (R&D). R&D is a general term that encompasses such things as scientists working in a lab to develop a new product and managers figuring out, through experience, how to motivate employees to work to their potential.

Incentives

Some economists have argued that economic growth appears first in areas that direct people to effective economic projects. In other words, economic growth develops where people are given the incentive to produce and innovate.

Consider two incentive structures: in one, people are allowed to keep the full monetary rewards of their labor, and in the other, they keep only half. Many economists would predict that the first incentive structure will stimulate more economic activity than the second, all other things being the same. Individuals invest more, take more risks, and work harder when the incentive structure allows them to keep more of the

monetary rewards of their investment, risk taking, and labor.

Two Worries About Future Economic Growth

Two worries commonly come up in discussions of economic growth. One concerns the costs of growth. Some individuals argue that more economic growth means more pollution, more factories, more crowded cities, more emphasis on material goods and getting ahead, more rushing around, more psychological problems, more people using drugs, more suicides, and so on. These individuals argue for less growth instead of more. Others maintain that no evidence indicates economic growth (or faster, as opposed to slower, economic growth) causes any or all of these problems. They argue that growth brings many positive things: more wealth, less poverty, a society that is better able to support art projects and museums, a society more likely to protect the environment, and so forth.

The debate between those who favor more growth and those who favor less growth is complex. Economists have joined in—as have psychologists, biologists, sociologists, and many others—and so the debate promises to continue for a long time.

The second worry concerns the relationship between economic growth and the future availability of resources. Some individuals believe that continued economic and population growth will hasten the time when there will be no more natural resources, clean air, or pure water and no more land for people to live on comfortably. These individuals advocate social policies that will slow growth and preserve what we have.

Critics of this position often charge that such "doomsday forecasts," as they have come to be called, are based on unrealistic assumptions, obvious oversights, and flimsy evidence. For example, economist Julian Simon pointed out that, contrary to popular opinion, population growth does not hinder economic growth, nor does it increase the incidence of famine. Furthermore, Simon points out, natural resources are not becoming increasingly more scarce. In fact, Simon had a wager with Paul Ehrlich, author and professor of population studies and biological sciences, about the relative prices of natural resources in the

period 1980–1990. Ehrlich said that natural resources were becoming increasingly more scarce and therefore would rise in price during this period. Simon, to the contrary, said that natural resources were becoming more plentiful and would actually fall in price. Simon won the bet easily.

Evaluating Data for Bias

As explained in the previous section, beliefs and theories based on economic data can be misleading. When you come across any economic information—whether it be economic data, an economic explanation, or an economic theory—it is always a good rule to evaluate and analyze for accuracy and bias. Is the data accurate? Is the explanation given by the person biased? With respect to bias, consider the fact that sometimes the point of view, or frame of reference, of the person presenting the explanation can tilt you in a direction of believing something that may not be true. Not only is it important to understand what a person says, but to make sure the context in which what is said is presented, and to understand why the person might have presented the explanation in one particular way and not another.

Assessment Book

You will find a quiz for this section in the *Assessment Book,* page 121.

Reteaching Activity

Use the Section Assessment to gauge which students may need reteaching on this section. Guide those students in examining Exhibit 12-9, and ask them what could make the PPF shift to the right? (*Answer:* an increase in resources.) What could make the PPF shift to the left? (*Answer:* a decrease in resources.) Have students reread the subsection "What Causes Economic Growth?" (pages 366–370).

Guided Reading

For further reteaching of the key concepts in this section, assign the Outlining Activity and the Just the Facts Handout from the *Guided Reading and Study Guide,* pages 213–216.

ASSESSMENT

Defining Terms

1. Define:
   a. absolute real economic growth
   b. per capita real economic growth
   c. human capital

Reviewing Facts and Concepts

2. Can real GDP rise as per capita real GDP falls? Explain your answer.

3. You put $1,000 into a savings account that pays an interest rate of 6 percent annually. How many years before your savings doubles?
4. Analyze and explain how productivity relates to economic growth.

Critical Thinking

5. "Natural resources are neither necessary nor sufficient for economic

growth." Explain what this statement means.
6. Can labor productivity decline as total output rises? Explain your answer.

Applying Economic Concepts

7. What do you see as the costs of economic growth? What do you see as the benefits?

SECTION 3

ASSESSMENT ANSWERS

Defining Terms

1. a. absolute real economic growth: an increase in real GDP from one period to the next; **b. per capita real**

economic growth: an increase from one period to the next in per capital real GDP, which is real GDP divided by population; **c. human capital:** the knowledge and skills that people use in the production of goods and services; also includes honesty, creativity,

and perseverance—traits that lend themselves to finding and keeping a job.

Reviewing Facts and Concepts

2. Yes. If the population rises by a greater percentage than real GDP, then per capita GDP will fall as real GDP rises.

3. According to the Rule of 70, it will take 11.67 years for the savings to double.
4. An increase in productivity signifies that more output can be produced with the same amount of resources. For example, an increase in labor productivity means that the same amount of labor can produce more output. So instead of 10 workers producing 100 units of a good in 1 hour, they can produce 120 unites of a good in 1 hour. As productivity rises, so does economic growth.

Critical Thinking

5. This statement means that a country doesn't need to have plentiful natural resources to grow and that a country that has plentiful natural resources isn't guaranteed to grow.
6. Yes. Labor productivity is equal to total output produced divided by the total hours it takes to produce the total output. If total output rises but total hours rises by a greater percentage, then labor productivity will decline.

Applying Economic Concepts

7. Answers will vary.

Your **Personal** Economics

Discussion Starter

Ask students if they have ever thought of themselves in terms of being human capital and what it means to them personally to do so. In other words, what is the value in thinking of oneself that way?

Research Activity

After students have read the section comparing specific and generic capital, have them research at least five jobs they might be interested in pursuing in the future. Have them chart the generic and specific human capital they would gain from each job. Then ask students to identify which jobs would provide them with the most generic human capital (allowing them to work in a variety of industries). Invite students to report their findings to the class.

Teaching with Visuals

Answers will vary.

Your Goal:
Generic, Not Specific, Human Capital

As you've learned in reading this chapter, human capital refers to the knowledge and skills that people use to produce goods and services. Economists talk about two types of human capital: specific and generic. What's the difference? An economist once explained it by saying that *specific* human capital is an employee knowing where the restroom is, whereas *generic* human capital is knowing how to read the signs on doors.

Specific Capital

Anybody who works for a business acquires certain specific human capital; he or she learns certain things that are useful and important in that particular business. Suppose you go to work for a company that produces movies. You may learn how movies are made, how they are distributed, and what makes some movies more profitable than others. You will also likely learn certain things about the people who work in the movie industry. No doubt, working in the movie industry will give you much more specific knowledge about it than many people have.

Now ask yourself how transferable that specific human capital will be. In other words, how hard will it be for you to transfer the knowledge and skills (the human capital) you acquired working in the movie industry to another job in another industry? If making that transfer is hard, then it's likely the human capital you acquired is specific—that is, it can be used only in that particular industry. If it is easy to transfer, then it's likely the human capital you acquired is generic and can be used in almost any industry.

Comparing Specific to Generic Capital

As another example, let's look at two jobs: one as a machine operator at a car manufacturing plant and the other as a computer programmer.

▶ Compare the two types of human capital—specific and general—that you would acquire as a pizza delivery person.

It's likely that the machine operator has specific human capital. He can operate a particular machine in the auto plant, but he can't transfer this knowledge and skill to operating a different kind of machine in the non-auto plant. On the other hand, it's likely that the computer programmer has generic human capital. She can transfer her knowledge and skills in computer programming to a number of different industries.

Human Capital and Unions

How might these differences between specific and generic human capital affect unionism in the United States? Unionism tends to be strong and visible in manufacturing, where it's likely workers have specific human capital. Unionism doesn't tend to be strong or visible in computer programming, where it's likely workers have generic human capital.

Why is unionism strong in one type of workplace and not in the other? Some economists say unionism appears where workers need strong bargaining muscle (the places where the workers have specific human capital). If you have generic human capital, having strong bargaining muscle is less crucial, because you can work for many different companies in many different industries.

In recent years, the percentage of the U.S. labor force that is unionized has declined. In 1983,

Cooperative Learning

After reading the section "Learning to Solve Problems," divide students into groups of three or four. Assign each group a different section of the required courses listed in your school's graduation plan—for example, mathematics, sciences, history, language arts, fine arts, and physical education. Have each group review the courses in its assigned section and create a list of human capital assets—both specific and generic—to be gained by taking these courses. After 15 minutes, ask the groups to report to the class.

▲ Why do higher level math courses contribute to your generic human capital?

20.1 percent of the labor force was unionized. By 2016, that percentage had fallen to 10.6 percent. Why the decline over the years? Some economists have linked the decline to a shift from manufacturing to service sector jobs. With such a shift, generic human capital became more important than specific human capital.

Learning to Solve Problems

This trend away from specific human capital and toward generic human capital is likely to continue. Now, perhaps more than ever before, it's important to acquire generic human capital.

While you're in school, you need to acquire as much generic human capital as possible. You need to acquire the skills and knowledge that more and more employers want: critical thinking skills, an ability in mathematics, and an ability to write and reason clearly. You want to acquire the knowledge and skills that are in high demand in a world that is coming to value

generic human capital more than specific human capital.

Sometimes, students take an algebra, trigonometry, or chemistry course in high school and wonder what good it will ever be to them in the real world. You might hear statements such as "I don't know what use algebra is going to be to me when I'm out in the real world working" and "I'll never use what I learned in chemistry. I don't plan to be a chemist." Well, you may not plan to be an algebra teacher or a chemist, but that doesn't mean the thinking skills you acquire learning algebra or chemistry won't be useful in the real world. Thinking

skills, after all, are what transfer easily among jobs.

For workers in the U.S. economy, it's becoming increasingly more important to know how to solve many problems, not just a single problem. But to solve many problems, you must have good thinking skills.

Your Personal Economics Activity

Analyze your current courses and identify what generic and specific human capital you are currently acquiring. Write a brief evaluation that examines each course and notes the skills for each. Support your evaluation with logical reasoning.

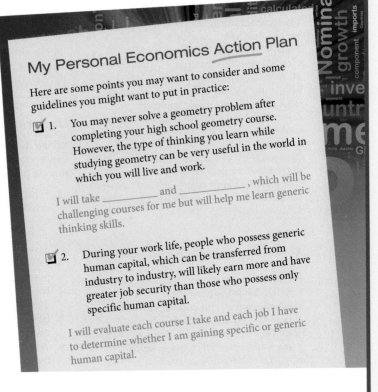

My Personal Economics Action Plan

Here are some points you may want to consider and some guidelines you might want to put in practice:

☑ 1. You may never solve a geometry problem after completing your high school geometry course. However, the type of thinking you learn while studying geometry can be very useful in the world in which you will live and work.

I will take _____ and _____ , which will be challenging courses for me but will help me learn generic thinking skills.

☑ 2. During your work life, people who possess generic human capital, which can be transferred from industry to industry, will likely earn more and have greater job security than those who possess only specific human capital.

I will evaluate each course I take and each job I have to determine whether I am gaining specific or generic human capital.

Discussion Starter

To help students realize the importance of human capital, ask them to create human capital profiles of themselves. Have them include knowledge and skills obtained from education, on-the-job training (if applicable), and experience they may have had. Also, have them include personal traits that lend themselves to finding work. After students have completed their profiles, ask them how doing this activity increased their knowledge of their personal human capital. How could having this human capital profile help them in applying for jobs?

My Personal Economics Action Plan Have each student survey several adults to determine how human capital is evident in their jobs. Students may need to ask follow-up questions to determine if a job has specific capital or generic capital. Allow students to report back to the class.

Differentiating Instruction

English Language Learners

To help students who are English language learners, use the following resources, which are provided as part of the *Economics: New Ways of Thinking* program:

- a Spanish glossary in the *Student Text*
- Spanish versions of the Chapter Summaries on an audio disk

Grading Rubric: Evaluation

1 2 3 4 5   Evaluations described skills learned in each course.

1 2 3 4 5   Evaluations were supported with logical reasoning.

Assessment Answers

Economics Vocabulary

1. demand-side inflation; **2.** supply-side inflation; **3.** velocity; **4.** simple quantity theory of money; **5.** Deflation; **6.** peak; **7.** expansion; **8.** trough; **9.** absolute real economic; **10.** per capita real GDP.

Understanding the Main Ideas

1. Inflation is an increase in the price level. Deflation is a decrease in the price level.

2. Yes. An increase in aggregate demand causes inflation, while a decrease in aggregate demand causes deflation.

3. Inflation is an increase in the price level, which lowers the purchasing power of money—each dollar buys less than it did before.

4. Suppose a firm produces good X with resources A, B, and C. If prices fall but the price of good X falls before the prices of A, B, and C fall, then the firm's total revenue will likely fall as its total costs remain constant. This situation will lower profits. As a result of having lower profits, the firm may reduce the number of workers it hires or go out of business altogether. Either way, some people will lose their jobs. In the interim, at least, unemployment will rise.

5. An increase in the money supply can cause inflation.

6. The assumptions are that velocity and the quantity of goods and services are constant. The theory predicts that changes in the money supply will bring about strictly proportional changes in the price level.

7. The inflation rate will likely be higher after year 4. The simple quantity theory of money holds that changes in the money supply bring about strictly proportional changes in the price level.

8. Yes. An increase in aggregate supply causes deflation, whereas a decrease in aggregate supply causes inflation.

9. With less aggregate demand or total spending in the economy, there is less buying of goods and services. When

---

Chapter Summary

Be sure you know and remember the following key points from the chapter sections.

Section 1

▶ Inflation is an increase in the price level.

▶ A positive change (rise) in the consumer price index means inflation has occurred.

▶ When an increase in the price level occurs because of increased demand, economists call it *demand-side inflation*.

▶ When an increase in the price level occurs because of decreased supply, it is called *supply-side inflation*.

▶ In the exchange equation, money supply (M) multiplied by velocity (V) equals price (P) times quantity of output (Q).

▶ Deflation is a decrease in the price level.

Section 2

▶ The recurrent swings in an economy's real GDP are known as a *business cycle*.

▶ Economists identify five phases of a business cycle: (1) peak, (2) contraction, (3) trough, (4) recovery, and (5) expansion.

▶ Economists use leading indicators (including stock prices, money supply, consumer expectations, and manufacturing labor hours worked) to forecast the direction the economy is heading.

▶ Economists use various theories to explain the phases of the business cycle, including changes in the money supply, levels of business investment and government spending, politics, innovation, and supply shocks.

Section 3

▶ Absolute real economic growth is an increase in real GDP from one period to the next, whereas per capita real economic growth is an increase in real GDP divided by population.

▶ Economic growth is the result of a number of factors, including the supply of natural resources, labor productivity, capital investment, human capital/experience, technological advances, and incentives to produce.

Economics Vocabulary

To reinforce your knowledge of the key terms in this chapter, fill in each of the following blanks on a separate piece of paper with the appropriate word or phrase.

1. Aggregate demand rises, and the price level rises. This scenario is an example of _____

2. Aggregate supply falls, and the price level rises. This scenario is an example of _____.

3. The average number of times a dollar is spent to buy final goods and services in a year is called _____.

4. The _____ predicts that changes in the price level will be strictly proportional to changes in the money supply.

5. _____ is a decrease in the price level or average level of prices.

6. Real GDP is at a temporary high if it is at the _____ of a business cycle.

7. The _____ of a business cycle refers to increases in real GDP beyond the recovery.

8. If real GDP is at the low point of the business cycle, it is in the _____.

9. An increase in real GDP from one period to the next is referred to as _____ growth.

10. Real GDP divided by population is called _____.

Understanding the Main Ideas

Review the main ideas in this chapter by writing answers to the following questions on a separate sheet of paper.

1. What is the difference between inflation and deflation?

2. Can both inflation and deflation be caused by changes in aggregate demand? Explain your answer.

3. How does inflation reduce the value or purchasing power of money?

4. Explain how deflation can lead to an increase in unemployment.

5. How might inflation be caused by events on the demand side of the economy?

6. What are the assumptions of the simple quantity theory of money? What does it predict?

---

fewer goods and services are bought, there is less need to hire people to produce these goods and services.

10. Inflation lowers the standard of living of people on fixed incomes by reducing their purchasing power. They can transfer fewer goods and services from others to themselves. Inflation hurts savers by lowering the purchasing power of the dollars they are saving.

11. The more incentive people have to produce and innovate, the more economic growth there will likely be.

12. The Fed alternates between increasing and decreasing the money supply. When it increases the money supply, people buy more goods and services, and there is an economic recovery or expansion. By alternately increasing and decreasing the money supply, the Fed influences

7. In year 1, the Fed increases the money supply 10 percent, and in year 4 it increases the money supply 20 percent. Following which year is the inflation rate likely to be higher, assuming the simple quantity theory of money is accurate? Explain your answer.

8. Can both inflation and deflation be caused by changes in aggregate supply? Explain your answer.

9. Explain why the unemployment rate might rise if aggregate demand falls.

10. Explain how inflation affects both individuals on fixed incomes and savers.

11. How do incentives affect economic growth?

12. Explain how activities by the Fed can cause a business cycle.

13. What is human capital, and how does it relate to economic growth?

Doing the Math

1. The CPI is 145 in year 1 and 154 in year 2. What is the inflation rate between the two years?

2. The money supply is $2,000, velocity is 2, and the quantity of goods and services is 500 units. According to the exchange equation, what is the average price of a good?

3. Real GDP is $4,233 billion in year 1 and $4,456 billion in year 2. The population is 178 million in year 1 and 182 million in year 2. What is the per capita real GDP in each year? Did per capita real economic growth occur from year 1 to year 2?

4. If positive absolute real economic growth and negative per capita real economic growth occur at the same time, what is the relationship between the change in real GDP and the change in population?

Working with Graphs and Tables

1. Illustrate the following:
   a. demand-side inflation
   b. supply-side inflation

2. In Exhibit 12-11, identify each of the following:
   a. point A   d. point A to D
   b. point B   e. point B to C
   c. point C to D

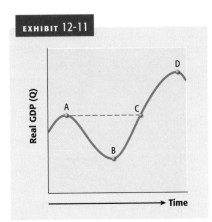

EXHIBIT 12-11

Solving Economic Problems

1. **Apply.** Explain how knowledge of the exchange equation can be used to explain both inflation and deflation.

2. **Analyze.** Can inflation occur after an increase in the quantity of goods and services? Explain your answer.

3. **Identify Cause and Effect.** Do higher interest rates cause higher inflation, or does higher inflation cause higher interest rates? Explain.

4. **Find the Main Idea.** MEDIA Find a newspaper article that discusses economic growth. Identify and discuss the details of the article, and explain how they are used to support the main idea.

5. **Analyze.** If one person can't have too much money, then how can all persons together have too much money?

Project or Presentation

Hyperinflation Board Game. In this chapter, we discussed hyperinflation in Germany in 1923. Work with a group to create a board game about life in a country that experiences hyperinflation. Exchange completed games with another group.

ONLINE emcp.com
Practice Tests and Study Guide

Go to www.emcschool.net/Economics2e and choose *Economics: New Ways of Thinking*, Chapter 12, if you need more help in preparing for the chapter test.

---

is greater in year 2 than in year 1, so there has been per capita real economic growth.

4. The percentage increase in population has to be greater than the percentage increase in real GDP.

Working with Graphs and Tables

1. **a.** See Exhibit 12-3(a). **b.** See Exhibit 12-3(b).

2. **a.** the peak of a business cycle; **b.** the trough of a business cycle; **c.** the expansion phase of the business cycle; **d.** an entire business cycle (peak to peak); **e.** the recovery phase of a business cycle.

Solving Economic Problems

1. Inflation and deflation deal with changes in the price level. Inflation is an increase in the price level, and deflation is a decrease in the price level. The price level (P) appears in the exchange equation: $M \times V = P \times Q$. Using the exchange equation, we can explain both increases and decreases in the price level. For example, an increase in the money supply will raise the price level, while a decrease in the money supply will lower the price level.

2. The question is really asking whether the price level can go up at the same time as the quantity of goods and services rises. This situation is certainly possible; an increase in aggregate demand that is greater than an increase in aggregate supply will bring this about.

3. Higher inflation causes higher interest rates. The text states, "If inflation persists, however, it is customary for financial institutions to compete for customers by offering an interest rate that has been adjusted upward by the inflation rate." If interest rates are being adjusted upward by the inflation rate, then the higher the inflation rate, the higher the interest rate. In other words, higher inflation causes higher interest rates.

4. Answers will vary.

5. One person having more money doesn't cause prices to rise. But if everyone has more money, prices will likely rise.

Project or Presentation

Answers will vary.

---

ups and downs in the economy.

13. Human capital is the knowledge and skills that people use in the production of goods and services. It also includes traits such as honesty, creativity, and perseverance that lend themselves to finding and keeping work. Economic growth relies on the human capital of a well-trained, educated, hardworking, and conscientious labor force.

Doing the Math

1. 6.2% (*calculation:* [(154 − 145) ÷ 145] × 100 = 6.2%).

2. $8 (*calculation:* If $2,000 × 2 = P × 500, then P = $8).

3. In year 1, per capita real GDP is $23,780.89 (*calculation:* $4,233 billion ÷ $178 million). In year 2, it's $24,484.51 (*calculation:* $4,456 billion ÷ $182 million). The per capita real GDP

Chapter 13 Planning Guide

	Learning Objectives	Reproducible Worksheets and Handouts	Assessment
SECTION 1 **Fiscal Policy** (pages 378–387)	▶ Explain what fiscal policy is. ▶ Identify the type of fiscal policy used to reduce unemployment. ▶ Identify the type of fiscal policy used to reduce inflation. ▶ Define *crowding out*. ▶ Explain Keynes's ideas on the best way to heal a sick economy. ▶ Explain how tax rates can affect the supply side of the economy.	Section 1 Activity, *Applying the Principles Workbook*, pages 139–142 Outlining Activity, *Guided Reading and Study Guide*, pages 225–227 Just the Facts Handout, *Guided Reading and Study Guide*, pages 228–230	Section Assessment, *Student Text*, page 387 Quick Quiz, *Annotated Teacher's Edition*, page 386 Section Quiz, *Assessment Book*, page 130
SECTION 2 **Monetary Policy** (pages 388–395)	▶ Identify the type of monetary policy used to reduce unemployment. ▶ Identify the type of monetary policy used to reduce inflation. ▶ Explain how monetary policy reduces unemployment and inflation. ▶ Explain the purpose of the exchange equation.	Section 2 Activity, *Applying the Principles Workbook*, pages 143–144 Outlining Activity, *Guided Reading and Study Guide*, pages 231–232 Just the Facts Handout, *Guided Reading and Study Guide*, pages 233–234	Section Assessment, *Student Text*, page 394 Quick Quiz, *Annotated Teacher's Edition*, page 358 Section Quiz, *Assessment Book*, page 131
SECTION 3 **Stagflation: The Two Problems Appear Together** (pages 398–401)	▶ Explain why the output of goods and services rises before prices when the money supply rises. ▶ Explain why the output of goods and services falls before prices when the money supply falls. ▶ Explain what causes stagflation.	Section 3 Activity, *Applying the Principles Workbook*, pages 145–146 Outlining Activity, *Guided Reading and Study Guide*, page 235 Just the Facts Handout, *Guided Reading and Study Guide*, page 236	Section Assessment, *Student Text*, page 400 Quick Quiz, *Annotated Teacher's Edition*, page 364–365 Section Quiz, *Assessment Book*, page 132

Reproducible Chapter Resources and Assessment Materials

📖 Graphic Organizer Activity, *Guided Reading and Study Guide*, pages 237–238

📖 Vocabulary Activity, *Guided Reading and Study Guide*, page 239

📖 Working with Graphs and Charts, *Guided Reading and Study Guide*, page 240

☑ Practice Test, *Guided Reading and Study Guide*, pages 241–242

📖 Critical Thinking Activity, *Finding Economics*, pages 35–37

☑ Chapter Test A, *Assessment Book*, pages 133–136

☑ Chapter Test B, *Assessment Book*, pages 137–140

Student Text Internet Links

Economics: New Ways of Thinking, Second Edition encourages students to use the Internet to find out more about economics. Given the wealth of current, valid information available on websites, students should be encouraged to use the Internet as a research tool. Doing so will likely increase students' interest in and understanding of economics principles and topics. In addition, doing Internet research can help your students form the habit of accessing and using economics information, as well as help them develop investigative skills they will use throughout their educational and professional careers.

To aid your students in achieving these ends, each chapter of *Economics: New Ways of Thinking, Second Edition* includes the addresses of several websites that provide engaging and relevant information. When students type in any of the addresses provided, they will immediately arrive at the intended site. The addresses have been modified so that EMC Publishing can monitor and maintain the proper links—for example, the website http://www.deposit accounts.com/ has been changed to http://econ.emcp.net/accounts. In the event that the address or content of a site changes or is discontinued, EMC's Internet editors will redirect the link to a site with equivalent information.

Activities in the *Annotated Teacher's Edition* often suggest that students search the Internet for information. For some activities, you might want to find reputable sites beforehand and steer students toward them. For other activities, have students do their own searching and then check out the sites they have found and discuss why they might be reliable or unreliable.

Passport® for Economics

Technology resources are available with the *Economics: New Ways of Thinking, Second Edition* program through Passport®. These include:

eBooks for *Economics: New Ways of Thinking, Second Edition*

▶ Student textbook eBook
▶ Interactive Applying the Principles eWorkbook
▶ Finding Economics eBook
▶ Guided Reading and Study Guide eBook
▶ Annotated Teacher's Edition eBook
▶ Lesson Plans eBook
▶ Assessment eBook

Passport® for Students

Students can access helpful resources through Passport® for Economics. Resources include:
▶ Study guides
▶ Practice tests
▶ Flash cards in English and in Spanish
▶ Word games in English and in Spanish
▶ Tutorials and key-concept videos
▶ Spanish print and audio summaries

Passport® for Teachers

Keep your course current and relevant by using the teacher resources provided through Passport® for Economics. In addition to all of the resources on the student side of Passport®, the teacher side contains:
▶ Link to the Annotated Teacher's Edition eBook
▶ Standards correlations
▶ Microsoft® PowerPoint® Lectures
▶ Current Events Lessons
▶ Additional Economics in the Real World features
▶ ExamView® Assessment Suite
▶ PDFs of all print supplements (student and teacher)

This chapter introduces the ways that government can intervene in the economy. Two principal means are through fiscal policy and monetary policy. Fiscal policy deals with changes in taxes and government spending. Monetary policy deals with changes in the money supply. The following statements provide brief descriptions of the major concepts covered in each section of this chapter.

SECTION 1 Fiscal Policy

Section 1 defines and describes fiscal policy. It also explains both expansionary and contractionary fiscal policies.

SECTION 2 Monetary Policy

Section 2 explores monetary policy. It discusses the different types of monetary policy, as well as how monetary policy is used.

SECTION 3 Stagflation: The Two Problems Appear Together

Section 3 deals with the definition and causes of stagflation.

Why It Matters

In the past, people in the United States thought that the government had no right to try to manage the economy. The government was simply there to provide goods and services (such as national defense) that the economy could not produce itself. Today, many people believe that if something is wrong with the economy, the government should get to work on it. They expect the government to manage the economy. Specifically, if inflation occurs, the government should get rid of it; if the level of unemployment is too high, the government should reduce it; if economic growth is weak, the government should give the economy a boost.

A worker inspects sheets of one-dollar bills at the Bureau of Engraving and Printing. As you learned in Chapter 10, paper currency is just one component of the nation's money supply. In this chapter, you will learn about the important decisions the Fed must make regarding the expansion and contraction of the money supply.

The government uses monetary and fiscal policy to try to manage the economy at times. Do monetary and fiscal policy always work as hoped? Not always. This chapter will help you understand the technical details and effects of monetary and fiscal policy.

376

Teaching Suggestions from the Author

In this chapter, we present students with an introduction to fiscal policy and monetary policy. One key point we make is that the effectiveness of fiscal policy depends on the conditions that exist. For example, fiscal policy is effective at changing total spending in the economy if there is no crowding out. One of the best things that you can do before teaching this chapter is to get students to think in terms of conditions. In other words, X will occur if Y happens first, or Z will occur if A happens first.

Economics Around the Clock

The following events occurred one day in February.

9:43 A.M. George and Michelle are talking about the tax bill that the president outlined the night before on TV. George says, "I think it's wrong to cut taxes right now. We have a huge budget deficit in this country, and lowering tax rates will just make the deficit worse. The government needs to raise more money, not less." Michelle says, "Yeah, but I really need a tax cut now. I've got a lot of bills to pay."

• **Is George right? Will lowering the tax rates end up decreasing tax revenues?**

1:12 P.M. Natalie is in her economics class learning about fiscal and monetary policy. Her teacher says, "Sometimes when the government spends more money, people end up spending less. It's like being in a family. When you spend more money, your father or mother or sister ends up spending less." Natalie thinks to herself, "I don't think my teacher has ever met my family."

• **If the government spends more, do people spend less?**

3:03 P.M. Mark and Carla are talking about their economics project. Mark says, "I don't see why the government doesn't simply print a lot of money and hand it out to people. That way, everyone could be rich." Carla asks, "But wouldn't that cause inflation?" Mark says, "I guess, but if everybody had more money, then they could afford to pay higher prices."

• **What kind of monetary policy is Mark advocating, and what are its likely effects?**

10:56 P.M. Carl is watching the nightly news on TV. The economics reporter says: "Signs indicate that inflation is moving upward and, oddly enough, the unemployment rate is too. It could mean that the economy is in for a dose of stagflation." Carl thinks, "What in the world is *stagflation*?"

• **What is stagflation?**

377

Introducing the Chapter

To introduce this chapter, write the words *fiscal policy* and *monetary policy* on the board. Explain to students that these terms represent two types of government policy designed to meet economic goals. Ask students what types of goals they think the government might try to meet.

Answers will vary. They might include reducing inflation, reducing unemployment, and promoting absolute real economic growth. Tell students to skim the Key Terms on page 378. Ask them to predict what they will learn in this chapter.

Teaching with Visuals

Direct students' attention to the photo on this spread of a worker inspecting one-dollar bills. Ask students if they think the government can increase the money supply simply by printing more paper currency. Students should understand that paper bills are only one component of the money supply and that the total amount of paper currency in circulation doesn't equal the total money supply. Technically, the government can increase the money supply by printing more paper currency. However, if the government prints too much money, each piece of currency becomes worth less and inflation results.

Ask students to give you examples of if–then statements. Here are some examples: if it rains, then we can't have the picnic. If you don't study for a test, then you won't do well. If you don't drive carefully, then you might have an accident.

Brainstorm a list of statements with students and write them on the board. Introducing this type of if–then thinking in advance will make it easier for all students to understand the material in this chapter.

Teacher Support

Section Objectives

After completing the section, students will be able to

▶ explain what fiscal policy is;

▶ identify the type of fiscal policy used to reduce unemployment;

▶ identify the type of fiscal policy used to reduce inflation;

▶ define *crowding out;*

▶ explain Keynes's ideas on the best way to heal a sick economy; and

▶ explain how tax rates can affect the supply side of the economy.

Kickoff Activity

Ask students the following questions: Why would the government want to increase spending in the economy? What can the government do to increase spending in the economy?

Activating Prior Knowledge

Allow students to discuss their answers to the questions in the Kickoff Activity. Answers will vary. Students might mention increasing government spending and cutting taxes.

Teach

Teaching with Visuals

After students examine Exhibit 13-1, ask for volunteers to explain the difference between expansionary and contractionary fiscal policies.

 Visit econ.myemcp.com/videos for videos that will help students better understand the key concepts found in this section.

Fiscal Policy

Focus Questions

▶ What is fiscal policy?

▶ What type of fiscal policy does the government use to try to reduce unemployment?

▶ What type of fiscal policy does the government use to try to reduce inflation?

▶ What is crowding out?

▶ According to Keynes, what is the best way to heal a sick economy?

▶ How can tax rates affect the supply side of the economy?

Key Terms

fiscal policy
expansionary fiscal policy
contractionary fiscal policy
crowding out
after-tax income
Laffer curve

Two Types of Fiscal Policy

Fiscal policy deals with government spending and taxes. If the government increases spending, reduces taxes, or both, it is said to be implementing **expansionary fiscal policy**. The objective of this type of policy is to increase total spending in the economy to reduce the unemployment rate. For example, suppose the government is currently spending $1.8 trillion a year and it increases its spending to $1.9 trillion a year. This act is an example of expansionary fiscal policy.

If the government decreases spending, raises taxes, or both, it is said to be implementing **contractionary fiscal policy**. The objective is to reduce total spending in the economy to reduce inflation. For example, suppose the government is currently spending $1.8 trillion a year and it reduces its spending to $1.7 trillion a year. This act is an example of contractionary fiscal policy. (The two types of fiscal policy discussed here are summarized in Exhibit 13-1.)

fiscal policy
Changes the government makes in spending or taxation to achieve particular economic goals.

expansionary fiscal policy
An increase in government spending or a reduction in taxes.

contractionary fiscal policy
A decrease in government spending or an increase in taxes.

EXHIBIT 13-1	Two Types of Fiscal Policy	
Type of fiscal policy	**Change in government spending**	**Change in taxes**
Expansionary	↑	and/or ↓
Contractionary	↓	and/or ↑

Expansionary Fiscal Policy and the Problem of Unemployment

Suppose the unemployment rate in the economy is 8 percent and the government sets the goal of getting the unemployment rate down to 5 percent. Does the government have any economic tools to help it reduce the unemployment rate? Some economists say that the answer is yes. The government can use the tool of expansionary fiscal policy. Here is how these economists explain it:

Differentiating Instruction

Visual Learners

To ensure that students understand the concepts of both expansionary and contractionary fiscal policies, ask each student to create two political cartoons that clearly illustrate these concepts. For example, the student might create a political cartoon about unemployment and the solution of expansionary fiscal policy. The student might create another cartoon showing prices or interest rates skyrocketing with the government trying to use contractionary fiscal policy to contain the problem.

- A high unemployment rate is the result of people not spending enough money in the economy. In other words, if people spend more money, firms will sell more goods, and they will have to hire more people to produce the goods (in the process, lowering the unemployment rate).
- To reduce the unemployment rate, Congress should implement expansionary fiscal policy—that is, it should increase government spending, lower taxes, or both. If Congress chooses to increase government spending instead of lowering taxes, the government can choose to spend more on health care, education, national defense, and many other needed programs.
- An increase in government spending means more spending in the economy. For example, suppose that at current prices, the government is spending $1.8 trillion, business is spending $1.2 trillion (buying factories, machines, and materials), and consumers are spending $6.0 trillion (buying TVs, clothes, computers, and other goods). Total spending at current prices is $9.0 trillion. If the government decides to increase its spending by $200 billion (to $2.0 trillion), then total spending increases to $9.2 trillion.
- As a result of the increase in total spending, firms sell more goods.
- When firms start to sell more goods, they have to hire more workers to produce the additional goods. The unemployment rate goes down as a result of more people working.

▲ The government builds submarines to bolster the nation's defense. What other reason might the government have for building submarines?

Suppose a person is feeling sluggish. The reason he is feeling sluggish is because he isn't getting enough vitamins. So, the doctor boosts his vitamin intake and he feels better. Expansionary fiscal policy works the same way. The patient (the economy) is sluggish (it has too high an unemployment rate). The doctor (the government) says the sluggishness will go away if vitamins (increased spending) are added to the diet. As a result, the patient (the economy) gets better (the unemployment rate drops).

A Student Asks

QUESTION: *Let me see if I have this right. The reason the unemployment rate is high is because there isn't enough spending (buying) in the economy. So, the government boosts spending and the unemployment rate comes down.*

ANSWER: *Yes, that's essentially how things work. An analogy comes to mind.*

The Issue of Crowding Out

Some economists do not agree that things will turn out the way they were just presented. They say that when the government spends more, total spending in the economy does not necessarily increase. They bring up the issue of **crowding out**, which occurs when increases in government spending lead to reductions in private spending (spending made in the private sector by consumers and businesses).

Suppose that currently in the economy, $60 million is spent on an average day. We'll say that $45 million is spent by the private sector (households and businesses buying such things as TVs, houses, and factories), and $15 million is spent by the government (paying for such things as defense and education). Suppose now that government

crowding out
The situation in which increases in government spending lead to reductions in private spending.

Teaching with Visuals

Answers will vary. Students might say that the parents will take advantage of the improved public education by reducing spending on private education. If enough people respond this way, the reduction in private spending will offset the increase in public spending.

Cause and Effect

Ask students to research the current fiscal policy of the U.S. government. To do so, they should look at recent fiscal policy decisions or study economic positions expressed in party platforms. Ask students the following questions: How would the economy be affected if Congress changed legislation to spend more? To spend less and cut government programs? Which of these actions would be expansionary fiscal policy, and which would be contractionary fiscal policy?

Discussion Starter

Students may be intrigued by the concept of crowding out. Guide them in a discussion of how and why this can occur. Have students examine other segments of the economy (besides education) in which crowding out might occur—for example, health care and public safety.

Prediction Activity

Stop students before they read the section "Contractionary Fiscal Policy and the Problem of Inflation." Have them use what they know about expansionary fiscal policy to predict how contractionary fiscal policy can be used to fight inflation. If students need a hint, remind them that contractionary fiscal policy involves reducing spending or increasing taxes.

▲ Suppose that to boost the economy, the federal government decides to increase its spending on preschool education by $2 billion. How might this young family and others like it spoil the government's strategy? What do economists call this sort of activity?

decides to increase its spending on education, raising its average daily spending to $17 million. What is the consequence? Does total spending rise to $62 million ($17 million in public spending plus $45 million in private spending)?

Not necessarily, say some economists. Because the government spends more on education, people may decide to spend less on education. Specifically, because the government spends more on public schools and public school teachers, people may decide they can spend less on private schools and private school teachers. As a result, private spending will drop from $45 million to $43 million. Total spending therefore will remain at $60 million ($17 million in government spending plus $43 million in private spending).

In this example, when an increase of $2 million in government spending causes a $2 million decline in private spending, we have *complete crowding out*; each dollar increase in government spending is matched by a dollar decrease in private spending. With complete crowding out, an increase in government spending does not lead to an increase in total spending in the economy. Thus, it does not affect unemployment.

As another example, if the government spends an extra $2 million and consumers and businesses spend less—but not $2 million less—*incomplete crowding out* will result. When a decrease in private spending only partially offsets the increase in government spending, increased government spending does raise total spending in the economy.

EXAMPLE Suppose the unemployment rate is high at 9 percent, and the government wants to bring it down to 5 percent. The government therefore enacts expansionary fiscal policy by raising its daily spending by $10 million. As a result, the private sector lowers its spending by $10 million a day. Did total spending in the economy go up? No. The increase in government spending was completely offset by less private sector spending. Because every added dollar of government spending was offset by one less private sector dollar, we have *complete crowding out*. ◆

A Student Asks

QUESTION: *Can you explain crowding out using the "vitamin" analogy?*

ANSWER: *Yes, but with a modification. Let's say that we can get vitamins in two different ways. The first way is by having your body produce vitamins itself, using the food that you eat. The second way is the way we all know: getting vitamins through a pill. Now let's say the patient is sluggish because he lacks vitamins. The doctor gives him some vitamin pills. Because the doctor gives the patient some vitamin pills, the patient worries less about nutrition and eats fewer vitamin-rich foods. Crowding out happens in the same way. The government does X, but because the government is doing that now, when it wasn't before, the private sector no longer does X, or it doesn't do as much X as it used to do.*

Differentiating Instruction

Kinesthetic Learners

Reinforce the meanings of the terms in this section by tossing a tennis ball to a student. If the student drops the ball, he or she must define a term, such as *fiscal policy, expansionary fiscal policy, contractionary fiscal policy, crowding out, incomplete crowding out, consumption, after-tax income, tax* *revenues,* or *Laffer curve.* If the student catches the ball, he or she chooses a classmate who must define the term. You might also ask students to give examples of terms or phrases. (For example, *complete crowding out* occurs when the government spends an additional dollar and the private sector then reduces its expenditures by a dollar.)

Do Voting Rules Matter to Taxing and Spending?

A voting rule is a mechanism to decide whether something is approved or not. Consider two voting rules – simple majority and supermajority. Under a simple majority rule, 51 percent of the voters must decide whether something is approved or not; under a supermajority voting rule – such as a 2/3rds supermajority voting rule – 66 percent of the voters must decide whether something is approved or not.

Now let's ask whether the voting rule matters to whether government spending and taxes are raised or lowered? Consider both the simple majority and supermajority voting rules in the U.S. Senate, where there are 100 senators. Suppose a Senate bill proposes that government spending be raised by $200 billion. Will government spending be raised by $200 billion? To

a large degree, it will depend upon which voting rule—simple majority or supermajority— is used. If the simple majority voting rule is used government spending is more likely to be increased by $200 billion because it is easier to get 51 senators to agree on a spending increase than to get 66 senators to agree. In other words, government spending is more likely to be raised under a simple-majority voting rule than a supermajority voting rule.

Now consider a Senate bill that proposes to raise income tax rates across the board. Is the bill more likely to be passed with a simple-majority voting rule or a supermajority voting rule? The answer is again a simple-majority voting rule. So, if the objective is to increase the probability of tax increases being passed, a simple-majority voting rule is more effective than a supermajority voting rule. If, however, one wanted to decrease the probability of passing a tax increase, the best way to proceed is with a supermajority voting rule.

So, again, we return to our original question: Does the voting rule matters to government spending and taxes are raised or lowered. The answer is that it does.

THINK ABOUT IT Suppose Jones is a U.S. Senator who has to vote on a bill that proposes to lower taxes. Jones does not want taxes to be lowered. Would Jones prefer a simple majority or supermajority voting rule? Explain your answer.

Contractionary Fiscal Policy and the Problem of Inflation

Chapter 12 stated that inflation (increases in the price level) can occur when the aggregate demand in the economy grows faster than the aggregate supply in the economy. In other words, inflation is the result of *too much spending* in the economy compared to the quantity of goods and services available for purchase. Some economists describe inflation as "too much money chasing too few goods." Many of these economists argue that the way to get prices down in the

---

Direct students read the feature and voice their opinions on whether or not it would be better to have a simple majority or supermajority vote rule in Congress.

ANSWERS TO THINK ABOUT IT Jones would prefer a supermajority voting rule because with it there is less chance that taxes will be lowered.

Thinking Like an Economist

Tell students that if they asked an economist a question, they would probably get a conditional answer. For example, suppose they asked an economist if expansionary fiscal policy will bring about more spending in the economy. The economist might say that it will, given the condition that complete crowding out doesn't occur. In other words, if complete crowding out occurs, then expansionary fiscal policy won't increase spending in the economy, but if complete crowding out doesn't occur, then expansionary fiscal policy will increase spending in the economy. Hearing this conditional answer will likely make some people think that the economist simply can't give a direct answer, but this isn't the case at all. The economist is simply specifying the conditions under which expansionary fiscal policy does and does not work. Put students in groups and assign each group to find examples of economists using conditional answers. Allow groups to present their findings to the class.

Background Information: Conditional Answers

Economists provide conditional answers because conditions change—often, quickly and frequently. Economists speak without stating conditions only if they can be certain that nothing else will change. (Economists use the Latin phrase *ceteris paribus,* or "all else being equal," to describe this state.) As students study fiscal policy, they need to remember that the success of any fiscal policy is conditional. Expansionary and contractionary fiscal policies are used to help keep the economy flowing as well as can be expected. Even so, economists keep in mind that *ceteris paribus* doesn't always exist in the real U.S. economy.

Encourage students to draw pictures that will help them remember the meaning of the terms *contractionary* and *expansionary*.

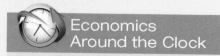

Economics Around the Clock

Direct students to the 1:12 p.m. scenario in Economics Around the Clock (page 377), and discuss their answers to the question provided there.

Students should note that when the government spends more, it's possible that people will spend less. If they do, economists say that government spending has "crowded out" some private spending.

Teaching with Visuals

The classical school of economics believed that the economy is self-regulating—in other words, it can "heal itself" if it "gets sick." Keynes disagreed. He believed that the government sometimes needs to step in and enact expansionary or contractionary policy to help the economy move in the right direction.

---

economy is to reduce spending, which they say can be done through contractionary fiscal policy. Here are the points they make:

- Inflation is the result of too much spending in the economy. So, if people spent less money, firms would initially sell fewer goods. The firms would end up with a surplus of goods in their warehouses. To get rid of their goods, they would have to lower prices.
- To get prices down, Congress should implement contractionary fiscal policy by decreasing government spending, raising taxes, or both. Let's suppose that government cuts its spending.
- The decrease in government spending means less overall spending in the economy. To illustrate, suppose that at current prices the government is spending $1.8 trillion, business is spending $1.2 trillion, and consumers are spending $6.0 trillion. Total spending at current prices is $9.0 trillion. Government decides to cut its spending by $200 billion. Now total spending decreases to $8.8 trillion.
- As a result of the decrease in total spending, firms initially sell fewer goods.
- When they sell fewer goods, firms end up with surplus goods on hand. The inventories in their warehouses and factories rise above a desired level, so to get rid of the unwanted inventory (the surplus goods), firms lower prices.

Fiscal Policy and John Maynard Keynes

The name John Maynard Keynes is closely connected to macroeconomics and fiscal policy.

Keynes was born on June 5, 1883, in Cambridge, England, and died on April 21, 1946, in Tilton (in Sussex) England. His father was John Neville Keynes, an eminent economist. John Maynard Keynes was educated at Eton College and then at King's College, Cambridge University, where he received a degree in mathematics in 1905. At Cambridge, he studied under Alfred Marshall, another well-known economist. In 1925, Keynes married the Russian ballerina Lydia Lopokova.

In 1936, Keynes published his major work, *The General Theory of Employment, Interest and Money*—usually called simply *The General Theory*. Many economists consider *The General Theory* to be one of the most influential economic treatises ever written.

Before *The General Theory* was published, Keynes presented its ideas in a series of university lectures between October 10, 1932, and December 2, 1935. Keynes's lectures were said to be both shocking and exciting. They were shocking because they pointed out what Keynes believed were the errors of the classical school of economics. They were exciting because they proposed something new.

The classical school view said the economy is self-regulating. A self-regulating economy is one that can "heal itself" if it "gets sick." For example, if an economy slips into a recession and unemployment begins to rise, there is no need to do anything. In time, the economy will cure itself from the recession and high unemployment. In other words, the economy reacts much like the body of someone who gets a common cold.

▲ British economist John Maynard Keynes (1883–1946). According to Keynes, is the economy self-regulating? Explain.

Differentiating Instruction

Visual Learners

Creating pictorial representations often helps visual learners focus on and retain information. Ask each student to create a cartoon that illustrates the concept of crowding out. Give students an opportunity to explain their cartoons to the class.

The body can cure itself of the cold, and nothing more than a little rest is needed to speed along the healing process.

Keynes disagreed with the classical school view. He said an economy can't always heal itself. Sometimes, an economy gets sick (contracts) and can't get well (expand) on its own. Its "immune system" isn't up to the job at hand. When the economy can't recover on its own, Keynes argued, government should step in and enact an expansionary fiscal policy.

But what exactly is the government supposed to do? Keynes's answer: stimulate spending in the economy. According to Keynes, an economy often experiences declining real GDP and rising unemployment because aggregate demand (AD) is not sufficient to bring about full employment. The government's job then is to increase its spending so that aggregate demand will rise, which will pull the economy out of its sickly state.

Keynes formulated his macroeconomic ideas and wrote his major work during the Great Depression, which started with the stock market crash of 1929. Throughout that period, real GDP fell and the unemployment rate rose dramatically. Keynes didn't think the economy of the Great Depression could heal itself. He saw it as sick and unable to get well without a dose of fiscal policy medicine administered by the government.

Keynes has never been without his critics. Not all economists believe that Keynes's diagnosis and recommended treatment are correct. Not all economists believe that economic problems often stem from too little aggregate demand or that the government must use expansionary fiscal policy to solve such problems. However, whether Keynes was right or wrong, there is little doubt that he has been a major influence on macroeconomic thought and policy in the United States and in many other countries around the world.

QUESTION: *So far in our discussion of fiscal policy, I've noticed that you say some economists think one way, but that other economists disagree with them. Is there much disagreement among economists?*

ANSWER: *Yes, economists frequently disagree—especially when it comes to macroeconomic issues such as what causes high unemployment and how fiscal policy works. Economists have different ideas about what will cure the economy's ills, in much the same way that doctors often disagree about a patient's illness and the best remedy for it. High school and college economics students have always yearned for their teachers to simply tell them how the economy works, in much the same way that a math teacher might teach them how to solve for X in the following equation:*
2X + 1 = 5. Things aren't quite as simple or as neat and tidy in economics.

Are economists simply not smart enough to figure out exactly how the economy works? It is probably not that. The economy, like the human body, is a complicated mechanism. We know a lot more about it today than we used to, but it still isn't easy to figure out exactly how it works.

Fiscal Policy and Taxes

The discussion so far has focused on either an increase or a decrease in government spending. Besides changing spending, the government can also change tax rates. Changes in taxes are different from changes in spending in that tax changes can affect two sides of the economy, not just one. Changes in taxes can affect the spending (demand) side of the economy and the producing (supply) side of the economy.

Problem Solving

Invite students to imagine that they are government officials who have some influence over fiscal policy. Tell students that inflation is high, and ask them how they would solve this problem and what conditions would have to be in place for the solution to work. Then tell students that the unemployment rate has skyrocketed. Ask them how they would solve this problem and why.

Cross-Curricular Activity

Invite a government teacher to your class to discuss fiscal policy. You might introduce the topic by quickly reviewing the aims of fiscal policy, along with the definitions of *contractionary fiscal policy* and *expansionary fiscal policy*. The government teacher can then discuss the mechanics of implementing fiscal policy, including the president's budget proposals, significant lobbies, congressional battles, and final adoption. You might ask the government teacher to stress how particular interest groups and party loyalties can influence fiscal policy.

Economics in the Real World

Economics *in the* Real World

ANSWERS TO THINK ABOUT IT Answers will vary, but students should recognize that economists mean that sometimes a good economic policy (one that will bring about certain desirable results in the long run) may not be popular with politicians or the public in the short run and that sometimes bad economic policy (one that will bring about undesirable results in the long run) may be popular with politicians and the public in the short run.

Economics *in the* Real World

What Did Keynes Overlook?

In 1977, two economists, James Buchanan and Richard Wagner, wrote a book called *Democracy in Deficit: The Political Legacy of Lord Keynes*, in which they argue that Keynes didn't fully account for the political setting in which Keynesian economics would be applied.

To illustrate, according to Keynes, when unemployment is high and the economy is slow, what's needed is a good strong dose of expansionary fiscal policy. In other words, increase government spending and/or cut taxes to stimulate aggregate demand in the economy. However, when inflation is high and the economy is a little too stimulated, the best thing to do is enact contractionary fiscal policy. In other words, cut government spending and/or raise taxes.

Now think about the effects of these two types of fiscal policy. The first, expansionary fiscal policy, requires the government to increase spending and cut taxes. Both higher spending and lower taxes will likely be politically popular measures. Politicians who promise to give voters more benefits and lower taxes are going to be very popular.

However, things don't play out that way when it comes to the second type of fiscal policy (contractionary), which, Keynes argued, needs to be implemented when inflation is too high and the economy is overstimulated. In this case, politicians will have to go before voters and say that they plan to cut government spending and raise taxes.

Applying this economic "medicine," Buchanan and Wagner argue in their book, is not politically popular. People will be angry that some of the money and services they are currently getting from the federal government are being cut *and* that they will have to pay higher taxes. This will certainly be some sour economic medicine to try and sell to the voters. So what will happen?

Buchanan and Wagner argue that what Keynes overlooked is that only half of Keynesian economics is going to be implemented in a country where people get elected to office. Which half? The half that supports raising government spending and cutting taxes—in other words, the expansionary fiscal policy part. That's the half that is politically popular. But the half that supports cutting government spending and raising taxes is politically unpopular, and so politicians will avoid running on that fiscal policy.

What is the consequence of politicians choosing the politically popular part of the Keynesian doctrine and rejecting the politically unpopular part? According to Buchanan and Wagner, it's big federal budget deficits. Think about it: If there is always upward pressure on government spending and downward pressure on taxes, then the government will likely end up running huge budget deficits. Or, as Buchanan and Wagner might put it (from the title of their book), we will end up with a "democracy in deficit."

THINK ABOUT IT Some economists have argued that good economics doesn't always make good politics and that bad economics sometimes makes good politics. What do you think they mean?

Cooperative Learning

Divide students into small groups, and assign each group to create a chart or other graphic illustrating the concept of crowding out. Also ask each group to prepare a brief presentation explaining its graphic. Encourage the groups to use multiple types of media, including audio and video. Post the results in the classroom or online, and allow time for each group to present its work.

How Taxes Can Affect the Spending (Demand) Side of the Economy

You may remember from Chapter 11 that economists designate four sectors in the economy: the household sector, the business sector, the government sector, and the foreign sector. For now, let's look at just the household sector (the spending of the household sector is called *consumption*) and assume that no crowding out occurs.

Members of the household sector get most of the money they spend on goods and services from their income. However, people do not get to spend all of the income they earn; part of it goes to pay taxes. The part left over is called **after-tax income**.

Let's say that the average household spends 90 percent of its after-tax income and saves the rest. (In other words, out of every $1 earned, it spends 90 cents and saves 10 cents.) Now suppose that the average household earns $60,000 a year and pays $15,000 in taxes. The household has an after-tax income of $45,000. If the household spends 90 percent of its after-tax income, then $40,500 ($45,000 $\times$ 0.90 = $40,500) is spent on goods and services. If the economy includes, say, 50 million households, the entire household sector spends the following on consumption: 50 million $\times$ $40,500 = $2.025 trillion.

What happens if the government lowers taxes? For example, suppose it lowers taxes such that the average household no longer pays $15,000 in taxes but rather pays $10,000 in taxes. After-tax income now rises from $45,000 to $50,000. If the average household continues to spend 90 percent of its income, it now spends $45,000 ($50,000 $\times$ 0.90 = $45,000) on goods and services. If we multiply this amount times 50 million households, we get $2.250 trillion. In other words, as a result of a decrease in taxes, consumption spending has risen from $2.025 trillion to $2.250 trillion. If no other sector's spending in the economy falls, then total spending in the economy rises as a result of a tax cut.

The increase in total spending means that firms sell more goods. When firms start to sell more goods, they hire more workers to produce the additional goods. The unemployment rate goes down as a result of more people working.

Would things work in the opposite direction if taxes were raised? Most economists think so. A rise in taxes would lower after-tax income, thus lowering consumption spending. A reduction in consumption spending would, in turn, lower total spending in the economy.

EXAMPLE Suppose the unemployment rate is high and the government wants to lower it. The government chooses to use expansionary fiscal policy; that is, it will raise government spending or lower taxes or do some combination of both. Let's say it decides to cut taxes. As a result of cutting taxes, individuals have more after-tax income. Suppose the average taxpayer ends up with an extra $100 a month in after-tax income. What does she do with this extra $100 after-tax income? She might save part of it, but she will probably spend some of it too. This extra spending means that businesses will end up selling more goods and services. As a result, they will have to hire more workers to produce the additional goods and services. In the end, the unemployment rate drops. ♦

A Student Asks

QUESTION: *When the government cuts taxes, does it cut the taxes for all income groups the same? For example, suppose one person earns $1 million a year and another person earns $50,000 a year. Do both persons have their taxes cut by the same percentage?*

ANSWER: *No, not necessarily. It could be that everyone's taxes will go down by, say, 5 percent, or it could be that some people's taxes will go down by 4 percent, others by 5 percent, and so on. Depending on how Congress writes the tax law, everyone could receive the same tax cut, or many different groups of people could all receive different amounts of cuts.*

after-tax income
The part of income that's left over after taxes are paid.

Teaching with Visuals

Tax revenues might fall as a result of raising the tax rate, because people might be less motivated to work and thus generate lower income on which to be taxed.

 Application Activity

After reading and discussing Section 1, you may want to assign the Section Activity in the *Applying the Principles Workbook,* pages 139–142.

Assess

Quick Quiz

The following true-or-false quiz will help you assess student understanding of the material covered in this section.

1. Increasing government spending and tax rates is an example of expansionary fiscal policy. (False)
2. Expansionary fiscal policy brings up the issue of crowding out. (True)
3. If the inflation rate is high, government should implement contractionary fiscal policy. (True)
4. Incomplete crowding out will make expansionary fiscal policy ineffective. (False)
5. Cutting taxes always leads to collecting lower tax revenues. (False)

 Assessment Book

You will find a quiz for this section in the *Assessment Book,* page 130.

How Taxes Can Affect the Producing (Supply) Side of the Economy

How much would anyone work if income taxes were 100 percent? In other words, if out of every $1 a person earned, he or she had to pay the full $1 in taxes, how many hours a week would the person work? Of course, no one would work if he or she had to pay 100 percent of earnings in taxes. It stands to reason, then, that people would work more as the income tax rate came down from 100 percent. For example, people might work more at a 40 percent tax rate than at a 70 percent tax rate.

> *"Congress can raise taxes because it can persuade a sizable fraction of the populace that somebody else will pay."*
> —Milton Friedman, twentieth-century economist

We can also look at this concept in terms of after-tax income. The higher your after-tax income, the more you are willing to work; the lower your after-tax income, the less you are willing to work. In other words, we would expect a much more industrious, hard-working, long-working labor force when the average income tax rate is, say, 20 percent than when it is 70 percent. It follows, then, that the supply of goods and services in the economy will be greater (the aggregate supply curve shifts rightward) when taxes are lower than when they are higher.

Tax Rates and Tax Revenues

Many people think that a tax rate cut results in lower tax revenues for the government, but that isn't necessarily true. Tax cuts can lead to lower or higher tax revenues.

If Smith is a representative taxpayer who earns $2,000 each month and pays an average tax rate of 40 percent, then he pays $800 a month in taxes. His after-tax income is $1,200:

▶ Most people assume that the higher the tax rates, the more tax revenues the government collects. Can you explain why this is not necessarily the case?

Tax revenue = Average tax rate × Income

Now suppose the average tax rate is cut to 35 percent. Does it follow that tax revenues will decline? Not necessarily. As was stated earlier, tax cuts often stimulate more work, and more work leads to more income. Suppose that, as a result of the tax cut, Smith works more and earns $2,500 a month—an increase in income of $500 a month. Now, he pays 35 percent of $2,500 in taxes, or $875 a month, and he is left with an after-tax income of $1,625.

Thus, at a tax rate of 40 percent, Smith paid $800 in taxes, but at a tax rate of 35 percent, he pays $875 in taxes. So, in this example, if Smith is the representative taxpayer, a *tax rate cut* will actually *increase tax revenues.* The government will take in more tax money with a tax cut, not less money, because the rise in income was greater than the tax cut. Income rose from $2,000 to $2,500 a month, which is a 25 percent increase. The tax rate cut was from 40 to 35 percent, which is a 12.5 percent cut. As long as income rises by more than taxes are cut, tax revenues will rise.

Consider what could have happened, though. Suppose Smith's income had risen from $2,000 to $2,100 (a 5 percent rise in income) instead of to $2,500. At a tax rate of 35 percent and an income of $2,100, Smith pays $735 in taxes. In other words, he pays less in taxes at a lower tax rate. If he is the representative taxpayer, it follows that lower tax rates generate lower tax revenues, because the rise in income (5 percent) is less than the tax rate cut (12.5 percent).

A group of economists called *supply-side economists* believe that cuts in high tax rates can generate higher tax revenues, whereas cuts in low tax rates can generate lower tax revenues. To illustrate, Exhibit 13-2(a) starts at a relatively high tax rate of 90 percent (point A). A tax rate cut to 80 percent raises tax revenues from $700 billion to $1,000 billion. Lower tax rates go together with higher tax revenues.

Alternatively, Exhibit 13-2(b) starts at a relatively low tax rate of 20 percent (point A). A tax rate cut to 10 percent lowers tax revenues from $1,000 billion to $700 billion. This time, lower tax rates are accompanied by lower tax revenues.

Background Information: Taxes in Different States

Individuals in some states pay a higher percentage of their income in state and local taxes than do individuals in other states. In 2011, here are the percentages for select states: California, 11.4 percent; Texas, 7.5 percent; West Virginia, 9.7 percent; Florida, 9.2 percent. To find the percentages for all 50 states, go to http://econ.emcp.net /statetaxes.

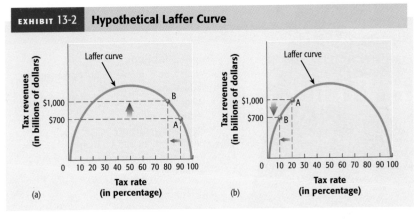

EXHIBIT 13-2 **Hypothetical Laffer Curve**

▲ The Laffer curve represents the relationship that some economists believe exists between tax rates and tax revenues. Starting at relatively high tax rates, a *tax rate cut* will generate *higher tax revenues*. For example, as shown in (a), the tax rate is cut from 90 percent to 80 percent and tax revenues rise. Starting at relatively low tax rates, a *tax rate cut* will generate *lower tax revenues*. For example, as shown in (b), the tax rate is cut from 20 percent to 10 percent and tax revenues fall. The Laffer curve is named after economist Arthur Laffer.

Laffer curve
The curve, named after economist Arthur Laffer, that shows the relationship between tax rates and tax revenues. According to the Laffer curve, as tax rates rise from zero, tax revenues rise, reach a maximum at some point, and then fall with further increases in tax rates.

The curve in Exhibit 13-2 is called the **Laffer curve**, after economist Arthur Laffer. The Laffer curve simply illustrates the relationship that some economists believe exists between tax rates and tax revenues.

In Exhibit 13-2, notice that tax revenue is maximized at a tax rate of 50 percent.

No one knows whether it is maximized at 50 percent; specific tax rates were added to the Laffer curve drawn here merely for explanatory purposes. As far as anyone knows, tax revenue may be maximized at some tax rate higher or lower than 50 percent.

SECTION 1 ASSESSMENT

Defining Terms

1. Define:
   a. fiscal policy
   b. expansionary fiscal policy
   c. contractionary fiscal policy
   d. crowding out
   e. after-tax income
   f. Laffer curve

Reviewing Facts and Concepts

2. What is contractionary fiscal policy, and why is it likely to be used?

3. Give a numerical example of complete crowding out.

4. "Even though changes in government spending mainly affect the demand side of the economy, a change in taxes can affect both the demand side and the supply side." Do you agree or disagree? Explain.

5. What did Keynes propose that the government should do if the economy is in a recession?

Critical Thinking

6. Is expansionary fiscal policy always effective at increasing total spending in the economy and decreasing unemployment? Explain your answer.

7. What does crowding out have to do with the ability of expansionary fiscal policy to increase spending?

Applying Economic Concepts

8. Someone says, "If the federal government cuts income tax rates, tax revenues will rise." Might this person be wrong? Explain your answer.

SECTION 1 ASSESSMENT ANSWERS

Defining Terms

1. a. **fiscal policy:** changes the government makes in spending or taxation to achieve particular economic goals; b. **expansionary fiscal policy:** an increase in government spending or a reduction in taxes; c. **contractionary fiscal policy:** a decrease in government spending or an increase in taxes; d. **crowding out:** occurs when increases in government spending lead to reductions in private spending; e. **after-tax income:** income that's left over after taxes are paid; f. **Laffer curve:** the curve that shows the relationship between tax rates and tax revenues.

Reviewing Facts and Concepts

2. It's a decrease in government spending and/or an increase in taxes. It's used to reduce total spending and thereby reduce inflation.

3. The government spends $10 billion more, and the private sector spends $10 billion less.

4. Students should agree. Government spending is one of the four components of total spending in the economy. If there is incomplete or no crowding out, an increase in government spending will raise total spending. A change in total spending affects the demand side of the economy. A change in taxes can affect the demand side by affecting after-tax income. It affects the supply side by affecting people's incentive to work and produce goods.

5. Stimulate spending through enacting expansionary fiscal policy.

Critical Thinking

6. No. Its effectiveness depends on whether there is complete crowding out. If for every $1 increase in government spending, private spending decreases by $1, then a rise in government spending won't decrease unemployment.

7. If there is no crowding out, more spending by government won't reduce spending by the private sector, so overall spending will rise. But if there is crowding out, more spending by government will reduce spending by the private sector, so overall spending may not rise.

Applying Economic Concepts

8. The person might be wrong. If the tax rate falls on the upward-sloping portion of the Laffer curve, then cutting income tax rates will lower tax revenues.

Reteaching Activity

Use the Section Assessment to gauge which students may need reteaching on this section. Give those students balloons, and ask them to inflate the balloons. This is expansionary. Instruct students to let the air out of the balloons, and explain that this is contractionary. Ask students to relate this activity to fiscal policy.

Guided Reading

For further reteaching of the key concepts in this section, assign the Outlining Activity and the Just the Facts Handout from the *Guided Reading and Study Guide*, pages 225–230.

Focus and Motivate

Section Objectives

After completing the section, students will be able to

▶ identify the type of monetary policy used to reduce unemployment;

▶ identify the type of monetary policy used to reduce inflation;

▶ explain how monetary policy reduces unemployment and inflation; and

▶ explain the purpose of the exchange equation.

Kickoff Activity

State the following at the beginning of class: In an earlier chapter, you learned that the Federal Reserve can increase or decrease the money supply. How do you think changing the money supply affects the economy?

Activating Prior Knowledge

Allow students to share their responses to the Kickoff Activity. Some of their responses may reflect the following: increasing the money supply will increase the amount of spending in the economy; decreasing the money supply will decrease the amount of spending in the economy.

Teach

Reinforcement Activity

American economist Milton Friedman is closely associated with the topic of monetary policy. Assign students to research the life and work of Milton Friedman and then present their findings to the class or turn in their work.

Monetary Policy

SECTION 2

Focus Questions

▶ What type of monetary policy is used to reduce unemployment?

▶ What type of monetary policy is used to reduce inflation?

▶ How does monetary policy reduce unemployment and inflation?

▶ What is the purpose of the exchange equation?

Key Terms

monetary policy
expansionary monetary policy
contractionary monetary policy

Two Types of Monetary Policy

Monetary policy deals with changes in the money supply. If the Fed increases the money supply, it is implementing **expansionary monetary policy**. Its objective is to increase total spending in the economy to reduce the unemployment rate. If the Fed decreases the money supply, it does so to reduce total spending and thereby reduce inflation. In this case, it is implementing **contractionary monetary policy**.

Expansionary Monetary Policy and the Problem of Unemployment

Many economists believe that expansionary monetary policy works to lower the unemployment rate in the following manner:

- The Fed increases the money supply.
- A greater money supply is usually associated with greater total spending in the economy. (There is more money to spend.)

monetary policy
Changes the Fed makes in the money supply.

expansionary monetary policy
An increase in the money supply.

contractionary monetary policy
A decrease in the money supply.

- As a result of increased spending in the economy, firms begin to sell more products.
- As firms sell more products, they hire more workers, thus lowering the unemployment rate.

The issue of crowding out doesn't arise in monetary policy. If the Fed increases the money supply, no one needs to spend less; there is simply more money to spend. Because crowding out is not an issue with expansionary monetary policy, many economists argue that an increase in the money supply will increase total spending in the economy, which will indirectly lower the unemployment rate.

EXAMPLE The Fed meets and decides that the nation's unemployment rate is too high. To lower the unemployment rate, the Fed decides to enact expansionary monetary policy—in other words, it decides to increase the money supply. In an earlier chapter, you learned that the Fed can increase the money supply by (1) lowering the reserve requirement, (2) undertaking

Differentiating Instruction

English Language Learners

Some terms and phrases in this chapter may be difficult for students to understand. Encourage students to rephrase, in their own words, these difficult words and phrases. For example, they might say that *expansionary fiscal policy* is "a plan for expanding the amount of money that people spend in the economy." Then review the concepts behind these terms and phrases. On the board, draw the three-way connections among the original terms, the students' phrases, and the concepts the terms and phrases represent.

Is Monetary Policy Sometimes Ineffective?

One way to stimulate spending in the economy is for the Fed to increase the money supply. As we learned in an earlier chapter, one way to increase the money supply is to have the Fed conduct an open market purchase—that is, to buy government securities from banks. Now let's go through this operation one more time and see where things might get stuck. The Fed buys government securities from banks, the banks hand over the government securities to the Fed, and the banks get more reserves. (Remember that a bank's total reserves equal deposits in the reserve account at the Fed plus vault cash.)

What do the banks do with any excess reserves? We would expect banks to create new loans or new checking account deposits with these reserves. It is this creation of new loans or new checking account deposits that ends up raising the money supply, since we know that the M1 money supply is equal to currency, checking accounts, and traveler's checks.

But a nagging question pops up: Is it possible that the banks will *not* take their excess reserves and create more loans and checking accounts? Could the banks simply hold the excess reserves?

The answer is yes. There are three main reasons that banks might hold on to their excess reserves. The first reason has to do with the interest rate banks can receive from the Fed by holding on to their reserves. It wasn't always the case, but today, the Fed actually pays banks interest on their reserves. So, banks have to compare the interest rate they would get on a new loan they create using the reserves with the interest rate they receive from the Fed holding on to the reserves. If banks can earn 4 percent interest by creating a loan and only 0.5 percent interest by holding on to reserves, they will have a monetary incentive to create a loan. Of course, if they percentages were reversed, the banks would hold the reserves.

The second reason banks may hold the reserves instead of create new loans with them is that they don't believe the economic environment is good enough to make it likely the loans will be repaid. It doesn't make sense to give a loan to someone who probably won't repay it.

The third reason has to do with how close a bank is to insolvency. At the end of 2008 and well into 2009, many banks were adding to their reserves, but they weren't turning them into loans largely because they were in poor financial shape. At the time, many banks were either insolvent (their liabilities were greater than their assets) or close to being insolvent. When banks are close to being insolvent, they are particularly wary of making loans, especially in an uncertain environment.

What does all this mean? It means that it's possible for expansionary monetary policy to sometimes be ineffective at raising aggregate demand. In short, the Fed may want to increase the money supply to raise aggregate demand in the economy, and to do this, it will undertake an open market purchase that ends up increasing banks' reserves. But there is no guarantee that the banks will use those reserves to create new loans and new checking accounts. In other words, there is no guarantee that the banks will transform those reserves into an increased money supply.

THINK ABOUT IT If the Fed wanted banks to lend their reserves instead of holding on to them, it could charge a negative interest rate on excess reserves. Suppose that for every $1 in reserves a bank holds beyond its required reserves, the bank has to pay the Fed an interest rate of 2 percent. Would this policy prompt banks to turn excess reserves into loans and new checking accounts? Why or why not?

ANSWERS TO THINK ABOUT IT Yes, it would. If the Fed charged banks a negative interest rate on bank reserves (beyond the dollar amount they are required to hold), it would penalize banks for holding excess reserves. Thus, banks would be encouraged to create new loans and checking accounts with their excess reserves.

 Visit econ.myemcp.com/videos for videos that will help students better understand the key concepts found in this section.

an open market purchase, (3) lowering the discount rate, or (4) reducing the federal funds rate target. In time, the money supply rises. People have more money to spend, and so they spend it. As a result, firms sell more goods and services. To produce the additional goods and services, the firms have to hire more people. In the end, the unemployment rate drops. ♦

A Student Asks

QUESTION: *Do the president or members of Congress have anything to do with monetary policy?*

ANSWER: *No, strictly speaking, monetary policy is under the jurisdiction of the Fed (which we discussed in Chapter 10). The president and the members of Congress deal with fiscal policy, and the Fed deals with monetary policy.*

Contractionary Monetary Policy and the Problem of Inflation

Many economists believe contractionary monetary policy works to reduce inflation in the following manner:

- The Fed decreases the money supply, perhaps by conducting an open market sale. (Open market sales are discussed in Chapter 10.)
- A smaller money supply is usually associated with lower total spending in the economy. (There is less money to spend.)
- As a result of the decrease in spending in the economy, firms begin to sell less.
- As firms sell fewer products, their inventories in the warehouses rise. To get rid of surplus goods, firms reduce prices (or they at least stop raising prices).

Monetary Policy and the Exchange Equation

The exchange equation, introduced in Chapter 12, states that the money supply

(M) times velocity (V) is equal to the price level (P) times the quantity of goods and services produced (Q):

$$M \times V = P \times Q$$

Some economists say that the objective of monetary policy, pure and simple, is to maintain a stable price level—in other words, to keep P constant in the exchange equation. If this objective is met, then neither inflation (P rising) nor deflation (P falling) occurs.

Suppose that maintaining a stable price level is the objective. How should the Fed go about meeting it? To answer this question, we must realize that if $M \times V = P \times Q$, then

$$\%\Delta M + \%\Delta V = \%\Delta P + \%\Delta Q$$

where Δ stands for "change in." In other words, the percentage change in the money supply plus the percentage change in velocity equals the percentage change in the price level plus the percentage change in the quantity of goods and services. For example, if the money supply grows by, say, 3 percent, and velocity rises by 1 percent, then it means a 4 percent change on the left-hand side of the exchange equation. Ask yourself how much the right-hand side must rise now (because the right-hand side will always equal the left-hand side). The answer is 4 percent.

The exchange equation can be rearranged in a way that shows how the percentage change in the money supply is calculated. Subtracting $\%\Delta V$ from both sides gives us this equation:

$$\%\Delta M = \%\Delta P + \%\Delta Q - \%\Delta V$$

With this equation in mind, suppose that the average annual changes in velocity and quantity of goods and services are as follows:

1. $\%\Delta V = 1\%$
2. $\%\Delta Q = 3\%$

Now let's assume that the objective is to hold the price level stable:

3. Objective: $\%\Delta P = 0\%$

Background Information: John Maynard Keynes

John Maynard Keynes (1883–1946) is considered one of the greatest economists of all time. Before Keynes, most economists thought it was impossible for insufficient spending within an economy to cause high unemployment. They believed that if people were spending too little, firms would simply lower prices and people would start buying more goods.

Keynes argued that even if people were not spending much money, firms such as car manufacturers might not lower prices because doing so would necessitate reducing wages. If wages couldn't be cut, the car manufacturer might not lower prices.

Why wouldn't wage rates decrease? You would think that a representative of the car manufacturer

What Is The Wizard of Oz Really About?

For most people, *The Wizard of Oz* is the story of a young girl, Dorothy, who travels a yellow brick road to Emerald City, where she encounters a wizard (who really isn't a wizard). But *The Wizard of Oz* is really a story about monetary policy in the United States around 1893.

At that time, the country had fallen into an economic depression. The stock market had crashed, banks had failed, and many workers had been laid off. Some people blamed the bad times on the gold standard: a monetary arrangement in which gold backed paper money. Based on this standard, a major way to get more paper money was to get more gold.

Many Americans believed that the bad economic times would disappear if people had more money to spend. But people didn't have any more money to spend because the government had already printed up all the paper money it could, given its gold supply.

What could the government do? Some suggested that it should use both gold and silver to back paper money, not only gold. With gold and silver backing the paper money supply, more money could be printed, turning the bad economic times into good economic times.

One of the champions of the so-called silver movement was William Jennings Bryan, who was the Democratic candidate for U.S. president in 1896. One of Bryan's big supporters was L. Frank Baum, the author of *The Wonderful Wizard of Oz*, which was the book that was the basis for the 1939 movie *The Wizard of Oz*.

In the book and movie, Dorothy represents William Jennings Bryan. Both Dorothy and Bryan were young (Bryan was 36 years old when he ran for the presidency). The cyclone in the book and movie transports Dorothy to Oz, in much the same way that the delegates at the Democratic convention lifted Bryan into the world of presidential politics. (Oz is the abbreviation for *ounces*, as in an ounce of gold or an ounce of silver, the common measurement for these two metals.)

As Dorothy begins her journey to the Emerald City (which represents Washington, D.C.) with her dog Toto (who represents the Democratic Party) to meet the Wizard of Oz, she travels down a yellow brick road. The yellow brick road represents the gold standard. On her way, she meets a scarecrow (who represents the farmers of the day), a tin man (who represents

the manufacturing workers of the day), and a cowardly lion (who represents the Populist Party of the day). The Populist Party was often represented in cartoons of the day as a lion. It was said to be cowardly because it didn't have the courage to wage an independent campaign for the presidency in 1896.

The message was clear, according to Baum: Jennings, along with the farmers, manufacturers, the Populist Party, and the Democratic Party, would travel along the road of the gold standard to Washington, D.C., and make things right.

Once Dorothy reaches the Emerald City, however, she and the others are denied their wishes, just as Bryan was denied the presidency. (He lost the election.)

Even so, the story isn't over. Dorothy must battle the Wicked Witch of the West, who wears a golden cap (the gold standard). When the witch sees Dorothy's silver shoes (they were ruby shoes in the movie but silver shoes in the book), she desperately wants them for their magical quality. However, Dorothy kills the Wicked Witch of the West and then clicks her silver slippers together. The silver slippers take her back home, where all is right with the world.

THINK ABOUT IT Analyze the decline in value of the U.S. dollar in the late 1800s and how abandoning the gold standard was supposed to help the economy. Do you think Baum had any knowledge of the exchange equation? Explain your answers.

Ask students whether they think the interpretation of *The Wonderful Wizard of Oz* that's provided in the feature is plausible. Clarify any parts of the interpretation that students find confusing.

ANSWERS TO THINK ABOUT IT Answers will vary. Students might say that Baum seemed to be aware of the role that the money supply part of the equation plays in the economy, even if he wasn't aware of the exact exchange equation.

Discussion Starter

Show clips from the movie *The Wizard of Oz* to illustrate the symbolism in Baum's book. After students have watched the clips, discuss the gold standard once again with the class.

could go to the workers and say, "I need to lower car prices so that people will buy more cars. That way, we can avoid layoffs." Keynes said that workers would initially resist wage cuts, thinking that the car manufacturer was trying to pay them less to earn higher profits.

If wages aren't coming down quickly and sellers aren't reducing prices, people might be laid off

from their jobs because consumers aren't spending enough for full employment to exist. Keynes argued that at this point, total spending in the economy had to be increased. Government had to increase its spending or lower taxes. However, critics argue that Keynes's proposal didn't take into account crowding out: if government spends more, consumers and businesses will spend less.

Reinforcement Activity

If students have trouble with the section "Monetary Policy and the Exchange Equation" (pages 390–392), have them review the section in Chapter 12 on the simple quantity theory of money (pages 349–351). Create several problems using various values for the percentage changes in money supply, velocity, price level, and quantity of goods and services produced. Call on students to work through the problems on the board.

Teaching with Visuals

If the Fed decreases the money supply, prices will likely drop to help firms sell their rising inventories. You will pay less for the goods you buy. If reform limits the Fed's power over the money supply, the Fed may not be able to respond as easily when prices rise. In this case, you will likely pay more for the goods you buy.

Given 1 through 3, how much should the Fed increase the money supply so that the price level does not change? The answer is 2 percent:

$$\%\Delta M = \%\Delta P + \%\Delta Q - \%\Delta V$$
$$\downarrow \qquad \downarrow \qquad \downarrow \qquad \downarrow$$
$$2\% = 0\% + 3\% - 1\%$$

Some economists propose that monetary policy should be implemented this way—that is, put on automatic pilot. The Fed should simply compute the average annual change in velocity and in the quantity of goods and services, set the percentage change in prices equal to 0 percent, and calculate the money supply change accordingly. The Fed should not fiddle with the money supply from month to month or year to year. It should not increase it sometimes and decrease it other times.

Will such a policy always yield stable prices? Probably not, because in some years, V and Q will change by more or less than the average annual rate. For example, if the average annual change in velocity is 1 percent, some years it might change by,

"In our time, the curse is monetary illiteracy, just as inability to read plain print was the curse of earlier centuries."
—**Ezra Pound, twentieth-century poet**

▼ Here is the room at the Federal Reserve in Washington, D.C., in which major monetary policy decisions are made. **How might decisions made by the Fed affect the price you pay for the goods you buy?**

say, 2 percent or by 0.5 percent. Economists who support this type of monetary policy, however, say that the changes in V and Q will be close enough to their average annual changes that we will come close to keeping prices stable if we simply put money supply changes (monetary policy) on automatic pilot.

A Student Asks

QUESTION: *It seems to me that you are saying that the president, the members of Congress, and the Fed can use economic policy (fiscal or monetary) to get rid of almost any economic sickness—high unemployment or high inflation. It's as if the government always has the right economic medicine to cure the economy of what ails it. But if it does, then why does the economy stay sick sometimes?*

ANSWER: *Well, think about these factors: First, not all economists agree that the government always has the right medicine. For example, go back to our discussion of fiscal policy. Some economists think the medicine of "expansionary fiscal policy" won't cure*

Internet Research

Tell students to use the Internet to learn about different economic theories of monetary policies. Students should search for sites that discuss Keynes, Friedman, and other prominent economists. Have students write papers comparing and contrasting at least two of these theories. They should be sure to discuss the differing views on the relationship of fiscal policy to inflation and unemployment.

the economy of high unemployment because of crowding out.

Second, sometimes economic policies are enacted too early or too late. Just like a medicine that won't cure a patient whose disease has gone too far, policies are sometimes put in place too late.

Third, sometimes economic policies aren't as precise as we need them to be. For example, suppose the unemployment rate is high and the Fed wants to lower it. We know that the Fed will enact expansionary monetary policy and raise the money supply. But suppose it raises the money supply too much. It could raise the money supply by more than is necessary and end up solving the high unemployment problem but causing a new problem—high inflation. This would be similar to giving a patient too much of a medicine and in the process of curing one health problem causing another. Think of it this way: the right amount of an antibiotic can make you well, but too much of an antibiotic can make you sick. Even the best doctors aren't always sure which antibiotic or how much of it is just the right amount for a particular patient.

A Gold Standard as Monetary Policy and the Value of the Dollar

The type of monetary policy we have discussed so far is implemented by the Fed. Increases and decreases in the money supply are mostly caused by the Fed. Moreover, the Fed has the ability to increase or decrease the money supply by as much or as little as it believes is appropriate to bring about the desired economic consequences (such as low inflation and low unemployment).

Although some economists argue that the money supply should be increased only by a low rate each year (as if on autopilot), others advocate a gold standard. These advocates often argue that during the years the United States was on a gold standard (1834–1933), the price level in the country was fairly stable and there was very little inflation. According to economist Michael Bordo:

> The great virtue of the gold standard was that it assured long-term price stability. Compare the aforementioned average annual inflation rate of 0.1 percent between 1880 and 1914 with the average of 4.1 percent between 1946 and 2003.[1]

How does a gold standard work? Effectively, it ties the (paper) money supply to the supply of gold that a government holds. And since the supply of gold (in the world) does not usually increase significantly from year to year, it is usually impossible for the money supply to increase significantly. There are some exceptions, though.

For example, the gold strike that occurred in California in 1848 caused a sharp increase in the supply of gold and the money supply, producing sharply rising prices, especially in the areas around where the gold was being mined. To illustrate, at the time, a loaf of bread sold for 4 cents in New York (which is the equivalent of about $1 today), but near the gold mines, it sold for 75 cents a loaf (the equivalent of about $16 today). In San Francisco, not far from the gold mines, land prices soared dramatically. In a period of 18 months, real estate that once cost $16 before gold was discovered suddenly cost $45,000.

To get some idea of how a gold standard works, suppose the monetary authority in a country (such as the Fed in the United States) holds 100 ounces of gold and states that for every ounce of gold it holds, it can issue $1,000 (paper money). The money supply will be $100,000. Now suppose the gold stock of the monetary authority rises to 103 ounces. Again, we remind ourselves that since the supply of gold usually rises by only a small percentage each year, the supply of paper money will also rise by only a small percentage each year.

---

[1] Michael D. Bordo, *The Gold Standard*, The Concise Encyclopedia of Economics.

Application Activity

After reading and discussing Section 2, you may want to assign the Section Activity in the *Applying the Principles Workbook*, pages 143–144.

Cooperative Learning

Divide the class into two groups. Have one group gather information that supports the idea that monetary policy should be put on "automatic pilot," as described in the text. Ask the other group to research counterarguments to this idea. Have both sides present their findings to the class. Then lead a class discussion about whether the Fed should continue its practice of adjusting the money supply from time to time.

Quick Quiz

The following true-or-false quiz will help you assess student understanding of the material covered in this section.

1. Expansionary monetary policy does nothing to reduce unemployment. (False)
2. Contractionary monetary policy does nothing to reduce inflation. (False)
3. Some economists believe that monetary policy should be placed on "automatic pilot." (True)
4. As a result of contractionary monetary policy, firms sell fewer goods. (True)
5. Decreasing the money supply is an application of expansionary monetary policy. (False)

Economic Facts *and* Fallacies

Money Supply and Velocity

Some people think that if the money supply is, say, $1,000, then the level of spending in the economy can't exceed $1,000. But that isn't necessarily true.

Remember, the total amount of spending is equal to the money supply times velocity. If velocity is 2 and the money supply is $1,000, there will be $2,000 worth of spending. If velocity is 3 and the money supply is $1,000, then there will be $3,000 worth of spending.

In fact, total spending in the economy is always greater than the money supply, as long as velocity is greater than 1.

Think of things in terms of the exchange equation ($M \times V = P \times Q$). If the money supply rises by only a small percentage (say, 1 percent) and the quantity of output rises by the same small percentage (1 percent), then if velocity is unchanged, the price level will remain unchanged.

Compare this gold-standard scenario with a pure paper money system—that is, one in which the supply of paper money is not held in check by the amount of gold. In this type of system, the monetary authority can raise the money supply as much as it wants.

There is another way to think of and discuss a gold standard (one we discussed in Chapter 10, but is worth repeating in the frame of monetary policy). Instead of thinking about and discussing the gold standard in terms of the supply of gold, we can think about and discuss it in terms of an official price of gold. Suppose the monetary authority states that it is willing to buy and sell gold for a set price of $1,000 an ounce and that this will be the only monetary policy it implements. This $1,000 price of gold is the *official price of gold*.

Now suppose that the *market price of gold*, which is the price of gold determined in the gold market, rises above $1,000 an ounce of gold—say, to $1,100 an ounce. What will members of the public do? They will go to the monetary authority and buy gold at the official price of $1,000 an ounce.

Then they will turn around and sell that ounce of gold in the gold market for $1,100. But, of course, as people buy gold from the monetary authority and sell it in the gold market, the supply of gold in the gold market will rise and we can expect the market price of gold to fall. The market price of gold will keep falling until no one has any incentive to go to the monetary authority and buy gold. In fact, the market price of gold will keep falling until it is $1,000, which is equal to the official price of gold.

As the price of gold falls, what will happen to the general price level (as, say, measured by the consumer price index)? It should fall too, and here is why: when the public buys gold from the monetary authority, it pays for that gold with money. That money leaves the economy. (Think of the public turning over 10 $100 bills for every ounce of gold it buys from the monetary authority.) Now, the monetary authority doesn't spend that money; it simply removes it from circulation. Doing so leads to a reduction in the money supply in the economy, and according to the exchange equation, what then happens to the price level? If nothing else changes, the price level will decline. That is, the price of gold and the general price level move down together.

Now let's reverse things. Suppose the market price of gold falls to $900. What will people do now? They will go to the monetary authority and sell their gold for $1,000. (They buy gold in the market at $900 an ounce before going to the monetary authority and selling it for $1,000.) But selling gold to the monetary authority takes gold out of the market (the supply of gold in the market declines), and thus the market price of gold will start to rise. When will it stop rising? When there is no longer any monetary incentive to sell gold to the monetary authority instead of to others— that is, when the market price of gold rises to the official price of gold at $1,000.

As the market price of gold rises from $900 to $1,000, what happens to the general price level? Well, as people sell their gold to the monetary authority, they get money in return. (Think of the monetary authority turning over 10 $100 bills for every ounce of gold it buys.) As a result, the money supply in the economy rises, and according to the exchange equation, as the money supply increases, assuming nothing else changes, the price level decreases. We conclude that both the price of gold and general price level decline together.

By stabilizing the price of gold, it's also possible to stabilize the general price level, since the general price level moves up and down with the price of gold. It follows that if the monetary authority stabilizes the market price of gold at $1,000, it will indirectly be very close to stabilizing the general level of prices throughout the market. This is why some economists argue that a gold standard stabilizes the price level, thus preventing a decline in the value of the dollar.

Defining Terms

1. Define:
   a. monetary policy
   b. expansionary monetary policy
   c. contractionary monetary policy

Reviewing Facts and Concepts

2. Explain how expansionary monetary policy can lower the unemployment rate.

3. The objective is to keep prices stable. Suppose the average annual change in velocity is 1 percent, and the average annual change in the quantity of goods and services is 4 percent. By what percentage should the Fed increase the money supply?

Critical Thinking

4. What evidence would be inconsistent with the theory that predicts lower inflation through contractionary monetary policy?

5. What evidence would support the theory that lower inflation results from contractionary monetary policy?

Applying Economic Concepts

6. Suppose the Fed sets as its single objective the stabilization of the price level. To this end, it decides to automatically increase the money supply by 2 percent each year based on an average annual change in velocity of 1 percent and an average annual change in the quantity of goods and services of 3 percent. If current-year velocity is above its average annual rate, what will happen?

7. Suppose that under a gold standard, the official price of gold is $1,000 an ounce and the market price of gold is $1,200 an ounce. What will happen to the supply of gold, price of gold, supply of money, and general price level? Explain your answer.

Assessment Book

You will find a quiz for this section in the *Assessment Book,* page 131.

Reteaching Activity

Use the Section Assessment to gauge which students may need reteaching on this section. Work with those students to create flowcharts that show what happens to the economy during times of expansionary monetary policy and during times of contractionary monetary policy.

Guided Reading

For further reteaching of the key concepts in this section, assign the Outlining Activity and the Just the Facts Handout from the *Guided Reading and Study Guide,* pages 231–234.

Critical Thinking

4. Inconsistent evidence would be for prices to remain the same after a decrease in the money supply.

5. A decrease in the price level would support the stated theory.

Applying Economic Concepts

6. If current-year velocity is above the average annual rate of 2%, then the price level will rise. In other words, inflation will occur.

7. If the market price of gold is $1,200 an ounce and the official price of gold is $1,000 an ounce, then the public will buy gold from the monetary authority for $1,000 and try to sell it for $1,200 in the market. As a result of this action, two things will happen: first, the supply of gold in the gold market will rise, and second, the supply of money in the economy will fall (since people will be buying gold from the monetary authority with money). When the supply of gold rises in the gold market, the price of gold will fall. Because the supply of money in the economy will fall, the price level will likely fall.

Defining Terms

1. a. monetary policy: changes the Fed makes in the money supply; **b. expansionary monetary policy:** an increase in the money supply;

c. contractionary monetary policy: a decrease in the money supply.

Reviewing Facts and Concepts

2. The Fed increases the money supply, which leads to greater total spending in the economy. Because of increased spending, firms sell more products. As firms sell more products, they hire more workers, and thus the unemployment rate drops.

3. Using the formula on page 390, the student should determine that to keep prices stable, the Fed should increase the money supply by 3%.

Discussion Starter

Ask students if they have any type of bank account. Some may have savings or checking accounts. Explain that you will be learning about the types of accounts that are available to them and that they should consider what accounts would help them with their financial goals.

Research Activity

Assign students with checking or saving accounts to identify the benefits and costs of their accounts. Students without accounts should compare and contrast two different accounts (two checking or two savings accounts) and identify the costs and benefits of each. Students should list any interest rates, restrictions, and fees associated with each account. Each group of students should evaluate and identify which account is the best choice for their financial goals.

Your Account Options

This chapter discussed monetary policy and the nation's money supply. But what about your personal money supply? Although it is much smaller than the nation's money supply, it is still important to you. What should you do with it? No doubt you will spend part of it, but you may want to save part of it too. If this is the case, both a checking and a savings account will be of use to you.

Establishing a Savings Plan

Usually, when people save money, they have a goal in mind.

The first step in devising a savings program for yourself is to identify what it is you are saving for and how much you need to save. For example, if you are saving to go to college, get an estimate of the costs of attending college (e.g., tuition, room and board, books, and so on). Then estimate how much you need to save each week or month to reach your goal in the desired time period.

A Good Habit

Some people argue that a good rule is to save 10 to 15 percent of whatever you earn. If you earn $100 a week, save $10 to $15 a week; if you earn $1,000 a week, save $100 to $150 a week. This habit makes future emergencies less catastrophic. When your car needs a major repair or you become unemployed for a number of months, you have an emergency fund to draw on.

Understanding Savings Accounts

Often, people are unaware of the variety of ways in which they can save their money. One way to save is with a certificate of deposit (CD), also known as a time deposit. A CD requires a minimum deposit and you cannot withdraw your money (without penalty) for a period of six months to a year. The benefit of CDs is that they usually pay a higher interest rate than some other savings options.

You can also save by using a money market account. A money market account invests your money in securities issued by the U.S. Treasury. These accounts require a minimum deposit and minimum balance and place a limit on the number of checks you can write per month on the account. Money market accounts also offer a relatively high interest rate.

The simplest way to save your money, however, is in a basic savings account. With this type of account, you can make deposits or withdrawals at any time while still earning a low rate of interest on the money in the account.

You can open a savings account in several ways. You can do so online, by calling the bank or savings institution (usually a phone number can be found on their websites), or by going to the bank in person. Opening a savings account (or any account, for that matter) requires

you to provide personal information, such as your full name, social security number, home address, and telephone number.

Although a savings account pays interest on the money you put into it, the rate of return is less than you could earn by investing your money in stocks, bonds, or real estate, which brings us to the topic of risk versus return. Low-risk investments usually yield low returns but have little to no potential for loss, while high-risk investments can yield high returns but also have the potential for much greater losses. You could buy several stocks for $4,000 and end up with a fraction of that money if those stocks fall in value, but you wouldn't have lost any of your $4,000 in a savings account. With interest paid on the savings account, you would actually end up with a little bit more than your original $4,000. If the account pays 4 percent annually, you would have $4,160 at the end of the year, less any fees or charges. Some savings accounts charge an annual fee. Transferring funds from your savings account to your checking account may also come with a fee. A major benefit of a savings account (as well as a checking account) is that it is insured by the Federal Deposit Insurance Corporation (FDIC) up to $250,000.

Background Information: Tracking Checks

One way to keep bank records current is to make sure bank statements are reconciled with personal records. Record all written checks (in a checkbook) and subtract the dollar amount of the check from the current balance. This indicates how much money is available in the checking account.

Current bank statements are also available to review online. The bank keeps a list of all the checks written from checking accounts (as well as deposits and withdrawals). Encourage each student to check his or her personal record (the record of deposits, withdrawals, checks written) against the record the bank is keeping. If there is a difference, he or she should find out who has made the mistake.

Understanding Checking Accounts

The purpose of putting your money in a checking account is to keep it in a safe place while still providing easy access to your funds by writing a check, using a debit card, or taking out cash at an ATM. As with any account, a checking account may come with certain restrictions and fees. For example, you may have to pay for paper statements unless you either maintain a certain average balance or are committed to monthly direct deposits of a certain dollar amount. Some checking accounts pay interest and others do not. Often the accounts that are advertised as "free" do not. Checking accounts that offer interest may require you to maintain a higher average balance (e.g., $1,500 or more). Because checking accounts usually pay lower interest than savings accounts, CDs, money market accounts, and other saving instruments, the forfeited interest is an opportunity cost. However, this opportunity cost may be unavoidable since you likely need to keep money in your checking account to meet everyday expenses.

Reconciling Your Bank Statements

Suppose your monthly rent needs to be paid by the fifth of every month. One day the check you wrote to the landlord bounces. That means you did not have sufficient funds in your checking account to cover the check. Your bank charges you a fee of $50 for writing a "bad check") and the landlord charges you $25 for the late payment. That

is a $75 mistake! How might it be prevented next time?

The key to not writing "bad checks" is to keep good personal records. Record every deposit, withdrawal, check written, and debit expense incurred against your checking account. Then check, or reconcile, your records against the bank's online or paper statements.

Your Personal Economics Activity

1. Research online or contact your local bank to identify the types of accounts that are available. Select an account and identify potential risks, monetary costs (fees), and benefits of maintaining your selected account.
2. Write a two-paragraph essay that analyzes the role of risk and return in choosing where to allocate money.
3. Summarize how you would begin a savings program.
4. Analyze and explain the positive and negative aspects of using a debit card.

My Personal Economics Action Plan

Here are some points you may want to consider and some guidelines you might want to put into practice.

☑ 1. Visit http://econ.emcp.net/accounts. There you will find a list of different banks and savings institutions and the interest rates they pay on CDs, basic savings accounts, and so on.

Before I open up a checking or savings account, I will visit the Deposit Accounts website and research savings accounts, interest rates, CDs, and so on.

☑ 2. It is important to have a savings plan. Identify what it is you are saving for, how much you plan to save each week or month, and how long it will take to reach your savings goal.

I will consider my savings goal. I will also consider adopting a savings rule, such as saving 10 to 15 percent of everything I earn.

☑ 3. It is important to keep good records of your deposits, withdrawals, checks written, and so on.

I will purchase a small notebook and record all my deposits, withdrawals, and checks written. I will reconcile my records with my bank statements on a regular basis.

Focus and Motivate

Section Objectives

After completing the section, students will be able to

▶ explain why the output of goods and services rises before prices when the money supply rises;

▶ explain why the output of goods and services falls before prices when the money supply falls; and

▶ explain what causes stagflation.

Kickoff Activity

Ask students the following question at the beginning of class: What do you think *stagflation* is?

Activating Prior Knowledge

Invite students to share their ideas about the term *stagflation*. Be sure they know that stagflation is the simultaneous occurrence of high inflation and unemployment.

Teach

Critical Thinking

Some people say that incumbent politicians at the national level are not likely to be reelected if stagflation exists. Ask students whether they think the state of the economy influences how people vote and if so, how. Students should understand that people dislike both inflation and unemployment, but when the two occur together, people have so much to dislike that they often take their anger out on incumbent politicians.

 Visit econ.myemcp.com/videos for videos that will help students better understand the key concepts found in this section.

Stagflation: The Two Problems Appear Together

Focus Questions

▶ When the money supply rises, why does the output of goods and services rise before prices?

▶ When the money supply falls, why does the output of goods and services fall before prices?

▶ What causes stagflation?

Key Terms

stagflation

stop-and-go, on-and-off monetary policy

Rising Unemployment and Inflation (at the Same Time)

For many years, economists believed that the economy would experience either high inflation or high unemployment but not both at the same time. Moreover, they believed that inflation and unemployment moved in opposite directions. As the inflation rate increased, the unemployment rate decreased, and as the inflation rate decreased, the unemployment rate increased. Economists thought that inflation and unemployment were on opposite ends of a seesaw.

Real-world data appeared to support this view. For example, during most of the 1960s, inflation and unemployment moved in opposite directions. But in the 1970s, the inflation–unemployment trade-off disappeared for a few years. Instead of moving in opposite directions, inflation and unemployment began to move in the same direction—specifically, both began to increase. The economy began to experience high inflation and high unemployment at the same time, or **stagflation**.

stagflation
The occurrence of inflation and high unemployment at the same time.

stop-and-go, on-and-off monetary policy
An erratic monetary policy.

How Money Changes Affect the Economy

Some economists believe that stagflation is the result of a **stop-and-go, on-and-off monetary policy**. Before we examine their position, though, we need to look at the sequence of effects that monetary policy has on the economy.

Most economists agree that changes in the money supply affect both prices and the output of goods and services but that output is affected before prices. For example, when the Fed increases the money supply, total spending in the economy increases. As a result, firms sell more goods, and consequently, they begin to hire more laborers and produce more output. Only later do prices rise.

Why does output rise before prices? When firms begin to sell more, they don't know at first whether this increase is temporary or permanent. Thinking it may be temporary ("It was a good sales week, but next week may not be so good"), firms hold off on changing prices. If they raise prices and later learn that the higher sales

Cross-Curricular Activity

Invite an American history teacher to class to discuss the political, social, and economic culture of the 1970s. Make sure she or he discusses the conflict in Southeast Asia, the Watergate scandal, the oil crisis, and other issues that may have contributed to the feelings of disillusionment experienced by Americans at that time. After the history teacher has established the historical context, connect it to the economic realities by using charts that show the inflation rate and unemployment rate over the same period. Discuss with students the relationship among governmental actions, political crises, and the economy.

▲ An increase in the money supply can cause an increase in spending, which can in turn cause an increase in production and employment. **In this scenario what usually happens to prices, and if so, when does it happen?**

were only a quirk, they may become less competitive.

Consider Yoko, who owns a pizza restaurant. In an average week, she sells 400 pizzas at an average price of $9. This week, she sells 550 pizzas. Yoko doesn't know why she did so well this week. People may be getting tired of hamburgers, or people may be getting tired of eating at home, or the Fed may have raised the money supply and increased total spending.

Yoko could immediately raise the price of her pizzas from $9 to $11, but suppose her higher-than-average sales don't last. If this week's higher sales are only temporary and Yoko raises her price to $11 (while her competitors keep their prices the same), she may lose customers. She is therefore likely to be cautious and wait to see what happens. If sales continue at 550 a week for a few weeks, maybe then she will raise her price. But if sales drop back to 400 a week, she will keep the price as it is. We can conclude that given an increase in the money supply, output is likely to go up before prices do.

Similarly, when the money supply decreases, output is affected before price. Suppose that instead of selling an average of 400 pizzas this week, Yoko sells only 250 pizzas. She doesn't know why sales are lower than average; she just knows they are. She reduces her output of pizzas and perhaps cuts back on overtime for her employees. She doesn't immediately reduce the price, though, because she can't be sure whether the lower-than-average sales will continue. She doesn't want to lower the price until she is sure that the demand for her good has fallen. We conclude that given a decrease in the money supply, output is likely to go down before prices do.

EXAMPLE Elizabeth owns a hair salon. Last week, she did better than she has ever done. Business seems to be booming, but she isn't quite sure why. She decides to take a wait-and-see attitude. She hires more stylists, but she doesn't raise prices—at least not yet. Now suppose that time passes and Elizabeth has the worst business week of her life. People canceled their appointments

Section 3 Stagflation: The Two Problems Appear Together **399**

Internet Research

The severe economic problems and the recession that most Asian nations experienced in the late 1990s had global implications. Have each student select a particular country in Asia and, using the Internet, learn how the recession affected it. The student should also address how economic problems in that country affected the United States.

Another option is to have students use the Internet to locate inflation and unemployment statistics and then determine whether the United States has experienced stagflation since the 1970s. If stagflation has occurred in recent years, what reasons explain why? If it hasn't occurred, what might have changed since the 1970s to help improve the U.S. economy?

Teaching with Visuals

Prices usually increase after firms conclude that the increase in their output will be permanent.

Economics in the Real World

Talk about the economy is everywhere around, but if you ask people what they know about economics, most will say, "Not much." Invite students to explore this phenomenon by going to www.emcschool.net/Economics2e, selecting Chapter 13, and reading the Economics in the Real World feature titled **"Why Does the Public Know So Little About Economic Policy?"**

After students have read this feature, ask volunteers to offer additional reasons that it would be worthwhile to understand the basics of economics.

ANSWERS TO THINK ABOUT IT Answers will vary. Most students will probably say that it's easier for politicians to say economically incorrect things to an ignorant public than to a knowledgeable public that can catch them making mistakes.

Discussion Starter

Students often begin their study of economics without understanding how economic policies affect them. Ask students to reflect on whether their views of the relevance of economics have changed during the semester.

Tell students that what happens in Washington, D.C., in terms of monetary or fiscal policy does indeed affect them. Economists believe that fiscal policy and monetary policy can affect the total spending in the economy. This, in turn, affects how many goods and services are bought. Students will eventually be producers of goods and services or will work for firms that produce goods and services, so these policies affect them.

Reinforcement Activity

Invite students to imagine that they are small-business owners in markets of their choice. Then have them imagine that demand suddenly increases or decreases. Ask what they will do and why they might wait before changing prices.

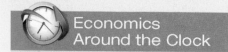

Economics Around the Clock

Direct students to read the 10:56 p.m. scenario in Economics Around the Clock (page 377), and tell them to write down how they would explain stagflation to Carl.

Answers will vary. Essentially, students should explain that stagflation occurs when inflation and high unemployment happen simultaneously.

Teaching with Visuals

Answers to the photo question on page 401 will vary. The unemployed workers might say that they were laid off to increase company profits. Economists might say that they were laid off because aggregate demand decreased.

 Application Activity

After reading and discussing Section 3, you may want to assign the Section Activity in the *Applying the Principles Workbook,* pages 145–146.

Assess

Quick Quiz

The following true-or-false quiz will help you assess student understanding of the material covered in this section.

1. Economists have always understood the concept and possibility of stagflation. (False)
2. Some economists believe that stagflation is the result of a stop-and-go monetary policy. (True)
3. Stagflation is a combination of inflation and low unemployment. (False)
4. Some economists believe that a marked decrease in aggregate supply can also cause stagflation. (True)
5. When there is a decrease in the money supply, output is affected before price. (True)

Economic Facts and Fallacies

FALSE
TRUE

Government Policy and Economic Results

Suppose that a TV economics reporter says: "The unemployment rate is high, inflation is picking up, and consumer sales are way down. Obviously, a free market economy cannot always produce good economic results." How might an economist respond to this statement? He or she might say that this person is observing the effects of poorly designed and implemented government economic policies.

For example, a too-rapid increase in the money supply can cause "inflation to pick up"; a contractionary fiscal policy implemented at the wrong time can cause consumer sales to drop; and a stop-and-go, erratic monetary policy can cause high unemployment and high inflation. The economist knows that sometimes the blame should be placed on poorly conceived government economic policies, and not on the free market economy.

right and left and didn't reschedule. Elizabeth isn't quite sure what happened. Again, she adopts a wait-and-see attitude. She reduces the hours of a few stylists, but she doesn't lower prices yet. ◆

What Causes Stagflation?

Some economists believe that stagflation is caused by a *stop-and-go, on-and-off monetary policy* (an erratic monetary policy), which was defined earlier. They describe what happens as follows:

- The Fed increases the money supply. It pushes the monetary "accelerator" to the floor, which first raises output and then raises prices.
- Time passes. The increased money supply raises the price level—that is, it causes inflation.
- At the same time that people are dealing with high inflation, the Fed reduces the money supply. It puts on the monetary "brakes." As a result, output is affected first, and it falls. Because of less output, fewer people are required to work in the factories. Unemployment rises.

Notice that in the economy, inflation is coupled with a cutback in output and an increase in unemployment. The previous monetary policy (money supply up) caused high inflation, and the current monetary policy (money supply down) caused high unemployment. The economy is experiencing the effects of both monetary policies, or stagflation.

Not all economists agree with this description of the cause of stagflation or believe it's the only cause. Some economists maintain that a marked decrease in aggregate supply (perhaps due to a fall in the market supply of a major resource, such as oil) can also cause stagflation.

EXAMPLE Think of the following events happening along a time line. It's January and the Fed increases the money supply. Let's say that prices are starting to head upward by April. Then in May, the Fed decreases the money supply. Soon after, in July, output is headed down and so the unemployment rate rises. (Less output means fewer people are needed to produce the output.) Does anything else happen in July? Yes, remember that prices started heading up in April, and they continue to rise in July. So, what does July look like? July is a month of rising unemployment (caused by the money supply decrease in May) and rising prices (caused by the money supply increase in January). ◆

A Student Asks

QUESTION: *It seems to me that monetary policy is important. If the money supply is too high, we seem to get inflation. If it is too low, we might end up with high unemployment. If it goes from up to down too quickly (stop and go, on and off), we get stagflation. Do I have this right? Is the money supply a big factor in what happens in the economy?*

ANSWER: *Most economists would say that it is. Think of it in extreme terms for a few minutes. Suppose the money supply were cut in half overnight.*

Background Information: Keynesian Economics and Stagflation

In the Keynesian view of the economy, stagflation could not occur. There could be a choice between high inflation and high unemployment, but the two would never happen together. The simultaneous high inflation and high unemployment experienced by the United States in the late 1970s and early 1980s partly discredited the Keynesian view.

Wouldn't that cut spending in the economy dramatically and result in high unemployment? Suppose the money supply were raised by 50 percent overnight. Wouldn't that lead to a high rate of inflation? Now, in reality, the Fed doesn't raise or lower the money supply by these large percentages, but that doesn't mean the smaller changes in the money supply that the Fed makes don't have consequences.

Most people are used to thinking that what the president does or what the members of Congress do is all that matters to the state of the economy. But what the Fed does is extremely important to the state of the economy. Some people call the chair of the Fed "the second most powerful person in the country," after the president, because that individual has a big part in directing the monetary policy of the country.

▲ These people (many of whom may have just lost a job) are now standing in a line to find a new job at a job fair. What are some of the reasons these people might give if asked why they lost their jobs? What reasons might an economist give?

ASSESSMENT
SECTION 3

Defining Terms

1. Define:
   a. stagflation
   b. stop-and-go, on-and-off monetary policy

Reviewing Facts and Concepts

2. In the past, how did economists view the relationship between unemployment and inflation? When did economic events begin to change this view?

3. Does a decrease in the money supply cause a change in output, prices, or both?

4. Explain in detail (and using economic-related terms correctly) how some economists believe the Fed causes stagflation. What is an alternative view of what causes stagflation?

Critical Thinking

5. Because firms adjust output before prices, what information do they lack?

6. When the money supply increases, output rises before prices. Why?

Applying Economic Concepts

7. Use the information from the chapter to make inferences and draw conclusions about what effect, if any, the occurrence of stagflation may have on the reelection prospects of the president of the United States?

Assessment Book

You will find a quiz for this section in the *Assessment Book,* page 132.

Reteaching Activity

Use the Section Assessment to gauge which students may need reteaching on this section. Make sure that those students understand that stagflation occurs when prices rise, causing inflation, and then aggregate demand falls, causing output to fall before price.

Guided Reading

For further reteaching of the key concepts in this section, assign the Outlining Activity and the Just the Facts Handout from the *Guided Reading and Study Guide,* pages 235–236.

monetary policy causes stagflation. The money supply increases, so firms sell and produce more. When higher sales appear to be permanent, firms raise prices, causing inflation. Then the Fed reduces the money supply. Firms sell less and cut back on production. They fire some workers; unemployment rises. Higher prices occur at the same time as higher unemployment. Some economists argue that a marked decrease in aggregate supply can also cause stagflation.

Critical Thinking

5. Firms don't know whether a rise or fall in sales is temporary or permanent. Only time will provide the company with this information.

6. When firms begin to sell more, they don't know whether this increase is temporary or permanent. Because it may be temporary, they don't want to change prices, so they adjust output instead.

Applying Economic Concepts

7. Answers will vary. Generally, bad economic times are thought to hurt an incumbent president's chances of reelection.

SECTION 3
ASSESSMENT ANSWERS

Defining Terms

1. a. stagflation: the occurrence of inflation and high unemployment at the same time; **b. stop-and-go, on-and-**

off monetary policy: an erratic monetary policy in which the money supply is increased, then decreased, and so on.

Reviewing Facts and Concepts

2. Economists believed that unemployment and inflation moved in opposite directions.

The concurrent appearance of the two in the 1970s changed this view.

3. A decrease in the money supply leads to lower output, which eventually leads to lower prices.

4. Some economists believe that stop-and-go, on-and-off

Economics Vocabulary

1. complete crowding out; **2.** contractionary monetary; **3.** expansionary monetary; **4.** Stagflation; **5.** Fiscal policy; **6.** Laffer curve; **7.** after-tax income; **8.** expansionary fiscal; **9.** contractionary fiscal.

Understanding the Main Ideas

1. The objective of expansionary fiscal policy is to increase total spending. If there is complete crowding out, an increase in government spending will simply be offset by a decrease in private sending, making expansionary fiscal policy ineffective.

2. Most economists believe the cause of stagflation is stop-and-go, on-and-off monetary policy. The inflation part of stagflation is caused by increases in the money supply. The unemployment part of stagflation is caused by decreases in the money supply.

3. The money supply increases. As a result, total spending increases, firms sell more goods and hire more workers, so the unemployment rate decreases.

4. The money supply decreases, which reduces total spending in the economy. Firms sell fewer goods; inventories rise. Firms decide to lower prices to rid themselves of their surplus goods, and inflation decreases.

5. A reduction in income tax rates leaves people with more after-tax income, so they end up spending more. This is how an income tax rate cut affects the demand side of the economy. A tax cut also motivates people to work more and produce more goods, affecting the supply side of the economy.

6. The demand side. Keynes would argue that high unemployment and recession exist because aggregate demand is too low. The solution is to increase aggregate demand, and government needs to enact expansionary fiscal policy to increase aggregate demand.

7. Rosa doesn't know if the demand for her hotel has gone up or if this week is

---

Chapter Summary

Section 1

▶ Government increases in spending and decreases in taxes are considered expansionary fiscal policy, whereas decreases in spending and increases in taxes are contractionary fiscal policy.

▶ Expansionary fiscal policy is believed to reduce the unemployment rate.

▶ Crowding out suggests that increased government spending reduces private spending.

▶ A contractionary fiscal policy is believed to reduce inflation.

▶ According to Keynes, the economy is not always self-regulating. Sometimes, the government needs to enact specific economic policies to move the economy out of a recession.

▶ Supply-side economists believe that cuts in high tax rates can generate higher tax revenues, whereas cuts in low tax rates can generate lower tax revenues, as demonstrated by the Laffer curve.

Section 2

▶ Monetary policy deals with changes in the money supply.

▶ Expansionary monetary policy can help reduce unemployment and does not involve crowding out because the money supply is increased.

▶ Contractionary monetary policy works to reduce inflation by reducing the money supply, which leads to a decrease in spending and a decrease in prices.

Section 3

▶ High inflation and high unemployment at the same time is known as stagflation.

▶ Most economists agree that changes in the money supply affect both prices and the output of goods and services and that output is affected before prices.

▶ Stop-and-go, on-and-off monetary policy is an erratic policy in which the Fed alternately increases and decreases the money supply.

Economics Vocabulary

1. The scenario in which government spending increases by $1 and, as a result, private spending decreases by $1 is called _____.

2. If the Fed decreases the money supply, it is implementing a(n) _____ policy.

3. If the Fed increases the money supply, it is implementing a(n) _____ policy.

4. _____ is the simultaneous occurrence of inflation and high unemployment.

5. _____ refers to changes the government makes in spending, taxation, or both to achieve particular macroeconomic goals.

6. The _____ expresses the relationship that some economists believe exists between tax rates and tax revenues.

7. Income minus taxes is _____.

8. If the government increases spending or lowers taxes, it is implementing a(n) _____ policy.

9. If the government decreases spending or raises taxes, it is implementing a(n) _____ policy.

Understanding the Main Ideas

1. Explain how complete crowding out affects expansionary fiscal policy.

2. In general, what causes stagflation?

3. Explain the process by which expansionary monetary policy reduces the unemployment rate.

4. Explain the process by which contractionary monetary policy reduces inflation.

5. How can changes in income tax rates affect both the supply side and the demand side of the economy?

6. Would Keynes be more likely to argue that economic problems (such as high unemployment and recession) emanate from the demand side of the economy or the supply side? Explain.

7. Rosa Jenkins, who owns a hotel, rented out a higher-than-average number of rooms this week. Why will she likely wait awhile before raising the room rent?

8. Describe the process by which expansionary fiscal policy reduces unemployment (assuming no crowding out or incomplete crowding out).

9. Explain why expansionary monetary policy is probably not a solution to stagflation.

---

simply an above-average week. If she raises the rent too fast, she may become less competitive.

8. Government increases its spending; thus, there is more spending in the economy. As a result of more spending in the economy, firms sell more goods and hire more workers, so the unemployment rate goes down.

9. Expansionary monetary policy would probably make the inflation part of stagflation worse.

10. Not necessarily. A cut in tax rates can increase or decrease tax revenues depending on whether the percentage increase in income (as a result of the tax cut) is greater than the percentage reduction in the tax rate. If it is, then tax revenues will rise; if it isn't, then tax revenues will fall.

11. The inflation part of stagflation is caused by increases in the money supply. The unemploy-

10. Do lower tax rates mean lower tax revenues? Explain your answer.

11. What causes the inflation part of stagflation? What causes the unemployment part?

12. Suppose the United States uses a gold standard and the official price of gold is $800 an ounce while the market price of gold is $1,000 an ounce. What will happen to the supply of gold, price of gold, supply of money, and general price level? Explain your answer.

Doing the Math

1. Suppose the average tax rate is 20 percent and tax revenues are $800 billion. What does (taxable) income equal?

2. Suppose the average tax rate is 25 percent and tax revenues equal $600 billion. If the average tax rate falls to 20 percent, how much will (taxable) income have to increase to keep tax revenues unchanged?

Working with Graphs and Tables

1. If the objective is to maintain price stability, by what percentage should the money supply change in cases A through D in Exhibit 13-3?

2. Using Exhibit 13-4, answer the following questions:
   a. What happens to tax revenues as the tax rate is lowered from E to D?
   b. What happens to tax revenues as the tax rate is increased from A to B?
   c. What is the tax rate at which tax revenues are maximized?
   d. What happens to tax revenues as the tax rate is increased from D to E?

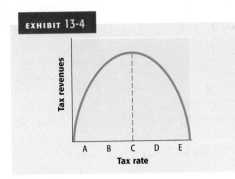

EXHIBIT 13-4

(Graph: y-axis "Tax revenues", x-axis "Tax rate", with points A B C D E along the x-axis, curve peaking at C.)

Solving Economic Problems

1. *Apply.* It's often said that making consistently accurate predictions in economics is difficult. Give an example that illustrates this point.

2. *Infer and Conclude.* WRITING Based on your reading of the chapter, write a one-page paper that addresses this question: *Why do economists differ in their views on the effects of fiscal policy actions?*

3. *Synthesize.* Suppose a country experiences continuous inflation but not stagflation. What can you infer about the country's monetary policy? Write a one-page paper explaining your thoughts to someone who hasn't taken this course. Be sure to explain (in your own words) any economic terms that your audience may not know.

Project or Presentation

Speaking of Money... Buchanan and Wagner argued that politicians have an incentive to increase government spending and cut taxes rather than decrease spending and raise taxes. Give a presentation that supports or opposes this claim. Use secondary sources (articles, TV reports, and so on) to support your viewpoint. Evaluate the validity of the information you use and acknowledge any known points of view or biases within sources.

ONLINE *Practice Tests and Study Guide*
emcp.com

Go to **www.emcschool.net/Economics2e** and choose *Economics: New Ways of Thinking*, Chapter 13, if you need more help in preparing for the chapter test.

EXHIBIT 13-3

	A	B	C	D
%ΔV	0	−1	+2	−2
%ΔQ	+2	+2	+3	+3

---

ment part of stagflation is caused by decreases in the money supply.

12. If the market price of gold is $800 an ounce and the official price of gold is $1,000 an ounce, then the public will sell gold to the monetary authority. As a result, the supply of gold in the gold market falls and the supply of money in the economy rises (because people are selling gold to the monetary authority and obtaining money

in exchange). When the supply of gold falls in the gold market, the price of gold will rise. When the supply of money in the economy rises, the price level is likely to rise.

Doing the Math

1. $4,000 billion (*calculation:* $800 billion = 0.20 × X; therefore, X = $4,000 billion).

2. $600 billion. If a 25% tax rate generates $600

billion in tax revenues, taxable income must equal $2,400 billion. An income of $3,000 billion is required before a 20% tax rate will generate $600 billion in tax revenues. The difference between $3,000 billion and $2,400 billion is $600 billion.

Working with Graphs and Tables

1. A. 2%; **B.** 3%; **C.** 1%; **D.** 5%.
2. a. tax revenues increase; **b.** tax revenues increase; **c.** tax revenues are maximized at tax rate C; **d.** tax revenues fall.

Solving Economic Problems

1. Answers will vary. It's difficult to predict what will happen to tax revenues if tax rates are lowered. The answer depends on whether the increase in taxable income (as people are motivated to work more) is greater than, less than, or equal to the cut in taxes. If we knew which of the three possibilities would materialize, we could make an accurate prediction. Because we don't know, we can't be sure that our "best guess" of which condition will hold will be the "right guess" and therefore give us an accurate prediction.

2. Answers will vary. Students may note: (1) Economists don't know whether there will be complete crowding out, incomplete crowding out, or no crowding out. Which condition exists can determine whether expansionary fiscal policy is effective at changing total spending or not. (2) Economists don't know whether a cut in tax rates will generate a proportionately larger or smaller rise in taxable income and therefore a rise or fall in tax revenues. In general, any time economists have several possible conditions to choose from, different economists will choose different options. Consequently, economists will have different views on what will likely happen to the economy in the future.

3. If stop-and-go, on-and-off monetary policy causes stagflation, then obviously there is no stagflation. There is also no stop-and-go, on-and-off monetary policy. The monetary policy that causes continuous inflation is continued rapid increases in the money supply.

Project or Presentation

Answers will vary.

Chapter 14 Planning Guide

SECTION ORGANIZER

Taxes
(pages 406–413)

Learning Objectives	Reproducible Worksheets and Handouts	Assessment
▶ List the three major federal taxes. ▶ List the three types of taxes people pay in addition to the three major federal taxes. ▶ Explain what a value-added tax is. ▶ Explain how proportional, progressive, and regressive income taxation differ. ▶ Discuss the idea of fair taxation.	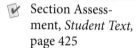 Section 1 Activity, *Applying the Principles Workbook*, pages 147–148 Outlining Activity, *Guided Reading and Study Guide*, pages 243–244 Just the Facts Handout, *Guided Reading and Study Guide*, pages 245–246	☑ Section Assessment, *Student Text*, page 413 ☑ Quick Quiz, *Annotated Teacher's Edition*, page 412 ☑ Section Quiz, *Assessment Book*, page 141

SECTION 2

The Budget: Deficits and Debt
(pages 416–425)

▶ Describe how the federal government spends its tax revenues. ▶ Define the terms *balanced budget, budget deficit,* and *budget surplus.* ▶ Explain the relationship between a budget deficit and the national debt. ▶ Identify some of the issues connected with budget surpluses.	Section 2 Activity, *Applying the Principles Workbook*, pages 149–150 Outlining Activity, *Guided Reading and Study Guide*, pages 247–249 Just the Facts Handout, *Guided Reading and Study Guide*, pages 250–251	☑ Section Assessment, *Student Text*, page 425 ☑ Quick Quiz, *Annotated Teacher's Edition*, page 424 ☑ Section Quiz, *Assessment Book*, page 142

Reproducible Chapter Resources and Assessment Materials

📖 Graphic Organizer Activity, *Guided Reading and Study Guide*, pages 252–253

📖 Vocabulary Activity, *Guided Reading and Study Guide*, page 254

📖 Working with Graphs and Charts, *Guided Reading and Study Guide*, page 255

☑ Practice Test, *Guided Reading and Study Guide*, pages 256–258

📖 Critical Thinking Activity, *Finding Economics*, pages 38–40

☑ Chapter Test A, *Assessment Book*, pages 143–145

☑ Chapter Test B, *Assessment Book*, pages 146–149

Student Text Internet Links

Economics: New Ways of Thinking, Second Edition encourages students to use the Internet to find out more about economics. Given the wealth of current, valid information available on websites, students should be encouraged to use the Internet as a research tool. Doing so will likely increase students' interest in and understanding of economics principles and topics. In addition, doing Internet research can help your students form the habit of accessing and using economics information, as well as help them develop investigative skills they will use throughout their educational and professional careers.

To aid your students in achieving these ends, each chapter of *Economics: New Ways of Thinking, Second Edition* includes the addresses of several websites that provide engaging and relevant information. When students type in any of the addresses provided, they will immediately arrive at the intended site. The addresses have been modified so that EMC Publishing can monitor and maintain the proper links—for example, the website http://www.deposit accounts.com/ has been changed to http://econ.emcp.net/accounts. In the event that the address or content of a site changes or is discontinued, EMC's Internet editors will redirect the link to a site with equivalent information.

Activities in the *Annotated Teacher's Edition* often suggest that students search the Internet for information. For some activities, you might want to find reputable sites beforehand and steer students toward them. For other activities, have students do their own searching and then check out the sites they have found and discuss why they might be reliable or unreliable.

Passport® for Economics

Technology resources are available with the *Economics: New Ways of Thinking, Second Edition* program through Passport®. These include:

eBooks for *Economics: New Ways of Thinking, Second Edition*

► Student textbook eBook
► Interactive Applying the Principles eWorkbook
► Finding Economics eBook
► Guided Reading and Study Guide eBook
► Annotated Teacher's Edition eBook
► Lesson Plans eBook
► Assessment eBook

Passport® for Students

Students can access helpful resources through Passport® for Economics. Resources include:

► Study guides
► Practice tests
► Flash cards in English and in Spanish
► Word games in English and in Spanish
► Tutorials and key-concept videos
► Spanish print and audio summaries

Passport® for Teachers

Keep your course current and relevant by using the teacher resources provided through Passport® for Economics. In addition to all of the resources on the student side of Passport®, the teacher side contains:

► Link to the Annotated Teacher's Edition eBook
► Standards correlations
► Microsoft® PowerPoint® Lectures
► Current Events Lessons
► Additional Economics in the Real World features
► ExamView® Assessment Suite
► PDFs of all print supplements (student and teacher)

This chapter introduces the taxing and spending activities of the federal government. It describes what taxes the government applies and how the government spends tax revenues. It also examines the national debt, as well as the effects of having a budget surplus and a budget deficit. The following statements provide brief descriptions of the major concepts covered in each section of this chapter.

SECTION 1 Taxes

Section 1 describes the types of taxes that exist. It also explains the differences among proportional, progressive, and regressive income taxation.

SECTION 2 The Budget: Deficits and Debt

Section 2 answers the following questions: What is a balanced budget? What is a budget deficit? What is a budget surplus? What is the relationship between a budget deficit and the national debt? What are some issues connected with budget surpluses?

Why It Matters

The federal government affects your life in many different ways. Two major ways result from the government's taxing and spending decisions.

If you have a job and your employer deducts taxes from your paycheck, then you have already felt the impact of federal taxes. The kinds of taxes the government imposes and the sizes of those taxes affect important parts of your life, such as what you buy and how much you work.

Most people would agree that the tax dollars spent for fire-fighting equipment and firefighters' salaries is money well spent. But much of the government's process of taxing and spending is subject to debate—a debate that you will participate in as a citizen and taxpayer throughout your adult life.

How the government spends the tax revenues affects you too. For example, how much it spends on education directly affects you now and in the future.

The more you know about the government's taxing and spending policies, the better able you will be to prepare for and deal with these policies.

404

Teaching Suggestions from the Author

Many students see this as a very practical chapter, because it discusses taxes and government spending. Students seem to have a natural interest in these two subjects. They want to know what taxes are paid, how much revenue selective taxes raise, how the federal government spends money, and so on.

Students also seem interested in the national debt and, perhaps to a lesser degree, social security. These topics are also discussed in this chapter.

It's a good idea to start off by talking generally with students about taxes. Do they think the average taxpayer pays too much in taxes? How much

Section 1: Taxes

Section 2: The Budget:
Deficits and Debt

Economics Around the Clock

The following events occurred one day in October.

5:30 P.M. As the Stevens family eats dinner, Mary Stevens tells them that she thinks the rich in the country don't pay their fair share of taxes. Frank Stevens says he doesn't think that is true.

- Who are the rich, and what percentage of federal income taxes do they pay?

5:32 P.M. Vernon and Maria Cole are eating dinner. Maria says, "I think we spend too much money in this country on national defense. We should spend less on national defense and more on education, health care, and environmental concerns." Vernon says, "How much do we spend on national defense?" "I don't know," Maria says, "but I'm sure it's a lot."

- How much does the federal government spend on national defense?

6:04 P.M. Clark and Eddie, two friends at college, are eating dinner together in the dining hall. "I find it interesting," says Eddie, "that Russia has a flat tax." "What's so interesting about that?" Clark asks. "Well," says Eddie, "Russia used to be part of the Soviet Union, a communist country, and a flat tax is usually associated with countries where low taxes are all the rage. It just seems that a flat tax and a formerly communist country don't go together. Of course, I heard recently that Russia is thinking of doing away with its flat tax."

- What is a flat tax, and what countries in the world have a flat tax?

7:16 P.M. The Martinez family is eating dinner. Elise Martinez says, "I heard today that the top federal income tax rate in the United States is around 40 percent." Ken Martinez, Elise's husband, says, "I don't think that's right. I think it's closer to 60 percent."

- What is the highest federal income tax rate?

405

Introducing the Chapter

To introduce Chapter 14, write this phrase on the board: *taxation without representation*. Ask, Where have you heard this phrase before? (*Answer:* Students should be familiar with this famous phrase from their study of U.S. history.) Stress that paying taxes is almost always seen as a burden. The types of unfair taxes that the British imposed on the American colonies were sufficient to spark the American War for Independence. Ask, Can you think of any other famous quotes regarding taxes? Answers will vary. Students might mention Benjamin Franklin's frequently quoted statement: "In this world nothing is certain but death and taxes." Explain that taxes, along with deficits and debt, are a main topic of this chapter. You might ask students to skim the lists of Key Terms for the chapter; then ask student volunteers to share what types of things they expect to learn.

Teaching with Visuals

Direct students' attention to the image on these pages. Ask students what government services they think are necessary.

do they think the average taxpayer pays? Do they think they will receive social security benefits when they retire? Why or why not?

Sometimes, it's a good idea to start off this chapter with a more philosophical discussion. Ask students what they think government should do. Should it provide roads and national defense only, or should it provide education, too? Should it provide health care, scholarships for college, and food for people with low incomes? Some students will think government should provide many services; other students will disagree. Before students read this chapter, try to get them to engage in a debate on the government's proper roles and responsibilities.

Teacher Support

Taxes

Focus and Motivate

Section Objectives

After completing this section, students will be able to

▶ list the three major federal taxes;

▶ list the three types of taxes people pay in addition to the three major federal taxes;

▶ explain what a value-added tax is;

▶ explain how proportional, progressive, and regressive income taxation differ; and

▶ discuss the idea of fair taxation.

Kickoff Activity

Ask students to explain what they know about taxes and to list as many different types of taxes as they can.

Activating Prior Knowledge

Invite students to share their responses to the Kickoff Activity. Create a list of taxes on the board from the information students provide. For every tax that students mention, ask them if they know how that tax is assessed, and write the correct response on the board next to the tax. For example, personal income tax is applied to income, and sales tax is applied to the purchase of goods and services.

Visit econ.myemcp.com/videos for videos that will help students better understand the key concepts found in this section.

Focus Questions

▶ What are the three major federal taxes?

▶ What are three types of taxes people pay in addition to the three major federal taxes?

▶ What is a value-added tax?

▶ How do proportional, progressive, and regressive income taxation differ?

▶ What is a fair tax?

Key Terms

value-added tax
proportional income tax
progressive income tax
regressive income tax

Three Major Federal Taxes

The government has three levels: federal, state, and local. At the federal level, there are three major taxes: personal income tax, corporate income tax, and social security tax. In 2016, the federal government took in tax revenues of $3,267 billion. Of this total, about 91 percent was from these three major taxes. Exhibit 14-1 shows estimates from the Congressional Budget Office of the tax revenues that these three taxes are projected to generate from 2018 to 2024.

Personal Income Tax

The personal income tax is the tax a person pays on his or her income. A federal personal income tax is applied by the federal government, and many states also have a personal income tax. At the federal level, the personal income tax raised $1,546 billion in 2016, which accounted for approximately 47 percent of total federal tax revenues that year. In other words, for every $1 the federal government received in taxes in 2016, 47 cents came from the personal income tax.

▶ Here are the federal tax projections made by the Congressional Budget Office for the years 2018–2024.

EXHIBIT 14-1 Federal Tax Projections, 2018–2024 ($ billions)

Taxes	2018	2019	2020	2021	2022	2023	2024
Personal income	$ 1,781	$1,871	$ 1,957	$2,052	$2,148	$2,249	$2,355
Corporate income	340	352	382	377	381	385	396
Social security	1,190	1,230	1,265	1,312	1,364	1,417	1,468
Other	293	280	274	278	284	295	308
Total	$3,604	$3,733	$3,878	$4,019	$4,177	$4,346	$4,527

Source: Congressional Budget Office.

Cooperative Learning

Divide the class into groups. Each group should research the taxing and budgeting process for one country other than the United States. Group members should decide which country to research and then find the following information for their country: What types of taxes does the government impose? How is the budget pre- pared? Does this country currently have a budget deficit or surplus? How do the taxing and budgeting in this country compare to those in our own country? Each group should present its findings in a brief oral report and use visual aids to enhance the presentation.

Corporate Income Tax

The tax corporations pay on their profits is the corporate income tax. The federal government applies a corporate income tax, as do many states. At the federal level, the corporate income tax raised $300 billion in 2016. This amount was about 9.2 percent of the total federal tax revenues for that year.

Social Security Tax

The social security tax is a federal government tax placed on income generated from employment. Half of the tax is placed on the employer, and half is placed on the employee. In 2016, at the federal level, the social security tax raised approximately $1,115 billion, or about 34 percent of the total federal tax revenues. (See Exhibit 14-2.)

A Student Asks

QUESTION: *Don't tax revenues steadily climb for the U.S. government? In other words, aren't tax revenues always higher in a later year than in an earlier year?*

ANSWER: *Over a long period of time, tax revenues rise, but tax revenues in a later year are not always higher than in an earlier year. For example, in 2007, federal tax revenues were $2,568 billion, but in 2008, they fell to $2,524 billion. One year later, in 2009, they fell again to $2,105 billion. Clearly, federal tax revenues can fluctuate.*

Three Other Taxes

The taxes just described are not the only taxes people pay. In most states, people also pay a state income tax. Other major taxes are sales taxes, excise taxes, and property taxes.

Sales Tax

Sales taxes are applied to the purchase of a broad range of goods—cars, computers, clothes, books, and so on—when they are purchased. State governments typically raise tax revenues through sales taxes. The federal government does not collect a (national) sales tax.

Sales taxes differ among states. For example, in Kentucky, the sales tax rate is 6

EXHIBIT 14-2 **Where the Money Comes From**

| Personal income tax | Corporate income tax | Social Security tax | Other taxes |

Source: U.S. Bureau of the Census.

▲ For each dollar the federal government raises from taxes, about 47 cents comes from the personal income tax, 9.2 cents comes from the corporate income tax, 34 cents comes from the social security tax, and 9.8 cents comes from other federal taxes. (These percentages are for 2016.)

percent, but in North Dakota, it is 5 percent. Although some states tax food sales at a rate that is lower than the regular sales tax, most states have no sales tax on food purchased at a grocery store.

Excise Tax

Excise taxes are taxes placed on the purchase of certain goods, such as tobacco products and gasoline. Every time people buy gasoline at a gas station, they pay an excise tax. The federal government applies excise taxes, as do many states.

EXAMPLE Edward goes to the gas station and fills up his car with gas. He looks at the price per gallon: $3.60. He might not realize it, but an excise tax is included in that price. Both federal and state excise taxes are applied on gasoline. While the federal tax is uniform across the country, state excise taxes vary. Generally, state excise taxes on a gallon of gasoline vary from 38 cents to 70 cents. ◆

"The hardest thing in the world to understand is the income tax."
—Albert Einstein, physicist

Property Tax

Property tax is a tax on the value of private property, such as a home. It is a major revenue source for state and local governments.

Teaching with Visuals

Exhibit 14-1 (page 406) shows the federal tax projections for the years 2018–2024. Ask students which tax brings in the most revenue for government. (*Answer:* personal income tax.) Ask, Did you notice that the dollar amounts for all the taxes increase each year? To what do you attribute the increase? Do you think taxes will be raised each year, or could there be other reasons for the increases shown? Students may suggest that the increases occur because there will be more taxpayers contributing to government revenues.

Teaching with Visuals

To help students better understand the breakdown of government revenues from taxes, create on the board or on an overhead transparency a pie chart that shows the information in Exhibit 14-2. If possible, color the segments of the pie chart differently, so that students can easily see the different percentages of taxes paid.

Discussion Starter

Ask students to list some of the things that are done with tax revenues. Possible answers include paying for schools, highways, national defense, and interest on the national debt. Suggest that although many people don't like to pay taxes, most do like the things that taxes buy. For instance, Julio may not want to pay taxes, but he likes the fact that tax money is used to provide national defense; Jane doesn't like to pay taxes, but she likes the fact that taxes provide some people with health care. Help students to see that the economist tries to look at both sides of the coin—both costs and benefits.

Reinforcement Activity

Ask students to review the six types of taxes discussed on pages 406–409. Instruct them to identify which taxes they have paid, either by working at jobs or by purchasing goods and services.

Differentiating Instruction

English Language Learners

One method of assisting English language learners is to read the chapter's Key Terms and their definitions aloud before assigning the chapter. Reading these words aloud will help students to "hear" them as they read the text. You might also use the Spanish glossary from the back of the *Student Text* and the Spanish versions of the Chapter Summaries on an audio disc, which are provided as part of the *Economics: New Ways of Thinking* program. Another way of helping English language learners is to go over all Section Assessment and Chapter Assessment answers orally.

Ask students if it occurred to them before reading this feature that the employers' social security tax burden is actually paid by employees, to some extent. Ask if students think that the way social security is funded should be modified, and discuss any ideas for change that they offer.

ANSWERS TO THINK ABOUT IT Yes, it can. Although the tax is placed fully on the employer (who purchases labor), it affects the demand for labor. And if the demand for labor is affected, the wage rate will be affected too, because the wage rate is determined by both the demand for and the supply of labor. The wage rate is earned by employees (the suppliers of labor), so indirectly, the suppliers of labor are affected by something that initially affected the demand side of the market.

Economics *in the* Real World

Are You Paying Someone Else's Taxes?

Since social security taxes were first collected in 1937, they have been split between the employer and the employee. For example, in 2017, the social security tax rate was 12.4 percent. Half of this tax, or 6.2 percent, was placed on the employer, and the other half was placed on the employee. In other words, the employee was expected to pay $6.20 per $100 of gross earnings (up to a limit), as was the employer.

It's commonly believed that if a tax is placed on someone, then that someone actually pays the tax. However, the *placement* of a tax is different from the *payment* of a tax. Just because the government places a tax on Anderson, it doesn't necessarily follow that Anderson will pay the tax. The same is true for the social security tax. Just because the government places half of the tax on the employer doesn't necessarily mean that the employer will pay the tax.

To better understand this concept, suppose that the social security tax is $2 a day and that $1 of the tax is placed on the

employer and $1 is placed on the employee. An earlier chapter explained that wage rates are determined by supply and demand. For example, the demand for labor and the supply of labor go together to determine the wage rate. Suppose that the equilibrium wage rate before the tax is placed on the employer is $10 an hour.

How will the tax that's placed on the employer affect the employer's demand for labor? The tax will lower the employer's demand for labor. Employers won't want to hire as many employees as they might otherwise, if they have to pay a $1 tax per employee per day.

So, as a result of the social security tax being placed fully on the employer, the demand for labor falls. And if the demand for labor falls and the supply of labor is constant, we know (through our supply-and-demand analysis) that the wage rate will fall—say, from $10 an hour to $9.35 an hour.

Going back to our example, have employees paid for any of the social security tax that was placed on the employer? Yes, they have paid in terms of lower wages. Without the tax, employees' wages would be higher ($10 an hour) than they are with the tax ($9.35 an hour). Some of the social security tax (in our example, 65 cents of the $1 tax) is paid by the employees in the form of lower wages, even though the tax was placed on the employer.

The first moral of the story is this: many people think that the employer pays half of the social security tax and the employee pays the other half when, in fact, the employee ends up paying more than half of the social security tax. The employee pays the employee half of the tax plus some of the tax in the form of employer part of the tax in the form of (earning) lower wages.

And here's the second moral of the story: the legislature can place a tax on anyone it chooses, but it's not the legislature that determines who pays the tax. The laws of economics (in this case, the laws of demand and supply) determine who pays the tax.

THINK ABOUT IT Every market has two sides: a demand side (buying side) and a supply side (selling side). If a tax is placed on one side of the market, can it affect the other side? Explain your answer.

Internet Research

Ask students to use the Internet to find information and additional resources that will enhance their study of this chapter. Direct students to search for sites that provide assistance in filing federal income tax returns and that provide tax advice. Ask them to list the types of services these sites offer and to explain what tax-related concerns people appear to have. Instruct students to locate IRS Form 1040 online and to assess whether they think it would be easy or difficult to prepare their own tax returns. If they have ever filed their own returns, ask what was easy or difficult about doing so.

EXAMPLE Yvonne buys a house. In the state in which she lives, the property tax rate is 1.25 percent of the market price of the house. She paid $300,000 for her house, so her property taxes each year amount to $3,750, or $312.50 a month. ♦

Value-Added Tax

In recent years, some individuals have recommended charging a value-added tax (VAT). Some people propose it as an additional tax. In other words, they want it added to the list of taxes that currently exist and that individuals and firms pay. Others suggest a VAT should replace the sales tax.

What is a **value-added tax**? It is essentially a multistage tax that is collected from firms at each stage in the production process and distribution process. The base of a value-added tax is the *value added* to a good at each state of production.

To illustrate, consider three firms: firm A, a manufacturer; firm B, a wholesaler; and firm C, a retailer. Suppose firm A buys materials and labor and produces a good that it sells to firm B for $700. The value added to the good by firm A is $700. Firm B then distributes the good to firm C for $900. The value added to the good by firm B is $200 (or the difference between what it paid for the good and what it sold the good for). Firm C then sells the good to a consumer for $1,000. The value added by firm C is $100. With a value-added tax in place, each firm is taxed on the value it adds to the good. Firm A is taxed on $700, firm B is taxed on $200, and firm C is taxed on $100. Notice that the total value added ($700 + $200 + $100) is equal to the sales price that the consumer paid for the good ($1,000).

Proportional, Progressive, and Regressive Income Taxes

Income taxes can be proportional, progressive, or regressive. (See Exhibit 14-3.)

Proportional Income Taxation

With a **proportional income tax**, everyone pays taxes at the same rate, whatever his or her income level. For example, if Kuan's taxable income is $100,000, she will pay taxes at the same rate as Arehart, who has a taxable income of $10,000. Suppose this rate is 10 percent. Kuan then pays $10,000 in income taxes, and Arehart pays $1,000 in income taxes. Notice that Kuan, who earns 10 times as much as Arehart, pays 10 times as much in taxes ($10,000 as opposed to $1,000). However, Kuan pays at exactly the same rate—10 percent—as Arehart. Sometimes, a proportional income tax is called a *flat tax*, because everyone pays the same rate. Interestingly enough, many (but not all) of the countries that today have flat tax systems were once communist countries. Exhibit 14-4 provides a list of 8 of the 25 or so countries with flat taxes.

value-added tax
A tax placed on the value added to a good at each stage of production and distribution.

proportional income tax
An income tax that everyone pays at the same rate, whatever his or her income level.

EXHIBIT 14-3 **Three Income Tax Structures**

Proportional	Progressive	Regressive
Same tax rate for every taxpayer. Tax rate remains constant as taxable income rises.	Tax rate rises as taxable income rises.	Tax rate falls as taxable income rises.

▲ Do you think that one of these types of income tax makes more sense or is more nearly fair than the others? If so, explain.

EXHIBIT 14-4 **Selected Countries with a Flat Tax**

Country	Rate
Estonia	21%
Hungary	16
Lithuania	15
Russia	13
Serbia	12
Bosnia and Herzegovina	10
Bulgaria	10
Macedonia	10

▲ A flat tax is the same type of tax as which of the three taxes described in Exhibit 14-3? If the U.S. government switched from its current tax structure to charging a flat tax, would it likely see tax revenues rise, fall, or stay the same? Explain.

Teaching with Visuals

Answers to the question with Exhibit 14-3 will vary.

Teaching with Visuals

A flat tax is the same as a proportional tax. Answers to the question accompanying Exhibit 14-4 will vary. Students might say that tax revenues will fall, because the tax rate will be lower for higher-earning individuals.

Cross-Curricular Activity

Throughout this text, we have discussed the roles and responsibilities of government many times. Opinions differ regarding the degree to which the government should be involved in the economy. You may want to invite a government teacher to your class to provide more insight into this subject.

Then divide your class into two teams. Ask one team to be in favor of more government control and the other team to be opposed. Give teams time to research the issue and to prepare to support their points of view in a debate. Encourage students to use primary source documents and visual aids in support of their arguments. Each team should select two speakers who will represent the team's perspective.

Invite students to discuss their answers to the questions following the 6:04 p.m. scenario in Economics Around the Clock (page 405).

Students may respond that a flat tax is another name for a proportional income tax. A flat, or proportional tax, is one in which all taxpayers pay the same rate no matter what their incomes. For example, the person who earns $1 million a year and the person who earns $50,000 a year will both pay the same tax rate of, say, 18%. Some countries include Estonia, Russia, Serbia, Iraq, Mongolia, and Paraguay. For a complete list see http://econ.emcp.net/flattaxesl.

Reinforcement Activity

Students may not be aware that the United States has a progressive income tax structure. They may not know the percentages for the tax rates and that the amount someone pays is based on his or her yearly taxable income. Ask students to do research to determine the following: the various tax rates; the income ranges associated with the various tax rates; and the tax rates paid by the smallest number and the largest number of Americans. Students can get this information from the Internal Revenue Service and the U.S. Bureau of the Census. The results of their fact-finding activity will provide a good basis for class discussion.

Teaching with Visuals

Exhibit 14-5 shows the number of days a taxpayer has to work to pay his or her taxes. Ask students if they think the time period for most years is too long or too short. Ask them to explain their answers. In what year did taxpayers work the most days to pay their taxes? In what year did they work the fewest days to pay their taxes? (*Answers*: most days – 2016; fewest days – 1900).

progressive income tax
An income tax in which the rate increases as the income level rises. Progressive income tax structures are usually capped at some rate.

regressive income tax
An income tax in which the rate decreases as the income level rises.

▼ This exhibit shows the number of days an average taxpayer has to work to pay his or her taxes in selected years. In 1990, it was 112 days. In 2016, it was 115 days.

Progressive Income Taxation

With a **progressive income tax**, people pay at higher rates as their income levels rise. Suppose that Davidson pays taxes at the rate of 10 percent on a taxable income of $10,000. When his income doubles to $20,000, he pays at a rate of 12 percent. A progressive income tax is usually capped at some tax rate—that is, it rises to some level and then stops rising. For instance, perhaps no one will pay at a tax rate higher than 35 percent, no matter how high his or her income.

The United States has a progressive income tax structure. For example, in 2016, the tax rates were 10, 15, 25, 28, 33, 35, and 39.6 percent.

Regressive Income Taxation

With a **regressive income tax**, people pay taxes at lower rates as their income levels rise. For example, Lowenstein's tax rate is 10 percent when her income is $10,000, and her tax rate is 8 percent when her income rises to $20,000.

EXHIBIT 14-5	How Many Days Do You Have to Work to Pay Your Taxes?	
Year	Number of days spent working to pay all federal, state, and local taxes	Time period
1900	22	January 1–January 22
1920	49	January 1–February 13
1950	91	January 1–March 31
1960	102	January 1–April 11
1990	112	January 1–April 21
2010	99	January 1–April 9
2016	115	January 1–April 24

Source: Tax Foundation.

QUESTION: *I know that the federal income tax in the United States is progressive, but aren't some taxes in this country regressive? Do some taxes "hit" poor people harder than rich people?*

ANSWER: *A state sales tax is an example of a tax that is regressive. To understand this concept, suppose the state sales tax is 6 percent. This means that for every $1 purchase, a person will pay 6 cents in state sales tax. Now suppose that two individuals, A and B, each buy a $1,000 TV. Each will pay a state sales tax of $60. Because A has a larger income than B, A will pay a smaller percentage of his or her income in sales taxes than B will. For example, if his or her income is $5,000 a month and B's income is $3,000 a month, then $60 is 1.2 percent of A's income but 2.0 percent of B's income.*

How Long Do You Have to Work to Pay All Your Taxes?

Individuals, then, pay an assortment of taxes to federal, state, and local governments. How many days each year does the average person have to work to pay all of his or her taxes? It was calculated that if a person began work on January 1, 2016, he or she would have to work until April 24, 2016, before earning enough to pay all taxes owed. Exhibit 14-5 shows how long the average taxpayer had to work to pay taxes in selected years.

We should mention that the number of days a person has to work to pay his or her entire tax bill differs between states, because taxes are higher in some states than in other states. For example, in 2016, in California, a person worked from January 1 until April 30; in Texas, until April 17; in Florida, until April 20; in New Mexico, until April 9; and in New York, until May 11.

Cooperative Learning

Exhibit 14-3 defines proportional, progressive, and regressive income tax structures. Divide the class into three groups, and assign each group one of the tax structures. Each group should research its particular tax structure to find information about where and how this tax structure has been used and how effective it has been. Cap off the activity by encouraging the three groups to debate the merits of the different tax structures.

Would a Soda Tax Cure Obesity?

What is the purpose of taxes? The answer that most people give is, "To pay for certain things provided by the government—such as national defense, roads, and schools."

No doubt, taxes do raise revenues that can be used to pay for goods and services used by the public. But taxes can also be used to influence behavior, and in recent years, some people have advocated using taxes for just that purpose.

To illustrate, in 2009, the Senate Finance Committee proposed a soda tax to raise revenues for health care reform—and to help fight obesity. The soda tax was supposed to apply to every 12-ounce serving of a sugar-sweetened beverage (any drink with added sucrose, or table sugar; high fructose corn syrup; or fruit juice concentrates).

There are two issues to discuss with respect to the soda tax and its possible influence on behavior. The first has to do with whether the tax would actually reduce obesity. The second has to do with whether it's right to use taxes to try to influence behavior.

So, first of all, would a soda tax reduce obesity? It might or it might not. Look at it this way: If a tax is placed on sugar-sweetened soda, the price of sugar-sweetened

soda will rise. As the price rises, individuals will buy less sugar-sweetened soda. And, we would expect, once people drink less sugar-sweetened soda, they will take in fewer calories, and therefore, obesity will become less of a problem.

But wait. Just because the price of sugar-sweetened soda rises, it doesn't necessarily follow that individuals will consume fewer calories. People may drink less sugar-sweetened soda but continue to consume the same amount of sugar. They may simply substitute one sweet product for another.

Remember, as we learned in Chapter 4 that if two goods are substitutes, and the price of one rises, the demand for the other rises. This means that as the price of soda rises, individuals may increase their demand for other sweet products and substitute them for soda. If people consume sugar-sweetened soda partly because it's sweet, then they may simply substitute one sweet product for another. Perhaps they will drink less soda but eat more cake, cookies, or candy.

Charging a soda tax would likely reduce the consumption of soda. However, we can't assume it would reduce the consumption of sweets or lower the number of calories people eat, so we can't assume it would reduce obesity.

The second issue is whether the government should use taxes to try to influence behavior. On this issue, there are definitely two different opinions. Some argue that the government denies citizens a certain degree of liberty or freedom when it gets into the business of using its taxing power to influence behavior. For example, these people might oppose a gasoline tax if the goal is to get the public to drive fewer miles or to buy more fuel-efficient cars.

Others argue that government should use taxes to influence behavior if that behavior is harmful to the person engaging in it or to others. These people might support taxing alcohol because drunk drivers sometimes cause fatal car accidents; taxing fast foods because they are often unhealthful, high-calorie foods that may contribute to serious medical problems; and taxing cigarettes because smoking is strongly tied to lung cancer.

THINK ABOUT IT Should taxes be used to influence behavior? Why or why not? Who or what should decide whether to use taxes to try to influence certain behaviors? Who or what should decide which behaviors to try to influence?

Invite students to suggest other types of behavior that the government might be trying to influence through different types of taxes. Tell students to choose one of those taxes and to do research to find out whether it was in fact intended to change behavior and whether it had the desired effect. Students might work in pairs or groups and present their findings.

ANSWERS TO THINK ABOUT IT Answers will vary.

Do some people work a little less to avoid moving into a higher income group and paying more taxes? To explore this question, invite students to go to http://emcschool.net/Economics2e, select Chapter 14, and read the Economics in the Real World feature titled **"Do Tax Rates Affect Athletic Performance?"** After reading the feature, ask each student to pick a professional athlete and compute his or her approximate federal tax liability for last year.

ANSWERS TO THINK ABOUT IT Answers will vary. Students may believe that a tax rate of 70% might act as a disincentive for these athletes to compete once they have earned $326,450.

Internet Research

Tell students that they will carry out research on regressive taxes. Have each student choose a state and find out that state's sales tax rate. Next, have the student find out whether this rate has increased, decreased, or stayed the same over the last 10 years. The student should provide the reason that the rate has or has not changed during this period. Allow students to present their findings to the class.

Teaching with Visuals

Exhibit 14-6 (page 413) shows which income groups pay the most taxes in the United States. The answers to the questions posed with this exhibit are as follows: The percentage of the total tax bill was higher than the percentage of total income for five groups, or all groups except the bottom 50%. The percentage difference was greatest for the top 5%.

It might help students understand the figures if you change some of the percentages to fractions. For example, the top 1% pays over ⅓ of the taxes, and the top 5% pays over ½ of the taxes. You might also create a pie chart with this information to help students get a visual understanding of the information.

Application Activity

After reading and discussing Section 1, you may want to assign the Section Activity in the *Applying the Principles Workbook*, pages 147–148.

Economics Around the Clock

You may want to refer students to the 5:30 p.m. scenario in Economics Around the Clock (page 405) and discuss their answers to the question that follows it.

Refer students to Exhibit 14-6 on the following page. Note that if we define the rich as the top 1% of income earners, we can see that the top 1% pays 39.48% of the federal income taxes. The top 50% covers 97% of the federal income taxes.

Reteaching Activity

Use the Section Assessment to gauge which students may need reteaching on this section. Ask those students to list and describe the three major federal taxes.

EXAMPLE The average worker puts in about 35 hours a week, 49 weeks a year, or about 1,715 hours a year. How many of those hours are spent working to earn enough money to pay his or her total tax bill (for the year)? The answer is about 490 hours, or slightly more than 28 percent of all working hours. Or you can look at it this way: If you start work at 9 a.m. each day, take an hour for lunch, and leave work at 5 p.m., you work from 9 a.m. to a few minutes before 11 a.m. to pay your taxes. After 11 a.m., what you earn is yours. ◆

Who Pays What Percentage of Federal Income Taxes?

Do wealthy Americans pay their fair share of taxes? Polls taken in the United States indicate that most people think the wealthy do not pay their fair share.

Several issues are important in the discussion of taxes and the shares paid by different income groups. First, it's important to explain what we mean by "wealthy Americans." Are wealthy Americans those persons in the top 1 percent of income earners, the top 5 percent, or the top 10 percent?

Second, it's important to explain what we mean by a "fair share" of taxes. For example, is it unfair if wealthy Americans pay only 5 percent of all federal income taxes but fair if they pay 20 percent?

Third, it's important to get some idea of what wealthy Americans pay in taxes compared with what they earn in income. Let's compare tax data for people in different income groups. (See Exhibit 14-6.) How does each group's share of income compare with its share of taxes? Do you notice a pattern in the average tax rates for the different groups? After studying the data, do you have an opinion about whether the wealthy pay their fair share of the total income tax?

▶ Property tax is a tax on the value of private property, such as a house or condominium.

Invite an American history teacher from your school to the class to discuss how taxation has affected various groups in society during the nation's history. Make sure she or he touches on the history of the income tax—why it was considered necessary and how people reacted to it. After the history teacher has presented the historical facts, you can connect these facts to economic realities by using charts to show how tax rates have changed throughout U.S. history.

EXHIBIT 14-6 Federal Individual Income Tax Categories

Income group	Income split point	Group's share of total U.S. income	Group's share of federal income taxes
Top 1%	above $465,626	20.58%	39.48%
Top 5%	above $188,996	35.96%	59.97%
Top 10%	above $133,445	47.21%	70.88%
Top 25%	above $ 77,714	68.91%	86.78%
Top 50%	above $ 38,173	88.73%	97.25%
Bottom 50%	below $ 38,173	11.27%	2.75%

Source: Internal Revenue Service, 2016.

▲ This exhibit compares the percentages of income earned to the percentages of taxes paid by selected income groups in 2014. *Income split point* (second column) is simply a term for the amount of income a person had to earn to be in a particular group. For example, a person had to earn *at least* $465,626 to be in the top 1% of earners. For how many groups was the percentage of the total tax bill higher than the percentage of total income? For which group was this percentage difference the greatest?

SECTION 1 ASSESSMENT

Defining Terms

1. Define
   a. value-added tax
   b. proportional income tax
   c. progressive income tax
   d. regressive income tax

Reviewing Facts and Concepts

2. What three federal taxes together account for approximately 91 percent of federal government tax revenues?

3. Which federal tax raises the greatest tax revenues?

4. How many days of the year did the average taxpayer work in 2013 to pay all of his or her taxes?

Critical Thinking

5. "It is possible for a high-income earner to pay more in taxes than a low-income earner under a regressive income tax." Do you agree or disagree? Explain your answer.

6. Give an example to illustrate the difference between "paying more in taxes" and "paying a higher tax rate."

Applying Economic Concepts

7. Is a sales tax regressive, proportional, or progressive? Explain your answer.

Section 1 Taxes **413**

SECTION 1 ASSESSMENT ANSWERS

Defining Terms

1. a. value-added tax: a tax placed on the value added to a good at each stage of production and distribution; **b. proportional income tax:** an income tax that everyone pays at the same rate, whatever his or her income level; **c. progressive income tax:** an income tax in which the rate increases as the income level rises; **d. regressive income tax:** an income tax in which the rate decreases as the income level rises.

Reviewing Facts and Concepts

2. Personal income tax, corporate income tax, and social security tax account for 93% of federal tax revenues.

3. According to Exhibit 14-2, the personal income tax raises the greatest revenues.

4. In 2016, the average taxpayer worked 115 days to pay all his

Assess

Quick Quiz

The following true-or-false quiz will help you assess student understanding of the material covered in this section.

1. There are five major taxes at the federal government level. (False)
2. The federal government applies an excise tax on some items. (True)
3. The regressive income tax is a tax that everyone pays on top of his or her regular income tax. (False)
4. With a proportional income tax, everyone pays at the same rate. (True)

Assessment Book

You will find a quiz for this section in the *Assessment Book*, page 141.

Guided Reading

For further reteaching of the key concepts in this section, assign the Outlining Activity and the Just the Facts Handout from the *Guided Reading and Study Guide*, pages 243–246.

or her taxes. That's 31.5% of 365 days (1 year).

Critical Thinking

5. Agree. Under a regressive income tax, a person's tax rate goes down as his or her income rises, but it's still possible for a high-income earner to pay more in taxes than a low-income earner. Suppose the tax rate for a person who earns $10,000 is 10%, and the tax rate for a person who earns $100,000 is 5%. The person with the lower income pays $1,000 in taxes, and the person with the higher income pays $5,000 in taxes.

6. *Sample answer:* Smith pays more in taxes if he pays $400 and Jones pays $140. Smith pays a higher tax rate if he pays 20 percent of every dollar he earns and Jones pays 10 percent.

Applying Economic Concepts

7. A sales tax is regressive. Consider two people, Smith and Jones. Smith earns $10,000 a year, and Jones earns $100,000 a year. Both Smith and Jones buy good X for $40. The sales tax is $5, which is a larger percentage of Smith's income than Jones's income, so it's regressive.

Discussion Starter

Ask volunteers to describe their experiences in preparing and filing federal income tax returns. (You might want to make clear to students that they do not have to volunteer this information.) Ask, Did you prepare the return yourself, or did you ask for the assistance of a tax preparer, accountant, or other adult? Did you use tax software? How did the difficulty of completing the form compare with the difficulty of taking an economics test?

Research Activity

Instruct each student to conduct an opinion poll on whether federal income tax forms are too complex. The student should survey several adults to learn both opinions and reasons for them. Students may want to search the Internet to learn about other people's opinions on this issue. Ask students to compile their data and then report back to the class.

Your **Personal** Economics

Filing an Income Tax Return

If you haven't already, you will soon have to file an annual federal income tax return. Is it hard to do? In most cases, it isn't hard at all. You have taken numerous tests in high school that are much harder than filing a tax return.

How should you proceed? New software programs are available for you to use, or you can complete your tax return yourself. Even if you use the software, make sure you understand the process behind filing your return.

An Overview

Let's look at the big picture of what you will be doing. First, you will identify all of the income you earned in a given year. Let's say this amount is $50,000. Second, you subtract certain dollar items from this $50,000. These items come with different names: *exemptions*, *deductions*, *adjustments*. Third, you end up with a certain dollar amount of taxable income. Let's say this amount is $40,000. Fourth, you simply consult an IRS tax table to see how much you are supposed to pay in taxes based on this taxable income.

Following these simple steps is really all there is to it. Filing a tax return involves using a little addition and subtraction and consulting one (fairly simple) tax table.

The Step-by-Step Process

Now let's outline the steps in more detail:

1. Gather together all of your tax documents. They include things such as your W2 statement (a form you receive from your employer stating how much you earned during the year).
2. Most likely, for the first several years that you file, you will be able to use Form 1040EZ, which is the simplest form. You can use this form if you earned less than $100,000 during the year, don't plan to claim any dependents (anyone who depends on you for some support), and have interest

income of $1,500 or less. If you are unsure of which form to file, go to http://econ.emcp.net/IRS_formstofile.
3. Go to http://econ.emcp.net/IRS_pubs and print one or two copies of the 1040 form.
4. Start filling out the form. Take things slowly, line by line.
5. You need to determine your filing status. You must file as one of the following: single person, head of household, qualifying widow, married filing jointly, or married filing separately.
6. You next claim an exemption for yourself and for any dependents you may have. You cannot claim a personal exemption for yourself if anyone, such as a parent or guardian, has claimed you as a dependent.
7. You must state the amount of income you earned in the last year. Refer to your W2 form. It identifies the dollar amount of income you earned working at your job.
8. You may also list certain adjustments to your income. These adjustments include expenses you had over the year (moving expenses, tuition and fees deduction, health savings account deductions, and more) that will lower your taxable income and thus reduce the amount of taxes you must pay.
9. You may take the standard deduction (which is something else that will lower your taxable income). The amount of the

Cooperative Learning

Divide students into groups of four or five. Assign each group a different portion of IRS Form 1040. Instruct each group to look for places in the form that might be difficult for taxpayers to understand. Ask each group what kind of information

the IRS is looking for in that portion of the form. Allow each group to make a presentation to the class, explaining the portion of Form 1040 it was assigned.

standard deduction you take depends on your filing status.

10. If you don't take the standard deduction, you may take certain itemized deductions instead. Like exemptions, adjustments, and the standard deduction, itemized deductions lower your taxable income and thus lower the amount of taxes you must pay.

11. At this point, add up all of your exemptions, deductions, and adjustments and subtract this total from your total income. The amount that's left is your taxable income.

12. To figure out how much you have to pay in taxes, consult a tax table. Tax tables can be found at http://econ.emcp.net/taxtables or in the tax booklet that you received from the IRS. The table shown at the right was for a single person filing in 2016. Using a tax table, you can figure out your tax liability. For example, suppose your taxable income in 2016 is $75,150. Your taxable income falls between $37,651 and $91,150 so that you would pay $5,183.75 plus 25 percent of the amount over $37,650. The difference between $75,150 and $37,650 is $37,500 and 25 percent of this is $9,375. If we add this amount to $5,183.75 we get $14,558.75, which is the total dollar amount of income taxes you would pay.

13. It's also likely that you paid taxes throughout the year. You have probably noticed that a certain amount of money is deducted from each paycheck to pay federal income taxes.

Let's say the total amount of taxes deducted from your paychecks over the year was $10,000. Because you had already paid $10,000 of the $14,558.75 you owed in taxes, you would need to write out a check to the IRS for $4,558.75.

14. If, by chance, the total amount of taxes deducted from your paychecks over the year was $15,000, then you paid more in taxes than you owed. You

would be entitled to a tax refund of $441.25.

15. Finally, you can file your tax return over the phone, online, or via regular mail.

Your Personal Economics Activity

Taxes exist on the federal, state, and local level. Write an essay that identifies the economic importance of income taxes and how you benefit. Support your work with logical reasoning.

Taxable Income	Tax Rate
$0–$9,275	10%
$9,276–$37,650	$927.50 plus 15% of the amount over $9,275
$37,651–$91,150	$5,183.75 plus 25% of the amount over $37,650
$91,151–$190,150	$18,558.75 plus 28% of the amount over $91,150
$190,151–$413,350	$46,278.75 plus 33% of the amount over $190,150
$413,351–$415,050	$119,934.75 plus 35% of the amount over $413,350
$415,051– or more	$120,529.75 plus 39.6% of the amount over $415,050

Source: Internal Revenue Service.

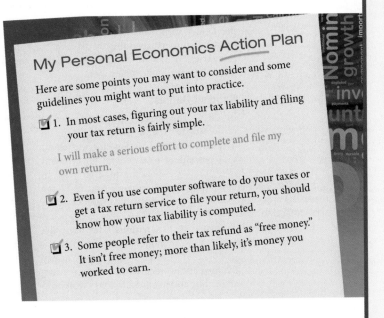

My Personal Economics Action Plan

Here are some points you may want to consider and some guidelines you might want to put into practice.

☑ 1. In most cases, figuring out your tax liability and filing your tax return is fairly simple.

I will make a serious effort to complete and file my own return.

☑ 2. Even if you use computer software to do your taxes or get a tax return service to file your return, you should know how your tax liability is computed.

☑ 3. Some people refer to their tax refund as "free money." It isn't free money; more than likely, it's money you worked to earn.

Discussion Starter

Remind students that when they work as employees, taxes will be taken out of their paychecks. If they are self-employed, taxes won't be taken out, but they will have to make quarterly payments to the federal government (assuming they earn more than a certain amount). Ask students why they think the government requires taxpayers to pay so far in advance of April 15, the day tax returns must be postmarked. Ask, What might be the downsides to paying taxes in advance? What might be the benefits to taxpayers and to the federal government?

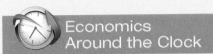 **My Personal Economics Action Plan** Lead students in brainstorming ways to prepare for paying federal income taxes. Ask students to consider the pros and cons of using tax software versus retaining the services of a tax professional. Ask students to suggest ways they might save money on their federal income taxes.

Economics Around the Clock

After students have read the information in the table, refer them to the 7:16 p.m. scenario in the Economics Around the Clock (page 405). Refer students to the table on this page to identify the highest federal income tax rate. The highest rate is 39.6% and applies to those with a taxable income over $400,000.

Teacher Support

Focus and Motivate

Section Objectives

After completing this section, students will be able to

▶ describe how the federal government spends its tax revenues;

▶ define the terms *balanced budget, budget deficit,* and *budget surplus;*

▶ explain the relationship between a budget deficit and the national debt; and

▶ identify some of the issues connected with budget surpluses.

Economics Around the Clock

Kickoff Activity

Direct students to read the 5:32 p.m. scenario in Economics Around the Clock (page 405) and to think about the question it asks.

Tell students that approximately one-fifth of the federal budget is devoted to defense and homeland security. Ask students to suggest reasons for this level of defense spending and to evaluate whether it's appropriate. In 2013, $675 billion was the projected spending on national defense.

Activating Prior Knowledge

Take time to have student volunteers share their responses to the Kickoff Activity. Tell them they will learn more about how the federal government allocates funds as they study this section.

Visit econ.myemcp.com/videos for videos that will help students better understand the key concepts found in this section.

The Budget: Deficits and Debt

Focus Questions

▶ How does the federal government spend its tax revenues?

▶ What is a balanced budget? A budget deficit? A budget surplus?

▶ What is the relationship between a budget deficit and the national debt?

▶ What are some issues connected with budget surpluses?

Key Terms

national debt
budget deficit
budget surplus

How Does the Federal Government Spend Money?

In 2016, the federal government was projected to spend $3,854 billion. How was this money spent? The federal government breaks down its spending according to categories, a few of which are briefly discussed on the following pages.

National Defense

In 2016, the federal government was projected to spend $595.3 billion on national defense. This amount was about 15.4 percent of total federal government spending for that year. In other words, out of $1 the federal government spent in 2016, 15.4 cents went to national defense. The money allocated to national defense goes mostly to pay the men and women in the armed services and to buy and maintain military weapons.

"It's a billion here and a billion there; the first thing you know it adds up to real money."
—Everett Dirksen, U.S. Senator (1951–1969)

Income Security

The term *income security* refers to government programs that provide assistance to people in need: for instance, low-income housing and food stamps for people who are poor; unemployment compensation for people who have lost their jobs; nutrition and education programs for children from disadvantaged backgrounds; payments to disabled federal employees; and so on. The federal government was projected to spend $514.6 billion on income security in 2016. This was approximately 13.3 percent of total federal government spending.

Social Security

The federal government was projected to spend $916.1 billion in 2016 on social security payments, which go mainly to retired persons. These payments were about 23.6 percent of total federal government spending.

Background Information: Social Security and Retirement

Students might question the importance of social security taxes, believing that they're too young to think about retirement. Tell them that during the past several years, however, there has been some concern about whether social security will run out of money or offer decreased benefits in the future. Most people agree that social security will still exist in the future but that the program may be changed.

Guide students to realize that in thinking about retirement, they should view social security as part of but not all of their income. They need to begin setting aside other funds to ensure having enough retirement income.

◀ Many of these senior citizens likely participate in the federal government's Medicare program. In 2016, the federal government spent $594.5 billion on Medicare.

Medicare

In 2016, the federal government was projected to spend $594.5 billion on Medicare, which is hospital and medical insurance for social security beneficiaries. This amount was 13.72 percent of total federal government spending.

Net Interest on the National Debt

When the government spends more money than it receives in tax revenues, it is said to "run a budget deficit." For example, if the government spends $3,000 billion and tax revenues are $2,800 billion, the budget deficit is $200 billion. The government has to borrow the $200 billion, in much the same way that people have to borrow money if their expenditures are greater than their incomes.

The federal government has borrowed a lot money over the years. On September 16, 2017, its total debt—referred to as the **national debt**—was $20.16 trillion. If you want to find out what the national debt is today, go to http://econ.emcp.net/nationaldebt. This website will show you the national debt to the penny for any date you enter.

The federal government has to pay interest on this debt, in much the same way that people have to make interest payments on their credit card bills (such as Visa and

MasterCard). In 2016, the interest payment the government had to make on the national debt was approximately $240.7 billion, or 6.2 percent of total federal government spending.

If we add up the amounts spent on national defense, income security, social security, Medicare, and the national debt, we will have accounted for 74.23 percent of all federal government spending. Just looking at spending on national defense and social security (plus Medicare) accounts for over half of all federal spending, or a total of 54.6 percent.

Exhibit 14-7 shows projected federal government spending for 2018–2023.

national debt
The total amount the federal government owes its creditors.

EXHIBIT 14-7	Projected Federal Government Spending, 2018–2023

Year	Projected spending (billions of dollars)
2018	$4,091
2019	4,334
2020	4,562
2021	4,816
2022	5,135
2023	5,346

Source: Congressional Budget Office, 2017.

Discussion Starter

In this section. students learn about the major categories of federal government spending. Ask students if they would allocate tax dollars differently and if so, why. Make it clear that there is no incorrect point of view and that differences in opinion are welcome.

Reinforcement Activity

Allow students to work in groups of four or five to learn about last year's national debt. Ask students to explore questions like these: What was the total dollar amount of the national debt? How did it rank historically with national debts of previous years? Why is the debt so large? Allow the groups to present their findings to the class.

Teaching with Visuals

As students look at Exhibit 14-7, ask them where the money for increased government spending will come from. (*Answer:* The money will come from tax revenues.) Do students think this means that taxes will go up? Why or why not?

Help students understand that even without raising taxes, the government receives more tax revenues in years when the U.S. economy is strong.

Background Information: Medicare

Medicare, which is the nation's largest health insurance program, is administered by the Centers for Medicare and Medicaid Services, which is part of the Department of Health and Human Services. Medicare provides insurance coverage for millions of Americans. In addition to insuring social security beneficiaries aged 65 and older, Medicare also provides for some people with disabilities under age 65 and for people with permanent kidney failure who are treated with dialysis or a transplant. To be eligible for Medicare, a person or his or her spouse must have worked for at least 10 years in Medicare-covered employment and be a citizen or permanent resident of the United States.

Taxing Peter to Pay Paul

We usually think of the act of spending money like this: someone takes money out of his or her pocket or bank account and uses it to buy some item—say, $20 for a book or $25,000 for a car. When it comes to government spending, though, things work somewhat differently.

Consider two examples of government spending. In the first, the government takes $10 million and buys some military equipment. In the second, the government taxes Peter $400 and then takes the money and gives it to Paul.

You might think that the second example isn't really government spending but rather *redistribution*: taxing one person and then turning the money over to another person. However, redistribution is considered an act of government spending. In fact, much of government spending today is redistributive.

The Costs and Benefits of Government Spending Programs

According to economists, a government spending program isn't worth pursuing unless the benefits of that program outweigh the costs. In other words, if the program generates $100 billion in benefits and costs $40 billion, then there is $60 billion in net benefits. This program is worth pursuing.

In reality, though, things don't always turn out this way. Sometimes, spending programs that have greater costs than benefits get passed in Congress. Why?

Let's look at an example. Five people, A–E, are represented in the table below:

Person	Benefit	Cost	Vote
A	$130	$100	Yes
B	120	100	Yes
C	102	100	Yes
D	50	100	No
E	10	100	No

Suppose these people are considering buying a statue for their town square, the total cost of which is $500. They have agreed that if they decide to buy the statue, they will split the cost equally, each member paying $100. Then they take a vote on whether to buy the statue.

How will each person vote? Each person has to compare his or her personal benefit from the statue to his or her personal cost. In this case, individuals' costs are all the same—$100. But to determine the benefit, each person must place a dollar value on what he or she thinks the benefit of having the statue is worth. This dollar amount is essentially what the person is willing to pay for the statue. If the person's benefit is greater than the cost, the person will vote yes for the statue; if the person's benefit is less than the cost, the person will vote no.

As you can see in the table, persons A, B, and C vote yes for the statue because for each of them, the benefit is greater than the cost. Persons D and E vote no because for each of them, the benefit is less than the cost; neither person believes he or she will receive $100 worth of benefit from the statue.

Having more yes votes (3) than no votes (2) means the community of five persons will buy the statue. Notice one thing, however: the total benefits to the community of five persons are less than the total costs to the community of five persons. Even though the total benefits ($412) are less than the total costs ($500), the community buys the statue.

On a personal level, you would never buy anything if the personal benefit to you was less than the personal cost. However, the government buys things every day for which the total benefits are less than the total costs, because its purchasing decisions are based on voting. And voting, as we have just shown, can lead to making purchases even when the total benefits are less than the total costs.

The Budget Process

Just as individuals may have budgets, in which they specify how they will spend their incomes—such as $300 a month for food and $100 a month for clothes—so does the federal government have a budget. In the federal budget, the federal government specifies how it will spend the money it has. It may decide to spend $250 billion on national defense, $100 billion on health care, and so on.

Cooperative Learning

Divide the class into groups, and ask each group to discuss how things might be different if there were no national debt. Ask groups to decide how they would spend an extra $12.59 trillion if they were the government. Would they spend it on education or on programs to help people who are poor? Would they return the money to the taxpayers to spend as they saw fit? Each group should itemize how it would redistribute the money and draw up a chart showing its spending plan. Then a representative from each group should present the group's ideas to the class.

Would We All Be Better Off Without Show-Offs?

Thorstein Veblen (1857–1929), an American economist, believed that people sometimes buy goods for the wrong reasons. He coined the term *conspicuous consumption*—that is, purchasing designed to show off or display one's status.

Consider the fact that today, you can buy several different makes of watches, two of which are a Timex and a Rolex. A Timex costs under $100, and a Rolex costs many thousands of dollars. Both brands of watches keep good time, but the Rolex does something else: it shows that you have the money to buy something expensive. In other words, a Rolex is a status symbol.

Does U.S. culture today promote status? Some economists believe that it does. The race for status, these economists contend, is a relative race and is wasteful.

Some economists argue that the race for status comes with certain opportunity costs, one of which is lost leisure. If we try to leapfrog each other, we work harder and longer to achieve a position that we could all achieve at a lower cost.

Another opportunity cost of the race for status may be that

society must do without certain goods that it wants. For example, suppose society wants the government to spend more money on medical research, education, and infrastructure. Currently, three individuals—A, B, and C—are locked into a race for status with the other two. A is richer than B, and B is richer than C, so A can buy more status goods (big houses, fancy cars, and so on) than B, who can buy more status goods than C.

Suppose the government proposes a 10 percent tax increase for each individual. A, B, and C argue against the higher tax rate, because it reduces their ability to buy status goods. They fail to realize, however, that even though paying higher taxes will reduce how much money they can spend on status goods, their relative positions in the race for status will not change. After the higher taxes have been paid, A will still have a higher after-tax income than B, who will have a higher after-tax income than C. Paying higher taxes won't

stop the race for status, nor will it prevent anyone from showing off. Paying higher taxes simply reduces the amount of money the individuals can spend in their race to show off.

Are any benefits derived from the higher taxes? According to some economists, the additional tax revenues can finance more medical research, education, and infrastructure. Thus, slowing down the race for status does produce some benefits.

One criticism of this reasoning is that the additional tax funds may not be used how people want them to be used. The funds may go for "public conspicuous consumption," such as expensive federal buildings and public art displays. Critics also point out that paying higher taxes reduces people's incentives to produce, which may lead to less economic growth and wealth in the future. Finally, critics point out that if the race for status is hobbled by higher taxes, the race will not slow down; it will simply take a different form. Instead of competing for status in terms of having goods, people will compete for status in terms of having power over others. In the end, critics argue, it may be better to have people compete over goods than over control.

THINK ABOUT IT Do people in your high school try to achieve status by purchasing certain goods? If so, what goods?

Before discussing this Economics in the Real World feature, ask students what the expression "keeping up with the Joneses" means. If students have not heard this expression, encourage them to ask parents or other adults the following questions about it: What does it mean? Is it intended as a compliment? Then discuss with students how the phrase relates to the topic of this feature.

ANSWERS TO THINK ABOUT IT Answers will vary. Students might mention certain types of clothing or shoes, electronic equipment such as MP3 players and video games, and even cars.

Internet Research

Have students locate websites that discuss the federal budget and online news articles that present politicians' views on how federal funds should be spent. Instruct students to read the articles for answers to these questions: What ideas are proposed? What are the general political leanings of the different groups that support various

proposals? Ask students to keep track of the proposals supported mostly by Democrats, those supported mostly by Republicans, and those supported mostly by other political parties. Hold a class debate in which students argue the pros and cons of one proposal for change.

Some countries have high taxes, and other countries have low taxes. For example, in the late 1990s, taxes in Singapore, Switzerland, Ireland, Chile, Ecuador, and the United States were relatively low compared with taxes in Finland, Denmark, Portugal, Greece, and Syria. Generally, economists find that countries with relatively low taxes experience more rapid economic growth than countries with relatively high taxes. However, countries with relatively high taxes often provide their residents with more government services.

Teaching with Visuals

Answers will vary.

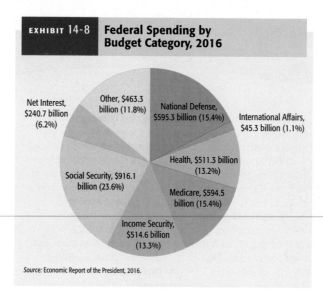

EXHIBIT 14-8   Federal Spending by Budget Category, 2016

- Net Interest, $240.7 billion (6.2%)
- Other, $463.3 billion (11.8%)
- National Defense, $595.3 billion (15.4%)
- International Affairs, $45.3 billion (1.1%)
- Health, $511.3 billion (13.2%)
- Medicare, $594.5 billion (15.4%)
- Social Security, $916.1 billion (23.6%)
- Income Security, $514.6 billion (13.3%)

Source: Economic Report of the President, 2016.

▲ For the 2016 federal budget, government spending totaled $3,881.1 billion. Major categories of spending are shown in this pie chart. Notice that 15.4% of the budget was for national defense. Do you agree with the decision to spend that percentage on defense? Explain your answer.

It Begins with the President

Preparing a budget and passing it into law is a long process. It begins with the president of the United States, who, with others in the executive branch of the government, prepares the budget. The president's budget recommends to Congress how much should be spent for things such as national defense and income security programs. (See Exhibit 14-8.) The president must submit the budget to Congress by the first Monday in February of each year.

Disagreements and Compromises

Once the president's budget is in the hands of Congress, it is scrutinized by the members of many congressional committees and subcommittees. The Congressional Budget Office advises committee and subcommittee members about technical details of the president's budget.

Members of Congress may disagree with the president about how money should be spent. For example, the president may want to spend more money for health care than do many members of Congress.

Disagreements may also arise over the amount of tax revenues likely to be raised over the next few months. Perhaps the president estimated that the federal government will take in $2,900 billion in tax revenues, but Congress estimated tax revenues to be $3,100 billion. Both the executive and legislative branches must estimate tax revenues, because no one knows for sure how the economy will perform. For example, if the economy is sluggish and many millions of people are out of work, less income is earned, and thus income taxes will be down. Many details of the president's budget may be changed to reflect compromises between the president and Congress.

Public Opinion Counts

Where are the American people in the budget process? Do they have a role to play? Once the president submits a budget to Congress, the people get a chance to hear about it. Usually, numerous newspaper articles and newscasts cover the president's proposals. The American people can write to or call their congresspersons and express what they would like to see in the president's budget. Also during this time, special-interest groups may lobby members of Congress and express their preferences for the president's budget.

The Budget Becomes Law

Congress is obligated to pass a budget by the beginning of the fiscal year, not the calendar year. (The calendar year begins on January 1 and runs through December 31; a fiscal year can begin on the first day of another month and run for the next 12 months. The fiscal year under which the federal government operates begins on October 1 and runs through September 30.) Once Congress passes the budget, the details of spending outlined in the budget become law for that fiscal year. Then, the whole process begins again in only a few months.

What Is a Fair Share?

Most people say that it's only right for everyone to pay his or her fair share of taxes. The problem is, how do we decide what a fair share is? And who decides? Historically, two principles of taxation touch on this issue: the benefits-received principle and the ability-to-pay principle.

Background Information: The President

Students have already learned that the president is responsible for preparing the nation's annual budget. But do they know that the president is also looked on as being the nation's economic leader? The public, Congress, and the business and labor communities look increasingly to the president to lower unemployment, fight inflation, keep down taxes, and promote economic growth.

The Employment Act of 1946 established the Council of Economic Advisors to give the president economic advice. Ask students how they think the current president is doing as the nation's economic leader and whether the president seems to be getting good advice from the Council of Economic Advisors.

Splitting the Check: Do You Order Lobster or a Hamburger?

Suppose you and five friends go out to dinner. In setting A, you and your friends agree to pay for your own meals. If you have lobster for dinner, you pay for lobster. If you have a hamburger for dinner, you pay for the hamburger. The same holds for your friends. In setting B, you and your friends agree to split the bill evenly. If the total bill comes to $150, then you split this bill six ways ($25 each).

Now, in which of the two settings, A or B, do you think (1) you will order more expensive food and (2) the total bill will be higher? Will you order a more expensive meal when you have to pay for what you order or when you pay one-sixth of what everyone orders? Also, will the total bill will be greater when everyone pays for what he or she ordered or when everyone pays an equal share?

We might think that a person would order the same meal in both settings, and so the total bill would be the same in both settings. However, some evidence indicates that people seem to buy more expensive things (food, clothes,

and so on) when they believe they are paying only a fraction of the cost.

Think of it this way: If you are considering the lobster and you know that you will have to pay for it, you consider the full price of the lobster—say, $35. If, however, you agree to split the bill, then the price (to you) of purchasing lobster is not $35 but one-sixth of $35, which is $5.83. Few people will choose the lobster at a price of $35, but many will at $5.83.

What holds for you holds for everyone at the dinner table. Because splitting the bill causes the items on the menu to appear cheaper (for each individual), each individual is more likely to buy an expensive meal. But if everyone buys a meal he or she wouldn't likely buy if paying the full price, the total bill for the dinner is likely to be high indeed.

Understanding individuals' behavior in these two different settings goes a long way toward explaining why government spending can zoom upward quickly. As you saw in Exhibit 14-7 on page 417, projected federal government spending in 2018 was $4,091 billion. But the people who lobby government for the various benefits it provides aren't paying for all of the benefits they receive.

For example, let's say that the farmers ask Congress for

subsidies. If Congress and the president agree to the subsidies, the taxpayers will have to foot the bill. Of course, farmers are taxpayers, so they will have to pay for some of the benefits they receive. But in the end, they will pay only for a fraction of the benefits they receive in a country with more than 100 million taxpayers. For the farmers, this is like going to dinner with 100 million people at the table, all of whom have agreed to split the check.

If 100 million people are going to split the check, then anything you order is going to be cheap! What does the lobster cost now? Dessert? I'll have 15.

In politics, almost everyone has an incentive to order big off the government "menu." And we know that if everyone does order big, the total "dinner" bill is going to be huge.

THINK ABOUT IT Why do people sometimes agree to split the check evenly rather than pay for exactly what they order? Does splitting the check result in having a higher total?

Ask students to think of other areas of government spending that benefit a particular group at the expense of the broad base of taxpayers. Encourage them to consider positive aspects of these situations, as well as negative aspects. For example, few of us have ever heard of Jumping Frenchmen of Maine, a rare disorder that causes an extreme reaction to unexpected noises or sights. Without government funds, it is unlikely that the very small percentage of the population suffering this condition would find the resources to search for a treatment or cure.

ANSWERS TO THINK ABOUT IT Answers will vary. Students might say that diners who are in a hurry will tend to agree to split the check evenly rather than take the time after the meal to identify each person's charges on the bill. Some might think that if people agree before the meal to split the bill, the total might be higher because people will feel more comfortable ordering expensive items knowing that the total will be divided evenly among everyone. Others might think the opposite—that people will want to be sure no one is overburdened by the cost of the meal, and will therefore order a less expensive meal in an effort to keep the total down.

Cooperative Learning

In many countries, the governments in power have had to take severe steps to curb runaway inflation, help decrease unemployment, and stabilize the economy. Divide the class into groups of three to four students. Have each group pick one of the following countries, in which this has occurred:

Argentina, Ecuador, Zimbabwe, or Germany following World War I. Ask each group to prepare a brief oral report outlining the government's actions to stabilize the country's economy and what the political, social, and economic results were.

People who drive on roads and highways often pay gas taxes, which are used to provide and maintain the roads.

budget deficit
The situation in which federal government expenditures are greater than federal government tax revenues.

budget surplus
The situation in which federal government expenditures are less than federal government tax revenues.

Benefits-Received Principle

The benefits-received principle holds that a person should pay in taxes an amount equal to the benefits he or she receives from government expenditures. For example, if you drive often on government-provided roads and highways, you should pay for the building and maintaining them. This goal is usually met through the excise tax on gasoline. People who drive a lot buy a lot of gas, so they pay more in gas taxes than people who drive only a little. Because gas tax revenues are used for the upkeep of the roads, the major users of the roads end up paying the bulk of these costs.

Ability-to-Pay Principle

With some government-provided goods, it's easy to figure out roughly how much someone benefits. For instance, in the roads-and-highways example, we can assume that the more a person drives on a road or highway, the more benefit he or she obtains from it.

With other government-provided goods, however, it isn't as easy to relate benefits received to taxes paid. For example, we could say that almost all Americans benefit from national defense, but we would have a hard time figuring out how much one person benefits compared to another person. Does Jackson, down the street, benefit more than, less than, or the same as Paul, who lives up the street? The benefits-received principle is hard to implement in such cases.

Often, the ability-to-pay principle is used instead. This principle says that people should pay taxes according to their abilities to pay. Because a rich person is more able to pay taxes than a poor person, a rich person should pay more taxes than a poor person. For example, a millionaire might pay $330,000 a year in income taxes, whereas a person who earns $50,000 a year might pay $8,000.

Budgets: Balanced and in Deficit

Adam Smith, the eighteenth century economist, said, "What is prudence in the conduct of every private family, can scarce be folly in that of a great kingdom." In other words, if it is right and reasonable for a family to do something, it is probably also right and reasonable for a great nation to do the same. So, if it is right for a family to save and avoid debt, then it is right for a nation to do the same.

For many years, this notion carried over to the discussions of U.S. federal budget policy. Most people believed that the federal budget should be balanced—that is, government expenditures should be equal to tax revenues. A **budget deficit**, which occurs when government expenditures exceed tax revenues, was acceptable but only during wartime. (As an aside, a **budget surplus** exists if tax revenues exceed government expenditures.)

The Great Depression

People's thinking began to change around the time of the Great Depression, a period of great economic distress in this country from 1929 to the early 1940s. During this time, unemployment skyrocketed, the production

Cross-Curricular Activity

Invite students to brainstorm questions about the history of, political implications of, and controversy about taxation according to the "benefits-received" and "ability-to-pay" principles. Then invite a history teacher and a government teacher to join you in a panel discussion in which you answer students' questions. Give the other teachers copies of the questions in advance so they can research answers to them.

▲ We would expect that the people living in the houses on the left are more able to pay taxes than the people living in the apartments on the right. Do you think the people living in the more expensive housing should have to pay a higher percentage of their income in taxes? Why or why not?

Teaching with Visuals

Answers will vary.

of goods and services plummeted, prices fell, banks closed, and companies went bankrupt.

Until this time, many people in the United States thought that free enterprise was a stable, smooth mechanism. The economic downturn of the Great Depression gave these people cause for doubt, however, and many previously accepted ideas of budget policy were slowly discarded. One idea in particular that fell by the wayside was that the federal budget should be balanced. People began to accept a budget deficit as a way of reducing unemployment.

Reducing Unemployment

What does a budget deficit have to do with reducing unemployment? Suppose the federal budget is balanced. Government spending is $2 trillion, and tax revenues are $2 trillion. However, unemployment is high—say, about 10 percent. The president, along with Congress, wants to reduce the unemployment rate by implementing expansionary fiscal policy (increase government spending or decrease taxes). Together, they decide to increase government spending to $2.2 trillion. Tax revenues, we'll assume, will remain constant at $2 trillion. In this instance, expansionary fiscal policy causes a budget deficit.

Many people came to see having a budget deficit as necessary, given the high unemployment that plagued the economy. According to them, the choice was simple: (1) either keep the federal budget balanced and suffer high unemployment (and the reduced output of goods and services that results), or (2) accept the budget deficit and reduce the unemployment rate. For many people, it was better to balance the economy than to balance the budget. Exhibit 14-9 on the next page shows projected budget deficits for 2018–2024.

> *"I'm not worried about the deficit. It is big enough to take care of itself."*
> —Ronald Reagan, U.S. president

A Student Asks

QUESTION: *Do all economists think that enacting expansionary fiscal policy (even if it causes a budget deficit) is the way to reduce the unemployment rate?*

ANSWER: *No. Remember what we said in the last chapter. Some economists believe that if the government spends more (enacts expansionary fiscal policy by raising spending), then members of the private sector (you,*

Differentiating Instruction

English Language Learners
Students sometimes have difficulty understanding the terminology used in this discussion, yet they clearly understand the concept of debt. Ask students what would happen if you charged them $5 for every imaginable minor rule violation (chewing gum, not having a pencil out when class begins, talking, etc.). Before too long, their debt to you would become so large that it would be unpayable. When the federal debt becomes unpayable, the government (unlike most consumers and businesses), can delay making payments until future years.

Critical Thinking

After students have read "Higher Future Taxes" (pages 424–425), ask whether they think it's fair or unfair to expect them to pay off the debt that their parents' and grandparents' generations incurred. Encourage students to consider the benefits they receive from the spending that contributed to the national debt.

You might encourage students to do more research on this topic and share their findings with the class. (See the Internet Research activity below.)

 Application Activity

After reading and discussing Section 2, you may want to assign the Section Activity in the *Applying the Principles Workbook*, pages 149–150.

Assess

Quick Quiz

The following true-or-false quiz will help you assess student understanding of the material covered in this section.

1. If the federal government spends more than it receives in tax revenues, it has to borrow the difference and incur a debt. (True)

2. To determine per capita national debt, we divide the national debt by the U.S. population. (True)

3. Higher interest rates are one effect of having a balanced budget. (False)

4. When overall spending exceeds tax revenues, the government has a budget surplus. (False)

5. All economists agree that it's better to have a budget deficit and reduce unemployment than to maintain a balanced budget. (False)

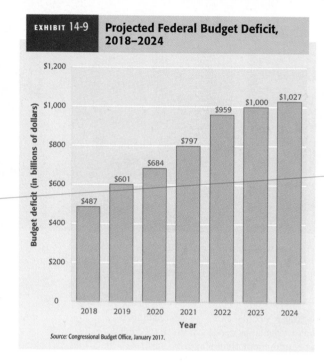

EXHIBIT 14-9 | **Projected Federal Budget Deficit, 2018–2024**

Budget deficit (in billions of dollars)

- 2018: $487
- 2019: $601
- 2020: $684
- 2021: $797
- 2022: $959
- 2023: $1,000
- 2024: $1,027

Year

Source: Congressional Budget Office, January 2017.

▲ These projections can change from year to year as economic conditions change and as Congress passes new tax laws.

for example) will spend less. In the case of complete crowding out (a term from the last chapter), $1 more spent by the government will lead to $1 less spent by the private sector. This means that no additional spending occurs in the economy to push down the unemployment rate,

National Debt

The only way an individual can spend more than he or she earns is to borrow the difference and incur a debt. (We are ruling out monetary gifts to this person.) For example, if Harry earns $30,000 a year and spends $32,000, he will have had to borrow $2,000. This $2,000 is Harry's debt.

What is true for Harry is true for the federal government. If it spends more than it receives in tax revenues, it has to borrow the difference and incur a debt. That is, every time the federal government runs a

deficit, it has to borrow money and incur a debt. In short, deficit leads to debt. The debt of the federal government is called the *national debt*.

In September 2017 the national debt was $20.16 trillion. If we divide the national debt by the U.S. population, we get *per capita national debt*, which is approximately $61,320. The per capita national debt is sometimes referred to as each "citizen's share" of the national debt.

Higher Future Taxes

When the government spends more than it collects in tax revenues, it has to borrow the difference. Deficit leads to debt. But what does debt lead to? Some economists argue that it leads to higher taxes in the future.

When the government borrows money to pay for the excess of its spending over tax revenues, it gets that money from people. Those people will have to be repaid one day, because the debt must be paid off. (If you borrowed money from a bank, you would have to repay the money with interest.) Where does the government get the money to pay off its debt? From tax revenues. This means that taxes have to be higher than they would have been had the debt not been incurred. Some economists say that as far as future taxpayers are concerned, running a budget deficit is a form of "taxation without representation."

Internet Research

Have students locate websites and news articles related to the budget deficit and the balanced budget debate. Direct each student to write an overview of the issues concerning the deficit and to explain viewpoints on the issue of whether there should be a constitutional amendment to balance the budget. Encourage students to become aware of differences between the positions of different political parties on this issue.

EXAMPLE Suppose that in a particular year, a government needs $3 trillion to pay for all of the things it provides and to pay interest on its national debt. The government calculates that it would need only $2.9 trillion in taxes were it not for interest on the debt. Taxpayers would be able to keep $0.1 trillion for themselves if the government had not run deficits in earlier years.

Is it ethical for one generation to buy things that another generation ends up paying for, at least in part? Some people say no, but others say it depends on whether what the first generation buys benefits the next generation. For example, suppose the present generation decides to build an interstate freeway system for $10 billion. The present generation decides to pay $2 billion itself through taxes and to borrow $8 billion. The present generation knows that the future generation will have to pay off the $8 billion (plus interest), but it reasons that the future generation will use the freeway system, so it should pay for some of it. If the current generation purchased $10 billion of something from which only it could benefit, the situation would be different. ◆

Thinking Like *an* Economist

Funding the Deficit

Suppose tax revenues are $2 trillion, but the government spends $3 trillion. Obviously, there will be a budget deficit of $1 trillion. You might say that since taxpayers paid $2 trillion of the $3 trillion that was spent, they got something for nothing ($1 trillion in spending benefits).

But an economist doesn't look at it that way. An economist knows that the $1 trillion budget deficit must be financed. This means that the U.S. Treasury has to borrow $1 trillion from people (taxpayers) by selling them Treasury bonds. Then one day, the Treasury will have to pay back the $1 trillion it borrowed—with interest. So who will pay back that $1 trillion plus interest? Future taxpayers.

In the end, the entire $3 trillion that the government spent will be paid by taxpayers. Some of it will be paid by current taxpayers, and some will be paid by future taxpayers. By considering current and future taxpayers together, the economist knows that taxpayers pay for every dollar the government spends.

SECTION 2 ASSESSMENT

Defining Terms
1. Define:
   a. national debt
   b. budget deficit
   c. budget surplus

Reviewing Facts and Concepts
2. How does the federal government spend tax revenues?
3. How is the current budget deficit linked to higher taxes in the future?
4. What was the national debt at the end of 2013?

Critical Thinking
5. What do people mean when they say, "It's better to balance the economy than to balance the budget"?
6. A person states, "The $100 billion program passed by Congress last week benefits thousands of people." What information is this person leaving out or ignoring?

Applying Economic Concepts
7. Suppose the Fed somehow created enough money to pay off the entire national debt. What would happen to prices? Explain your answer.

SECTION 2 ASSESSMENT ANSWERS

Defining Terms
1. a. national debt: the total amount the federal government owes it creditors; **b. budget deficit:** the situation in which the federal government's expenditures are greater than its tax revenues; **c. budget surplus:** the situation in which the federal government's expenditures are less than its tax revenues.

Reviewing Facts and Concepts
2. A few of the key spending categories are national defense; income security, retirement, and disability; social security; Medicare; and net interest on the national debt.
3. A budget deficit increases the national debt, which needs to be paid off in the future. Taxes will have to be higher in the future to pay off the debt incurred now.

Assessment Book

You will find a quiz for this section in the *Assessment Book*, page 142.

Reteaching Activity

Use the Section Assessment to gauge which students may need reteaching on this section. Instruct those students to draft a $2,000 billion budget that shows how they would allocate government revenues for the next year. Then ask them to explain what would happen if they needed more than $2,000 billion or less than $2,000 billion to meet all expenses.

Guided Reading

For further reteaching of the key concepts in this section, assign the Outlining Activity and the Just the Facts Handout from the *Guided Reading and Study Guide*, pages 247–251.

4. $17.2 trillion. (To find this answer, follow the links from http://econ.emcp.net/nationaldebt, mentioned on page 377.)

Critical Thinking
5. They mean that when unemployment is high, it's better to run a budget deficit, stimulate spending in the economy, and (hopefully) bring the unemployment rate down than to maintain a balanced budget at the expense of continued high unemployment.
6. This person is ignoring the fact that benefits rarely come without costs. While thousands of people might benefit from the program, thousands of other people might have to pay for its costs.

Applying Economic Concepts
7. If the Fed created enough money to pay off the national debt, the increased money supply would lead to a rise in demand. As a consequence of the increased demand, prices would rise.

Assessment Answers

Economics Vocabulary

1. budget deficit; 2. flat; 3. regressive; 4. ability-to-pay principle; 5. benefits-received principle; 6. benefits-received; 7. corporate income; 8. budget surplus; 9. progressive.

Understanding the Main Ideas

1. The three major types of federal taxes are personal income tax, corporate income tax, and social security tax.

2. State governments typically collect sales taxes.

3. A budget deficit can be reduced or eliminated if government spending falls, tax revenues rise, or both occur.

4. If the current generation spends $100 billion in one year and taxes itself just $75 billion, it runs a budget deficit of $25 billion. This $25 billion has to be borrowed and paid back at a later date. The future generation ends up paying back the $25 billion plus interest.

5. Smith meant that if it's right and good to do X in a family, then it's also likely to be right and good to do X in the nation.

6. *Sample answer:* Firm A buys materials and produces good X, which it sells to firm B for $40. Firm B adds a few things to good X and sells it to a customer for $50. The value is added in two places: (1) firm A adds the value of $40 and (2) firm B adds the value of $10.

7. A calendar year runs from January 1 to December 31; a fiscal year may run from the first of any month through the end of the month preceding it.

8. Personal income tax, corporate income tax, and social security tax raise more than 90% of federal tax revenues.

9. It's impossible to tell. To tell, we would have to know the tax rate and the taxable income for each person.

10. The benefits-received principle holds that a person should pay in taxes an amount equal to the benefits he or she receives from government spending.

11. With a flat tax, everyone pays taxes at the same rate.

Chapter Summary

Section 1

▶ A value-added tax is placed on the value added to a good at each stage of production and distribution.

▶ The three main forms of federal taxes are personal income tax, corporate income tax, and social security tax.

▶ Personal income tax is the tax a person pays on his or her income.

▶ Corporate income tax is the tax corporations pay on their profits.

▶ Social security tax is a tax placed on income generated from employment.

▶ With a proportional income tax, everyone pays taxes at the same rate, whatever his or her income level.

▶ With a progressive income tax, the form of income tax used in the United States, people pay at higher rates as their income levels rise.

▶ With a regressive income tax, people pay taxes at lower rates as their income levels rise.

Section 2

▶ The federal government breaks down its spending according to categories. The major categories include national defense, income security, social security, Medicare, and interest on the national debt.

▶ According to economists, a government spending program is not worth pursuing unless the benefits of that program outweigh the costs, but because spending is decided by voting, the costs of approved projects are sometimes greater than the benefits.

▶ The government prepares a budget that indicates how it will spend its tax revenues.

▶ A budget deficit occurs when government expenditures exceed tax revenues; a budget surplus occurs when revenues are greater than expenditures.

▶ When the government borrows money to pay for excess spending, it gets that money from people who will have to be repaid.

Economics Vocabulary

1. A(n) _____ exists when government spending is greater than tax revenues.

2. A proportional tax is sometimes called a(n) _____ tax.

3. A tax rate that falls as income rises is a(n) _____ tax.

4. The _____ is the idea that each person should pay taxes according to his or her ability to pay.

5. The _____ is the idea that each person should pay taxes according to the benefits that he or she receives from government expenditures.

6. A gas tax is consistent with the principle of _____ taxation.

7. The _____ tax is applied to corporate profits.

8. A(n) _____ exists if the federal government spends less than it receives in tax revenues.

9. A tax rate that rises as income rises is a(n) _____ tax.

Understanding the Main Ideas

1. What are the three major types of federal taxes?

2. Which level of government—federal, state, or local—typically collects sales taxes?

3. In what ways can a budget deficit be reduced or eliminated?

4. Explain how a budget deficit can cause a future generation to pay for what a current generation buys.

5. What did Adam Smith mean when he said, "What is prudence in the conduct of every private family, can scarce be folly in that of a great kingdom"?

6. Give an example that illustrates the value added to a good.

7. What is the difference between a calendar year and a fiscal year?

8. What three federal taxes raise approximately 91 percent of all federal tax revenues?

9. Lyons paid $40,000 in federal income taxes, and Abuel paid $20,000. Is the income tax progressive, proportional, or regressive, or is it impossible to tell? Explain your answer.

10. Explain the benefits-received principle of taxation.

11. What is a flat tax?

Doing the Math

1. The personal income tax will account for $2,052 billion of the total tax revenues of $4,019 billion, or 51%.

2. To pay off 1960 taxes, the representative taxpayer worked 102 of 365 days, or 27.9% of the year.

3. From 2020 to 2021, spending is expected to increase from $4,562 billion to $4,816 billion, or by $254 billion. The increase of $254 billion is 5.56% of $4,562 billion, so the correct answer is 5.56%.

Solving Economic Problems

1. Reducing the property tax makes it more beneficial to own property. The demand for

UNDERSTANDING AND APPLICATION

Doing the Math

1. According to Exhibit 14-1, what percentage of total taxes is the personal income tax projected to account for in 2021?
2. According to Exhibit 14-5, approximately what percentage of a year did the average taxpayer work to pay his or her taxes in 1960?
3. According to Exhibit 14-7, what percentage increase in government spending is expected from 2020 to 2021?

Solving Economic Problems

1. **Apply.** Suppose a local government lowers the property tax from 1.25 percent of the assessed value of property to 0.75 percent. How might this affect housing prices?
2. **Identify Cause and Effect.** Do you think a proportional tax or a progressive tax is more likely to lead to unequal after-tax pay? Explain.
3. **Infer and Conclude.** WRITING Write a one-page paper outlining your argument either for or against the benefits-received principle of taxation. Include evidence and draw conclusions based on that evidence.
4. **Find the Main Idea.** MEDIA Find an article in the local newspaper that addresses the current state of the federal budget, personal income taxes, sales taxes, or the national debt. Identify the major ideas of the article.
5. **Analyze.** Countries A and B are alike in every way except that the national debt in A is three times the national debt in B. In which country would you want to live 10 years from now? Why?
6. **Analyze.** Identify the costs and benefits of U.S. federal government spending and policies related to the economic goals of security and equity, such as personal, economic, and national security.

Working with Graphs and Tables

1. Look at Exhibit 14-10(a). Each bar represents a type of federal income tax in 2016. Identify the kind of tax that goes with each bar.

EXHIBIT 14-10

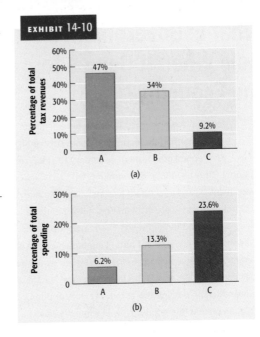

(a)

(b)

2. Look at Exhibit 14-10(b). Each bar represents a federal spending program in 2016. Identify the program that goes with each bar.

Project or Presentation

Flat Taxes. Do an Internet search using the key term *flat tax*. Then write a one-page paper answering this question: "Would a flat tax promote or hinder economic growth in the United States?" Discuss your opinion with a partner. Your paper should be free of spelling and grammatical errors and should be supported by your research. Make sure that your sources are reputable and are free from bias and propaganda.

ONLINE
emcp.com

Practice Tests and Study Guide

Go to www.emcschool.net/Economics2e and choose *Economics: New Ways of Thinking*, Chapter 14, if you need more help in preparing for the chapter test.

Working with Graphs and Tables

1. Bar A is the personal income tax; bar B is the social security tax; bar C is the corporate income tax.
2. Bar A is net interest on the debt; bar B is income security; and bar C is social security.

Project or Presentation

Answers will vary.

---

property will increase, and therefore, the price of property will rise. It may not rise by the amount of the tax reduction, though. In other words, if the property tax reduces taxes by, say, $5,000 on a given piece of property, it doesn't follow that the price of the property will rise by $5,000.
2. A progressive tax is more likely to lead to unequal after-tax pay, because tax rates increase as income rises.

3. Answers will vary.
4. Answers will vary.
5. The greater the national debt, the higher future taxes will need to be to pay it off. Future taxpayers in A will end up paying more in taxes than future taxpayers in B. All other things being equal, it would be better to be a future taxpayer in B than A.
6. Answers will vary.

Debating ← the Issues

Discussion Starters

1. Ask students if they know of anyone who benefits from government-provided services. If so, ask what services those people receive. (Caution students not to name names or otherwise identify the people they are talking about.) Allow students to share with the class what they know and understand about these services.

2. Invite students to consider and respond to the following scenarios:

Student A's grandmother lives alone and receives a modest social security pension. The pension barely covers her living expenses. What will happen to student A's grandmother if she doesn't receive a social security pension from the government?

Student B is the oldest child in a family of two parents and four children. The combined household income is below the poverty level, and the family must depend on food stamps to feed themselves each month. What will happen to student B's family if they don't have food stamps?

Student C's uncle had a serious accident and is unable to hold a full-time job. He receives a disability check from the government each month, but it isn't enough to cover his household expenses. What will happen to his family if he doesn't receive the disability check from the government?

If you were a government official, what would you say to people who want to cut social services that benefit people who are underprivileged and elderly? How would you decide which social services to limit to stay within the budget?

3. Ask students the following questions: How much help should the government provide to its citizens? Could providing national defense be considered help for a nation's citizens? Should the government have an emergency fund for citizens who suffer from natural disasters?

Debating ← the Issues

What Is Government's Role When It Comes to the Economy?

People often disagree about the federal government's role regarding the economy. Some people argue that the federal government should try to stabilize the economy. They say that if the economy is in a recession, the government should implement expansionary monetary and fiscal policy to stimulate growth. This may mean increasing the money supply and cutting taxes to stimulate spending. Others argue that if the government hadn't implemented the wrong monetary and fiscal policies in the past, there would be no recession to fix. So, here's the question: does the government mainly make the patient (the economy) sick, or does it mainly make the patient (the economy) well when it's sick?

Another hotly debated topic is what goods and services the federal government should provide to the citizens. Is it government's role to deliver the mail and care for the sick and elderly, or should government limit itself to building roads and providing a national defense? How much or how little should government do? Let's listen in to what some people have to say.

Hamid,
computer consultant

It seems to me that the Great Depression settled the issue of government's role in the economy. I believe that if government hadn't come to the rescue, and provided people with jobs, and stimulated spending in the economy, that the Great Depression would have gone on much longer than it did.

Before the Great Depression, many people used to think that a free enterprise economy could take care of itself. It wouldn't produce too much inflation, and it wouldn't bring on an economic contraction. Well, then, how do you explain the Great Depression? The unemployment rate rose to 25 percent during that time. The government had to do something.

Francine,
registered nurse

I'm not sure that Hamid has the explanation of the Great Depression correct. I don't think it was free enterprise that failed. I think it was government doing the wrong things. It was the government overspending in the 1920s and planting the seeds of the economic contraction. It was the government placing high tariffs on imported goods and making the contraction worse than it would have been. It was the Fed cutting the money supply too much. If anything, the Great Depression was a failure of government, not free enterprise.

The way I see it, government makes more problems for the economy than it solves. Sure, the government can do some things right, but government today is into more things than it can do. I am in favor of the government limiting itself to doing what individuals or businesses can't do. For example, I don't believe that either individuals or businesses can supply the country with the national defense that it needs. National defense then should be left to government. Use the tax money to provide for the national defense, not to subsidize the farmers. And in my opinion, it doesn't make sense for the government to be involved in programs such as Medicare and social security.

Differentiating Instruction

Enrichment and Extension

Hold a mock political election in which student "candidates" campaign on positions regarding the government's involvement in the economy. Begin by deciding what type of political office the class will fill: U.S. president? state governor? city mayor? Then ask students to write campaign speeches and deliver them to the class. After all speeches have been given, allow the class to vote for the candidate who gave the most convincing speech. Consider rewarding the winner with a seat of honor in front of the class and with the power to grant a small favor to the class, such as allowing five minutes of free talk.

Yong, retired attorney

Here's what I would like to know: if government is so bad—as Francine seems to imply—why has this country been so militarily and economically strong for so long? We have one of the largest economies in the world and the strongest and most capable military in the world. And we've developed both of these things at the same time that the federal government has been getting bigger. If government bigness is so bad, then explain to me why our economy is as strong and as big as it is?

Nancy, college student

I think Yong is making a mistake here. Just because two things occur at the same time, or nearly the same time, it doesn't mean that one is the cause and the other is the effect. There are more dogs in the United States today than there were in 1950. Does it follow that a rising dog population is what causes the economy to be strong? Not at all. There are a lot of things that happen at around the same time that have nothing to do with each other.

But I have a better point to make with respect to Yong's comment. Isn't it possible that we would have an even stronger economy, and a mightier military, if the government hadn't grown so large? With a smaller, less intrusive government, perhaps our economy would be even larger than it is today. And perhaps our military would be even stronger.

Blanca, physician

I think what we are talking about here is that neither free enterprise nor government is perfect at doing everything. Sometimes, the free enterprise economy does need government to help it out. For instance, when the economy is slumping or we need something that free enterprise won't produce, such as protection against terrorists, government needs to step in.

But certainly, this doesn't mean that government has been perfect. Government can make mistakes. I think government can implement the wrong monetary policy—perhaps causing high inflation. I believe that government may implement a particular fiscal policy that doesn't work because of, say, complete crowding out. My guess is that sometimes, government does more to make things worse than to make things better.

Maybe what we are learning over time is what government should and should not do and what free enterprise should and should not do. In other words, maybe the last 50 years have been a learning period for us.

What Do You Think?

1. What is your opinion about the proper role for government, especially when it comes to economic issues?
2. What goods and services should the government provide (using taxpayer money)? What, if anything, does the government currently do that it shouldn't do? Explain your answers.

Activities for What Do You Think?

1. Divide students into two groups to debate the following proposition: the government needs more control over the economy.

Allow students time to organize their points in the debate and to decide who will present each side. Give each side five to seven minutes to present its case. Allow enough time for debriefing and closure at the end of the class period.

2. Have students create posters of services they think the government should provide. (These can be services currently provided or not currently provided.) Display the posters at the front of the class. Also ask students to create separate posters on services the government provides that they think it shouldn't. Display these at the back of the class. Compare the two groups of posters. Are some services included in both groups? If so, you might hold a class vote to decide where those services should remain.

Closure

Instruct students to write one-page papers describing how their opinions on this issue were affected by reading and discussing Debating the Issues. Students should include what information from the text or discussion influenced their thinking.

Differentiating Instruction

Enrichment and Extension

Divide students into groups of three or four. Tell each group to decide on a position for or against greater government involvement in the economy. Then ask each group to compose a cheer for its position. Allow the groups to present their cheers to the class.

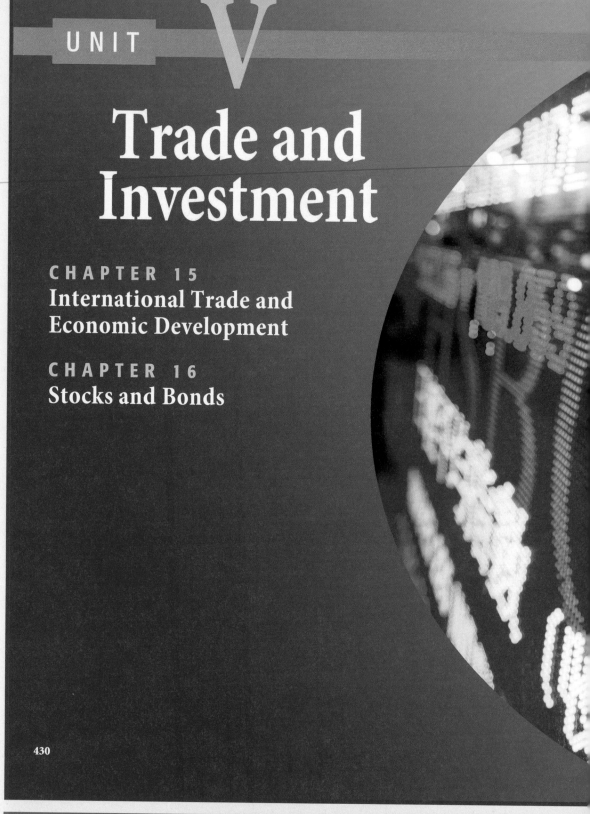

Listed below are the chapters included in this unit.

Foundations for the Unit

In Unit V, we enlarge our focus to study the world through economics. Increasingly, because of technological breakthroughs in science, communication, and other areas, the world seems to be a smaller place. Today, economic events in one part of the world can affect economic events in another part of the world almost instantaneously. All of us—economists, politicians, businesspeople, teachers, and more—are quickly discovering that the Disney song is accurate—"It's a small world after all." This unit will help students begin to understand the realities of our new global economy.

UNIT V

Trade and Investment

CHAPTER 15
International Trade and Economic Development

CHAPTER 16
Stocks and Bonds

430

Resources for the Unit

Books

Ashworth, William. *A Short History of the International Economy Since 1850.* London: Longman, 1987.

Heilbroner, Robert L. *The Making of an Economic Society.* Englewood Cliff, NJ: Prentice-Hall, 1962.

Mantle, Jonathan. *Car Wars: 50 Years of Greed, Treachery and Skullduggery in the Global Market.* New York: Arcade, 1996.

Articles

Cohen, Warren. "Up, Up, and Away," *U.S. News and World Report,* November 2, 1998.

"The Ragged March to Markets," *New York Times,* November 11, 1999.

Rohter, Larry. "Outlook 2000: International: After a Hard Year, Latin America Looks for Better Times," *New York Times,* December 20, 1999.

> **"An investment in knowledge always pays the best interest."**
>
> —Benjamin Franklin,
> statesman and inventor

431

Introducing the Unit

To introduce Unit V, read aloud the following: "Many economists define *globalization* as a process by which individuals and businesses in any part of the world are much more affected by events elsewhere in the world than they used to be." Ask your students where they might have heard this before. Students might recall that this definition of globalization was presented in Chapter 2. Stress to students that the material in this unit should help them to get a better economic view of our world. Point out that the more we know about the other "players" in the global economy, the better equipped we will be to succeed in it.

Performance Project

The performance task for Unit V can best be performed cooperatively. Working in groups, students should identify countries to study. For its country, each group should develop an economic atlas, including such data as pertinent economic statistics (data might include real GDP for the country and other selected neighboring countries, currency, and other statistics relating to economic health and standard of living); a brief summary of the country's economic history; a brief description of the country's governmental and economic systems; and maps showing important natural resources, crops, and industries for the country. Each group should present an oral report of its findings to the class. Encourage students to discuss the cultures of their chosen countries in their reports. Additionally, students might want to prepare and share with the class selected foods native to the countries they have studied.

Multimedia

Interest Rates and Exchange Rates. In *Introductory Economics*. VHS. Films for the Humanities and Sciences.

Is America Number One? Understand the Economics of Success. VHS. Films for the Humanities and Sciences.

Stabilization Policy for a Small Open Economy.

In *Introductory Economics*. VHS. Films for the Humanities and Sciences.

Thinking Globally: Effective Lessons for Teaching about the Interdependent World Economy. CD-ROM. National Council on Economic Education.

Chapter 15 Planning Guide

	Learning Objectives	Reproducible Worksheets and Handouts	Assessment

SECTION 1

International Trade

(pages 434–446)

Learning Objectives
- ▶ Describe what goods are major U.S. exports and imports.
- ▶ Explain what comparative advantage is.

Reproducible Worksheets and Handouts
- 📖 Section 1 Activity, *Applying the Principles Workbook*, pages 151–155
- 📖 Outlining Activity, *Guided Reading and Study Guide*, pages 259–261
- 📖 Just the Facts Handout, *Guided Reading and Study Guide*, pages 262–263

Assessment
- ☑ Section Assessment, *Student Text*, page 446
- ☑ Quick Quiz, *Annotated Teacher's Edition*, page 445
- ☑ Section Quiz, *Assessment Book*, page 150

SECTION 2

Trade Restrictions

(pages 447–454)

Learning Objectives
- ▶ Define the terms *tariff* and *quota*.
- ▶ Explain how tariffs and quotas affect prices.
- ▶ Explain why the government imposes tariffs and quotas if they make goods more expensive for U.S. consumers.
- ▶ Describe the effect that tariffs had on the Great Depression.
- ▶ Identify the arguments for and against trade restrictions.

Reproducible Worksheets and Handouts
- 📖 Section 2 Activity, *Applying the Principles Workbook*, pages 156–159
- 📖 Outlining Activity, *Guided Reading and Study Guide*, pages 264–266
- 📖 Just the Facts Handout, *Guided Reading and Study Guide*, pages 267–268

Assessment
- ☑ Section Assessment, *Student Text*, page 454
- ☑ Quick Quiz, *Annotated Teacher's Edition*, page 453
- ☑ Section Quiz, *Assessment Book*, page 151

SECTION 3

The Exchange Rate

(pages 455–459)

Learning Objectives
- ▶ Define the term *exchange rate*.
- ▶ Explain what it means to say that a currency "appreciates" in value.
- ▶ Explain what it means to say that a currency "depreciates" in value.

Reproducible Worksheets and Handouts
- 📖 Section 3 Activity, *Applying the Principles Workbook*, pages 160–161
- 📖 Outlining Activity, *Guided Reading and Study Guide*, page 269
- 📖 Just the Facts Handout, *Guided Reading and Study Guide*, pages 270–271

Assessment
- ☑ Section Assessment, *Student Text*, page 459
- ☑ Quick Quiz, *Annotated Teacher's Edition*, page 458
- ☑ Section Quiz, *Assessment Book*, page 152

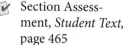

SECTION 4

Economic Development

(pages 462–465)

Learning Objectives
- ▶ Explain what a less-developed country is.
- ▶ Explain why some countries are rich and others are poor.
- ▶ Explain the vicious circle of poverty.
- ▶ Explain why savings accounts are important to economic development.
- ▶ List factors that aid economic development.

Reproducible Worksheets and Handouts
- 📖 Section 4 Activity, *Applying the Principles Workbook*, pages 162–164
- 📖 Outlining Activity, *Guided Reading and Study Guide*, pages 272–273
- 📖 Just the Facts Handout, *Guided Reading and Study Guide*, pages 274–275

Assessment
- ☑ Section Assessment, *Student Text*, page 465
- ☑ Quick Quiz, *Annotated Teacher's Edition*, page 464
- ☑ Section Quiz, *Assessment Book*, page 153

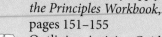

Reproducible Chapter Resources and Assessment Materials

- Graphic Organizer Activity, *Guided Reading and Study Guide*, pages 276–278
- Vocabulary Activity, *Guided Reading and Study Guide*, pages 279–280
- Working with Graphs and Charts, *Guided Reading and Study Guide*, page 281
- ✔ Practice Test, *Guided Reading and Study Guide*, pages 282–284
- Critical Thinking Activity, *Finding Economics*, pages 41–43
- ✔ Chapter Test A, *Assessment Book*, pages 154–157
- ✔ Chapter Test B, *Assessment Book*, pages 158–162

Student Text Internet Links

Economics: New Ways of Thinking, Second Edition encourages students to use the Internet to find out more about economics. Given the wealth of current, valid information available on websites, students should be encouraged to use the Internet as a research tool. Doing so will likely increase students' interest in and understanding of economics principles and topics. In addition, doing Internet research can help your students form the habit of accessing and using economics information, as well as help them develop investigative skills they will use throughout their educational and professional careers.

To aid your students in achieving these ends, each chapter of *Economics: New Ways of Thinking, Second Edition* includes the addresses of several websites that provide engaging and relevant information. When students type in any of the addresses provided, they will immediately arrive at the intended site. The addresses have been modified so that EMC Publishing can monitor and maintain the proper links—for example, the website http://www.deposit accounts.com/ has been changed to http://econ.emcp.net/accounts. In the event that the address or content of a site changes or is discontinued, EMC's Internet editors will redirect the link to a site with equivalent information.

Activities in the *Annotated Teacher's Edition* often suggest that students search the Internet for information. For some activities, you might want to find reputable sites beforehand and steer students toward them. For other activities, have students do their own searching and then check out the sites they have found and discuss why they might be reliable or unreliable.

Passport® for Economics

Technology resources are available with the *Economics: New Ways of Thinking, Second Edition* program through Passport®. These include:

eBooks for *Economics: New Ways of Thinking, Second Edition*

- ▶ Student textbook eBook
- ▶ Interactive Applying the Principles eWorkbook
- ▶ Finding Economics eBook
- ▶ Guided Reading and Study Guide eBook
- ▶ Annotated Teacher's Edition eBook
- ▶ Lesson Plans eBook
- ▶ Assessment eBook

Passport® for Students

Students can access helpful resources through Passport® for Economics. Resources include:
- ▶ Study guides
- ▶ Practice tests
- ▶ Flash cards in English and in Spanish
- ▶ Word games in English and in Spanish
- ▶ Tutorials and key-concept videos
- ▶ Spanish print and audio summaries

Passport® for Teachers

Keep your course current and relevant by using the teacher resources provided through Passport® for Economics. In addition to all of the resources on the student side of Passport®, the teacher side contains:
- ▶ Link to the Annotated Teacher's Edition eBook
- ▶ Standards correlations
- ▶ Microsoft® PowerPoint® Lectures
- ▶ Current Events Lessons
- ▶ Additional Economics in the Real World features
- ▶ ExamView® Assessment Suite
- ▶ PDFs of all print supplements (student and teacher)

This chapter discusses international trade and introduces the information necessary to answer such questions as these: Why do people in different countries trade with each other? Is it bad economic news if a country buys more from other countries than it sells to other countries? What causes the value of the U.S. dollar to rise and fall in foreign exchange markets? The following statements provide brief descriptions of the major concepts covered in each section of this chapter.

SECTION 1 International Trade

Section 1 explores what imports and exports are. This section also explains the concept of comparative advantage.

SECTION 2 Trade Restrictions

Section 2 explains the concepts of tariffs and quotas, as well as how tariffs and quotas affect price.

SECTION 3 The Exchange Rate

Section 3 discusses the exchange rate and what it means when a currency appreciates or depreciates in value.

SECTION 4 Economic Development

Section 4 explores economic growth and the ways in which less-developed countries become developed.

International Trade and Economic Development

Why It Matters

We live in a global economy. Precision ice hockey equipment is designed in Sweden, financed in Canada, and assembled in Cleveland, Ohio. An advertising campaign is conceived in Great Britain, and footage for it is shot in Canada, dubbed in London, and edited in New York. A sports car is financed in Japan, designed in Italy, and assembled in Indiana, Mexico, and France using advanced electronic components invented in New Jersey and fabricated in Japan. A jet plane is designed in the state of Washington and in Japan and

assembled in Seattle, with tail cones coming from Canada, special tail sections from China and Italy, and engines from England.

As Americans interact more and more with people in other nations, they may learn things about other people that they didn't know before or didn't stop to think about. This chapter considers an increasingly important activity of people in a global economy: trade.

In an increasingly global economy, the chances are good that the products these workers are loading for shipment will be used by people on the other side of the world. In this chapter, you will learn why people specialize and why they trade with people in different countries.

432

Teaching Suggestions from the Author

One thing that helps pique student interest in international trade is learning about different countries and their people. When students realize that other countries are fascinating places and that other people can be interesting, exciting, and unique, they develop an appreciation for what international trade is all about.

You might want to have each student choose a country that he or she is interested in and do a little research to find out what its products are and what its people are like. Usually, once a student learns about a country and its people, he or she is much more receptive to the idea of trading with the people of that country. What a student

Economics Around the Clock

The following events occurred one day in November.

12:04 P.M. Samantha Lawrence is packing for a trip to Paris. Tomorrow at 5:30 p.m., she will leave from JFK Airport in New York. She will spend five days in Paris and then go to England, where she will spend two days in London and one day in Oxford. After that, she will take a train to Scotland, where she will spend four days in Edinburgh and one day in Glasgow. Although the dollar has been falling in value relative to the euro and the pound, Samantha is still going on her trip.

• What does the value of the dollar have to do with taking a trip overseas?

3:04 P.M. In Jacob's family, each person has certain duties and responsibilities. His mother and father share responsibilities for the family finances, shopping, and meal preparation. His younger sister takes care of the family pets. Jacob's job is to take out the trash, keep his room clean, and mow the lawn. Right now, he is mowing the lawn. As he mows, he thinks, "I wonder why it's always my job to mow the lawn."

• Why do family members often specialize in performing certain tasks?

5:45 P.M. Marianne is watching a TV news report on offshore outsourcing (or offshoring) in the United States. The reporter is telling the story of Adam Evans, who was fired after working 10 years for a local company. The reporter ends her report by saying, "That's just one more job that has left our shores and gone to China."

• What is offshoring, and is it something U.S. residents should worry about?

433

Introducing the Chapter

A good way to begin study of Chapter 15 is to ask students to list the many foreign-made products that they or their families own. Allow only two minutes for this exercise. Call on volunteers to read their lists to the class. After students have begun to see the tremendous number of foreign products that are available in our country, ask them another question: which U.S.-made products do you think are exported? Allow students to share their responses. Emphasize that international trade is one of the most important aspects of the global economy. Explain that in this chapter, students will study international trade.

Teaching with Visuals

Because of international trade, many items are shipped around the world. Huge container ships are loaded down with cars, appliances, electronic parts, clothing, and food. The goods eventually find their way to us, coast to coast.

learns about one country can then be generalized to other countries around the world.

You might ask students to prepare maps of their selected countries, showing major cities, geographical features, and natural resources.

Teacher Support

Focus and Motivate

Section Objectives

After completing this section, students will be able to
▶ describe what goods are major U.S. exports and imports; and
▶ explain what comparative advantage is.

Kickoff Activity

Write the following on the board for students to answer:"Why do you think that countries produce only some goods and not all the goods they need or want? For example, the United States produces cars but not bananas. Why doesn't it produce both cars and bananas?"

Activating Prior Knowledge

Invite students to share their responses to the Kickoff Activity. Some students will say that the reason the United States doesn't produce bananas is that it doesn't have the proper climate. Remind students that bananas can be produced in the United States under hothouse conditions. The point is, though, that raising bananas this way would be very expensive. Try to communicate to students the idea that countries produce and export those goods that they can produce more cheaply than other countries. Countries import goods that they can buy more cheaply than they can produce themselves.

 Visit econ.myemcp.com/videos for videos that will help students better understand the key concepts found in this section.

International Trade

Focus Questions
▶ What goods are major U.S. exports?
▶ What goods are major U.S. imports?
▶ What is comparative advantage?

Key Terms
exports
imports
balance of trade
absolute advantage
specialize
comparative advantage
outsourcing

Why Do People in Different Countries Trade with Each Other?

We have international trade for the same reason we have domestic trade (trade within a country). Individuals trade to make themselves better off. Frank and Nate, who live in Fargo, North Dakota, trade because each values something the other has more than he values something of his own. For example, perhaps Frank trades $10 for Nate's book. On an international scale, Elaine in the United States trades with Cho in China because Cho has something that Elaine wants and Elaine has something that Cho wants.

Obviously, different countries have different terrains, climates, and resources. It follows that some countries can produce goods that other countries cannot produce or can produce only at extremely high cost. For example, Hong Kong has no oil, and Saudi Arabia has a large supply of oil. Bananas do not grow easily in the United States, but they flourish in Honduras. Americans could grow bananas if they used hothouses, but it is cheaper for them to buy

exports
Goods and services produced in the domestic country and sold to residents of a foreign country.

bananas from Honduras than to produce bananas themselves.

Sometimes, we forget how many of the goods we use each day are purchased from people living in other countries. Our alarm clock might be produced in Belgium, our shoes in China, and our watch in Switzerland. Take a look sometime at all of the goods you use each day. How many are produced in foreign countries?

What Are Exports and Imports?

Exports are goods and services that are produced in the domestic country and sold to residents of a foreign country. For example, if residents of the United States (the domestic country) produce and sell computers to people in France, Germany, and Mexico, then computers are a U.S. export. For 2016, the value of U.S. exports was $2.2 trillion, which means that U.S. residents produced and sold $2.2 trillion worth of U.S. goods and services to people in other countries. Major U.S. exports include automobiles, computers, aircraft, corn,

---

Differentiating Instruction

Visual Learners

Assign students to make collages that can be used as a bulletin board display. You could assign each student to make an individual poster, or you could ask students to bring in copies of photos of both consumer items and raw materials and then create a large cooperative collage. Each collage should be divided into two sections: imports and exports. On the import side, students can display pictures of goods imported by the United States. On the export side, students can display goods exported by the United States.

wheat, soybeans, scientific instruments, coal, machinery, and plastic materials.

Imports are goods and services produced in foreign countries and purchased by residents of the domestic country. For example, if residents of the United States (the domestic country) buy coffee from Colombia, then coffee is a U.S. import. For 2016, the value of U.S. imports was $2.7 trillion. U.S. residents bought $2.7 trillion worth of goods from people in other countries. Major U.S. imports include petroleum, clothing, iron, steel, office machines, footwear, fish, coffee, and diamonds.

Exhibit 15-1 shows the annual values of U.S. exports and imports for 2000–2016.

imports
Goods produced in foreign countries and purchased by residents of the domestic country.

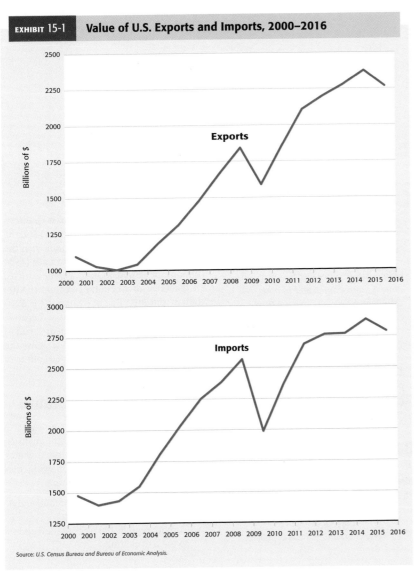

EXHIBIT 15-1 **Value of U.S. Exports and Imports, 2000–2016**

Source: U.S. Census Bureau and Bureau of Economic Analysis.

◀ Which had the bigger percentage increase from 2000 to 2016: exports or imports? Based on your earlier study of GDP, did this difference contribute to an increase or decrease in the GDP?

Discussion Starter

Ask students why they think people in different countries trade with one another. In short, what is the motivation behind international trade? The answer is that people trade with people in other countries for the same reason they trade with people in their own countries: to make themselves better off.

Teaching with Visuals

Percentage wise, exports increased at a greater rate than imports increased during the period, but still in terms of absolute dollar amounts, import spending was greater than export spending. We know that GDP is equal to consumption plus investment plus government purchases plus net exports (or export spending minus import spending). When export spending is greater than import spending, net exports are negative, which makes GDP smaller than it would be if export spending equal import spending or if export spending were greater than import spending.

Internet Research

Instruct students to look at the website for the Export-Import Bank of the United States. Ask them to determine the function of the bank. Divide students into groups to prepare brief presentations that highlight two small business ideas they believe should qualify for the support of the U.S. Export-Import Bank.

Analyzing

If the last 6 months of 2016 the balance of trade with France is the same as it was for the first 6 months of 2016, what will be the annual balance of trade with France? *Answer:* –$25 billion

Background Information

After students have read the section on the balance of trade, explain that this applies to all countries (including the United States). The imports and exports that a country makes has a direct impact on that country and its trading partners since the more a country imports the more likely it will have a balance of a trade deficit and the more it exports, the more the trade deficit will change from a deficit to a surplus.

Reinforcement Activity

Ask students to analyze the following scenarios and consider the impact to the country/countries involved.

1. The U.S. begins to import more foreign-produced goods. (The U.S. shifts toward a balance of trade deficit.)
2. The U.S. begins to export more foreign-produced goods. (The U.S. shifts toward a balance of trade surplus.)
3. The U.S. buys more goods from China. (The U.S. shifts toward a balance of trade deficit and China shifts toward a balance of trade surplus.)
4. The U.S. sells more goods to Canada. (The U.S. shifts toward a balance of trade surplus and Canada shifts toward a balance of trade deficit.)

▶This exhibit shows the balance of trade that the United States had with selected countries in the first seven months of 2017.

EXHIBIT 15-2 **U.S. Balance of Trade, Selected Countries, First Seven Months of 2017**

Country	Balance of Trade (billions of dollars)
Brazil	3.9
Canada	–10.9
China	–204.2
France	–8.0
Germany	–36.0
Hong Kong	18.7
India	–13.5
Italy	–17.2
Japan	–39.7
Korea, South	–13.1
Mexico	–41.2
Saudi Arabia	–2.8
Singapore	6.2
Taiwan	–9.4
United Kingdom	1.0

Source: U.S. Census Bureau

A Student Asks

QUESTION: *I noticed that in 2016, the value of exports was less than the value of imports. In other words, Americans bought more from people in other countries than the people in other countries bought from Americans. Does this happen most months?*

ANSWER: *Yes, in the recent history of the United States, Americans buy more from people in other countries than people in other countries buy from Americans.*

Balance of Trade

A country's **balance of trade** is the difference between the value of its exports and the value of its imports:

balance of trade
The difference between the value of a country's exports and the value of its imports.

Balance of trade =
Value of exports − Value of imports

For example, if the value of a country's exports is $300 billion (for the year) and the value of its imports is $200 billion, then the country has a positive balance of trade ($100 billion), or is said to have a *trade surplus*. If the value of a country's exports is $100 billion and the value of its imports is $210 billion, then the country has a negative balance of trade (–$110 billion), or is said to have a *trade deficit*. Exhibit 15-2 shows the U.S. balance of trade with selected countries in 2016.

Absolute and Comparative Advantages

Suppose that using the same quantity of resources as Japan, the United States can produce either of the following two combinations of food and clothing:

- Combination A: 150 units of food and 0 units of clothing
- Combination B: 100 units of food and 25 units of clothing

Background Information: Specialization

Government officials don't sit down with piles of cost data and determine what their country should specialize in producing and then decide to trade. Similarly, countries don't plot production possibilities frontiers on graph paper or formally calculate opportunity cost. Instead, it's the desire of individuals to make a dollar, a franc, a pound, or a yen that determines the pattern of international trade. It's the desire for profit that determines what a country specializes in and trades.

Suppose that Japan, using the same quantity of resources as the United States, can produce either of the following two combinations of food and clothing:

- Combination C: 30 units of food and 120 units of clothing
- Combination D: 0 units of food and 180 units of clothing

When a country can produce more of a good than another country using the same quantity of resources, it is said to have an **absolute advantage** in the production of that good. In our example, the United States has an absolute advantage in producing food, because the maximum amount of food it can produce (150 units) is greater than the maximum amount of food Japan can produce (30 units). Japan, in contrast, has an absolute advantage in producing clothing, because the maximum amount of clothing it can produce (180 units) is greater than the maximum amount of clothing the United States can produce (25 units).

Suppose that in year 1, Japan and the United States do not trade with each other. Instead, each nation decides to produce some quantity of each good and consume it. The United States produces and consumes combination B (100 units of food and 25 units of clothing), and Japan produces and consumes combination C (30 units of food and 120 units of clothing).

In year 2, things change. Each country decides to **specialize** in the production of one good and then trade some of it for the other good. Which good—clothing or food—should the United States specialize in producing? Which good should Japan specialize in producing?

In general, a country should specialize in production of the good for which it has a **comparative advantage**—the good it can produce at a lower opportunity cost.

Determining Opportunity Cost

Recall from Chapter 1 that the opportunity cost of producing a good is what is given up to produce that good. For example, if Julio gives up the opportunity to produce three towels if he produces a blanket, then the opportunity cost of the blanket is three towels.

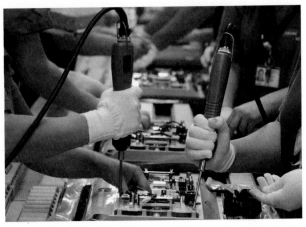

What is the opportunity cost of producing food for the United States? For Japan? We know that the United States can produce either combination A (150 units of food and 0 units of clothing) or combination B (100 units of food and 25 units of clothing). Suppose it is currently producing combination B. What will be the benefits and costs of producing combination A instead? The country will make itself better off by producing 50 additional units of food, but it will have to give up 25 units of clothing to do so. In other words, for every 1 extra unit of food, it will have to give up ½ unit of clothing. In economic terms, for the United States, the opportunity cost of 1 unit of food is ½ unit of clothing.

The tradeoff is similar for Japan. We know that Japan can produce combination C (30 units of food and 120 units of clothing) or combination D (0 units of food and 180 units of clothing). Suppose it is currently producing combination D. What will be the benefits and costs of producing combination C instead? By producing combination C, Japan will make itself better off by having 30 additional units of food, but it will have to give up 60 units of clothing to do so. In other words, for every 1 extra unit of food, it will have to give up 2 units of clothing. In economic terms, for Japan, the opportunity cost of 1 unit of food is 2 units of clothing. Thus, the opportunity cost of producing 1 unit of food (F) is ½ unit of clothing (C) for the United States and 2 units of clothing for Japan:

▲ These workers are assembling TVs at a Samsung plant in Kaluga, Russia. The United States imports millions of dollars' worth of TVs and related electronic products each year.

absolute advantage
The situation in which a country can produce more of a good than another country can produce with the same quantity of resources.

specialize
To focus or concentrate on a particular activity or product.

comparative advantage
The situation in which a country can produce a good at a lower opportunity cost than another country.

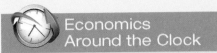
Reinforcement Activity

Direct students to look through newspapers and magazines to find stories about the international economy and international trade. Ask students to write one-page papers on the stories of their choice. Allow students to read their papers aloud in small groups, and encourage other students in the groups to ask questions and make comments.

Cooperative Learning

Divide the class into small groups. Each group should choose two imports and research where these products originated. The group should then find price data, so they can compare the price of the imported product with its American-made counterpart. Each group should try to answer the following questions about the imports they research: How much does it cost? How does this cost compare to an American-made counterpart, if any exists? Invite groups to share their findings with the class in oral reports. Encourage each group to include a map of the country of origin of each of its imported products, as well as any other visual aids to support its presentation.

Reinforcement Activity

Remind students that they first learned about the concept of opportunity cost in Chapter 1. Here we come across this concept again. Stress to students how important the concept of opportunity cost is in economics. Ask students to list all of the different ways that opportunity cost has affected their study of economics thus far.

Opportunity cost of 1 unit of food
United States: 1F = ½C
Japan: 1F = 2C

We conclude that the United States can produce food more cheaply than Japan. In other words, the United States has a comparative advantage in food production. Food, then, is what the United States should specialize in producing. If we followed this procedure for clothing production, we would find that Japan can produce clothing more cheaply than the United States. The opportunity cost of producing 1 unit of clothing is 2 units of food for the United States and ½ unit of food for Japan:

Opportunity cost of 1 unit of clothing
United States: 1C = 2F
Japan: 1C = ½F

Therefore, Japan has a comparative advantage in clothing production. Clothing, then, is what Japan should specialize in producing.

EXAMPLE Country A can produce either (1) 40X and 20Y or (2) 80X and 0Y. Country B can produce either (1) 20X and 20Y or (2) 40X and 0Y. What is the opportunity cost of producing 1X for each country, A and B? To find it for country A, we realize that when it goes from producing 40X to 80X, it ends up not producing 20Y. So, country A gets 40 more X at the cost of 20 fewer Y. In other words, for every 2 more X it gets, it gives up 1Y. Or, to state it differently, for every 1 more X it gets, it gives up ½Y. In short, the opportunity cost of 1X is ½Y.

Now let's look at things for country B. When it goes from producing 20X to 40X it gives up producing 20Y. In other words, to produce 20 more X, it must give up 20Y, or for every 1 more X, it has to give up 1Y. In short, the opportunity cost of 1X is 1Y.

Who is the low-cost producer of X: country A or B? It is country A, because it gives up less (½Y) to produce 1 more X. ◆

"No nation was ever ruined by trade."
— Benjamin Franklin, statesman and inventor

Benefits of Specialization and Trade

Suppose we look at two countries, Japan and the United States. Currently, we assume that each country can produce some food and some clothing. Here are the combinations of the two goods that each country can produce:

United States	Japan
A: 150 food, 0 clothing	C: 30 food, 120 clothing
B: 100 food, 25 clothing	D: 0 food, 180 clothing

Now let's consider two cases for both the United States and Japan. In the first case, Exhibit 15-3(a), neither Japan nor the United States specializes in the production of either good (thus, both produce some amount of each good), and the two countries do not trade. In this case, the United States produces combination B (100 units of food and 25 units of clothing), and Japan produces combination C (30 units of food and 120 units of clothing):

No specialization and no trade
United States: 100F + 25C
Japan: 30F + 120C

In the second case, Exhibit 15-3(b), each country specializes in the production of the good in which it has a comparative advantage, and then it trades some of that good for the other good. The United States produces combination A (150 units of food and 0 units of clothing), and Japan produces combination D (0 units of food and 180 units of clothing). Then the countries decide that the United States will trade 40 units of food to Japan in return for 40 units of clothing:

Countries trade
40F for 40C

After trade, the United States ends up with 110 units of food and 40 units of clothing. Japan, in turn, ends up with 40 units of food and 140 units of clothing:

Background Information: Foreign Trade Data

The U.S. Census Bureau is a useful, easily accessible resource for information about imports and exports and the current dollar amount the United States gains from exports. According to the bureau's website, the United States exports billions of dollars' worth of agricultural products each year.

These exports include wheat, grains, corn, fruit, cotton, beef, pork, poultry, dairy products, and fish. To find current figures, check the full report on U.S. international trade at http://econ.emcp.net /aboutforeigntrade.

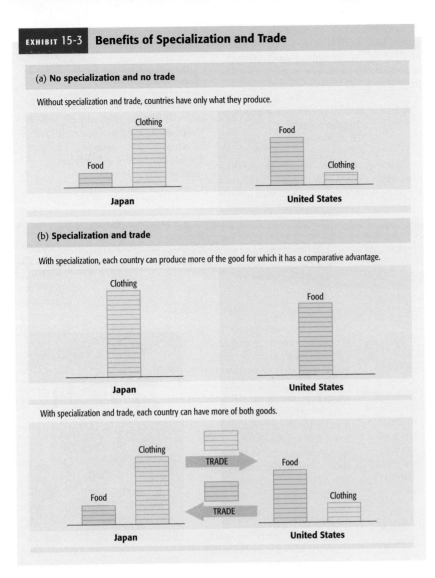

EXHIBIT 15-3 Benefits of Specialization and Trade

(a) No specialization and no trade

Without specialization and trade, countries have only what they produce.

Japan
Clothing
Food

United States
Food
Clothing

(b) Specialization and trade

With specialization, each country can produce more of the good for which it has a comparative advantage.

Japan
Clothing

United States
Food

With specialization and trade, each country can have more of both goods.

Japan
Clothing
Food
TRADE

United States
Food
Clothing
TRADE

▶ Countries can have more of both goods if they specialize in producing the good for which they have a comparative advantage. They can then trade some of that good for other goods.

Specialization and trade
United States: 110F + 40C
Japan: 40F + 140C

In which case are both Japan and the United States better off? The answer is the second case, in which they specialize and then trade. In the first case (no specialization and no trade), the United States ended up with 100 units of food and 25 units of clothing, whereas in the second case, it ended up with 110 units of food and 40 units of clothing. In other words, through specialization and trade, the United States ended up with more of both food and clothing.

Benefits to United States of specialization and trade
10 more units of F
15 more units of C

Teaching with Visuals

Assign students the task of re-creating the information in Exhibit 15-3, substituting Mexico or a European country for Japan. Students should show the goods most often involved in trade between that country and the United States. Students should also show comparative advantages in their visuals.

Reinforcement Activity

Ask students to respond in writing to the following question: How do opportunity costs relate to the concept of comparative advantage? The answer is that comparative advantage is the situation in which one country can produce a good at a lower opportunity cost than another country.

Ask students if, before reading this feature, they had ever thought of dividing chores in this way. Ask, Might any of you try to figure out the comparative advantages of various tasks with a sibling?

ANSWERS TO THINK ABOUT IT Answers will vary. Comparative advantage may play a role in deciding who does which chores, but in the past, household tasks have often been divided along gender lines. Women have been expected to cook and clean, and men have been expected to mow the lawn and fix things. Today, other factors may play bigger parts.

The same is true for Japan. In the first case, it had 30 units of food and 120 units of clothing. In the second case, through specialization and trade, it ended up with 40 units of food and 140 units of clothing:

Benefits to Japan of specialization and trade
10 more units of F
20 more units of C

Thus, if countries specialize in the production of the goods in which they have a comparative advantage and then trade some of these goods for other goods, they can make themselves better off.

A Student Asks

QUESTION: *Suppose one country in the world is better at producing all goods. In other words, it can produce more of all goods with a given amount of resources. Would this country still be better off trading with other countries?*

Economics *in the* Real World

To Mow, or Clean, or Both?

Fourteen-year-old Steve and twelve-year-old Danny are brothers. Their father just told them that each week, they must complete two tasks: clean their rooms and mow the lawn. The following table shows how many minutes it takes each brother to do each task:

	Time to clean both rooms	Time to mow lawn
Steve	100 minutes	60 minutes
Danny	100 minutes	120 minutes

Although both Steve and Danny take the same time to clean both rooms, Danny is slower mowing the lawn than Steve. Danny takes a lot more breaks than Steve does.

Steve and Danny wonder how they should go about doing what their father told them to do. They realize they could each do half of each task or they could simply split the tasks and each do one. Which is the better way to proceed?

Suppose each brother does half of each task. Steve spends 50 minutes on his half of cleaning the rooms, and Danny spends 50 minutes, which is a total of 100 minutes to clean the rooms. Then Steve spends 30 minutes mowing his half of the lawn, and Danny spends 60 minutes mowing, a total of 90 minutes of mowing. To complete both tasks, it takes 100 minutes plus 90 minutes, or 190 minutes.

Now suppose that Steve only mows the lawn (he specializes), and Danny only cleans the rooms (he specializes). It takes Steve 60 minutes to mow the lawn, and it takes Danny 100 minutes to clean the rooms, which is a total of 160 minutes.

The choice is between 190 minutes or 160 minutes. To save time, the brothers should do what each has a *comparative advantage* in doing and specialize in one task. That way, they will get their duties completed 30 minutes faster and

have much more time to do what they want.

THINK ABOUT IT In many families, people have certain things that they do and no one else does. For example, one person may cook and the other may wash dishes; or one may mow the lawn and the other may pull weeds. Do you think the jobs that family members do are the result of comparative advantage or something else? Explain your answer.

Cooperative Learning

Divide the class into groups of three or four students. Tell each group to research a different U.S. trading partner. Each group should conduct research to answer the following questions: In what types of goods does the nation specialize? Does it carry on a significant level of trade in these items with the United States? Ask students to find the most current data on what types of goods are traded between their nations and the United States. Allow groups to present their findings to the class.

ANSWER: *Yes. Instead of thinking of this example on a country basis, let's think of it on an individual basis. Suppose a person is a brain surgeon. She is a very good brain surgeon, but then she is good at almost everything she does. For example, not only is she a good brain surgeon, but she's also good at changing the oil in her car, washing her clothes, cleaning her house, mowing the lawn, fixing the faucet in the bathroom, and so on. Does it follow that because she is, say, better than most plumbers when it comes to fixing bathroom faucets, that she should fix her own bathroom faucet instead of calling a plumber? Not at all. Most likely, she can benefit from calling a plumber and devoting her time to brain surgery instead of fixing the faucet.*

Our point is a simple one: even if you find a person who is better at doing everything than everyone else, that person is made better off by doing the one thing he or she is best at doing and purchasing the services of other people to do other things.

The same thing is true for a country. Even if one country could produce everything better than other countries, it would benefit that country to do what it does best and then trade with other countries.

A Student Asks

QUESTION: *I have another question about trade. If we (in the United States) don't produce as many different goods as we can, won't we simply be shipping jobs out of the country? For example, although it might be costly to produce bananas in the United States, some Americans would be working in the banana industry in this country if we produced bananas. Now, no one works in the banana industry in the United States, but people in Honduras are working in the banana industry. Isn't it better for Americans to keep jobs at home?*

ANSWER: *First, you shouldn't assume that if Americans aren't working in the banana industry that they aren't working at all. Americans who aren't working in the banana industry might be working in some other industry. Second, it isn't so much a matter of "keeping jobs at home" as it is making sure Americans are doing the jobs they are best at doing. It may be relatively costly for Americans to work at producing bananas but relatively cheap—in terms of opportunity cost— for Americans to work at producing computer software, cars, or movies.*

Even without international trade, the types of jobs available in the United States changes. For example, in 1929, 22 percent of the workforce was made up of farmers. That percentage was down to 16.2 percent in 1945, and today it is about 1.2 percent.

No doubt someone in the 1940s, complaining about the declining employment of farmers in the United States, said something like, "We can't have people leaving the ranks of the farmers; it will be the end of America." But it wasn't the end of America. Agricultural production in the United States boomed at the same time as the number of farmers decreased (in both absolute and relative terms) in America. Many of the people who would have been farmers instead became teachers, doctors, accountants, engineers, plumbers, construction workers, taxi drivers, and so on.

Again, our point is a simple one: even without any international trade, the composition of the labor force will change. At one time in the United States, no one worked in the computer software industry because there were no computers. Today, thousands are employed in this industry. At one time in the United States, no one was employed in the auto industry because there were no cars. Today, thousands are employed in this industry.

Prediction Activity

Present the following scenario to the class: Carlos and Kim are married. Carlos can wash the dishes in 20 minutes and cut the lawn in 30 minutes. Kim can wash the dishes in 40 minutes and cut the lawn in 40 minutes. If Carlos and Kim decide to specialize in doing certain tasks, who should cut the lawn and who should wash the dishes? Ask students to predict who will do which task.

Carlos has a comparative advantage in washing the dishes. We predict that Carlos will therefore wash the dishes and Kim will cut the lawn. If they specialize this way, Carlos will spend 20 minutes washing the dishes and Kim will spend 40 minutes cutting the lawn, for a total of 60 minutes. This is less than the 70 minutes it would take if Kim washed the dishes and Carlos cut the lawn.

It is also less time than if Carlos and Kim decided to split tasks. In that case, Carlos would spend 10 minutes washing the dishes and complete half the dishes, and Kim would spend 20 minutes completing the other half. Carlos would then spend 15 minutes cutting half the lawn, and Kim would spend 20 minutes cutting the other half. The total time it would take to do the dishes and cut the lawn would be 65 minutes.

To recap, specializing in the task in which you have a comparative advantage minimizes the time it takes to complete tasks.

A Student Asks

Use the A Student Asks that begins on page 440 to make sure students understand the analogy between the brain surgeon and a nation that is good at producing all goods.

Internet Research

The International Trade Administration (ITA) of the U.S. Department of Commerce compiles trade statistics. Have students go to the ITA website at http://econ.emcp.net/trade and click on "Data & Analysis," then "Trade Stats Express," then "National Trade Data," and finally "Global Patterns of U.S. Merchandise Trade." On this web page, students will see the trade balance and imports and exports displayed on a map. Ask students what the U.S. balance of trade was for the latest year published.

Economics Around the Clock

Invite students to discuss their answers to the questions that follow the 5:45 p.m. scenario in Economics Around the Clock (page 433).

The answer to the first question is that offshoring occurs when a domestic company hires people in another country to do certain work activities. Should U.S. residents worry about offshoring? Answers will vary. Students may say that offshoring comes with benefits and costs. It definitely involves some costs for American workers, but it also provides benefits for American consumers.

ANSWERS TO THINK ABOUT IT They would be more likely to specialize and trade. Economic freedom is an important part of free enterprise; people have the right to choose what kind of work they want to do. Because specialization and trading commonly benefit individuals more than self-sufficiency and not trading, we can expect people in a free enterprise economic system to exercise their freedom in a way that makes them better off: through specialization and trade

Economic Facts and Fallacies

Self-Sufficiency Versus Specialization

FALSE TRUE

Some Americans insist that the United States should produce everything it consumes. That way, we'll be self-sufficient, they argue. If a country produces everything it consumes, then it won't have to depend on people in different countries to produce anything that it needs.

Producing everything you consume *can* lead to becoming self-sufficient. But ask yourself this: how many people want to be self-sufficient?

What about you, for example? Do you produce everything you consume? If you have a smart phone, did you produce it? If you use a computer, did you produce it? Did you produce the car you drive, the food you eat, or the TV you watch? Probably not.

The fact is, most individuals realize that it's more advantageous to them to specialize in producing one thing (accounting, teaching, cutting hair, laying carpet, building houses) and then sell that thing to others.

People (and countries) specialize for a reason: it's in their best interest. Being self-sufficient, it seems, isn't beneficial enough to overcome the benefits that come from specialization and trade.

THINK ABOUT IT Would people living in a free enterprise economic system be more likely to specialize and trade or to be self-sufficient and not trade? Explain your answer.

Outsourcing and Offshoring

Many Americans are concerned with the effects of outsourcing and offshoring. Before examining this issue, let's make sure you know the difference between these two terms.

Understanding the Difference

Suppose a company called "Adams Software" is located in Greensboro, North Carolina, and has 100 employees. One day, the president of Adams Software decides to hire some people in, say, Seattle, Washington, to do some work for the company. Because the president is hiring workers who are not formal employees of the company in Greensboro, he is said to be *outsourcing* jobs. In short, **outsourcing** is an arrangement in which work is done for a company by another company or by people other than the original company's employees.

outsourcing
An arrangement in which work is done for a company by another company or by people other than the original company's employees.

Recall from Chapter 2 that when a company outsources certain work to individuals in another country, it's said to be engaged in *offshore outsourcing* or *offshoring*. For example, if a computer company in Texas hires people in India to answer customers' calls, then the company is offshoring.

Sometimes, people use the word *outsourcing* when the correct word is *offshoring*. For example, it isn't uncommon to hear a person say, "Yes, many U.S. companies are outsourcing jobs to India and China." Once again, if we are talking about individuals being hired in another country (a country other than the United States), the correct word is *offshoring*.

Jobs Are Lost

Many Americans are upset by the loss of jobs that is caused by offshoring. Think of an extreme case: a person in Montana goes to college to learn software engineering. After studying four or five years in college, she gets her degree and is ready to work. Then, just as she enters the job market, she finds out that many of the companies she is seeking employment with are hiring software engineers in, say, India. Why? Because software engineers in India earn lower salaries than software engineers in the United States.

It's easy to see why our software engineer from Montana might be frustrated by what has happened. Here she went to college, thinking that a job would be waiting for her when she graduated, but instead, many of the jobs were "shipped" overseas.

Will these kinds of things happen in a free market, global economy? Yes they will. In fact, they have already happened. Are these personal disappointments for some people, such as our software engineer from Montana? No doubt they are. What happens to the software engineer isn't the full story, though. There is more to tell.

Some Benefits

First, offshoring isn't something that only happens in the United States. Yes, U.S. companies can and do hire individuals who live in other countries. It's also the

Differentiating Instruction

Enrichment and Extension

Encourage students to read *The World Is Flat: A Brief History of the Twenty-first Century,* by Thomas L. Friedman (New York: Farrar, Straus and Giroux, 2005). Challenge them to take notes on issues related to the topics of this chapter as they read. Also instruct each student to write three or four questions about these issues that would be good for discussion in a book club—for example, What does Friedman mean when he says the world is flat? When students have completed their reading and questions, gather them in a circle for a discussion of the book. You might host this discussion outside class in a relaxed environment with refreshments.

Indian employees at a call center in India provide service support to international customers. Why would a company in Germany, Russia, or the United States, for example, hire Indian workers, rather than workers in their own country to handle these calls?

Reinforcement Activity

Tell students that although many workers in India are willing to work for lower wages than workers in the United States, there may be other reasons that U.S. companies prefer to offshore jobs there. Ask students what some of those reasons might be. Answers will vary. Students might suggest reasons such as the presence of an educated workforce and low political barriers.

case, however, that foreign companies hire individuals who work in the United States. In short, offshoring is a two-way street.

Second, offshoring often benefits consumers. How so? U.S. companies offshore certain work activities only if it's less costly for them to hire foreign labor than U.S. labor (assuming the quality of the labor in the two countries is the same). That is, the motivation behind offshoring is the attempt to lower costs (and thus raise profits). As we know from an earlier chapter, lower costs shift the supply curve (of the good) to the right. Do you remember what happens if the supply curve shifts to the right? The price of the good falls. In other words, consumers end up paying lower prices.

Opportunity Costs Play a Role

Offshoring is nothing more than people producing the things they can produce at a lower cost than other people can. It is simply *comparative advantage* at work.

Looking at offshoring this way sheds some light on the case of the Montana software engineer. Recall that the job she was seeking had been offshored to India, because Indian software engineers earn less than American software engineers. But couldn't the software engineer from Montana have offered to work for the same wage that the Indian software engineer agreed to work for? Let's say this wage was $600 a week. The answer, of course, is yes. So why didn't she offer to do this? Why didn't she simply say that if the Indian software engineer is willing to work for $600 a week, then so is she?

The Montana software engineer must have had a better alternative open to her than working for $600 a week. If she didn't, then she would have offered to work for the same wage as the Indian software engineer. Here is her "priority list":

Top choice:
Work as a software engineer for $1,000 a week

Second choice:
Work at job X for $700 a week

Third choice:
Work as a software engineer for $600 a week
(which is the same wage an Indian
software engineer is receiving)

She initially goes after her top choice and learns that it is no longer open to her. She doesn't go for her third choice, though, because she has a second choice that is better.

In other words, our software engineer from Montana doesn't choose to work at the same wage as the Indian software engineer because her opportunity costs are greater than his. We are not suggesting that offshoring doesn't hurt her. Her hurt comes in the form of earning $700 a week instead of $1,000 a week. It's just that now, we understand her options are not between

Cooperative Learning

Remind students that offshoring doesn't occur only in the United States. Divide the class into groups of four or five students. Instruct each group to choose a company that offshores jobs to the United States. Each group should research the following questions: What product or service does the company offer? When and why did it begin offshoring jobs to the United States? Has the offshoring produced any sort of political backlash in the company's home nation? Invite groups to present their findings to the class.

The offshoring of these jobs means that some U.S. engineers might not land jobs that pay as highly as they had hoped. Other engineering jobs that still pay better than the jobs in other countries are probably still available.

A Student Asks

Use this A Student Asks to remind students that U.S. companies don't automatically send jobs overseas if wage levels are slightly lower in other nations. Companies have to consider other factors, such as political barriers, language barriers, and the costs of relocating personnel.

Reinforcement Activity

Tell students to work in groups of three or four to find newspaper or magazine articles about offshoring. Ask, What kind of jobs are being lost, and where are the jobs going? Urge students to think about how the offshoring of these jobs might affect consumer prices. Allow groups to present their findings to the class.

Thinking Like an Economist

ANSWERS TO THINK ABOUT IT The world economic growth rate would likely be lower. Offshoring often leads to lower costs (which is part of the reason for offshoring in the first place), and lower costs often lead to greater output of goods and services. Remember that we are considering the world economic growth rate and not the growth rate of a particular country.

Teaching with Visuals

The consumer in the photo on page 445 might not be aware that the item she is about to buy is made more affordable by offshoring. Offshoring helps to keep the cost of goods low by keeping labor costs low.

▲ Although some companies have chosen to offshore software engineering jobs, it doesn't necessarily follow that U.S. software engineers have no jobs at all. Explain.

(1) working for $1,000 a week and (2) not working. Her options are between (1) working for $1,000 a week and (2) working for $700 a week. Her options are not as clearcut or as extreme as we perhaps thought at first.

One final point to consider is that even though offshoring lowers our Montana software engineer's income by $300 a week, it lowers the U.S. company's costs by $400 a week (per software engineer hired in India instead of the United States). In other words, costs of the company fall by more than income falls. And, as we said earlier, if the company operates in a competitive environment—where prices tend to fall to a level just sufficient enough to cover costs—then we can expect a decline in prices to follow.

A Student Asks

QUESTION: *I think part of this story is unrealistic. You say that if the software engineer from Montana wanted to work for $600, she could have told the U.S. company offshoring jobs to India. Then she would have worked at $600 a week. But I've never heard of a person going into a company and offering to work for the same wage as a person in India, or China, or any other country. Isn't this unrealistic?*

ANSWER: *In a way, you are right. Very few, if any, people would send the following email to the president of a company that is offshoring jobs:*

Dear President:

I know you have been offshoring jobs to India because you can hire labor there at a lower wage than you can hire labor here in the United States. I also know that the wage isn't the only thing that matters to you—productivity matters too. So, it must be the case that Indian labor is as productive as U.S. labor—but just costs less. I can see why you are doing what you are doing. If I were in your shoes and had to answer to the stockholders, I would probably do the same thing.

So, here's the deal: I will work for the same wage you are paying the software engineers in India. Here are my phone number and email address.

I hope to hear from you soon.
Signed,
Software engineer from Montana

Even though emails like this one are rarely sent, if the message it contains is the same message on the minds of enough American software engineers, you can be sure the president of the company is going to hear it. He or she might not hear it in an email or on the phone, but he or she will hear it in board meetings. U.S. companies have a monetary incentive to learn what wages they have to pay. If many American software engineers will work for the same wage as Indian engineers, then U.S. companies will know this and hire Americans. Also, the cost of setting up an operation overseas is often expensive and problematic (especially if foreign government issues must be worked out).

Differentiating Instruction

English Language Learners

To help students who are English language learners, use the following resources, which are provided as part of the *Economics: New Ways of Thinking* program:

- a Spanish glossary in the *Student Text*
- Spanish versions of the Chapter Summaries on an audio disc

The Costs of Offshoring Are Easier to See Than the Benefits

In our economic discussion of offshoring, we have mentioned some benefits and costs. One huge cost came to the software engineer who ended up earning $700 a week instead of $1,000 a week. One huge benefit came in the form of lower prices for consumers. In addition, we learned that offshoring is a two-way street.

The biggest practical problem with offshoring is that the costs are much easier to see than the benefits. For this reason, many people think offshoring is nothing but costs.

Think of yourself watching the TV news one night. A news reporter tells you the story of our software engineer from Montana who went to college and then couldn't get a job as a software engineer earning $1,000 a week because so many U.S. companies hired Indian software engineers instead. The news report makes the picture easy to see. The software engineer from Montana on your screen is a real person—just like you. If you are an empathic sort of person, you can feel some of the pain and heartbreak that she must be going through.

What you don't see in the TV news report or perhaps read about in the newspaper the next day is that just as U.S. companies offshore jobs to India, some foreign companies offshore jobs to the United

States. But you don't see the American who is working for a foreign company. His or her story is rarely told in the news.

You also don't see the lower prices that often result from offshoring. As far as you know, prices just keep going up and up and up. So where are the lower prices that offshoring is creating for American buyers? The problem here is that two things are happening at the same time, It's difficult to see what is happening to prices because of

Thinking Like an Economist

The Costs and Benefits of Offshoring

Economists know that costs and benefits can be viewed from different perspectives. For example, when it comes to offshoring, costs and benefits can be viewed on an individual level and on an aggregate (combined) level.

It may very well be true that on an aggregate level, the country receives net benefits from offshoring. (The benefits are greater than the costs.) Of course, this doesn't mean that every person in the country receives net benefits from offshoring. Some people will likely incur a net loss from offshoring. (The costs are greater than the benefits.) For example, think of the person who might lose her current job because of offshoring.

THINK ABOUT IT Would the world economic growth rate be higher or lower if there were no offshoring? Explain your answer.

◀ As this American consumer shops, why might she fail to realize that she will benefit from offshoring if she decides to make this purchase?

After reading and discussing Section 1, you may want to assign the Section Activity in the *Applying the Principles Workbook*, pages 151–155.

Assess

Quick Quiz

The following true-or-false quiz will help you assess student understanding of the material covered in this section.

1. Exports are goods that are produced in foreign countries and sold to residents of the domestic country. (False)
2. The balance of trade is the difference between the value of a country's exports and the value of its imports. (True)
3. An absolute advantage means that one country can produce more of a good using the same quantity of resources than another country. (True)
4. Opportunity costs are very important in determining comparative advantage. (True)
5. Countries with comparative advantages in goods should not specialize in any one product. (False)

Assessment Book

You will find a quiz for this section in the *Assessment Book*, page 150.

Reteaching Activity

Use the Section Assessment to gauge which students may need reteaching on this section. For those students, write the term *balance of trade* on the board. Then draw a traditional scale. Tell students that the right side of the scale represents exports and the left side represents imports. Invite students to come to the board to draw weights on the scale to represent both favorable and unfavorable trade balances.

Guided Reading

For further reteaching of the key concepts in this section, assign the Outlining Activity and the Just the Facts Handout from the *Guided Reading and Study Guide*, pages 259–263.

Cooperative Learning

Divide the class into two groups, and tell them that they will need to prepare for a debate about offshoring. At issue: Is offshoring good for the United States? Give the groups several days to research the pros and cons of their sides. Then

act as a moderator for the debate. Make sure that most of the students have input. When the debate has concluded, ask students whether their opinions about offshoring changed while they prepared for or participated in the debate.

Defining Terms

1. a. exports: goods produced in the domestic country and sold to residents of a foreign country; **b. imports:** goods produced in foreign countries and purchased by residents of the domestic country; **c. balance of trade:** the difference between the value of a country's exports and the value of its imports; **d. absolute advantage:** the situation in which a country can produce more of a good than another country with the same quantity of resources; **e. specialize:** to focus on a particular activity or product; **f. comparative advantage:** the situation in which a country can produce a good at a lower opportunity cost than another country; **g. outsourcing:** an arrangement in which work is done for a company by another company or by people other than its employees.

Reviewing Facts and Concepts

2. 1 orange (*calculation:* The opportunity cost of producing 10 more apples isn't producing 10 oranges; $10 \div 10 = 1$).
3. Country A is the low-cost producer of computers, or country A can produce computers most cheaply.

Critical Thinking

4. No. Just because Jones is better at gardening than Smith, it doesn't follow that he should do his own gardening instead of hiring Smith. Jones may have a higher opportunity cost of gardening than Smith. He may have to give up one-half hour of work as an attorney (at $150 a half hour) if he does his own gardening. If it takes Smith one hour to garden and he charges $30 an hour, then Jones would be better off working as an attorney for one-half hour, earning $150, paying Smith $30, and keeping $120.
5. No. The benefits of offshoring are often harder to see than the costs. In short, what one perceives to be true may be different than what is true, and economic policies may more closely reflect the former.
6. It follows that the United States, by importing goods for which it does not

offshoring. The first thing that is happening is that the Fed, which we discussed in an earlier chapter, is busy raising the money supply (most months). The increased money supply is putting upward pressure on prices. At the same time, offshoring is putting downward pressure on prices. The problem, however, is that net prices keep rising because the money supply effect of pushing prices upward is stronger than the offshoring effect of pushing prices downward. It's as if the money supply raises the price of a good $3 at the same time that offshoring lowers the price $1. What will be the result? The price is going to rise by $2. (Think of a person throwing buckets of water on a fire. The fire is still burning, but the flames aren't as high as if no water had been applied.)

If all Americans can see the costs of offshoring, then many of them will likely rally against it. They might vote for politicians who speak out against it, or they might march in the streets against U.S. companies that practice it. Would their behavior be different if they saw the whole picture instead of only the cost side of the picture?

SECTION

1

ASSESSMENT

Defining Terms

1. Define:
  a. exports
  b. imports
  c. balance of trade
  d. absolute advantage
  e. specialize
  f. comparative advantage
  g. outsourcing

Reviewing Facts and Concepts

2. Suppose the United States can produce either 90 apples and 20 oranges or 80 apples and 30 oranges. What is the opportunity cost of producing 1 apple?

3. What does it mean to say that "Country A has a comparative advantage in the production of computers"?

Critical Thinking

4. Jones is an attorney, and Smith is a gardener. Jones, however, is better than Smith at gardening. Essentially, Jones can do what needs to be done in the garden in 30 minutes, whereas it takes Smith one hour. Should Jones do his own gardening instead of hiring Smith to do it? Explain.

5. Suppose the benefits of offshoring are $400 billion and the costs are $300 billion. Will all of the elected officials support economic policies that favor offshoring? Explain.

6. What is the impact of U.S. imports on the United States? What is the impact on U.S. trading partners of U.S. imports?

Applying Economic Concepts

7. How would you go about computing the opportunity cost (in dollars) of studying for a test?

have a comparative advantage, is buying those goods at a cheaper price than it would cost to produce those goods. This is a net gain for the United States. As to the trading partners of the United States, they benefit by selling goods to the United States. We know this because they would not enter

into these voluntary trades with the United States unless they were being made better off.

Applying Economic Concepts

7. Estimate how many hours of study it takes to achieve a certain grade on the test. For example, suppose it takes John two hours of study to get a B

on a test, and it takes Karie one hour of study to get a B on the same test. Find out what each could earn in an hour. Suppose John and Karie could each earn $5 an hour. The opportunity cost (in dollars) of studying to get a B is $10 (2 hours ⊠ $5 an hour) for John and $5 (1 hour ⊠ $5 an hour) for Karie.

Trade Restrictions

Focus Questions
► What is a tariff?
► What is a quota?
► How do tariffs and quotas affect prices?
► Why does the government impose tariffs and quotas if they make goods more expensive for U.S. consumers?
► What impact did tariffs have on the Great Depression?
► What are the arguments for and against trade restrictions?

Key Terms
tariff
dumping

Trade Restrictions: Tariffs and Quotas

Tariffs and quotas are the two major types of trade restrictions. A **tariff** is a tax on imports. For example, some Americans buy cars made in Japan, which are considered imports. Let's say each car sells for $22,000. Now, suppose the U.S. government places a $1,000 tariff on each car, raising the price of a Japanese car from $22,000 to $23,000. As a result, Americans will buy fewer Japanese cars. (Remember the law of demand: as price rises, quantity demanded falls.)

A *quota* is a legal limit on the amount of a good that can be imported. Suppose Japan is sending 300,000 cars into the United States each year. The U.S. government decides to set a quota, or legal limit, on Japanese cars at 200,000 per year. In short, the U.S. government says it is legal for Japan to send 200,000 cars each year to the United States but not one car more.

The effect of the quota is to raise the price of Japanese cars. With a smaller supply of Japanese cars and with demand for Japanese cars constant, the price of Japanese cars will rise. (Recall that when the supply of a good falls and the demand for the good remains the same, the price of the good rises.) In effect, then, both tariffs and quotas raise the price of the imported good to the U.S. consumer.

The U.S. Government and Producer Interests

If tariffs and quotas result in higher prices for U.S. consumers, why does the government impose them? The government is sometimes more responsive to producer interests than consumer interests. In other words, the government may be more responsive to U.S. car manufacturers than to U.S. car consumers.

To see why, suppose 100 U.S. producers produce good X and 20 million U.S. consumers consume good X. The producers want to protect themselves from foreign competition, so they lobby for and receive tariffs on foreign goods that compete with what they sell. As a result, consumers end up paying higher prices. We'll say that consumers end up paying $40 million more,

tariff
A tax on imports.

Focus and Motivate

Section Objectives

After completing this section, students will be able to
► define the terms *tariff* and *quota;*
► explain how tariffs and quotas affect prices;
► explain why the government imposes tariffs and quotas if they make goods more expensive for U.S. consumers;
► describe the effect that tariffs had on the Great Depression; and
► identify the arguments for and against trade restrictions.

Kickoff Activity

Present students with the following questions: In the United States, who asks for the tariffs and quotas that we see placed on some foreign goods? What do they want to accomplish with these tariffs and quotas?

Activating Prior Knowledge

Allow volunteers to share their responses to the Kickoff Activity. Answers will vary. Some students will probably say that U.S. producers of goods may ask for tariffs and quotas on their foreign competitors' goods. Some students may say that, at times, labor unions will ask for tariffs and quotas on foreign goods to secure their members' jobs.

 Visit econ.myemcp.com/videos for videos that will help students better understand the key concepts found in this section.

Differentiating Instruction

English Language Learners

English language learners may have trouble with the concepts presented in this chapter. To help these students understand the information, call on student volunteers to take turns reading the chapter aloud. Each time a volunteer comes across vocabulary that may be unfamiliar to English language learners, stop him or her and ask the class to help you define the word. At the end of each section, you might also call on class members to help summarize that part of the text. By explaining new vocabulary and providing summaries, you will aid those students for whom English is a second language.

Teaching with Visuals

The government might place tariffs on imported steel in response to pressure from the steel industry. Answers will vary as to whether students would vote for tariffs.

Critical Thinking

Ask students if producers and consumers share an interest in having tariffs and quotas applied to important goods. The answer is no. Whereas producers may want tariffs and quotas, consumers will not. As we show in this section, domestic producers are helped by tariffs and quotas, but consumers end up paying higher prices.

Background Information

Explain to students that in economics, *efficiency* is achieved when net benefits have been maximized. This means that a U.S. policy is only efficient if the benefits of the policy are greater than the costs. Explain that economists almost all agree that the benefits of tariffs and quotas to domestic producers of goods that compete with the imported goods are far less than the costs of the tariffs and quotas, tariffs and quotas are often placed on foreign imports. In short, sometimes U.S. policies (tariffs and quotas being one example) would be considered economically inefficient.

Research Activity

Ask students to consider what other U.S. policies might be considered economically inefficient. Assign students to research their selected policy and to analyze whether it would be considered efficient by an economist.

▲ Why might the U.S. government place tariffs on imported steel? If you were a member of Congress, would you vote for or against such tariffs? Why?

avoid paying the small additional amount added by tariffs.

Politicians, who generally respond to the most vocal interests, hear from those people who want the tariffs but not from those people who are against them. Politicians may thus mistakenly assume that consumers' silence means that they accept the tariff policy, when in fact they may not. They may simply not find it worthwhile to do anything to fight the policy.

and producers end up receiving $40 million more, for good X than they would have if the tariffs had not been imposed. If we divide the additional $40 million received equally among the 100 producers, we find that each producer receives $400,000 more as a result of tariffs. If we divide the additional $40 million paid equally among the 20 million consumers, we find that each customer pays $2 more as a result of tariffs. A producer is likely to think, "I should lobby for tariffs, because if I am effective, I will receive $400,000 more." A consumer is likely to think, "Why should I lobby against tariffs? If I am effective, I will save myself only $2. It is not worth my lobbying to save $2."

In short, the benefits of tariffs are concentrated on *relatively few producers*, and the costs of tariffs are spread over *relatively many consumers*. This situation makes each producer's gain relatively large compared with each consumer's loss. Producers will probably lobby government to obtain the relatively large gains from tariffs, but consumers will not lobby government to

A Student Asks

QUESTION: *Can you give me an example of producer interests getting the tariffs they seek?*

ANSWER: *In 2002, the federal government placed tariffs on imported steel, and in 2009, it imposed tariffs on Chinese tires. The tariffs were in response to what the domestic (U.S.) steel and tire industries were asking for at the time. As a result of the tariffs, consumers ended up paying more for cars. A USA Today article made this statement about the steel tariffs: "The tariffs will undoubtedly be passed on to consumers. Critics say the action will raise prices to consumers on items ranging from cars, houses, and appliances. One critical study suggested the average family of four would spend up to $283 more a year."*

A Student Asks

QUESTION: *Don't tariffs sometimes save American jobs, though? Didn't the steel tariffs save some American jobs?*

ANSWER: *Yes, the tariffs might have saved some American jobs, but at what cost? That's the question an economist would ask. For example, the Institute for International Economics estimated that the steel tariffs saved 1,700 jobs in the steel industry but at the cost to consumers (in the form of higher*

Internet Research

In the fall of 1999, the World Trade Organization (WTO) held its Ministerial Conference in Seattle. Thousands of protesters also went to Seattle to demonstrate against the WTO. Instruct students to use the Internet to find at least two websites or articles in favor of the WTO and two opposed to this organization. Ask students to imagine that their parents or friends have asked them to explain what happened in Seattle and to write papers summarizing what they have learned. Each student should conclude by explaining whether he or she would have joined the protesters or the contingent supporting the WTO.

prices) of $800,000 per job. In other words, U.S. consumers ended up paying $800,000 in higher prices for every one job that was saved in the steel industry. Or look at it this way: the average job saved in the steel industry was a job that paid $50,000 to $55,000 a year. In short, because of the tariffs, American consumers paid $800,000 in higher prices to save a $50,000–$55,000 job.

One of the lessons we introduced in the first chapter of this book is that economists want to look at the entire picture, not only part of it. Tariffs can save jobs, which is certainly part of the picture of tariffs. But another part is that tariffs drive up prices for consumers. Tariffs can also make it more expensive for other American producers to produce goods. For example, even though tariffs on steel might have helped the U.S. steel industry, they certainly hurt the U.S. car industry (because car producers buy steel). When discussing tariffs and quotas, it's important to make sure to identify all of their effects.

Tariffs and the Great Depression

In January 1929, many members of Congress became disturbed over the increase in imports into the United States. Willis Hawley, chairman of the House Ways and Means Committee, introduced a bill to deal with this apparent problem. That bill, which came to be known as the Smoot-Hawley Tariff Act, proposed substantially higher tariffs on many imported goods. It was thought with higher tariffs on imported goods, Americans would buy fewer imports and more goods produced in the United States. This would be good for the country, some thought.

Although the Smoot-Hawley Tariff Act was not signed into law until June 17, 1930, its passage was likely, and many Americans suspected it would become law long before it did. Some people believed it would be bad for business in the United States. They thought that other countries would retaliate

with their own high tariffs (which they did) and that global trade would diminish, thus hurting the U.S. economy. (If other countries imposed high tariffs on U.S. goods, then Americans would not be able to sell as much abroad.)

Some economists blame the sharp decline in the stock market in 1929—which some say dates the beginning of the greatest economic decline in the nation's history, the Great Depression—on the foregone conclusion that Congress would pass and that the president would sign the Smoot-Hawley Tariff Act. Many economists today believe that this legislation not only served as one of the catalysts of the Great Depression but that it also made the Great Depression last longer than it would have otherwise.

Arguments for Trade Restrictions

Do tariffs and quotas exist only because the government is sometimes more responsive to the interests of producers than consumers? Not at all. They exist for other reasons too.

The National-Defense Argument

It is often argued that certain industries—such as aircraft, petroleum, chemicals, and weapons—are necessary to the national defense and therefore deserve to be protected from foreign competition. For example, suppose the United States has a

▼ Why might a country that produces oil place a tariff or quota on imported oil?

When some people talk about free trade, tariffs, and quotas, they sound as if it's "us" against "them." Often, this isn't the case. For example, suppose there is a Toyota dealership in a U.S. city. Americans work for that dealership. Ask students to suppose that U.S. auto manufacturers lobby government to have tariffs placed on Japanese imported cars. Ask, Is this really a matter of "us" against "them"? Some students might suggest that it's a case of "us" against "us." For example, aren't the U.S. auto manufacturers hurting the people in the United States who work for the Toyota dealership?

Teaching with Visuals

The country might place a tariff or quota on imported oil to keep the cost of oil high, or it might do so because it believes that the production of oil is imperative to its national defense.

Reinforcement Activity

Instruct students to look through newspapers and magazines for articles about the arguments for trade restrictions that are mentioned in the text. Divide students into small groups or partnerships to share their findings, or ask them to turn in their work for evaluation.

Economics *in the* Real World

Question students about the pros and cons of offshoring grading. Ask, Will your school district save money? How might these savings be used?

ANSWERS TO THINK ABOUT IT Answers will vary. Students might reply that jobs that require personal interaction are less likely to be offshored.

---

comparative advantage in the production of wheat, and China has a comparative advantage in the production of weapons. Should the United States specialize in the production of wheat and then trade wheat to China in exchange for weapons? Many Americans would answer no; they maintain it is too dangerous to leave weapons production to another country, whether that country is China, France, or Canada.

The national-defense argument may have some validity, but even valid arguments may be overused or abused. Industries that are not necessary to the national defense may still want trade restrictions placed on imported goods. For example, in the past, the national-defense argument has been used by firms in the following industries: pens, pottery, peanuts, candles, thumbtacks, tuna fishing, and pencils. It is difficult to believe that these goods are necessary to the national defense.

Economics *in the* Real World

Might Someone in India Grade Your Homework?

A person walks into a hospital to have a magnetic resonance imaging (MRI) test. In an MRI, the area of the body being studied is positioned inside a strong magnetic field. The MRI detects changes in the normal structures and characteristics of organs and other tissues. These changes may indicate diseases caused by a trauma, infection, inflammation, or tumor.

The information from an MRI is often saved and stored on a computer. Then it's sent electronically to someone who studies the scan and reports what he or she sees. The person who examines the MRI scan can be anywhere in the world. Often, the person is located in another country.

What happens with MRIs today might happen with your five-page essays and homework assignments in the future. Imagine this: A high

school teacher spends most of the day teaching and discussing the material—economics, history, mathematics. At the end of the day, the teacher scans homework assignments, essays, tests, and all other student work and then sends a digital version of the materials to graders in India, Ireland, or even Russia. For the graders, the only requirements are to know the material students are being tested on and to read and write in English.

By the way, this same process is essentially what happens when you write the essay for the SAT. Your essay is scanned into a computer and sent to a grader who might live anywhere in the United States. Well, if your essay can be sent to anyone in the United States, it can also be sent to anyone in the world.

It may actually be cheaper to grade your work this way than to have your teacher take the time to do it. Of course, if you had a problem with your grader in India or Ireland, the teacher in your high school would be the one to speak with. He or she could change the grade if need be.

The combination of digital technology and the Internet make

some things commonplace today that weren't even possible before, such as separating teaching from grading. The teacher doesn't have to be the same person as the grader when the grader can receive your work in the time it takes to scan and send a document.

In the future, we might see a greater specialization of tasks than ever before. Instead of a teacher having to teach and grade papers and record grades, a teacher may just teach. Others will grade, and still others will record grades, and so on.

THINK ABOUT IT What kinds of jobs or tasks aren't likely to be offshored? For instance, is an accountant's work more likely to be offshored than a medical physician's work?

Background Information: European Union

The European Economic Community was created in 1957 and merged with several other groups in 1993 to form the European Union (EU). In 2014, the EU consisted of 28 countries and more than 500 million people. In June 1998, the European Monetary Institute became the European Central Bank. A major economic development of the EU was the adoption of a single currency, the euro. In 2002, the euro became the currency used by many of these countries.

The Infant-Industry Argument

Alexander Hamilton, the first U.S. secretary of the Treasury, argued that "infant," or new, industries often need to be protected from older, more established foreign competitors until they are mature enough to compete on an equal basis. Today, some persons voice the same argument. The infant-industry argument is clearly an argument for only temporary protection from foreign producers. Critics charge, however, that once an industry is protected from foreign competition, removing the protection is almost impossible. The once-infant industry will continue to argue that it isn't yet old enough to go it alone.

The Antidumping Argument

Dumping is selling goods in foreign countries at prices below their costs and below the prices charged in the domestic (home) market. For example, if Germany sells a German-made car in the United States for a price below the cost to produce the car and at a price below what the car sells for in Germany, then Germany is said to be dumping cars in the United States. Critics of dumping say that dumpers (in our example, Germany) seek only to get into a market, drive out U.S. competitors, and then raise prices. However, some economists point out that such a strategy isn't likely to work. Once the dumpers have driven out their competitors and raised prices, their competitors are likely to return. The dumpers, in turn, will have obtained only a string of losses (by selling below cost) for their efforts. Opponents of the antidumping argument also point out that U.S. consumers benefit from dumping by paying lower prices.

The Low-Foreign-Wages Argument

Some people argue that U.S. producers can't compete with foreign producers because U.S. producers pay high wages to their workers and foreign producers pay low wages to their workers. U.S. producers insist that free trade must be restricted or they will be ruined.

What the argument overlooks is the reason U.S. wages are high and foreign wages are low: productivity. High wages and high productivity usually go together, as do low

wages and low productivity. Suppose a U.S. worker who receives $20 per hour produces 100 units of good X per hour; the cost per unit is 20 cents. A foreign worker who receives $2 per hour produces 5 units of good X per hour. The cost per unit is 40 cents—twice as high as for the U.S. worker. In short, a country's high-wage disadvantage may be offset by its productivity advantage. (See Exhibit 15-4 for the hourly compensation paid to manufacturing workers in different countries in 2011.)

Look at it this way: if firms always sought out the lowest-cost labor in the world (and didn't account for the productivity of the labor), then almost nothing would be produced in countries such as the United States, Belgium, and Australia.

dumping
The sale of goods abroad at prices below their costs and below the price charged in domestic (home) markets.

▼ Hourly compensation includes wages; premiums; bonuses; vacation, holidays, and other leave; insurance; and benefit plans.

EXHIBIT 15-4	Hourly Compensation for Manufacturing Workers, Selected Countries
Country	**Hourly compensation for manufacturing workers (in dollars)**
Australia	$ 46.29
Austria	43.16
Belgium	54.77
Canada	36.56
Denmark	51.67
Finland	44.14
France	42.12
Germany	47.38
Ireland	39.83
Italy	36.17
Japan	35.71
Korea, South	18.91
Mexico	6.48
Netherlands	42.26
New Zealand	23.38
Norway	64.15
Portugal	12.91
Singapore	22.60
Spain	28.44
Sweden	49.12
Switzerland	60.40
Taiwan	9.34
United Kingdom	30.77
United States	35.53

Source: U.S. Bureau of Labor Statistics, 2012.

Teaching with Visuals

Ask students to compare the hourly wages of workers in the United States with those of workers in Mexico, Singapore, and Taiwan. Discuss with students how these differences might lead to offshoring.

Reinforcement Activity

Instruct students to find the hourly compensation for production workers in some countries not listed in Exhibit 15-4. One place to look is the *Statistical Abstract of the United States.*

Internet Research

Assign students the task of going online to find the most recent wages (hourly compensation) reported for workers in the countries listed in Exhibit 15-4. Then tell students to create charts showing both the figures given here and the newer figures. Ask, Is there a difference? Has there been real growth in income? Have workers' wages held steady, according to the CPI? Allow students to present their findings in small groups, and then guide the class in a discussion of the results of their research.

Answers will vary.

Critical Thinking

Some people suggest that we are moving toward more and larger free trade areas in the world. Others say that we will soon be moving in the other direction, toward greater protectionism. Ask students what they think. Allow them to discuss or debate the issue and give reasons for their positions.

Reinforcement Activity

Ask students to research one of the following: the European Union (EU), the North American Free Trade Agreement (NAFTA), or the General Agreement on Tariffs and Trade (GATT). They should investigate the following questions: Who belongs to this group? What is the group's purpose?

Discussion Starter

Ask students if they would be willing to move to another country if the jobs there paid more money. Ask, Why doesn't it necessarily follow that a high hourly wage makes for a good standard of living?

Discussion Starter

Some people have made the argument that the United States has a moral obligation to provide economic support to poor countries. Other people disagree. Ask students to research and debate this issue.

Teaching with Visuals

Answers to the photo question on page 453 will vary. Students may say that countries want to protect their shoe industries from Chinese competitors. China might respond by passing tariffs of its own.

Reinforcement Activity

During the last half of 1993, there was much debate in the United States over the advantages and disadvantages of NAFTA. Assign students to look at newspapers from this time period and then write two- to three-page papers outlining the debate. Students should address these questions: What did proponents of NAFTA believe? What did opponents of NAFTA argue?

▲ Suppose tariffs have been imposed on these goods. Do you think there is a good reason to impose tariffs? Explain your answer.

The Tit-for-Tat Argument

Some people argue that if a foreign country uses tariffs or quotas against U.S. goods, the United States should apply equal tariffs and quotas against that foreign country, in the hope that the foreign country will lower or eliminate its trade restrictions. According to this tit-for-tat argument, we should do to them as they do to us.

Critics of this type of policy argue that a tit-for-tat strategy has the potential to escalate into a full-blown trade war. For example, suppose China places a tariff on American-made microwaves. The United States retaliates by placing a tariff on Chinese-made microwaves. China then reacts by placing a tariff on American-made clothes, the United States retaliates by placing a tariff on Chinese-made clothes, and so on. At some point, it might be difficult to figure out who started what.

"Protectionism [trade restrictions] will do little to create jobs and if foreigners retaliate, we will surely lose jobs."
— Alan Greenspan, economist

A Student Asks

QUESTION: *Shouldn't the United States be concerned with what other countries do? After all, if other countries impose tariffs on U.S.-made goods or dump goods in the United States, won't the United States have to retaliate? It's sort of like having someone hit you in the face and you just say, "Hit me some more." Don't you have to defend yourself?*

ANSWER: *If you look at it in terms of the United States and other countries being individuals, then you come to the conclusion you have reached. But that comparison may not be the best one to use here. Take tariffs, for example. If China imposes tariffs on the United States, you say that the United States should retaliate and impose tariffs on China. Certainly, the United States can do that, but it won't just hurt Chinese producers. It will also hurt American consumers. Simply put, if the United States retaliates against other countries for the tariffs they have imposed, American consumers will get hurt in the crossfire.*

Consider what happens if Japan dumps some goods in the United States (sells at a price below cost). That action might hurt U.S. producers (that compete with Japan), but it will help U.S. consumers because they will pay lower prices. So dumping is like a slap in the face to our producers, but it's also a pat on the back to our consumers. The issue of international trade and trade restrictions isn't quite as black-and-white as it might first appear.

EXAMPLE Suppose Kelly is a domestic producer of good X. Currently, the United States imposes a high tariff on good X if it's produced in any foreign country. Kelly benefits from the tariff because it makes any foreign-produced good X less competitive with the good X that she produces. Now suppose a study comes out showing that American consumers are paying an extra $400,000 a year to increase Kelly's profits from $10,000 a year to $100,000 a year. This news is broadcast all over the TV and radio news, and finally, Congress decides to

Cooperative Learning

Divide the class into groups of four or five students. Direct each group to research one facet of the European Union (EU) that interests it, such as the history and struggles of the group or how a nation joins it. Groups should prepare reports on their findings. You might schedule time in the school library for groups to conduct research.

consider eliminating the tariff on good X. Kelly may know that the country, as a whole, benefits more from eliminating the tariff than keeping it, but she certainly doesn't benefit more. Kelly may lobby to keep the tariff, even though more Americans are hurt by it than helped by it. ♦

International Economic Integration

One of the hallmarks of a global economy is economic integration: the combining of nations to form either a *common market* or a *free trade area*. In a common market, the member nations trade without restrictions, and all share the same trade barriers with the outside world. For example, suppose countries A, B, C, D, E, and F formed a common market. They would eliminate all trade barriers among themselves (free trade would exist), but they would have common trade barriers with all other nations. Thus, any tariffs placed on country Z's goods would apply to all member countries.

A major common market is the European Union (EU), which consists of 28 countries (as of this writing). Currently, the euro is a common currency in 19 of the 28 countries of the EU.

In a free trade area, in contrast to a common market, trade barriers among the member countries are eliminated, and each country is allowed to set its own trade rules for dealing with the rest of the world. For example, if both country G and country D are part of a free trade area, country G might place tariffs on country Z's goods (country Z is not a member of the free trade area), while country D does not.

A major free trade area created by the North American Free Trade Agreement (NAFTA) includes Canada, Mexico, and the United States. NAFTA took effect in 1994. In 2005, the U.S. Congress passed the Central American-Dominican Republic Free Trade Agreement (CAFTA-DR). The CAFTA-DR is a free trade agreement between the countries of the United States, Costa Rica, El Salvador, Guatemala, Honduras, Nicaragua,

and the Dominican Republic. CAFTA-DR reduces barriers to trade between its member countries.

Although there are many benefits to international free trade organizations, there are sometimes costs for participating in international free trade agreements. Costs can include the displacement (or loss) of jobs and the possibility of unbalanced agreements between countries. For example, some economists have argued that NAFTA has created a U.S. trade deficit with Mexico, leading to the displacement of U.S. jobs. In other words, these are jobs that would have been in the United States had NAFTA not been implemented. There are, of course, benefits to some free trade agreements, one of which is that often domestic customers can buy goods at lower prices.

International Organizations

Many economists predict that countries are likely to join in common markets and free trade areas in the near future. Increasingly, countries of the world are finding that it's in their best interests to lower trade barriers between themselves and their neighbors.

The World Trade Organization (WTO) provides a forum for its member countries (164 countries in mid-2017) to discuss and negotiate trade issues. It also provides a system for adjudicating trade disputes. For example, suppose the United States claimed that the Canadian government was preventing U.S. producers from openly selling their goods in Canada. The WTO would look at the matter, consult trade experts, and then decide the issue. A country that is found engaging in unfair trade can either desist from this practice or face appropriate retaliation from the injured party.

Two other prominent international organizations are the World Bank and the International Monetary Fund (IMF). The World Bank, officially known as the International Bank for Reconstruction and Development (IBRD), is the biggest development bank in the

> *"Trade barriers are chiefly injurious to the countries imposing them."*
> — John Stuart Mill,
> **philosopher and economist**

Internet Research

Students are probably not familiar with the workings of the International Monetary Fund or the World Bank. Ask each student to search the Internet for an example of how one of these organizations is assisting a particular nation. Then assign a one-page paper in which the student summarizes his or her findings, including background information about the particular challenges facing the nation.

Teaching with Visuals

The answer to the question with the photo on page 454 is that the major economic purpose of the European Union is to provide a common market, in which member nations trade freely among themselves and enforce the same barriers to trade with nonmember nations.

 Application Activity

After reading and discussing Section 2, you may want to assign the Section Activity in the *Applying the Principles Workbook*, pages 156–159.

Assess

Quick Quiz

The following true-or-false quiz will help you assess student understanding of the material covered in this section.

1. A quota is a tax on imports. (False)
2. Tariffs and quotas exist only because government is sometimes more responsive to producer interests than consumer interests. (False)
3. Alexander Hamilton argued that "infant" industries often need protection from established foreign competitors.
(True)
4. In a common market, all member nations trade without restrictions.
(True)
5. Dumping is selling goods in foreign countries at prices below their costs and below prices charged in the domestic market. (True)

 Assessment Book

You will find a quiz for this section in the *Assessment Book*, page 151.

Reteaching Activity

Use the Section Assessment to gauge which students may need reteaching on this section. For those students, write the words *tariff* and *quota* on the board. Ask which term refers to a legal limit on the amount of a good that may be imported. (*Answer*: quota.) Then ask which term refers to a tax on imports. (*Answer*: tariff.)

▶ A meeting of the European Parliament in Strasbourg, France. This body of the European Union cannot initiate legislation, but it can amend and veto policies. **What is the major economic purpose of the European Union?**

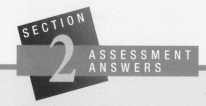
world. Its primary function is to lend money to the world's poor and less-developed countries. The money for lending comes from rich member countries, such as the United States, and from selling bonds and lending the money raised through bond sales. The World Bank usually makes loans for economic development projects that are expected to produce a return sufficient to pay back the loan.

The IMF is an international organization that, among other things, provides economic advice and temporary funding to nations with economic difficulties. It has been referred to as a "doctor called in at the last minute." When a country is in economic difficulty, the IMF might submit a list of economic reforms for it to follow, such as cutting excessive government spending to reduce budget deficits and decreasing the growth rate of the money supply. The IMF often lends funds to a country in economic trouble on the condition that its economic advice is followed.

A country's acceptance of IMF reforms is usually a signal to other international organizations, such as the World Bank, that the country is serious about getting its economic house in order. The World Bank may then provide long-term funding.

SECTION 2 ASSESSMENT

Defining Terms

1. Define:
  a. tariff
  b. dumping

Reviewing Facts and Concepts

2. What effect does a tariff have on the price of an imported good?

3. State and then evaluate the infant-industry argument for trade restrictions.

4. State and then evaluate the tit-for-tat argument for trade restrictions.

Critical Thinking

5. Consider a policy that effectively transfers $100 million from group A to group B. Group A is made up of 50 million people. Is the policy more likely to be passed and implemented if the number of people in group B is 50 million or 500,000? Explain.

6. Would domestic producers be more likely to lobby government to place tariffs on imported goods during good or bad economic times? Explain.

7. Evaluate the costs and benefits of participating in international free trade agreements.

Applying Economic Concepts

8. How might domestic producers of a good abuse the antidumping argument for restricted trade?

government for tariffs during bad than good economic times. In good economic times, a domestic producer can more easily survive without hampering foreign competition.

7. One of the key benefits is that trade restrictions between countries that have signed the agreement are lowered. One of the costs could be that members to the agreement don't have as much flexibility when dealing with countries outside the agreement.

Applying Economic Concepts

8. Domestic producers have a monetary incentive to restrict the importing of goods that compete with the goods they produce. For example, U.S. shoe manufacturers are better off if Americans cannot buy foreign produced shoes or if shoes produced overseas are very expensive. To this end, domestic producers may claim that a foreign competitor is dumping, when in fact it is not.

The Exchange Rate

Focus Questions
▶ What is an exchange rate?
▶ What does it mean to say that a currency "appreciates" in value?
▶ What does it mean to say that a currency "depreciates" in value?

Key Terms
exchange rate
flexible exchange rate system
fixed exchange rate system
depreciation
appreciation

Section Objectives

After completing this section, students will be able to
▶ define the term *exchange rate*;
▶ explain what it means to say that a currency "appreciates" in value; and
▶ explain what it means to say that a currency "depreciates" in value.

Kickoff Activity

Ask students the following question: What do you think it means if a person "buys currencies"?

Activating Prior Knowledge

Allow volunteers to share their responses to the Kickoff Activity. They may answer that there is a foreign exchange market. In this market, currencies of different countries are bought and sold.

What Is an Exchange Rate?

The **exchange rate** is the price of one nation's currency in terms of another nation's currency. Suppose you take a trip to Italy. To buy goods and services, you will need to have the currency used in Italy, the basic unit of which is the euro. (The monetary symbol for the euro, €, simply looks like a C with two lines through the middle.) Therefore, you will need to exchange your dollars for euros.

Suppose you want to exchange $200 for euros. How many euros you get will depend on the exchange rate, which may be determined in two ways: by the forces of supply and demand under a **flexible exchange rate system** or by the government under a **fixed exchange rate system**. Suppose the exchange rate is currently $1 for €0.80. For every $1 you have, you will get €0.80 in exchange, so you will receive €80 in exchange for $100. (Exhibit 15-5 on the next page shows the value of the U.S. dollar in terms of eight foreign currencies on April 21, 2017.)

EXAMPLE Just as people buy goods (like chairs and TVs), people can buy foreign money too. Americans can buy euros, pesos, yen, and so on. When Americans buy, say, euros, they have to pay some price. The dollar price they have to pay for a euro is called the *exchange rate*. Suppose an American is in Italy and sees an item for sale. Its price: €100 (100 euros). The American asks himself how much this is in dollars. If the exchange rate is, say, $1 = €0.80, he knows that for every $1 he has, he will get €0.80 in exchange. To get 100 euros, then, the American will have to pay $125. ♦

A Student Asks

QUESTION: *How did €100 turn out to be $125? Will you go over the calculation?*

ANSWER: *Keep in mind that any exchange rate can be expressed two ways, not just one. For example, here is one way to express the dollar-euro exchange rate: $1 = €0.80.*
This expresses the exchange rate between dollars and euros in terms of one dollar. Instead, suppose we want

exchange rate
The price of one country's currency in terms of another country's currency.

flexible exchange rate system
The system whereby currency exchange rates are determined by the forces of supply and demand.

fixed exchange rate system
The system whereby currency exchange rates are fixed, or pegged, by countries' governments.

Teach

Discussion Starter

Lead students in a discussion about their experiences in traveling to other countries. Ask, How did you handle money during your travels? Did you convert the value of a dollar to the value of the foreign currency with a calculator, or did you do the calculations in your head?

Visit econ.myemcp.com/videos for videos that will help students better understand the key concepts found in this section.

Section 3 The Exchange Rate **455**

Internet Research

Ask students to imagine that they have just found a wallet in the street. It's full of money but from several different countries—perhaps it belongs to someone on a world tour. Of course, students are going to turn in the wallet to the police. But in case it isn't claimed, they want to know how much money they will get to keep.

Direct students to a currency-exchange website (such as CNN's Currencies page) to find out how many dollars they would have if they exchanged the money today and the wallet contains 1,200 Japanese yen, 500 euros, 55 British pounds, 200 Australian dollars, and 450 Mexican pesos. Answers will vary depending on current exchange rates.

to express the exchange rate between dollars and euros in terms of one euro: we simply divide $1 by the number of euros it takes to obtain that one dollar. Here is the arithmetic: $1 ÷ 0.80 = $1.25. In other words, €1 = $1.25. We are saying, then, that (a) $1 = €0.80 and (b) €1 = $1.25 are exactly the same thing.

If you want to find out how much you'll have to pay to buy a foreign good, follow three simple steps:

1. Find the current exchange rate. (Exchange rates are often quoted in the daily newspaper and online.)
2. Figure out how much of your money it takes to buy 1 unit of the foreign money.
3. Multiply the number of units in the price of the foreign good by your answer to #2.

> "Local currencies are all logical. Each system is decimalized just like ours. There are a hundred 'little ones' (cents, pence, groszy, stotinki) in every 'big one' (euro, pound, złoty, lev)."
> -Rick Steves, world traveler

EXHIBIT 15-5 Exchange Rates

Country/ region	Currency	Currency units per U.S. dollar
China	yuan renminbi	6.88
European Union	euro	0.91
Australia	dollar	1.31
Sweden	krona	8.79
India	rupee	64.65
Mexico	peso	18.65
Japan	yen	110.58
Great Britain	pound	0.77

▲ If you travel outside the United States or invest in foreign businesses, you will want to know exchange rates for U.S. currency. The values in the table above are for selected currencies on April 21, 2017. On that day, it took 18.65 Mexican pesos to buy 1 U.S. dollar. The rate is probably different today, because exchange rates change constantly.

Let's rework the previous example, showing each step:

1. We identified the current exchange rate as $1 = €0.80.
2. We need to identify how much of our money (U.S. money) it takes to buy 1 unit of the foreign money. In other words, we need to know how many dollars and cents it takes to buy 1 euro. We can figure this out from the exchange rate identified in #1. We currently know that $1 buys €0.80, but we don't know how many dollars and cents it takes to buy 1 euro. To find out, we simply divide $1 by the number of euros it takes to buy $1: $1 ÷ 0.80 = $1.25. In other words, it takes $1.25 to buy 1 euro.
3. We now multiply the number of units in the price of the foreign good (100) times our answer in #2 ($1.25), and we get $125.

Let's consider another problem. Suppose someone from Italy comes to the United States and wants to buy an American good priced at $200. If the exchange rate is $1 = €0.80, how may euros does the person have to give up to buy a $200 item? Let's calculate things from the perspective of the Italian:

1. We know the exchange rate is $1 = €0.80.
2. We know how much it takes of our currency ("our currency" this time is the euro, because we are the Italian) to buy $1. It takes €0.80.
3. We multiply the number of units in the price of the American good (200) times our answer in #2 (€0.80). This gives us €160.

Note: These calculations aren't hard; you're just not accustomed to making them. Going between currencies is a little like translating from one language into another. You have to listen to the foreign language, understand what is being said, and then find the words in your native language that correspond to the foreign words. Just as it takes some time to learn how to translate a language, it takes some time to learn how to go from one currency to another. Go over the examples a few more times to get the hang of it.

Differentiating Instruction

Visual Learners

To expose students to different currencies, ask individuals in your school who have traveled to foreign countries to bring samples of the currencies from those countries to class. Ask, What do you notice about other countries' currencies? What do you find most similar and most different about the foreign currencies? Why do you think has the United States been so hesitant to move new coins into its own economy?

Can Big Macs Predict Exchange Rates?

In an earlier chapter, we explained why goods that can be easily transported from one location to another usually sell for the same price in all locations. For example, if a candy bar can be moved from Atlanta to Wichita, then we would expect the candy bar to sell for the same price in both locations. Why? Because if the candy bar is priced higher in Wichita than Atlanta, people will move candy bars from Atlanta (where the price is relatively low) to Wichita to fetch the higher price. In other words, the supply of candy bars will rise in Wichita and fall in Atlanta.

These changes in supply in the two locations affect the prices of the candy bars in the two locations. In Wichita the price will fall, and in Atlanta the price will rise. This price movement will stop when the price of a candy bar is the same in the two locations.

Now consider a good that is sold all over the world: a McDonald's Big Mac. Suppose the exchange rate between the dollar and the yen is $1 = ¥100 and the price of a Big Mac in New York City is $3 and ¥400 in Tokyo. Given the exchange rate, is a Big Mac selling for the same price in the two cities?

The answer is no. In New York it's $3, but in Tokyo it's $4 (the price in Tokyo is ¥400 and $1 = ¥100). Stated differently, in New York $1 buys one-third of a Big Mac, but in Tokyo $1 buys only one-fourth of a Big Mac.

Will Big Macs be shipped from New York to Tokyo to fetch the higher price? No. The exchange rate will likely adjust in such a way that the price of a Big Mac will be the same in both cities.

Now ask yourself what the exchange rate has to be between the dollar and yen before a Big Mac is the same dollar price in New York and Tokyo. Here are three different exchange rates. Pick the correct one:

(a) $1 = ¥133.33
(b) $1 = ¥150.00
(c) $1 = ¥89.00

The answer is (a), $1 = ¥133.33. At this exchange rate, a Big Mac in New York is $3 (as we stated earlier), and a Big Mac in Tokyo that is ¥400 is $3 (once we have computed its price in dollars). Here are the steps: (1) The exchange rate is $1 = ¥133.33; (2) 1 yen is equal to $0.0075; (3) $0.0075 × 400 yen is $3.

The *purchasing power parity theory* in economics predicts that the exchange rate between two currencies will adjust so that, in the end, $1 buys the same amount of a given good in all places around the world. This means that if the exchange rate is initially $1 = ¥100 when a Big Mac is $3 in New York and ¥400 in Tokyo, it will change to become $1 = ¥133.33. That is, the dollar will soon appreciate relative to the yen.

The Economist, a well-known economics magazine, publishes what it calls the "Big Mac index" each year. It shows what exchange rates currently are and what a Big Mac costs in different countries (just as we did here). Then it predicts which currencies will appreciate and depreciate based on this information. *The Economist* doesn't always predict accurately, but it does in many cases.

So, if you want to predict whether the euro, pound, or peso is going to appreciate or depreciate in the next few months, looking at exchange rates in terms of the price of a Big Mac will be useful information.

THINK ABOUT IT Suppose a Big Mac costs $3 in New York City and 4.25 Swiss francs in Zurich. Also, suppose $1 = 1.25 francs. Based on our discussion, do you expect the franc to appreciate or depreciate? Explain your answer.

Ask students why they think *The Economist* chose the Big Mac as a way to compare currencies.

ANSWERS TO THINK ABOUT IT At $1 = 1.25 francs and a price of 4.25 Swiss francs for a Big Mac, a Big Mac costs $3.40 in Zurich—40 cents more than in New York City. The exchange rate would have to be $1 = 1.42 francs for a Big Mac to cost the same in New York City and Zurich. The dollar will appreciate, and the franc will depreciate.

Reinforcement Activity

Instruct students to find the current numbers for the Big Mac index on *The Economist's* website. Create a chart in class to show the purchasing power parity theory to all of your students. Ask, Where is a Big Mac the cheapest in U.S. dollars? Where is it the most expensive? How might you use this index to predict the appreciation or depreciation of the foreign currency listed in Exhibit 15-5 over the next year?

Reinforcement Activity

After discussing "Appreciation and Depreciation" (page 458), instruct students to look through newspapers and magazines to find mentions of the terms *appreciation* and *depreciation*. Invite students to explain what is being discussed in the articles.

Differentiating Instruction

Enrichment and Extension

The text presents several scenarios related to the appreciation and depreciation of the dollar. Direct students to Exhibit 15-5 (page 456) and propose several problems for them to solve. For example, a book costs $22 in the United States, in U.S. dollars. How much will a consumer pay in euros for the same book? How much would someone using Australian dollars have to pay for the same book? Create several problems for students to solve that address both appreciation and depreciation.

Discussion Starter

Guide students in a discussion of appreciation and depreciation using numerical examples. After solving a few problems, students will better understand these two concepts.

Application Activity

After reading and discussing Section 3, you may want to assign the Section Activity in the *Applying the Principles Workbook*, pages 160–161

Assess

Quick Quiz

The following true-or-false quiz will help you assess student understanding of the material covered in this section.

1. The exchange rate is the price of one nation's currency in terms of another nation's currency. (True)

2. A government can fix the exchange rate for its currency. (True)

3. Appreciation is an increase in the value of one currency relative to others. (True)

4. When domestic currency depreciates, it is cheaper to buy foreign-produced goods. (False)

5. To buy goods in foreign countries, you usually need to exchange your dollars for pounds. (False)

▲ Many people speculate in currencies, attempting to make profits by buying and selling certain currencies at opportune times. Most people, however, are interested in exchange rates only when they travel to foreign countries.

Appreciation and Depreciation

Suppose that on Tuesday, the exchange rate between euros and dollars is $1 for €0.80. By Saturday, the exchange rate has changed to $1 for €0.70. On Saturday, then, a dollar buys fewer euros than it did on Tuesday. When this situation occurs, economists say that the dollar has "depreciated relative to the euro." **Depreciation** is a decrease in the value of one currency relative to other currencies. A currency has depreciated if it buys less of another currency.

Appreciation is the opposite—an increase in the value of one currency relative to other currencies. A currency has appreciated if it buys more of another currency. For example, if the exchange rate goes from $1 for €0.80 to $1 for €0.90, the dollar buys more euros and therefore has appreciated in value.

depreciation
A decrease in the value of one currency relative to other currencies.

appreciation
An increase in the value of one currency relative to other currencies.

EXAMPLE Suppose the exchange rate between the U.S. dollar and the Mexican peso is $1 = 10 pesos on Wednesday. So, if you have $1, you can get 10 pesos in exchange for it. Suppose two days later, on Friday, the exchange rate is $1 = 9 pesos; if you have $1, you can get 9 pesos for it. The dollar got more pesos in exchange on Wednesday than on Friday. We would say, then, that the dollar depreciated between Wednesday and Friday. ◆

If the Dollar Depreciates, Foreign Goods Are More Expensive

Suppose you and a friend take a trip to Mexico City this summer. While there, you come across a jacket you want to buy. The price tag reads 1,000 pesos, but what is the price in dollars? To find out, you need to

Background Information: Financial Stability

Some economists believe that the countries most prone to financial crises and instability have three major flaws in their economies. First, they have insufficient cash reserves to defend or support the nation's currency. Second, the banks are weak, and finally, they have a recent history of sharp currency inflation.

know the current exchange rate between the dollar and the peso. Suppose it is $1 = 10 pesos; for every dollar you give up, you get 10 pesos in return. This means you will pay $100 (which is the same as 1,000 pesos) to buy the jacket. You decide to make this purchase. Here are the steps in the calculation: (1) the exchange rate is $1 = 10 pesos; (2) if we divide $1 by 10, we learn how much we have to pay for 1 peso, which is 10 cents; (3) we multiply 10 cents times 1,000 pesos, which equals $100.

A week passes, and you and your friend are still in Mexico City. Your friend likes your jacket so much that he decides to buy one too. You and your friend return to the store and find the exact jacket for sale, still for 1,000 pesos. You tell your friend that he will have to pay $100 for the jacket. You are wrong, though, because the dollar-peso exchange rate has changed since last week. Now, it is $1 = 8 pesos. In other words, the dollar has depreciated relative to the peso, because this week, each dollar buys fewer pesos than it did last week.

What will the jacket cost in dollars this week? The answer is $125. Here are the steps

in the calculation: (1) we know the exchange rate is $1 = 8 pesos; (2) if we divide $1 by 8, we learn how much we pay to pay for 1 peso, which is 12.5 cents; (3) we multiply 12.5 cents times 1,000 pesos and get $125. Your friend says that he was willing to buy the jacket for $100 but he is not willing to pay $125.

The economic concept illustrated by this example is simply that when one's domestic currency depreciates (as the dollar did in the example), it becomes more expensive to buy foreign-produced goods:

Dollar depreciates → Foreign goods become more expensive

The flip side of this concept is that when one's domestic currency appreciates, it becomes cheaper to buy foreign-produced goods. Suppose the dollar-peso exchange rate changes to $1 = 12 pesos. Now, a jacket with a price tag of 1,000 pesos will cost $83.33:

Dollar appreciates → Foreign goods become cheaper

Defining Terms

1. Define:
   a. exchange rate
   b. flexible exchange rate system
   c. fixed exchange rate system
   d. depreciation
   e. appreciation

Reviewing Facts and Concepts

2. If the exchange rate is $1 = ¥129 (yen) and the price of a Japanese good is ¥7,740, what is the equivalent dollar price?

3. If the exchange rate is $1 = £0.6612 (pounds) and the price of a U.S. good is $764, what is the equivalent pound price?

Critical Thinking

4. Steve, an American in London, wants to buy a British-made sweater. The price of the sweater is £40. Will Steve be better off if the exchange rate is $1 = £0.87 or $1 = £0.77? Explain.

5. Suppose you have $4,000, and you are trying to

decide whether you can afford a trip to Spain. How might the exchange rate affect your decision?

Applying Economic Concepts

6. Are more Americans likely to travel to Mexico when the peso has appreciated relative to the dollar or when the peso has depreciated relative to the dollar? Explain.

Defining Terms

1. a. exchange rate: the price of one country's currency in terms of another country's currency; **b. flexible exchange rate system:** the system whereby currency exchange rates are determined by the forces of supply and demand; **c. fixed exchange rate system:** the system whereby currency exchange rates are fixed by countries' governments; **d. depreciation:** a decrease in the value of one currency relative to other currencies; **e. appreciation:** an increase in the value of one currency relative to other currencies.

Reviewing Facts and Concepts

2. $60 (*calculation:* ¥7,740 ÷ 129 = $60).

Assessment Book

You will find a quiz for this section in the *Assessment Book*, page 152.

Reteaching Activity

Use the Section Assessment to gauge which students may need reteaching on this section. In particular, try to ascertain that students understand how to calculate exchange rates. Give struggling students five to ten problems to solve, and allow them to work in pairs to find the correct solutions.

Guided Reading

For further reteaching of the key concepts in this section, assign the Outlining Activity and the Just the Facts Handout from the *Guided Reading and Study Guide*, pages 269–271.

3. £505.16 (*calculation:* $764 ⊠ 0.6612 = £505.16).

Critical Thinking

4. Steve will be better off if the exchange rate is $1 = £0.87. At this exchange rate, he will pay $45.97 for the sweater. If the exchange rate is $1 = £0.77, he will pay $51.95 for the sweater.

5. The exchange rate tells how many dollars you will pay for one unit of a foreign currency. Suppose the exchange rate is 1 dollar = 1 euro (the currency used in Spain), and you can afford the trip at that rate. If the exchange rate changes to 2 dollars = 1 euro, expenses such as hotel rooms, taxis, and meals will be twice as much.

Applying Economic Concepts

6. More Americans are likely to travel to Mexico when the peso has depreciated. If the peso has depreciated relative to the dollar, then the dollar has appreciated relative to the peso. This means that Americans get more pesos for their dollars than before, which makes Mexican goods less expensive. Point out that when the dollar is strong against a foreign currency, U.S. travelers to that country benefit.

Your **Personal** Economics

Discussion Starter

Ask students if they know anyone who has had his or her job offshored. Ask, What kind of work did the person do? Do you know why the job was offshored? Has the person found other employment, and if so, is it in the same field?

Research Activity

After students have read the feature, ask them to pick one of the 10 professions discussed. Have each student update the figures given in the text, including the number of people working in that profession, their median annual salary, and the predicted number of people in that profession in 10 years. Divide students into small groups to report their data.

Teaching with Visuals

Medical specialists may perform some tasks from a distance; in this case, the X-rays might have been sent through the mail or Internet and read by specialists in another location. Lawyers must be present in court to present their cases, but they review legal documents and prepare their cases at other locations.

Jobs: Location Matters . . . Sometimes

When it comes to some jobs, location matters. When it comes to other jobs, location doesn't matter. Let's look at some examples of both situations. Understanding the difference may help you choose a career with greater job security.

Location Matters

If you are sick and need a doctor, you prefer to have a doctor close to you. If you live in Salem, Virginia, you will probably want a doctor who works in Salem, Virginia, not in Bangkok, 8,914 miles away. If you need a plumber, you will probably want a plumber close by, not one on the other side of the world. If you want to go out to eat, you will most likely go to a restaurant near where you live, not one on the other side of the world.

When it comes to some services, you want the provider to be near you. So if you are at point X, you want your provider to be near point X too.

Location Doesn't Matter

When it comes to buying a book, it may not matter to you where the book seller resides, as long as you can get the book fairly quickly. When it comes to someone answering your technical computer questions, it may not matter where the technician is. As long as the technician speaks your language, listens well, and gives clear and concise instructions, you probably don't care where he or she is located.

Offshoring/Outsourcing

When a provider's (supplier's, worker's) location is important to you, you can be fairly sure that the kind of job the provider performs will not be offshored to another country. When a provider's location isn't important to you, the probability of the provider's job being offshored goes up.

Here is a list of 10 professions that are unlikely to be offshored:

1. **Top Executive.** In 2014, there were 2,467,500 top executives in the United States (including chief

executive officers of companies). That number is expected to rise to 2,614,500 by 2024. Although many top executives earn million-dollar salaries, the median salary in 2016 was $103,950. Why won't the jobs of top executives be offshored? Essentially, because they are at the top positions of the companies.

2. **Physician and Surgeon.** In 2014, physicians and surgeons numbered 708,300, and an increase to 807,600 is expected by 2024. The median pay in 2016 was $208,000. (Within the medical field, salaries vary widely. For example, an orthopedic surgeon may earn $200,000–$300,000 more than a psychiatrist.) Why won't such jobs be offshored? It's hard to perform surgery at a distance of greater than a few feet.

3. **Pilot, Co-Pilot, and Flight Engineer.** In 2016, the median annual salary for the 119,200 pilots, co-pilots, and flight engineers was $105,720. Why won't these jobs be offshored? Because you need someone in the cockpit to fly the plane.

4. **Lawyer.** In 2014, 778,700 lawyers earned a median annual salary of $118,160. In 2024, the number of lawyers is predicted to increase to 822,500. Today, many aspects of the legal profession can be outsourced or offshored (research,

◀ Does location matter for these occupations?

Cooperative Learning

Divide students into groups of four or five. Ask each group to research two professions that experts think are likely subjects for outsourcing in coming years. Allow groups to present their findings to the class. Once all the groups have completed their presentations, lead a class discussion of common characteristics among the professions that make them likely candidates for outsourcing. Write these characteristics on the board as students identify them.

transcription, document preparation), but the actual practice of the law—for instance, trying a case in front of a judge—is something that cannot be outsourced or offshored.

5. **Computer and Information Systems Manager.** In 2010, 348,500 individuals were employed in this profession. By 2024, that number is expected to be 402,200. The 2016 median annual salary was $135,800. It's true that software development has been offshored (to some extent), but the people who make strategic decisions and oversee day-to-day operations are staying put so they can be of assistance to higher-level executives when making key company decisions.

6. **Sales Manager.** Total employment of 376,300 in 2014 was predicted to increase to 395,300 in 2024. The 2016 median annual salary was $117,960. Many companies need a sales staff and an on-site person to manage them. Often, customers in one country like to deal with salespeople in the same country, who have a familiarity with the language, customs, business practices, and so on.

7. **Pharmacist.** The number of pharmacists employed (297,100 in 2014) is expected to rise to 306,200 in 2024. The 2016 median annual salary was $122,230. Although you can today buy drugs from other countries, it's unlikely the U.S. government will allow too much drug importation. In addition, in many cases, the role of the pharmacist is becoming increasingly consultative. People

like to ask him or her about their new medicine and its interactions with other medicines, about suggestions concerning various health issues, and so on.

8. **Chiropractor.** Total employment in 2014 was 45,200; in 2024, it is expected to be 53,100. The 2016 median annual salary was $67,520. Obviously, it's difficult to get someone to fix your back if you are thousands of miles apart

9. **Physician's Assistant.** In 2014. 94,400 physician's assistants were employed. This number is predicted to rise to 123,100 by 2024. The 2016 median annual salary was $101,480. Because physicians' assistants function like quasi-doctors, they need to be near their patients. Performing physical exams is difficult at a distance.

10. **Education Administrator, Elementary and Secondary School.** In 2014, education

administrators numbered 240,000; in 2024, the number is predicted to be 254,000. The 2016 median annual salary was $92,510. Although some electronic learning (e-learning) is occurring at the college level, not much is found at the elementary and secondary school levels. Especially for the lower grades, it seems critically important to have live teachers in the classroom. These teachers will continue to report to on-site education administrators.

Your Personal Economics Activity

How does U.S. economic policy affect the full employment of its citizens? Answer this question in an analytical essay, and use articles you find online to support your analysis. Be sure to attribute ideas to source materials.

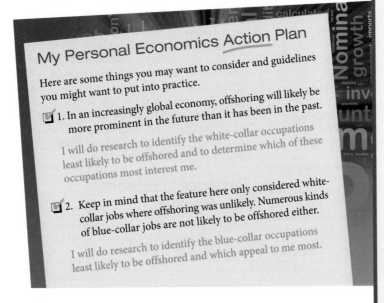

My Personal Economics Action Plan

Here are some things you may want to consider and guidelines you might want to put into practice.

☑ 1. In an increasingly global economy, offshoring will likely be more prominent in the future than it has been in the past.

I will do research to identify the white-collar occupations least likely to be offshored and to determine which of these occupations most interest me.

☑ 2. Keep in mind that the feature here only considered white-collar jobs where offshoring was unlikely. Numerous kinds of blue-collar jobs are not likely to be offshored either.

I will do research to identify the blue-collar occupations least likely to be offshored and which appeal to me most.

Chapter 15 Your Personal Economics **461**

Grading Rubric: Analytical Essay

1 2 3 4 5   Student used articles effectively to support his or her analysis.

1 2 3 4 5   Student cited his or her sources and attributed ideas correctly.

Focus and Motivate

Section Objectives

After completing this section, students will be able to

▶ explain what a less-developed country is;

▶ explain why some countries are rich and others are poor;

▶ explain the vicious circle of poverty;

▶ describe why savings accounts are important to economic development; and

▶ list factors that aid economic development.

Kickoff Activity

Write the following question on the board for students to answer: "What do you think life would be like in a poor country?"

Activating Prior Knowledge

Invite students to share their responses to the Kickoff Activity. Tell them that in economics, a poor country is more often referred to as a "less-developed country" (LDC) or an "underdeveloped" country.

Teach

Discussion Starter

Help students brainstorm obstacles to economic development. Ask each student to prepare an individual list to share with the class. Then allow students to share their ideas in a group discussion and write their lists on the board. Tell students that in this section, they will learn some of the obstacles that less-developed countries face as they move toward becoming developed countries.

Focus Questions

▶ What is a less-developed country?
▶ Why are some countries rich and others poor?
▶ What is the vicious circle of poverty?
▶ Why are savings accounts important to economic development?
▶ What factors aid economic growth and development?

Key Terms

developed country
less-developed country
population growth rate

How Countries Are Classified

People often talk about "rich" countries and "poor" countries. For example, the United States is often said to be a rich country; Ethiopia is said to be a poor country.

Economists talk about rich and poor countries too, although they don't always use the terms *rich* versus *poor*. More often, they talk about **developed countries (DCs)** or more-developed countries (MDCs) versus **less-developed countries (LDCs)**. A developed country is one that has a relatively high GDP per capita; a less-developed country is one that has a relatively low GDP per capita. The United States is a developed country, whereas Haiti and Ethiopia are less-developed countries.

Obstacles to Economic Development

Why are some countries poor while others are rich? Here are some factors to consider.

developed country
A country with a relatively high per capita GDP.

less-developed country
A country with a relatively low per capita GDP.

population growth rate
The birthrate minus the death rate.

Rapid Population Growth The population growth rate is typically higher in less-developed countries than in developed countries. The population growth rate in developed countries has been about 0.5 to 1 percent, compared with about 2 to 3 percent for less-developed countries.

The **population growth rate** is equal to the birthrate minus the death rate:

Population growth rate = Birthrate − Death rate

If in country X, the birthrate is 3 percent in a given year and the death rate is 2 percent, the population growth rate is 1 percent.

What causes the relatively high population growth rates in less-developed countries? First, the birthrates tend to be higher than in developed nations. In countries where financial assistance (such as pensions and social security) do not exist and where the economy revolves around agriculture, children are often seen as essential labor and as security for parents in their old age. In this setting, people

Differentiating Instruction

Visual and English Language Learners

To help visual learners and those who have difficulty comprehending English to better understand the information in this section, bring in pictures of street scenes from around the world. These are readily available in newspapers and magazines and sometimes on the Internet. Show each picture to the class and ask students to identify any indications of the image coming from a more-developed country or a less-developed country. Ask for markers such as population, the presences (or absence) of capital goods, and evidence of civil unrest. This conversation should be handled carefully. Ask students to limit their points to what actually appears in each picture and to avoid stereotyping.

tend to have more children. Second, in past few decades, death rates have fallen in less-developed countries, largely because of medical advances. The combination of higher birthrates and declining death rates explains why the population grows more rapidly in less-developed nations than in developed nations.

Is a faster population growth rate always an obstacle to economic development? The fact that many of the countries with the fastest-growing populations are relatively poorer on a per capita basis than those countries with the slowest-growing populations isn't proof that rapid population growth causes poverty. Many of the developed countries today had faster population growth rates when they were developing than the less-developed countries do today.

Low Savings Rate A farmer with a tractor (which is a capital good) will likely be more productive than one without a tractor, all other things being equal. Now consider a farmer who cannot afford to buy a tractor. This farmer may decide to borrow the money from a bank. The bank gets the money it lends from the people who have savings accounts at the bank. Savings, then, are important to economic growth and development. If the savings rate is low, banks will not have much money to lend, and capital goods such as tractors (which increase productivity) will not be produced and purchased.

Some economists argue that less-developed countries have low savings rates because the people living in them are so poor that they cannot save. In short, they earn only enough income to buy the necessities of life—shelter and food—leaving no "extra income" left over to save. This situation is called the *vicious circle of poverty*: less-developed countries are poor because they cannot save and buy capital goods, and they cannot save and buy capital goods because they are poor.

Other economists argue, though, that being poor is not a barrier to economic development. They say that many nations that are rich today, such as the United States,

were poor in the past but still managed to become economically developed.

Cultural Differences Some less-developed countries have cultures that retard economic growth and development. For example, some cultures are reluctant to depart from the status quo (the existing state of affairs). People may think that things should stay the way they always have been; they view change as dangerous and risky. In such countries, it isn't uncommon for people's upward economic and social mobility to depend on who their parents were, rather than on who they are or what they do. Also, in some cultures, the people are fatalistic by Western standards. They believe that a person's success or failure in life depends more on fate or the spirits than on how hard the person works, how much he or she learns, or how hard he or she strives to succeed.

Political Instability and Government Seizure of Private Property Individuals sometimes don't invest in businesses in less-developed countries because they are afraid that the current government leaders will be thrown out of office or seize their private property. People are not likely to invest their money in places where the risk of losing it is high.

High Tax Rates Some economists argue that high tax rates affect economic development.

▲ This family lives in Bangladesh. The per capita GDP in Bangladesh is $2,100 a year, and 31.5 percent of the population live below the poverty line. About 45 percent of the people work in agriculture. Some of the key agricultural goods produced are rice, jute, tea, wheat, and sugarcane.

Reinforcement Activity

Instruct students to check the *Statistical Abstract of the United States* to find countries with low per capita GDPs and then list 10–15 countries and their per capita GDPs. Let volunteers report their findings to the class.

Problem Solving

Remind your students that all countries face economic obstacles—not only less-developed countries. Instruct students to research five countries, including at least one country that exhibits one of the obstacles presented on these pages. Then ask students to determine whether these countries are developed or less developed. Ask, Are all of these obstacles apparent in all of these countries? How do the statistics used to measure developed countries versus less-developed countries compare among these five countries? Which of these countries should truly be considered developed? Allow students to present their findings to the class or in small groups.

Analyzing

Some less-developed countries have cultural traditions and values that retard economic growth and development. In a way, this might sound like a criticism of these countries, but in fact, might a country's particular traditions be more important than its economic growth? The answer to this question is subjective. Ask students to discuss the issue. For example, suppose the tradition in one country is to take every other day off to rest and relax. In such a country, economic growth would be lower than in a country in which people work five or six days a week. Ask, What is the economic trade-off of having a lot of time off work? What are the costs versus the benefits?

 Visit econ.myemcp.com/videos for videos that will help students better understand the key concepts found in this section.

Internet Research

Direct students to the IDB Population Pyramid site of the U.S. Census Bureau to find the population pyramids for three less-developed countries (such as Angola, Nepal, and Honduras) and one developed country (such as the United States). Students will see that a population pyramid shows a country's age distribution for men and women. Ask each student to compare and contrast the three population pyramids and to explain what each country's pyramid indicates about its future economic growth potential. Ask, What might having a youthful population today predict about a country's future economic circumstances and needs?

Discussion Starter

Review with students the ways that tax rates can benefit or hurt economic conditions. Ask them to explain why low tax rates, like those in Hong Kong, encourage economic growth. Governments that need more capital might need or want to demand higher tax rates, resulting in low per capita income growth.

Reinforcement Activity

Assign students to make lists of where their 10 favorite or most-used items were produced. Many electronic products come from China and Japan. Shoes and clothing are produced worldwide and then imported into the United States. Remind students that a major benefit of free trade is that these products are available to them at affordable costs.

 Application Activity

After reading and discussing Section 4, you may want to assign the Section Activity in the *Applying the Principles Workbook*, pages 162–164.

Assess

Quick Quiz

The following true-or-false quiz will help you assess student understanding of the material covered in this section.

1. Free trade allows residents of a country to buy inputs from the cheapest supplier. (True)
2. Paying high taxes provides a greater incentive for workers to be productive. (False)
3. Allowing investment by foreign countries promotes growth and development. (True)
4. The more difficult it is to obtain a business license, the more new businesses will develop. (False)
5. Protecting private property stimulates economic growth. (True)

Economist Alvin Rabushka studied the tax structures of 54 less-developed countries between 1960 and 1982 and categorized each country as a high-, low-, or medium-tax-rate nation. Rabushka found that Hong Kong, with the lowest tax rate, had the highest growth rate in per capita income during the period under study. Generally, low-tax countries had an average growth rate in per capita income of 3.7 percent, and high-tax countries had a per capita income growth rate of 0.7 percent.

Factors That Aid Growth and Development

Can a poor country follow a certain "recipe" and become a rich country? Some economists believe so. They argue that poor countries can become rich countries if they do certain things. Here are some of the factors that economists emphasize.

Free Trade Countries can hinder or promote international trade. For example, they hinder it when they impose tariffs or quotas on imports. They promote it when they eliminate tariffs, quotas, or anything else that prevents the free flow of resources and goods between countries. Free trade promotes the production of goods and services in a country and therefore spurs growth and development in two ways: free trade allows residents of a country to buy inputs from the cheapest supplier (no matter where in the world it's located), and free trade also opens up a world market to domestic firms.

Low Taxation Generally, a country that has relatively low taxes provides a greater incentive for workers to work and more incentive for investors to invest than does a country with relatively high taxes. As discussed earlier in the chapter, low-tax countries tend to have average growth rates in per capita income that are substantially higher than average growth rates in per capita income of high-tax countries.

Absence of Restrictions on Foreign Investment Some countries prevent foreigners from investing in their countries. For exam-

ple, country X may pass a law stating that no one from any other country can invest there. Such restrictions on foreign investment often hamper economic growth and development. Allowing foreigners to invest in a country—to start or expand businesses—promotes growth and development.

Absence of Controls on Bank Lending Activity Banks channel funds from those who save to those who want to invest and produce. In some countries, the government tells the banks to whom they can and cannot lend. For example, banks may not be able to lend to automobile manufacturers but be permitted to lend to steel manufacturers. Such restrictions may arise because the nation's government is trying to promote a particular industry.

Controls of this type often hinder growth and development. Banks have a monetary incentive to search out those individuals, firms, and industries that can repay any loans received. Often, these individuals, firms, and industries are the ones likely to be successful at producing goods and services and at generating employment.

Absence of Wage and Price Controls The free market determines equilibrium prices and wages. When government overrides the market and imposes controls on prices and wages, production usually suffers. Suppose the market wage for workers in a particular industry is $10 an hour, and the market price for the good produced in the industry is $40. At current wages and prices, firms are earning just enough profits to stay in business. Now suppose government says that these firms have to pay a minimum of $12 an hour to their workers and that they can't charge more than $38 for their goods. The firms will likely go out of business, and the goods and services they once produced will no longer exist.

Simple, Easy Business Licensing Procedures Most countries require a person to have a business license before starting a business. In some countries, obtaining a business license is easy, involving the filling out of a few papers and payment of a

Cooperative Learning

Divide students into small groups, and assign each group four or five different countries. Each student in the group should research one of the factors that aid economic development and growth for the assigned countries. Groups should address the following questions: If all the factors for economic development aren't in place in a country, is it doomed to economic failure? How many of these factors might a country need to implement to achieve economic success? If a country has already implemented these strategies, has it achieved or will it achieve economic success? Have each group prepare a chart showing each country's economic development strategies and the group's predictions for the country's future.

nominal fee. In other countries, it involves visiting government offices, filling out numerous documents, bribing government officials, and so on. The easier and cheaper it is to obtain a business license, the more new businesses will start up. Historically, new businesses have often promoted economic growth and development.

Protecting Private Property People will not work hard or invest in a business unless they are reasonably sure that the property they acquire from doing so is protected from expropriation (seizure by the government). Countries that protect private property often develop faster than those that do not.

Incentives Some individuals think that people in other countries are poor because they are not as motivated or as smart as people with greater incomes. Obviously, people are different when it comes to level of motivation and intelligence. However, when it comes to poverty in certain countries, economists usually place more emphasis on the incentive structure in the country than on the people themselves. Economists know that the incentive structure that people face

often affects how motivated they are.

To illustrate, suppose your economics teacher tells you that there will be an economics quiz tomorrow and it will account for 1 percent of your overall grade. Ask yourself how much time you will devote to studying for the quiz. Will you spend 30 minutes? 45 minutes? Now suppose your teacher says that there will be an economics quiz tomorrow and that anyone who earns a grade of 90 or above will receive $500. Again, ask yourself how much time you will devote to studying for the quiz. Will you spend more time studying now that the benefit from getting a good grade on the quiz is $500?

If your answer is yes, then you have proven that incentives matter to you and that you behave differently given different incentives. In fact, the greater the incentive to learn economics, the more you are deeply motivated to study. It is the same when it comes to starting a business, completing school, going to college, developing a new product, and so on. Under some incentive structures, a person will choose leisure over work; under others, a person will choose work over leisure.

Assessment Book

You will find a quiz for this section in the *Assessment Book*, page 153.

Reteaching Activity

Use the Section Assessment to gauge which students may need reeteaching on this section. Instruct those students to work in groups to create a list of the ways that less-developed countries can develop. Students should include specific examples to illustrate the steps these countries should take to further economic growth and development.

Guided Reading

For further reteaching of the key concepts in this section, assign the Outlining Activity and the Just the Facts Handout from the *Guided Reading and Study Guide*, pages 272–275.

ASSESSMENT

SECTION 4

Defining Terms
1. Define
   a. developed country
   b. less-developed country
   c. population growth rate

Reviewing Facts and Concepts
2. Why might people in less-developed countries have more children than people in developed countries?
3. What are some of the benefits of free trade to a less-developed country?

Critical Thinking
4. In country A, the government doesn't protect private property, taxes are high, and quotas and tariffs are imposed on imported goods. In country B, the government does protect private property, taxes are low, and free trade is practiced. In which country do you expect economic growth and development to be stronger? Explain your answer.

Applying Economic Concepts
5. In this section, we defined a poor or less-developed country as one with a low per capita GDP. Does it follow that the people in a country with a low per capita GDP are not as happy as the people in a country with a high per capita GDP? Explain your answer.

SECTION 4 ASSESSMENT ANSWERS

Defining Terms

1. a. developed country: a country with a relatively high per capita GDP;
b. less-developed country: a country with a relatively low per capita GDP; **c. population growth rate:** the birthrate minus the death rate.

Reviewing Facts and Concepts

2. In less-developed countries, the economy is often based on agriculture, and there are no pensions or social security programs to speak of. Children are more likely to be seen as necessary to help work on farms and to take care of their parents in old age.

3. Free trade allows residents of a country to buy inputs from the cheapest supplier, no matter where it's located; free trade opens a world market to domestic firms.

Critical Thinking

4. Economic growth and development is likely to be stronger in country B. According to most economists, there is ample evidence to support the view that countries grow and develop when private property is protected, taxes are low, and free trade is practiced.

Applying Economic Concepts

5. No. Happiness involves more than a high per capita GDP.

Economics Vocabulary

1. tariff; **2.** quota; **3.** comparative advantage; **4.** balance of trade; **5.** Dumping; **6.** Absolute advantage; **7.** Appreciation; **8.** exchange rate; **9.** Depreciation; **10.** less-developed country; **11.** population growth rate.

Understanding the Main Ideas

1. The peso will appreciate. For example, instead of 1 peso = $0.25, 1 peso = $0.30. When a peso is worth more of another currency, it has appreciated in value.
2. The United States has a comparative advantage in producing food and Japan, in producing clothing.
3. The low-foreign-wages argument states that U.S. producers cannot compete with companies in other countries that pay lower wages.
4. It means that the United States is the low-cost producer of computers or that the United States produces computers the most cheaply.
5. Fewer cars. A tariff raises the price of imported goods, so consumers would be expected to buy fewer imported goods.
6. Agree. To illustrate, suppose the exchange rate goes from £1 = $1.75 to £1 = $2. The pound has appreciated, because it now fetches more dollars and cents. It follows that the dollar fetches fewer pounds. At the first exchange rate, $1 exchanges for £0.57 (that is, if £1 = $1.75, then $1 = £0.57), whereas at the second exchange rate, $1 exchanges for £0.50.
7. Critics of the low-foreign-wages argument say that producers care about more than simply wages; they care about productivity too. If foreign workers earn low wages and are less productive than U.S. workers who earn high wages, a company may decide to pay high wages to a productive workforce rather than pay low wages to a less productive workforce.
8. –$107 billion (*calculation:* Exports – imports = balance of trade). The United States has a negative balance of trade.

Chapter Summary

Be sure you know and remember the following key points from the chapter sections.

Section 1

▶ Exports are goods that are produced in the domestic country and sold to residents of a foreign country.
▶ Imports are goods produced in foreign countries and purchased by residents of the domestic country.
▶ A country's balance of trade is the difference between the value of its exports and imports.
▶ Countries specialize in the production of goods in which they have comparative advantage.

Section 2

▶ Tariffs and quotas are the two major types of trade restrictions.
▶ A tariff is a tax on imports; a quota is a limit on the amount of a good that may be imported.

Section 3

▶ The exchange rate is the price of one nation's currency in terms of another nation's currency.
▶ Depreciation is a decrease in the value of one currency relative to other currencies.
▶ Appreciation is an increase in the value of one currency relative to other currencies; this means that it buys more of another currency.

Section 4

▶ A developed country is one with a relatively high GDP per capita; a less-developed country is one with a relatively low GDP per capita.
▶ Obstacles to economic development include rapid population growth, low savings rate, cultural beliefs, political instability and seizure of property, and high tax rates.
▶ Factors that aid economic development include free trade, low taxation, few restrictions on foreign investment or control on bank lending, absence of wage and price controls, easy business licensing procedures, protection of private property, and incentives.

Economics Vocabulary

1. A(n) _____ is a tax on imports.
2. A legal limit on the amount of a good that may be imported (into a country) is called a(n) _____.
3. Country A has a(n) _____ in the production of a good if it can produce the good at lower opportunity cost than country B.
4. The _____ is the difference between the value of exports and the value of imports.
5. _____ refers to the sale of goods abroad at prices below their costs and below the price charged in the domestic market.
6. _____ refers to the situation in which a country can produce more of a good than another country can produce with the same quantity of resources.
7. _____ refers to an increase in the value of one currency relative to other currencies.
8. If one dollar buys two pesos, it is called the _____ between dollars and pesos.
9. _____ refers to a decrease in the value of one currency relative to other currencies.
10. A _____ is a country with a low per capita GDP.
11. The birthrate minus the death rate equals the _____.

Understanding the Main Ideas

1. If exchange rates under a flexible exchange rate system are determined by the forces of supply and demand, will an increase in the demand for pesos cause the peso to appreciate or depreciate? Explain.
2. The United States can produce either combination A (100 units of food and 0 units of clothing) or combination B (80 units of food and 20 units of clothing). Japan can produce combination C (80 units of food and 0 units of clothing) or combination D (75 units of food and 10 units of clothing). Which country has a comparative advantage in the production of food? Which country has a comparative advantage in the production of clothing?
3. State the low-foreign-wages argument for trade restrictions.
4. What does it mean to say that "The United States has a comparative advantage in the production of computers"?

9. The national-defense argument states that certain industries should be protected because they are essential to the security of the United States.
10. A culture that would foster economic development would be one that was not afraid to depart from the status quo, took risks, and was not fatalistic. A culture that might hinder economic development would be the opposite. It would not want to move away from the status quo, it would shun risks, and it would be fatalistic. (That is, it would believe that a person's good or bad fortune in life depend more on fate or the spirits than on such things as how hard he or she works.)
11. No, many of today's developed countries had higher rates of population growth when they were developing than is true of less-developed countries today. Also, some countries with high-density populations are richer than some countries with low-density populations.

5. After a tariff is imposed on imported cars, would you expect consumers to buy more or fewer imported cars? Explain your answer.

6. If the pound appreciates relative to the U.S. dollar, the dollar must depreciate relative to the pound. Do you agree or disagree? Explain.

7. What do critics of the low-foreign-wages argument for trade restrictions say?

8. If the value of U.S. exports is $103 billion and the value of U.S. imports is $210 million, what does the balance of trade equal?

9. State the national-defense argument for trade restrictions.

10. Describe a culture that would foster economic development. Describe a culture that would hinder economic development.

11. Is a fast-growing population necessarily an obstacle to economic development? Explain.

12. Evaluate and explain the benefits and costs of participating in international free trade agreements.

13. What is the impact of U.S. exports on the United States? What is the impact on U.S. trading partners of U.S. exports?

Doing the Math

1. If the price of an Irish sweater is €30 and the dollar-euro exchange rate is $1 = €0.70, what does the sweater cost in dollars?

2. If the price of a U.S. car is $20,000 and the dollar-yen exchange rate is $1 = ¥129, what does the car cost in yen?

3. If the United States can produce either 20 units of clothing and 40 units of food or 60 units of clothing and 0 units of food, what is the opportunity cost of producing 1 unit of food?

4. If Brazil can produce either 100 units of clothing and 0 units of food or 30 units of clothing and 50 units of food, what is the opportunity cost of producing 1 unit of clothing?

Solving Economic Problems

1. **Apply.** Suppose the United States buys 1 million cars from Japan each year. If the dollar depreciates relative to the yen, will Americans buy more or fewer cars from Japan? Explain.

2. **Analyze.** Suppose that U.S. imports currently equal U.S. exports. Explain how a fall in the value of the dollar in comparison to other currencies can affect the current U.S. balance of trade.

3. **Identify Cause and Effect.** Over a six-month period, you notice that the dollar appreciates in value compared to other currencies and that the U.S. balance of trade goes from zero to −$30 billion. You suspect there is some relationship between the change in the value of the dollar and the U.S. balance of trade. Did the change in the balance of trade cause the change in the value of the dollar, or did the change in the value of the dollar cause the change in the balance of trade? Explain.

4. **Infer and Conclude.** WRITING Suppose the people in Houston buy more goods from the people in Los Angeles than vice versa. This is not "news." Write a one-page paper that answers this question: Why is a city-to-city trade balance not news but a country-to-country trade balance is?

Project or Presentation

Debating the Issues: Offshoring. Do an Internet search for "offshoring" and "outsourcing." Read a few primary sources and secondary articles on the subject. Analyze and evaluate the validity of each source by identifying any propaganda, bias, or frames of reference that should be acknowledged. When you are finished, write a two-page paper identifying the writer that you think made the strongest points. Address in your paper why those particular points were strong and persuasive. Discuss your paper with a group of classmates who chose different sources.

ONLINE emcp.com — *Practice Tests and Study Guide*

Go to **www.emcschool.net/Economics2e** and choose *Economics: New Ways of Thinking*, Chapter 15, if you need more help in preparing for the chapter test.

---

12. One of the key benefits is that trade restrictions between countries that have signed the agreement are lowered. One of the costs could be that members to the agreement don't have as much flexibility when dealing with countries outside the agreement.

13. When the United States exports a good, some other country imports that good. When a country buys a good from the United States (imports that good), it benefits by buying that good for a lower price than the cost the country would incur to produce the good. The United States benefits from voluntary trade. It would not sell a good to someone in another country unless it could be made better off.

Doing the Math

1. $42.85 (*calculation:* £30 ÷ 0.7 = $42.85).
2. ¥2.58 million (*calculation:* $20,000 × 129 = ¥2.58 million).

---

3. 1 unit of clothing (*calculation:* 20 ÷ (60 − 40) = 1).
4. 0.71 unit of food (*calculation:* 50 ÷ (100 − 30) = 0.71).

Solving Economic Problems

1. Americans will buy fewer cars from Japan. If the dollar depreciates relative to the yen, the price of Japanese cars will increase for Americans. As a result, Americans will buy fewer cars (according to the law of demand).

2. If the dollar depreciates in comparison to other currencies, it follows that other currencies will appreciate in value. A depreciated dollar makes foreign-produced goods more expensive for Americans and makes U.S. goods less expensive for foreigners. As a result of more-expensive foreign goods, Americans will buy fewer imports. As a result of less-expensive U.S. goods, foreigners will buy more U.S. goods. Conclusion: U.S. exports will rise, and U.S. imports will fall. Thus, the United States will have a positive balance of trade.

3. The change in the value of the dollar caused the change in the balance of trade. To understand this concept, remember that if the dollar appreciates in value, foreign (imported) goods become cheaper for Americans, who therefore buy more of them. In contrast, because the dollar has appreciated, some foreign currencies have depreciated (relative to the dollar). This makes it more expensive for foreigners to buy U.S. goods; therefore, they cut back on their purchases. As a result, the United States exports fewer goods. In sum, the appreciation of the dollar stimulates import buying and restrains export selling. We started with a zero balance of trade (where value of exports equals value of imports). Now, the value of imports must be greater than the value of exports, so the United States is running a negative balance of trade.

4. Answers will vary. Students may suggest that different currencies are involved when different countries are involved. Thus, no one cares if some Americans buy more from some other Americans. They do care, however, if Americans buy more from the Japanese, Mexicans, or English.

Project or Presentation

Answers will vary.

Chapter 16 Planning Guide

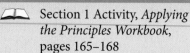

SECTION ORGANIZER

Learning Objectives	Reproducible Worksheets and Handouts	Assessment
Stocks (pages 470–481) ► Explain what stocks are. ► Describe where stocks are bought and sold. ► Explain what the Dow Jones Industrial Average is. ► Explain what it means to "buy the market."	 Section 1 Activity, *Applying the Principles Workbook*, pages 165–168 · Outlining Activity, *Guided Reading and Study Guide*, pages 285–288 · Just the Facts Handout, *Guided Reading and Study Guide*, pages 289–291	☑ Section Assessment, *Student Text*, page 481 ☑ Quick Quiz, *Annotated Teacher's Edition*, page 480 ☑ Section Quiz, *Assessment Book*, page 163
Bonds (pages 482–489) ► Explain what bonds are. ► Identify the factor that determines the rating of a bond. ► Explain the relationship between interest rates and the price of bonds. ► Identify various types of bonds. ► Explain the relationship between risk and return. ► Explain why financial markets are important.	Section 2 Activity, *Applying the Principles Workbook*, pages 169–171 · Outlining Activity, *Guided Reading and Study Guide*, pages 292–294 · Just the Facts Handout, *Guided Reading and Study Guide*, pages 295–296	☑ Section Assessment, *Student Text*, page 489 ☑ Quick Quiz, *Annotated Teacher's Edition*, page 488 ☑ Section Quiz, *Assessment Book*, page 164
Futures and Options (pages 492–497) ► Explain what a futures contract is. ► Explain why people enter into futures contracts. ► Explain a currency futures contract. ► Explain an options contract. ► Describe the difference between a put option and a call option. ► State the major reason an investor would use a put or call option.	Section 3 Activity, *Applying the Principles Workbook*, pages 172–174 · Outlining Activity, *Guided Reading and Study Guide*, page 297 · Just the Facts Handout, *Guided Reading and Study Guide*, pages 298–299	☑ Section Assessment, *Student Text*, page 497 ☑ Quick Quiz, *Annotated Teacher's Edition*, pages 496–497 ☑ Section Quiz, *Assessment Book*, page 165

Reproducible Chapter Resources and Assessment Materials

 Graphic Organizer Activity, *Guided Reading and Study Guide,* pages 300–302

Vocabulary Activity, *Guided Reading and Study Guide,* page 303

Working with Graphs and Charts, *Guided Reading and Study Guide,* page 304

Practice Test, *Guided Reading and Study Guide,* pages 305–307

Critical Thinking Activity, *Finding Economics,* pages 44–46

Chapter Test A, *Assessment Book,* pages 166–168

Chapter Test B, *Assessment Book,* pages 169–172

Student Text Internet Links

Economics: New Ways of Thinking, Second Edition encourages students to use the Internet to find out more about economics. Given the wealth of current, valid information available on websites, students should be encouraged to use the Internet as a research tool. Doing so will likely increase students' interest in and understanding of economics principles and topics. In addition, doing Internet research can help your students form the habit of accessing and using economics information, as well as help them develop investigative skills they will use throughout their educational and professional careers.

To aid your students in achieving these ends, each chapter of *Economics: New Ways of Thinking, Second Edition* includes the addresses of several websites that provide engaging and relevant information. When students type in any of the addresses provided, they will immediately arrive at the intended site. The addresses have been modified so that EMC Publishing can monitor and maintain the proper links—for example, the website http://www.deposit accounts.com/ has been changed to http://econ.emcp.net/accounts. In the event that the address or content of a site changes or is discontinued, EMC's Internet editors will redirect the link to a site with equivalent information.

Activities in the *Annotated Teacher's Edition* often suggest that students search the Internet for information. For some activities, you might want to find reputable sites beforehand and steer students toward them. For other activities, have students do their own searching and then check out the sites they have found and discuss why they might be reliable or unreliable.

Passport® for Economics

Technology resources are available with the *Economics: New Ways of Thinking, Second Edition* program through Passport®. These include:

eBooks for *Economics: New Ways of Thinking, Second Edition*

- Student textbook eBook
- Interactive Applying the Principles eWorkbook
- Finding Economics eBook
- Guided Reading and Study Guide eBook
- Annotated Teacher's Edition eBook
- Lesson Plans eBook
- Assessment eBook

Passport® for Students

Students can access helpful resources through Passport® for Economics. Resources include:
- Study guides
- Practice tests
- Flash cards in English and in Spanish
- Word games in English and in Spanish
- Tutorials and key-concept videos
- Spanish print and audio summaries

Passport® for Teachers

Keep your course current and relevant by using the teacher resources provided through Passport® for Economics. In addition to all of the resources on the student side of Passport®, the teacher side contains:
- Link to the Annotated Teacher's Edition eBook
- Standards correlations
- Microsoft® PowerPoint® Lectures
- Current Events Lessons
- Additional Economics in the Real World features
- ExamView® Assessment Suite
- PDFs of all print supplements (student and teacher)

Stocks and bonds are important commodities for both businesses and individuals. This chapter describes the different kinds of stocks and bonds and discusses their roles in the economic

SECTION 1 Stocks

Section 1 of this chapter discusses the stock market: how to buy and sell stocks, how to predict changes in stocks' value, and what it means when changes

SECTION 2 Bonds

This section will answer questions about bonds and the bond market. Students will learn how to buy and sell bonds and the relationship between interest rates and bond prices.

SECTION 3 Futures and Options

The final section of this chapter covers investments known as futures and options. It will discuss the differences between futures and options and the risks and benefits of investing in each.

Stocks and Bonds

Why It Matters

Wall Street is a narrow street that extends only seven blocks, from Broadway to the East River, in Manhattan, in New York City. It was named for a wall built by Dutch settlers in 1653 to repel an expected English invasion. As you probably know, some of the chief financial institutions in the United States—the New York Stock Exchange, investment banks, the Federal Reserve Bank of New York, and commodity exchanges—are located here. As a result, "Wall Street" has become shorthand for investing, especially in stocks and bonds.

More and more people are buying stocks and bonds and want to know what futures and options are and how they work. Will this information be useful to you? Most likely, it will. The day will come (if it hasn't already) when you have some extra money that you want to invest. Should you buy stocks or bonds? Are some stocks better than others? What does the price of a bond have to do with interest rates?

Every day, stock exchanges around the world process countless "buy" and "sell" transactions. This chapter will introduce you to the whys and hows of investing in stocks and bonds.

It will be important for you to know the answers to these questions and more. In a nutshell, you should be informed about the markets you might want to invest in before you start investing. In this chapter, you will learn some investment basics.

Teaching Suggestions from the Author

Students of today are somewhat different from students of 20 or even 10 years ago. Today, students hear much about the stock market, the bond market, and futures and options. Every night on the news, the anchor reports whether the Dow (Dow Jones Industrial Average) is up or down. Every night, the anchor reports on the NASDAQ (National Association of Securities Dealers Automated Quotations). Students know that investing in the stock market has become a booming business in the United States. They know that thousands of people today invest online.

Students come to this chapter with a natural curiosity. They want to know what the Dow is and

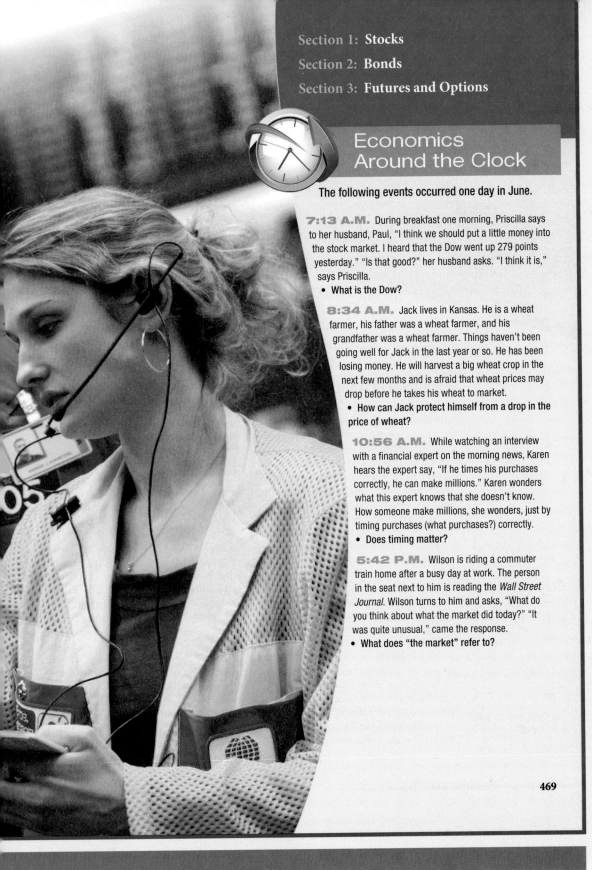

Economics Around the Clock

The following events occurred one day in June.

7:13 A.M. During breakfast one morning, Priscilla says to her husband, Paul, "I think we should put a little money into the stock market. I heard that the Dow went up 279 points yesterday." "Is that good?" her husband asks. "I think it is," says Priscilla.

- **What is the Dow?**

8:34 A.M. Jack lives in Kansas. He is a wheat farmer, his father was a wheat farmer, and his grandfather was a wheat farmer. Things haven't been going well for Jack in the last year or so. He has been losing money. He will harvest a big wheat crop in the next few months and is afraid that wheat prices may drop before he takes his wheat to market.

- **How can Jack protect himself from a drop in the price of wheat?**

10:56 A.M. While watching an interview with a financial expert on the morning news, Karen hears the expert say, "If he times his purchases correctly, he can make millions." Karen wonders what this expert knows that she doesn't know. How someone make millions, she wonders, just by timing purchases (what purchases?) correctly.

- **Does timing matter?**

5:42 P.M. Wilson is riding a commuter train home after a busy day at work. The person in the seat next to him is reading the *Wall Street Journal.* Wilson turns to him and asks, "What do you think about what the market did today?" "It was quite unusual," came the response.

- **What does "the market" refer to?**

469

Introducing the Chapter

Over the lifetime of your students, the Dow Jones Industrial Average—a leading indicator for the New York Stock Exchange—has risen more than 10,000 points. People have become very excited over the rising stock market, and in fact, overexcitement has caused the stock market to have huge fluctuations, much larger than the so-called crash in 1929. Reading this chapter should give students a sense of how the stock market works.

Teaching with Visuals

The trading floor of the New York Stock Exchange is a hectic place. People working on the floor carry out the many stock purchases and sales that take place each day.

why it goes up and down. They want to know what the NASDAQ is. They want to learn how to buy stocks (even if they don't have the money right now to do so.) They want to know the difference between a bond and a stock and between a futures contract and an option.

I've often thought that we can do our students a big service if we get them to develop the habit of keeping track of financial matters. We can instill that habit in them if we present the material in this chapter in an interesting and exciting way.

Teacher Support

Focus and Motivate

Section Objectives

After completing this section, students will be able to

▶ explain what stocks are;

▶ describe where stocks are bought and sold;

▶ explain what the Dow Jones Industrial Average is; and

▶ explain what it means to "buy the market."

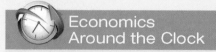

Economics Around the Clock

Kickoff Activity

Refer students to the 7:13 a.m. scenario in Economics Around the Clock (page 469) and tell them to guess the answer to the question, using their prior knowledge of the stock market.

Activating Prior Knowledge

Discuss students' guesses about what the Dow is. Invite volunteers to share any experiences with the stock market that they have had themselves or through their parents. Tell students that "the Dow" refers to the Dow Jones Industrial Average (DJIA), a weighted average of 30 widely traded stocks on the New York Stock Exchange. The Dow is viewed as an indicator of day-to-day stock market activity.

Visit econ.myemcp.com/videos for videos that will help students better understand the key concepts found in this section.

Stocks

Focus Questions

▶ What are stocks?

▶ Where are stocks bought and sold?

▶ What is the Dow Jones Industrial Average?

▶ What does it mean to "buy the market"?

Key Terms

stock
Dow Jones Industrial Average (DJIA)
initial public offering (IPO)
investment bank
dividend
index

Financial Markets

Everyone has heard of stocks and bonds, and that stocks and bonds can be sold and purchased. But not everyone knows the economic purposes served by stocks and bonds. Buying and selling stocks and bonds occurs in a financial market. Financial markets serve the purpose of channeling money from some people to other people.

Suppose Jones has saved $10,000 over two years and Smith is just starting a new company. Smith needs some money to get the new company up and running, and Jones would like to invest his savings and receive a return. Jones and Smith may not know each other; in fact, they may live on opposite sides of the country. They can be brought together, though, by a financial market. It will allow Jones to invest in Smith's company or to lend Smith some money. For example, Jones might buy stock in Smith's company or buy a bond that Smith's company is issuing. In this chapter, you will learn more about the ways in which people like Smith and Jones help each other through the use of financial markets.

stock
A claim on the assets of a corporation that gives the purchaser a share of the corporation.

What Are Stocks?

What does it mean when someone tells you that she "owns" shares of a particular stock? For example, suppose Jane owns 100 shares of Yahoo! stock. It means that she is a part owner of Yahoo!, Inc., which is a global Internet media company that offers a network of World Wide Web programming. A **stock** is a claim on the assets of a corporation that gives the purchaser a share in the corporation.

Jane, in this example, is not an owner in the sense that she can walk into Yahoo! headquarters (in Sunnyvale, California) and start issuing orders. She cannot hire or fire anyone, and she cannot decide what the company will or will not do over the next few months or years. Still, Jane is an owner, and as an owner she can, if she wants, sell her ownership rights in Yahoo! All she has to do is find a buyer for her 100 shares of stock. Most likely, she could do so in a matter of minutes, if not seconds.

Background Information: New York Stock Exchange

For more than 100 years, the main measuring stick for the New York Stock Exchange has been the Dow Jones Industrial Average. For the first 50 of those years, the Dow grew relatively slowly. In fact, with a starting index of 40.94 points on May 26, 1896, the Dow had only gained 460 points by March 12, 1956. In the next 40 years, the Dow increased from 500 points to almost 6,000 in October 1996. In December 2005, it was over 10,000.

Where Is Stock Bought and Sold?

You know where groceries are bought and sold—at the grocery store. You know where clothes are bought and sold—at the clothing store. But where are stocks bought and sold?

Let's go back in time to help answer this question. In 1792, 24 men met under a buttonwood tree on what is now Wall Street in New York City. They essentially bought and sold stock (for themselves and their customers) at this location. Someone might have said, "I want to sell 20 shares in company X. Are you willing to buy these shares at $2 a share?"

From this humble beginning came the New York Stock Exchange (NYSE). Every weekday (excluding holidays), men and women meet at the NYSE in New York City and buy and sell stock.

Suppose you own 100 shares of a stock listed on the NYSE. Do you have to go to the NYSE in New York to sell it? No, you simply contact a stock broker (over the phone, in person, or online) and have him or her represent you in selling the stock to a person at the NYSE. That person at the NYSE then executes your order.

In addition to the NYSE, other stock exchanges and markets also serve as places to trade stocks and bonds, including

▲ The interior and exterior of the New York Stock Exchange.

the NASDAQ (pronounced NAZ-dak) stock market. NASDAQ stands for National Association of Securities Dealers Automated Quotations. Buying and selling stock on NASDAQ doesn't take place the same way it does on the NYSE. NASDAQ is an electronic stock market, so trades are executed through a sophisticated computer and telecommunications network. Trading doesn't occur in one central location. The NYSE might change to this kind of market in the near future. Instead of people meeting on Wall Street to buy and sell stock, they could simply make trades electronically.

Increasingly, Americans are buying and selling stocks not only in U.S. stock exchanges and markets but in foreign stock exchanges and markets too. For example, an American might buy a stock listed on the German Stock Exchange, the Montreal Stock Exchange, or the Swiss Exchange.

The Dow Jones Industrial Average (DJIA)

You may have heard news commentators say, "The Dow fell 302 points after heavy trading." They are talking about the **Dow Jones Industrial Average (DJIA)**. It first appeared on the scene more than 100 years ago, on May 26, 1896. It was devised by Charles H. Dow, who took 11 stocks, summed their prices on a particular day, and then divided by 11. The "average price" was the DJIA. Some of the original

Dow Jones Industrial Average (DJIA)
A weighted average of 30 widely traded stocks on the New York Stock Exchange. The most popular, widely cited indicator of day-to-day stock market activity.

Section 1 **Stocks** **471**

Charles H. Dow created the Dow Jones Industrial Average in 1896 to convey information about what was happening in the stock market. The Dow serves the same purpose today.

Discussion Starter

Ask students if they think there is a need for multiple stock exchanges. Encourage them to identify advantages and disadvantages of having multiple exchanges and also of having a single exchange. Students might mention that if all stocks were sold on a single exchange, the list of offerings would be enormous, and buyers and sellers might be more likely to overlook small offerings from small companies.

Reinforcement Activity

Journalist Charles H. Dow was co-founder of Dow Jones & Company and creator of the Dow Jones Industrial Average. He began his career as a reporter with the *Springfield* (MA) *Daily Republican* and soon became an assistant editor. In 1875, he left Springfield to join the Providence (RI) *Morning Star and Evening Press*. There he met Edward Jones, and in 1882, they formed Dow Jones & Company. In 1896, Dow came up with the idea for the Dow Jones Industrial Average.

Allow students to work in groups to research more information about Charles Dow and Edward Jones. Groups can present their information to the class in oral presentations.

Prediction Activity

Invite students to consider the following scenario: It has just been announced that personal income in the United States is higher than expected. Do you predict that this announcement will have any effect on the Dow? Explain your answer.

Students should understand that a higher-than-expected increase in personal income often causes the Dow to rise. Stock investors think that higher incomes will cause people to spend more, and more spending is good for business. Therefore, investors think this is a good time to buy stock, and stock prices rise as demand increases.

EXHIBIT 16-1 **The 30 Stocks of the Dow Jones Industrial Average**

3M	Johnson & Johnson
American Express	JPMorgan Chase
Apple	McDonald's
Boeing	Merck
Caterpillar	Microsoft
Chevron	Nike
Cisco Systems	Pfizer
Coca-Cola	Procter & Gamble
E.I. du Pont de Nemours	The Travelers Companies
Exxon Mobil	United Technologies
General Electric	UnitedHealth Group
Goldman Sachs	Verizon
Home Depot	Visa
Intel Corp	Wal-Mart Stores
IBM	Walt Disney

▲ Why did Charles Dow create the Dow Jones Industrial Average? What purpose does it serve today?

---

companies on the DJIA included American Cotton Oil, Chicago Gas, National Lead, and U.S. Rubber.

When Dow first computed the DJIA, the stock market was not highly regarded in the United States. Prudent investors bought bonds, not stocks. Stocks were thought to be the area in which speculators and conniving Wall Street operators plied their trade. It was thought back then that Wall Streeters managed stock prices to make themselves better off at the expense of others. A lot of gossip surrounded what was and was not happening in the stock market.

Dow devised the DJIA to convey some information about what was actually happening in the stock market. Before the DJIA, people had a hard time figuring out whether the stock market, on average, was rising or falling. Instead, they only knew that a particular stock went up or down by so many cents or dollars. Dow decided to find the average price of a certain number of stocks (11) that he thought would largely mirror what was happening in the stock market as a whole. Given this number,

people would have some sense of what the stock market was doing on any given day.

Today, the DJIA consists of 30 stocks, which are widely held by individuals and institutional investors. (See Exhibit 16-1.) This list can and does change from time to time, as determined by the editors of the *Wall Street Journal*.

You might assume that the DJIA is computed by summing the prices of stocks and dividing by 30, but it isn't quite that simple today. A special divisor is used to avoid distortions that can occur, such as companies splitting their stock shares.

In addition to the DJIA, other prominent stock indices are cited in the United States. A few include the NASDAQ Composite, the Standard & Poor's 500, the Russell 2000, and the Wilshire 5000. Other prominent stock indices around the world include the Hang Seng (in Hong Kong), the Bovespa (Brazil), IPC (Mexico), BSE 30 (India), and CAC 40 (France).

Different economic consulting firms attempt to find out what influences the Dow: What causes it to go up? What causes it to go down? According to many economists, the Dow is closely connected to changes in such things as consumer credit, business expectations, exports and imports, personal income, and the money supply. For example, increases in consumer credit are expected to push up the Dow. The expectation is that when consumer credit rises, people will buy more goods and services, which means more business for companies that sell goods and services. When consumer credit falls, the reverse is expected to happen. Exhibit 16-2 shows the ups and downs of the Dow during the period 2013 to early 2017.

A Student Asks

QUESTION: *I own a few stocks as a result of gifts I received from my grandparents. None of these stocks is included in the Dow Jones Industrial Average, but are they affected when the Dow goes up or down? Am I somehow affected?*

Differentiating Instruction

Kinesthetic Learners

Show students a videotape of the floor of a stock exchange, with people flashing hand signals to each other. Ask students why flashing hand signals is so important on the stock market floor. (*Answer:* Brokers need to be able to commu-

nicate across distances in a loud environment.) Have some of your kinesthetic learners research the hand signals of the trading floor and their meanings. These students can come to class and demonstrate the signals for the rest of the class.

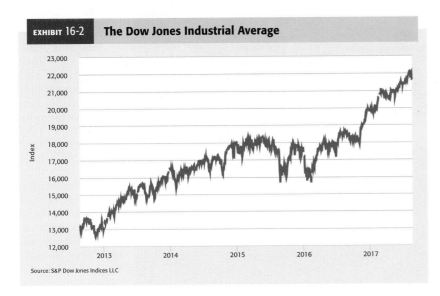

EXHIBIT 16-2 **The Dow Jones Industrial Average**

Source: S&P Dow Jones Indices LLC

◄ Based on this graph, when would have been a good time to purchase shares in the companies making up the DJIA? When would have been a good time to sell shares? (There's more than one answer to each question.)

ANSWER: *You aren't affected if we are looking at daily changes, but if we are talking about a long decline or a long rise in the DJIA, then you are indirectly affected. Many economists say that what happens in the stock market— or to the DJIA—is a sign of future economic events. So, if the DJIA goes down over time, it indicates that the economic future is somewhat depressed; if it goes up over time, it indicates that the economic future looks good. The economic future, good or bad, is something that definitely affects you. It affects the prices you pay, how easy or hard it is to get a job, how large or small a raise in income you get, and so on.*

How the Stock Market Works

Suppose that a company wants to raise money so it can invest in a new product or manufacturing technique. It can do one of three things to get the money. First, it can go to a bank and borrow the money. Second, it

can borrow the money by issuing a bond (a promise to repay the borrowed money with interest; you will learn more about bonds later in Section 2). Third, it can sell or issue stock in the company, or put another way, it can sell part of the company. Stocks are also called *equity* because the buyer of the stock has part ownership of the company.

When a company is formed, the owners set up a certain amount of stock, which is worth little. The owners of the company try to find people (usually friends and associates) who are willing to buy the stock (in the hope that one day, it will be worth something). In the early days of a company, it would be nearly impossible for anyone who owned stock to sell it. For example, if Alvarez owned 100 shares of some new company that almost no one had heard of, she would have trouble finding someone who would be willing to buy the stock.

As a new company grows and needs more money, it may decide to offer its stock on the open market. The company can offer

> *"Everyone has the brainpower to follow the stock market. If you made it through fifth-grade math, you can do it."*
> —Peter Lynch, investor

Section 1 Stocks **473**

Teaching with Visuals

Have students study Exhibit 16-2 and then answer the questions. Answers will vary. Students should understand that it makes sense to buy stocks when values are low and to sell stocks when values are high.

Reinforcement Activity

The Dow Jones Industrial Average is an average of 30 stocks. Assign students to research how these stocks have been determined over the years and answer the following questions: Have any stocks remained the same through the entire history of the Dow? Which of the current stocks has been part of the Dow for the longest time? For the shortest time?

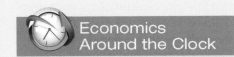

Economics Around the Clock

After reading and discussing financial markets, refer students to the 5:42 p.m. scenario in Economics Around the Clock (page 469) and discuss their answers to the question provided there.

Students should recognize that in the context of financial issues, "the market" usually refers to a stock index, such as the Dow or the Standard & Poor's 500. When the Dow goes down, someone might say, "The market is down today."

Differentiating Instruction

Kinesthetic and Visual Learners

Play a stock market game: Tell students that each of them has a fixed amount of play money to invest, and set an end date at which the game will be over. Ask students to research companies and buy imaginary stocks with their money. To add more interest to the game, allow students to set up their own imaginary companies and then buy

capital, monitor their investments over the course of the game, and sell and trade stock (with you serving as the broker) to increase their holdings. Give students a certain amount of time each day (and perhaps before and after school) to make their trades. On the last day of the game, students will sell their stocks at that day's values, and the one with the most money wins a prize.

Teaching with Visuals

Answers will vary. Students may deduce that the owners of Twitter determined that selling stock of their company was the best financial decision at the time.

Reinforcement Activity

In the last few years, the initial public offerings (IPOs) of some companies have been so eagerly anticipated that their prices have skyrocketed past usual numbers. Some companies have raised their IPO prices several times before their stocks were actually sold because the demand for them was perceived as being very high. Ask students to research some recent IPOs and answer the following questions: What is the highest IPO stock price you found? Would you be willing to spend that kind of money for one share of stock that had never been traded before? What information would influence your decision?

Background Information

Ask students whether events in other countries might influence the Dow. Give them this example of one way that foreign events influence the index: Suppose we learn that one of the companies currently listed in the Dow will face stiff competition in Spain next year because of the emergence of a new company there. As a result, the market value of the U.S. company's stock falls, and because it is one of the 30 stocks that compose the Dow, the Dow ends up dropping.

▲ Twitter founders (first three on the left) and Twitter CEO (right) celebrate the Twitter IPO on the floor of the New York Stock Exchange. Why do you think the owners of Twitter decided to sell stock in their company?

initial public offering (IPO)
A company's first offering of stock to the public.

investment bank
A firm that acts as an intermediary between the company that issues the stock and the public that wants to buy the stock.

its stock to anyone who wants to buy it. By this time, the company may be better known, so people may be more willing to buy stock. The company makes what is called an **initial public offering (IPO)** of its stock. The process is quite simple. Usually, an **investment bank** sells the stock for the company for an initial price—say, $10 a share. How do you find out about an IPO? IPOs are announced in the *Wall Street Journal.*

When an IPO occurs, the stock is usually traded on a stock exchange or in an electronic stock market. Sometimes a stock that initially sold for $10 will rise in price, and sometimes the price will fall like a rock. It all depends on whether people in the stock market think the company that issued the stock will do well in the future. If they think the company is destined for big earnings, the stock will likely rise in price. If they think the company is destined for losses or only marginal earnings, the stock will likely fall in price.

In a way, trading stock is a lot like trading baseball cards, or paintings, or anything else. The price depends on the forces of supply and demand. If demand rises and supply is constant, then the price of the stock will rise. If demand falls and supply is constant, then the price of the stock will fall.

Sometimes people buy a certain stock because they hear that other people are buying it and because they think the stock is "hot." In other words, it's popular and everyone wants it. In the 1990s, some of the Internet stocks fit this description. People bought the stocks of companies such as Yahoo!, Amazon.com, and eBay because they thought the Internet was the wave of the future and almost anything connected with it was destined for great profit.

More often, though, people buy a particular company's stock if they think the company's earnings are likely to rise. Remember that a share of stock represents ownership in a company. The more profitable that company is expected to be, the more likely people will want to own its stock, and therefore the greater the demand for that stock.

EXAMPLE Suppose that William Welch started a company in 1895, and through the years, his company has been passed down to family members. In 2018, the family members running the company want to expand it to two, three, or four times its current size. Where might they get the money for this expansion? One way is by selling shares in the company—that is, by issuing stock in the company. But once they issue shares in the company to the public, the company is no longer solely family owned. "Going public" means that people outside the family own part of the company too. ♦

The Language of Wall Street

People who work on Wall Street often use their own "language." For "translations" of some of that language, see Exhibit 16-3.

Cooperative Learning

Divide students into groups of three or four. Tell them that each group is a financial advisory board that wants to help Kirk (the investor) with his investment portfolio. Kirk has $50,000 to invest and no previous experience with the stock market.

Instruct groups to prepare different strategies for Kirk, detailing how he can invest his money

and how much he can expect in returns. Tell groups that the more specific their suggestions for the investments Kirk should make and the higher the returns, the more likely Kirk will hire them as his financial advisor board. Have each group prepare and turn in a summary of its advice to Kirk.

EXHIBIT 16-3　Translating Financial Talk

after the bell	Refers to the time after the bell sounds and the stock market is closed until the next trading day.
air pocket stock	A stock that plunges quickly and furiously, much like an airplane that hits an air pocket.
Bo Derek	A slang term used to refer to a perfect stock or investment; named after the movie actress who starred in the 1979 movie *10*.
big board	The nickname for the New York Stock Exchange.
bull and bear markets	Terms used to describe the direction the market is moving. A bull market is one in which prices are expected to rise. A bear market is one in which prices are expected to fall. The terms *bull* and *bear* come from the way these animals attack their opponents: the bull puts its horns up in the air and a bear moves its paws down (across its opponent).
casino finance	An investment strategy that is considered extremely risky.
deer market	A flat market where not much is happening and investors are usually timid. It is neither a bull nor a bear market.
eat well, sleep well	A phrase describing two different strategies for investing. If you want a high return, you usually have to assume some risk. If you don't want to take on much risk, then you will likely have a low return. "Eat well, sleep well" captures this idea: do you want a risky investment that may end up feeding you well, or do you want a safe investment that lets you sleep at night?
falling knife	A stock whose price has fallen significantly in a short time. Someone might say, "Don't try to catch a falling knife" because you can hurt yourself).
Goldilocks economy	An economy that is not too hot or too cold but is just right. People often referred to the economy in the mid- to late 1990s in the U.S. as the Goldilocks economy.
lemon	A disappointing investment.
love money	Money given by family or friends to a person to start a business.
Nervous Nellie	An investor who isn't comfortable with investing, mainly because of the risks.
sandwich generation	A phrase that refers to people usually of middle age who are "sandwiched" between their children and their parents and obligated to provide care and support for both groups of people.
Santa Claus rally	A jump in the price of stocks that often occurs during the week between Christmas and New Year's.
short selling	A technique used by investors who are trying to benefit from a falling stock price. For example, suppose Brian believes that stock X will soon fall in price. He borrows the stock from someone who currently owns it with the promise to return the stock later. He then sells the (borrowed) stock, hoping to buy back enough shares later at a lower price to return to the original owner.
war babies	A name given to stocks issued by companies that produce military hardware (tanks, airplanes, etc.).

Why Do People Buy and Sell Stock?

Millions of people, in countries all over the world, buy stock every day. Why do they do it? People invest in stocks for a couple of reasons. Some people buy stocks for the **dividends**, which are the payments made to stockholders based on a company's profits.

EXAMPLE Suppose company X issued 1 million shares of stock purchased by different people. Each year, the company tabulates its profit and loss, and when it earns a profit, it divides up much of the profit among the owners of the company as dividends. This year's dividend might be $1 for each share of stock a person owns. So, if Florian owns 50,000 shares of stock, she will receive a dividend check for $50,000. ♦

The other reason to buy stock is for the expected increase in its price. Stockholders can make money if they buy shares at a lower price and sell them at a higher price.

EXAMPLE Kristor buys 100 shares of Microsoft stock today. He thinks that the company is going to do well and that a year from now, he will be able to sell the stock for as much as $50 more a share than he purchased it. In other words, he hopes to earn $5,000 on his stock purchase. ♦

People also sell stock for many reasons. Smith might sell her 100 shares of IBM because she needs the money to help her son pay for college. She also might sell the stock to help put together a down payment on a house. Another common reason for selling stock is the belief that the stock will soon go down in price. Obviously, it's better to sell today at $25 a share than to sell one week from now at $18 a share.

dividend
A share of the profits of a corporation distributes to stockholders.

Section 1　Stocks　**475**

Discussion Starter

Buying and selling stocks online has become one of the most popular pastimes of Americans. It can be very risky, however. Ask students to think about what problems might occur if an uninformed person trades stocks without getting advice.

Background Information

Knowing a stock's history is very important in predicting what will happen with the stock in the future. Brokers often look at a stock's previous performance over a certain period of time to get a sense of how its price will change in the near future.

Reinforcement Activity

Allow students to demonstrate understanding of the material presented in this section by writing one or two sentences to define the term *stock*.

Discussion Starter

Allow students to watch or listen to financial news, and ask them to keep track of things that they understand because they have read this section—that is, things they wouldn't have understood before reading this section. Ask students to comment on how the stock market is related to the economic health of the United States.

Internet Research

Many Internet sites provide information that can help investors predict the stock market. Remind students that the best way to predict the future of a stock is to be informed about the current nature of the company and its history in the market. Some companies are seasonal, and by looking at a chart of the company's earnings, you may be able to predict when its stock will be most profitable. Charting websites offer all kinds of free information on the recent history of stocks and their industries.

After students have read this feature, ask them to share what they know about the Great Depression. Ask students to answer questions like these: Suppose you were a wealthy teen living on October 24, 1929. How would your lifestyle have changed had your family lost its fortune in the stock market crash? How might the Great Depression have changed the psychological mind-set of people living at the time?

ANSWERS TO THINK ABOUT IT Answers will vary. Students will probably say that it's impossible for economists to make long-term predictions about the stock market because stock prices are affected by many events—some of them impossible to predict.

Discussion Starter

Ask students if they ever traded anything, like sports memorabilia or food at lunch. If so, were they certain they were getting the best end of the deal? How could they tell? Remind students that when stocks are traded, their value does not always increase.

Reinforcement Activity

To make sure students understand how the price of a stock is determined, have them write one or two sentences explaining the process. If they have trouble, direct them to page 474.

Was the Great Crash the Culprit?

On Thursday, October 24, 1929, the *New York Times* ran a headline that read "Prices of Stocks Crash in Heavy Liquidation." Elsewhere in the *Times*, a headline read "Many Accounts Wiped Out." These headlines referred to the stock market crash (sometimes simply called the Great Crash) that began on that October day in 1929 and continued through October 28 and 29.

In some historical accounts and in the minds of many members of the public, the stock market crash in 1929 was what caused the Great Depression that followed. However, this cause-and-effect assumption is not true. In fact, it's an example of the logical fallacy *post hoc ergo propter hoc* (which is Latin for "After this, therefore as a result of this"). Stated differently, it means "That which comes before another must be its cause." For example, if X comes before Y, then X is the cause of Y. This statement isn't necessarily true.

Think of some simple examples. The teacher gives you a test and then it rains, but the teacher's giving you a test didn't cause the rain. Similarly, just because the stock market crash occurred before the many years of the Great Depression doesn't necessarily mean that the crash caused the depression. In fact, most economists believe that both the stock market crash and the Great Depression (along with such trends as rising unemployment and falling incomes) were effects of the same causes. In other words, the same factors caused both the stock market crash and the Great Depression.

Nonetheless, the stock market crash changed the psychological mind-set of the people living in the late 1920s. Gone were the good times of the Roaring Twenties; a dark economic cloud seemed to hang over the United States. It's interesting how many people failed to see that cloud on the horizon. Irving Fisher, perhaps the best-known American economist of the day, said just a week before the crash, "Stock prices have reached what looks like a permanently high plateau. I expect to see the stock market a good deal higher than it is today within a few months." Fisher ended up losing a fortune in the stock market crash.

Other people who didn't see the crash coming were Myron Forbes, president of Pierce Arrow Motor Company, and E. H. H. Simmons, president of the New York Stock Exchange. Also, Winston Churchill had just visited the United States and written to his wife about how well they were doing in the stock market. Ironically, Churchill had just ended a five-year term as chancellor of the exchequer, an important financial position in Great Britain.

On October 24, 1929, when word got out that the stock market was crashing, thousands of people gathered on Wall Street to witness events. Among them was Churchill (who became prime minister of Great Britain in 1940), who watched from the visitors' gallery of the New York Stock Exchange as his fortune disappeared on the trading floor below.

THINK ABOUT IT Predicting stock market movements is often difficult. Why do you think it is difficult?

Differentiating Instruction

Kinesthetic and Visual Learners

Students may not realize that it's possible to buy and sell stock in foreign stock markets. We have discussed in earlier chapters how interrelated countries are economically and how fluctuations in one country's economic stability can have far-reaching effects. Tell students to track stocks of companies that produce substitutes for U.S. goods. Students might track Peugeot as an example of a foreign automobile manufacturer and compare the value of its stock to General Motors stock. Visual learners can reflect their learning in the form of a chart or graph.

A Student Asks

QUESTION: *Suppose I buy 100 shares of stock at a price of $40 a share. The stock goes down in price to $32. Should I wait until the share price rises to $40 or higher before I sell it?*

ANSWER: *When it comes to stock, what goes down isn't guaranteed to go up. Even if the stock's price has gone down by $8, it might go down more. You should always look forward to the future (not backward to the past) when deciding whether to sell a stock. If you suspect the price will fall even more, you should probably sell. It would be better to sell at $32 (and take an $8 per share loss) than to sell at $25 (and take a bigger loss). If you believe the price will eventually rise, then you should hold on to the stock.*

How to Buy and Sell Stock

Buying and selling stock is relatively easy. You can buy and sell through a full-service stock brokerage firm, a discount broker, or an online broker. With any type of broker, you usually open an account by depositing a certain dollar amount into it, most commonly between $1,000 and $2,500. Once you open an account, you can begin to trade (buy and sell stock).

With a full-service broker, you may call and ask him or her to recommend some good stock. Your broker, usually called an *account representative*, might say that you should buy X, Y, or Z stock. You may ask why these stocks are good ones to buy. The broker may say that the research department in the firm has looked closely at these stocks and believes they are headed for good times. The analyst's reasons might be based on the current economic situation in the country, the level of exports, the new technology that is coming to market, and so on.

If you don't want or need help to buy stocks, you can go to a discount broker or an online broker. You can call a discount broker the same way you would call a full-service broker and tell him or her that you want to buy or sell so many shares of a given stock. The broker will simply execute the trade for you; he or she isn't there to make recommendations or offer advice.

You can follow the same process to buy stocks online. Go to your broker's website, log in by entering your username and password, and then buy or sell stock. For example, if you submit an order to buy 100 shares of stock X, your online broker will register your buy request and then note when it has been executed. Your account, easily visible online, will show how much cash you have in it, how many shares of particular stocks you hold, and so on.

Deciding Which Stocks to Buy

You can use various methods to decide which stocks to purchase. One way is to simply buy shares of stock that you think are going to rise in price. So, you might buy 50 shares of Microsoft, 100 shares of General Electric, and 500 shares of Disney.

▲ It's fun to check your stocks each day in the paper or on your computer—when they're going up. It's not much fun, though, if your stocks are going down.

Background Information

Ask students whether they have ever saved something of value and, if so, how long they saved it, why they did so, and how difficult it was to do so. Point out that it's sometimes very hard to be patient with stocks, but patience and the use of long-term investment strategies are the keys to being successful in the market. Explain that if you own stock in a company and the price triples in two weeks for some reason, it may seem like a great time to sell. But it's possible that the price could continue to rise—or it could fall just as quickly. Historically, stock prices have gone up over the long term. However, investing in the stock market isn't a reliable way of making a lot of money in the short term.

Reinforcement Activity

Assign students to watch the markets for four or five countries in addition to markets in the United States and to track whether fluctuations in one market affect the other markets. You might want to check the markets in class every day and perhaps graph them as time progresses.

Internet Research

Direct students to visit the Dow Jones Industrial Average website to learn more about the Dow. Have them create reports with text, charts, and other visual aids that explain to beginning investors what the Dow is all about. Students' reports should answer the following questions: What does the Dow show? How does the Dow differ from other indices? How much has the Dow fluctuated in the past century? What stocks are currently traded? What stocks were originally traded? What do the types of stocks originally and currently traded reveal about changes to the economy since the Dow was created?

Background Information

Some students might think that they can make millions on the stock market overnight. Remind students that literally millions of people have invested in the stock market based on the same information they have and not made millions of dollars.

Buying stocks is a long-term investment. Some stocks open at a low price and then shoot up over the next week, but many of them slip below their initial values in a matter of months.

Reinforcement Activity

There are many mutual funds companies to choose from in the stock market. Ask students to research the leading mutual fund companies and then track their successes and failures over a period of time. Then encourage students to look at the companies' websites to determine how accurately they present their track records.

Reinforcement Activity

Many people invest in mutual funds through company retirement accounts or individual retirement accounts (IRAs). Assign students to interview adults to find out how various retirement programs work. Students might talk with parents or other relatives, teachers, family friends, bankers, human resource professionals, or financial advisors. Students might also consult popular financial books, such as those by Suze Orman. Allow students to share their results with the class or in small groups.

▲ Rather than trying to select the biggest winners, some investors "buy the market." If the market as a whole does well, so these investors do well.

"Anyone who thinks there's safety in numbers hasn't looked at the stock market pages."
— Irene Porter

index
A portfolio of stocks that represent a particular market or a portion of it; used to measure changes in a market or economy.

Mutual Funds

Another way to buy stock is through a mutual fund, which is a collection of stocks. The fund is administered by a fund manager who works for the mutual fund company. For example, Smith may manage mutual fund Z at mutual fund company Z. If you put, say, $10,000 in mutual fund Z, you are in effect buying the stocks in that fund. Let's say the fund consists of stocks A, B, C, W, and X at the current time. The fund manager may, on any given day, buy more of A and sell some of B or sell all of C and add stock D to the fund portfolio.

It's up to the fund manager to do what he or she thinks is best to maximize the overall return from the fund. As a buyer of the fund, you put your money in the fund manager's hands. Mutual fund companies often advertise the records of their fund managers. They might say, "Our fund managers have the best record on Wall Street. Invest with us, and get the highest returns you can." You may be prompted to put your money in the hands of the "experts," because you feel they know better than you what stocks to buy and sell and when to do each.

Buying the Market

You could also use another strategy and buy the stocks that make up a stock index. An **index** is basically a portfolio of stocks that represent a particular market or a portion of it. Indexes are used to measure changes in a market or an economy. Earlier, we discussed the DJIA. The DJIA is a stock index. It gives us information on the performance of the 30 stocks that make up the Dow. Another index is the Standard & Poor's 500. This index is a broad index of stock market activity, because it is made up of 500 of the largest U.S. companies. Another broad-based stock index is the Wilshire 5000, which includes all stocks that have readily available prices.

A particularly easy way to get a composite type of fund is to buy what are called "Spyders." Spyders—or SPDRs, which stands for "Standard & Poor's Depository Receipts"—are securities that represent ownership in the SPDR Trust. The SPDR Trust buys the stocks that make up the Standard & Poor's (S&P) 500 index. Spyders are traded under the symbol SPY. When this book was being written, Spyders (or Spiders) were selling for about $239 a share. Spyders cost one-tenth of the S&P index (the total of the share prices of the stocks in the S&P). For example, if the S&P index is 2,390, then a Spyder will sell for $239.

When you buy Spyders, you are buying the stocks of 500 companies. Because you are buying the stocks of so many companies, you are said to be "buying the market."

EXAMPLE Jack has decided to "buy the market" instead of buying a few individual stocks. He checks on the current price of Spyders and sees that it's $239.00 per share. He decides to buy 100 shares, for a total of $23,900. His online broker charges him a small commission for making this stock purchase. ◆

How to Read the Stock Market Page

Suppose you purchased some stock, and now you want to find out how it's doing. Is it rising or falling in price? Is it paying a dividend? How many shares were traded today?

One of the places you can find the answers to these questions and more is the newspaper, whether in print or online.

Differentiating Instruction

Kinesthetic and Visual Learners

Economic concepts such as the "bull" and "bear" markets have often been represented in political cartoons. Cartoons can present difficult subjects in clear ways. Have an art teacher come into your class and assist students in creating economic cartoons about various facets of the stock market. After students have finished their cartoons, invite volunteers to explain their work to the rest of the class. Display the cartoons around the room. With permission, you may also create transparencies of some cartoons for use in future classes.

Picking Stocks: Darts or Analysts?

Let's say that you just inherited some money and would like to buy some stock. What's your investment strategy?

- You could pick and buy certain individual stocks yourself.
- You could buy shares in a mutual fund, which means investing your money in a fund created by the so-called Wall Street experts.
- You could buy a stock index fund, such as the 30 stocks that make up the DJIA or the 500 stocks that make up the Standard & Poor's 500.

Most people think stock mutual funds do better than stock index funds because the experts pick the stocks that make up mutual funds. These experts make it their business to study stocks day and night. Right?

Enter Burton Malkiel, a professor emeritus of economics at Princeton University. He has shown that a person who invested $10,000 in 1969 in the Standard & Poor's 500 stock index fund (which is not managed by the experts) would have seen its value increase to $310,000 by mid-1984. But the person who invested $10,000 in 1969 in the average actively managed fund would have seen its value increase to $170,000, or $140,000 less than in the stock index fund.

Many rigorous studies have confirmed Malkiel's results. For now, though, consider a rather informal study done by editors at *Forbes* magazine. Their "study" involves pinning the stock market page of the newspaper to the back of an office door and throwing darts at it. Then they invest "play money" in each stock hit by a dart. At the same time, they invest the same amount of "play money" in the stock picks of some of the best-known stock pickers on Wall Street. At the end of the year, they check to see which group of stocks (dart-picked or expert-picked) did better. Over the years, few of the highly trained professionals have done as well as the darts.

To understand why throwing darts often beats the experts, consider the stocks of two companies, IBM and Ford. Suppose that on a given day, each stock sells for $100 a share. Then one day, IBM announces a major breakthrough in computer technology. On the same day, Ford has to recall one of its best-selling cars. In other words, the IBM news is good and the Ford news is bad.

What will happen to each company's stock? No doubt, the IBM stock will be bid up in price and the Ford stock will be bid down in price. At the end of the day, IBM will sell for more than $100 and Ford will sell for less than $100. Over time, the prices of the two stocks will keep adjusting until it's no better to buy IBM stock than Ford stock. In the end, buying

Ford at the lower price will come out about the same as buying IBM at the higher price.

As long as stock prices adjust quickly—and evidence indicates that they do—then no stock will be better or worse than any other stock. If all stocks are alike once their prices have adjusted to good and bad news, then even a monkey throwing darts can pick stocks as well as Wall Street experts.

You can test this yourself. Pick 10 stocks using the dart method, and invest $100 play money in each stock. Next, go online and search for "top stock picks." Invest $100 play money in the same number of top picks as dart-picked stocks. Compare the results.

THINK ABOUT IT If stock pickers can do no better (and sometimes do worse) than throwing darts at the stock market page, then why do some people still pay the experts to pick stocks for them?

After students read this feature, allow them to test the dart method using $100 of play money, as suggested in the feature. When students have completed the test, ask them whether they would use the dart method to invest in stocks.

ANSWERS TO THINK ABOUT IT Answers will vary. Students will probably say that experts have valuable knowledge to use when choosing stocks.

Background Information

People who have stocks usually watch NASDAQ reports closely, because a rapidly declining market might be an economic indicator of a larger problem.

Internet Research

Tell students to select one or two companies that are listed on the New York Stock Exchange or NASDAQ and track their stock prices in the newspaper for a week. Also have students track the prices of the same stocks online for the same period. Then have students answer the following questions: Which source gave them the most up-to-date information? Which was easier to use? Were the figures reported the same? Which source would they likely use if they were intending to purchase or monitor stock prices? Why?

Reinforcement Activity

Invite students to bring to class the financial or business section of a newspaper and locate the stock reports. Ask which market seems to have the most stocks listed in it. Direct students to compare the amounts and types of information presented for the different markets.

Discussion Starter

Ask students the following questions after they have read through this section: How would they invest their money in stocks? Would they put their money into individual stocks, or would they rather use a mutual fund? Would they invest it themselves, or would they have someone manage their money for them?

Application Activity

After reading and discussing Section 1, you may want to assign the Section Activity in the *Applying the Principles Workbook*, pages 165–168.

Assess

Quick Quiz

The following true-or-false quiz will help you assess student understanding of the material covered in this section.

1. The New York Stock Exchange is the largest market for the sale and purchase of stocks in the world. (True)
2. There are still 11 companies in the Dow Jones Industrial Average. (False)
3. One reason to buy stock is for the expected gain in value. (True)
4. Spyders are stock guides that give information to stockholders. (False)
5. The yield of a stock is the dividend divided by the closing price. (True)

Economic Facts *and* Fallacies

The Importance of Timing

Over the long run, stock prices generally go up. Some people think this means that if they invest their money in a Dow Jones Industrial Average (DJIA) index fund, they will earn a positive return. They are confident that the price of stock in the DJIA fund will always be higher at the end of the year than at the beginning of the year and that the value of the stock will go up and up and up.

That isn't true, though. In the 42 years from 1975 to 2016, the DJIA went up in 31 years and down in 11 years. Sometimes it went up by a large percentage, and sometimes it went up by a small percentage. Other times it went down by a large percentage, or by a small percentage. For example, in 2003, the DJIA went up 25.32 percent, and in 2008, it went down 33.84 percent. In 2013, it went up 26.50 percent, and in 2015, it went down 2.23 percent.

Overall, whether the stock you buy increases in value depends, at least in part, on when you buy it and when you sell it. Timing is more important than many people realize.

Go to the stock market page, and you will see something similar to what's shown in Exhibit 16-4. The descriptions that follow focus on the last stock (in bold type) as an example:

1. **52W high.** This column provides the high price of the stock during the past year, or 52 weeks. For our example stock, you see the number "51.25," which is $51.25.

2. **52W low.** This column provides the low price of the stock during the past 52 weeks. For our example stock, you see the number "27.69," which is $27.69.

3. **Stock.** In this column, you see "Rockwell," which is either an abbreviation of the name of the company or the full name of the company whose stock you are studying. The company here is Rockwell Automation Incorporated.

4. **Ticker.** In this column, you see "ROK," which is the stock or ticker symbol for Rockwell Automation.

---

5. **Div.** In this column, the number (in this case "1.02") indicates that the last annual dividend per share of stock was $1.02. For example, a person who owned 5,000 shares of Rockwell Automation stock would have received $1.02 per share, or $5,100 in dividends. (If this space is blank, then the company does not currently pay out dividends.)

6. **Yield %.** The **yield** of a stock is the dividend divided by the closing price:

$$\text{Yield} = \frac{\text{Dividend per share}}{\text{Closing price per share}}$$

The closing price of the stock (shown in column 11) is 47.54, or $47.54. If we divide the dividend ($1.02) by the closing price ($47.54), we get a yield of 2.1 percent. A higher yield is better than a lower yield, all other things being the same.

7. **P/E.** The PE ratio, or price-earnings ratio, is obtained by taking the latest closing price per share and dividing it by the latest available net earnings per share:

$$\text{PE} = \frac{\text{Closing price per share}}{\text{Net earnings per share}}$$

A stock with a PE ratio of 14.5, like the one here, means that the stock is selling for a share price that is 14.5 times its earnings per share. What does this number tell us about the stock? Let's suppose that most stocks have a PE ratio of 14.5. In comparison, let's say stock X has a PE ratio of 50. What would make stock X have a PE ratio so much higher than most stocks? A high PE ratio usually indicates that people believe the stock will experience higher than average growth in earnings. Whether they are right remains to be seen.

8. **Vol 00s.** Volume in the hundreds, or 6412 here, translates to 641,200. In other words, 641,200 shares of this stock were traded (bought and sold) on this particular day.

Differentiating Instruction

English Language Learners

Some of the terms and phrases in this chapter may be difficult for some of your students. Encourage students to state in their own words the meanings of some of the more difficult words and phrases in this chapter. Then, using students' definitions, review the concepts behind the terms and phrases. On the board, draw a three-way connection among the original word or phrase, the students' definitions, and the concept the term or phrase represents.

EXHIBIT 16-4 **Reading the Stock Market Page of a Newspaper**

◀ The text on the previous page and this page explains how to read and understand the information about stocks that's provided in the newspaper and online.

(1)	(2)	(3)	(4)	(5)	(6)	(7)	(8)	(9)	(10)	(11)	(12)
52W high	52W low	Stock	Ticker	Div	Yield %	P/E	Vol 00s	High	Low	Close	Net chg
45.39	19.75	ResMed	RMD			57.5	3831	42.00	39.51	41.50	−1.90
11.63	3.55	Revlon A	REV				162	6.09	5.90	6.09	+0.12
77.25	55.13	RioTinto	RTP	2.30	3.2		168	72.75	71.84	72.74	+0.03
31.31	16.63	RitchieBr	RBA			20.9	15	24.49	24.29	24.49	−0.01
8.44	1.75	RiteAid	RAD				31028	4.50	4.20	4.31	+0.21
38.63	18.81	RobtHall	RHI			26.5	6517	27.15	26.50	26.50	+0.14
51.25	**27.69**	**Rockwell**	**ROK**	**1.02**	**2.1**	**14.5**	**6412**	**47.99**	**47.00**	**47.54**	**+0.24**

9. **High.** This number, 47.99, stands for the high price the stock traded for on this particular day, which translates to $47.99.

10. **Low.** This number is the low price the stock traded for on this particular day. The number is 47.00 and translates to $47.00.

11. **Close.** The number here—47.54, or $47.54—is the share price of the stock when trading stopped this particular day.

12. **Net chg.** Net change is the difference between the current closing price and the previous day's closing price. The number here is +0.24, which translates to $0.24. This means that the price of the stock on this particular day closed 24 cents higher than it did the day before.

> *"Wall Street is the only place that people ride to in a Rolls Royce to get advice from those who take the subway."*
> — Warren Buffett, businessman and philanthropist

SECTION 1

ASSESSMENT

Defining Terms

1. Define:
   a. stock
   b. Dow Jones Industrial Average (DJIA)
   c. initial public offering (IPO)
   d. investment bank
   e. dividend
   f. index

Reviewing Facts and Concepts

2. What information did Charles Dow provide with the DJIA?

3. What does it mean to "buy the market"?

4. Does the likelihood that you will earn a positive return by buying (and selling) stocks go up or down the longer you hold the stocks (before selling)?

Critical Thinking

5. Suppose that share prices for 500 stocks rise on Monday. Does this mean everyone in the stock market believes those share prices are headed even higher? Explain.

6. Is it possible for the yield of a stock to rise without the dividend per share rising? Explain.

Applying Economic Concepts

7. Which stock has a bigger gap between its closing price and net earnings per share: stock A with a PE ratio of 17 or stock B with a PE ratio of 45?

SECTION 1

ASSESSMENT ANSWERS

Defining Terms

1. **a. stock:** a claim on the assets of a corporation that gives the purchaser a share of the corporation; **b. Dow Jones Industrial Average (DJIA):** a weighted average of 30 widely traded stocks on the New York Stock Exchange; **c. initial public offering (IPO):** a company's first offering of stock to the public; **d. investment bank:** a firm that acts as an intermediary between the company that issues the stock and the public that wishes to buy the stock; **e. dividend:** a share of the profits of a corporation distributed to stockholders; **f. index:** a portfolio of stocks that represent a particular market or portion of it.

Reviewing Facts and Concepts

2. He conveyed information on how the stock market was doing on average.

Assessment Book

You will find a quiz for this section in the *Assessment Book*, page 163.

Reteaching Activity

Use the Section Assessment to gauge which students may need reteaching on this section. With those students, create a large chart that resembles the stock market page, with columns for the stocks, symbols, and so on. Guide students as they identify each column in their own words and then describe what the number in the column represents. Make another chart that shows the applicable equations.

Guided Reading

For further reteaching of the key concepts in this section, assign the Outlining Activity and the Just the Facts Handout from the *Guided Reading and Study Guide*, pages 285–291.

---

3. It means to invest in a composite fund, which represents the stocks of many companies.

4. The likelihood goes up, because stock prices generally increase over the long run.

Critical Thinking

5. No. The stock market is made up of buyers and sellers. If one person buys 100 shares of stock, then someone must have sold 100 shares of stock. The people who sold probably thought that share prices were going to fall. If they had thought otherwise, they would have waited to sell to get a higher return.

6. Yes, yield can rise without the dividend per share rising. Since yield is equal to the dividend per share divided by the closing price per share, it will rise if the closing price per share declines and the dividend per share remains constant.

Applying Economic Concepts

7. Stock B has a bigger gap. The PE ratio is the closing price of the stock divided by the net earnings per share. Stock B has a closing price 45 times larger than net earnings, while stock A has a closing price 17 times larger than net earnings.

Teacher Support

Focus and Motivate

Section Objectives

After completing this section, students will be able to
▶ explain what bonds are;
▶ identify the factor that determines the rating of a bond;
▶ explain the relationship between interest rates and the price of bonds;
▶ identify various types of bonds;
▶ explain the relationship between risk and return; and
▶ explain why financial markets are important.

Kickoff Activity

Encourage students to think about these questions at the beginning of class: We have learned in this course that economists have their own definitions for many words. What meanings do you know for the word *bond*? How might this word relate to financial markets?

Activating Prior Knowledge

Discuss students' answers to the questions in the Kickoff Activity. Encourage students to think about how the word *bond* sometimes implies a trust relationship. In an economist's way of thinking, a bond is an IOU (or promise to pay) that's typically issued by companies, governments, or government agencies as a way of borrowing money.

Teach

A Student Asks

To help students understand how someone who buys a bond is a lender, invite two volunteers to act out the transaction described in A Student Asks.

Bonds

Focus Questions
▶ What are bonds?
▶ What factor determines the rating of a bond?
▶ What is the relationship between interest rates and the price of bonds?
▶ What are the various types of bonds?
▶ What is the relationship between risk and return?
▶ Why are financial markets important?

Key Terms
bond
face value (par value)
coupon rate
yield

What Is a Bond?

Suppose a company in St. Louis wants to build a new factory. How can it get the money to build the factory? Recall that companies can raise money in three principal ways. First, they can go to a bank and take out a loan. Second, they can issue stock, or in other words, sell ownership rights in the company. Third, they can issue bonds.

A **bond** is simply an IOU, or a promise to pay. Typically, bonds are issued by companies, governments, and government agencies. In each case, the purpose of issuing a bond is to borrow money. The issuer of a bond is a borrower, and the person who buys the bond is a lender.

bond
An IOU, or a promise to pay, issued by companies, governments, and government agencies for the purpose of borrowing money.

face value (par value)
The dollar amount specified on a bond. The total amount the issuer of the bond will repay to the buyer of the bond.

A Student Asks

QUESTION: *I don't quite understand how a person who buys something (like a bond) can be called a "lender." I thought that when you lend money to someone, you just turn it over to that person and he or she pays you back later.*

ANSWER: *Suppose a friend asks to borrow $10 and tells you that he will pay you back $11 next month if you lend him the money today. You say okay and hand over $10. Now suppose your friend takes out a piece of paper and writes the following on it: "I owe the person who returns this piece of paper one month from today a total of $11." Then he signs his name and gives the piece of paper to you. For all practical purposes, that piece of paper is a bond (an IOU statement), and you, by purchasing the IOU, have become a lender.*

The Components of a Bond

The three major components of a bond are face (par) value, maturity date, and coupon rate. The **face value**, or **par value**, of a bond is the total amount the issuer of the bond will repay to the buyer of the bond. For example, suppose Dawson buys a bond from company Z, and the face value of the bond is $10,000. It follows that company Z

Background Information: Bonds and the Military

During the crisis of the American Revolution, the colonial government needed to build funds to support its struggle against the British. The government tried to raise money by selling bonds: pieces of paper that people buy at a set price knowing that they can exchange their bonds for a profit after a certain amount of time. This practice wasn't as successful as it is now, and the government had to look to other means to finance its military.

promises to pay Dawson $10,000 at some point in the future.

The *maturity date* is when the issuer of the bond must pay the holder of the bond the face value. For example, suppose Dawson buys a bond with a face value of $10,000 that matures on December 31, 2020. On that date, he will receive $10,000 from the issuer of the bond.

The **coupon rate** is the percentage of the face value that the bondholder receives each year until the bond matures. For example, suppose Dawson buys a bond with a face value of $10,000 that matures in 5 years and has a coupon rate of 10 percent. He will receive a coupon payment of $1,000 each year for 5 years.

EXAMPLE Jackie buys a bond with a face value of $100,000 and a coupon rate of 7 percent. The maturity date of the bond is 10 years from today. Each year, for the next 10 years, Jackie will receive 7 percent of $100,000 from the issuer of the bond. This amounts to $7,000 a year for 10 years. In the tenth year, Jackie also receives $100,000 from the bond issuer. ◆

Bond Ratings

Bonds are rated or evaluated. The more likely the bond issuer will pay the face value of the bond at maturity and will meet all scheduled coupon payments, the higher the bond's rating. Two of the best known ratings are Standard & Poor's and Moody's. A bond rating of AAA from Standard & Poor's or a rating of Aaa from Moody's is the highest rating possible. A bond with this rating is one of the most secure bonds you can buy; the bond issuer is almost certain to pay the face value of the bond at maturity and meet all scheduled coupon payments. ◆

Bonds rated in the B to D category are lower-quality bonds than those rated in the A category. In fact, if a bond is rated in the C category, it may be in default (the issuer of the bond cannot pay off the bond), and if it is rated in the D category, it is definitely in default.

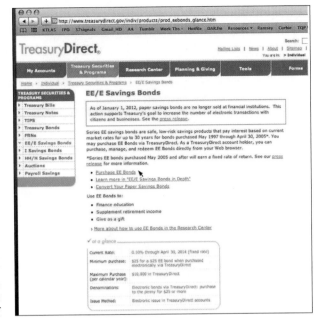

▲ One way for young people to begin saving and investing is to buy U.S. savings bonds. Issued by the U.S. government, these bonds can be purchased in smaller, more affordable denominations than most other bonds. Beginning in 2012, the U.S. Treasury discontinued the sale of paper savings bonds and began selling bonds exclusively online at TreasuryDirect.gov (shown here).

A Student Asks

QUESTION: *Suppose I want to buy a bond issued by some corporation. Would I buy the bond from the corporation or from someone else (say, a person who purchased a bond from the corporation at an earlier time)?*

ANSWER: *If the corporation is currently issuing (selling) bonds, you could buy the bond from it. Actually, you would purchase the bond through a broker who is finding buyers for the bonds the corporation wants to sell. If the corporation is not currently issuing bonds, you could buy a bond from someone who owns one that was purchased from the corporation at an earlier date.*

coupon rate
The percentage of the face value that the bondholder receives each year until the bond matures.

Reinforcement Activity

Students may be aware of bonds as they relate to school bond issues or education bonds voted on in state or local elections. Have some students interview school, local, and state government officials to find out what school or education bonds really are and how they are used. Have other students talk to local corporate leaders to discuss how bonds are used in the corporate world. Allow students to report their findings to the class and answer the more applicable of the following two questions: Is selling education or school bonds a good way of raising money? Do corporations make money by selling corporate bonds?

A Student Asks

Use this A Student Asks to make sure students understand the difference between primary and secondary markets.

Discussion Starter

Ask students the following questions: Which would you rather buy: a B-rated bond with a $10,000 face value and an 8% coupon rate or an AAA-rated bond with a $10,000 face value and a 4% coupon rate? Why?

Visit econ.myemcp.com/videos for videos that will help students better understand the key concepts found in this section.

Differentiating Instruction

Visual Learners

Have the class participate in the InvestSmart Market Simulation on the Internet. Students can first review stock market basics and view the "real life examples." Then register the class as a group, and have them go through the simulation. This site also includes lesson plans. If you don't have Internet access in your classroom or school, develop a stock market game using the information found here and the daily newspaper.

Reinforcement Activity

Have a student come to the board and show how market forces affect the prices of bonds. He or she should be able to create a graph that shows that the price of a bond goes up in response to rising demand relative to supply. Invite another student to the board. As a class, assign a face value and a coupon rate to a bond. Then ask the student to find the yield on that bond over one year.

▲ Two of the best known bond ratings are Standard & Poor's and Moody's, both of which have informative websites.

Primary market and secondary market are the terms that apply here. If you are buying a bond that is newly issued, you are buying it in the primary market; if you are buying a bond from someone who already owns it, you are buying it in the secondary market. By far, most bond and stock purchases occur in the secondary market.

Bond Prices and Yields

The price that a person pays for a bond depends on the market conditions. The greater the demand for the bond relative to the supply, the higher the price. The price is important because it determines the yield that the bondholder receives on the bond.

Let's suppose that Sonya is currently the owner of a bond with a face value of $1,000

yield
Equal to the annual coupon payment divided by the price paid for the bond.

and a coupon rate of 5 percent. She decides to sell this bond to Joshua for $950. Now, we know that the coupon payment on this bond will be 5 percent of $1,000 each year, or $50. This means that Joshua can expect to receive $50 each year. However, the **yield** on the bond is the coupon payment divided by the price paid for the bond:

$$\text{Yield} = \frac{\text{Annual coupon payment}}{\text{Price paid for the bond}}$$

In this example, it is $50 ÷ $950, or 5.26 percent. For the bond buyer, a higher yield is better. (Sometimes, in everyday language, people talk about the yield on the bond as being the same as the interest rate. For example, someone might ask "What is the yield on that bond?" when he or she is actually referring to the interest rate.)

Now suppose that Joshua paid $1,100 for the bond instead of $950. In this case, the yield would be $50 ÷ $1,100, or 4.54 percent. As the price paid for the bond rises, the yield declines.

When are the coupon rate and yield the same? Obviously, they are the same when the price paid for the bond equals the face value. For example, consider a bond with a face value of $1,000 and a coupon rate of 5 percent. If the bond is purchased for $1,000, then the yield ($50 ÷ $1,000), which is 5 percent, is equal to the coupon rate.

EXAMPLE Robin buys a bond with the face value of $10,000 for $9,000. The coupon rate on the bond is 4 percent. Because the coupon rate is 4 percent, Robin receives 4 percent of $10,000 (the face value of the bond), or $400, each year through the time the bond matures. Because Robin bought the bond for a price lower than the face value, the bond's yield will be higher than the coupon rate. To find the yield, we divide the annual coupon payment of $400 by the price of the bond ($9,000), giving us a yield of 4.4 percent. ◆

Background Information: Financial Journalists

Financial journalists work at newspapers, magazines, TV networks, cable TV stations, and many other places. Most attended college and majored in journalism, with perhaps a second major or a minor in business or economics.

Networking can be an important part of getting a job in financial journalism, as it can be for many jobs. Many financial journalists serve as interns at newspapers or TV networks while in college. They also work on college newspapers to gain experience and publish work that can be submitted when interviewing for their first postcollege jobs. When interviewing financial journalists, employers look for the ability to write well, a solid knowledge

Are Economists Poor Investors?

You might think that an economist would do pretty well in the stock market compared with the average person. After all, an economist's job is to understand how markets work and to study key economic indicators.

So, how do you explain a *Los Angeles Times* article titled "Experts Are at a Loss on Investing"? The article looked at the investments of four economists—all Nobel Prize winners in Economics. Not one of them said that he invests the way he should invest, and none seemed to be getting rich through his investments. So, it seems there can be a big difference between knowing what to do and actually doing it.

Harry M. Markowitz won the Nobel Prize in Economics in 1990. He was honored for his work in financial economics; he is known as the father of "modern portfolio theory," which suggests that people should diversify their investments.

Did Markowitz follow his own advice? Not really. Most of his life, he put half of his money in a stock fund and the other half in a conservative, low-interest investment. Markowitz, who was 77 when he won the prize, said, "In retrospect, it would have been better to have been more in stocks when I was younger."

George A. Akerlof, who won the Nobel Prize in Economics in 2001, invested most of his money in money market accounts, which tend to have relatively low interest rate returns (but are safe). When confronted with this fact, Akerlof said, "I know it's utterly stupid."

Clive W. J. Granger, who won the Nobel Prize in Economics in 2003, was asked about his investments. He said, "I would rather spend my time enjoying my income than bothering about investments."

Daniel Kahneman, who won the Nobel Prize in Economics in 2002, said the following about his investments: "I think very little about my retirement savings, because I know that thinking could make me poorer or more miserable or both."

Keep in mind what we said in an earlier chapter: almost every activity comes with both benefits and costs. Benefits can come from investing wisely, but certain costs are involved too. It takes time to find out about various investments, to research them, and to keep informed on how they are doing.

The actions of our four Nobel Prize winners also point out something else. As we said before, many people think that economics is simply about money and money issues. It isn't. It's about utility and happiness and making oneself better off. Each of our four Nobel Prize winners might not have been doing the best thing for his wallet, but certainly, each knew it and continued on the same path anyway. It seems that each was willing to sacrifice some money to live the lifestyle he preferred.

What is the lesson for you? Should you care nothing about your investments and hope that your financial future will take care of itself? Or should you spend time regularly watching, researching, and evaluating various investments that you have made or plan to make? Neither extreme is very sensible. It isn't a matter of one or the other. It's possible to learn enough about investments to protect yourself from the financial uncertainties of the future but not spend so much time worrying about the future that you don't enjoy the present.

THINK ABOUT IT Sometimes people choose not to learn about investing because they think the information is too difficult to understand. A person might say, "Learning about stocks and bonds and other such things is just beyond me." What do you think?

After students have read this feature, ask them why they think the economists interviewed have, in their own opinions, invested badly. Invite students to consider how much time they want to devote to investing when they have the money. Ask students to explain what it means to say that economics is about "utility, happiness, and making oneself better off." Then ask whether they agree and why or why not.

ANSWERS TO THINK ABOUT IT Answers will vary. Invite volunteers to share their answers with the class.

Reinforcement Activity

To give students a good idea of how stocks and bonds differ, have them create a chart with stocks on one side and bonds on the other. Then have them answer the following questions for both stocks and bonds:
1. What does the investment represent?
2. How is the price determined?
3. How is profit gained?
4. Is there a chance to lose the principal investment?
5. How do interest rates affect the price?

Cause and Effect

Tell students that they are going to buy bonds from a corporation. They have $10,000 to spend. What should they check next? (*Answer:* The interest rate.) Why is this information important? (*Answer:* The coupon rate should match or exceed the interest rate.) What would happen if they buy the bonds and interest rates go up 2%? (*Answer:* As the interest rate rises, the price of old or existing bonds falls. Interest rates and the price of old or existing bonds move in opposite directions.)

of economics and business, strong initiative, good ideas, and the ability to work as part of a team.

With the increasing use of the Internet for investment, many people are investing their money from home. TV financial journalists such as Louis Rukeyser have become mainstays for these at-home investors. Ask students to research some financial journalists and determine their qualifications to report investment and financial news.

Reinforcement Activity

Ask students why timing is so important in buying and selling bonds. They should say that bond prices are based on interest rates, so to make a profit on the buying and selling of bonds, you need to understand the relationship between bond prices and interest rates. As interest rates rise, the prices of old or existing bonds fall.

Critical Thinking

After students read A Student Asks, which deals with the relationship between coupon rates and interest rates, have them consider the following scenario: Vera buys a $10,000 corporate bond with a 5% coupon rate. The next year, interest rates on savings accounts go up to 7%. What will this mean for the company if it wants to issue more $10,000 bonds? (*Answer:* It will need to offer a coupon rate of at least 7%.) What will it mean for the value of Vera's bond? (*Answer:* She won't be able to sell it for the full $10,000, because people can buy $10,000 bonds from the company at a 7% coupon rate. She will have to sell it for less money than she paid for it.)

A Student Asks

Use this A Student Asks to make sure students understand the concept of coupon rates, how they are set, and the role of the bond issuer.

Teaching with Visuals

Answers will vary. Students may say the trader needs to know the face value of a bond, maturity date, current yield, volume, close, net change, and tax liability.

▲ If one of these traders was buying bonds for you, what information would he need about the bonds being considered for purchase?

A Student Asks

QUESTION: *Can a bond issuer set the coupon rate at anything he or she wants? If so, why wouldn't the bond issuer always set the coupon rate at something like 1 percent?*

ANSWER: *The answer has to do with competition. Suppose company A needs to borrow $1 million and decides to issue $10,000 bonds. The only way anyone will be willing to buy one of these bonds (that is, to lend the company $10,000) is if the company promises the buyers a rate of return comparable to the interest rate they would get if they put the money in a savings account. In other words, the company has to set the coupon rate at a level that will attract people to the bonds. If people are earning, say, 5 percent, on their savings accounts, they won't lend money to the company unless the company pays a coupon rate of at least 5 percent. In short, the coupon rate is set at a competitive level—not at any level the company wants to set it.*

Types of Bonds

As stated earlier, bonds are typically issued by companies, governments, and government agencies. This section briefly describes some of the many types of bonds that these entities issue.

Corporate Bonds A corporate bond is issued by a private corporation and typically has a face value of $10,000. Corporate bonds may sell for a price above or below the face value depending on the current supply and demand conditions for the bond. The interest that corporate bonds pay is fully taxable as income.

Municipal Bonds Municipal bonds are issued by state and local governments. States may issue bonds to help pay for a new highway. Local governments may issue bonds to finance a civic auditorium or a sports stadium. Many people purchase municipal bonds because the interest paid on them is not subject to federal taxes.

Treasury Bills, Notes, and Bonds When the federal government wants to borrow funds, it can issue Treasury bills (T-bills), notes, or bonds. The only difference among bills, notes, and bonds is their time to maturity. Although called by different names, they are all bonds. Treasury bills mature in 13, 26, or 52 weeks, Treasury notes mature in 2 to 10 years, and Treasury bonds mature in 10 to 30 years. Treasury bills, notes, and bonds are considered safe investments because the federal government won't likely default on its bond obligations. After all, the federal government has the power to tax to pay off bondholders.

Inflation-Indexed Treasury Bonds In 1997, the federal government began to issue inflation-indexed bonds. The first indexed bonds issued matured in 10 years and were available at face values as small as $1,000. The difference between an inflation-indexed Treasury bond and a Treasury bond that is not indexed is that an inflation-indexed bond guarantees the purchaser a certain real rate of return, but a nonindexed Treasury bond does not. For example, suppose you

Cooperative Learning

Divide students into four groups, and assign each group a type of bond (as listed on page 486). Each group should research what the bond is, how to buy it, and what tax liability is associated with it. Then the group should identify five examples of its assigned bond and chart out the symbol, coupon rate, maturity date, current yield, volume, close, and net change. The group can present this information to the rest of the class.

purchase an inflation-indexed, 10-year, $1,000 bond that pays a 4 percent coupon rate. If no inflation occurs, the annual interest payment will be $40. However, if the inflation rate is, say, 3 percent, the government will "mark up" the value of the bond by 3 percent—from $1,000 to $1,030. Then it will pay 4 percent on this higher dollar amount. So instead of paying $40 each year, it will pay $41.20. By increasing the monetary value of the security by the rate of inflation, the government guarantees the bondholder a real return of 4 percent.

How to Read the Bond Market Page

If you turn to the bond market page of the newspaper, you will find information about the different types of bonds. If you want to invest in bonds, you will need to know how to read the information that relates to both corporate bonds and Treasury bonds. Let's start by looking at corporate bonds.

Corporate Bonds

Not all publications present information about corporate bonds in exactly the same format. The format we show you here is most common:

(1) Bonds	(2) Cur. Yld.	(3) Vol	(4) Close	(5) Net Chg.
Co. X 6⅝ 34	6.7	115	99½	−¾

The first column contains three pieces of information. The first is the abbreviation for the company that issued the bond. Here, we have written Co.X to stand for Company X. Next, to that you see "6⅝," which indicates the coupon rate of the bond. Next you see "34," the year the bond matures, which in this case is 2034.

In the second column, you find the current yield. (We showed how to compute the yield on a bond earlier.) This current yield means that if the bond is purchased today (hence, the word *current*), it will provide a yield of 6.7 percent.

In the third column, you find the volume of sales in dollars for a particular day. The number here is 115, so the dollar volume today is $115,000.

The fourth column indicates the closing price for the bond on this particular day: 99½. Bond prices are quoted in points and fractions; each point is $10. Thus, 99½ is $999.50 (99.5 × 10 = $999.50).

In the fifth column, we see the net change for the day. The "−¾" means the price on this day was $7.50 lower than it was the day before.

▲ At City Hall in New York City, the government might decide to build a new football stadium and to finance construction of the stadium by selling bonds. What do we call the type of bonds that the city would sell?

Section 2 Bonds **487**

Reinforcement Activity

Invite the financial journalist from your local newspaper, radio, or TV station into your class to discuss the bond market. Students should prepare questions ahead of time to give the visitor the chance to prepare answers for the class.

Application Activity

After reading and discussing Section 2, you may want to assign the Section Activity in the *Applying the Principles Workbook*, pages 169–171.

Assess

Quick Quiz

The following true-or-false quiz will help you assess student understanding of the material covered in this section.

1. The face value of a bond is also called the par value. (True)

2. The more likely the bond issuer will default on the face value of the bond, the higher the bond's rating. (False)

3. Coupon rate and yield are the same when the price paid for the bond equals the face value. (True)

4. Bond issuers can set any coupon rates they like. (False)

5. Inflation-indexed treasury bonds guarantee bondholders a real return based on inflation. (True)

▼ Storing your valuables in a lock box is safe and secure but offers no return on your assets. Buying high-risk stocks and bonds, on the other hand, offers an opportunity for high returns—and high losses. **What sort of investment strategy do you think is the wisest?**

Treasury Bonds

Not all publications present Treasury bond information in exactly the same format. The following format is common:

(1) Rate	(2) Maturity	(3) Bid	(4) Ask	(5) Chg	(6) Yield
7¾	Feb. 23	105:12	105:14	−1	5.50

In the first column, we find the coupon rate of the bond. This Treasury bond pays 7¾ percent of the face value of the bond in annual interest payments.

In the second column, we learn when the bond matures. This Treasury bond matures in February 2023.

In the third column, we learn how much the buyer is willing to pay for the bond (the price you will receive if you sell it). The number here is 105:12. The number before the colon is multiplied by 10, and the number after the colon stands for 32nds of $10. Therefore, first multiply $105 \times \$10$, which gives you $1,050. Then, since $^{12}/_{32}$ is 0.375, multiply 0.375 times $10, giving you $3.75. Add the $3.75 to $1,050 to get $1,053.75.

The fourth column indicates how much the seller is asking for the bond. In other words, it is the price you will pay to the seller if you buy the bond. In this case, it is $1,054.37.

In the fifth column, the change in the price of the bond from the previous trading day is quoted in 32nds. It follows then that a −1 means that the price of the bond fell by $^{1}/_{32}$ of $10, or approximately 32 cents, from the previous day.

Finally, yield, which is based on the ask price, is the return realized by a person who buys the bond today (at the ask price) and holds it to maturity. For this bond, the yield is 5.50 percent.

Risk and Return

We discussed stocks in the first section of this chapter and bonds in the second. The common denominator between these two sections is that people buy stocks or bonds for the return. Simply stated, they buy stocks and bonds in the hope that they will make money.

We need to keep in mind that stocks and bonds often come with different risk and return factors. For example, it might be much riskier to buy stock in a new company than it is to buy a Treasury bond issued by the U.S. Treasury. You can be fairly sure that the U.S. Treasury is going to pay off that bond; after all, the U.S. government has the ability to tax people. However, you can't be so sure you'll have a positive return on the stock you buy in a new company. You might buy the stock for $10 one day, see it fall to $1 three days later, and then stay at that price (or thereabouts) for 10 years.

Differentiating Instruction

English Language Learners

To help students who are English language learners, use the following resources, which are provided as part of the *Economics: New Ways of Thinking* program:

- a Spanish glossary in the *Student Text*
- Spanish versions of the Chapter Summaries on an audio disc

Back in Chapter 1, you encountered a well-known principle in economics: there is no such thing as a free lunch. Applied to stocks and bonds (or any investment), this means that you never get something for nothing. In short, higher returns come with higher risks and lower returns come with lower risks. Treasury bonds, for example, often pay (relatively) low returns because they are relatively safe.

What Would Life Be Like Without Financial Markets?

In Section 1, you learned that the purpose of a financial market (such as the stock or bond market) is to channel money from some people to other people. Now you have a better idea of how that happens. People with saved funds might buy stock in a company that wants the money to buy a piece of machinery or a new plant. Similarly, people with saved funds might buy bonds from a company (and therefore lend it money) that wants to borrow the money to buy a piece of machinery or a new plant.

To see just how important financial markets are, imagine a world without them. Suppose that in this world, you are a person with a great idea for a new product. The only problem is that it's almost impossible for you to save enough money (on your current salary) to develop, produce, and sell the new product. In a world without

▲ A Chinese clerk counts renminbi (RMB) and U.S. dollar bills.

financial markets, you have nowhere to turn. You can't issue stock in your new company because no stock market provides a place of trade. You can't borrow the funds because no bond market provides a place of exchange. So, your good idea is never acted on. Society never gets the new product.

In a world of financial markets, though, the people with the good ideas can be matched up with the people who saved funds they would like to invest. As a result, society ends up with more goods and services than otherwise would have been the case.

SECTION 2 ASSESSMENT

Defining Terms
1. Define:
   a. bond
   b. face value (par value)
   c. coupon rate
   d. yield

Reviewing Facts and Concepts
2. a. Is the issuer of a bond a lender or borrower?
   b. Is the buyer of a bond a lender or borrower?

3. If the face value of a bond is $10,000 and the annual coupon payment is $600, then what is the coupon rate?
4. If the annual coupon payment is $500 and the price paid for the bond is $9,544, then what is the yield?

Critical Thinking
5. "If you can predict interest rates, then you can earn a fortune buying

and selling bonds." Do you agree or disagree? Explain your answer.
6. Do you think some products that currently exist would not exist if there were no financial markets? Explain.

Applying Economic Concepts
7. Why might a person purchase an inflation-indexed Treasury bond?

SECTION 2 ASSESSMENT ANSWERS

Defining Terms

1. a. bond: an IOU issued by a company, government, or government agency for the purpose of borrowing money;

b. face value (par value): the dollar amount specified on a bond; **c. coupon rate:** the percentage of the face value that the bondholder receives each year until the bond matures; **d. yield:** equal to the annual coupon payment divided by the price paid for the bond.

Reviewing Facts and Concepts

2. a. borrower; **b.** lender.
3. 6% (*calculation*: $600 ÷ $10,000 = 6%).
4. 5.24% (*calculation*: $500 ÷ $9,544 = 5.24%).

Assessment Book

You will find a quiz for this section in the *Assessment Book*, page 164.

Reteaching Activity

Use the Section Assessment to gauge which students may need reteaching on this section. Show those students a single line of a bond market page from the newspaper. Have them identify aloud what each column means and how it is calculated.

Guided Reading

For further reteaching of the key concepts in this section, assign the Outlining Activity and the Just the Facts Handout from the *Guided Reading and Study Guide*, pages 292–296.

Critical Thinking

5. Students should agree. As interest rates rise, bond prices fall, and as interest rates fall, bond prices rise. The objective is to buy bonds when they are low and sell them when they are high. If a person can predict interest rates, he will buy bonds when he thinks interest rates are at their highest (because at this time, bonds will be at their lowest), and he will sell bonds when he thinks interest rates are at their lowest (because bonds will be at their highest). Buying low and selling high consistently is the way to earn a fortune.

6. Students should say yes. Without financial markets, there would be much less lending and borrowing activity. It follows that individuals with good ideas (say, for new products) wouldn't be as able to borrow and put those good ideas into effect. Products that individuals today take for granted (especially products that require high research and development costs) might not exist.

Applying Economic Concepts

7. Inflation-indexed Treasury bonds guarantee the purchaser a certain real rate of return. The government increases the monetary value of the security by the rate of inflation, thereby guaranteeing the bondholder a real rate of return.

Discussion Starter

Ask students if any of them have considered saving for retirement. Many students may not have even begun saving for college, let alone retirement; however, it is important that they are aware of their options once they begin to earn an income.

Discussion Starter

Before reading the section on charitable giving, ask students if any of them volunteer their time for charities or have ever given money to a charity. Ask, Which charities are important to you? Which do you think best help the community in which you live?

How Will You Invest in the Future?

Personal finance requires that you be aware of your money, including how much you earn and where you spend it. By now you may have made your own plans for post-secondary education and investments in stocks, bonds, or business ventures. There are, however, other ways to invest your money. One is by saving for your future with a retirement account and another is by helping to secure the future of your community through charitable giving.

Personal Retirement Plans

Many full-time workers in their early to mid-twenties think that it is far too early to begin planning for their retirement. "Retirement is such a long way off," they say. "I'll start thinking about that when I get into my forties," they say.

The truth is that it is never too early to start planning for your retirement. Yes, retirement may be a long way off, but the earlier you start, the more financially secure your retirement years will be. People in their late-forties, fifties, and early-sixties often regret not having started saving for their retirement earlier in their careers.

In the past, people often described retirement planning as a "three-legged stool." The three legs consisted of pensions, social security, and personal savings. Let's take a look at each of these factors.

A pension is a defined retirement contribution plan that a company provides its employees. While

pensions were a common benefit for workers in the mid-twentieth century, company pensions are no longer offered as often as they once were. For the most part, pensions have been replaced by 401(k) plans that place the responsibility of saving for retirement back on the individual employee. The company will sometimes provide assistance by matching a percentage of the employee's contributions.

Social security is another retirement benefit on which today's workers may not be able to rely. For people who are 50 years or younger, there are serious concerns about whether sufficient social security funds will be available. In the future, the social security benefits provided to each individual may decrease, the age at which one can collect social security payments may increase, and the program may become means-tested, which means payments would be allocated based on income.

Personal savings has always been, and will continue to be, a reliable option for retirement planning. While in the past personal savings were seen as a supplement to pensions and social security, in the future they may become the primary means of retirement income. What this means is that the three-legged stool of retirement planning has become a little shakier in recent years. Because of this, it is more important than ever before to understand how to save for retirement and to begin doing so early in your career.

Individual Retirement Accounts

An important first step for retirement planning today is to set up an individual retirement account (IRA), which is a retirement account that individuals create (sometimes with the assistance of their employers) and control themselves. The Internal Revenue Service has set up a website (access it at http://econ.emcp.net/IRSRetire) to assist individuals in learning about individual retirement accounts. There are several types of individual retirement accounts, including:

- Traditional IRA
- Roth IRA
- SEP IRA
- SIMPLE IRA (Savings Incentive Match Plan for Employees)
- Self-Directed IRA

The monies deposited into individual retirement accounts can often be invested in stocks and bonds, among other options. However, the law does prohibit IRA funds from being invested in certain collectibles (such as artwork, rugs, antiques, stamps, alcoholic beverages, and so on). The expectation of these accounts is that they will support the account holder upon his or her retirement.

Charitable Giving

In 2015, Americans gave $373.25 billion to their favorite causes. The greatest portion of charitable giving in 2015 ($268.28 billion) was donated by individuals or

Cooperative Learning

Break students into groups of three to four. Have each group research social security in the United States and answer the following questions: How does it work? Who pays social security? Who benefits from social security? After they have identified the answers to each of these questions, ask each group to discuss whether they are for or against the use of social security in the United States. Benefits and costs of the program should be discussed and then shared with the rest of the class. Note that all views should be supported with logical reasoning.

households, and the highest percentage of the money was given to religious organizations. The next highest recipient of charitable giving was educational institutions.

Giving money is not the only way people can make charitable contributions. They can also donate goods (e.g., food and clothing) and time or labor (e.g., working at a homeless shelter). Whatever form donations come in, recipients use them to run their organizations and to support their causes, whether they advocate for specific topics (like cancer research) or groups (like homeless youth). Charitable giving is meant to support the community.

The Costs and Benefits of Charitable Giving

The benefits people receive from charitable giving are both tangible and intangible. People may experience social or emotional advantages, such as impressing employers and peers and gaining happiness through doing good for others (e.g., giving to victims of a natural disaster) or assisting in achieving a particular goal (e.g., helping underprivileged teens pay for college). There is also a tax benefit connected with charitable giving. For example, if you give $10,000 to a charity and pay a tax rate of 35 percent of the last dollar of income earned, then your tax bill will be $3,500 less than it would have been without the $10,000 charitable contribution. Of course, to lower your taxes by $3,500 you had to make the $10,000 charitable contribution. More goes in one direction (toward the charity) so that less can go in the other direction (toward paying taxes).

The cost of charitable giving is best understood in opportunity cost terms. Suppose an individual chooses to make a charitable contribution of his or her time. The cost of the charitable contribution is what the person would have been doing with his or her time had he or she not made the charitable contribution. If the person were to make a monetary charitable contribution instead, then the cost would be what the person would have used the money for had he or she not made the contribution.

Your Personal Economics Activity

1. Examine investment options available in a personal retirement plan using the information you can find online. Review your options and identify which type of plan seems the most appealing.
2. Consider a local, national, or international charity that you would like to support, either now or in the future. Write an informative essay that identifies the charity, its mission, and why and how you would choose to support it. Finally, evaluate and explain the costs and benefits of giving to this charity.

My Personal Economics Action Plan

Here are some points you may want to consider and some guidelines you might want to put into practice.

☑ 1. In this feature we discussed some of the benefits of charitable giving.

I am going to think deeply as to what benefits I might experience (or do already experience) through charitable giving. Are the benefits different if I give to a person rather than an organization? What are my reasons for giving; i.e,. do I give to receive, to impress others, to help others, etc.?

☑ 2. As stated in this feature, there are different types of individual retirement accounts.

I am going to do some research on the various types of individual retirement accounts. I want to know the best type of IRA for me. I want to find out how much per year I can contribute to my IRA. I also want to find out when the money can be withdrawn from the account.

My Personal Economics Action Plan Encourage students to complete the personal economics plan and report the results of their investigation.

Brainstorming Activity

Explain to students that there are costs and benefits associated with donating your personal property to a charitable organization. Tell students to brainstorm a list of costs and benefits of disposing of their personal property in this manner. Ask them to use the Internet if they have difficulty thinking of ideas. (Costs include the time to research an organization and its donation practices, delivering the items [although students will find that some organizations have their own collection services], and the loss of the income they would have if they sold the item. Benefits may include tax deductions for charitable giving, the ease of disposal, and the benefit of knowing they are supporting their community.)

Grading Rubric: Retirement Plan

1 2 3 4 5 Student identified a plan and supported his or her choice with logical reasoning.

Grading Rubric: Essay

1 2 3 4 5 Student identified a favorite charity and described its mission.

Chapter 16 Your Personal Economics 491

Futures and Options

Section Objectives

After completing this section, students will be able to

▶ explain what futures contracts are;

▶ explain why people enter into futures contracts;

▶ explain a currency futures contract;

▶ explain an options contract;

▶ describe the difference between a put option and a call option; and

▶ state the major reason an investor would use a put or a call option.

Kickoff Activity

Invite students to predict the economic meanings of the following terms: *futures* and *options*. Allow students to discuss their answers. Remind students that in an economic way of thinking, many words have definitions that are different from the definitions with which they are familiar. Have students preview the definitions of these terms on pages 492 and 495 and use each term in a sentence that illustrates its economic definition.

Activating Prior Knowledge

To review previous sections, direct students to compare stocks and bonds, noting their similarities and differences.

Discussion Starter

As you discuss with students what a futures contract is, ask them why someone would want to buy or sell a product at today's prices in the future. What chances are the buyer and seller taking? What is each hoping for? Ask students whether they would be willing to take these kinds of chances.

Focus Questions

▶ What is a futures contract?

▶ Why do people enter into futures contracts?

▶ What is a currency futures contract?

▶ What is an options contract?

▶ What is a put option?

▶ What is a call option?

▶ What is the major reason that an investor would use either a put or call option?

Key Terms

futures contract

option

Futures

Myers is a miller. He buys wheat from the wheat farmer, turns the wheat into flour, and then sells the flour to the baker. Obviously, he wants to earn a profit for what he does. But how much, if any, profit he earns depends on the price at which he can buy the wheat and the price at which he can sell the flour.

Now suppose Myers enters into a contract with a baker. He promises to deliver to the baker 1,000 pounds of flour in six months. At the current wheat price, $3 a bushel, Myers knows he can earn a profit on his deal with the baker. But he doesn't need the wheat now; he needs it in about six months. What will the price of wheat be then? If it is, say, $2 a bushel, then Myers will earn more profit on the deal with the baker. But if it is, say, $4 a bushel, then he will lose money on the deal. Myers's problem is that he doesn't know what a bushel of wheat will sell for in six months.

Myers decides to enter into a **futures contract**: a contract in which the seller agrees to provide a particular good (in this case, wheat) to the buyer on a specified future date at an agreed-on price. For example, Myers might buy bushels of wheat

futures contract
An agreement to buy or sell a specific amount of something (commodity, currency, financial instrument) at a particular price on a stipulated future date.

now for a price of $3 a bushel to be delivered to him in six months.

Who would enter into a futures contract with Myers? A likely possibility would be a speculator: someone who buys and sells commodities to profit from changes in the market. A speculator assumes risk in the hope of making a gain.

Suppose Smith, a speculator, believes that the price of wheat six months from now is going to be lower than it is today. She may look at things this way: "The price of wheat today is $3 a bushel. I think the price of wheat in six months will be close to $2 a bushel. Why not promise the miller that I will deliver him as much wheat as he wants in six months if, in return, he agrees today to pay me $3 a bushel for it? Then, in six months, I will buy the wheat for $2 a bushel, sell it to the miller for $3 a bushel, and earn myself $1 profit per bushel."

Myers (the miller) and Smith (the speculator) enter into a futures contract. Myers agrees to buy 200 bushels of wheat for delivery in six months; Smith agrees to sell 200 bushels of wheat to Myers for delivery in six months.

Internet Research

Direct students to use the Internet to research the job of floor trader. Students should write one- or two-page essays answering the following questions: Would you like this type of job? Do you have the type of personality to be an effective trader? Students should also list the things they would and wouldn't like about the job. Then they should list the additional topics they would want to learn about before feeling prepared to become a trader.

What does each person get out of the deal? Myers gets peace of mind. He knows that he will be able to buy the wheat at a price that will let him earn a profit on his deal with the baker. Smith takes a chance, which she is willing to take, for the opportunity to a profit.

EXAMPLE Wilson is a farmer who grows primarily corn. The current price of corn is $2.34 a bushel. Wilson doesn't have any corn to sell right now, but she will in two months. She hopes that between now and then, the price of corn won't fall, say, to something under $2. She decides to enter into a futures contract in corn. She promises to deliver 5,000 bushels of corn two months from now for $2.34 a bushel. Johnson, a speculator in corn, decides that this deal is a good one for him because he believes that in two months, the price of a bushel of corn will rise to $3.14. So, Wilson and Johnson enter into a futures contract. Two months pass and the price of corn drops to $2.10. Johnson turns out to be wrong about the price rising. Wilson delivers 5,000 bushels of corn to Johnson, for which Johnson pays Wilson $2.34 a bushel (total: $11,700) as agreed. Then Johnson turns around and sells the corn for $2.10 a bushel (receiving $10,500). Johnson loses $1,200 on the deal. ♦

A Student Asks

QUESTION: *In the example, the price of corn went down. It could have gone up, though. In this case, would Wilson, the farmer, have lost money?*

ANSWER: *Let's suppose that the price of corn rose to $4. In this case, Wilson would have delivered 5,000 bushels of corn to speculator Johnson for $2.34 a bushel, and then Johnson would have turned around and sold the corn for $4 a bushel. Johnson would have earned the difference between $4 and $2.34— or $1.66—for every one of the 5,000 bushels, for a total of $8,300.*

Did Wilson, the farmer, lose this $8,300? In a way, she did. She didn't lose it in the sense that it was once in her pocket and now it isn't. She lost it in the

sense that it could have been in her pocket (if she hadn't entered into the futures contract with Johnson) and now it isn't.

This situation might be okay with Wilson. Remember, she might not want to be in the speculating business. She might want to worry only about growing and selling corn and nothing else. Maybe she doesn't want to be involved in speculating on the price of corn. In other words, maybe she is willing to "give up" $8,300 now and then so that she can sleep soundly at night and not worry constantly about possible price declines.

Thinking Like an Economist

Trading Uncertainty

For the economist, economics is principally about exchange, or trade. People trade money for goods and services; they trade labor services for money; and they trade "more money tomorrow" for "some money today." (Think of lending someone $100 today and being paid back $110 tomorrow.) People can also trade uncertainty.

Suppose a farmer is uncertain what the price of a bushel of wheat will be when it's time to harvest and sell his crop. A speculator removes that uncertainty by telling the farmer that he will guarantee a price for the wheat (say, $5 a bushel) when it's time to sell. When it comes time for the farmer to sell his wheat, the speculator pays the guaranteed price. Then the speculator turns around and resells the wheat on the open market. The speculator hopes that the market price (at which he can now sell the wheat) will be higher than the price he paid for the wheat (for example, $6 a bushel instead of the $5 a bushel he paid the farmer).

Where is the trade here? It's between the farmer and the speculator. The farmer sells uncertainty over the future price of wheat to the speculator, and the speculator buys the uncertainty from the farmer. Why does the speculator make this purchase? He thinks that when it comes time to sell the wheat in the market, the market price will be higher than the price he paid the farmer.

THINK ABOUT IT Suppose your neighbor has agreed to pay you $20 for shoveling her walk each time it snows this winter. You know that in an average winter, it snows 10 times. You really need to earn $200 this winter. How might a speculator help you?

Thinking Like an Economist

ANSWERS TO THINK ABOUT IT A speculator might agree to pay you $200, if in return you give the speculator $20 each time it snows during the winter. If it snows fewer than 10 times, the speculator will lose money; if it snows more than 10 times, the speculator makes money. Either way, you get the $200 you need and your neighbor pays the price that he or she agreed to.

Problem Solving

Invite students to suppose that they are looking to trade in some type of agricultural future for a product commonly produced in your area. Ask students what they would need to know before trading futures for that product. Allow students to work on this problem on their own and then come together as a class to discuss their thoughts.

Answers will vary. Students might mention that they should know the current price of the product, the factors that affect the supply of the product (weather, insects, seed supply) and the demand for the product (dietary trends), and any other information that might help them predict the supply and demand for the product and thus the equilibrium price in the future.

 Visit econ.myemcp.com/videos for videos that will help students better understand the key concepts found in this section.

Background Information: Futures and Options

If students question the importance of learning about futures and options, tell them that these are two of the riskiest ways to invest money. Professional advisors and brokers want investors to be aware of the following key rules of investing:

1. Never invest more than you are able to lose. No one can completely predict the market, especially not in terms of futures and options.

2. Be aware of costs attached to the trade itself, such as commissions.

3. Make sure you know where your money is; don't assume the broker is working in your best interests.

Instruct students to read this feature. Then ask them how likely it is that anyone would make $1.3 quadrillion on a $1 investment. Ask students whether they think that making any investment—whether small or large—is better than making no investment at all.

ANSWERS TO THINK ABOUT IT Answers will vary. Students should see that there are no guarantees in investing and that the future won't look exactly like the immediate past.

Reinforcement Activity

Because of the highly volatile nature of the futures market, trading without the help of an advisor or broker isn't recommended. The general policy of "buying low and selling high" can be even trickier in futures, because as a speculator, you set your own prices for buying and selling. This means that you make your buying and selling decisions ahead of time, not at the time of the purchase or sale. It's very important to keep a constant eye on your portfolio and to know what's happening in the market. Ask students to monitor the futures market in the newspaper for three days, or if possible, have them check the market on the Internet twice a day. Ask, How much do the prices for futures change over a three-day period?

Activating Prior Knowledge

Recall that in Chapter 3 you learned about the various characteristics of a free enterprise system. Two benefits of the U.S. free enterprise system is that it allows for and supports investment opportunities and the creation of wealth. Ask students to explain how investment and the creation of wealth are benefits of free enterprise.

Economics *in the* Real World

Want to Make $1.3 Quadrillion?

At the close of the twentieth century, the editors of the financial magazine *The Economist* identified the highest returning investment for each year, beginning in 1900 and ending in 1999. For example, the highest-returning investment in 1974 was gold; in 1902 it was U.S. Treasury bills, and in 1979 it was silver.

The editors then asked how much income a person would have earned by the end of 1999 if he or she had invested $1 in the highest-returning investment in 1900, taken the return from that investment and invested it in the highest-returning investment in 1901, and so on for each year during the century. After taxes and dealer costs, this investor would have earned $1.3 quadrillion. (Quadrillion comes after trillion. In September 2013, Bill Gates, the richest person in the world, had $72 billion, and $1.3 quadrillion is 18,055 times what Bill Gates had.)

What is the lesson here? With perfect foresight (or with a crystal ball that correctly tells you what the highest-returning investment of the year will be), a person would become rich beyond his or her wildest imagination.

After the editors ran their experiment, they changed it. They went back and asked themselves what a person would have earned over the twentieth century if instead of investing in the highest-returning investment in a given year, he or she invested in it one year later. In other words, if X was the best investment in 1956, then he or she would invest in it in 1957.

Why did the editors choose to proceed this way? They believed that many people invest in "hot" investments only when it's too late. That is, they invest in something after they have heard about it, which is usually too late to get a big return.

Think of an investment as a mountain. Going up the mountain is comparable to increasing the return on the investment; going down the mountain is comparable to decreasing the return. It's only when the investment is near its peak that many people hear about it. Then it's too late, with no place to go but down.

Here's an example. A person with a crystal ball (or with perfect foresight) would have invested in the Polish stock market in 1993, when no one was talking about it, and reaped a 754 percent gain. The typical investor would have invested in it one year later, in 1994, when everyone was talking about it. The problem is that the Polish stock market fell by 55 percent in 1994.

So, what would the person who is always one year late have earned over the twentieth century? After taxes and dealer costs, $290.

What are the economic lessons here? First, the best investments are often the ones that you don't hear about until it's too late. Second, ignoring the first lesson and thinking that a popular investment is necessarily a good investment often results in low returns.

THINK ABOUT IT Many people seem to think that when it comes to investments, whatever an investment did last year will be what it does this year. If it went up by 30 percent last year, then it will go up this year by 30 percent. But consider the words of Warren Buffett, one of the most successful investors of all time: "If past history was all there was to the game, the richest people would be librarians." What do you think? Does anything guarantee that the immediate future will look exactly like the immediate past?

Background Information: Online Trading

According to leading sources, U.S. families are managing an increasing number of online accounts. Right now, most American investors are passive investors, allowing their financial advisors and 401(k) fund managers to move their investments. Soon, analysts believe, more people will take control of their own investments through on-line brokerages. The lure of big payoffs has more and more Americans checking their investments every day and moving their money in the hope of having a "big score." However, in the long run, it's more likely that the people who move their money will lose rather than make money.

Currency Futures

A futures contract can be written for wheat, as we have seen, or for a currency, a stock index, or even bonds. Here is how a currency futures contract works.

Suppose Bill owns a Toyota dealership in Tulsa, Oklahoma. It is currently May, and Bill is thinking about a shipment of Toyotas he plans to buy in August. He knows that he must buy the Toyotas from Japan with yen, but he has a problem. Right now, the dollar price of yen is $0.012. Bill wonders what the price of yen will be in August when he plans to make his purchase. Suppose the dollar price of yen rises to $0.018. If the price of the yen goes up, then instead of paying $30,000 for a Toyota priced at 2.5 million yen, he will have to pay $45,000.

What can Bill do? He can purchase a futures contract today for the needed quantity of yen in August. Who is willing to sell this contract? Obviously, someone who thinks the dollar price of yen will go down between now and August. For example, Julie may think to herself, "I think the dollar price of yen will go down between now and August. Therefore, I will enter into a contract with Bill stating that I will give him 2.5 million yen in August for $30,000, the exchange rate specified in the contract being 1 yen = $0.012. If I am right and the actual exchange rate at the time is 1 yen = $0.011, then I can purchase the 2.5 million yen for $27,500 and fulfill my contract with Bill by turning the yen over to him for $30,000. I will walk away with a $2,500 profit."

EXAMPLE Suppose you check the dollar price of a euro today and find that it is 83 cents. In other words, for every 83 cents, you get 1 euro in return. Let's say that you believe that in three months, you will have to pay $1.10 to buy a euro. With this in mind, you enter into a futures contract: essentially, you say that you are willing to buy $10 million worth of euros three months from now for 83 cents a euro. Who might be willing to enter into this contract with you? Anyone who thinks the dollar price of a euro will be lower (not higher) in three months. Suppose you and this other person enter into a contract. You promise to buy

$10 million worth of euros in three months (at 83 cents a euro), and this other person promises to sell you $10 million worth of euros in three months (at 83 cents a euro).

Three months pass and you learn that it takes 97 cents to buy a euro (not 83 cents and not $1.10). What happens now? The person who entered into the contract with you has to buy $10 million worth of euros at an exchange rate of 97 cents = 1 euro. For $10 million, he gets 10,309,278 euros. He then turns these euros over to you and gets 83 cents for every euro, which gives him $8,556,701. Obviously, this person has taken a loss; he spent $10 million to get $8,556,701 in return—a loss of $1,443,299.

What about you? You now have 10,309,278 euros for which you paid $8,556,701. How many dollars will you get if you sell all of those euros? Well, since you get 97 cents for every euro, you will get approximately $10 million. Are you better off or worse off now? You are better off by $1,443,229. ◆

Options

An **option** is a contract that gives the owner of the option the right but not the obligation to buy or sell shares of a stock at a specified price on or before a specified date. The two types of options are *calls* and *puts*.

Call Options

A call option gives the owner of the option the right to buy shares of a stock at a specified price within the time limits of the contract. The specified price at which the buyer can buy shares of a stock is called the

▲ You may remember from Chapter 8 that this wheat farmer is a price taker. He has to sell his wheat at the equilibrium price—not a penny more or less. How might a farmer reduce the uncertainty in the wheat market?

option
A contract that gives the owner the right but not the obligation to buy or sell shares of a good at a specified price on or before a specified date.

Reinforcement Activity

Ask students the following questions: When would a buyer exercise a call option? When would a buyer exercise a put option? (*Answer:* A buyer would exercise a call option if the price of the specified stock increases. A buyer would exercise a put option if the price of the specified stock decreases.)

Cause and Effect

In today's business market, employees commonly receive stock options as bonuses. Ask students to predict what would happen to the stock price if employees exercised their option, or purchased stock. Students might point out that demand for the stock would rise—and that if demand rose while supply stayed the same, the price of the stock would rise.

Reinforcement Activity

Guide students in reviewing the different kinds of investing. Ask if they would like to invest and what kinds of investments they would make. Remind them that when they invest, they should do so wisely and under the supervision of a qualified professional.

Teaching with Visuals

To answer the question with the image on page 497, no, clients don't already own the stock in question. Answers will vary. Students should see that a call option gives clients a chance to watch a stock's performance without spending a lot of money.

 Application Activity

After reading and discussing Section 3, you may want to assign the Section Activity in the *Applying the Principles Workbook*, pages 172–174.

Assess

Quick Quiz

The following true-or-false quiz will help you assess student understanding of the material covered in this section.

1. In a futures contract, the seller would be someone who does not mind assuming the risk of a change in price. (True)

▶ Thousands of people work in the financial industry helping people trade almost anything they want to trade—stocks, bonds, wheat, gold, or money, for example. Would you enjoy this type of work?

strike price. For example, suppose Brown buys a call option for $20. The call option specifies that she can buy 100 shares of IBM stock at a strike price of $150 within the next month. If the price of IBM stocks falls below $150, Brown won't exercise her call option. She will simply tear it up and accept the fact that she has lost $20. If she still wants to buy IBM stock, she can do so through her stockbroker, as she normally does, and pay the going price, which is lower than $150. If the price rises above $150, she will exercise her call option. She will buy the stock at $150 a share and then turn around and sell it for the higher market price. She will have made a profit.

If Brown buys a call option, then someone must sell it to her. Who would sell her a call option? Anyone who thought the option wouldn't be exercised by the buyer. For example, if Jackson believed that the price of IBM was going to fall below $150, then he would gladly sell a call option to Brown for $20, thinking that the option would never be exercised. That would be $20 in his pocket.

Put Options

A put option gives the owner the right but not the obligation to sell (rather than buy, as in a call option) shares of a stock at a strike price during some period of time. For example, suppose Martin buys a put option to sell 100 shares of IBM stock at $130

during the next month. If the share price rises above $130, Martin will not exercise his put option. He will simply tear it up and sell the stock for more than $130. But if the price drops below $130, then he will exercise his option to sell the stock for $130 a share. Who buys put options? Anyone who thinks the price of the stock is going to decline.

Who sells put options? Obviously, the people who think the price of the stock is going to rise. Why not sell a put option for, say, $20, if you believe the price of the stock is going to rise and the buyer of the put option isn't going to exercise the option?

A Student Asks

QUESTION: *I've heard some people talk about getting part of their pay or a bonus in the form of stock options. Some people seem to make a lot of money through stock options. What are these options?*

ANSWER: *A stock option gives an employee the right to buy a specific number of shares of stock at a price specified by the employer. The price specified by the employer is often the current market price of the stock when the stock option is issued. The hope for the employee is that the market price will rise over time. For example, if the stock option specifies the price of $10*

Cooperative Learning

Divide students into small groups. Have half of the groups write scenarios in which someone might want to enter into a futures contract. Have the other half of the groups write scenarios in which someone might want to purchase an option.

Encourage students to write some scenarios that focus on the speculator and some that focus on the other party. Then have groups trade scenarios and explain what each party hopes for in each transaction.

a share, the employee has the right to buy the stock at $10. Now suppose time passes and the market price of the stock rises to $40. What can the employee do now? He or she can buy the stock for $10 a share and then turn around and sell it for $40 a share.

How You Can Use Call and Put Options

Suppose you think a certain stock is going to rise in price during the next few months. Currently, the stock sells for $250 a share. You don't have enough money to buy many shares of stock, but you would like to benefit from what you expect will be a rise in the price of the stock. What can you do? You can buy a call option. A call option will sell for a fraction of the cost of the stock. So, with limited resources, you decide to buy the call option, which gives you the right to buy, say, 100 shares of the stock at $250 anytime during the next three months.

Wait a minute. If you don't have the money to buy the stock at $250 a share now, why does anyone think you will have the money to buy the stock at $250 in a few months? Well, you don't have to buy the stock. If you are right that the price of the stock will rise, then the call option you are holding will become worth more to people. In other words, if you bought the option when the price of the stock was $250 and the stock rises to $300, then your call option has become more valuable. You can sell it and benefit from the uptick in the price of the stock.

Alternatively, let's say you expect the price of the stock to fall. Then, you can buy a put option. In doing so, you buy the right to sell the stock for $250 anytime during the next three months. If the price does fall, then your option becomes more valuable. In fact, the further the price falls, the more valuable your put option becomes. People who have the stock and want to sell it for a price higher than it currently brings on the market will be willing to buy your put option for some price higher than the price you paid.

EXAMPLE Suppose the current price of a call option for AT&T stock is $10, while the current price of the AT&T stock is $100. Ginny decides to buy a call option for $10. This call option gives her the right to buy AT&T at a price of $100. Five months pass and the price of AT&T shares has risen to $150. If Ginny wants to, she can exercise her call option to buy AT&T stock at $100. In other words, she can spend $100 to buy a share of stock, which she can turn around and immediately sell for $150, making a profit of $50 per share. ♦

 ▲ If these traders are buying call options, do their clients already own the stock in question? Why would someone buy an option on a stock rather than the stock itself?

2. It isn't possible to create a currency futures contract. (False)

3. There are two types of options: call options and push options. (False)

4. A call option gives the owner the right to buy shares of a stock at a strike price during some period of time. (True)

5. You can make money with options without having to buy the stocks. (True)

 ### Assessment Book

You will find a quiz for this section in the *Assessment Book*, page 165.

Reteaching Activity

Use the Section Assessment to gauge which students may need reteaching on this section. Divide students into groups, and have them research the differences between futures and options. Why aren't these investments as steady as bonds or stocks?

Guided Reading

For further reteaching of the key concepts in this section, assign the Outlining Activity and the Just the Facts Handout from the *Guided Reading and Study Guide*, pages 297–299.

SECTION 3 ASSESSMENT

Defining Terms
1. Define:
   a. futures contract
   b. option

Reviewing Facts and Concepts
2. Why might a person buy a futures contract?

3. Why might a person buy a call option?

Critical Thinking
4. "The currency speculator who sells futures contracts assumes the risk that someone else doesn't want to assume."

Do you agree or disagree? Explain your answer.

Applying Economic Concepts
5. If you thought the share price of a stock was going to fall, would you buy a call option or a put option? Why?

SECTION 3 ASSESSMENT ANSWERS

Defining Terms

1. a. futures contract: an agreement to buy or sell a specific amount of something at a particular price on a stipulated future date; **b. option:** a con-

tract that gives the owner the right but not the obligation to buy or sell shares of a good at a specified price on or before a specified date.

Reviewing Facts and Concepts

2. A person might buy a futures contract to lock in a price. In

the text, Myers, a miller, buys a futures contract for wheat delivery at a certain price. Myers buys the futures contract because he wants to be assured of the price he will pay.

3. A person might buy a call option because she or he thinks a particular stock will rise

in price in the future but doesn't have enough money to buy the stock. Buying a call option is a way to benefit from an expected increase in price at a fraction of what it would cost to actually buy the stock.

Critical Thinking

4. Students should agree. The following illustrates the point: Jack sells Japanese TVs. He expects to buy a shipment of TVs in four months. The price he pays for them will depend on the exchange rate between the yen and the dollar. Jack doesn't want to take a chance that the exchange rate will turn against him—that the dollar will depreciate and he will have to pay more for yen—so he buys a currency futures contract. The seller of the contract locks in a price per yen for Jack and, by doing this, assumes the risk of the exchange rate changing.

Applying Economic Concepts

5. Students should say they would buy a put option.

Economics Vocabulary

1. the market; **2.** yield; **3.** bond; **4.** yield;
5. municipal; **6.** Treasury notes;
7. futures contract.

Understanding the Main Ideas

1. Financial markets serve the purpose of channeling money from some people to other people.

2. You are buying ownership in the company.

3. The New York Stock Exchange (NYSE) and the National Association of Securities Dealers Automated Quotations (NASDAQ) are three places where stocks are bought and sold.

4. Charles Dow created the Dow Jones Industrial Average to convey information about what was actually happening in the stock market.

5. The Dow Jones Industrial Average (DJIA) can be seen as an average price of 30 key stocks. When the DJIA rises by 100 points, it means this average price has risen by $100. In general, when the DJIA rises, it costs more to buy the 30 stocks that make up the DJIA.

6. Earning dividends and making gains in a stock's price are two reasons to buy stock.

7. The price of a stock is determined by the forces of supply and demand. If demand rises and supply is constant, then the price of the stock will rise. If demand falls and supply is constant, then the price of the stock will fall.

8. If you invest in a mutual fund, you are buying the stocks of the companies that make up the fund. For example, if mutual fund A is made up of companies that sell Internet technology and you invest in it, then you are buying the stocks of Internet technology companies. If you invest in a stock index fund, you are investing in the companies that make up the stock index. For example, if you buy Spyders, you are buying stock in the 500 companies that make up the Standard & Poor's 500 index.

Chapter Summary

Be sure you know and remember the following key points from the chapter sections.

Section 1

▶ Financial markets serve the purpose of channeling money from some people to other people.

▶ A stock is a claim on the assets of a corporation that gives the purchaser a share (ownership) in the corporation.

▶ Stocks are bought and sold on exchanges and markets such as the New York Stock Exchange.

▶ People may buy stocks to earn dividends, which are payments made to stockholders based on a company's profits, or to make money by buying shares at a lower price and selling them at a higher price.

Section 2

▶ A bond is simply an IOU, or a promise to pay; bonds are typically issued by companies, governments, and government agencies.

▶ The three major components of a bond are the face or par value, maturity date, and coupon rate.

▶ The price that a person pays for a bond depends on the market conditions: the greater the demand for the bond relative to the supply, the higher the price.

▶ The yield on the bond is the coupon payment divided by the price paid for the bond.

Section 3

▶ In a futures contract, a seller agrees to provide a particular good to a buyer on a specified future date at an agreed-on price.

▶ An option is a contract giving the owner the right but not the obligation to buy (a call option) or sell (a put option) shares of a particular good at a specified price on or before a specified date.

Economics Vocabulary

1. A person that buys Spyders is buying a stock index, which is sometimes referred to as buying _____.

2. The _____ of a stock is the dividend divided by the closing price.

3. A(n) _____ is an IOU, or a promise to pay.

4. The _____ on a bond is equal to the annual coupon payment divided by the face value of the bond.

5. A(n) _____ bond is issued by a state or local government.

6. The federal government issues bonds of different maturities. Bonds with maturities of 2 to 10 years are called _____.

7. A(n) _____ is a contract in which the seller agrees to provide a particular good to the buyer on a specified future date at an agreed-on price.

Understanding the Main Ideas

1. What is the purpose of financial markets?

2. If you buy a stock, are you lending money to the company issuing the stock or are you buying ownership in the company?

3. Name two places that stocks are bought and sold.

4. Why did Charles Dow create the Dow Jones Industrial Average?

5. What does it mean if the Dow Jones Industrial Average rises by, say, 100 points in a day?

6. What are the two reasons to buy stock?

7. What determines the price of a stock?

8. What does it mean if someone invests in a mutual fund? In a stock index fund?

9. "The stock market may not be the best place to put your money in the short run, but it is a pretty good place to put your money in the long run." What does this statement mean?

10. The PE ratio of a stock is 33. What does this number mean?

11. List and define the three major components of a bond.

12. Name two of the best-known bond ratings services.

13. What determines whether a bond will have a good rating or a poor rating?

14. What is the yield of a bond?

9. The statement refers to the fact that over the short run, the stock market goes up and down. You could buy stocks with an average price of $100 in year 1, and in year 2 see the average price fall to $76. Yet despite the short-term ups and downs in the stock market (say, from one year to the next, or even over a 5- to 10-year period), the trend for the stock market has been up. If you buy stocks in year 1 and sell them in year 25, you can be fairly sure that you will make a profit.

10. It means that the stock is selling for a share price that's 33 times higher than its earnings per share.

11. The three components of a bond are face value, or the total amount the issuer of the bond

15. Would you buy or sell bonds if you expected the interest rate to rise? Explain your answer.

16. If your city needed to raise money, what kind of bond would it issue?

17. What is a Treasury bill?

18. Suppose you are the type of person who likes to take chances and is not afraid of risk. Will you likely receive higher or lower returns on your investments? Explain.

19. What is a futures contract? Give an example of a situation in which someone might buy such a contract. Why would this person buy the contract?

20. What is a call option? Why might someone buy a call option rather than shares of stock?

Doing the Math

Do the calculations necessary to solve the following problems.

1. Assume that you own 1,250 shares of stock X. You just read in the newspaper that the dividend for the stock is $3.88 per share. What did you earn in dividends?

2. The closing price of a stock is $90.25. The stock is paying a dividend of $3.50. What is the yield of the stock?

3. The closing price of the stock is $66.40, and the net earnings per share is $2.50. What is the stock's PE ratio?

4. The face value of a bond is $10,000, and the annual coupon payment is $850. What is the coupon rate?

5. Let's say that a person buys a bond that matures in 10 years and pays a coupon rate of 10 percent. The face value of the bond is $10,000. How much money will the bondholder receive in the tenth year?

Solving Economic Problems

Use your thinking skills and the information you learned in this chapter to find solutions to the following problems.

1. **Apply.** In Chapter 10, you learned how the Fed decides to change the money supply. Suppose that the Fed decides to increase the money

supply. How do you think this action will affect the stock market?

2. **Analyze.** If bonds and stocks are substitutes, then what should we see happen when bonds offer high returns?

3. **Identify Cause and Effect.** Suppose that there is no cause-and-effect relationship between the current condition of the federal budget (deficit, balance, or surplus) and the Dow Jones Industrial Average. If so, what would we expect to see in the real world?

4. **Infer and Conclude.** WRITING Write a one-page paper discussing the factors that you think will influence the stock market over the next several years. Explain how the factors you have identified will cause people to want to buy more stocks, sell more stocks, or turn to other types of investments.

5. **Identify Cause and Effect.** Would you expect the return on a Treasury bond to be higher or lower than the return on a corporate bond? What does your answer tell you about the cause-and-effect relationship between risk and return?

Project or Presentation

Predicting Stock Prices. Research stocks online or in a newspaper. Choose 10 stocks at random, and list them on a piece of paper. Then choose 10 stocks you think will rise in price during the next two weeks, and list them on another sheet of paper. For both lists, identify the price of each stock at the beginning of the two-week period and at the end of the two-week period. Did one list perform better (in terms of more stocks rising in price) than the other? If so, which list did better? How much better did it do? Were you a good predictor of which stocks would gain value? Why or why not? Present your findings to the class.

ONLINE emcp.com — *Practice Tests and Study Guide*

Go to **www.emcschool.net/Economics2e** and choose *Economics: New Ways of Thinking*, Chapter 16, if you need more help in preparing for the chapter test.

17. A Treasury bill is a bond issued by the federal government. The government issues Treasury bills when it wants to borrow funds. Treasury bills mature in 13, 26, or 52 weeks.

18. You will likely receive higher returns. Higher returns come with higher risks.

19. A futures contract is a contract in which the seller agrees to provide a particular good to the buyer on a specified future date at an agreed-upon price. Examples will vary.

20. A call option is a contract that gives the owner the right to buy shares of stock at a specified price within the time limits of the contract. Call options usually cost less than stock shares.

Doing the Math

1. $4,850 (*calculation:* 1,250 × $3.88 = $4,850).

2. 3.88% (*calculation:* $3.50 ÷ $90.25 = 3.88%).

3. 26.56 (*calculation:* $66.40 ÷ $2.50 = 26.56).

4. 8.5% (*calculation:* $850 ÷ $10,000 = 8.5%).

5. $10,000 plus a $1,000 coupon payment, for a total of $11,000.

Solving Economic Problems

1. When the Fed increases the money supply, there is more money in the economy. Some of this added money will stimulate buying activity in the stock market, driving prices upward.

2. We should see people getting out of stocks (selling stocks) and into bonds (buying bonds).

3. We should see that changes in the Dow are unrelated to changes in the state of the budget. In other words, the Dow will rise or fall regardless of whether the budget is balanced, in deficit, or in surplus.

4. Answers will vary.

5. The return on a Treasury bond is likely to be lower than that on a corporate bond. A Treasury bond is safer because it is more likely to be repaid. The greater the safety, the less the risk—and the less the risk, the lower the return. This answer suggests that a higher risk causes a higher return and a lower risk causes a lower return.

Project or Presentation

Answers will vary.

will repay to the buyer of the bond; maturity date, or the date the issuer must pay the buyer the face value of the bond; and coupon rate, or the percentage of the face value of the bond that the bondholder receives each year until the bond matures.

12. Standard & Poor and Moody are two of the best-known bond ratings services.

13. The rating is determined by the likelihood that the bond will be paid off. The more likely

the bond will be paid off, the better the rating.

14. The yield of a bond is the coupon payment divided by the price paid for the bond.

15. You would sell. Interest rates and bond prices move in opposite directions. If you expect interest rates to rise, then you will expect bond prices to fall. If you own bonds you should sell them before the price falls.

16. It would issue municipal bonds.

Discussion Starters

1. Ask students to define the terms *tariffs* and *quotas* in their own words. Ask them why the United States would impose tariffs and quotas on goods produced in other countries.

2. Ask students if they know of someone who lost his or her job because of an influx of imported goods. How did the loss of job affect the person and his or her family? (Advise students not to use people's names.)

3. One perception is that tariffs and quotas protect American workers, producers, and consumers. Is this true? Ask students how they think American workers, producers, and consumers are protected through tariffs and quotas.

4. Ask students to think of the benefits of free trade for American workers, producers, and consumers. Does free trade offer benefits for students and their families personally? Have students share that information with the class.

Debating the Issues

Is Free Trade the Best Policy for the United States?

Oklahoma can't impose a tariff or quota on goods produced in Wisconsin, but the United States can and does impose tariffs and quotas on goods produced in other countries. For example, the United States currently imposes tariffs on garments, textiles, sugar, and many other goods produced in other countries. This means that free trade exists between the states of the United States but not between countries of the world. Do you think there should be free trade between countries, as there is between states? This issue has both opponents and proponents.

One day in November, two high school debate teams met and debated the issue of free trade. The question before each team was, Is free trade the best policy for the United States? Here is what four of the debaters, two from each team, had to say.

Alycyn, Addison High School Debate Team

When I go to the store to buy something new, whether it be a pair of running shoes or a cell phone, I want to buy the best product for the lowest price. That's my objective, plain and simple. I have a better chance of meeting that objective living in a world of free trade than living in a world where countries impose tariffs and quotas on each other's goods. Free trade maximizes competition, which is what guarantees me the highest-quality goods at the lowest possible price.

Suppose there are 40 running shoe companies in the world: 10 in the United States and 30 in other countries. Am I, as a consumer, better off if all 40 companies sell

their shoes in the United States or if only the 10 U.S. companies sell their shoes in the United States? The answer is obvious. I am better off when 40 companies, domestic and foreign alike, compete for my business, than when only 10 domestic companies compete for it. Free trade is the policy that maximizes choice for the consumer. It guarantees high-quality goods at reasonable prices.

Mike, Spring Valley High School Debate Team

If every country in the world practiced free trade, then perhaps free trade would be the best policy for the United States. But that's not the case. That's not the world we live in, and we shouldn't pretend that it is. When other countries impose tariffs and quotas on our goods, that hurts our industries and our workers, and we should retaliate in kind.

Suppose the German government places a tariff on American cars imported into Germany. As a result, the price of American cars rises in Germany and Germans buy more German cars and fewer American cars. Since U.S. car companies sell fewer cars, they will have to lay off some of their workers. The people who are laid off are Americans, not Germans. In other words, some Americans will lose their jobs because the German government decided to impose tariffs on American cars.

Is this fair? Should the U.S. government practice free trade when another country doesn't? Should our government sit back and do nothing as the German government puts Americans out of work?

I, for one, don't think so. A policy of "give and take" would be more acceptable to me. If Germany practices free trade with us, then we should practice free

Differentiating Instruction

Enrichment and Extension
Divide students into groups of three or four. Ask each group to imagine that it's a business that produces a particular good. Then ask each group to decide if its business profits from a free trade policy or would do better with a tariff and quota system. The group should provide reasons for its decision. Have groups share their decisions with the class.

trade with Germany. But if Germany doesn't practice free trade with us, then we shouldn't practice free trade with them. We have to be realistic, and we have to protect ourselves.

Sylvia, Addison High School Debate Team

I disagree. I think that practicing free trade is a little like practicing honesty: you should do it even if others don't. If 10 people tell lies, it doesn't follow that the best thing you can do is tell a lie too.

If most countries impose tariffs and quotas, it doesn't follow that the United States should do likewise. The United States should practice free trade even if every other country in the world imposes tariffs and quotas on all products being imported. That's because the United States prospers through free trade, even when other countries do not practice it.

Suppose there are five countries in the world. Four of the countries impose tariffs and quotas; one country, the United States, does not. Certainly, foreign tariffs and quotas hurt U.S. producers and workers, but the U.S. government can't make things better for our producers and workers by making our consumers worse off. And that is exactly what the U.S. government would be doing if it retaliated by imposing tariffs and quotas on foreign goods. Then, not only would U.S. producers and workers be hurt by foreign tariffs and quotas, but U.S. consumers would also be hurt by U.S. tariffs and quotas on foreign goods. If the choice is between hurting producers and workers or hurting producers, workers, and consumers, then it's better to hurt as few people as possible.

Here's what it comes down to: The best policy is for every country in the world to practice free trade. The second best policy is for the United States to practice free trade, even if no other country in the world does. The worst policy is for the United States to impose tariffs and quotas on foreign goods simply because other countries impose tariffs and quotas on our goods.

Madison, Spring Valley High School Debate Team

The United States' policy shouldn't protect the interests only of consumers; it should protect the interests of consumers, producers, and workers. When other countries impose tariffs and quotas on U.S.-produced goods, they hurt our producers and our workers and should have to bear the economic consequences. There must be a price for taking such actions, or these countries will continue to make themselves better off at the expense of American producers and workers. The higher the price of imposing tariffs and quotas on U.S.-produced goods, the less likely foreign countries will do so.

The way to ensure free trade is for the United States to give other countries a taste of their own medicine. If they practice free trade with us, then we should practice free trade with them. If they impose tariffs and quotas on our goods, we should do the same to their goods.

What Do You Think?

1. Should the United States practice free trade even if other countries do not? Explain your thinking.
2. Is the world moving toward or away from greater free trade? Give some examples from recent news stories to support your answer.

Activities for What Do You Think?

1. Label two points in the room with "Yes" and "No." Then ask students to "vote with their feet" by moving to one of the two labels in the room to answer this question: should the United States practice free trade even if other countries do not? Allow the groups five minutes to compile their reasons for voting for that opinion. Then have each group spend one minute presenting its reasons to the class. Conduct another class vote to see if there is any change in the voting.
2. Divide students into groups of three or four to discuss whether the world is moving toward or away from free trade. Require that students cite specific examples to substantiate the group's opinion. Each group can then create a skit to share its opinion with the class.

Closure

Direct students to write paragraphs describing how their opinions on this issue were affected by reading Debating the Issues and discussing it with the class. Ask those students whose opinions changed what information influenced their thinking.

Pacing

This multimedia project can be covered as a separate unit at the end of a semester, or as an ongoing assignment throughout the semester. Use the following guidelines to conduct the project as a separate 2-week unit:

Overview, Phase 1, and Phase 2: 1 day
Phase 3: 2 days
Phase 4: 2 days
Phase 5: 2 days
Phase 6: 1 day
Phase 7: 1 day
Phase 8: 1 day

Skills Covered

This project provides ample opportunities for students to master the **twenty-first-century skills** they need to succeed in today's world:

1. *Core subject and twenty-first-century theme:* economics
2. *Learning and innovation skills:* creativity, innovation, critical thinking, problem solving, communication, and collaboration
3. *Information, media, and technology skills:* information literacy, media literacy, and information and technology communication (ICT) literacy
4. *Life and career skills:* flexibility and adaptability, initiative and self-direction, social and cross-cultural, productivity and accountability, and leadership and responsibility

In addition, the project addresses the eight **multiple intelligences** (Linguistic, Logical-Mathematical, Interpersonal, Intrapersonal, Spatial, Bodily-Kinesthetic, Musical, and Naturalist) and the six levels of **Bloom's taxonomy** (Knowledge, Comprehension, Application, Analysis, Synthesis, and Evaluation).

Project Outcome

Before beginning the project, decide what will be the final outcome and audience. (Or you might work with your class to make these decisions.) Consider the following outcomes and audiences, or come up with ideas of your own.

In this project, your class will research how the financial crisis of 2007–2009 affected and was affected by four broad sectors of the economy: housing, financial, governmental or quasi-governmental, and global. You will work in small groups to study the sectors and then work together as a class to draw conclusions, make recommendations, and present your findings in a multimedia format.

The Crisis: An Overview

The financial crisis of 2007–2009 was a series of events that had both serious immediate effects and long-term consequences for the U.S. and world economies. Why were the effects of the crisis so widespread? To answer this question, let's start with the formula for gross domestic product (GDP):

$$GDP = C + I + G + X$$

where

C	=	Consumer spending
I	=	Investments, or business spending
G	=	Government spending
X	=	Net exports (imports minus exports)

All these factors played a role in the crisis. Consider consumer spending, which accounts for two-thirds of the U.S. economy. When people have more money, they spend more, thus increasing GDP. And how do people get more money? One way is through borrowing.

The nature of borrowing during the early 2000s had far-reaching and long-term effects. Let's look at one kind of borrowing—taking out a mortgage—and how it affected the four sectors of the economy.

Traditional Versus Nontraditional Mortgages

Banks make profits by lending money and being repaid with interest. For example, for a $100,000 mortgage at 7 percent over 30 years, a bank will earn $139,508.90 in interest (plus get back $100,000 in principal). However, this will take 30 years. How much risk is involved for the bank? It depends on how likely it is the borrower will pay back the loan.

Let's say you're buying a house for $100,000. You make a 20 percent down payment (the standard for many years) and borrow $80,000 for 30 years. If your house increases in value by 5 percent over the next year, your equity will be more than $25,000. (*Equity* is the value you own free and clear—in this example, the $20,000 you put down, plus the $5,000 the house has gone up in value, plus the amount of the loan you've paid back.) If house prices don't decline more than 20 percent this first year, you and the bank will have almost no risk. If you can't make the payments, the bank will sell the house for more than what you owe.

Suppose you can't afford a down payment. The bank might lend you the full amount. In this case, your payments will be higher and you will earn less equity than with a traditional mortgage. As long as house prices stay even or go up, everyone will be happy. But if house prices fall and you can't make your payments, the bank won't be able to sell your house for enough to get back what you owe.

In the early 2000s, borrowers who couldn't afford the standard down payment were given mortgages with high interest rates. For banks, charging higher rates helped offset the risk in lending to these borrowers by bringing a greater return. For borrowers, paying a higher interest rate increased the monthly payment, the length of the mortgage, or both.

As a borrower, if you can't afford a down payment, then you probably can't afford a high interest rate either. Your lender might get around this by offering you an adjustable-rate mortgage (ARM) with a *teaser rate*: an artificially low rate that can help you qualify for a loan. For example, if the market rate on your $100,000 mortgage is 7 percent, you will owe $665.30 a month. If you can't afford that, you might be offered a teaser rate of 5 percent, lowering your payment to $536.82. However, a teaser rate is good for only a short time—often, three years. After that, the rate will go up to the higher market rate.

ARMs with low teaser rates were popular in the early 2000s. But when these rates expired in the mid to late 2000s, many borrowers found themselves facing substantially higher and sometimes unaffordable payments.

Mortgage Investments

Suppose a bank needs cash right away and doesn't want to wait for your mortgage to be paid off. It can sell your loan to someone who will package it with thousands of others and sell off shares like stock. This is how *mortgage-backed securities (MBSs)* work. Each investor gets an equal share in the MBS.

Collateral debt obligations (CDOs) are similar, except investors own unequal shares. An investor who wants low risk will buy the highest share, or tranche. He or she will earn a lower return, however. An investor who wants a higher return will buy one of the lower tranches, but he or she will have more risk. This trade-off is known as the *risk-reward trade-off*.

Because the default rate on mortgages was traditionally low, MBSs and CDOs became very popular. Many people in the financial sector earned incredible salaries and bonuses. But how could banks and others issuing the original mortgages determine the level of risk and decide whether to make the loans and at what interest rates? In the 2000s, people called *quants* used sophisticated computer models to show what was and wasn't risky. These financial models were untested, however, and extremely complex, so few people understood them.

Another factor was the *credit default swap (CDS)*, a type of insurance contract. An MBS or CDO investor who wanted to limit risk could make monthly payments to a mortgage default insurer. Doing this was intended to guarantee the investor would get paid if the borrower on the original mortgage defaulted. But after many borrowers had defaulted, some default insurers didn't have enough money to pay the investors. The CDS insurers weren't regulated, unlike traditional insurance companies, which are required to have enough money to pay claims.

Global Repercussions and Government Intervention

The MBS market was backed, in part, by two quasi-governmental companies: Fannie Mae and Freddie Mac. Both ended up in serious trouble, as did a number of companies in the mortgage lending industry. Some went out of business or were sold, and thousands of people lost their jobs. This happened not only to Americans but also to people worldwide.

The U.S. government decided it couldn't let all these companies fail, so the Fed lent them money. Also, in late 2008, the Bush administration persuaded Congress to pass the Troubled Asset Relief Program (TARP). Among other things, TARP was designed to free banks from *toxic assets*: loans on which borrowers had defaulted and for which the value of the asset (usually, a home) was less than the amount of the loan. The Obama administration also got Congress to pass a number of measures to help homeowners. In 2009, President Obama signed into law a major expansionary fiscal policy measure, the American Recovery and Reinvestment Act.

Multimedia Project   **503**

Produce a Pamphlet and Workshop

Write a multilanguage pamphlet for audience members. Distribute it during a community workshop in which groups take turns presenting information on their assigned sectors.

Teach Another Class

Teach a unit on the financial crisis to another economics class. Each group should spend one class period presenting information on its assigned sector.

Create a Website

Create a comprehensive website that includes video, audio, and slide presentations; text with charts, graphs, and other images; and a booklet in the form of a downloadable PDF document. If you choose this option, the following websites offer free tools that you can use:

- keepvid.com, at http://econ.emcp.net/keepvid, easily captures many types of flash video and other files from the Internet.
- zamzar.com, at http://econ.emcp.net/zamzar, converts a wide variety of files, including flv (Flash video files), and captures YouTube video.
- Google.com, at http://econ.emcp.net/google, offers account holders free websites and tools for creating them.

Project Overview

Begin the project by asking students to read the introductory paragraph and "The Crisis: An Overview" individually. Then quickly outline the project and decide on an end product and target audience for the project.

Phase 1: Form Groups

Divide the class into four equal groups, and assign each group one of the four economic sectors outlined in the textbook. Ensure that each group chooses a leader and a note taker. Encourage the groups to identify members' strengths and interests and to divide tasks so that each member contributes according to those strengths and interests.

Phase 2: Learn the Terms

In this phase of the project, each group researches, defines, and provides sample sentences for terms specific to its sector and then presents this information to the class. Have one or two volunteers from the class combine all the terms into a glossary for distribution to the class and for use later in the presentation. (**Bloom's levels:** Knowledge and Comprehension)

Phase 3: Research the Issues

Next, each group researches its economic sector. Have the groups do the following:

- Read the sections recommended in the textbook.
- Conduct Internet research using the suggested links as well as sites found by typing the key terms into an Internet search engine.
- Interview community members who were involved in the crisis or have expert knowledge of economics during that period.
- Review audio and video files covering news of the crisis.

As students research their assigned sectors, have them find answers to the questions posed in the textbook and discover and answer additional questions. Also have them define any additional terms they think might be unfamiliar to their audience. (**Bloom's levels:** Knowledge, Comprehension, Analysis, and Synthesis)

The Project

This project has eight phases. Read the directions carefully, and ask your teacher for help as necessary.

Phase 1: Form Groups

Divide the class into four groups to research how the financial crisis of 2007–2009 affected and was affected by these broad sectors of the economy: housing, financial, governmental and quasi-governmental, and global. Your group should choose a leader, a note taker, and other roles as necessary.

Phase 2: Learn the Terms

The lists of terms below relate to the four sectors of the economy. Use Internet and library sources to research the terms on your group's list. Write a definition for each term, and use it in a sentence.

Each group will present its terms to the class. One or two volunteers will then compile all the terms in a glossary for all the groups to use. The same glossary can be given to the audience during the class presentation at the end of the project.

Housing Sector
adjustable-rate mortgages (ARMs)
collateralized debt obligations (CDOs)
credit default swaps (CDSs)
equity
fixed-rate mortgage
foreclosure
leverage
mortgage-backed securities (MBSs)
prime loan
secondary market
securitization
subprime loan
teaser rate
tranche

Financial Sector
asset
balance sheet
Bear Stearns
capital (net worth)
Goldman Sachs
insolvent
Lehman Brothers
leverage
liability

Morgan Stanley
return
risk
solvent
toxic assets

Governmental/Quasi-governmental Sector
American Recovery and Reinvestment Act
Community Reinvestment Act (CRA)
conforming and nonconforming loans
Fannie Mae
FDIC
Federal Reserve (Fed)
FHA
Freddie Mac
Making Home Affordable program
regulatory capital
regulatory capital arbitrage
"too big to fail"
Troubled Asset Relief Program (TARP)

Global Sector
AIG
domino effect
international savings glut
real sector (consumption plus investment)
saving rate
"too big to fail"
unemployment rate

Phase 3: Research the Issues

In this phase, you will research how your sector of the economy was affected by the crisis of 2007–2009. Begin by reading the following features in your textbook:

- What Happened to U.S. House Prices between 2001 and 2009? (page 153)
- What Gives Money Value? (page 302)
- Could You Lose Your Job If Your Bank Loses Money? (page 336)
- Taking Out a Mortgage (pages 524–530)

Research on the Internet, in the library, and in your community—reading books and articles, viewing and listening to news reports, and interviewing people. The following links provide information for all groups. You will also find links listed for each sector. Locate other useful sites by typing the key terms for your sector into an Internet search engine.

Grading Rubric: Participation

1 2 3 4 5   Student was committed to group and its work.

1 2 3 4 5   Student completed group assignments on time and with acceptable quality.

1 2 3 4 5   Student cooperated with and supported group members in completing tasks.

1 2 3 4 5   Student contributed to group discussions and was respectful of other members' contributions.

General Information

Links

http://econ.emcp.net/generalinfo (General financial information)

http://econ.emcp.net/econterms (Economic terms)

Focus your research by answering the questions listed for your sector. As you work, take notes, record sources, and think about how best to organize and present the information.

Housing Sector

Links

http://econ.emcp.net/mortgageinfo (Mortgage information)

http://econ.emcp.net/homesales (Home sales and building data)

Questions

1. Why did lenders start making so-called subprime loans?
2. How did making subprime loans affect the housing market and the prices of houses?
3. What incentives did brokers and lenders have to make adjustable-rate versus fixed-rate loans?
4. How did refinancing homes and "cashing out" the equity affect the economy as a whole?
5. How did the fall in house prices affect the housing market as a whole?
6. How did the fall in house prices affect borrowers?
7. How did the fall in house prices affect the economy in general?
8. What happened in communities where a lot of homeowners defaulted on their mortgages?

Financial Sector

Links

http://econ.emcp.net/SECbondrules (Securities and Exchange Commission's mortgage bond rules)

http://econ.emcp.net/mortgagecalculator (Mortgage calculator)

Questions

1. Is banks' lending money essential to the proper functioning of the economy? Explain.
2. Traditionally, what was the difference between a bank and an investment bank? How and why did the distinction become blurred, and what were the consequences?
3. What was the purpose of the Glass-Steagall Act?

4. How did investment banks such as CitiCorp, Lehman Brothers, Bear Stearns, and Goldman Sachs operate? How were their employees paid?
5. What are mortgage-backed securities (MBSs), and how did they provide money for home loans?
6. What are collateralized debt obligations (CDOs), and what part did they play in the crisis?
7. What are credit default swaps (CDSs), and what part did they play in the crisis?
8. What happened to MBSs, CDOs, and CDSs when housing prices declined and borrowers couldn't pay back their loans? How did the failure to pay back mortgages affect the credit market and the economy as a whole?

Governmental/Quasi-governmental Sector

Links

http://econ.emcp.net/FannieMae (Fannie Mae)

http://econ.emcp.net/FreddieMac (Freddie Mac)

http://econ.emcp.net/federalreserveeducation (Federal Reserve)

http://econ.emcp.net/FDIC (FDIC)

http://econ.emcp.net/BLS (Bureau of Labor Statistics, current and historical data)

http://econ.emcp.net/MakingHomeAffordable (Making Home Affordable program)

http://econ.emcp.net/SECbondrules (Securities and Exchange Commission's mortgage bond rules)

Questions

1. What happened after Congress encouraged Fannie Mae and Freddie Mac to buy subprime mortgages from banks?
2. What actions did the Bush and Obama administrations take to ease the financial crisis? How did these actions affect the economy, in general, and the financial sector, in particular?
3. How did the approaches of the Bush and Obama administrations differ? Discuss each approach in terms of general economic theory.
4. What happened to Bear Stearns, Lehman Brothers, and Morgan Stanley? What did the government do in response?
5. What steps did the Fed take to help fix the crisis?
6. What long-term effects (positive and negative) have been identified regarding the actions of the Fed and the federal government?

Phase 4: Organize Your Part

Once each group has analyzed and synthesized its information, have it decide how to focus that information and present it to the audience for the project. During this phase, encourage the groups to be creative and to use the skills of their members. Different members can work on different parts of the group's presentation—for example:

- Students with audio and journalism skills can present some of the information as a radio news show. (**Multiple intelligences:** Linguistic, Logical-Mathematical, Interpersonal)
- Artistic students can create a cartoon strip, graphic novel, illustrated pamphlet, or billboard. (**Multiple intelligences:** Linguistic, Spatial)
- Students who enjoy writing can write a play or story, and students who enjoy performing can act it out. (**Multiple intelligences:** Linguistic, Bodily-Kinesthetic)
- Students who enjoy interacting with others can conduct an interview or hold a debate. (**Multiple intelligences:** Interpersonal)
- Students who enjoy introspective and reflection can share personal experiences of the financial crisis, either their own or those of a fictional or real person. (**Multiple intelligences:** Intrapersonal, Spatial)
- Musically inclined students can write and perform a song or rap. (**Multiple intelligences:** Linguistic, Musical)
- Math whizzes can study and explain formula, and/or organize data in charts, diagrams, and graphs. (**Multiple intelligences:** Logical-Mathematical, Spatial)
- Students who enjoy being outdoors can discover ways that an economic principle applies to the natural world and share that discovery. (**Multiple intelligences:** Naturalist) (**Bloom's levels:** Knowledge, Comprehension, Application, Analysis, and Synthesis)

Grading Rubric: Product

1 2 3 4 5	Material was accurate and easy to understand.
1 2 3 4 5	Group followed accepted rules for grammar, punctuation, and style in written work and corresponding rules for other work.

1 2 3 4 5	Presentation was creative, attractive, and informative.
1 2 3 4 5	Presentation method and amount of work done were appropriate for the information.

Phase 5: Rehearse, Draw Conclusions, and Look to the Future

As part of this project, have the class draw a set of general conclusions and make recommendations for the future. To accomplish this, the groups need to present their findings to each other and discuss their presentations. The groups' presentations can also serve as a dress rehearsal for the class presentation of the project to the designated audience.

Use the Grading Rubrics in the bottom margins of these teaching notes to evaluate students' work on the project. For each criteria, assign a score between 1 (Did not meet expectations) and 5 (Exceeded expectations). Add the scores from both rubrics together to get a total score for the project.

Evaluate students on both their participation and the product that resulted from their contribution. Also have students use the rubrics to evaluate themselves, their fellow group members, and other groups' presentations. Ask students to jot down questions and suggestions during and after each group's presentation and to give that information to the group to help it polish the presentation.

Using the Grading Rubrics, you might collect and average three scores for each student: your own evaluation, the student's self-evaluation, and evaluations from the other members of student's group or the class. (**Bloom's levels:** Analysis, Synthesis, Evaluation)

Phase 6: Assemble the Parts

In this phase, the class regroups to form three "directorate" teams, which organize and craft the presentation for your audience. Their goal is to pull together the work of the four topic groups into one presentation. Depending on the end product you have chosen for the class project, you may want to modify these teams. (**Bloom's levels:** Application, Analysis, Synthesis)

Global Sector Links

http://econ.emcp.net/BLS (Bureau of Labor Statistics, current and historical data)

http://econ.emcp.net/Icelandeconomy (Iceland financial crisis)

http://econ.emcp.net/USsavingsrate (U.S. personal savings rate)

http://econ.emcp.net/Chinasavingsrate (Chinese savings rate)

http://econ.emcp.net/USChinasavingsrates (U.S. and Chinese savings rates)

Questions

1. How did the financial crisis in the United States affect other countries? Did the crisis have a "domino effect"? Explain your answers.
2. Were certain countries hit harder than others by the crisis? If so, which ones and why? For instance, what happened to the banking industry in Great Britain and in Iceland?
3. What role did China play in the international savings glut?
4. What does the phrase "too big to fail" mean? How does it apply to the financial crisis?
5. What role did AIG play in the crisis?
6. How did the crisis affect unemployment?
7. How did the crisis affect the real economy, such as home builders, restaurants, hotels, and stores?
8. How is the economy doing now in your area or state? Has it fully recovered? Has the crisis had any long-term effects? Explain your answers.

Phase 4: Organize Your Part

Once your group has completed its research, think about the best way to present the information. Your contribution to the class presentation should include definitions of key terms, presentations of data, and a list of sources. Consider the following formats:

- Slide, video, or audio presentation
- Play, skit, role-play, or reader's theater
- Article, booklet, or brochure
- Web page, blog, or podcast
- Graph, map, diagram, or other visual
- Song, rap, poem, story, or other literary work
- Painting, drawing, collage, or other artwork

Phase 5: Rehearse, Draw Conclusions, and Look to the Future

A key part of this project is to present your work to the class. After all the groups have presented, work as a class to draw general conclusions. What caused the crisis? Which sector or sectors were most

responsible? What could have been done to avoid the crisis? Finally, consider the future:

1. What have we learned from this chapter of economic history?
2. What can individuals, the nation, and the world do to prevent another crisis?
3. Will the U.S. and global economies have permanent or long-term scars from the crisis? Explain.
4. What can be done to ensure the strength of the U.S. and world economies?

Phase 6: Assemble the Parts

Your class will now form two teams to organize the four group presentations into one complete class presentation. All students will take part in this process. Choose the team that best matches your skills:

- *Organizers* will create the overall structure for the presentation and make sure the project is coherent and appealing. They will develop an outline or plan and fit each part into the plan, prepare introductions and conclusions, and develop an advertising plan and materials (such as posters or Web announcements).
- *Technologists* will put together the presentation. If it will be presented live, this team will set up computers, audio and video equipment, and other technology. If it is offered on a website, this team will collect and post materials and test and maintain the site.

At your first team meeting, select a leader and secretary, divide up the assigned tasks, and set up a schedule for completing them.

Phase 7: Present to Your Audience

When the project has been completed, your class will present it to the chosen audience, post it on a website, or both. If the presentation is given live, each group should select a leader to introduce its part, and the class as a whole should select students to introduce the presentation and present the class's conclusions and suggestions. The presentation might end with a panel discussion of these conclusions and suggestions, and audience members might be invited to join in.

Phase 8: Debrief

After presenting the project, evaluate what went well and what didn't go well, as well as what you learned about the topics and the process of presenting to others. Your teacher might conduct this debriefing as a class discussion or ask you to write about your experiences individually, with a partner, or with your original group.

Phase 7: Present to Your Audience   Phase 8: Debrief

Encourage students to take responsibility for the presentation and to accomplish the organization and logistics themselves, offering support and guidance as needed. Consider passing out evaluation sheets to audience members or posting an evaluation sheet on the website. (**Bloom's levels:** Application, Analysis, Synthesis)

Lead the class in a debriefing session, or ask individual students to write about the experience. If you have collected evaluation sheets from audience members, review the results. Be sure to congratulate students on work well done and to encourage them to continue improving their knowledge and skills. (**Bloom's levels:** Evaluation)

Personal Finance Handbook

In this handbook, you will find background information and tips that will help you get the most from your money. You will also find guidelines to help you begin planning for your future, with a focus on the years immediately following your graduation from high school.

The topics covered in the handbook, appearing alphabetically, are:

You will find additional information and tips on practical, day-to-day issues in the *Your Personal Economics* features that appear throughout this text. Your teacher may have already assigned some of the features. If, at a particular point, you wish to refer back to the information contained in these features, here is a list of the features with corresponding page numbers:

While you will find the information and tips in this handbook useful, keep in mind that you have easy access to the most up-to-date information available through the Internet (that's the topic of the *Your Personal Economics* feature on page 166). As you know, in a world of scarcity, it's crucial that we make the most of our limited resources, and taking time to acquire all the relevant information is necessary if you hope to maximize your own personal resources.

Avoiding Telemarketing Frauds and Swindles

Each day in the United States, thousands of telephone calls are made in attempts to sell something. Some of the offers are legitimate; others are not. It's important for you to be able to separate the two. When dealing with companies that sell products or services over the telephone (telemarketers), listen for the following tactics, which are frequently used by unethical telemarketers who want to trick you out of your money.

- **They know more about you than they should.** If your name and number came from a mailing list, the caller may know such personal information as your age, income, and occupation. Telephone callers may tailor their comments to what they know about you in an attempt to hold your interest and to gain your trust.
- **They will say anything.** They are always ready with an answer, no matter what you ask. Don't assume that every telephone salesperson is as honest as you are. Be skeptical.
- **They sound legitimate.** Good telephone swindlers (people who earn money by trickery or deceit) do not sound like telephone swindlers—that's what makes them good at what they do. If they sound believable, it's probably because they have had a lot of practice lying.
- **Their offer sounds too good to be true.** If the deal they are offering sounds almost too good to be true, it probably is too good to be true. Be very skeptical of these offers.
- **They will use high-pressure sales tactics.** Legitimate salespersons will respect your decision not to buy their products. Swindlers, on the other hand, will try to pressure you into making a decision. The harder they push, the more you should resist.
- **They insist that an immediate decision is necessary and in your best interest.** They might say "There are only a few left" or "This offer is only good today." Be wary of this tactic. It often means that the telemarketer wants to prevent you from researching the product or service he or she is trying to sell you.
- **They often advertise in recognized magazines and newspapers.** You may see an ad in a magazine and return a card asking for more information, and days later, you receive a call. Don't assume that just because you requested information, the telemarketer works for a legitimate business.
- **They are unwilling to provide written information or references.** When you ask for written verification, swindlers will make excuses. This is a sure sign that something is wrong.
- **They will ask for your credit card number.** Be very careful about providing a credit card number to an unknown company or individual.
- **You are unlikely to get your money back.** Government agencies and consumer protection groups will try to bring swindlers to justice, but once you give the dishonest telemarketers your money, you are unlikely to get it back.

Practicing Your Skills

1. A person calls you on the telephone and tells you that you have won a prize. The person knows your age and occupation. He says that he needs to know your Social Security number before he can send you the prize. What would you do?
2. In recent years, some people have been receiving recorded messages on their phone stating that the caller is from the IRS (Internal Revenue Service) and that you owe a certain dollar amount of taxes, which you must send in immediately or be penalized. What would you do if you received such a message?

Budgeting

A budget is an organized plan for spending and saving money. Creating a budget isn't a cure-all for your money problems; it is simply an organized way of looking at your costs and goals and at what you are doing about them. Your budget records your efforts, successes, and failures—information that's useful for planning and decision making.

What you do with the information in a budget is up to you. If you write out a budget and don't follow it successfully at first—if you don't save as much as you wanted to, perhaps—don't worry. Few people immediately succeed at following a budget. Like practicing good study habits, following a budget takes willpower. Only you can decide whether your goals are important enough for you to exercise the willpower necessary to achieve them. And as a student of economics, you may understand better than others that all of your decisions and actions mean that trade-offs have been made and opportunity costs incurred.

Here is a five-step process for making a budget.

Step 1. Determine your income over the past year. Figure out dollar amounts for both your income and your expenditures over a year. To find your annual income, check your pay stubs.

Step 2. Determine your average monthly expenses. To figure out your expenses, keep a list of what you spend for a month or two. An easy way to keep track of your spending is simply to ask for receipts for everything you buy and keep them in one place. Another way is to record your expenses in a journal each night. You might want to break your expenses down into four or five categories, such as the following:

- School
- Clothes
- Entertainment, including movies, CD purchases, eating out, and so on
- Transportation
- Miscellaneous

Each day, register the dollar amount you spent in each category. After you have done this for a month or two, add up the dollar amounts you've spent. Then ask yourself if these two months are typical. Take into account any unusual expenses. The point is to come up with your best estimate of your *average* monthly spending.

Step 3. Calculate your annual expenses. Once you have found your typical monthly cost in each category, multiply by 12 to find your yearly cost in each category.

Step 4. Decide how much you want to save. Refer back to the *Your Personal Economics* feature on page 24 to remind yourself of the value of saving. You want to carve out a spot in your budget for some savings. The only question is how much. You will need to make this decision based on your long-term goals. Obviously, if you have not already allowed for savings, you will need to take money from your other categories (school, clothes, etc.) to make up your savings.

Step 5. Write out a monthly budget. Exhibit PF-1 below shows the main elements of a monthly budget.

Column 1, which lists expense categories, can contain as many or as few categories as you want. Often, a person's stage of life determines the number of categories in this column. For example, a high school student may have fewer expense items than a 30-year-old who is employed. The 30-year-old may have such expenses as health insurance and mortgage insurance that the high school student doesn't have.

Main Elements of a Monthly Budget

(1) Expense	(2) Budgeted	(3) Actual	(4) Difference
School	$10	$15	+$5
Clothing	33	37	+4
Entertainment	25	30	+5
Transportation	60	62	+2
Savings	37	20	–17
Miscellaneous	12	13	+1
Total	**177**	**177**	**0**

Column 2 lists the dollar amounts the person plans to spend in each category— the budgeted amounts.

Column 3 lists the actual dollar amounts the person ends up spending in each category.

Column 4 records the differences between the budgeted and actual expenses. To determine each difference, subtract the dollar amount in column 2 from the dollar amount in column 3. A plus sign before the dollar amount means the person spent more in this category than planned. A minus sign means he or she spent less.

Buying and Financing a Car

If you are like most people, you will buy many cars in your lifetime, and these purchases will probably be among your major expenses. Also, the costs don't end with the purchase of the car. You will need to buy gasoline for the car, maintain it, and repair it from time to time—all factors that you should consider when buying a car. Here are some tips to keep in mind when buying a car, whether new or used.

1. **Know the type of car you want before you go shopping.** Think about the type of car you want before you set out to shop for one. Otherwise, a salesperson may sell you a car that doesn't really meet your needs—perhaps one that costs too much, is not fuel efficient, or doesn't have the safety features you want. If you like to "window-shop" for cars before you start talking to a salesperson, then tell the salesperson that you are only looking so you can walk around the lot at your leisure.

2. **Do your homework.** Study articles in *Consumer Reports* before setting out to shop for a car. This magazine (available in print and online) is full of information about such topics as safety, maintenance, and fuel economy for all the major makes and models. Some people take their *Consumer Reports* magazine with them to dealerships so the car salespersons will know that they have done their homework and are serious about getting a good car at a reasonable price. You can also find valuable information online at http://econ.emcp.net/car_pricing.

3. **Investigate the competition.** Suppose you have decided that you want to buy a Ford. If there are two Ford dealerships in your town, visit both of them. The two dealerships then may compete for your business, perhaps by offering you a better price or more features on the car.

4. **Watch out for certain sales tactics.** Some car salespersons use sales techniques that will make you end up paying more than you need to. Here are a few commmon techniques to watch out for.

    Lowballing is the practice of quoting an unusually low price to get you interested. Later, when you sit down to do business, the salesperson says she made a "mistake" and forgotten to include some costs or that her managers won't let her sell the car for that price.

Highballing is the practice of promising you an unusually high price for a trade-in (the used car you give to the dealer in partial payment for the car you are buying). Later, the salesperson says that the car has been checked out and isn't really worth as much as he thought.

Determining your income level, or the income level of your parents, is something many a salesperson try to do. For example, a salesperson who learns that a customer is a physician may be less likely to bargain on the assumption that physicians are wealthy. If you are a teenager looking for a car, the salesperson might ask what your parents do for a living.

Where you live can also affect how a salesperson deals with you. If you live nearby, she may be less likely to offer a lower price than if you live farther away. The salesperson assumes that the farther away you live, the less likely you will return after shopping around.

Intimidation is another tactic you may encounter if you are a teenager seeking to buy a car. A salesperson may think he can take advantage of you because he is older and because this is the first time you have bought a car. Remember, though, that you are the customer, and that means you are in charge. The salesperson wants your business. Do not act intimidated (even if you feel that way), and do not be afraid to walk out of the car dealership at any time. There are other places you can buy a car.

5. **Your attitude matters.** If you act thrilled at seeing exactly the car you want, the salesperson won't likely lower the price. If you act as if you could take the car or leave it, you will be in a better position. Don't give the impression that there's only one car in the world for you.

6. **Determine the value of the car.** If you're buying a new car, you need to know the wholesale price (dealer cost) of the vehicle you want to buy. Some newsstands carry publications that list the wholesale prices of most makes of cars; you can find the same information online. If you are buying a used car, you can obtain estimates of the current market value of the car at several websites, such as Kelley Blue Book and Edmunds (http://econ.emcp.net/car_pricing). You will greatly increase your chance of getting the best price possible for the car you want if you know what the dealer paid for it or what the "going rate" is for a used car.

7. **Know the value of your trade-in.** You may have an old car that you want to trade in when you buy your new car. To find out its value, look in the Kelley Blue Book Market Report or go to http://econ.emcp.net/car_pricing. Car dealerships have this information, but they won't give it to you. Banks, credit unions, and libraries usually carry the Blue Book and will let you see it.

8. **Drive the car.** Make sure you drive the car you are thinking about buying. Test-drive it without using the radio or air conditioner, which can sometimes mask car sounds you need to be aware of. The salesperson often goes with you on a test-drive and talks to you while you're driving. If you want to drive in silence so you can hear the car, just say so.

9. **Find out if there is a warranty; if there is, understand it.** New cars, as well as some used cars, come with warranties. A warranty is a guarantee or an assurance given by a seller stating that a product is in good working order. It may also state that the seller will provide certain types of service for a period of time. For example, a car seller may provide a warranty specifying that if anything goes wrong with the engine in the next five years, the seller will fix it free of charge. It's important to know what the warranty says, so make sure to ask about it and to read it carefully. Many dealers sell service contracts, or extended warranties, which frequently cost $1,500 to $2,000. Whether

these contracts/warranties are good investments depends on the condition of the car and the reliability of the dealer. If you are buying a new car, be sure to distinguish between the new car's warranty and the extended warranty by asking the following questions:

- What is the difference between the coverage under the warranty and the coverage under the service contract?
- What repairs are covered?
- Who pays for the labor? The parts?
- Who performs the repairs?
- How long does the service contract last?
- What is the policy on cancellation and refund?

10. **Shop for the best rates when financing the purchase.** If you decide to borrow money to finance your car purchase, be sure to compare the interest rate the car dealership offers with the rates offered by banks, credit unions, and savings and loan institutions. Interest rates on car loans vary, so shop around for the best rate.

11. **Be extra careful when buying a used car.** A new car loses about 25 percent of its value during the first year. This is partly why used cars are much less expensive than new cars, and, if you get the right one, a much better value. Buying a used car always involves some risk, however. If you are buying the car from a dealer, you probably won't know who the previous owner was or why he sold or traded in the car. Obviously, this is one advantage of buying a used car from the owner—you can ask questions and decide for yourself whether the owner has taken care of the car and is telling you the truth. Here are some additional points to keep in mind when buying a used car:

- Don't buy a used car that's no longer in production. It will be hard to get parts for the car.
- Don't buy a used car without taking it for a test-drive.
- Watch out for used cars that are loaded with options, such as power windows, power seats, and so on. Such things need replacing as a car gets older.
- Find out if the used car you want to buy has been recalled. A manufacturer will recall a car model if it finds out something is wrong with it. The owners of the cars are notified of the recall and asked to bring their cars in to be fixed (at no charge). Almost half of car owners don't respond to recalls, however, so the used car you want to buy might have been recalled but never fixed. To learn about recalls and other safety information, call the Department of Transportation Auto Safety Hotline at 1-888-327-4236 or go online to http://econ.emcp.net/SaferCar.
- Have an auto mechanic inspect a used car you are thinking about buying. This inspection is particularly important, because a $100 to $200 inspection fee may save you hundreds of dollars and endless problems later on. In addition, it may put your mind at ease.
- Look for the Buyer's Guide sticker on the window of the used car. The sticker, which is required by the Federal Trade Commission, gives you important information on the car, such as whether it comes with a warranty and what major problems may occur in any used car.
- Be alert to those things on the car that you can check. For example, are the tires slick, with very little tread? Are there oil spots under the car?

Practicing Your Skills

1. How would you go about calculating your annual expenses?
2. Suppose you deem that your annual expenses are too high. How might you go about trying to decrease those expenses?
3. Suppose you are thinking of buying a new car. How might you go about determining a good price to offer for the car?
4. What is a warranty?

Buying Insurance

Insurance is a guarantee against loss. When you buy insurance from a company, you enter into a contract with it. Your part of the contract says that you will make regular payments (called *premiums*) in exchange for the promise that the company will pay you for a certain kind of loss or damage should it occur. The type of insurance you are buying (car, life, health, personal property) and the amounts of money involved are spelled out in the contract.

Some people buy insurance and then, when they don't use it, say that they spent their money for nothing. The fact is, everyone buys insurance and hopes not to use it. No one buys car insurance hoping to have an accident; no one buys fire insurance hoping that his or her house will catch on fire; and no one buys health insurance hoping to get sick and go to the hospital. The best we can hope for is not to have to use the insurance we buy. But we still buy it because having it usually gives us peace of mind. We buy insurance because we aren't sure what the future holds.

Automobile Insurance

You should be aware, if you are not already, of your state's laws regarding automobile insurance. For example, if your state requires all drivers to have liability insurance, you can be assessed heavy fines and your license can be revoked if you drive without insurance. Know what coverage you must have, and then make the best decisions you can about the other types of coverages. For example, if you purchase an older model used car with lots of miles and some body damage, you might decide that collision coverage isn't something you need.

Types of Coverage The following are brief descriptions of the different types of coverages.

Liability Insurance *Bodily injury* liability insurance pays for losses due to death or injury in a car accident that is the insured driver's fault. It covers people both inside and outside the car. Injured persons can make a claim against this coverage to pay for medical bills, lost wages, and damages due to pain and suffering. *Property damage* liability insurance covers damage done to another person's car, building, fence, and so on.

Medical Payments Insurance Medical payments insurance pays for medical expenses resulting from a car accident, no matter who is at fault. Some people don't purchase medical payments insurance because their health insurance pays for injuries caused by an accident.

Uninsured Motorist Protection Insurance Some people drive their cars without having any automobile insurance. If one of them hits you with his or her car and causes injury or damage, you may not be able to collect any money from the person. To guard against this possibility, you may choose to purchase uninsured motorist coverage. This insurance will cover you if you are in an accident with an uninsured motorist or harmed by a hit-and-run driver.

Collision Insurance Collision insurance pays for the damage to your car if it's in an accident, no matter who is responsible for the accident. Your coverage is limited by the amount of the deductible, which usually ranges from $100 to $250. As always, the higher the deductible, the lower the premium.

Comprehensive Insurance Comprehensive insurance is the companion of collision insurance. While collision insurance covers damage to your car if it's in an accident, comprehensive insurance covers just about everything else that can happen to a car. For example, it covers damage if the car is stolen, is vandalized, or catches fire. As with collision insurance, the coverage is limited by the deductible.

Factors Determining Premiums An automobile insurance policy is a package of several types of coverage, each with its own premium. The sum of these premiums is what you pay for the policy. The following are some of the factors that determine how much you will pay.

- **Your Age** In most but not all states, a person's age affects his or her automobile insurance premium. Statistics show that drivers under the age of 25 have a higher accident rate than drivers between the ages of 25 and 35. For this reason, their premiums are higher. In many cases, your premiums will be lower if you are listed on your parents' or gurardians' policy.

- **Where You Live** If you live in a densely populated area, where vandalism and car theft are common, you will pay a higher premium than if you live in a sparsely populated area, where these crimes are relatively uncommon.

- **Your Driving Record** If you have a history of car accidents and speeding tickets, your premium will likely be higher than if you don't have such a history. This is why it's important for you to drive carefully and avoid accidents.

- **The Car You Drive** If you drive a new, expensive car that is difficult and costly to repair, you will pay a higher premium than if you drive an older car that is easy and inexpensive to repair.

- **How Much You Drive** If you drive only a few miles a week, you are likely to pay a lower premium than a person who drives many miles a week.

- **Whether or Not You Have Had a Driver Education Course** Many insurance companies will give you a discount on your premium if you have taken a driver education course. The discount is usually 5 to 10 percent.

- **Whether or Not You Have Air Bags in Your Car** Some insurance companies will give you a discount on the medical insurance part of your automobile insurance coverage if you have air bags in your car.

- **Whether or Not You Have Antitheft Devices in Your Car** Many insurance companies will discount the comprehensive part of your automobile insurance coverage if you have installed antitheft devices in your car.

What to Do in an Automobile Accident Here are the steps to take if you have a car accident.

1. **Check to see if anyone is injured.** Next, call the police. When you call the police, state where the accident occurred (the nearest cross streets). If someone has been injured, ask that an ambulance or rescue squad be sent immediately.

2. **Do not move injured persons.** If you move injured persons, you could harm them. Cover an injured person with a blanket or coat if one is handy.

3. **When police officers arrive, cooperate fully.** Be sure to answer police officers' questions honestly, but state only what you know to be the facts. It's natural to be shaken up after an accident, and some people in this condition quickly conclude that they must have been at fault. Remember to stay calm and state only the facts, rather than guesses, assumptions, or beliefs.

4. Ask a police officer where you can obtain a copy of the police report. You may need a copy of the police report for insurance purposes or for a court case. Ask a police officer on the scene where you should go to obtain the report.

5. Make sure you obtain the following information: the names and addresses of all drivers and passengers in the accident; the license plate numbers, makes, and models of the cars involved; other drivers' license identification numbers; insurance identification numbers; the names, addresses, and telephone numbers of any witnesses to the accident; and the names of the police officers at the scene. This information may come in handy later, and your insurance agent may ask for it. Get into the habit of carrying a pencil or pen and paper in the glove compartment of your car so that you are always ready to write down the information you may need.

6. If possible, take pictures of the accident scene. Use a camera or phone to photograph the damage done to the cars; skid marks, if there are any; and so on. If you can't take photos, then make a sketch of the accident. You may need it later to refresh your memory.

7. If you run into an unattended car, leave your name and telephone number on the windshield so that the owner can get in touch with you. This response is simply the right thing to do.

8. Get in touch with your insurance company as soon as possible. Make sure you tell your insurance agent exactly what happened, and let the agent advise you as to what to do next. The insurance company will probably want to have an insurance adjuster inspect your car before you get it repaired. It's a good idea to keep the name and telephone number of your insurance agent in the glove compartment of your car. That way, if you are out of town and have an accident, you can easily and quickly get in touch.

9. Keep a record of your expenses. Make sure to keep a record of all the expenses you incur as a result of an accident. This list might include lost wages, the cost of a rental car, and so on.

10. Keep copies of all your paperwork. There is a good chance that you will have to refer to certain papers later.

These are general guidelines. It's also important to know the laws of your state in dealing with motor vehicle accidents.

Health Insurance

Medical costs for major illnesses and injuries are often far beyond what the average family can pay. That's why most people feel the need to have health insurance. Because the premiums for health insurance are high, you, as a young adult, will want to be covered by your parents' or guardians' policy for as long as possible. Many employers provide health insurance and pay a large portion of their employees' premiums, so you will want to find a job that includes these benefits if at all possible.

If and when you need to purchase your own health insurance, you may want to explore local HMOs (Health Maintenance Organizations). These organizations offer members comprehensive medical care for a monthly or yearly fee. In exchange for the regular fee, members receive medical care from a selected group of doctors and hospitals. While many people prefer flexibility in choosing their medical providers, an HMO is usually one of the more economical options for health insurance.

Life Insurance

At some point, you will probably want to consider buying life insurance. Many people first consider purchasing life insurance when they begin a family. Life insurance guarantees payment to a specified person (the *beneficiary*) if the policyholder dies or reaches a certain age. People buy this type of insurance to financially protect loved ones in case of an unexpected, untimely death. There are two major types of life insurance:

Term Life Insurance   With term life insurance, you pay premiums to the insurance company, and in turn, the beneficiaries you name are paid a certain sum of money if you die during a specific period. When the specific period ends, your coverage ends, and you receive no payments from the insurance company. When you buy term insurance, you are buying nothing but life insurance for the *term* of the policy. For this reason, term insurance is considerably cheaper than whole life insurance.

Whole Life Insurance   As the name implies, whole life insurance covers a person for his or her whole life, until death. One important feature of whole life insurance is its cash value: the amount of money policyholders will receive if they decide to redeem, or cash in, their policy. Some people see the cash value that's accumulated in a whole life policy as a form of savings to be drawn on (borrowed) in later years. When a policyholder makes a withdrawal from the cash value in an insurance account, however, he or she gives up insurance protection. Because of the cash values involved, whole life insurance is more expensive than term insurance.

Practicing Your Skills

1. What is the difference between automobile collision insurance and comprehensive insurance?
2. What are some of the factors that can determine how much your premiums are for automobile insurance?
3. You are in a car accident, and while you are not hurt, the person driving the other car is. What should you do?
4. Why is it important to have health insurance?

Career Planning

If you haven't yet decided what you are going to do after you graduate from high school, the following information might be of assistance. Looking ahead, thinking about your future, and making some plans, even if you change them later, will increase your chances of leading a happy, fulfilling life.

Education

As you already know from reading this text, education and income are closely related, and education is becoming increasingly important in the era of globalization. You may want to review some of the features in the text that discuss the importance of education:

Investing in Yourself (page 138)
Education—It's Like Multiplying Yourself (page 258)
Your Goal: Generic, Not Specific, Human Capital (page 372)

Matching Your Abilities, Educational Interests, and Job

Ideally, we all would like to work at a job that is interesting, that we are able to do, and that pays relatively well. Protecting your future requires you to be aware of many things. When it comes to getting a job, you must consider what you are good at doing, what you are interested in, and what pays an income you will be comfortable with. Talk to your school counselor about taking some interest and aptitude inventories to find out more about yourself.

How do you know if what you are interested in will be in demand and pay well when it's time for you to go job hunting? The U.S. Department of Labor makes predictions about the outlook for jobs and earnings. Two useful sources of information about jobs are the *Occupational Outlook Handbook* and *Occupational Projections Data* (both available on the Bureau of Labor Statistics website: http://econ.emcp.net/BLS). Additional information can be obtained from state job service centers, which can be found online or in the telephone book in the state government section.

Getting a Job

There's a good chance you have applied and been hired for part-time jobs while you have been in high school. So, you know something about finding and getting a job. As you look for full-time work, whether it be after high school or after college, the process will become more competitive and more important. Here are some tips to help you increase the chances of getting the job you want.

Application Forms When you apply for a job, you will have to fill out an application form. It's important that you do a good job filling out the form, since often there are more applicants than open positions, and the applications are used to decide who will be hired. It's not just the information you provide but also the neatness and accuracy (including spelling and grammar) of the form that impacts the employer's decision about hiring. Following are some things to consider when filling out an application form:

1. **Photocopy the form, if you can, before you start to fill it out.** Most people make mistakes when filling out application forms. A neat, clean application is what you want. If you can, fill out a photocopy of the application first, check it for mistakes, rewrite it where necessary, and then use it as a guide to fill out the actual application form that you will submit to the employer.

2. **Be prepared.** Come to an interview prepared to fill in an application form when you visit an employer's premises. Suppose you visit a local company and ask if there are job openings. The personnel manager says yes and hands you an application form to fill out immediately. You need to be prepared with some information about yourself. For example, you may need (1) the names, addresses, and telephone numbers of former employers; (2) your social security number; and (3) previous home addresses. Keep this information with you when you visit prospective employers.

3. **Don't leave anything blank.** If something doesn't apply to you, simply write "n/a," which stands for "not applicable." If you leave some lines of an application form blank, the person reading the form won't know if you missed something.

The Résumé A résumé is a document you create that contains the following information: (1) your name, address, and telephone number; (2) the job you are seeking or your career goal; (3) your education; (4) your work experience; (5) honors you have received; and (6) any other information relevant to your ability to do the job you are seeking. A résumé should be well organized, easy to read, and no longer than two pages. Exhibit PF-2 on the next page shows a standard way to organize a résumé.

The Interview The job interview is your best opportunity to present yourself in a favorable light to an employer. Keep in mind that you represent a risk to the employer, who doesn't know what type of employee you will be. Will you be consistently late to work or on time? Will you be a good worker or not? Will you get along with others? To be equipped for an interview, keep these things in mind:

1. **Learn something about the company before the interview.** You will want to know information such as what the company produces, how long it has been in business, and

Alison Brandon
1976 Jackson Drive
San Marcos, CA 92069

(760) 555-7777

Job sought: Manager trainee at Vernon Building Supplies Company

Skills, education, and experience

Working with people: Both in high school and in my jobs, I have worked well with people. As treasurer of the senior class and as vice president of the junior class, I worked on school projects that required me to argue my positions convincingly, listen to the arguments advanced by others, and find suitable compromise positions. I realize that I cannot always get my way, but I continue to state what I believe, accept that people may disagree with me, and move on to see if we can work together.

In my work experience I have enjoyed dealing with the public. I have learned to be patient, listen attentively, and recognize that if people get "hot under the collar," I should try to work things out in a cordial way.

Effective communication: In high school, I played a leadership role in my junior and senior classes. I learned that a part of good leadership is being able to communicate your views and opinions to others in a cordial way. I have developed this skill, which I believe will help me throughout my life.

Hard work and attention to detail: In my school courses, activities, and jobs, I have learned the need to work hard and attentively. I have learned that it is better to do something right the first time than have to re-do it.

Chronology

September 2014–2018	Attended Clarksville High School in San Marcos, California. I was treasurer of the senior class and vice president of the junior class, played on the tennis team for 3 years, worked as a member of the yearbook staff for 1 year, helped to raise $10,000 for the school library, and was on the honor roll for 5 semesters.
March 2015 to present	I worked as a salesperson in the women's clothing department at Dixon's Department Store in Carlsbad, California.
May 2015 to August 2015	I was camp counselor at Fire Valley Girls' Summer Camp in Fire Valley, California. I was voted "Best Counselor for Summer 2015."

Recommendations available upon request.

how many employees it has. You want to be able to give a knowledgeable answer if an interviewer asks, "Do you know what we do at our company?" You can usually obtain general information about a company at the local library, at the company's website, or from persons who work for the company. You can also call the company before the interview and ask a few questions.

2. **Rehearse the interview.** One of the best ways to prepare for an interview is to rehearse with a friend or two. Let your friend be the interviewer and you be the interviewee. Before you start the rehearsal, write down a list of questions the real interviewer is likely to ask you. Here is a possible list:

- Why did you apply for this job?
- What do you know about this job or company?
- Why should I hire you?
- What are your strengths and weaknesses?

- What would you like to tell me about yourself?
- What accomplishment has given you the greatest satisfaction?
- What courses did you like best in school?
- What courses did you like least in school?
- Why did you leave your last job?
- What do you hope to be doing in three to five years?
- What are your hobbies?
- What would you change about yourself?
- How do your education and work experience relate to this job?
- What salary do you expect?

3. **Arrive for the interview on time.** Arriving early or late makes a bad impression. When you arrive early, you may interrupt the person who will interview you. When you arrive late, you signal that you are not dependable.

4. **Mention your strengths and achievements without bragging about them.** Sometime during the interview, tell the interviewer why you think you would be a good person to hire. The interviewer may give you this chance by simply asking, "Why do you think you are right for this job?" You have to be careful, however. It's one thing to state the truth and tell someone that you would be a good person to hire; it's another thing to brag. No one wants to hire a bragger, but almost everyone wants to hire people who are confident about themselves and know how to tell others of their strengths in a positive, polite manner.

5. **Ask questions when you have a chance.** At the end of the interview, the interviewer will often ask if you have any questions. Here are some suggestions:

- What would a day on this job be like?
- To whom would I report?
- Would I supervise anyone?
- Why did the last person leave this job?
- What is that person doing now?
- What is the greatest challenge of this job?
- Is this company growing?

6. **Listen carefully.** Many people get nervous in interviews. They wonder if they look right, if they are smiling enough, if they should not have said what they just said, or if the interviewer likes them. Feeling nervous is natural, but try your best to put such concerns aside and listen to what the interviewer is saying and asking. If you don't listen carefully—and if you don't respond directly and specifically—the interviewer may get the feeling that your mind is somewhere else and that perhaps you really don't want the job.

7. **Write a thank-you letter.** Soon after the interview, send a letter to the interviewer expressing your appreciation for the interview. If you need to follow up on something you said during the interview, do it in this letter.

Practicing Your Skills

1. Why is it important to rehearse before a job interview?
2. Identify a job that you might be interested in obtaining. Next, what do you think would be good answers to the following questions:
   a. Why did you apply for this job?
   b. What are your strengths and weaknesses?
   c. What would you like to tell me about yourself?
   d. What do you hope to be doing in three to five years?
3. What might your arriving late to a job interview signal to your prospective employer?

Consumer Rights and Responsibilities

As a consumer, you have some rights and responsibilities. Here are some of the most fundamental rights and responsibilities.

Consumer Rights

In general, as a consumer, you have four basic rights: the right to be informed, the right to be safe, the right to choose, and the right to be heard.

The Right to Be Informed You have the right to the information you need to make a good consumer decision.

The Right to Be Safe You have the right to a safe product—one that will not harm your health or threaten your life.

The Right to Choose A consumer has the right to choose from among a variety of products offered at competitive prices. Choice isn't usually present if competition is prohibited, so firms can't legally band together to prevent consumers from paying a lower price for a good.

The Right to Be Heard Consumers with complaints have the right to be heard. They can bring their complaints to various government and private agencies that deal with consumer affairs, or they can go to small-claims court.

Consumer Responsibilities

Just as you have rights as a consumer, you also have responsibilities.

The Responsibility to Obtain Information Yourself If you are going to buy a car, a pair of shoes, or anything else, you have to ask questions to get the information you need. You can't simply wait for the seller to tell you everything there is to know about the subject. Also, when you are planning to make a purchase, especially a large one, it's your responsibility to call the Better Business Bureau and ask whether it has received any complaints about the seller from whom you are planning to buy.

The Responsibility to Learn How to Assemble or Use the Products You Buy Some consumer goods come with instructions. In particular, most items that can be used incorrectly come with instructions telling you what to watch out for, how to use the product safely, and so on. Read the instructions carefully, and learn how to assemble or use the product.

The Responsibility to Make Fair Complaints and to Be Honest Consumers feel they have a right to expect honesty from sellers. In turn, sellers feel they have a right to expect honesty from consumers. When making a consumer complaint, you have a responsibility to provide the seller, or any government agency or court that gets involved, with the whole truth as you know it. This consumer responsibility should not be taken lightly.

The Responsibility to Act Courteously A consumer has the responsibility to be courteous. You have probably seen people in restaurants who treat servers rudely, order them about, and complain when their every request isn't instantly fulfilled. Remember that a seller is simply there to sell you a product, not to be put down, to be argued with unnecessarily, or to do your full bidding.

The Responsibility to Seek Action Through Government Organizations If you have a complaint that you can't settle with the seller, you have a responsibility to report this fact to the appropriate government agency. Don't hesitate to report a seller to a government agency if you feel that you have been wronged. Remember, as a consumer, you have the right to voice your complaints, and you also have a responsibility to exercise that right.

1. When it comes to product safety, a consumer has both rights and responsibilities. What are they?
2. Identify two rights and three responsibilities that you have as a consumer.

Paying for College

If you plan to attend college but don't have the resources to pay for it, you may want to apply for financial aid. Following are brief descriptions of some of the best sources of aid and some tips on how to get more information.

Grants, Loans, and Work-Study Programs

The U.S. Department of Education offers the following major student financial aid programs. These six programs fall into three categories: grants, loans, and work-study programs. A grant is financial aid that you do not have to pay back. A loan is borrowed money that you must pay back with interest. A work-study program gives you the chance to work and earn money to help you pay for your college education.

If you need more information on the different kinds of grants, loans, and work-study programs than is given in this section, you can go to the U.S. Department of Education site on the World Wide Web (http://econ.emcp.net/financialaid). Once there, click on "Student Financial Aid" and then "Funding."

Pell Grants A Pell Grant is an award to help first-time undergraduates pay for their education after high school. To obtain a Pell Grant, a person must show financial need and must be attending school at least half time, which for most colleges means being registered for at least six semester hours. Applications for Pell Grants can be obtained from financial aid offices of colleges and universities and sometimes from high school guidance counselors' offices. The amount of a Pell Grant award depends on the degree of financial need and the cost of the school.

Federal Supplemental Educational Opportunity Grants A Federal Supplemental Educational Opportunity Grant (FSEOG) is an award to help first-time undergraduates with exceptional financial need, as determined by the school. Like a Pell Grant, an FSEOG does not have to be paid back.

Federal Work-Study The Federal Work-Study (FWS) program provides jobs for first-time undergraduates; it lets students earn money to help pay for their education. The student's job may be on or off campus, and the student receives at least the federal minimum wage. A student's work schedule and number of hours worked are determined by the school, not the student.

Federal Perkins Loans Federal Perkins Loans are low-interest loans for first-time undergraduates with exceptional financial need, as determined by the school. The student can borrow up to $4,000 per year for each year of undergraduate study. The student must repay this loan but may be allowed up to 10 years to do so.

Stafford Loans Stafford Loans are low-interest loans to students attending school at least half-time. These loans must be repaid.

PLUS Loans PLUS Loans (Parent Loans for Undergraduate Students) are for parents who want to borrow to help pay for their children's education. These loans must be repaid.

Practicing Your Skills

1. What is a major difference between a Pell grant and a Stafford loan?
2. What is Federal Work-Study?

Getting Needed Information

The federal government has a toll-free number to call with questions about financial aid (1-800-433-3243), and information is also available at the Federal Student Aid website (http://econ.emcp.net/StudentAid). Use one of these resources to inquire about the default rate of the college you are thinking about attending (the percentage of loans that are not repaid), because there may be restrictions on borrowing money to attend a college with a default rate of 30 percent or more. Other places to obtain information on financial aid are the financial aid office of the college you want to attend, the guidance counselor's office at your high school, and the Internet.

Renting an Apartment

Many young adults rent apartments. Here are some factors to consider if you are thinking of renting an apartment in the near future.

Location Most people consider it important to rent an apartment near their workplaces or schools. Being in a convenient location cuts down on transportation costs.

Neighbors Find out about the people who will be your close neighbors before you move into an apartment. Simply asking the apartment manager to tell you about your neighbors may yield information. If quiet is particularly important to you, tell the apartment manager; he or she may rent you an apartment among some of the quieter tenants.

Safety Features Before you rent an apartment, make sure the apartment complex has fire escapes, smoke detectors, and safe stairs. Also important are such safety features as good lighting outside, good locks on the doors and windows, and no large shrubbery near windows where people can hide.

Crime in the Area You may want to know the amount and nature of crime in the area where an apartment is located. The local police department will usually provide this information.

Common Areas Most apartment complexes have common areas—areas that are shared by the tenants, such as a common TV area, recreational facilities, and meeting rooms. Check the condition of common areas. You may not want to live in an apartment complex where these areas aren't kept in good repair.

Lease A lease is a contract that specifies the terms under which property is rented. The lease sets the rent for a period of time. The apartment owner or manager will ask you to sign a lease. Read it carefully—every word. Leases often contain formal language that you might find difficult to understand if you have not read many leases before. If you don't understand the terms of the lease, ask the apartment owner or manager to carefully explain them to you. If you don't believe that the apartment manager will correctly explain the lease, seek out a friend, relative, or attorney. Before you sign, be sure you know the conditions under which you can sublease the apartment and the conditions for renewing and ending the lease.

Condition of the Apartment Before you accept an apartment and begin paying rent, carefully inspect the premises with the owner or manager. If things need to be fixed (such as a shower rod or stove), urge the owner or manager to fix them promptly, and ask the manager to state in the lease that the repair will be made by a specified date. It's also a good idea to take a few photos of the inside of the apartment before you move in (as well as after you move out). The photos can be important if, after you move out, you and the apartment owner or manager disagree on the condition of the apartment when you moved in or out. Without photos, you may find that you get back less of your security deposit than you think you should.

Shopping for Food and Clothes

When you are first out on your own, much of your shopping will be for food and clothing. So, here is some basic information and a few tips to help you get the most for your money.

Food

Food buying involves many decisions and strategies. Let's look at where you can buy and the differences between those stores, as well as some tips for buying food.

Where to Shop People buy food from three principal types of stores: supermarkets, discount warehouse food stores, and convenience stores. There are some basic differences that you should be aware of.

Supermarket Supermarkets within the same area often differ in the prices they charge for specific items. A loaf of brand X bread may be $1.25 at one supermarket and $1.55 at the supermarket down the road. Make a list of the food items you buy on a regular basis and check the prices at different supermarkets to find out which gives you the lowest weekly total for the same quality of service and convenience.

Discount Warehouse Food Store Discount warehouse food stores don't usually carry as large a variety of foods as supermarkets, but they do sell most items for less. Also, they tend to sell things in large quantities. For example, a 1-pound jar of mayonnaise at a supermarket will have a higher price per pound than a 5-pound jar of mayonnaise at a discount warehouse food store. Of course, the 5-pound jar may not be your best buy if you normally use only a small amount of mayonnaise.

Convenience Store Most convenience stores, such as 7-Eleven stores, are open 24 hours a day. They charge more than supermarkets and don't carry as large a selection. But for some people, what they lack in selection and price, they make up for in convenience. Do you need to pick up a few food items in a hurry? The nearest convenience store could be your best bet. Just keep in mind that you will be paying more than you would in a supermarket for most items.

What to Consider While Shopping If you are like most people, you will do most of your grocery shopping at the supermarket. You should think about a number of things while you shop at the supermarket.

Have a list. Going food shopping without a written list of things to buy often leads to impulse buying (buying things you didn't plan to buy). Writing out a list takes time and thought, but using it can cut down on impulse buying and thus help you get some control over your food budget. A list can also help if you are trying to cut down on buying junk food, which you are more likely to buy when you don't make and follow a list.

Don't shop hungry. It's also a good idea to do your food shopping on a full stomach. If you are hungry, many foods will look good to you, and you may end up buying more than you should.

Know unit prices. To get the most for your money, compare unit prices, which show prices per unit of measurement (such as ounces and pounds). Suppose your supermarket offers two sizes of the same laundry detergent, one small (40 ounces) and the other large (120 ounces). The small one is priced at $1.97, and the large one at $5.45. To compute the unit price—the price per ounce, in this case—you need to divide the price of each item by its volume (number of ounces).

In this case, the small size costs 4.9 cents per ounce, while the large size costs 4.5 cents per ounce. Many supermarkets provide the unit price along with the total price for a product. If your supermarket does not, you may want to carry a calculator to compute unit prices.

Use coupons. Food coupons often appear in newspapers, magazines, and shopping circulars and on product and shopper websites. Using them can lower your grocery bill. Keep in mind, though, that a time cost is involved in clipping or finding coupons and gathering them before your shopping trip. You have to decide whether having a lower grocery bill is worth spending this time.

Try the private and generic brands. Products in food stores may carry national brand names, private brand names, or generic brand names. A national brand is a brand name owned by the maker of a product, such as Kellogg's and Coca-Cola. A private brand is a brand name often produced for a specific supermarket chain and includes the name of that chain. A generic brand is simply a brand name that identifies the product (for example, "Corn Flakes"). National brands are more expensive than private brands, and private brands are more expensive than generic brands.

Review your selections before checking out. It's a good idea to quickly look over the food selections in your cart before you enter the checkout line. Nutritionists say that to maintain a good diet, you should regularly eat lots of grains, fruits, and vegetables. If you find that most of the items in your grocery cart are prepared foods and snacks, you may decide to exchange the potato chips for fresh fruit and the ice cream for yogurt.

Clothes

This section discusses some of the things you should keep in mind when you buy clothes.

Be aware of trade-offs. When you buy clothes, be aware of dollar price and durability. Durability refers to how long the clothing item will remain in good condition. Usually, the higher the quality, the more durable an item is and the higher its price. A low price doesn't necessarily mean a better buy. But you aren't getting more for your money if you buy the cheaper, less durable item and then have to replace it in the near future. In short, consider the trade-offs in price versus quality.

Pick your spots to shop. We can buy clothes in a variety of places that differ in terms of selection, price, quality, and service. For example, consider both the upscale department store and the manufacturer's outlet. In the upscale department store, you will likely find high-quality clothing items at relatively high prices and receive good to excellent service. At the manufacturer's outlet, you will find many items of the same quality at lower prices and get little service. You have to be aware of the price you pay for the service and decide whether it's worth this price.

Comparison shop but not too long. An economist would never advise you to shop for clothes for as long as it takes to find exactly what you want at the lowest possible price. Some comparison shopping is good, but too much can be costly in terms of the time you spend and what else you could be doing.

Practicing Your Skills

1. What are some of the safety features you should consider when renting an apartment?
2. Why is it important to take photos of an apartment (inside and out) when you move in.
3. There are two sizes of product X. One is 40 ounces and the other is 15 ounces. The 40 ounce-sized product is $4 and the 15 ounce-sized is $2. What is the unit price of each?

Taking Out a Mortgage

Suppose it's 10 years into the future, and you are ready to buy your first house. Congratulations! Unless you just won the lottery or are sitting on a large inheritance, you probably need a mortgage. Here's how a mortgage works:

- The *lender* loans money up front to buy a house (or condominium or other piece of real estate).
- The *borrower* (that's you) signs a legal agreement to pay back the loan, plus interest, over a term of years.
- If the borrower doesn't make the payments, the lender can *foreclose* (take the real estate and sell it to pay off the loan).

The legal agreement between the lender and borrower is the *mortgage*. The amount of the loan is the *principal*. The house (or other real estate) is the *security* or *collateral* for the mortgage.

Where to Go for a Mortgage

If your mom is a rock star with a gigantic bank account, she can lend you the money and hold the mortgage on your house. If not, you will need to look for a mortgage lender.

Banks or Savings and Loans Your bank or savings and loan is a good place to start looking for a mortgage. As you learned on pages 299–303, banks are interested in making loans because they use loans to generate money. To ensure the loans they make are profitable for the lenders, these institutions look for borrowers who are likely to pay their mortgages on time. If you have had a checking or savings account, a car loan, or a credit card, your bank has some record of who you are and how reliable you are.

Many banks sell their loans. If your bank decides to do that, your mortgage amount and monthly payment will stay the same, but you will make your payments to a different place. Do you care whether your lender sells your loan? Maybe not. But if you get sick or are laid off from work, you might need to renegotiate your mortgage. It might be easier to renegotiate with a lender in your community than with some giant finance company halfway across the country.

Why do banks sell their loans? Sometimes, they need the money for other investments. For example, say that the Middletown Bank has $1 million in mortgages. Over the next 30 years, those mortgages will pay nearly another $1 million in interest to the bank. But Middletown Bank wants to get cash now to invest in a new shopping center, so it sells the mortgages to Giant Investment Firm (GIF). GIF pays the bank $1.05 million—the cost of the mortgages plus $50,000. Now Middletown has cash to invest, and GIF will earn the interest on the mortgages over the next 30 years.

Sounds simple, right? Actually, this is where things start to get complicated. GIF decides that it wants cash to invest in other enterprises, so it puts together a package of mortgages from all over the country with a value of $10 billion. Then GIF sells shares in this package to other investors. This is called a *mortgage backed security (MBS)*, and it's one kind of derivative investment.

Now things get even more complicated. The other investment firms decide they want to make cash too. They slice and dice a lot of different mortgage packages, selling some parts of them as collateralized debt obligations (CDOs) and others as credit default swaps (CDSs). These complicated derivative investments are largely unregulated and not backed by insurance. Also, all the slicing and dicing makes it impossible for investors to claim any right to the real estate that secured the original mortgages. These very risky investments were a big part of the real estate, financial, and economic crisis that began in 2007.

Credit Unions Credit unions will sometimes offer better interest rates than banks or savings and loans, and they are more likely to keep your mortgage and service it throughout the life of the loan. Unlike banks, credit unions are member owned. You have to be a member of the credit union to borrow money there. People qualify for a credit union membership through their employer, an affiliation with an organization such as a church or social group, or a community-chartered credit union. Becoming a member is usually as simple as opening a checking or savings account.

Mortgage Lending Companies and Brokers Mortgage lending companies and brokers are available all over the country and all over the Internet. Some mortgage companies make loans themselves, while others act as mortgage brokers. A broker places the loan with a bank and gets its income by charging fees to you or the bank. Brokers claim that they can get you a lower interest rate or save you the trouble of finding a bank. A mortgage broker may be able to find you a loan if you have a tough time finding one on your own, perhaps because you have a less than perfect credit history.

Some mortgage brokers are good, legitimate businesses, and some are unreliable or predatory. (*Predatory lenders* take unfair advantage of borrowers who lack either information or good credit.) If you decide to work with a mortgage lending company or broker, find out all you can about its business practices.

What About VA and FHA Loans?

The Veterans Administration (VA) and the Federal Housing Administration (FHA) are government agencies that help individuals obtain mortgages. The VA and FHA don't actually make mortgage loans, but they can help you get a mortgage through their mortgage guaranty programs. A guaranteed VA or FHA loan is made by a regular lender. The VA or FHA protects the lender by paying off the mortgage if you fail to do so.

You may be able to get a better rate or lower down payment if you qualify for an FHA or VA loan. For more information about VA loans, see http://econ.emcp.net/VeteransUnitedLoans. For more information about FHA loans, see http://econ.emcp.net/FHAmortgage.

What's in a Mortgage?

When you are looking for a mortgage, you should balance these four numbers:

- *Mortgage principal amount:* the total amount borrowed
- *Down payment:* the amount paid in cash at the time of purchase
- *Interest rate:* the percent of interest paid on the mortgage
- *Term:* the number of years to pay off the mortgage

Changing any of these numbers will change the amount that you pay, both in your monthly payment and in the total you pay over the life of the mortgage. For example, if you are buying a $200,000 home and your down payment is $30,000, then the mortgage principal will be $170,000.

Down Payment The down payment is typically 10 percent to 30 percent of the purchase price. Making a larger down payment will save money over the long term. Let's look at three down payment amounts on a $200,000 home, with the same 5 percent mortgage interest rate over a 30-year term:

- If you put down 10 percent, or $20,000, you will pay $167,860.80 in interest over the life of the mortgage.
- If you put down 15 percent, or $30,000, you will pay $158,536 in interest over the life of the mortgage.
- If you put down 20 percent, or $40,000, you will pay $149,207.60 in interest over the life of the mortgage.

Interest Rate The interest rate is the percentage of the mortgage that's charged for servicing the loan. The interest rate will vary depending on market conditions, your creditworthiness, and whether you qualify for a government loan guaranty program.

Your interest rate will make a huge difference in the amount you pay each month and over the life of the loan. Consider the difference between paying 5 percent and 7 percent interest on a mortgage of $170,000 to be repaid over 30 years:

- At 5 percent interest, your monthly payment is $912.60. Over the life of the mortgage, you will pay $328,536 in principal and interest.
- At 7 percent interest, your monthly payment is $1,113.31. Over the life of the mortgage, you will pay $400,791.60 in principal and interest.

In other words, a 2 percent increase in the interest rate will cost you more than $200 each month and more than $72,000 over the life of the mortgage.

Term The term of the mortgage is the number of years you have to repay the loan. Having a shorter repayment term will mean a higher monthly payment but less total interest paid. Let's go back to your $200,000 home with a $170,000 mortgage at 5 percent interest:

- At a term of 20 years, your monthly payment is $1,121.92. Over the life of the mortgage, you will pay $269,260.80.
- At a term of 30 years, your monthly payment is $912.60. Over the life of the mortgage, you will pay $328,536.

Other Fees and Charges

In addition to the mortgage and down payment, you will pay some other fees and charges:

- Points, or loan origination fees, are paid to the bank at the time of closing. (*Closing* means the actual signing of papers to transfer ownership of the home.) Points are usually a percentage of the loan, and they can be substantial. For example, one point on a $170,000 loan means $1,700. Points increase the amount of the money the bank makes up front and generally reduce the interest rate charged on the mortgage. For example, one point paid up front might reduce the interest rate by 0.25 percent—say, from 6 percent to 5.75 percent.
- Processing fees paid to the lender cover the cost of putting together the necessary paperwork. These fees may amount to hundreds of dollars.
- Fees for appraisals, title searches, housing inspections, and credit reports may also be charged.
- Life insurance or mortgage insurance is sometimes one of the extra costs. This insurance protects the lender, not you, although you pay for it. The lender might require mortgage insurance if you make a very small down payment.
- Property taxes and home insurance are usually paid as part of your monthly mortgage payment. Sometimes, this charge is called *PITI*, which stands for *principal, interest, taxes,* and *insurance.* You should check to see if the amount quoted by the lender for your monthly payment includes PITI. If it doesn't, look into the lender and the mortgage terms you are being offered.

Ask for an estimate of additional fees before agreeing to the mortgage. Compare the fees charged by one lender with those charged by others, and include these costs when comparing mortgages. The differences in fees charged by different lenders can be large. If a lender's fees are high, that's a warning sign that you might be dealing with a predatory lender. (See the paragraphs on predatory lending at the end of this section.)

Kinds of Mortgages

Prime and Subprime Mortgages A prime mortgage is a standard, fixed-term mortgage with the best available interest rate. If you have good credit and your income is high enough to make the mortgage payments, you should be eligible for a prime mortgage.

A subprime mortgage has a higher interest rate, larger fees, or other terms that are more favorable for the lender and less favorable for the borrower. Lenders stand to make more money from subprime mortgages. Because they make more money, they can take more risks, lending to people with lower credit ratings or people whose incomes are barely high enough to make the mortgage payment. Subprime mortgages can make it possible for people without great credit to buy homes.

Fixed-Rate Mortgages A standard mortgage has a fixed interest rate over a fixed term of years. The payments are the same each month over the life of the mortgage. Prime mortgages are typically fixed-rate mortgages. A fixed-rate mortgage with a higher than prime interest rate can be a subprime mortgage.

Adjustable-Rate Mortgages (ARMs) An adjustable-rate mortgage begins with a lower interest rate, but the rate increases over time. Sometimes the rate adjusts upward after three or five years, and sometimes it changes more often. An increase in the interest rate means a bigger monthly payment for you—sometimes double or triple your original payment.

For example, a lender might offer a teaser loan with a 2 percent interest rate. If your mortgage is $200,000, that means your monthly payment will be only $739.24. But if the interest rate adjusts upward to 5 percent, your monthly payment will go up to $1,073.64. Five percent is still a relatively low mortgage interest rate, so your payments could go even higher.

Several different types of ARMs are available. An interest-only ARM is a special kind of ARM that allows you to make only interest payments during the first years of the mortgage. A payment-option ARM is another variation that allows you to pay even less than the interest payment on your mortgage for a period of time. The unpaid interest is added to the principal. With a payment-option ARM, the *amount you owe* actually increases each month. Then at some point, your payments go up a lot.

Choosing an ARM can be a good financial decision if your income is rising steadily or if you will be able to sell or refinance easily in a few years. Choosing an ARM can also be dangerous. During the economic crisis that began in 2007, refinancing became difficult. Many people with ARMs lost their homes because they couldn't make the increased payments or refinance.

Graduated Payment Mortgages A graduated payment mortgage starts with a smaller monthly payment to principal and interest. Then the payment increases each year up to a set amount. This type of mortgage is different from an ARM, because the interest rate remains the same—only the payment amount changes. For example, you could have a beginning mortgage payment of $800 per month with an adjustment upward to $1,200 in three years.

Why would you want a graduated payment mortgage? Maybe you are finishing medical school, and you know that your income will go up in a few years. You want to buy a house now, and you need lower payments right now, but you are sure that you can make higher payments in five years.

Balloon Payment Mortgages A balloon payment means that the full amount of the loan comes at the end of a certain number of years. For example, you might pay $800 per month for five years, at which time your mortgage "balloons"—requiring you to pay the entire balance at once.

Perhaps you buy a home for $200,000. You make a $20,000 down payment and take out a mortgage with a 5 percent interest rate and a balloon at the end of five years. For the first five years, you pay $966.28 per month on the mortgage. At the end of five years, you owe $166,257.93. To pay off that remaining balance, you will need to refinance or sell the house.

Why would you want a mortgage with a balloon payment? You might know that you are going to be transferred to another city in two years, so you plan to sell the house before the mortgage balloons. In the meantime, you have lower payments. Or you might only be able to get a mortgage with a balloon payment, because you don't have great credit or you have only one income in the household. You believe that in a few years, your income will increase or your partner will get a job. Your plan is to refinance with a traditional mortgage when the balloon comes due.

Sometimes refinancing is easy. Sometimes it's not—and you end up paying a much higher interest rate or large fees to get a new mortgage. If you can't refinance when the mortgage balloons, you will lose your home to foreclosure.

Refinancing

Refinancing your home means getting a new mortgage that will pay off the old mortgage. Getting a new mortgage with a lower interest rate can save you a lot of money, both in monthly payments and over the term of the mortgage. If interest rates drop, refinancing is a good option for you as a borrower.

A second reason for refinancing is to "cash out" the equity in your home. Maybe you bought your home 15 years ago for $150,000. You still owe $100,000 on the mortgage, but home values have increased in your area and now your home is worth $250,000. You could refinance your home with a new $150,000 mortgage. Here's how it works:

- You owe $100,000 on the original mortgage.
- You borrow $150,000 with a new mortgage.
- You use $100,000 to pay off the original mortgage.
- You now have $50,000 in cash—and a new mortgage debt of $150,000.

Taking cash out of your home equity may sound good, but if home values drop, you may end up owing more than your home is worth. Many people faced this situation when house prices dropped in mid-2006.

Sometimes, predatory lenders or brokers persuade you to refinance repeatedly. This is called *loan flipping* or *churning*. Each time you refinance, you pay additional points, origination fees, and closing costs. Paying these charges means a big profit for lenders but a big cost to you.

Second Mortgage

A second mortgage is just that—a new mortgage that's secured by your home as collateral. A second mortgage is completely separate from a first mortgage and will have its own mortgage principal, down payment, interest rate, term, and additional fees and charges.

Lending institutions typically require that the total amount of money owed on the first and second mortgage not exceed the market value of the home. So if your home is worth $200,000 and you owe $100,000 on your first mortgage, the lender will limit a second mortgage to $100,000. Second mortgages are often used to finance home improvements.

Predatory Lending

Predatory lenders and brokers use a wide array of unethical business practices when dealing with home buyers and home owners. These lenders and brokers may just overcharge you and take your money, or they may trick you into taking out a mortgage that will end up costing you your home. The Department of Housing and Urban Development (HUD) warns that predatory lenders commonly do these things:

- Use false appraisals to sell properties for much more than they are worth.
- Encourage borrowers to lie about their income, expenses, or cash available for a down payment when trying to get a loan.
- Knowingly lend more money than a borrower can afford to repay.
- Charge high interest rates to borrowers based on their race or ethnicity, not their credit history.
- Charge fees for unnecessary or nonexistent products and services.
- Pressure borrowers to accept higher-risk loans, such as balloon loans, interest-only payments, and steep prepayment penalties.

- Target vulnerable borrowers with offers of cash-out refinances when they know these borrowers are in need of cash due to unemployment, illness, or debt.
- "Strip" homeowners' equity from their homes by convincing them to refinance again and again when there is no benefit to the homeowner.
- Use high-pressure sales tactics to sell home improvements and then finance them at high interest rates.

Predatory lenders and brokers also often try to "pack" the mortgage with overpriced single premium–financed credit life, disability, and unemployment insurance. Your best defense against predatory lending is to shop around for a mortgage, asking several lenders for their best offers.

Practicing Your Skills

1. If a 15 percent down payment is required for a mortgage loan, what does this mean?
2. If someone tells you that the term of the mortgage loan is 30 years, what does this mean?
3. What is the difference between a fixed-rate mortgage and an adjustable-rate mortgage?
4. Why might a person want to refinance his or her home?

Verifying Your Credit Report and Your Credit Score

Anwar has finally saved up enough money to buy his first car. He's sure he can cover the down payment, taxes, and fees, plus the first six months of insurance, and he earns enough money to take care of maintenance, repairs, and fuel. The local dealer that has the car Anwar wants to buy is advertising 0 percent loans for qualified buyers. "That's me!" Anwar thinks and asks his dad for a ride to the car lot.

A few hours later, Anwar drives home in his new car—with an 8 percent car loan. What happened? It turns out that he didn't qualify for the 0 percent loan because his credit score was too low. Anwar can't understand why his credit score is so low. He knows he missed a few payments on one credit card, but that was more than a year ago. Otherwise, he has made timely payments on his credit accounts and loans.

How can you avoid an expensive surprise like this? Review your credit report and credit score regularly and correct any errors that you find.

Your Credit Report

Just like you need to be careful in using credit, you need to be careful in ordering a credit report. Federal law requires each of the three nationwide reporting companies—Experian, Equifax, and TransUnion—to give you one free credit report a year. You can order reports from all three companies at the same time and compare them. Or you can order one report from one company every four months to get updates throughout the year.

The best place to order your credit report is from AnnualCreditReport.com at http://econ.emcp.net/CreditReport. Other websites will automatically enroll you in expensive monthly reporting plans. Even at AnnualCreditReport.com, you need to be careful. All three credit-reporting companies deliver their free reports through that site, but first they will try to sell you other products. Read each web page carefully, and click only on the lines that say something like "No, I don't want your other offers. Just give me my free credit report."

Once you get your credit report, read it carefully and compare what it says against your own credit records. You should keep records of all your credit cards, loans, mortgage information, and bank information. These records are important to use in verifying credit information, charges, payments, and tax deductions, in some cases.

Your credit report will tell you about any negative credit information, as well as your current accounts, your payment histories, some personal information, and who else has requested your credit report. Negative credit information includes things such as late payments, bounced checks, and bankruptcies.

If you have made one late payment, that won't ruin your credit rating. Context is important. For example, if you made one late payment two years ago but have made all the other payments on your six credit cards on time, then the single late payment won't likely be a problem. However, if you made two late payments per year on each credit card, that will damage your credit.

Looking at who else has requested your credit report may alert you to possible identity theft. If there are requests from several companies where you have never applied for credit, you may want to investigate further.

If any of the information on the report is wrong, contact the agency directly to request a correction. If you have been a victim of identity theft, also ask the agencies to put a "fraud alert" on your file. This will warn potential lenders to take extra precautions to protect you, but it may also delay your ability to get credit.

Your Credit Score

Your credit report does *not* tell you your credit score. To get your credit score, also called your FICO score, you have to pay for it. *FICO* stands for *Fair Isaac and Company*, a private company that calculates credit scores. This is the company used by all three major credit-reporting bureaus. Each credit bureau reports your FICO score differently, but the differences should be small.

FICO scores range from 300 to 850. The higher the score, the better your credit rating. Having a higher score will get you lower interest rates on loans.

When you order your FICO credit score, you will also get an explanation of some of the factors that go into the scoring process. In addition, you will get advice from FICO on how to improve your score.

Some companies advertise that they can improve your credit score for a fee. The Federal Trade Commission (FTC) warns that these companies can't do anything that you can't do yourself at little or no cost. The FTC and state attorneys general have sued many so-called credit clinics for fraud.

Practicing Your Skills

1. If you order a credit report and something on the report is incorrect, what should you do?
2. What is the range of FICO scores and how does a FICO score of 600 compare with one of 800?

Economic Skills Handbook

Learning and practicing some basic skills will help you better understand economic principles and apply them to real-world situations. Listed below are the skills covered in this handbook.

Illustrating Ideas with Graphs and Charts

A picture is worth a thousand words. It is with this familiar saying in mind that economists construct charts and graphs. With a few lines and some curves, much can be said. Make sure you know how to read and understand the graphs and charts most commonly used in economics. Before learning about specific kinds of graphs and charts, study the following list of general steps:

1. Read the title of the graph or chart to find out what information is being presented.
2. Find the labels for both the vertical and the horizontal axes to make sure you understand the two types of information being discussed.
3. Look for any legends that might be necessary for understanding the graph or chart.
4. Look at the graph or chart as a whole and try to state in your own words what the graph or chart "says."

Pie Charts

A pie chart is a convenient way to represent the parts of something that, added together, equal the whole. Suppose we consider a typical 24-hour weekday for Danny Chen. On a typical weekday, Danny spends 8 hours sleeping, 6 hours in school, 2 hours at football practice, 2 hours doing homework, 1 hour watching TV, and 5 hours doing nothing (hanging out). It is easy to represent the breakdown of a typical weekday for Danny in pie chart form, as in Exhibit ES-1.

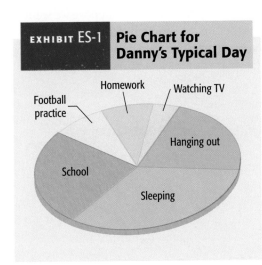

EXHIBIT ES-1 Pie Chart for Danny's Typical Day

Football practice · Homework · Watching TV · Hanging out · School · Sleeping

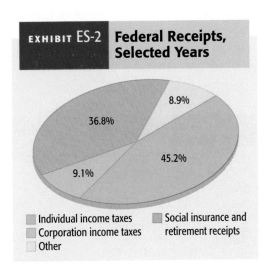

EXHIBIT ES-2 Federal Receipts, Selected Years

36.8% · 8.9% · 9.1% · 45.2%

Individual income taxes · Social insurance and retirement receipts · Corporation income taxes · Other

As you will notice, a pie chart gives you a quick visual message that shows rough percentage breakdowns and relative relationships. For example, in Exhibit ES-1, it's easy to see that Danny spends much of his time sleeping (the "Sleeping" slice of the pie is the largest slice). He spends the same amount of time at football practice as doing his homework and twice as much time doing his homework as watching TV.

Now look at Exhibit ES-2 to see how an economist would use a pie chart to show how the total amount of money collected by the federal government is divided into four major categories.

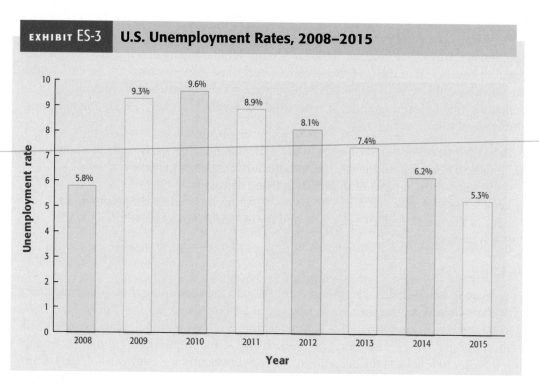

EXHIBIT ES-3 U.S. Unemployment Rates, 2008–2015

Bar Graphs

A bar graph is another graphic that economists use to convey relationships. Suppose we want to represent U.S. unemployment rates over a 10-year period, as shown in Exhibit ES-3. The bar graph helps you see at a glance how the rates fluctuate over this time period. You can also quickly identify the year with the highest rate and the year with the lowest rate.

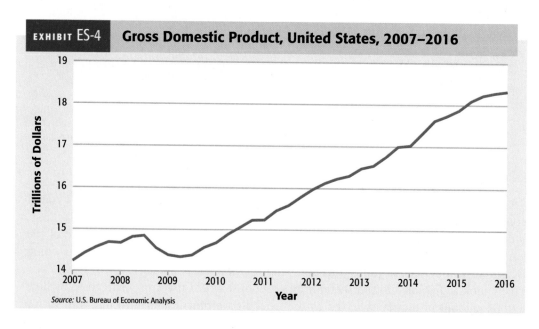

EXHIBIT ES-4 Gross Domestic Product, United States, 2007–2016

Source: U.S. Bureau of Economic Analysis

Line Graphs

Sometimes information is best and most easily displayed in a line graph. Line graphs are particularly useful to illustrate changes in one factor over some time period. Suppose we want to show the changes in real GDP over time. Follow Exhibit ES-4 from left to right. What do you see happening to real GDP? It mainly rises, but then around mid-2008, it begins to fall.

Practicing Your Skills

1. Does Danny spend more time at school or hanging out?
2. Which produces more federal tax revenue: corporate taxes or individual taxes?
3. Was the unemployment rate in the years 2008–2010 trending up or down?
4. In which year(s) during the period 2007–2016 was real GDP the highest?

Thinking the *Ceteris Paribus* Way

To illustrate the law of demand, an economist might say, "As the price of coffee falls, people will buy more coffee." Suppose, however, that at the same time the price of coffee falls, people learn that coffee causes cancer. Someone might say to the economist, "People aren't going to buy more coffee just because its price has fallen if they know that coffee can give them cancer."

Who is right? You might think that the economist is wrong and this person is right. It seems only reasonable to believe that people won't run out and buy more of a cancer-causing product just because it's cheaper than it used to be.

While your thinking here is good, the economist and the law of demand are not wrong. When economists state the law of demand they assume that when price changes, *nothing else changes*. In Latin, the term used to denote that nothing else changes is *ceteris paribus* (pronounced "set eris pair ibus"). All economic laws assume nothing else changes, *ceteris paribus*.

Why would economists want to assume that when the price of coffee falls, nothing else changes? After all, other things change in the real world all the time. So why should we assume things that we know are not true?

Economists do not specify *ceteris paribus* because they want to say something false about the world. They specify it because they want to study what they believe is the real-world relationship between two variables, such as price and quantity demanded.

Suppose you were explaining the law of gravity to someone and you said, "If I drop a ball off the roof of a house, it will fall to the ground." Everyone would accept this as a true statement. But couldn't someone reach out and catch the ball before it hit the ground, thus making your statement false? Of course this could happen. But when you made your statement about the ball hitting the ground, you implied that nothing else would change—that nothing else would interfere with the ball falling. In this case, you were thinking the *ceteris paribus* way.

Practicing Your Skills

A person has been eating one bowl of regular ice cream every day for 20 days. After the twentieth day, the person realizes she has put on 2 pounds. In her attempt to lose weight, she switches to low-fat ice cream. After 20 more days, she has gained 2 more pounds. Does this mean that low-fat ice cream adds as much weight as regular ice cream? Explain your answer, based on your knowledge of how the *ceteris paribus* assumption is used in economics.

Thinking Critically in Economics

There is a right and a wrong way to conduct an economic analysis. To do it the right way, you must avoid certain fallacies, or errors in thinking. The following explanations will help you avoid making some of the more common critical thinking errors.

Cause and Effect

Suppose you are listening to your teacher explain the economic concept of scarcity. You look out the window and notice that it has started to rain. Three minutes later, your teacher says, "All right, that is enough about scarcity. Let's get out pencil and paper and take a pop quiz."

Two events occurred: (1) it started to rain and (2) your teacher announced a pop quiz. The two events occurred close together in time, so we could say that the two events are associated. But did the first event cause the second event? Did the rain cause the quiz? Obviously not—it was just coincidence that they occurred a few minutes apart.

While this seems like a simple idea, it's an example of the kind of mistake many people make regarding cause and effect. The simple fact that two events are associated in some way does not make one event the cause of the other. In short, association is not causation.

The Fallacy of Composition

John is in the football stadium cheering on his team. Suddenly, he stands up so that he can see better. Does it follow that if everybody stood up, everybody could see better? No. The principle we learn from this observation is that what is good for the individual isn't necessarily good for the group. The fallacy of composition is the erroneous view that what is good (or true) for the individual is necessarily good (or true) for the group.

Now suppose that Mary moves to the suburbs because she dislikes the crowds in the city. Does it follow that if everyone moved from the city to the suburbs, everyone would be better off? If your answer is yes, you have committed the fallacy of composition. If Mary moves to the suburbs because she dislikes crowds, she makes herself better off. But if everyone moved to the suburbs, not everyone would be better off, because the suburbs would become as crowded as the cities were.

Fact and Opinion

There is a difference between fact and opinion. A *fact* is something that is objectively true. It is a fact that you are reading this sentence at this moment. There is no room for doubt. An *opinion*, in contrast, is not necessarily objectively true. An opinion expresses a subjective, or personal, judgment, preference, or belief. For example, your friend may say that Thomas Jefferson was the most intelligent U.S. president. You may disagree with your friend's statement. The matter can never be proved, because you are both making subjective evaluations.

Practicing Your Skills

1. Explain what it means to say that "association is not causation."
2. Give an original example that illustrates the fallacy of composition.
3. For each of the following, state whether it is a fact or opinion:
   a. The inflation rate in 1960 was 3.5 percent.
   b. Alan Greenspan was the most successful Federal Reserve chairman ever.
   c. High income tax rates are not good for the country.
   d. During the Clinton administration, the federal deficit declined.

Writing an Economics Paper

Here are some guidelines to help you develop and write an effective economics paper.

Finding a Topic

Before you start to look for a topic, take a moment to think about the purpose of the paper and your intended audience. Is your assignment to report the factual information that you have learned about your topic or to express an opinion and develop an argument that will support your case? Who is going to read your paper? Your choice of topic might be very different if you are writing for the school newspaper than if you are writing for your teacher.

There are a number of ways to find a topic. You might make a list, as you read, of questions you would like answered. Economics topics can be found in print and online versions of news and business magazines (such as *Time, Newsweek, Forbes,* and *Fortune*), newspapers, and encyclopedias. You might even discover an idea in a textbook. For example, you might want to go back to a topic that you found interesting in this text, and as you reread the pages, write down a question after every two or three paragraphs. Here are some questions that might come to mind as you read about business firms:

1. Why do some business firms earn higher profits than others do?
2. What determines where business firms will locate?
3. Do U.S. business firms face much competition from foreign business firms?
4. Do business firms do things differently today than, say, 20 years ago?

Keep in mind that it's important to find questions that you find interesting. You're the one who will be spending the time to research and write the report. If you aren't interested in the topic of your report, what you have to say won't likely be of interest to your readers.

At this stage, you shouldn't be concerned with whether your questions make sense. You should simply write down the questions that come to mind. Ask anything you want. Then, once you have written down a few questions, go back to see if any of them contains a topic to write about. For example, look at question 3 above. This question contains a topic: "U.S. businesses and foreign competition." This phrase, then, could be the title of your economics paper.

Perhaps you have trouble coming up with questions as you read. If so, think about the fact that newspaper reporters often think in terms of the following questions:

- Who?
- What?
- Where?
- When?
- How?
- Why?

You might ask, "What is the world's largest business firm? What does it produce? Where is it located? How did it become so large?"

A common mistake of many students is to choose a topic that is too broad. For example, a student might consider writing about the topic "competition." That is an enormous topic about which many people have written entire books. You couldn't begin to address that topic within the scope of a brief paper, and any attempt would be very frustrating. Try to narrow down the question to one that you can realistically expect to answer.

Doing the Research

Let's assume that you have chosen "U.S. businesses and foreign competition" as your paper topic. The next step is to do your research.

Finding the Information The place to begin your research is on the Internet. First, locate informative websites on your subject and try to identify if the source contains any bias, propaganda, or specific point of view that may influence the information presented there. Be sure to locate a variety of sources so that the information you gather is well-rounded and so you can fact-check claims made by each source.

Another place to do research is the library, and a key person to speak with there is the librarian. You might tell the librarian, "I want to write a paper on U.S. businesses and foreign competition. Here are a few of the questions I would like to answer in my paper. Where would you suggest I begin my research?" Librarians are experts at finding information; they are some of the best investigators around.

Search the library catalog using the subject index. To do this, you need to identify a couple of key words that pertain to the topic—perhaps *foreign competition, U.S. businesses,* and *foreign firms in the U.S.* The librarian might be able to suggest other key words for your search.

Locate the books, and examine them to see if they have information relevant to your topic by checking the index at the back of the book. Look for the same key words you used to search the subject index of the card catalog.

You can also search for information in newspapers and magazines using a database, information in electronic form that can be accessed through a computer. If your library subscribes to a database service on newspapers, type in key words pertaining to your topic and a list of articles will come up that contain information on your subject.

Other excellent sources of information are encyclopedias and dictionaries of economics, such as the *International Encyclopedia of the Social Sciences* and the *Fortune Encyclopedia of Economics,* edited by David R. Henderson.

Taking Notes As you conduct your research, be sure to take clear and detailed notes. Each time you find some information that pertains to the topic, write down a summary of what you have found. Also note where you found your information. Keep detailed bibliographic references, including the name of the source, the author, the publisher, the city of publication, the date of publication, and the page where you found the information. This information will help you when it comes time to write the paper. If you copy passages from any source, be sure to note that they are quotations so you can give proper credit in your paper. If you use someone else's words or ideas, you must let your reader know that you are doing so.

Working Hard Finally, keep in mind that research often requires a lot of tedious work. You might spend hours looking for a source that ends up being of little use to you when writing your paper. Research isn't about finding the source or coming across the person who can give you all the answers. It's about making the best use of all the resources available to you.

Writing and Rewriting

Before you begin writing, spend some time prewriting, or generating and organizing ideas. One way to prewrite is to brainstorm, writing down everything that comes to mind about the topic. Once you have written down as many statements or ideas as you can, look at them to identify links that suggest a theme.

Once you have identified that theme, begin to structure your paper. Structuring your paper involves figuring out the best way to tell your story. One useful way to organize your thoughts is to use index cards. Follow this procedure:

1. Write down each of the main points you want to make in your paper on a separate index card.
2. Organize the cards in the order in which you want to discuss each point.
3. Using your index cards, pretend you are giving an oral report. You may either say the words out loud or silently to yourself. The important point is to "hear" yourself "write" the paper.
4. Consider reordering your main points so your paper is better organized. This is where the use of index cards makes things easy. Now repeat step 3. Continue reordering your main points and orally presenting your paper until you have found the best way to present the information.
5. Using your sequenced index cards as your guide, write the paper. And remember, *writing* requires *thinking* and *preparation*—the free, unconstrained thinking used in prewriting and the focused thinking used in structuring.

If you remember only one thing about writing, let it be this: good writing is the result of rewriting. The process of rewriting begins with reading your paper sentence by sentence. After reading each sentence, ask yourself whether you have clearly communicated what you intended.

After reading each paragraph, try to identify its main message. Then ask yourself if you have communicated that message clearly.

Now go back and rewrite the sentences and paragraphs that need to be rewritten. Try to use as few words as possible to communicate your message. Much of rewriting is getting rid of unnecessary words. Next, go through the paper again, sentence by sentence, correcting any grammatical, punctuation, or spelling errors.

Finally, read the paper from beginning to end without stopping. Then ask yourself whether a person picked at random would find it clear, organized, and interesting. If it fails this test, ask yourself why.

Practicing Your Skills

1. Skim the chapters of this text and find a topic that interests you. Then write three or four questions about that topic that you would like to answer. Remember, free up your mind to ask any question that is interesting to you. Now choose the most interesting question and turn it into a topic for a paper.

2. Go online or visit your school (or city) library and write a list of five sources that seem relevant to your topic. If any of your sources are books, identify the pages you think will be most useful. (Check the index.) Identify the sources that were the most useful.

3. Make notes on your topic using the identified sources. Arrange the notes in a way that tells a story.

4. Write your paper using your notes as a guide. Revise your paper as necessary.

Identifying Economic Trends

A *trend* is a general tendency in a particular direction. To illustrate, suppose Robert is just about ready to graduate from high school. During his four years in high school, his grade point average, or GPA, has looked like this:

Freshman year GPA = 2.45
Sophomore year GPA = 3.33
Junior year GPA = 3.45
Senior year GPA = 3.89

Robert's GPA has been rising during his time in high school. Here, then, is the trend: an upward trend in Robert's academic performance.

Consider another example. Suppose that this year, in a city in the Midwest, 2 feet of snow fell in the winter. Last year 3 feet of snow fell. Three years ago 4 feet of snow fell, and four years ago 5 feet of snow fell. There is a trend toward less snow.

Economists often try to identify trends in economic data. Here are four of the many variables for which they try to identify trends:

1. the money supply
2. the average annual growth in the economy
3. the unemployment rate
4. the inflation rate

For example, the average annual growth rate in the money supply in the 1960s was 3.86 percent. It was higher in the 1970s, at 6.51 percent, and even higher in the 1980s, at 7.66 percent. Was there a trend in the average annual growth rate in the money supply? Yes, and the trend was upward.

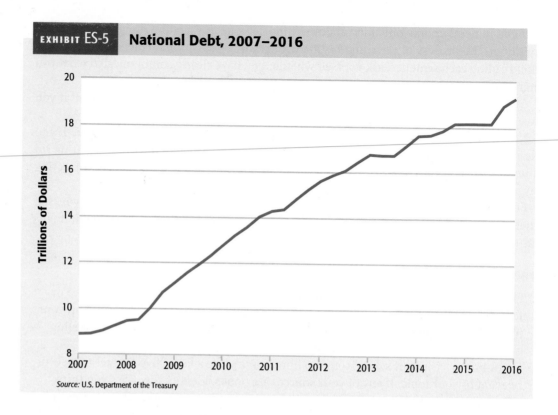

Source: U.S. Department of the Treasury

When an economist identifies a trend in economic data that is going in the "wrong" direction, one of his or her jobs is to figure out how to reverse the trend. If a trend in a variable is going in the "right" direction, an economist will figure out what is causing this desirable trend. For example, the average annual inflation rate was relatively high in the 1970s, lower in the 1980s, and still lower in the 1990s. An economist is interested in knowing what happened to bring about this desirable trend.

Practicing Your Skills

1. *Global warming* is defined as "an increase in the earth's average atmospheric temperature that causes corresponding changes in climate and that may result from the greenhouse effect." Is there anything in the definition of global warming that indicates a trend? If so, what?
2. Harry has promised himself that he will exercise three to four times each week. Today is the first day he's exercised. Is this a trend? Explain your answer.
3. Look at Exhibit ES-5. Identify the trend.

Using Percentages to Make Comparisons

You have probably heard that you "can't compare apples to oranges." For example, it probably wouldn't be meaningful to compare an increase in the price of aspirin from $3.50 a bottle to $3.89 to an increase in the price of steaks from $10.99 a pound to $11.99. However, it would be meaningful to say that medical care prices rose by 80 percent, while food prices increased by 39 percent. This type of comparison—comparing the percentage changes rather than the price changes—can be useful. This is why it's important to be able to work with and understand percentages—so you can compare apples to apples and oranges to oranges.

Suppose you are a farmer and you produce certain food goods to sell. You also buy certain goods and services in your role as consumer. What might be of interest to you is the percentage change in the price of what you sell (food products) compared with the percentage change in the price of what you buy (all kinds of consumer goods and services).

To compute the change in the prices of what the farmer buys, we can look at the consumer price index (CPI) in different years. For example, one year the CPI was 160.5, and the next year it had risen to 163.0. Using the following formula, we can compute the percentage change in prices:

$$\text{Percentage change in CPI} = \frac{\text{CPI in later year} - \text{CPI in earlier year}}{\text{CPI in earlier year}} \times 100$$

$$= \frac{163.0 - 160.5}{160.5} \times 100$$

$$= \frac{2.5}{160.5} \times 100$$

$$= 1.56\%$$

The first year the price index for food goods that farmers sell was 107, and the next year it had fallen to 101. We can use the formula that follows to compute the percentage change in prices:

$$\text{Percentage change in prices of food goods that farmers sell} = \frac{\text{Price index in later year} - \text{Price index in earlier year}}{\text{Price index in earlier year}} \times 100$$

$$= \frac{101 - 107}{107} \times 100$$

$$= \frac{-6}{107} \times 100$$

$$= -5.61\%$$

Having made our computations, we see that the prices of the goods that farmers buy increased (1.56 percent) and the prices of the goods that farmers sell fell (–5.61 percent) during the two-year period.

Practicing Your Skills

1. Valerie's objective is to cut back on buying clothes and entertainment so she can save money. Last month, she spent $136 on clothes and $98 on entertainment. This month, she has spent $129 on clothes and $79 on entertainment. Compute the percentage change in spending for each good, and then compare the changes. Is Valerie cutting back more in spending on clothes or entertainment?
2. Suppose the price index for the goods Juan sells is 132 in year 1 and 145 in year 2. The price index for the goods he buys is 124 in the first year and 135 in the second year. How much have prices increased between the two years for the goods he sells? For the goods he buys?

Converting Currency

Different nations, of course, have different currencies. The United States has dollars, Mexico has pesos, most countries of the European Union have euros, Japan has yen, and so on. It's important to know how to convert from one currency to another.

Suppose you are in England and see that a sweater has a price tag of £20. How much does it cost in U.S. dollars? To answer this question, you need to know the exchange rate between dollars and pounds. You can get this information by looking at the business section of many newspapers, finding a conversion website online, or calling almost any bank.

Let's say the exchange rate is $2 for £1. To find out what the English sweater costs in U.S. dollars, simply use this formula:

Price of sweater in dollars	=	Price of sweater in foreign currency	×	Number of dollars needed to buy 1 unit of foreign currency

Let's find the price in dollars of the sweater costing £20, given an exchange rate of $2 for £1:

Price of sweater in dollars = £20 × $2 (per £1) = $40

The answer is $40.

Suppose you knew the price of the sweater in dollars and wanted to find out its price in some other currency. You could use this formula:

Price of sweater in foreign currency	=	Price of sweater in dollars	÷	Number of dollars needed to buy 1 unit of foreign currency

Let's find the price in pounds of the $40 sweater, given an exchange rate of $2 for £1:

Price of sweater in foreign currency = $40 ÷ $2 (per £1) = £20

The answer is £20.

Practicing Your Skills

1. The price of an Indian shirt is 4,300 rupees, and the exchange rate is 1 rupee = $0.02. What does the Indian shirt cost in dollars?
2. The price of a Swedish lamp is 500 kronor, and the exchange rate is 8 kronor = $1. What does the lamp cost in dollars?
3. Suppose you are working in Mexico, and you earn 2,000 pesos a week. The exchange rate is 1 peso = $0.25. What is your weekly pay in dollars?

Building Decision-Making Skills

As a consumer, citizen, and voter, you will make many economic decisions every day. One of the best ways to improve your decision-making skills is by learning and using a decision-making model. The steps in the decision-making model are listed and described below using the hypothetical example of choosing a major for college.

Step 1. Define your need or want. The first step in the decision-making process is to define the need or want that requires a decision. When working through this step, be as specific as possible. For instance, define your need or want as follows: I want to choose a major that I will enjoy and that will help me to fulfill my long-range goal of a happy, productive career.

Step 2. Analyze your resources. Your resources will vary according to the decision you have to make. In this case, your resources might include your parents and guidance counselors. For example, many guidance counselors can provide you with interest inventories and other tools that can help you to determine your main areas of interest. You might also talk with college representatives or friends or family members who are attending college.

Step 3. Identify your choices. The fact that a decision needs to be made implies that choices exist. Brainstorm to come up with as many alternatives as possible. Don't discard any possibilities at this point. Regarding your major, you may feel that you are interested in art, art history, anthropology, sociology, and music.

Step 4. Compare the choices. At this point, you need to determine which choice is the best by using your available resources to gather information. Let's say that your guidance counselor tells you that you should look at the career opportunities associated with each major. Then you should try to imagine the outcome of each choice.

Step 5. Choose the best alternative. After you have compared your choices, choose the best one. This can be difficult if no one alternative stands out as the best. Suppose, for example, that all the majors have basically the same appeal. You finally choose art history because it seems to combine your other interests and because it might lead to a career as a museum curator, which sounds exciting and rewarding.

Step 6. Make a plan to get started. You must make a plan of action. Your plan of action might include obtaining college catalogs, completing applications, and writing letters to art history departments for information about curricula.

Step 7. Evaluate your decision. Just because you have made a decision doesn't mean that you can't change your mind. Look at the results of your decision. If the outcome is not what you had hoped, perhaps it's time to start over with step 1. Continue to evaluate your decision as you learn more about your first choice.

Notice that the decision-making model contains words such as *choices, wants,* and *resources.* As you have learned, scarcity exists and, as a result, choices have to be made. Decision making is part of economics, and using the decision-making model is a good way to think like an economist.

Practicing Your Skills

Identify a real-world situation in which you will need to make a decision in the near future. Use the seven-step process just described to make a decision for that situation. Compare the process used to your usual method of decision making. Do you think using the seven-step process led you to a different decision than you would have made otherwise? Did following the process result in making a better decision?

Databank

On the following pages, you will find historical data for selected economic and economic-related topics, such as real GDP, money supply, population, and velocity. The data will be of use as you study the principles of economics. Following is a list of the data included in this databank.

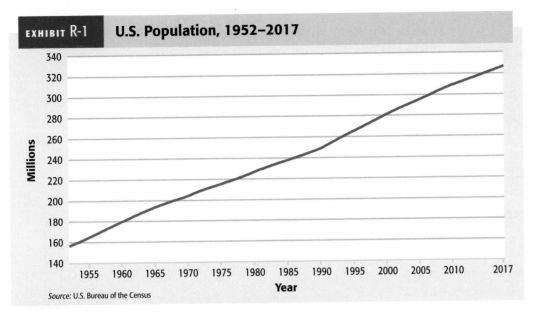

EXHIBIT R-1 U.S. Population, 1952–2017

Source: U.S. Bureau of the Census

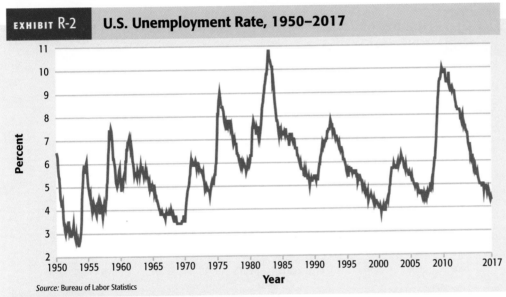

EXHIBIT R-2 U.S. Unemployment Rate, 1950–2017

Source: Bureau of Labor Statistics

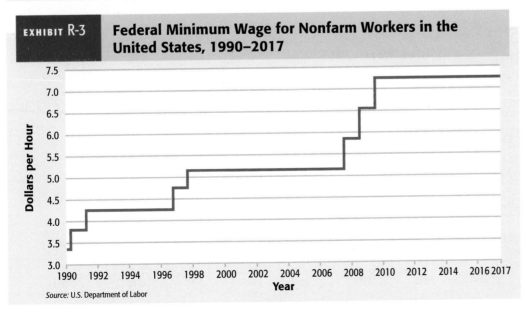

EXHIBIT R-3 Federal Minimum Wage for Nonfarm Workers in the United States, 1990–2017

Source: U.S. Department of Labor

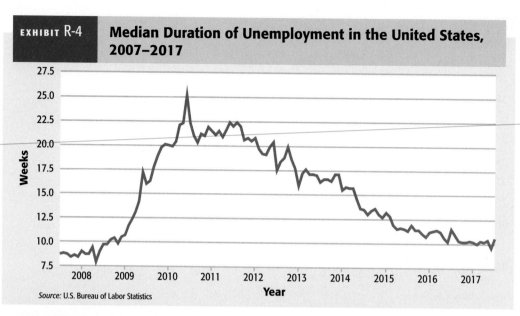

EXHIBIT R-4 **Median Duration of Unemployment in the United States, 2007–2017**

Source: U.S. Bureau of Labor Statistics

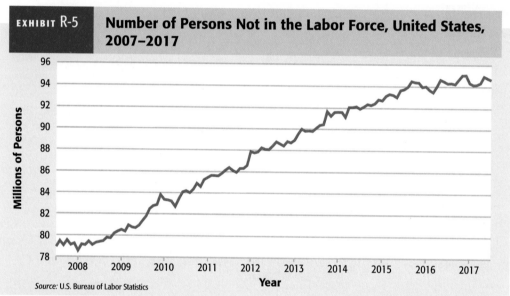

EXHIBIT R-5 **Number of Persons Not in the Labor Force, United States, 2007–2017**

Source: U.S. Bureau of Labor Statistics

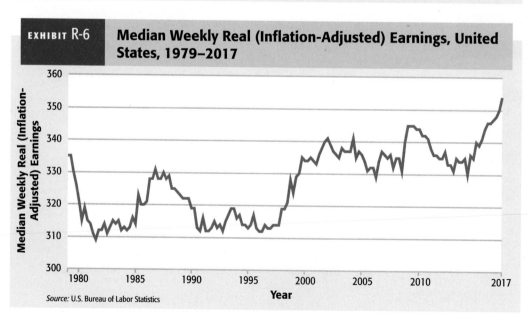

EXHIBIT R-6 **Median Weekly Real (Inflation-Adjusted) Earnings, United States, 1979–2017**

Source: U.S. Bureau of Labor Statistics

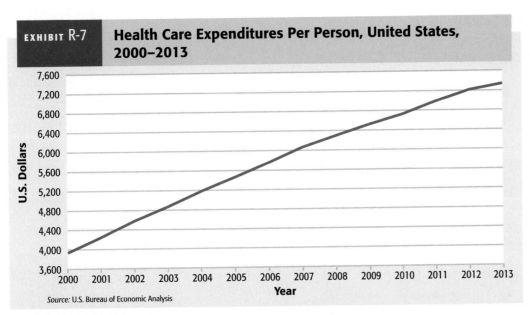

EXHIBIT R-7 — Health Care Expenditures Per Person, United States, 2000–2013

Source: U.S. Bureau of Economic Analysis

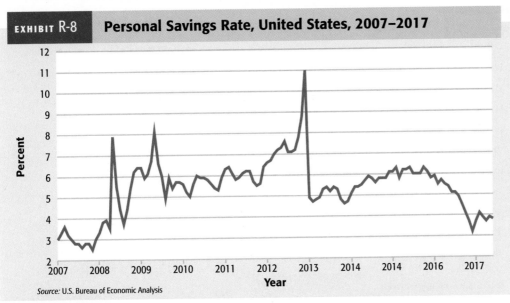

EXHIBIT R-8 — Personal Savings Rate, United States, 2007–2017

Source: U.S. Bureau of Economic Analysis

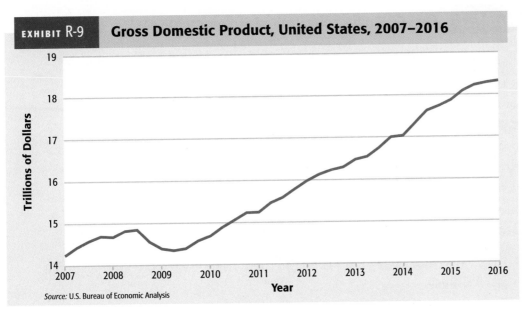

EXHIBIT R-9 — Gross Domestic Product, United States, 2007–2016

Source: U.S. Bureau of Economic Analysis

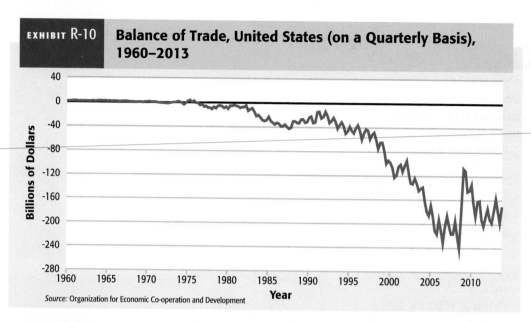

EXHIBIT R-10 Balance of Trade, United States (on a Quarterly Basis), 1960–2013

Billions of Dollars

Year

Source: Organization for Economic Co-operation and Development

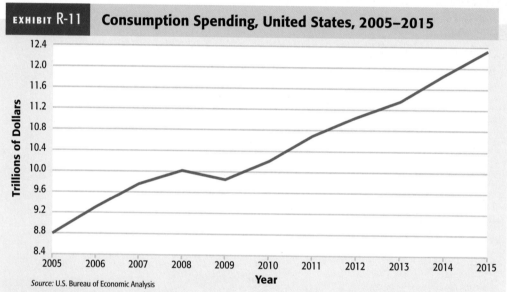

EXHIBIT R-11 Consumption Spending, United States, 2005–2015

Trillions of Dollars

Year

Source: U.S. Bureau of Economic Analysis

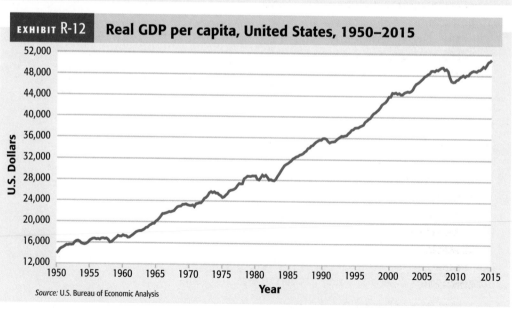

EXHIBIT R-12 Real GDP per capita, United States, 1950–2015

U.S. Dollars

Year

Source: U.S. Bureau of Economic Analysis

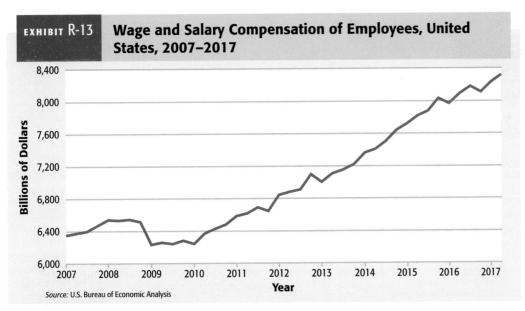

EXHIBIT R-13 Wage and Salary Compensation of Employees, United States, 2007–2017

Source: U.S. Bureau of Economic Analysis

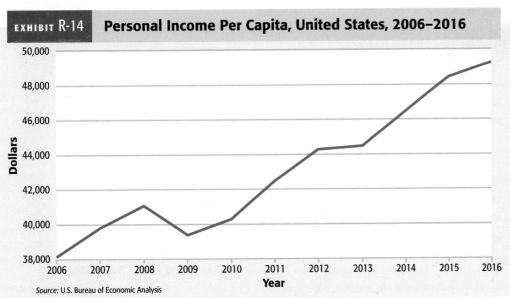

EXHIBIT R-14 Personal Income Per Capita, United States, 2006–2016

Source: U.S. Bureau of Economic Analysis

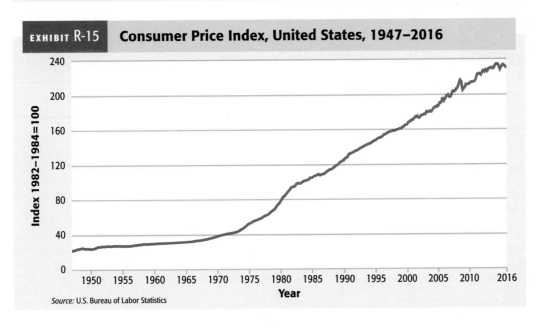

EXHIBIT R-15 Consumer Price Index, United States, 1947–2016

Source: U.S. Bureau of Labor Statistics

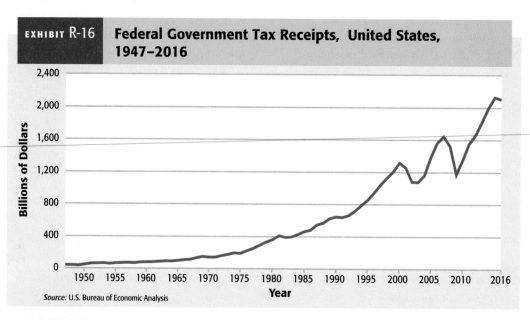

EXHIBIT R-16 **Federal Government Tax Receipts, United States, 1947–2016**

Source: U.S. Bureau of Economic Analysis

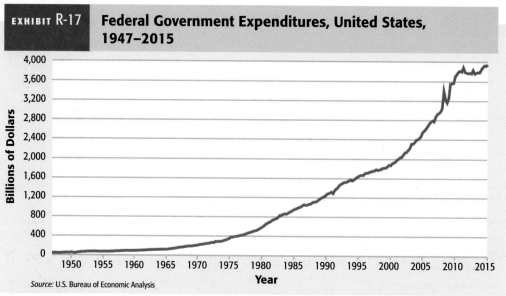

EXHIBIT R-17 **Federal Government Expenditures, United States, 1947–2015**

Source: U.S. Bureau of Economic Analysis

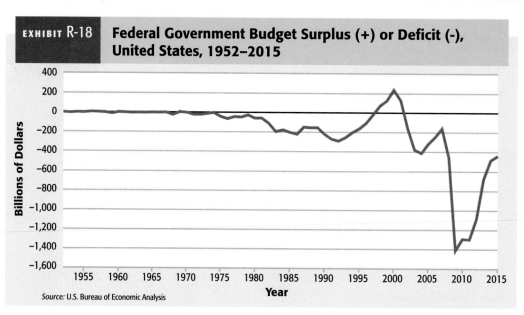

EXHIBIT R-18 **Federal Government Budget Surplus (+) or Deficit (-), United States, 1952–2015**

Source: U.S. Bureau of Economic Analysis

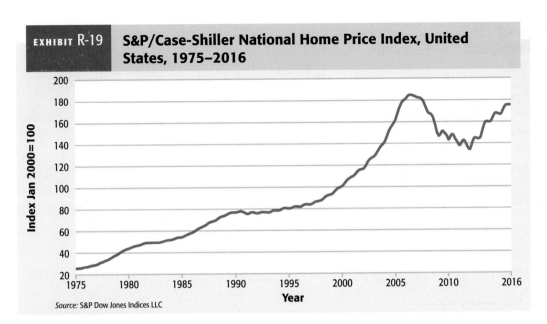

EXHIBIT R-19 S&P/Case-Shiller National Home Price Index, United States, 1975–2016

Source: S&P Dow Jones Indices LLC

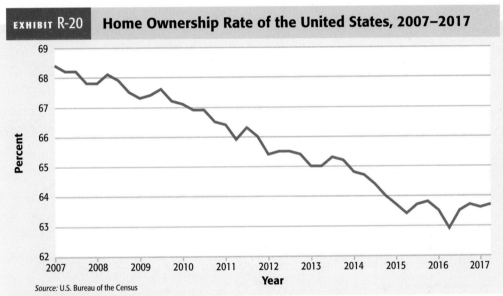

EXHIBIT R-20 Home Ownership Rate of the United States, 2007–2017

Source: U.S. Bureau of the Census

EXHIBIT R-21 10-Year U.S. Treasury Bond Rate, 1962–2016

Source: Board of Governors of the Federal Reserve System (US)

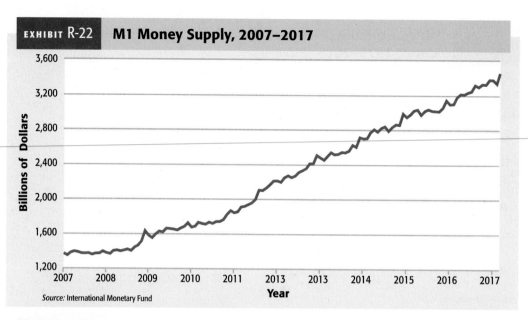

EXHIBIT R-22 **M1 Money Supply, 2007–2017**

Source: International Monetary Fund

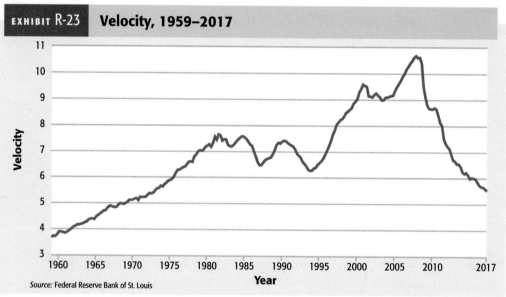

EXHIBIT R-23 **Velocity, 1959–2017**

Source: Federal Reserve Bank of St. Louis

Glossary

absolute advantage The situation in which a country can produce more of a good than another country can produce with the same quantity of resources. (p. 437)

absolute real economic growth An increase in real GDP from one period to the next. (p. 364)

advancement in technology The ability to produce more output with a fixed amount of resources. (p. 130)

after-tax income The part of income that's left over after taxes are paid. (p. 385)

aggregate demand curve A curve that shows the quantity of goods and services that buyers are willing and able to buy at different price levels. (p. 333)

aggregate supply curve A curve that shows the quantity of goods and services that producers are willing and able to supply at different price levels. (p. 333)

antitrust law Legislation passed for the stated purpose of controlling monopoly power and preserving and promoting competition. (p. 220)

appreciation An increase in the value of one currency relative to other currencies. (p. 458)

asset Anything of value to which the firm has a legal claim. (p. 181)

asymmetric information Exists when one party to a transaction has information that another party does not have. (p. 187)

average total cost The total cost divided by the quantity of output. (p. 191)

balance of trade The difference between the value of a country's exports and the value of its imports. (p. 436)

barrier to entry Anything that prohibits a firm from entering a market. (p. 215)

barter economy An economy in which trades are made in goods and services instead of money. (p. 278)

base year In general, a benchmark year—a year chosen as a point of reference for comparison. When real GDP is computed, the outputs of different years are priced at base-year levels. (p. 327)

board of directors An important decision-making body in a corporation. It decides corporate policies and goals, among other things. (p. 184)

Board of Governors of the Federal Reserve System The governing body of the Federal Reserve System. (p. 294)

bond An IOU, or a promise to pay, issued by companies, governments, and government agencies for the purpose of borrowing money. (p. 482)

budget deficit The situation in which federal government expenditures are greater than federal government tax revenues. (p. 422)

budget surplus The situation in which federal government expenditures are less than federal government tax revenues. (p. 422)

business cycle Recurrent swings (up and down) in real GDP. (p. 358)

business firm An organization that uses resources to produce goods and services that are sold to consumers, other firms, or the government. (p. 176)

capital Produced goods that can be used as resources for further production. Such things as factories, machines, and farm tractors are capital. (p. 27)

cartel agreement An agreement that specifies how the firms that entered into the agreement will act in a coordinated way to reduce the competition among them. (p. 235)

circular flow of economic activity The economic relationships that exist between different economic groups in an economy. (p. 65)

closed shop An organization that hires only union members. (p. 261)

comparative advantage The situation in which a country can produce a good at a lower opportunity cost than another country. (p. 437)

complement A good that is consumed jointly with another good. With complements, the price of one and the demand for the other move in opposite directions. (p. 108)

consumer price index (CPI) The most widely used price index. (p. 331)

consumption Expenditures made by the household sector. (p. 321)

contract An agreement between two or more people to do something. (p. 80)

contractionary fiscal policy A decrease in government spending or an increase in taxes. (p. 378)

contractionary monetary policy A decrease in the money supply. (p. 388)

corporation A legal entity that can conduct business in its own name in the same way that an individual does. (p. 181)

coupon rate The percentage of the face value that the bondholder receives each year until the bond matures. (p. 483)

crowding out The situation in which increases in government spending lead to reductions in private spending. (p. 379)

currency Coins issued by the U.S. Treasury and paper money (called Federal Reserve notes) issued by the Federal Reserve System. (p. 285)

deflation A decrease in the price level, or average level of prices. (p. 353)

demand The willingness and ability of buyers to purchase different quantities of a good at different prices during a specific time period. (p. 98)

demand curve The graphical representation of the law of demand. (p. 101)

demand deposit An account from which deposited funds can be withdrawn in currency or transferred by a check to a third party at the initiative of the owner. (p. 285)

demand schedule The numerical representation of the law of demand. (p. 100)

demand-side inflation An increase in the price level that originates on the demand side of the economy. (p. 348)

depreciation A decrease in the value of one currency relative to other currencies. (p. 458)

derived demand A demand that is the result of some other demand. (p. 252)

developed country A country with a relatively high per capita GDP. (p. 462)

direct relationship A relationship between two factors in which the factors move in the same direction. For example, as one factor rises, the other rises too. (p. 124)

discount rate The interest rate the Fed charges a bank for a loan. (p. 306)

disutility The quality of bringing dissatisfaction or unhappiness. (p. 26)

dividend A share of the profits of a corporation distributes to stockholders. (p. 474)

double counting Counting a good more than once in computing GDP. (p. 317)

Dow Jones Industrial Average (DJIA) A weighted average of 30 widely traded stocks on the New York Stock Exchange. The most popular, widely cited indicator of day-to-day stock market activity. (p. 471)

dumping The sale of goods abroad at prices below their costs and below the price charged in domestic (home) markets. (p. 451)

economic plan A government plan specifying economic activities, such as what goods will be produced and what prices will be charged. (p. 37)

economic system The way in which a society decides what goods to produce, how to produce goods, and for whom goods will be produced. (p. 34)

economics The science that studies the choices of people trying to satisfy their wants in a world of scarcity. (p. 13)

elastic demand The type of demand that exists when the percentage change in quantity demanded is greater than the percentage change in price. (p. 112)

elastic supply The kind of supply that exists when the percentage change in quantity supplied is greater than the percentage change in price. (p. 135)

elasticity of demand The relationship between the percentage change in quantity demanded and the percentage change in price. (p. 112)

elasticity of supply The relationship between the percentage change in quantity supplied and the percentage change in price. (p. 135)

employment rate The percentage of the noninstitutional adult civilian population that is employed. (p. 337)

entrepreneur A person who has a special talent for searching out and taking advantage of new business opportunities. (p. 77)

entrepreneurship The special talent that some people have for searching out and taking advantage of new business opportunities and for developing new products and new ways of doing things. (p. 29)

equilibrium In a market, the point at which the quantity of a good that buyers are willing and able to buy is equal to the quantity that sellers are willing and able to produce and offer for sale (quantity demanded equals quantity supplied). (p. 145)

equilibrium price The price at which a good is bought and sold in a market that is in equilibrium. (p. 145)

equilibrium quantity The quantity of a good that is bought and sold in a market that is in equilibrium. (p. 145)

ethics The principles of conduct, such as right and wrong, morality and immorality, good and bad. (p. 72)

excess reserves Any reserves held beyond the required amount. (p. 299)

exchange rate The price of one country's currency in terms of another country's currency. (p. 455)

excludable public good A public good that individuals can be excluded (physically prohibited) from consuming. (p. 80)

expansionary fiscal policy An increase in government spending or a reduction in taxes. (p. 378)

expansionary monetary policy An increase in the money supply. (p. 388)

export spending The amount spent by the residents of other countries on goods produced in the United States. (p. 321)

exports Goods produced in the domestic country and sold to residents of a foreign country. (p. 434)

face value (par value) The dollar amount specified on a bond. The total amount the issuer of the bond will repay to the buyer of the bond. (p. 482)

federal funds rate target The rate the Fed would like the federal funds rate to be. (p. 308)

federal funds rate The interest rate one bank charges another for a loan. (p. 306)

Federal Open Market Committee (FOMC) The 12-member policymaking group within the Fed. This committee has the authority to conduct open market operations. (p. 295)

Federal Reserve note Paper money issued by the Federal Reserve System. (p. 285)

Federal Reserve System (the Fed) The central bank of the United States. (p. 294)

fiscal policy Changes the government makes in spending or taxation to achieve particular economic goals. (p. 378)

fixed cost A cost, or expense, that is the same no matter how many units of a good are produced. (p. 190)

fixed exchange rate system The system whereby currency exchange rates are fixed, or pegged, by countries' governments. (p. 455)

flexible exchange rate system The system whereby currency exchange rates are determined by the forces of supply and demand. (p. 455)

fractional reserve banking A banking arrangement in which banks hold only a fraction of their deposits and lend out the remainder. (p. 284)

franchise A contract by which a firm (usually a corporation) lets a person or group use its name and sell its goods in exchange for making certain payments and meeting certain requirements. (p. 186)

franchisee The person or group that buys a franchise. (p. 186)

franchiser The entity that offers a franchise. (p. 186)

free enterprise An economic system in which individuals (not the government) own most, if not all, the resources and control their use. The government plays only a small part in the economy. (p. 34)

free rider A person who receives the benefits of a good without paying for it. (p. 82)

futures contract An agreement to buy or sell a specific amount of something (commodity, currency, financial instrument) at a particular price on a stipulated future date. (p. 492)

globalization A phenomenon by which economic agents in any given part of the world are affected by events elsewhere in the world; the growing integration of the national economies of the world to the degree that they could merge and operate as a single worldwide economy. (p. 43)

goods Anything that satisfies a person's wants or brings satisfaction; also, tangible products. (p. 26)

government purchases Expenditures made by the government sector. Government purchases do not include government transfer payments. (p. 321)

gross domestic product (GDP) The total market value of all final goods and services produced annually in a country. (p. 316)

hedge To try to avoid or lessen a loss by taking some counterbalancing action. (p. 353)

household An economic unit of one person or more that sells resources and buys goods and services. (p. 65)

human capital The knowledge and skills that people use in the production of goods and services; also includes honesty, creativity, and perseverance—traits that lend themselves to finding and keeping a job. (p. 369)

import spending The amount spent by Americans for foreign-produced goods. (p. 322)

imports Goods produced in foreign countries and purchased by residents of the domestic country. (p. 435)

incentive Something that encourages or motivates a person to take action. (p. 15)

income distribution The way all the income earned in a country is divided among different groups of income earners. (p. 37)

index A portfolio of stocks that represent a particular market or a portion of it; used to measure changes in a market or economy. (p. 478)

inelastic demand The type of demand that exists when the percentage change in quantity demanded is less than the percentage change in price. (p. 113)

inelastic supply The kind of supply that exists when the percentage change in quantity supplied is less than the percentage change in price. (p. 135)

inferior good A good for which the demand falls as income rises and rises as income falls. (p. 105)

inflation An increase in the price level, or average level of prices. (p. 346)

initial public offering (IPO) A company's first offering of stock to the public. (p. 474)

intangible Not able to be felt by touch. For example, an economics lecture is intangible. (p. 26)

inventory The stock of goods that a business or store has on hand. (p. 145)

investment Expenditures made by the business sector. (p. 321)

investment bank A firm that acts as an intermediary between the company that issues the stock and the public that wishes to buy the stock. (p. 474)

labor The physical and mental talents that people contribute to the production of goods and services. (p. 27)

labor theory of value The belief that all value in produced goods is derived from labor. (p. 41)

labor union An organization that seeks to increase the wages and improve the working conditions of its members. (p. 260)

Laffer curve The curve, named after economist Arthur Laffer, that shows the relationship between tax rates and tax revenues. According to the Laffer curve, as tax rates rise from zero, tax revenues rise, reach a maximum at some point, and then fall with further increases in tax rates. (p. 387)

land All the natural resources found in nature. Acres of wheat fields, mineral deposits, and water in a stream are all considered land. (p. 27)

law of demand A law stating that as the price of a good increases, the quantity demanded of the good decreases, and that as the price of a good decreases, the quantity demanded of the good increases. (p. 98)

law of diminishing marginal returns A law that states that if additional units of one resource are added to another resource in fixed supply, eventually the additional output will decrease. (p. 199)

law of diminishing marginal utility A law stating that as a person consumes additional units of a good, the utility gained from each additional unit of the good will eventually decrease. (p. 99)

law of supply A law stating that as the price of a good increases, the quantity supplied of the good increases, and as the price of a good decreases, the quantity supplied of the good decreases. (p. 124)

less-developed country A country with a relatively low per capita GDP. (p. 462)

limited liability A condition in which an owner of a business firm can lose only the amount he or she has invested (in the firm). (p. 182)

loanable funds market The market for loans. There is a demand for loans (stemming from borrowers) and a supply of loans (stemming from lenders). The loanable funds market is where the interest rate is determined. (p. 288)

loss The amount of money by which total cost exceeds total revenue. (p. 68)

macroeconomics The branch of economics that deals with human behavior and choices as they relate to the entire economy. (p. 21)

marginal In economics, marginal means "additional." (p. 15)

marginal cost The cost of producing an additional unit of a good; the change in total cost that results from producing an additional unit of output. (p. 191)

marginal revenue The revenue from selling an additional unit of a good; the change in total revenue that results from selling an additional unit of output. (p. 196)

market Any place people come together to buy and sell goods or services. (p. 98)

market structure The setting in which a seller finds itself. Market structures are defined by their characteristics, such as the number of sellers in the market, the product that sellers produce and sell, and how easy or difficult it is for new firms to enter the market. (p. 208)

medium of exchange Anything that is generally acceptable in exchange for goods and services. (p. 282)

microeconomics The branch of economics that deals with human behavior and choices as they relate to relatively small units—individuals, business firms, and single markets. (p. 21)

minimum wage law A federal law that specifies the lowest hourly wage rate that can be paid to workers. (p. 254)

mixed economy An economy that is neither purely capitalist nor purely socialist; an economy that has some elements of both capitalism and socialism. Most countries in the world have mixed economies. (p. 39)

monetary policy Changes the Fed makes in the money supply. (p. 388)

money A good that is widely accepted in exchange and in the repayment of debt. (p. 279)

money supply The total supply of money in circulation, composed of currency, checking accounts, and traveler's checks. (p. 285)

monopolistic competitive market A market structure characterized by (1) many buyers and many sellers, (2) the production and sale of slightly different products, and (3) easy entry into and exit out of the market. (p. 228)

monopolistic market A market structure characterized by (1) a single seller, (2) the sale of a product that has no close substitutes, and (3) extremely high barriers to entry. (p. 215)

national debt The total amount the federal government owes its creditors. (p. 417)

natural monopoly A firm with such a low average total cost (per-unit cost) that only it can survive in the market. (p. 219)

negative externality An adverse side effect of an act that is felt by others. (p. 84)

neutral good A good for which the demand remains unchanged as income rises or falls. (p. 105)

nonexcludable public good A public good that individuals cannot be excluded (physically prohibited) from consuming. (p. 80)

normal good A good for which the demand rises as income rises and falls as income falls. (p. 105)

offshoring The term used to describe work done for a company by persons other than its employees in a country other than the one in which the company is located. (p. 51)

oligopolistic market A market structure characterized by (1) few sellers, (2) the production and sale of identical or slightly different products, and (3) significant barriers to entry. (p. 233)

open market operations Buying and selling of government securities by the Fed. (p. 305)

opportunity cost The most highly valued opportunity or alternative given up when a choice is made. (p. 8)

option A contract that gives the owner the right but not the obligation to buy or sell shares of a good at a specified price on or before a specified date. (p. 495)

outsourcing An arrangement in which work is done for a company by another company or by people other than the original company's employees. (p. 442)

partnership A business owned by two or more co-owners, called partners, who share profits and are legally responsible for debts. (p. 180)

per capita real economic growth An increase from one period to the next in per capita real GDP, which is real GDP divided by population. (p. 364)

per-unit cost The average cost of a good. For example, if $400,000 is spent to produce 100 cars, the average, or per-unit, cost is $4,000. (p. 130)

perfectly competitive market A market structure characterized by (1) many buyers and many sellers, (2) all firms selling identical goods, (3) all relevant information about buying and selling activities being available to buyers and sellers, and (4) easy entry into and easy exit out of the market. (p. 209)

population growth rate The birthrate minus the death rate. (p. 462)

positive externality A beneficial side effect of an action that is felt by others. (p. 84)

price ceiling A legislated price—set below the equilibrium price—above which buyers and sellers cannot legally buy and sell a good. (p. 151)

price discrimination The practice by which a seller charges different prices to different buyers for the product it sells when the price differences do not reflect cost differences. (p. 236)

price floor A legislated price—set above the equilibrium price—below which buyers and sellers cannot legally buy and sell a good. (p. 151)

price index A measure of the price level, or the average level of prices. (p. 331)

price searcher A seller that can sell some of its output at various prices. (p. 215)

price taker A seller that can sell all its output at the equilibrium price but can sell none of its output at any other price. (p. 210)

private good A good for which one person's consumption takes away from another person's consumption. (p. 80)

private property Any good that is owned by an individual or a business. (p. 63)

production possibilities frontier A graphic representation of all possible combinations of two goods that an economy can produce. (p. 10)

profit The amount of money left over after all the costs of production have been paid. Profit exists whenever total revenue is greater than total cost. (p. 68)

progressive income tax An income tax in which the rate increases as the income level rises. Progressive income tax structures are usually capped at some rate. (p. 410)

proportional income tax An income tax that everyone pays at the same rate, whatever his or her income level. (p. 409)

public franchise A right granted to a firm by the government that permits the firm to provide a particular good or service and excludes all others from doing so. (p. 218)

public good A good for which one person's consumption does not take away from another person's consumption. (p. 80)

public property Any good that is owned by the government. (p. 63)

quantity demanded The number of units of a good purchased at a specific price. (p. 99)

quantity supplied The number of units of a good produced and offered for sale at a specific price. (p. 124)

quota A legal limit on the number of units of a foreign-produced good (import) that can enter a country. (p. 130)

rationing device A means for deciding who gets what portion of the available resources and goods. (p. 12)

real GDP Gross domestic product (GDP) that has been adjusted for price changes; GDP measured in base-year, or constant, prices. (p. 327)

recession A slowdown in the economy marked by real GDP falling for two consecutive quarters. (p. 358)

regressive income tax An income tax in which the rate decreases as the income level rises. (p. 410)

required reserves The minimum amount of reserves a bank must hold against its deposits, as mandated by the Fed. (p. 298)

reserve account A bank's "checking account" with its Federal Reserve district bank. (p. 295)

reserve requirement The regulation that requires a bank to keep a certain percentage of its deposits in its reserve account with the Fed or in its vault as vault cash. (p. 298)

resource Anything that is used to produce goods or services. For example, a person's labor may be used to produce computers, TV sets, and much more; therefore, a person's labor is a resource. (p. 6)

right-to-work law A state law that prohibits the practice of requiring employees to join a union to work. (p. 261)

savings account An interest-earning account. (p. 286)

scarcity The condition in which our wants are greater than the resources available to satisfy them. (p. 6)

services Tasks that people pay others to perform for them. (p. 26)

shirking The behavior of a worker who is putting forth less than the agreed-to effort. (p. 177)

shortage The condition in which the quantity demanded of a good is greater than the quantity supplied. Shortages occur only at prices below the equilibrium price. (p. 145)

simple quantity theory of money A theory that predicts that changes in the price level will be strictly proportional to changes in the money supply. (p. 350)

socialism An economic system in which the government controls and may own many of the resources. (p. 34)

sole proprietorship A business that is owned by one individual, who makes all of the business decisions, receives all of the profits or takes all of the losses of the firm, and is legally responsible for the debts of the firm. (p. 178)

specialize To focus or concentrate on a particular activity or product. (p. 437)

stagflation The occurrence of inflation and high unemployment at the same time. (p. 398)

stock A claim on the assets of a corporation that gives the purchaser a share of the corporation. (p. 470)

stockholder A person who owns shares of stock in a corporation. (p. 181)

stop-and-go, on-and-off monetary policy An erratic monetary policy. (p. 398)

store of value Something with the ability to hold value over time. (p. 282)

strike A work stoppage called by union members to put pressure on an employer. (p. 261)

subsidy A financial payment made by government for a certain actions. (p. 130)

substitute A similar good. With substitutes, the price of one and the demand for the other move in the same direction. (p. 106)

supply The willingness and ability of sellers to produce and offer to sell different quantities of a good at different prices during a specific time period. (p. 124)

supply curve A graph that shows the amount of a good sellers are willing and able to sell at various prices. (p. 126)

supply schedule A numerical chart illustrating the law of supply. (p. 125)

supply-side inflation An increase in the price level that originates on the supply side of the economy. (p. 349)

surplus The condition in which the quantity supplied of a good is greater than the quantity demanded. Surpluses occur only at prices above the equilibrium price. (p. 144)

surplus value The difference between the total value of production and the subsistence wages paid to workers. (p. 41)

Taft-Hartley Act An act, passed in 1947 by the U.S. Congress, that made the closed shop illegal and allowed states to pass right-to-work laws. These laws prohibit employers from making union membership a condition of employment. (p. 261)

tangible Able to be felt by touch. For example, a book is tangible: you can touch and feel it. (p. 26)

tariff A tax on imports. (p. 447)

technology The body of skills and knowledge concerning the use of resources in production. (p. 130)

theory An explanation of how something works, designed to answer a question for which there is no obvious answer. (p. 21)

total cost The sum of fixed costs plus variable costs. (p. 191)

total reserves The sum of a bank's deposits in its reserve account at the Fed and its vault cash. (p. 298)

trade-off A situation in which having more of one thing necessarily means having less of something else. (p. 8)

transaction costs The costs associated with the time and effort needed to search out, negotiate, and complete an exchange. (p. 278)

unemployment rate The percentage of the civilian labor force that is unemployed. (p. 337)

union shop An organization that requires employees to join the union within a certain period after being hired. (p. 261)

unit of account A common measurement used to express value. (p. 282)

unit-elastic demand The type of demand that exists when the percentage change in quantity demanded is the same as the percentage change in price. (p. 113)

unit-elastic supply The kind of supply that exists when the percentage change in quantity supplied is equal to the percentage change in price. (p. 135)

utility The quality of bringing satisfaction or happiness. (p. 26)

value-added tax A tax placed on the value added to a good at each stage of production and distribution. (p. 409)

variable cost A cost, or expense, that changes with the number of units of a good produced. (p. 190)

velocity The average number of times a dollar is spent to buy final goods and services in a year. (p. 349)

vision A sense of how the world works. (p. 40)

wage rate The price of labor. (p. 246)

want Something that we desire to have. (p. 6)

yield Equal to the annual coupon payment divided by the price paid for the bond. (p. 484)

Glosario

absolute advantage / ventaja absoluta
Situación en la que un país puede producir una mayor cantidad de un bien que lo que puede producir otro país con la misma cantidad de recursos. (p. 437)

absolute real economic growth / crecimiento económico real absoluto Aumento del PBI real de un período a otro. (p. 364)

advancement in technology / avance tecnológico Capacidad de obtener una producción mayor con una cantidad fija de recursos. (p. 130)

after-tax income / ganancias luego de la deducción de impuestos Parte remanente de las ganancias luego de abonarse los impuestos. (p. 385)

aggregate demand curve / curva de demanda total Curva que muestra la cantidad de bienes y servicios que los compradores desean y pueden adquirir a distintos niveles de precios. (p. 333)

aggregate supply curve / curva de oferta total Curva que demuestra la cantidad de bienes y servicios que los productores desean y pueden ofrecer a distintos niveles de precios. (p. 333)

antitrust law / ley antimonopolio Legislación dictada para controlar el poder de los monopolios y preservar y promover la competencia. (p. 220)

appreciation / apreciación Aumento en el valor de una moneda en relación con otras. (p. 458)

asset / activo Cualquier objeto de valor al cual una empresa tiene un derecho legal. (p. 181)

asymmetric information / información asimétrica Existe cuando una de las partes en una transacción tiene información que no tiene la otra. (p. 187)

average total cost / costo total promedio El costo total dividido por la cantidad de producción. (p. 191)

balance of trade/ balanza comercial Diferencia entre el valor de las exportaciones de un país y el valor de sus importaciones. (p. 436)

barrier to entry / barrera de entrada Cualquier disposición que prohíba el ingreso de una empresa a un mercado. (p. 215)

barter economy / economía de trueque Economía en la que el comercio se lleva a cabo mediante el intercambio de bienes y servicios en lugar de dinero. (p. 278)

base year / año base En general, un año de referencia, es decir, elegido como punto de referencia para realizar una comparación. Al calcular el PBI real, se asignan precios a las producciones de los distintos años al nivel del año base. (p. 327)

board of directors / directorio Importante órgano a cargo de la toma de decisiones en las sociedades anónimas. Establece las políticas y objetivos societarios, entre otras cosas. (p. 184)

Board of Governors of the Federal Reserve System / Junta de Gobernadores del Sistema de la Reserva Federal Cuerpo directivo del Sistema de la Reserva Federal. (p. 294)

bond / bono Vale o promesa de pago, emitida por empresas, gobiernos o agencias gubernamentales a fin de tomar dinero en préstamo. (p. 482)

budget deficit / déficit presupuestario Situación en la que los gastos del gobierno federal son mayores que sus ingresos fiscales. (p. 422)

budget surplus / superávit presupuestario Situación en la que los gastos del gobierno federal son menores que sus ingresos fiscales. (p. 422)

business cycle / ciclo económico Fluctuación regular (de aumento y descenso) del PBI real. (p. 358)

business firm / empresa comercial Organización que utiliza recursos para producir bienes y servicios que son vendidos a los consumidores, a otras empresas o al gobierno. (p. 176)

capital / capital Bienes producidos que pueden utilizarse como recursos para una nueva producción. Por ejemplo, las fábricas, máquinas y tractores agrícolas constituyen un capital. (p. 27)

cartel agreement / acuerdo de cartel Acuerdo que especifica el modo en que las empresas que lo han suscripto actuarán en forma coordinada a fin de reducir la competencia entre ellas. (p. 235)

circular flow of economic activity / flujo circular de la actividad económica Relaciones económicas que existen entre los distintos grupos económicos dentro de una misma economía. (p. 65)

closed shop / empresa de sindicalización obligatoria Organización que sólo contrata a individuos afiliados a los sindicatos. (p. 261)

comparative advantage / ventaja comparativa Situación en las que un país puede producir un bien a un coste de oportunidad menor que el de otro país. (p. 437)

complement / complemento Bien que se consume en forma conjunta con otro bien. En el caso de los complementos, el precio de uno y la demanda del otro se mueven en direcciones opuestas. (p. 108)

consumer price index (CPI) / índice de precios al consumidor (IPC) El índice de precios más utilizado. (p. 331)

consumption / consumo Gastos efectuados en el sector doméstico. (p. 321)

contract / contrato Acuerdo entre dos o más personas de hacer algo. (p. 80)

contractionary fiscal policy / política fiscal contraccionista Disminución en el gasto gubernamental o aumento de los impuestos. (p. 378)

contractionary monetary policy / política monetaria contraccionista Disminución de la oferta monetaria. (p. 388)

corporation / sociedad anónima Entidad legal que puede llevar a cabo una actividad comercial en su nombre, como si fuera un individuo. (p. 181)

coupon rate / tasa del cupón Porcentaje del valor nominal que el titular de un bono recibe por año hasta la fecha de vencimiento. (p. 483)

crowding out / efecto desplazamiento Situación en la que el incremento del gasto público provoca una reducción del gasto privado. (p. 379)

currency / moneda Monedas emitidas por el Tesoro de los Estados Unidos y billetes (llamados billetes de la Reserva Federal) emitidos por el Sistema de la Reserva Federal. (p. 285)

deflation / deflación Disminución del nivel de precios o del nivel promedio de precios. (p. 353)

demand / demanda Voluntad y capacidad de los consumidores de adquirir diversas cantidades de un bien a distintos precios durante un período determinado. (p. 98)

demand curve / curva de demanda Representación gráfica de la ley de la demanda. (p. 101)

demand deposit / depósito a la vista Cuenta de la que se pueden retirar fondos depositados, ya sea en efectivo o por medio de una transferencia por cheque a un tercero, según lo disponga el propietario. (p. 285)

demand schedule / diagrama de demanda Representación numérica de la ley de demanda. (p. 100)

demand-side inflation / inflación del lado de la demanda Incremento en el nivel de los precios, emergente del sector de la demanda dentro de la economía. (p. 348)

depreciation / depreciación Disminución del valor de una moneda en relación con otras. (p. 458)

derived demand / demanda derivada Demanda que resulta de otra demanda. (p. 252)

developed country / país desarrollado País con un PBI relativamente alto por persona. (p. 462)

direct relationship / relación directa Relación entre dos factores en la que dichos factores se mueven en una misma dirección. Por ejemplo, al subir un factor, también sube el otro. (p. 124)

discount rate / tasa de descuento Tasa de interés que cobra la Junta de la Reserva Federal del Banco Central de los Estados Unidos a los bancos por el otorgamiento de préstamos. (p. 306)

disutility / de utilidad La calidad de generar insatisfacción o infelicidad. (p. 26)

dividend / dividendo Parte de las utilidades de una sociedad anónima que se distribuye entre sus accionistas. (p. 474)

double counting / doble contabilidad Contar un bien más de una vez para calcular el PBI. (p. 317)

Dow Jones Industrial Average (DJIA) / Índice promedio industrial Dow Jones (DJIA) El indicador más popular y utilizado de la actividad diaria bursátil. El DJIA es el promedio ponderado de 30 acciones de gran comercialización en la Bolsa de Comercio de Nueva York. (p. 471)

dumping Venta de bienes en el extranjero a un precio inferior al de su costo y al que se cobra en el mercado interno. (p. 451)

economic plan / plan económico Programa del gobierno que especifica las actividades económicas, tales como los bienes que deben producirse y los precios que se cobrarán. (p. 37)

economic system / sistema económico Modo en el que una sociedad decide qué bienes producir, cómo producirlos y para quién producirlos. (p. 34)

economics / ciencias económicas Ciencia que estudia las elecciones de las personas en un intento por satisfacer sus necesidades en un mundo de escasez. (p. 13)

elastic demand / demanda elástica Clase de demanda que existe cuando el cambio porcentual en la cantidad demandada es mayor que el cambio porcentual en el precio. (p. 112)

elastic supply / oferta elástica Clase de oferta que existe cuando el cambio porcentual en la cantidad ofertada es mayor que el cambio porcentual en el precio. (p. 135)

elasticity of demand / elasticidad de la demanda Relación entre el cambio porcentual en la cantidad demandada y el cambio porcentual de precio. (p. 112)

elasticity of supply / elasticidad de la oferta Relación entre el cambio porcentual en la cantidad ofertada y el cambio porcentual de precio. (p. 135)

employment rate / tasa de empleo Porcentaje de la población civil adulta no institucional que posee un empleo. (p. 337)

entrepreneur / empresario Persona con un talento especial para buscar y aprovechar nuevas oportunidades comerciales. (p. 77)

entrepreneurship / iniciativa empresarial Talento especial que poseen ciertas personas para buscar y aprovechar nuevas oportunidades comerciales, así como también para desarrollar nuevos productos y formas de hacer las cosas. (p. 29)

equilibrium / equilibrio En un mercado, el punto en el que la cantidad de un bien que los compradores desean y pueden adquirir es igual a la cantidad que los vendedores desean y pueden producir y ofrecer para la venta (la cantidad demandada es igual a la cantidad ofertada). (p. 145)

equilibrium price / precio de equilibrio Precio en el que se adquiere y vende un bien en un mercado en equilibrio. (p. 145)

equilibrium quantity / cantidad de equilibrio Cantidad de un bien que se adquiere o vende en un mercado en equilibrio. (p. 145)

ethics / ética Principios de conducta, tales como lo correcto e incorrecto, lo moral e inmoral, y lo bueno y lo malo. (p. 72)

excess reserves / reservas en exceso Toda reserva que supere la cantidad requerida. (p. 299)

exchange rate / tasa de cambio Precio de la moneda de un país expresado en la moneda de otro país. (p. 455)

excludable public good / bien público excluible Bien público de cuyo consumo puede excluirse (prohibirse físicamente) a los individuos. (p. 80)

expansionary fiscal policy / política de expansión fiscal Incremento del gasto público o reducción de los impuestos. (p. 378)

expansionary monetary policy / política de expansión monetaria Incremento de la oferta monetaria. (p. 388)

export spending / gastos en exportaciones Monto que gastan los residentes de otros países en la compra de bienes producidos en los Estados Unidos. (p. 321)

exports / exportaciones Bienes producidos dentro del país y vendidos a residentes de otro país. (p. 434)

face value (par value) / valor nominal (valor a la par) Monto en dólares consignado en un bono. Monto total que el emisor del bono debe abonar al comprador del bono. (p. 482)

federal funds rate / tasa de los fondos federales Tasa de interés que cobra un banco a otro por un préstamo. (p. 306)

federal funds rate target / objetivo de tasa de fondos federales La tasa de la fed sería como la tasa de fondos federales para ser. Es la tasa a la cual el banco central le gustaría que los fondos federales tuviese. (p. 308)

Federal Market Open Committee (FOMC) / Comité para las Operaciones de Mercado Abierto de la Reserva Federal (FOMC) Grupo de 12 miembros a cargo del dictado de políticas dentro de la Junta de la Reserva Federal del Banco Central de los Estados Unidos. Este comité está autorizado a efectuar operaciones en el mercado abierto. (p. 295)

Federal Reserve note / billete de la Reserva Federal Billete emitido por el Sistema de la Reserva Federal. (p. 285)

Federal Reserve System (the Fed) / Sistema de la Reserva Federal Banco central de los Estados Unidos. (p. 294)

fiscal policy / política fiscal Cambios efectuados por el gobierno en los gastos o impuestos a fin de lograr determinados objetivos económicos. (p. 378)

fixed cost / costo fijo Costo o gasto que permanece invariable, independientemente de la cantidad de unidades de un determinado bien que se produzcan. (p. 190)

fixed exchange rate system / sistema de tipo de cambio fijo Sistema en virtud del cual la tasa de cambio es determinada o fijada por el gobierno del país. (p. 455)

flexible exchange rate system / sistema de tipo de cambio flexible Sistema en virtud del cual la tasa de cambio es determinada por el juego de la oferta y la demanda. (p. 455)

fractional reserve bank / sistema bancario de reserva fraccionaria Arreglo bancario en virtud del cual los bancos sólo conservan una fracción de los depósitos y otorgan el resto en préstamo. (p. 284)

franchise / franquicia Contrato por medio del cual una empresa (por lo general, una sociedad anónima) permite a una persona o a un grupo utilizar su nombre y vender sus productos a cambio de ciertos pagos y requisitos. (p. 186)

franchisee / beneficiario de la franquicia Persona o grupo que adquiere una franquicia. (p. 186)

franchiser / concesionario de la franquicia Entidad que ofrece una franquicia. (p. 186)

free enterprise / libre empresa Sistema económico en el que los individuos (no el gobierno) son propietarios de la mayoría, si no de la totalidad, de los recursos y controlan su uso. El gobierno desempeña tan solo una función menor en la economía. (p. 34)

free rider / oportunista Persona que recibe los beneficios de un bien sin pagar por él. (p. 82)

futures contract / contrato de futuros Contrato que establece la compra o venta de una cantidad determinada de un bien (productos primarios, divisas, instrumentos financieros) a un precio específico y en una fecha futura estipulada. (p. 492)

globalization / globalización Fenómeno en virtud del cual los agentes económicos de cualquier parte del mundo se ven afectados por los hechos que tienen lugar en otro lugar del mundo; integración creciente de las economías nacionales del mundo hasta un grado tal que permite suponer que podamos estar siendo testigos del surgimiento y funcionamiento de una única economía mundial. (p. 43)

goods / bienes Toda cosa que satisfaga los deseos de una persona o le produzca satisfacción; también productos tangibles. (p. 26)

government purchases / compras gubernamentales Gastos efectuados por el sector gubernamental. Las compras realizadas por el gobierno no incluyen pagos de transferencia del gobierno. (p. 321)

gross domestic product (GDP) / producto bruto interno (PBI) Valor total de mercado de la totalidad de los bienes y servicios producidos anualmente en un país. (p. 316)

hedge / cobertura Intento de evitar o disminuir una pérdida que resulte de medidas de contrarresto. (p. 353)

household / hogar Unidad económica de una o más personas que venden recursos y compran bienes y servicios. (p. 65)

human capital / capital humano Conocimientos y habilidades que los individuos obtienen de la educación, la capacitación en el trabajo y la experiencia laboral, y que utilizan en la producción de bienes y servicios. Comprende también la honestidad, la creatividad y la perseverancia, características adecuadas para obtener un empleo. (p. 369)

import spending / gastos en importación Monto que gastan los estadounidenses en la compra de bienes producidos en el extranjero. (p. 322)

imports / importaciones Bienes producidos en países extranjeros y adquiridos por residentes del país. (p. 435)

incentive / incentivo Algo que fomenta o motiva el actuar de una persona. (p. 15)

income distribution / distribución de las ganancias Modo en el que las ganancias obtenidas en un país se dividen entre los diversos grupos de generadores de ingresos. (p. 37)

index / índice Cartera de acciones que representa un mercado en particular o una parte de él, utilizada para calcular los cambios registrados en un mercado o en una economía. (p. 478)

inelastic demand / demanda inelástica Clase de demanda que existe cuando el cambio porcentual en la cantidad demandada es menor que el cambio porcentual del precio. (p. 113)

inelastic supply / oferta inelástica Clase de oferta que existe cuando el cambio porcentual en la cantidad ofertada es menor que el cambio porcentual del precio. (p. 135)

inferior good / bien inferior Bien cuya demanda disminuye a medida que las ganancias aumentan y se incrementa a medida que las ganancias disminuyen. (p. 105)

inflation / inflación Incremento en el nivel de precios o en el nivel promedio de precios. (p. 346)

initial public offering (IPO) / oferta pública inicial (OPI) Primera oferta de acciones al público por parte de una sociedad. (p. 474)

intangible / intangible Que no puede sentirse mediante el tacto. Por ejemplo, una lección sobre economía es intangible. (p. 26)

inventory / inventario Existencias de bienes que un negocio o local tiene disponibles. (p. 145)

investment / inversión Gastos efectuados por el sector empresarial. (p. 321)

investment bank / banco de inversión Empresa que actúa como intermediario entre la sociedad que emite acciones y el público que desea adquirirlas. (p. 474)

labor / mano de obra Talento físico y mental que aportan los individuos a la producción de bienes y servicios. (p. 27)

labor theory of value / teoría laboral del valor Creencia de que el valor total de los bienes producidos surge de la mano de obra. (p. 41)

labor union / sindicato Organización que procura incrementar los salarios y mejorar las condiciones de trabajo de sus afiliados. (p. 260)

Laffer curve / curva de Laffer Curva así denominada en honor al economista Arthur Laffer, que muestra la relación entre las alícuotas y los ingresos fiscales. De acuerdo con esta curva, a medida que las alícuotas se incrementan desde cero, también se incrementan los ingresos fiscales, hasta llegar a un nivel máximo, luego del cual los ingresos disminuirán ante cualquier otro incremento de las alícuotas. (p. 387)

land / tierra Recursos naturales que se encuentran en la naturaleza. Tanto un acre de terreno como los depósitos de minerales y el agua de un arroyo se consideran tierra. (p. 27)

law of demand / ley de la demanda Ley que establece que a medida que el precio de un bien aumenta, disminuye la demanda de dicho bien, mientras que, a medida que el precio de un bien disminuye, aumenta la demanda de dicho bien. (p. 98)

law of diminishing marginal returns / ley del rendimiento marginal decreciente Ley que establece que si se agregan unidades adicionales de un recurso a otro recurso fijo, la producción adicional obtenida disminuirá con el tiempo. (p. 199)

law of diminishing marginal utility / ley de la utilidad marginal decreciente Ley que establece que, a la medida que una persona consume unidades adicionales de un bien, la utilidad obtenida de cada unidad adicional de dicho bien disminuirá con el tiempo. (p. 99)

law of supply / ley de la oferta Ley que establece que, a medida que el precio de un bien aumenta, también aumenta la oferta de dicho bien, y que, a medida que el precio de un bien disminuye, también disminuye la oferta de dicho bien. (p. 124)

less-developed country / país menos desarrollado País con un PBI per cápita relativamente menor. (p. 462)

limited liability / responsabilidad limitada Condición en virtud de la cual el propietario de una empresa puede perder solamente el monto que ha invertido (en dicha empresa). (p. 182)

loanable funds market / mercado de fondos para préstamos Mercado para préstamos. Existe una demanda de préstamos (que se origina en los prestatarios) y una oferta de préstamos (que se origina en los prestamistas). Es en el mercado de fondos para préstamos donde se determina la tasa de interés. (p. 288)

loss / pérdida Suma de dinero por la que los costos totales superan los ingresos totales. (p. 68)

macroeconomics / macroeconomía Rama de las ciencias económicas que estudia la conducta y las elecciones humanas en relación con la totalidad de la economía. (p. 21)

marginal / marginal En economía, marginal significa adicional. (p. 15)

marginal cost / costo marginal Costo de producción de una unidad adicional de un bien; cambio que tiene lugar en el costo total como consecuencia de la generación de una unidad adicional de producción. (p. 191)

marginal revenue / ingreso marginal Ingresos obtenidos de la venta de una unidad adicional de un bien; cambio que tiene lugar en los ingresos totales como consecuencia de la venta de una unidad adicional de producción. (p. 196)

market / mercado Todo lugar en el que los individuos se reúnen para comprar y vender bienes o servicios. (p. 98)

market structure / estructura de mercado Marco dentro del cual se encuentra un vendedor. Las estructuras de mercado se definen según sus características, tales como el número de vendedores dentro del mercado, el producto que los vendedores producen y venden, y el grado de facilidad o dificultad con el que nuevas empresas pueden ingresar al mercado. (p. 208)

medium of exchange / medio de cambio Todo aquello que generalmente es aceptado a cambio de bienes y servicios. (p. 282)

microeconomics / microeconomía Rama de las ciencias económicas que estudia la conducta y las elecciones humanas en relación con unidades relativamente pequeñas, tales como un individuo, una empresa o un mercado único. (p. 21)

minimum wage law / ley del salario mínimo Ley federal que establece el salario mínimo por hora que puede abonarse a los trabajadores. (p. 254)

mixed economy / economía mixta Economía que no es puramente capitalista ni absolutamente socialista; economía que posee tanto elementos del capitalismo como del socialismo. La mayoría de los países del mundo poseen economías mixtas. (p. 39)

monetary policy / política monetaria
Cambios introducidos por el gobierno respecto de la oferta monetaria. (p. 388)

money / dinero Bien ampliamente aceptado para fines de intercambio y amortización de la deuda. (p. 279)

money supply / oferta monetaria Oferta total de dinero en circulación, compuesto por divisas, cuentas corrientes y cheques de viajero. (p. 285)

monopolistic competitive market / mercado competitivo monopólico Estructura de mercado caracterizada por (1) numerosos compradores y numerosos vendedores; (2) la producción y venta de productos apenas diferenciados; y (3) fácil ingreso y egreso del mercado. (p. 228)

monopolistic market / mercado monopólico
Estructura de mercado caracterizada por (1) un único vendedor; (2) la venta de un producto que no posee sustitutos cercanos; y (3) barreras extremadamente altas para el ingreso al mercado. (p. 215)

national debt / deuda nacional Suma total que el gobierno federal debe a sus acreedores. (p. 417)

natural monopoly / monopolio natural
Empresa con un costo total promedio tan bajo (costo por unidad) que sólo ella puede sobrevivir en el mercado. (p. 219)

negative externality / externalidad negativa
Efecto colateral adverso de un acto que es experimentado por terceros. (p. 84)

neutral good / bien neutro Bien cuya demanda permanece invariable, independientemente de que las ganancias aumenten o disminuyan. (p. 105)

nonexcludable public good / bien público no excluible Bien público de cuyo consumo no puede excluirse (prohibirse físicamente) a ningún individuo. (p. 80)

normal good / bien normal Bien cuya demanda aumenta a medida que aumentan las ganancias, y disminuye a medida que se reducen las ganancias. (p. 105)

offshoring / relocalización Término utilizado para describir el trabajo efectuado para una compañía por personas distintas de los empleados originales de la compañía, en un país distinto de aquél en el que la compañía está localizada. (p. 51)

ogopolistic market / mercado oligopólico
Estructura de mercado caracterizada por (1) pocos vendedores; (2) la producción y venta de productos idénticos o apenas diferenciados; y (3) barreras considerablemente altas para el ingreso al mercado. (p. 233)

open market operations / operaciones de mercado abierto Compraventa de títulos públicos por parte de la Junta de la Reserva Federal del Banco Central de los Estados Unidos. (p. 305)

opportunity cost / costo de oportunidad La oportunidad o alternativa de mayor valor perdida al realizar una elección. (p. 8)

option / opción Contrato que otorga al propietario el derecho, pero no la obligación, de comprar o vender acciones de un bien a un precio determinado, en una fecha determinada o con anterioridad a ella. (p. 495)

outsourcing / tercerización Término utilizado para describir el trabajo llevado a cabo para una compañía por otra compañía o por individuos distintos de los empleados originales de la compañía. (p. 442)

partnership / sociedad de personas
Sociedad que pertenece a dos o más copropietarios, llamados socios, quienes comparten las ganancias y son responsables por sus deudas ante la ley. (p. 180)

per capita real economic growth / crecimiento económico real per cápita Incremento de un período a otro del PBI real per cápita, el cual consiste en el PBI real dividido entre la población. (p. 364)

perfectly competitive market / mercado perfectamente competitivo Estructura de mercado caracterizada por (1) numerosos compradores y numerosos vendedores; (2) todas las empresas venden bienes idénticos; (3) toda información pertinente a las actividades de compraventa se encuentra disponible para los compradores y vendedores; y (4) un facuk ingreso y egreso del mercado. (p. 209)

per-unit cost / costo por unidad Costo promedio de un bien. Por ejemplo, si se gastan $400,000 para producir 100 automóviles, el costo promedio o costo por unidad es de $4,000. (p. 130)

population growth rate / tasa de crecimiento de la población La tasa de nacimientos menos la tasa de defunciones. (p. 462)

positive externality / externalidad positiva Efecto secundario positivo de una acción que beneficia a terceros. (p. 84)

price ceiling / precio máximo Precio establecido por ley—inferior al precio de equilibrio— por sobre el cual los compradores y vendedores no pueden comprar ni vender bienes de forma legal. (p. 151)

price discrimination / discriminación de precio Práctica en virtud de la cual un vendedor establece distintos precios (para distintos compradores) respecto del producto que vende, y las diferencias de precio no reflejan las diferencias de costo. (p. 236)

price floor / precio mínimo Precio establecido por ley—superior al precio de equilibrio— por debajo del cual los compradores y vendedores no pueden comprar ni vender bienes de forma legal. (p. 151)

price index / índice de precios Cálculo del nivel de precios o del nivel promedio de precios. (p. 331)

price searcher / buscador de precios Vendedor que puede vender parte de su producción a diversos precios. (p. 215)

price taker / tomador de precios Vendedor que puede vender la totalidad de su producción al precio de equilibrio pero no a otro precio. (p. 210)

private good / bien privado Bien que al ser consumido por una persona no podrá ser consumido por otra. (p. 80)

private property / propiedad privada Todo bien que sea de propiedad de un individuo o negocio. (p. 63)

production possibilities frontier / frontera de posibilidades de producción Representación gráfica de la totalidad de las combinaciones posibles de dos bienes que pueda producir una economía. (p. 10)

profit / ganancia Suma de dinero que resta luego de que hayan sido pagados los costes de producción. Habrá una ganancia siempre que el ingreso total sea mayor que el costo total. (p. 68)

progressive income tax / impuesto a las ganancias progresivo Impuesto a las ganancias cuya alícuota aumenta a medida que aumenta el nivel de ganancias. Las estructuras progresivas del impuesto a las ganancias tienen por lo general una alícuota máxima. (p. 410)

proportional income tax / impuesto a las ganancias proporcional Impuesto a las ganancias en virtud del cual todos se encuentran sujetos a la misma alícuota, independientemente de sus ganancias. (p. 409)

public franchise / franquicia pública Derecho otorgado a una empresa por parte del gobierno, que permite a dicha empresa brindar un determinado bien o servicio, mientras que excluye a todos los demás de la provisión de dicho bien o servicio. (p. 218)

public good / bien público Bien cuyo consumo por parte de una persona no quita a otro la posibilidad de consumirlo. (p. 80)

public property / propiedad pública Todo bien de propiedad del gobierno. (p. 63)

quantity demanded / cantidad demandada Número de unidades de un bien adquiridas a un precio determinado. (p. 99)

quantity supplifed / cantidad ofrecida Número de unidades de un bien producidas y ofrecidas para la venta a un precio determinado. (p. 124)

quota / cuota Límite legal del número de unidades de un bien producido en el extranjero (importación) que pueden ingresar a un país. (p. 130)

rationing device / mecanismo de racionalización Medio para decidir quién recibe y qué parte recibe de los recursos y bienes disponibles. (p. 12)

real GDP / PBI real Producto bruto interno (PBI) ajustado de acuerdo con los cambios de precios; PBI calculado sobre los precios de un año base o constantes. (p. 327)

recession / recesión Desaceleración de la economía como consecuencia de la disminución del PBI real durante dos trimestres consecutivos. (p. 358)

regressive income tax / impuesto a las ganancias regresivo Impuesto a las ganancias cuya alícuota disminuye a medida que las ganancias aumentan. (p. 410)

required reserves / reservas obligatorias Monto mínimo de reservas que debe poseer un banco respecto de sus depósitos, según lo determinado por la Junta de la Reserva Federal del Banco Central de los Estados Unidos. (p. 298)

reserve account / cuenta de reserva Cuenta corriente de un banco en el banco del distrito de la Reserva Federal. (p. 295)

reserve requirement / requisito de reservas Disposición que establece que los bancos deben conservar un cierto porcentaje de los depósitos en su cuenta de reserva en la Junta de la Reserva Federal del Banco Central de los Estados Unidos, o en su bóveda, como efectivo de caja. (p. 298)

resource / recurso Todo aquello que se utilice para producir bienes o servicios. Por ejemplo, la mano de obra de un individuo puede utilizarse para producir computadoras, televisores y muchas otras cosas y, por lo tanto, la mano de obra constituye un recurso. (p. 6)

right-to-work law / ley contra la filiación sindical obligatoria Ley estatal que prohíbe requerir la afiliación de los empleados a un sindicato para poder trabajar. (p. 261)

savings account / caja de ahorro Cuenta que genera intereses. (p. 286)

scarcity / escasez Situación en la que nuestras necesidades son mayores que los recursos necesarios para satisfacerlas. (p. 6)

services / servicios Tareas cuya realización ciertos individuos encargan a otros a cambio de un pago. (p. 26)

shirking / holgazanear Conducta de un trabajador que trabaja con menor esfuerzo que el acordado. (p. 177)

shortage / desabastecimiento Situación en la que la cantidad demandada de un bien es mayor que la cantidad ofertada. Dichos desabastecimientos sólo tienen lugar cuando se establecen precios menores al precio de equilibrio. (p. 145)

simple quantity theory of money / teoría simple cuantitativa del dinero Teoría que predice que los cambios en el nivel de precios serán estrictamente proporcionales a los cambios en la oferta monetaria. (p. 350)

socialism / socialismo Sistema económico en el que el gobierno controla y puede poseer muchos de los recursos. (p. 34)

sole proprietorship / empresa unipersonal Empresa que pertenece a un individuo, quien toma todas las decisiones comerciales, recibe la totalidad de las ganancias o afronta deudas en nombre de la empresa, y es legalmente responsable de las deudas de dicha empresa. (p. 178)

specialize / especializarse Dedicarse a una actividad o a un producto en particular. (p. 437)

stagflation / estanflación La coexistencia de inflación y un alto desempleo. (p. 398)

stock / acción El derecho a los activos de una corporación que tiene un comprador para tener parte de una compañía. (p. 470)

stockholder / accionista Persona que posee acciones de una sociedad. (p. 181)

stop-and-go, on-and-off monetary policy / política monetaria de pare y arranque, intermitente Una política monetaria errática. (p. 398)

store of value / reserva del valor Aquello que tenga la capacidad de conservar el valor con el transcurso del tiempo. (p. 282)

strike / huelga Suspensión del trabajo convocada por miembros de sindicatos a fin de ejercer presión sobre un empleador. (p. 261)

subsidy / subsidio Pago financiero efectuado por el gobierno respecto de ciertas acciones. (p. 130)

substitute / substituto Bien similar. En el caso de los substitutos, el precio de uno y la demanda del otro se mueven en la misma dirección. (p. 106)

supply / oferta Voluntad y capacidad de los vendedores de producir y ofrecer a la venta diversas cantidades de un bien a distintos precios, durante un período determinado. (p. 124)

supply curve / curva de oferta Gráfico que demuestra la cantidad de un bien que los vendedores desean y pueden vender a distintos precios. (p. 126)

supply schedule / diagrama de oferta
Cuadro numérico que ilustra la ley de oferta. (p. 125)

supply-side inflation / inflación del lado de la oferta Incremento en el nivel de precios que se origina en el lado de la oferta de la economía. (p. 349)

surplus / superávit Situación en la que la cantidad ofrecida de un bien es mayor que la cantidad demandada. El superávit sólo tiene lugar cuando existen precios superiores al precio de equilibrio. (p. 144)

surplus value / plusvalía Diferencia entre el valor total de producción y los salarios de subsistencia abonados a los trabajadores. (p. 41)

Taft-Hartley Act / ley Taft-Hartley Ley aprobada en 1947 por el Congreso de los Estados Unidos, la cual determinó la ilegalidad de las empresas de sindicalización obligatoria y otorgó a los estados el derecho de aprobar leyes contra la filiación sindical obligatoria. Dichas leyes prohíben a los empleadores requerir la pertenencia a un sindicato como condición para obtener un empleo. (p. 261)

tangible / tangible Que puede sentirse o tocarse. Por ejemplo, un libro es algo tangible: puede tocarse y sentirse. (p. 26)

tariff / arancel Impuesto a las importaciones. (p. 447)

technology / tecnología Cuerpo de técnicas y conocimientos vinculados con el uso de recursos para la producción. (p. 130)

theory / teoría Explicación acerca del funcionamiento de algo, a fin de responder a una pregunta para la cual no existe una respuesta obvia. (p. 21)

total cost / costo total Suma de los costos fijos más los costos variables. (p. 191)

total reserves / reservas totales Sumas de los depósitos que los bancos conservan en sus cuentas de reserva en la Junta de la Reserva Federal del Banco Central de los Estados Unidos y el efectivo en caja. (p. 298)

trade-off / compromiso Situación en la que más de una cosa significa necesariamente menos de otra. (p. 8)

transaction costs / costos de transacción Costos asociados con el tiempo y esfuerzo necesarios para buscar, negociar y llevar a cabo un intercambio. (p. 278)

unemployment rate / tasa de desempleo Porcentaje de la fuerza laboral civil que está desempleada. (p. 337)

union shop / empresa de sindicalización obligatoria posterior a la contratación Organización que requiere a los empleados afiliarse al sindicato dentro de un período determinado luego de haber sido contratados. (p. 261)

unit of account / unidad de cuenta Medida común utilizada para expresar valores. (p. 282)

unit-elastic demand / demanda elástica unitaria Clase de demanda que existe cuando el cambio porcentual de la cantidad demandada es igual al cambio porcentual del precio. (p. 113)

unit-elastic supply / oferta elastica unitaria El tipo de suministroque existe cuando el cambio porcentual en la cantidad suministrada es igual al cambio porcentual en el precio. (p. 135)

utility / utilidad Calidad de proporcionar satisfacción o felicidad. (p. 26)

value-added tax / impuesto al valor agregado Impuesto agregado al valor que adquiere un bien en cada etapa de su producción y distribución. (p. 409)

variable cost / costo variable Costo o gasto que varía según el número de unidades de un bien producido. (p. 190)

velocity / velocidad Número promedio de veces en que se gasta un dólar para adquirir productos y servicios finales dentro de un año. (p. 349)

vision / visión Sentido de cómo funciona el mundo. (p. 40)

wage rate / salario Precio de la mano de obra. (p. 246)

want / necesidad Algo que deseamos tener. (p. 6)

yield / rendimiento Es igual al pago anual de un cupón, dividido por el precio abonado por dicho cupón. (p. 484)

Photo Credits

Index

stagflation, 398–400
supply-side, 348–349, 348 (exhibit)
velocity concept and, 349
inflation-indexed Treasury bonds, 486–487
information
asymmetric information, 187–188
in perfectly competitive market, 209
validating, 371
initial public offering (IPO), 474
injunctions, 265
innovation, business cycle and, 363
institutions, importance to economic systems, 84
insurance
automobile insurance, 194
buying, 194
health insurance, 194–195
life insurance, 195
premiums and deductibles, 194
value of, 194–195
intangibles, 26
interest, paid on national debt, 417
interest rates
determination of, 288–289
discount rate, 306
federal funds rate, 306, 307–308
primary credit rate, 306
for savings accounts, 396
short-term vs. long-term, 289
intermediate goods, 317
International Bank for Reconstruction and Development (IBRD), 453
International Monetary Fund (IMF), 453–454
international trade. See trade
Internet
commerce and monopolistic market, 219
monopoly of first-class mail and, 222
price information from, 166–167
inventory, 145
investment bank, 474
investments
bonds, 482–489
foreign investment and economic development, 464
futures, 492–495
in GDP measurement, 321–322, 322 (exhibit)
housing as, 339
options, 495–497
risk and return, 488–489
stocks, 470–481

in yourself, 138–139
invisible hand, 41, 75
issuing debt, 184

J

Japan
economic freedom score, 39 (exhibit)
exports of, 51 (exhibit)
GDP of, 318 (exhibit)
jobs
changing demand and, 106
loss of, to offshoring/outsourcing, 51, 442
Occupational Outlook Handbook (OOH), 267
physical location and job security, 460–461
professions unlikely to be offshored, 460–461
Jobs, Steve, 29

K

Kahneman, Daniel, 164, 485
Keynes, John Maynard, 382–383
Knights of Labor, 264

L

labor
defined, 27
economic growth and productivity, 367
government regulation, 266–269
job loss, and offshoring/outsourcing, 51, 442
Occupational Outlook Handbook (OOH), 267
as resource, 27
unemployment, 335–337, 337 (exhibit)
labor theory of value, 41
labor unions, 260–269
American Federation of Labor (AFL), 264–265, 266
closed shops, 261
Congress of Industrial Organizations (CIO), 265–266
defined, 260
demand for union labor, 260
early court decisions and, 265
historic development of, 264–266
human capital and, 372–373
Knights of Labor, 264
Landrum-Griffin Act, 266
National Labor Relations Board (NLRB), 265
Norris-LaGuardia Act, 265
productivity and efficiency, 262–264

public employee unions, 266
right-to-work laws, 261–262, 261 (exhibit)
Sherman Antitrust Act, 265
strikes and, 261, 265
supply for union labor, 260–262
Taft-Hartley Act, 261, 266
union shop, 261
wages and effect on, 262
Wagner Act, 265
Laffer, Arthur, 387
Laffer curve, 386–387, 387 (exhibit)
lagging economic indicator, 359–360
land
defined, 27
as resource, 27
Landrum-Griffin Act, 266
law of demand, 98–101
law of diminishing marginal returns, 199–201, 200 (exhibit)
law of diminishing marginal utility, 99
law of supply, 124–126
leading economic indicator, 359–360
legal systems
antitrust laws, 220–225, 221 (exhibit)
ethical economic activity, 76
free enterprise and, 65
importance to economic systems, 84
labor unions and, 261, 265
minimum wage laws, 254–255
negative externalities and, 86
price discrimination and, 241
right-to-work laws, 261–262, 261 (exhibit)
lenders, 289
less-developed countries (LDCs), 462
leverage, banks and financial crisis of 2007-2009, 336
Lewis, John L., 265
liability
bank, 307, 336
corporations, 182
partnership and, 181
sole proprietorship and unlimited liability, 180
liability insurance, 194
licensing procedure, economic development and, 464–465
life expectancy, globalization and, 48 (exhibit), 49
life insurance, 195